ADLAI STEVENSON
OF ILLINOIS

BY JOHN BARTLOW MARTIN

THE PANE OF GLASS
THE DEEP SOUTH SAYS NEVER
BREAK DOWN THE WALLS
WHY DID THEY KILL?
MY LIFE IN CRIME
BUTCHER'S DOZEN
INDIANA
CALL IT NORTH COUNTRY
OVERTAKEN BY EVENTS

JOHN BARTLOW MARTIN, born in Ohio, became one of America's most distinguished journalists in the late 1940s and 1950s. He wrote extensively for *Harper's* and *The Saturday Evening Post,* winning four times the Benjamin Franklin and twice the Sigma Delta Chi awards for best article of the year. Many of his prodigiously researched pieces became important pioneering books on such subjects as prison reform, desegregation, and mental health care. He worked as a writer for and adviser to Adlai Stevenson and was twice a presidential envoy—for John Kennedy and Lyndon Johnson. Mr. Martin was U. S. Ambassador to the Dominican Republic from 1962 to 1964, and out of this dramatic experience came his classic ambassador's report, *Overtaken by Events.* He is a professor at Northwestern University's Medill School of Journalism.

ADLAI STEVENSON OF ILLINOIS

The Life of
Adlai E. Stevenson

JOHN BARTLOW MARTIN

ANCHOR BOOKS
ANCHOR PRESS/DOUBLEDAY
GARDEN CITY, NEW YORK
1977

To Fran

ACKNOWLEDGMENTS

Adlai E. Stevenson died in July of 1965. In December of that year I undertook to write his biography. I have worked at it ever since, at Princeton, Washington, New York, Lake Como, Springfield, Chicago and its suburbs, and other places he frequented. When we began the research, my family and I lived for a few months in the house in Libertyville that he loved. We had visited him there often during his lifetime, and that winter it was at first hard to realize that we would not see his slightly dumpy figure waddling up the sloping field from the Des Plaines River, picking up dead tree branches as he came; to enter through the sun porch, blue eyes wide, cross the living room and, looking slightly perplexed, hesitate by the fireplace; then, grumbling about "this appalling task," go into his study to work on a speech.

The place was not quite the same that winter as when he left it. For one thing, the sheep were gone. He had raised sheep on his seventy acres (to save the cost of cutting hay and grass, I suspected). Adlai III, his eldest son, had had the sheep butchered and given to his father's friends that first Christmas of his father's death, a hard thing for him.

Well, to work. A researcher and I catalogued his library. It was a working library—reference books and bound copies of his own speeches nearest his desk. But genealogies and family histories were not far away, nor were the Lincoln shelves. He was a man of Illinois, always; even after he belonged to the world, Illinois history, the Illinois prairies, and above all these seventy acres held him. Scattered about were gorgeous pictures of a cruise on a private yacht during the UN years; a bust of President Kennedy and an autographed photograph of President Johnson; plaques and awards, gavels and a collection of plaster donkeys; exotic mementos of his travels. (He used to have a basement room full of travel mementos and at Christmas gave them to friends—keys to cities, spears, oriental bric-a-brac.) Under his desk blotter was a scrap of paper containing in his handwriting a notation that Artie, his Dalmatian, was buried by a tree outside his study window.

The living room, like the study, was comfortable. The upholstered chairs and sofa that flanked the fireplace were frayed. Yet the whole house was light and airy, filled with sunshine, cheering. The house was bigger than it looked from the outside, where trees and shrubbery screened it. It sat far back from a gravel road. In later years hundreds of tourists found their way here, and even if he was working in seclusion, he received them courteously. He always called the place "the farm" and dutifully reported its profit or loss on his income tax returns.

We searched the house, a search, really, for Stevenson. And, merely in using it, found traces of him, too—his highball glasses were decorated with Princeton's orange and black tiger and "22," his class. He was only somewhat less a Princetonian than an Illinoisan. The freezer was full of lamb and mutton. Over the big double bed in the master bedroom hung two gilded cupids, melancholy when one reflected on his disastrous marriage. On the night table beside his bed lay a book—the Social Register. So many of his Social Register friends voted against him for President.

On a telephone note pad Stevenson had written "Penelope is 21," a reminder. Lifelong he was good to his friends' children, helped raise them, in a way. He was thoughtful and affectionate. Forgetful, too—we found nine identical trench coats in a downstairs closet, bought no doubt while traveling, having forgotten to bring a coat.

On the wall of the basement stair was a lithograph from the campaign of 1892, when Stevenson's grandfather and namesake was elected Vice President, the running mate of Cleveland. And another from the campaign of 1900, when he lost with Bryan. In the basement we found an old filing cabinet. One drawer was stuck tight. I finally pried it open—and found Stevenson's daily appointment books covering his entire four years as Governor.

One wintry day Adlai III and I sat in front of the fireplace with my agent and publisher and worked out the contracts for the biography. As a writer and lawyer, Stevenson would have enjoyed that. Then we had a drink, and he would have enjoyed that too. Soon I moved on, to Washington, and he would have approved.

Stevenson was a string-saver; he almost literally never threw anything away. Among his papers one can find not only the longhand first drafts of famous speeches but also football game ticket stubs and old dance programs. His archive is enormous. We copied several hundred thousand pages of his papers. We indexed the copies, making an average of perhaps a thousand index cards on each of the sixty-five years of his life. To fill in gaps, I interviewed about a hundred people who had been close to him. In using the material, I have usually let it speak for itself, though occasionally I have felt it necessary to intervene. It has not always been possible to unravel all the complexities and resolve all the ambiguities of his life, for he was a complex and sometimes ambiguous man. But I think the important questions have been answered.

A great many people helped in the making of this book.

I had the cooperation of Stevenson's family—his sister, Mrs. Ernest Ives, and his three sons, Adlai III, Borden, and John Fell. They gave me free access to Stevenson's private papers. I consulted them at various stages of the project. It is only fair to them, however, to absolve them of any responsibility for the book that has resulted. It is my book, not theirs; its interpretation of Adlai Stevenson is mine, not theirs. I am deeply grateful for their help.

For supporting the project in various ways, I wish to express my gratitude to Lake Forest College, the Woodrow Wilson School of Princeton University, the Graduate Center of the City University of New York, the Medill School of Northwestern University, and the Rockefeller Foundation—and to their presidents, deans, professors, and librarians. And to the First National Bank of Highland Park, Illinois.

I am grateful to the memory of Louis A. Kohn and to his widow, Mary Jane Kohn, for introducing me to Adlai Stevenson in the first place, while he was still Governor.

Many people kindly gave me permission to quote from their own letters, private journals, or other writings.

A few fragments of this book—a part of the Acknowledgment section and material on isolationism, Chicago politics, and the Centralia mine disaster—were originally published, in different form, in *Harper's Magazine,* the *Saturday Evening Post,* and *Life.*

The reader should know that the passage on Stevenson's feelings about Richard Nixon was written long before Nixon's disgrace and resignation.

Quotations from unpublished letters, journals, and other writings are reprinted by permission of their authors (or their authors' estates), as follows:

Jacob M. Arvey, William Attwood, Edwin Austin, George W. Ball, William Benton, William McCormick Blair, Chester Bowles, Kenneth F. Burgess, William J. Campbell, Cass Canfield, Benjamin V. Cohen, Norman Cousins, John Cowles, Henry Crown, Beth Currie, Harry S. Truman, Mrs. Clifton Daniel, Jane Warner Dick, Paul H. Douglas, William O. Douglas, James Doyle, Roxane Eberlein, Carol Evans, Mrs. Kellogg Fairbank, Ruth Field, Gay Finletter, Thomas K. Finletter, Dorothy Fosdick, J. W. Fulbright, John Kenneth Galbraith, Lloyd Garrison, Averell Harriman, Barnet Hodes, Chester Holifield, Evelyn Houston, Hubert H. Humphrey, Walter Johnson, Clay Judson, Murray Kempton, George Kennan, Robert F. Kennedy, Louis A. Kohn, Henry Lax, David Lloyd, Archibald MacLeish, Donald MacPherson, Mercedes McCambridge, Nan McEvoy, Carl McGowan, Davis Merwin, Loring Merwin, Louis Merwin, Agnes Meyer, Eugene Meyer, John S. Miller, Newton N. Minow, Charles Murphy, Jacqueline Kennedy Onassis, Mrs. Walter Paepcke, Francis T. P. Plimpton, David Riesman, James Reston, William Rivkin, Eugene Rostow, James Rowe, Dean Rusk, Dore Schary, Arthur M. Schlesinger, Jr., R. Sargent Shriver, William Sidley, Hermon Dunlap Smith, Mrs. Smith, John Steele, Richard K. Stevens, Roger Stevens, Adlai E. Stevenson and Ellen Stevenson, Adlai E. Stevenson III, Borden Stevenson, John Fell Stevenson, Nancy Stevenson, Stuart Symington, Robert W. Tufts, Barbara Ward, Jacob Weinstein, Harriet Welling, Theodore White, Wilson W. Wyatt, Suzie Zurcher.

Francis S. Nipp served as Research Director of the project for the first two years. Roxane Eberlein, who was formerly Stevenson's private secretary, took over thereafter. Alton B. Smith arranged the typing of various drafts of the manuscript. My wife helped research and edit the book through all the years. To their fidelity, I owe much. And to my understanding and patient and skillful editors and agents—Samuel S. Vaughan, Kenneth McCormick, and Eric Larrabee, all of Doubleday, and Ivan Von Auw and Dorothy Olding of Harold Ober Associates.

I am grateful to Stevenson's friends and associates who submitted to interviews, most of them more than once. I am not listing them here because they are quoted in the text. I am grateful, too, to several private citizens and to several of my own graduate students who volunteered help with research and other chores—I especially want to mention Cynthia Brilliant, Dave Gollust, William King, Lee Knauerhaze, Suzanne Meldman, and Nancy Szokan.

PHOTO CREDITS

CONTENTS

CONTENTS

PART ONE
GROPING

CHAPTER ONE

A Boy in a Midwest Town
1900-1916

Adlai E. Stevenson was born February 5, 1900, on the threshold of the twentieth century. He lived through nearly two thirds of the century and died on July 14, 1965. He was a wanderer and happened to be born in California and to die in England, but his roots were in Bloomington, Illinois.

On the next to last Christmas of his life, ambassador of the United States to the United Nations, he went home to Bloomington to visit his sister Buffie in the big old house on East Washington Street where they grew up. He had just come from the UN and he was tired and late in the afternoon lay down on the green velvet sofa in the bay window in the living room and went to sleep. Outside it got dark. His sister came in and quietly lit the lights on the Christmas tree, then stepped into the adjoining library and sat and watched him. The living room was Victorian, filled with Dresden lamps their mother had bought in Germany and an ornate table she had bought in New Orleans, a Japanese sword and a carved elephant tusk their father had bought in Japan. After a while Stevenson shook himself a little, raised his head, then said, "Buffie?"

His sister said, "Yes, here I am."

He said, "Why did they fight so much?"

"Who?"

"Mother and Father."

"I don't know, Adlai. Lydiard Horton told me once they were lovers' quarrels."

"Hmph," he said.

He lay there quietly a little while. Then: "Father was so violent."

"Yes, he was a violent man."

He said nothing for a while. Until, "Well, I guess we ought to go see some people."

"Why don't you just rest?"

"No, we ought to go see Bud Merwin. And Joe Bohrer. Shouldn't we go see Bud and Joe? Of course we should. Let's go," and he got up quickly—he always moved quickly, in bursts of energy, as it were, though a little ponderously now that he was fat—and as they went out to pay a few calls, she asked, "How do you feel about coming back?"

He said, "Oh, I don't know. The old shack looks pretty good. But I don't feel too much. There's nothing here any more, is there? It's all changed."

Bloomington *had* changed, but not so much as he.

2

Bloomington is a town of about 36,000, about 25,000 when Stevenson was a boy, situated approximately a hundred and twenty-five miles southwest of Chicago on the rich swelling prairie of Illinois. Once it was a railroad town, and their shops were the biggest industry; but the railroads declined. Bloomington is located on the rim of Illinois's underground coal basin and it had a coal mine—the Stevensons owned an interest in it—but it has long been abandoned. Bloomington has become an insurance town and its twin town, Normal, a college town of 28,000. But today, and when Adlai Stevenson was born, and always, Bloomington's wealth has rested at bottom on the land—the black Wisconsin drift that runs across Illinois and Indiana into Ohio, topsoil fifteen feet deep, some of the richest land on earth. McLean County has long been reckoned one of the most fertile farm counties in the United States. Always the talk in town has been of the weather—"Sure could use some rain"—and of the crops. Bloomington has a number of wealthy families. Their wealth comes from owning land.

The new spires of the university rise to the sun, and traffic is thick now on Main Street, and Bloomington has an airport but, like all Midwest farm towns, Bloomington is past-haunted. Buildings on Main Street have new false store fronts on the first floor; up above they bulge with Victorian bay windows. The court house is three stories high capped by a round green dome. The streets are asphalt but in places the bricks show through. A parking lot occupies the site where Abraham Lincoln spoke. A sign on a bus reads "Stevensonville"; Stevensonville is a section of town on the other side of the tracks where the Stevensons owned land; it was settled by Germans, Irish, Swedes, and Hungarians who worked at the railroad shops, the buggy factory, and the Stevenson-Scott coal mine; the Stevensons once had a Hungarian laundress and a Swedish maid from Stevenson-ville. Out Jefferson Street stands the grand square brick and stone mansion of Judge David Davis, appointed to the United States Supreme Court by Abraham Lincoln, elected to the United States Senate to represent the people of Illinois. Over there, at the corner of Chestnut and Clinton streets, is an empty lot where once stood the house of W. O. Davis, owner of the Bloomington *Daily Pantagraph,* grandfather of Adlai Stevenson. Stevenson's parents were married in that house; his sister was born in it. Their preacher and their doctor lived down the street. In that little house with a turret room once lived L. B. Merwin, married to Jessie Davis, Stevenson's aunt. The Merwins always had a way of keeping their houses back from the street.

When Adlai Stevenson was young, East Washington Street, where he lived, was considered the best section of town. At that time there were a board sidewalk and a hitching post in front of the Stevenson house, and the streetcar line ended there; the children knew the conductor. Great elm trees arched over the street. That old house across the way usually had cows behind it. On Halloween Stevenson and his friends dumped over outhouses and soaped the streetcar tracks and pulled off the streetcar trolley.

To go to school, Adlai Stevenson used to walk a block or two down Washington Street. On the way he would pass the new house where his friend, Hesketh Coolidge, lived and the home of a girl who did his sister Buffie's arithmetic, and a brick house that belonged to Cousin Spencer Ewing. He walked this way to school; later Buffie's grandchildren would.

Sometimes he would walk on down Washington Street and cross the tracks and go to the home of his grandfather, Adlai Ewing Stevenson, who had been elected Vice President of the United States with Grover Cleveland in 1892. Grandfather Stevenson's home faced Franklin Park. Young Adlai's family took him there to dinner on Sundays to listen to the old man's stories. In that same block were the homes of Frank Funk, Bull Moose candidate for governor in 1912 and member of one of the great landowning families of the region, and Joseph W. Fifer, elected Republican Governor of Illinois in 1888. "All this in a little dinky town like Bloomington," Joe Bohrer, Governor Fifer's grandson and a lifelong friend of Adlai Stevenson, once said. Winters, as a boy, Adlai Stevenson and his friends went sledding in front of Vice President Stevenson's house. In 1948, Stevenson, campaigning for Governor, rode in a torchlight parade that started here in Franklin Park. Bloomington is strongly

Republican. Though Stevenson carried this county for Governor, he lost it for President. A man who knows has said, "Stevenson couldn't have been elected here. He never was fully accepted here until he was brought back for burial."

Out South Main is the Evergreen Memorial Cemetery, a quiet shaded place. On the slope of a hill is a large plain stone marker: "Adlai Ewing Stevenson 1900–1965." The slab marker is shaped a little like the United Nations building. Now and then a tourist comes and takes pictures. Some bring flowers and lay them on a little plot of grass in front of the marker; his sister comes out and removes them when they die—they'll kill the grass. To the east is the grave of his grandfather, the Vice President. Adlai Stevenson's mother and father are buried here too. On the other side of the hill lie his forebears on his mother's side, Jesse Fell and W. O. Davis. In an older part of the cemetery is the grave of Jesse Fell's father, born in 1776. Adlai Stevenson is the fifth of his line to lie here. This is about as far back as it is possible to go in central Illinois.

3

Great streams of migration built this Midwest, this American heartland, this "unique America" that early travelers remarked. One, Quaker and Republican, came through Pennsylvania across the mountains from New England and New York. Another, Presbyterian and Democratic, came up the Cumberland Gap through Kentucky from the Carolinas. These were the two strains that produced Adlai Stevenson. His Quaker Republican ancestors from Pennsylvania were on his mother's side—Fells and Davises; his Carolina-Kentucky Democratic Presbyterian ancestors were on his father's side—Stevensons.

Adlai Stevenson often said, "I have a bad case of hereditary politics." All his life Stevenson was interested in his ancestors. After he became famous, people sent him mementos of his Grandfather Stevenson's campaigns. He treasured them. From early childhood through manhood Stevenson was constantly reminded of his distinguished ancestors. His wife derided his interest in them.

His mother's side of the family arrived in Bloomington first. And his mother's grandfather, Adlai's great-grandfather, Jesse W. Fell, lawyer, publisher, abolitionist, tree planter, land developer, town booster, dabbler in politics, friend of Abraham Lincoln, was par excellence the Midwest local leader and Stevenson's favorite ancestor.

4

Jesse W. Fell was born November 10, 1808, of Quaker parents in a stone house in New Garden, Chester County, Pennsylvania. His parents proposed to apprentice him as a tailor but he wanted education, worked to pay his way through boarding school, and in 1828 went West. He sold books, worked for an abolitionist newspaper, worked for a law firm and studied law, was indoctrinated with Whig views, and entered Illinois in 1832. In Jacksonville he was admitted to the Illinois bar; in Springfield he called on a lawyer named John T. Stuart, who later became Abraham Lincoln's law partner. Stuart told him that Bloomington, seat of the newly created county, McLean, had no lawyer and advised him to go there.

Bloomington's first house had been built in 1826; when Fell arrived in 1832, Bloomington contained about a hundred people, no lawyer, no newspaper, and no clergyman. Fell decided to become its lawyer. He prospered but the law did not hold him. Much of his early work was connected with land titles; people were taking up the prairie. Quickly it became the land, not the law, that interested Fell—the land and growth of the West. He interested himself in Bloomington's fortunes, in growing with it. He became a speculator in land, a promoter of towns, and a Bloomington booster.

Bloomington had about 800 people in 1845; ten years later, 5,000. The railroads came in 1853—Fell helped bring them. He led the movement to establish a state teachers' college, or "normal" school, at North Bloomington, and North Bloomington was renamed Normal. Fell bought in and sold out of a newspaper that in 1853 became the Bloomington *Daily Pantagraph,* using it to campaign for popular education, prohibition, firefighting equipment, sidewalks, sewers, pavements, and Republican candidates.

Though he never ran for public office, Fell was active in Illinois Republican politics. In the spring of 1856, when the Whig Party was disintegrating, Fell helped lead a movement to establish the Republican Party of Illinois. At the ˜1858 convention Fell offered a resolution that Abraham Lincoln "is our first, last and only choice" for election to the U. S. Senate. That year Lincoln and Stephen A. Douglas held their debates. It is said that Fell or his associate, Judge David Davis, proposed the debates. Fell went East to seek support for Lincoln. He found Eastern anti-slavery men interested in Lincoln but knowing little about him. Therefore, when Fell returned to Illinois he urged Lincoln several times to provide him with a sketch of Lincoln's life, and Lincoln finally did, three sheets of longhand written here in Bloomington. (Adlai Stevenson was extraordinarily proud of this document and hung facsimiles of it in his home and in the Governor's Mansion.) Fell realized that Lincoln, though popular in the West, needed Eastern votes to be nominated for President. Pennsylvania was the key. Fell used the autobiography in an effort to get the Pennsylvania convention delegation for Lincoln. (The Pennsylvania delegation would be crucial for Adlai Stevenson in the Democratic Convention of 1952.) He succeeded.

The day after the fall of Fort Sumter, Jesse Fell called a meeting of leading citizens of Bloomington to solidify support for Lincoln. Lincoln appointed him a paymaster in the Union Army at Louisville. He died February 25, 1887, and five hundred people, including the Governor, attended his funeral.

5

When Jesse Fell went to Louisville as army paymaster, he took with him as a clerk his young protégé, W. O. Davis (no relation to Judge David Davis). Like Jesse Fell, W. O. Davis was born in Pennsylvania, was a Quaker, and traced his ancestry back to William Penn's time. His father was a prosperous farmer. Like Jesse Fell, W. O. Davis did not want to become a farmer, refused to settle for a country family school, attended several boarding schools, and became a teacher. In August 1858 he went to Bloomington at Fell's invitation to teach in a school Fell had established in his home. Fell was then nearing fifty; W. O. Davis was twenty-one. Davis became Fell's protégé, married one of Fell's daughters, Eliza, and their daughter Helen became the mother of Adlai Stevenson.

The fall that W. O. Davis arrived in Bloomington, 1858, was the year of the Lincoln-Douglas debates. He went to Springfield on a campaign train and met the Governor. His father bought a farm outside Bloomington for Davis and his brother. (Davis later bought out his brother.) In the spring of 1860 Davis joined some thirty-five others from Bloomington in going to the Colorado goldfields. They found little gold but profited by selling their supplies. From Louisville during the Civil War, in his letters to "My dearest little Elsie," Davis complained of his poor health and enjoined her to guard her own health, recurrent themes—one hears much of illness and headaches on both sides of Adlai Stevenson's family. Through Jesse Fell and a Pennsylvania politician, W. O. Davis was appointed a clerk in the federal Internal Revenue Service. He and Eliza Fell were married

on June 17, 1863. Davis found wartime Washington "full of interest" but his health "would not stand the confinement of office work"
and after a few months he resigned and with his bride returned to
his farm.

Eliza Davis was a little less than five years younger than her
husband. She had finished the high school course of State Normal.
She was interested in gardening and riding. A picture of her shows a
round pretty girlish face with gray eyes and hair brushed back
plainly. Her later correspondence with her children and husband is
rather barren and unimaginative. That of her husband, W. O. Davis,
is rich, showing wide-ranging interests. He was a distinguished-look-
ing man, with big eyes and a spade beard. He operated his farm successfully. He, Fell, and a Pennsylvania man bought the *Daily Pantagraph* for $15,000. Davis and his wife Eliza moved to town and
Davis bought sole control. W. O. Davis proved to be a good businessman and newspaper proprietor. The *Pantagraph* is today the only
survivor among some 140 newspapers that have been published in
the Bloomington-Normal area. Most were purely political party or-
gans. "Davis, though a staunch Republican, turned the *Pantagraph*
into a community newspaper *first* and a Republican exponent *last,*"
according to Loring Merwin, who along with his cousin Adlai Stevenson, and their families, inherited the paper and who ran it after the
mid-1930s. "He ran it alone—W. O. Davis, Sole Prop.—for forty
years. He turned it from a struggling country daily into a strong, respected regional newspaper. By the time of his death it had the largest downstate circulation in Illinois." Bloomington, the *Pantagraph,*
and W. O. Davis all prospered. At about the time W. O. Davis
bought the *Pantagraph,* his daughter Helen was born. It was she
who married into the Stevenson family and became the mother of
Adlai E. Stevenson. The *Pantagraph* became a key factor in his life.

6

The first Stevenson to come to America, William Stevenson, came
from the north part of Ireland about 1748. He settled in Pennsylvania, married there, and moved to what later became Iredell
County, North Carolina, near Statesville. Here he raised his family
—he fathered twelve children—and in 1809 died. One of his sons,
James, born March 10, 1768, married Nancy Brevard, related to
the reputed author of the Mecklenburg Resolves of 1775 "suspend-
ing" the authority of the King and Parliament a year before the Continental Congress declared independence. (Of his ancestor's Meck-

lenburg connection, Adlai Stevenson was always very proud.) James Stevenson took his family West in 1813 through the Cumberland Gap and settled in Christian County, Kentucky. They built a log house for school and church. Jefferson Davis, later President of the Confederacy, lived nearby. Abraham Lincoln had been born near Hodgenville. This was not pioneering as Daniel Boone had known it but life was not easy and illness was common. One family letter says, "Must I be the means of conveying to you the melancholic tidings of your father's death? Yes, my sister, he is no more. . . . He did not die as you may suppose with his old complaint but was taken with the common fever of our country, which is the bilious. He was taken the 18th of August and died the 22nd after a violent chill. The fever never rose until the icy hand of death fastened on him and he fell asleep without a struggle or a groan. My dear sister, death has made wide breaches in our three families since we left our native land." Their letters to relatives back in Iredell County, North Carolina, speak their praise for Kentucky. One wrote, ". . . . Brother William, if I could have my wish, a part of it would be to have you situate about two miles west of us . . . where you could get lands plenty . . . at three dollars per acre with an excellent spring on it. . . . There is a friendship among neighbors here that the people in Carolina know nothing about. . . ." And speak, too, of the wrench of parting from their Carolina families. Their letters frequently mention religion, crops, the weather, and the misfortunes of wilderness life. One letter ends, "Clarisa has another son and Tobithe has a son and Malinda has had a son since she came here and the one she brought with her is dead and she is on the way again."

James Stevenson died in 1850. His son, John Turner Stevenson, married Eliza Ann Ewing. She too had been born in Iredell County, North Carolina, and raised in Christian County, Kentucky. Her father had been named Adlai Ewing for his uncle Adlai Osborne; it is here that the name Adlai enters the family.[1] Eliza's second child of seven, Adlai Ewing Stevenson, was born in Christian County, on October 23, 1835. It was he who later became Vice President of the United States. He grew up on his father's farm in Kentucky. He went to school in the same log schoolhouse his father had attended. When he was sixteen, his father lost his tobacco crop to frost; he took his family to Bloomington, Illinois, arriving July 7,

---

[1] It is a biblical name and occurs in I Chronicles 27:29, thus: "And over the herds that fed in Sharon was Shitrai the Sharonite: and over the herds that were in the valleys was Shaphat the son of Adlai."

1852. According to one source, he had owned a few slaves and set them free before leaving Kentucky.

The first Adlai Ewing Stevenson worked at his father's sawmill in Bloomington and taught school to earn money to go to college. He attended Wesleyan University in Bloomington, then with his cousin, James S. Ewing, he went to Centre College at Danville, Kentucky. The president of Centre College was the Rev. Dr. Lewis Warner Green, a distinguished, widely traveled Presbyterian preacher and classical scholar whose wife traced her lineage to a well-known scholar and pre-Revolutionary War soldier, Joshua Fry.[2] Green condemned the French Revolution as "sensational and infidel," deplored "the array of labor against capital," and defended slavery. Green's daughter Letitia and young Adlai Ewing Stevenson fell in love while Stevenson was a student at Centre, but his father died and he was in no position to marry. He returned to Bloomington, studied law, was admitted to the bar in 1858, and set up in practice in Metamora. It is believed that in 1860 he ran for state's attorney on the Regular Democratic ticket, though records have disappeared. The Democratic Party was split three ways that year, and Stephen A. Douglas of Illinois was the presidential candidate of the "Regular" wing. Lincoln carried Illinois and was elected President; Douglas lost both Illinois and the presidency; young Stevenson lost. Stephen A. Douglas died the next year and Stevenson delivered the eulogy at Metamora on July 4. He was only twenty-five but the oratorical flourishes and clichés of his later life seem already set. He closed by saying that Douglas, near death, was asked if he wanted to send his sons any message and replied, "Tell them to obey the laws and support the Constitution." In 1864, Stevenson again ran on the Democratic ticket for prosecuting attorney. That year the Democratic candidate against President Lincoln was General George B. McClellan. Stevenson was identified with him. Worse, he was running in a Republican district. Illinois went Republican that year. Nevertheless, Stevenson was elected. Two years later he married Letitia Green in the home of her married sister, Mrs. Matthew Scott, at Chenoa, some thirty miles from Bloomington.

[2] In 1749, Fry was commissioned, with Peter Jefferson (father of Thomas), to run part of the Virginia-Carolina boundary line. He was commander-in-chief of the militia sent in 1754 to stop French encroachments at the head of the Ohio River but died at Will's Creek and was succeeded by the second in command, George Washington. Fry had made a "Map of the Inhabited Parts of Virginia" (1751), one of the first maps of Virginia, and given an account of frontier settlements. Adlai Stevenson kept the map, or a facsimile of it, on his office wall and often showed it to visitors.

Stevenson's pay as prosecutor was small, his law practice was not rewarding in Metamora, and in 1869, after his term as prosecutor ended, he moved back to Bloomington and formed a law partnership with his cousin, James S. Ewing. Almost from the start their practice prospered. Ewing, too, was a Democrat and he worked to advance Stevenson's political career. After Stevenson became prominent in national politics, Ewing was appointed minister to Belgium. Frequently a two-man law firm contains one politician and one lawyer. In this firm Stevenson was the politician, Ewing the lawyer.

Stevenson's first child, Lewis Green Stevenson, was born August 15, 1868; he became the father of our subject. (He fathered three other children, one of whom died young.) Stevenson made numerous speeches and became a famed raconteur. When he and Ewing gave a banquet for the bench and bar at the close of a term of court in 1873, the *Pantagraph* called it "the social event of the season." In 1874, Stevenson ran for Congress. For a Democrat, the auguries were not good—this was a strong Republican district, Grant was President, Reconstruction had been running its powerful bitter course, the Republicans had controlled Congress by lopsided majorities ever since the war. Republican newspapers attacked Stevenson as "a vile secessionist." Such charges were dangerous to Democrats, fighting to return as a national party for the first time since the war. A former Union Army officer wrote a letter to the editor refuting the charges. Stevenson had many friends, and they worked hard for him. He won—carried even his own Republican county, McLean.

Stevenson was elected twice to Congress—in 1874 and 1878. Both were off years, and both were years in which, although a Republican was in the White House, the Democrats won control of Congress. In Congress, he opposed federal intervention in Texan-Mexican frontier troubles, played a prominent role in the dispute over the Hayes-Tilden election of 1876, and in effect opposed the filibuster (later, as Vice President, he supported the filibuster).

During these years Stevenson was speaking frequently back home. Sometimes his themes reached far beyond the borders of Illinois. On one occasion he said, "I believe that the recent settlement of our controversy with England, by arbitration at Geneva, is the beginning of a new era in the world. Long before another century shall have passed, International Courts will have been established for the adjustment of controversies amongst nations, and war will be known only as a relic of the barbarism of the ages gone by."

Sometimes he sounded like a Populist. Twice, in 1878 and 1880, he ran for Congress on both the Democratic and the Greenback tickets. And in 1878 he won. That year, a depression year, he said, "The cause of this state of affairs, in my judgment, is the ill-advised, vicious, *criminal* legislation of the party in power since the close of the war, in the interest of money-lenders and against the rights and interests of the people." [Applause.] Strong stuff for Bloomington. It enabled him to tread carefully on "the rights of labor"—he ended by promising to appoint a study commission. While attempting to appease Republican voters with appeals to non-partisanship, he launched a heavy attack on Republican monetary policy (though limiting his attack to that policy); and he cloaked the whole in Populist rhetoric which made it seem a good deal more radical than it really was. In winning, he carried his home county by only 19 votes out of 10,000 cast. He received more votes than any other Illinois candidate for Congress. He always got Republican votes. A politician once said of him, "Hundreds of Republicans will vote for him, hundreds of men who hold allegiance to neither party will vote for him, and every Democrat will vote for him, because all know him to be an incorruptible man." The case for his grandson, running for Governor in 1948, as his supporters saw it, could hardly have been better put.

Yet Stevenson was a strong party man. At a Democratic rally he delivered a speech that his grandson would have both admired and scorned: "I firmly believe that your interests, the interests of all the people of these United States, are bound up in the success of that grand old party which came in with Jefferson in the very infancy of our Republic; the party which for fifty-two years of our existence has stood at the helm of State; the party which in all periods of our history has been the bulwark of our Constitution and the faithful guardian of the rights of all the people; the party under whose broad banner the men of all nationalities have been welcomed to share with us this God-given heritage. . . ."

When not politicizing, Stevenson was practicing law and civic affairs in Bloomington. He and Ewing won a $50,000 damage verdict in 1882 for "a young woman of rare beauty" who claimed that a physician in Bloomington during her visit there had "accomplished her downfall through the use of a drug." The Bloomington *Bulletin,* a Democratic newspaper, reported that Stevenson and Ewing "made the most eloquent and able arguments." In 1875, Stevenson delivered the Fourth of July oration from the Bloomington Court House steps "to an immense concourse of people," an oration that must have been duplicated in style and substance on uncounted thousands of courthouse steps. In 1878, Stevenson was petitioned to run for

the Board of Education, the newspaper declaring there was no office
of greater importance "within the gift of the people," a phrase his
grandson would use later. In 1881 he gave a reception at his home
for former President Grant that was called by the Democratic *Bulletin* brilliant and "one of the most delightful" of social events. W.
O. Davis' Republican *Pantagraph* was more restrained. The *Bulletin*
also reported at length a reception the Stevensons gave in 1882 for
their young cousins and nieces—"about 35 of the invited couples of
young ladies and gentlemen of the city's best society" attended, and
so did two members of the landowning Funk family and Mrs. Stevenson's wealthy sister, Mrs. Matthew Scott. Stevenson was combining
politics and society. The coal mine in which the Stevensons were interested became Bloomington's second biggest industry, next to the
railroad shops, employing between two and three hundred men. Its
prime movers were Matthew Scott and Stevenson and his brothers.
In 1871 the miners organized one of the town's first unions and
struck, demanding their own weighman. The company's weighman
is said to have been one of Stevenson's brothers.

In 1881, Bloomington faced a dark crisis, a lynching. On the night
of October 1 a prisoner in the county jail charged as a horse thief
shot and killed the jailor. The leaders of a mob of five thousand broke
into the jail and hanged the prisoner on a nearby elm tree. After it
was over, Stevenson, asked what he thought, said, "I have no hesitation in pronouncing it the most outrageous affair that has ever occured in McLean County. It has brought disgrace upon the fair name
of this city, that only time will wipe out." He condemned the mur-
derer but said he was confident he would have been punished by the
courts—"in a land of law, of courts of justice, there is, there can be,
no excuse for mob violence." The interviewer asked, "Is there any
foundation for the charge that criminals are not punished in this
county?" Stevenson replied, "The charge is without foundation," and
said in no county in the United States had the criminal law been
"more uniformly" enforced. The interviewer asked, "Don't you think,
Mr. Stevenson, that there are many legal technicalities that stand in
the way of the punishment of crime?" Stevenson replied, "The criminal law is the outgrowth of centuries of human experience. . . .
While it has provided for the sure punishment of guilt, it has likewise
reared bulwarks of defence to the innocent. . . . What are the technicalities of which there is complaint?" and he elucidated the Bill of
Rights. "These are some of the safeguards which surround every
citizen. Is there a sane man who would strike down one of them?
They are more precious by far than jewels. And yet these safeguards, as old as our civilization, and as priceless as woman's honor,

are to be brushed like cobwebs from the pathway of those who yearn for speedy justice!" The interviewer asked if disrespect for law and its administrators wasn't increasing. Stevenson said, "I fear this is true, and it is one of the saddest signs of the times." His partner, Ewing, concurred and said, "I have great respect for the men who did what they could to assist the sheriff and other officers of the law on Saturday night. Their names should be remembered," and he named them, including Stevenson.

Stevenson was greatly interested in his genealogy. In 1876, having just completed his first term in Congress, he visited the old Stevenson home in Iredell, North Carolina, and wrote a long letter to his mother about it. It began: "My dear Mother: The dream of my life has been realized. Faith has at length ended in sight. Wings palpable and familiar have succeeded the golden exhalation of the dawn. (I hope you understand just what that is; if you do, I will get you to explain it to me sometime.)" He described "Old Iredell" and Statesville, its buildings, paths, church, cemetery, stores; its people. Stevenson met other men named Adlai. With one he spent an hour or two reading the inscriptions on tombstones. He visited his ancestors' homes. He found the ruins of "the old Ewing place." He collected souvenirs—a piece of pine, a rosebud. He traced lines. "Passing down the street, I saw a sign of 'Wallace Brothers.' Taking it for granted that they were my uncles, I rushed over and found myself in a Jew Clothing Store! It was a different family." He collected family lore and found people who remembered his grandfather. "They are all Presbyterians, most of them well fitted to be ruling elders from the very cradle. . . . These kindred have dwelt upon the same spot, tilled the same old fields, drunk from the same spring and worshipped in the same church their fathers and our fathers did, while we for sixty years have been absent, one generation at rest in the old church yard in Kentucky, another in Illinois, and the third far advanced toward the period of middle life. . . . I saw the identical house in which Brevard and [others] wrote the Mecklenburg Declaration." In this letter we can see portents of his grandson's character—a penchant for rather arch overblown prose yet perspective enough to laugh at it; traces of Toryism and remarks about Jews; reverence for the American past and sensitivity to the places of history; indefatigable tourism; and an abiding interest in genealogy, not simply for its own sake but for what it reveals about one's self and one's nation. Adlai Stevenson got more than his name from Grandfather Stevenson.

Grover Cleveland, elected President in 1884, appointed Stevenson First Assistant Postmaster General. Here he proved his partisanship. The Democrats had not held the presidency since before the Civil War; they were hungry for jobs. The largest reservoir of political patronage was the post office. Stevenson began firing Republican postmasters and replacing them with Democrats so energetically that he became known as "the Headsman." In all, Stevenson replaced some 40,000 Republican postal employees. It is for this that he is, unfairly, principally remembered. Old friends asked him to establish post offices near their scattered homes; he complied, and on at least one occasion established not only a post office but a town to go with it.

In 1888, Stevenson campaigned vigorously for Cleveland, making at least ten speeches in New York and many more in Illinois and North Carolina. Cleveland lost. A lame-duck President, he nominated Stevenson for a federal judgeship. But Republican Senators resented Stevenson's partisan ardor at the post office and refused to confirm him. Stevenson went home to Bloomington.

The year was 1889, and he was fifty-four. Photographs at that time show him round-faced, getting bald, with piercing eyes and a bushy mustache. He was as fair-skinned as a woman. His manners were courtly, his everyday speech rather ornate. He wore a Prince Albert coat (though finally was persuaded to doff it during the hot Bloomington summers) and addressed his wife as "Mrs. Stevenson." One of his daughters once referred to his "dual nature"—his "extreme sensitiveness" and "extreme pain" in adversity and yet his enjoyment of "the most violent political battles, hurling and receiving terrific blows." His granddaughter Buffie has said, "When he lost an election, his wife had to toughen him up. He was hurt. He couldn't understand why they hadn't voted for him." In photographs he looks anxious. He also looks somewhat pompous, and some people in Bloomington considered him so. Though churchgoing and abstemious, he "nipped now and then," as it was called. His friends esteemed him as a "great raconteur," his detractors called him "windy but amusing." He was a Mason and delivered orations at the installation of officers.

His wife, Letitia Green Stevenson, born January 8, 1843, was nearly eight years younger. She was a formidable woman, self-contained, a strong figure who sustained her husband in political vicissitude. Though she looked impressive, she suffered from migraine headaches and, in later years, rheumatism. (The family story is that her son Lewis, the father of our subject, inherited migraine from her.) She was forever training Irish immigrant girls as household servants. She descended from a distinguished family and she became, during the time her husband was Vice President, president general of the National Society of the Daughters of the American Revolution, succeeding Mrs. Benjamin Harrison, the DAR's first president general. She was also an early leader in the National Congress of Mothers which became the National Congress of Parents and Teachers. She was fond of saying that "all nursing mothers should read Robert's Rules of Order," preparing themselves for participation in the DAR and PTA. Her father's home was always filled with books. She herself appears to have been an amateur of the arts, in the manner of ladies of that day, and gave "readings" on such subjects as "Gleanings from Greek Art."

Back from Washington, Stevenson suffered the derision of some of the townspeople. A woman who knew him has remembered, "The Republicans laughed at how Mr. Stevenson was out of office. He had a way of hunching up his shoulders and glowering—they thought he did this because he was being parked in Bloomington again. He had no real occupation here except in the law office—and Mr. Ewing was the main lawyer. The coal office, as we called it, was in the old Gridley Bank. We'd gather in the bank building to wait for the streetcar to [school in] Normal. Mr. Stevenson would come out of his office and come down and wait there with us." He had little more to do.

7

Bloomington by now was a rather spacious, sizable place. The principal club, the Bloomington Club, was founded in 1886 for the announced purpose of promoting "the business interests of the city of Bloomington, and the social enjoyments of the members"; Adlai E. Stevenson and W. O. Davis were members from the beginning, Davis on the first board of directors. Photographs of the period show broad shaded streets, the proud domed courthouse, buggies and blocky brick office buildings and factories, a mahogany-barred saloon, bewhiskered high-collared gentlemen and ladies in forbidding black alpaca. There were several severe churches and a grandiose opera house, and parks, and in them the holiday crowds and public gatherings of a Midwest America that was still young and proud, confident and innocent. The lawns were clipped, the porches wide, the horses sturdy, the carriages handsome, the men imposing. No self-consciousness inhibited these men from adding spires and gingerbread and cupolas and mansard roofs and round bay windows to their homes; the interiors were filled with ornate chandeliers and fringed upholstered furniture; china stood on plate rails and bold framed portraits of ancestors adorned the walls. It was the time of the hitching post and shaded streets, of roll-top desk and garden club. It was a time of great expectations.

By this time, the end of the 1880s, W. O. Davis was certainly one of the town's most prominent citizens. Owner of the *Pantagraph,* he had prospered, and he lived in a splendid ornate Victorian house near Franklin Park. Summers he went to Charlevoix, Michigan, a resort favored by wealthy Chicagoans and people from other Midwest towns. A photograph shows him sitting in a rocker, wearing a sailor cap, bearded, a smile of satisfaction on his face. His face looks kind; it also looks confident and betrays none of Stevenson's anxiety. (But his granddaughter Buffie said, "He was a great neurasthenic—worried about his health all the time.") Over the years he carried on a remarkable correspondence with his wife and children. It shows him to be a literate man, modest in expression, and sensible. Threads run through his letters—a genuine love of children; concern, sometimes too much concern, for their health and safety; and encouragement of cultural interests; an interest in travel; a sure knowledge of the price of everything.

He was strongly Republican; so was the *Pantagraph.* Between elections it liked to appear independent but it never supported a Democrat for President. Davis' health was, in the phrase of those days, "delicate." His granddaughter has written, "Mr. Davis' intense sensitiveness and nerves forced him to live as retired and quiet a life as possible. . . . As the care of the *Pantagraph* increased and taxed his strength, he had a long black leather couch in his office where he could stretch himself out to rest. . . . He read poetry. . . . He was very careful of his expenditures. . . . Among these Quaker families in early Illinois there was a close, warm bond of loving friendship." W. O. Davis was neat almost to mania. Even collar buttons had their place in his bureau drawers. The pencils on the night table had sharp points; his bow tie was always in place, his shirt always spotless.

Davis' wife, Eliza, the daughter of Jesse Fell, had a long nose, pursed lips, and looked patrician and superior. She was a person of less culture than he, with fewer interests and more traces of snobbism, race prejudice, and religiosity. One of her nieces wrote: "She was in every way created to care for the sick. . . . Her husband's father was nursed in his last illness by her; by her own strength and care she brought her husband through a serious fever; for two years her son's critical illness took her every thought."

W. O. Davis and his wife had three children. The first was Hibbard, called Bert. As a young man he fell seriously ill and thereafter walked with a slight limp. He went East to boarding school but did not attend college and succeeded his father in running the *Pantagraph*. He is remembered for his profanity and is said to have been the only man in Bloomington who could swear in the middle of a word.

The second child was Helen, born September 17, 1868. She married Lewis Stevenson and became the mother of Adlai.

Jessie was the third child. She married Louis B. Merwin. In the twentieth century the fortunes of the Stevenson and Merwin cousins intertwine through their joint ownership of the *Pantagraph*.

The Davis sisters, Helen and Jessie, were of different temperaments. Jessie Merwin was slender, retiring, not social, quiet. Helen, Adlai's mother, was strong-willed and could be overbearing. She had a deep sense of honor. She was an accomplished mimic who enjoyed doing take-offs on people. She had a quick wit and a sharp tongue; she could easily do injury with it. In later years Helen was heavy, a large woman with a somewhat queenly look. "She always had positive ideas and there was not much doubt in her mind," a relative recalls. Her parents sent her East to school, to Dean Academy near Boston, and sent her to Europe with an aunt. They stayed more than a year. Helen and her father exchanged long letters. He instructed her to number the pages of her letters and include the day of the week in dating them. He planned to publish some of her letters in the *Pantagraph*. He suggested she bring home "a fine German or French [maid], remember though, I do not want a Count."

That year, 1888, was an election year—Benjamin Harrison defeated Grover Cleveland for President—and a few days after the election Helen's mother told her the political excitement "wore papa out so he remained at home all day yesterday resting and will probably go down to the office again today; his head aches, and he is nervous." W. O. Davis and Adlai E. Stevenson held strong loyalties to opposing political parties. W. O. Davis went to Chicago to rest. He declined to go to Governor Fifer's inaugural—"too much crowd for comfort." Early in 1889 Helen planned to travel to Turkey; her father told her, "You must go over to Scutari so that you may be able to say that you have been in Asia." Helen's father's letters were literate and interesting; her mother seemed preoccupied with food and servants, and her prose is filled with errors. Davis urged Helen to visit Robert Burns's birthplace; his wife wrote, "Some say to wear paper over the stomack is a good thing to keep off sea sickness."

W. O. Davis himself went to Europe early in 1890 for several months. He wrote in June that he had caught cold in Paris and so

been obliged to curtail his sightseeing in London, and he quoted a
Byron poem on London.

8

Helen went abroad with her sister Jessie in 1892. That was the
year the Democratic Party nominated Adlai E. Stevenson for Vice
President of the United States. By that time, Helen and Stevenson's
son Lewis were engaged to be married. They had corresponded
while he was at Exeter and afterward, become secretly engaged in
August of 1891, and had had some sort of understanding for a year
before that. In 1892, Helen decided to let their engagement be
known, not by formal announcement but by openly wearing a gift
from him; and Lewis sent her a discreet hairpin. She exchanged it
for a bracelet, to his joy but also to his consternation—he felt he
himself should select the gift. When Helen returned from Europe in
1893 they were married. In view of all this, it seems odd she would
have chosen to be out of the country when his father was running
for Vice President.

Stevenson led the Illinois delegation to the Democratic National
Convention at the "Wigwam" in Chicago on June 21. The keynote
speaker said, "This mission of the Democratic Party is to fight for
the underdog." Powerful currents were working for change in the
nation. On Western farms, men formed the Populist Party; in Eastern
cities, they organized labor unions; in Chicago, the Haymarket
Riot[3] of 1886 had shaken "the best people." Nor was unrest confined to "a handful of agitators"; demands were rising everywhere
for regulation of the railroads and public utilities and for an end to
corrupt government. The contrast is strong between the turmoil in
the nation and the placid life of "the best people" at Bloomington.

The political parties felt the winds of change. The Democratic
platform denounced centralized government, high tariffs, trusts, corruption in Washington, land giveaways to railroads; it came out in

---

[3] During the eight-hour labor movement in Chicago, conflicts arose between
strikers and police. In protest against the shooting of several workmen, August
Spies, editor of the semi-anarchist *Arbeiter-Zeitung,* announced a mass meeting
at the Haymarket on May 4, 1886. A heavy force of police demanded that the
crowd disperse. Someone threw a bomb among the police, and seven were
killed and many injured. Eight supposed anarchists were convicted and four
were hanged. One killed himself. Governor Altgeld pardoned the three surviving prisoners in 1893, declaring that the trial had been a farce, a view
widely shared.

favor of bimetallism, civil service reform, and rigid enforcement of the Chinese exclusion laws. Grover Cleveland of New York was nominated on the first ballot. Adlai Stevenson delivered Illinois's 48 votes to him, the third biggest delegation. Stevenson himself was nominated for Vice President on the first ballot partly because of party loyalty to the efficient headsman and partly to carry Illinois and hold the silverite vote farther west (minimizing the vote of the new Populist Party). Thus did he fulfill his role as a bridge between the splintered postwar Democratic Party and the Populism of William Jennings Bryan that led to the Bryan-Wilson-Roosevelt mainstream of twentieth-century Democratic liberalism. When Stevenson went home to Bloomington, a big crowd gathered at the railroad station and escorted him home to Franklin Park.

Cleveland and Stevenson were "notified" of their nomination in New York in Madison Square Garden; the audience was estimated at 20,000. On the flag-draped platform the names of Cleveland and Stevenson were arranged in light bulbs; when the names were lit the crowd rose to salute the "illumination." A few minutes later Stevenson went to the platform, nearly bald, his remaining hair white; then Cleveland joined him. Stevenson said: "In the contest upon which we now enter we make no appeal to the passions, but to the sober judgment of the people," words that would echo sixty years later when his grandson accepted a nomination. One newspaper thought Stevenson's nomination "by far the wisest act of the convention." The New York *World* published a campaign jingle:

> *Then up and sing hosannas*
> *And shout them very gladly*
> *For victory is certain*
> *For Grover and for Adlai.*

His son Lewis, then twenty-four, managed his campaign in Bloomington and ran a headquarters in the family home. Stevenson opened his campaign in Bloomington on August 27. His wife went campaigning with him to Indiana. He went down to Christian County, Kentucky, September 2 for a Stevenson Barbecue at the "old Blue Water Spring," on the farm where he was born. He arrived late because his train was derailed. More than 7,000 people attended. The speakers' stand fell down. With the help of a local prompter, he managed to recall men by their first name whom he had not seen for forty years. He sent Cleveland an optimistic report. Cleveland, who had not "the least idea of making a political trip away from home during this campaign," congratulated Stevenson "on the good work you are doing."

Helen Davis, in Europe during the campaign, received a letter from her mother in October. "Mrs. Sterling said she saw Lewis S. [Stevenson] yesterday and he was looking very well—I told her if the campaign lasted long enough he would forget to be sick." Helen's brother Bert wrote: "I met Lou [Lewis Stevenson] on the car one evening some time ago and the way he talked surprised me greatly, and if one has to judge him by that he could be termed very vindictive and unreasonable. Now the idea of him expecting all his republican friends to vote for his father is absurd. I told him that there would be a good many of them vote for his father that would say nothing to them about it, and because a man didn't rush up and tell him so, was no reason why he wouldn't vote for his father. But he flew off the handle and called them hypocrites . . . he said [his father] was sure of election. . . . He thinks the *Pantagraph* is not treating his father right. If you read the paper you can see we very seldom mention his name and when we do we usually say something good."

The last big Democratic rally in Bloomington took place November 4. Stevenson spoke and so did John Peter Altgeld, Democratic candidate for Governor. Stevenson spent Election Day at home. That night when word came that he had won, crowds gathered at his house. Altgeld was elected governor over the incumbent, Fifer; Cleveland and Stevenson carried Illinois (as well as New York); they were elected by a plurality of 372,736. Stevenson said that in Bloomington it was the Swedes and other immigrant workingmen who voted for him, not his well-to-do social friends. His grandson would have cause to make the same lament.

9

When the Vice President-elect left for the inauguration in Washington, "a whole trainload" of his friends went with him. W. O. Davis was not among them. On March 5, the day after the inaugural, Davis wrote Helen this brief decisive paragraph: "The Stevensons are in a blaze of glory this last week and are now in possession of the earth and the fulness thereof. The papers are full of their doing, and their retinue. Most likely four years later they will be in a cave of gloom. It is the pretty certain fate of politicians. *Le roi est mort, vive le roi*—is a cry they must become familiar with—Jeffersonian simplicity has taken to the woods. Still I hope they will enjoy their triumphs. We in Bloomington cannot but feel pleased at their success."

Western farmers who had voted for Cleveland could find little comfort in his inaugural address; he called for "prompt and conservative precaution" to protect a "sound and stable currency." Three months later the panic of 1893 began, an economic disaster unmatched until 1929. Next year Pullman workers struck in Chicago, and Eugene V. Debs came to lead them; Cleveland sent the troops; Governor Altgeld protested; Debs was jailed; the strike was broken. To some it seemed that American society was breaking up. But the impression one gains from memorabilia preserved by the Stevenson family is that these great events hardly rippled the smooth surface of family life. Most of the memorabilia is social. A writer for the *Washington Sketch Book* wrote, "Mrs. Letitia Green Stevenson, the wife of the Vice President, is descended from a long line of distinguished patriots. One of her colonial ancestors was John Washington, the progenitor of George Washington." A photograph of her at that time shows her with hair swept tightly up from her neck and piled high on her head; her eyebrows are raised; she is heavy; she wears a gown with ornate floral collar; her husband, with his bald head and bushy mustache and rather narrow shoulders, scarcely looks a match for her.

The Vice President and his family lived in a suite at the Ebbitt House. He went to the Capitol about 10 A.M., an hour before the Senate convened, to work on his mail, mostly from job seekers and people who wished to lay petitions before the Senate. When the Senate convened, he presided. His terms in Congress had made him familiar with parliamentary procedure. His son Lewis served as his clerk for a time. In his first year he drew unusual attention to his office by refusing to shut off debate on the silver question, and in his final speech to the Senate he said, "In this chamber alone are preserved, without restraint, two essentials of wise legislation and good government—the right of amendment and of debate."

Vice President Stevenson traveled a good deal in the United States during his term. He already knew many wealthy and socially prominent Chicagoans; as Vice President he met more. He made an official visit to San Francisco accompanied by his family, a Chicago judge and his family, the Chief Justice of the Illinois Supreme Court, and the general counsel for the Wabash Railroad and his family. They traveled by private railroad car, passing through the territories of New Mexico and Arizona, stopping at Los Angeles, and, after leaving San Francisco, going home by way of Oregon, Montana, North Dakota, and Minnesota. The Vice President said he had gained "an adequate idea of the vastness" of the nation. San Francisco's greeting was spectacular—a reception flotilla in the bay, a nineteen-gun salute, a formal reception, calls on and from the Governor, sightseeing and visits with friends. George Hearst and his family were friends of the Stevensons. Having made his money in mining, he was laying the foundations of a newspaper empire and had been appointed and elected to the Senate. Their sons, William Randolph Hearst and Lewis Stevenson, were friends.

During the Vice President's first year in office his son Lewis married Helen Davis. Helen returned from Europe that spring; and when their engagement was announced, newspapers called the marriage a "triumph of love over politics." The wedding, large and elaborate, took place in the evening on November 21, 1893, in the Second Presbyterian Church. Governor Altgeld attended; the Secretary of the Navy came from Washington. Nearly all the "better families" of Bloomington were present—Funks, Fifers, Scotts, others. Lewis' best man was from Washington, not Bloomington. Snow and sleet had fallen during the day but the weather turned fair by evening. After the wedding a reception for four hundred was held at the home of the bride's parents, and a mandolin orchestra played for dancing. At the same time Vice President Stevenson gave a reception of his own for the daughter of the Secretary of the Navy, and guests at the "Davis mansion" moved on to the "Stevenson mansion," as the Chicago *Tribune* put it. That night fourteen Bloomington homes were burglarized, "a night when all the city was astir because of the wedding, theatre and balls."

10

The marriage of Helen and Lewis Stevenson was not a happy one. And their problems, and their characters, contain striking parallels to the unhappy marriage of their son Adlai and his own wife.

Helen Stevenson, twenty-five at the time of her wedding, was almost beautiful, with a high forehead, a long neck, a long nose, large rather deep-set eyes with long heavy eyelids. She had a long oval face. She wore her hair piled high. She dressed beautifully in clothes she bought in Paris. She stood tall and dark and straight.

A photograph of Lewis Stevenson taken at that time shows him wearing a wing collar and ascot tie with stickpin and high-buttoned coat and flaring white pocket handkerchief, the clothes, one might say, of a dandy. His forehead was high, his eyes wide and bold, his nose a bit heavy. He wore a mustache. He was twenty-five, handsome, and looked as though he thought so. Somehow in such pictures, and in others taken later in their life, Lewis Stevenson never looked as impressive as his wife Helen.

Lewis Green Stevenson had attended Phillips Exeter Academy in New Hampshire but had not gone to college. His shoulder had been injured by a shotgun recoil or explosion and thereafter his health was always considered "very delicate." His mother had spoiled him.

A woman who knew Lewis and Helen Stevenson well recalls, "Helen was a brilliant girl. Very high-strung. No one ever thought she and Lewis would get along together—and they didn't. They were too much alike. Helen had nervous prostration for a while after she was first married, and her mother took care of her." Lewis journeyed to Japan. Helen's father, W. O. Davis, bought the house at 1316 East Washington Street in Bloomington and gave it to them, saying, in effect, that he would do no more for them. Helen and Lewis were childless for nearly four years. Mrs. George Hearst, by now a widow, hired Lewis to manage the Santa Rita copper mine in New Mexico for the Hearst estate. On July 16, 1897, Helen bore their first child, Elizabeth Davis Stevenson, called Buffie, in her parents' home in Bloomington. A few months later, Helen, the baby, and a nurse joined Lewis in New Mexico. Lewis told her not to bring finery or bric-a-brac to the mining country. New Mexico's climate was thought to be good for Lewis' health, too. During their first year there, Helen wrote to her father, "Lewis has given his daily duties the slip and gone hunting with some 'half-breed' neighbors. I am glad, for the change will do him good. His only trouble now is occasional headache which I think is caused largely by nervousness." Helen's mother wrote to her frequently that winter—advice on the baby's health and her own, advice on how to comport herself with her husband ("I hope you will always go to your meals with a pretty waist on and never neglect your personal appearance when your husband is around this is one mistake I made"), complaints about the maid, advice that Helen "try to procure a Chinaman or a Jap," as a cook. Early in 1898, Helen's mother visited Helen and Lewis, and Lewis' father, the Vice President, now out of office and back in Bloomington, wrote, "We find our house all right—but oh! how empty! Not a child with us." Lewis traveled a good deal in the West. His mother, addressing him as "Precious Boy," wrote to him in Albuquerque, "We were so relieved to know that you are well and contented. We are also glad that you had decided not to be separated any longer than necessary from Helen and [the baby] Elizabeth.

But all these questions you must decide for your own dear self and for your loved ones. I do want you, though, to be much with the wonderful Elizabeth. She will need the tenderest and most careful training. The child has inherited so much from both parents, that they can hardly hold her responsible but themselves for her intense nature. She had unusual strength in many directions. She has physical, mental, nervous, strength, great self-will, energy beyond degree, self confidence, absolute [?] and patience, forbearance, gentleness beyond expression should be used in her rearing." The child Buffie was then only a year old.

Lewis told W. O. Davis he had been prospecting and, confidentially, was making profits on the side from smaller mines in which he owned interests without interfering with his Hearst position—"There will be big money in it." By early 1899 he told Davis he was "making several hundred dollars a month besides my salary" and had "salted" away $10,000. But, he wrote, he was not "strong," and he hoped Davis and his own father would intercede with President McKinley to get him appointed an army paymaster—"I don't want to spend my life in mining camps."

Helen and Lewis appear to have been separated intermittently for some time. In 1899, Helen wrote to Lewis:

I do love you and so much that sometimes I think I cannot wait to *see* and *talk* and feel your presence! Today, being obliged to remain in bed, I have had a long sweet dream of all we want to do next winter. If only you can manage to have us in Silver City and yet to be with you. If not, I am about tempted to go out to the mine. . . .

The [letter] I had last nite [from you] written the day before your birthday was written in a tone I don't quite understand. . . . I regret indeed, my love, if you are feeling old and dissatisfied. [He was then thirty-one.] For it is the first step to inquietude and irritability that will cause you much more age than the years. Now I am feeling very young and I am not going to allow years to age me—nothing but unhappiness or wrong doing will be able to do that.

I wish my love could compensate you somewhat for all you feel you have lost in life, but if it can't—dear, tender, beautiful little Elizabeth's life and love ought to. . . . Perhaps, and I pray with all my heart it may be so—your real happiness and pleasure in life is just commencing.

Please do not grieve or resent the years already gone. It will only make them more unsatisfactory and the Christian way to do is "to look up and not down", you know. So God bless you dear and believe with me in a golden future all of your making. With all good heart, your wife.

In 1899, Hearst transferred Lewis to Los Angeles. He and Helen lived in a rented house there. Helen's mother, Eliza Davis, died January 21, 1900. Helen could not return for the funeral; she was pregnant. There in Los Angeles, on February 5, 1900, the child was born and named Adlai Ewing Stevenson. Grandfather Stevenson wrote to the baby March 9, six pages of praise of Helen and Lewis and their ancestors and affection for the infant. In it can be seen the adoration that formed so important a part of Adlai Stevenson's early years, one of the forces that shaped him.

11

That year, 1900, Grandfather Stevenson was again nominated for Vice President by the Democratic Party. This time the presidential candidate was William Jennings Bryan. Bryan and Stevenson, in their acceptance speeches, struck a new note—foreign affairs. While Stevenson demanded laws to repeal Spanish-American wartime taxes, restrain trusts, curb monopolies, and end railroad rate discrimination, he made it clear, as did Bryan, that "the paramount issue" of the campaign was foreign policy. Stevenson denounced imperialism forthrightly. He denounced the new Puerto Rican law and Republican policy toward the Philippine Islands. He urged "wise," not "aggressive," territorial expansion. He campaigned on the issue he declared paramount, "Republic or Empire?" It was a position of which his grandson could have been proud.

The Republicans gladly accepted the challenge. With William McKinley and Theodore Roosevelt their candidates, they cried, "Don't haul down the flag." Stevenson campaigned hard, and in a major address at Madison Square Garden in New York in mid-October drew the line clearly: "The Republican Administration is upon trial. Shall imperialism, the policy of aggression and conquest, receive the indorsement of the American people?" As the historians Morison and Commager have noted, however, the real issue was not imperialism but prosperity: the Republican Party was in power, the country was prosperous and contented and weary of idealism.

One thinks of 1952 or 1956.

12

During the next six or seven years the infant Adlai's father Lewis changed jobs and moved often, living in, among other places, Los Angeles, Berkeley, Denver, and Battle Creek, Michigan (where he was interested in a health food venture). In 1904 he was a delegate to the Democratic National Convention from Michigan. Sometimes Helen accompanied him; more often she did not. In 1906 he went alone to Europe, entered a sanitarium in Germany, changed doctors and went to Lausanne for treatment to "keep all unpleasant thought of you out of my mind," and, before returning home, bought miniatures for "our art treasures" and visited Cairo, telling Helen, "Your last letter pleased me greatly. It was really the first evidence of affection you have shown in a long time & made me very happy. It's all been so strange, so unnatural & untimely. We can never go through such an ordeal again & I hope to God it may never start. I love you my Helen with all my heart. . . . I'll soon be home. We will then begin anew." He worked on Hearst's San Francisco paper for training in the newspaper business, then was made assistant manager of Hearst's Los Angeles paper, the *Examiner*. Once, living in Berkeley while Lewis was in Los Angeles, Helen told her father, "I'll agree to [live] any place so that I may be settled in my own house." Summers she and the two children visited her father in Bloomington and Charlevoix. He bought a farm for her, 158 acres in Indiana along the Wabash River. His letters indicated that he was aware that Lewis did not appear to be settling down, that he was sympathetic, and that he was trying to be helpful. Grandfather Stevenson's letters indicate little more than his own adoration for his grandson.

After the San Francisco earthquake in 1906, Helen and the children returned to Bloomington to stay, and after his trip to Europe, Lewis joined them. Adlai was then six years old. Although his parents took him traveling a good deal during the ensuing ten years, he spent most of his time in Bloomington. He played there, he went to school there, he was surrounded by grandfathers and aunts there, he grew up there.

He lived in the house at 1316 East Washington Street. It was about a mile straight out shaded Washington Street from the courthouse, a big roomy two-story clapboard house, later stuccoed, set back from the street on a lot about 100 feet wide by 750 feet deep. At the end of the back yard was a fence and beyond that a cow pasture and creek; today the cow pasture has become the country club golf course. Adlai used to crawl through the fence and go looking for crawfish in the creek. His mother had a certain creative bent (so, later, did Adlai's wife) and it came out in landscaping, decorating, and choosing clothes. She curved the straight front walk, moved the steps to the end of the porch, curved the driveway and its shrubbery border. Helen was a tree planter (as her grandfather, Jesse Fell, had been, and as her son Adlai became) and planted the driveway with Russian olive and Lombardy poplars. She put a gingko tree and a pine by the front porch. In the back yard were raspberry bushes and a vegetable garden, an enormous elm near the garage where Adlai and his playmates built a tree house. One of Adlai's chores was to pump rainwater from a back-yard cistern for his mother to wash her hair.

Indoors, the rooms were dark, the woodwork dark, the portieres dark, the ceilings high, the furniture heavy. The living-room walls were covered with gray grass cloth. The living room had a big bay window with stained glass panes, a white-tiled gas grate fireplace, a long red runner, and in front of the fireplace a monkey skin and a tiger skin that Lewis bought in Japan. The living room was cluttered with objects of art, bric-a-brac, and furniture Lewis and Helen brought back from their travels—a Florentine miniature that Helen brought home before she married, an oil painting that Lewis brought from Europe, a Buddha, candelabra. The sofa in the bay window had come from the Davis house in Pennsylvania. The Stevensons were very proud of their belongings, as they were of their travels. Adlai's sister Buffie has said, "My early recollections are of those stairs," gesturing toward the dark stair well near the front door, "and of trunks going up and down those stairs." One receives the impression the Stevensons were somewhat apart from the rest of the town.

The library behind the living room was lined with books, especially "sets" of books, the collected works of Goethe, Kipling, Burns, Prescott, Parkman; and books from the library of the Rev. Dr. Lewis Warner Green, some in French. Pictures of ancestors adorned the walls. On one wall was a coal- or wood-burning fireplace of green tile and black iron with a wooden mantel. At Christmas, 1909, Grandfather Stevenson presented Lewis and Helen with a thirteen-volume set, *The Real America in Romance,* edited by Edwin Markham; the legend arose that young Adlai read all thirteen volumes; it is doubtful. Summers in Charlevoix, Grandfather Davis read poetry to Adlai and Buffie; in Bloomington, Helen read to them. This reading aloud made of Adlai an aural man: lifelong he learned far more from listening than from reading, and when he read he sometimes moved his lips.

The dining room was decorated with prints Lewis brought from Japan. Ornate china stood on a plate rail. The walls were covered with canvas, the woodwork was pine, the floor oak. A silver service and silver candelabra stood on the sideboard. In an upstairs hall was a chest, a Fell heirloom filled with genealogical books and family memorabilia. Helen and Lewis occupied separate bedrooms.

The attic was capacious, finished, and varnished. The maid slept up there; young Adlai and his sister Buffie played there. It was filled with trunks and the effluvia of Helen's and Lewis' life—rock samples Lewis brought from Colorado, Helen's wedding gown (Buffie as a child dressed up in it), a sewing machine, rugs and draperies, a marble statue of a naked lady on a lion that Grandfather Stevenson gave to Helen, a discarded dressing table (though the Stevensons never really discarded anything with finality), and, later, Helen's finery—a Parisian evening cape of velvet and moleskin and chiffon, a moleskin hat to match, a blue net sequined evening dress, handmade silk dresses, ostrich plumes, hats of straw and velvet.

The Stevensons always had a maid, sometimes imported. One was French. A Bloomington woman, Alverta Duff, was a housekeeper and a member of the household most of her life; she was part Indian and part Negro, and family legend had it that her father had been brought to Bloomington from the South on the underground railroad by Jesse Fell. The Stevensons usually had a Negro man working for them. One was called Sambo; Helen brought him up from New Orleans; in the winter he slept in the basement and in the summer he slept outdoors under the trees. Once Lewis plotted to frighten him by wrapping himself in a sheet to resemble a ghost. The Stevensons thought of their servants as "faithful family retainers." Marietta Tree, a liberal intimate of Adlai, years later said, "He told me all about the 'family retainers,' the Negroes. They conditioned his attitude toward Negroes for a long time." (Eleanor Roosevelt's upbringing taught her similar attitudes. Her commitment to civil rights did not appear until after her husband became President. Furthermore, it must not be forgotten that, whatever Stevenson's early upbringing, in public policy when he became assistant to the Secretary of the Navy and Governor of Illinois, he made a strong pro-civil rights record.)

A picture of the mature Helen makes her appear patrician. She was wearing a blue tweed suit and an Irish lace blouse and a lorgnette on a chain. Her eyes were a mixture of gray, blue, and green. (Lewis' eyes were pure blue. So were Adlai's.) She sang and played the piano, took horseback riding lessons, bought lace abroad and brought it home to have a seamstress sew it. She was very orderly. If it rained, she hurried out to lower the awnings. She let nothing appear "run down," deteriorating. If something broke, she had it repaired at once. One kept one's property up. She kept her bank account in her head, always knew how much money she had and in which bank. She was, her daughter said later, "careful and tight," traits her son inherited. She took a long time to dress for dinner; Adlai and Buffie used to watch her don her jewelry, her switch and puffs. Though raised a Quaker, she became interested in Christian Science. She worried a great deal about her "nerves." She spent weeks and months in various sanitariums, health resorts, which were "all the rage" at that time; later she spent months in mental institutions. Somehow her surviving belongings carry an air of delicacy, an ethereal quality, an aura of electric automobiles and smelling salts. She wore high lace collars. She tended to dominate conversations, to be flighty, to hold the center of the stage. She had a bad temper and hurt people. A relative has said, "Helen was a terrible snob. As far as I know, she was not artistic or poetic—she was interested in the arts, though not involved." She was considered by some "brilliant but unpredictable and not too reliable." She has been called "very striking and handsome and dashing" but not beautiful.

During Adlai Stevenson's political years, his sister Buffie (and he) drew a happy picture of their parents' marriage, understandably enough; but after his death Buffie said with considerable courage, "My parents were both too high-strung for it ever to be a smooth marriage. They were always moving around, too. My father was struggling for financial security. When Father was angry, Mother would go to her bedroom and be sick, lying in her bed, and I'd nurse her. I'd keep the others out and make her cocoa. Adlai was quick, like Father. I am, too. I've seen Adlai yank a horse back. Later he learned to control his temper. My mother's happiest years were at Charlevoix. Her husband was jumpy and flying from one thing to another." Marietta Tree recalled, "Adlai talked to me about his mother and father, about his mother especially. He said she always talked about how ill she was all the time. About how he had to chew every mouthful a certain number of times when he was a boy. Of course, that's why he never chewed anything when he grew up. From what he told me, she strikes me as a pampered Southern belle. She used to be massaged every day. He told me how she was massaged in her bed and he used to watch her. Then once in Lausanne he showed me the hotel room they had occupied on those trips. He loved those trips. She had ideas about how ladies and gentlemen should behave. She lived—there is a phrase in French for it—you know, above one's station. There doesn't seem to be anything genuine about her."

Perhaps one of the most revealing things ever said about Helen's relationship to her children is to be found in a letter Buffie wrote to Adlai at the time their mother died. Buffie had said many years earlier she hoped she herself would die when her mother died; her mother's death crushed her. She told Adlai that the three of them —Adlai, Buffie, and their mother—had had a relationship so intimately binding that no one could break into it. She reminisced about her childhood—how she used to touch her mother's things, get into her bed at night when she was afraid, sit on her bed to watch her dress for a party, watch her brush her long hair, dress up like a nurse and nurse her when she was ill, marvel at the care she took of her belongings. But the most telling sentence in the letter is the one about the intimate binding relationship that no outsider could penetrate. It not only says much about their relationship and about Adlai Stevenson's mother's influence on him; it also says much about his parents' relationship to each other.

Lewis Stevenson never really "amounted to much." In his early adult life, in "delicate" health, he had been dependent: had clerked for his illustrious father and worked in his father's coal office and worked for Hearst and dabbled in politics. In Bloomington as an adult, he managed farms, mainly for his wife and his mother's wealthy sister, Mrs. Matthew Scott. The Scott farms were operated on a tenant system. The tenant provided the tools and labor; the landlord provided the house and half the seed corn; they divided the crop equally. Or the arrangement might be a straight rental. The manager visited the farm periodically to see how the tenant was getting along, make plowing contracts, help plan crop rotation, collect the money when the corn was sold, audit the accounts, disburse the money. This was Lewis Stevenson's work. He came to dislike it. A neighbor boy who drove for him for a time has recalled, "He always told me to drive fast and he just stopped a few minutes at each farm." Sometimes he would camp out overnight on a farm, taking young Adlai with him. Occasionally Lewis felt rewarded: he once wrote that he wanted his aunt to know what he had done with her farms, for "I am very proud of it." He acquired something of a reputation as an early "scientific farmer" but the truth was that he hired a young man as his assistant and, at least in later years, the young man did much of the work. He detested Lewis.

Lewis suffered from migraine headaches which sometimes lasted three or four days. "He was always getting into things," Buffie remembers. "He was a promoter." Helen's farm on the Wabash River flooded; Lewis lobbied in the Illinois legislature for a bill to change the course of the river. He started one promotion scheme after another—health food at Battle Creek, a theatrical venture, a proposal to publish cookbooks, a scheme to create a cultural center or opera house in Chicago, and a scheme to promote Zeppelins in the United States. He was stage-struck all his life.

Lewis Stevenson never made much money. When he died he left an estate of $174,333, nearly half of which consisted of a farm in McLean County his father had given him, the farm in Indiana that Helen's father had given her, and a farm in Iowa. Buffie has said, "We didn't get to Europe until Grandfather Davis died and left Mother some money." Helen paid the household bills. Lewis was extravagant. He had his shirts and suits handmade. He would return from a trip East or to Chicago with a gold bracelet or a silver pincushion for Helen; she would tell him she didn't need it.

Like his father, Lewis was considered a great raconteur. A relative has recalled, "His wife led him on, though she had heard all the stories. He was always repeating himself to different sets of guests. He could keep a crowd chuckling. The kids liked him. But he had a bad temper. So did Mrs. Stevenson. He never stayed in any one school or any one thing very long. He early became bemused with politics. From then on his life consisted of politics or temporary family jobs or semi-political jobs. He'd get an appointment to some commission or other. He was a completely spoiled only son. He was a charmer, he was entertaining as all get-out—but the next morning he'd be swearing at Helen like all get-out. If you were in the neighborhood you'd hear it. But he was nice to the children."

Lewis was not well liked by his fellow townsmen, and he disdained the small town and left it whenever possible. He had, after all, lived in Washington while his father was Vice President, as well as in California. Through his father's political connections, he knew people around the country, and he preferred their company to that of Bloomingtonians. Buffie later recalled, "Mrs. Lewis [the wife of J. Hamilton Lewis, United States Senator from Illinois] was a very good friend of Father's. Father went to Washington and Mrs. Lewis adored seeing him there. She always said there was nobody like that Lewis Stevenson. Father was very keen about knowing the key people, the right people—one thing led to another—one person led to another—he had learned this. When I came home from a trip and said that I had been with Mrs. McCormick, Father was very interested. This is the big world. Adlai learned to use people from Father."

Lewis had a cleft chin and a bald head. In nearly all his photographs he seems to be making an effort to look "distinguished." Somehow there is something almost untrustworthy about his appearance. Perhaps it is because of what he was—a promoter. In photographs with the children he looks authoritarian; in photographs with his wife he looks less so. She was probably abler than he. She was probably also disappointed in him. "She came from a family where accomplishment mattered a great deal," a relative has said. Once Lewis brought a mummy home from Egypt; Helen thought it dirty and revolting, refused to have it around the house, and gave it to the local historical society. Lewis had a shoe collection he assembled while traveling—shoes from Japan, Egypt, Korea, Holland.

He appears to have been ridden by fears. He kept a gun under the bed and at least once, when someone rang the doorbell late at night, he opened the window and fired. One night somebody took his Locomobile out of the garage and drove it away, then brought it back. Lewis became convinced that a boy who lived two doors away, Hesketh Coolidge, whom Lewis paid thirty-five cents an hour to drive for him, had "stolen" the car; he took his gun and went to the Coolidge house and accused Hesketh. Hesketh was innocent. The incident ended in no more than angry words but it did not improve relations between the Stevensons and their neighbors.

Helen and Lewis Stevenson often made Helen's sister, Jessie Merwin, the butt of their wit; her elder son, Dave Merwin, resented it. They turned their ability to wound on each other. In later years Lewis may have given up the battle; a man who knew them then has recalled that Helen was "flighty, the center of things, an actress type, she had a flair," but that Lewis was quiet—"after twenty years of living with her you learn to be quiet." A woman who knew them much of their lives has said, "I always felt sorry for Buffie and Adlai —their parents were so uncongenial. I don't think those two children were very happy. Their mother and father did not live together a great deal." A relative has said that their sexual life together ended "very early."

Adlai Stevenson himself late in his life once told a confidante that his parents "fought all the time." He talked more about his grandparents and about Bloomington than about his own parents.

At the same time, the picture drawn during his lifetime of a home "filled with love" in a tranquil town cannot be wholly without truth. The letters that Helen wrote to her son show she loved him deeply. Indeed, if anything, she loved him too much. Furthermore, his grandparents adored him. They not only said so; they showed it— spent countless hours with him while he grew up. Nor is there any evidence whatsoever that his father did not love him; on the contrary, some evidence shows he did. Just as his parents' quarrels must have had some effect on him, so must the love surrounding him.

Many parallels exist between his parents' life and his own. Everyone spoke of the charm and the lack of serious purpose of Lewis Stevenson; Adlai Stevenson too learned to use charm and sometimes seemed frivolous. Lewis knew the importance of "connections"; so did Adlai. Lewis and Helen had a brilliant society wedding followed by a miserable married life; so did Adlai. Adlai's mother wrote poetry, struck poses, wore high-fashion clothes, seemed flighty, held the center of the stage; so did his wife. His mother came from a more locally distinguished family, though less famous nationally, than did his father; just so with Adlai's wife. In Adlai's childhood he caught the scent of public greatness and private misery; his own life went much that way.

One mystery, though, is difficult to explain: the strength of character, the immense courage, that carried Adlai Stevenson whole through great adversity in his manhood. Where did he get that? One thinks first of his grandfather, W. O. Davis. Looking to the atmosphere of his boyhood is less rewarding—unless it came from the unremitting adoration he received from his family and their almost tribal certitude that he was marked for greatness.

What was the position in Bloomington of his family during his boyhood? Unquestionably the Davises and Fells had been among the first families of Bloomington. Lewis' father, though less wealthy, had been nationally known so he too must be ranked with the Fells and Davises. A knowledgeable Bloomington man has said, "Helen and Lewis Stevenson were in the top select circle not because of money but because of Fell and because Lewis Stevenson's father was Vice President. That's enough for a town this size." But the Stevensons, Helen and Lewis, were less wealthy than such large landowning families as the Funks, David Davis, and the Matthew Scotts. One family owned on the order of 40,000 acres—40,000 acres of the richest farmland on earth. Such a holding could have been worth something like $28 million by the time Adlai Stevenson died.

Helen and Lewis Stevenson considered themselves superior to Bloomington. Buffie once said, "When I was a child the other children kidded us—'She says cahn't and shahn't and so on.' Maybe their parents said, 'That Helen Stevenson's a snob.' Now," with a trace of bitterness, "they all go abroad and sign 'Bloomington, Illinois,' on the hotel registers and everyone recognizes it," meaning that she believed Adlai had made Bloomington world-famous but, like his parents, been unappreciated in his home town. Of Buffie, Lewis Stevenson always said, "For God's sake don't let her stay in Bloomington and marry a Funk."

Helen's and Lewis' friends in Bloomington were well-to-do people, nearly all Republicans. They were businessmen, lawyers, bankers, landowners. One of them once said of Paul Douglas, the liberal intellectual Democratic Senator from Illinois, "Douglas has always been for the underdog, not for the people that think." He said it without rancor, offhandedly; it is the sort of "social" remark one makes at a social gathering, a comfortable, if rather idiotic, axiom universally accepted within that closed Republican upper-class society. Newton N. Minow, a liberal Democrat, a law partner of Adlai Stevenson in the 1950s, once said, "He always said he was a small-town boy, he always said he felt in Lake Forest like a country bumpkin, but I never believed it until I saw the house and the life there in Bloomington."

To know Bloomington, to know his home and his family, is to raise large questions about Adlai Stevenson. Why as a man did he constantly ask for solitude and peace and yet not really seek them? Because he had learned as a child they were unattainable? Why in politics did he swim upstream, against the Bloomington current? Inherited membership in the Democratic Party, in part; but was it also because he felt rejected by Bloomington—his father a disappointment, his mother regarded as a snob, their private life unhappy, his sister loving but strong and sometimes domineering, and he himself, as we shall see, hurt by the meanness of the small town, scarred by a fatal accident, and unable as a young man to gain control of the prize he wanted, the *Pantagraph?* The small town gave him little. His parents traveled restlessly, seeking the great world. He too sought his place there.

13

The strongest impression one receives from studying the family papers is that his family's frequent travels, usually separately, had one demonstrable consequence for Adlai Stevenson, intermittent schooling, and one plausible one, alienation of affection. A picture emerges of a devoted but sometimes absent and often unwell mother, a frequently absent father, a doting histrionic Grandfather Stevenson, and a loving practical Grandfather Davis. Adlai's own earliest letters, written between the ages of ten and thirteen, show how often his mother and father were, separately, away from him and how much he missed them. His sister Buffie as an adult once recalled, "If they wanted to take us out of school and go South for the winter, they did. They knew how to do things. Sometimes they got teachers fired." Often a maid or nurse traveled with them. Adlai's first letter—or at least the one his mother called his first—was written from New Orleans and says, in full:

> Dear Mrs. Stone: —
> I am going to school.
> Buffie has a cold, and can't go to school.
> We are coming home soon.
> How is the weather there?
> I wrote it myself.
> With much love
> Adlai

His father went to Europe in 1906 to consult a "famous" neurologist he had heard of about his severe, recurring, mysterious headaches; Adlai and Buffie and their mother went to Winter Park, Florida, with Grandfather Davis. There Adlai's mother was sick with a lingering cough; Grandfather Davis blamed it on the cold damp night air. (Changes of air and their effects on health figure prominently in family correspondence.) Adlai started school in Florida. His grandfather wrote, "He was a pretty raw scholar, had no idea of the rules. . . . On his return home at noon, he felt quite a little chesty, and told of his experience chiefly in the rough house, at the recess at 10 o'clock—He said, 'there is one boy I must get rid of, so I swatted him some good ones on the slats and soaked him a warm one in the face and was oftener on top than I was under.'" Buffie had a private tutor. Helen's health did not improve, and she ended in a Southern sanitarium, but its regime was too rigid, and Grandfather Stevenson sent her with a nurse to a relative in Augusta. Grandfather Davis told Lewis, "Helen is a good deal better, chiefly nervously weak now from the excitement of her destructive illness." Adlai himself wrote to his father about this time:

> Dear Father
> I hoped you will come home soon?
> I will make you a pictire[4] of a cow.

He drew the cow, which takes more space than the letter itself, and signed himself "Adlai E. Stevenson." Now he was seven.

---

[4] Stevenson was, lifelong, a poor speller. We shall omit the word "sic"; the reader should understand that misspellings and other errors in corresponence are not typographical errors but appeared in the original text.

Summers, in those years, Adlai went to Grandfather Davis' cottage at Charlevoix, Michigan. Joseph Bohrer, who grew up with him in both Bloomington and Charlevoix, has said that women took their children to Charlevoix for the summer and their husbands visited them when they could. As the children grew older they played tennis all morning, swam all afternoon, went boating, and attended dancing school. Bohrer recalls, "Adlai as a kid was not a very good tennis player or golfer or baseball player. But he kept improving. I could beat him at golf and tennis easily when we were kids, but by the time he became Governor I couldn't." Buffie has said, "We went to Charlevoix every summer until [Grandfather Davis] died. Then Mother didn't want to go back. When she did go back, she rented. Adlai loved Charlevoix." Yet as a man he stopped going there. One summer his mother took a Bloomington teacher to Charlevoix whose duty it was to take Adlai and Buffie on "nature walks." Adlai was also given "carpenter lessons." Family photographs show him playing in a sandbox, show sailboats and pine trees, shirtwaist dresses and wooden cottages and wooden piers. Every Thursday night there was a picnic, with as many as ninety Bloomington people present and a Negro servant to plank the fish. At Charlevoix, Adlai first met Hermon Dunlap Smith and James Douglas; Smith became a wealthy Chicago insurance executive, a principal supporter of Stevenson for Governor and President, and lifelong friend; Douglas became a college friend, a wealthy Chicago lawyer, government official in the Hoover and Eisenhower administrations. At Charlevoix, Buffie played with a girl who later married Dean Acheson, Truman's Secretary of State.

Grandfather Davis spent some of his winters in New Orleans, sometimes taking Adlai and Buffie and their mother with him. In 1910, Adlai wrote to his mother from a train on which he and Buffie were traveling to New Orleans: "The train is a very nice one and my sister and my selfe are having a fine time altho I did not wont to go at first." He sounded a little sad.

Grandfather Davis' letters to Helen were filled with concern about her health. Many years later Adlai Stevenson corresponded with a person who described himself as a consulting psychologist, Lydiard H. W. Horton. Adlai addressed him as "doctor" but his stationery did not show him to be a physician. Horton attempted psychotherapy with both Helen and Lewis in 1908–9. He saw them in Bloomington and Charlevoix and kept in touch with the family intermittently through the years. In discussing Helen Stevenson's case he wrote a good deal about hysteria. He may have attempted hypnosis on Lewis. Helen preserved for at least twenty-five years a clipping from a 1908 issue of the *Ladies' Home Journal* containing an article on mental health Horton recommended. In later life, in 1927, Helen and Lewis visited a clinic together. Horton told Adlai Stevenson Helen had been under chronic mental strain since 1908.

Lewis wrote a letter to Helen in September of 1908 accusing her of flirting with Horton. It said, "I can stand this no longer. . . . You have deceived me persistently & with deliberate intention. I have known—felt it instantly all the time & I was never with Horton for one moment without feeling the deepest loathing for him for being a party to this. Unless I know the truth I shall punish him relentlessly and regardlessly. As for you my love made me feel the time would come when you would see all in a different light. That you haven't & that you let me go away after all that had passed between us is too much for me. I can forgive & forget anything willingly but the thought that you want to and believe you are deceiving me & want to continue it. This has determined me on my course. . . . I found at the Annex your letter. . . . That immediately after writing such a letter you should select a dark night to spend from 4 to 9:30 p.m. alone on the Beach with H. is to me bad. No, Helen, you don't flirt—'only a little bit'. . . . I shall be satisfied with nothing but a full, frank & complete statement from you. . . . I valiently promised your father I would not quarrel & I will not but I'll get at the truth of this matter regardless of appearances, anyone's feelings, or legal code. I never felt so in my life, Helen. Write to me *honestly* for God's sake."

He wrote again: "I am ill. With my mind full of our trouble I am unable to sleep at all & I can't keep this up long. Buffie can give me what I most need & I beg you to let her come. If I had her in my arms this minute it would be everything to me. . . . I am determined to know everything—cost what it may, & God knows it has cost enough already. . . . That you should have spent three nights on the beach with [Horton] is bad. I don't recall an occasion when I was able to get you to go with me rather than put the children to bed. No, you didn't flirt! I can't but believe Horton hypnotyzed you."

14

While Grandfather Davis read to Adlai and took him on long summer and winter vacations, Grandfather Stevenson wrote him doting letters and, when Adlai was in Bloomington, told him endless tales, mostly about his forebears and his term as Vice President. Years later Adlai said, "We went there for Sunday dinner as a rou-

tine. Grandfather sat at one end of the table in the Prince Albert
coat and white tie and Grandmother at the other end in a black silk
dress. . . . There was always grace—I felt unreasonably long. . . .
Invariably the discussion of the sermon slipped into stories by
Grandfather and Mother, and the dinner became so lively that even
small boys could sit still until the inevitable vanilla ice cream arrived." Grandfather Stevenson's library contained many "historical
treasures," as the phrase went—curios from Alaska; a photograph
of President Cleveland and Vice President Stevenson; Grandfather
Stevenson's framed commission as First Assistant Postmaster General; the cedar box that contained the electoral vote cast for McKinley; a silver plate commemorating his vice-presidential visit to San
Francisco. Adlai Stevenson thought later that the disposition of the
library was "something of a mystery"—parts of it were at the McLean
County Historical Society, parts scattered among the family, but
most, apparently, had been thrown away. But it all entered Adlai's
consciousness as a boy and stayed there. He learned history from a
man who had helped a little to make it and who enjoyed relating it.

During these early years of the twentieth century, Grandfather
Stevenson delivered such occasional orations as one on Stephen A.
Douglas to the Illinois State Historical Society, and he occupied such
honorific positions as an incorporator of the Lincoln Centennial Association. Now in 1908 he ran for Governor of Illinois on the Democratic ticket. The auguries seemed good—the Chicago *Daily News*
endorsed him in the primary, the party was united, he campaigned
hard. But it was a Republican year—William Howard Taft won the
presidency and carried Illinois by 179,122 votes. Stevenson's Republican opponent for Governor won by only 23,164. It was Grandfather Stevenson's last campaign. Adlai was eight years old.

His early childhood in Bloomington seems uneventful. His playmates' and his sister's memories could describe the boyhood of almost any boy at that time and place—a fair scholar, a pupil in Miss
Coleman's dancing class, a boy shooting rats in the alley with a .22-
caliber rifle. And a boy in motion: Joe Bohrer has recalled, "At
about the age of eight, Adlai was very nervous. Always charging
around, he had a runny nose—my grandfather said it would be a
miracle if young Ad ever grew to maturity, the way he charged
around. He changed, though, after he grew up past ten or so. He
was just a normal kid—too much nerve, maybe, bustling around.
Fairly gullible, never a leader, at least up to the age of fifteen—
never captain of a team or anything. Always a nice kid. Not bookish.
I really think he never started doing things until he went to Chicago
and into the law firm there and then into the Council on Foreign

Relations"—he was about thirty-five then—"that's where his vision started to increase. Once he started, he never stopped growing. Most of us do stop, but he didn't."

Among his playmates were his cousins, Davis Merwin, born about a week before Adlai Stevenson and living almost next door, and Dave's younger brother Loring, born in 1906 and called Bud. A more important figure was Buffie. As a young woman, she was very pretty, with a long face, long nose, and the long heavy eyelids of her mother and of Adlai. Her attitude toward Adlai when they were children was possessive, almost competing with her mother while her father was away for possession of Adlai. She kept it up all his life, competing with his wife, his friends, and even his political associates. Early she displayed a metaphysical bent; she never lost it. It attracted her to Christian Science. In later life she wrote Adlai extremely long letters quoting poets and metaphysicians. As a woman she was tall and erect and rather patrician in appearance, with a tense manner, an explosive temper, a rapid swinging broad-bottomed walk like Adlai's own. She had a quick tongue and a quick temper and could be charming or cutting as she chose. Buffie inspired both resentment and admiration, dislike and something approaching pity. Like most brothers and sisters, she and he had moments of tension; but lifelong they loved each other deeply. After he became famous, he sometimes asked her to do things for him, and this on occasion aroused resentment or envy among others.

The years between 1911 and 1914 were crucial in Adlai's development. On May 22, 1911, Grandfather Davis died. His mother, inheriting a share of the *Pantagraph,* as well as other valuable properties, took the family off to Europe. She took a Bloomington schoolteacher along to tutor the children. Lewis, who stayed home, wrote to young Adlai on June 14, saying, "I was out camping 7 nights last week. Weather & roads fine. Missed my old Scout. So did the rabbits." (Adlai used to shoot rabbits while visiting farms with his father.) He enclosed a letter from Grandfather Stevenson, saying, "Wish you would keep this letter from Gaga always. Write to him. . . . I sometimes feel his mind and hopes are centered entirely on you—his only namesake, that you will be worthy of him I have no doubt." Throughout his boyhood Adlai was adjured to be worthy —and throughout the rest of his life, he would travel.

They returned in July. Lewis met them at the dock, took them to New Jersey, and took Adlai to call on Woodrow Wilson, recently nominated for President. That winter one of the truly crucial events of Adlai Stevenson's life occurred.

It happened on December 30, 1912, when he was not quite thirteen

years old. On that evening his sister Buffie had a party at the house
on East Washington Street. Most of her friends who attended were
older than Adlai; he was not really a guest at the party, just a
younger brother hanging around. One of the guests was home from
school where he had learned the manual of arms; he offered to demonstrate it. Adlai got a .22 rifle. The other boy demonstrated the
manual of arms, then handed the gun to Adlai. It was, of course,
presumed to be empty. According to most versions, while Adlai was
putting the gun away it went off. But an eyewitness says that Adlai
took the gun from the other boy, pointed it at one of the girls, Ruth
Merwin, and pulled the trigger. The gun had been loaded; the bullet
struck her in the forehead; she fell to the library floor dead.[5]

Afterward, Adlai went upstairs to his room alone. It was snowing
outside. One of the young guests went to get Ruth Merwin's parents.

Helen took Adlai to Chicago the day of the funeral; Lewis and
Buffie attended, then went straight to Chicago, joined Adlai and
Helen, and stayed with a relative there for four days. They returned
to Bloomington and Adlai's father went off on a trip. On January
20, Adlai wrote to his father in Urbana. It was a childish letter; it
made two mentions of the Merwins, both entirely casual as though
nothing had happened. It said:

> Dear Father:
> I was over at Dave's [almost surely Dave Merwin's, his cousin's]
> house this afternoon. Betty Coolidge and Tip . . . and Mary
> Fredrick and Hester and Dave and I were there. We made pop
> corn balls, and had lots of fun in the attick.
> We had consibrel snow to day it is freezing so I think we will
> have some costing. When you called up from Urbana Mother and
> Aunt Jessie were at Normal in Aunt Jessie's electric. I made a big
> Wind Mill with my American Model builder, it works fine. I am
> going to attach my motor and see how fast the fan will go round.
> I am going to school to morrow and day after to morrow they
> have the Geography test and I dont have to go because I dont have
> to take it.
> I hope you are well.
>
> > > yours
> > > Truly

---

[5] The witness believes pure chance led Adlai to point the gun at Ruth Merwin.
No other evidence disputes this. He knew her only casually; though her name
was Merwin, she was not directly related to him. She was the daughter of a
brother-in-law of Jessie Davis Merwin, Adlai's and Buffie's maternal aunt. Thus
Ruth Merwin was a cousin of Loring and Davis Merwin on their father's side,
while Adlai and Buffie were their cousins on their mother's side.

A little later he again wrote to his father in Urbana, beginning by saying, "We are going to have a circus in Dave's attick next Saturday." These letters give an impression of an extraordinarily self-contained boy so soon after so terrible an accident—or of one heavily repressed by his parents—or of one almost frighteningly unfeeling —or of one blocking, unable to face it. Except for two notes in Buffie's diary, so far as can be learned, the accident was never mentioned in the Stevenson family.

What effect did it have on Adlai? His sister has said she thinks that writers attempting amateur psychoanalysis have overemphasized the accident, adding that his divorce from his wife had a more profound effect on him. Loring Merwin says that the incident was forgotten until it was suddenly discovered[6] during the spring of 1952, when Stevenson was being propelled toward the presidential nomination. Merwin adds that for years after the accident there were no guns in the Stevenson household and Adlai gave up hunting, though in adult life he hunted enthusiastically. Rather late in Stevenson's life a woman friend suggested he see a psychiatrist to delve into the incident. His old friend Joe Bohrer has said, "Maybe that's why he wasn't mean—even in politics. Maybe that's why he was doing good for other people." Some have suggested that guilt caused by the accident may account in Stevenson's later life for his spirit of public service. Some have suggested he seemed to feel he was on earth under sufferance and therefore obligated to live a life exemplary and useful. This, however, suggests a nobler character than his—perhaps nobler than any human's. A more modest thesis is that a touch of guilt may explain his self-doubts and his protestations of unworthiness. At the 1952 convention he told the Illinois delegation he was not fit for the nomination and in his acceptance speech he told the world, "I accept your nomination—and your program. I should have preferred to hear those words uttered by a stronger, a wiser, a better man than myself." Of course, an American tradition of humility in public men descends from George Washington through Abraham Lincoln—Washington, accepting command of American forces at the Second Continental Congress, said, "I do not think myself equal to the command I am honored with." And any suggestion of boasting or even exulting would have been foreign to a man so mannerly as Stevenson.

When his friend Lloyd Lewis died, Stevenson made one of the most touching, eloquent speeches of his life; but he told his intimate friend, Alicia Patterson, "I choked up like a silly ass and made a fool

---

[6] By a *Time* magazine reporter, William Glasgow.

of myself on top of everything else." It may have been this same
feeling that so often made him protest that honors which came to him
must be tarnished, worthless. He wrote to Alicia Patterson shortly
after his election as Governor, "Darling—It is very late and I am
propped up in bed desolate, weary, harassed and sad. Its been a
ghastly six weeks. The boys are all home and I've had a few good
hours with them, but this job is murder and I need help, understanding and encourgement & I have none. . . . The Inaguaration is the
10th; the smoke will clear away soon and then I'll settle down to my
hideous ordeal—alone. . . . ."

It may even be that this accident of 1912 was the root origin of
Stevenson's lifelong habit of grumbling at his circumstances, a habit
which misled his acquaintances upon occasion, as when shortly before his death he told journalists he could scarcely bear the burden of
supporting policies he did not believe in at the UN, a habit which his
close friends were familiar with and were inclined to dismiss as a
superficial mannerism; but a habit which in fact, if it originated in
this accident, may have served the necessary unconscious function of
turning triumphs into disasters, honors into burdens, as unconscious
penance for his deed. In the 1948 campaign for the governorship he
wrote Alicia Patterson, "Dear—Its midnight again & the last of the
politicians and professors has just left. I'm about to topple into bed.
Up and away for Danville at 8—and so on and on to the end of
time or until my sins are expiated—or until the morning comes when
I just can't get up again. I wonder what the hell I'm doing and why
—and then I think of you and that you think its good and worth
while and wouldn't love me if I didn't behave this way." And again,
"You've made a great success—in the very field [of publishing] I
had once dreamed of working. And there is enough of responsibility
and opportunity for useful, interesting, important living for you to
fill me with a little awe and much hope. I don't suppose love and
envy can meet—but I can't help wishing I was on the beam as you
are. Maybe I'm confused with wanting any direction. . . . And why
the hell do I want to win and get into that hideous mess for 4 years
of solitary agony & heartbreak. I must be nuts. . . ."

To link all this to a gun accident that happened when he was
twelve is, of course, sheer speculation. Yet several hard facts support
it. First is the fact that nobody in his family ever mentioned the incident after it happened, so far as can be learned. Second, Stevenson
himself never, or at least almost never, mentioned it, not even to
Marietta Tree or Alicia Patterson. The evidence indicates he did
not even mention it to his wife—she once told a friend of theirs about
it, and this friend told Stevenson, and he responded with something
near shock, "I didn't know she knew about that." His silence on the

accident even to those who shared his life most intimately says more eloquently than any words how painful the accident was to him. Third, we know that about 1955 Stevenson wrote to a woman who was a stranger to him and whose son had had a similar experience, "Tell him that he must live for two."

15

In the fall of 1913, Adlai, in University High School at Normal and his mother away, implored her not to "make" him change his English class—the proposed one was too big—"please, please!, please!" Three days later he wrote that the change had nevertheless been made but his mother need not worry. He also wrote: "Please telegraph father to let me play football as you said you would. . . . I have been deprived of that pleasure for so long you ought to let me play this year, as I have been asked to. Hope you are better and will be home soon. I am having a fine time and like Normal pretty well. . . . P.S. Please dont forget about the football. Please." A few days later he wrote again: "Buffie got your letter this morning in which you said you would not let me play football for another year, that is what you and father have been telling me for so long, and anyway you promised me . . . you would let me play this fall. If I wait another year I will not be able to play. All doctors say its a bad game but all doctors havent played it, and more than that they did not play like we play at Normal. . . . Just because they have read of accidents in for instance a *Harvard* or *Yale* game this is a third Normal team. . . . P.S. All the games you mencioned in your letter are out of season."

On Christmas Day his Grandmother Stevenson, the wife of the former Vice President, died. Adlai's and Buffie's parents had just taken them to California. Lewis hurried home, leaving Helen and the children in California. Part of that winter they were at Las Encinas in Pasadena, of which Buffie has said, "It was like a rest cure. Mother was always looking for some place to do what she called rest. The sanitarium habit which we all had." A Harvard teacher and his wife tutored Adlai. Buffie wrote often in her journal about Adlai and about her mother's ill health. When her father returned, Buffie wrote in her journal that she hated him; she blamed him for her mother's poor health. She hoped that when her mother died she too would die.

Grandfather Stevenson lived only six months after his wife died. The year was 1914; World War I began in Europe. Young Adlai

Stevenson was fourteen. Within only a little more than three years, he had lost both his grandfathers, his only grandmother, and had himself accidentally shot a child.

16

In October the Secretary of State of the state of Illinois died. The Democratic Governor, Edward F. Dunne, had already appointed Lewis Stevenson chairman of the state Board of Pardons; he now appointed Lewis Secretary of State. Helen began to divide her time between Springfield and Bloomington (as Adlai's wife later divided her time between Springfield and Libertyville while he was Governor). In Springfield the Stevensons lived in a house once owned by a former governor. Adlai went to high school briefly in Springfield. Donald Funk, a man from Bloomington who had moved to Springfield, has recalled, "While his father was Secretary of State, they were prominent here. They knew a lot of people in Springfield before they came here, of course. In those days it was hard to get between small towns in Illinois and there was a lot more staying overnight than there is now. The Stevensons knew bankers and lawyers in Peoria, Decatur, Bloomington, and Springfield—people that knew each other in a business way. There was one group of people in each town," that is, one small upper class. As a girl, Dougie Hay, the woman Funk married, lived in Springfield and went to high school there with Stevenson. Legend has made her his childhood sweetheart but her own recollection is that he was merely a boy she went out with occasionally.

Adlai went to a camp at Oxford, Maine, in the summer of 1915. On July 25 he wrote to his mother, "When you telephoned me you said you might come over tomorrow or soon but I advise you not to as the weather is pretty bad." It is the first of several letters that suggest he was trying to grow up and escape his mother's domination. Adlai wrote to her again: "When I got back yesterday afternoon I found your letters in which you did not want me to go on the White Mountains hike, but I had already returned when I received them. I am certainly glad I went now," and he described the hike with zest.

A fellow student at University High in Normal saw Stevenson as well dressed and serious and purposeful—"he always seemed to have a mission." He debated the question, "Resolved, that the President of the United States should be elected by direct vote." His classmate remembers, "I was a country boy and I stood in awe of this scion of a grandfather who was a Vice President, as we prepared for this debate. He soon put me at ease. I was amazed at his studious approach to this question. He was an excellent student." His grades at U High averaged 82.

Buffie went away to school in the fall of 1915 and, on October 15, Adlai, by now a junior in high school, wrote her, showing a new flip attitude toward his parents and an adolescent insouciance: "I just wrote the 'old man' asking for fifty seeds (dollars) I am expecting a hot reply. I am going over to Decatur tomorrow with the football team." He was growing up. He wrote to "Buff" on December 4 that he had attended a basketball game that afternoon, was going to see a play that night, had received a "bid"—invitation—to "the Iota B Ø dance" on New Year's Eve, thought she should invite someone to the dance when she came home for the holidays, and said his own "Frat" was not giving a winter dance but "the dance next spring during the convention will be a peach." He added, "The old man is going to Washington today and wants me to go with him but I dont believe I will." He was attending dancing school and told Buffie he was "becoming some artist in the manily sport." He was dating several girls in Bloomington (one of whom later played in George White's *Scandals*). Sometimes his mother sent her chauffeur to pick him up at U High; it mortified him; the other boys rode bicycles or the streetcar.

That summer of 1916, Adlai's father took him and Buffie to the Republican and Bull Moose national conventions in Chicago. His father was running to succeed himself as Secretary of State of Illinois, and Adlai accompanied him to Democratic rallies. In the fall Adlai, having gone three years to University High, went away to a college preparatory school. At Choate, in Wallingford, Connecticut, he was, for the first time in his life, on his own. He was sixteen. Childhood had ended. From now on, with one brief exception, Adlai Stevenson spent little time in Bloomington.

CHAPTER TWO

East to School
1916-1927

A photograph of Adlai Stevenson taken at about the time he entered Choate shows him in stiff collar and heavy wool suit, a somewhat superior expression on his face. His upper lip was long; so were his eyelids and his nose. His forehead was rather broad and high but lacked the high-domed effect of later life; it is not merely that later he became bald; it is that, as an adolescent, he did not have the appearance of intellectuality that later came to be associated with his name.

His cousin Dave Merwin had gone to Choate. Choate was a good school at that time though not yet, as it became, one of the handful of the best private secondary schools in the United States. Young Stevenson was accepted for the fourth form, the sophomore year. He roomed alone. His letters home at the time do not indicate unhappiness but the following year he wrote, "I am feeling fine and like school far better than I did last year. . . . I am never going to room alone again." That first year he joined St. Andrew's Society and the Dramatics Club, played tennis, and made grades that were fair or worse—English 67 "work erratic," Latin 56 "very poor," French 76, geometry 75 "work fair," Bible 75—an average for the year of 70. No doubt because of the *Pantagraph,* he worked hard on the school newspaper, the *News.* A man who went to school with him has recalled, "The secret of Adlai's success was that he always tried to bring out the best in others. . . . When I approached Adlai at school with a problem, things looked pretty gloomy. But after his kindliness, tactfulness, and encouragement, I went away lighthearted." Stevenson himself, acting as toastmaster at a Choate function in 1935, said, "My debt to Choate is formidable. Starting with something very fresh from the prairie and somewhat deficient in everything except appetite, the magic alchemy of Choate produced an accomplished actor, a promising writer, and a passable athlete with revivalist tendencies who sailed into college—on the wings of war—all in two years! . . . If you believe as I do that the capacity to distinguish the gods from the half-gods—to want what's worth having—is life's most precious endowment, then the function of private school education assumes new importance." The gods and half-gods—it was an Emersonian phrase his mother used.

His father, running for Secretary of State of Illinois, found the primary contest abrasive. He said, "I never had a more unpleasant time. It cost me a great deal of money for detectives" to keep watch on "tough factors" in the Chicago machine. He won the primary and campaigned hard in the general election. He was alone— Adlai was at Choate; Buffie and her mother were in New Jersey. Lewis lost (so did Governor Dunne; President Wilson, though re-elected, failed to carry Illinois). At Thanksgiving time Lewis took his family to the Army-Navy football game as guests of the Secretary of the Navy. Closing out his office in Springfield, he reassigned low auto license numbers to his friends. (Adlai kept his father's low number all his life.) Governor and Mrs. Dunne invited Lewis and Helen to dinner at the Governor's Mansion December 29 and asked them to spend "the last two or three days" at the Mansion. This (1916) was the end of the Stevenson family's high official life at Springfield until Adlai Stevenson was elected Governor in 1948.

His mother's letters to Adlai at Choate show her to be an adoring mother forever eager to state her love for him; a proud mother forever praising his accomplishments and glossing over his academic shortcomings; a protective mother forever counseling him to get plenty of sleep and not tire himself. She almost invariably addressed him as "My darling Laddie" and signed herself "Mud." In February of 1917: "You are certainly doing well to get on the dramatic club. Even to have them consider you shows you are making a place for yourself. . . . You are growing to be a big boy—seventeen years! They have been the most precious years to us and you have blessed us beyond our deserts." And again: "That we have a genius in our midst is becoming more and more apparent." He attended a dance at a girls' school; his mother wrote, "Do write us all the particulars of your trip, where you stayed, whom you met, etc.," and adjured him to write his hostess a thank-you note—"be careful that it is written well and properly *spelled.*" He wrote to his mother faithfully. She complimented him on his letters: "You are acquiring a real talent for letter writing." It was true: Stevenson would turn out to be an almost compulsive letter writer. He must have written hundreds of thousands of letters in his lifetime. He took great pains with them, sometimes dictating a draft, then rewriting it extensively, sometimes writing in longhand on ruled pads of paper, crossing out words, changing sentence structure, writing as a writer writes. His letters are, in a real sense, Adlai Stevenson's literary legacy. Into them, and into speeches and occasional papers, he, a natural writer, poured his writing ability and energy. His books were all compiled from speeches and occasional pieces. Moreover, many hands touched those manuscripts. But the long letters, especially the travel letters, were Stevenson's alone and are throughout his life the most reliable guide to what he thought, what he saw, what he did. He often annotated letters, with a sense of history.

The United States declared war on Germany that first spring he spent at Choate. His father and Buffie went to California in March. Their relationship was still somewhat strained. "She is meeting nice people," he told his wife, "& I am trying to have her cultivate those that will be of advantage to her in the future. . . . My own great sorrow is her quickness and determination to call me down so often. . . . She is some better now that she sees I am not altogether a fool." Lewis was trying to get a political job in Washington. Things were not going smoothly between him and his wife either. From California, he told her he knew how hard for her separation from the children had been, "for you must recall you were entirely dependent upon them. I counted for little as your thought seemed to be to repulse me rather than encourage our trying to get closer together which I have always longed for. Possibly it will be different in the future. I hope so." She had taken the management of her farms out of his hands; he offered to resume responsibility. "In fact I'll do any and everything I can for you if you will only let me." He would continue to manage the Scott farms for another year. After that, perhaps they would move to Chicago "if you felt the climate would suit you."

At the end of the school year Adlai wrote to his mother, "Well in four more days I will be travelling toward the best home in all the world. . . . I am pretty nervous about my exams." He felt certain he would fail at least one. The good student had become a marginal student and knew it. He barely passed and was tutored in French that summer. When he and Buffie went to the H F Bar Ranch at Buffalo, Wyoming, he fell in love with the West. He went back several times; so did such friends as Hermon Dunlap "Dutch" Smith. Other guests there also went to Charlevoix. On this first visit he wrote, "It certainly is a beautiful place. . . . Buffie's cottage is in or rather on the edge of a little grove of cottonwoods which border a very pretty and fast flowing mountain stream. Almost directly back of us the ground rises into the first range of the Big Horns, beautiful mountains. . . .

The horses are not very good, in fact quite rotten so tell father he does not need to worry about any accidents from bucking bronchos etc."

Adlai went back to Choate that fall, 1917, and he enjoyed it more and performed a little better academically—an average for the year of 74. In extracurricular activities he blossomed—was elected secretary-treasurer of his class, became business manager of the *News* and associate editor of the *Literary Magazine* and board member of the school Friendship Fund, remained a member of St. Andrew's Society and the Dramatic Club, and made the varsity tennis team. He liked the other boys. His letters were filled with news of the school—athletic scores, a motion picture, midnight meals in his room, the football schedule, an issue of the *News* ("I am quite proud of it"), holiday plans, a dance after the Taft game with a girl from Hartford. He seemed quite interested in religion. He was beginning to show in his letters the fondness for long and elegant words that later distinguished and sometimes disfigured his speeches. Sometimes his prose sounded arch—"Your delightful letter of Thursday just arrived." Most of his letters sounded happy and unremarkable. One began, "Yesterday and today have been wonderful days."

Secretary of the Navy Josephus Daniels appointed Adlai's father a special investigator for the Navy at a salary of $200 per month and assigned him to Washington. His duties were to enforce contracts, ensure prompt deliveries, and prevent fraud.

Choate was planning a dance; Adlai invited his mother, his sister, and a girl from home, Dougie Hay, who attended a girls' school nearby. She declined. His mother encouraged him to write a story and an editorial, adding, in that curious anticipation of failure which recurs in her and her husband's letters to Adlai, "It is good practice even if they aren't accepted."

Tennis occupied a great deal of Adlai's time and thoughts that spring; he reported his triumphs to his mother, and she exulted: "To think of your winning both singles and doubles. It's glorious!" She added, "It would be a great relief if you could pass off your Spanish but to prepare for the examination, go slowly, sleep all you can, and be confident and calm, relying always for help on a higher power." He spent spring vacation with his parents in Washington and, returning, told his mother, "It is a very great relief to know that my visit did you some good. Certainly my ten days with you all this Spring were the happiest of my life and it is certainly a great gratification to think that you enjoyed them. . . . I do hope and feel sure that you will improve steadily now." In this letter is foreshadowed a role that Adlai Stevenson was soon increasingly called upon to play: that of looking after his mother.

His cousin Louis E. Davis, a military flier, was killed in a plane crash in Texas. Louis Davis was the son of Bert Davis, who, along with his sisters Helen Stevenson and Jessie Merwin, had inherited the *Pantagraph.* Later Louis Davis' death had an important influence on Adlai Stevenson's career since it affected ownership of the paper. Adlai's mother wrote him a rather religious letter. He replied, "Please don't worry about his death as he generously sacrificed his life for a cause that should inspire in us all the spirit of sacrifice which alone can unite us in a general endeavour to maintain our countrys standards, which have so many times in the past proved so high. . . . We have lost seven of our alumni now and have 136 in service, which I think is a very good showing." It was a long letter. His election as editor-in-chief of the *News* was relegated to a single factual sentence in a postscript.

If he returned to Choate for his senior year next fall, he would be, in addition to editor of the *News,* vice-president of his class, president of St. Andrew's, secretary of the Athletic Association, and captain of the tennis team. But he wanted to try to enter college next fall, and, despite his mother's misgivings, did. He did not graduate from Choate. Instead of returning for his senior year he enlisted in the U. S. Navy as an apprentice seaman, passed his college entrance examinations, and entered Princeton. Nonetheless, he was declared officially a member of the Choate class of 1918. It had been a good two years, especially at the end.

2

Adlai spent the summer in Bloomington and at Choate studying for his college entrance examinations. A letter written near the end of summer foreshadows his letter-writing style of years later: "I am each day gaining in erudition and sincerely believe that you will not recognize me in my present intellectual disguise when next we meet. I really am working pretty hard this week, in fact everyone is, as the exams come next week. I am going to leave here Sunday morning and go directly to P [Princeton]. We have engaged a room at the Nassau Inn for the period of the exams and so do not have to worry about accomodations. I think, if the Gods are with me, that I may pass my exams. . . . I shall leave [my belongings] here and request the office to send them when I find it advisable. In the meantime I will drift around with my trunk and suitcase. . . . Well I must close and seek a few hours repose." He adjured his mother not to worry about his "going into the service." She need not; the war ended two months later; his service was to be spent entirely at Princeton.

He was admitted to Princeton on September 24, 1918. He had been nervous about his physical examination for the Navy but he told his mother, ". . . thanks to your unceasing care I passed the physical exam pretty high." He was five feet nine and weighed 131 pounds. He was drilling in the Navy and arranging his courses—advanced French, Spanish, chemistry, American history, and naval discipline and administration. John Harlan, an older student and campus leader, chairman of the *Princetonian* (and later a justice of the United States Supreme Court), was his lieutenant commander. Stevenson came to admire Harlan greatly, and Harlan was for a time interested in Buffie. Adlai wrote, "There are quite a few fellows around here that I have seen or met before," some at boarding school, some at Charlevoix, some elsewhere. Some became lifelong acquaintances or friends, such as Bill McIlvaine, Don Lourie, James Douglas, Ogden West. On October 22 he wrote, "Well I have taken the oath of allegiance for 4 years service anywhere in the world and am now a real 'gob' in the U. S. Navy. Believe me I am certainly one hot looking little 'Jack' and you will just about split when you see me." Like most of his friends, he considered the government-issue uniforms inferior and bought a privately made one.

He was very proud to be at Princeton; he made it clear, and described Princeton life, in a long letter on October 27:

Dearest Mum:
Yesterday was quite a gala day here for the freshmen. But before explaining it all you must remember that all the fellows who are here in the freshman class are not freshmen, but only those that entered by examinations, as I did. In other words all the fellows that came in on certificate etc. to join the military organizations are not ranked as Princeton men and are not included in the class of 1922. I certainly am glad that I came in by exams and am a real Princeton man. Although it is very difficult to maintain all the old college customs etc. the difference between the regular Princeton men and the others is very obvious. For instance whenever Old Nassau or any of the other P. songs are sung the non-regular men are not allowed to sing and have to stand at attention.

Well to go on with the events of Saturday. At 3:00 all the regular freshmen assembled in front of Witherspoon hall for the annual freshman P-rade. We P-raded around the campus sing-

ing Princeton songs and cheers led by John Harlan. . . . We then
went to the steps of Whig Hall for the freshman picture. . . .
[Then we] went to the big assembly room in McCosh hall to elect
officers for the 1st term.

The election of officers was a matter of great interest to me.
It is all done by the various big prep schools. Each one nominates
a fellow for certain of the offices, and some of the schools like Hill
have a man up for all 3 offices, and the school with the most representatives or the one that can induce the most 'non-prep,' (fellows
that did not go to some big prep school and don't know who to
vote for), fellows to vote for their man wins. It is all graft but very
interesting. . . . And then when it came to electing a Sec. Tres.
much to my surprise and inquietude, I was nominated and then,
with the other 5 or 6 nominees, had to get up and stand before the
whole assembly and then walk into an adjoining room during the
balloting. Of course I felt like a fool coming from such a small prep
school and knowing so few fellows. However, I afterwards learned
that I got a good many more votes than I had expected. . . . I
had a Spanish exam yesterday which I "killed." I am rather doubtful about my chances to pass the chemistry and History exams
tomorrow.

It is all there in that letter, both the young man and his university—
boyish enthusiasm, school spirit, snobbery, ambition, campus politics,
a touch, but little more than a touch, of the academic. Princeton is a
beautiful and historic university, its Nassau Hall now the university
president's office, once the seat of government of the United States.
The town of Princeton is a lovely place, then a quiet college town,
later a college and New York commuters' town, bearing a striking
resemblance to Lake Forest, Illinois, the wealthy suburb north of
Chicago which drew Adlai Stevenson after he finished college. Princeton looks pleasant, wealthy, conservative, untroubled. It is obvious
from his letters that Adlai Stevenson fell in love with Princeton
University at first sight; he never lost his love for it; he returned
often; he made one of his most moving speeches to its senior class in
1954; the highball glasses in his home in Libertyville, Illinois, when
he died were inscribed with the Princeton tiger and "Class of '22";
he went back for football games; he strove mightily to gain ad-
mittance of his sons to Princeton; he made friends there who remained his friends throughout his life and who helped him greatly
in his early career; before he died he gave some of his private papers
to Princeton's great Firestone Library (stipulating orally that they
not be housed in the John Foster Dulles wing) and after his death

his sons gave the remainder of his papers to Princeton (except those relating to his governorship, which were given to the Illinois State Historical Library).

His four years there as an undergraduate reached from the very end of World War I to the beginning of the 1920s—1918 to 1922. Merely to name two young writers who went to Princeton at about the same time, F. Scott Fitzgerald and Richard Halliburton, is to suggest the atmosphere. It was a time of innocence and insouciance, of gaiety and pretense, of postwar disillusion and withdrawal, of raccoon coats and flappers' skirts, and the emphasis was more on motorcars than on minds. The tragedies of Woodrow Wilson and the League of Nations were little heeded. The disasters of the Great Depression were unthinkable. Young men were going into the bond business; young heiresses were marrying European counts. Prohibition prevailed.

Stevenson was not much more a scholar at Princeton than he had been at Choate. The university ranked students by their grades into seven groups; the first group held highest scholastic standing, the second high, the third fair, the fourth low, the fifth passing, the sixth failure, the seventh bad failure. Stevenson was in the fifth group his first year, the fourth group his second year, and the third group his last two years. When he graduated he had a grade average of 3.45, almost dead center, and he ranked 105th in a graduating class of 250. He never failed an academic course. As he had at Choate, he improved as time passed; his worst year was his first. He was always a late bloomer.

Why did he not get better grades? Because it was beyond his intellectual capacity? Because he didn't try? More likely because it was not fashionable. Classmates have recalled that students then disdained a boy who was too much the intellectual; it was considered fashionable to "get a gentleman's third"; this is precisely what Stevenson did. Adlai Stevenson was always more interested in people and in going places and doing things and engaging in activity of almost any sort than in purely intellectual pursuits (though when he became prominent many of his admirers thought otherwise). Don Lourie, at Princeton with Stevenson, said, "Sure, Adlai's grades were a gentleman's third. If you got more you were a bookworm. Also you couldn't be a big politician. You had to conform. As I look back, a fellow didn't have much chance to be brilliant." Stevenson had always been inclined to conform. Another Princeton and Lake Forest friend, James Douglas, has recalled that at Princeton Stevenson was "not colorful—he was likable. He really developed very slowly." At Princeton Stevenson acquired the nickname of Rabbit. At least three legends purport to explain it—that he had big ears, that he ate salad with a rabbit's enthusiasm, and that he was sexually promiscuous. The last seems most unlikely. He dated the usual number of girls but much later in life he told one of his most intimate and reliable friends that he never had had sexual intercourse until he married.

At Princeton boys lived in dormitories and belonged to the "eating clubs" which line Prospect Street. Club life was important at Princeton. It was a gentleman's life and a comfortable one. The clubs maintained staffs of servants, mostly Negroes. Some were luxurious, heavily endowed. Considerable social status attached to one's club. Boys took their meals there and gave parties there. The clubs were, traditionally, ranked into a hierarchy of three groups ranging from most to least desirable socially. Stevenson wanted to join the Ivy Club, a top-ranking club; he did in fact, however, join Quadrangle, ranked in the middle group.

Stevenson was also a member of Whig Hall, a debating society. Whig met every Friday for a debate and on other occasions to hear "fireside talks" by faculty members. Stevenson became an active member his first year; he was taking an English course in oratory and argument rather than the usual freshman English course. He enjoyed speaking and listening to speeches. In his last year he was a member of the Senior Council and the Class Movie Committee and the Class Day Committee. He tried out for freshman baseball but got nowhere. He played tennis and golf. His principal extracurricular activity was in the school's newspaper, the *Daily Princetonian*. He became a member of its board during his second year and its managing editor his last year. On that occasion he rebuked his father sharply: His father had told the Chicago *Tribune* he was editor-in-chief, a higher post, and it had published the item. "Once more . . . I protest (as usual in vain, I suppose) against your assumption of the duties of my publicity manager. As in the past, when I have strenuously objected, you have nevertheless gone ahead and, with the apparent interest of pleasing a mere child, put things in papers which were altogether wrong in point of fact & most embarrassing to me. And now again. . . . Please desist and do me a real favor." He addressed the letter "Dear Father" and closed with nothing but his signature. (He remembered the incident all his life and as late as 1951 referred to it in a letter to a friend.)

A reading of his letters shows Stevenson was deeply interested in "The Prince," as he called the *Princetonian;* struggled with his studies and examinations; was keenly interested in sports, in several girls, in football weekends and club parties and trips to New York, in getting ahead; and maintained throughout his four years the love and enthusiasm he originally felt for his university. What the letters do not show a trace of is intellectuality.

Once a girl from home went to Princeton as Stevenson's date for a big dance. Years later he wrote, "I recall taking Dougie Hay to a prom at Princeton I think my sophomore year, and I recall vividly breaking down in that old Hudson car I had there for a couple of years out in the country somewhere in the middle of the night going to or from a party at somebody's house. It was a harrowing experience trying to be nonchalant in a dinner jacket with a girl I hardly knew in a car I knew all too well." He took a Vassar girl, Harriet Cowles from Spokane, to another dance and became seriously interested in her.

The most extraordinary thing about his college years was that his mother lived there during them. She and Buffie visited him briefly during the fall of his first year. Later, in the fall of 1919, they took a house in Princeton and Stevenson spent much of his time there. Finally, they took another house during his last year, 1922—Buffie remembered they were there from February or March until his graduation in June. One of Stevenson's classmates regarded his mother as "overzealous" in her affection for Stevenson and thought she "overprotected" him. "She embarrassed him often." A close friend of Stevenson has said, "I think the cruelest thing a mother could do to a boy was what she did—go to Princeton when he did." Buffie said, "I think Mother took me to Princeton to expose me to Princeton young men. Father wanted wider horizons for me. He'd seen it in Washington." Matchmaking between Buffie and John Harlan may indeed have taken Helen Stevenson to Princeton that first year but could not have during Stevenson's senior year—by then Harlan had graduated. From what we know of her feelings for Adlai we may surmise that her primary purpose was to be near him.[1]

What did Adlai himself think of her presence? It is perhaps significant that although in his later years he told Marietta Tree a great deal about himself, as much, probably, as he ever told anyone, he never mentioned two things to her: that he had killed a child accidentally, and that his mother had lived at Princeton while he was there. From his letters it appears he welcomed his mother's visit during his first year but by his senior year he opposed it. In that year he wrote to his father rather curtly, "I don't believe you would have

[1] Franklin D. Roosevelt's mother went to live in Boston during part of the time he was at Harvard.

been so preremptory in your demands about looking for houses if you fully appreciated the exacting demands for time on an active senior in the 'two big game' weeks of his senior year. . . . Personally I can see no reason for coming to Princeton—if you want to come at all— until after Christmas—about the first of February. There is nothing doing here now & I thought perhaps the family would like to go south somewhere for Christmas—Pinehurst, Southern Pines, Camden, or some other place where mother would enjoy the weather."

When she was not with him, his mother continued to send letters filled with religion, moralizing, advice, love, and concern about his health. She urged him strongly not to smoke, but he smoked anyway. In February of 1920—she was still addressing him as "my darling Laddie"—she congratulated him upon some college success and said: "Is there no chance of you coming over Saturday [to Lakewood, New Jersey, where she was staying]? Remember this is your natal day and it would be nice to have a celebration!" Nearly all her life she wrote a birthday letter to him.

Stevenson was always conscious of his physical surroundings and it shows in his early Princeton letters: "This is the most beautiful winter day I've witnessed—with the first snow of the season, the winter has been ushered in most gloriously. I wish you could have seen McCosh walk and the trees around Prospect embedded in snow —about two inches on the smallest twig." He always had a penchant too for being "charming," for meeting "the right people," and all this showed in the same brief letter: "Went to dinner at Mayor McClellan's the other night and had a perfectly delightful time. Sat on Mrs. McClellan's right and had for a dinner partner Princess Ruspigliosi (something like that)." Lifelong, too, he was gregarious; he loved parties; he could hardly bear to be alone for long; his was an almost compulsive seeking-out of people, all sorts of people.

3

That year, 1920, Stevenson's father went to Europe to promote one of his grander schemes, the Zeppelin deal—negotiated for the American rights to the German patents on lighter-than-air aircraft. He spent months on it. Helen was not well enough to go. Once he wrote her that he had been the guest of a German who was "head of one of the largest concerns in the country" and that "we may close a satisfactory deal." Another time he wrote, *Have secured a number of desirable contracts,* or at least have their promise, & am now struggling with the different Boards of Directors & the lawyers, about the most trying job I ever tackled. It is an interminable number of meetings, conferences, etc." But nothing ever came of the Zeppelin deal, no more than had come of Lewis' other schemes.

Adlai Stevenson went to Europe too that summer, the end of his second college year, with college friends. Buffie also went. At times they and their father met in Europe. But on the whole for the first time in his life Adlai Stevenson was on his own abroad.

He wrote often to his mother, who spent the summer in Charlevoix, Bloomington, and in a Battle Creek sanitarium. His letters to her are the literary antecedents of the long travel letters he wrote in later life in longhand to women friends. They are filled with excellent descriptions of places he visited, clogged with irrelevant detail, contain his thoughts on important and on minor matters. Adlai Stevenson was a tireless traveler and an insatiable sightseer. On trip after trip he wore out companion after companion. He had almost a lust for travel; it was as though he was either compulsively running away from something or compulsively searching for something. His adult life was crammed with travel; the pattern was set now in 1920.

Aboard ship he met other Princeton men and men from Harvard and Yale, some working for their passage, and he described them and their boarding schools and collegiate attainments to his mother. He did not suffer "from that horrible malady—mal de mer"—Stevenson never could bring himself to use one word when seven would do. He and his companions visited London, then went to Oxford and toured England, in part afoot. All his life Adlai Stevenson had a fondness for and admired British aristocracy, British history, British traditions. British locutions found their way into his speech. Of all the many honorary degrees he received he was proudest of that from Oxford and never passed up an opportunity to wear his scarlet Oxford robes. This trip in 1920 may be where all that started.

Back in London, he watched guests arriving at Buckingham Palace and had fittings on several suits. "The next morning Bill and I left for Paris by AIRPLANE! . . . The airplane passage cost us $42—about 2½ times as much as it would have cost on the train. It sounds pretty extravagant but it was, I think, altogether worth it. . . . The plane . . . carries 10 people and is fitted up with windows, wicker chairs etc. There was even a lavatory in it. . . . As it was my first time up everything was, of course, most interesting," and he described the Channel crossing. In that letter, dated "Paris, le 26 Juillet 1920 Monday," Stevenson apologized for not having written sooner—he had been in Paris several days—and explained, "I haven't been able to come down to realities. . . . Paris is the most fascinating city I have ever been in and I almost believe I should like to live there

As for the French people, I wasn't particularly attracted by the men but the women are, for the most part, very good looking and awfully well dressed."

He took a night train to Coblenz and wrote from there, "Last night . . . when a couple of miles out of Chateau Thierry I could [see] the ruins of walls and houses on the surrounding hills standing out against the sky and bathed in the brilliant white of the moon. A little further down the track we passed a great field of neat little white crosses arranged in symmetrical rows and stretching away over the hills—the final resting place of some 30,000 American soldiers and Marines. It also occured to me that it was almost exactly 2 years and 1 week ago that the Chateau Thierry offensive was begun, which lended a kind of subconsciously romantic air to the scene. All this, augmented by the brilliant moon, the ruins sillouetted against the sky, the desolation of the landscape and the fact that it was the 6th anniversary of the war gave a most effective atmosphere of tragedy and at the same time hilarity to the night. In the next compartment to me a girl started to play a violin—this was the middle of the night as we were following the Marne—and before long the whole car had assembled to hear and how she could play."

From Berlin on Sunday, August 1, he noted that the trip up the Rhine had been "beautiful." He noted the cost of a meal at Wiesbaden—he was always conscious of costs. He considered German an "extremely ugly language." He related a headwaiter's views: "He was extremely nice and said the same thing that all Germans say, namely, that Germany would have won the war had not America entered and again like all Germans he could not understand why America entered against Germany." He thought Berlin "beautiful" and the people surprisingly happy, the women "quite unattractive" and abominably dressed. They had considerable difficulty arranging transportation through Belgium to a town on the French border. In recounting this, Stevenson had one of those inexplicable, opaque lapses of sensitivity he occasionally showed throughout his life. He wrote:

We left in the afternoon on the first leg of our journey to Rheims and at 12 o'clock we had to get out at a small town on the border. Here we had to go thru the douance etc and also stay until 5:30 when we could get a train which would take us thru Belgium to a town on the French border. Frank and I had a very novel walk thru the devastated remains of the town in the middle of the night and then at last we lay down on a grave stone & tried to go to sleep, however, that proved anything but comfortable and sleep was quite impossible so we walked back to the station and at last managed to get a few winks on the station platform. . . .

I shan't attempt to recount the viscissitudes of our trip to Rheims —suffice it to say that it was an astonishingly hard place to reach and that we changed trains exactly 8 times in all. We spent several hours in Soissons on the way and hired a car to take us over the Chemin des Dames battlefield. It was over the possession of this road that we rode along that the severest fighting of the entire war occurred. It was intensely interesting and the complete devistation and destruction of the countryside and the little villages surpassed all the powers of description. I was told by a very delightful Frenchman, whom I met later, that the country surrounding Soissons was the best agricultural country in France and he also added that, in his opinion, the region would never be repopulated again for the constant shelling had left the land so rough and uneven that it would be impossible to cultivate it.

We visited a number of other completely demolished towns. . . . The train . . . ran on a newly constructed bed thru a almost totally bare country with trenches & barbed wire stretching away on both sides of the track.

We arrived at Rheims in the evening, secured rooms and had a very acceptable cleaning up as you may imagine after 2 days & nights in those dirty trains. As we were having dinner who should arrive but 5 other Princeton fellows on bicycles. We all had a big party together and then walked around the town for a while. They went on to Paris in the morning by train and we got a car and went out to inspect the battlefields around Rheims. We spent several hours walking thru the remains of Fort Pompellis and the very well preserved trenches that surround it. The ground was practically paved with iron and, although it has been thoroughly cleaned up, I found lots of unexploded shells, hand grenades etc. I also found a French bayonet which I am bringing home and many other souvenirs which are a little bulky to carry about. It was all extremely interesting. . . . I also was told that in 1914 there were 16,000 houses in Rheims and that on Nov 11, 1920 there were exactly 14 that remained intact. From this you can roughly estimate what the town looks like. However they are rebuilding it very rapidly.

This is a very cool, detached, self-contained young man. He has all the facts and figures straight; none of the horror. If the scene moved him, he concealed it carefully. Adlai Stevenson always did. And he always romanticized.

He continued, "We got to Paris that evening. . . . That night we all, about 12 of us, had a big party together and in the course of the evening we found ourselves at the Folies Bergere. Imagine my astonishment to see Father walk in all of a sudden. Of course he said he was just looking for me but it certainly looked as though he had started out on a little party of his own and that I had accidentally interrupted it."

There was more to the incident than that. He related it many years later to an intimate friend. The facts were that he and his companions went to the Folies Bergère and after drinks his friends decided to go off with some prostitutes. Stevenson felt he should go too, though he had never had sexual intercourse. A girl took him to her room and undressed. It revolted Stevenson; he slipped away, leaving the customary fee behind, and fled back to the Folies Bergère. There he found his father. Next day he met his father and Buffie for lunch. He "hung around with them most of the time for the next few days until we started for Switzerland."

On August 9–10 his father wrote to his wife from Paris, "We have had two glorious days with the Brute," as he referred to Adlai. "I never saw him more cheerful or communicative. Talks all the time & most interestingly. What he doesn't know about Paris ain't. . . . He has had a wonderful trip & it has done him a real good. He now keeps his nails perfectly clean & carries a stick which he would have frowned upon a month ago. . . . Buffie now has her string of pearls & is radiantly happy. They cost 1995.00 & are beautiful. Bought at Cartier, Paris. Please follow my advice & say nothing—not a word—about them, because they are not yet *delivered in New York*. See?" (One wonders whether he was evading United States customs duties.) He wrote that he had "slight arthritis & vericose veins" and did not yet feel "equal" to going to Berlin. He urged her to "get well & join Buffie here for winter" and asked her to send him "at once" a "N.Y. draft for $2000.00 for Buffie & don't fail to endorse it this time."

From Geneva, Adlai wrote to his mother, "Father was going to Berlin and I equipped him with a letter of introduction to my German friends." It is the first patronizing note about his father. Lewis wrote to his wife from Berlin on August 20: "Have been beautifully received & entertained at dinner by several delightful people. The American Commissioner (would be Ambassador but for war) gave me a beautiful luncheon at which he had 15 guests including a great German political scientist . . . also prof. of political economy at Harvard & others of note." Poor Lewis—so often he mistook the appearance of power for its reality. He set great store by whom he met and how he was received. Soon he was fretting about money and fearing that his young assistant back home might be scheming to take the management of Mrs. Scott's farms away from him. His wife wrote blithe chatty letters to Buffie. She cautioned her son in Switzerland that mountain climbing might strain his heart and back. Before he received that letter, Adlai had climbed the Breithorn near Zermatt. He described it in a letter to her:

"I found the glacier most interesting and the ice formations were intensely beautiful. . . . We reached the cabane in the late afternoon, had supper and, after witnessing a glorious sunset, went to bed for those of us that were going up had to get up at 4.

"I shall never forget that night. It was intensely cold, the moon full and brilliant and not a cloud in the sky. I found it quite impossible to sleep and actually sat or rather lied spellbound looking out of the window until time to get up. My window faced the Matterhorn which rose like a jagged column of granite out of a sea of sparkling white. Down below me, glittering in the moonlight, lay a vast glacier which occasionally uttered a reverberating groan as the ice cracked or moved slightly. In every direction great jagged peaks shot up and stood out black against the unearthly blue of the sky and over all was a choking and almost maddening silence. The intense cold and clearness of the atmosphere made the stars unbelievably brilliant and everything seemed magnified and brought closer while the real vastness of the scene was unconceivable. It was a sight that I shall never forget and I know hardly whether to call it beautiful or horrible for there was something about it that was awe inspiring and at the same time fascinating, frightful and supernatural. . . . I could not determine whether it was nature—whether I should thank God or Satan and in fact I feel sure there was more of the latter in it—an awful grandeur that was really not beautiful but rather magnetic and fear-inspiring. Anyway I lay their enthralled and at last got up and went out to look some more—it fascinated me and I stood there stiff from [cold] and unable to realize that this was merely a 'clear night in the Alps'. . . . The descent was accomplished in an hour and a quarter which the guide said was the best time he had ever heard of."

They left Zermatt next day and met their father in Montreux, living in what Adlai called the "criminal luxury" of a hotel. Lewis wrote to Helen September 9 saying he was glad she had had some of Adlai's letters published in the *Pantagraph* and recommended she publish the one on climbing the Breithorn—"the boy has a real gift in this direction." Lewis made use of the gift: "I am anxious that it be known in Bloomington that I was successful in Berlin & I wish you would add the enclosed to Adlai's letter. It is about the only way I see of getting it published, & it will be of value to me. Do it please, & send me a copy." "The enclosed" was an addition to

Adlai's letter, written by his father, describing his father's triumphs in Berlin, and added to Adlai's letter without Adlai's knowledge. One recalls that Lewis "used" people; here he "used" his own son. It is all rather sad.[2] In sending the "addition," Adlai's father told Helen, "Better publish the letter before Adlai comes or he will not want it done. He does not realize what good they [the letters] do him. They will help him more than he knows in B. [Bloomington]."

Adlai went home. His father and Buffie stayed on in Switzerland. Buffie spent part of that fall studying psychoanalysis with Carl Jung. At various times in her life she showed an interest in psycho-analysis, Christian Science, and other methods of healing. Lewis wrote to Helen, "Don't tell any one she is studying psycho analysis, say psycology & the languages, & above all things do not mention that she is studying with Mrs. McCormick. I know best about this & I can't urge it too strongly. . . . Mrs. McC. has already sensed B.'s inherited disposition to 'punish' & I think is convincing her of the horrors that follow in the wake of such a course." The rest of that letter, written September 24, was an angry diatribe: "I have not the time nor am I in the mood to write more than a line. If you could possibly have conceived a more absurd thing to do than send Buffie's money in the way you did I can't guess it. Think of her doing business with a bank which has no branches, & besides I can buy franks at far better rate here than there—any one should know that. It surely was a brilliant thought to have her pay by stocks, too. She is so experienced in this sort of thing. My God if you knew all the trouble caused by your not endorsing that draft to N.Y. & now all the effort & complete loss of time this latest thing has caused! I simply won't take more time to explain it. I said send her a *draft*. The draft for $1000.00 was O.K. & she is now using it. I am broke. My legs—not feet now—are in a bad way—bandaged to the thighs—& I've

---

[2] The "addition" reads: "Father joined us here last week after a three weeks stay in Germany. He was successful in his business efforts and is much elated. While in Berlin he was the guest of a general of the General Staff—a Division Commander—and met many prominent people. The American Commissioner gave a dinner [it was a lunch, not a dinner] in his honor. In Mannheim he was the guest of a former Admiral. Going it a bit strong wasn't it, but running true to form for he was always a good chooser. With one of his friends he flew from Berlin to Leipzig making trip in less than two hours. A former German ace drove the plane and did a few funny stunts much to fathers discomfort. Fathers legs are much better but he still goes a slow pace for him. He returns to Berlin in ten days and will sail home soon as he can secure passage. Mrs. Stanley McCormick is here with her Fiat car. She is unusually charming and we drive with her a great deal. Love to all. See you soon. Adlai."

had to walk all over this place of no cabs until near dead trying to straighten out this affair. Don't now, for God's sake, write & worry."

He wrote again, "I am not altogether pleased with her study of psycho-analysis. . . . You complain, Helen, in a letter & cards received by B. [Buffie] today that I haven't written for two weeks. I haven't done so because you sent B. [Buffie] a letter I wrote you . . . & complained bitterly about it. It was written after midnight when I was completely exhausted & was only supposed to be a goodbye note, & didn't require punishment. *There is to be no more punishment.*"

4

Adlai Stevenson was not unaware of the difficulties between his mother and father. Yet only the most veiled hints ever appeared in his letters, as when he wrote: "Do hope you all are well and things are serene." He had somehow erected a barrier between himself and this trouble. It may explain why in adult life he so often seemed to place a screen between himself and others. Robert Oppenheimer once said, "He was a man you felt you knew intimately almost instantly, on first meeting—and after a time you realized you never did really get to know him any better." He had defenses that almost nobody, perhaps nobody at all, ever penetrated; depths almost nobody reached.

That fall the presidential candidates were Warren G. Harding and James M. Cox. The *Princetonian,* and Adlai Stevenson, were deeply interested. Stevenson helped organize a Cox-Roosevelt club. The *Princetonian* endorsed the League of Nations and Cox. Readers protested, and the *Princetonian* published a statement signed by fifteen of the twenty-seven members of its board, all Republicans and including three good friends of Stevenson, saying that the endorsement was the work of the chairman of the board of editors and that the signers favored Harding. On March 1, 1921, the first issue listing Adlai E. Stevenson as managing editor appeared.

On his birthday, February 5, 1921, his mother wrote:

My darling Laddie:[3]

---

[3] A variant version of this letter gives the salutation as "My Precious Son," not "My Darling Laddie." Such uncertainty surrounds some of Stevenson's early letters and those of his forebears because his sister in later life, in a laudable effort to preserve the family documents, had them typed. They were not always transcribed literally.

Twenty-one years old, 21 years young, 21 years wise, 21 years beloved! I telegraphed today and told you the best wish one could make for you was that the next 21 might be as fine as these first 21—and so it is, my dear boy!

Your babyhood, boyhood, and young-manhood have been a natural, sweet unfolding and gradual developement. Round upon round. There are no dark, muddy spots thus far in your career. . . . You have never wanted something for nothing nor anything that was not rightfully yours. And so whatever in rewards come to you, you can rejoice over Right for the sake of Right! . . . So you may know how grateful and happy your little family is, on this your blessed birthday. May God remain with you always.

Buffie joins me in congratulations, love and all good wishes.

Your proud and adoring
Mother

We have no way of knowing how the twenty-one-year-old Princeton junior reacted to the love, deep and cloying and possessive, of this unfortunate woman with her own unsatisfactory marriage, or how he felt about what can only be called her attempts to hide reality, as when she said, "There are no dark, muddy spots thus far in your career."

In March, Buffie and her mother went to Europe. Adlai had a good spring. He was one of five men chosen by his club to "bicker" —talk—with sophomores seeking membership. He used the word "bicker" thereafter. In April, Stevenson wrote to his mother, "The house parties come on the 14th of May and I am seriously considering having Harriet Cowles down [from Vassar]. I have found Miss Green and have weekly treatments from her . . . in order to get my hair in good shape for the summer. . . . The weather is beautiful and the trees are in full blosom. However, I suppose the beauty of Montreux in the spring beggars anything else." "Beggars"—it is another word he used all his life. He was nominated for next year's Senior Council. He went to a convention of the Eastern Intercollegiate Newspaper Association at Columbia, representing the *Princetonian*. He described the convention as "a frightful bore," another phrase he would use. "As a representative of one of the larger colleges and better papers, I had to sit by the hour and answer the questions of an endless number of befogged but hopeful journalists from the smaller colleges."

He went back to Europe that summer with friends, toured Spain. His letters were briefer, fewer, and less "written" than last year's. He went back to Princeton in the fall. That was the year he resisted, unsuccessfully, his mother's intention to settle down in Princeton. She stayed till he graduated, in June of 1922. Princeton was over.

5

Stevenson went West that summer and considered buying a ranch, but his father insisted he go to law school, and so in the fall he began. On September 26 he sent his first impressions to his mother: "This Harvard Law School is the most feverish place Ive ever seen —everyone works *all* the time and still about 25–35% get dropped every year. All we've heard since we arrived were gruesome tales of disaster from our friends and staggering stories of astonishing hours of work when the big reviews begin in March. Until then it is a comparative loaf. Just do your work from day to day—and it can be done easily in about 8 hours. Oh the news is certainly encouraging and I'm looking forward to a very delightful winter. Everyone around here insists that the Harvard Law School is the hardest graduate school of any kind in America. . . . I don't like Boston or Cambridge but it doesn't make much difference because we apparently are not going to have time for an enjoying of the urban communities. . . . The law school is sort of like being in business, not college."

He never liked Harvard Law. The academic work was hard, allowing little time for play. He remained—in a sense he remained for a long time—the Princeton undergraduate of the time of Scott Fitzgerald, the clubman who got no more than a "gentleman's third" and traveled abroad in the summer to "inspect" battlefields and perform feats of derring-do on Alps. The hard serious grind of the law repelled him. He had not wanted to study law at all; his father had virtually forced him to. As for Harvard University, its atmosphere was entirely different from Princeton's—he described it as "a city club rather than a country club."

He was going with Harriet Cowles, called Hite; from a friend he learned she had a new boy friend and he had "fallen most completely." A time or two his letters showed a flicker of interest in the law. But his heart still lay in Princeton—"Harvard has a splendid team and I'm afraid we'll have a hard time beating them this year" —and even in Bloomington—"Buff seems to be quite gay in Bloomington. . . . Its realy not such a bad place after all." Buffie visited him for the Harvard-Princeton football game. The night before he went to a Princeton smoker and "had a great time," then to Boston for a big party at the Copley Plaza. "I've never seen such a frightful crowd in my life." The game itself was an unmitigated triumph—

Princeton won: "The Princeton team—all green and without experience—simply beat Harvard by spirit and fight alone. It was a glorious day for us." Of a Sunday he and his friends slept late, read the
papers, talked about football, "and loafed luxuriously," then in the
afternoon borrowed a Ford and drove to suburban Milton to see the
"attractive young sister" of a friend. "We had tea in the demure and
chaste confines of the young ladies seminary and came back along the
river at sundown. . . . To discover that there really were trees and
grass after all was a pleasant revelation to me after being cooped up
in this God-forsaken city for 3 weeks."

His mother tried to encourage him:

> Dearest Laddie:
>
> As the time draws near for your argument, I wonder if you are in
> doubt about your success? Success as regards your equanimity? Let
> go your hold (as W. James says) resign your destiny to higher
> powers and you will get a perfect inward relief—and again—"re-
> laxation not intentness should be the rule"—and Virgil says, "They
> can because they *think* they can." So it all comes to *right* thinking
> —or right suggestion. The Coué[4] formula I gave of auto-suggestion
> (self suggestion) is the latest thing and a powerful thing. . . . Rest
> and sleep have always been your best medicine and please take my
> advice and get it now.

But for him, all, or nearly all, was drudgery. Or, rather, the prospect of drudgery: most of his law textbooks are lightly marked and
show little signs of having been read. A 1924 novel, *Nina,* by
Susan Ertz, is heavily marked. Francis T. P. Plimpton, a New York
lawyer who roomed with Stevenson and Charles Denby at Harvard
Law and who later became Stevenson's first deputy at the United
Nations, has recalled that, "If there had been a vote of the Class of
1925 at Harvard Law for who would be likely to be President, it
would probably have been Denby. It certainly wouldn't have been
Adlai. Adlai was delightful, pleasant, unassuming. He used to moan
about the difficulties of the law. He worked fitfully and complain-
ingly. He was conscientious about his work but he grumbled, 'What
am I doing all this for?' At law school he was never taken seriously."

That Thanksgiving was, his mother pointed out, the first she and
her son had spent apart since he had left home for boarding school
six years ago. She wrote: "I know you are thinking of us and wishing

---

[4] The so-called Coué Method was a popular self-improvement method of that
period; its leader recommended that one repeat endlessly to oneself the formula,
"Day by day, in every way, I am getting better and better."

we were all together. . . . Without this love of *home* and our desire to get together—to love and protect one another—where would be the use of living?" It seems a strange letter, considering the amount of time the members of this family spent apart. But Helen Stevenson had a way of idealizing things. In this same letter she wrote, "We are so happy in the thought that you are well and doing so splendidly." He was not doing splendidly at all, was barely passing.

He spent Christmas at home, then went to Lake Placid. His mother thought him changed and did not like the change—he seemed brusque and impatient. From the Lake Placid Club at Essex County, New York, Stevenson wrote to his mother, "If there is a heaven on earth I've found it at last." He was with Princeton friends, skiing, going on a sleigh ride with girls, playing bridge, hiking. He met "one of the best of the ex-debs of N.Y.'s 400."

Back to the grind: he had a case to prepare. He wrote a letter to Buffie and their mother at Southern Pines, North Carolina, that is a good example of his early prose style, a style he never quite shook off: "I was delighted to hear that you are comfortably installed and that the rejuvenation under salubrious southern skies had already commenced."

He stopped smoking for Lent. One night he "did society," as he put it, attending a "Junior Supper" dance at the Copley but not enjoying it. He went to Maine for a Washington's Birthday weekend, "probably the best week-end I ever had," with Plimpton, other college friends, several girls, all chaperoned by the parents of Lorna Underwood. They spent the weekend playing bridge, tobogganing by moonlight, cross-country skiing, playing hockey, sleigh riding, dancing at a fancy dress ball, skating, with "large and hilarious meals thrown in." He wrote: "All 14 of us ate at one table so the conversation was fast and furious." They returned to Boston in "a car reserved *exclusively* for us," a "riotous 5 hour ride." The girls were "all knockouts." But he mentioned none that he had courted. A little later he and his friends visited the Underwoods at their home in Belmont, a Boston suburb, and subsequently he dated Lorna Underwood. Plimpton says, "He pursued her hard but she never caught fire though I'm sure he did." Lorna herself, however, recalled years later that she had cared about him. After Stevenson's death his sister asked Lorna why she never married him; she replied, "He never asked me." On this first visit he wrote, "The Underwoods have a very nice house; apparently not tremendously wealthy, but very aristocratic, refined and cultured. . . . The daughters very attractive—one came out 2 or 3 years ago & the other last year I believe." The eight young people "set out for a tramp across the slushy countryside," struggling through "bottomless snow," returning in time for tea. "After tea we sat around & amused ourselves until supper, at which Mr. Underwood presided and constructed a Welsh rabbit of rare delicacy. Then followed a session of bridge and conversational jesting." Stevenson had begun a pattern of spending weekends at the country homes of friends. Even this early, his personality seems to have made him a welcome house guest.

Harriet Cowles was about to sail for Europe; he sent flowers and a telegram to her aboard ship. In New York, he "called on some of my business friends around town," then joined others for lunch at the Yale Club. He went to a matinee with Aunt Letitia Stevenson "and had a really delightful time with her." One of Stevenson's enduring and endearing traits was an ability to have "a really delightful time" with almost anyone—or so he said. After the theater he met "some more of 'the boys'" and they discussed their futures and went to Delmonico's for dinner. Next day he went down to Princeton to the Cap and Gown Club. "We're motoring up to New York"—lifelong, Stevenson said "motoring," not "driving," a locution alien to Midwest ears—"after dinner in time for me to catch the midnight back to Boston & the books."

He had received a $792 dividend from the *Princetonian* and speculated in stocks, but their value declined and he asked his father for money. He was planning to lease an eight-room house the next year with five others, including Francis Plimpton. He spent at least two weekends at the Plimptons' farm at Walpole, Massachusetts, that spring, "his ancestral manor" filled with pre-Revolutionary family relics, autographs of George Washington "and other celebrities."

As the term ended Stevenson wrote that he was worried about his marks. He had reason: at the end of this, his first year at law school, he scored 58 in Civil Procedure, 70 in Contracts, 65 in Criminal Law, 65 in Property, and 62 in Torts, an average of 64, equivalent to a C.

He returned next fall for his second year. Now his letters showed less distaste for Harvard, Cambridge, and Boston. He had not learned to like them; rather, he had learned to escape them by going to New York, Princeton, the Plimpton farm, or elsewhere. His letters do not show either that he had mastered the law school work; he simply did not write about it much. Many of his letters were lengthy, discursive, chatty, sometimes striving to be charming. Sometimes they contained a hard jarring note of bad taste or cruelty of which he was totally unaware. In a letter about a weekend trip to New York to meet Buffie, he described a man they met as "loquacious like most of his race," said he had met three friends in the evening for "a jolly old bicker," said he had gone shopping and "we Jewed them down from $35 to $25"—a phrase rather common at the time—for a book for the Underwoods. "At this juncture in the day's activities I removed from Buff's wing to the Princeton club." He went down to the financial district "for luncheon with some of the younger financiers." A young man and woman joined Stevenson and Buffie for dinner, then the couples went separately to different plays. He left Buffie in New York to go to the Plimptons' for several days of homework, riding, golf with Lorna Underwood, lunches at the clubhouse. Patterns were forming—patterns that recur throughout Stevenson's life: the house guest, the clubman, the tireless party-goer, the inability to be alone, the urge to meet the right people and get ahead; a girl and the theater, escape from his sister's wing, long courtly words to describe his obligation to weekend host and hostess; a sudden hint of prejudice. Stevenson's father visited him one year at Harvard, inspected the school, attended a class, "and seemed very impressed with the display of erudition not to mention the thirsty intellects of the semitic element," as Stevenson wrote.

The remark about Jews just noted is not an isolated instance. It flawed Stevenson's attitudes for years. In considering it, one must remember that Stevenson was, like all of us, a product of his time and his place. His place was the Midwest, plus Eastern schools attended largely by the sons of the wealthy, white, Protestant, and well-born; during those years, and in those places, and among those people, such utterances were simply made heedlessly.[5]

On October 15 he described a long weekend in New York at the home of Norman Davis, a prominent Democrat and financial adviser to President Wilson and the father of one of Stevenson's Harvard roommates. A girl and her mother from Cuba were also house guests. "The girl was very attractive and what with Irene & Maria from Memphis & Martha Davis who came down from Vassar for the week-end we were well supplied with attractive girls. On Saturday we motored to Princeton for the game." It was a typical Princeton day—lunch at the Quadrangle Club, the game, tea at Ivy, driving back to New York. But that evening in New York was not typical of a Princeton weekend; it was typical of a Stevenson weekend: "I sat up & listened to Mr. Davis talk about democracy etc. until about

[5] Again, a biographer of Eleanor Roosevelt has written that as a young woman she too "did share society's prejudice against Jews."

12:30—as you can imagine he is quite fascinating & has a tremenduous fund of information." There was always a measure of serious conversation buried somewhere in any Stevenson weekend. One Saturday he went to Lancaster with Haven Parker, "a Harvard student of the better class," whose father was "a very distinguished old member of this august commonwealth." Saturday night they dined on pheasant and played mah-jongg. They spent Sunday "at the ancient country place of the Fullers who reside in that locality." The engagement of Miss Anna Fuller was announced to "Mr. C. J. Hubbard, captain of the Harvard footballers during the past season." Stevenson wrote, "There was a large crowd of select Boston damsels and Harvard students."

His mother urged him to read Emerson and to go to church. She passed on advice that he practice law in Chicago. Apparently Stevenson said something derogatory about someone during Christmas vacation in Bloomington; his mother adjured him never to hate—but as always she quickly absolved him. She went back to the Battle Creek sanitarium and wrote to him from there January 23: "Our children have accomplished beyond our fondest dreams; my debts are paid, our income is more than we ever looked forward to; Father has had a vindication in this little 'boom' and can now, I hope, see himself going daily up in his own self-respect and sense of achievement."

That spring Stevenson was dating Lorna Underwood but he was also still interested, perhaps more seriously, in Harriet Cowles. He mentioned both in letters home. Curiously, he usually described occasions when he was with Miss Underwood and others, not alone with her. So begins a penchant for seeing a woman in the company of other men or women. Once that spring he described how he, Plimpton, Denby, Lorna Underwood, and two other girls had gone slumming in Boston. Next day they went riding and in the evening went to someone's house for supper and parlor games (which he disliked). He described another weekend at the Underwoods': "As always in the bosom of that most natural of families we had a riotous time. After lunch we spread rugs on the terrace and drank our coffee and bathed in the sun. Thus went the whole afternoon; a few neighbors dropped in and as tea time approached the usual delegation came out from Cambridge to pay homage." He might have been describing a weekend ten years later in Lake Forest or his own home in Libertyville or, for that matter, his weekend in somebody's country house during the 1950s or 1960s. This aspect of his way of life—a love of pleasure with attractive wealthy people in elegant country surroundings—was formed in college.

That spring Harriet Cowles jilted him. He told his mother, "The crumbling of the air castles is about over now. It did leave me a little bewildered for a couple of days and then unconsciously I found myself unconsciously forgetting all about it and quite as merry as usual—a little mortifying to myself in my self imposed role of the martyred lover! In calm, collected and dispassioned retrospect I feel quite sure that she suddenly made up her mind to marry this long suffering swain just this winter—she's always known him."

His mother told him it was God's will and all for the best. And, "Are you looking after that old head, putting in lots of tonic and oil and occasionally washing well and rinsing well? Be careful not to take cold. The instant you have any stoppage, take care of it at once —rest, sleep and lots of drinking water—eight glasses a day."

His mother repeated tales told by his cousins that he and his roommates drank heavily in their rented house at Harvard, and Stevenson wept, angrily denied the accusation, and said it was his cousin who drank too much: "[I] hope I shall never become so il-liberal as to object to entertaining ones friends with cocktails before a dance or dinner party—providing always that no one [such as his cousin] doesn't know when to stop." Stevenson did in fact drink sparingly, at least until the last few years of his life. He had a curious horror of drunkenness. Examinations were approaching; Stevenson was apprehensive and told his mother, "The last week is upon us and the fear of God is strong within me! I always seem to get worried before exams and wonder how I can possibly get thru." Lifelong, before a speech as before an exam, he was always stricken with nervousness and felt sure (or said he felt sure) he would fail at it.

He failed two courses, Agency and Evidence, scoring 51 in each, and his over-all grades averaged 58, a D—59 in Equity, 62 in Property II, 61 in Sales, and 62 in Trusts. This meant that he flunked out of Harvard Law and was not eligible to return as a student the following September. He could have returned in 1925, taken examinations in the subjects he had failed, and if he passed them been re-admitted. But he never went back. Some of his friends thought he had flunked out; others were not sure. Stevenson himself later tended to cloud the question of why he left Harvard.

6

After school ended, Stevenson attended the races at New London "& had the time of my life," he wrote. He and Plimpton spent a day on a yacht with Lorna Underwood. They had lunch aboard and returned for supper after a dance. "And then [the owner] put his beautiful launch with a crew of two at our disposal to take us way up the harbor to our hotel. Well all in all it was the best & most luxurious day of my life." He dined at the Davises' with the Democratic whip in the House and a Senator. He was in New York to attend the Democratic National Convention in Madison Square Garden, the famous long convention. Stevenson was an assistant sergeant at arms; so were Plimpton and two other friends. Stevenson's father had arranged it. His father was promoting the dark-horse compromise candidacy of David F. Houston, Wilson's Secretary of Agriculture and Treasury. Stevenson himself thought Houston had little chance and thought John W. Davis would be nominated. He was right, his father wrong.

Stevenson went home to Bloomington. Now, twenty-four years old, with two years of law school behind him, it was he who began to look after the family, not the other way around. Increasingly, his parents and sister looked to him. He was indeed the ablest and most sensible among them. That summer of 1924 they put him into the *Daily Pantagraph* to look after the Stevenson family interest.

The *Pantagraph* was a valuable property. When incorporated in 1907, its 800 shares of stock were valued at $250 per share, a total of $200,000. In 1911, when W. O. Davis, its owner, died, its value was appraised for inheritance tax purposes at $78,900, an extremely low figure. In 1929 the *Pantagraph* earned a net profit of $169,933; calculating valuation at ten times net earnings, as was customary then, its value would have been $1,699,330; evidence indicates that a tentative offer was made to purchase the paper in 1930 for $2 million.

When W. O. Davis died, ownership passed to his son, Bert Davis, and Bert's two sisters, Helen Stevenson and Jessie Merwin, in life estate. Bert ran the paper. By 1922 or 1923, however, his health was failing and he spent most of his time in California, handing management of the paper over to Davis Merwin, the elder son of Jessie Merwin, for by that time Bert Davis' own two sons were dead; it appeared that after his death ownership would devolve upon the Stevenson and Merwin families. Dave Merwin was an intelligent, difficult, somewhat erratic man with a quick mind, a hair-trigger temper, tremendous energy, and an almost compulsive drive to work. His younger brother Loring Merwin, called Bud, once said, "I don't think he really had a taste and temperament for newspapering, but he did a tremendous job while he was at it." The *Pantagraph* had gone into decline under Bert Davis. An opposition paper, the *Bulletin,* Democratic and evening, had begun to gain. Bert was glad to hand over control to Dave Merwin. Merwin, challenged by the *Bulletin,* plunged into building up the *Pantagraph.* He knew little of publishing but he learned everything. He took armloads of out-of-town newspapers home to study weekends. He worked day and night. His brother Bud said that when he came in the *Pantagraph* was going downhill. In four or five years he had it reorganized and going and he persuaded the *Bulletin* owner to sell out.

One of Bert Davis' sons had left his shares of *Pantagraph* stock to his own widow; the Stevensons and Merwins got together and bought and divided them. They could get together on little else. They feuded constantly. Lewis Stevenson often upbraided Merwin's mother, his wife patronized her. Merwin did not want Helen Stevenson at directors' meetings. Representing the Stevenson family interest in the *Pantagraph* would not be easy.

Dave Merwin ran the business side of the paper, Stevenson worked in the news room. He wrote articles on the famous monkey trial of John T. Scopes at Dayton, Tennessee. He covered a tornado in southern Illinois, describing the "bleeding smoking world" he saw. He and Merwin disagreed on nearly everything. "Dave and Ad had a lot of friction from their own different temperaments," Bud Merwin said. "Those two couldn't see anything alike. Adlai saw the arrangement was not going to work." After Bert Davis died in California a year later, July 16, 1925, the question became real: Who would control the *Pantagraph,* the Stevensons or Merwins? With Bert and both his sons dead, Grandfather W. O. Davis' will was ambiguous. The two families started a lawsuit to construe the will. The suit is usually described as "friendly" but the feeling between the two families was anything but friendly. The Stevensons took the view that the stock should be divided equally between Helen Stevenson and Jessie Merwin and, upon their death, their children. The Merwins took the view that it should be divided in proportion to the number of children each had.

The suit dragged on for two years (and the family acrimony for longer). It was heard in the Circuit Court at Bloomington in 1926. The court ruled for the Merwins. The Stevensons appealed, and the Appellate Court reversed the lower court in October 1927, and held for the Stevensons—divided the stock equally, 395 shares to each family. By that time, however, the question was moot: the Merwins had purchased the only ten outstanding shares from an elderly long-time employee. This purchase gave them control. It was made without the Stevensons' advance knowledge, and more than anything else exacerbated relations between the two families. Adlai Stevenson's father drafted a letter for Adlai to send to Dave Merwin, accusing the Merwins of perfidy. As far as can be determined, Adlai Stevenson never sent the letter. He was far less likely than his father to employ rhetoric and recrimination in business matters.

At one point Stevenson tried to settle the lawsuit—proposed that each family take half the stock but give Dave Merwin managerial control: Merwin refused. Stevenson's further relations with Dave Merwin can perhaps best be described as "businesslike." In their long correspondence over ensuing years they addressed each other by their first names; they were courteous; only occasionally did they collide head on; for the most part, they maintained a distant and correct relationship. Stevenson was on much better personal terms with Bud Merwin; they were more frank with each other; therefore, they were at the same time both friendlier and more frequently in open disagreement than Stevenson and Dave Merwin. Stevenson's true feelings showed in a letter he wrote to Bud Merwin in 1945, opposing "large salaries" from the *Pantagraph* "for members of the family and stockholders": "My view on these matters, as you know, springs from the purchase of [the old employee's] stock when I thought we were in good faith trying to resolve our family dispute by orderly recourse to the courts . . . this anxiety to get control of the paper by any means."

7

If the Merwins had not purchased the critical ten shares of stock, Adlai E. Stevenson might have remained in Bloomington, Illinois, as co-publisher of a downstate daily. Still, Stevenson and Dave Merwin could never have worked together. That he really wanted to become a publisher is clear, however. Throughout his life he made various attempts to buy newspapers. He seems to have thought of himself sometimes as a newspaperman. He had a journalist's curiosity; but he aspired to a publisher's power and money.

In any case, this was the last time he lived in Bloomington. On September 27, 1925, he entered Northwestern University Law School. At Northwestern Law his grades were much better than at Harvard. He took fourteen courses and made an A in five of them and a B in the other nine. He received his law degree in 1926 and was admitted to the Illinois bar.

Ill health, whether or not of psychosomatic origin, continued to plague his mother. She wrote to Buffie, "My first mistake was insufficient education in physocology, physics, hygiene, and physio-

analysis! The first study of mankind is man! and I can only pray that
many of my mistakes may not be visited upon my children." On
Stevenson's twenty-sixth birthday, February 5, 1926, his mother
wrote to "My darling *little* boy!" and dated the letter, "February 5—
the Natal Day." She recalled his childhood and said that now, she
supposed, "matrimony is intriguing you." She did not oppose his
marrying. Buffie, she wrote, wanted to marry an Italian actor and go
on the stage.

That summer Stevenson went to Europe with his mother and Buffie.
During the trip Buffie met a United States Foreign Service officer,
Ernest L. Ives, and later married him. Armed with press credentials
obtained by the *Pantagraph,* Stevenson made a trip alone to Russia,
crossed the Black Sea on a tramp steamer, and in Moscow walked
the streets and waited interminably—and fruitlessly—for an interview with the Foreign Minister. He viewed it as a great adventure,
nonetheless.

He spent a good deal of time in Italy where Mussolini was in
power, and wrote two articles about it which the *Pantagraph* published. In them he summarized Italian history and described the rise
of Mussolini and Fascism, which he viewed as "the only counter-
force to bolshevism." Of Mussolini's 1921 electoral success, he wrote:
"Here was the first conquest of the new spirit of Italy and the first
great manifestation of the new feeling of hope and accomplishment
that has radiated from Italy thru all Europe—the restless spirit of
youth which is everywhere supplanting the old order with its faith
and its passion. Thenceforth Fascism was no longer simply a movement of reaction against bolshevism; new and greater roles suggested
themselves to its tireless leader. . . . Italians have always preferred
to follow personalities rather than principles. This is the primary
reason why the rank and file of Italians are working with a spirit that
is altogether new. For its dynamic, dramatic qualities, Mussolini's
character has few historical counterparts, Italy presents a cleaner,
a more vigorous and enthusiastic atmosphere than ever before. . . .
Those incidents and measures in his career which to us as Americans,
bred in the democratic tradition, are hardest to condone have all been
eloquently if not altogether convincingly explained by Fascists whom
the writer has interviewed. . . . As the Fascist government has become more firmly entrenched . . . the right of free speech has pro-
portionately been denied. The process has finally culminated . . . in
the total abolition of the opposition press. This combined with other
repressive measures, such as the dissolution of all opposition parties
and organizations has created a situation which finds a counter-part
only in Russia. . . . One wonders just how much liberty you can

take away before you begin to tyrannize. . . . What the future of
Italy is no one can say. . . . One thing is clear, that Fascismo has
done great things for Italy. . . . Mussolini ranks with Lenin as
one of the great national idols of all time, but Italy must have peace
and tranquility if the vigorous tree that he has planted is to bear all
its potential fruit."

Playtime and schooltime were over. At the end of 1926, not quite
twenty-seven years old, Adlai Stevenson returned to Chicago and began his career as a lawyer. He did so without enthusiasm. He wrote
in a letter at the time, "I must confess, heretical and un-American as
it may seem, that I view the prospect without the least eagerness. . . .
I know perfectly well that if I am to make a 'success', sooner or
later I must 'sell out'—I mean chuck most of my ideas and my acute
sympathy for the less fortunate. A stony and obedient loyalty to class
and vested interests seems to be the necessary adjunct of a life time
of hard and imaginationless work."

CHAPTER THREE

A Career and a Marriage Begin
1927-1934

Stevenson went to work for Cutting, Moore & Sidley, now called Sidley & Austin, one of the oldest and most respected law firms in Chicago, organized in 1866. Stevenson himself always referred to it as "the old Sidley firm." It was a conservative firm with a general law practice. Most of its members were Republicans but it was non-political and, one of its former partners has said, "rather frowned on politics." Another associate said, "The Sidley firm was very social," and gave the impression he left because, not being a member of a prominent family, he felt he would not rise high in the firm. Edwin C. Austin, who later became the senior partner, has said, "The best thing then and now about our practice was variety. Some firms spend fifty or ninety per cent of their time on one client. We have a very varied practice. We do a great deal of corporate financial work—a considerable volume of trial work—a great deal of probate work—a fair amount of real estate. A very general practice with professedly no criminal or divorce practice—but even there we get involved on the prosecuting side of criminal work, thefts from our corporate clients. And with so many statutes providing fines and imprisonment in connection with matters of taxation, business, and employment and so forth, every businessman is a potential criminal."

Stevenson went to work for the firm as a clerk. A clerk was a young lawyer who worked for a law firm for a salary instead of sharing in the firm's profits, as the partners did; today clerks are called "associates." A few of the partners are "underwriting partners," senior partners who share more fully in the profits and also personally underwrite the risk of loss. Stevenson never became an underwriting partner in the Sidley firm, though he did become a partner on January 1, 1936. Ed Austin has said, "In his time a clerkship in this office was quite highly prized. We were rather strong on Princeton men. We had Donald McPherson and Bill Bangs, young partners, and Ed McDougal and Jim Oates, clerks. Dwight Dickinson and I, young partners, were from Midwestern universities. It was a small office. Cutting, Moore, and Sidley were the senior partners." Members of that firm became closely associated with Stevenson for many years, socially or in the law or in politics, or all three—Ogden West, Donald McPherson, James Oates, Ed McDougal, Wally Schaefer, George W. Ball.

In the 1870s the forerunner of the Sidley firm represented Western Union Telegraph. People sued the company for late or erroneous delivery of telegrams in various parts of the United States. The Sidley firm would pick a good local attorney to handle the matter locally. In Bloomington, they used the law firm of Stevenson & Ewing. Vice President Stevenson was a close friend of Sidley's founder. In the 1920s when Stevenson was hired, Sidley was the "internal head" of the firm, though Cutting was nominally its head. Stevenson once emphasized to a journalist that he got the job without his father's help, but his family background did him no harm. It was, however, by no means the only factor. Princeton counted. Donald McPherson, a partner in the firm who was interested in bringing young men in, was related to Ogden West, whom Stevenson had known at Princeton. West was a close friend of Stevenson during the late 1920s and early 1930s. In sum, a combination of family and Princeton ties, personal friendship, acceptable education and social position brought Adlai Stevenson to the Sidley law firm. It was a combination he used—later adding political ties—all his life.

His first full year, 1927, the firm paid him $1,450. This was about average for a clerk in those days.[1]

His income tax return for 1927 shows that in addition to his salary he received $1,659 in interest and $3,305 in dividends, mostly from *Pantagraph* stock—a total gross income of $6,414, of which he earned only $1,450 in salary. In the next year his salary was even more substantially overshadowed by other income—he not only received his usual *Pantagraph* dividends and his interest but he made more than $25,000 by speculating in the stock market; that year, of his

[1] His earnings from the firm in his first six years were as follows:

1927	$1,450	1930	$4,100
1928	$2,158	1931	$4,379
1929	$3,400	1932	$4,847

total gross income of nearly $30,000, he earned from salary only $2,158.

At the law firm, Stevenson performed the chores of any clerk. Austin has said, "All our clerks do a considerable amount of library work, research, preparing the basis for giving opinions. One of the traditions of this office is that we try to put young men in contact with the clients directly so that they get the experience of getting the client's story and advising him. Also there is a certain amount of small litigation that they handle—small claims cases. It gives the boys a little court experience."

2

A photograph of Stevenson taken at about this time shows a strong resemblance to his mother; his expression was rather authoritative, with even a touch of disdain. He was living in the area called the Gold Coast—a thin slice of Chicago along Lake Michigan not far north of the Loop. Here on Michigan Avenue and Lake Shore Drive and such streets as Astor Street, in mansions and apartments, dwelt the wealthiest, most powerful people in Chicago. A few blocks farther west lay a criminal slum. In the summers, Stevenson and other young bachelors lived in cottages in Lake Forest, the most opulent of all the North Shore suburbs, a village of vast estates and mansions, the home of the presidents and chairmen of the boards of Chicago's great mercantile and industrial establishments.

Not every ambitious educated young man who goes to Chicago from the small towns scattered around the Midwest to make his career is immediately accepted into the top layer of Gold Coast and Lake Forest society. What linked Stevenson to it?

Many of his friends, if asked when and how they first met him, are likely to look puzzled and say, "I can't honestly say. It seems as though I'd always known him." He simply turned up, a part of the scenery. It is the best measure of his instant, his automatic, acceptance into this society. Yet there are discoverable links. Family was one. For example, his sister Buffie Ives has said, "They were Father's friends. Margaret Farwell was a Welling, we met them first at Lakewood, New Jersey. Then Father was a friend of Medill McCormick. Then Francis Peabody, the coal man, was a friend of Father. Harriet Welling was a Walker—they went to Ephraim, Wisconsin, and she knew the older Adlai Stevenson, the Vice President, at Ephraim when she was seventeen. You meet a young man, he's a good name, you invite him. Mrs. James McAlvin, she was Joan Stuart, daughter of John T. Stuart, president of Quaker Oats—Adlai knew her at Charlevoix." Although Stevenson's father made great point of cultivating people who could be useful to him or his children, Buffie said that Stevenson was uncomfortable when his father tried to promote him. Princeton and Harvard were other links—Jim Douglas, Og West, Jim Oates, Bill McIlvaine. Harriet Welling, seven years older than Adlai Stevenson, who became one of his closest as well as most sensible lifelong friends, knew Buffie before she knew Adlai, had met her in 1925, when she was spending a summer at a ranch in Wyoming. Once Mrs. Welling's family rented a house at Charlevoix. Dutch Smith of Lake Forest said, "Adlai went to the H F Bar ranch in Wyoming. Groups from here used to go there. I went to the ranch in 1919. I knew Adlai a little at Charlevoix—saw him maybe twice in a summer. He and I were both there in 1900. He was four months old and I was two months old. For a while he lived in Lake Forest with Nig Bowen. Nig was Hotchkiss and Yale. They probably met through Og West. Where he went to school is very important. He'll get on every party list you could think of. Then it's up to him." At the H F Bar Ranch, too, Adlai met Elizabeth Nitze, a sister of Paul Nitze and nicknamed Pussy, who married Walter Paepcke and became an elegant leader of Chicago society. Edison and Jane Dick became two of Stevenson's closest lifelong friends. A friend who knew them in those days has said, "Both Adlai and Buffie were very socially conscious. VIP-itis—Ad and Buffie had it." It may be said that Stevenson made the transition from Bloomington to the Gold Coast with the help of family, Princeton, Harvard, Charlevoix, and the H F Bar Ranch, and that he made the secondary move from the Gold Coast to Lake Forest because his bachelor friends on the Gold Coast spent their summers in Lake Forest.

On the estate of Graham Aldis in Lake Forest—Aldis had preceded Stevenson at Princeton—was a building called Red Bird Cottage. Stevenson spent his summers there, and in another cottage called the Chateau, with several other bachelors. One, Stephen Y. Hord, who would become a partner in Brown Brothers Harriman & Co. and advise Stevenson on investments, came to this society in 1921 from Terre Haute, Indiana, with family and background similar to Stevenson's. "We were all kind of on hire to the social secretary lady at the debutante parties and if you had a dinner coat and kept your neck and ears clean you could go to those things. The hostesses would call in, say, 'We need four men for the day after tomorrow.' There was another bachelor cottage in Lake Forest called the Stagger Inn. They drank all the time. We were the nice, clean all-American boys." Hord, a few years older than Stevenson, was an assured, careful, respected man. As young bachelors they rode bicycles to the Lake Forest suburban station and took the commuter train to their offices in Chicago's LaSalle Street financial district. They inhabited a world of investment banking and corporate law and finance, or horsy weekends and debutante parties, a world where the men used a kind of locker-room humor and called each other by their last names. It all seems quite unlike the Adlai Stevenson the world knew in the 1950s and 1960s. But it was his world in the 1920s. One of the most interesting things about Adlai Stevenson is that he inhabited several worlds at different periods of his life—indeed, at times he inhabited several worlds simultaneously—yet he seems for the most part to have managed with aplomb the stresses of moving from one to another. His friends in those days were young lawyers, bankers, businessmen, and, a little later, university people. Those people remained his friends for many years. Soon he joined the Wayfarers Club, described by Ed McDougal as "a small exclusive coterie of men who had had some unusual experience, usually in the form of travel"; the Commonwealth Club, for younger business and professional men; and, later, the Commercial Club, for business leaders who were also interested in public service. The Commercial Club contained, a member's widow has said, "the leading capitalists" of Chicago. Most were Republican (as, indeed, were nearly all of Stevenson's Gold Coast and Lake Forest friends).[2]

Stevenson, an "eligible young bachelor" as the phrase went, was much in demand among the young society girls. Most memories of him in those years, 1927 and 1928, revolve around dances and parties. Og West's widow, Ruth Winter, has said, "He was a gay blade, very gay. There seemed to be no signs of anything serious in him at the time." Along with the other young bachelors on the social secretary's list, he attended the Assembly Ball, society's great event of the year. (One had to be in the Social Register to attend the Assembly Ball, according to one who attended.) Some-

---

[2] The reader will find various passages where the parochial, frivolous outlook of Lake Forest people at that time is criticized, together with their sometimes bad influence on Stevenson as he moved into politics. It must be understood that a number of individuals—for example, Hermon Dunlap Smith, called Dutch, and Jane W. Dick—are always excepted from the category of "the Lake Forest crowd." While they did live there, they were serious people, not frivolous; they took politics seriously, they were intelligent and able and interested in issues; and they had a breadth of vision that enabled them to see far beyond Lake Forest. They were, moreover, devoted to Stevenson and were of immense help to him in his political enterprises.

thing of the quality of that life can be found in the recollections of
the women who were young when he was. Jane Dick has recalled,
"I made my debut in Chicago in 1925. A little later Adlai came up
from Bloomington, he was single, he was six years older than I. If
the older men paid any attention to us, we thought this was really
exciting. I can't remember when I first met him. The parties—those
were glorious days. He was delightful and charming and always
courteous. He made you feel that you were the person that he was interested in. I'm sure he found lots of boring people. But he always
had a natural courtesy and natural kindness."

Some of these people felt a responsibility to society; more often
than not it took the form of private charity. Hermon Dunlap Smith's
grandmother had been a friend of Jane Addams, the social worker
who founded Hull House in the Chicago ghetto. Smith's grandmother also helped establish Juvenile Court and once took a found-
ling to the Cook County Board and dumped the child into the
board members' laps. Jane Dick's father, though a conservative Republican businessman, entertained what were considered advanced
liberal views on labor questions and felt, as his daughter has put it,
"one's responsibility to society—it was not exactly *noblesse oblige*
but something like that, the idea that we who were so lucky had great
obligations." His sister was also a friend of Jane Addams and helped
start Hull House. So was the grandmother of William McCormick
Blair, Jr., son of another wealthy and social family who later became
Adlai Stevenson's close associate. Jane Dick said, "I thought it was
romantic that my uncle proposed to his wife on a cracker barrel in
the basement of Hull House. As little children we went to Christmas
plays at Hull House. Having been brought up with a gay, lighthearted
mother and this father, I had a feeling that fun and frivolity were all
right but at the same time I was brought up with a more serious
strain. So I found Adlai very sympathetic when I was young. He
didn't just make table talk. I realized he had much more, despite the
gay humor that bubbled up."

Harriet Welling became active in the 1930s in the Chicago Council on Foreign Relations. Here we find a crucial interest of Adlai
Stevenson's life—the Chicago Council on Foreign Relations.

Of the late 1920s, Mrs. Welling said, "Chicago was more colorful
in those days. The first Mrs. John Carpenter was a talented amateur
who decorated the first Casino Club and designed big benefits like
the famous Streets of Paris. In the twenties there were lots of fancy-
dress parties, lots of black face—it was a gay era. A booming era,
with men like Samuel Insull having enormous prestige. Adlai was
married in 1928 and then along came 1929."

Ruth Winter has recalled, "It was a strange period. Debuts, coming out—introduction to friends of family—but then came months or sometimes years of social life. It seems now to belong to a different age and a different planet. I'd been to college," unlike many of the young girls, "but my family wanted me to go through this business anyway. At that time Adlai aroused a great deal of curiosity—he was new here. It wasn't very long until everyone was drawn to him. Ellen Borden and I grew up together on Bellevue Place in Chicago. She lived in the big house on the corner. She was an imaginative, sensitive person with a sense of humor. Then we separated—I went to college, she went to a school and led a very protected life. I don't think she ever went out with a man until she came out at the age of nineteen. She was presented at court [of England]—that was the thing certain people did. Then we met again, meeting eligible young bachelors. At first Adlai was not interested in Ellen or me. He was interested in older women with experience in the world. That made him all the more desirable."

What had set him apart? Jane Dick once recalled sitting out a dance to talk politics with him. She said she thought the "campaign ballyhoo was disgusting" and, to be elected, a candidate need only lay down "a few clear-cut ultimatums about what he'd do and wouldn't do." Stevenson replied with a lengthy discourse on compromise as the essence of democracy. Ruth Winter said, "He had done more traveling, especially in Russia."

Buffie Ives said that Stevenson proposed to at least three girls before he proposed to the girl he would marry. One of them was Claire Birge of Connecticut, whom he had met at Charlevoix in 1923. He was then twenty-three, she seventeen. Though separated by distance, they corresponded and saw each other intermittently until 1928, when he married; and in 1925 he asked her to marry him. Years later their friend Dutch Smith asked why she had refused, and she said she had been too young for marriage, still trying to find herself, and had looked upon him as an older brother to whom she was greatly devoted. Stevenson was also interested in Alicia Patterson, daughter of Captain Joe Patterson, the swashbuckling co-editor of the Chicago *Tribune* with his cousin, Colonel Robert R. McCormick, and founder of the New York *Daily News*. Alicia Patterson made her debut about that time. Jane Dick recalls, "I adored her. A great person. A good astringent liberal, very downright." The Pattersons lived in Libertyville, where Stevenson later built a house. "She had a lot of brains and a lot of Patterson in her. She was individualistic and headstrong." Alicia Patterson was married three times, the last time to Harry Guggenheim, and they remained married until she died.

She knew Stevenson intimately at various periods of his life. A
friend of both said, "I always thought Adlai was a little afraid of
Alicia." Whether or not he was, the girl he finally married was
Ellen Borden.

3

Ellen Borden Stevenson was the daughter of John and Ellen
Borden. John Borden's father had made a fortune in mining. His
wife Ellen "was always spiritual," a friend has recalled. "She was
in Moral Rearmament," an ethical movement begun in the late
1930s, "and theosophy." Borden was wiped out in the stock market
crash. Later he and his wife were divorced. He remarried twice.
His first wife, Ellen's mother, was also remarried, to John Alden Carpenter, the composer. John and Ellen Borden had two daughters.
One, Betty, died years later in mysterious circumstances. In the
mid-1920s the Bordens lived in a mansion at 1020 Lake Shore
Drive. Mrs. Borden and Mrs. Potter Palmer were the two "so-
called Queens of Society" in Chicago. Mrs. Borden was "very social"
but "devoted to her children and very outgoing. Ellen was devoted
to her mother. As a child, she used to write poems and put them under her mother's pillow. She came out in 1926 or 1927 and married Adlai in 1928. At her coming-out party at the Blackstone,
Ethel Waters did the latest dance called the Black Bottom."

In December 1926, as Chicago "society" prepared for the horse
show, a major event, Ellen's mother gave a small tea at her Lake
Shore Drive home, and a newspaper published a picture of Ellen
and another girl with a champion polo pony, describing them as
"two of the season's most popular debutantes." The picture showed
her as what was then called "dark blonde," with wide eyes and wide
mouth and a curiously childish expression on her face.

Young Ellen Borden was beautiful or at the least extremely attractive. Over and over people who knew her used the words "fey"
and "glamorous." She was "charming-looking, not very educated,
but bright, quite a glamor girl." A friend whose wife was in the
wedding party once said, "Ellen was attractive and capable and
bright but highly competitive. She was enthusiastic about Adlai as
long as she had a picture of herself as the outstanding person and
intellect and a picture of Adlai as a nice convenient person for
whom she had affection. Ad wasn't 'running for anything' with his
friends—Ellen always was. She dominated." Another friend has recalled, "I remember when Adlai met Ellen. I can hear him saying,

'I like that round face.' She had a very open face. She was a gay person, like a butterfly coming out of a cocoon. Everything was a delight. Everything was new. She had been so protected. She had no relationship with the world. Here she was receiving an awful lot of attention. And I don't think she was spoiled by it—she had a naïve response to it. There was a freshness about her that was appealing. She had a real gift for writing poetry. That was another thing that appealed to Adlai. She had a whimsical turn of mind. She and I would give joint house parties at Lake Geneva—both our families had houses there, so we'd both invite these gentlemen we met in Chicago there. Adlai was one of them. During that time he really and genuinely fell in love with Ellen. She had many beaux but she was interested in this man of the world."

Jane Dick: "Ellen was completely self-centered. She was pretty, not beautiful but pretty, and she had an intriguing fey quality about her. She was spoiled. I have the impression that her father was a rather frivolous man who played polo and all that sort of thing. She had been brought up to believe that she was a sort of princess."

Why did Ellen and Adlai Stevenson marry? Mrs. Welling has said, "She told me much later that she thought he could give her a more interesting life." Jane Dick said that Stevenson, upon arriving in Chicago, had not acted so much the grandson of a Vice President as a small-town boy come to Chicago. She said Ellen believed she had "picked off this attractive and interesting young bachelor from downstate." Stevenson was somewhat dazzled and overwhelmed by Ellen, who appeared glamorous, pretty, interesting, and well read. "Ellen gave the appearance of being well read but I don't know how much she actually read. I heard her quote for years from the life of Henry Adams as though she had just read it the other day." For Stevenson, Ellen opened up a whole vast new world, Chicago, with all its power and wealth. Jane Dick vigorously denied he was "marrying money," as others have suggested. Similarly, she believed, it was Ellen's "fey" and "literary" qualities rather than her society "glamour" that attracted Stevenson. "He was very proud of her because she was pretty and a charming hostess and good at décor."

Stevenson's parents opposed his marriage to Ellen. Many years later he told one of his few confidantes, Marietta Tree, that his parents had "done everything they could to stop the marriage." Buffie Ives has recalled, "When our father met Ellen, he told Mother and me, 'He's got the wrong girl.'" Their engagement was announced at Lake Geneva, Wisconsin, in the summer of 1928. At that time Stevenson told his mother, "Ellen's quiet reassuring way which I so long thought dreamy indecisiveness, is resolving itself into an ordered calmness and is exceedingly good for an intense 'planner' like we are. My happiness & certainty envelop me & I feel already her calming effect."

They were married at four o'clock on Saturday afternoon, December 1, 1928, in the small chapel of the Fourth Presbyterian Church on the Gold Coast. Greenery covered the chapel's walls and ceiling. The chapel holds only about thirty people. The reception afterward in Mrs. Borden's home at 1020 Lake Shore Drive was huge, and a man who attended has said that "the top of society in Chicago" was there. Buffie had been married to Ernest Ives, the Foreign Service officer, for nearly two years and, from Turkey, sent Adlai and Ellen a rug. (Her father predicted Buffie and Ernest would be happy, and they did stay married and had one son, Tim, who became manager of the *Pantagraph*'s radio station in Bloomington.)

4

The Stevensons moved into a small apartment on the Gold Coast. Stevenson's mother wrote, "And you, Ellen dear, must take care of your health, get lots of out-of-doors, and inspirational interests! Won't you please encourage Adlai to go to Dr. Irons, and you should go too. . . . How about his new clothes? His evening clothes were all too small & I would be relieved to know he has gotten some new ones! Please relieve my agony on this score! . . . A coming statesman must look the part!" Two months married, Stevenson wrote to his mother, "I feel very guilty for not having written in detail long ago but we've been suffering from a severe attack of society—wedding, engagement parties & then just parties. . . . Nig Bowen is engaged to Kay Throne—I distinguished myself with a speech on the homelife of the Stevensons at the announcement dinner! We are contemplating a house in Lake F[orest] for the summer & have been out once to look them over." They had gone to the opera with friends and entertained Ellen's mother and uncle at dinner. "That's the extent of our entertaining—no teas for 150 yet—or ever I hope!" In another letter he said, "We are having lots of quiet evenings now—good reading and bitter chess & checker contests!"

During these years the Stevensons rented apartments and a house in town in the winter and, in the summer, a house in Lake Forest. Ruth Winter has recalled, "I saw them a lot. They were very happy and gay. They did not entertain a lot. He was working awfully hard. I don't remember parties. I remember more of them as a family—her being absorbed in her babies." Their first child was born

October 10, 1930, and they named him Adlai Ewing Stevenson III. They had two more boys, Borden Stevenson, born July 7, 1932, and John Fell Stevenson, born February 7, 1936. "Ellen was terribly excited about that first little boy, so huge and comical-looking. She was a sort of model mother. He took pride in this. They lived quite simply. Adlai hated to spend money. It used to drive Ellen wild. She would complain to me about some piece of furniture she wanted and he wouldn't let her buy. Even food. So they went out more than they entertained. But they did the things everybody did. Once a year to the Assembly Ball—get dressed up. With Adlai making fun of her in front of her and she enjoyed it. He'd tease the life out of her about spending money on flowers. She was gay, she'd laugh a great deal. He was proud of her beauty—oh, she was pretty. She had a kind of inward grace. She'd come into a room rather quietly, with poise, and would be charming. She was a very good hostess."

Among the couples they saw were the following men and their wives—Walter Paepcke, who became chairman of Container Corporation of America; Stephen Hord, the investment counsel; Don Lourie, who became president of Quaker Oats; William McIlvaine, a lawyer with whom Stevenson had gone to college; Robert Hutchins, the precocious president, later chancellor, of the University of Chicago. To a considerable extent their friends were his rather than hers and some were several years older than she. Occasionally the Stevensons entertained in Ellen's mother's big house—Steve Hord recalled a costume party there at which everyone was supposed to dress as his or her "suppressed desire." In the country they went fox hunting, the Onwentsia Hunt. Once the Stevensons, the McBrides, the Otises, the Hords, the Kelloggs, and the Dicks went on a skiing trip to Michigan.

One of their friends recalls, "Other wives got along together but Ellen was a little bit, oh, high-hatted. She couldn't remember other people's names. She was not a part of that group as he was." Jane Dick mentions an incident in her living room. Ten or twelve people were present, all listening to Stevenson, "enthralled." Seeing this, Ellen monopolized a man's attention, though he preferred listening to Stevenson. This stratagem failing, Ellen rose abruptly and said, "Adlai, we are going home," and he "jumped up," Jane Dick recalled, "and they left." Many of their friends note that Ellen "had a way of either making or breaking a party." Entering a room, she "made an entrance" and dominated the group; thereafter, she would be charming or nasty, as she chose, and on this choice depended the gathering's success. Their friends recall that as Stevenson's prominence rose Ellen increasingly chose to be nasty. Jane

Dick has said, "He was basically very much of a family man. When he lost his home base, it was a terrible thing," that is, his divorce. "He was rooted there. His security was lost. People who saw him in later life in New York didn't see him the way he really was. He was basically monogamous."

We have another glimpse of the Stevensons' family life. Their first son, Adlai III, has said, "We *never* demonstrated affection in our family. We were not a demonstrative family. We were not a close family. Dad was in London or somewhere. The children were away in school or on trips. It's not hard to understand why he was flattered by women [later] and always helping out with [other people's] children. He never felt confident that he had done a good job with his own children. His marriage failed. He loved the ladies and the children, and he needed them. They probably gave him a sense of family he lacked in his own." Most of the people they were seeing were businessmen or lawyers with few concerns beyond their work and social life, with little interest in ideas or public affairs, though most voted Republican. As the men got on, it was a life revolving around the office on LaSalle Street and the commuting train to Lake Forest weekdays, Saturday hunts and Saturday night parties and Sunday brunches. Stevenson appeared to fit himself comfortably into it. Jane Dick said, "He liked people. Mickey Kellogg was a rock-ribbed Republican but he didn't discuss politics with her—he enjoyed and adored her, he played tennis with her, he and Ellen and the boys stayed with the Kelloggs in British Columbia, fishing. She was about as interested in discussing politics or philosophy as— well, let's say Mickey was very engaging. Adlai simply responded and enjoyed her. She never saw the other Adlai," that is, the serious public man.

Over and over, talking with these people, one is impressed with the essential frivolity of life in Lake Forest in the late 1920s and the 1930s. And impressed with Stevenson's rise above it. Wealth, family, position—these helped him but handicapped him too. This was a closed society that he had broken into. It was a pattern throughout his life. Time and again, in Lake Forest, in the United States Government, in Cook County machine politics and Democratic national politics, among the floating international set in his last years, he broke into a society hermetically sealed off from the rest of life and somehow fit himself into it.

A number of times Stevenson took Ellen to Bloomington but the visits were not a success. Bud Merwin thought Ellen hated coming to Bloomington, felt she had married beneath herself. Mrs. Merwin said, "I remember a summer party for Adlai and Ellen. Ellen came here with tremendous reluctance, and she always turned up in something that looked like she had just come from doing the kitchen dishes. Everyone else was dressed for the party. People here felt that she felt that they were not worth putting on a dress for." One night at Joe Bohrer's Ellen said she couldn't abide parties in Bloomington. People who knew the Stevensons during those years say that Buffie represented "a problem" to Ellen.

Summers during those years, and in fact throughout their life together, they had no vacation place of their own but, rather, spent holidays with friends. They went to the Wausakee Club in northern Wisconsin to which Ed Austin belonged. In 1930 they began what became almost annual visits to the summer place of the Dutch Smiths at Desbarats, Ontario, near Sault Ste. Marie.

Stevenson's private letters written during the 1930s still had a rather boyish ring, not unlike his letters from Princeton. Once he wrote to Buffie and Ernest Ives, "How's it going? At the moment you must be approaching your new domicile & we hope it will be all you anticipate. . . . I'm frantically busy with office work—on the day and night shift again—and on top of it all I've been commanded to act as General Chairman of the President's Birthday Ball for Chicago —ain't that hell! . . . Ho hum, its Sat. night & I'm still at the d— office." Jane Dick thought he was not entirely happy in his inner life in those years. He once told her, "I can make myself believe almost anything."

Perhaps the most striking thing about this period of his life, however, is the parallel between his mother and his wife. His mother tended to dominate social gatherings by being stagy and "always on," as an actress is; so did Ellen. His mother pretended to considerable taste and ability in the arts but actually was neither very talented nor interested in intellectual things; so with Ellen. His mother was a snob; so was Ellen. His mother could make things difficult for her husband; so could Ellen. (Ellen once said, in the presence of Stevenson and Jim Oates and Ed Austin, the senior partner in his law firm, "No gentleman should work." Austin has said, "It threw a little light for me upon what he was up against at home.") Both his wife and mother were, if not real beauties, close to it. Both dressed beautifully—when they chose to—and were conscious of it. Both dominated, or tried to dominate, their husbands.

5

Stevenson had been married less than five months when his father died. The previous summer, in 1928, at the time of the Democratic National Convention, Lewis Stevenson had been briefly mentioned as a possible vice-presidential candidate with Al Smith. During the campaign, Lewis joined with George Peek, who later became head of the Agricultural Adjustment Administration under President Roosevelt, and others in running a "corn belt" committee for Al Smith. Afterward, Lewis and his wife went abroad to visit Buffie Ives and her husband. His wife stayed with them; Lewis, returning home in February of 1929, wrote a long letter to Buffie, upbraiding her for saving $1,000 he had given her instead of spending it to improve her health, adjuring her to take care of her mother, telling her to make her husband quit smoking, discussing at length some obscure problem about a dog ("seems odd that such matter as a dog would have been allowed to upset an entire family"), and imploring her not to ruin her life: "Observe your mother & me & our unhappy lives as examples to be avoided. . . . I have been denied many of the real pleasures of life & I am afraid there is always in me a feeling of resentment on account of it. . . . I like E[rnest Ives] greatly. . . . He can do much & I believe will if you help him *in the right way.* And that is not by running around to teas and cocktail parties with people who do not count. . . . One word more B & Listen to it. Do not harbor *resentment,* nor *punish.* They *never* fail to react *horribly. I know.* . . ."

Various arrangements had gone awry, he wrote to his wife: "It's all so unfortunate." He had seen Adlai: "Adlai, believe me, was never better nor have I ever seen him so happy. He has been made President of some sort of Charity Ball and is full of that to overflowing now. Ellen too. They may give a 'Night in Hollywood' and if they carry it out as they are now planning it will be a hit." The maid, Alverta Duff, had not yet opened the house in Bloomington; he was living in one room of it, his bedroom. He wrote to his wife on March 24 from Adlai's apartment: "Will send you a hurried line while waiting for Ad & Ellen's dinner guests. . . . We have just come in from a bully time. Ad, Ellen & I visited the zoo & had lots of fun. Apartment is lovely & they seem very happy." He expressed relief that she was staying with Buffie "to recuperate."

Helen's trip to Europe was a failure. On March 26, Adlai wrote to his mother, "We've naturally been somewhat alarmed about . . . vissicitudes you & Buff have encountered. I'm afraid yours has been an ill omened trip & instead of a pleasant visit with Buff, all you've had was dysentery & a sore finger!" He related his father's visit: "Our first family party was a pronounced success. . . . I've sent the LaSalle down to Bloomington where it awaits you—and we are using our Graham-Paige."

That day his father had a heart attack while reading at the Bloomington Club, entered the hospital at Normal, and ten days later, on April 5, 1929, died. He was sixty years old. Before he died, he advised his son never to go into politics—it was an ungrateful business.

Among Lewis Stevenson's papers was a document he had written more than two years earlier: "Notes for Adlai to help him in case of my death." It began, "I want to be buried next to my father. Your mother should be buried in her father's lot." His will and directions for his funeral could be found in his "brown colored tin box. *Read directions at once.*" (Lewis had always been a little imperious.) His assistant, Fred Robinson, he wrote, could explain the records on the farm properties. "As the years pass he will realize what I did for him, feel differently I'm sure, & help you if you ask him. But do not put him in charge. He is old, fat & lazy." The document was long, containing advice on how to handle the most minute details. Lewis had a final piece of advice: under no circumstances was Adlai or his mother to allow the tax collector into the house to make his annual inventory of personal property. Instead, Adlai should simply copy Lewis' previous schedule, take it to the assessor in the basement of the courthouse, sign it and swear to it, and let it go at that.

Adlai, Ellen, and Ellen's mother went to Bloomington for the funeral, held in the Second Presbyterian Church. The Rev. Martin D. Hardin, Lewis' brother-in-law and pastor of a church in Ithaca, New York, delivered the eulogy. Governor Louis L. Emmerson, former Governor Fifer and former Lieutenant Governor John G. Oglesby of Springfield attended the funeral as honorary pallbearers.[3] As so often in his lifetime, Lewis and Helen had been apart when he died—she was still abroad. Lewis was buried as he wished, in the Bloomington cemetery beside his parents. Helen did not learn he was dead until Adlai met her at the boat and told her.

6

Adlai Stevenson spent months meticulously settling his father's estate. Even before his father's death, Stevenson had been assuming management of the family affairs. Now he was virtually in full

[3] Also in the long list of honorary pallbearers were Frank H. Funk, Fred B. Capen, Chester Davis, former Mayor William E. Dever of Chicago, former Governor Edward F. Dunne, David F. Houston, two former United States ministers, Senator J. Hamilton Lewis, and Mayor Carter H. Harrison of Chicago. Among those attending, the *Pantagraph* listed V. Y. Dallman, editor of the *Illinois State Register* in Springfield; Logan Hay; George N. Peck; and various relatives.

charge. Buffie gave him her power of attorney. His mother's health was failing; increasingly he became responsible for her care.

Lewis' death precipitated a great uproar over the family silver. When Grandfather Stevenson left the vice presidency, the Senate had given him a silver tray with an elaborate inkwell. This was "the great family possession," Buffie Ives said. The Stevensons were careful about their flat silver, too—"I remember that every time we left the house that brown wooden box that looked like a coffin was taken to the bank and put there for safekeeping—every trip we made Mother would say, 'Lewis, did you take the silver?'" The great family treasure had been inherited by Letitia Stevenson, Lewis' sister. Adlai's mother had taken it to Princeton with her, then taken it back to the bank in Bloomington. After Lewis died, nobody could find it. "Aunt Letitia made a terrible row over this," Buffie recalled. "She suspected that Lewis had sold it or that I had it. Once she threatened to go to court about it. They even dug up the basement looking for it. Mother went to Chicago to see a medium about it. I came home from Europe and Adlai met me and took me over to make an affidavit because Joe Bohrer thought that I had taken the silver to Europe. They had detectives watching the bank." Stevenson tried to trace the silver through a national silversmiths' association. The affair went on and on. Years later a man at the bank called Joe Bohrer and said, "We looked up on the balcony and found it." The family divided the silver. Stevenson at first refused to accept any but finally accepted one piece while he was governor.

In December of 1929, Stevenson engaged in a dispute over the *Pantagraph* salary of Dave Merwin. Merwin had raised the question at the December directors' meeting but, since Stevenson was unable to attend, had deferred it. He believed he deserved a raise because he had almost singlehandedly operated the *Pantagraph* "to the very marked benefit of the stockholders," other men in similar jobs received as much as $60,000, he himself had been offered more elsewhere. There could be no doubt that in the five years he had been running the paper its circulation, advertising, prestige, and profits had increased greatly. He wanted $15,000. Stevenson asked an outsider for advice. Merwin wanted to discuss the matter with Stevenson but was unable to see him. Stevenson did not attend the postponed directors' meeting on December 14. It raised Merwin's salary as of January 1 to $15,000. Stevenson was "surprised" and compelled "to assume that your request for my acquiescence as a director was only a perfunctory gesture." The dispute sputtered on, Stevenson saying he hadn't known they intended to settle the matter at the December 14 meeting—"if you had that in mind, why didn't you say so in so many words?"—and Merwin responding with similar acerbity. They came to no open break, however.

Dave Merwin did indeed build the *Pantagraph*. He corresponded regularly with Stevenson, going into great detail to keep him informed of all its operations, emphasizing its business operations much more than its editorial policies. Clearly, during these early years, not only Merwin but Stevenson too was far more interested in the *Pantagraph*'s profits than its policies. Stevenson left the running of the paper to Merwin. He seldom attended directors' meetings, picnics, or ceremonial functions. A few times Stevenson gave Merwin legal advice (and was paid for it), but for the most part Merwin relied on a Bloomington law firm. The paper was a moneymaker; even in the first ten months of the depression year, 1930, it showed a net profit of $119,177. As the depression deepened, advertising declined, and Merwin began cutting costs. He brought the paper through the depression.

7

In 1929, Stevenson's total income was $13,400, of which $3,400 came from his earnings at the law firm. After Ellen's father lost his money in the stock market crash, Stevenson teased his wife at parties, "And I thought I was marrying an heiress." Stevenson and Ellen kept separate accounts. At least once in the early 1930s they followed the investment advice of her father, John Borden. Sometimes Stevenson and his father-in-law quarreled, but more often their correspondence was friendly and it continued through the 1930s. Mr. Borden fell on hard times, and Ellen contributed to his support, and Stevenson arranged for other members of the family to contribute, devoting much time to the effort. Ellen's mother, by then married to John Alden Carpenter, made a large gift to Ellen in 1936, and Stevenson, building a new house in Libertyville, thanked her. Ellen repeatedly overdrew her bank account, and Stevenson arranged to have her dividends sent to him so he could keep track of them. His relationship with Borden was sympathetic and patient.

Both Stevenson and his wife had been speculating during these years. In later years Stevenson became conservative in his investments. He was not a plunger. One of his law partners, Newton N. Minow, once tried to persuade him to invest heavily in a business venture; he put up only a modest amount; had he plunged, he could have made a fortune. Throughout his life Stevenson was tight-fisted, "a hard man with a dollar," one who seldom picked up a luncheon check, one who spent a great deal of time and energy avoiding spending. Wasteful spending, public or private, pained him. Some of his closest friends considered him miserly. William Benton, who in later years became a business associate and personal friend of Stevenson, said that love of money was Stevenson's worst weakness. Stephen Hord considered Stevenson a shrewd investor, with innate sense of values and potential. "Horse sense. He calculated the degree of speculation. Stevenson liked money."

Ed McDougal, who had joined the Sidley law firm earlier, said, "He did the things the ordinary law clerk would do—made motions in court, handled minor matters, real estate matters, replevin suits," that is, suits to repossess articles whose purchasers had defaulted on their payments. "That was in the depression and there were a lot of replevin suits. One of our clients made motion picture projectors and Adlai repossessed a good many." Once when Stevenson went to a motion picture theater to repossess the projector, the manager asked permission to show the film which was about to start; Stevenson consented, watched the movie, then picked up the projector. This work did not please Stevenson: The minutes of a firm meeting on December 15, 1931, show that he asked to be relieved of it. McDougal has said, "In the six years from 1927 to 1933, he did the ordinary mine-run things. He did not immediately emerge," smiling, "as a Daniel Webster or a Henry Clay. He worked hard, he was assiduous, he was very conscientious."

Ed Austin added, "Stevenson was always a hard worker. I remember one situation we put him into, a corporate financial deal, that was a little over his head. We had to send someone to help him; he lacked experience. But I would say that Stevenson was an excellent lawyer and would have developed into one of the outstanding lawyers of the country if he had concentrated on his law practice and stayed out of public life." Austin can recall only one case Stevenson ever tried in court (though Stevenson in a letter to his mother mentioned another). "I held his hand in that one. It involved a leasehold that one of our clients had given. The corporate lessee had let the building go to pot, then he wanted to liquidate and leave the lessor holding the bag. We enjoined them. Stevenson won it. It was tried before a judge without a jury. I told the other partners that Stevenson would make a great trial lawyer if he would stick at it. He had great talent—not merely adequate talent." Another lawyer has said, "He was not good at corporate finance but on any general legal problem, he had a good instinct for what the important point was."

These early years, from 1927 to 1933, were almost Stevenson's longest continuous attention to the law. Even during that period, however, he devoted a good deal of time to other matters. Ed Austin once said, speaking of Stevenson's entire career, "My major impression was that he never did himself justice as a lawyer. His interest in public life—he kept getting involved in outside affairs." Stevenson himself wrote in 1941, "I have had a good many outside interests, probably too many." As early as 1930 one of those interests turned up, the one that was to dominate the rest of his life: foreign affairs. He mentioned it in a letter to his mother January 17, 1930: "Last night Ellen & I went to the League of Nations Assoc. dinner." And he joined the Chicago Council on Foreign Relations.

8

The Council was started in 1922 and incorporated in 1933. Ed McDougal, one of the men active in it, says, "Chicago was a hotbed of isolation. There was no TV, the Council was the only place there was for discussion of foreign affairs or authentic information on U.S. foreign policy. Georges Clemenceau was an early speaker. In those early days the Council was an elite group. It was the fashionable thing to do." The Council met weekly for luncheon, usually on Saturdays at the Palmer House, to hear speakers from the outside world. Its functions were usually reported on the society pages of the newspapers. It was natural that Stevenson join. Though the Council was social, it had intellectual content. Some of the people active in it were the same people whom he had known at Princeton and Lake Forest, people whose travels had given them a broader view of the world than was usual in the Midwest at that time. By 1932, Stevenson was secretary of the Council. At that time its president was his friend, Graham Aldis, and among the members of its executive committee were Steve Hord, John P. Kellogg, William P. Sidley, Clay Judson, and Mrs. Harriet Welling. Stevenson wrote a short article to explain the Council on Foreign Relations. "The war introduced international politics to interior America. It revealed problems, names, and places which few people west of the State Department had ever suspected. But the war was just a prelude. When the thunder of guns ceased, the rattle of voices commenced. Out of the clamorous meeting of the international creditors in Paris emerged the Versailles Treaty and a host of problems and perplexities. . . . Our comfortable frontier isolation was irrevocably shattered once we began imbibing international politics with our morning coffee."

The Council on Foreign Relations was young Stevenson's training ground. It was the place where he first made a public reputation in Chicago. It was where he learned to make speeches in public. From its membership came many of the people who helped him during his campaign for Governor, during his governorship, and during his two campaigns for the presidency. It represented Adlai Stevenson's first real move upward and outward from the world of Bloomington-Princeton-Lake Forest-LaSalle Street, the schoolboyish frivolous monied world he had heretofore inhabited all his life. The Council was his launching pad.

9

Ernest and Buffie Ives had been transferred to Copenhagen and soon would be transferred to Pretoria, South Africa. Late in the spring of 1931, when their first child was about six months old, Ellen and Adlai Stevenson went to Copenhagen and toured Scandinavia. Stevenson, the indefatigable sightseer, described in letters to his mother visiting ancient cities and churches and ruins, going swimming "in the icy Baltic," taking "a delicious sun bath on the mighty wooded cliffs under a cloudless sky & read the history of old Vishy." At Stockholm Stevenson called on a man at the legation who invited them to tea, where they met various American diplomats and military men, went to "a most elegant dinner," and "had a gay time & finally ended up at the Czech minister's legation drinking highballs & dancing at 2 A.M. It was an amusing evening for a couple of corn fed provincials!" On this trip Stevenson learned something about travel he never forgot: to make all possible use of diplomatic connections. He wrote, "I never realized before how much is lost to the conventional tourist." Ernest Ives was trying to get the support of Senator J. Hamilton Lewis of Illinois to get a promotion, and Stevenson became involved, but because of the approaching presidential election the matter was dropped for the time being.

10

That year, 1932, a presidential year, Stevenson engaged in politics. Even earlier he had shown some interest. Jane Dick, his longtime Lake Forest friend, said that her father, Ezra J. Warner, had first suggested to Stevenson that he run for public office about 1930. One of her father's business associates was Colonel A. A. Sprague. Sprague was a bridge between the world of Democratic organization politics and the world of LaSalle Street and Lake Forest society. He was a director of the Continental Illinois National Bank, chairman of the board of Sprague, Warner & Company, a member of the Onwentsia Club, and a resident of Lake Shore Drive—but he was also a leading Democrat and in 1924 had been the Democratic candidate for United States Senator. Stevenson had told his mother early in 1930, "Last night we went to the opera with Col. & Mrs. Sprague. It appears that the gods have been busy weaving plans over my innocent head. I broached the subject of the legislature to him only to discover that he has talked to all the democratic 'big shots' & has been to see Mr. Sidley—who has eagerly consented. He has talked with the ward boss Mulcahy (not French!) who is at outs with O'Brien, the present representative, & Mulcahy is at present finding out what the chance is of giving me the organization support instead of O'Brien. Unless he can assure me of that Sprague says he wasn't going to speak to me about it."

In another letter at about that time, Stevenson had described to his mother a lunch at which he had had "a long talk with J. Ham Lewis re politics, one with Col. Sprague in the morning & in the afternoon had a back room conf. with Alderman Crowe and Committeeman Connors! The latter eloquent Irishman tried earnestly to persuade me to run for the State Senate with extravagant assurances of success. But I told them I didn't 'choose to run'." These were important figures in Democratic politics in Chicago at that time. Lewis was the Democratic Senator from Illinois. Dorsey R. Crowe was the alderman in the City Council from the 42nd Ward, Stevenson's ward on the Gold Coast. William Connors, almost universally called Botchy Connors, was the ward committeeman. There are fifty wards in Chicago. Each elects an alderman to the City Council. Each party has a committeeman, the ward boss, in each ward. Together—often they are the same man—the alderman and ward committeemen control patronage and favors in their wards. Their power rests, ultimately, upon their ability to win elections. They do this through their precinct captains. In "machine wards" their power is overwhelming. Stevenson's ward was a machine ward. True, it contained the Gold Coast of the East Side, where he lived; but the great mass of voters lived in the slums on the west side of the ward, near the Chicago River; this was the power base of the organization. As alderman and committeeman, Crowe and Connors were powerful in the Democratic machine, as some people call it, or Democratic organization, as others say. That organization was born in the Great Depression in 1931. That year Negroes, workingmen, and the middle class elected a Democratic Mayor of Chicago, Anton Cermak, breaking the Republican hegemony that had lasted through the 1920s.

It was a harbinger of the upheaval of 1932 that propelled the Democrats into national power and kept them there for twenty years. It began in Chicago in 1931. From that time until long after Adlai Stevenson's death, Illinois politics was dominated by the Chicago organization. Stevenson, through his father, had previously been acquainted with Senator J. Hamilton Lewis. In 1930 he had met Alderman Crowe and Committeeman Connors. That luncheon is the earliest evidence we have of Stevenson's relationship with Democratic organizational politics. What makes this series of events curious is that Stevenson, having been approached by Jane Dick's father, having himself made a tentative approach to Sprague, when he received the offer of endorsement for state Senator, rejected it. It is a pattern that recurs in the later 1930s and 1940s, that nearly recurred in 1947–48 when he was nominated for Governor. Viewed in this perspective, what seemed indecision to some in 1952 looks far more like a deliberate political tactic. He was testing the water.

Stevenson became active in the spring of 1932 in party affairs. A friend wrote to Senator Lewis in April, "Adlai is busily engaged in soliciting funds for the Victory Campaign drive but, I am afraid, with discouraging results." (Stevenson may have drafted the letter himself.) Ed Austin has recalled, "In 1932, he was Western treasurer for the Roosevelt campaign. I remember his telling me before the convention that the Democratic nomination was a shoo-in for John W. Davis or someone else—not Roosevelt. George Dern and McAdoo came out for Roosevelt the next day. He spent a lot of time in that campaign."

Stevenson attended the Democratic National Convention that year but was unable to get a press badge. At the convention Stevenson saw Gardner Cowles, called Mike, and his brother, John Cowles, then publishers of the Des Moines *Register and Tribune,* later of *Look* magazine and other publications. Stevenson was on a first-name basis with them. He asked them to evaluate the *Pantagraph*'s situation. Shortly after the convention John Cowles told Stevenson that Dave Merwin and his associates had done "a magnificent job" in continuing to earn a sizable net profit.

During that 1932 campaign Stevenson involved the *Pantagraph* in politics more than ever before. In August he brusquely complained about an editorial and said support of Judge Henry Horner, Democratic candidate for Governor, "must be forthright and vigorous when the time comes." On the same day Stevenson told Judge Horner that "the editorial was frivolous, but I am confident in no way intended to indicate any change or changing heart of the *Panta-*

graph." He was staunch in his support of Horner. He wrote to him, "I am utterly unable to understand how any independent honest newspaper proprietor could think twice before making his decision, and you may rest assured that toward the end of the campaign your candidacy will receive vigorous support in the *Pantagraph.*" He was learning something of Illinois politics. He suggested to Horner that in his campaign he emphasize his "intimate acquaintance with the historical panorama of the whole State" in order to dispel downstate mistrust of a Chicago candidate. In two sentences that foreshadowed his own subsequent political methods, Stevenson wrote, "I wish you could have some one write a series of articles about your non-political activities, largely Lincoln and the Probate Court. To be saturated with Lincoln is to be saturated with Illinois."

Henry Horner, of Jewish faith, was a respected Lincoln scholar and probate judge. He was regarded as a "blue ribbon candidate," not a Democratic organization hack. He was elected Governor that year and served two terms, the second time defeating the Democratic organization in a bitter primary fight. A senior partner in Stevenson's law firm, Charles S. Cutting, had been Cook County probate judge for many years; Horner succeeded him. Horner was on a first-name basis with a number of the law firm's partners and knew Stevenson as a young lawyer who brought probate cases before him and belonged to a fairly prominent Illinois Democratic family. Their relationship continued for a number of years, though it never became really close. The *Pantagraph* endorsed Horner but not Franklin D. Roosevelt, running for President for the first time that year.

After the election Stevenson found himself being asked by friends to solicit Horner for jobs. On December 3, 1932, he promised to speak to Horner on behalf of Frank H. Funk of Bloomington, who wanted to go on the Tax Commission, and James Clark of Bloomington, who was seeking reappointment to the Commerce Commission. He wrote to Horner the same day, saying only of Funk that he "was a friend of my father's and . . . has long been prominent in central Illinois" and of Clark that he was "a popular and respected Bloomington citizen" and Stevenson's law firm associates considered Clark "capable, accommodating . . . an especially useful servant." But he added, "I have assured them that my family and I could and would ask for no favors and that I would merely pass the applications along for you to consider on their merit alone. I hope you will take me at my word and any disposition you make of the matters will be agreeable with me." All the rest of his life, Stevenson's endorsement was sought by men seeking appointive political jobs. In some cases he gave his endorsement with alacrity and enthusiasm. More often he was guarded. In later life he learned to handle the guarded endorsements more gracefully than he handled these first ones.

Stevenson's mother-in-law spent Christmas Eve with him and Ellen, talking and listening to the radio; they had Christmas dinner with her. In a letter to his own mother, Stevenson described in an almost boyish way the gifts he and Ellen and Adlai III received. He told his mother on January 3, 1933, "New Years eve was a big night in Lake Forest but we finally did get to bed & slept until noon on Sunday. Had 6 to lunch & a very merrie time. Thanks to the fact that Anna had her *worst* hangover from her own New Year's eve celebration & the lunch reflected her bewilderment. The turkey came in upside down etc!"

Ernest Ives told Stevenson in a buoyant letter about all the ambassadorships and ministries which would fall vacant with the change of administration in Washington and hoped Stevenson could intercede for him—"if Mr. Norman Davis should be Secretary of State you could possibly discuss it first with him. . . . You may deem it advisable to approach the Secretary first and then the President."

Stevenson and Ellen gave a large costume party at 1020 Lake Shore Drive, Ellen's mother's home, about forty to dinner and eighty afterwards. Jane Dick once recalled, "It was a terrific party. Adlai adored to dress up."

Stevenson considered joining the new Democratic Administration. He wrote to his mother, "There are opportunities in Wash for the younger men of independent means etc etc. But I don't believe I'll press for anything now—unless it is offered & they never are! There will be plenty of opportunities & with things as uncertain here I think it would be best to stand by for the present." He and Ellen went to Washington to attend the inauguration and stayed with the James Douglas—Douglas had been Assistant Secretary of the Treasury under President Hoover. Stevenson himself was unable to attend the inaugural ball because of a painful ear infection. He attempted unsuccessfully to see Senator Lewis—Lewis was in committee hearings "all the while" and Stevenson "left cards on" him. He had "a very pleasant interview" with Harold Ickes, of Chicago, President Roosevelt's Secretary of the Interior, who had known Stevenson's father—he "seemed much interested in my vague suggestion that I might be interested in government employment!"

Fifteen years later, in 1948, when Stevenson was nominated for Governor, it seemed to most people in Illinois—as in 1952 it seemed to most people in the nation—that he was a well-to-do public-spirited lawyer interested in good government who had only then become interested in politics; and to many people for many years, indeed, all his life, it was difficult to think of Stevenson as a politician or as politically ambitious. But his activities in 1930 and in the 1932 campaign, and his indication at Roosevelt's first inauguration that he "might be" interested in joining the New Deal, make it clear that Adlai Stevenson entertained political ambition at least from 1930, when he was thirty years old.

From Washington the Stevensons went with the Iveses to Southern Pines, North Carolina, which Buffie had first visited with their mother. The Iveses bought land and a cabin there and later divided their time between it and the house in Bloomington.

On April 2, 1933, the nominating committee of the Chicago Council on Foreign Relations nominated Stevenson for its president. He was then thirty-three, younger by at least five years than most Council presidents. It was the most important post he had received. But he left it almost immediately to go to Washington to join the Agricultural Adjustment Administration under his father's friend, George Peek. On July 17, Stevenson told Governor Horner he had just arrived in Washington, had been told earlier by Peek that political sponsorship was unnecessary, but now found he needed formal letters recommending his appointment—would Horner provide one? "I am sorry to bother you with this troublesome detail, but I suppose such things are necessary in the Federal Service."

11

Stevenson was one of many young Democratic lawyers drawn to Washington in the first explosion of the New Deal. He himself said he joined the AAA "largely because I was much interested in the agricultural problem," adding that he owned several Midwest farms, but beyond this he was drawn by the excitement of New Deal politics and the opportunity to advance his career by gaining experience in administrative law, a field that was burgeoning because of New Deal agencies. Nothing in his correspondence indicates any deep commitment to New Deal liberalism at that time.

In his brief time at the AAA—he stayed less than a year—he played a relatively minor role. His principal duty was drawing marketing agreements for various crops, starting with the California fruit trade. He was working long hours. He told his mother, "Affairs of state manage to keep me & everyone else busy all day & most of the night." George W. Ball, another young New Deal lawyer who later became Stevenson's close political associate and Undersecretary of State in the Kennedy and Johnson administrations, knew Stevenson slightly during this period. Francis Plimpton, his friend from Harvard Law, had gone to Washington with the Reconstruction Finance Corporation before Stevenson arrived on the scene. Stevenson did not impress them at this time as having an extraordinarily bright future. Arthur Krock, the New York *Times* political writer, met him through a mutual friend, Wayne Chatfield Taylor; the three of them and another man played bridge together; and Krock remembered him later as a pleasant companion, no more. According to Krock, he met several people who later were to become important in his life, including James Rowe, a Democratic lawyer and politician; Mike Monroney, later senator from Oklahoma and a strong Stevenson supporter; and Dean Acheson, who became Truman's Secretary of State.

Stevenson said that his first job was a marketing agreement for the California deciduous tree fruit industry. The delegation from California was only a little upset when he asked what "deciduous" meant. He learned the difficult economics of perishable commodities, "working night and day against the rapidly maturing crop—and the highly perishable crop can't wait to go to market." At that time, agricultural surpluses threatened ruin, he said, but it was never contemplated that crop reduction should be continued indefinitely. He recalled he had "negotiated with producers, processors or handlers of everything from Atlantic oysters to California oranges, and from Oregon apples to Florida strawberries. Walnut and asparagus growers from California, rice millers from Louisiana, lettuce shippers from Arizona, shadegrown tobacco handlers from Connecticut, potato merchants from Maine, candy manufacturers from Pennsylvania, chicken hatchers from everywhere, date and grape shippers and olive canners from California, pea canners from Wisconsin, peanut processors from Virginia and the Carolinas—all these and dozens more came to confess their sins and beg for help. We laughed a little when the wintergreen trust appeared, and more at the pimento magnates who wanted an embargo on Spanish pimentos. The mayonnaise people won an endurance contest with the cotton seed crushers with three continuous months on the doorstep, and the Boston mackerel fishermen arrived in the Potomac in a Gloucester schooner. But the big laugh came the morning a Georgia delegation led by a Senator and a couple of congressmen arrived and calmly announced that the Packaged Bees Industry was going to hell!! . . . Of course, few of the proposals got beyond the stage of perfunctory consideration. . . . Law, economics and hotel bills usually wore them out and after one last round of highballs on the bed at the Mayflower, they would fade out and make room for the next one."

Of Jerome Frank, general counsel to AAA and Stevenson's supervisor, Stevenson said, "I have never encountered a more agile, rapacious mind." The "intellectual atmosphere" at the AAA, Stevenson said, was such that "I didn't have the least idea what they were talking about most of the time. . . . The A.A.A. legal division attracted some exceptionally able men." (One of them was Alger Hiss, who later became involved in a sensational dispute with Whittaker Chambers over whether Hiss had been a Soviet agent.)

Ellen did not accompany him to Washington immediately. He lived briefly at the Wardman Park Hotel, then with friends. All his life while away from home—and he was away from home almost more than he was home—Stevenson stayed with friends, not in hotels, partly to save money, partly because he always wanted people around him. Ellen chid him, "I think it is one thing staying in an empty house when its owners are away—but visiting so permanently as you are considering it—'til Sept—embarrasses me a little."

Almost immediately after arriving in Washington, Stevenson wrote a long revealing letter to his wife. Addressing her as "Lambkin," he said he had left the office at 7 P.M., "the earliest yet and I feel now as tho I had only done a half days work!" He had received formal notification of his appointment at $6,500 a year (about $5,600 after deductions under the Economy Act, he thought) and been sworn in. He wrote, "Our Gen. Counsel is a Jew named Jerome N. Frank—who is as smart and able as he can be. There is a little feeling that the Jews are getting too prominent —as you know many of them are autocratic and the effect on the public—the industries that crowd our rooms all day—is bad. Don't mention this to anyone—I've noticed it from the start and my cell mate Mr. Woodward, an older man and a very able rate lawyer, agrees with me. Frank has none of the racial characteristics and has done a dreadfully difficult job as well as could be hoped for—he's indefatigable & literally works most all night every night but he's brought several other Jews down who, tho individually smart and able, are more racial. Woodward tells me that Frank was handed to Peek without the latter's having anything to say about it & there's been some friction from the start. Apparently Felix Frankfurter who has the Pres. confidence persuaded him to appoint Frank at the same time he appointed Peek and even then Frank's confirmation was held up two months! This is all confidential."

Many years later Ellen said she had helped Stevenson become a success in those early years so that she could leave him. Her letters written at the time do not sound at all that way. The day he arrived in Washington, she sent him a postcard, described a party she had attended at which several Italian fliers were the guests of honor, said she had been "seated between two capitanos who spoke *no* English—My Italian had them in a constant state of hysterics & I arrived home slightly before 3," and said, "I believe I miss you already *and* I am giving you mental treatments beginning Monday. . . . Love from the kiddies and wifie!"

When she received his letter about his salary and Jerome Frank, and another in which he seemed discouraged, she said they "made me want to come right down!! If your salary is $5,000 you *must* have one of the more important jobs, because certainly the drudges and drones aren't payed that much. After all your first day you obviously wouldn't be given the most important work. Think that this is a test period and *please* don't get discouraged." One recalls his mother's similar adjurations when he was in school. "Anyway it is an adventure and there is something to be gotten out of it—even if it isn't as you expected? Is Wayne [probably Wayne Chatfield Taylor] sold on his job? How does it compare with yours? Perhaps I'd better come down and vamp the Jews! I'm just blond enough to do some good, mayhaps." She asked him to describe his "cubicle" minutely so she could visualize him at work. She again told him, "If you are discouraged keep your discouragement to *yourself!!* There is no use in getting your family upset or having it get around particularly *as it is all going to be for the best!!* . . . The tone of your letter worried me. Also please buy yourself an electric fan or shall I send you one. All my love dear. The children keep talking about Da Da. . . . I shall come down in about two weeks—about the 10th or 11th of August—which is not so far away."

Next day, July 20, she wrote again: "Today your second letter— and so much more cheerful. At a moment when having glanced at the most recent stock market quotations I need a little cheer!" She had taken the children to the beach; Adlai III had gone in "up to his chin and swam while I held one hand under his tummy. We could hardly get him out!—and he was very proud." She felt, she said, "very serious and man of the familyish when I am alone—I read politics and agriculture & I have sent $1 to subscribe to the 'Financial News'!! which will surely solve all my problems. . . . I haven't slept very well since you left—quite to my surprise—I thought your absence might have a soothing effect—but alas—I roll and toss—and spill over into your bed—which I certainly never did before." She closed the letter, "Goodbye—My beloved Pig—

you!" It was a nickname used many years later by another girl who was in love with him.

The World's Fair was taking place in Chicago that summer, and Ellen was having a gay time but she missed him. When he had been gone a week she wrote, "I have gone back to all the old and glorious foibles of my youth and find myself again—an independent virgin! Therefore as befits my present status—last evening I *caroused* with two young men and that wench named Ruth—'til it was indeed late. . . . Dinner in the Belgian Village [at the World's Fair] and . . . ending up at the Streets of Paris—I finally sailed into an alien port at about 14 bells. . . ." She signed the letter, "Adios—Tutti Frutti."

She wrote to him every few days that summer, sometimes more than once in a single day. She addressed him variously as "Dear Adlai," "Adlai dear—Assistant Agrarian," "Dear Ad," "Adlai, my love." Her letters were pert, chatty, witty, coquettish, and loving. She was gambling in wheat and urged him, *"Don't* worry about it." Stevenson did, though. She wrote to him, "Forget about the money— I am doing juggling tricks with my wheat. It makes me nervous, I don't approve, I dislike it intensely but I want *money."* Once she wrote, "Can you send me 250. or 300. . . . Don't impoverish yourself but send me as much as is convenient—I'll make it up next month if I can—At the moment I have only 150. in my special account— and none in my other. . . . I have sacrificed so much of my income that I may have to do something about it. I'll scrape along somehow. Some dividends will come in later in the month. *Please* don't worry about finances—If only you are being paid your salary Signed —The Business Woman." Once her broker told her she had a profit of $5,000 "in my wheat—which is pretty good for an investment of a day and a half. . . . My losses on margin stocks are enough to keep me from getting out but not enough to worry about."

She asked if he thought inflation would occur, as her father thought, and said, "But isn't it almost crooked to float a bond issue —suck the public in—and then inflate? How can they do it?" Once she wrote, "If I could only make enough money in wheat to pay all our expenses in Washington!!" She went to many parties, and sometimes her descriptions of them seemed designed to arouse his jealousy. She wrote, "Day after [tomorrow] in to spend the nite with Muriel & go on a bat. So the week goes—I quite enjoy being girlish again. . . . [I send] this resumé that you may know I am not utterly deserted & desolate." She went to the Fair again and stayed until two-thirty— "and how I love it." After a party, she wrote, "I am enclosing my place card to impress you—Champagne, lobster—and a gold dinner service." She wrote of dinners, movies, cocktail parties—"Betty [her sister] says she has an irresistible man for me. Ahmmmmmmmm!" Somebody gave a party and "served pre-war gin in my honor." She had lunch with her father and his new wife: "She immediately ordered a 1.50 lobster salad and of course I felt just as though I had been robbed! Daddy was a dear and she seemed very sweet to him. . . . It goes against the grain to see your father with a wife younger (and dumber) than you." She went to a dinner at the Arthur Meekers' in honor of the Italian ambassador, who asked her and another woman "to show him the Fair—so we ended up at the Streets of Paris. . . . The Ambassador is quite young and attractive. Grant Smith . . . told me just how to cope with Washington—& that I had a lovely mouth—an exquisite profile. . . . I lost my gloves and found them in the Ambassadors hat. My place card went home in Tomasi's pocket. The Ambassador says he will give a dinner for me in Washington. Madeline & I were escorted home by Tomasi & the Amb. at 2 o'clock in his special car with policemen on motorcycles clearing the way—It was a very amusing evening!"

Not all the parties were raucous. She spent a quiet evening with friends after listening to a speech by President Roosevelt. The Wellings took her and Adlai III to a horse show for children— "Ponies. Pony carts. Goats . . . ice cream." One evening Jim Oates and his wife took her to a movie, then to their home to talk. "It was very sweet of them—People are sorry for the derelict wife! and so am I especially if I don't hear from you soon! Soon! Soon! I can hardly wait to hear. . . . I have had innumerable people tell me they thought going to Washington was the smartest thing you ever did. I hope and pray so—Last night Jim [Oates] stressed again how blue he was about your leaving & how much he hoped you'd come back—also McPherson." She seemed proud of her husband, though she sometimes masked pride with mild derision: the *Pantagraph* was "going to give you a big write up . . . 'country boy makes good.'" She asked him to tell her about his work: "People ask me about it so often and I'd like to make it as impressive as possible." She asked for ammunition to defend the Democrats.

She wrote often about the children—"adorable," "splendid." She was solicitous of his health and she asked for letters which were "something other than a legal document. I want full details—all emotions minutely described . . . tell me about your ankle—state of nerves—quantity of nosedrops." At times she seemed lonely and loving. Once she wrote, "I am now developing all the characteristics of a prima donna—I lounge in my bath—my food is cooked and ordered to my taste alone—and yet—? . . . I am in bed writing on a telephone book and eating cherries—alone again—in my old room." She sent love and "wifely solicitude." She wrote, "I would call you up if I knew your telephone number."

Her mother had written to her saying she did not approve of their being separated—"one so easily forms other habits," and Ellen added, "And its true—I can see already—other habits creeping upon me— I am getting very independent—I'm afraid that you will have to break me in all over again!—or raise my wages!!—" and she signed the letter with four initials, "S.M.R.A.," then wrote what must have been an explanation of the initials, then crossed it out heavily and added, "I'm shocked at myself." What she crossed out read, in part, "(Stevenson Matrimonial Recovery Act) will put [illegible] back to [back?]"

Once she wrote, "It seems to me in retrospect that your presence has a very soothing effect. . . . Now on my own I become aggressive, nervous, eager for excitement—all the things." She closed one letter by printing in large block letters "LOVE ELLEN," turning the last "N" on its side and printing "Addie" on the last stroke of the "N" then added an arc on which she printed "baby." Once she wrote, "I don't think I *do* approve of long separations—it is disillusioning to find that I am quite *capable* with you away. The house remains intact—The children still laugh and play and all in all I think—we need a reunion—to convince me that I can't do without you!! . . . As for you I'm sure you're revelling in your bachelor independence—

"1. Read the paper all you want

"2. Eat all you want

"3. Using whatever method you prefer

"4. Make all the noise you want while shaving—*etc*. What memories it all brings back—Oh to hear the blissful tone of your early morning rituals! Till we meet again," and she signed it "She Who Got Left."

Stevenson visited her at least once. She was making plans to join him in Washington. She was trying to sublease their house; prospective tenants were few. Stevenson asked the owner's real estate agent to reduce the rent to a hundred dollars a month and hoped Ellen could rent it furnished for seventy-five but feared it unlikely. Ellen's mother was living with her husband, John Alden Carpenter, in Massachusetts, and Ellen visited them, leaving the two children with a governess. From there on August 16 she wrote to Stevenson, *"Please Please* try to sleep & don't let yourself get nervous and *please* don't smoke too much All those things worry me so I can't relax and be happy—and it makes me feel so spoiled & selfish—not to have you enjoying it too." She hoped he would not fly when he came to see her. *"Please again*—remember that your the father of a family that doesn't approve of aeroplanes but *does* like its Da Da—!!" Throughout their married life his flying—and later the boys'—was a point of contention between them. Their correspondence indicates they were eager to reunite. For her part, Ellen wrote on August 22, "Adlai dear: One more letter from you at *last*—and one more from me—I think I shall leave Thurs—and arrive Fri morning. I will wire exact details." For his part, he told his mother, "Ellen & the babes arrive tomorrow morning & am I happy!" They found a house in Georgetown, at 30th and 0 streets. He said, "The house is really too large & we may rattle a bit—tho I guess it will fill up a little when the gang arrives." His mother sent Negro servants by car from Bloomington, members of the family which Stevenson once said had served his family for four generations. At least at first, Ellen was happy in Washington.

Years later, after Stevenson came to prominence, after he and his wife were divorced, the world caught glimpses of Ellen Borden Stevenson that made her seem vindictive, sharp-tongued, unpredictable, even unbalanced. But the letters she wrote during those happy early years of their marriage reveal her as an extremely appealing young wife.

12

While in Washington, Stevenson continued to interest himself in Bloomington and *Pantagraph* affairs. Earlier, Dave Merwin had written a bitter letter to Stevenson protesting a proposal to "adjust" his salary, presumably downward: "I have overworked myself for several years for the extraordinary gain of *Pantagraph* stockholders, with an obvious lack of appreciation and minimum thanks from you & your family; so I was not as surprised as I might have been by the ingratitude of your suggestion." But when a Public Works Administration appropriation was needed to finish building an airport at Bloomington, Merwin wrote to Stevenson asking him to "put in a good word at the right place." A Bloomington man went to Washington and Stevenson accompanied him at an appointment with Harry Hopkins, Federal Emergency Relief administrator. Like many publishers, Merwin wanted to exempt newsboys from the NRA (National Recovery Act) code, which would have raised their wages. Publishers took the position that their business was different from all others and that any attempt to regulate them abridged freedom of the press. Their critics said they were really worrying about their profits, not their freedom, and accused them of exploiting child labor. Merwin told Stevenson that the *Pantagraph* was not directly affected, since its newsboys bought papers from the *Pantagraph* at wholesale and sold them at retail, but Merwin "felt it advisable to cooperate in the general movement" of opposition by publishers. He also feared the government would regard the newsboys as *Pantagraph* employees, not independent contractors, despite the "Little Merchant Plan," and he suggested that Stevenson use his judgment on whether to "say something on the subject to the right person." Stevenson replied that he saw no need to do anything for the time being and added, "I feel confident that newsboys in the position of ours will be exempted." During this period, as the New Deal intervened more and more in the economy, Dave Merwin became increasingly at odds with it, and so with Stevenson, and henceforward to the old disputes over ownership, salaries, dividends, and profits was added the new dispute over editorial policy.

13

Early in 1934, Stevenson transferred to the Federal Alcohol Control Administration and on April 18 he was officially appointed its chief attorney at $7,500 a year. He told his mother, "Ten or 12 hours a day will just about handle the mail—with 5 assistants—without giving me any time for the important work." He and Ellen were going to New York where Plimpton was giving "a stag party of all my old law school friends" while their wives would "foregather" with Ellen. They would stay with friends. Stevenson was "feeling fine—hair clean & nose clear!"

In a speech a year later Stevenson recalled his move from the AAA to the FACA. Late in 1933, he said, it became evident that the repeal of prohibition was imminent and that the gigantic liquor industry would resume business before Congress convened to enact regulatory legislation, and so FDR's "Brain Trust" hastily devised six Codes of Fair Competition under the Industrial Recovery Act and by executive order created the FACA. "When I arrived I found I had a couple of able men from the Prohibition and Industrial Alcohol Bureaus, one boy just out of law school, several more with an average of two years' experience answering court calls, an expert on aviation law, and a famous gentleman jockey!" They had to answer inquiries, write regulations to protect the public, organize the industry for self-policing, and work out a quota system for imported liquor. He hoped that eventually the states would leave these matters wholly to the federal government, a position that might surprise those familiar only with Stevenson's later tendency toward federalism and insistence on states' rights and responsibilities, and his misgivings about the increasing growth of the national government.

Characteristically, even as he was accepting the job at FACA, Stevenson was considering leaving it. As early as March his mother wrote to him saying that "perhaps" he should "stay on in Wash. with the New Deal. The field there is more amusing and wider in scope . . . also the opp. for acquaintances. . . . I have never been very keen about Chi for you." But she went on to say she did not wish to "influence" him. She returned to Bloomington from Florida late in the spring. He was seriously concerned about her health—she had been in a sanitarium for several months, and he later told a doctor that she had had "a nervous breakdown" during that spring. He wrote to her often, advising her in June, "So glad you've found the road back—don't wander—and we'll have a big time this summer."

Stevenson, Ellen, and both boys went up to Massachusetts for the long Fourth of July weekend at the Carpenters, (though the Carpenters were away temporarily). Stevenson returned to Washington alone and told his mother, "I had three glorious days in Mass with Ellen & the babes & hosts of servants. The days were hot, the water cold and the nights cool. I can't but believe that, with the exception of occasional foggy days, you would find the climate warm enough & the cool nights invigorating. The house situation seems good—some nice roomy well furnished ones, of course not on the sea, for $300 for the season up."

At about this time he decided to return to private law practice. He was offered better jobs in Washington but refused them. He told his mother, however, "I feel sure I'll come back here again sometime to do some more government work." He proposed to return to the law firm October 1—that would enable him to wind up his affairs and take a vacation. Ellen would rent a house in Massachusetts, Buffie would arrive from abroad, and Stevenson and his mother would join them all in Massachusetts shortly after August 1, bringing the maid Alverta Duff along.

Donald McPherson of the law firm wrote to him July 10, "It will be entirely agreeable to us to have you return on October 1 next. . . . Do not come back with the impression that your work will be confined to routine tax matters. We have no such thought in mind. It will be our desire to have you take full advantage of your recent experiences in administrative law and to do other important work." Kenneth F. Burgess, another partner, wrote, "In my opinion you are making a wise decision, although I think you will have yearnings to be back in Washington after you leave. In my own work it frequently seems to me as though I am doing little of a really worthwhile nature, and there are times when all of us get discouraged. I suppose that is a human tendency. It is given to the lot of very few people to do anything really outstanding for the good of humanity; perhaps only two or three of a generation do anything that is really of permanent value. On the other hand, if we do our day's work and live a family life so that we and our children are good citizens, I suppose that is as much as we can do. As you know, I have greatly feared that if you stayed too long in Washington you might unfit yourself for a more routine existence such as is called for in the practice of law. You have a fine personality, many friends, ability and industry. It seems to me that you can make out of yourself what you will, and that your future lies largely in your own hands. I am glad that you are coming back." Burgess was entirely right—right in saying that the choice lay between a life as family man and lawyer or public figure, right in saying that to only a very few in a generation was it given to accomplish much of lasting value for humanity, and right in saying that Adlai Stevenson's future lay "largely" in his own hands (though "largely" is a heavy qualifier).

Why did he leave the New Deal? Other men his age stayed and made important public careers. Some have suggested he left Washington because his wife did not like it, but no evidence supports this. Some have said he "got fed up with the work he was doing" but no evidence supports this either. The simplest explanation seems the most likely: that he went home to make a living and make a place for himself in Chicago. For the time being, he was choosing private life. But he left the door open.

He broke the lease on the house in Georgetown as of August 15 but told the owner that Wayne Chatfield Taylor and James Alley, who had moved in with him after Ellen went to Massachusetts, might want to keep the house. His plans were changed suddenly: the FACA sent him to Hawaii August 3 on a final assignment. He took Ellen with him, spending a few days in San Francisco and arriving in Honolulu by ship on August 16. The Hawaii trip replaced the Massachusetts vacation. By early September he was back in Washington, winding up his affairs. He took advantage of his departure to make the rounds of important people he had met in Washington. Some he called on in person, some he wrote. Secretary Ickes responded, "I am sorry to learn that you are going back to Chicago. . . . It is almost unbelievable how extraordinarily busy we all are here in Washington. One would have thought that we would have seen each other on many occasions during your stay here, and for one I am sorry that this was not so." Arthur Krock wrote, "I feel that the government is losing a damned good man. . . . I shall miss the occasional sight of the lovely Ellen." Robert Jackson, who later became a Supreme Court justice, wrote that "It was with real regret that I read your letter. . . . We shall all miss you and Ellen." Among others who wrote to him were the Solicitor General, a special assistant to the Secretary of State, several lawyers, men at the AAA and the State Department. Some obviously did not know him well; one spelled his name "Stephenson." (About the same time he received a letter addressing him as "My dear Miss Stevenson." This misapprehension that his first name was feminine plagued him for a time; he had his calling cards printed "Mr. Adlai E. Stevenson.")

Several months after he had left Washington, Stevenson delivered a speech to Chicago lawyers on the proper role of government. The role of government and of administrative law was expanding rapidly, he said. It was futile for lawyers to protest. The administrative system was for better or worse "the inescapable medium through which government must work if it is to meet the demands of our society." The Supreme Court had had "its day of power" under Marshall, the Congress under Taft, and now the executive branch was in the ascendancy. Rather than resist, we should strive to improve the quality of administration—and able young lawyers could go to Washington and help. "I can look forward mistily to the time when government service will be one of the highest aspirations of educated men," one of his great themes. And another: "Bad government is bad politics and good government means good men." The New Deal represented "the use of the power of government to preserve private enterprise by regulating its abuses and balancing its deficiencies." In that 1935 speech can be found several of the ideas and even some of the phrases that later caught the attention of Illinois and the nation.

CHAPTER FOUR

Courage Under Fire
1934-1941

Somehow, in retrospect, Adlai Stevenson's first foray to Washington, 1933–34, appears a continuation of his going away to Choate and Princeton. Now, after he returned to Chicago in the fall of 1934, his whole life changed. He was thirty-four years old. He was gathering up the threads of young manhood and striking out in new directions. Within a little more than a year he would become a partner in his law firm, he and his wife would build their first home, the house in Libertyville, his oldest child would come of school age, his mother would die, the management of the *Pantagraph* would change, and Stevenson would develop his career as a public speaker. Moreover, this period from 1934 to the outbreak of war was one of wrenching change in the Midwest, for Hitler's rise called into question United States isolationism, and Stevenson became deeply engaged in that bitter controversy.

2

The minutes of the law firm's meeting on October 9, 1934, show that Sidley would talk to Stevenson about his duties. Henceforward, Stevenson handled tax work and chancery litigation, especially litigation under the federal bankruptcy statute, and various matters relating to Washington. (Chancery litigation did not involve trials; it consisted in foreclosing mortgages, asking for an accounting of business associates, and so on.) He accepted appointment as the non-industry member of two NRA Code Authorities, one for the wine industry and one for the wheat flour milling industry. Legal work for them took up a good deal of his time.

As in the past, Stevenson tried to find jobs for friends. The son of a *Pantagraph* reporter wanted a job with the National Park Service. Stevenson told him he was unable to get an endorsement from either Illinois Senator "for you or any one else" but wrote to Secretary of the Interior Ickes. A former colleague of Stevenson's at the AAA asked him to solicit the endorsement of Senator Lewis for John Abt for a job in the Justice Department. Abt, a Chicago lawyer, was years later involved in testimony about an underground Communist apparatus in the AAA that included Alger Hiss and others. Stevenson replied, "I remember John Abt at least by name, and his cousin, Dr. Abt, Jr., is our pediatrician. I would like to do what you suggest except that I have had some unsatisfactory experiences in similar situations with Senator Lewis—mostly indirectly." He suggested that Abt see William L. O'Connell, who handled patronage for Lewis in Chicago.

Though Stevenson did not say so, he was reluctant to approach Lewis on Abt's behalf because he himself was seeking appointment as United States district attorney. He discussed it with a friend in Chicago who leaked it to a newspaper. When the story appeared in a political column, Stevenson promptly sent copies of the clipping to Senator Lewis, George Peek, Stanley F. Reed, and Secretary Ickes, saying, "I suspect that it was as much of a surprise to Mr. Cummings as it was to me." Homer Cummings was Attorney General. Stevenson asked Peek and Ickes to speak to Cummings or Lewis. He sent the same clipping to Louis FitzHenry of Bloomington, a federal judge of the Circuit Court of Appeals. Judge FitzHenry told him, "Don't let anybody fool you about this appointment. The positions of United States Attorneys are purely senatorial patronage." Mike Igoe, the judge thought, would be appointed. Ickes said roughly the same thing, adding, "I suspect also that Senator Lewis is far from pleased when he learns from the newspapers that someone else is proposing a candidate." Stanley Reed, the Solicitor General, said, "Hope the newspaper comment is more accurate than you admit." (As he did with other letters from important persons, Stevenson showed this one to Kenneth F. Burgess, a senior partner in his law firm.)

Senator Lewis told Stevenson, "Of course I understand newspapers and their method of writing as soon as they can, whatever they hear, but I beg to assure you that there is nothing that indicates that you have been presented for any office and therefore there will be no record that you were defeated or denied anything for which you have applied or as to which you are being mentioned." End of episode. It was his first lesson in upper-level politics.

He missed Washington. It was only the first time that he (like many others) would find it difficult to return to humdrum private life in Chicago after the excitement of official life in Washington.

The atmosphere in the law firm was not entirely congenial. Many of its members were conservative Republicans, and by now Republican distaste for President Roosevelt was turning into hatred of "that man in the White House." Kenneth F. Burgess, the partner who appreciated Stevenson's worth as much as any member of the firm, was conservative in his political views. The day after he returned to Chicago, Stevenson told a friend, "I am so incensed with the current critical attitude generally that it is difficult for me to do anything except defend on the same [emotional] basis." Being a New Deal Democrat in a LaSalle Street law office and a Lake Forest country club required courage as well as agility. Considering his real interests versus his legal work, it is not surprising that, as his friend and fellow lawyer, Ed McDougal, once said, "He seemed to get most of his satisfaction out of other things."

His involvement in Chicago civic affairs began almost immediately after he returned from Washington. He spoke at the Legal Club, preparing his speech carefully, and helped draft a resolution that the Metropolitan Housing Council proposed to submit to the City Council. Its director wrote, "You did an admirable job. . . . The Mayor . . . was well pleased."

Stevenson again became a resident member of the Onwentsia Club in Lake Forest. The club was exclusive, in the sense that a member had to be socially acceptable and also in the sense that it excluded Jews. He and Ellen decided to live in town—that is, in Chicago proper, on the Gold Coast. One of his law firm colleagues, leaving for Washington to join the FACA, offered them his apartment, but they declined, and the colleague wrote jokingly: "I wish it had been big enough and elegant enough for you and Ellen and your numerous offspring, maids, chauffeurs, butlers, etc." They stayed for a time in Ellen's mother's house at 1020 Lake Shore Drive, then rented a smaller house at 1246 North State. He engaged in a dispute with the owner of the house he had rented in Washington. She wanted to collect rent from August 15 to September 15 and sent a list of household furnishings missing or damaged. Stevenson computed the rent carefully and as to her belongings wrote, "Mrs. Stevenson is returning your vacuum cleaner and carpet sweeper. They were packed by the moving company by mistake and Mrs. Stevenson apologizes." He quoted his wife's comments on other items: "All of these shades were old. Furthermore there are only four shades in this room, not six. . . . Deduct $2.00. . . . My recollection is that the plate had a small chip on the back where it was not noticeable, for which Mrs. Mayo is charging $12.50!" The owner had claimed he owed her $167. He sent her a check for $20.65. Time and again, Stevenson spent much time and energy on such financial house-keeping.

Mrs. Kellogg Fairbank, a wealthy leader of "society" in Chicago and a neighbor of Stevenson's at 1244 North State Street, wrote to him, "Yesterday when I looked down the alley . . . it was a beautiful unbroken expanse. . . . I think we have made history by having the Mayor intervene personally about garbage collection. . . . I think it would please the Mayor, if you would write him on your office stationery so that he realizes that you are a valuable Democratic friend." Mayor Edward J. Kelly had succeeded Anton Cermak, assassinated in Miami at Franklin Roosevelt's side; it was Ed Kelly who, with Tom Nash and later Jacob M. Arvey, built the powerful Democratic organization that dominated Chicago politics for more than forty years. The "Kelly-Nash machine" was the object of vilification by the Chicago *Tribune,* many of whose Republican readers were Stevenson's neighbors. Stevenson wrote to Kelly, "Your prompt and effective response was very gratifying. To a good Democrat, it is cumulative evidence of the fine service your administration is rendering in even the smallest details." Kelly thanked him and said he earnestly hoped that in the future the residents on North State Street would find the condition of their alley satisfactory.

3

His principal concern at this time was his mother. Indeed, his deep involvement in her worsening condition during the next year became a primary factor in his life. Many years later he told Marietta Tree that his mother had "gone insane toward the end of her life." In his middle years he worried about his wife's mental condition. Not the least of the agonies of Adlai Stevenson's life was that both his mother and his wife, beautiful and talented and loving though they started out, ended unable to manage their affairs.

His mother had hoped for a family reunion in Charlevoix the summer before. Instead, she had been obliged to go to a rented house in Manchester, Massachusetts, and when she arrived had found only Buffie and Stevenson's children and the Carpenters—Stevenson and Ellen were on their Hawaiian trip. It was during this Manchester episode that his mother suffered what Stevenson once described as "a severe nervous breakdown."

Buffie asked Lydiard Horton of Boston to examine her, and he did, at length. Horton had tried to help Lewis and Helen Stevenson some twenty-five years earlier. He was given to writing long screeds to

Stevenson explaining his "Bio-psychic" theories. He thought ill of Freud and once denounced the takeover of psychology by Jews. Horton considered himself a psychologist and said he had been connected with various hospitals. About September 12, Stevenson and Ellen arrived at Manchester from Hawaii. It was only ten days before Mrs. Stevenson was due to sail for Algiers with Buffie, but, after family counsel, Stevenson decided to send her not to Algiers but to the Battle Creek Sanitarium in Michigan. Horton prepared a "Bio-psychic Assay" of Mrs. Stevenson, twelve single-spaced typewritten pages, much of it given over to defending his psychosomatic theories. Today it reads like pseudo-science, if not gobbledygook.

This episode at Manchester and his mother's departure for Battle Creek was the beginning—consultation after consultation with physicians and other healers, family meeting after family meeting, decisions to move his mother from one place to another, visits to her at place after place, and always heavy expense. It was in truth, as Stevenson sometimes said with hyperbole of other things, a "dreadful burden." But he bore it without complaining, was ever conscientious, spared neither effort nor expense to find the best treatment and care. A photograph of him and Buffie taken with their mother in Manchester makes him look near death himself.

Buffie went to Algiers. Stevenson and his family went back to Chicago. The doctor at the Battle Creek Sanitarium that fall reported that his mother required constant attention from an attendant, was beset by fears, feared Horton was "hypnotizing her at long distance." Buffie urged the doctor to disregard her mother's hostility toward Horton and to heed Horton's Assay. Horton continued to correspond with Stevenson. The Battle Creek doctor reported that Stevenson's mother complained about nurses, frequently said she wished she were some place else, "fusses occasionally about her heart" without reason, "treated" her throat constantly. The doctor agreed with Stevenson that she should go to a warm climate for the winter, perhaps the Southwest, which she seemed to prefer.

On November 1, Dr. John A. P. Millet of New York wrote to Stevenson at the request of a cousin of Stevenson. Dr. Millet thought "the difficulty is almost entirely nervous in origin" and she should be examined "by somebody used to dealing with functional nervous disorders"—going South for the winter was no solution to the underlying problem. He recommended three New England institutions that were among the best in the country. What Dr. Millet was proposing was that Mrs. Stevenson be taken out of a sanitarium that relied mainly on rest, sedatives, and sympathy and be given thoroughgoing psychiatric examination and treatment. Stevenson responded promptly and gratefully and said, "I feel confident that your suggestions are correct." He hoped to bring his mother to Chicago, have her see a psychiatrist there whom Dr. Millet recommended, and then persuade her to go to Dr. Austen Riggs' institution at Stockbridge, Massachusetts, instead of going South, although "she is so supersensitive to climate that I may not get that done until spring." Whether Stevenson fully realized it or not, this was a radical break with Horton and the sanitarium regime which Helen Stevenson had pursued most of her adult life; this made a sharp turn to psychiatry.

Stevenson brought his mother to Chicago. She saw her old doctor, Dr. Ernest Irons, went briefly into Presbyterian Hospital, then moved to a small apartment in the Whitehall, an apartment hotel. She had her maid with her in the daytime and at night Viola Van Valey served as a nurse. Viola, a McLean County girl, was with the Stevensons off and on over the years, first as a companion to Mrs. Stevenson, then with Stevenson in Libertyville, and finally with Stevenson while he was United States ambassador to the UN in the 1960s. Stevenson was getting advice from various quarters—Horton, Dr. Millet, the Battle Creek doctor, Dr. Irons. Stevenson wrote to a physician in Phoenix, Arizona, wrote to Horton for advice on Arizona and on a doctor and a nurse, wrote to a woman who operated an institution in Scottsdale, Arizona, wrote to a man who operated a sanitarium in Tucson, corresponded with a cousin about a nurse, received a prospectus from a hotel in Arizona addressing him as "Miss Stevenson," corresponded with a doctor in Louisville who suggested a sanitarium in Miami Springs, Florida, run by "a Yale man." In his inquiries he merely described his mother as suffering from "nervous exhaustion" and added she would have a maid and nurse with her. In one letter responding to a prospectus he wrote: "[I] note on the floor plans what appears to be a two room bungalow. This might be convenient for my mother and her maid," and asked for monthly rates starting in January. Horton gave silly advice. An Arizona "sanatorium and institute of research" sent an elaborate brochure which listed a staff with impressive titles but no psychiatrist, and Stevenson wrote out a telegram asking the director to "please reserve quiet corner room with porch" for his mother and her maid but changed his mind.

By now he had opened negotiations with Dr. Austen Riggs of Stockbridge, Massachusetts, who operated what was almost surely the best psychiatric institution Stevenson had considered. The tone of his letter to Dr. Riggs was quite different from that of his other inquiries. "In short, she has been deprived of all the active interests of her past life, and . . . suffered a nervous breakdown. At present her condition suggests the necessity of competent psychological attention. . . . Her blood pressure is a little high. . . . But her trouble is principally functional and not organic."

Dr. Riggs replied by telegram on New Year's Eve: he believed his institution probably appropriate, reserved final judgment pending the medical report, and would have a vacancy January 7. But Stevenson's mother was apprehensive about going to the Riggs institution, and so Stevenson sent her to her home in Bloomington, expecting she would go to Dr. Riggs in February. It was not easy—in a letter to another doctor, Stevenson spoke of "a series of crises and 'final decisions' in the last few days." And all the while, Stevenson was practicing law, participating in civic affairs, and carrying on a social life with Ellen.

On January 19, Stevenson told the Riggs clinic he thought he had "finally" persuaded his mother to go there. She would leave January 27. She would take her maid with her. "My mother's means will not permit her to stay very many months and I sincerely hope that you will find it possible to do something for her within a reasonable time. I understand, of course, and I think she does, that these things are very slow." He asked relatives in Bloomington to help her board the train, and they did, with some difficulty—even at the railroad station she implored them to let her go home. From Riggs's institution, Stevenson's mother wrote:

> My boy without price—Soon you will have passed another milestone—oh how terrible it is that my health is not your gift! . . .
>
> My blessing is always upon you but I am too humiliated to write now. I recall you as a wee boy & as a upstanding fine young man— & now on the threshhold of successful manhood—with only your mother as a detriment or deterrent.
>
> So how can I write—
>
> May God bless & keep you—
Mother

After only nine days Riggs told Stevenson that "the pace was too fast" there for her and recommended he send her to Craig House in Beacon, New York. Expenses at Riggs's, by Stevenson's reckoning, came to $807.16. Craig House was a little cheaper. It was a sanitarium on an estate in the Hudson highlands. Stevenson's mother was admitted there February 4, 1935. She stayed a little over five months at a cost of about a thousand dollars a month. On February 14 the physician in charge of Craig House gave Stevenson the nearest thing to a clinical psychiatric diagnosis theretofore made: "Since your mother's admission she has at all times represented an agitated

depression, probably of an involutional type and with a possible pre-
senile reaction slowly developing." He said she fretted about the
windows, the atmosphere in her apartment, "and all kinds of
imaginary disturbances. . . . If we prescribe a rest period for her,
she immediately thinks that she should get up. Whatever medication
we prescribe for her she thinks is the wrong kind. . . . She believes
that we are endeavoring to 'dope' her." He warned Stevenson not to
"expect too much."

His mother wrote to him, now sorely disappointed at having left
the Riggs institution "which was so perfect for me," full of advice
about Stevenson's children, urging him to spend time with them in
the evening. On the back of the letter Stevenson wrote, "This is the
best letter I've had from her in months—for a few minutes she really
thought about something beside herself." He wrote to her, reassuring
her of his confidence in Craig House. They sent him weekly reports.
Some weeks she seemed to be improving, some she was severely
agitated about her throat and ears and the temperature of the room.
Stevenson told Dr. Irons, "She has been there a month and seems to
have made some improvement. I believe that in time they will
gradually break many of the bad habits." "Bad habits"—Stevenson
showed little insight into her real problems, or concealed it.

Stevenson and Ellen had bought a piece of land west of Lake
Forest outside the village of Libertyville and were planning to build.
He wrote:

Dear Maw—
This morning we had a riotous easter egg hunt and then took
the bears [the children] out for the Easter parade!—and had not
a little difficulty warding off the photographers—Ellen being afraid
of kidnappers! Then to Lake Forest for a big lunch at the Larry
Williams—then the inevitable visit to the farm. . . .
We are going to rent our house for $175 a month from May 15
to Sept. 15 & take a small box on the [Graham] Aldis place in Lake
Forest—with their swimming pool and tennis court always available! It sounds too good to be true & comfortably economical.
Plans for development of the [Libertyville] property are still amorphous with some misgivings as to whether we can afford to do anything. . . .
Governor Horner has appointed me to the state of Child Welfare
Commission—which is something tho not much in my line! Work
at the office has been pretty intense lately, but Ellen says I seem to
thrive on it. . . . Courage & down with the body and up with the
spirit!
Ad

May reports from Craig House was mixed. Once she seemed much better. At other times she was severely agitated, and for the first time the doctor used the word "psychosis" to describe her condition. She became severely disturbed, probably because Craig House had, at Stevenson's suggestion, dropped one nurse. Stevenson visited her on June 9, a successful visit until shortly before he left, when the doctor told her Viola would have to take a few nights off to rest; she became agitated. The doctor advised against sending her home—"she will carry her present symptoms wherever she goes." But Stevenson nonetheless said, "Mother is at present so homesick and dissatisfied that I suspect it may be best for her to come home shortly." Stevenson brought her home early in July.

4

That spring Mayor Ed Kelly was running for re-election in his own right. On March 28, Stevenson wrote, endorsing him for re-election: "This is the first political endorsement I have ever written. . . . Under most trying circumstances, you have somehow managed to restore Chicago's safety, self-respect and solvency. . . . As a citizen, I am happy to acknowledge my debt for what you have already done and my confidence that your usefulness to Chicago has only begun." Kelly thanked him cordially if formally. James B. Alley, whom Stevenson first had known at Harvard Law School and later in Washington, was appointed general counsel of the RFC. Stevenson congratulated him, and Alley suggested that Stevenson seek the political endorsement of the two Illinois Senators, Lewis and Dieterich, so that Alley could designate him special counsel for the RFC in a pending railroad matter.

Stevenson replied at once: "I will ask the Illinois senators to write appropriate letters to you. I have little doubt that Senator Lewis will respond, but I do not know Senator Dieterich as well." Stevenson, though he developed into a skillful politician, never entirely lost the streak of political naïveté that led him to assume, despite past experience, that Senator Lewis' endorsement would be easy to obtain. He wrote on April 2 to both Senators. Senator Dieterich responded by return mail with his endorsement. But Senator Lewis referred Stevenson to O'Connell, his patronage man in Chicago. Stevenson went to see O'Connell and on April 9 thanked him for the interview, adding, "I hope to have a further opportunity to renew my acquaintance with you and incidentally to learn something about local politics, in which I hope to take a more active part—thanks to an—irresistable, congenital urge!" He had erred—had asked O'Connell to write to Alley, not to Senator Lewis. On April 12, prompted by Alley, he corrected it. After seemingly endless correspondence, Lewis gave Stevenson his endorsement, Stevenson thanked him profusely, and one of Alley's subordinates sent Stevenson his first assignment: to represent the RFC in the reorganization of the Chicago Great Western Railroad Company. It was the first important piece of legal business he had brought the firm. But only a week later the firm decided he could not handle the case after all because of a possible conflict of interest.

When Stevenson returned to Chicago from Washington the preceding fall, he had begun giving more time to *Pantagraph* affairs. Dave Merwin proposed to construct a new building. Stevenson approved but wanted to cut out frills to save money. He went over the plans carefully—"a modest exterior seems in keeping with the community and our functions. The mezzanine floor impresses me as desirable but not essential." Now Dave Merwin was leaving the *Pantagraph*—John and Gardner Cowles, Jr., owners of the Des Moines *Register-Tribune,* had bought the *Star* of Minneapolis and made Dave Merwin publisher. His brother Bud took his place. Bud Merwin was quite different from Dave. He was firm, not stubborn; even-tempered, not excitable; reasonable, not irascible; patient, not hot-tempered; and both hard-working and steady. Bud had worked at the *Pantagraph* as a boy, had worked on the Harvard *Crimson* and as a string correspondent for Boston newspapers. When he left college in 1928, his family felt that because of the ancient feud he had best not work at the *Pantagraph*—it would have had two Merwins and no Stevenson—and, moreover, as Bud had put it, "Dave was a very take-charge guy," implying he himself would not have been comfortable working under his older brother. He worked in California for a tile manufacturing company his father had started, went around the world, and marked time until 1935, when he replaced Dave at the *Pantagraph*. "So then I had the uncomfortable job here of learning the business from the top down. Joe Bunting helped me over the hump. Since then I've been the executive head of the paper. Adlai and I were always personally friendly. I made it clear that I was not here to represent the Merwin family to the exclusion of the rest of the ownership. I was here to represent everybody." Sometimes, as he mediated among his brother and sister and Stevenson, and Buffie Ives, who occasionally telephoned to complain about something in the paper and once had a great row with the society editor, Bud Merwin's work seemed more like diplomacy than publishing.

Dave Merwin left the *Pantagraph* in good condition. Bud Merwin continued to build it. Stevenson had permitted Dave, the professional, to run the paper; Stevenson's principal interest had been in profits, not policy. On the contrary, Bud and Stevenson were friendlier and less businesslike and, while Stevenson still watched the profits closely, he became increasingly concerned with the newspaper's editorial policies—when he and Bud disagreed, it was more likely to be over politics than money.

Bud Merwin has said, "Frankly, I never considered that in lots of ways Adlai was a hell of a liberal sort of fellow. He'd come to our directors' meetings and ask if it was true that we'd made a new contract with the unions; I'd say we gave them ten cents across the board; he'd say, 'Couldn't you get by with a nickel?' We started a retirement program and a profit-sharing program for executives and others. I don't recall his ever taking a leading part in it and I do recall a lot of questioning." Stevenson had some knowledge of the business side of publishing, little knowledge of news-gathering, an increasing interest in editorial policy, and always a somewhat exaggerated idea of the importance of a newspaper which, while it returned handsome profits and enjoyed local respect, was after all not the New York *Times*. That he took it so seriously was characteristic of him. Whatever he was involved in was important to him.

5

Stevenson had been elected president of the Chicago Council on Foreign Relations for the next two years. It was a milestone in his life. It was as president of the Council that he first emerged as a public figure. What attracted attention was his way of introducing guest speakers. Sometimes his graceful introductions were more arresting than the speeches that followed. "Adlai raised the level of performance at the Council," Ed McDougal said, just as he later elevated political debate. Ruth Winter has said, "Gosh, you'd go to those meetings and in two minutes that man had his audience. There wasn't anybody who was anybody who didn't go to the Council luncheons—it was the same as the Chicago Symphony," that is, the thing to do, socially. "That must have been the time he first had the sense of power with audiences. After him, everybody was a comedown."

Harriet Welling, who had helped nominate him for president, once said, "This was a very rapid rise for him. Here he had graduated from law school in 1926 and only eight years later he was president. We tried to get the Council off the society page and on to the news pages." At the Council, Stevenson met many people who later played important roles in his life. Many of his most ardent supporters when he ran for Governor and President had been his associates there. As Governor, he appointed Council people to important jobs. His work at the Council drew him to the attention of Frank Knox, publisher of the Chicago *Daily News,* who would later take Stevenson back to Washington. Among others active on the Council were William Sidley, John Kellogg, Graham Aldis, Edison Dick (Jane Dick's husband), Jim Douglas, Steve Hord, and Carroll Binder of the Chicago *Daily News.* Under Stevenson the Council changed from a small elitist group of like-minded people to a larger, more public and more diverse group. During his first year Council membership increased from 1,606 to 2,141. The change was due not only to him but to the board members, the salaried director, Clifton Utley, and the times—menacing events abroad were forcing themselves on Midwesterners' attention. Stevenson worked hard at getting new members, and at Council finances, as well as at obtaining and introducing speakers. The first fall luncheon meeting, on September 27, 1935, was attended by 1,159 people. Two other meetings that fall were attended by more than a thousand.

Stevenson always asked to be briefed on the speakers four days in advance. He wrote out his introduction and memorized it. Most people thought Stevenson's introductions were extemporaneous but his close friends knew better. Once, about an hour before he was to introduce a speaker, Mrs. Welling asked him to insert something into his introduction and he replied, "I'll try, Harriet—but you know I learn these things by heart." He wrote out the introductions in longhand on yellow legal-size lawyer's pads. He worked hard, doing a great deal of crossing out and interlining. They were usually brief, limited to the speaker's background and subject, with as little as possible on the dull affairs of the Council, on the whole sober, but with occasional flashes of wit, especially during his second year as president. Occasionally he indulged in the self-deprecation that marked his later speeches.

What is most interesting about these luncheons in the Palmer House is that the speaking style which during the 1952 presidential campaign came to be thought of as uniquely Stevensonian—not merely the wit and self-deprecation but the long complicated sentences, the complex syntax and high level of diction, the seriousness of thought, the use of parallelisms and other devices to impart an inner rhythm to the prose—all of this seems to have been developed during the two years he served as Council president from 1935 to 1937. And it was here too that he developed his choppy delivery, a delivery that seemed halting and irritating to some people but to others arresting, brilliant, and eloquent.

Stevenson's work at the Council made heavy demands on his time and infringed on his law practice. Ed McDougal has said, "The law took second place in his own interests to the Council and the William Allen White Committee," formed a few years later. "He was always more interested in public questions and international affairs. It was the urge of his political inheritance." Preoccupation with the Council did not, however, impair his relations with his wife. "During this period, Ellen didn't mind it," Mrs. Welling said. "It was always a sort of 'spectator sport'—but of increasing importance, of course, as the nation's attention was forced to foreign affairs."

6

He and Ellen were building a house on the forty acres of Libertyville land they had bought from the Insull estate. (They later bought an adjoining thirty acres.) The post office address was Libertyville but the land itself was farmland. At that time it could not be reached by road; St. Mary's Road was built later. The surrounding countryside is gently rolling fertile Illinois prairie, some of it wooded, some crop land, some pasture land for large dairy farms. Even by the time of Stevenson's death in 1965, houses were scattered thinly and landholdings were large, and the area was by no means one of suburban development but, rather, estates given over to the pleasures of outwardly simple but actually expensive country living. Stevenson's land lay low and somewhat swampy on the east, rose to a slight knoll where he built his house, and sloped gently westward down to the Des Plaines River, a small pretty stream. The larger portion of his land, some forty acres, where the house stood, Stevenson kept in grass, with wide-spaced great maples and oaks. The thirty acres to the north Stevenson in some years planted to soybeans, corn, and vegetables, and he kept a flock of sheep that used to sweep en masse across the grassland near the house, to the astonishment of the distinguished visitors who came there in later years. The whole establishment resembled more a modest country estate than a Midwest farm, but Stevenson always referred to it as "the farm." Fences were few thereabouts in those days; it was excellent horseback-riding country, and in those years Stevenson loved to ride. He and his wife originally used the house only as a summer place. It was their first home of their own. Stevenson noted once that they were moving to the country and Ellen was "reconciled" to it. Some of Adlai III's earliest memories are of visiting the homesite on weekends.

Stevenson's original house was built of prefabricated steel; he referred to it as his "mechanical house." It burned in 1938 and Stevenson rebuilt it of frame. It was set far back from St. Mary's Road, and from a white mailbox at the roadside a long lane, first straight, then curving slightly, ran up the knoll to a gravel turnaround and the house. The house was low and white, rectangular and boxlike. Off to the right stood the farmer's house, garage and a barn with three horse stalls, a tack room, and a workshop. Behind the barn was a white-fenced corral.

The house itself looked smaller than it was. The small foyer inside the front door was wood-paneled and tile-floored. On its wall hung two water colors by Diego Rivera. To its left was a sizable guest bedroom with parquet floor, private corridor, and bathroom. Ahead of the foyer and two steps down was the living room, twenty-nine feet by eighteen, parquet floor, yellow walls, white ceiling, french doors opening to the porch overlooking the land sloping down to the river. Many of the original furnishings had been brought from Europe. The living room looked quiet, lived-in, comfortable—leather armchairs at the fireplace, kidney-shaped end tables, an antique burl walnut desk, a grand piano, odd tables and chairs, some rickety. Some of the furniture needed reupholstering. Subdued pictures hung on the walls, and green plants stood in a brass "Imperial standard half-bushel" made in London long ago. The dining table was antique; the walls and ceiling were white. A tiny light burned down from the ceiling to supplement candlelight at dinner. The sideboard was small and old; a high cupboard was filled with old china. The wall facing the river was nearly all glass.

Beyond the living room was Stevenson's study, a light room with a fireplace, corner windows overlooking trees and rolling grassland and woods, bookshelves and cabinets covering one wall and most of two more. In the early years it contained an early American walnut chair, poker chips and backgammon sets. Later his desk was an old table six feet long and two and a half feet wide; his swivel chair was upholstered in brown leather. The floor was hardwood, partly covered with thick rugs. A bookshelf and cabinet held record-playing equipment. The library was a working library. The books closest to his desk were the books one needs to write speeches—an encyclopedia, a Bible, an anthology of quotations, plus three shelves of books on Lincoln. Nearby were numerous family books, including campaign biographies of President Cleveland and Vice President Stevenson; a book Grandfather Stevenson wrote, *Something of Men I Have Known;* a *Life of L. W. Green, The Life of Jesse W. Fell,* books on genealogy, a brief history of the Daughters of the American Revolution by Grandfather Stevenson, and other family memorabilia. In later life, Stevenson's library became encrusted not only with his own speeches and books by and about him, but also with a disorderly collection of books, mostly on current foreign affairs, sent to him by publishers or authors, written by such people as James Byrnes, Barbara Ward, Thomas K. Finletter, Chester Bowles, Theodore H. White, James P. Warburg, and Walter Lippmann. Stevenson was not a great reader, and few of the books, except the "working" books, show much evidence of having been read.

The stairs to the second floor were of oak, with a carpet runner. The master bedroom was large and light and airy. The floor was wood, the rug was white, the walls were light blue, a fireplace took part of one wall, a chaise longue and chairs were scattered about as were family pictures and old French prints, and doors opened to a sun deck and porch with outside stairs down to the ground. He indulged his wife. Adjoining the bedroom was an unusually large dressing room with two washbowls. The appointments were rather luxurious—thick oversize towels, thick rugs, scale, full-length mirror, many closets and drawers, monogrammed leather cases and silver brushes, elegantly framed photographs of family and friends. Many of these things were gifts. The master bedroom and dressing room took up the entire south end of the upstairs. The other half contained three bedrooms.

Stevenson loved the Libertyville farm and house. He loved the sun and spent hours sun-bathing in the grass or on the deck outside his bedroom. He took long walks on his property, observing wild flowers, picking up fallen tree limbs. He was not parsimonious about this place; he spent much time and money caring for his maples. From the porch, he loved to watch, with his children, the sun setting red over the prairie and the river. This was his Illinois. Few people got more pleasure out of the things in life than Adlai Stevenson—sunsets, dogs, children, vegetables from his own garden, the blue sky, the warm prairie winds. "His love of life," Adlai III once said, "that was the great thing. The incredible joy he got out of those little things. Except they weren't little to him."

Stevenson lived in the Libertyville house longer than he lived any other single place except his growing-up years in Bloomington, yet his residence even in Libertyville was rather spasmodic. He and Ellen were there in 1936 and 1937, then, after rebuilding the burned first house, lived there until 1941. Stevenson spent the war years in Washington and abroad, and when he finally returned to Libertyville he had scarcely settled in before he ran for Governor. As Governor, he lived in Springfield. During the 1950s he made his home in Libertyville but spent a great deal of time traveling, both in the United States and abroad, and in the 1960s he lived in New York at the United States Embassy to the United Nations. All in all, he probably actually lived in the house at Libertyville less than ten years. It was, however, home to him, and the name Libertyville became known to countless people around the world as Adlai Stevenson's home.

7

Stevenson's mother had hoped to go home to Bloomington in the fall but on August 12, accompanied by Buffie and Viola, she arrived at the Milwaukee Sanitarium in Wauwatosa, Wisconsin. The doctor there told Stevenson she arrived in an agitated condition. The doctor advised her to stay with him and let Buffie return to Charlevoix. He felt it had been a mistake to leave Craig House: she had not improved enough to be outside of a sanitarium.

So the weary round began again; the institution was different but the story much the same. Three days after she arrived the doctor wrote that she continued to be "restless and dissatisfied" and Buffie still was "standing by." Stevenson thought Buffie should not stay— it would be hard on her and would not do their mother much good. He objected to the charge for the day nurse; the doctor offered to consider adjusting it. Stevenson paid about $900 a month. He visited his mother September 3 and told the doctor she was "vastly improved." He was still talking about her going South for the winter.

Taking up his duties as president of the Council on Foreign Relations that September, Stevenson asked Secretary of State Hull to address the Council. Hull said he could not make a definite commitment but would "keep the matter under consideration." Stevenson urged on him the importance of his speaking in the Middle West, where ignorance of Administration foreign policy was widespread. A Chicago lawyer, Newton Jenkins, refused an invitation to join the Council because he believed it was "a training school for treason to our country." Stevenson replied, "I am going to take the liberty of asking you the following three questions: 1. Have you ever attended a meeting of the Council? 2. If so, what did you hear that convinced you that the Council was a training school for treason to the United States? 3. If you have not attended a meeting, on what evidence do you base your quoted conviction?" A charter member of the Council told him that Stevenson's grandfather, the Vice President, and his own grandfather had been "very intimate friends." At the bottom of the letter Stevenson penciled, "It's always pleasing to pick up my grandfather's threads." All the rest of his life Stevenson received letters about his grandfather from people he had never met. It pleased him.

That fall Stevenson's mother's letters worsened. Stevenson visited her, and she reacted very well. Stevenson told the Peoples Bank in Bloomington his mother wanted to give her thirty-four shares of bank stock to him and Buffie. He suggested the sanitarium take her for "a short motor ride" each day and offered to send her car up. It was difficult, the sanitarium reported—after the car was ordered she would change her mind. Julia Hodge of Bloomington asked Stevenson's mother to contribute to the Art Association in Bloomington; Stevenson replied she would like nothing better but could not because of the expenses of her institutionalization. Julia Hodge understood but suggested "a plain one dollar membership" for her instead of life membership—"I can't bear to have her name taken off the rolls." Stevenson acquiesced.

On November 7 the sanitarium told Stevenson his mother was "about the same" but added a new note: at times she had "a low grade fever," a little over 100° the day before; a nose and throat specialist had found nothing. Nonetheless, the sanitarium curtailed her activities a little.

On November 11 the Milwaukee Sanitarium told Stevenson his mother's condition was essentially unchanged—better nights but refusal to get out of bed by day, at times "very abusive" toward nurses. She was seen by a throat specialist, and her fever subsided. Stevenson went to Milwaukee on business November 13, visited his mother briefly, told the doctor her failure to show improvement was "disconcerting," and said, "I am wondering if you are still as confident of her ultimate recovery as formerly." He asked about her teeth, suggested a consultation with a psychiatrist, and said he hoped to visit her again on Sunday. The sanitarium reported that she "seemed to react fairly well" to his visit. "She has been worried a good deal recently about being changed to another building, as she is quite aware that she is disturbing." On November 15 the sanitarium replied to Stevenson—she was too agitated to undertake dental work. That morning she suddenly developed a high fever, 104°, and her pulse rate became somewhat more rapid than usual; an internist examined her and found nothing to explain the fever. However, before the next morning she was dead. The cause of death was given as "fever of unknown origin perhaps acute endocarditis" and a contributory cause was given as "manic depressive depression." Her body was shipped to Bloomington November 17. Helen Stevenson's long struggle with life was ended.

Her funeral was held Monday afternoon, November 17, at the Unitarian Church in Bloomington. The *Pantagraph* offices closed. The pallbearers were all *Pantagraph* employees. Buffie was in Algiers at the time but has since recalled that Ellen went through the house on Washington Street and said there was nothing there she'd want— "maybe some kitchen things." Buffie went on, "But then she took four chairs from the living room, the piano, and an iron couch for the garden, a bedroom set, a chair and sofa out of the library, a chest, a marquetry table, and Mother's wedding china." It may be taken more as a measure of the bitterness between the two women than as a strictly factual account.

At the time of their mother's death, Buffie's thoughts were of her mother and brother. She wrote a long anguished letter to Stevenson that seemed to sum up how she felt about their mother and their family life—the letter saying that the three of them had forged a ring, a circle so tight it closed everyone else out. Now she had been rereading her mother's letters since her father's death, and it suddenly seemed to her that her mother had in recent years been terribly lonely, and she reproached herself and Stevenson for having been blind to that loneliness. Buffie's own husband and son Tim had sympathized with her grief over her mother's death but nevertheless she longed to be once more beside her mother and Stevenson. Nearly all of Buffie's letters to Stevenson showed a religious fervor, a deep affection for him, and a sense of the quiet desperation in which those three had lived a part of their lives.

That his mother had died of ambiguous causes troubled Stevenson. On December 9 he asked the sanitarium for a copy of her last blood examination report, and any conclusion as to the cause of death. Many a child whose mother dies in an institution feels the guilt Buffie seemed to feel. If Stevenson felt it too, it did not show. He had erected a barrier to guard his innermost self. And frequently he showed a certain obtuseness, an opaque quality, in his judgment of friends and associates, overvaluing some and undervaluing others. It may have been the price he paid for guarding his own intimate feelings so carefully. Recalling now his mother's and father's storms during his childhood, his relationship with his sister and mother, his accidental shooting of the girl, the long agony of his mother's illness and his responsibility for her, and later, the disastrous course his own marriage took, one does not wonder that he erected the barrier. It gave him fortitude to endure the gravest adversity, both public and private, adversity that has broken others but did not break him. The wrenching final year of his mother's life must have helped strengthen that barrier.

8

Glenn McHugh of Equitable Life sent Stevenson Washington gossip and a speech by the president of Equitable, and in commenting on the latter, Stevenson expressed in embryonic form a view of the proper role of government that he later developed at length. He thought it true that, as the speaker had said, the first duty of government was "to provide security for the results of enterprise" but, he argued, business enterprise had a corresponding responsibility to the people—"After all, government in a way is the common meeting ground of all interests in the interest of all, and there can be no enduring security provided by government for enterprise without the accompanying provision of security *by* enterprise."

Arthur Krock of the New York *Times* planned to be in Chicago December 6 and asked Stevenson to arrange a lunch of opinion leaders there. After a good deal of juggling names, Stevenson invited eight men, mostly bankers, lawyers, and business executives. It was hardly the "cross-section of the political and economic thought of Chicago" Krock wanted. It included no labor leaders, no politicians, no university professors, no journalists or editors or publishers. (He may, however, have had in mind Krock's own rather conservative views. A few months later he assembled a more literate and liberal group for a New Dealer.)

At a Council luncheon on December 18, Stevenson introduced the man who had served as Undersecretary of State under President Hoover, William R. Castle. Castle attacked the Roosevelt administration's foreign policy. He criticized remarks on the export of oil to Italy by Secretary of the Interior Ickes and asked, "What satisfaction can there be in being Secretary of State when the White House or the Department of Agriculture or the head of some alphabetical bureau is liable at any moment to lay down foreign policy with the apparent acquiescence of the President? . . . Poor Mr. Hull had to begin his usual series of explanations that things were not what they seemed." Stevenson sent newspaper clippings to Sec-

retary Ickes and Secretary Hull, said the speech had embarrassed
the non-partisan Council, and requested Hull to speak in rebuttal
or to send someone to do so. He asked Ickes to help persuade Hull.
The matter came up at a cabinet meeting and it was decided not to
dignify the incident by sending Secretary Hull to Chicago in person
but rather to send some other department official. The upshot was
that Stevenson for the first time was able to induce a high State Department official to address the Council, William Phillips, Undersecretary of State. In introducing him on February 15, 1936, Stevenson made no mention of former Undersecretary Castle's speech.
Afterward, Stevenson thanked Secretary Hull for sending Phillips
and told him, "The press of course was apathetic, which, as you
know, is always the case in Chicago when the subject matter is cred-
itable to the Administration." The incident prefigured the controversy over isolationism into which Stevenson was drawn deeply a
few years later.

9

On the first day of 1936, Stevenson was made a partner in the
Sidley law firm. He had been there nine years, with about a year
out in Washington. This was the usual amount of time young law
clerks needed to become partners. His income from the law firm in
1935 had been $5,655. In 1936 it was $9,838.12.

This was an election year, when President Roosevelt ran for a
second term, and Stevenson became involved. Politics and the Council on Foreign Relations took up Stevenson's spare time. He concerned himself rather closely with *Pantagraph* affairs. And although
only now a partner in his law firm, he made another ambiguous
move to rejoin the federal government. An assistant attorney general told him the Attorney General had informed him that Stevenson
wanted to join the Justice Department staff. He said no vacancy
existed in his division but he would like to meet Stevenson for later
consideration. Stevenson promptly replied that he was not interested and recommended a lawyer friend in Washington, John Paulding Brown, whom Stevenson had repeatedly recommended for various jobs. This episode is one of several in which he seemed to
have put out a tentative feeler for a job, then, when it appeared he
could not get the job, quickly disclaimed interest, as though anxious
to make it appear, as Senator Lewis once had put it, that no record
existed of his having been "defeated" in seeking a position.

At this time Stevenson made a first serious try at joining Democratic organization politics in Chicago. On February 17, R. J. Dunham, a well-to-do Democratic politician who lived on the Gold Coast in Stevenson's own ward, wrote a letter to the ward committeeman about Stevenson. Dunham was, like Colonel A. A. Sprague, a bridge between the worlds of politics and monied "society." At that time, the Democratic committeeman in the ward was Mathias Bauler, almost universally called Paddy, a troglodytic machine politician whose beer-drinking celebrations of his own birthdays in his own saloon became famous and who has been immortalized by the Chicago press as the man who said during one of several efforts at political reform in the 1950s, "Chicago ain't ready for reform." Bauler's ward was a stronghold of the organization; its strength lay in the slums on the west side of the ward near the Chicago River, and Bauler had little but contempt for the East Side, the Gold Coast where Dunham and Stevenson lived. Now Dunham wrote to Bauler to introduce Stevenson as the grandson of the former Vice President and a prominent young lawyer interested in politics, to propose that Bauler enlist Stevenson for organizing work on the east side of the ward, and to suggest that Bauler interest Stevenson by considering him as a candidate for alternate delegate to the 1936 National Convention. Bauler replied promptly and decisively. In the stilted idiom that unlettered Chicago politicians employ when called upon to draft an official document, Bauler said that experience showed that trying to get out the vote from the luxury apartments and hotels of the east side was an unrewarding task, that the signal honor of alternate delegate had already been bestowed upon a loyal party worker, and that investigation revealed that this Adlai Stevenson was not even registered to vote. He might, however, Bauler added graciously, attend a ward meeting if he wished.

It was the first time Adlai Stevenson had brushed up against the ponderous bulk of the Chicago machine. He did not like it. In longhand, crossing out and rewriting many sentences, Stevenson framed a letter to "Mr. Dunham":

> Thank you very much indeed. . . . You more than did your part and I appreciate it. Bauler's reply is, I presume, a characteristic commentary on our current municipal politics. While, insofar as it affects me personally, I am disappointed at his complete indifference, I am far more concerned with the implication of thoughtless disregard of long range party welfare.
>
> The attitude of too hell with him & the east end of the ward is a brief and eloquent answer to the familiar question as to why more men like yourself don't take an active part in our municipal politics.

And, as you know, in spite of its apparent popular strength the Dem party locally & nationally never needed active sympathy on the East side as much as it does today.

I will, of course, continue my missionary work among the heathen, a familiar role in my family for several generations, but of course it can never be very useful unless the party leaders occasionally recognize and thus enlist some of these younger men in the active Dem party. Of course our salvation is that the Republicans have likewise always overlooked this potential advantage in enlisting some of the "other half."

Few of the later Illinois Democratic leaders knew Stevenson was interested in politics this early (though as we have seen he was interested at least five years before this). All his life Stevenson had trouble with the Paddy Baulers of the Illinois Democratic Party. He never fully understood them nor they him. Governor Otto Kerner of Illinois, who while winning votes from good-government groups was always able to work with the machine, once said, "That was the wrong way to approach Paddy. If you want to see Paddy you go to see him—you don't send someone else." Colonel Arvey once said, "That was the main fight I had as [Cook County] chairman—to get the committeemen to open ranks to good people." Arvey added that Stevenson was a "Roosevelt Democrat" and that one of President Roosevelt's "great attributes" was his ability to attract good new people to the party, an attribute that also later distinguished both Stevenson and John F. Kennedy. It was also true, as an old friend of Stevenson said, that Stevenson never fully experienced the low-level politics on which high-level politics rests. "Ambition was very deep in him, but he always masked it by a very casual manner. He was terribly interested in politics—politics and government and people—but Adlai III will know more about politics than his father did," since Adlai III started young at the bottom, running for the state legislature in 1964 and for state Treasurer in 1966 before running for the United States Senate, whereas Stevenson's first campaign for elective office had been for Governor. "He could inspire people. But I remember a line from Lord Acton: 'I don't hate humanity. I just don't know them personally.' This was true of Adlai."

10

Buffie was ill. On March 10 her husband, Ernest Ives, wrote Stevenson from Algiers, "You must not worry too much about

Elizabeth's health. She gets fed up and tired like the rest of us. I will let you know should her troubles get really serious." Ives commented on Undersecretary of State Phillips' speech to the Council and related his own unhappy experiences with Phillips. He went on to recount difficulties Buffie had had at various diplomatic posts, transfers and treatment he considered unfair, promotions denied, concluding, "It has all been rather discouraging. On the other hand this is a damn good post. It is practically independent, the climate is excellent, we have a lovely place and for foreigners a position second to none. The work is normal and from the political angle is getting more interesting as time goes on. Tim is getting French and Elizabeth is happier here than she would be anywhere else." Ives never did receive an appointment as ambassador and later retired somewhat disappointed. If he did not make the most brilliant career in diplomatic history, he made a thoroughly respectable one, and he was a kind man and a devoted friend during Stevenson's governorship and presidential campaigns. (He died in 1972.)

That spring Governor Henry Horner was running for renomination in the Democratic primary. He had quarreled with the Cook County machine over patronage and had built his own personal downstate machine (and downstate politics can be at least as corrupt as Cook County politics). It was one of the nastiest primary fights in recent Illinois history. Horner asked Stevenson to serve as treasurer of his primary campaign. If he did, he would alienate the Chicago machine. Stevenson dodged—told Horner he was taking his wife South soon. A few days later he wrote to Bud Merwin, "In connection with the primary campaign, I feel we should vigorously endorse Horner in the Democratic primary." They did. Horner won the primary and went on to win re-election. (The *Pantagraph* supported him but opposed Roosevelt again.)

Francis T. P. Plimpton, Stevenson's friend at Harvard Law School and by now a partner in the New York law firm of Debevoise, Stevenson, Plimpton & Page, wrote, "It has been far too long since we have had an orgy of the Kent Club Marching and Chowder Association," said March 28 and April 4 were under consideration for "this matchless event," and told Stevenson to bring William McIlvaine "and your respective spouses." Stevenson replied with a letter similar in tone, saying he could not go because of a Mexican trip and inviting Plimpton and his wife to join them in Cuernavaca and Acapulco. Before leaving, Stevenson sent a physician a check for $250 on account, saying he was "a little short of cash at present." Returning on April 14, Stevenson congratulated Governor Horner on his primary victory, reflecting his own resentment of

Paddy Bauler's rebuff. "As a Democrat with downstate background, I hope that this stinging rebuke to Cook County leadership will serve a useful purpose." He offered to serve Horner in the fall campaign.

Opening the Council's annual meeting on May 12, Stevenson said, "For the last couple of days I have searched in vain for some way of relieving the monotony of this annual meeting. Even stockholders' annual meetings are sometimes enlivened with questions about the president's salary, et cetera, and I thought of reversing the tables this time and asking you for a salary for your overworked president—but I dismissed that one hastily with the certain knowledge that you would probably rise indignantly and say the question is not 'why a salary' but 'why a president.' . . . I've observed that most all presidents have been reporting successful years lately and I'm happy to say that the Council is no exception—like the armament industry, the Council thrives on trouble." The Council had held twenty luncheon meetings, five of which dealt with U.S. foreign policy, five with the Ethiopian war, three with Germany, and the rest with various problems in Europe and the Far East. The nominating committee reported. "I admit I appointed this nominating committee" Stevenson said, and asked its spokesman "to see this thing through as presiding officer while I tremble in my chair." Once his own re-election was accomplished, Stevenson said, "It's always gratifying to witness the democratic process—to see the sovereign people exercise their considered will after a fair and vigorous contest!" Clay Judson, a law partner of William McIlvaine, wrote, "Have I told you recently what a splendid job I think you do as a presiding officer? . . . It should be on your conscience that you are not serving your country by going into politics." It is one of the earliest unsolicited specific suggestions that Stevenson enter politics.

On May 12, Governor Horner appointed Stevenson a delegate to the National Conference of Social Work in Atlantic City, regretting the state could not pay Stevenson's travel expenses. Stevenson declined the appointment. On the eighteenth Stevenson made a speech to the Junior Association of Commerce on foreign trade. He began with self-deprecation, saying at length he knew nothing about foreign trade and then, having done his homework well from documents sent him by Wayne Chatfield Taylor, delivered a 4,000-word masterly advocacy of the Administration's reciprocal trade policy, buttressed solidly by statistics, couched in terms acceptable to this audience of young Midwest businessmen. Why, having mastered his subject and drafted a skillful logical argument and a few lines of graceful rhetoric, had he begun by disparaging his effort and himself? He did it all his life. Some who knew him thought he lacked self-confidence, perhaps because of personal hurt, failure, and disappointment. But Mrs. Welling once said, "He didn't lack confidence in himself," and most people who knew him best agreed. Self-deprecation seemed reinforced now—seemed the sort of mannerly, graceful thing one would say in a Lake Forest drawing room, masking what really was self-confidence. In politics, it became a tactic, one designed to disarm, ingratiate, win sympathy, encourage help, inspire affection. The trouble was that it was better understood at a Lake Forest dinner party than in the political crucible. Just so with two other tactics of his—that of asking someone's advice long after he had made up his mind, and that of stating a view he did not really hold simply in order to provoke a reaction and hear the arguments. He did both, repeatedly, throughout his career, and while it was harmless enough in Lake Forest, it led to endless misunderstanding in public life.

11

On July 27 a St. Louis lawyer invited Stevenson to attend a meeting of "Constitutional Democrats" who opposed the re-election of Roosevelt "and his . . . collectivist policies." Stevenson reacted promptly and strongly: he believed Roosevelt deserved re-election and gratitude although he did not approve of everything he had done. Stevenson sent a copy of his letter to S. E. Thomason, publisher of the Chicago *Times*. This was the year Governor Alfred Landon of Kansas ran against Roosevelt. The campaign was embittered by such groups as the Liberty League, which Al Smith and other conservative Democrats joined. Stevenson became state finance director of the Democratic National Campaign Committee and performed well. Thus his entry into national Democratic politics was as a fund raiser. Mayor Kelly asked Stevenson if the National Committee could use his name as a businessman supporting Roosevelt.

At the season's first meeting of the Council on Foreign Relations that fall, Stevenson said that interest in foreign affairs was rising "here in the midlands. To promote and satisfy that interest has been our educational function in this community, and that we have succeeded in some measure is attested by the gathering you see here today and by the fact that our membership has increased from a handful to almost twenty-two hundred. Perhaps in time *all* of Chicago newspapers will even realize that the Council is not a club but an im-

portant Chicago institution—an active adult educational institution."
It is a revelatory passage, foreshadowing Stevenson's conception of
a political campaign as an exercise in adult education and his attacks
on the "one-party press." The society editor of the *Daily News,* referring to his "quip" about the press—the earliest use of the word
which was later used *ad nauseam* to describe his wit and humor—told
him the *News* had begun covering the Council adequately only
after the society reporters had become interested and now printed
faithfully advance notices of the time and place of meetings. "And
should you or your treasury committee be saddened if your membership grows because we describe hats rather than economic conditions?" Stevenson agreed and said, "By aspiring to the news pages,
I do not mean to disparage the society pages—or bite the hand
that feeds us."

That season of 1936–37, Stevenson's second and last term as president, the Council held twenty-six luncheon meetings, and he introduced nearly all the speakers. Introducing the journalist Edgar Ansel
Mowrer, Stevenson said, "Last year at this time we were occupied
with war in Ethiopia—this year it is war in Spain—what it may be
next year no one can foretell. Last year we witnessed a disheartening
rebuff to the age-old ambition to subject to the reign of law not only
men but states. Today we are witnessing something even more sinister—a bloody conflict between brothers which many people suggest
is but a ghastly prelude to the more ghastly drama to follow. Because we are destined to hear much of the conflict between fascism
and socialism we are devoting two consecutive meetings to Spain."
Perhaps as presiding officer he felt he must be impartial—but so
bland were his comments that they revealed none of the passion
most American liberals felt about Spain. But after all, at that time
the Council was, as one of its leaders once said, only a spectator
sport.

In domestic policies, he was firm in his support of Roosevelt, and
on October 2 he told a woman in California who feared Communist
influence in the United States, "I do not share your misgivings."

On October 23, Stevenson went up to Carleton College in Minnesota and made a speech for Roosevelt that began: "I want to pref-
ace my remarks by assuring you that this is not intended as a political speech. I say that for several reasons: in the first place, it will
effectively prevent you from saying it is the worst political speech
you have ever heard; secondly, I have never made a political
speech and I confess, without shame, that it is all I can do to listen
to most of them, let alone make one; and, finally, were I to attempt

one it would not be before an intelligent academic audience without any single dominant interest which I could seize upon for my excursion into the familiar wonderland of irrational praise and intemperate damnation. . . . In this atmosphere, we can, perhaps, step aside from the sound and fury and reason together quietly and tolerantly. I believe that you and I by education have a great responsibility to democracy." It was disarming, and it sought to identify him with the vast body of Americans who mistrust politicians, a tactic he employed throughout his political career.

And he went on in words that anticipated some of his best-known speeches in the 1952 presidential campaign: "Whether you vote for Governor Landon or President Roosevelt is not so important, but that you pay your debt to democracy soberly and intelligently is important; for you, the discriminating and enlightened electorate of tomorrow, are the burden bearers of democracy and the continuing insurance of the survival of our system of things at a time when political and economic freedom is everywhere being challenged and engulfed. . . ." Independents, he said, usually vote negatively, not affirmatively; and so he examined the reasons for voting against Roosevelt. He stated the Republican case, dismissing some of it as beneath serious argument, conceding some of it, and concluding that Roosevelt's re-election might ensure against "a union of the more radical elements behind irresponsible leadership," America's greatest danger. Then he switched to the attack and, characteristically, attacked on the foreign front—said the Republican Party was once more advocating "a policy of aloofness, isolation, and narrow nationalism." It was the kind of reasoned partisanship that in 1952 almost automatically drew to Stevenson the intellectual liberals of the Democratic Party.

On October 29, Stevenson bet $200 against $100 that Roosevelt would win. He put the bet in writing, in the form of a lawyerlike letter of agreement to a third party, a LaSalle Street friend, who held the money (and who wrote: "I don't care so much about Roosevelt but I would like to see you win as a just reward for your good sportsmanship"; many of Stevenson's Lake Forest-Gold Coast-LaSalle Street friends took good sportsmanship more seriously than national politics). Stevenson's brother-in-law, Ernest Ives, bet against Roosevelt. A Washington friend praised Stevenson for his work in the campaign. "You spoke deprecatingly of it as not of great importance but you were cultivating a very strong and barren field." He knew only one other Chicago lawyer who had worked hard for Roosevelt. "I would like to see you in some high position in this administration and you are certainly entitled to such a place if you want it."

Stevenson accepted an invitation to go on the board of the Immigrants' Protective League, a non-controversial and somewhat old-fashioned charity popular with Lake Forest people. He was becoming increasingly involved with various organizations around the country interested in international affairs, including the Institute of Pacific Relations.

At the annual Christmas luncheon of his law firm, Stevenson gave a speech reminiscing about his first years with the firm and poking gentle fun at the senior members: "Judge Cutting and Mr. Moore had already achieved some little standing at the bar—although I always suspected they were both unwholesomely addicted to night life—in the library. Mr. Sidley was a very promising young man. . . . But it was a couple of years before I ever saw him, i.e., saw him standing still—as he was then living in rather modest circumstances—in a . . . suitcase, for the most part somewhere between New York and Chicago." And so on—it was all somewhat vapid and verged on the precious; but, considering the awe with which law clerks looked upon senior partners in this austere firm, it was no doubt considered daring and very funny. More, it illustrated an important side of Stevenson. Increasingly, he was becoming what his father had wanted him to become—a "personality," to use the term of gossip columnists: that is, to overstate it, a performer with no particular ability but with great charm and style, an articulate witty man who could be counted on to enliven a party or introduce a speaker with wit and grace and enough substance to satisfy people who demanded substance. There was, of course, more, much more, to Stevenson; but his quality of being a "personality" carried him a long way in politics and was, in the mid-thirties, gaining him recognition among Chicago's business and professional leaders.

A week before Christmas, Stevenson wrote to Mrs. Ives, "[Christmas] is causing the usual harrowing confusion—but I suppose the children do enjoy it enough to justify the effort." Stevenson was sending Christmas gifts to the Iveses at Stockholm, where they were being transferred from Algiers. Ives seemed pleased with the transfer. Stevenson computed income tax returns for him and Buffie, and they corresponded a good deal about it, figuring closely. Stevenson, for example, claimed as a deduction the expense of Buffie's trip to the United States before her mother died, though he thought Internal Revenue would disallow it. Like his father, Stevenson was as eager as most Americans to avoid the tax collector. That year Stevenson's own income tax return showed a total income of $42,165 and a net of $40,235. (His income from the *Pantagraph* increased greatly that year—to $23,600 from $3,716—because he inherited *Pantagraph* stock.) On the last day of the year the name of his law firm was changed to Sidley, McPherson, Austin & Burgess; Stevenson commented to his sister, "Sounds like a trunk falling downstairs, doesn't it?"

12

He spoke on foreign affairs to the Advertising Men's Post of the American Legion in Chicago on January 4, surveying the world "with reference to the impending war." He reviewed the conquests of Hitler, Mussolini, and the Japanese and the "disastrous retreat" of the democracies, discussed the likelihood of a firm alliance between Hitler and Mussolini and a resulting "grim" future for the democracies. He thought "if the Germans do not provoke a war, no one will." He considered a Fascist victory in Spain impossible unless Germany sent "a large expeditionary force" and in that case "it is hard to see how France and England could remain passive." It was not a particularly impressive performance but the Legionnaires were pleased. The *Christian Science Monitor* published an article on the Council on Foreign Relations, and Stevenson said, "As Middle Westerners you will be most gratified to hear, from Boston, that you as members of the Council are the spearhead of this attack on the lines of provincialism."

He was working hard—a letter to Mrs. Ives enclosing her income tax return was dated on a Saturday night, March 27. He spent a good deal of time as co-chairman, with A. A. Sprague and another man, of the President's Birthday Ball in Chicago. He and Ellen were "contemplating" a vacation in Ireland, he wrote—"quick & cheap & motivated at this time by the possibility that Aunt Lucy Porter may sell Glenveigh Castle & it will be too late next year." The house in Libertyville was almost finished. They would occupy it in the summer; they moved now to a house on Astor Street in Chicago, one of the most fashionable addresses on the Gold Coast. He told Mrs. Ives, "I'm in the dog house again working most every night for the last three weeks." Ellen's father's "damn oil refinery came within an ace of the wringer & I had to jump in & do some heavy negotiating on that last week in the middle of everything else. . . . We talk about war in Europe constantly—do you [in Stockholm]?" Two relatives had died and he had not been able to go to the funerals. "Our family is vanishing rapidly & it gives me a wistful, lonely feeling—but I suppose it happens to everyone & that we must realize that we've suddenly become the older generation now."

On April 3, Stevenson opened another long, awkward, ambiguous correspondence with Senator Lewis. The matter dragged on for months. Stevenson was elected to the Commonwealth Club. He performed a chore for the Immigrants' Protective League. He acted as moderator at a symposium on collective security. His introductions at the Council that year were filled with forebodings about war.

Secretary of Labor Frances Perkins offered him appointment as Commissioner General of Immigration and Naturalization. He declined but indicated interest in some other government job. Governor Horner again appointed him a delegate to the National Conference of Social Work; again Stevenson declined.

He was restless, curiously unfocused, eager to be diverted from the law. All his negotiations with Senator Lewis, all his efforts at appointive office, came to nothing. He was still groping for a career—and he was in his late thirties.

13

When Secretary Perkins "summoned" him to Washington (as he put it) he took Ellen. They borrowed a car and drove down to Virginia, exploring the land of his ancestors. To Mrs. Ives he wrote, "The country was glorious—fruit trees in blossom—woods spattered with white dogwood and purple judas trees! And as we rolled along a road a few miles beyond Monticello we passed an historical sign saying that the house was the oldest in Albermarle County and was built by Gen. Joshua Fry! We stopped and walked in across the blood red fields and there stood an ancient frame house of glorious proportions—but not 'grand'—weather beaten & neglected these many, many years. It is occupied by a poor tenant farmer now who showed us around—the old oft painted wooden wainscotting, the ancient locks on the doors from England, the heavy blacksmith made nails. Its all dreadfully run down, but the property—300 acres—is beautiful and the location perfect, just 9 miles from Charlottesville on the main road south, with fine views, a stream, woods—and of course worn out soil! . . . . We made inquiry when we got back to town & were told that it could be bought for about $6000! It looks to me like a great possibility."

Stevenson was always interested in real estate. More than once he considered buying a house in the Georgetown district of Washington. He had his eye on three things—price, beauty, and historical association. He was drawn to the land. But, like his father, he viewed the farms he owned as income-producing properties and watched them closely.

When they returned, Ellen "threw herself into our next move," as Stevenson put it, "& over this last week end we got installed in our mechanical house" at Libertyville, the weekend of May 8. They hired a new nurse for the children, "a wizened little old Austrian woman" who "speaks excellent French, is intelligent & gentle & we hope will have a cultivating effect on our roughnecks—if she lives! I have some doubts as to whether she will be able to handle the monster John Fell!" They were building the combined garage and stable and expected to finish it by July 1. "If you've never seen a 'moderne' stable you've something in store," he told Mrs. Ives. Stevenson went down to Bloomington on "Decoration Day," as many Midwesterners refer to May 30, Memorial Day, and put "bushels" of flowers "from our own garden" on the graves of his parents and forebears.

On June 16, Stevenson wrote to Mrs. Ives that he was leaving for his fifteenth reunion at Princeton. "Its hard to believe it all happened so long ago. Do you remember that heavenly spring in the [Princeton house] when Mother was so happy—at least I thought she was—and you were having your usual beaux trouble! I am going to Pittsburgh to spend tomorrow at the Rolling Rock Club as Dick Mellon's guest —along with some 20 others invited from all over the country." Stevenson was considering returning to government but not very seriously. "J. Ham [Lewis] has been after me to be appointed Assistant Att'y General which would mean moving back to Wash. But I'm getting lazy & I like our country place so much that I find it easy to resist—so I wonder if perhaps the time isn't approaching when I might say 'no thanks but how about a ministry for Ernest.'"

The Stevensons had to postpone their trip to Ireland for two weeks because of his work. The weather was hot and humid, the boys had had "pink eye," probably from a swimming pool infection. "I wish Ellen could have taken the older boys away somewhere for a few weeks," he wrote, "—the change would do them good, but we can't do everything & I really need my vacation more this time than ever before." The previous Saturday night Ellen had gone to the

Villa Venice, a roadhouse outside Chicago, and stayed until 3:30 A.M. with another man while Stevenson was home in bed. Stevenson was still "struggling desperately to salvage something" of Ellen's father's refinery. His one consolation seemed to be that the Libertyville house was a success. They finally canceled their trip to Ireland because Aunt Lucy Porter rented her castle.

Governor Horner appointed Stevenson to the Northwest Territory Celebration Commission; he accepted. He was elected to the Board of Trustees of the Chicago Latin School, a private grammar school on the Gold Coast. On August 11 he told Mrs. Ives, "I've had bad luck this summer," but John Fell was "wonderful—big & rough—waddling, & squirming & chattering all the time. . . . Happiness seems to bear a direct relation to nervous equilibrium with us. . . . The 'farm' is developing rapidly & expensively. . . . I get up every morning at 6 & ride before breakfast! . . . Ellen has now taken on a job doing some experimental decoration for the Stevens Hotel & what with new servants, the farm, the children etc is busy as a bird dog."

Stevenson and several other lawyers, including his friends Walter T. Fisher and Clay Judson, met to discuss the Wagner Labor Act. They reported that they "for the most part" favored a minimum wage in principle but felt it should not be attempted by the federal government. They felt that "in time" the states would eliminate labor exploitation. They favored amendments to "mutualize" the Wagner Act. These positions were contrary to trade union policy and to the Roosevelt administration's policy.

Ernest Ives was in trouble in Stockholm. He wrote to Stevenson on October 11 that he was "so knocked off my pins that I have had little interest in anything." He did not say precisely what had happened but the State Department, acting on a report from Ives's former superior at Stockholm, had declined to promote him, thus jeopardizing Ives's career. He would come home in November, stopping en route at Belfast where he was being transferred, and talk things over with Stevenson. He would retire as soon as possible, probably in June 1939. Stevenson tried unsuccessfully to help.

Stevenson declined to join the board of the Lawson YMCA—he lacked the time required. By now he was vice president of the Princeton Club of Chicago. He was becoming what is usually called "a young civic leader." On November 12, Senator Lewis, in return for a favor, proposed to personally introduce Stevenson to Attorney General Cummings and suggested Stevenson come to Washington "to look the situation over." By December 2 the FBI was making a security check on him. But Stevenson indicated doubts, and on

December 9, Senator Lewis asked him to state plainly whether he preferred a State Department appointment. Stevenson at last closed the door to an assistant attorney general appointment—or almost closed it. On December 16 he told Lewis, "I am afraid I did not make myself altogether clear. Of course, I do not know what the Attorney General or the State Department might have in mind for me and it is difficult to decline appointments that have not been offered, but I do not feel that I want to or can afford to go back to Washington [at this time] and interrupt the very satisfactory progress I am making here both professionally and in the community." Evidently Stevenson, as he had done before, had stimulated a suggestion that he return to public life but then, when no job that he wanted was firmly offered, withdrew. In any case, it is clear that he constantly, from the time he left the AAA and FACA, entertained the notion of returning to public life. Moreover, his political activities and his reference to his progress in Chicago "both professionally and in the community" suggest that he was also thinking of running for public office in Illinois.

Stevenson was seeing university people as well as "society" friends. At the home of a Russian professor, Sam Harper, whose advice on Russia he frequently sought, he met Louis Brownlow, political scientist at the University of Chicago, and asked him to speak to the Commonwealth Club in January on the New Deal's reorganization of the federal government, describing the membership as "active middle-aged business and professional men . . . with the usual conservative flavor." Brownlow accepted, and Stevenson was "delighted." He never abandoned his efforts to bridge the gap between the enlightened business community and Democratic liberalism.

14

The Ives family came to Bloomington, Chicago, and Libertyville for the holidays. On the night of January 13, 1938, Stevenson's house in Libertyville burned. He and his family were in Chicago at the time. Glen Lloyd, his next-door neighbor, has recalled, "I got here about eleven o'clock. The Half Day Fire Department was here, waiting around for someone to bring the keys. I told them to go on in. I went over to my house and telephoned the Lake Forest Fire Department, then called Ad. I told him that the house was so much on fire that he might as well go to sleep. I asked if there were any heirlooms and told him we'd see what we could do. He told me to get into the study if I could and on the north wall behind his desk there were some family Bibles and papers. I went over there and went in and saved what I could." According to legend and a society columnist at that time, Stevenson himself watched the blaze and, when a friend seeing him with an unlit cigarette offered him a light, he replied, "No, thanks, I've got one," then, lighting his cigarette from a burning ember, said, "We're still using the place." Writing to John Paulding Brown, Stevenson said, "It was a dreadful catastrophe," and in later years he frequently bemoaned the fire, especially the loss of irreplaceable family papers and memorabilia; but Adlai III, who was seven at the time, has recalled visiting the scene with his parents and has said, "It wasn't a dreadful family tragedy." Stevenson often used hyperbole. The house, though built of steel and considered fireproof, was a total loss and so were most of the furnishings. In his income tax return, Stevenson valued the house at $30,000, of which $18,000 was insured, and the contents, not insured, at $20,018—a total uninsured loss of $32,018. (Internal Revenue disallowed $6,710 of this.) The Stevensons started rebuilding the house almost at once.

That Stevenson had attained some recognition in Chicago is attested by the fact that when his house in Libertyville burned the Chicago newspapers reported it, describing him as a lawyer and grandson of the former Vice President.[1]

Stevenson and Bud Merwin considered buying a radio station in Bloomington. The Bloomington League of Women Voters invited him to speak but he declined—he was too busy. On March 14 a state legislator from Chicago, Benjamin S. Adamowski, asked Stevenson for his support as a candidate for renomination in the coming primary election—he had been refused endorsement by the regular Democratic organization. Adamowski, an ambitious man of Polish extraction who was for many years an insurgent Democrat and who finally became a Republican, addressed Stevenson by his first name but his letter sounded like a form letter. It said the machine had refused him endorsement because he had supported Governor Horner and other insurgents. Stevenson replied, "I . . . wish you would send me about twenty-five of your campaign cards, which I think I can use to good advantage in your district. I also enclose a personal contri-

---

[1] That year he reported gross income of $50,412, the highest yet. Of this $33,127 came from dividends; $15,433 from his law practice; and $1,108 from stock market transactions, mostly short-term and mostly in his wife's account. His farms showed a loss of $380; oil leases brought him, before depletion allowance, $822.

bution. I wish it were more!" For some years they maintained an acquaintanceship. A group of lawyers formed a committee to work for the Democratic senatorial nomination of Michael L. Igoe against the organization candidate, Scott W. Lucas. Stevenson contributed $35. Lucas was elected and later became President Truman's floor leader in the Senate at the time Stevenson was Governor of Illinois. Stevenson and Lucas never developed a close relationship, perhaps because of this long-ago primary of 1938. It is interesting that, just ten years before Stevenson himself became the Democratic machine's candidate for Governor, he was supporting, albeit rather tentatively, two rebels against the machine.

Stevenson was losing touch with Washington. Recommending a young man for a job there, he told his friend Ben Thoron, "It occurred to me that you would know what is going on around town. . . . I find I no longer know any one in the legal division of the R.F.C." Washington had changed greatly in the four years since Stevenson had left it. The ferment of the New Deal was giving way to the danger of war.

Stevenson, speaking on April 11 to the American Legion, blamed the rise of Nazism on British and American isolationism and France's understandable but unwise determination to dismember Germany and ring her with states allied to France. By now it was clear that the victor's best hope for peace lay instead in his rehabilitating the vanquished—thus Stevenson foreshadowed support for what came to be the Marshall Plan after the 1941–45 war.

At one point he seemed to say that collision was inevitable, at another that Germany would probably not risk war for the present. France still had "the finest army in Europe" but suffered internal turmoil and was unwilling to move without England. England vacillated, ruled by conservatives whose single concentration was on the menace of Bolshevism and some of whose sympathies lay with Nazi Germany. Only recently had the British upper classes come to realize that Fascism, not Communism, was the danger; to prove it he cited a recent London by-election. He thought there was hardly room in our small world for both democracy and an "aggressive antagonistic philosophy" like Fascism. The Napoleonic wars had commenced as a crusade for the principle of individual liberty. "My hope and my guess is that before it is too late the liberal democracies will realize that there is something worse than war—slavery! —and that Fascism will retreat into history . . . and that the twentieth century will be saved!"

Stevenson's views were clearly "liberal" within the meaning of the word at that time. What is remarkable is that he could deliver such a speech at that time and place. It was a speech presuming a certain knowledge of and a considerable interest in events far away; it supported a point with an obscure London by-election; and it was delivered to an American Legion audience in the heart of the isolationist Midwest at a time when nearly the whole force of public opinion there was setting in favor of peace and isolationism.

Circuit Judge Chalmer C. Taylor of Bloomington asked Stevenson to use any influence he had with friends in Springfield in behalf of Taylor's candidacy for election to the state Supreme Court. Stevenson wrote to Governor Horner but knew nobody else well enough to write to. He had not yet established contact, really, with the Democratic Party in his own state. Governor Horner did not reply for two weeks and then it was to say that another judge had been nominated. Mayor Kelly on May 21 invited Stevenson to become a member of an "all-Chicago civic group" authorized by the City Council to "sponsor a program of civic activity and business stimulation." Stevenson accepted with "great pleasure." A Chicago bankers' society was to debate United States isolation and sent a tentative definition of isolationism to Stevenson, asking him to interpret it, an indication of Stevenson's local reputation as an expert on foreign affairs.

He and Ellen and John Fell had been living in the stable-garage at Libertyville and the two older boys in a tent while the house was being rebuilt. He noted, "It has been surprisingly comfortable, and I have even enjoyed sharing my wash basin with my horse!" Such remarks enlivened Stevenson's correspondence and conversation and accounted for a good part of the feeling of ebullience and well-being so many people found so attractive. They expected to move into the new house late in August and postpone furnishing it indefinitely. Adlai III was busy catching "bullheads" (catfish) in the Des Plaines River. A dog, Frisky, "continues to entertain us. . . . So far, he has almost bitten off my first finger, lacerated the houseman to the extent of three stitches and yesterday killed a kitten which we had just acquired for mouse consumption purposes." Stevenson nearly always had pets.

He and Ellen decided to stay in Libertyville all winter because of the expense of rebuilding and to see the job finished. Stevenson sublet their Near North Side house, telling its owner that the new occupants were "very nice people" and belonged to Onwentsia—"we have no misgivings about leaving all of our precious things in their care." He resigned from the Board of Trustees of the Chicago Latin

School, saying they were spending the winter in "the country," as he often referred to Libertyville, and they put the boys into the Bell School, a private school in Lake Forest. Adlai III's early memories are of his father's driving him to school mornings. Stevenson would make the ten-minute drive from the house in Libertyville to Lake Forest, drop Adlai and his brother Borden at school, then park at the Northwestern Railroad station in Lake Forest and catch a commuter train for an hour's ride to Chicago and his law office. Ellen or the caretaker would pick the children up after school.

From Adlai III's memories, and from other sources, it is possible to reconstruct life at Libertyville and harbingers of trouble ahead. "I remember the river—skating on the Des Plaines River. Taking the horse and the sleigh out on the river, which Dad liked to do. I did a lot of riding with him. I started early hunting pheasants and rabbits. Dad went along occasionally. He never was a compulsive hunter—he thought of it as an opportunity to be with the boys and to get outdoors. He loved to ride, especially a big horse called Jeb.

"My memories of our mother are not all pleasant. I don't know when it all started—and I suppose a certain amount of it is normal for any mother with boys—she had all sorts of notions how to raise children—strict diets, eating regularly, cold showers every morning before breakfast. We were not allowed to read the newspapers because we might be infected by the evil in the world. Radio and the comics were strictly out. She was very strict about taking risks with the family safety. There was no flying in airplanes unless all five of us were together. Borden bore the brunt of her discipline. Dad rarely got involved in it. I can remember only once being spanked by him. We were rarely if ever permitted to go to movies. There was a time when only French was spoken around the house. We usually had French governesses in Libertyville. We didn't have a great deal of contact with Dad. He was a compulsive worker. We'd see him in the morning when he took us to school. Evenings he'd read to us before we went to bed or they went out. I remember he read a biography of George Washington, novels by Walter Scott, Mark Twain, Kipling—we were always a little too young for whatever it was he read to us. It was something of a ritual, the reading in the evening, after our dinner and before theirs. We did not eat with them very much. They went out often. Then nights, if they were home, I remember the light burning in that library. I remember Sunday lunches—that was always a big meal, a family occasion. Weekends we saw the most of him, skating, riding, trap shooting, and lots of tennis at the house. He was constantly trying to make tennis players and golfers and horseback riders out of us. He encouraged the social life of the kids—having parties, having friends over.

"I have a vague memory of quarrels, bitter quarrels. I guess we weren't very happy as children. There was the terrible discipline, few friends, living on the farm which we loved but which made us isolated. All these constraints started breaking down as Borden and John Fell came along. We were always closer to Dad, and sympathized with him. We didn't like to see him hurt all the time.

"In many ways she was a great mother. She worked hard. She had servants, but she drove us to town and worked in the house and gardened. The diets, cold showers, and so on, must have been, although often misguided, out of concern for her children."

Stevenson probably saw his children more during these years in Libertyville than at any other time—and that was not much, commuting as he did and working late. But he loved his children, and they him. Adlai III's governess once told Stevenson that the boy used to, "while getting undressed, tell me about the things you had told him. I often wished that you and Mrs. Stevenson could listen to him, you would have enjoyed it ever so much. Especially when he would start to whisper about a secret 'that was not even in the papers!' "

Life in those days on St. Mary's Road was rather quiet, horsy, taken up with evening work through the week and, on the weekends, fox hunting, tennis, sun-bathing, canoeing on the river, and, on Saturday night, parties in the neighborhood or in Lake Forest or "in town," that is, Chicago. Dress was informal, and on weekends Stevenson tended to wear baggy old slacks and sport shirts and sneakers. Glen Lloyd, next door, Republican lawyer given to wearing sports clothes, once said, "A hunt went right through his property. I remember he called me one day about 1938 and said a fellow wanted to sell him a horse, a jumper, and would I go up and look at the horse. It was about twenty miles north of here. Great hunt country. It was a big horse named Jeb. Adlai bought him. It was in the fall and the leaves were beautiful. People gathered in various houses for stirrup cups. It wasn't the Virginia hunt but—" and he gestured, indicating it was pretty good. "Bill McIlvaine was the master of the hunt for a time. Most everybody rode—Stuart Otis here, a lot of Lake Forest people like the Kelloggs—Mickey Kellogg used to ride sidesaddle and jump." Ellen Stevenson, however, did not ride, Lloyd said.

Stevenson built a tennis court at his house; it drew the Libertyville and Lake Forest players. Stevenson was a "good average tennis player," most of his partners recall, one saying, "He had a wicked forehand." He was good at placing shots. He played a cutting game, not a driving game, especially in later years. He and Ellen gave New Year's Eve parties. "It was a relaxed, fairly informal kind of a country life," Lloyd recalled. "On Sundays they'd have tables out here and we'd come over and be on the porch." One of his near neighbors was Lloyd Lewis, a writer for the *Daily News* and author of several serious books. Stevenson's confidante of later years, Marietta Tree, had the impression that Lewis had been Stevenson's best friend.

The Stevensons were in demand at parties—she was pretty, he was funny. On birthdays or other "occasions," when the Lake Forest-Libertyville crowd gathered, it was Stevenson who was called on to "do the honors" or "say a few words," as was said at the time. That year Ellen's sister Betty and her husband Robert Pirie, of the extremely wealthy department store family, were moving to New York, and a gathering was held in their honor. Stevenson's notes for his remarks on that occasion have survived and, with their puns and vulgarities and in-group jokes, are almost incomprehensible to outsiders but provide a glimpse into the life of the period.

The text of my carefully prepared address this evening is taken from the familiar old war song entitled "Of all my wife's relations I love myself the best." With that exception I confess I share the prevailing partiality for the Piries. Even the name is verse, terse verse—Pirie, weary, dreary, a Pirie is never dreary or even a weary Pirie is never dreary. Something cavalier can be done with dearie—I used to try it on Betty until she went Republican on me! Possibilities with Erie.

But I'm digressing and my purpose is to repeat to you the real undisclosed reasons for their heartless desertion. My investigation reveals that the facts have been misrepresented. The fact is that L. F. [Lake Forest] is no fit place for an ambitious sanitary commissioner—it is completely drained say the rich and too flush say the poor. And N.Y. with its teeming millions offers Betty more fertile soil for research in sewage disposal. Besides, I understand from the Nat. Geo. [*National Geographic*] that N.Y. offers singular and sundry diversions for wives whose husbands don't go out nights.

Now the reason for Bob's departure is even clearer. The fact is that after long search CPS & CO [Carson Pirie Scott & Co., the great department store] discovered that the only man who could play tag with the Jews in the N.Y. wholesale district was wee Bobby—the two word merchant—yes and no—usually no. In business he's like his compatriot the Scotchman who said to the young lady, "I'm a mon of few words, will you or won't you?" "Andrew," she said, "you've convinced me, I will." Indeed I understand that since his arrival in N Y anti-semitism has all but disappeared and everyone is cheering for the embattled Jews!

During these years in the late 1930s, Ellen Stevenson appeared frequently on the society pages of the Chicago newspapers. She went to a society costume ball in a pink faille gown, blue velvet jacket, and flower-trimmed hat that she found in a trunk in the attic of her mother's home. The photographs were oddly disparate. One taken of her at a costume ball in 1938 shows her very pretty, with wide eyes, dimpled cheeks, a pert upturned nose, a long jaw and rather sharp chin and wide white-toothed smile, altogether a look of freshness and a little of coquetry. But a photograph at Easter the same year, showing her entering the fashionable Casino Club on the Gold Coast, made her look almost plain and even sad, in dark dress, fur boa, small mouth and long jaw. It was the mouth and eyes that changed. A picture taken when they were building their Libertyville house shows the eyes wide, the mouth open, her face framed by a white snap-brim hat, a liveliness in her expression; another picture of her arriving in floor-length dress at the Assembly Ball shows her with mouth open in surprise, neck taut, head oddly turned as though peeking provocatively around a corner. It was as though something inside her turned on a light or turned it off; she could look radiant or pouty. She was photographed visiting sick children in a hospital as a member of the Community Fund's women's division; at lunch planning a benefit performance of the Ballet Russe; entering a dance at the Arts Club dressed in long fur-trimmed evening cape; at the 1940 Democratic National Convention; having tea with Mrs. Walter Paepcke and Mrs. John R. Winterbotham at a fashionable restaurant in the Stevens Hotel (later the Conrad Hilton Hotel), where they had decorated some rooms, thus having "expressed" themselves, as the society writer put it.

A photograph of her having lunch at the fashionable Pump Room of the Ambassador East appeared in *Harper's Bazaar*. She wrote verse and went to the Arts Club. One season she was president of The Scribblers, whose luncheons were at the homes of such leaders of Chicago society as Ellen's own mother, Mrs. Carpenter; Mrs. A. H. Patterson; Mrs. Chauncey McCormick; Mrs. Potter Palmer; Mrs. Clay Judson; Mrs. Walter Brewster; and Mrs. Donald M. Ryerson. She attended a concert and poured tea wearing "the first of the large picture hats." A society writer said: "It was a large fuchsia straw hat with navy blue bands and navy blue core. Ellen uses her makeup so well that one wonders whether she uses even powder; no rouge, of course, and but very little lipstick. She has a very fresh unpainted look, which is a great relief." She gave a lunch at Libertyville and the menu was printed—iced whole tomatoes with "1,000 island caviar dressing," halibut ring with seafood newburg, vegetable platter, rolls, crepes Suzette, and coffee.

Ellen had good taste in interior decoration, liked doing it, and Stevenson "appreciated it," Mrs. Ives has recalled. Ruth Winter said, "There was great excitement when they moved to Libertyville. They did more entertaining there. Ellen did it very well, with taste and informality and charm. Adlai enjoyed this because he knew people enjoyed going there. She had a good relationship with the people working there. They loved her." Certainly Stevenson's correspondence of the period makes it sound as if he were happily married. He referred to Ellen as "my war department," affectionate slang of the period.

Jane Dick once recalled, "Ellen liked to think that she was living on a farm when they were out in Libertyville—cows—out there, she often wore dirndl dresses and was doing little things about the house. In a way she enjoyed it. In a way she felt it made her a more interesting person. In the first years they seemed very happy, though it was hard to tell what Ellen thought. She was brittle." Was she in love with Stevenson? "I don't know. I'm sure *he* was in love with *her*. We saw a lot of them in the thirties. Ellen, Laura Magnuson, and so on. We got up a current events class and got Clifton Utley to come out every week and discuss current events. Later we tried to carry it on ourselves—tried to tell each other about some great event," laughing. "We did this up to the time of the war. We saw a lot of the Stevensons— we'd go there for dinner, sleigh ride, or they'd come over here, or Dutch Smith's and so on—this place or that. Within a group that was congenial. Our children were schoolmates at Lake Forest. All the children were friends. All our children adored Adlai." Mrs. Paul Magnuson recalled, "I knew Ellen but I don't understand her." When the house in Libertyville burned, Ellen said, "Maybe I was never supposed to have possessions." John Fell once said, "I can remember fights between them going back pretty early. When they would be going out to dinner he would be sitting in the front hall with his coat on and reading the newspaper, waiting. He was patient. I don't know what they argued about. But I always thought Dad was on the rational side. Looking back, I don't know—Dad was not easy to live with."

A friend of Ellen's once said, "In the late thirties she had 'crushes' on two other men—both also friends of Adlai's. They were flirtations which the men took lightly, but Ellen was quite intense about them." As far as the friend knew, Stevenson himself had no affairs during those years. But Stevenson himself told another intimate friend many years later, "Ellen scared hell out of —— once by telling him she was going to divorce me and marry him. There was nothing to it." In retrospect, a friend of Ellen's thinks she can recall signs that Ellen was "cracking up" as early as the late 1930s. "I remember my husband telling me that I looked terrible and that I must have been talking to Ellen Stevenson. She would say terrible things to me about people close to me. She thought other men were in love with her. She had illusions of martyrdom." Another friend thought later, "She was a classic case of paranoia. She seemed to make sense but didn't."

15

On September 10, Mrs. Henry Goddard Leach of New York wrote to Stevenson and his wife, saying that the Duchess of Atholl, a Conservative member of Parliament, was coming to the United States, was eager to talk with "influential Americans" whose opinion counted, and might be willing to speak on the Spanish Civil War; and she invited Stevenson and his wife to become members of a committee to welcome her. Stevenson accepted.[2] She would speak to the Chicago Council on Foreign Relations on October 15. Stevenson introduced the duchess gracefully to the Council and said of her book, *Searchlight on Spain*, "I recommend [it] to anyone who is still on the fence—if there is a fence or anyone still on it." (He had not read it.) The affair was a success. The secretary for the New York committee told Stevenson later that the duchess was more impressed

---

[2] Among other members of the committee were Hamilton Fish Armstrong, Margaret Culkin Banning, Carrie Chapman Catt, Mrs. Allen W. Dulles, Marshall Field, Thomas Lamont, Henry R. Luce, Mrs. Dwight W. Morrow, Mrs. Paul Scott Mowrer, Francis T. P. Plimpton, Mrs. Samuel Seabury, Gerard Swope, Harold Urey, William Allen White, Quincy Wright, and Henry M. Wriston.

with her visit to Chicago than any other place. Nicholas Murray Butler, president of Columbia University in New York, asked Stevenson to join a committee to aid in resettling refugees from the Sudentenland. Stevenson declined—said the responsibility belonged to France and Britain. Stevenson was not yet a national figure but his name was becoming known to people who were.

Near the end of the congressional campaign that fall, Stevenson asked Bud Merwin to carefully consider endorsing T. V. Smith, a University of Chicago professor who was the Democratic candidate for Congressman-at-large. Merwin replied that the *Pantagraph* would express its high regard for Smith's ability but since the Republicans had "two good candidates," one of whom was from Bloomington, "I think that we would normally endorse these on the grounds of needed conservatism and strengthening the minority party in the house." It was a viewpoint often expressed on the North Shore among Stevenson's friends there—independence, two-party system, good government, good candidates.

On November 3, Stevenson, substituting for the Council president, introduced Edward R. Murrow, who had broadcast from Munich that fall. Stevenson called radio propaganda "the air raid of ideas" and said, "Contrary to the prevailing impression, there were two triumphs at Munich—Hitler's and Columbia Broadcasting's. . . . It was Mr. Murrow's ingenuity and indefatigable efforts that recreated the historic drama of those fateful September days and brought to America the voices of the principal actors, Hitler, Mussolini, Chamberlain, Daladier, Beneš, Eden, and others. . . . But more important than these spectacular demonstrations of the reportorial possibilities of radio are the implications in radio propaganda—the weapon of the twentieth century which knows no frontiers, no obstacles in time, space, and expense; which has been used with such telling effect already and is destined to play such a significant part in the world of tomorrow." It was good early Stevenson, containing the arresting phrasing and graceful sentences that became his hallmarks, the detached view of portentous events and the broad vision of the future which at once attracted the thoughtful and raised in the minds of others the suspicion that somehow Stevenson would always be a cool spectator, not a perspiring actor, on history's stage.

16

In 1939, the year war began in Europe, Stevenson went to Ireland on vacation and continued on course in Chicago, practicing law, participating in civic affairs, widening his reputation as a speaker, dabbling in politics, and watching his investments. He was short of cash—told Bud Merwin in January he needed the *Pantagraph*'s extra dividends.[3] He was still on the executive committee of the Council on Foreign Relations and tried to get speakers who would defend Nazism and Italian Fascism. He said the Council was "having some lively times"—had heard a Nazi and one of Franco's representatives. He attended a speech by Charles G. Dawes, a leading Republican financier and former Vice President of the United States, and wrote him a letter, praising the speech, disagreeing with parts of it, seeking common ground.

Stevenson served for several months as the first chairman of the Civil Rights Committee of the Chicago Bar Association. His work there revealed a natural civil libertarian point of view but no crusader's zeal in handling cases. His interest was more in principles than people.

He sent a message on Brotherhood Day to a Jewish weekly published in Chicago. After he became famous, Stevenson sent hundreds of such messages, often to Jewish or Negro groups. They thought he had a deep commitment to civil rights and civil liberties. He did have a deep private commitment to civil liberties but a much shallower one to civil rights. He was, however, a public advocate of both and as early as 1939 was acquiring a reputation for it. On February 22, Stevenson spoke on civil rights and liberties (using the terms interchangeably) to the Chicago Women's Club. He explained his committee's three kinds of activity. First, it helped defend persons whose rights were violated. Second, it hoped, after study, to recommend changes in present law and practice to reduce the violation of civil rights. Everyone was outraged by police brutality, but at the same time the police were under constant attack and pressure to suppress crime—perhaps the remedy lay in making laws "more workable" so that violations of civil rights no longer would have the "justification" of practical necessity as they did now. Third, the committee hoped to educate the public in the value and meaning of civil liberties. He then made a transition to foreign affairs: we should indoctrinate the young as Communism and Fascism did, teaching them "the simple precious guarantees of the freedom of free

[3] In March he paid $4,000 on a note dated the previous June, leaving a balance due of $10,000. (He may have borrowed to rebuild his house.) He reported income of $48,967 for the year, including $14,435 from the law firm and nearly three times as much, $41,262, from dividends, including $26,662 from the *Pantagraph*.

men" and warning that law and order could not be provided by mistreating criminals, Communists, and Fascists "in an illegal and disorderly way." It was a curiously unformed, almost uninformed, speech. He misquoted Voltaire, his peroration was confused, his fundamental position on civil liberties was sound but he seemed not to fully understand its implications, and his conservative remarks about the police, who at that time in Chicago were notorious for their flagrant disregard of civil liberties, would today offend any leader of the American Civil Liberties Union (many of whom adored him in later years). One might think he had not prepared his speech with his usual care—yet filed with it were six pages of typewritten notes on freedom of speech containing numerous citations from Supreme Court decisions and a page of well-reasoned speech language. The speech does make clear his advocacy of fundamental civil liberties and it provides an early illustration of what became a pattern in his presidential campaigns: moving from domestic to foreign affairs.

His friend Harriet Welling was running a committee called "Stop Arming Japan"; Stevenson lent his name to it, as did many of his friends. At Mrs. Welling's request, he wrote to his Congressman and Senator, urging that the export of scrap iron to Japan be stopped.

Dutch Smith, a serious collector of Americana, acquired a letter of Grandfather Stevenson's and sent it to Stevenson. A woman offered to sell him five letters of his grandfather; he declined. A letter to Stevenson from Ernest Ives sounded isolationist and even proGerman. On February 25, Stevenson introduced Eduard Beneš eloquently. Senator Lewis died, and Stevenson sent condolences to his widow and recommended to Governor Horner that he appoint T. V. Smith to the vacancy. Horner appointed James M. Slattery, a Chicago Democrat.

On March 16 the State Department posted its promotion list. Ernest Ives was not on it. He said he was through, he would go home in June and retire from the Foreign Service. Mrs. Ives was privately pleased. They would leave Belfast at once, storing their belongings here. In May, Stevenson and Ellen went to Ireland, visited the Iveses, and toured England and Scotland and Ireland, borrowing the Iveses' car. Stevenson said he learned more about the Derby than about the international crisis. Young Tim Ives, always devoted to his uncle, showed them around. Stevenson took Tim to Parliament. The Iveses had a dancing party with an Irish singer; it pleased Mrs. Ives enormously that her brother enjoyed it, and she prayed to live long enough to serve him.

Back in Chicago in June, Stevenson thanked Walter Paepcke

for the pedigree of a Dalmatian dog named Merlin which the Paepckes had given or sold to the Stevensons Stevenson said he wished his own pedigree were as good.

He told Laird Bell he had "found the British pulse very firm and the appeasers are not in evidence!" and said he had witnessed "a very gentile skinning" of Sir John Simon in Commons. He declined to become a member of the board of the Juvenile Protective Association of Chicago, pleading "the pressure of other responsibilities." His friend John Miller proposed him for membership in the prestigious Commercial Club in Chicago and asked Donald McPherson to second him; he accepted membership. Mrs. Ives and her family visited in Libertyville. Mrs. Ives thought the new house attractive but Ellen's life disorganized. Stevenson was still paying rent on the house in Chicago and trying to sublease it He asked the owner to consider offering a prospective tenant a four-year lease and offered a complicated computation intended to demonstrate the advantages to her and himself. He was still spending a good deal of time on the details of such matters.

Stevenson and George Ball went to Omaha together to work on the financing of a gas company. Ball recalls, "We were there about a month and it was hotter than hell. This was a technical reorganization matter involving the SEC. Stevenson was bored but extremely conscientious. He was always conscientious and hard-working. We went back to Chicago and he went on to New York to put the finishing touches on the matter. He called me from New York and said 'I've just spent a magnificent morning with the bankers. The greed ran down their faces like sweat.'" Stevenson took Ball to a Council lunch and afterward said the speaker was "a prissy rat." They lunched together often, and Ball recalls, "He was always saying even then that so-and-so was talking to him about running for something. I didn't take it seriously. I thought it was fantasy." Ball visited the Stevensons in Libertyville He saw no hint of marital trouble. "Ellen was very gay and charming and vivacious "

Stevenson spoke to the Unitarian Church in Bloomington on "Civil Liberties and Religion," causing the chairman of the church's board to remark that the speech was "outstanding" and "we should send him some place . . . maybe to the Senate."

17

Germany declared war on Poland September 1, and on September 8, President Roosevelt proclaimed a limited emergency. On September 25, Stevenson protested to the *Pantagraph* about its editorial position against repeal of the arms embargo. Merwin was "sincerely sorry" Stevenson felt as he did but the editorial represented the view of the editorial committee after two months' reading and discussion. The debate over isolationism had been sharpened by the opening of hostilities.

Stevenson's life went on much as before. He was appointed to the "Secret Committee" (membership) of the Wayfarers' Club which elected members. He doubled his contribution to the Legislative Voters League but declined to contribute to the League of Women Voters, pleading the demands of other organizations. The Francis Plimptons visited the Stevensons on their way West, and afterward Plimpton wrote a long warm letter in which he introduced a young lawyer named Carl McGowan. Plimpton explained that McGowan was leaving Plimpton's New York law firm to go on the faculty of Northwestern University Law School. McGowan came from down-state Illinois, had attended Dartmouth where he had been a member of both Phi Beta Kappa and Delta Kappa Epsilon, "a very unusual person indeed," had attended Columbia Law School "and did very well," and at Plimpton's law firm for three years had helped on important cases. "I think he is a really first class lawyer," Plimpton wrote. "He is an unassuming sort of a person, but gets along well with other people, and clients have spoken very highly of him. . . . I have a feeling that, at least after a year or two, he could be tempted into private practice again, for my hunch is that he will find academic life a little too tranquil in the long run." Stevenson took McGowan to lunch, introduced him to Kenneth F. Burgess, who was president of Northwestern's Board of Trustees, and asked him to help the Bar Association's Civil Rights Committee examine the Illinois Constitution's Bill of Rights.

Stevenson had been asked to speak on October 28 to the Bar Association on lawyers in government but instead he introduced a film on the Russian Revolution and, in emphasizing the propaganda power of film, anticipated the television age and his own deep interest in educational films. Later, when Stevenson came to national prominence, he did not like television and used it poorly himself. Some of his aides thought he did not understand it. Television may be like other things in Stevenson's ambit: he understood it intellectually but could not accommodate himself to it.

Mrs. Ives engaged in a quarrel over a servant with Bud Merwin's wife, reopening old family wounds; Stevenson sent her a nasty letter, but nonetheless the Iveses spent Christmas with the Stevensons. Stevenson began another long difficult correspondence over the sublease of the house at 1434 Astor Street. He bargained closely with the owner, Mrs. Vesta Channon, over the rent; he bargained closely with the tenant when the tenant, pleading illness and misfortune and bad plumbing, reduced her rent; one night a mirror fell down in the hall and broke; Stevenson's monthly profit on the sublease dropped to $12.50. Considering his notorious parsimony, he was surprisingly indulgent of this tenant. Moreover, his relationship with the owner, Mrs. Channon, remained cordial. He was a hard bargainer and a man of property who expected property to yield a profit; but he was a compassionate man too.

On January 31 he addressed a Zionist mass meeting. He began, "I must confess at the outset that I hardly know why I am here, and I suspect that before I have finished my brief remarks, you will wish I wasn't here. I am not a Zionist and I am not distinguished in any way, but I *am* a practicing lawyer in Cook County and when your friend and my friend, Judge Harry Fisher, suggests that I do something, I generally find it convenient to do it with alacrity!" Stevenson continued, "I am a Gentile and, what is worse, I am a Scotch Presbyterian—on my father's side. But on my mother's side I am a Unitarian. I shall never forget a conversation between my devout and aggressive grandparents. The Unitarian said acidly that the Scotch Presbyterians kept the Ten Commandments and everything else they could lay their hands on. The Scotch Presbyterian replied that he had made some study of the Unitarian faith and would be obliged if the Unitarian could enlighten him as to how it differed essentially from the Jewish! So I guess I cannot claim to be a religious purebred. But I don't see why the Jews are so exclusive about their Zionism and in so far as it represents the aspiration for a national home, I am a Zionist." But he defended the British policy of delaying establishment of a Jewish "national home."

He discussed the war in Europe: "It may well be, as many have foreseen, that before the fury has spent itself the fire of hate and fear and intolerance will engulf the Catholics and other groups as well as the Jews. Perhaps even we here in America are in for a period which will test our restraint and fidelity to our ancient ideals of tolerance and civil liberty on which the precious democratic tradition rests. At least one detects unpleasantly familiar symptoms—the restless unemployed, growing anti-Semitism, Red scares, intolerance, and a quickening nationalist feeling—all in the name of Americanism. But I cannot help but feel that the civilization of our times is destined to survive the present challenge. . . . I foresee that the garden the Jews have wrested from the wasted sands of Palestine must and will flourish; and in large part because inscrutable Providence has given them a great leader [Chaim Weizmann] in this dreadful hour of trial. And perhaps sometime when the Hebrew scholars and scribes of latter days continue the chronicle of their imperishable race, they will find an illumined page for the man who, after two thousand years of troubled wandering, led them back to their promised land—led them back with an example and an ancient admonition: 'To do justice and to love kindness and to walk humbly with thy God."

Twelve years later, in 1952, Stevenson used the same biblical quotation from Micah when he accepted the nomination for President (quoting it accurately that time, as he did not this time).

On February 23, Stevenson spoke at a lunch of the Town Meeting of the Air, a popular radio program which discussed serious issues. He declared the Town Meeting made "a major contribution to American adult education." He suggested other ideas and even used phrases that would recur—democratic self-government was "the most difficult and most dangerous form of government"; "the problems . . . are going to get harder and not easier"; "as an Englishman said, 'Your public servants serve you right!' "; American elections were decided by "the small minority of independent voters that oscillates back and forth between the inert masses of partisanship and prejudice"; "free discussion, free combat of ideas with the people as the jury is the essence of our scheme of things."

The primary election was coming up. On April 2, Stevenson sent his recommendations to the *Pantagraph*.[4] The *Pantagraph* had already published its choices and they coincided with Stevenson's in all but one instance: the *Pantagraph* endorsed C. Wayland Brooks for the United States Senate. Stevenson did not seem greatly disturbed.

---

[4] For Governor, among the Republicans, he thought Dwight H. Green "better qualified" than his opponent. (Green was nominated and elected; Stevenson ran against him eight years later.) For Governor, among the Democrats, Stevenson was opposed to John Stelle, a downstate politician with whom Horner had been obliged to make an alliance. For Senator, among the Republicans, Stevenson opposed C. Wayland Brooks. (Brooks was nominated and elected.) For Senator, among the Democrats, Stevenson favored Adamowski against the organization's candidate. (Adamowski lost.) Stevenson thought T. V. Smith should be kept in Congress.

18

The war was going badly for the democracies. Dormant during the winter, it suddenly came alive that spring of 1940. German panzer divisions were sweeping everything before them. Hitler declared war on Norway and Denmark April 9 and on the Netherlands, Belgium, and Luxemburg on May 10. France fell June 22. The British Expeditionary Force was evacuated at Dunkirk between May 26 and June 4, and the German bombing of Britain began July 10. But war was still a long way from the Midwest. On May 17, Stevenson, writing to Mrs. Ives about her investments and about a weekend he and Ellen were planning, tucked into the letter a paragraph: "Isn't the war dreadful? I can see you down there hanging on the radio and groaning. I suppose the cabin [at Southern Pines] is finished now and I wish I could see it. We are all well and the country is beautiful, but the weather too cold and gloomy." That same day Stevenson acted as master of ceremonies at a Legal Club entertainment making fun of the national political conventions, which were not far away.

When the great German attack in the west began in the spring of 1940, William Allen White, editor of the Emporia (Kansas) *Gazette,* Clark Eichelberger, director of the League of Nations Association, and others who had struggled to amend the Neutrality Act met in New York to form the Committee to Defend America by Aiding the Allies. They believed that a Nazi victory in Europe would imperil America and that therefore we should now arm ourselves and give all aid to the western European democracies short of war. They would mobilize public support for this view. They wrote, telephoned, or telegraphed people all over the country. White would head the committee—he was from the Midwest stronghold of isolationism but he was also a liberal Republican with ties to President Roosevelt. Eichelberger was executive director. The executive committee included Thomas K. Finletter, a partner in the big New York law firm of Coudert Brothers, and Mrs. Emmons Blaine, a wealthy Chicago woman. Leaflets went out telling people how to organize local committees and publicize the committee's purposes.

On May 18, the day after White sent out his first circular telegram around the country, the Chicago committee met—twelve men and women including Stevenson; Mrs. Blaine; Walter Dill Scott, president emeritus of Northwestern University; Quincy Wright, whose wife had been active in the Council of Foreign Relations and the League of Women Voters; and Colonel Frank Knox of the Chicago *Daily News*. The committee immediately sponsored a mass meeting at the University of Chicago attended by 1,100 people, Clifton Utley made a radio broadcast which produced some 500 letters, the committee issued press releases announcing its formation and purposes. Stevenson probably became chairman at a meeting on June 21. He was a natural choice—an internationalist, former president of the Council on Foreign Relations, prominent socially with access to large contributors, and known as a speaker, organizer and master of ceremonies.[5] It was a major turning point in his career. In his work with the White Committee, Stevenson for the first time in his life confronted a great national issue that clove him from many of his friends as it split the nation. It was his first serious political fight. It was so almost from the start. The pressures on him were great.

During the 1930s the people of the United States had shown little interest in affairs abroad and no desire to become involved. The outbreak of war in September 1939 had shocked them, and President Roosevelt said, "When peace has been broken anywhere, the peace of all countries everywhere is in danger." With the support of a non-partisan citizens' committee launched by Clark Eichelberger, and headed by William Allen White, the Democratic majority in Congress had amended the Neutrality Act on November 3, 1939, to permit belligerents to purchase war materials in the United States on a "cash and carry" basis—if they had the money and the ships and

---

[5] An early letterhead of the committee showing him as chairman listed more than fifty names, including several friends or associates of Stevenson—Graham Aldis; Bill Blair; Paul Douglas, then a University of Chicago professor and alderman, later United States Senator; Judge Harry M. Fisher; Walter Johnson, instructor in history at the University of Chicago; Frank Knox; Robert Merriam of the University of Chicago, a student of government and later an alderman; William P. Sidley, head of Stevenson's law firm; Colonel A. A. Sprague; Clifton Utley; and Quincy Wright. A later letterhead added Ronald P. Boardman as treasurer, John A. Morrison as staff director, Lucy McCoy as secretary, and the following names of Stevenson's friends or acquaintances: Ben Adamowski; Ralph Bard; Laird Bell; L. E. Block; Mrs. Morton Bodfish; Mrs. John A. Carpenter; Edwin R. Embree; John V. Farwell; Mrs. John F. Fenn; Judge John Gutknecht; Mrs. John Holabird; Mrs. J. L. Houghteling; Paul Scott Mowrer; James F. Oates, Jr.; Judge George L. Quilici; Clarence B. Randall; Carroll H. Sudler, Jr. Several omissions of his friends are noteworthy—Edison Dick, Dutch Smith, the Kelloggs, Mrs. Kellogg Fairbank and Janet Fairbank, Harriet Welling, Ed McDougal, George Ball, Glen Lloyd, Don Lourie, Don McPherson, and Kenneth Burgess of his law firm.

could get them here, they could buy material and take it home. This was a cautious first step toward United States involvement. The quiet of the "phony war" that winter reassured the American people. They may have desired the victory of the democracies and the defeat of Hitler but more than either they wanted peace for themselves. Then in the spring and summer of 1940 the rush of events changed everything. In his great speech at the time of Dunkirk, Winston Churchill said, "We shall fight on the beaches, we shall fight on the landing grounds, we shall fight in the fields and in the streets, we shall fight in the hills; we shall never surrender, and even if, which I do not for a moment believe, this island or a large part of it were subjugated and starving, then our Empire beyond the seas, armed and guarded by the British Fleet, would carry on the struggle, until, in God's good time, the new world, with all its power and might, steps forth to the rescue and liberation of the old."

Whether and when the New World would come to the rescue depended upon the outcome of the great debate that now reached climax—a debate that divided the country into two camps, that of the "interventionists" and that of the "isolationists." It was a debate carried on in the midst of the 1940 presidential contest between President Roosevelt and Wendell Willkie, a campaign that the historians Morison and Commager have called in many respects the most important since 1860, a debate that they termed "one of the great debates in American history." It was carried on in Congress, in the press, over the radio, in town halls and on street corners and in factories and saloons and homes and churches all across the United States. It cut across party lines—Wendell Willkie was a Wall Street lawyer and president of a public utility which had fought the TVA but he was also an internationalist and had won the Republican nomination from three then isolationists, Senators Robert Taft of Ohio and Arthur Vandenberg of Michigan, and District Attorney Thomas E. Dewey of New York. This debate split labor unions, divided friends, and produced editorials and campus quarrels as bitter as those produced nearly a generation later by the Indochina war. Its crucial battleground was the Midwest, for the Midwest was the heartland of American isolationism, and Chicago was the capital of the Midwest. Shortly before France fell, the Chicago *Tribune* said, "Inflamed by commercial radio commentators, the east has fallen into a complete state of hysteria."

Isolationism was nothing new. Its creed was stated by Senator William E. Borah of Idaho, in 1934: "In matters of trade and commerce we have never been isolationist and never will be. In matters of finance, unfortunately, we have not been isolationist and never will be. When earthquake and famine, or whatever brings human suffering, visit any part of the human race, we have not been isolationists, and never will be. . . . But in all matters political, in all commitments of any nature or kind, which encroach in the slightest upon the free and unembarrassed action of our people, or which circumscribe their discretion and judgment, we have been free, we have been independent, we have been isolationist."

The roots of isolationism have been traced to many sources, from Washington's Farewell Address to pro-Germanism of World War I to anti-Semitism of World War II. No single explanation satisfies. Geography alone is not enough: although by 1940 the principal stronghold of isolationism was the Midwest, and although the insularity of the Midwest far from any coast undoubtedly reinforced isolationist sentiment, such worldly Easterners as Norman Thomas were isolationist. Political party does not explain it—Herbert Hoover was an isolationist, but so were Senator Bennett Champ Clark of Missouri and Congressman Louis Ludlow of Indiana, both Democrats—and so was Senator Borah of Idaho, quite a different Republican from Herbert Hoover, and so were the La Follettes of Wisconsin and Gerald Nye of North Dakota, heirs of the great Progressive tradition of the upper Midwest. Samuel Lubell, the astute political analyst, once sought to account for isolationism on an ethnic basis, showing that isolationism flourished in areas populated by people with pro-German and anti-British ethnic prejudices. But isolationism flourished elsewhere too.

Isolationism was both a political principle and a state of mind. The political principle was that the United States should avoid foreign entanglements (to the extent possible, some would have added) and should at all costs (not quite all, some would have added) stay out of war. The state of mind was both harder to define and more important since it provided the canopy broad enough to gather under it men of very diverse stripe. This state of mind was a Muncie, Indiana, Chamber of Commerce manager's saying as late as 1944, "We want to avoid foreign entanglements. Of course we can't stand for somebody who's a rabid isolationist—that's foolishness, like being an ostrich. But we've got to watch the other nations or they'll get the big end of the swag." It was a county agricultural agent saying, "Postwar world affairs? I have not heard anybody mention world affairs for weeks or months. The farmer is too busy to worry about things like that." It was a small-town newspaperman: "I'll always stay here now, I guess. Been here too long." Postwar international affairs? "I never hear any talk about that. People here don't care about other countries. They're strong isolationists. A few people think we'll have to fight Russia some day. You hear a lot of anti-British talk. People think that every time Churchill and Roosevelt get together, Churchill steals something else from him." Isolationism was a young Wisconsin farmer who saw no point in worrying about things far away; it was a little old lady in a flowered dress in Indiana, content with the peaceful pleasures of Sunday afternoon church picnics in the park, undisturbed by things abroad because things at home never change; it was a Chicago businessman who had no time for affairs of state; it was a Chicago broker who feared a market break if war came; it was a Michigan auto worker up from Kentucky to work in a war plant for high wages and to keep out of the draft; it was a university professor who argued that, while aggression and barbarism anywhere were to be deplored, America would be far less endangered by war with Japan than by war with Germany, since an Asiatic war would never be fought on the ground and could be fought alone, without the entangling alliances with Britain and France that a European war would entail; it was, simply, a pacifist who rejected war as an instrument of national policy; it was, simply, a patriot who quoted President Washington and said, "If you're not for America first, then who are you for?"

In 1940 numerous organizations sprang up on both sides of the debate but the most important ones were, on the isolationist side, America First and, on the interventionist side, the White Committee.[6] America First, founded in Chicago in September of 1940, had as its chairman General Robert E. Wood, chairman of the board of Sears Roebuck & Company; its principal mouthpiece was Colonel Robert R. McCormick's powerful Chicago *Tribune;* and among its diverse members were its director, R. Douglas Stuart, Jr., of Quaker Oats, its treasurer, J. Sanford Otis, Charles A. Lindbergh, Norman Thomas, Chester A. Bowles, Alice Roosevelt Longworth, Kathleen Norris, Henry Ford, Father Coughlin. One historian has written, "Socialist intellectuals shared the views of the American Legion. The

[6] White, born in 1868 in Emporia, Kansas, had bought the Emporia *Gazette* in 1895, had used it to attack the Populists and help elect McKinley, had used it later to promote liberal movements inside and outside the Republican Party, and had used it to support the League of Nations. He powerfully supported much of the New Deal as descending from the programs of Theodore Roosevelt and Woodrow Wilson; he attacked as Fascists such extremists of the 1930s as Father Coughlin, warned in 1938 that the United States was in danger of becoming completely isolated, denounced Fascist aggression, and by 1940 had made his newspaper and himself national symbols of liberal "grassroots" political thought.

Chicago Federation of Labor agreed with Henry Ford. Midwestern Progressives who had spent their lives fighting against Eastern banking interests espoused ideas on neutrality legislation first expounded by Bernard Baruch. Herbert Hoover's arguments were supported in the pages of the *New Republic.*"

In Illinois in 1940, isolationist sentiment, heavily influenced by the *Tribune,* was very strong, and a Republican tide was running. True, Franklin Roosevelt carried the state, but only by 51.2 per cent of the popular major party vote, and only after he had pledged to keep us out of war unless attacked—and the Republicans elected the Governor, Dwight Green, and a Senator, "Curly" Brooks. In Chicago, many, if not most, of Adlai Stevenson's personal friends and business associates were isolationists critical of the Roosevelt foreign policy. His leadership of the William Allen White Committee was therefore an act of considerable personal and political courage. If the Council on Foreign Relations had been a spectator sport, the White Committee was a free-for-all fight. The Council had been non-political and tried to be non-controversial. The White Committee was highly political and its cutting edge was the most trenchant of controversies. The Council had been social; the White Committee was deadly serious.

Noting the many organizations Stevenson had already joined and his reputation as a master of ceremonies, one might have expected him to become an "organizational tramp," as did so many lesser men who possessed only his more superficial abilities. That he did not was due to his own character—and that character was brought to the surface by the White Committee. George Ball has dated Stevenson's liberal coloration first from his baptism in the early New Deal and second from his battle against isolationism and the *Tribune*—though adding, "but Adlai was never a real liberal." Mrs. Welling, who opposed America First but voted for Willkie that year, has said, "Adlai was always a little old-fashioned, he wanted to conserve values, he was not rashly liberal—yet he went pretty far on the William Allen White Committee." Heretofore unfocused, flirting with various appointments and organizations, Adlai Stevenson now suddenly stood at the heart of a great and searing national issue, and he focused all his energies on it. He had found his issue—and found himself.

Both the America First-White Committee controversy and the Willkie-Roosevelt campaign divided Stevenson from some of his friends. That summer and fall were perhaps the most difficult yet for Stevenson. There was no passing this issue off lightly in Lake

Forest drawing rooms: people felt strongly; Stevenson had made a deep commitment and a difficult one, the deepest and most difficult of his life up till now. He paid for it. His friend Robert Hutchins was a leader of America First. So were his friends R. Douglas Stuart, Jr., and J. Sanford Otis, Clay Judson, Sterling Morton, Lessing J. Rosenwald, and Edward L. Ryerson, Jr. Mrs. Welling has said, "I was terribly impressed with Adlai. It took a lot of courage." Ed McDougal's wife later recalled, "Ernest and Buffie had a little cocktail party at Charlevoix and Adlai was there and I remember the coolness toward him," because of the White Committee. Many of the Stevensons' closest North Shore friends stayed with him through the White Committee, out of conviction, and some stayed simply because "they liked Adlai, no matter what he was doing," Jane Dick has said; a telling sentence: their loyalty was to him personally, not always to the causes he espoused.

A White Committee supporter expostulated with Mrs. Kellogg Fairbank because she supported America First; she had been a friend of Stevenson. Clifton Utley, director of the Council on Foreign Relations while Stevenson was president, became a leader of the White Committee. He was also a radio news commentator and said he lost an important sponsor because an official of the sponsoring company was an America Firster.

Friends of Stevenson had the impression that Stevenson came under pressure from clients of the Sidley law firm who disapproved of his work with the White Committee. Ed Austin, a senior partner at the Sidley firm, has said, "I recall no such pressure. Ken Burgess and I were concerned that the clients might resent it—the William Allen White Committee was anathema to some of our clients—but I don't think it ever came up." Stevenson himself, however, on December 17 wrote to Mrs. Stanley McCormick of 209 Lake Shore Drive: "Yours was the kindest letter I think I have ever received. I have never really felt that I was doing or had done in the past more than what I thought my simple duty as a citizen with some convictions. But recently, in connection with this White Committee work, I find that there has been considerable pressure brought to bear on my firm. I think suppression of thought by indirect commercial coercion is despicable, but of course I must consider not only myself but the others that may be injured by what I do. It is all very unpleasant, and your letter makes me feel much better."

Ed Austin later said, "Some of us here disapproved of his taking that job. I remember arguing with him one day. I told him he was wrong and the William Allen White Committee was wrong. I said, 'How can FDR keep us out of war?' Adlai said that FDR was saying it to get elected. Adlai always said that I had a wrong conception of world affairs. A lot of us were pro-America First until it got into the hands of the Nazis. The William Allen White Committee was Roosevelt-dominated. An editorial writer on the Louisville *Courier-Journal* started a committee that said simply, 'This is our war, let's get into it.' I was more sympathetic with this than trying to get us in through the White Committee. Burgess believed, as I did, that the policies urged by the committee would inevitably involve the United States in war and that the committee should have been honest enough to say so." It must, however, be noted that William P. Sidley, senior partner of the firm, was a member of the White Committee. Stevenson and Sidley remained friendly throughout the years. During the 1950s, while leader of the Democratic Party, Stevenson used to call on Sidley, by then an elderly man, and Sidley took pride in Stevenson's accomplishments.

An early leaflet signed by Stevenson as chairman of the White Committee asked "Are you willing to do YOUR part?" and began, "The Blitzkrieg has struck—the awful crisis reaches its decisive stage!—The outcome of this struggle will affect your life, your liberty, your property. If Britain falls, tyrants who detest democracy will rule the world," and urged people to write or wire the President or their Senators and Congressmen, requesting them to "release destroyers to Great Britain NOW." It also asked for contributions. The committee circulated for signatures a petition to the President and Congress, asking them to, among other things, supply Great Britain with planes, guns, ships, and food; expand our own preparedness program; and "guard against war materials reaching aggressor nations either directly or through neutral powers." Privately Stevenson told Bud Merwin, "That does not mean intervention or an army in Europe —yet."

Stevenson wrote to Senator Claude Pepper of Florida "to applaud what you are doing"—Pepper was an outspoken opponent of isolationism—"and to assure you that even in this benighted middlewest many people are hoping and praying that, thanks to you, the Senate will see the light before it is too late." He urged Senator Scott Lucas to support a resolution Pepper introduced. (He also asked Lucas to obtain the reappointment of a postmistress who was being blocked by a precinct committeeman.) He opened a headquarters and a bank account for the committee. Stevenson hoped Clarence Randall of Inland Steel could come to the next meeting. He was trying to find a list of contributions that had already gone from Chicago to the national committee in New York. He was running the committee almost single-handed; he asked his fellow members if they knew anybody who could help. Bill Blair, later his close assistant, came to help. He sent them a draft statement which he proposed to release to the press together with a list of prominent citizens he hoped would sign it, observing, "The list is merely preliminary and is designed to appeal to labor, etc.—'the common people.'" The committee approved the statement. It went out July 2 to a long list of prominent Chicagoans provided by Stevenson together with a letter from him: "I do not know what your views are on the question of aid to Britain, but I know you appreciate the implications for us in defeat of England. . . . Isolationist sentiment in this section of the country is the principal obstacle to more effective material aid to Britain now—while it can do some good." This was the opening of the Chicago committee's campaign. Stevenson was using his own personal prestige—he accompanied the statement with a personal note in many instances.

The response was mixed—and revealing. People were wary. One of Stevenson's friends cautioned against unauthorized use of his name. Sidley endorsed the statement with a note to Stevenson: "I heartily endorse the statement & have written my Congressman accordingly." So did William McCormick Blair, father of Bill Blair, Stevenson's aide. On the other hand, Edward L. Ryerson, Jr., told him that, while he was generally in accord with the statement, before he could endorse it confusion about the meaning of isolationist and non-intervention should be cleared up. He also wanted to know what Stevenson planned to do with the endorsements.

R. Douglas Stuart replied that he was not in sympathy with the White Committee and said that, while his sympathy was with the Allies, in his view America could help them more by remaining neutral than by doing anything that would be likely to involve her in the European war. A bond broker friend of Stevenson's refused to endorse the statement—he thought we were being asked to pull England's chestnuts out of the fire after we warned her at Versailles not to put them in. William H. King, Jr., a lawyer, declined to sign because he questioned the committee's competence to make the military judgment that England could win. Stevenson replied courteously. A rabid isolationist told Stevenson his statement constituted "treason to your own country." One man returned the statement with a note: "Are you personally available for, and would you make good cannon fodder."

The *Daily News* published the statement on July 10 under the headline "More Join Drive to Help Britain 'Fight for U.S.'" Few of Stevenson's close friends had signed and almost none of his friends who were wealthy businessmen or LaSalle Street lawyers.

Important support had come instead from labor, the colleges, and certain civic leaders.

On July 5, Stevenson asked Colonel Frank Knox, publisher of the *Daily News,* for permission to use his name as honorary chairman of the Chicago chapter. Chicagoans had been speaking of the "battle of the two colonels," Knox of the *News* and McCormick of the *Tribune;* and Roosevelt, creating a coalition Cabinet, appointed Knox Secretary of the Navy and Henry L. Stimson Secretary of War, both Republicans. Knox replied to Stevenson that he thought it best to decline to head the White Committee for the time being. But he assured Stevenson of his continuing approval of and cooperation with the committee.

The Democratic National Convention in Chicago was coming on, and Stevenson and Ellen moved into town to her mother's house on Lake Shore Drive for the week. He submitted a platform plank on foreign affairs, took part in discussions with Senator Pepper and others on whether to precipitate a floor fight over the platform, gave a luncheon for Secretary Henry Wallace (who was nominated and elected Vice President), and gave a large party at Mrs. Carpenter's house. Subsequently Stevenson told Senator Pepper, "My participation—thanks to you—on the fringes of high political strategy was intoxicating, and I would be tempted to run for county commissioner if I didn't live in such a nest of Republicans!"

Stevenson's proposed foreign affairs plank differed markedly from the statement Clark Eichelberger made to the platform committee for the White Committee. Stevenson's plank was shorter and more political. With an astute politician's instinct, he avoided commitment to specific programs, avoided attacking isolationism, avoided reference to the neutrality law, and emphasized America's peaceful intentions. The legislative core of the entire debate was the neutrality law; the political core was how to keep America safe and at the same time keep her out of war.

19

After the convention Stevenson went back to work for the White Committee. Laird Bell, a wealthy lawyer friend of Stevenson, sent a hundred-dollar contribution, telling Stevenson he was filled with admiration for the good works Stevenson found time for. Several others sent fifty or a hundred dollars; Stevenson replied with literature and petitions and asked them to solicit their friends for more. He sent an emissary to Milwaukee and concluded that a small group of sympathizers existed there but no leadership; a stockbroker said, "In this Germanized town people are very much afraid of 'getting their necks out.'" Stevenson asked Charles R. Walgreen, Jr., his friend who was president of the drugstore chain, for permission to put a committee poster in every Walgreen drugstore, which would cover Chicago thoroughly. Walgreen refused—if he permitted one organization to do it he could not refuse others. The Marshall Field estate too refused permission for the lobby of the Field Building in the heart of LaSalle Street, a prize location. On August 12, Stevenson had lunch with several LaSalle Street men to discuss raising $15,-000. Max Epstein, a merchant, sent $200, and Stevenson said he hoped Epstein could provide more. Studying Stevenson's heavy daily correspondence for the committee that summer and fall, one wonders if he did not shirk the law. If so, his firm did not penalize him; his income from the firm in 1939 had been $14,435; in 1940 it rose to $18,006.[7] Mrs. Ives wrote that she was organizing a White Committee in Charlevoix but it was hard going—many of her friends hated Roosevelt and the war. Stevenson would find the same thing throughout his political career—support among the masses, not in Lake Forest. And he would find something else too—Mrs. Ives, however disagreeable she could sometimes be, was always loyal to his public projects.

Secretary of the Navy Knox told Stevenson on August 1 that he had suggested to Harry Hopkins, then Secretary of Commerce, that Stevenson take over Knox's duties as chairman of the Citizens Aviation Training Committee; Hopkins was receptive and suggested Stevenson go to Washington the following week. Stevenson went and saw Hopkins but nothing was decided. He saw Hopkins again that fall. Propelled by the great issue, he was moving closer to the center of United States power.

Those who opposed the committee held a rally in Soldier Field on August 4. It was sponsored by the "Citizens' Committee to Keep America out of War." Charles Lindbergh and Senator Pat McCarran spoke. Stevenson thought it was "a dismal failure"—although the *Tribune* estimated attendance at 35,000 to 40,000, he thought the crowd looked small in the vast arena.

In response, the Chicago White Committee decided to hold a large public mass meeting September 18, probably at the Coliseum, an auditorium on the South Side which seated 13,000.

On August 23, Stevenson and his wife left for Desbarats, Ontario.

---

[7] This considerable increase resulted from two circumstances: the firm's overall business improved so that his share of its profits rose by about $2,000; Sidley increased the share received by Stevenson and two other partners by $2,000 each.

While he was away, the committee's leaders made him chairman of the Coliseum mass meeting. It was his greatest public challenge to date. He returned to Chicago and organized the rally himself, though he had been reluctant to risk it. The total cost would be $3,500 including $600 to rent the Coliseum and $2,900 to promote the rally. Stevenson would preside. It was proposed that the pastor of St. James Church deliver the invocation but Stevenson made a marginal note, "too English." Dorothy Thompson, a columnist, Mayor Maury Maverick of San Antonio, Texas, Clark Eichelberger, and others would speak. Beside the item, "band music prior to and for exit after meeting," he wrote, "has it been engaged—Is there an organ." He drafted a letter to priests inviting them to attend the rally. He asked the English Speaking Union to circularize its members. He asked Judge Harry Fisher to arrange to circularize members of the Covenant and Standard clubs, both Jewish.

Stevenson told Clark Eichelberger in the New York office, "I hope that these speakers have all been cautioned not to overreach or to talk about intervention or immediate participation in the war. The label of 'interventionist' is, as you know, very dangerous in this community and we do not want to give the *Tribune* or the America First Committee any ammunition." He also hoped Eichelberger could persuade Douglas Fairbanks, Jr., the actor, and "some important opera singer" to participate. "Names of this kind have, of course, the best box office appeal." When Maury Maverick sent him a draft of his speech, Stevenson wrote, "It is splendid! I have nothing to suggest, unless possibly a note of warning toward the end against the influence of defeatists, isolationists and appeasers in Chicago and elsewhere." Stevenson asked the Mutual Broadcasting System to broadcast the rally over WGN, the *Tribune*'s radio station which was affiliated with Mutual, and over Mutual network itself, inasmuch as it had recently broadcast the Lindbergh rally at Soldier Field. He rewrote a leaflet to be distributed at the rally, sharpening it. He invited Rabbi Solomon Goldman to sit on the speakers' dais: "I am anxious to have a representative of the Jewish people." He asked a Chicago politician of Polish descent to introduce Dorothy Thompson at the rally, telling him, "My purpose in asking you and other leaders of European ancestry to participate is to indicate that the Committee is *American* and not English or anything else." He asked Judge John Gutknecht (misspelling his name), of German ancestry, to introduce Maury Maverick. He was using the Chicago politician's traditional system of "balancing the ticket."

The evening of the rally was hot. In the large Coliseum, with spotlights and banners and bunting and more than 13,000 strangers facing the speaker's dais, Stevenson confronted a setting far different from the quiet luncheons of the Council on Foreign Relations in the Palmer House, a setting much more like the huge political rallies he would one day address. (The *Tribune* said only 11,000 to 12,000 attended.) He introduced Monsignor Thomas V. Shannon, who pronounced the invocation, and George Chaplicki of the Chicago Opera Company, who sang "God Bless America." Douglas Fairbanks, Jr., Maury Maverick, Admiral Standley, Dorothy Thompson, and others spoke, including Stevenson. The program was a huge success. After it was over, Stevenson and his wife, most of the speakers, the Chicago staff, and others went to Ellen's mother's home on Lake Shore Drive to celebrate, and, Stevenson said, Dorothy Thompson "entertained us until a quarter after two" in the morning. Stevenson received many congratulations on the meeting. It had been a personal triumph, his first public one. He had organized it, presided over it, and put his reputation on the line for it, and it had succeeded. After it, a committee staff member told him, "Sometime I'll send you over some of the many letters we have gotten saying that 'anything Adlai Stevenson is connected with must be a good cause'—or words to that effect." Stevenson knew the Coliseum meeting was important to him. George Ball once said, "He thought he was moving into the big time." He was.[8]

20

Stevenson spoke at a rally in Milwaukee, at a Federal Union meeting in Chicago, at the Chicago Bar Association. He repeated the same basic speech, a speech he had prepared for the League of Women Voters when he debated with Clay Judson, who put the case for America First. In November the national White Committee announced new objectives—increased emphasis on arms production, determination to maintain "the life line" by sea between Great Britain and the United States, a "firm policy" in the Pacific including aid to China. The controversy intensified. Clifton Utley recom-

[8] One speaker, Admiral Standley, had given the *Tribune* the opening Stevenson had feared, and the *Tribune* did not overlook it. In a long lead editorial on September 20, the *Tribune* quoted Standley as saying, "To wait for war to come to our shores when we know it to be inevitable is the greatest crime in history," and said editorially, "War between the United States and Germany is inevitable if the men in power in the United States or Germany are determined to have a war." It was the "interventionist" label, the one Stevenson had most feared. "The Committee to Defend America by Aiding the Allies is, in reality, the Committee to Get the United States into the war."

mended investigation of "the Nazi sympathies" of a prominent America First member. The committee discussed investigating America First and the local Bund and issuing news releases on them. Stevenson did not concur.

Most of the committee's big contributions were coming from Jews. M. J. Spiegel, Jr., president of a Chicago mail order house, sent Stevenson a check for $2,461, by far the largest contribution to date, which Spiegel had raised among his company's executives (who had decided against soliciting employees because of "the religious aspect"). Stevenson, thanking him profusely, said he had considered announcing the contribution at a committee luncheon "but in view of the religious aspect, I concluded not to do it. I hope you agree that it is probably best, at least at this stage, to keep the large Jewish support feature in the background. I am very apprehensive that, as time goes on, the 'enemy within' may try to couple up anti-Semitism with appeasement with a consequent increase in confused thinking."

He was worried too about "the hypocrisy accusation"—that the committee really wanted to intervene but was afraid to say so. He cautioned Herbert Agar of the Louisville *Courier-Journal* "not to go too far toward actual intervention, in view of the 'delicate' state of opinion in this area." A man asked Stevenson if the committee was "a mere adjunct of the New Deal cloaked in our national alarm in war hysteria." Stevenson stood his ground: "Unfortunately, too many people are more interested in political suspicion than in national policy." A partner in the law firm of Stevenson's friend, William B. McIlvaine, Jr., attended a committee meeting and wrote, "May I suggest . . . that the presence of a large number of Jewish people at the speaker's table was a surprise to me and I think it is a mistake even if they make contributions." He feared the public would think that the White Committee was supported by Jews who wanted to push the United States into war because of Hitler's persecution of the Jews. This, he thought, would ruin the committee. Stevenson agreed: "You are quite right about the conspicuous number of Jews the other night. This is the sort of thing that is always happening, but I just cannot find time to attend to every detail."

As the debate grew more shrill and the cleavages more cruel, Stevenson and Clay Judson, who debated several times, maintained their friendship even though they disagreed. Judson once sent Stevenson a *Daily News* cartoon showing two men astride a horse jumping over a fence labeled "Mutual Understanding"; Judson labeled the men Stevenson and Judson and in a penciled note to Stevenson said, "How about a poster like this as advance publicity for our appearance on the Keith-Orpheum Circuit? . . . You did a grand job yesterday, as you always do,—(with a *bum* cause)." It was one of the few ameliorative notes that autumn. Carl McGowan, Stevenson's young friend and later close associate, attended one of their debates and later recalled, "He needed courage to do it. Judson lived in Lake Forest and was a prominent lawyer. I thought Stevenson did himself proud. He showed he was good and natural, eloquent, pointed, handled himself extremely well under difficult conditions— and the audience was ninety per cent against him."

Senator Scott Lucas, put in charge of the Chicago regional branch of the Democratic presidential campaign by President Roosevelt, asked Stevenson to help. Stevenson said he would be glad to talk to Lucas "but I am afraid I cannot be of much help as I have been devoting practically all of my time" to the White Committee. This was true enough; but Stevenson had another reason for expending his energy on the White Committee rather than on the Roosevelt campaign: he admired Wendell Willkie. Willkie came out for aid to Britain, and Stevenson wrote, "He must have been under considerable pressure, and I think it speaks well for his courage." Stevenson never forgot this campaign; twelve years later when he himself was running for President he constantly worried about getting "the independent vote" that he thought Willkie had attracted. Because he was a good Democrat, the 1940 campaign plagued him considerably.

The *Pantagraph* endorsed Willkie early in September, and Stevenson wrote Bud Merwin, "I have no objection to the endorsement of Willkie, but I do have strenuous objection to endorsement without my knowledge and in advance of the usual time. . . . The directors should be consulted." Merwin replied that he was "distressed"—it "never had occurred" to him to consult Stevenson because editorial policy had always been made by the editorial committee, not by the directors. Stevenson replied that "matters of major policy" should be decided by the directors.

Late in October the *Pantagraph* completed its endorsements and they were all Republican. One of its candidates for Congressman-at-large, Stephen A. Day, was an America Firster. It opposed T. V. Smith, whom Stevenson admired. (He was defeated.) It endorsed C. Wayland Brooks for the Senate, terming him "independent." Stevenson protested vehemently that Brooks was controlled entirely by the *Tribune* and was "violently isolationist." Merwin replied that the editorial committee had been split on Brooks, and Merwin himself had favored no endorsement. Merwin added that the *Pantagraph* would endorse Dwight Green, the Republican candidate, for Governor. Stevenson immediately protested. Merwin replied, "I shouldn't try to answer your letter today. I ought to lay it over until the palms of my hands have a chance to dry and I can be sure that I can approach it without any risk of ill temper." Stevenson was not mollified. He wrote, "I am sorry my letter made you angry" but denied it had been written in anger—"and now I read that you are endorsing [William] Stratton for congressman at large—26 years old and without experience of any kind—in lieu of [T. V.] Smith, a distinguished scholar, experienced in politics, notoriously independent, and an incumbent with perhaps the best first term record in the entire House. . . . Did you know, by the way, that Stratton has refused to endorse Willkie's position on aid to Britain," and he pointed out that in endorsing Les Arends for Congress the paper had cited with apparent approval Arends' votes against revision of the Neutrality Act, against the draft law, and for a sixty-day delay in putting the draft into effect. Stevenson asked, "Is this consistent with the position of the paper? I am confounded!" The exchange between them lasted almost to Election Eve. Douglas Fairbanks saw President Roosevelt and told Stevenson the President was "very pleased" with the Coliseum rally.

General Robert E. Wood, of America First, addressed the Council on Foreign Relations at the invitation of Walter Lichtenstein, a banker and Stevenson's predecessor as president of the Council who had differed with him on several occasions. General Wood was introduced by Clay Judson. Wood sought common ground with non-isolationists—the necessity of a strong defense, the determination to prevent any foreign nation from obtaining possession of any part of the Western Hemisphere, and the belief that Great Britain should be able to purchase munitions from private United States manufacturers.

Stevenson's personal affairs went on as always. He finally wound up the long and difficult relationship with the tenant in the house on Astor Street. The tenant sent a last check with a letter saying, in spite of all their difficulties, "Might I say, how glad I feel to have met with such understanding and tolerance as in you; the world may not be in such agony if we had more of it." Stevenson replied, "I appreciate the sincere efforts you have made in the unfortunate situation, and wish you every good fortune." It is remarkable that throughout his life most, though not all, of Stevenson's personal relationships, however strained they became at times, concluded amicably. Ambassador William C. Bullitt spoke to the Council on Foreign Relations in reply to General Wood, and Stevenson wrote to President Roosevelt, "I cannot resist the temptation to thank you personally for permitting Ambassador Bullitt to speak." The President replied: "Dear Adlai: I appreciated very much your nice note of October twenty-second. I agree with you as to the importance, not only in your section but in other parts of the country, of the matter of our foreign policy and it is good to have your favorable opinion of Bill's presentation."

Toward the end of the campaign, Stevenson sent a contribution to the state Democratic campaign fund, saying, "I wish it could be more but I am also contributing to the city, national and Norris-LaGuardia Independent Committee, in the last of which I am active." On the same day he sent a contribution to Mayor Kelly. On October 25 he made a frankly political speech in suburban Skokie, acting as master of ceremonies at a rally of "independent voters" for Roosevelt. Barry Bingham, president and publisher of the Louisville *Courier-Journal* and the Louisville *Times,* corresponded with Stevenson about holding a nationwide White Committee rally in Louisville. This was the beginning of a long friendship between Stevenson and Bingham.

Almost at the close of the campaign, on October 30, Arthur Krock wrote a column in the New York *Times* deploring the fact that the isolationist debate was being drawn into the presidential election. Krock wrote that in Chicago, the center of the debate, the protagonists on both sides were pro-American and anti-Hitler, and he mentioned Stevenson, General Wood, and Mrs. Kellogg Fairbank by name, writing, "It happens that while Mr. Stevenson expects to vote for the President, his chief interest in life at the moment is to furnish that aid to Great Britain which he believes is vital to the survival of the American system. He is fully satisfied that Mr. Willkie occupies the same position and expresses admiration [for Willkie]." Stevenson thanked Krock for "the gracious and accurate advertising."

Stevenson was working hard for the National Committee of Independent Voters, called the Norris-LaGuardia Committee, a group intended to rally to Roosevelt's side Republicans and independents. He helped stage a rally for LaGuardia at the huge Chicago Stadium. The names of Stevenson, Charlotte Carr of Hull House, and other members of the Norris-LaGuardia Committee appeared on a pro-Roosevelt ad in the newspapers. Stevenson's good friend, Dutch Smith, objected: he felt that Stevenson was not really an independent at all, but a Democrat. He wrote to Stevenson and Miss Carr, "Several people have asked me, and I have also asked myself, how two people who have for many years actively supported the New Deal and President Roosevelt, as have you and Adlai Stevenson, could permit your names to appear under an advertisement with the title, 'Sorry, Mr. Willkie, this is where we get off the fence.' To get off a fence which you were never on, is a piece of gymnastics which I am unable to explain. Having the greatest confidence in the integrity of both of you, I cannot believe that there is not some explanation for your names appearing in this manner. Perhaps it was done without your knowledge or consent. I will certainly reserve my judgment until I hear from you."

Stevenson, who respected Dutch Smith and valued his friendship highly, replied:

1. I did not see the advertisement or know anything about it.

2. However, I see no "gymnastics" in stating that I am off the fence—unless you *assume* that I have no independent judgment on political candidates. I did not decide to vote for Roosevelt until after the Elwood speech when Willkie endorsed the New Deal both domestic and foreign, and then ridiculed the conduct of foreign affairs in what seemed to me a foolishly contradictory way.

3. That I have generally supported Roosevelt in the past, does not seem to preclude me from having any independent judgment now. If it does, then you should ask a lot of "No Third Term Democrats" who have never supported him about *their* gymnastics— and I can give you their names.

4. I don't understand your use of the words "integrity" and "judgment," unless you deem me dishonest for stating that I have decided to vote for Roosevelt.

5. I agree with you on one thing—that traditional partisans should not identify themselves with "independent" committees. Perhaps I am such a partisan, though I had never so considered myself, and should not have helped this committee even in the meager way I have.

But let me ask you this: If mine was not a Democratic "name," would you have written that letter? I am afraid my "integrity" suffers from my ancestry!

Their relationship was unimpaired. But that it was imperiled at all indicates the cruel divisiveness of this campaign.

21

A Gallup poll shortly after the election showed that the people were uniting behind more aid to England if she appeared about to be defeated. But the great debate went on. An isolationist publication said the White Committee was now "openly urging Americans to consider immediate entry into the war." The Chicago *Times* deplored editorially that decent men "find themselves calling each other 'fascist,' 'warmonger,' and 'appeaser,'" and described as "preposterous" a statement of John T. Flynn of America First that the Roosevelt administration was "conspiring" to get the country into the war.

Boake Carter, a radio commentator, said the White Committee was "virtually advocating immediate United States entry into the war" and asked "what sinister interests are backing them?" V. Y. Dallman told Stevenson this was libelous.

On November 22, Stevenson wrote a letter to the editor of the *Tribune,* complaining that it had carried a story saying that the White Committee was "urging an outright declaration of war against Germany" and saying that "this flagrant misstatement was deliberate." A writer for a new liberal newspaper in New York, *PM,* accused America First of appeasement, anti-labor bias, traces of anti-Semitism, and "some of the appearances of incipient American fascism." A Chicagoan wrote a letter to the *Tribune* suggesting that General Wood of America First was Hitler's "advance man." Notorious native American fascists and anti-Semites became involved with the isolationist movement. On December 12 the *Tribune* published a long front-page story saying Senator Rush Holt, a leading isolationist, had disclosed who had paid for an interventionist advertisement. Stevenson asked the Anti-Defamation League of B'nai B'rith, a Jewish organization to combat anti-Semitism, to draft a letter of protest and it did, and he rewrote it extensively. It protested that the *Tribune* article was "not news," that the facts had been published in the Congressional Record in July, and that the same material had appeared in *Liberation,* which was published by William Dudley Pelley of the Silver Shirts, a fascist and anti-Semite. Stevenson became rather close to some of the people at the Anti-Defamation League.

A Notre Dame professor attacked the White Committee as a "mass murder committee," whereupon a White Committee supporter denounced Catholic organizations for trying to push the United States into intervention in Mexico a few years earlier. Stevenson wrote a letter to the *Times* pleading for "dispassionate and rational discussion" of issues, a plea he would make, usually fruitlessly, many times. Near the end of the year Stevenson declined an invitation to go on the advisory board of the Chicago Civil Liberties Committee, saying he had "more to do than I can properly attend to."[9]

President Roosevelt warned the country that it faced an emergency

---

[9] Whether he knew it or not, that organization—which included such men as Paul Douglas, Arthur Goldberg, Edgar Bernhard, Robert T. Drake, Charles Liebman, Melville J. Herskovitz, Robert Morss Lovett, and T. V. Smith, most of them later Stevenson supporters—was going through an agony of its own and soon would divide on policy issues concerning both isolationism and Communism; out of it would emerge the Illinois division of the American Civil Liberties Union, some of whose individual members became his most ardent supporters.

comparable only to war, pledged increased aid to Britain, and declared, "We must be the great arsenal of democracy." William Allen White asked Stevenson and other local committee chairmen to wire the President and their Senators and Congressmen; Stevenson did so.

White, on New Year's Day, resigned as chairman of his committee—he was old and tired and he differed with other committee leaders. Just before his resignation was announced publicly, Stevenson, Utley, and John Morrison (the Chicago staff director) held a conference telephone call with White, Eichelberger, and a man who represented the New England branches; Stevenson and all the others except Eichelberger asked White to continue as chairman. He refused. Stevenson himself was considering resigning as chairman of the Chicago committee. He was disturbed by the degeneration of the debate into name-calling. Further, he had misgivings about what some considered the committee's hypocrisy. Again, as American entry into the war came to seem inevitable, he wanted to return to government in Washington. Finally, his law firm was under pressure. For weeks in the house in Libertyville he asked his friends in harried tones, "What am I going to do?"

Stevenson was considered as a replacement for William Allen White. Representatives of sixteen Midwest committees met early in January. White and Eichelberger attended; Stevenson presided. They voted to move national headquarters to Chicago. They drew up a list of candidates to succeed White, including Stevenson. His request that his name be withdrawn was refused. He left the chair while his qualifications were discussed. "Among his favorable qualities," the minutes of the meeting read, "are tact, great efficiency, excellent and agreeable as a public speaker, quiet, moderate, is a man of mature judgment which would be an asset in drafting and giving out statements of policy, middle westerner, young, could be readily built up in national prominence because the family name Adlai Stevenson has long been known in American history. . . . The only criticism of him that could be found is the fact that he is an ardent new dealer." At length the delegates decided that their first choice was Willkie, their second Senator Gibson of Vermont, their third Stevenson, their fourth Lewis W. Douglas, and their fifth Governor Lloyd Stark of Missouri. Stevenson, Morrison, and other Midwesterners would take this slate to the National Committee in New York a few days hence.

Stevenson sent an account of the meeting to Lewis W. Douglas, argued that national headquarters should be in the Midwest, and asked Douglas to help persuade Willkie to address a large mass meeting in Chicago. Douglas replied that the geographical importance

of the Midwest would merely be weighed against other factors, Willkie or Landon would be almost fatal, and someone else should approach Willkie.

Stevenson went to the meeting in New York on January 9.
There Senator Gibson was elected to succeed White, and Douglas
was elected chairman of the national board. (Six vice presidents
were also elected, none from the Midwesterners' preferred list.)
Stevenson and John Morrison strenuously opposed all this. Returning home, Stevenson apologized to Lewis Douglas "for my mis-
behavior" at the meeting. John Morrison resigned. Clark Eichelberger told Morrison, "The question of the successor to Mr. White
was debated for at least two hours after everybody in the room had
come to one opinion except yourself and Adlai Stevenson." Stevenson had made up his mind to resign as chairman of the Chicago
committee.

This was the first time Adlai Stevenson had come up against the
high wall of what was later called the Eastern establishment—the
coterie of Wall Street lawyers, bankers, financiers, foundation heads,
corporate executives, and rich men that has for so many years
exerted so much influence on American political life, in the nominating conventions of both political parties, in the financing of campaigns, in presidential appointments, and in the formulation of Administration policy, especially foreign and defense policy, no matter
which party has been in power. Stevenson, perhaps because of his
European travel as a child and his Eastern education, was more at
home in their clubs and homes and conferences than many Midwesterners. And they came closer to accepting him than they did
to accepting most Midwesterners. A few became his ardent supporters as did another wing of the establishment—publicists,
broadcasters, publishers. But on the whole the hardheaded men
from Wall Street never really accepted him, and indeed at several
points in his career they fought him on policy questions. This split
over the successor to White was his first rebuff at the hands of the
Eastern establishment, and though he took it with good grace, he
never again resumed the intense activity on behalf of the White Committee he had shown. Instead, he resumed his long-neglected law
practice and looked for a job in Washington.

22

Seeking a job in the State Department, he enlisted the aid of
Secretary Knox, Louis Brownlow, and Arthur J. Goldberg, then a

Chicago labor lawyer. Knox wrote that he would inquire about Stevenson's joining Navy's legal staff. It was beginning to look as though Stevenson would return to government. This was January 31, six months before it actually happened. William Sidley sent Stevenson a longhand note and said, "I find my chief satisfaction and reward in my present practice of the law in the regard and companionship and, in many cases, the affection of my associates in this office, and in the pride I feel in heading up such an outstanding group of good lawyers and good citizens."

Opposition to the Lend-Lease bill disturbed Stevenson, and he aroused himself to plan a mailing campaign to a half million people that would cost $10,000. A test mailing brought discouraging results. Stevenson said Senator Brooks's mail was running about eighty per cent against Lend-Lease and even Senator Lucas' mail was three to one against. He urged redoubled efforts to deluge Brooks with mail and himself sent a caustic letter to Brooks.

On February 22, Stevenson made a direct move to re-enter government—wrote to Harry Hopkins. "I hope you will remember me," he said. "My work here as Chairman of the [White] Committee . . . is largely finished, and I am anxious to help in any other way I can." Could he see Hopkins in Washington? Hopkins replied that he would be "tied up" for the next ten days but would be glad to see Stevenson after that. Stevenson again made inquiry of his friend Wayne Chatfield Taylor. Taylor replied that he hoped to see Secretary Knox soon. Vacancies existed at the SEC; would Stevenson be interested? No; but working for Knox interested him.

Mrs. Ives sent Stevenson a letter full of Washington gossip. She had gone to the State Department to inquire about having her belongings shipped to the United States from Belfast, where they were in storage, and discovered the government would pay the freight but not the expensive wartime insurance. Later that spring their belongings were destroyed by German bombing. Several years later Stevenson tried to get the United States government to compensate them for the loss.

On March 8, Lend-Lease passed the Senate and on March 11 the House. Stevenson issued a statement applauding it. Wayne Chatfield Taylor told him on March 10 that he was making slow progress in bringing Stevenson's name to the attention of important people and counseled patience. Stevenson replied his patience was "more than adequate"—he was taking Ellen to Phoenix, Arizona, for a vacation and expected to be in Washington about April 1. The White Committee declined rapidly—by March, the switchboard had gone dead and mail had fallen off to practically nothing. Stevenson undertook one final chore for the committee—he went to Rushville, Indiana, on April 23, to persuade Wendell Willkie, who lived there, to speak at a Chicago rally. The rally was held June 6. Stevenson put far less time and energy into it than into the earlier Coliseum rally. Still, the rally was a success.

Meanwhile, Stevenson, job-hunting, corresponded with Lowell Mellett of the Office of Government Reports, Fiorello LaGuardia of the Office of Civilian Defense, Vice President Wallace, and his friend Thomas H. Woodward, head of the U. S. Maritime Commission. Woodward asked if he had anything particular in mind. He did not—he would consider anything. Finally, about June 23, he made a trip to Washington. Both John Lord O'Brien, general counsel of the Office of Production Management, and Oscar Cox, of the Office of Emergency Management, offered him jobs, but so did Secretary Knox, and he took the job with Knox, though the pay was less than Cox offered. Characteristically he told a friend, "I was probably a fool not to accept" Cox's offer but "I feel that Colonel Knox and Ralph Bard need some help, even of my modest quality." On June 30, Knox signed the official commission appointing Stevenson principal attorney in the office of the Secretary of the Navy at a pay rate of $5000 per year, effective that day. Stevenson arranged with his partners for a leave of absence until October, "at which time we can all look the situation over again." The leave of absence did not work out; Stevenson's partners feared that his work for Knox might create a conflict of interest, since some of their clients had government contracts. (The fear proved well grounded: one of Stevenson's first assignments from Knox was to help settle a strike of Western Electric workers; the Sidley firm represented Western Electric.) On July 15, Stevenson wrote a letter to Sidley, terminating his partnership as of July 21 with "reluctance and misgivings." The firm paid him something less than he would have received for a full year's compensation. He wrote to his senior partner, Burgess, who had always been interested in him, "I should like to add something about how sensitive I am to one who seems to understand my depth of conviction about the war and my restless anxiety to help in some way. Your prompt approval of this adventure did not surprise me— but it did reassure and comfort me enormously." Ed Austin wrote, "I hope, very sincerely, that your absence will not be for long. At the same time, I rather have a feeling that the lure of public service will be quite strong and you will stay beyond the time now anticipated. I am confident that you will do a good job."

When news of Stevenson's appointment was published, he received many congratulations from relatives and friends in Chicago and Bloomington, associates at the Council on Foreign Relations and the White Committee, and political acquaintances, some of whom wanted Washington jobs themselves. To one who congratulated him he wrote, "I look forward to my assignment with lively interest— but the prospect of a summer in Washington in the heat, confusion and congestion, fills me with dismay!" Barney Hodes, Jack Arvey's law partner, was "thrilled" at the appointment and told Senator Lucas "to keep a generous eye on" Stevenson. Stevenson replied, "I would prefer to have stayed right here if I could work without re-strictions." All his life he sought jobs, then pretended reluctance when he got them. Mayor Kelly congratulated him on the "patriot-ism" which prompted him to serve the nation "in this crucial period." He told a municipal judge, "I doubt if I will be of much help," but he told the state Senator from his own district, with whom he was on a first-name basis, "I think the work will be an interesting—and ex-hausting—experience." Two women he had known a long time con-gratulated him and said they agreed "that you are good 'presidential timber' and isn't this exactly the way both Roosevelts got their start?"

For the time being, Ellen would not go to Washington. Stevenson wound up his affairs. He recommended two young sons of friends in his law firm for naval commissions, not failing to mention that he was about to become "personal legal advisor" to Secretary Knox. Finally, on July 21, 1941, Stevenson reported for duty.

It had been seven years since he worked in Washington. During his first time there, the New Deal was just getting under way. Now it was preparing for war. The years in Chicago had been important ones in Adlai Stevenson's life. He had established a home. He had made a place for himself in the city's civic and social life. His work at the Council on Foreign Relations and the White Committee had launched him as a public figure, trained him as a public speaker, and in many ways prepared him for a public career. The White Com-mittee especially had helped. Not only had he been drawn to the at-tention of important national figures; not only had he learned to or-ganize large public enterprises; even more important, he had for the first time stepped into the searing fire of a great national controversy that cut across party lines, friendships, business and even family relationships. While he had not always enjoyed it, he had stuck to his guns. He had learned (or should have learned) a good deal, in-cluding the fact that money for such an endeavor came by and large from Chicago, not from Lake Forest, came not from his own

wealthy friends but from wealthy Jews, and that support came from
the masses. He had learned the difficulty of educating the public. He
had learned who his friends were. He had learned that he preferred
public life to the law. From the day he went to work for Frank Knox
until the day he died, he never really returned to private life.

CHAPTER FIVE

Washington at War
1941-1946

Stevenson went to work in Secretary Knox's office July 21, 1941. He told Dave Merwin, "I wish I could tell you what my job is, but at the end of the first week I have not found out myself—perhaps legal maid servant to Frank Knox would be accurate." His title was principal attorney in the Secretary's office. Early in the next year he was promoted to special assistant to the Secretary of Navy and his salary raised from $5,000 to $5,600 per year. His wife once said after their estrangement that she always thought of Stevenson as somebody's assistant. A special assistant to a high government official, however, can be far more important than that disparaging remark implies. He may advise his chief on policy, determine whom he sees and whom he does not see, decide what mail he reads and what he ignores, write his speeches, arrange his meetings, do his infighting in the bureaucracy, speak for him publicly and inside the government, slow down projects and speed up others, influence promotions and assignments, and a thousand other things. Much depends on the relationship between the assistant and his chief.

Stevenson, at the White Committee, had powerfully advocated the anti-isolationist views of Frank Knox's *Daily News*. Stevenson was a friend of Laird Bell, attorney for the *News*. He belonged to the small Chicago establishment of well-to-do liberals. Stevenson felt later that the hardest job he did for Knox was working on desegregating the Navy. Shortly after joining Knox, Stevenson told Mrs. Ives, "I've got a grand job tho I confess I don't know yet precisely what my duties are—apparently most anything the Secretary wants to unload. I've played golf with him, been down the river for the evening on his beautiful yacht with a company of distinguished guests, lunched with him in his private dining room at the Dept. most every day and heard all the low down on what's going on & his troubles in the Dept. in a very confidential & disarming way. So I feel I'm in an interesting spot & only hope I'll be able to be of some real service to him."

A special assistant to the wartime Secretary of the Navy was close to the center of American power, and one would expect that Stevenson's work was important. He did a little of everything— negotiated the lease of a naval oil reserve, helped settle a defense plant strike, traveled with Knox, wrote Knox's speeches. Stevenson's Princeton and Lake Forest friend, James Douglas, a wartime Air Force officer, has said, however, "He never got hold in the Navy Department. I was always somewhat surprised." On the other hand, a columnist has recalled, "As far as talking about the grand strategy of the war is concerned, it was better to talk to Stevenson than to Knox." Archibald MacLeish said, "Everyone who had to do with him in the days when he was working for Knox soon learned that the best way to move topside in the Navy was through Adlai."

Stevenson stayed briefly at the Hay-Adams Hotel, a pleasant place overlooking the White House, then moved into the home of a friend in Georgetown who was out of town on a government mission and who also loaned him a servant. A friend from his Princeton days offered "Rabbit" hospitality in Baltimore for weekend visits. Of a Sunday he visited friends in the country "for sun and swimming."

He and his wife were following the pattern established by his own mother and father: living apart. Nevertheless, a letter Ellen wrote was a loving one, commencing, "Darling" and saying, "The evening after you left I rode after an early supper—there was a beautiful sunset & it was cool—We should do that often." She urged him to guard his health: "The doctor gave me some salt pills. *Please* get yourself some! No one loses valuable salts more profusely than you do!" Their youngest son, John Fell, was going to visit Ellen's mother in Massachusetts. Ellen herself was preparing to leave for British Columbia to visit the Kelloggs, taking Borden and Adlai. "Please write me a lot. . . . I think I'd better come to see you when I get back!" On August 5, from British Columbia, Ellen sent him a postcard bearing a sexy photograph of a girl swimming in a transparent bathing suit and a man parachuting to join her with the legend, "Hope you'll drop in soon." (She enclosed the postcard in an envelope.)

Stevenson must have carried this postcard and its envelope around with him for several days. For on August 16, only a month after he had gone to work for Knox, Knox sent him on a mission to President Roosevelt, and he scribbled some notes on the back of Ellen's envelope, either in preparing for his meeting with the President or while or just after talking with him. Stevenson had been working on the strike at the Kearny, New Jersey, yard of the Federal Shipbuilding and Dry Dock Corporation. The company had refused to accept recommendations of the National Defense Mediation Board, and government agencies had recommended that the federal government take over the plant. At 10:30 A.M. on the sixteenth, Knox told Stevenson to fly to Rockland, Maine, to meet the President aboard the *Potomac*—he was returning from a meeting at sea with Winston Churchill where they had signed the Atlantic Charter—and deliver to the President not only his papers on the Kearny strike but also a highly secret intelligence message. That night, having completed his mission, Stevenson described it to Ellen (but told her he could not reveal the secret message):

Darling—Its Saturday night—7.36 EST to be exact—and guess where I am! Your wrong. I'm alone in a ten passenger Lockheed bomber south bound from Portland, Maine, and we must be almost exactly over John Fell—at this—no—this instant!

And so the story of the most exciting day of my life—(except for 12/1/28, 10/10/30, 7/7/32 and 2/7/36) [the dates of his marriage and the births of his three sons] begins. . . . At 10:30 it was decided that I should fly in a Navy land plane to the great naval air base at Quonset Point, R.I. there transfer to a seaplane and fly up to Rockland, Maine, to meet the President on the Potomac. . . .

I was whisked out to the field in a navy car in a welter of last minute instructions from the secretaries—in the air at 11:45, then across the Chesapeake, over Philadelphia, over Newark and Manhattan and down at the Quonset air base at 1:45—to be told by the commandant who was waiting with his staff at attention that the weather reports north of Portland were bad. So we debated ways and means for awhile & then off again in the great Lockheed for Portland, hoping somehow to get from there to Rockland before the President. Portland at 2:55—passing exactly over the tennis court of your mothers house en route. . . . At Portland airport I telephoned Rockland to inquire if the Pres. had docked and when his train would leave. The stationmaster was agitated to say the least—said he didn't know where the Pres was but that most of Maine was surging around his station & the train was due in 3 minutes at 3, and would arrive in Portland at 6:30. I was in despair —the President had wired us his train would not leave until 4. At the airport they told us our big ship could never land in the 'cowpasture' at Rockland even if we wanted to go on and take a chance on the Pres. being late. Just at that moment Admiral Bristol's small

Navy plane landed. They threw me in it, bag and baggage, and at 3:35 the pilot and I were circling over Rockland—remember it? And that lovely early American print you picked out in the dark?

Below we saw the train & masses of people—the train started, moved 6 or 8 yards and stopped—we circled the 'field' again— and again—trying to decide whether it was worth trying to land and get thru the traffic to the train. We did—with an awful bump—I sprang out with brief case & satchel—jumped in a car—whose I don't know, but we careened thru the town, got hopelessly enmeshed . . . in the traffic & never saw the train! Back to the little Navy plane, bounced into the air and off over Booth Bay for Portland again—with your versatile lover at the controls for 15 minutes!!

We reached Portland again at 5—the President's train was not due until 6:30. I was whisked by a petty officer off to the USS Prairie, a great destroyer tender; sent a wire to the Secretary explaining my misadventures; dined in solitary splendor with Admiral Bristol's chief of staff—the Admiral was away. . . .

Then back to the Ry Station with commander Rawlins and my swell pilot, Lieut Easton and who do I run into in the station waiting for the President's train but Senator Pepper and wife, Gov. Brand, the mayor [of] Portland, Mr. X & Mr Y. We had gay conversation waiting for the train to arrive while Mildred Pepper wilted before the charms of Comdr. Rawlins. And when the train arrived we were ushered through the crowd, but who was taken aboard first? You're right—old Dada was ushered into the presence while the crowd seethed and the dignitaries languished! He was at dinner with Harry Hopkins, an Admiral, a lady & another gentleman. As I walked thru the door he looked up, said, 'Hello Adlai, sorry I missed you at Rockland. Do you know all these people— Mr. Hopkins, (who remembered me), Ad. X, Mr. Y Mrs. Z'— while I stuttered something like 'Hi Folks'—explained my mission, delivered my papers—hoping he would deem it important enough to ask me to stay on the train & talk with him en route to Wash. He didn't, but he took my memoranda, said he would read them tonight . . . whereupon I backed out gurgling some inarticulate sounds. I should have added that just as I was leaving I handed him my secret message scribbled on a slip of paper while confusedly saying it was for him alone. . . .

So ends my saga—or it [will] in an hour when I get to Anacosta and report to the boss by telephone that I accomplished very little.

President Roosevelt returned to Washington next day, and the New York *Times,* reporting that the recommendation of plant seizure at Kearny had been placed before him said, "The importance of the case to officials here [in Washington] was demonstrated by the fact that Adlai Stevenson, special assistant to Secretary of the Navy Frank Knox, who has been drafting a proposed executive order for seizure of the plant, hurried to Portland, Me., yesterday and boarded the Presidential special train. . . . It was assumed that the President and Mr. Stevenson began at once a discussion of the Federal Shipbuilding controversy." Twenty years later, on August 18, 1961, Stevenson told Marietta Tree that twenty years ago that day his name had appeared for the first time on the front page of the New York *Times.*

The secret message which Stevenson told his wife he had carried to Roosevelt but could not reveal to her was this: "Comdt. 3d Nav. Dist—Admiral Andrews—informed Admiral Nimitz that he has heard from a source previously reliable that Stalin is negotiating with Hitler today." In later years Stevenson, embroidering the story and telling it in various versions as a joke on himself, said that he had been instructed to deliver the message orally, that he told the President so, that the President said he could speak freely in front of Hopkins and the others, but that Stevenson instead scribbled the message on a menu and handed it to the President, who read it, then said, "Adlai, do you believe this?" Stevenson stammered, "Why, I don't know, Mr. President." Roosevelt said, "I don't believe it. I'm not worried at all. Are you worried, Adlai?" Stevenson said he guessed not, and turning to leave, bumped into a door.[1] In the letter to Ellen, the note of boyish adventure, missing since the AAA days, returned.

2

Stevenson was thinking of running for the Senate next year. Arthur Goldberg, then a Chicago labor lawyer, later a Supreme Court justice and ambassador to the United Nations, suggested it in July and introduced Stevenson to Illinois labor leaders. On September 11, Paul Scott Mowrer, editor of the Chicago *Daily News,* told him that

[1] Stevenson's various versions of the episode also say that the President did not even open the envelope containing "my precious Kearny shipyard papers." The copy of the message about Stalin given here is in Stevenson's handwriting on a sheet of notepaper headed, "Office of the Secretary of the Navy," not on a menu; it was in Stevenson's papers after his death. Stevenson's various versions make better yarns but the letter he wrote to Ellen that same night, plus the scribbled note about Stalin, are probably nearest the truth.

Thomas J. Courtney, Cook County state's attorney, was "about out of the picture." Democrats were talking now about A. A. Sprague and Otto Kerner but "I think both of them will eliminate themselves. So the coils are closing in on you." Paul Douglas saw Secretary Knox, who told him that Stevenson wanted to run for the Senate but had no political experience. Douglas went back to Illinois to campaign for the nomination himself, working hard downstate. On September 23, Lloyd Lewis of the *Daily News,* Stevenson's friend and neighbor in Libertyville, told Stevenson that he had talked to Democratic leaders in East St. Louis and Peoria and they said if Courtney did not run Stevenson was "the man." The East St. Louis leader had spoken to Mayor Kelly. Another friend of Lewis' had seen Al Horan, a powerful ward leader in the Cook County machine, and Horan had said Stevenson should be the man if Courtney did not run. V. Y. Dallman, the Springfield publisher, believed Stevenson could win. Barry Bingham of the Louisville *Courier-Journal* promised to "start agitating for you." In view of all this, Lloyd Lewis suggested Stevenson go to Chicago October 27, Navy Day, and make a speech and talk things over privately with downstate leaders. He asked Stevenson to send his autobiography to an East St. Louis political leader, emphasizing his downstate origin.

Lewis, though he knew politics, was an amateur, not an insider in the Democratic machine. Things began to sound more serious October 15, when Barney Hodes, an insider, wrote Stevenson, "I have been thinking of the coming senatorial campaign and would like to talk to you about the general situation and your relation thereto—if you are in Chicago sometime." Stevenson replied, "This senatorial business confounds me and I would welcome your comments and advice. I had hoped to come to Chicago this coming weekend to stay over Navy Day, and I still may be able to make it. If I do, rest assured I will be on your door step."

He did go to Chicago that weekend, and a few days later Mayor Kelly complimented him on a recent nationwide radio network speech supporting Roosevelt's policy. Kelly said, "The people cannot be told plainly enough or often enough what the true picture is— plain, every day down-to-earth talking right to them will rouse them." The Mayor, however, said nothing about the senatorial nomination.

The party, led by Kelly, would be slating its candidates late in December, as usual. On December 17, Lloyd Lewis told Stevenson that Brooks seemed sure of renomination by the Republicans and Courtney was an "odds-on favorite" among Democrats, though some downstaters thought Stevenson might emerge in case of stalemate. Stevenson replied, "To be candid—a difficult role for me—I am not disappointed. In the first place I have something to do here that needs doing, secondly I never fancied myself as a combatant politico. . . . But I am concerned as much as ever about beating Brooks and all he represents." As it turned out, the Democrats slated Raymond S. McKeough. Stevenson told Dutch Smith a little later, "The political pot has been boiling and I have been conferring with a stream of Illinois statesmen. But the organization wouldn't have me—'not well enough known', so they took McKeough who is one of the boys. But there were other reasons against me—most of which I'm proud of!" Lloyd Lewis suspected McCormick of the *Tribune* had maneuvered the selection of McKeough because he would be a weak opponent for Brooks. Dutch Smith told Stevenson, "Under the circumstances, I can see why you are proud of being 'not available.'" Paul Douglas ran in the Democratic primary against McKeough and lost. Douglas, who had campaigned hard, has recalled primary election night: "One by one my supporters left the headquarters. Finally Emily [his wife] and I went home in a taxicab and I said, 'I'm going to enlist in the Marines tomorrow.'" He did—at the age of fifty—rose from private to lieutenant colonel, and returned a wounded war hero to win the Senate seat in 1948, the year Stevenson was elected Governor.

3

At the end of that September, Ellen and the children went to Washington to join Stevenson. They lived in a house at 1904 R Street. Young Adlai III attended J. Q. Adams Public School his first year in Washington and a private school, Saint Albans, his second. He recalls spending weekends with his parents in a Potomac River cabin which belonged to one of Stevenson's friends, and walking along the canal towpath with his father. John Fell remembers his father's taking him in a kayak on the canal. Mrs. Ives visited them. She thought he had realized his parents' hopes for him (and, as she often did, she adjured him to guard his health).

Serious marital difficulties seem to have begun during this period in Washington. Ellen was not happy there. She did not stay but went to and fro between Washington and Libertyville, between Washington and her mother's house at Beverly, Massachusetts. Harriet Welling has recalled that at the end of their first year in Washington Ellen returned for the winter in order to write poetry, which upset Stevenson. Ellen told Mrs. Welling at the time that she

" 'couldn't stand all those terrible people in Washington'—the 'terrible people' included people like Walter Lippmann!" Once she took the boys for a vacation with her mother in Massachusetts and, preparing to drive back to Chicago, impulsively bought a Buick; it annoyed Stevenson. When several years later Glen Lloyd, their next-door neighbor in Libertyville, tried to persuade Ellen not to divorce Stevenson, she told him, "I've wanted out of this since 1941 in Washington." Lloyd reminded her that he had attended a party at their house in Washington in 1941, and she had seemed to enjoy it. She said, "You don't know how miserable it was. I hate it. The duplicity of politics." Their friend Ruth Winter has said, "When he went with Knox, that's when things started falling apart. Something happened to her. It was a terrible thing. She became suspicious. She became terribly jealous of his position. She thought he was not paying attention to her. She felt that she was responsible for everything that he was and that he didn't appreciate it. I had known her so well that I was extremely concerned. She told me he was thoughtless and inconsiderate. Possibly the fact that he was getting a lot of attention in Washington and she was only his handmaiden, she was entertaining not for herself but for him, because it was part of his business—she resented it and lost her taste for doing for him. Adlai must have seen this happening too and it must have been hard on him. She seemed to lose her identity, which was very important to her. She was trying to write poetry but not writing it as well as she thought she should have because of all this going on and so she took it out on him and blamed him for interfering with her poetry." The Stevensons quarreled frequently in Washington. The boys sympathized with their father. Stevenson knew something was wrong and he was trying to put it right. Once he visited Ellen for a weekend, then returned to Washington and wrote a long revealing letter:

> Darling—
> I am back at the old stand on R street and, despite the usual frenzied day and a bulging brief case, my heart is still surging after that glorious week end. I can still see you on the [railroad] platform— all three smiling and waving me good bye. I don't know why I am so immoderately sentimental but I almost cried as the train pulled away—until I got engrossed in the Daily News!
> I have told Cora about the rugs, curtains etc. She says she has been using the carpet sweeper but I will have her take the smaller rugs and give them a beating. She says she can't take down the big curtains. . . . I guess I'll have to take them down on Sunday. What should I do with them? . . .

I am so glad we had those nice long quiet talks. I feel immeasure-
ably better and I guess they were long overdue. I do hope you
will write me . . . that you are having a thorough check up including a basic metabolism. Please don't feel that you *must* come down
here soon if you feel strongly that staying there next winter is
best. . . .

I have implicit confidence in your judgment and I know what
ever you decide about next winter will be best for all of us. My
heart is so full I am in danger of verbosity!—but I am sure you
know how thankful I am for the tolerant, uncomplaining and for-
giving way you talked to me and explained everything—how it
wasn't what I had done but what happened within you etc! I see
everything much more clearly and I pray that somehow I can prove
worthy of you. We are getting older now and the fever of youth is
subsiding—don't be alarmed by it & please don't feel that I can't
understand your anxiety to find yourself and peace and the feeling
of urgency. Your happiness is as important to me as my own, for
they are the same, they are inextricably intermingled. Time more
often plays good tricks than bad ones at our age & somehow I can't
believe that with self control patience and wisdom we can't be
everything we want to be. But one must want to be. I have never
had a moment's doubt—(my behavior to the contrary notwith-
standing)—I get so damnably confused and you're so damnably
clear minded.

Just one more thing. I felt mortified about my cross examination
regarding [a man] afterward. It was an unworthy business and,
believe me, I didn't ask all those questions to embarrass you or
solely out of gratuitous curiosity. I was selfishly trying to protect
myself, trying to give you advice—when I obviously could only
give you *selfish* advice. As I say, I have implicit confidence in you
and if you can forgive me, I promise you I will never do that
again—

I should like to continue this conversation but you are probably
nauseated already and my bulging brief case is beckoning—and
there I am, unrepentent, confessing my sins! But if you were here I
would chuck it out the window—because I love you and the boys
even more than the brief case!—Ad

It was characteristic that he prefaced the intimate passage of his
letter with housekeeping chitchat and that he feared even as he
wrote she might be laughing at what he wrote. Later he told Jane
Dick that during the war years he and Ellen had talked about
separating but that "they got over that hump." He seemed to feel

that, while his marriage had not turned out to be perfect, he and Ellen had reached a *modus vivendi*. Stevenson's suggestion that Ellen have "a thorough checkup" reminds one, of course, of correspondence between his own mother and father. The "basic metabolism" test he suggested was fashionable in the 1940s. Stevenson first consulted a psychiatrist about Ellen during the Washington period. He and Ellen went to a psychiatrist together there; Ellen would agree to go only if Stevenson went too. Ellen herself once said, many years later, that Stevenson had told their children that she was "a paranoid type in 1941." Mrs. Welling once told Stevenson that Ellen was "a case of classic paranoia" and read to him a description of it from a medical dictionary. Many years later, Stevenson told his children that the Washington psychiatrist had told him she was suffering from "persecutory paranoia" and there was "little hope for the marriage." He took them into the library and opened the Encyclopaedia Britannica to a well-worn spot and almost recited the passage on paranoia from memory.

4

On December 8, 1941, the day after Pearl Harbor, Stevenson drafted a "suggested statement to Navy yards": "The enemy has struck a savage, treacherous blow. We are at war, all of us! There is no time now for disputes or delay of any kind. We must have ships and more ships, guns and more guns, men and more men—faster and faster. . . . Speed up—it's your Navy and your Nation!" The use of the phrase "speed up," an odious phrase among labor unions, betrayed a lack of sensitivity to, or ignorance of, the hagiography of the unions Stevenson was dealing with. He complained about an editorial in the *Pantagraph:* Bud Merwin explained it had been written before the declaration of war and said, "I can assure you that there will be nothing in our editorial expressions during this total war to encourage complacency."

Stevenson's sense of urgency did not prevent him from taking his family to Mrs. Ives's place at Southern Pines for Christmas, despite the extreme difficulty of wartime travel—with planes and railroad cars pressed into service to carry troops, plane and train reservations were hard for civilians to obtain, and one always ran the risk of having one's reservation pre-empted by someone with a higher travel priority. Stevenson could stay at his sister's only a day and a half. Mrs. Ives was grateful for even so short a visit, as a mother is grateful.

Carl McGowan went to Washington after Pearl Harbor to see Stevenson about joining the Navy. Stevenson helped, and McGowan ended up in the Bureau of Aeronautics. "One afternoon I was sitting there doing nothing and the phone rang and it was Stevenson. He asked, 'What the hell are you doing that you can't stop for two or three weeks?' I said nothing. He said, 'We've got a crisis.' It was something about the navy petroleum bill, I think. He said he needed help with legal problems. So I said all right. I spent the rest of the war there with him. I had a little office across the hall from his office," Room 2048. George Ball has said, "Stevenson was the God-damnedest man I ever saw for running a one-man employment agency. If somebody mentioned some casual interest in a job, he spent hours and days working to get it for him. I've never known a man who was so generous that way." Stevenson suggested Ball come to Washington, and he did. To Room 2048 came a steady stream of applicants and letters of applicants. He wrote in his diary, "Ah God these people who want commissions! Will it ever stop." Some wanted commissions, some wanted promotions, some wanted disabilities waived, some wanted overseas duty. They were friends from Bloomington, from Princeton, from Chicago; they were friends of politicians. They included a publicity man for the Ambassador Hotel in Chicago, a judge, a state legislator, a law clerk at Stevenson's old firm. More often than not Stevenson was successful, and he won the thanks of scores of people.[2] He helped Illinois State Senator Abraham Lincoln Marovitz, a protégé of Jack Arvey, obtain overseas duty. Paul Douglas, then preparing to run against McKeough in the Democratic senatorial primary, told Stevenson he himself preferred Stevenson as the candidate but the organization probably would slate neither of them, and if Douglas was not nominated he would "like to be admitted as a private or a plain seaman into the armed forces"; and he asked Stevenson's help in getting the age limitation waived. Stevenson sent a memo to Undersecretary James Forrestal asking if he knew "of anything that can be done with an over-age destroyer like this," adding that Douglas was a "very distinguished" professor, an alderman, and a friend of Secretary Knox. After he was defeated in the primary, Douglas telegraphed Stevenson, asking him to try to get the age qualification waived for entry into the Marine Corps as an enlisted man. Stevenson suggested he

---

[2] Among them were a Congressman from Illinois; Stanley Reed, Jr.; Undersecretary of State Ed Stettinius; his senior partner William P. Sidley; Circuit Judge Cornelius J. Harrington of Chicago; Robert S. Pirie; the writer Struthers Burt; and Walter Lichtenstein, the Chicago banker and Stevenson's predecessor as president of the Council on Foreign Relations.

send a note to Knox, since "special dispensation" was not easy. Knox sent a letter to the Marine Corps commandant, and Stevenson sent a copy to Douglas. Finally, on April 28, Douglas thanked Stevenson—he had passed the physical examination and been accepted. Only now did Stevenson and Douglas, despite their former association at the Council on Foreign Relations, the White Committee, and politics, address each other by their first names. They continued to correspond intermittently throughout the war.

5

When Stevenson registered for the draft on February 16, 1942, he was forty-two years old, weighed 180 pounds, and stood five feet ten inches tall. A caricature drawn by Robert Sherwood, the playwright come to Washington to help Roosevelt and Hopkins, showed him long-nosed, getting bald, and serious. Stevenson wrote a long legal memo for the Undersecretary of the Navy on the modern history of legislation limiting wartime profits. He wrote a memo to Secretary Knox recommending that the Navy and War departments develop a common policy on labor relations in companies taken over by the government. In later years Stevenson was fond of telling how he was sent to treat with a Soviet emissary who had complained about delays in delivering war matériel; Stevenson told the Soviet emissary that deliveries were behind because of Soviet delays, not American, whereupon the Russian replied, "I have not come here to talk about my behind but your behind." He represented the Navy on an interdepartmental committee—Navy, Army, State—which met weekly to coordinate public information policies at the behest of Archibald MacLeish, the poet in the Office of Facts and Figures, a forerunner of USIA. (John J. McCloy represented the Army.) Stevenson and MacLeish became fast friends, and, because of her interest in poetry, Ellen came to know MacLeish too.

Stevenson was writing speeches for Knox. The diction and syntax were Stevenson's own; he made little attempt to adapt them to Knox's style. Stevenson himself addressed the Chicago Council on Foreign Relations February 17. He fell back at the outset into the relaxed manner he had employed at the Council long ago, beginning by saying he had come prepared "to divert you for a moment with an amusing story" only to discover that his boss, Secretary Knox, had already told the story in Chicago. (Stevenson himself had no doubt written the story into Knox's speech.) In the main body of the speech he paraphrased (and sometimes used without paraphrasing) passages he had written for Knox. The way of the speech writer who is also making speeches himself is hard.

He gave the Council a world-wide survey of the war, emphasizing that "it is all one war." It was an attack on complacency, a long sober speech, concluding with a warning that the war could be lost. "[Hitler] knows that if we have the will to do it we and we alone can beat him. This year, perhaps the next six months, will tell the story. Can we do it? I submit, not in our present frame of mind. Not until we get mad, fighting mad. . . . And when it's over, please remember that if the four freedoms of the doctrine of the Atlantic Charter is to have a chance, peace must be guaranteed and there will be worthy work for your mighty Navy on the long journey to the promised land—in the *American age!*" Thus did Stevenson, at a time when there was talk about both a postwar "American century" and a postwar world organized by nations united, adopt the more imperialistic of the two ideas.

He maintained his Chicago ties—saw friends on LaSalle Street, accepted a suggestion of R. J. Dunham that he run on the Democratic ticket for trustee of the University of Illinois (it turned out to be impossible—he would have had to resign his navy post); declined an invitation (with hyperbole—"I am still dizzy from your flattering invitation") from Jane Dick to address the Immigrants' Protective League. In Washington he was making numerous friends who were or would become important. He partially filled out an application for a commission in the uniformed Navy but Secretary Knox told him his effectiveness would diminish in uniform—as Knox's civilian special assistant he dealt with high-ranking officers but a commission consistent with his age would lower his rank. He remained a civilian.

On May 1 he went West with Knox on an inspection trip to New Orleans, Corpus Christi, El Paso, San Diego, Monterey, Alameda, Sand Point, Billings, and Glenview, covering 6,542 miles in eleven days, quite a feat in those days. Knox gave a series of speeches written by Stevenson in May and June, including a thoughtful one at Harvard accepting an honorary degree and a militant lurid one at the Boston Garden—"we are all Americans fighting like hell to obliterate these wolves who are tearing the world apart . . . these bloodthirsty jackals . . . the wily Jap . . . the brutal Nazi."

On June 24, Stevenson left on an official two-week trip, mostly by commercial plane, to the Caribbean, stopping at Balboa, Panama; Port of Spain, Trinidad; San Juan, Puerto Rico; Camagüey, Guantánamo and Havana, Cuba; and, en route home, Miami, Jacksonville, Charleston, and Norfolk. Stevenson made notes as he traveled.

They showed his insatiable curiosity and his irritable impatience with customs formalities and inefficient travel arrangements. Returning to Washington, he wrote a report on each place he had visited and nearly every navy officer he had met. It was a good report, and he had worked hard gathering material for it.

Bud Merwin was going into the Navy; Stevenson helped him get a commission. Ellen was in Libertyville, having a bad summer. On August 7 she wrote, "Dear Adlai," not, as previously, "Darling," and said, "When I start writing you letters—you'll know I've reformed! And you insist on air mail too—and what shall I say now that I'm writing you? . . . You started worrying just about when I stopped. . . . I sold the wool [from the sheep] and they paid me $40.66—which doesn't quite pay for my trip to Washington." Stevenson noted that Ellen had "finally decided" to go East for the winter.[3]

He spent a good deal of time that fall at the Metropolitan Club. He met foreign diplomats and spent evenings in their homes, sometimes with journalists. At that time people were trying to define what the United States was fighting for. In a speech that Stevenson probably wrote, Secretary Knox said we were fighting for democratic self-government and for the doctrine that all men are created equal and deserve equal opportunity. Stevenson proposed to Knox that he appear voluntarily before House and Senate committees to improve the Navy's congressional relations. He received a reply not from Knox but from Undersecretary Forrestal: "I think your suggestion about the new Congress has merit." Knox asked Forrestal, Bard, Gates, and Stevenson to list members of Congress with whom they had good relations so that each could be assigned to keep in touch with their friends. Stevenson listed fifteen Representatives and ten Senators—Pepper, Guffey, Lucas, Barkley, Bridges, Austin, Connally, Green, Glass, and Nye.

Again, when Stevenson took Ellen and the boys to Southern Pines for two weeks at Christmastime he could stay only briefly. He looked tired. It is noteworthy that, in her journal, Mrs. Ives referred to the Christmas tree as Stevenson's, not as the children's. Mrs. Ives recalled much later, "Ellen told me at Southern Pines that she'd like to change their lives. She didn't like Washington. She liked the woods."

Ellen and the boys returned to Washington January 3, 1943.

---

[3] Stevenson's rent in Washington was $300 a month. He paid Saint Albans School $1,178. He paid a caretaker in Libertyville about $110 a month. He was paid only $5,840 that year by the Navy and received $21,223 in dividends, plus $2,468 in farm income.

Stevenson, who started to keep a diary January 1, wrote, "Wonderful to have them back. . . . Sincere and flattering letter to Ellen from Struthers Burt about her poetry. She *must* find time or *organize* her time to write more. Her quality is so high but her output so low." He had a "gay dinner" with Ellen and the boys and read a Negro dialect story aloud to the boys and noted in his diary later, "Rather pleased with my negro accent even if the boys weren't."

6

Congress convened January 6, and Stevenson sat in the executive gallery while President Roosevelt delivered his address. Mrs. Henry Morgenthau and Mrs. Robert Sherwood sat alongside Stevenson. Mrs. Roosevelt and Mrs. Henry Wallace were nearby. Stevenson thought the speech "good" and noted in his diary that Roosevelt "used one sentence in almost [verbatim form] from speech I wrote for K about a month ago." Afterward Stevenson had lunch with Knox and Senator Harry Byrd. Jim Oates and John Kellogg came to dinner that night. Three days later, Saturday, January 9, Stevenson left with Secretary Knox for the South Pacific.

They were gone about three weeks. Various naval officers accompanied them on different legs of the trip, including Admiral Chester W. Nimitz, Commander-in-Chief of the Pacific Fleet. Stevenson kept a diary. They stopped overnight at Dallas, where Stevenson wrote to Ellen, in a fine display of his surprising naïveté, "I find that this trip by the Secretary is secret so *please* don't tell anyone ELSE where I am. I'm afraid I have already talked too freely. . . . Also caution the boys and the servants." He described their long flight to Los Angeles and up the Central Valley to San Francisco Bay. There they stayed overnight at the St. Francis Hotel, and Stevenson wrote to Ellen, "I'm filled with memories. But the Secy has even more palatial quarters than we did 8 yrs ago!" He dined at an Italian restaurant with several naval officers, one of whom had lost his ship in the Solomons—"good food & fascinating yarns of the real war." He told her, "Get a lot of poetry written & after I've done my talking I'll criticize it for you. . . . Get a lot of rest for I'm going to run you ragged when I get back."

About 10 P.M. on January 11 they took off for Hawaii, having visited men wounded at Guadalcanal—"some harrowing cases." A painful shoulder prevented Stevenson from sleeping during the long flight. They inspected Pearl Harbor, and Stevenson saw "no evidence of Dec. 7 damage anywhere." Driving about, he noticed the barbed wire along the beaches and everywhere else, a "waste of steel." He noted endless details—the length of runways, a dispersal of parked aircraft, manpower shortages, natural beauty. He and Nimitz took a swim surrounded by barbed wire and he passed a ranch where he and Ellen had had lunch in 1934. They held decoration ceremonies, had drinks in the officers' club, were presented with leis. "The airmen are the best talkers, salesmen, personality, good looking devil may care boys. (Only Navy Cross was won by a Jew named Rothenburg!)." On January 14 they arose at six, breakfasted at daylight with Admiral Nimitz, then took off in two PBY flying boats, Stevenson in one with Knox, Nimitz, and four others. Stevenson wrote in his diary that his plane took off first: "long taxi—2 trys—difficult course—long taxi—she's on the step—she rocks—long bounces (weight about 63,000)—she's up—30 ft, 50 ft—I crave to peer out of port window for view of P.H. . . . Motors suddenly cut, coming down steep, hit water hard, bad list to Port—look out, wing tip under, Ah! Ah! Blue jacket hands me life belt. . . . Main hatch door opened. Water . . . below the edge on port side. Ordered up topside & out on starboard wing. . . . We almost fall off! Everyone sort of gay—enjoying it thoroughly. (McCloud, pilot, explains that No 2 engine failed, tried to right, slipped to port, motor tore off portion.) Much excitement—Sec Nav & Cincpac almost crack up in middle of Pearl H! Small boat takes us in tow. Adm N. very calm; no need of criticism of pilot—tells him to take charge; that we wanted to get started for Midway as soon as possible." They transferred to the other plane.

Stevenson wrote that he could neither sleep nor work aboard the plane. He described the "blue Pacific" and the islands they flew over. About four-thirty they landed at Midway, twelve hundred miles west of Hawaii, and inspected it: "Hangar only sign of damage. Goonies everywhere, bowing and dancing, sitting on their nests, awkward takeoffs and landings; always proud and dignified. Black more animated than white. Strange and lovable birds, must be lonesome when they go." He could not get over these strange birds and referred to them time and again. He did not neglect his work, noting construction in progress, praising the work of the Seabees (construction workers), inspecting underground gun emplacements, observing that it was difficult to keep fighter pilots "on edge" with little to do at Midway. There was a party at the officers' club. Next morning they visited another of the Midway islands, "much more primitive. . . . Marines looked the best as always. . . . Seem to have plenty of everything —except women. . . . Adm N. constantly concerned with fuel storage—wants a lot more out here."

Their departure for Johnston Island was delayed by damage to a plane; waiting for it to be repaired, they went aboard a submarine in from forty-seven days of patrolling, its crew pale. Next day they flew south-east to tiny Johnston Island with a quonset hut for an officers' club, officers and men wearing nothing but pants and burned almost black by the sun. Johnston was blacked out—"after groping about in the pitch darkness thru a series of black baffles into a brightly lighted room full of chattering American boys is a very cheering experience. . . . After a little experience you learn how to get up in the dark, shave in the dark with cold blackish water, pack in the dark, find your way to the mess hall."

They continued south to inspect Canton Island, almost on the equator: "Messy, disorderly looking place. Life is hard here. Officers call it Isle of Atonement; you are not assigned to Canton, you are condemned. Plane crews lying under wing for shade." An engine on one of their planes had failed; they went on in one plane, over-loaded: "She struggles up while we—I—hold my breath." They reached Suva that afternoon, a large rugged island with a huge palm plantation. American soldiers mingled with New Zealand sol-diers and natives. "Natives make fine jungle fighters, quiet, can see in the dark," Stevenson wrote. "Many malaria and battle damage cases from Guadalcanal." The dinner table at the residence was decorated with ferns and flowers, and they used napkins, and Steven-son wrote of the "easy, graceful way [the] English entertain." They left next morning, island-hopping in the New Hebrides, not far from Guadalcanal and the Solomons, and Stevenson noted the natural beauty and the people, Micronesians, "small black husky haired, g string . . . shell or bead necklases, bows & arrows, beads of boar tusks." On Espiritu Santo they found troops drawn up in formation by a shrine where the names of casualties were painted, and Knox spoke to the troops, and they sang, "Oh, we'll hang the Old Mikado to the cherry blossom tree. . . ." Everybody was talking about Guadalcanal, not far away to the northwest on the route to Japan. An admiral told Stevenson the Japanese must have lost 20,000 men there. He slept aboard ship on deck. "Ships blinking at each other but blacked out. Shadowy figures creeping all around with bed clothes to escape heat inside. Its beautiful moonlight & one could hardly believe the turmoil behind those peaceful, graceful silent palms along the moonlit beach. . . . A typewriter is still chattering slowly in the communication room on the deck just above and be-hind us. It happened all of a sudden. I don't believe I was awake but 1 distinctly heard a series of 5 or 6 rapid and distant thuds. I thought I could feel the concussion a little. It sounded like anti air-craft fire." A nearby airfield had been bombed.

Stevenson, left behind at Espiritu Santo while Knox went to Guadalcanal, went by jeep to a forward hospital. On the way, in-quisitive as ever, he talked to the driver, a welder from Mississippi who could make $150 a month at home and had a wife and two children. Up forward, "almost passed out from heat, smell and horror in one surgical hut. All the boys with fixed glazed eyes staring at the ceiling, half naked; brave smiles; no complaints. Boy wounded in neck, breathing into his tissue, inflated, scrotum as big as a grape-fruit. His body [illegible] to the stomach as tho his bones were smashed. He'll recover. Amputated leg on another; 36 shrapnel wounds. Intake of about 2000 per mo. here and only lost 7 so far! Blood plasma, sulfa drugs and rapid evacuation from the front by air before the [illegible] gangrene sets in is the explanation. Negro had shot 4 inches of bone out of his leg cleaning his rifle—what to do! I reeled out into the sunlight. But I didn't fool the doctor—they sat me down just in time, pushed my head between my knees and spirits of ammonia under my nose."

He talked to many others that afternoon, soaking up tales of war in the South Pacific, and wrote, "You can't write about a day like this one when everything from heroism stories on Guad. to laundry machinery to cannibalism has tumbled into your head like the topsy, turvy cargoes in the merchant ships." He thought that "this war is going to do wonders for a lot of privileged Americans of my genera-tion—but can we count on more political maturity as a result of these experiences?"

Next day, January 22, Stevenson went to Efati to wait for Knox and the others, thinking, as he flew over a surf-ringed beach, of Ellen. The Secretary's party arrived about four-thirty. They had been bombed repeatedly during the night on Guadalcanal. "Wished I dared write all I've heard about operations in the last few days," Stevenson wrote, "but one still wonders how island by island we can ever do the enormous job ahead out here. But of course I don't know the grand strategy of the Pac. I wish I did."

On January 23 they were in Noumea, "the first real town we have seen since P.H.," off the Australian coast. Newspapermen complained that their air transport was inadequate, and Stevenson interceded with Admiral Nimitz on their behalf, with little success. (Perhaps because of the *Pantagraph,* Stevenson was always more sensitive to the press than most people he dealt with.) Next day, heading home-ward, they flew back to Suva, and Knox distributed medals, "a fine show in a beautiful setting," and Stevenson talked with a native chief who "speaks perfect Oxonian English." Dinner was "gala," and after it Stevenson suggested to the Governor that someone should write a history of Fiji—"there is no good one." Upalo was "the tropical paradise at last!" Stevenson's curiosity was insatiable; he even described how Samoan venetian blinds were made. They flew to Tutuila, in American Samoa, and the pilot circled the home of Robert Louis Stevenson, "spacious, white, green roofed," and the "storied harbor of Pago Pago." After a cocktail party in a general's quarters at Pago Pago, Stevenson played the role of honored guest at a siva dance. The dancing girls were bare-breasted, he wrote, a special compliment.

Next day, after driving past the hotel made famous as the abode of Sadie Thompson in Somerset Maugham's story, they left for Canton, "bare & desolate as ever," then, heading back north to Hawaii, went on to Palmyra, having engine trouble en route and inspecting the defenses there. They rose at daybreak but both planes were "out of order," so Nimitz organized a fishing trip. On January 28 they took off for Pearl Harbor. There Stevenson prepared suggested answers to questions the press would ask Knox—"but of course he won't use them," a despairing phrase that Stevenson's own speech writers and press officers would later utter many times.

At Pearl Harbor, Stevenson found Ensign Robert Crown, the son of Henry Crown, one of the wealthiest and most influential industrialists of Chicago and, though a Republican, a close friend of Jack Arvey and a Democratic Party campaign contributor. Crown had been told that his wife probably would not recover from an illness. Crown had asked Knox or Stevenson to get his son transferred so he could return home before his mother died. Stevenson arranged it, and Crown remained grateful to Stevenson the rest of his life and was his powerful supporter.

Stevenson wrote, "It was 18 nights and a life time of adventure." They arrived in Washington about 6:30 P.M. on February 1.

7

He had accumulated the names of a score of people to call with messages from friends or relatives in the South Pacific, including Will Clayton, a wealthy Houston cotton man, later an Assistant Secretary of State; Frank Murphy, Associate Justice of the Supreme Court; a Congressman; a Senator; Robert Patterson, later Secretary of War; Robert Lovett, New York banker and Assistant Secretary of War, later Secretary of Defense. In February and March he wrote several speeches for Knox and made some himself. Both drew on their experiences of the trip. Knox delivered a Stevenson speech on Lincoln's birthday at Springfield, Illinois, which foresaw the necessities of peace. The United States must stay strong militarily. The old system of balance of power bred war and must be replaced. Political security required economic cooperation. We could not maintain our standard of living in a world of want. We should not meddle in everybody's affairs; liberty, freedom, and opportunity for all were not to give—they must be won. But we could help create a world where other peoples could win their freedom. We must lead the world in defense of the peace that victory would bring. We must supply the major part of the military power that could enforce the peace against aggression. We must contribute greatly to establishing an economic system that would permit "undeveloped" peoples to raise their standards of living. This was not popular talk at that time in the Midwest. In writing Knox's speech, Stevenson made skillfull obeisance to lingering isolationism but at the same time tried to bring people to think about postwar world affairs and, in doing so, expressed some thoughts that one day he would develop fully, especially about rich and poor nations.

In June, Ellen and two of the children were home in Libertyville. She sent Stevenson a letter full of family chitchat—Mrs. Ives and Tim had visited her and "I think they had a very good time I know we did"; they had had a buffet party "that almost tore the house down"; the children had been swimming "and I never saw boys enjoy themselves more"; she was going in to Chicago to dinner with the Paepckes.

Stevenson seriously considered buying the Chicago *Daily News*. In May or June he asked his investment adviser, Steve Hord, for financial data on the *News*.[4]

And he was interested too in running for Governor of Illinois next year, 1944. Gubernatorial aspirants began maneuvering for the nomination now, a full eighteen months before the election. Richard Folsom, attorney for the Chicago Board of Education, sent Stevenson a clipping from the June 7 issue of the *Daily News* containing a review of the downstate political situation and mentioning Stevenson. Stevenson replied, "I suspect Charlie Wheeler's reports on my availability from downstate were largely imaginary which your lis-

---

[4] The figures showed that the *News'* profits per share of common stock had declined from $2.76 in 1933 to 58¢ in 1942, that its preferred stock was valued at $3,755,518 and its common stock at $4 million, that its profit margin after taxes had declined from 14.8 per cent in 1933 to 4.9 per cent in 1942, and that the current market price of the stock was 10 bid, 10¾ asked.

tening posts will confirm. But anyway it was flattering and nice to feel that after almost two years here I am not altogether forgotten in Illinois. I admire John Cassidy very much and I should think he would make a splendid candidate. I suppose you are concerned about the Catholic angle. Some day we must talk about these things —but not about me!" It was the note of reluctance and self-deprecation which in the spring of 1952 irritated President Truman and others. A man from Hinsdale, a Republican suburb west of Chicago, asked if Stevenson had seen the piece in the *News* and said, "I am an independent Republican, but if you do run for Governor I will support you." (Stevenson had helped a young friend of his get a navy commission.) Stevenson thanked him and said, "I doubt if you will have to subordinate your Republican principles in my cause." Stevenson did not let the matter die, however. He wrote to Wheeler, the *News* political writer, directly: "I have just seen your story. . . . You were very kind to me and it made me feel like a statesman—almost! Some day you must tell me all about those big shots in the hinterland who think I look like a possibility. I suspect Lloyd Lewis is all of them." He also wrote directly to John E. Cassidy in Peoria: "I report in haste that I am highly flattered to share a column with you. You should keep better company!" Stevenson wrote to Barney Hodes and, on June 22, Hodes said the Democrats might have a real chance next year to unseat the incumbent Replican Governor, Dwight Green, providing "the proper ticket" could be put together: "If you are interested I do not think that you have too much time to lose although it might seem a little early." Mrs. Ives thought his being considered for Governor a high honor and one that would make his parents proud.

8

Knox and Stevenson made a series of speeches in June. At the Annapolis graduation exercises, Knox delivered some lines that sounded more like the later Stevenson than the present Secretary of the Navy: "Remember, too, that one of the obstacles to human progress, or to individual progress, is the closed mind" and "Your generation will be the custodians, with your brothers in arms in other nations, of an expanded freedom in a contracted world." Speaking at commencement at Northwestern University, Knox said, "Beyond the war lies a new era of hope. . . . The concept of the United Nations is both noble and realistic. . . . It is broad, liberal education that fits men to be and to stay free. . . . When states have agreed to submit their sovereign interests to judicial determination of occasions for the privileged and unprivileged use of force, it will be time to establish a truly international police force to guarantee stability and peaceful change." This was not mere commencement rhetoric. Earlier, and to the end of his life, Stevenson kept saying that the solution to most problems was education and that the way to world stability and peace was through international coopera- tion, backed by effective peace-keeping machinery, including force, to direct inevitable social change into peaceful channels.

Stevenson negotiated for the Navy with Standard Oil of California over the development and operation of the naval oil reserve at Elk Hills, California, an issue that threatened to blow up into a public scandal. The chairman of a House subcommittee investigating the progress of the war, Congressman Lyndon B. Johnson of Texas, re- leased one of his subcommittee's reports which criticized Stevenson for treating Standard too leniently. Some years later Johnson criti- cized Stevenson for being unsympathetic to the oil industry.

Stevenson kept his eye on Illinois politics. In a letter of August 5 he told Struthers Burt that he detected growing sentiment against the re-election of Roosevelt to a fourth term next year, though Roosevelt would be re-elected anyway, but thought a Republican House and perhaps a Republican Senate would be elected: "This confusing situation has personal implications for me. I have been beset of late to run for Governor of Illinois next spring and you would not blame me for eschewing certain defeat." Burt had asked Stevenson's view of Senator Scott Lucas of Illinois. Stevenson wrote, "I have known him a long while but never intimately. . . . He has the looks and the manners and the agility, but there is certainly something wanting in profundity and that odd thing called 'leader- ship.' . . . Scott is a small town boy . . . who has made good in a big way without any real distinction anywhere along the route. . . . In short, he seems to me a good, steady, well-balanced guy who'll never set the world on fire—but can and has done a workmanlike, conscientious and enlightened job in public life." He asked Burt to send him a magazine article of his: "God knows there never was a time when we needed more cogent, pointed writing in popular peri- odicals. As for the liberal sheets, I'm getting thoroughly fed up on them and their constant sniping at this and that."

"The local scene," he told a Winnetka friend, "interests me a good deal as I have been undergoing one of my periodical political flirta- tions—this time relating to the Governorship. Frankly, I don't know what's developing, if anything, but I believe some exploratory talks are being held with [Mayor] Kelly. . . . Marshall Field [publisher of the Chicago *Sun*] purports to be interested, also Sam Levin, Lloyd Lewis, et al. As for Stevenson, he is not sure whether he is interested or not and certainly doesn't seem to have any time to do much about it."

The editor of a small political weekly newspaper in Chicago told Stevenson he had talked with Charles Wheeler of the *Daily News* about suggesting Stevenson's name for governor to "the powers that be" and said, "I believe I will 'shoot' some publicity in [my newspaper], unless you are averse to it." He enclosed a clipping from the Chicago *Times* saying that "certain Democrats" close to the White House and Secretary Knox were promoting Stevenson for Governor. Stevenson told him, "It was all very interesting and I am much indebted to these anonymous Democrats who are interested in my candidacy. I suspect it will be something of a surprise to Colonel Knox as I doubt if he has heard about it before!" He did not, however, tell the editor to desist. Almost simultaneously Richard Folsom said he wanted to talk to him about the political situation. Stevenson replied he looked forward eagerly to canvassing the political situation—he would be in Chicago in September.

He received a letter from Mrs. Ives about Ellen and his political future, the first hint of trouble with her over politics. After telling him that Mrs. Bohrer of Bloomington thought he ought to go to the Senate, not the Governor's Mansion, Mrs. Ives wrote that he now needed, above all, Ellen's help—and he did not have it. Ellen, she thought, was approaching middle age and should long since have put away all childish things and developed mature values, but she had not. She did not know what she wanted. Mrs. Ives thought a man's career should come first and his wife should adapt to it. She could not, she said, understand women who were not content to be simply wives, mothers, women. The maid Alverta, she said, advised him not to run for office unless his wife wanted him to.

Paul Douglas, by now a captain with the First Marine Amphibious Corps, wrote to Stevenson on September 30 from the Pacific: "I am glad you are thinking of running for office. The state and the party need men like you. You know, however, what I think about the K-N [Kelly-Nash] crowd not wanting to have the Democrats win in the state, and I think their hold will have to be broken before we can build up a serious party in the state as such. . . . I have not given up all hope of getting into a combat outfit. . . . The usual objection is of course my age. . . . [He was fifty-one.] To be overseas and yet not see battle is a frustrating experience." Stevenson advised Douglas to apply for duty as a regimental adjutant and offered to help. (Douglas succeeded in getting combat duty and was badly wounded.) Stevenson wrote, "I appreciate your flattering comments regarding politics. I am still in a very indecisive state of mind and look forward to the possibility of being chosen as the candidate for Governor with grave misgivings and, unhappily, active disinterest. I feel that what I am doing here is wholly satisfying and the pros- spect of undertaking an ordeal like that is not attractive to me, particularly in war time. However, I have decided to coast along without saying anything definitely and see what transpires." He thought all possible candidates possessed liabilities; his own was that he was not well known. Milburn P. Akers, called Pete, political editor of the Chicago *Sun,* wrote that Stevenson wanted to run for Governor and had told prominent Illinois men in Washington so and that they in turn were writing about him to friends back home. Akers thought he was too little known.

On September 29, Stevenson gave Secretary Knox a memorandum which began: "I feel very emphatically that we should commission a few negroes." The Navy already had more than 60,000 Negroes and was getting 12,000 more each month. Ultimately the Navy would have Negro officers. "It seems to me wise to do something about it now." Specifically, he recommended commissioning ten or twelve Negroes selected from among civilians, as white officers were pro- cured, and a few from the ranks.

Ellen was in Libertyville that summer, and Stevenson gave up the house on R Street in Washington and shipped their belongings to Libertyville.

Ellen wrote to him from Libertyville September 23—she was getting a new maid; she and the help had made twelve pounds of but- ter and would send him some "if you're interested"; she would visit him in Washington when she had settled her servant problems. (Twelve pounds of butter was several weeks' ration.) Stevenson paid tuition at the Bell School in Lake Forest that fall. In Novem- ber, Adlai III told him his marks were improving, the barn was filled with alfalfa for the cows, and he had shot a rabbit, a pheasant, a pigeon, and a squirrel. It was the first wartime winter Ellen and the boys had spent in Libertyville.

Stevenson's speech October 8 to the Chicago Council on Foreign Relations was reported briefly in the New York *Times.* While in Chicago, Stevenson spent the weekend at the farm and saw Edison and Jane Dick and Richard Folsom. A few days later Folsom sent him an editorial from the Chicago *Sun* and told him that the ques- tion of a postwar world organization "may well be paramount" in next year's election—Stevenson's advocacy of one had been well re- ceived. Stevenson replied, "I only hope that popular approval of

post-war participation is sustained in Illinois in spite of the Tribune."
Isolationism was always much on Stevenson's mind. His uncle, Louis
Merwin, congratulated him on the Council speech and said he noted
that Stevenson was "being groomed for our future Governor." Stevenson replied, "If my occupancy of the Governor's chair is a matter
of personal inclination, it will be cold as far as I am concerned."
Jane Dick thanked him for the Council speech; he had sent her a
copy, as he sent copies of most of his speeches to a good many people. A lawyer friend in Chicago, David Bazelon, a man quietly active in Democratic fund raising (later Chief Judge of the United States
Circuit Court of Appeals in Washington), reported that a downstate
friend had told him Stevenson's candidacy for Governor was "a natural." Bazelon agreed and thought "spontaneous" committees should
be formed, and he asked Stevenson if such a committee was contemplated. Stevenson replied, "I have done nothing about encouraging
any voluntary, spontaneous committee organization and I really
don't know whether I should or not. . . . Nor do I know if anyone
else has it in mind tho sundry people have suggested something of
the kind. I would be glad to have your views. I had a fine talk with
Judge Igoe. He indicated that, although the Mayor was not too favorable, he was going to make some other inquiries and bring it to his
attention by other indirect methods again. For my part, I am still in a
quandary as to what I should do should the opportunity arise. I
wish I had a little more enthusiasm." This letter was written November 1. The slate-making committee would meet in December. But all
Stevenson's political maneuvering came to nothing. Courtney ran for
Governor (and lost); Lucas ran for Senator (and won).

Stevenson told Robert Sherwood that "my evenings with you are becoming the lamp-posts on my journey through Washington!" He went
out to Illinois again to speak November 26 at Great Lakes, and an
old friend stationed there said, "It hardly seemed as though you
were the Adlai I had known in time gone by." He was growing.

9

Stevenson had shown signs of restlessness during the year. Now he
obtained his third wartime mission outside the United States and the
first of which he himself was in charge: he led a special Foreign Economic Administration mission to survey the economic situation and
the problems of reconstruction in the parts of Italy that had been
taken by Allied troops. This meant a leave of absence as Knox's assistant. He became an employee of the Foreign Economic Adminis-

tration, where he had friends—Leo Crowley, administrator; Lauchlin Currie, Crowley's deputy; and George Ball, associate general
counsel. The New York *Times* said, "It will be the task of the mission to develop the first United States program for coordinated economic operations in a major liberated area." Stevenson's companions
would be an industrial engineer, an agricultural expert, and David
D. Lloyd, a member of the State Department's Italian Area Committee, who would be Stevenson's own assistant. (Lloyd later joined President Truman's White House staff and was involved in presidential
politics when Stevenson ran.)

Italy was the first territory on the mainland of Europe recaptured
by the Allies. Allied troops had landed in Sicily in July; Italy had
surrendered in September; Mussolini had fled; the new Badoglio government had declared war on Germany; but the Germans had occupied central and northern Italy, including Rome, and the Italian
campaign from October of 1943 to the end of the war in 1945 was
hard and costly. By December, when Stevenson arrived, the Allies
had taken Salerno and Naples but were stopped north of Naples at
Monte Cassino. Stevenson was following close on the heels of the
advancing Allied troops.

He and his companions left on December 7, 1943, and returned on
January 15, 1944. They spent a week in North Africa and about
three weeks in Sicily and Italy. Stevenson kept a diary for a time.
They flew to Miami and on through the night across the Caribbean to
British Guiana and then to Natal, Brazil. "God, what vast areas of
unused & useless land I've seen in the last couple of years!" he wrote.
They slept in a barracks and spent several hours "examining the hideous little town" of Natal—"all Latin American places look alike"
—then headed for Dakar "across the moonlit sea" to the western
hump of Africa, arriving about noon on December 10. President
Roosevelt, homeward bound from the conference at Teheran with
Stalin and Churchill, had left Dakar only the day before. On December 11, Stevenson arose at five and his plane took off at seven-thirty
across the desert, deviating from its course to search for a missing
military plane. Stevenson wrote a good description of the Atlas
Mountains, taking pains to erase a word in order to improve a sentence.

Next day was awful: "Up & off in darkness. The weather is thick
and we can see little of the ground. . . . As we approach Oran and
the sea the weather gets worse—bumpy, high wind, white fog rolling
in from the sea. All of a sudden we're across the water & then there
followed the worst hour I've ever had. The pilot was lost. The coast
is dangerous flying—mountains & valleys. He had to pull her nose

up sharp several times and almost turned me inside out & all the while the big plane was shaking like a leaf & the wind was howling as I've never heard it. It was raining torrents and the ceiling was 0. They put up a smoke screen on the ground that finally gave the pilot a fix & at last we landed." Stevenson traveled by plane a great deal all his life and had several near accidents but he always remembered that flight.

Once down, they had to stay overnight. They were sent to a French air force barracks but an OSS man "rescued" them and a colonel put them up handsomely in a villa. On the fourteenth he presented himself at General Dwight D. Eisenhower's headquarters but despite his letters of introduction, including one from President Roosevelt, he was unable to see Eisenhower and instead saw General W. Bedell Smith. Smith was helpful, telling him much about Italian politics. The billeting officer put him up in a hotel he called fourth rate—"no sheets, no hot water, tiny cell, dirty. What kind of reception is this for Pres. emissary!" He talked with other American officials about Italy. Harry Hopkins was there "with tales of the Pres. trip to Teheran." Stevenson spent two more days in Algiers, "endless conferences and planning," a meeting with Henri Bonnet, Minister of Information in the Free French Committee, meetings with intelligence officers and State Department people, and a visit to navy headquarters where he felt "more at home" and moved into a "beautiful villa."

On December 17 he left on the last leg of his trip, taking with him, he told Mr. and Mrs. Ives, "a bedding roll and a knapsack for luggage." That day Ellen sent him news of home: "The river is frozen solid and as smooth as glass. The boys' [Christmas] vacation started yesterday. . . . Adlai has muskrat traps set up & down the river under the ice. Yesterday he caught a muskrat and sold him for 1.50 —some night we can have muskrat 'stew'. Aren't you glad you're not home." The night before, the Kelloggs, Mowrers, Magnusons, and another woman had come to dinner and stayed till 1:15 A.M. "It was a *great* success! Alma, the new cook, *couldn't* be nicer (so far). . . . *Now* I'm going on a health cure—I'm going to be so sensible you'll be surprised. . . . We are all going in town to mother's on Xmas day. And where will you be??—Love from us all—and we miss you." She added a drawing and verse.

Stevenson reached Palermo, Sicily, December 18 and set to work interviewing people. He found forty per cent of the houses and large sections of most public buildings wrecked. The main problem was food. The harbor had been patched up by army engineers. Hoarding and black marketing were serious. The police were inadequate. Politics was confused and trouble seemed possible when the Badoglio government took over. Counterfeiting was widespread. The American Military Government (AMG) employed Fascists. Tactical forces had liberated eighty-five political prisoners who were also criminals. There was "a multiplicity of orders & regulations & no one" in charge.

He spent three days in Palermo, neglecting neither his sightseeing nor his work, then on December 21 set out on a survey of Sicily in a command car with a trailer for luggage. His diary described the scenery; his brown spiral notebook recorded conversations about the country's problems—shortages of materials and food, black marketing, expectation of chaos when government was turned over to the Italians.

On December 22 he crossed to mainland Italy with a Princeton classmate now an AMG officer. He found a scene of "devastation and destruction and utter defeat." Up the coast to Naples: "We land on the beach & churn up a rocky path thru a fishing village to main road where a British MP orders us south to Reggio Calabria to be checked in at the traffic control post and then we start the long journey N to Naples full of good spirits, K rations and expectations. The road rises and falls along the rocky coast around terraced vineyards past Scilla where we bid farewell to Charybdis and the Straits of Messina—the funnel of Greco-Roman history. The road & the rivers are incredibly beautiful—in the distance across the blue sea Stromboli lifts his conical smoking head out of the sea as he has always done and one thinks a little sadly of all the wars and all the legions that have passed before him along these shores. Everywhere the ragged smiling urchins beg for . . . anything to eat & the boys of any age shout—'Hello Joe, Gimme cigarette.'"

They spent the night at Nicastro, four in a room, with the bedbugs; they had breakfast on K rations on a deserted road. Seeing poverty, he wondered, "How is the Am. taxpayer to be persuaded that to help Italy at his expense is to help himself & perhaps his grandchildren." Even at that, things were better than they had been. In Naples, an officer told him, "When we came, no electricity, no kerosene, no candles, no water, no sewage, no transport, no telephone, no banks, Germans opened all prisons, no police, no fuel, no fire dept, no hotels except one—mined, streets closed, 500 babies, mayor had fled, no prefect, no government, no law courts. Most all now restored." Under Mussolini, everything had emanated from Rome. Now the country must be rebuilt region by region—and not the least of the problems was finding able experienced people untainted by Fascism. The difficulties of reorganizing a society torn to pieces by war come through vividly in Stevenson's notes.

One page of his diary, dirty and at one time wet, suggests he visited the front, or at least Caserta, forward headquarters below Cassino. He wrote: "Bridges all out—nothing but gulleys—signal wires hanging on trees along road like vines. People living in caves for months. . . . Town 98% destroyed." In a speech after he returned, he said, "I spent a day at the front and came away with a healthy respect for that war along the muddy, bloody, mountainous road to Rome. I wish I could describe that mud that has to be shovelled off the roads like snow and the cold penetrating rain, the stench of those ruined towns with the unburied dead in the rubble, the conditions in which the doughfeet—as they call them—live and fight, up and down those stony rugged mountains, supplied by donkeys, with the Germans and their machine guns and screaming mortars always above them on the next hilltop. . . . On the valley floor the olive groves have been shaved off close to the ground and the shell holes merge into one another. It looks like the western front in the last war. I stood on the rubble of what was San Pietro, only a few miles south of Cassino to watch our shell bursts. Cassino is just about half way from Salerno to Rome—and we landed at Salerno 6½ months ago."

In later years it became part of the Stevenson legend that he made his decision to go into politics during this mission to Italy. This is, as we now know, hyperbole—he had wanted to go into politics for at least thirteen years. Nevertheless, this mission to Italy made a deep impression on him. He himself once wrote, in an introduction to the book of speeches published after his 1952 campaign:

"I think it was in Naples on a wet, cold night in that ugly winter that I naively asked Ernie Pyle if the G.I.'s up at the front were much interested in the soldier-vote legislation I had just been working on in Washington. He looked at me incredulously. 'No,' he said, 'I don't think so, but I can tell you what they *are* thinking about. They're thinking about a dry spot where they can place their bottoms and wring out their socks.' Later I went up there in the mud and blood of the Liri Valley and saw for myself. He was right.

"Somewhere, there in Italy, I think, I read about a public-opinion poll which reported that some seven out of ten American parents disapproved their sons going into politics or public service, or something like that. From what I had already seen of the war at home, in the Pacific, in the Mediterranean and from what I was still to see in Europe, I've often thought of that little morsel of news: fight, suffer, die, squander our substance, yes; but work in peacetime for the things we die for in war, no! Small wonder, I thought, that our 'politics' is no better, and great wonder that it is as good as it is. It seems to me sad that 'politics' and 'politician' are so often epithets and words of disrespect and contempt, and not without justification, in the land of Jefferson and in a government by the governed."

Back home he submitted a report to Leo Crowley, head of FEA. "Italy presents a far greater burden upon Allied resources for relief and sustenance than had been expected." Unemployment, typhus, inflation, agriculture disrupted, much of industry destroyed by the German scorched-earth policy, governmental administration feeble —until now, all these problems had been handled by AMG. Soon the area would be restored to the Italians—the Badoglio government—under supervision of the Allied Control Commission. While the AMG had "done a remarkable job in Italy," military government had a "limited objective"—maintaining civil order in the rear of the advancing troops and prevention of disease among the civilian population. AMG did not import supplies to restore agriculture and industry and create employment, all urgent necessities. "The net effect of this policy has been to defer the major economic questions for future handling." The economic situation was bound to worsen. Italy would need Allied help. Increasingly the British were assuming control. While Britain had obvious objectives in the Mediterranean, the United States also had interests there. Russia had already shown an interest in U.S. and British policy toward Italy. This might increase. For all these reasons, close consultation among the Allies was essential after the war. No agency of the United States Government could assume sole responsibility for economic operations in Italy—the Army was busy with the war and the State Department with policy, the FEA could not handle currency and budgetary matters, Treasury could do the latter but no more. Therefore, the Allies must maintain in Italy a combined supervisory body as comprehensive in scope as the Allied Control Commission, with experts covering almost all aspects of the Italian economy and administration, responsible, first, to the Combined Chiefs of Staff and, after hostilities, to some other combined agency. The Allied Control Commission had already been established as a transition mechanism under the military theater commander. Stevenson recommended that the commission be gradually demilitarized and put under an Allied agency. Presumably we wanted to transfer to the Italians as rapidly as possible the burden of feeding and clothing the people and keeping them healthy. Presumably Congress and public opinion would support such measures. "If this is the present limit of policy decision, it should be made clear. And then the subsidiary questions should be clarified," and he listed several. He discussed Italian politics and detailed Italy's needs. He concluded: "The only safe assumption is that the factors of devastation, hunger, inflation, confusion and demoralization of economy and administration which have characterized Italy will be found in varying degrees behind the retreating German armies throughout Europe. Food and civil order will be the first requirement, but beyond this limited military objective are the other goals. Delay in planning and initiating essential rehabilitation will only injure local morale, multiply our burdens, prolong the period during which we must feed the populations, and impair our larger interest in laying the foundations of enduring peace."

Stevenson's report is noteworthy for several reasons. First, during the 1952 presidential campaign, Senator Joseph R. McCarthy would accuse Stevenson of having connived at bringing Communists into the Italian government. Stevenson would reply that on the contrary he had warned in his report against the spread of Soviet influence in the Mediterranean, and the report bears out what Stevenson said. Second, the report was an early harbinger of what became the Marshall Plan to reconstruct postwar Europe. Moreover, Stevenson saw this task as an essential ingredient of building an "enduring peace" and a system of world order. Characteristically, he broadened his mission from one to study Italy's economy to one to study the reconstruction of a society and, furthermore, he looked beyond Italy's borders to all Europe. Third, he instinctively favored taking reconstruction out of the hands of the military and giving it to civilians. Fourth, he criticized, though gently, AMG for using Fascist officials. While pointing out that AMG officers' directives instructed them not to sacrifice administrative efficiency to political ends and to retain Fascists if they thought them necessary, Stevenson reported "that in some cases at least AMG might have done better to ignore considerations of administrative efficiency. . . . [By retaining Fascists] they may have lost some goodwill and aroused misapprehensions among the population more damaging in the long run than inefficiency." This was a sensitive issue at the time. John J. McCloy, then Assistant Secretary of War, said in a speech in New York on March 5, 1944, that AMG had made great progress in removing Fascists: "The distinction which we have made . . . is the distinction between the active and notorious Fascists and those who were only nominal in their attachment to Fascism for the purpose of holding their jobs or keeping out of internment camps or some other such human motive." It is striking how many times over the years McCloy, a member of the Eastern establishment, and Stevenson disagreed— and also striking how successfully they worked together during at least one crisis.

Finally, the Italian report added a new dimension to Stevenson's concern with the shape of the postwar world. In a speech to the

Decalogue Society of Lawyers in Chicago in March, he closed with a paragraph that foreshadowed the idea he later developed as "the revolution of rising expectations": "I've traveled during this war in the Pacific, the Caribbean, South America, West Africa and the Mediterranean, and . . . no one has enough food, enough clothing, enough anything—except in the United States of America. And now all these people—black, brown, yellow, white—have seen our forces move thru; have seen our healthy boys, their clothes, their food, and their equipment. It makes you wonder about tomorrow. Are they envious; is more and worse trouble in the making, or is there a great opportunity to improve their lot and ours at the same time? The demand is there; is the wisdom here?"

10

Stevenson's report was widely circulated inside the government. A friend in the U. S. Embassy in London told him it was "by far the best job of this kind." Lauchlin Currie, deputy administrator of FEA, congratulated him. On January 27, Leo T. Crowley, head of FEA, asked Secretary Knox to release Stevenson to take charge of all FEA relief and rehabilitation activities. Crowley told Knox, "The President himself has indicated the importance he attaches to the work by authorizing me to select—and get—the most suitable man in Washington. Adlai Stevenson is uniquely qualified for the work." Another aide to Knox showed the letter to Stevenson, and Stevenson immediately wrote to Knox, who was ill, "I doubt if I care to go there at this time unless you think I should. . . . While you and Jim Forrestal are both away I think it would be well for me to be here. So I suggest you write him a note at least delaying any decision until you have returned." Knox did as Stevenson suggested. This ended the matter.

At about this time Stevenson had dinner with Barney Hodes and said he was unhappy working for Knox, talked about his political heritage from his grandfather, and asked if he had any political future. Hodes thought he might have if he returned to Illinois. Stevenson made other speeches in Chicago at this time, to the Legal Club and the Council on Foreign Relations, drawing on his Italian experiences. The Council's staff director, Louise Wright, told him, "You can run for any office any day now!" After one speech, a friend described the dilemma of "high-class" Republicans in Illinois: they opposed the *Tribune* but did not speak out for fear of helping

Roosevelt. Stevenson thought his letter "about as lucid a picture of the eternal morass . . . as I have seen. But what does one do?"

Ellen had spent the winter with the children at Libertyville. In February they had been snowed in briefly—"the children love it and so do I." She wrote, "When the weather clears, and my head clears —! I'll hope to pay you a visit—I'll write you a long letter soon—& don't *you worry*—I have enough faith to think that things will work out the *right way*—if we all try hard enough." On March 24 she wrote that she had been in bed with a cold and had used Christian Science. Adlai III was in his last year at the Bell School in Lake Forest, and Ellen had talked to its director about preparatory schools. He said "Exeter was tops" and did not require much Latin, Adlai's worst subject. "So," she wrote, "please do something about Exeter as soon as possible . . . and I will visit it and talk to the principal as soon as I can get away. . . . Adlai is doing very well at school and *is happy*—I had a long talk with him." She added, "I hope you aren't 'worrying'—it just makes everything worse—doesn't it?" On the back of the letter Stevenson penciled the name of the admissions director at the Phillips Exeter Academy in New Hampshire. It was Stevenson's start at a distressing effort to get his children into the schools and colleges he wanted.

It is doubtful, however, that the children's early lives were happy. In his early photographs, Borden looks sad. His mother picked on him. John Fell was her favorite. In later years Stevenson himself turned to Adlai III for advice and help. John Fell amused him and gave him pleasure. Borden he did not understand. In Stevenson's eyes, Borden was the one who was chasing girls, staying out late, sleeping all day, not working on the farm.

Stevenson met Ellen in Boston on April 21 and they visited Exeter and Milton Academy, then went to Washington together. Ellen had intended to stay only a few days but, on April 28, Secretary Knox died after a series of heart attacks. Mrs. Ives wrote in her diary that Stevenson's future was suddenly uncertain. Indeed it was. Undersecretary Forrestal was appointed Secretary. On May 19, Stevenson sent a note to Forrestal, saying he assumed Forrestal would want to reorganize his office and "I am, accordingly, submitting my resignation as Special Assistant to the Secretary to you herewith to take effect at your pleasure." It was the kind of resignation that one submits who feels that his relationship with his former chief cannot be re-established with his new one but who hopes that some new post will be found for him.

He may have known it was a vain hope. Although his letter of resignation to Forrestal was addressed "Dear Jim," they did not get along well together. When Forrestal moved up to Secretary, Stevenson hoped to move up to Assistant Secretary. Carl McGowan has recalled, "He kept waiting around to see if he'd be appointed. President Roosevelt wanted to appoint him, but when he proposed it to Forrestal, Forrestal opposed and said, 'He's too diffuse.' It's the beginning of this Eastern establishment view that Stevenson was a softhead. Forrestal, McCloy, Lovett, and Acheson thought of themselves as sharp and sophisticated intelligences. They believe that power, not kind words, decides things. This group was always anti-Stevenson, especially in private conversation. It gets down to the idea that they can't understand a guy that started Harvard Law School and didn't finish. They think of themselves as what intellectuals should be in government. Stevenson lacked the hard intelligence that big Wall Street lawyers had. He couldn't rise to be a leading partner in Dillon, Read. It turned out that Stevenson was an infinitely tougher guy than Forrestal. Forrestal cracked after a few months. Stevenson never did, even after the most terrible disappointments."

Stevenson himself once told George Ball that, before Knox died, Knox told him he was going to appoint him Undersecretary and had drawn up the papers, but died before signing them. After Knox's death, Forrestal stopped the promotion. George Ball says, "Stevenson was disappointed. He and Forrestal were different, that's all. Forrestal was brisk. He had come up Wall Street the hard way. He fancied himself tougher than hell. Forrestal really hated Stevenson. They were completely different temperaments. Forrestal was brutal and a son of a bitch. He made a fetish of being tough-minded—the kind of thing Adlai most abhorred. Forrestal made a cult out of being ruthless."

The admissions director at Exeter told Stevenson that Adlai III should take entrance examinations on May 31 and said he felt confident he would do well at Exeter. Stevenson told him May 8 that Knox's death had "complicated" his situation. If he was obliged to return to Chicago "it may be that we will have to make some adjustment in our plans." Stevenson was seriously considering Milton Academy, whose headmaster told him, "We should not like to put the slightest pressure upon you in the matter of reaching a decision and as you know we should be very happy if it eventually turned out to be in favor of Milton."

With no future at the Navy Department, Stevenson was trying to decide what to do. Four possibilities were open—to return to the Sidley law firm, to start a new law firm, to take another job in government, or to try to buy the Chicago *Daily News*. He talked about forming a new law firm with Ed McDougal but told him, "It would have to be temporary because I have politics in my blood and eventually I'll get into it."

Stevenson probably could have remained in government. He had lunch on June 28 with Archibald MacLeish and Raymond Gram Swing to discuss the problem of educating the American people on the need for the United Nations. He told Ed Austin he had received an offer from the Securities and Exchange Commission. Eugene Rostow of the State Department asked him to become general counsel and adviser to the French Supply Mission. Another State Department official, impressed by his report on Italy, asked him on June 27 whether he would be interested in becoming the Department's adviser on economic operations in China, working in Chungking.

As he had done leaving Washington ten years earlier, Stevenson wrote numerous farewell letters to friends. They were dated June 13, although his resignation did not become effective until September 13. Among those who replied cordially were men of high station, both in and out of official life.[5] Stevenson took with him a list of more than 300 people which he titled, "People I helped while in the Navy Dept." He had kept careful records of what he had done for each.

By the time Stevenson left, many of his Washington friends knew he was going home to try to buy the *Daily News*. George Ball wrote to him on June 15, "I can think of nothing better for Chicago and for the country generally than to have your plans work out. . . . If, however, your Chicago project doesn't materialize, I certainly hope you will return to Washington."

The long-awaited invasion of France on June 6 did not deter Stevenson. Indeed, the day before it occurred he sent an analysis of the *News* to Jesse Jones, the Texas capitalist and politician, and, the day after, he told an associate at his old law firm, "I hope to get away from here by the middle of next week to see if anything can

[5] Edward B. Burling of the prestigious law firm, Covington and Burling, in which Dean Acheson was a partner; Thomas M. Woodward; various people in the Navy, War, and State departments; Secretary Forrestal; Arthur Krock; Walter Lippmann; George Ball; John J. McCoy; Undersecretary of State Edward Stettinius; Byron Price; Raymond Gram Swing; Nelson A. Rockefeller; Ernest K. Lindley; William C. Bullitt; Supreme Court Justice Stanley Reed; Archibald MacLeish. All praised his work; many predicted he would return.

be done about the Daily News situation. . . . [Government] jobs can wait, but the News can't as the executors will want to do something within a reasonable time." It showed a single-minded purpose. From June until October he did little else, even though there was not only a war but a presidential and Illinois election going on (and the Democratic Convention was held in Chicago).

Stevenson himself always said that a group of long-time *Daily News* employees and executives urged him to form a group, that would include them, to buy the *News*. Among them were Lloyd Lewis, Paul Scott Mowrer, and Carroll Binder. He had known these men at the Council on Foreign Relations. They belonged to the *Daily News* of great tradition, the *News* which had built up one of the best foreign correspondent staffs in the world, had built a reputation as a forthright newspaper of independent judgment, one of the most articulate and intelligent papers on foreign affairs in the isolationist Midwest. The *Daily News* was something more than a businessman's property; it had a legendary aura about it. Mowrer, Lewis, Binder, and four other executives, in a letter to Stevenson formalizing their wish, spoke eloquently of the *News*'s tradition, their association with it, and their deep concern about its future. At this time Chicago was torn by the contest between Colonel McCormick's *Tribune* and Marshall Field's liberal Democratic *Sun*. Many Chicagoans hoped that the *News,* which had declined somewhat under Knox, would, under new management, regain its old high standing. It was in this spirit that Stevenson approached the purchase of the *News;* but it was in the spirit of a hardheaded businessman that he lost it to a harder-headed one, John Knight.

The negotiation was complicated, delicate, and protracted. Stevenson proposed to form a syndicate of men who would subscribe from $25,000 to $100,000 each (in most cases) to buy the *News*. He himself would subscribe about $250,000, borrowing most of it from Marshall Field. The *Daily News* employees would subscribe $235,-000. In his voluminous correspondence on the project, the phrase recurs that he was trying to put together a group of "the right kind of people," Chicagoans who would allow him to publish an independent paper. Once he assured Laird Bell, Stevenson's friend and an executor of the Knox estate, that the fact that he and Jesse Jones might be the only principals—as he intended at one stage—did not mean that the *News* would become a Democratic organ: "I can assure you . . . that partisanship is the antithesis of my view of a newspaper's responsibility for public enlightenment." For backers, Stevenson turned just where one would expect him to turn—to his Lake Forest and LaSalle Street friends and, additionally, a few people in the East.[6] Steve Hord and others helped raise the money. Lessing Rosenwald, whose immense wealth originally had come from the Sears Roebuck company, subscribed $400,000, the largest single amount.

Stevenson asked John Cowles's opinion of the *News*'s value. Cowles said that as a purely business proposition other newspapers might be sounder investments but that the *News* possessed an intangible prestige similar to that of the Washington *Post,* Washington *Star,* New York *Times,* or New York *Herald Tribune.* Cowles wrote, "There is an extremely heavy load of debt ahead of the Knox equity in the Daily News, and with tax rates what they are one could argue that it would not be sound business to pay a million and three-quarters, or possibly as much as two million, for that equity. On the other hand, a million and three-quarters and even two million may not be too high a price to pay for the control of such a fine and influential publication. If you want, more than anything else, to be head of the Chicago Daily News, I would advise you as a friend to go ahead and buy it if you can, on the theory that you might get deeper satisfaction from heading the Daily News than you could in any other way." It seemed like good advice but Stevenson in the end did not take it.

All summer long and into the fall, Stevenson traveled and wrote letters and held meetings ceaselessly, raising money, seeking advice, making computations. He was able to raise enough money to make what he considered a prudent bid. He originally had thought $1.8 million was all that was justified, and his first bid was $12 per share. In the end, he bid $13 per share, or $1,935,000. By October 1 the Knox executors had his bid of $13 and several higher bids, and Laird Bell told him a decision would be made that week. Stevenson believed the Knox executors, who were not bound to accept the highest bid, would prefer to sell to someone who lived in Chicago and would preserve the independent character of the *News,*

[6] The list of subscribers included William P. Sidley; Donald P. Welles, Edward K. Welles, Edison Dick, Dutch Smith, and William Burry, Jr., all of Lake Forest; Walter J. Cummings of the Continental Illinois National Bank; Ralph Bard; Henry Crown; Max Ascoli of New York, who was married to a Rosenwald and who later became editor and publisher of the *Reporter,* a liberal magazine; T. O. Thackrey, editor of the New York *Post* who was married to its owner, Dorothy Schiff; Lewis L. Strauss, then in the office of the Secretary of the Navy; Edward B. Burling, head of the Acheson law firm; Ronald P. Boardman, vice president of the City National Bank and Trust Company.

a belief supported by Knox's will. Stevenson told a friend the executors would have to choose between virtue and money and identified himself with virtue. At the critical juncture on October 4, although some of his backers would have authorized him to bid higher, he told Laird Bell he did not feel justified in raising his bid above $13. He did, however, ask Bell to give him a second opportunity if the executors declined his bid. Bell did—according to Stevenson, the executors received three bids at $15 per share, considered none of them desirable purchasers, and persuaded John Knight to match the $15 bid; and at that point Bell so informed Stevenson. But Stevenson told him on October 6, "I have thought over and discussed your proposal to sell to my group at the top price others have offered, and I must decline. I do not feel justified in asking my associates to go up and up. Nor do I feel justified, myself, in going to $15, or $16 if I could, merely to compete with someone else and to take possession of the paper by force of money. There is something more involved. If local ownership, continuity of control, and staff support are calculated to preserve the character and traditions of the paper and fulfill Colonel Knox's purpose, then I assume any merit in the project I have worked up has had your careful consideration and has been properly weighed against the advantages of more money elsewhere." He wrote Jesse Jones, "Mrs. Knox insisted on the full amount she could get elsewhere. Using other people's money, I did not feel disposed to go further." He told a closer friend, "I contemplate putting so much of my own money in this that I cannot afford to pay too much." Years later, campaigning in Texas, Stevenson encountered Jesse Jones, who told him he should have bid higher. More than once Stevenson expressed disappointment at having been unsuccessful.

11

The Stevensons decided to send Adlai III to Milton. Stevenson told Exeter they would either keep him home or send him to a smaller school. Adlai III received the impression that the decision to send him to Milton was largely his mother's. He has said, "She had friends with children at Milton, including Mrs. Graham Aldis, probably her closest friend in Lake Forest, and one of the Kellogg kids was there too. It was a training ground for Harvard. I was just *sent* there." Stevenson told the Milton registrar, "Adlai is a conscientious, diligent boy, quite self-reliant I think but perhaps a little immature. He is somewhat reserved. . . . He seems to me awkward at this stage. He is much interested in shooting and a fine shot for his age. His habits are normal, with a taste for reading which has not been well organized. . . . I suspect he will conform to the rules." Adlai III did not like Milton and felt confined and lonely. He saw little of his parents. "I had few contacts with Dad there except he would take us to a football game or two when he was in the East. I was always a passing student; the parents never had a great deal of concern over my academic problems. Dad always wrote—he was a great correspondent. Birthdays were a ritual—I received long tender letters from him and the same number of dollars as I was years old. The other boys did too. He was always generous with us about finances. To a fault. We never had an allowance—we just told him what we wanted. It was different with mother. I remember her extravagance, and his concern about it. I remember myself being shocked by it." At the end of his first quarter, Adlai III was passing everything except music.

Stevenson took little part in the election campaign that year, when Roosevelt defeated Thomas E. Dewey. After the Democratic Convention, Struthers Burt told Stevenson he thought Henry Wallace, dropped as the vice-presidential candidate, had a deep appeal to young people and would end up as President or as another William Jennings Bryan. Stevenson agreed, adding, "I don't even feel badly about his defeat in Chicago. It just seemed to me that in a way he was what this interval of history has all been about."

12

On November 2, George Ball telephoned him from Washington and said he was going to France the next day on a government mission and wanted Stevenson to go as his deputy. Paris had recently been liberated. Stevenson agreed (according to Ball), then called back an hour later and said, "What are we going to Paris for?" Ball replied, "You come on down here and I'll tell you." Stevenson said, "All right but I have to be back by Christmas because of Ellen." Ball promised he would. Stevenson noted in a journal, "Dreadful last minute scramble to get off. Ellen took me to Lake Forest. Hard to say goodbye in spite of all the practice I've had."

Ball's mission was a part of the Strategic Bombing Survey—an effort to determine the effects, military, economic, political, and social, of strategic bombing. After a briefing in Washington on November 3, the party left by plane November 4. It was headed by Franklin d'Olier. In it were Ball, Stevenson, Paul Nitze, and eight others. En route, Stevenson wrote in his journal, "We are advance noticed as V I P S—very important personages." In London he observed bomb damage in Berkeley Square, passed the hotel where he and Ellen had stayed in 1939, dined on pheasant with a friend "in his super elegant apt. at Claridges & almost broke my neck in blackout getting there. Home with flashlight." He found all American military and naval activities centered around Grosvenor Square, near where twenty-one years later he died. He ran into his cousin, Bud Merwin, on the street. He lunched or dined with such people as Lester Armour, Jan Masaryk, and members of the British aristocracy, jotted down wartime gossip and jokes about the famous—Eisenhower, Patton, Stalin, Churchill, Roosevelt, Goebbels—noted that the House of Commons had been "destroyed" and Westminster Hall hit. He spent a Sunday in the country, noting carefully the titles and accomplishments of the British guests. He and Ball were working together to "conspire" against what they considered bureaucracy that might smother the Survey. They went to Paris to evaluate tactical bombing during the Normandy invasion, landing "at shattered le Bourget," and took a bus into town: "Constant uncomfortable feeling that 'only yesterday' the Germans were everywhere as the Americans are today." They went to St. Germain, where they were quartered with a general "in a good, tasteless house," Stevenson wrote, "no coal, very damp & cold. . . . Indeed sleeping in that house was the most discomfort I had on the whole duty. . . . Very poor mess."

After a week's work, Stevenson and a general on Thanksgiving Day, November 23, headed toward the front with a "helmet, gas mask, bedding roll." They crossed the Marne, entered Château-Thierry in the rain, and walked through the Rheims cathedral. It had been little damaged, and they observed a wedding. Stevenson wrote in his journal, "Lunch at a transient mess—corned beef sandwiches and black coffee out of soup bowls with the G.Is. Thru beautiful, rolling country soaked with rain, streams flooded. . . . All bridges blown. Roads lined with abandoned vehicles, mostly German, but roads fine. . . . Thru the bunkers and pill boxes of the Maginot line along the Luxembourg frontier . . . into Luxembourg." He had a good dinner at the officers' mess in the hotel. The front was eight miles away—"gun flashes against low lying clouds. Went to concert by Lux. band with Major Charles Kindelberger and drank very weak war beer. Discussed our affairs relating to tactical bombing during battle of France."

He spent next morning at conferences with Air Force officers and in the afternoon went sightseeing. Next day he went on to Metz, still dangerous, noting bomb damage. He encountered General George S. Patton, Jr., "pearl handled pistols and all."

On November 26, Stevenson returned to St. Germain and spent two weeks there and in Paris and environs. His notes describe gay cocktail and dinner parties, theaters, the opera with French diplomats, British ladies, American admirals and generals, American journalists. George Ball came over from London from time to time, and one night when they were walking home in Montmartre about 2:30 A.M. they came upon American military policemen raiding an off-limits house of prostitution. Stevenson wrote in his diary, "Out emerged fine assortment of Am. officers all very angry and irritable and one Britisher, quite philosophical and good humored about it all. Very entertaining performance." Ball had recalled that the house was located—appropriately, as Stevenson observed—"on the rue Casanova. . . . Adlai and I, although civilians, were in uniform (we each had the assimilated rank of colonel) and hence were indistinguishable from the culprits. This created a situation of some hazard, for Adlai was enchanted with the spectacle of so many chagrined and choleric officers 'whose expectations and consummations' as he said, had been abruptly interrupted. He insisted on seeing the show, and at least twice his curiosity led him so far into the crowd that he found himself shoved into a paddy wagon. It took all the advocacy my colleague and I could muster to establish Stevenson as a noncombatant."

It must not be imagined that Stevenson regarded his mission as a lark. His travel diaries written on official missions always read like tourist diaries. What he did not put into them was the work he was doing. But he kept a separate notebook in which he scribbled notes on his interviews about bombing. They are almost meaningless today—names and figures and organizational details to buttress the impressions he formed. But they were important at the time. Ball himself has said, "He did a hell of a job. Worked very hard. He interviewed everybody. When he undertook any job like that he was absolutely tireless." If, in the 1960s, United States planners in Vietnam had paid more heed to the World War II Strategic Bombing Survey, they might not have been led so deeply into the morass of Vietnam, including the bombing of the North. Indeed, it was, in part, George Ball's experience with the 1944 Strategic Bombing Survey that led Ball, as Undersecretary of State in the 1960s, to argue before President Johnson that strategic bombing of North Vietnam never could bring Hanoi to its knees.

There is a jarring note in Stevenson's diaries, as there had been in his letters to his mother many years earlier when he "inspected"

Word War I battlefields. Now, touring the Ardennes Forest in a snowstorm on December 9 just before the Battle of the Bulge, he wrote, "Like fairyland. Will never forget that lovely winter scene—with the lines only a few miles east."

Adlai III wrote to him from Milton—he had passed his examinations, his work was "coming along all right." Ellen wrote November 19, enclosing a letter from Borden and saying, "Where are you—and what are you doing??—I wish a letter would hurry up and come." She had sat next to Marshall Field at dinner in town, and Field said that Stevenson would "do well' in the State Department, that President Roosevelt "thought very highly" of him, and that he regretted Stevenson had been unable to buy the *News*. John Fell added a note, "Dear Daddy, I miss you very much. love John Fell S. I hope you bring lots of souvenirs." Ellen signed her letter "love." She wrote again on November 27, saying his first letter had arrived and relieved her and the children. The maid was sick but "anyway, I guess, I was born to be a housewife." She had gone to the Saddle and Cycle Club with the John Farwells and danced till 2 A.M. She and a man had "cut quite a figure on the dance floor. What a funny little man." The Milton reports on Adlai III were good. "Everything is really fine—so don't worry about us. . . . I'm so sleepy most of the time (except when I go out!) I go to bed at 9:30—Will you be able to wake me up when you get home??—Take care of yourself—and don't do anything rash!! Goodbye, darlink. If you keep on going away I'll really have to turn myself into a letter writer—and that will be difficult!" Stevenson, despite travel difficulties and baggage restrictions, saved the letters.

George Ball has described their quarters in France: "We shared a large apartment in a run-down villa in Saint-Germain-en-Laye, which, a few weeks before, had housed the generals commanding the veterinary corps of the Wehrmacht—and, Adlai strongly suspected, 'their horses and other patients as well.' The winter of 1944–45 was unusually cold and we had no heat. At night we faced a tough decision. Should we spend the evening with an American general who had a coal stove but who, in Adlai's words, was a '14-carat bore,' or should we make out as best we could in our Arctic quarters? One evening with the general provided a definitive answer. 'I'd rather,' said Adlai, 'be frozen stiff than bored stiff.' During the nights that followed, we pursued a consistent ritual. We put on our overcoats and placed a bottle of gin on the table before us. There was nothing to drink with the gin but tap water purified with halazone tablets. Yet we made out. . . . Our conversation ranged widely, not limited to the work we were doing or the events of the day. We talked about our personal problems, our hopes and aspirations. Characteristically, Adlai asked as many questions as he answered." Stevenson was thinking about his future. "He was at loose ends, the *News* deal had fallen through, he was bored with the law—the firm gave him $6,000 a year and an office, but what he really was doing was making speeches. He talked about getting into politics— running for Senator or Governor. He said Ellen hated it all. He was keen to get home for Christmas to see her. He used to read letters from Ellen to me. He seemed to be confidential with you, but you never really got through to him."

Stevenson went back to the front December 10 for a few days. He passed through "the dragons teeth of the Siegfried line" and into Germany. "The big push is on. . . . Much supressed excitement and nervousness. . . . On to Aachen and thru the utter ruins of that ancient city of 150,000 and out on the bloody broad auto bahn to Eischwiler past woods shattered with shell fire and thru shell packed sodden ground. Every fox hole & every crater level with water." He conferred with General Terry Allen who was attacking from his forward command post in the basement of a bank. "Artillery banging away on all sides." He met with General Omar Bradley and other generals and thought them "very, very impressive." He toured radar installations and witnessed an experiment in blind bombing by automatic radar release. He studied engineering and transport problems in the battle of France. He went to Brussels and conferred with SHAEF officers about the Bombing Survey. In a plane to London they found England "utterly fogbound"—the pilot tried several airports and finally, with only thirty-five minutes of fuel left and night coming on, found a hole in the fog over a runway and miraculously landed at an RAF training station. "Tea! No customs or immigration formalities and then a 5 mile bus ride . . . thru the fog." Returning home after Christmas, Stevenson brought with him another long list of people to telephone or write about their husbands or friends whom he had met in Europe.

13

The new year, 1945, began; Stevenson was almost forty-five years old; what would he do? It was becoming a perennial question. Early in the year he wrote to, telephoned, and talked with many people in Chicago and Washington, opening possibilities, considering them, trying to keep himself loose to do what ultimately seemed best. He once made a list of jobs he had been offered in 1945.[7] The related correspondence leaves the impression, as he would have hoped, that it was always a case of "the job seeking the man," not of the man seeking the job. Both things are true—he sought the job and it sought him.

In 1945 he did not really want to return to law practice but wanted a public career; yet he did not formally ask for a public job and if one was offered he feigned reluctance. The fact is that government needs able men; Stevenson was an able man, and by early 1945 he had good connections and a good record, he saw important people and let it be known he was available though he felt he should return to the law and to Ellen at Libertyville. And in 1948 the Democratic Party needed him in Illinois and in 1952 it needed him nationally. In 1948 he wanted to be Governor but would have preferred to be Senator; in 1952 he wanted to be President but did not want to run that year; and so he hesitated. From all this arose two impressions: among his friends, he was forever answering the call to public service; among his enemies, he was indecisive. The fact seems to be, rather, that Stevenson was a man with a driving ambition to go as far as he could in public life, that he explored as many avenues as possible, that he kept himself available and yet was careful not to burn his bridges—the law—behind him, that those in power recognized his ability and needed and wanted him, and that at each fork in the road he made up his mind which to take only after he had thoroughly explored all and when events finally forced a decision.

Some jottings he made at about this time indicate his state of mind about returning to the law:

Too old
Time
Bench
College
DA

[7] Chief, Economic Mission to Italy with rank of minister and member of Allied Commission; chief, Economic Mission to United Kingdom with rank of minister; chief, Office of War Information, London, with rank of minister; general counsel, Surplus Property Board; member, Securities and Exchange Commission; deputy director general, United Nations Relief and Rehabilitation Administration, London, in charge of all operations on Continent; assistant to Dean Acheson, Assistant Secretary of State in charge of legislative matters and international conferences; assistant to Archie MacLeish, Assistant Secretary of State in charge of information; Assistant Attorney General, Lands Division or Criminal Division; member, Federal Communications Commission.

Dull practice—"don't know what it is"
Unhappy
Have a right to come back
Wouldn't be content to do Wassling's work—estates
Get clients because competent—not on basis of friendship.

Perhaps he made those notes in connection with a conversation with Ed Austin. Austin has recalled, "He was torn badly between external interest in world affairs and a sense of frustration in doing things that bored the hell out of him. To a man with his background in public life and his age, it must have been frustrating to be doing work for other partners. He did not have his own clientele. Once he came in to talk to me about his appointment as an alternate delegate to the United Nations. He said, 'How did you develop your clientele?' I told him it was luck. He said, 'Hell no. You've told me and the other young men that the way to get a clientele is to do the most excellent work and do your best for your client and stick to high ethics.' I said yes. Stevenson said, 'I don't have any list of clients and I'm sure you did from the time you left law school.' I said, 'That's true but you've done nationally important public service and I haven't.'"

Now in January Stevenson was back in Chicago, ostensibly to resume his practice. He made a trip to Bloomington to talk to Joe Bunting of the *Pantagraph* about the Farm Bureau's dissatisfaction with the paper's farm policy. Bunting was negotiating for the *Pantagraph* to buy a half interest in radio station WJBC for $40,000; Stevenson became involved. Until Bud Merwin returned from the war in October, Stevenson interested himself considerably in *Pantagraph* affairs. On February 16, Archibald MacLeish, by now Assistant Secretary of State for Public and Cultural Relations, asked Stevenson to come to work for the State Department to help MacLeish inform the American people about foreign affairs and to promote communication among the peoples of the world. It was an eloquent letter, indicative of how people felt at that time about building a better world when peace came, pleading with Stevenson to help.

American and Allied planning for the shape of the postwar world had been going on a long time. Even before Pearl Harbor, Roosevelt and Churchill had signed the Atlantic Charter. On January 1, 1942, the nations at war with the Axis had signed the Declaration by United Nations, affirming their adherence to the principles of the Charter. Various groups had met to discuss postwar world organization, most importantly at Dumbarton Oaks in Washington from

August 21 to October 7, 1944. In early February of 1945 the Yalta
meeting was held; from it came the agreement to meet at San Francisco on April 25, 1945, to write the charter of the United Nations
Organization.

On January 23, Edward Stettinius, by then Secretary of State,
wrote, "Dear Adlai, If there is any possible way in which you can
arrange your affairs to join us in the Department, move Heaven
and earth to do so." (The letter was signed simply "Ed"; Stevenson,
proud of it, noted at the bottom, "Edw. R. Stettinius, Sec'y of State."
He often identified letters from prominent people.) On January 25,
Stevenson wrote to MacLeish, "This is the hardest letter I've ever
written! The answer is no." He pleaded the need to meet his family
obligations and to make a living. Perhaps he could return to government when the children were grown. "Don't say, 'It will be too late
—now is the time!' because you might be right." And he added a
postscript: "Reading this over leaves me as confused as you will be.
In short, I want to come but I don't feel I should." The letter contained more than a hint that Ellen opposed his going. On January
29, perhaps not having yet received that letter, MacLeish telegraphed him, "Please wire me that you are coming and soon." On
the bottom of that telegram Stevenson drafted a reply declining but,
once more, hedging the refusal: "But my conscience is also troubled
and it has been a difficult decision. I hope to be in Wash. next week
and will talk to you." MacLeish did not give up. On February 12 he
telegraphed Stevenson—he was writing Sidley asking him to arrange
things so Stevenson could come. On the bottom of the telegram
Stevenson penciled a reply, "Will report next Tuesday I hope you'll
be sorry! Regards." Why he changed his mind we do not know.
Perhaps another job he wanted worse failed to materialize. Perhaps
he finally obtained Ellen's agreement. Perhaps he simply wanted to
clarify his duties or his title—his initial appointment gave him the
title of "Special Assistant to Assistant Secretary Mr. MacLeish" at
$8,000 a year but later his title became "Special Assistant to the
Secretary" and "Deputy to Mr. Stettinius," much higher rank. Stevenson by now was wise in the ways of the bureaucracy.

He went to Washington on or about February 19 and went to
work in MacLeish's office (he was in fact MacLeish's assistant,
though he sometimes jumped the track and worked directly for the
Secretary). He told people it was a "temporary emergency job in
the State Department." He received the usual congratulations from
friends and admirers. Ellen stayed in Libertyville and wrote to him
about the boys, the servants, her social life, the farm. Still her letters
sounded much the same as they had many years earlier. His had

lost their boyish quality; hers were still girlish. In one letter she wrote:

Dear Ad—

Sunday night—I've washed the last child and the last dish—at last! Yesterday and today were beautiful days—Temp. 42—almost all the snow has disappeared—our pregnant sheep & pregnant Beatrice [Beatrice Holland, wife of Frank Holland, 'the farmer'] wander about the pregnant fields—Frank sees that the ewes (and Bea) take a walk every day—a good expectant father—& shepherd —don't you think? Lots of love, darling. The boys *really* miss you—and the fire hasn't been lit since you left.

She closed, "Love, Ellen." She was trying to make plans for Adlai III to come home for Easter vacation and wished Stevenson could come too. She wrote, "I feel as though you were in Tibet. Love, Ellen." It is hard to reconcile these letters with the tales about their quarrels and the fact that four years later she divorced him. Possibly she wrote other letters less loving which he destroyed.

On April 4 the Secretary of State spoke to the Chicago Council on Foreign Relations, an occasion which Stevenson arranged. He wrote the speech and accompanied the Secretary. Ellen went to Washington. President Roosevelt died on April 12, 1945. Archibald MacLeish wrote the proclamation for President Truman on Roosevelt's death with, Stevenson noted, "very little help from AES" the night of April 12. (When President Kennedy was assassinated in 1963, Stevenson recalled this occasion.) MacLeish inscribed a copy to Stevenson. Ellen stayed on briefly in Washington. Returning, she wrote, "Darling, I had a good time—It's nice to be married!! I won't feel like a spinster again—for at least a month! Take care of your *health* (or they may be mistaking me for your granddaughter *next*)." They were as usual trying to make plans to send the children somewhere for the summer. (A friend has suggested their purpose was to get rid of them.) Stevenson wanted them to go to Culver Military Academy in Indiana but it could not take them.

The conference in San Francisco to establish the United Nations would begin April 25. MacLeish went there in advance, intending to stay for the first week of the conference, when Stevenson would replace him. Stevenson had lunch with Ed Austin and told Mrs. Ives he now thought he could work out a satisfactory arrangement with the law firm which would give him freedom for outside activities. He told Bud Merwin, "It has been interesting, and I hope, useful, but I expect to get home for keeps this summer—it has been four years now and it's high time."

Stevenson did not go to San Francisco on schedule. Instead, on May 1, with the surrender of Germany imminent, he became involved in the State Department's public relations problems. He sent a memorandum to Acting Secretary Joseph Grew anticipating questions the press would ask the State Department upon surrender. Next day, after enlisting the help of Assistant Secretary Dean Acheson, Stevenson strongly urged Grew to release the full story of surrender negotiations immediately—doing so would show the world we were quick to reject Himmler's proposal to go on fighting the Russians, would debunk Hitler's martyred death; and would tell the story authoritatively once and for all instead of letting it dribble out piecemeal from Churchill, Eisenhower, and others. In the first days of May, as the American army captured Field Marshal Karl von Rundstedt of Germany and Stalin proclaimed the fall of Berlin, as the Germans surrendered in Italy and finally all German military forces surrendered officially at General Eisenhower's headquarters, Stevenson continued to bombard Grew with memos urging authoritative disclosure. He once said it was at this time, in fending off the press, that he learned to answer questions with "yo," a combination of yes and no. (Years later, as ambassador to the UN in the 1960s, Stevenson pretended he had invented "yo" only recently.)

The eight American delegates to the San Francisco Conference, led by Secretary Stettinius, had met first on March 13 in the State Department. Over the weeks that followed they worked out a United States position. They also chose their advisers, including five "principal" advisers from State—John Foster Dulles was one of these. In addition, the delegation was joined in San Francisco by MacLeish, two other assistant secretaries, and Stevenson, who was listed as a special assistant to the Secretary. Seventeen advisers were appointed from other departments and agencies, including Abe Fortas, then Undersecretary of Interior; Harry D. White, Assistant Secretary of Treasury; Charles F. Brannan, Assistant Secretary of Agriculture; and John J. McCloy, Assistant Secretary of War. In addition the delegation had four more members of Congress; fourteen political and liaison officers, including Dorothy Fosdick, who was special assistant to the Secretary General of the delegation. The Secretary General was Alger Hiss. Hiss signed Stevenson's identification card at San Francisco.

The United States delegation stayed at the Fairmont Hotel, high atop Nob Hill in San Francisco, which was and always remained Stevenson's favorite San Francisco hotel. In later life Stevenson recalled those days fondly. The work, however, was hard and grinding. Stevenson drafted a statement for Secretary Stettinius asserting the right of any nation to a hearing in the Security Council. He and John Foster Dulles drafted a proposed statement on the veto for the five permanent members of the Security Council. On behalf of Mac-Leish he dealt with a memorial from the press proposing that the human rights enumerated in the Charter include freedom of speech, press, communications, and exchange of information.

But Stevenson's principal function at San Francisco was to inform the press unofficially about what was going on—to "leak" information to them. According to two New York *Times* reporters who were present, Arthur Krock and James Reston, the official spokesmen for the United States delegation at the outset told the press little, while the Soviet, British, and other delegations talked freely. On behalf of the press at large, Krock and Reston complained to Stettinius and proposed "a leak office" run by Stevenson. After this, Reston has recalled, Stevenson, Thomas K. Finletter, or another man would see the press informally every day and tell them what was happening. "This was one of the few conferences," Reston has said, "where the press was handled really well." Stevenson told the press so much, in fact, that he got in trouble with United States delegates. Once, the American position was published in the New York *Times* before the delegation had even acted, and at a meeting delegates wrathfully protested poor staff work and threatened to call the President while Stevenson cowered in a corner; but as the delegates left, Vandenberg and Stassen winked at him approvingly. Stevenson thought it foolish to negotiate diplomatic arrangements that required the support of Congress and the people without enlisting the aid of the press. Stevenson, in later years as a candidate and public official, was often critical of his own press officers.

Stevenson was in San Francisco almost two months. He and Mac-Leish lived together for a time. Ellen visited him briefly. After she went home, Stevenson wrote, "Yesterday was the top drama—the Big 5 met for 2½ hrs in the AM and 2 hrs, in the PM—& I got to bed very late & very tired after a long [and] futile struggle trying to work out a Big 5 statement with the Russians, British et al. . . . It's an awful spot to be on—backgrounding Big 5 meetings when negotiations are at such a delicate point with our Russian friends. I'm getting awfully tired & never getting out of doors is depressing. . . . Poor Gromyko can't spit without permission from Moscow."

The impasse was broken, the conference adjourned. Secretary Stettinius thanked Stevenson for his work. On June 28, Stevenson spoke to the annual meeting of the Chicago Bar Association. After explaining the press's role and his work, he discussed the Charter's substance. (The Senate commenced consideration of the Charter that same day.) He anticipated and rebutted criticisms of the Charter—that the Security Council's tools were inadequate for its task, that the General Assembly was only a debating society, that the World Court could not compel member states to accept its jurisdiction, that the trusteeship system was a fraud. He said the veto was essential given the present condition of the world. He thought the Charter superior to that of the League of Nations. He said the press had emphasized the disagreements, not the agreements, at the conference and said that while "it *is* difficult to work with the Russians," one must understand why—their negotiators lacked the latitude ours had, they were only now emerging from a long isolation, they were understandably suspicious of the Western states. He pleaded for understanding of the Russians. They would insist on surrounding their borders with friendly governments but would make use of the UN to advance their interests. Moreover, they needed peace to restore and develop their shattered, backward country. "I have no illusions that there will be many years of difficulties, misgivings, and contentions, which only patience, firmness, and organized reason in the forum of the world can resolve. . . . The Charter. . . is only paper and no better and no worse than the will and intentions of its five major members . . . particularly the United States, Russia, and Britain." For twenty years he worked to persuade people of the UN's worth—and during part of that time he enhanced its worth considerably himself.

14

He returned to Washington June 29. James F. Byrnes was sworn in as Secretary of State July 3, replacing Stettinius. Once again Stevenson's chief had been replaced. Byrnes was not as close to MacLeish and Stevenson as Stettinius had been but he did not dislike Stevenson as Forrestal had. Stevenson told Byrnes he was briefing witnesses appearing before the Foreign Relations Committee and when the Charter was ratified he would have fulfilled his commitment to Stettinius and MacLeish and intended to resign and return to Chicago. Stevenson received the Distinguished Civilian Service Award. People congratulated him, including Sidley, and Stevenson replied, "It was good of you to write me and it made my meager honor seem much more significant." The Washington *Post* published a photograph of Grandfather Stevenson, mislabeling it one of Stevenson. Stevenson told Clay Tate of the *Pantagraph* he might be back in Chicago "for keeps" before the summer was over. He still considered starting a new law firm in Chicago—talked about it to Ed McDougal, Jim Oates, and Stephen A. Mitchell, a Chicago lawyer who had just opened his own law firm and who, later, managed Stevenson's 1952 presidential campaign. Ed Austin wrote, "I hope you will canvass the subject of coming back here very fully with all of us before deciding on any other course." It was another of the periodic decision points in Stevenson's life. On July 26 he wrote a revealing letter to Archibald MacLeish:

I don't think I "rate" your job should the Secretary accept your resignation—that is, I have no distinction and little experience in the field of information, cultural relations, etc. I'm just a low order of country lawyer with a congenital taste for public service, politics, politicians and the public trough where my family have been nibbling, frugally, albeit, for several generations. My only other attributes are acquaintance around Washington, agreeable, inoffensive manner untarnished with aggressive ideas (in spite of my Navy citation!), and a long, if superficial, familiarity with foreign relations —with a slight predisposition for the economic.

Add to the foregoing, restlessness, ambition (wholly undirected) and a strong feeling that after four years here I should get back to the prairies and act like a responsible husband, father and breadwinner instead of a piecework man in Washington. Having no other talents or opportunities, I suspect I'll have to do my winning at the law—ho hum! But then maybe after several years of being a good citizen and a *good* Democrat in a town not over endowed with either, perhaps I'll get another chance when the boys are grown and off to school. (But I hope the Secretary doesn't press me—I can resist anything but temptation, as you know.)

Meanwhile, I hope the Department will keep me in mind as an "expert" on most anything, should there be opportunities to serve on missions, commissions, conferences, etc., for private citizens for limited periods. Maybe it would help to fool the clients and the politicians—and it would make life on LaSalle Street tolerable!

MacLeish replied that Stevenson's description of himself reminded him of the old British travel books about America—landscape was always recognizable and the natives picturesque but "the only trouble was that the distinguished authors had never seen the things they looked at."

Stevenson went home to Libertyville. But he left behind time bombs. The San Francisco Conference which wrote the UN Charter had established a Preparatory Commission to bridge the gap between the signing of the Charter and the convening of the first session of the UN. The Preparatory Commission would meet in London next fall. Stevenson wanted to become a member of the United States delegation. Later he told Ed Austin he had "succumbed to considerable pressure to go to London" for the Preparatory Commission. But the fact is that when he left Washington he left behind a letter he himself drafted; it was addressed to Secretary Byrnes by Undersecretary Grew and it began, "Archie MacLeish has asked me to bring to your attention a matter which weighs rather heavily on his mind." It recited how Stevenson had reluctantly joined MacLeish with the understanding he would leave when the Charter cleared the Senate and would not be pressed to stay. "MacLeish considers this a personal obligation on his part, and one on which he must make good and so do I. But"—and this was where Stevenson made the real point—"Stevenson is more than anxious to meet your wishes, so instead of separating from the Government, he has gone home on leave without pay to see his family and will be available if and when you want to see him on short notice. He is on his farm at Libertyville, Illinois, telephone—233-J and does not intend to resume his business in Chicago immediately in any event."

Stevenson stayed in Libertyville only briefly, then went back to Washington to maneuver his own appointment to the United States delegation to the Preparatory Commission. MacLeish resigned from the government and was replaced by William Benton, chairman of the board of the Encyclopaedia Britannica, and Stevenson advised him on press relations. By August 22, Stevenson's appointment was assured: he received a travel order from the Department of State authorizing him to go to London with the United States delegation; and on September 4, President Truman appointed Stevenson deputy United States representative on the Preparatory Commission with the personal rank of minister. Secretary Byrnes announced Stevenson would be the alternate delegate for Stettinius and his "first deputy."

Stevenson had already drafted the "pressure" letter to Ed Austin, giving his formal title and rank, saying he would direct a staff of twenty-five to fifty, anticipating that the commission's work could be completed by Christmas. "I hope then to come home and pick up where I left off. Meanwhile, in view of my prolonged absence and indecision, I feel that I must say to you and through you to the firm that I consider you no longer in any way obligated to me as a former partner; that I am full of gratitude for all the consideration and genuine friendship you have shown me. . . . You can be sure that when I return to Chicago for keeps, the office will be the first place I will go. If there is then no position for me, I will be neither surprised nor hurt. . . . So please consider this a 'mutual release.'" Although he drafted the letter on August 31, he seems not to have sent it until September 4, the day his appointment became official. It was the first clean break with the Sidley law firm, and he did not make it until he was sure of the government job.

Ed Austin replied, "Speaking as your friend rather than as your partner, my main concern is that you do not detract from your career by trying to ride too many horses." He pointed out that Stettinius had been a distinguished steel corporation executive before entering public life and said if he had tried to continue both he would not have done well in either. "I would like to see you carry on whole-heartedly either as a public man, or—with our firm—as a law-yer. . . . I am skeptical as to how you will come out if you try to 'play in both leagues.'" He called Stevenson's tender of a full release to the firm generous and said he was glad that Stevenson intended to make the office his first stop when he returned to Chicago—and he would be delighted if in the end he returned to the firm "on a really fulltime basis." Stevenson's senior partner, William Sidley, wrote a warmer letter: "[I] have great sympathy with you in the ordeal which you are undergoing with reference to a career. If it will be of any comfort to you, I will say that I think you did the right thing in accepting this London assignment. . . . Much as I would like to have you return here for a full time partnership, I am even more interested in your making the right decision in your own interest. You have a wealth of ability, character and intelligence which I wish to see put to the fullest possible use, and if the diplo-matic or public field is likely to bring you greater distinction and happiness, then I am for it. . . . You will always find a warm wel-come in this office, whether you come as a permanent resident or a transient guest."

Ellen would join him in London with Adlai III and Borden on September 15. They would leave John Fell with Ernest and Buffie Ives at Libertyville. Stevenson told Jim Oates he had insisted: "That I wasn't going to be separated from my family any longer with the war over was the one resolution on which I never wavered." He would be paid at the rate of $9,800 per year, plus $25 per diem, he told Oates, "so taking the family won't be too disastrous."

Alone in an army plane Stevenson left Glenview Naval Air Sta-tion outside Chicago at 8:30 A.M. on September 3, 1945. After a Washington stopover, he went on board the *Queen Elizabeth* in New York with Secretary Byrnes and his party. He shared a cabin with an expert on waterways but immediately found more convivial company—Anne O'Hare McCormick of the New York *Times;* a correspondent for the Philadelphia *Bulletin;* Robert Kintner, vice president of the American Broadcasting Company, and his wife—and they all went ashore for a sandwich and champagne at the fashionable Stork Club, encountering en route difficulty with army security officers and being joined by Turner Catledge of the New York *Times* and others, returning to the ship late and sailing at 5:30 A.M.

Stevenson received the usual congratulations from friends in Chicago, Washington, and New York. One of his law partners said Mayor Kelly thought highly of him. Clearly his new prominence, not as "somebody's assistant" but as an alternate delegate to the commission, was not doing him any harm in Chicago if he wanted a political career. If one feels a twinge of sympathy for his friends there who took at face value his statements that he had "succumbed" under pressure to his country's call to duty when in fact one knows that he called his country, one must admire the skill with which he kept his lines open to Chicago and at the same time threaded the maze of appointive politics in Washington. In doing so, he showed a real politician's flair, manipulating people and events so they came out where he wanted. He knew what he wanted and he knew how to get it.

15

The crossing on the *Queen Elizabeth* was pleasant. Charles E. ("Chip") Bohlen, a State Department Russian expert and later ambassador to Russia and France, moved into Stevenson's cabin. Stevenson enjoyed "much hilarity in the evenings at cocktails in the [James] Dunns' cabin" and played checkers late into the night with Ben Cohen. Once during the crossing he had lunch with Secretary Byrnes. Byrnes's attitude toward Russia seemed to Stevenson "emphatic and firm." Byrnes and Stevenson talked politics, too—Byrnes thought Stevenson probably should return to Chicago after the Preparatory Commission meetings if he was not going to do anything politically.

They arrived at Southampton September 10, and Stevenson was driven to London in a car sent by Stettinius, was lodged at Claridge's, and had dinner with Stettinius and several others. Next morning he went to work. Three issues consumed much of their time: whether the commission should proceed rapidly, whether the first meeting of the General Assembly should be largely organizational, and whether the permanent site of the UN should be in the United

States or Geneva. Stevenson found himself aligned with the Russians and Chinese and opposed to the British in wanting to proceed rapidly, keep the first Assembly organizational, and locate the UN in the United States. The discussions went on day after day. Stevenson wrote in his diary, "Interminable talk—am constantly amazed by the prolixity of international discussions." At the same time he was hunting a house for Ellen, the children, and himself. One night he dined as P. J. Noel-Baker's guest at the Ritz with Stettinius; John G. Winant, U.S. ambassador to Great Britain; and Gladwyn Jebb, executive secretary of the Preparatory Commission; and he noted in his diary, "Good food, wine and talk, and notable progress with Noel Baker" on proceeding rapidly. (Noel-Baker was a British cabinet minister.) So the days passed—official Executive Committee meetings, private talks with ambassadors and other delegates, lunches and dinners with them and with journalists and British friends, cocktail parties, receptions: indeed, Stevenson's crowded journal of that fall is remarkably similar to his calendar during the years in the 1960s when he was ambassador to the UN in New York. Work proceeded not only in official meetings but at lunch, cocktails, dinners, and on into the evenings. He saw Lady Mary Spears, Ellen's aunt, and her British husband, General Spears. He visited Ronald Tree at his great country house, Dytchley. Ronald Tree had been born in England of American parents and had married a niece of Lady Astor and lived in the United States in the early 1920s. His mother was Ethel Field, daughter of Marshall Field I. He inherited wealth from Chicago real estate. Lambert Tree, his grandfather, was a judge and ambassador, was involved in Democratic politics, and once ran on the same ticket as Stevenson's grandfather. In the mid-twenties Tree went to England to live and became a member of Parliament. During the war he was in Churchill's junior cabinet and worked hard at bringing Americans and Englishmen together. Thus he had met Stevenson, and Stevenson now visited him several times at Dytchley. Later Tree's second wife, Marietta, became Stevenson's intimate friend.

When he could, Stevenson went walking in Kew Gardens "in a cool wind and fleeting sunshine." He attended an "impressive" service at Westminster Abbey commemorating the Battle of Britain. He dined with Byrnes and Dulles and talked about the Foreign Ministers Meeting being held concurrently and going badly—the U.S.-U.S.S.R. division was widening, the cold war was about to begin. He met with the Big Five—"Gromyko, Massigli, Noel-Baker and Victor Hoo. Found Noel-Baker hostile to any Big Five agreements, but the others pleased. . . . Gromyko seems to be getting more cordial and agreeable. . . . Long meeting of the committee on permanent site, at which I was happy to be able to contribute a few simple sentences here and there that somewhat perceptibly seemed to speed up the procedure. Drafting among fourteen people in two languages was not easy. . . . Dinner with !" Who "!" was we do not know; but a friend has recalled that when Ellen arrived she was jealous of Stevenson's British secretary, and Dave Merwin in a letter at the time said Stevenson had "the most beautiful secretary in all England." On the other hand, an entry in Stevenson's diary a little later reads, "Dorothy leaves for week" and another, "Theatre— Arms & the Man with F," suggest that he was seeing Dorothy Fosdick, who later became his intimate friend.

Ellen and the boys arrived September 29. Stevenson had found a house at 2 Mount Row in Berkeley Square. They put Adlai III and Borden in Harrow and they got along well. Young Adlai has recalled, "We commuted to school and spent weekends sightseeing in the country, calling on Lady Astor and Ronny Tree." Stevenson told Mrs. Ives about Ellen's arrival, saying, "But with the problems of coal, food, servants, etc., she has ended up right in the kitchen again and will have her hands full." Stevenson had read a letter to Ellen from Beatrice Holland, the wife of the farmer at Libertyville; she complained about the way Mrs. Ives treated her. Stevenson told Mrs. Ives, "Please understand that we have literally used every possible device to keep this couple with us for the last five years and it would be most disturbing if anything should happen while we are gone. . . . I hope you will do your *level best* to keep this in mind and treat them with the utmost friendliness and cordiality and try to preserve the situation even if you don't get the service or attention that you want. . . . Believe me, it's a matter of prime importance to me and my peace of mind." It was not the only time that Stevenson felt obliged to mediate between his sister and his servants or friends.

Ellen joined Stevenson in the social life attendant upon his work. The day after she arrived they entertained three Chicago *Daily News* correspondents at cocktails. In ensuing days they dined at the Ritz with General and Lady Spears, had James Dunn and his wife for cocktails, went to a dance at the Dorchester, had cocktails at Claridge's with Settinius, several times went to the theater.

Stevenson did not neglect correspondence with people back home. Samuel Levin, manager of the Chicago Joint Board of the Amalgamated Clothing Workers, referred to their last conversation about Stevenson's running for Governor or Senator and said he still hoped he would. Stevenson replied that the Preparatory Commission work was going well, that it should end in December, and "Not long thereafter I hope to be home for keeps and will look forward to more enlightenment from you!" Stevenson, leaving Chicago, had telephoned or written notes to many people there. One of them, Federal Judge William J. Campbell, a prominent Chicago Democrat, wrote, "Please accept my hearty congratulations upon your high appointment. The publicity on it has been wonderful. I have carefully gone over all of the clippings. I think it fits very well into the program which we discussed regarding your personal future." Ed McDougal wrote at length about forming a new law firm with Stevenson.

When Stettinius fell ill on October 16 and had to return to the United States, Stevenson, as his alternate, took charge of the United States delegation—became the chief U.S. spokesman. This was the period in his life when his luck was running good—a period that lasted until 1952. Among his opposite numbers from other countries were Andrei A. Gromyko, of the Soviet Union; H. V. Evatt of Australia; Paul H. Spaak of Belgium; Dr. V. K. Wellington Koo of China; Jan Masaryk of Czechoslovakia; Luis Padilla Nervo of Mexico; P. J. Noel-Baker of Great Britain. Nearly all held the rank of Ambassador or higher (Masaryk was Foreign Minister). Some became or already were Stevenson's friends. (During the 1952 campaign a reporter remarked that Stevenson was the only person he knew who was on a first-name basis with Gromyko.) He was by no means a world figure himself but he was working with world figures daily. It is not surprising that in 1961, when Stevenson was appointed Ambassador to the United Nations, he felt he was returning to where he had begun.

His new eminence received attention in the Chicago press. Steve Mitchell, the Chicago Democrat and lawyer, told Stevenson the *Daily News* was being extremely complimentary and the *Tribune* churlish, which made it clear that Stevenson had assumed a role in Illinois politics. Dutch Smith told Stevenson that "we were all very much excited to see your name in the headlines" and enclosed a *Tribune* editorial which referred to "Mr. Adlai Stevenson, all for England and nothing for America." Stevenson told Smith, "Sometimes I share the incredulity of people I meet and talk to about that newspaper around the world." Stevenson talked by telephone with Kenneth F. Burgess and the head of the Chicago Association of Commerce, both interested in bringing the UN to Chicago. Later Mayor Kelly led a delegation to London to press Chicago's case, and the Stevensons had them to supper.

Stevenson replaced Stettinius just as it became the United States' turn to preside over the Executive Committee. Moreover, the committee began at that time to meet daily instead of weekly. Stevenson told Burgess, "It was an ordeal but a fine experience and I really enjoyed it. And I think the United States emerged without any serious disasters. . . . We have created the organizational structure. . . . I feel that on the evidence to date the Russians are entirely sincere about the United Nations, but it's a slow and tedious process."

The Executive Committee adjourned October 27. The New York *Times* quoted Stevenson as praising its work. The full Preparatory Commission itself would not meet for nearly a month. Stevenson spent the interval dining with his UN colleagues and the British aristocracy, making a brief trip to Paris, and making a few speeches on the UN and peace: "The twentieth century has been the bloodiest in history, but we can retrieve it." Stevenson told Mrs. Ives he enjoyed his work immensely and Ellen was content, though she missed John Fell.

The Preparatory Commission met November 24 and worked nearly a month, with Stevenson the United States' acting delegate. Tension was increasing between the Soviet Union and the Western powers. Noel-Baker sent Stevenson a note: "The full onslaught of the Soviet campaign fell on you, and I wish we had been able to share it better. But at least it makes it easier for me to congratulate you on the fair & public spirited work you did & on the amazing patience & skill you showed. No one could have done it better!" Stettinius told Stevenson, "I hear nothing but praise."

The principal of the Lake Forest Day School reported that John Fell, though of normal ability, was doing poor school work. He had been seeing a teacher "with a rich background in psychology" daily. That teacher thought his parents' leaving him, the youngest, behind, made him feel "rejected or not wanted." This in turn suggested to him that he may have done something to merit rejection; guilt resulted. "When I started working with him over a month ago, he was utterly defeated before attempting to answer a comprehensive question or in attempting anything new. He evidenced a great need for praise. Had this need been supplied sufficiently in the past it might not be so outstanding now. His actions also indicated that at some time he had been humiliated. . . . In commenting one day on how well he had done in his work, his face lighted up as he replied, 'Did I really; do you think so?' Then rather helplessly he added, 'Mother would not think so.' When asked to tell me something about his home and what he did there, he said, 'There is nothing to tell.'" Stevenson marked several passages in the report. But he abandoned plans to return to Chicago by Christmas—he wanted to stay on for the first

General Assembly. Nor did he send Ellen and the other two boys home for Christmas, as he had intended. The teacher said John Fell was "bravely accepting" that. John Fell himself has said that, while his childhood was "basically happy," he did not enjoy staying with the Iveses in Libertyville while his family was in London—"I spent quite a bit of time with the caretaker when Buffie was around, I'd stay at their house until I had to go over for dinner." On December 12, Stevenson, in a long letter to Mrs. Ives, referred briefly to John Fell: "Please assure John Fell that his father hasn't forgotten him and that it's going to be a dismal Christmas without him. I have no doubt you will make his a happy one." He complained that he saw little of Adlai III and Borden "due to the pressure on my time."

Stevenson told William Sidley he had expected to be home by the first of the year. "But then, of course, the Secretary asked me to continue [as Senior Advisor] during the General Assembly." This was disingenuous. The fact is that, on December 7, Stevenson wrote to Secretary Byrnes and asked him directly to appoint him one of the official delegates to the January meeting of the first General Assembly. He said he had agreed to serve only during the Preparatory Commission but "I suppose" the Department would want him to continue through the Assembly and "I am willing to do this and can arrange it at home, but it would give me a sense of justification professionally and politically if I could be appointed as one of the delegates. . . . I have never before asked for any personal consideration and I am loath to do so now, but I feel, somehow that I should not go on indefinitely if I am ever to resume my practice in Chicago."

At that time the President was about to make his appointments. On December 11, Undersecretary Dean Acheson told him how much the Department appreciated the "magnificent" job he had done—he had heard nothing but the highest praise. But on December 19, Acheson cabled that it was impossible to appoint Stevenson a delegate—the President himself had taken charge of the appointments. President Truman sent to the Senate the names of Stettinius, Connally, Vandenberg, and Mrs. Roosevelt as delegates and of others, including John Foster Dulles, as alternates. Secretary Byrnes would be the fifth delegate. Acheson asked Stevenson to serve as "one of the senior advisers" to the delegation.

Despite this, Stevenson took the unusual step of cabling Senator Lucas of Illinois to seek appointment. On December 26, Lucas told him his cable had arrived too late. On December 29, Stevenson thanked Acheson and told him he was resigned to his lot. Even then the matter did not end—Stevenson tried to get appointed alternate delegate. Finally Secretary Byrnes told him it was impossible. Stevenson said he intended to return to law practice in Chicago when the Assembly ended (adding "I suppose," almost wistfully), and took the opportunity to say directly to the Secretary, "I hope I will have other opportunities as a private citizen to serve the State Department on temporary missions and that you will bear in mind my availability."

Clearly Stevenson's "first interest" lay in public office, especially foreign affairs. He pursued his ambition with utmost vigor—although at pains to conceal it. Just as in the 1960s he regarded John F. Kennedy and his close advisers as young upstarts, he himself would be in rather the same position in 1952—he was nominated for the presidency by a Democratic Convention to which Byrnes was a delegate from South Carolina.

The Preparatory Commission finished its work December 23. In The New York *Times* of December 31, Stevenson reviewed its accomplishments and said he was optimistic about prospects for the General Assembly. Walter Lippmann and others congratulated him, and Gromyko sent him a New Year's card.

Stevenson spent New Year's weekend at Cliveden. A few days later the United States delegation arrived, and that same night Stevenson dined with Alger Hiss, who was principal adviser, a rank one level below Stevenson's. (Dorothy Fosdick was another adviser.) The next day he went to lunch at Cliveden with Senators Vandenberg and Connally, John Foster Dulles, and their wives, and that night he entertained Mrs. Roosevelt at dinner at his house at 2 Mount Row. He and Mrs. Roosevelt saw each other frequently and began a friendship, both personal and political, that continued strong to the end of her life. Most of his luncheon and dinner companions, however, were newspaper and magazine correspondents, foreign ambassadors or American staff members, not American policy makers. When he saw Byrnes or Stettinius it was usually at large receptions, at private staff meetings, or at public sessions of the General Assembly.

The General Assembly convened January 10. Stevenson, as senior adviser, sat behind the delegates. William Stoneman, a Chicago *Daily News* correspondent in London whom Stevenson saw frequently, wrote: "While the professional diplomats and professional politicians monopolize the limelight and contribute the oratory, it is Adlai Stevenson . . . who actually does much of the legwork and no small part of the brainwork. . . . Time and again he broke *impasses* between the powers when agreement seemed impossible. In the process he earned the full respect of large and small powers alike. . . . Foreign diplomats were slightly surprised when Stevenson was made senior adviser to the American delegation at the assembly, instead of being made a full delegate or an alternate. Americans who had watched his work during earlier meetings were not only surprised, they were slightly disgusted." One can infer that Stevenson himself had sown the seed that sprouted in that story.

Stettinius wrote a mollifying letter to Stevenson, as Acheson had: "I hope that some day I will be in a position to see that you are properly rewarded for the great contribution you have made." Stevenson caused the letters to be placed in a file marked "Very Special Letters." He received congratulatory letters from friends back home, including one from the president of Princeton. On January 19, Stevenson gave a cocktail party at his London home and preserved cartoons depicting it. Lifelong, Stevenson's parties were attended by jokes, skits, or costumes, perhaps a carry-over from the 1920s. Lifelong, too, he carefully labeled and saved such memorabilia. Ellen took the boys home, then returned to England. A friend remarked that their house was "quite the most fascinating that London had to offer." Some who knew her recall that Ellen began to seem irrational or erratic at about this time. Her relationship with Mrs. Ives, never good, worsened. "They were both picking on each other," a family member once said. A friend of Ellen's has recalled that Ellen began to drink more now. Her father had drunk heavily.

The General Assembly adjourned February 14. Its last formal act was to choose the United States as its permanent headquarters. Stevenson in a radio broadcast spoke of this "great honor and the great responsibility." On February 21 he went through his familiar routine of saying good-by—sent letters to, among others, Jan Masaryk, Noel-Baker, Ralph Bunche, Gladwyn Jebb, Dorothy Fosdick, Wellington Koo, and members of various foreign delegations. Nearly all responded generously. Stevenson told Dorothy Fosdick, "Among the bright spots in these months of our travail in London there have been no brighter for me than my acquaintance with you." He and Ellen gave a cocktail party at 2 Mount Row on February 22. On February 24 they sailed aboard the *Queen Mary*. Stevenson spent the crossing sleeping, eating, playing shuffleboard, reading, working on forthcoming speeches, and talking over "our adventures" of the last six months, as he wrote in his diary. They landed at New York February 28. Ellen left for Libertyville; Stevenson visited Adlai III at Milton, then went to Washington. There, he once said, Secretary

Byrnes offered him the post of ambassador to Argentina. He resigned from the delegation to the UN and went home to Illinois.

16

Back in Libertyville that spring, Stevenson once again confronted the question: What next? Ed McDougal still wanted to form the new law firm. Stevenson was not prepared to commit himself. He wrote to Secretary Byrnes on March 13 and said he would spend a month in Chicago getting his affairs in order, then take a "long postponed holiday" before making any final commitments to resume law practice. "If you still have in mind positions where you think I could be of real service I will gladly come down to see you at the end of April. . . . I particularly hope that I can be of some use at the General Assembly in September." Byrnes saw no need for him to come to Washington.

Stevenson turned down a suggestion that he go to New York and become president of the Foreign Policy Association. He was considered for president of the Carnegie Endowment for International Peace by John Foster Dulles, chairman of the board, and others; he indicated he would reluctantly decline and discussed, among others, Alger Hiss for the job; a little later Hiss got the job. Stevenson declined the vice-presidency of a liberal political movement in Chicago. He advised Mayor Kelly to inform Secretary General Trygve Lie of Chicago's facilities as UN headquarters. He was maneuvering for other political preferment through Dutch Smith.

Friends at the Northwestern University law school, including Dean Leon Green, asked Stevenson to organize a series of lectures on foreign relations for the law school. Stevenson hesitated to commit himself. Northwestern offered him the honorary degree of Doctor of Laws; he accepted eagerly. He finally agreed to organize a monthly series of lectures on the United Nations to be called the Julius Rosenthal Foundation Lectures, delivered by guests and attended by lawyers and students. Stevenson's job was to write, telephone, visit, and cajole people into giving the lectures. It was the kind of thing he enjoyed and did well and it was good for him—kept him in touch with important people and on the fringe of foreign affairs, gave him an academic coloration and a base in Illinois, all without tying him down. Having undertaken the job, he threw himself into it with characteristic energy. The second lecture was given by Alger Hiss. Six years later, when Stevenson was running for President, the *Tribune* charged that Stevenson had arranged for Hiss to lecture at Northwestern and had introduced him. This was only partly true. Stevenson did arrange for Hiss to speak but he did not introduce him—he was in New York when Hiss spoke. Stevenson ran the lectures for a year and a half.

That spring and summer Stevenson was making family plans—a vacation, sending Borden to summer camp in Canada, sending Adlai III to Canada on a canoe trip, corresponding with Milton about Adlai's math. He was reviewing his investments. He was helping the children of friends get navy assignments. He took Ellen and John Fell to the Pacific Northwest and there saw Richard L. Neuberger, then a journalist, whom he had met at the San Francisco UN Conference and who later became United States Senator from Oregon. He declined an invitation to join an organization to promote U.S.-Soviet understanding. He declined an invitation to speak in Philadelphia but he declined few in Chicago. He made at least two speeches a month during the spring—to the Commercial Club, Chicago Council on Foreign Relations, Wayfarers' Club, Chicago Bar Association, Illinois Wesleyan University, all places where he already had a base. The speeches were essentially the same—he traced the UN's development, described his own UN experiences, stated his view of U.S.-Soviet relations. As the cold war developed, he repeatedly tried to explain Soviet grievances against the West. Over and over, he said that hope for the UN depended on cooperation among the U.S., U.S.S.R., and Great Britain. "There have alway been competing ideologies. There is room for their system and ours to exist side by side."

Thus Stevenson, home from the war and far-off places, spoke to his old audience, the Chicago Council on Foreign Relations. A little later, to the Chicago Bar Association, he extended his Russian thought. We had been engaged, he said, in "a global war of ideas with the Soviet Union" for many years. Since the war began, he said, Soviet power had been extended over at least 160 million more human beings. Europe was stabilized. But South America and dependent colonial areas were not—"this is the battleground in the new thirty years' war of ideas." He briefly criticized the Truman administration for demobilizing too fast, then said, "Food is a better weapon than cannon, or atomic bombs, right now." (Eleven months later, a speech by Undersecretary of State Acheson would launch the Marshall Plan.) He returned to rhetoric, including a phrase he later made famous—"This is a time for greatness"—and to other ideas he later gave wide currency, including this: "There is room for us all, but in the new era that dawned over Hiroshima we will have to wage peace with all the zeal and urgency of war—all of us."

Those who attempted to make Stevenson appear "soft on Communism" when he ran for President would find these speeches odd reading. Instead they show him in 1946 as rather more a cold warrior than some of his critics, and he seemed to feel this himself, for in the Bar Association speech he remarked, "I hope you don't feel that I have been unfair to the Russians. I am not anti-Russian." The speeches also foreshadow themes Stevenson later developed at length —a deep interest in the third world and concern at Soviet successes there, the appeal to reason and insistence on the importance of ideas, the view that the struggle was not with bullets but with ideas and food, the insistence that both sides must learn to co-exist or perish, and, finally and always, the plea for the UN. They show something else too—a politician's keen awareness of his audience, as when he protected his flank by saying to this Midwest audience, "We must be independent—friendly with all and entangled with none"; a basic stance of not being a politician himself, of being independent, and of criticizing politicians; the crucial importance of an informed electorate that would elect good public servants and promote democracy's chances of success. One cannot find in these speeches a program or even a policy, or even sustained criticism of programs and policies. Rather one finds a survey of recent events, a pinpointing of what he considered the heart of the difficulty, and a rhetorical affirmation of faith and exhortation to greater effort. These speeches stand midway between those he had given at the Council before the war, when he merely surveyed events, and those he would give later when obliged to come to grips with specific issues, concrete programs, and policy decisions. But his basic stance was already here established, and from it he almost never departed.

17

On July 18, President Truman appointed Stevenson one of four alternate representatives to the second part of the first session of the UN General Assembly scheduled to meet in New York in September. This was a step up, at least in title. The chief representative was Senator Warren R. Austin; the other representatives were Senator Tom Connally, Senator Arthur Vandenberg, Mrs. Roosevelt, and Congressman Sol Bloom. Other alternates, in addition to Stevenson, were Congressman Charles A. Eaton, Congressman Helen Gahagan Douglas, and John Foster Dulles.

Awaiting the opening of the Assembly, Stevenson asked George Ball, now with a Washington law firm, to help find a tax lawyer for

Stevenson's own proposed new firm. He made a speech on foreign policy to the American Veterans Committee in Chicago, and its officers thanked him on stationery on which was printed, "Citizens First . . . Veterans Second," a phrase Stevenson picked up and later made famous. He went campaigning downstate in this off-year election, speaking to Democratic County committeemen at Springfield on October 4. He worked hard on that speech. It was his first speech to professional politicians, to "the organization," during a political campaign; and it was very Stevensonian, employing a complex syntax and high diction level, using parallel sentence structure, quoting Kant, embodying themes he later made familiar—politics was respectable, politics was education, citizens must be informed and public servants responsible, what America did at home affected the world and the peace, bigotry would win America no friends, the Democratic Party's progressive tradition—and themes that he and, later, John F. Kennedy, made familiar—competitive peaceful coexistence with Russia; America was great abroad when she was great at home. It caused little stir but several downstate politicians congratulated him on it, and the state chairman of the Illinois Democratic Women's Division wrote, "It was a real inspiration to hear a new voice and a new subject." In another year and a half, a great many other people would be saying the same thing.

A few days later, on October 16, Stevenson went to New York. Ellen would join him later.

The United States delegation had the fifth floor of the Pennsylvania Hotel. The delegates and alternates were given position papers prepared by the State Department; Stevenson thought the staff work excellent and gave credit to several Department officers, including Dorothy Fosdick. He considered Senator Vandenberg "the ablest man in the Senate and certainly in our Delegation, if only he wasn't so acid and partisan." Austin made committee assignments. Stevenson would sit on the committee to select the UN's permanent site in the United States. He would also coordinate the work of eight political officers and, he noted, do "trouble shooting for Austin generally." Soon he was also appointed to the Economic and Financial Committee. Several permanent sites in Westchester County were under consideration, and Stevenson visited them. He set to work on a speech draft for Austin on the veto, the most vexatious question in the Assembly. He wished the United States could favor reconsideration of the veto but Department policy was fixed—we could not assent to any modification of the veto because of strong Russian feelings. Stevenson made a brief radio network speech, explaining the UN to the American people.

On October 23, Stevenson wrote in his journal, "This is the day the Assembly opens! All Delegates to assemble at Waldorf. Drove up with Dulles. Big crowd and saw many old friends. Automobile cavalcade from Waldorf to City Hall for the city reception ceremonies. . . . Found myself seated next to Vyshinsky with Gromyko behind me. . . . After luncheon drove to Flushing Meadows in automobile cavalcade with police escort. . . . President's arrival, accompanied by surprisingly little dramatics. . . . Truman's [speech] delivery was atrocious. He looked tired and sick. I met Mrs. Carpenter and Betty[8] afterward. . . . Took [them] down the line to meet the President. Introduced them to Byrnes, Molotov, Vyshinsky, Gromyko, Manuilsky, and assorted Delegates and Americans. They had a big time."

The next day he attended the opening of the general debate in plenary session of the General Assembly, saw newspaper friends, lunched "in very elegant and too-expensive Delegates Restaurant" with Senator Connally and Dorothy Fosdick, and afterward listened to speeches all afternoon. All the American delegates and alternates drifted away, he noted in his journal, except Mrs. Roosevelt and himself. He wrote, "Drove back with her afterward and she explained that [she] felt it was only polite to stay and listen to the speeches of other countries and 'moreover I have been doing nothing while our other Delegates have been so busy all summer.' Told me about Christmas parties at Hyde Park for the soldier guards stationed there. Discussed politics, languages, and education. Everything confirms conviction that she is one of the few really great people I have known." All his life Stevenson listened courteously to dull speeches, as he and Mrs. Roosevelt had done that afternoon.

All his life, too, he appraised people, sometimes indiscreetly. He would listen attentively to the mouthings of a fool; later he would tell a confidante, "What an ass!" His private judgments on people were not always good but he made them constantly and seemed unable or unwilling to suspend the critical faculty. If he suffered fools he often knew it but had his reasons. During this General Assembly he wrote that he had gone to dinner with "some uninteresting English people . . . and [a woman] who has recently been divorced from her very dull husband, Bill." And, "Helen [Gahagan] Douglas very emotional but most interested and intelligent." And Zuleta Angel of Colombia was "a very foxy man and trustworthy only when it serves his own interest."

In the Economic Committee he took up the question of whether

---

[8] Mrs. Carpenter was, of course, his mother-in-law. Betty Pirie, his sister-in-law, Ellen's sister, had recently lost her husband in a plane crash.

future United States contributions to the reconstruction of Europe should be made directly or through some international organization— the Department favored direct relief but Stevenson thought Congressman Bloom opposed, and he expected trouble. He also expected trouble over how strongly the United States would support economic aid to Europe. (Both these questions were resolved the following spring by the Marshall Plan.) On October 26, when Stevenson made another brief radio network speech, he wanted to say something about the veto but the State Department again forbade it. Marshall Field's Chicago *Sun* reported the speech on the front page. Stevenson's wife heard the speech and wrote, "You did very well, as usual, and sounded more genial than last time—not so clipped and impatient," and she offered to come to New York at any time "on the sit up train." She had telephoned Stevenson the morning he made his speech, and he noted in his journal, "First I have heard from her. All well at home, thank God."

Ed McDougal, still looking for a tax lawyer for the proposed new law firm, suggested Stevenson call on a New York lawyer for advice and interview a tax lawyer working in Washington. Stevenson had already interviewed one man: "He was [warmly recommended] to me by the former Solicitor General who is a friend of mine, but he is Jewish." The Washington lawyer McDougal had suggested went to New York to see Stevenson, and Stevenson's reaction was "very favorable." The lawyer was prepared to leave government, wanted a partnership in the firm, and would talk to his wife— a Vassar graduate, Stevenson noted.

At this time Stevenson was receiving requests for speeches or statements from a widening collection of people and institutions— the National Education Association, the United Auto Workers, the Woodrow Wilson Foundation. Reinhold Niebuhr, the liberal theologian, invited Stevenson to come to Washington to meet with a group of American liberals in what turned out to be the founding meeting of the Americans for Democratic Action. They were meeting in the wake of what Niebuhr called "the political disaster of November 5." Among them were Walter Reuther, James B. Carey, and A. Philip Randolph, labor leaders; James G. Patton, a farm leader; and Mrs. Roosevelt. James Loeb, Jr., was the executive secretary. It was Stevenson's first brush with a politically oriented and formally organized national group of labor leaders and liberal intellectuals. Later he drew some of his most fervent support from such people. But though he knew them personally, listened to them, agreed with many of their views, and was considered one of them, he never himself actually joined their organizations—Americans for Democratic

Action, Independent Voters of Illinois, or American Civil Liberties Union.

He did not attend that founding meeting of ADA. And thereafter he was "very careful" about his relationship with ADA, as Jim Loeb has said, "to the point where some of us were quite angry." Once when Stevenson was Governor, ADA held its national convention in Chicago and two other governors, Chester Bowles of Connecticut and G. Mennen Williams of Michigan, attended but not Stevenson—"Adlai was 'cute' about the meeting," Loeb has said. "He couldn't find time to welcome the Convention or address it. But he did find time to come to the hotel to greet his gubernatorial colleagues and, I think, to meet privately with some key members of the Independent Voters of Illinois."[9]

The 1946 mid-term election was indeed a disaster for the Democrats. Just as had the voters in England, American voters repudiated the party that had led them through the war. The Democrats lost control of both houses of Congress. This was the 80th Congress against which Truman later campaigned in 1948. Of the twenty-six Congressmen elected from Illinois, the Democrats were able to save only six. Neither Senate seat was up for decision that year in Illinois nor was the governorship. But the worst blow of all befell the Chicago Democratic machine. They lost most of their county ticket in Cook County (Chicago) for the first time since they had elected Anton Cermak mayor in 1931. Even Richard J. Daley, running then in 1946 for Cook County sheriff, was defeated, his only defeat. Nationally, the old Roosevelt coalition that had carried the country for fourteen years seemed to be breaking up. The powerful Cook County machine seemed run down. Ironically, it was this debacle which made possible the launching, only a little more than a year later, of the political career of Adlai Stevenson.

Jane Dick's daughter was attending school in the East, and Mrs. Dick visited her, and Stevenson arranged for them to attend a UN meeting at Lake Success. Louis A. Kohn, a well-to-do lawyer with a leading Chicago law firm—Mayer, Meyer, Austrian and Platt— whom Stevenson knew, was in New York at the time and escorted them to Lake Success, and, driving back to Manhattan, Kohn told Mrs. Dick, as she later recalled it, "That's the man we've got to have for our next Senator. I was out in the Pacific during the war,

[9] Some years later it was said that Stevenson once signed an ADA membership card and that when he became the presidential nominee in 1952 the ADA "lost" the card in order to protect him from gratuitous conservative criticism.

and I got to thinking about the home front so I determined to come back and try to persuade Adlai Stevenson to run for office. . . . I guess he thinks I'm nuts. I call him up all the time, and try to get to see him and talk to him, but he's awfully busy and I think he thinks I'm a sort of crackpot with a crazy idea." Kohn became one of Stevenson's most loyal friends and did, indeed, help to launch him politically.

That fall of 1946 in New York during the Assembly, Stevenson saw again another man who became important to him, Carl McGowan. McGowan had stayed in Washington after the war. Now he called on Stevenson in New York, and Stevenson told him he was "drifting toward running for office in Illinois." That fall, too, Stevenson met the woman who was to become Marietta Tree—Mrs. Ronald Tree—and who became important in both his personal and political life. Ronald Tree was seeing her now in New York. She belonged to an illustrious New England family, a tall striking blonde woman then twenty-nine years old, divorced, the mother of a daughter. She had met Stevenson's sister, Mrs. Ives, in the 1930s. She had been going to school in Italy and visited Algiers, where she went to tea at the home of the American consul, Ernest Ives. Ronald Tree took her, her first husband, and Stevenson to dinner in New York this fall of 1946 and Stevenson went to Ronald Tree's for dinner several times, and they played charades, a game in which the players act out roles that their opponents must divine. Marietta has recalled, "He was rather difficult about that and reluctant." Marietta and Ronald Tree were married the next year.

Stevenson's life that fall was faintly reminiscent of his college days—work, town luncheons, and country weekends. He noted in his journal that he met Mr. and Mrs. John D. Rockefeller at a cocktail party before a banquet of the American Association for the United Nations, that at the banquet he sat at the speakers' table next to General Romulo of the Philippines, that next day he drove out to Pocantico Hills to "Nelson's gigantic luncheon for 300–400 assorted guests," that he had a champagne lunch with friends at the Plaza one Sunday, then drove to Norman Davis' house at Chappaqua for the afternoon, then had supper at someone else's "fine house in Rye," then drove back to the hotel and "worked late on the veto portions of Austin's speech to the General Assembly." He saw old friends from school days, including Francis Plimpton and a pretty girl he had known in San Francisco, Nan Tucker (McEvoy). He visited his sister-in-law, Betty Pirie, and his Aunt Letitia and such New Yorkers as Max Ascoli and Archibald MacLeish and Tom Finletter. Once he "motored to New Haven" for a Yale game. Dutch

Smith and his wife came to town and Stevenson went to dinner and the theater with them. Ellen was preparing for a trip to New York and asked if she would need "a dressy dinner dress." She sent him a book with passages marked for his use in speeches. She asked him to write to friends in San Francisco to introduce a young Chicago friend—"and please don't groan, you're doing a very good deed!" She asked Stevenson how many cigarettes he was smoking a day. He evidently had told her that his apartment had two bathrooms; she wrote: "I am very much impressed by your two bathrooms. How long does it take you to decide which one to use?" She could be acid. But affectionate too: "I'm writing this on my lap—in front of a very cosy fire—I shall probably be in bed by 9:30 and up at eight—I'm just as agreeable and attractive as can be—a nice harmless vegetable waiting to be fed to a carnivorous U.N. delegate—what a fate! Love from us all."

On October 29, Molotov delivered a vitriolic cold war speech in the General Assembly, and Stevenson noted that everybody in the delegates' lounge looked "a little incredulous and stupefied." But back at the Hotel Pennsylvania, Stevenson found Austin "almost happy" about the "constructive aspects" of the Molotov speech. Late that evening Stevenson found Vandenberg indignantly drafting a tough reply to Molotov to insert in Austin's speech. About midnight Stevenson started on a new speech, finished at 2 A.M., and went to bed exhausted. The speech "evoked much applause," Stevenson wrote. Stevenson lunched and dined with his colleagues and went home at 11 P.M. "very tired," only to find another colleague "waiting for me for another midnight session." Yet he found time during the day to call on a New York lawyer in search of a tax lawyer for his proposed new firm. He noted in his journal a jingle that a man had repeated to him as descriptive of the UN: "I live in a sea of words where the nouns and the adjectives flow, where the verbs speak of actions that never take place and the sentences come and go." In later years Stevenson used the jingle so frequently that he came to think he might have written it himself.

During November and December, Stevenson was assigned to state the official United States position before the General Assembly on restoring representative democracy in Franco's Spain and on feeding the world's hungry after UNRRA expired. On November 14, Stevenson and the Australian ambassador to the United States appeared on a national radio program called the "Town Meeting of the Air" to discuss the veto. He handled himself well but received at the time only six fan letters, three of them from relatives. On November 21 he delivered a long sober speech at the University of Chicago, saying the world was "not ready" for an international professional standing army, navy, and air force, and discussing disarmament and atomic energy.

Stevenson returned to New York next day and Ellen joined him there shortly. Adlai III went to New York from Milton to spend Thanksgiving with them, and they all went to the Plimptons' for lunch and played touch football and shot clay pigeons. Stevenson was trying to get Ernest and Buffie Ives's son Tim into Princeton (unsuccessfully, it turned out).

The General Assembly adjourned December 16. If it had not produced lasting harmony among the great powers, it had at least provided a safety valve for their disagreements. Stevenson, after his customary good-bys, left two days later. He noted in his calendar on December 20, "At Home!" The Sidley law firm issued an announcement that he was returning to practice. At the law firm's annual luncheon on December 21, Stevenson made a speech. That night he and Ellen gave a party. He spent Monday at home addressing Christmas cards. The Iveses came to Libertyville, and Stevenson took Ernest Ives to lunch and Mr. and Mrs. Ives to dinner. Christmas afternoon they gave a big dinner party at Mrs. Carpenter's. On December 27, Stevenson wrote in his calendar, "Day with the boys on the farm!" He loved those days, yet somehow did not contrive to have many. Next day he took part in a national radio broadcast commemorating Woodrow Wilson's birthday. Stevenson was by then a director of the Woodrow Wilson Foundation. He was and he remained a Wilsonian.

He spent the rest of the week at luncheons and cocktail parties and supper parties except for one day in the office. He declined an invitation to address an ADA dinner. On New Year's Eve he took Ernest Ives to a club for lunch, went home in midafternoon, and that night went to a New Year's Eve party at Stuart Otis' in Libertyville that was reminiscent of the old prewar days. Nothing much had changed there. He was back home.

CHAPTER SIX

The Run for Governor:
A Star Is Born
1947-1948

On February 5, 1947, Adlai Stevenson wrote in a diary, "Am 47 today—still restless; dissatisfied with myself. What's the matter? Have everything. Wife, children, money, success—but not in law profession. Too much ambition for public recognition; too scattered in interests; how can I reconcile life in Chicago as lawyer with consuming interest in foreign affairs and desire for recognition and position in that field? Prospect of Senate nomination sustains, & some time troubles, even frightens me. Wish I could at least get tranquil & make Ellen happy and do go[od] humble job at law. Lunched with Princeton 1922 people . . . to talk about reunion plans."

This was for him a winter of discontent. On January 31 he wrote: "Kellogg's for dinner—some old friends—pleasant, easy, relaxed feeling. Sad how little most of them have lived; done for their generation. Left early." And on February 1 and 2: "Sunday supper-cocktail party at Tom Connors'—the implacable entertainers. Left early." The Chicago *Herald-American* published a photograph of him and Ellen giving a large cocktail party. It was not enough. An old political story says that a Senator, defeated after several terms and asked about his plans, said, "I don't know—but they never go home to Pocatello."

A close friend once said, "He never wanted to give up Illinois—but he thought that living in Lake Forest, those would be the people he'd see, businessmen, lawyers, bankers—and watching them get drunk at so-and-so's on Saturday night was not his idea of a good time—he's been seeing awfully interesting people." What he really wanted at the time was to run next year for the U. S. Senate seat held by the Republican Brooks. But he also wanted to be ambassador to London, a post then open, and wrote in his diary, "How

I wish it was me and I had the money to do it. I *know* I could & its one of the few things I do *know* I could do. Maybe the time will come when Ellen would like to do something like that on a scale we could afford. But will I ever get the opportunities again—the way I have in the last year?" Although he noted in his diary, "Ride in cutter in afternoon with John Fell on tobogan. Beautiful winter day," his discontent infected his private life: "John Fell's birthday—and he was so late at breakfast I drove away without him! Now I'm miserable. After talking about his birthday for days & all Ellen's planning for the big party tomorrow, I even forgot to congratulate him this morning!" And he went on to mention two people who had died, saying, "I've met a lot of the significant people of this generation," an almost elegiac note.

Before this year was out, this year that began with so many self-doubts, he would be launched on an Illinois political career that would change his life completely and would help change American politics of the next two decades. In January he had no way of knowing this. But something kept him in Illinois—either the hope of being nominated for the Senate, or sheer instinct, or a need to salvage his deteriorating marriage to Ellen, or all three. For, whatever the reason, early in January he turned down an offer to become a full-time deputy to Trygve Lie, Secretary General of the United Nations, at a tax-exempt salary of $24,300, plus a house. Declining, he noted, "I must stay at home now & get family situation straightened out. Also might as well try out political situation there."

2

During this spring and indeed during most of the year Stevenson was back at the old law firm but he was also as usual deeply involved in other endeavors: planning his own law firm, organizing the Rosenthal Lectures at Northwestern, making a good many speeches of his own, and talking politics.

He noted in his diary in January, "Lunch with Steve & Ed re new firm. Little progress as usual. I'm getting skeptical about ever doing this." Nonetheless, he continued to pursue it. He drew up a tentative budget of $72,240 per year for a firm containing six partners, including himself, Ed McDougal, Glen Lloyd, and three other lawyers; he jotted down a list of four prospective clients with total fees of $21,200. He looked for office space. Friends in New York and Washington helped in the search for lawyers. Stevenson was carrying out the enterprise discreetly—he did not approach Chicago lawyers directly for fear his own partners would get wind of his plans. His efforts continued until December, when the file was marked, "Law Firm 1947—Plans Abandoned."

He declined several invitations that spring to speak outside Illinois but accepted invitations in Illinois. He was staking out a position as the leading Chicago exponent of the UN and the leading Chicago expert on foreign affairs. A Chicago *Daily News* writer said that Stevenson and Mrs. Roosevelt had "measured up to their jobs excellently" at the UN General Assembly. Mrs. Roosevelt, speaking at the Council on Foreign Relations, praised Stevenson's work at the UN, saying, "In all but name he was a full delegate." Introducing Mrs. Roosevelt, he said, "With goodness an American woman has won the respect, the confidence and the love of more people, great and small, at home and abroad, than, I venture to say, any living person," then went on, "It is better to light candles than to curse darkness," a phrase he used in eulogizing Mrs. Roosevelt after her death fifteen years later.

At the Lincoln Library Forum in Springfield in January, Stevenson discussed U.S.-Soviet relations and the United Nations, said "the price of permanent peace is permanent effort" to perfect the UN, said America must rid herself of bigotry, for the world was watching, and must overcome the obstacles James Bryce had mentioned—"private self-interest, excessive partisanship and the sin of indolence," of which he considered the last most important: citizens must inform themselves on public issues and must vote; good men must not shun public office. Reading his speeches during this period, one is struck by the fact that much that seemed so fresh when he ran for office he had been saying for a good many years. The speeches that made his reputation in the state and nation grew naturally out of these earlier speeches.

On April 27 he debated on the radio with Governor Kim Sigler of Michigan the question, "Should the Communist Party be banned in America?" Governor Sigler, a Republican, argued that it should— the Communist Party was not a political party but an alien conspiracy to bring about a bloody revolution and had no right to be on the ballot. Stevenson opposed, and in arguing his case bespoke civil libertarian ideals more forthrightly and eloquently than at any previous time: "In the first place you would drive the Communist Party underground, and surely everyone knows it is best to keep your adversary where you can see him. In the second place, it would be a confession of weakness. Democracy is strong; let's act that way. . . . And thirdly, suppression is a dangerous precedent. If in a moment of nervous anxiety we outlaw a political party to protect democracy, who knows what liberties may be sacrificed to the same end and then where is our freedom, our democracy? Let us not adopt Fascism to defeat Communism." He argued that repression could not put down ideas. Only better ideas could do that. Discontent bred Communism; if discontent were deprived of a voice, it would multiply. "But even more important than these common-sense reasons for opposing this legislation are some fundamental principles. This is the land of the free." We believed in human wisdom and the power of inquiry. Our great strength was that we could discuss anything openly. Conformity could lead to secret police, hysteria, witch hunts, book burning. We must not adopt the very methods of suppression we despised. "Let's not throw out the baby with the bath water."

On May 13, Stevenson went downstate to Pontiac, to speak to a Democraic Party Jefferson Day dinner and, after a long opening passage identifying himself through Jesse Fell with downstate Illinois, delivered his standard UN speech. On May 20 he went to French Lick, Indiana, and spoke to the Investment Bankers Association of America; the speech was a long paste-up of several he had already given on the UN, U.S.-Soviet relations, and the consequences of economic crisis at home and abroad, but because Stevenson and the association broadcast copies, it created more stir than previously. Ben Cohen, counselor to the State Department, told Stevenson it was "a ripping good speech." George Ball told him it was "both penetrating and eloquent." Laird Bell thought it "exceedingly good." William Benton, Assistant Secretary of State, asked if he "could prevail on you to come back into the Department."

Stevenson became involved in a number of other projects—soliciting contributions for the War Orphans Appeal and the Emergency Committee of Atomic Scientists, lending his name to a fund-raising drive of the Foreign Policy Association in New York, talking with Arthur M. Schlesinger, Jr., who was writing a piece on Eleanor Roosevelt for *Life,* talking with people who wanted him to become involved in the editorial direction of Marshall Field's *Sun,* which was floundering under a succession of editors.

He noted in his journal in January, "Another wonderful, quiet week end at home. But find it very hard to do creative writing there. Too many diversions." He visited Ellen's sister Betty and noted, "She wanted to talk about my situation with Ellen; told her all was well." But all was not well—their relationship was worsening. And Stevenson was bored—he wrote, "Big tea or cocktail party at apt. before Emerson House benefit dinner dance. Too old & tired for these people—or something! Couldn't wait to leave." Applying to Milton Academy for Borden's admission, Stevenson said his scholastic record was "disappointing" but he was improving. "He is a most engaging boy, full of personality and good spirits, but he has gotten along entirely too well on personality!" Milton said Borden could not be considered for a grade below ninth, for which he did not qualify scholastically—during the past two years all his grades, except for English for one year, were failing grades—but Milton was willing to await Borden's summer school performance at Exeter before rejecting him. Stevenson replied, "We are much troubled." Borden did poorly in summer school at Exeter, and Milton rejected him, and his parents sent him back to school in Lake Forest. Adlai III, already at Milton, did better work that spring and by June all his marks were satisfactory, and Stevenson sent him to Europe that summer with a school friend. He was by now sixteen. His father had been twenty when he first went abroad without his parents. As for John Fell, his parents sent him away for the summer for the first time, to a camp in northern Wisconsin, from which he wrote, "I am still having a medium time."

3

Stevenson's principal preoccupation during 1947 was politics. It was a year of deep and far-reaching ferment in Illinois politics and American politics, particularly in the Democratic Party. For this reason, it was the crucial year in Stevenson's political career. Indeed, without the ferment, he would almost surely have had no political career. But in this year, and in the year that followed, 1948, everything fell out exactly right for him.

Following the elections of 1946, liberal Democratic intellectuals and like-minded independents had set about organizing to defend the New Deal-Fair Deal, endangered by the resurgent Republican Party. They were aiming at 1948, the next presidential year. They met in Washington on January 4, 1947, and organized the Americans for Democratic Action (ADA). Wilson Wyatt, former mayor of Louisville, became chairman and Leon Henderson, former OPA administrator, became chairman of the executive committee. Other leaders included Franklin D. Roosevelt, Jr., Hubert H. Humphrey, Louis H. Harris, Joseph Rauh, Jr., James Loeb, Jr., David Dubinsky, William Evjue, Reinhold Niebuhr, Paul A. Porter, Arthur M. Schlesinger, Jr., Schlesinger's father, and David D. Lloyd (who had gone to Italy with Stevenson). In Illinois a similar group, the Independent Voters of Illinois, had already sprung up. In all this there was an element of youth-returned-from-war challenging the old guard.

Important as these groups were, however, in Illinois in 1947 change took a different course. While the leaders of the Cook County Democratic machine welcomed the IVI—so long as it posed no third-party threat—they themselves retained control of the nominating, or slate-making, process, and so any real change would have to come from within the machine itself. Most IVI and ADA leaders were young amateurs. Yet the need for change was no clearer to them than to the older professionals of the Democratic machine. Indeed, since the professionals must have winners to exist, they had a greater personal stake in successful change than the amateurs. When in 1946 the Democratic machine lost not only congressional seats but part of its Cook County ticket, nobody was more keenly aware of the need for change than Colonel Jacob M. Arvey, the maximum leader of the machine.

Arvey was a small man, short and slight with a bulging forehead and large bald head. He had been born November 3, 1895, in Chicago of Russian (now Polish) immigrant parents. He had grown up in what came to be called "the poor Jew ward," the 24th, and had taken the slum boy's political ladder upward, becoming 24th Ward committeeman and finally county chairman, as well as a lawyer who made a great deal of money, in part because of politics. In later years Arvey ascended to Democratic national committeeman and finally, as Dick Daley gained strength, to elder statesman of the party and doer of good works. But at this time, 1947, he was the Democratic leader of Cook County, the very incarnation of a big-city boss, vilified mercilessly by the *Tribune*. He was, however, intelligent as well as shrewd, a man of flexibility and imagination, a man of certain principles, one interested in ideas as well as votes, one who kept his word, and one who did not ignore the public welfare whether for pragmatic or idealistic reasons. He once said, "When I was in the Army I was determined that if I went back into politics it would be on my terms—with good candidates. If I were selling beer and I wanted to sell it to Negroes, and a Negro could sell beer better, I'd hire him. If I were selling to Jews, I wouldn't send an Arab. It's the same with politics. The precinct captains have a better line to sell when they've got a good man on the ticket."

In 1947—indeed, almost immediately after the polls closed in November of 1946—Arvey knew he needed something new and good to sell to the voters if he was to save the machine in 1947 and 1948. Years of hammering at the Kelly-Nash machine as corrupt had helped produce the 1946 disaster. So had Mayor Kelly's firm stand for open housing—the Irish resented it. Kelly—and all fifty aldermen—would be up for re-election in the spring of 1947. (City elections in Chicago are held every fourth spring in odd-numbered years, thus divorcing the local election entirely from presidential, congressional, and state-wide elections. The primary is held in February, when cold weather helps ensure a small controllable party vote; the nomination is actually decided in advance of the primary by the fifty ward committeemen and their chairman, at that time Arvey.)

Arvey has recalled, "My lieutenants told me that they wouldn't go for a Kelly man for Mayor in 1947. I wanted to know the reasons. I had a man that Kelly trusted"—Arvey did not say so but it was Spike Hennessey, for many years a Democratic press agent in City Hall—"take the poll lists and take voters that were Irish, Poles, Jews —call them and say he was making a survey of movie stars from Los Angeles and at the end of the conversation say 'By the way there in Chicago, how's your Mayor doing, pretty good?' We learned from the Irish that Kelly was very low in popularity. He had suffered less among the Jews, Germans, and Poles. Among the Negroes he was stronger than before. I called the committeemen together. They made it even worse. So I waited upon the Mayor one day. I prefaced my remarks by telling him that I'd be for him alone if he decided to run but I owed it to the Democratic Party to give him the result of the poll I had taken. Kelly was stunned. I told him who had taken the poll. Then Kelly believed it. We knew we couldn't afford to lose the mayoralty—the Governor and Senator and Congress and President were coming up next year. The momentum would carry over. We needed the patronage and the news advantage of City Hall. This is the test of Kelly's greatness. He said, 'I wouldn't be in this chair without the support of the Democratic Party. If I can't win, I have no right to drag the party down. And if I can't win, then no man close to me can.' He said—remember, Kelly said—'Say, how about this fellow Kennelly? He opposed us in 1936—he was for Horner— he's a Democrat but not an organization Democrat.' I didn't know Kennelly. Kelly called him, not me."

Martin Kennelly was a businessman with a reputation for being honest and civic-minded, a white-thatched man who looked more like a pastor than a politician. That he turned out to be a poor mayor is, for our present purposes, beside the point. When at Arvey's urging the Democratic ward committeemen slated him and their precinct captains duly got out the primary vote to formally nominate him, he gave the Democratic Party of Cook County, so long besmirched as the corrupt creature of Ed Kelly and Pat Nash and Jack Arvey, what was then called a new look. It may very well be that he saved the machine.

Stevenson had been in New York at the UN General Assembly in December of 1946 when the decision to drop Kelly and slate Kennelly was being taken. His friend Louis A. Kohn, the Chicago lawyer, sent him clippings about it, and Stevenson wrote a letter indicating he hoped Arvey would not re-slate Mayor Kelly. When in December Kennelly was announced, Stevenson congratulated Arvey, and Arvey thanked him and predicted that Kennelly would make "a great Mayor." Arvey's letter to Stevenson was addressed "Dear Adlai" but actually Arvey did not know Stevenson at that time, never called him "Adlai" to his face, and did not sign the letter —it was a form letter signed for him by his secretary.

At the start of 1947, Stevenson had no direct connection with all this, and his own political ambitions seemed stalled. He noted in his journal on January 13, "Lunch with Louis Kohn—my most ardent backer for Senate. Still has hope for me in 1948."

On January 21, Stevenson had a conference with Barney Hodes, Arvey's law partner, about a law case and wrote in his journal, "Much talk of politics. . . . Not a word about me. Think he's for Douglas for Senate." In March, Stevenson sent a contribution to Kennelly's campaign fund. On March 19 he made a brief speech, not the main speech, at an IVI dinner for Kennelly, saying that government "must be the positive business of all of us, and beneath the dignity of none of us. It must be the honorable calling the founders of a government by the governed meant it to be. 'Your public servants serve you right,' as somebody said." Kennelly was elected mayor in April. It was this event, more than anything else, that made possible Stevenson's move only nine months later. As one politician put it, "If the Kennelly formula had not worked, Stevenson wouldn't have been slated." Arvey, pleased that his strategy of turning to a good-government candidate had succeeded, would repeat the formula next December. All this was not, however, so clear in April.

Stevenson was not yet doing anything openly to seek nomination, perhaps because the machine had rebuffed him years earlier, perhaps because he felt some inner hesitation. And in any case, it would have been suicidal for Stevenson to have openly sought machine support that spring and summer. His strength as a candidate— and therefore his value to the machine—lay in his very lack of connection with the machine. He had somehow to get its endorsement— without that, he could hardly be nominated—yet at the same time maintain his independence of it.

Louis A. Kohn had come to Chicago from Missouri. He was then thirty-nine, short, stocky, energetic, with boundless energy and good will. He and his pretty wife lived on the Near North Side, the old Gold Coast, attended numerous social and intellectual functions, entertained a good deal, kept in touch with influential Eastern journalists who visited Chicago, and had a way of bringing people together and changing their lives. Kohn, having met Stevenson years earlier on legal matters and heard him speak at the Bar Association and Council on Foreign Relations, had returned from the war determined to promote Stevenson for the U. S. Senate. Now he talked to Stevenson and telephoned him repeatedly. Few men can be as persistent as Lou Kohn. Stevenson's Lake Forest friend, Dutch Smith, has recalled, "Adlai called me and said, 'Lou Kohn is driving me crazy. He's determined that I run for the Senate. You talk to him.'" Smith and Kohn had lunch together, and while they agreed that Stevenson ought to be nominated for the Senate, neither had close political connections, though Kohn had important friends in legal and Smith in financial circles.

Stevenson himself knew few important politicians well. He did, however, know Steve Mitchell, and on June 20 at a lunch at the Union League Club Stevenson broached the Senate candidacy to him. Now Mitchell, a Chicago lawyer whom Stevenson had consulted about his proposed new law firm, had been on the fringe of Chicago Democratic politics but never at its center. This was a curious time for Stevenson to approach Mitchell as a conduit to the Democratic organization. For Mitchell was in trouble with the organization—he had tried to go around it and persuade the President directly to appoint him United States district attorney in Chicago.[1]

---

[1] The United States district attorney in Chicago had just resigned. This is a presidential appointment, made upon recommendation of the U. S. Senator and the national committeeman; the recommendation was considered the patronage prerogative of the national committeeman. Former Mayor Ed Kelly was national committeeman at the time, and upon learning that the vacancy would occur, Jack Arvey called on Kelly. Kelly said, as Arvey recalled it, "Find a Democrat but one that's not too close to the organization." (Several embarrassing income tax indictments were expected.) Arvey had heard that Steve Mitchell was Kelly's candidate for U.S. attorney; he asked Kelly if it was so. Kelly denied it. A little later Senator Lucas told Arvey he understood that Mitchell had been endorsed by Kelly and the organization. Arvey decided Mitchell had lied—had told Senator Lucas and others in Washington that the Cook County organization endorsed him. This angered Arvey and he told Lucas that the county organization would not endorse Mitchell and asked Lucas not to. Thereupon, as Arvey later recalled it, Mitchell sent friends to Arvey soliciting his support. Arvey rebuffed them bluntly and began seeking another candidate. On a Saturday, he and David Bazelon, then an

This episode, which opened a split between Arvey and Mitchell that never healed, had important effects on Stevenson's 1952 campaign for the presidency. It has another curious aspect. During the maneuvering, Arvey went to Washington, and Senator Lucas gave a lunch for him attended by James F. Byrnes and Senator Alben Barkley, then Senate Democratic leader. Lucas said Arvey was looking for a U.S. attorney, and Byrnes said, "Why don't you grab this fellow Stevenson—he's a gold nugget." It was, Arvey says, the first time he had heard of Stevenson. But he picked Otto Kerner instead.

In any case, now Stevenson asked Steve Mitchell's help in seeking the senatorial nomination, and Mitchell agreed. Thenceforward the principal movers of the Stevenson-for-Senator movement were Lou Kohn, Dutch Smith, and Steve Mitchell. (Kohn was the most active during the summer and did not work directly with Smith until a little later.)

It would be tedious to trace every move they made. A sampling will indicate their method. On June 26 a man in downstate Carlinville wrote to Lou Kohn (misspelling his name): "Thank you very much for sending me the address given by Mr. Stevenson. Of course I feel that all good Democrats and good citizens should rally to the support of Mr. Stevenson for any important office he may seek, and I will be glad to do anything I can to promote his interests." On July 7, Steve Mitchell talked about Stevenson to Morris Leibman, a

---

assistant U.S. attorney in Chicago, had lunch at Fritzel's, a restaurant in the Chicago Loop favored by politicians, racetrack people, and people in show business. Bazelon reported that Mitchell was putting on pressure through a protégé of Ed Kelly's and through the Catholic Church and that President Truman sent word that Arvey must find a candidate quickly. "So," Arvey has recalled, "we went back to my office and took down Sullivan's directory," a book listing all Chicago lawyers, "and started going through it. We got to the Ks and found Otto Kerner. We remembered his background." Otto Kerner had married the daughter of Anton Cermak, the Democrat whose election as mayor of Chicago in 1931 had commenced the rise of the Cook County machine. Arvey went on, "I called up Kerner's father and asked what his son was doing. He was up in Wisconsin fishing. I asked, 'How would he like to be U.S. attorney?' His father said he didn't know. When he got back from Wisconsin he came to see me and said fine. I took him to see Kelly and he was appointed." This launched a career that took Kerner to the two-term governorship of Illinois and the Federal Circuit Court of Appeals in Chicago. (In 1973, while a sitting judge, Kerner was convicted of accepting a bribe while Governor, and of evading income taxes.) Arvey has said, "If Mitchell had gone to Kelly or me it would have been all right. His credentials were good. We needed somebody like him. But he tried to use the pressure of the Catholic Church. We couldn't take him when he was trying to go around us by subterfuge."

liberal lawyer, and to a Catholic leader. Lou Kohn wrote to V. Y. Dallman, of the *Illinois State Register* in Springfield, and on July 8 Dallman replied that he would gladly work for Stevenson for senator. On July 15 a man from Pontiac told Kohn he would meet with him soon to discuss Stevenson and added, "Mr. Stevenson appeared at the Livingston County Jackson Day Dinner and made what I thought was one of the finest talks I have ever heard." A law partner of Kohn's wrote to an attorney in Effingham, who replied, "As to the Stevenson candidacy, I do not believe he is very well known in this area. As is every one else, we have been so busy I have given little thought to politics." Another man wrote, "Among those who know him the response is encouraging. However, he is not well known except among lawyers." And another, "The reaction in this area to the possibility of his being a candidate is rather neutral but certainly not unfavorable." And there was more, much more, of the same.

On July 22, after conversations with Stevenson and Dutch Smith, Bud Merwin sent a letter to various newspaper friends downstate, saying that his Republican and independent friends in Chicago, "fed up with" the isolationist record of Senator Brooks and the Chicago *Tribune,* were "trying to interest" Stevenson in running for senator on the Democratic ticket. They thought Stevenson would attract "many" Republican voters. Merwin enclosed a biographical sketch of Stevenson, said Stevenson had never sought political office but had long worked for good government, said he did not adhere to the left wing of the party, and asked "how well, if at all, Stevenson is known in your district" and whether he might draw Republican and independent votes. "Please be completely frank as Mr. Stevenson is in no way seeking this job, and I suspect he might even prefer discouraging reactions to those which sound hopeful!" (The language of the last sentence suggests that Stevenson, not Merwin, drafted the letter.) Most of the editors replied that Stevenson was not well known but had no opposition. Smith spoke several times to Mayor Kennelly about Stevenson and arranged for them to meet on July 31. Kennelly gave Stevenson no help whatsoever.

On July 21, President Truman announced he was appointing Stevenson once more as an alternate delegate to the General Assembly of the UN, due to convene that fall. The Chicago *Sun* on July 24 editorially praised Stevenson as "one of the state's most valuable citizens." Lou Kohn, an inveterate clipper of newspapers, broadcast the editorial. On August 1, Kohn and Mitchell met to discuss establishing a formal Stevenson-for-Senator Committee. Kohn began sending out a form letter claiming that Stevenson was "the leading candidate for the Democratic nomination," a bold tactic characteristic of Kohn. Kohn's ebullience, vigor, and tenacity caused some people to think him brash and others to think him unimportant but he was neither. The impression one gains from all this is that Stevenson's supporters were poorly coordinated, that Lou Kohn was leading the campaign, and that the response was not unfavorable but not particularly favorable either.

Stevenson himself was doing what he could—making speeches, attending a Democratic picnic in Springfield, telling Secretary of State Marshall that Judge Harry Fisher and Jack Arvey were concerned lest Jews prevented from entering Palestine be returned to Europe. He told his friend V. Y. Dallman, the Springfield editor, "I am not taking the talk about me as the candidate for something seriously. I even doubt if I would attempt such a new and unfamiliar enterprise if I had the opportunity. My only ambition, for the present at least, is to live quietly with my family, which I have neglected for years, and get re-established in practice here in Chicago. Some day I hope to feel free enough and still be useful enough to do something more for the government, but not in competitive partisan politics."

4

The UN General Assembly opened September 16 in New York. Stevenson went East alone a few days ahead of time, stopping in Washington. There he resisted what he called "the heaviest pressure" from Secretary of State George Marshall to take the job of Assistant Secretary that Archibald MacLeish had had and that William Benton was now resigning. Doing so, he told Marshall he hoped Marshall would not "write me off all together." Ellen stayed in Libertyville.

At the UN, Stevenson worked diligently in the committee dealing with the UN's budget. He drafted replies to citizens who wrote to U. S. Representative Warren Austin. On November 7 and 10, in the important political committee, Stevenson stated the U.S. position on applications for UN membership, arguing for the admission of all states that met the requirements of the UN Charter. But on November 17, in a plenary Assembly meeting, he defended U.S. opposition to the admission of Albania, Mongolia, Hungary, Rumania, and Bulgaria.

One of the most difficult questions confronting the General Assembly was Palestine. Stevenson became involved, though not in policy-making—policy was made at the top level of government. After World War II—indeed, since the Balfour Declaration of World

War I—Zionists had wanted unlimited Jewish immigration into Palestine and the establishment of a Jewish state. The Arabs had opposed. The British, to whom Palestine had been entrusted by the League of Nations, restricted immigration, fearing that unlimited Jewish immigration in the face of Arab opposition would "set aflame the whole Middle East," as Prime Minister Attlee put it. The Jews went anyway, particularly European Jews. Terrorism began. Truman and the British tried to bring Jews and Arabs together and, failing, handed the problem over to the UN. A UN commission recommended that the British mandate be ended, that two independent states, one Jewish and one Arab, be established under UN auspices, and that the city of Jerusalem be placed under UN trusteeship. The United States now supported this plan. Bitter debate ran through the Assembly all fall, through the United States, too. President Truman wrote in his memoirs, "I do not think I ever had as much pressure and propaganda aimed at the White House as I had in this instance."

On November 5, Mrs. Roosevelt asked Stevenson to participate in a nationwide radio discussion of the Palestine question, and he accepted. Marshall Field IV, the son of the founder of the *Sun,* told Stevenson he "might have made a mistake in voting for partition" of Palestine. Stevenson replied that he too was rather pessimistic about trusteeship but, on the other hand, "I get very cold comfort out of the conclusion that there is nothing to do about Palestine except to let the Jews fight it out to a bloody conclusion." UN action was, he thought, the only course possible once the British had decided to leave.

5

That fall Lou Kohn, indefatigably promoting Stevenson, had lunch with a reporter in the Chicago bureau of *Time* who was favorably disposed. Stevenson's friend Dick Bentley was receiving favorable responses from LaSalle Street lawyers who lived in the North Shore suburbs. Kohn reported to Stevenson a rumor that the Democrats would not try hard to elect Democrats for Governor and Senator in 1948. Stevenson found it hard to believe. Kohn visited Stevenson in New York and met with Steve Mitchell in Chicago and the next day, October 4, Stevenson issued a statement saying that if he was offered the nomination for the Senate to run against Curly Brooks he would accept.

Stevenson told Adlai III in October, "I am deferring any decision about the political situation until I can get back to Chicago. Senator Lucas is very eager to have me run for the Senate but I am sceptical about my chances of election and very reluctant to make a 'sacrifice hit.'" It was the beginning of a habit Stevenson developed of consulting young Adlai about his political moves. Mrs. Roosevelt advised him to run for public office in Illinois. He told a woman, "The ticket seems to be Douglas-Meyer, but my friends still continue to agitate and I have not called them off for the reason that it might be desirable for that group to develop some influence in the party councils for a later date." (Meyer was Dr. Karl Meyer, a respected physician, civic leader, and medical superintendent of Cook County Hospital.) Stevenson persuaded Secretary Marshall to speak to the Chicago Council on Foreign Relations and introduced him gracefully. Thanking Marshall, Stevenson wrote, "I know you will not hesitate to call on me if you think I can ever be of any service. . . . And I suspect the time is not far distant when home and family will be moveable." The program had been broadcast over radio, and a man who heard it told Stevenson, "It seemed that the professional [Democratic] party men here . . . ought to be saying to themselves, 'There is a fellow who can campaign all right.'"

Lou Kohn went to Washington and, returning on October 9, told Stevenson that Senator Lucas and David Bazelon looked on Stevenson's candidacy with favor and that Bazelon thought Arvey did too. Other Democrats asked Kohn about Kelly's and Kennelly's position, and Kohn set about influencing them. Kohn suggested to Dutch Smith that he speak to Marshall Field about getting publicity for Stevenson in the *Sun.* Smith did, successfully. On October 23, Lou Kohn met with Steve Mitchell and William Harshe, a public relations man, to discuss publicizing the Stevenson-for-Senator Committee. On November 4, Milburn P. Akers, by now national political writer and editorial writer on the *Sun,* preparing to leave for Japan, told Dutch Smith he thought Stevenson's chances of being nominated for the Senate were "quite favorable" and that Stevenson could "certainly" be nominated for Governor. Akers said that the Democrats feared to have Paul Douglas, who had made a reputation as a maverick in City Council, elected Governor—he would control some 30,000 patronage jobs—and, further, Douglas, with his war record in the Marines, would make a strong candidate against the Republican Brooks, who always campaigned on his own World War I record. Akers wondered if the strongest ticket would not be Douglas versus Brooks, and Stevenson versus Green. This was the first suggestion from an influential person that Stevenson might better run for Governor than for Senator. Dutch Smith passed it on to

Stevenson. Stevenson replied that he regretted Akers had gone to Japan, since he had hoped "to counsel with him" upon his own return to Chicago, and told Smith, "I have never felt that [the governorship] was my 'dish' and still don't. However, perhaps I should not be too emphatic and I won't for the present." He added, "The organization of the Harshe Committee took me a little by surprise as I had not assumed he was planning any formal project of this kind. I suspect the best role for me is to continue to act surprised. So please consider me very surprised indeed!" A little later he told Jane Dick he suspected his political promoters were really out "to improve their bargaining position to increase their influence in the party."

Many people later claimed to have "discovered" Stevenson, or to have set him on the road to political greatness. Abraham Lincoln Marovitz, Arvey's protégé, has recalled taking Stevenson to see Arvey in New York that fall during the World Series. Barney Hodes has recalled helping Scott Lucas persuade Stevenson to accept nomination for Governor. Arvey remembers Judge Harry Fisher's talking to him about Stevenson, and Arvey's suggesting that Stevenson's supporters call on Arvey. All those things, and more, may have happened and probably did—Stevenson was filling a vacuum, and it would not be surprising if several people close to Democratic politics had the same idea that fall. The crucial approach to Arvey, however, was made on November 15.

On Lou Kohn's call, Stevenson's principal backers had met the day before at the Bar Association with a number of Democrats from around the state. On the fifteenth a delegation waited on Jack Arvey—Lou Kohn, Laird Bell, Dutch Smith, and Steve Mitchell. By now, Arvey had heard of Stevenson from James Byrnes, Abe Marovitz, Judge Fisher, and others. As they were ushered in, the delegation had no way of knowing what was on Arvey's mind. This is what Arvey himself has said was on his mind: "I used to go to bed every night thinking about 'the ticket.' The polls showed that President Truman would be beaten badly in 1948. When the head of the ticket is weak, you need a good state ticket. I didn't think President Truman could win. But I was sure that Governor Green could be beaten and I thought Brooks could if we got the right man. I thought I had Brooks—I had made up my mind in 1946 that it should be Paul Douglas against Brooks. In 1946, Douglas came to a mass meeting in uniform. He did not make a speech but he waved a greeting to the crowd. I saw his withered hand [wounded in the war]. Brooks never made a speech without saying, 'I got shrapnel in my back at Chateau-Thierry and I learned what it means to serve our country.' I knew the shattered hand would dispose of that."

Arvey was, therefore, already committed in his own mind to running Paul Douglas for Senator when the Stevenson-for-Senator Committee waited on him in November of 1947. He received them in his small, soft-lit, wood-paneled law office on LaSalle Street. Arvey, though raised in the bare-knuckled 24th Ward, could be as courteous, even courtly, as anyone. He heard them out and then, as Dutch Smith remembers it, said, "I would agree that Stevenson would make a very good Senator but you've got to get elected. Douglas is much better known. Douglas has been working—'campaigning'—all summer downstate. He is much better known than Stevenson and I feel he would make a better candidate." Smith and his friends left, feeling that they were amateurs and this was a professional's business. Arvey did not mention the possibility of running Stevenson for Governor, as they recalled it.

When Stevenson came to Chicago to introduce Secretary Marshall at the Council on Foreign Relations on November 18, he had lunch next day with Mitchell, Kohn, probably Smith, and several others. Returned to the UN, Stevenson wrote to Kohn on November 21: "Yesterday Judge Fisher telephoned me about the Palestine business and added that he was meeting Arvey, Kells [George Kells, Democratic state chairman], et al soon; and seemed surprisingly optimistic with respect to myself. I hardly know why unless it has to do with larger campaign contributions. The latter is not a wholly reassuring basis for selection." In a postscript he added, "I wish I wasn't getting so cold on this whole political business." Ellen was cool toward it.

Arvey, after his conversation with Stevenson's supporters, remained unmoved in his determination to run Douglas for the Senate. "But this crowd kept urging Stevenson for Senator." Arvey asked Smith to bring Stevenson to lunch with Arvey and Senator Lucas. Smith did, though Stevenson protested he already had a lunch engagement. Arvey suggested he might run for Governor: Stevenson replied, "It's not my field. All my experience has been at the UN and in the State Department. I've never given it a thought. I don't think I'd be interested." So, Arvey later recalled, "I didn't think I had a candidate. So I started looking for someone else for governor." It was at this time he considered Dr. Karl Meyer. And he also was reported considering Thomas J. Courtney, a Democrat who had opposed the machine in the Horner primary, a perennial candidate, later Cook County state's attorney, and still later a judge, not notably a "good-government" candidate yet not notably a "machine man" either. Actually, it was Mayor Kennelly who urged Courtney on Arvey. But Arvey thought that this year he needed a candidate "without scars"—and Courtney had scars from his years in public life.

In the absence of other workable candidates, Arvey checked further on this Adlai Stevenson. He telephoned Henry Crown, the industrialist, and Edward Eagle Brown, the banker. They spoke well of Stevenson. Steve Mitchell was making telephone calls to various politicians, including George Kells. Mitchell and Kohn met frequently at the Bar Association, sometimes with others. William McCormick Blair, Jr., who had been drawn to Stevenson during the William Allen White Committee days, said at one of these meetings, "I'd like very much to help but I really don't know any Democrats." This was literally true of a good many of Stevenson's Lake Forest supporters.

Stevenson returned to Chicago and on December 1 had lunch with Lou Kohn, Steve Mitchell, and two others. They agreed on a form letter to be broadcast widely and immediately. It urged Stevenson's nomination and election to the Senate, set forth his qualifications, said, *"The time is short,"* and asked people to mark an enclosed card saying they favored Stevenson or authorizing the use of their names on the Stevenson-for-Senator Committee. Signed by Mitchell, Smith, and Kohn, it was the first formal piece of literature promoting Stevenson for any office.[2]

The committee members were drawn largely from the lawyers and financial men of LaSalle Street, from Lake Forest and other North Shore suburbs, from old college friends, and from the Council on Foreign Relations. This, not labor unions or ethnic groups or Negroes or others of the Democratic coalition, was the Stevenson base. The committee opened headquarters at 221 North LaSalle Street. The letter was dated December 3, 1947. It was late indeed —the slate-making committee would meet at the end of December. They mailed about 8,000 copies of the letter; about 1,000 replied endorsing Stevenson, a good return.

But everywhere they turned, Stevenson and his supporters ran head on into Jack Arvey's determination to run Paul Douglas for

[2] Among those listed as members of the organizing committee were Graham Aldis, Ernest S. Ballard, Ralph A. Bard, Laird Bell, Richard Bentley, William McCormick Blair, Mrs. John Alden Carpenter, John Dern, Edison Dick, Marshall Field IV, Walter T. Fisher, Raymond J. Friend (a law partner of Kohn), Meyer Kestnbaum, Ferd Kramer (head of a large mortgage house), Morris I. Leibman, Ed McDougal, William McIlvaine, Loring Merwin, John S. Miller, Nathaniel Owings, Ernst W. Puttkammer, Walter V. Schaefer, Leo T. Tierney, Carl Vrooman, Mrs. John P. Welling, Hubert L. Will, Samuel W. Witwer.

1. Presidential campaign image-making before the days of radio and television: the posters of the rival tickets in 1892, when Adlai Stevenson's grandfather, for whom he was named, was elected Vice President.

2. As a boy Adlai Stevenson went to family Sunday dinners in his grandfather Stevenson's stately old home on Franklin Park in Bloomington to
listen to his tales. The former Vice President is shown here with his wife

and children: standing—Letitia, Julia, and Lewis (father of Adlai Stevenson); seated—the Vice President, his wife, and Mary.

3. In this photo Vice President Adlai Stevenson (1835–1914) appears to be a stern man but a just one. Dignified, he wore a Prince Albert coat; just, he denounced a Bloomington lynch mob. Twice elected to Congress, he was a famed orator and raconteur, took liberal positions on issues, always ran well in the workingmen's section of Bloomington, and, although a staunch Democrat, always received independent votes.

4. Adlai Stevenson's father, Lewis Green Stevenson (1868–1929), traveled widely, frequently to little purpose. He was photographed in Japan in 1894.

5. In 1892, the year the first Adlai Stevenson was elected Vice President as a Democrat, his son Lewis became engaged to marry Helen Davis (1868–1935), daughter of the publisher of the Republican Bloomington *Pantagraph*. Then twenty-four, she went to Europe, where this photograph was taken. Next year she married Lewis and in 1900 became the mother of Adlai Stevenson.

6. This photograph of Elizabeth Stevenson Ives (1897–   ), sister of Adlai Stevenson and called Buffie, and their father was made on February 5, 1900, the day Stevenson was born. Their father was then working on the Hearst newspaper in Los Angeles.

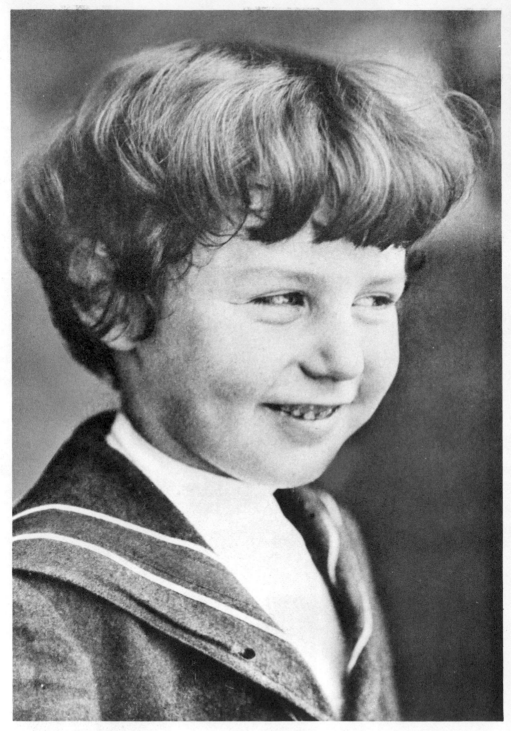

7. Adlai E. Stevenson (1900–1965) was three years old when this picture was taken. At about that time his parents were living in California, where he himself was born.

8. Adlai Stevenson at about the age of ten. By then his family had moved back home to Bloomington to stay.

9. Formal portrait of the future Governor of Illinois, presidential candidate, and ambassador to the United Nations at the age of fifteen, when he was a student in University High School at Normal, Illinois, adjacent to Bloomington.

10. In 1920, for the first time in his life, Adlai Stevenson, then a Princeton junior, went abroad alone—tramped through England, flew to Paris, toured Germany and the battlefields, climbed an Alp. In Switzerland he met his father and his adoring sister Buffie, shown with him here in Montreux.

11. Stevenson's sister Buffie and her husband, Ernest L. Ives, a career Foreign Service officer, are shown here with their son Timothy in Bloomington in 1928.

12. Adlai Stevenson's lovely wife, Ellen Borden Stevenson, during the early happy years of their marriage. The picture was taken for a Chicago *Tribune* society page.

13. Stevenson loved to "dress up," as the saying went. Here he is (left) with his wife and two friends at a Gay Nineties party given in 1936.

Senator and Stevenson for Governor if for anything at all. Ed Kelly liked the idea of Stevenson for Governor, partly because he wanted to foil his old enemy, Tom Courtney. Clifton Utley believed the Democratic machine refused to slate Douglas for Governor because, being experienced as an alderman, Douglas knew the workings of machine politics and would interfere with it as governor; Stevenson was safe since he was inexperienced. Utley and others thought the machine wanted to get rid of Douglas by sending him to the Senate, where he would have little patronage and little influence over state and Cook County politics. This idea may contain some truth but surely was not the only consideration. Yet Stevenson himself, and to some extent Douglas too, subscribed to it (though Douglas exempted Arvey).

Stevenson was reacting badly to the efforts to sidetrack him to the governorship. He asked the advice of many people. Arthur Krock urged him to stand fast for the senatorial nomination. His next-door neighbor, Glen Lloyd, said, "I hate to see somebody do something he doesn't really want to do but maybe if you really think about it you'll change your mind." Stevenson asked Harriet Welling whether it would be better for his "domestic situation" if he ran for Governor or Senator—he had in mind his strained relationship with Ellen. Mrs. Welling advised him to do what he thought right for him. He asked his old law partner, Ed Austin, to save a whole afternoon for discussion. Austin has recalled, "He said Arvey and the rest insisted that he run for Governor. I asked why not for the Senate. He said, 'I think because they want Douglas out of their hair. Anyway they'll support me for Governor but not for Senator and I've got to decide.' I said, 'Adlai, in the first place you're now twenty years out of law school and you've never quite decided if you want to be a lawyer or be in public life. You should make up your mind. I think it's public life though I think you could be a great lawyer. If you want public life, this is the opportunity of a lifetime. [Governor] Pete Green is in trouble with Republicans and independents. You'll be elected. And if you retain your health you'll be an outstanding candidate for President in 1952.' He guffawed. I said, 'I am sure that you're basically a very honest person—that you'll do your best to give Illinois an honest administration—and by 1952 the Democratic Party will be ready to turn to an honest man.'" Austin added years later, "As Governor he gave Illinois an honest and pretty good administration."

At about this time Dutch Smith went to New York on business and in the club car of the Twentieth Century Limited found Arvey alone. Smith has recalled, "I'd only seen him that one time. But I went over and sat down beside him and recalled myself to him and said, 'I'd like to talk to you a little more about him.' I made it sound casual. We'd been breaking our necks trying to get five minutes alone with Arvey. He invited me to go ahead and I did. Colonel Arvey said, 'Well, I don't know—a fellow was telling me the other day I'd better lay off Stevenson, that he went to Oxford.'" (Anglophobia was an important Chicago *Tribune* trait, as was contempt for "striped pants diplomats" and "the effete East.") Smith has said, "I told him I knew Adlai pretty well and I was pretty sure he hadn't gone to Oxford but I suggested the best thing to do would be to ask Adlai. Colonel Arvey said that'd be fine. We talked awhile and he asked when I was going back to Chicago. I told him Thursday. He said he would be on the same train and invited me to have dinner with him."

In New York, Smith wired Stevenson. Stevenson replied, "Never went to Oxford not even to Eton." On the return train trip Smith reported this to Arvey. Arvey said he had two good candidates for Senator, Douglas and Stevenson, but none for Governor. He wanted "a Kennelly type," a businessman, a man who was not a Republican but was not closely identified either with the Democratic organization. Smith suggested a man on the train, James Knowlson, president of a manufacturing company. He asked Arvey if Arvey wanted him to ask him and Arvey said, "Sure," so Smith went over to Knowlson and asked, "Do you want to be Governor of Illinois? Arvey's looking for a candidate." Knowlson replied, "I'm not going to be a Democrat this year—we need a change." Another man was sitting with him, so Smith asked him too, but he was a Republican. He reported to Arvey, who said, "That's the trouble." They continued talking about Stevenson, and Arvey asked if Stevenson was married. Smith suggested Arvey come to lunch next Sunday to meet Ellen and talk to Stevenson.

Smith lived in an impressive home on an estate fronting on Lake Michigan. Arvey recalled many years later, "I got lost on the way. Stevenson was playing tennis when I got there so I sat and talked to Ellen. I said, 'Mrs. Stevenson, this is an opportunity for public service. What difference does it make which office it is? What matters is that he has an opportunity for public service and this will put him into the political picture, project him into the limelight. As far as the Governor's office being a dead end goes, it's just the opposite. Move governors have gone to the presidency than senators. Senators have to vote on issues. The Governor is an administrator and doesn't have to get tangled up in these controversial issues. He can run a clean slate government and an efficient one. He can do a good job and attract national attention.' I had no more idea of Stevenson being President at that time than I have of that"—pointing to an object on his desk—"jumping up and turning a somersault by itself. But I used it with Mrs. Stevenson. He came in from playing tennis and asked me, he said, 'Jack, I'm a little worried about this Governor thing. What's expected of me? Everybody says you don't trust Douglas on patronage.' I said, 'I will tell you the same thing I told Kennelly in 1947. The only thing I ask of you is that you help the Democratic Party as much as you can in a decent way. We want the patronage when a Democrat can fill the job. I am not talking about cabinet appointments or your own personal appointments. Get the best men you can for those. We want you to get the best. That's the way you can help the party the most. You're our showcase. If you do well, then we'll look good. All I ask is that you be loyal to the party—don't make an alliance with the Republicans.' "

Time was running out. Arvey held a key meeting of his associates on December 23 and asked Stevenson about the position of the Chicago *Daily News*. Stevenson consulted Lloyd Lewis and reported that the *News* would not commit itself but its owner was "very friendly" toward Stevenson. Stevenson consulted his son Adlai III, home from Milton for Christmas. Adlai III has recalled, "It was on one of these walks along the river. I asked some silly question such as was he sure he'd be nominated in the primary. He was terribly calm and man-to-man about it, sounding a little reluctant and weighing both sides. I think as always he was making sure the kids had no objections. He did it on the presidency and on the governorship. I always said, 'Whatever you think you should do.' " Adlai thought his father had already made up his mind to run for governor.

Now, between Christmas and New Year's, the time of decision had come. The statewide slate-making committee gathered in the Morrison Hotel. Arvey asked Smith to bring Stevenson to Arvey's office to talk with Arvey and Senator Lucas. The meeting went well but no decisions were reached. In the next few days Arvey asked Smith several times why Stevenson seemed reluctant. Finally he told Smith flatly that Douglas was going to run for the Senate and Stevenson could have the nomination for Governor. Smith suggested Arvey offer it to him directly. Arvey did, on a Saturday morning, December 27. Stevenson said he didn't know what to say and asked to think it over during the weekend. Arvey called Smith and asked if he thought Ellen was objecting. Smith didn't but would ask Stevenson immediately. He telephoned but Stevenson was attending a performance of the Princeton Triangle Club. Smith asked Ellen directly how she felt; she said she preferred Springfield to Washington. "So I called Arvey back and reported this. I thought I'd better not tell Arvey that Adlai was at the Triangle Club or he'd think he was a cream puff for sure so I just told Arvey he was at the theater and couldn't be reached."

Stevenson kept insisting on party unity and in particular on obtaining the support of Mayor Kennelly, with whom he was greatly impressed. The case of Kennelly was curious. Henry Tenney, a lawyer and friend of both men, said Kennelly never "warmed up" to Stevenson. "Kennelly was brought up in Bridgeport. He was a different breed of cat—he had worked for a living—a newsboy type. He looked on Stevenson as a striped-pants diplomat Johnny-come-lately." Tenney tried unsuccessfully to persuade Kennelly to support Stevenson. Of all the people whose endorsement Stevenson or his friends sought, Kennelly was the one man who held out against Stevenson.

Dutch Smith has recalled, "It was a last-minute thing. The night before the decisive meeting Arvey called me and said he still didn't have an answer. And couldn't I do something about it. I went to Adlai's office at nine in the morning and told him, 'If you turn this down you're not going to have another chance.' He said, 'Can I get Kennelly's support?' I said, 'If you get the nomination he'll have to support you.' He wanted it checked. I said, 'I don't know him well but Ned Brown does.' So I went over to First National and tried to get Brown. He was away. Jim Forgan, a Republican, called Kennelly. Kennelly was in a City Council meeting until 1:00 P.M. The state committee decision was due by noon. I went back to Adlai's office and said, 'We can't get to him but you've made an effort and left a message and he'll have to support you.' So he called Arvey—I was with him—and he said okay."

That day, Tuesday, December 30, the slate-making committee nominated Douglas for Senator and Stevenson for Governor. (They telephoned Douglas just as he was about to begin a speech on the theory of production.) Kathryn Lewis, widow of Lloyd Lewis, has recalled that she and her husband went home on the commuter train to Lake Forest with Stevenson that evening. He was elated. Ellen was supposed to meet the train at Lake Forest but she did not, and, after waiting for her awhile, Stevenson let the Lewises drive him home. They all went in to celebrate. Lewis had the newspapers announcing the nomination; John Fell grabbed them and ran to tell the cook. Stevenson called to Ellen upstairs and went to get ice cubes for drinks. After some delay, Ellen came down in a hostess gown. She said nothing about the nomination. Instead she read aloud to Lloyd Lewis a poem she had just written. Lewis said it was good and suggested publishing it. Conversation languished. Mrs. Lewis later recalled, "It was so awkward we finally left."

The next day was December 31. For many years Stevenson's Lake Forest and Libertyville crowd had gone to a New Year's Eve party at the home of John and Mickey Kellogg on Little St. Mary's Road north of Stevenson's. During the war, when the men were away, the wives had gathered there and gone skating on the Des Plaines River and drunk champagne and cooked hamburgers in a riverbank cottage the Kelloggs had. After the war the parties resumed, becoming larger as Mrs. Kellogg added relatives and the growing children of guests. Sometimes the guests wore costumes and put on charades. It was this sort of party that had begun to bore Stevenson. Now, with Stevenson nominated, the guests converted the annual party into a mock torchlight parade and political rally. They did so to prevent the party from becoming a wake—they could not believe that Stevenson had a chance to beat the powerful Green machine. One of them composed a song, "Stevenson for Governor," to the tune of "Wintergreen for President" from *Of Thee I Sing.* Others contrived and assembled costumes, flares, and noise-makers. Jane Dick has recalled, "That evening there took place perhaps the smallest and most skeptical, but certainly the most affectionate, political demonstration that this country has ever seen." Some of Stevenson's social friends never did quite shake the habit of regarding his political ventures as something of a lark.

6

Now at last, after so many years of trying, Adlai Stevenson was in politics. Born with money, reared in luxury, traveled, Princeton-educated, member of a conservative Republican LaSalle Street law firm, friend of the bankers and lawyers and businessmen who dwelt on Lake Forest estates, diplomat, friend of the British aristocracy, Chicago socialite and clubman, after-luncheon and after-black-tie-dinner speaker, he had at last found the political support he needed —found it among the slab-faced men from the slums of the Cook County Democratic machine. That machine was one of the most powerful in the nation, exercising at least as much control over its area as the Hague machine's over Jersey, Tammany's over New York, the Crump machine's over Memphis, Pendergast's over Kansas City. Indeed, as later events proved, it outlasted all the others. It had been called the Kelly-Nash machine; now it was being called the Arvey machine. (Later it would be called Daley's machine.)

The 1946 defeat had hurt it badly but had not smashed it, and now in 1948, having recouped with the election of Mayor Kennelly, it was once more strong. Many times the machine, or some of its leaders, had been accused of possessing ties with the Syndicate, as the criminal heirs of Al Capone were called. Many times the machine, or some of its leaders, had been accused of appointing district police captains who permitted gambling and prostitution, with the payoff divided between the police captain and the ward committeeman. Many times the machine, or some of its leaders, had been accused of graft and vote fraud. Little was ever proved though much was doubtless true. None of this, of course, was new: corruption in Chicago goes back to the last century and characterizes both political parties. The politicians kept dead men on the election poll books. They registered imaginary voters from vacant lots. They arranged for voters to vote several times on a single day—"chain voting." They "short-penciled" some voting booths—tied a pencil on a string too short to reach the Republican column on the ballot —and stuffed voting boxes with Democratic ballots hours before the polls opened. (When voting machines came into use, the politicians simply set the dial on the machine to give the Democrats a landslide lead several hours before the polls opened.) Counting paper ballots with a pencil lead under the fingernail, they spoiled Republican ballots. They rolled up enormous Democratic majorities.

Some men will work for a political party because they deeply believe in its programs or candidates. But not many will, and even fewer can afford to work for principle or for free. Most want to get paid. They want jobs working for the city, the County Board, the state's attorney, Municipal Court, Circuit Court, the Sanitary District, the sheriff, and so on. In the 1930s, one machine man once recalled, the machine had the Governor, the Mayor, the county offices, everything. (By 1948, city and county jobs totaled an estimated 31,000.) One politician recalled, "We also in those days had more of what you might call the sinews of war. There was a handbook on every street corner, and a man could work in the bailiff's office in the morning and in a handbook in the afternoon. In the 24th Ward, people used to think that sheet writing"—posting odds on horses in an illegal handbook—"was civil service." The old way of winning an election was to load the public payrolls with temporary appointees at election time and open up the gambling houses so the gamblers could afford heavy campaign contributions.

The machine contained everything—black men and white, Irish and Jews, Poles and Lithuanians. It was composed of such diverse elements that it was always in danger of flying apart. When newspapers attacked it, it closed ranks. Sometimes attack helped, not hurt, it.

Jack Arvey once said, "What do they do over at the Morrison?" —the hotel that was machine headquarters at the time. Smiling, he said, "It's a crime to tell the truth—the legend is much more interesting. Most people think when politicians meet they go to a corner and figure out deep diabolical schemes to outwit the enemy. Actually, the Morrison is just like any sales organization trying to sell its product and straighten out its problems. Setting up an organization in a ward where we're weak. Then there's the matter of literature— deciding on it, distributing it, getting it into the hands of four or five thousand precinct captains. Then there's organized labor. Labor and fraternal groups are for you but you've got to see to it that they do the work, get special literature, and so on. You try to find out where you're weak. When Daley first ran, he was a little weak among Jewish voters so you set to work running cocktail parties and mass meetings in Jewish sections. I had a cocktail party for him for three hundred Jewish men and women, mostly heads of organizations. I'd tell them, 'I don't know if you're a Democrat or a Republican but I want you to meet Dick Daley so when he's your mayor you'll understand what kind of a man he is.' In politics people want to know the candidate, they like to be able to say, 'Oh yes, I know him.' So the Morrison guides that sort of thing. It straightens out matters of conflicting interests. We may have rival men in a certain ward; we iron out the differences. We take weak men out. We see that the polls are manned—see that no vacancies arise among the election officials so the opposition can fill 'em. It's a full-time job, eight-thirty to six at night. That's what makes an organization. It does no good to win the 24th Ward by 20,000 and lose in the 49th and 50th by 21,000."

Long before a campaign begins, billboards have to be rented and copy prepared for them; radio (and now television) time has to be bought. Every major rally requires countless man-hours of planning: men must plan ward by ward how to get their people downtown to the rally, they must decorate the hall and see that the proper dignitaries find seats on the stage. During a campaign, thousands of circular letters must be mailed, perhaps a letter to all precinct captains, a special letter to members of Italian-American groups, another to Greek-Americans. ("This is a big town, you know.") Several carloads of literature go out during a campaign. The headquarters sets up a speakers' bureau and sends the sheriff, the state's attorney, aldermen, and other party leaders out to the wards nightly.

But at bottom the machine depends upon the individual ward organization and its precinct captains. A precinct captain is usually thought of as a rather seedy character with a lowly job in the Sewer Department. Sometimes he is. But he often turns out to be a well-dressed man in a convertible coupe who owns a couple of two-flat apartments and employs several paid assistant captains. A precinct captain is a man of power and standing in his community. He is the man the citizen telephones if the garbage is not collected or a dead tree needs cutting down or a traffic ticket has to be paid (or fixed) or a set of complicated Social Security forms has to be filled out. The City Hall government is remote; the precinct captain lives down the street. He *is* the government. A precinct captain once said, "When I go around to see you just before the election, I don't say vote for Daley—I say vote for *me*. Daley's *my* candidate. He's the guy gives me my job. Give me a vote and you'll protect my job. And if I'm a good precinct captain, you'll do it, because you know me, I've done favors for you, I'm on the job three hundred and sixty-five days out of the year, I walk around house to house, I'm making myself conspicuous, I'm asking if there's anything I can do for you."

One of Congressman Dawson's men once said, "The function of a captain in a precinct is much like a mayor in a village in France. There are a lot of things that happen, they go to the precinct captain and he solves it. He'll get in jail, the captain has to go down and get him out, go get him a lawyer. If his wife has to get to the hospital to have a baby, the captain will get an ambulance. If he gets paid on Saturday night he'll spend all his money and on Monday the captain will lend him six dollars to get through the week." Housing and jobs—those were the overriding issues on the South Side ghetto because among Negroes they were the overriding personal problems. "People can't get a job, can't pay the rent—the captain helps. People were kicked out of their tenements when the tenements were torn down around here and they went to Hyde Park and bought homes and then they were kicked out again. They are displaced persons, displaced over and over. But a displaced person from Europe can get a job when a Negro can't. Listen, they're suffering. Most Negroes are Democrats because the Democrats have given them a welfare program." Dawson himself once said, "This headquarters functions three hundred and sixty-five days in the year. The people in here are poor people, they have many problems, they bring their problems here and we do what we can. Getting people into the hospital, getting Aid to Dependent Children for mothers—a thousand and one problems that will come up to the poor people who are easily shoved around. If a problem comes up that the captain can't solve he refers it in here. The captains take care of the people when they're sick, when a person dies they are there, and when a child is born they are there. That is the only secret to it. Three hundred and sixty-five days in the year. He does not wait till Election Day. If you help them the rest of the year, they will help you on Election Day."

But mere aimless neighborliness is not enough. How does the precinct captain convert favors into votes on Election Day? Dawson's man said, "Well, you hire workers. In a big apartment building you have a worker for each section to get the vote out. To knock on the door and say, 'Have you voted yet?' and bring 'em on down. To get people to get out of bed and vote. Each place in the precinct where there are a lot of people living, you get workers in there, pay them five, ten, twenty dollars apiece for the day. So a hundred dollars per precinct goes pretty quick that way. You might have ten workers per precinct." The Dawson organization, he said, spent a hundred dollars per precinct on Election Day—about ten thousand dollars per ward. "Of course where Mr. Dawson gets the money I do not know. He gets it from all those he created, I presume." In addition to the workers, the party has watchers in each polling place. "As people come in the watcher checks them off. Then two hours before the polling place closes you know who has not voted in your precinct. So you send out runners to get the people out. 'Come out here and vote, the polling place is closing, when you wanted your light bill paid I did it for you.' The last two hours is the busiest time. That's the effectiveness of an organization. And a man who hasn't got an organization is just in a hell of a fix. Because the majority of the people are not going to come out and vote unless they are urged and coerced."

The pre-eminent Democratic ward in Chicago is the 24th Ward, on the West Side. This is the birthplace of the machine, Jack Arvey's home ward. Its leaders call it "the famous 24th." On its membership cards is printed, "The Champion Democratic Organization of Chicago." When its residents move to the North Side they tell their new precinct captains, "You don't have to worry about us—we're from the 24th Ward, we're broke in good." In 1922, when the 24th Ward was established, Arvey became its first alderman. Since then many other men who learned their politics in the 24th have moved out over Chicago to bolster the machine. The 24th Ward has never gone Republican. The 24th performed its most remarkable feat in 1936, when the machine decided to dump the Democratic Governor, Henry Horner. Horner was Jewish and the 24th was almost entirely Jewish. But he lost the 24th by some 7,000 votes. *"This,"* said one admirer, "is organization." The Republican ward committeeman in the 24th once said, "In 1930 we could get 30 or 35 per cent of the vote. But in 1932 we got murdered. Unemployment did it." During the 1930s many of the best Republican precinct captains swung over to the Democrats. "You can't blame them—that's the way they make their living, it's a profession with them, no more degrading than any other. This got to be a tough ward to get *any* Republican votes. We read in the papers about how the Democrats steal votes. Gosh all fishhooks, they don't have to do a damn thing here. Any more than the Republicans have to in Vermont or Evanston."

The 24th Ward is a small West Side ward, a workingman's neighborhood and an old neighborhood, full of once fashionable apartment buildings fallen into decay, of cottages and two-flats and factories. It was carved out of two wards, one of which had been the home ward of Mayor Anton Cermak. When Arvey became the ward's first alderman in 1922, the ward was still predominantly Bohemian but the Jews were already moving in, and soon the ward was almost entirely Jewish. When Arvey went into the army in 1941, his secretary and protégé, Arthur X. Elrod, took over, and he remained ward committeeman for many years, even long after he himself moved away to an expensive apartment on Lake Shore Drive overlooking Lake Michigan. Elrod was a compact, smart, expressionless man who smoked big cigars and wore black suits and a black hat and spent winters in Florida and summers in Michigan. He had been a precinct captain twenty years. The story that he most enjoyed telling concerned the 1948 election. President Truman came to Chicago near the end of that campaign, and nearly everyone thought he was losing, but Elrod told him he would carry the 24th by 25,000 votes. Truman, almost alone, had thought he was going to win but even he could not credit such optimism. Elrod attended the inaugural and attempted to go to the presidential box. Guards stopped him, but he sent a note to Truman showing him the 24th Ward result: 26,400 for Truman, 3,600 for Dewey. The President ordered the guards to stand aside and greeted him. Elrod liked to recall, "I put out my hand to put the note back in my pocket and he said, 'Oh no, I'm going to keep this—this I must show to people who'll come to me and say they did such a great thing for me in this campaign.'"

For years the 24th Ward went 24,000 to 3,000, no matter who was running—Mayor Kelly beat his two opponents in 1935 by 24,489 to 453 in that ward, Mayor Kennelly beat his opponent in 1947 by 26,017 to 3,111, Stevenson, running for Governor in 1948, beat his opponent 27,295 to 3,264, President Truman carried the ward that same year 26,497 to 3,638, Stevenson in 1952 beat Eisenhower 23,681 to 3,099 in the 24th Ward. The 24th Ward was a banner ward. When in a single year in the 1950s it switched from being nearly all Jewish to being nearly all Negro, the machine rolled on: Mayor Daley in 1955 beat his opponent in the 24th Ward by 18,329 to 1,658.

With huge majorities like those, the machine elected its candidates. The 24th was not the only one that consistently turned in lopsided majorities. So did the 1st Ward, comprising the downtown Loop. So did the Negro wards on the South Side and later the West Side. So did the "river wards"—those fronting on the Chicago River as its two branches curved around the Loop and sliced through the Southwest and Northwest sides—the Northwest Side wards that were heavily Polish and German, the Southwest Side wards inhabited by Irish and Poles and Lithuanians and Bohemians, the West Side Italian wards, the poor Jewish wards first on the West, then on the North Side. As you moved out toward the edges of the city, where homes are better and incomes higher, the machine's control diminished sharply. Republicans carried several wards on the city's fringes. And the Democratic machine was weak in white-collar Evanston to the north and all but helpless in such executive suburbs as Winnetka.

In all fairness, it must be said that the Republican machine in Chicago was equally corrupt if less successful than the Democratic machine. In the 1920s, the Prohibition years, the years of Al Capone, when Chicago was controlled by the Republican machine's Big Bill Thompson, that machine employed all the chicanery that the Democrats used later. In the 1930s and 1940s, and later, in some wards Republican leaders made deals with Democratic leaders and, in return for jobs or money, made no effort to contest the election but let the Democrats win by default.

As its strength increased, the Cook County Democratic machine had little need to resort to vote fraud in order to win. The Democrats, controlling City Hall and the County Building—both were housed in the same block-square stone structure—controlled enough patronage jobs to put on the city and county payrolls enough men to put a precinct captain and an assistant precinct captain in each one of Chicago's precincts. Each of Chicago's fifty wards had a Democratic and a Republican ward committeeman; they were the party leaders of their wards. (Sometimes they also had themselves elected aldermen to represent the ward in City Council but their power stemmed from being ward committeemen.) The committeeman handed out city and county jobs that his party controlled; he appointed the precinct captains and assistant precinct captains. Often the city or county jobs entailed little work; the precinct captain devoted most of his time to politics—doing favors for his constituents. Sometimes he stretched his influence into less legitimate areas—ignored fire hazards that violated the building code in a slum building, helped obtain by bribery a zoning variation, meddled in police matters and even serious criminal cases, not excluding murder. For some services, fixed prices existed—it used to cost $5,000 to "cut a curb," that is, to get a permit to construct a driveway over a curb. Such important matters went up to the ward committeeman himself. But with the day-to-day problems, the precinct captain was the man who straightened things out. A week before the election, and again on the Sunday before, the precinct captains canvassed their precincts. Sunday night they reported to their ward committeemen how many votes they would get on Tuesday. These reports went in to the Central Committee headquarters at the Morrison Hotel. There they were tabulated, compared with registration lists and previous votes, and, if the tally seemed low, the machine's leaders gave the precinct captains extra money to hire election workers and ordered them to increase their efforts. By the day before the election, the Morrison Hotel leaders knew pretty well how many votes they would get. On Election Day the precinct captain got out his vote. If he did not deliver, he was fired—fired as precinct captain, fired from his city or county job.

Now, one must remember that the machine was at its strongest in the most dismal slums. To become a precinct captain, to climb the political ladder, was, for many a slum boy, the best and indeed almost the only way to rise from the gutter. The powerful leaders of the machine, the hard-faced men who sat in dinner jackets at huge banquets honoring, or raising money for, Governors and Senators and Presidents, had come up this way from the slums. They might be ward committeemen, they might be aldermen, they might have delegated those jobs to others. They might be city or county officeholders, they might be judges. They might have gone into the insurance or real estate business and become rich—a ward committeeman in either of those businesses can hardly avoid riches. They wore silk suits and white-on-white shirts and pearl-gray neckties. They went to Miami Beach in the winter and the Wisconsin lakes in the summer. They spent hours under the sun lamp and were always tanned in the winter; they always looked as if they had just spent two hours in their private club being massaged, manicured, shaved. They lunched at Fritzel's and rode in Cadillacs and went to the fifty-dollar window at Arlington Park race track. Their wives wore mink and diamonds. The few who, growing older, assumed the role of elder statesman devoted themselves to good works, traveling, if they were Jewish, to Israel, where buildings and parks were dedicated to them, and selling bonds for Israel. On the walls of their private lux-

uriously furnished offices were photographs of their parents; autographed photographs of dignitaries, of Presidents, even, had come
later to the walls, nearly covering them. They were sentimental men
among themselves, and, grown older, liked to reminisce about the
teachings of their immigrant parents, about the old days in the
ward, boxing in the sporting clubs of the West Side, a Jew telling a
story about an Irishman who "used to make rosaries for me." Talking to each other, they touched each other—the hand on the arm,
on the shoulder, plucking at the sleeve. They told long stories, "So
I said to him, 'Listen, you son of a bitch,' and he said to me," and
so on, acting it out, seizing the listener by the lapels to dramatize the
story. Their relationships were very personal. They were almost
embarrassingly intimate with each other; to outsiders they were invariably granite-faced, suspicious, rude, or silent. They observed, or
always claimed to observe, their own code of honor—camaraderie
and loyalty and honesty with their own, hostility to outsiders. They
never forgot the quarrels they had with rivals when younger, quarrels over place, money, power, even issues—Abraham Lincoln Marovitz, who was in the legislature during Stevenson's time and later
became a federal judge, liked to recall how he had fought Mayor
Ed Kelly because Kelly favored a bill to bar foreign physicians
from medical practice: "So I said to Kelly, 'We give you thirty thousand votes to seven or eight hundred—why are you with people
like the American Medical Association that are against you?'" They
all had one thing in common: wherever they dined and wintered
today, however they and their wives dressed today, they all had
come up from the gutter in the slums, a dog-eat-dog jungle, and
they never forgot it. Some, as they fought their way up, had committed indictable offenses, though few ever had been indicted. The
best had done nothing dishonorable by their own code. Each knew
all about the others. They formed indeed a closed ring no one
could break.

What could Adlai Stevenson have in common with them, or they
with him? Not much, except a desire to win elections. He knew
nothing of the world they came from. Except as a lawyer who had
gone there occasionally, he knew nothing of the old blocky City-
County Building, with its dirty windows and brass spittoons, with
seedy-looking men trudging in and out, the fortress of the machine;
he knew nothing at all of the dingy ward headquarters where the
deals were made and the cases fixed and the votes secured. His
first brush with the ponderous bulk of machine power, his effort in
1936 to join the ward machine of Paddy Bauler, one of the more

raucous of the ward committeemen, had been bluntly rebuffed. Now years later he was the machine's candidate for Governor of Illinois.

Jack Arvey was his friend. Arvey, although still under heavy *Tribune* attack, had by now begun to ascend toward the level of elder statesman. He was by nature as well as learning a gentler man and one with broader horizons than most of his colleagues. Arvey and Stevenson formed a genuine friendship, founded on mutual respect. Arvey had an almost fatherly attitude toward Stevenson. He served, or tried to serve, as a buffer between Stevenson and some of the blunter, cruder powerful ward and county leaders, such as Al Horan and Tom Keane. These men, and their colleagues, got the vote out for Stevenson; that was their job. (The statistics do not show, as some have claimed, that they "cut" him—that is, ordered their precinct captains to tell voters to vote for the county ticket but not for Stevenson, both in the 1948 governorship election and in the two later presidential elections.) But though they got him votes, they had no use for him. He was not their sort. Many of them, and many of their voters, were Catholics; these appear to have especially disliked Stevenson. Arvey has said, "They thought he was a narrow-minded Presbyterian from Lake Forest." Many actively disliked him. Once at a fund-raising dinner after he had run for President, a dinner in Chicago at which both Stevenson and former President Truman spoke, and where the expensive tables were bought by the machine leaders, one of the most powerful and toughest of the ward leaders, Tom Keane, talked to his table partner throughout Stevenson's speech and pointedly neither rose nor applauded when Stevenson finished speaking. One can remark a curious justice in the instinctive anti-Stevenson reaction of the ward committeemen and precinct captains and, ultimately, their voters. For Stevenson *did* upon occasion suffer lapses of taste, he *did* on occasion utter unworthy remarks about Jews. To a limited degree— and it is necessary to limit the degree sharply—he *did* seem "a narrow-minded Presbyterian from Lake Forest"; and somehow these people sensed it.

About half the total vote in Illinois was cast in Cook County. It ought not be thought that all vice resided in Cook County, all virtue downstate. The second biggest Democratic stronghold in Illinois, after Cook County, was the glob of industrial cities lying just across the Mississippi River from St. Louis—East St. Louis and other towns nearby. No more corrupt area existed anywhere in the United States. Moreover, many Democratic leaders from other downstate areas were every bit as corrupt as those in Cook County and some were worse. The Republicans too held whole tiers of counties in central Illinois where vote fraud was traditionally as common as in Cook County and where Republican majorities were as implausibly lopsided as Democratic majorities in some Chicago wards. In one such polling place, when a voter in the primary asked for a Democratic ballot, something like consternation ensued, and a Democratic ballot was produced only after considerable effort. Numerous Republican leaders and officeholders were notorious, and some had ties to downstate gangsters every bit as noxious as the Chicago Syndicate. Indeed, Republican corruption gave Stevenson, running for Governor in 1948, one of his best issues.

His opponent was the incumbent Republican, Dwight H. Green. Green was running for a third term. He had made his name earlier as one of the prosecutors who convicted Al Capone of income tax evasion. Once he had run for Mayor of Chicago and had lost to Ed Kelly, presenting himself as a vigorous young crime fighter and reformer. During the second term of the Democratic Governor, Henry Horner, the Democrats had become corrupt, and Green had won the governorship as a reformer. During his own second term, however, he had become distracted by visions of the presidency— or at least the vice-presidency—and his own administration had become corrupt. He became known as the *Tribune*'s puppet. The state payroll increased greatly as Republican politicians put men on it who did no work but drew their pay—building "the Green machine," as it came to be called. Scandals occurred in state purchases of land and supplies. Highways and state institutions deteriorated. Money was extracted from businessmen. The Centralia mine blew up, killing 111 men, after months of warnings that it was unsafe and a direct appeal by the miners to Governor Green to "please save our lives," and in the ensuing investigation it transpired that some of Green's coal mine inspectors (not the one at Centralia) had solicited campaign contributions from coal mine operators. During the 1948 campaign, a downstate gangster was murdered at Peoria. In the subsequent uproar and investigation, politicians affiliated with Green indicted Ted Link, a reporter for the St. Louis *Post-Dispatch* (which opposed Green), on trumped-up charges of kidnapping and conspiracy, thereby raising the issue of freedom of the press; several Republican newspapers deserted Green. Although long since forgotten, "the Green machine" at that time had a reputation at least as bad as that of the Cook County Democrats.

It was against the Green machine and in favor of good government that Stevenson made his basic campaign for the governorship in

1948. He said, "I am not a politician; I am a citizen." He presented himself as the man of probity with an impeccable past of civic rectitude and good works come down from high estate, surrounded by "independents" like Dutch Smith, to rescue Illinois from spoilsmen. Judge Marovitz has said, "Stevenson was naturally not at home with the average guy in politics. He'd try but it was difficult. He had a facial reaction, a forced smile. But once during the campaign he came to our ward party at the Chez Paris," a gaudy Near North Side night club famed years earlier for its gambling, "and charmed everyone." Arvey has recalled a ward meeting, possibly in the Near North Side river ward of Paddy Bauler, which Stevenson attended. Bauler, a heavy red-faced man, ran the ward out of his saloon, and at parties for his precinct captains handed out free steins of beer and stood on a table hoarsely singing a song called "Chicago." Arvey has recalled that Stevenson, observing the festivities, said, "My long-haired friends wouldn't approve—but I'm having a hell of a good time here." Stevenson's later law partner, Newton Minow, once said, "He liked the pols." One of the most telling criticisms made during his later presidential campaigns, however, was that as he traveled the nation he spent too much time working on speeches and not enough talking to local politicians. It seems likely that Stevenson, basically a gregarious man, would like to have been closer to the pols but his own background kept getting in his way—and the clannishness of the Chicago machine made it no easier. This, then, was the setting for his first try for elective public office. To this summary must be added that this was also the year that President Truman was running for President in his own right. His opponent, Governor Thomas E. Dewey of New York, was expected to beat him. Indeed, a good many of Stevenson's friends, and other people too, suspected that the Democratic machine had slated Stevenson and Douglas only because they thought they had no chance of winning.

Arvey, of course, could not singlehandedly appoint Stevenson the Democratic candidate; the state Central Committee had to approve Arvey's choice. It is a measure of Arvey's great power that the committee did so with few murmurs. Arvey has recalled, "When Stevenson was slated, only one ward committeeman walked out— Babe Connelly, Dick Daley's predecessor. Several did not vote. One said to me, 'I know what you're doing and it's all right.' He meant that he knew I believed that the Democrats had no chance that year and they might as well lose with a good-looking candidate. One committeeman even thought I had a deal with Dwight Green. A good many of the politicians didn't think Stevenson could win. I was sure he would. The week before the election Al Horan and Joe Gill and I each bet a thousand dollars on Stevenson at three to one. Got back nine thousand dollars."

7

On New Year's Day, January 1, 1948, Stevenson, just slated and nearly forty-eight years old, rapidly growing bald but still looking young, wrote from Libertyville to Mrs. Ives and her husband, "Well, I'm in it, after several dreadful days of indecision & stalling. I'm still a little stunned by the enormity of the task I've undertaken. Whether I've the strength, thick skin & capacity to at least make a good race I don't know, but at least I've got to try now for 10 fearful months." He told Mrs. Ives to send money "if you want to" to Dutch Smith. He added, "And if you really *want* to do some work I suppose the most useful thing would be a biography You might write such ancestral portions as you can from the material you have & it can be fitted into something more complete later I don't feel very gay this New Year's day!"

Stevenson had indeed gotten himself into a bewildering undertaking. A state-wide political campaign in a big state is a vast enterprise, entailing the collaboration of almost unnumbered wildly disparate elements, hurling the candidate, particularly such a fresh and inexperienced candidate as Stevenson, into the most unfamiliar settings. There were numberless tasks to be performed—raising money, preparing and distributing brochures and buttons and other campaign paraphernalia, buying advertising space in newspapers and radio, organizing special groups such as conservationists, getting out press releases and statements and speeches, doing research on issues and writing speech drafts, scheduling speeches throughout the state, making contact with county Democratic organizations and groups of independents, soliciting the support of important groups such as labor—endless tasks

Stevenson was not alone The Stevenson-for-Senator Committee led by Lou Kohn, Steve Mitchell, and Dutch Smith swiftly converted itself into the Stevenson-for-Governor Committee. By January 8 it had sent out its first mailing to its original list and by February 17 it had leased a headquarters at 7 South Dearborn Street. The lease was signed by Kohn, Smith, and Ed McDougal, who had become the committee's treasurer. During January, February, and March, Steve

Mitchell's time sheets show many meetings.[3] All this activity indicates efforts to coordinate the Stevenson "independents," the regular Democratic machine, and the Paul Douglas campaign.

Stevenson assembled a small personal staff to work on issues, speeches, and publicity. Carol Evans came to work with him in the campaign as his private secretary on February 1 and remained with him for thirteen years, until 1961. James W. Mulroy, a heavy-set Irish Chicago newspaperman who had won a Pulitzer Prize for a story on the Leopold-Loeb murder case, became the nearest thing to a campaign manager Stevenson had. Mulroy had left the *News* some years previously, had become managing editor of Marshall Field's *Sun,* and in 1948 when the *Sun* merged with the *Times* had found himself out of a job. In January of 1948, probably at the instigation of Marshall Field, Mulroy joined Stevenson's staff. The Stevenson campaign had no money and was not paying its public relations man, and he was doing little for the campaign; Mulroy asked William I. Flanagan, another Chicago Irishman, who was working for another public relations firm, to help out, and Flanagan did, giving his nights and weekends. Flanagan later became Stevenson's press secretary during his governorship and first presidential campaign. Lloyd Lewis wrote speech drafts. Stevenson, knowing little about state government, asked the advice of Carl McGowan. McGowan had decided to teach at Northwestern Law School. Stevenson asked him to join the campaign but McGowan felt committed to Northwestern and said he could not. He recommended Walter V. Schaefer, a lawyer who had worked in the Illinois Legislative Reference Bureau, was by now a professor of law at Northwestern, a member of Stevenson's old law firm and a resident of Lake Bluff, not far from Libertyville. During the spring Schaefer had to stay in Washington but in July he returned to Chicago and spent most of his time writing position papers and speech drafts for Stevenson. Jim Mulroy's brother-in-law was Don Walsh, also formerly with the *News* and *Sun* as "circulator," in charge of circulation, a hard-boiled job in Chicago; he now helped run Paul Douglas' campaign.

Stevenson and Douglas did some campaigning together. Douglas was expert at sidewalk campaigning, standing at factory gates early

---

[3] With Stevenson, Kohn, Smith, Dick Daley, Mike Greenebaum, a close associate of Paul Douglas; State Chairman George Kells; Bob Merriam, a young University of Chicago professor who held the 5th Ward aldermanic seat given up by Paul Douglas and who was the son of a distinguished professor friend of Stevenson; Mayor Kennelly; Bill Harshe, the publicity man; Marshall Field; Bill Blair; Jack Arvey; Henry Tenney.

in the morning, shaking hands. He was a burly vital man, stronger physically than Stevenson. Stevenson studied his technique but never learned to do it so well as Douglas. Douglas would move into a crowd, shake a voter's hand, say a word or two, then move invincibly on, like a tank, smiling, listening, speaking a few sentences to each, making sure he missed no one but spending little time with any. If, on the other hand, something a voter said struck Stevenson as interesting, he would stop and carry on a long conversation with him, while the rest of the voters waited and his campaign aides fidgeted.

One might have expected that Stevenson and Douglas, presenting similar good-government appeals, enjoying the machine's support but standing apart from it, interested in ideas, would have hit it off well. They did not, however. Through the years their relationship never became genuinely close, and several times they clashed. The root of their difficulty lay, Carl McGowan believes, in that first 1948 campaign. Douglas proposed to Stevenson that they pool their campaign contributions. Stevenson refused, probably feeling that he had access to more money than Douglas, and pooling would disadvantage him. Douglas resented it and said Stevenson was not a real Democrat—was more interested in his rich friends in Lake Forest than in the Democratic Party or Douglas. During the campaign itself, both the Chicago *Daily News* and the *Pantagraph* endorsed Stevenson but opposed Douglas; Douglas thought Stevenson could have prevented it. Little things happened—Ellen was rude to Mrs. Douglas. Douglas and Stevenson were never close comfortable allies.

The nucleus of Stevenson's personal campaign staff became Mulroy, Flanagan, and Schaefer, plus Lloyd Lewis and Carol Evans. Gradually other young men gravitated to it, some to work on speeches, some to perform purely political chores. Indeed, the Stevenson-Douglas campaign of 1948 brought into Democratic politics a leavening of good young men who stayed. William R. Rivkin, a lawyer and lecturer at Northwestern, joined the Stevenson campaign, became president of the Young Democrats of Cook County, worked in Stevenson's and Kennedy's presidential campaigns, and became a Kennedy and a Johnson ambassador. Daniel Rostenkowski joined the campaign and went on to become a Congressman from Illinois. Angelo Geocaris helped Douglas that year and for many years thereafter. Richard J. Nelson got into the Stevenson campaign, went on his staff when he became governor, and became national president of the Young Democrats. Perhaps because so many of the people in it were young, perhaps because Stevenson himself was new and stood apart from the machine, the 1948 campaign had the air of an adventure. Lou Kohn has recalled, "We were all new and enthusiastic. We had some good issues. We had a bad administration to defeat. It was an ideal campaign. The Governor enjoyed it—he was young and vigorous then."

Parallel to the staff working with Stevenson on issues and speeches was the Stevenson-for-Governor Committee. They wanted Harriet Welling to be the chairman of the Women's Division but she declined because of her husband's health. Jane Dick took the job, though she could not become active until after a spring trip to Europe. Stevenson's friends from Lake Forest and Libertyville and North Shore suburbs volunteered to work in the headquarters. Many were Republicans; the rest considered themselves independents; almost none was a Democrat. Stevenson encouraged this independent coloration. Many of them considered his candidacy amusing, not taking it with the seriousness the professional politicians took it. They seemed to think it the most natural thing in the world that Stevenson should be nominated; after all, they themselves held powerful positions in the financial and legal and business life of Illinois; why shouldn't Stevenson be called on to put things right politically? Many of these people differed greatly with Stevenson on national issues but supported him for Governor. Glen Lloyd once said, "As a neighbor we never had one difference. If we had to rebuild the fence, we'd each pay half of it. If the river needed attention—the dam went out once, it was an illegal Insull dam in the first place—we did it together. But I didn't agree with Adlai on many things. Once just before or during the 1948 campaign—we were sitting in front of the fire in his house —he said he couldn't see what was wrong with getting rid of the price system and controlling prices. I couldn't disagree more." As the campaign moved on, new people came to the headquarters to work, and Stevenson's socialite friends sometimes found themselves outnumbered by strangers. One, Mrs. John Miller, recalled, "I worked in the office sending out circulars and acting as receptionist, pushed around by a lot of Jewish women." Kathryn Lewis once said, "Election night in the headquarters Blair turned absolutely white—he came in and said, 'Harry Truman is winning.' He was shocked."

As the campaign progressed, young people from all over Chicago flocked to the headquarters, drawn by Stevenson's attractive "new look" in politics. A few of Stevenson's Lake Forest or Gold Coast friends still came in occasionally to help out, some on regular schedules. But by the end of the campaign, of the fifty-odd volunteers who appeared daily, on any given day one would probably find, in addition to Jane Dick and Dutch Smith, no more than one or two of his socialite friends.

Ellen made appearances for Stevenson during the campaign, though not so regularly as most candidates' wives. Mrs. Lewis has recalled that a woman in suburban Barrington invited some two hundred people to her home with Ellen the guest of honor. "Ellen was supposed to pick me up but she didn't show up till four-thirty, an hour and a half after the party was supposed to start. Instead of apologizing she said, 'Whoever heard of having tea before five?' By the time we got there, most of the guests had left." Others observed that Ellen was of little help to Stevenson during the campaign.

Some of Stevenson's downstate friends went to work for him. Donald Funk of Springfield, president of Sangamo Electric, though a Republican, was active in the campaign there, and so were Mary Jane Masters and Edna MacPherson and others. Stevenson had known them all from long ago. At least once, campaigning downstate, Stevenson stayed with the Funks. Don Forsyth, a Springfield insurance man, has said, "I have always been active in Democratic politics here but I've never had anyone inspire me as Stevenson did. I gave him hundreds and hundreds of hours away from my business."

The Stevenson-for-Governor Committee was reconstituted to make it statewide and tie it into Stevenson's personal staff. Its leaders were Stevenson's old friends and associates at law and the Council on Foreign Relations. There was little or no infusion of new blood, not much from the academic world, none from labor.[4]

From the outset, Stevenson had the support of Marshall Field III and his son, Marshall Field IV. With that went the endorsement of the Chicago *Sun-Times.* The Chicago *Daily News* also supported him. So did the St. Louis *Post-Dispatch,* influential in the southern half of Illinois, particularly in the coal-mining counties where it constantly reminded readers of the Centralia mine disaster. The Chicago

[4] James A. Cunningham of Chicago was the committee's general chairman; its director was James W. Mulroy. Its treasurer was Ed McDougal, the chairman of its finance committee was Carroll H. Sudler, Jr., and the co-chairmen of the Women's Division were Jane Dick and Mrs. Eric W. Stubbs. Its twelve vice-chairmen included two men from Chicago—Dutch Smith and Floyd E. Thompson, a lawyer—and ten from downstate, including Florence Fifer Bohrer of Bloomington, Donald Funk of Springfield, and Harry Hershey of Taylorville. The long list of the Chicago executive committee included Graham Aldis, Richard Bentley, Edgar Bernhard, young Bill Blair, Edward Eagle Brown, Mrs. John Alden Carpenter, Edison Dick, the young Marshall Field, Walter T. Fisher, Fred K. Hoehler, Meyer Kestnbaum, Lou Kohn, Ferd Kramer, John A. Lapp of the American Civil Liberties Union, Lloyd Lewis, William B. McIlvaine, Jr., Steve Mitchell, George W. Overton, Walter Schaefer, William P. Sidley, Sydney Stein, Jr., Clifton M. Utley, Harriet Welling, Jay N. Whipple, Quincy Wright.

Tribune, of course, opposed Stevenson vigorously, as did Hearst's *American.* Several downstate papers supported Stevenson, including V. Y. Dallman's *State Register* and Stevenson's own *Pantagraph.*

Stevenson's old friend and fellow Princetonian, Don Lourie, who was president of Quaker Oats, said years later, "He blossomed during that campaign. He did a wonderful job against Green. Ice cream socials, fairs, he worked the territory hard. He was not well known then. But he surprised a lot of people." During the campaign Kenneth F. Burgess sought out Henry Crown and said, "You know a lot of Democrats—will they agree to reward Stevenson's yeoman service to the party with a judgeship?" He expected Stevenson to lose the governorship. Jack Arvey has recalled encountering William Sidley at a barbecue at Stevenson's Libertyville farm. Sidley asked Arvey, "Jack, you're not hurting my boy too much, are you?" Arvey asked, "What do you mean?" Sidley said, "He won't be beaten so badly he'll be disgraced, will he?" Arvey said, "He's going to win." Clay Tate, editor of the *Pantagraph,* once recalled that when Stevenson had spoken in Bloomington on the UN about 1946 he had made "a lousy speech," his delivery hesitant, his manner uncertain, but that he became a good speaker while running for Governor because he was his own man.

The winters are long and cold in Illinois. To be officially nominated as the Democratic candidate for Governor, Stevenson would have to run in the primary, then held in April, albeit without opposition. Moreover, since he was not well known throughout the state and faced an incumbent Republican who was very well known, he must start campaigning immediately, in inhospitable January and February, with the election day, November 2, a long ten months away. Such a campaign is a grinding, wearing experience. Stevenson grumbled about it—he always grumbled—but he bore up well.

The campaign had started slowly. They always do, but it always troubles the candidate. One candidate said, "In January and February you're slogging around in the slush and ice, nobody at the meetings, who but a lunatic would go to a political meeting on nights like that; but then it gets to be March and April, the sky gets blue and it warms up a little, and pretty soon you're beginning to feel pretty good about how it's going."

On January 6, Stevenson spoke at a Junior Association of Commerce lunch, and the *Tribune* was quick to note that although he was a candidate for Governor of Illinois his topic was the Marshall Plan. After the speech Stevenson took a train with Arvey and other politicians to Springfield, where the state Central Committee was meeting to receive his acceptance of their nomination. Stevenson wrote out his speech in longhand on telegram blanks and gave it to Arvey and Spike Hennessey, the Democratic press agent, inviting them to revise it. "We didn't change a word of it," Arvey has said. The committee met, as it traditionally did, in the St. Nicholas Hotel at Springfield. These were professional politicians, looking him over.

He opened with a somewhat nervous joke, told them "how much I appreciate the honor" they had done him "in this fateful election year of 1948," then launched into his speech with complicated sentences that must have sounded strange to some of them: "I accept your endorsement sensible not only of the great and undeserved honor you have done me but also of your flattering confidence that my stable mates—and I know they will agree with me—and I can and will conduct the state campaign in a manner befitting the best traditions of the Democratic Party in Illinois. But even more than these, I am sensible of the solemn responsibility you have given me —a responsibility not alone to you as the organized, militant shock troops of the Democratic Party in Illinois, who have carried the standards of the people's party for so long, in adversity as well as triumph, but also the responsibility you have assigned me to the people of Illinois, regardless of party, who are not content with things as they are."

It was not a great speech but it was Stevensonian—he was addressing an audience of professional Democrats but talked about winning Republican and independent votes; he laid down the basic line of the campaign, an attack upon Republican corruption and a promise of good government, and he linked good government to the broader issue of the survival of the democratic system in a hostile world; he denounced inflation and rising prices and materialism and spoke of "the free way of life"; he spoke better of Mayor Kennelly than of the Democratic Party that elected him; and finally he bespoke eloquently his love for Illinois.

The *Tribune* identified him as "a delegate in the United Nations general assembly," somehow making the phrase sound as if it were a criminal record. The Democratic State Central Committee decided that their candidates would launch their primary campaign with two "caravans" led by Stevenson and Douglas that would tour the state, unusual for an uncontested primary, evidence that the party would make a serious effort to unseat Green and Brooks and that it needed to make its candidates known. Next night Stevenson introduced the Netherlands' ambassador to the United States at a huge formal dinner party at the Casino Club, an event reported on the society pages.

A cousin had written Stevenson on January 4, "Heartiest congratulations from us all, Adlai. How this would warm the hearts of those who have gone before you in the family as outstanding political figures from our state in the two preceding generations!" During the first faltering weeks, however, the campaign limped along. Henry Tenney said, "We'd call a meeting and have twelve people there." Illinois labor was split; the CIO supported Stevenson but the AFL supported Green. Even CIO support was in some quarters lukewarm. One day a CIO leader, Joe Germano, came storming in to Arvey and said, "We wanted to give him a contribution and get him to appoint our man Director of Labor and he refused." Arvey promised to talk to Stevenson and did. Arvey recalls, "They had asked him to promise this job to their man, Frank Annunzio. Stevenson had said he was not going to commit himself to any man. I agreed with him. I went back to Germano and told him, 'You think he's honest and fair and decent, don't you? Then why don't you take his word that he'll do the honest and decent and fair thing?' Well, Germano sulked throughout the entire campaign. Nevertheless Stevenson did not hesitate to appoint Annunzio. And a few years later when Annunzio got in trouble, Stevenson did not hesitate to fire him either."

In January, Stevenson was still doing some legal work. He did not resign from the Sidley law firm until February 4, telling Sidley, "I must tell you again how deeply I appreciate the generous financial settlement." This was, it turned out, his final break with the Sidley law firm.

Before long, campaigning absorbed his every waking hour. He had no time at all for social life and almost none for his family. He was away from home for weeks at a time; he was always surrounded by political people. He became increasingly remote from Ellen.

Henry Crown, the industrialist, told his son, "Stevenson doesn't have a chance in hell of being elected but let's show our appreciation," and sent his son to Stevenson with a check. Hughston McBain, a friend of Stevenson and president of the Marshall Field department store, sent him a contribution, and Stevenson wrote, "I have been much worried about how I was going to finance this fantastically expensive project without accepting help I don't want." Solicited by Dutch Smith, Edison and Jane Dick contributed $250 in March and more later. Dutch Smith talked with Marshall Field IV and Field contributed $3,000 and Stevenson, thanking him, said, "Money is our principal problem." Field would contribute more. William Sidley gave a "token" $250, saying he knew little of such matters, would give more if needed, and though a lifelong Republican hoped Stevenson would win. The Stevenson-for-Governor Committee received many contributions from Republicans who were anxious that their money be used to help Stevenson but not the rest of the Democratic ticket. Stevenson reassured them.

Few of Stevenson's Lake Forest friends made large contributions. Dutch Smith, who gave $1,000 in addition to a great deal of time and effort, once said, "Adlai gave Lou Kohn the names of three old friends of his and said we could get a thousand dollars from each. They didn't give a penny. For years they had been telling him that if he'd get into politics they'd support him financially. It was all cocktail party talk. In 1952 he gave me those same three names. I was embarrassed to tell him. I'd just nod and forget it. Adlai's so sort of trusting."

An audit—Ed McDougal insisted on it—of the Stevenson-for-Governor Committee's books was completed long after the election and included some post-election money raised to pay off an anticipated deficit. It showed that the total expenditures of the committee were only $154,215.44 (including $3,319.51 for the inauguration). This is an astonishingly small sum. Contributions totaled $172,840.10. This does not, of course, include any money the regular Democratic organizations spent on Stevenson's behalf, or any money that other organizations such as labor groups spent. Few campaigns for governor or senator in big states in recent years have spent so little. Of the total contributed, Stevenson personally received $10,200, including $1,000 from the Peabody Coal Company—one is reminded of the Centralia miner who said that if a coal company gives a politician $1,000 it expects something in return. Stevenson loaned the committee $3,000 at the outset, as did Mrs. Ives; they reimbursed themselves. Lou Kohn was repaid $1,000 he loaned it. The audit showed that the Cook County machine as such contributed $10,-000, the largest single sum. And individual leaders of the machine contributed heavily—$2,500 each from Joe Gill and Al Horan (but only $75 from Stevenson's friends John and Mickey Kellogg). Moreover, various ward organizations contributed—Dick Daley sent $250 on behalf of the 11th Ward Regular Democratic Organization. Steve Mitchell wrote years later that Arvey and the machine had made it clear that "we were on our own financially." This is not fair to Arvey and the machine. The machine did contribute. Moreover, the practice of the machine was to exact a large campaign contribution from each candidate to be spent on behalf of the entire ticket. For example, it was said to cost $50,000 to be slated for Circuit Court judge. In the case of Stevenson, the Cook County machine levied no assessment. (Mitchell said the state committee extracted $2,400.) Moreover, the Cook County machine launched a program for Stevenson in the suburbs, something unusual. Labor unions contributed substantially—$2,000 from Sam Levin's Amalgamated Clothing Workers, $2,500 each from the United Auto Workers and the United Steel Workers. Stevenson accepted large contributions from several companies doing business with the state or local governments. He obtained small sums from a good many wealthy liberal Jews whom he did not know. He received surprisingly little money from the East.[5]

8

Stevenson spoke at the Chicago Athletic Club, an illustration of his efforts to get Republican and independent votes. He began with his disquisition upon Lord Bryce's three hindrances to democracy—indolence, private self-interest, and excessive partisanship—and praised the audience for holding meetings such as this, then said, "Because I saw a lot of the war, of its waste, its horrible destruction and ghastly suffering; because I saw a lot of the peace making, its difficulties and frustrations; because I've seen rather intimately the policies and methods of our Communist competitors unfold; I have developed a holy passion for our democratic system and the free way of life which, like many of us, I am afraid, I had taken for granted. Hence, I've become more and more interested in these hindrances to good citizenship, these divergencies between the professions of democracy and its practice. I even like to think that I was moved by some such noble motive when I agreed to run for Governor, and not just vanity! But, Mr. Chairman, I promised you that I would not impose upon your good Republican membership and make a political speech. I won't, and as you suggested I'll take in a little more territory than Illinois and talk about foreign affairs." The rest of the long speech was devoted to foreign trade, the UN, Soviet relations, and the Marshall Plan.

On Stevenson's forty-eighth birthday, February 5, the Democrats gave him a birthday party at the Morrison Hotel, their headquarters. The next night he went downstate into the corrupt, squalid Democratic stronghold, East St. Louis and nearby towns.

On February 7, Governor Green spoke to a Chicago rally in what the *Tribune* called the "kickoff rally of the 1948 campaign," saying that New Dealers wanted to raid the state treasury and make "huge" state expenditures. (Stevenson was always sensitive to the Republican charge that Democrats were big spenders.)

[5] Detailed contributions will be found in Appendix A.

On February 11, Stevenson spoke to the Citizens Schools Committee, an important civic group formed years earlier to take the Chicago school system out of politics. It was a "good-government" audience, a good one for Stevenson, and he made a long, thoughtful, serious speech which at the same time made a campaign issue: Governor Green's neglect of the schools. The 1947 legislature, he said, had appropriated only 6 per cent of its total budget for Chicago schools—only about 8 per cent of the Chicago school budget. But he carefully refrained from promising flatly to increase state aid to common schools. And, characteristically, he set the problem in a wide context, terming education "our greatest resource and our greatest need as a self-governing people." Addressing a Republican audience of Lions and Rotary clubs in Quincy on February 17, he mentioned the difficulty of persuading good men to go into government and said, "They even had trouble getting a suitable man to run for Governor of Illinois—and I'm not sure they succeeded." Sometimes his speeches sounded almost like those of a Republican, as when at Quincy he said, "Our nation's well-being and healthy growth—terms I prefer to 'security'—rest upon many other considerations than the purely military. Sound finances, a sound economy, taxes which are not destructive of business enterprise and individual savings, development of our own resources and access to raw materials—these are part of the problem of security." It was far different from the "give-'em-hell" speeches President Truman would deliver in this campaign year.

Stevenson asked Mrs. Ives to go to Bloomington and open the house on Washington Street so he could officially launch his campaign there. She and Ernest Ives drove to Bloomington from Southern Pines, North Carolina, "through snow and ice and high water," as Ives later put it, taking three and a half days instead of two. On Saturday, February 21, Ives went to Springfield to attend a Jackson Day dinner for more than a thousand Democrats which Stevenson addressed. "He made a fine forceful speech," Ives later reported, "and sold himself to the entire gathering." The *Tribune* reported, "Adlai E. Stevenson, Democratic candidate for governor, who recently wore the striped pants of the State Department, said tonight in a prepared speech that he is 'happy to be in the heart of the corn and Bible belt.'" Throughout the campaign the *Tribune* and Governor Green used the epithet "striped-pants diplomat." Stevenson began by introducing himself, recounting his Grandfather Stevenson's and his father's political careers, and saying, "I have a bad case of hereditary politics, and I hope by associating with veterans like you to contract an equally bad case of practical politics!" He declared that

resentment of the present state leadership was mounting among
Democrats and Republicans alike. He said, "That Governor who
once with righteous fervor and missionary zeal decried machine
politics has become the master political machinist of all time! He
has created a political octopus, whose tentacles spread over the
state like a Cape Cod fog, and reach into every crack and crev-
ice where there is money for political—or other—purposes." He
promised if elected to "emancipate" state employees from being obliged to contribute a percentage of their salary to the party—"I
want servants, not solicitors on the state payroll." If Illinois was
to "regain her rightful position" of leadership among the states, "the
first order of business on the agenda must be to banish from
Springfield the unconscionable spoils machine. . . . Its foundations
must be uprooted and the earth scorched so that another can't arise
in its place—whether it bears the trademark of the over-fed elephant or the lean donkey." He promised if elected to restore Illinois's reputation as "one of the most progressive commonwealths of
the Union," a leader in social legislation, education, and government of high quality, and to "act as the servant of all the people,
without regard to race, color, creed, or political affiliation. I have no
ambition and no other interest in politics than to do what I can to
clean up Illinois," a reference to Governor Green's supposed presidential ambitions; "to administer its affairs in the interest of all the
people, be they downstaters from whence I come or Chicagoans
where I work; and to put Illinois in the forefront as the best-gov-
erned state of this Republic."

It was his most partisan attack yet. After it, Ernest Ives drove him
to Bloomington, arriving past midnight. On Sunday, Stevenson rested
and worked on speeches in the old house on Washington Street.
Ellen came down from Libertyville that evening. Her visit was no
more successful than her other visits to Bloomington. Next day Mrs.
Ives gave a reception in the house for 400 people and, her husband
reported, "There was [radio] broadcasting from the house—his old
high school teacher, the grandson of the late Governor Fifer (a good
Republican), and Alverta Duff, the old family maid. Then Adlai
spoke for seven minutes." Stevenson said, "Many of you are the oldest friends I have. . . . Although I have practiced law in Chicago for
more than twenty years, except for intervals of government service,
Bloomington and this house have always been 'home' for me. . . .
Here, too, my family have lived and labored for generations. My
great-grandfather, Jesse Fell, settled here a hundred and fifteen years
ago; my grandfather, Adlai Stevenson, for whom I was named, was
a citizen of this community when he was elected Vice President of

the United States; and here my mother and father were born, married, and are buried." He said he had not sought the nomination—it had sought him. "I was told that they selected me because they respected my record in private life and my public service in the war and the peace, knew I could win, and that as Governor I could be a credit to the party. I remember that one of the leaders said to me that the best government was the best politics," a phrase Stevenson used for many years, "and that if any politicians were skeptical, Mayor Kennelly's conduct of Chicago's affairs was rapidly convincing them." Thus to a downstate audience in a heavily Republican area did Stevenson divorce himself from the Cook County Democratic machine. He said he had accepted nomination because "politics is in my blood" and because he felt "a little guilty" about having taken free institutions for granted. "Already too many people think of state elections as merely the quadrennial struggle"—a phrase he used in the presidential campaign, to the dismay of some politicians—"to decide which set of politicians will dispense the patronage for the next four years. I think that government is more than the sum of all the interests; it is the paramount interest, the public interest."

After that everybody went downtown to the Illinois Hotel for a dinner for 300 (200 more arrived after dinner). In his speech there, also broadcast, Stevenson repeated what he had said at the house and raised several specific issues: the schools, juvenile delinquency, mine safety, charitable and correctional institutions. He praised farmers and farming and promised to work to harmonize relations between Chicago and downstate. He promised if elected to experiment with new ideas. (The *Tribune* called this "a willingness to attempt New Deal experimentation with the government of Illinois.") He ad-libbed further attacks on Green. For a radio speech in a Republican area so early in the campaign, the speech contained more partisan bile than one might expect; yet at the same time he blunted accusations of partisanship by divorcing himself from the Cook County Democratic machine, appealing for support from Republicans and "independents," and ranging himself on the side of honesty, probity, and good government. It was in a real sense a "kickoff" speech, keynoting his entire campaign.

V. Y. Dallman told Stevenson, "Your triumphs in Springfield Saturday night and in Bloomington last night have gripped the imagination of central Illinois." Mrs. Donald Funk of Springfield wrote an enthusiastic letter to Mrs. Ives: "Aren't you proud of him? His talk tonight was just right—and I understand that he was a sensation Saturday night." *Time* said that machine men had feared "their gentlemanly candidate" would not do well at his debut but "needn't have been so nervous." It said, "Stevenson, a novice in campaigning, was completely at ease in Bloomington," handshaking, reminiscing with boyhood friends, and talking with local politicians, and delighting the dinner crowd with his attack on Green. "The diners went wild. 'Go get 'em, Ad!' screamed jubilant party functionaries. When it was all over, veteran Chicago newsmen knew that a dazzling political star had been born." John Dreiske, political editor of the *Sun-Times,* wrote, "He was a smash hit. There once were those who gloomily opined he should not travel in the same caravan with Paul H. Douglas because of the danger he would be eclipsed by that brilliant orator. Put away your handkerchiefs. Don't cry for Stevie."

9

To those on the inside, however, all was not well. Stevenson and Ellen drove back to Chicago, where he had to speak at 11 A.M., the morning after the speech in the Illinois Hotel. That same day Ernest Ives, a reserved man, wrote what was for him a remarkable letter to Ellen's mother, Mrs. Carpenter. Ives said:

I have always tried to steer clear of family entanglements but the situation seems to me so serious that I am appealing to you to ask you to give a helping hand to Ellen and Adlai. . . . Adlai's speech last evening was delivered in a very tired and seemingly discouraged vain. His winning smile was even lacking and while he had had a tiring day I *know* that the principal reason was the discouraging attitude evinced by Ellen and [her] complete lack of interest and cooperation here at the reception and at the dinner. She evinced boredom to such a point that the TIME correspondent, Mr. Bell, during the afternoon, was prompted on two occasions to ask, once of me and once of someone else—"Is Mrs. Stevenson sick?" There will not be much need, as I see it, with the exception of an occasional reception, such as the reception and dinner yesterday, for Ellen to take an active part in the campaign, but on such occasions if she would, for only an hour or two, exert herself and show some helpful interest. . . . You well know how vulnerable a politician is and that his family also comes in for its share of inspection by the press and public, and it would seem rightly so. Adlai and his running mates, all of whom have fine records, have excellent prospects . . . but they will need all possible aid and support. Adlai . . . is getting this from most everyone, even many dyed in the wool republicans, but [it] is manifestly lacking in Ellen whose attitude seems to take all the fire and vim out of him. I don't for a moment mean to whitewash Adlai for I am sure he has his shortcomings. But in public life . . . one must play the game. I have talked to and endeavored to encourage Ellen to be helpful to Adlai, not to belittle his efforts and his aspirations but to play her role. . . . That I feel so strongly the need of your help is the only excuse for this long letter.

Ives's letter was only a hint of serious trouble to come. At this same time close friends of the Stevensons were attempting to help ward it off. In October of 1949 the widow of Donald MacPherson, the lawyer who had years earlier played a part in bringing Stevenson into the Sidley law firm, told Stevenson that "in the last year or so I have done everything in my power to try and help Ellen to see things differently. . . . I am so deeply fond of you both." And the wife of Clay Judson, who had opposed Stevenson's internationalist policy but remained his friend, wrote, "I still cling to the hope that now that circumstances have changed for her something might happen to give her a different perspective. To have the wandering eye during the age that she has just been thru is practically a universal experience—for both sexes I guess—like the measles—and *should* not cause a permanent rift." The Stevensons' marital troubles, however, were known to only a very few during the spring of 1948.

10

The Stevenson-for-Governor Committee, by now the All-Illinois Stevenson for Governor Committee, published a leaflet extolling Stevenson's virtues and emphasizing his statement at Bloomington, "I want to say right now that this is a campaign to revive the people's faith in the integrity of democratic government." On March 1 the two Democratic "caravans" set forth on their three-week state-wide tour. The candidates would speak in more than 125 towns and villages, splitting up for the daytime meetings and appearing jointly at a rally each night. Though the caravans were led by Douglas and Stevenson, the rest of the state ticket went along. The first day the caravans fanned out from Herrin, in the far south coal fields. During the day Stevenson visited several small towns, then joined Douglas and the others for a night rally at Herrin. The *Tribune*'s reporter, Thomas Morrow, wrote, "He had his introduction to practical politics in the rainy gloom of Union county. . . . Stevenson, with his background of wealth and diplomatic service, fitted easily into the role of folksy candidate. Hands in pockets, he warmed Democratic audiences in Anna and Jonesboro by making a 'friendly talk' to 'you folks,' and employing such phrases as 'neat as a whistle.' . . . On the debit side, seasoned Democratic campaigners were concerned by a weak voice and a certain lack of fire in their candidate. Some deplored his mention of many Republican friends. . . . If he has too many Republican friends, it's no good for the guys who need the jobs." That night at Herrin, a coal town with a history of gang warfare, Ku Klux Klan violence, and bloody labor disputes, Stevenson spoke on the mine inspection service and the "plight" of the common schools. As he nearly always did, he began by mentioning Illinois's place in "the troubled world of today" and his own experience of government in war and peace, then connected it up with Illinois issues. He said the Administration had ignored mine safety precautions and accepted contributions from mineowners, a sale of governmental favor. "This barter at the risk of human lives and safety must stop. I ask you here and now to join with me in a vow that there will be no more Centralia tragedies." He pledged that if elected he would appoint mine inspectors on merit alone, would forbid them to solicit campaign funds for him. "I want on the payrolls of Illinois servants, not solicitors!" He quoted at length from an article on the Centralia disaster in *Harper's* magazine, reprinted in *Reader's Digest*.[6] "Here lies Green's responsibility—not that, through a secretary's fumble, he failed to act on the miners' appeal to 'save our lives' but rather that, while the king-makers were shunting him around the nation making speeches, back home his loyal followers were busier building a rich political machine for him than in administering the state for him." Stevenson quoted from the article many times and made coal mine safety a major issue of the campaign. He went on to strike his familiar theme that "the best government is the best politics," to deplore Illinois's loss of reputation, to predict that "the fury of the outraged citizenry" would "blow the Green machine and all that it represents clear out of the State House."

The campaign caravan moved through the far south. On March 2, the *Tribune* reported, the candidates were cheered by an overflow crowd in Carmi, "where 500 persons filled the seats and lined the walls" and heard Stevenson accuse Governor Green by name of piling up dollars in the state treasury so he could present himself

[6] It was written by the present author, who did not know Stevenson at that time.

as an expert in economy and thus be eligible for the vice-presidential nomination. The caravan moved to East St. Louis, the Democratic downstate stronghold, where on March 4 Stevenson demanded that the state payroll be cut (hardly an issue that would endear him to party workers) and Douglas attacked the Republican record on labor. Already the candidates had visited 49 towns and 14 counties and, the *Tribune*'s Morrow estimated, spoken to about 14,000 persons. He wrote, "Stevenson is gaining confidence as he travels the vote-seeking circuit, is making better use of his voice, but needs a loudspeaker. Audiences yield to his personality but those seeking burning utterances are disappointed. Only Paul Douglas . . . seems able to cope with Stevenson's first name. . . . The rest of the candidates kick the name around with a long 'I' ending to rhyme with gadfly." They went to Taylorville and near there Stevenson donned miner's clothing and went down into a coal mine owned by a Lake Forest friend of his. The caravan moved north and east, and on March 6 at Urbana, seat of the University of Illinois, Stevenson tried out the "third term" issue—Green had campaigned earlier against FDR's attempt to win a third term but now was seeking one himself. Morrow wrote, "Stevenson, tired after a week's campaigning, admitted his lack of fire. . . . 'I am no corn stalk orator,' he said, 'but I plan to discuss the issues calmly thruout the state.'" He was getting into midstate Republican territory. At a lunch meeting in Pontiac on March 8 he said the Republicans had not planned a primary caravan but now were about to launch one. He visited a shoe factory and a farm sale, shook hands on the street, then went to Kankakee, the site of a large state mental hospital, and said that, under Green, Illinois state hospitals had declined from national leadership to "a state of neglect and abuse . . . the same cynical indifference, waste and graft." Inadequate staffing, overcrowding, brutality, and graft were widespread. Attendants were underpaid and appointed politically. Little attempt was made to "cure" patients. With an adequate program, Illinois could discharge two out of three patients. (Few psychiatrists would have been so optimistic at that time—the new drugs were not yet in use—and none would have used the word "cure.")

He was keeping a grueling schedule, starting out early in the morning and campaigning far into the night, constantly on the move, writing speeches in the back seat of a speeding car, eating hastily or not at all, never alone, no time to himself, traveling all day, getting to a hotel with only enough time to change his shirt before commencing the round of evening meetings. It was the hardest kind of work.

The Stevenson campaign was hurting Governor Green, and Green felt obliged to return from a vacation to reply. On March 10, in a major speech opening his downstate campaign at Fairfield, Green said that the people of Illinois "are in no mood to extend the power and the scope of the New Deal Democrats and bunglers" and referred to Stevenson as a man "apparently on leave from the striped pants brigade of the Roosevelt-Truman state department while he carries the New Deal torch in Illinois." Green called the United Nations "the most dismal failure" in United States history. He opposed the creation of "a little New Deal" in Illinois, and recited his record.

Next day Stevenson crossed the state to Rock Island on the Mississippi River and replied to Green's speech, which the press had referred to as "Green's Uppercut." Stevenson said, "The uppercut was, I suppose, intended for Stevenson's jaw. It didn't land, so here I am sticking my chin out again tonight. My chin feels all right and I haven't suffered any body blows. Honestly, and I make this statement in all modesty, I believe that in the last two weeks I have done a great public service to Illinois—at least we now have a Governor within the territorial limits of the state." Green, he said, had damned him as being on leave from the "striped-pants brigade." He said, "Pretty strong words with which to damn a Democrat. But damned or striped I will keep my pants on. . . . I would remind Mr. Green that Centralia is located in Illinois and that it didn't blow up or explode in Moscow or Arizona. One hundred and eleven Illinois miners didn't die on the steppes of Russia. They were killed right here in Illinois. I don't propose to use the language of diplomacy in this campaign. A diplomat would say 'perquisites of office.' As an amateur in politics I have already learned that 'graft' is a more descriptive word. A diplomat might say the gentleman labors under a misapprehension of the facts. But an amateur political realist says the same thing when he says the man lies. That's enough about diplomacy and my pants; let's get down to business." He then undertook to rebut Green's speech point by point, addressing Green directly. He concluded: "I am just an amateur at politics, and, frankly, I am looking for advice. Shall I stick to Illinois in this campaign? Do you think perhaps that all this discussion about international issues and the 'striped-pants brigade' is just an effort on the part of the professional politician to take advantage of an amateur? Is Mr. Green trying to divert my attention and yours away from, shall we say the shame and the hypocrisy, from the graft and corruption of his administration? . . . I think I ought to stick to Illinois. I am not running against Dwight Green for Vice President. . . . Power-drunk political spoilsmen, pseudo-Republicans with temporary authority created the issue of this campaign. The issue is Illinois."

He told Jane Dick the speech was "good" but "too subtle & much of the satire went over the heads of the audience. I went to bed, however, with an unhappy feeling that you would not have approved—too much 'unworthy' sarcasm about Green. . . . If I only had a little more facility with the political manner of speaking—showmanship, oratory & the mysterious something that excites people —I would worry no more. . . . But I just haven't got that something—impress them, yes, but not excite them."

Next day in Decatur, Governor Green said it was no wonder Stevenson knew so little about Illinois's accomplishments—for the last ten or twelve years he had been out of the state. On the same day, Stevenson in Peoria repeated the attack—said he had expected to debate Illinois issues and was surprised "when I was informed that Mr. Green had opened his campaign downstate, had marshalled his forces at Fairfield and was marching on the United Nations—at the head of 2,000 words." Then he added a "deadly solemn" defense of the United Nations, "the law of our land," "the cornerstone of United States foreign policy," "the hope, the only hope, of countless millions." He called Green's remarks "dangerous and irresponsible chatter."

The New York *Times* wrote of Stevenson's "lively" campaign, saying, "Political observers with the caravan report that Mr. Stevenson's chatty, persuasive style of delivery and his infectious grin have introduced a 'new look' in Illinois campaigning that is winning audiences." On March 18 the Democratic caravan ended its three-week downstate tour with a meeting in the Waukegan courthouse, seat of Stevenson's home county. Stevenson began, "I'm glad to be back home. . . . And I'm also heartened to see so many Democrats in one room in Lake County. I hope we're not raided as an unlawful assembly." He then delivered what was becoming his standard attack on Green—boss of a corrupt "Statehouse gang," misleading claims about the sales tax and state aid to common schools, the Centralia mine disaster, state hospitals, illegal campaign contributions, Governor in absentia—and what was becoming his own standard defense of the United Nations and promise to give Illinois good and honest government in order to restore her high position among the states. Although he spoke of "the immortal Franklin Roosevelt," he did not mention President Truman's name.

At that time the Democratic Party was deeply divided over whether to renominate President Truman for re-election. Basically, the question was whether he could win. Many Democratic Party leaders thought not. Moreover, his Palestine policy disaffected them. A delegation of University of Chicago professors visited Arvey and said they wanted to talk to him not as county chairman but as a human being with sons and as a Jew. They disapproved of Truman's Palestine policy. They feared the atomic bomb. Nations were jealous and suspicious. The world was in danger. The United States must lead. But if Truman could win at all, it would be by the narrowest of margins. They said, as Arvey later recalled it, "It's time now that the parties ought to forsake personal ambitions and pick a man who can get eighty per cent of the vote and speak for the majority of the people. Eisenhower. He's not a Democrat or a Republican, he's a war hero, he's a liberal." "Well," Arvey continued, "it got me thinking. They sent me to a number of people to contact. I sought out others. Phil Murray," president of the United Steel Workers and the CIO, "was one of them. And various other people. In fact, some of Truman's closest friends encouraged me to be for Eisenhower."

Back in January, a newspaper publisher in New Hampshire had proposed that Eisenhower be nominated by the Republican Party, and a National Draft Eisenhower League had been formed. But Eisenhower declared he could not accept the nomination and expressed the view that a military man was not qualified for the presidency. Nonetheless, Arvey and others sent an emissary to Eisenhower privately to broach the subject of his being nominated by the Democrats, and did not at first receive an unequivocal refusal (though a little later they did). This encouraged Arvey and other party leaders.

Although the General Assembly of the United Nations had adopted a resolution to partition Palestine, it had not provided any blueprint for ending the British mandate and carrying out partition. In December the British had announced they would pull out May 15, 1948. In January and February both Arabs and Jews made bellicose moves. In February, President Truman appealed to Arab leaders to preserve the peace. They rejected his appeal; Truman approved presenting the issue to the Security Council. But a little later his ambassador told the Security Council the United States would favor temporary trusteeship pending a decision on Palestine's permanent status. To many Zionists, this looked like a reversal of U.S. policy and a betrayal of those Jews who wanted to set up an independent state of Israel.

The domestic political repercussions were loud, especially in the Democratic Party. If Truman was already a weak candidate, he was far weaker if he could not command the votes and money of Jews in New York, Illinois, California, and other states. New York

City Democratic leaders revolted against Truman almost immediately and expressed the hope that Eisenhower could be persuaded to run. Franklin D. Roosevelt, Jr., rejected Truman and urged that Eisenhower be drafted. So did Elliott Roosevelt. Southern Democratic leaders were reported backing Eisenhower. In Chicago a long protest march paraded through Jack Arvey's own 24th Ward. On April 2, Paul Douglas issued a statement rejecting Truman and favoring Eisenhower. The New York *Times* reported on April 4, "Ramblings of dissension in the powerful Cook County . . . Democratic organization, described by some observers as a 'dump-Truman' movement, have been recorded in the stories of political writers here recently." The *Public Service Leader,* a small political newspaper published by Frank Keenan, a maverick Democratic machine leader, declared that "many powerful influences in the streamlined party organization are convinced that the party, its hopes and its ideals would go down to sure defeat in November if President Truman is nominated to succeed himself." The *Times* reported that Arvey hoped Eisenhower would become available. "This elicited from Mr. Arvey the following explanation: 'I'm no more for Eisenhower than for any of the other men who might be considered. I consider him the kind of a liberal I could vote for. . . . When the Convention comes in July, I'll vote for the man who gives the most hope of carrying out the ideals of the Democratic party.' "[7]

In the midst of all this, after the Waukegan meeting winding up their downstate "caravan," Stevenson and the other candidates brought their campaign into Chicago. They began on March 20, the very day that the explosive new Truman Palestine policy was announced, at a $25-a-plate luncheon with Senator Barkley, the principal speaker, asking for united support of President Truman. Stevenson spoke, establishing his Democratic antecedents, mentioning his kinship with Barkley. (Barkley was a distant cousin.) He said, "I regret that I could not appear before you in that mythical attire which has received so much publicity. The simple truth is that I do not own a pair of striped pants. . . . The only pair of striped pants I ever expect to own is the pair I'll jerk off Mr. Green next November. . . . Since [his Fairfield speech] the august Governor has been racing up the turnpike with his shirttail on fire." He praised Barkley, Roosevelt, Paul Douglas, Ed Kelly, Mayor Kennelly, the other state candidates, but again he did not mention President Truman.

The primary was less than a month away, the Cook County organ-

---

[7] The Palestine issue subsided in May when Truman recognized the provisional government of Israel a few minutes after it was proclaimed.

ization was setting to work. Night after night Stevenson and the other candidates went to ward headquarters all over Chicago to shake hands and speak briefly to meetings of precinct captains. The Speakers' Bureau of the Cook County Democratic Central Committee, with headquarters in the Morrison Hotel, sent him almost daily a mimeographed form telling him what meetings he was assigned to attend. He saw parts of Chicago new to him, for the ward headquarters were where Chicago's millions lived and worked—empty stores in the Negro ghetto, offices huddled amidst warehouses and tenements and factories, Paddy Bauler's saloon.[8] Most were solid wards; in a few a party fight for control was going on. Before he visited Paddy Bauler's 43d Ward, an aide gave Stevenson a notation: "There is a big fight going on in this Ward. The IVI is sponsoring someone other than Bauler for Committeeman. . . . but the organization is backing him." It was hard work. Sometimes his schedule carried driving instructions: "California is 2800 West—Take Division (which is 1200 North) all the way out to California and turn North 1½ blocks for #1335." Sometimes he simply was unable to keep all his commitments. On April 1, when he was scheduled to appear at seven meetings all over town between 8 and 10 P.M., he missed the last one and apologized to its committeeman. When it was over, Barney Hodes advised Stevenson to send a letter to the ward committeemen and county chairmen he had met. Stevenson did.

Once, campaigning downstate, Stevenson had written to Jane Dick from a motel in Carmi, "It's been an amazing experience, and I've come to wonder how anyone can presume to talk about 'America' until he has done some political campaigning. Perhaps it's the secret, perhaps the curse, of American political success—the illusive business of finding your way to the heart of the average man, when there is no such thing, and when, unhappily, the human heart is often an organ encased in a pocketbook, and not a textbook, let alone a Bible. I've seen Illinois in a capsule—the beauty of the south, the fruit belt, the coal fields, the oil fields, the great industrial area around East St. Louis—and everywhere the rich, black, fecund

---

[8] Party records show that, on March 19, Stevenson went to three North Side meetings, on March 22 he went to three South Side meetings, on March 23 to two on the far South Side, on March 25 to one on the North Side, on March 25 to five on the South Side, including one run by the IVI; on March 30 to three in industrial southwest suburbs, on March 31 to seven. The names of the ward committeemen made a roster of Democratic Party power in Chicago—Tom Nash, Paddy Bauler, Barney Hodes, Artie Elrod, Frank Keenan, Dick Daley, Al Horan, A. J. Cilella, John J. Touhy, Walter Orlikowski, Joe Gill.

earth stretching away and away. It gives you a great feeling of pride and power. Shut your eyes a moment and let the fetid, hot places, the scorched islands, the arid, the cold, the small—all the places of the world where men struggle to live and love and breed—dance through your head. Then open your eyes and look at Illinois, and murmur 'thrice blessed land.' Exult in the power, majesty, wealth, might of it—and then come back to life with a start when a political pal with a cigar says 'Pardon me, Governor, but—.' " He told Carl McGowan, still in Washington, that his downstate campaigning had been "a wonderful experience, and I am mortified to confess that I knew but little of Illinois before. . . . The progress of the campaign so far is rather better than we had any right to expect. We forced Green to come back from his vacation and he is now campaigning violently and talking incessantly. . . . It has been an exhausting business, but I have enjoyed it and I am learning slowly."

It was developing into a strange governorship campaign, with Governor Green complaining that Stevenson was discussing state issues to conceal Democratic failures in Washington, while Stevenson defended the UN and talked about his pants and accused Green of discussing national issues to conceal Republican failures in Springfield. Once he said that if the law were enforced, "Green and his pals might each get a pair of striped pants, but the stripes would be running the other way."

Stevenson kept in touch with his Republican friends—told John Nuveen, an investment banker who was running in the Republican primary against an entrenched conservative Congressman from Winnetka, "I am very hopeful that you can beat [Congressman] Church. . . . I have urged many people to vote in the Republican primary in that district. (Not to be published.)" Nuveen replied, "I might tell you, off the record also, that I have explained to a number of people how it is not inconsistent for them to vote for me for Congress and you for Governor. Best wishes in the splendid campaign which you are making."

Early in April, a few days before the primary, Stevenson's campaign confronted a financial emergency—it had $800 in the bank and commitments to the first of May amounting to $13,550. Stevenson suggested to Dutch Smith that Henry Tenney, their lawyer friend, meet with "a few people" to explain the problem. About $18,000 had been contributed. The monthly staff payroll was $1,550. Stevenson, despite his heavy speaking schedule, continued to send notes to Smith, suggesting the names of wealthy friends such as Ralph Bard, who he was confident would make substantial contributions. Not much came of many of his suggestions, although Bard and his wife contributed $150.

In the primary election Green and Brooks were nominated by the Republicans to run for Governor and Senator, Stevenson and Douglas by the Democrats. Republicans were heartened by the vote, for Green received some 200,000 more votes state-wide than Stevenson. In Cook County, despite the power of the Democratic machine, Stevenson had received only 113,500 more votes than Green out of 740,000 cast, which in most general elections of that period probably would not have been enough to elect him—the Republican candidate usually carried downstate and the Democrat had to win by a large margin in Cook County. Paul Douglas ran ahead of Stevenson in Cook County, receiving 443,600 votes to Stevenson's 426,700. It was not an auspicious start. If he was to win in November, Stevenson needed to do much better. Stevenson himself, however, in a letter to Adlai III, said, "We did well in the primary. . . . I am very optimistic. The hazards are Wallace, Truman's unpopularity and the enormous and ill-gotten Republican campaign funds."

11

Two days after the primary Stevenson spoke at a luncheon of the Immigrants Protective League, deploring as "demagogic" the political tactic "of appealing to citizens on the basis of national origin rather than as Americans," a line he used with increasing frequency and broadened to include not only citizens of national origin but groups of all kinds, including veterans, labor unions, businessmen, Negroes, Jews, and many more. He used another gambit that became one of his favorites, especially with a friendly audience: "I don't know whether I appear here today as a candidate for Governor or as a member of the Board of Directors of the Immigrants Protective League, or as a member of the Chicago Committee on Displaced Persons, or as a plain citizen. . . . I'm telling you all this just to get some sympathy for my unhappy and unfamiliar predicament. It's so bad that I can't even talk to old friends without my feeling that they feel that I'm trying to get their vote, or a campaign contribution. And, of course, the worst of it is that both are true!" He also adopted a familiar pose, that he was an amateur politician: "My advisers have been reminding me . . . that a statesman thinks of the next generation, but a politician thinks of the next election, and that the next election is my present and exclusive business."

He used, too, another idea that he continued to use and that, sharpened up, electrified the convention and the nation in 1952—the idea that Illinois had had but three Democratic Governors since the Civil War: John Peter Altgeld, who was born in Germany; Edward F. Dunne, who was only one generation removed from Ireland; and Henry Horner, whose father was born in Bavaria. Altgeld, he went on, was a Protestant, Dunne a Catholic, and Horner a Jew. "Here truly is the American story, written in the last fifty years here in our city of Chicago and here in our state of Illinois."

Stevenson went off for a ten-day holiday with the Iveses at Southern Pines. Returning on May 2, Stevenson dealt with his children's plans. He told Adlai that he might spend the summer working at the *Pantagraph* and at the Chicago campaign headquarters "but I think Mother will want you to go away somewhere for a holiday." Borden was failing in school in Lake Forest, and the headmaster at Choate wrote that to take on Borden would be to take on a big job but he would do it. He recommended summer school. Stevenson replied, "We have concluded to follow your advice. . . . I am frank to say that in view of some seven years of government work and the unhappy effect that has on one's earnings, and now with this campaign on my drooping shoulders, I can ill afford Choate, not to mention sumer school. But this, after all, is our first obligation." Despite his difficulties through these early years, Borden grew into an attractive young man and later, toward the end of his father's life, established a strong relationship with him and more than repaid him for his early support.

On May 5, after three days in the Chicago headquarters, Stevenson left on a downstate campaign trip, expecting to be gone most of May. His staff had provided him with a speech draft for Peoria that contained a rather mild attack on the Green administration. Stevenson inserted a stronger one. He did so frequently, both in this campaign and in 1952. Stevenson traveled on—Kankakee, Urbana, Danville, Shelbyville, speaking endlessly, shaking hands, talking to local politicians. It was a wearing schedule.

And Stevenson was a man in private torment. Although his wife gave an occasional interview to the press or appeared with Jane Dick at social political gatherings, the truth was that Stevenson's marriage was approaching dissolution. Moreover, he was seriously in love with a woman who was married to someone else. She was Alicia Patterson, the third wife of Harry F. Guggenheim, member of the Guggenheim copper family, financier, philanthropist, horseman, former ambassador to Cuba, founder in 1940 with his wife of *Newsday,* a Long Island daily newspaper.

Alicia Patterson was a handsome, thin-faced, dark-haired forceful woman from Chicago, the daughter of Joseph Medill Patterson, who had been co-editor of the Chicago *Tribune* with his cousin, Colonel Robert R. McCormick, had in 1919 founded the sensationally successful tabloid, the New York *Daily News,* and in 1925 had moved to New York to run it. Patterson had been a war correspondent in China in 1900 and in Europe in 1914–15; he had been a captain in the Rainbow Division after the United States entered World War I and had fought at the second Battle of the Marne and Argonne; he had been a legendary figure around Chicago in the 1920s. His daughter Alicia inherited some of his strong-willed character. Born in 1906, she and Adlai Stevenson had known each other when he first came to Chicago in the late 1920s and some of their friends had thought him taken with her but afraid of her; and he had married Ellen Borden instead. Alicia had been married twice earlier and had married Guggenheim July 1, 1939. She and Stevenson saw each other during the 1940s when he was in New York at the UN and she was at *Newsday.* One piece of evidence suggests that she and Stevenson fell in love in the fall of 1947, when he was in New York at the UN shortly before he was slated for Governor— he mentioned her in a letter to Jane Dick on October 20, and in April of 1949 he referred in a letter to their relationship as "this mysterious dream that's enveloped me for a year and a half," which would date it at the fall of 1947, although Marietta Tree once said she thought it began a year earlier, during the winter of 1946–47.

Stevenson was unusually attractive to women all his life, and they attracted him. The ones who became close to him—and many more who tried—were nearly all bright, pretty, and rich, and several of them had newspaper connections. They were, most of them, also strong-willed, as his mother and sister had been. Unlike some political leaders, such as John F. Kennedy, Stevenson did not separate his political or official life from his private life. Kennedy had two sets of friends: those he worked with in politics or government, and those he saw socially, and to a considerable extent they were different people. Stevenson was inclined to mingle the two. The women in his life, except for his wife, gave him political advice. His most private letters to women are likely to contain his frankest views on public men and public issues—he confided more fully in women than in men.

Alicia Patterson was one of the two or three most deeply felt relationships of his life. Marietta Tree, who became one of Stevenson's few confidantes in later years, has said, "He often said that Alicia was the one he should have married," after his divorce from Ellen, that is. "When they were young she had proposed marriage to him and he had said no." Others who knew him best agree. Now, campaigning downstate the week of May 10, 1948, he wrote to Alicia the first surely datable letter we have in the collection she later returned to him. He wrote it from the Urbana-Lincoln Hotel in Urbana, Illinois, where the University of Illinois is located.

Dear—

Its midnight again & the last of the politicians and professors has just left. I'm about to topple into bed. Up and away for Danville at 8—and so on and on to the end of time or until my sins are expiated—or until the morning comes when I just can't get up again.

I wonder what the hell I'm doing and why—and then I think of you and that you think its good and worth while and wouldn't love me if I didn't behave this way—and then I get up and go at it again.

I'm going to catch a train back to Chicago from Shelbyville Sunday night and I'll be in Chicago all of next week, leaving Sunday a week (May 23) to resume the torture at Belleville— And then I'll be back in Chicago June 5 for most of the month of June with a few trips for a day downstate.

I've been hoping for a telephone call from you & a report on the Washington adventure. It all seems so much more significant than my aimless wandering—and . . . I love you—A.

Sometime that spring, probably immediately after the primary, when he went off on a holiday to Southern Pines, North Carolina, he visited Alicia at her plantation in Georgia and, returning aboard a plane, wrote:

Alicia dear—You asked for a bread & butter letter—instead you'll get the disordered reveries of a drowsy, contented man high in the clouds. There is something fitting about coming to you on wings of wind and floating away from you into the clouds. You are an earthy person. Yet, just as long ago, I never quite touch the earth when I'm with you—in spite of all your rude reminders! It may not make for very mature, sensible, helpful, companionship, but I hope you don't mind my happy idiocy. I hope you don't mind the abandoned way I shed my shackles, and float away half conscious dreaming dreams and seeing visions and, like a wraith, you're always dancing away in front of me beckoning me on—with a satirical little smile that should warn me that that way lies

Nirvana and the never never land, posted to trespassers from the land of affairs and reality.

Anyway I enjoyed my little walk hand in hand down tobacco road—and I'm still there. Indeed, I'm afraid I'll be there for days to come—even after this bird plunges down thru the white wool and sets me gently on earth again. I'll see you striding in that solid straight legged way along the bank and thru the pines, all white in sunlight, looking quizically here and there—half sinking, half panting—but I'll be very circumspect, very casual, very courteous, very banal. I'll resist the awful temptation to sweep you up into a soft white ball, that, magically, unfolds a sharp, savage little tigress. That is, I'll resist until I'm very much alone and its very late and very still. Then the cocoon will unfold in the moonlight—very soft, very tender, and my heart will stop—

But what carryings on for the Governor! He liked the bread, he liked the butter—he liked everything but Buzz! And I guess he was really just a little jealous of Buzz. I hope you'll come out to Libertyville after this summer. I want you to know the boys. I want them to grow to love you like their father—well not just like their father. And I want you to know Ellen better. You can probably help me a lot in that direction—not that you're good, but because you are wise; because you are half man and half woman and probably understand both more than anyone else I know. The wise have to correct the errors of the good. No, I didn't say I was good!

I must say farewell again, again, again—and pull myself together for Raleigh. It's only taken 5 minutes to get here—4 for reverie and one for a bread and butter note to a wicked enchantress who likes the same things I like but whose found compartments for reason, for sentiment, for living, for loving, for dreaming, while for me its all a disordered melange. I learn so much from you—I love you—

Altitude—Heaven
Temperature—sublime
Visibility—perfect
Condition—contented.

And, again, he sent a note "To the Queen of Kingsland," (her Georgia plantation):

Your devoted, faithful subject is passing by the post office in a moment, which occasions this absurd note for no better purpose than to report—

1. Each day, all day, I think of a thousand things—important, interesting, revealing things—I wanted to talk about with you.

2. Each night, all night, I'm tormented by memories and moonlight.

3. I must get back home and break this lovely spell in turmoil and travail.

. . . I'll hope for a letter—an adolescent letter—if you are still an adolescent.[9]

12

Back in Chicago on schedule, Stevenson spent the week of May 17 at his headquarters working with his staff, writing a major speech for the State Convention at Springfield, and talking to such politicians as Mayor Kennelly, Judge Igoe, Tom Courtney, and the leaders of the County Committee and to such amateurs as Mrs. Clifton Utley, Mrs. John Miller, Floyd Thompson, Louise Wright, and Henry Tenney. On Friday night, May 21, he met with Jack Arvey to discuss supporting Eisenhower for the Democratic presidential nomination. At headquarters, Lou Kohn tried to get free radio time to match that given by WGN to the Republican State Convention, recommended that Stevenson stress the reactionary isolationist control of the Republican Party in Illinois in order to attract Republican voters sympathetic to Stassen, Dewey, and Vandenberg, and wrote to friends in various towns, trying to set up local branches of the Stevenson Committee. Thanking Judge Fisher for speech material, Stevenson said, "I find so little time for the kind of creative writing to which I am accustomed and I have so little competent help that your contributions are precious indeed." It was a complaint that became chronic throughout Stevenson's life henceforward—no time to write himself and no competent help.

Stevenson had long since written to a friend at Princeton to arrange for young Adlai to visit Princeton and had strongly resisted a suggestion by the Milton registrar that Adlai was not ready for college. On May 24 the Princeton director of admissions rejected Adlai's application for admission, though he put him on a list of alternates. He wrote to Stevenson, saying they had turned Adlai down "because of his low school standing" but adding, "Adlai has plenty of ability. His school reports that he once made an I.Q. grade of 137 which is considerably above the average. He also did very well indeed in three out of his five College Board tests. On the other hand, he gets nothing better than C's and D's[10] in school and stands

---

[9] It is possible that the last letter was written later.
[10] Actually, Adlai III never received a D in school.

in the fourth quarter of his class. I have never met Adlai, but this record would seem to indicate immaturity or at least an immature attitude toward the important problem of education."

It was a stuffy letter, and Stevenson did not let it pass. He wrote to the director: "You are bedeviled with plaintive letters from so many Princeton fathers that I don't want to add another. However, I do want to call your attention to some considerations that may be relevant as I am, of course, anxious for him to go to Princeton where my family have been educated since the 18th Century." He agreed that Adlai's Milton record indicated immaturity but laid it to his preoccupation with athletics and other extracurricular activities and the fact that he had attended several different grade schools. "I am confident he can do whatever he puts his mind to. . . . He has had exceptionally broad worldly experience and has everywhere shown a mature sense of responsibility and judgment. . . . I have presumed to write you because if anything could be done to relieve the suspense it would be most helpful. . . . He is under great pressure [at Milton] to go to Harvard. . . . The uncertainty with the resultant hesitation about making commitments elsewhere is the more awkward because I am running for Governor here in Illinois and must be away from home most of the time."

At the same time, Stevenson sent copies of the correspondence to a friend at Princeton for his "advice," though Stevenson undoubtedly wanted help more than advice. The friend told him the admissions director was giving Adlai "the most serious consideration." The admissions director told Stevenson he could not consider the alternate list until July. He wrote, in a passage Stevenson marked, "I regard my office as a doctor's office and I must tell the truth in regard to all our applicants and must try to be particularly helpful to boys who are the sons of Princeton graduates. On this basis your boy has excellent ability, but has never performed to the level of that ability and were he to come to Princeton at this time, before gaining a more mature attitude toward his work, he might easily do badly himself and exert very little influence for good on others. I, personally, would like to see him take another year in school or go to some small college and adjust himself enthusiastically to his work. He needs to punish himself and the fact that he has not been successful in the competition to gain admission to Princeton this year may constitute the shock that is necessary to impress upon him the necessity of constant work. I think that it should be impressed upon him that he has done poorly at Milton and stood low in his class simply because he has not chosen to apply himself. . . . I need hardly tell a man of your experience that a boy must learn to face facts and this is a good time for Adlai, III, to think out the situation for himself."

It was a punitive and presumptuous letter. Stevenson, busy as he was with his campaign, asked the registrar at Milton to speak to the Princeton admissions director. He did, recommending Adlai unreservedly. But the admissions director merely said Adlai III was on the alternate list. The Milton registrar recommended that Adlai III accept the place offered him at Harvard promptly. Instead, Stevenson wired the registrar and asked for a copy of the admissions director's letter. Receiving it, Stevenson wrote to John Stuart of Quaker Oats, an important Princeton alumnus: "I did not especially relish the 'punishment' tone in this letter, particularly for a boy who, if anything, takes life and responsibility very seriously indeed." He also enclosed a letter from Milton reporting Adlai III's "marked improvement," described conversations and correspondence he had had with Milton and Princeton, and said icily of the admissions director's letter to Milton, "[He] said he could hold out no encouragement whatever, and that in this year's severe competition they could not put Adlai ahead of scores of 'others who have infinitely better *general* record.' I gather from this that the original objection of immaturity has now been abandoned and he is being rejected because his record is not good enough, although his examinations were." Stuart was willing to help, though he wanted to meet Adlai III first. In the end, however, Princeton did not relent, Stevenson surrendered, and Adlai III went to Harvard. Stevenson was deeply disappointed. But he did not in the long run permit his disappointment to undermine the abiding love he felt for Princeton. More important than this, however, the whole episode, coming as it did in the midst of his campaign for high political office, shows Stevenson's devotion to his son, his thoroughgoing faith in him, his resentment of what he rightly regarded as rigid if not unfair treatment, and his tenacity and willingness to use pressure in a cause he thought was just and knew was dear to him.

13

Stevenson set out again on May 22 for downstate. He went to St. Louis that night and the following morning spoke across the river in East St. Louis and Belleville and the following day in Alton and Edwardsville. On Wednesday he moved northward to Carrollton and Jacksonville. The Democratic State Convention met in Springfield on Thursday, May 27, and he went there, and so did Mrs.

Ives and Ellen. The most important topic at the convention was President Truman's renomination, but Jack Arvey announced that resolutions to bind the Illinois delegation to Truman—or to Senator Lucas or Mayor Kennelly as favorite sons—had been withdrawn, and Stevenson and Douglas in radio speeches avoided the Truman subject. It was doubly embarrassing because Truman was to speak in Chicago the following week as he started his famous cross-country whistle-stopping tour, seeking renomination and re-election in the face of opposition within his own party. To the State Convention Stevenson made a straight party speech, praising Paul Douglas and other candidates, asking the party's help, attacking Green on familiar issues, and promising to "restore Illinois to the place of vigorous leadership." As usual, too, he sought to present himself as the state-wide counterpart of the good-government Mayor of Chicago, Kennelly. Even in this routine speech, however, he characteristically broadened the subject. In praising the practice of the two parties in choosing candidates, he said: "It is fitting that we meet as free men to participate freely in the deliberations of our freely chosen parties. It is peculiarly fitting that we do so in this 1948th year of the Christian Era when so much of the modern world cannot do so; when a large segment of the human race has no free choices, no choices whatever; when the shadow of a medieval, pagan darkness is creeping across the earth, and tyranny, the most ancient form of government, again envelops so many of our fellow men. Ours is a sad, disillusioned world. Too many people on this blood-soaked, battered globe live in constant fear and dread; fear of hunger and want, dread of oppression and slavery. Poverty, starvation, disease, and repression stalk the world and over us all hangs the menace of war like a gloomy shroud. But everywhere people cling to their hope and their faith in freedom and justice and peace—though fear, anguish, even death, are their daily lot. Why? Because the Master's teachings forever nourish the soul and the spirit of men. And westward the land is bright. Amid this mounting misery the United States is the symbol of hope. America stands out as an earthly paradise, a land of plenty where freedom, justice, and democracy flourish, and no one rattles a saber and no one drags a chain," a line that electrified the nation when he used it at the 1952 National Convention which nominated him for President. It was, again, a very Stevensonian speech. He told Barney Hodes he had written it himself.

On June 1, Stevenson made a foray into northwestern Illinois, returning to Chicago Friday, June 4, the day Truman came. Truman has written that he felt he had to "make a fight" for re-election. His main issue would be the 80th Congress, Republican controlled.

In May, confronted with "the Republican-controlled press," unfavorable public opinion polls, and a divided Democratic Party, he decided to "go directly to the people." The most dangerous split in the party, he thought, was over civil rights, with Southerners threatening to bolt the party. The Henry Wallace movement on the left was a danger too. And so was an Eisenhower draft. Truman's cross-country whistle-stopping trip, one of the great episodes in American political history, was officially labeled non-political. The first stop was Chicago. For several days before his arrival, considerable maneuvering attended arrangements. Mayor Kennelly, not Jack Arvey, arranged the dinner. The guest list was limited to forty. It included Governor Green and only five Democratic politicians—Senator Lucas, Mayor Kennelly, Ed Kelly, Jack Arvey, and George Kells. Stevenson was not invited. Of those who were, only Kelly still supported Truman. The other guests were newspaper publishers, churchmen, and leaders of industry, business, and labor. In his speech at the huge Chicago Stadium, which Stevenson attended, Truman said his formula for uprooting Communism was "more and better democracy" and indicated he would veto the Mundt bill to establish controls over Communists. The *Times* said that Chicago gave Truman "an enthusiastic welcome." The *Tribune* called the welcome "respectful if not tumultuous" and added that the hearty applause caused Democratic leaders to reconsider their determination to oppose him at the convention.

Except for a weekend at Milton for Adlai's graduation and a few minor appearances downstate, Stevenson spent the rest of June and the first half of July—the remaining six weeks before the national convention—in Chicago. Instead of making public appearances, he was engaging in backstage politicizing—raising money, soliciting the support of politicians and churchmen and others, giving interviews, making plans with the professional politicians. He met, sometimes singly and sometimes in a group, with the party leaders, sometimes at the Morrison, sometimes at private clubs. He saw leading businessmen. He saw the editor of the Chicago *Defender,* the Chicago Negro newspaper, seeking its support (he got it). He courted such indifferent or hostile politicians as Tom Courtney and Mayor Kennelly. Repeatedly he telephoned or called on Kennelly. Indeed, as early as June 5, Lou Kohn recommended that veterans pressure Kennelly to work for Stevenson. On July 5, Stevenson and Dutch Smith talked about "the Kennelly problem" as it was coming to be called, and Stevenson proposed that a small group of businessmen and civic leaders call on Kennelly to make it clear that they were working for Stevenson. Despite all this and much more, Kennelly hardly budged.

Stevenson was trying to improve the campaign staff and to organize material and speeches on issues. It was at this time that Walter Schaefer joined the staff to do "brain-trusting" on the issues and "editorial work," as Stevenson put it. (He never could bring himself to refer to a speech writer as a speech writer; he always used such circumlocutions as "brain-truster" or "editorial work" or "speech research." His aides recognized this sensitivity and usually referred to their work as "editorial research.") Stevenson told Schaefer he wanted several speeches designed for urban audiences, rural audiences, and labor audiences, combining attack with constructive proposals. He also "hoped to develop paragraphs which could be inserted from time to time for press release purposes, bringing in new matter as I travel along."[11] Another staff member outlined a dozen major speeches and recommended that the Central Committee schedule Stevenson's major appearances to fit them. (It is nearly always done the other way around—politicians decide where the candidate will go and when; the candidate's staff then writes a speech suitable for the occasion.) Stevenson painstakingly went over the topics and suggested authors, some on the staff, some outside. He conferred at length with various experts, learning about such state issues as juvenile delinquency and unemployment compensation—"is this something that I should be concerned about?" Bill Blair came to work as a volunteer.

From all this activity, results began to show—paragraphs, bits and pieces, background material on issues, complete speech drafts. Some were used, some were not; some were good, some were hopeless. Stevenson rewrote all he used. The speech writing of few campaigns ever gets properly organized. At the outset, various people draw up lists of what they think the issues are, write position papers, collect research material, and draft. But politics moves fast, issues recede, new ones appear, and in the end it usually turns out that the speech that gets delivered is written by the candidate or someone close to him just before delivery. Nonetheless, when a campaign starts, the candidate usually has a staff organized. It is a measure of the amateurish quality of Stevenson's 1948 campaign that only now in June and July, and on into August, were he and

11 He thought his affirmative program should include constitutional reform, taking the Conservation Department out of politics—and perhaps the state police, Boxing Commission, and Racing Commission as well—and providing more state aid to schools. He went on to mention other issues vaguely—deteriorating roads, housing, taxes, agriculture.

his cohorts doing what one might have expected them to have done in January. That he won, and won so largely, is a great personal tribute to Stevenson's own campaigning—and a powerful indictment of Green.

Fund raising, too, was lagging. On June 18, Stevenson told a friend who gave him $100 that "the big money is still conspicuous by its absence." He tore up a check for $250 that his friend Lloyd Lewis sent him—he felt Lewis could ill afford it and was already doing too much, but he warned Lewis he might call on him if things got desperate. The committee sent out mailings and gave a fund-raising luncheon July 1. Thanking Bill McIlvaine for $100, Stevenson said, "If you see any more money about, keep your foot on it until I get there!"

On the whole, Stevenson felt optimistic at this point. Returning from a brief trip to Rock Island and Moline—"perspiring through southern Illinois"—he told John S. Miller he had found Green "so unpopular" downstate that "there should be little difficulty in beating him if I can only put on a proper campaign to overcome the probable handicap of the Democratic national ticket. As you know, a proper campaign, using radio, billboards, advertising, etc., is fearfully expensive."

Virtually every town in Illinois had some pet project, and candidates for high office are under heavy pressure to espouse it. Stevenson, campaigning for good government and against special interests, tried to avoid making promises. In a speech at Peru, Illinois, on June 14, however, he promised, or virtually promised, to build a bridge. Before doing so, he had the project checked carefully, evidence of good staff work. But as Governor he did not make good on his commitment—work was not begun on the bridge until two years after Stevenson left the governorship, and the bridge was not completed until 1962.

Alicia Patterson visited him at Libertyville the week of June 7. (It is not clear where Ellen was.) On June 15, on a train returning from speeches at Peru and LaSalle, he wrote:

> E my love—[he often called her Elisha and sometimes spelled it out but more often simply wrote E]
>
> Was it all a dream? Were you really here last week; did we really walk along the river bank together; did we really sit on the deck [sun deck outside his second-floor bedroom] beneath the sky; did we cook supper together; did we conspire, plan, talk, worry, laugh—? Did we, did we, did we? I've relived it all—every instant, every word, wise and foolish, every gesture, sharp and

tender. And now I don't believe it ever happened and I like to think my patience will be rewarded; that it will be next week. But it did happen and it is a memory, not a dream—and it was bright, and good and warming, and I left you better, stronger, more self confident and purposeful. But something was wrong and haunts me. I did nothing for you and for your problems. I was an ogre of egoism and ever since I've felt uneasy, dissatisfied. I took & took & took and didn't give when giving is what makes one happiest—and what will make A-A enduring and good.

But it will be different in Phila[delphia]![12] . . .

Flew to Boston Friday—worked all the way—dinner in Cambridge, night in Beverly (after Mrs. C[arpenter] had us 50 miles off the course), Saturday at Milton—Adlai very handsome, sharp paternal pangs of pride—and the best commencement address I've ever heard, by a Unitarian minister. Sunday—Beverly—rain, rain, rain and home with Ellen by train yesterday. A few hours at the office with so much to do, to decide etc that I was glad to escape to LaSalle for last nights ordeal—speaking first at a dinner, then in a ball park to acres of empty seats. They seem to have a way of sitting in their cars and listening to the amplifier—but it's tough on the speaker. . . .

"Chicago!—this way out" So farewell—I'm off to a dinner by Cardinal Stritch to grin and smirk and try to make myself contagious to a lot of rich catholics—and how I hate it all—when I might be walking along river banks with you—A

14

The Democratic National Convention met at Philadelphia on July 12. Illinois had 60 delegates led by Mayor Kennelly and including Stevenson.[13] Before the convention, a good deal of backstage maneuvering had gone on among the Illinois delegates. The Republican Convention nominated Governor Thomas E. Dewey of New York for President and Governor Earl Warren of California for Vice President; this made it doubtful Eisenhower would run, the *Tribune*

---

[12] The Democratic National Convention was to meet in Philadelphia—and so, evidently, were Stevenson and Alicia.

[13] Among the others were Senator Lucas, Jack Arvey, Paul Douglas, Harry B. Hershey, Paul Powell, George Kells, Joe Gill, Congressman William L. Dawson, Barney Hodes, Richard J. Daley, Al Horan, Henry Sonnenschein, Pete Fosco, William J. "Botchy" Conners, Ben Adamowski, P. J. Cullerton, William J. Tuohy, Frank Keenan, Edward J. Barratt, John Stelle.

thought, since he would feel that the Dewey-Warren ticket would support the Marshall Plan. But Arvey predicted openly that Eisenhower would stampede the Democratic Convention unless he plainly refused nomination and would have a much better chance of election than Truman. Arvey was one of the signers of telegrams inviting all delegates to meet in a caucus in Philadelphia, two days before the convention opened, at the Illinois delegation's headquarters in order "to achieve an open and free Democratic convention," according to the *Tribune*. While the telegrams did not mention either Truman or Eisenhower by name, they plainly indicated that the signers considered Eisenhower both available and a stronger candidate than Truman.[14]

On July 4 the draft-Eisenhower boom seemed to be moving: Frank Hague of New Jersey, Democratic national vice chairman, and the New Jersey delegation joined it. Arvey said openly that Eisenhower, not Truman, might win on the first ballot unless he took his name out. Eisenhower was reported to have told an emissary of James Roosevelt, California Democratic national committeeman, that he would accept the nomination only if he got it without a fight. But next day, July 5, Eisenhower stopped the movement cold: he said he "could not accept nomination for any public office" and would not identify himself with any political party. George Tagge of the *Tribune* reported that "confusion" reigned among anti-Truman forces in Chicago and "some political necks [were] sticking out." Arvey left for New York on July 6 to talk to Mayor O'Dwyer. One Chicago machine leader said, "There's nothing to do now but swim even if the water is colder than supposed." Senator Lucas said the Illinois delegation now would swing behind Truman. An Arvey man said, "We've been in much tougher spots. This isn't nearly as big a job as replacing Kelly with Kennelly for the 1947 mayoralty." The *Tribune* reported next day, "Arvey was beginning to find words of solid praise for Mr. Truman when he got off a train in New York City."

The Illinois delegation left for the convention on a special train July 9. Aboard it, Arvey issued a joint statement with Mayor O'Dwyer, switching to Truman. Thus by the time the delegates gathered at the convention Truman was almost certain to be renominated.

The principal issue was civil rights. A minority report of the Cre-

[14] Among the signers were Senator Lister Hill, Chester Bowles, Arvey, Mayor Hubert Humphrey of Minneapolis (then a senatorial candidate), Mayor William O'Dwyer of New York, and seven Southerners.

dentials Committee recommended throwing out the Mississippi delegation because it was not bound to support the party's nominees if Truman or anybody else supporting his civil rights program was nominated, or if the convention adopted a platform plank advocating that program. Stevenson was one of ten delegates who signed the minority report. "He entered the civil rights fight joyfully at the convention," Carl McGowan said.

When the majority and minority reports came to the floor Tuesday night, the Illinois delegation, led by Arvey and Paul Douglas and Ed Kelly, tried to force a roll-call vote but the temporary chairman gaveled them down and seated all delegations, including Mississippi. The best they could do was persuade him to announce the names of states that opposed seating Mississippi—Illinois, New York, and ten other states plus the District of Columbia, with a total vote of 292, far short of enough to throw Mississippi out. The civil rights fight did not end there. Next afternoon the platform committee reported a civil rights plank that satisfied neither Mississippi nor the Northern liberals, and both filed minority reports. After a stormy fight the Northern liberals, led by Hubert Humphrey and supported on a close roll-call vote by Illinois, won adoption of their plank. Mississippi and Alabama walked out. That evening Truman was nominated for President and Senator Barkley for Vice President. Stevenson, in seconding Barkley's nomination, said, "Long before the great era of the Roosevelt revolution, Alben Barkley stood and battled with the Southern courage we all know so well, for the new freedom of another great Democrat, Woodrow Wilson. My fellow Democrats, Alben Barkley never surrendered. The Democratic Party never surrendered. We have not begun to fight, and I am proud to be able to call him my kinsman, and we will all be proud to call him Vice President of the United States in the second administration of Harry Truman."

Stevenson had prepared, in haste, for a five-minute seconding speech. As he was being introduced, Sam Rayburn, the crusty permanent chairman of the convention, muttered: "Not over a minute." This scared Stevenson to death, he told Wilson Wyatt later, but what he said differed little from what he had intended to say.

It had been a difficult spring of politics and a difficult convention. Stevenson had played it well. Considering Truman a handicap, he had hardly mentioned him during his spring campaigning. On the other hand, he had stayed clear, at least publicly, of Arvey's attempt to dump the President. At the convention, he took a strong civil rights position, which was also a strong Truman position. And by seconding Barkley, using the words "Southern courage," he protected both his Truman flank and his Southern flank. For an amateur, he was doing nicely.

15

During the summer and early fall it became apparent to some of their friends that Ellen Stevenson intended to divorce him. Frayn Utley, wife of Clifton Utley, recalled, "I went through a hell of a summer with Ellen Stevenson. She would come over to the house all the time. Dutch Smith and I tried to tell her to go to see a psychiatrist. So did others. She simply could not tolerate Adlai's achieving anything on his own. She had to feel that everything was her doing. She couldn't take it. So the only thing to do was flee from it. She came over to my house six or eight times in the summer of 1948 and said she was going to divorce Adlai. She said he couldn't do anything without her help. She had started him. Her contacts made everything possible." Memories are not entirely reliable, but if Mrs. Utley's and Jane Dick's are correct, Stevenson's friends knew his wife's intentions before he did. For while Mrs. Utley places her own conversations with Ellen in the summer, Mrs. Dick recalls, "One day either in September or October Adlai came into the office where our headquarters were and his face was absolutely ashen. He said, 'She is going to divorce me.' He had known their marriage was in trouble—but that she really meant to divorce him came as a complete surprise to him." Mrs. Dick and other friends tried to persuade Ellen not to go ahead with the divorce, at least then— "You can't do this to him at this time." A divorce in mid-campaign would be, in their opinion, disastrous politically. Mrs. Dick thought Ellen chose this time precisely because it was the time of maximum damage.

During the remainder of July and first part of August, Stevenson continued to concentrate on backstage politicizing, with only occasional public appearances. Sometimes when he went campaigning Adlai III drove him, and Tim Ives went along. Adlai III said, "We'd drive into a town, Tim and I would pass out literature, sit in the audience, size up the audience response. I remember that blue Chevrolet, batting around from one place to another, he in the back seat with the politicians and writing speeches. He campaigned hard. I have a blurry memory of county fairs and barbecues. I wasn't in the headquarters or the brain trust. He wanted me to be along with him on that campaign. He was criticized later for not enjoying campaigning but he did a lot of handshaking and talking at county fairs, and he liked it. He spent more time in his later years reminiscing about the 1948 campaign than the '52 and '56 presidential campaigns. Partly it was because his roots were in Illinois—and it was a grass-roots campaign. Dad told a story about how once he went to a town square, the old men were sitting on a bench on the courthouse lawn, whittling and chewing. They'd say, 'Well, Adlai, where you been—I ain't seen you since you was here in 1908.'[15] He really got a kick out of that."

Once a staff aide scouted a Republican meeting and reported that Senator Brooks was speaking only about ten minutes to small-town crowds, and the state office candidates were merely introduced. Stevenson said, "Oh, my gosh—maybe we're giving them too much." But he kept it up. Lou Kohn, sometimes accompanying Stevenson downstate, was shocked to see him leave a twenty-five-cent tip for lunch; Kohn left the dollar that a politician was expected to leave. Repeatedly Kohn, Mulroy, and Mike Howlett, who maintained liaison between the Cook County organization and the Stevenson headquarters, schemed to persuade Stevenson to dress better. Once Mulroy surreptitiously dropped Stevenson's battered hat out of the car; Stevenson retrieved it and reproved Mulroy.

August—the time for fairs in Illinois, county fairs and the state fair, and for candidates to visit fairs. Stevenson made the circuit. When he went to the county fair in Libertyville with Adlai III and Lloyd Lewis and Mrs. Lewis, they had to pay to get in, and fair officials refused to allow Stevenson to speak though Governor Green would speak a few days later "as Governor." Stevenson shook a few hands, then left. "It was awful," Mrs. Lewis once recalled. "We walked back to the car through the dust. Lloyd tried to cheer little Adlai up. Now they've named a school for him in Libertyville." (Actually the school is in Prairie View, near Libertyville.) He did better elsewhere. He developed, writing and rewriting as he went along from county to county, a standard county fair speech. At a town called Farmer City he began, "You all came out here today to have a good time, and I doubt if listening to me is what any of you would call a good time. I think I know how you feel because a long time ago I used to work on the *Pantagraph* over in my home town of Bloomington and during the summer one of my jobs as a reporter was to come over here to Farmer City to write up some of the events in this famous fair. It was always my hard luck to have to listen to some estimable gentleman make a political speech, and it

---

15 Grandfather Stevenson, having been Vice President, had run for Governor in 1908.

never seemed quite as interesting or important to me as the trotting races. But maybe that was because those speakers were usually Republicans!" And he went on and on, telling jokes and yarns, poking fun at himself, describing himself as a farmer, reminding them of the depression when "corn was so cheap some of you were burning it for fuel" and of what Roosevelt had done for the farmers. Only after long preliminaries did he discuss price parity, soil conservation, and other problems of agriculture.

Alicia Patterson apparently was in Chicago the weekend of August 6, and so was Stevenson; he wrote to her on Monday: "E my sweet—I wish I had time to write you and tell you all thats in my heart and head. Instead I'll have to content myself with that everlasting vision of Peter Pan in pink pants & a sun hat leaning against an old crooked elm by a lazy summer stream—dreaming of what might have been, what is and what may be. I didn't like Sat night— I wanted to talk, to quote, to be gay. I couldn't. But I'm glad it happened, that you were there and caught a little of the panorama. . . . I'm off for the feverish prairies now. I'll be back Aug 14 and here until the 28th when the horror starts in earnest." At the bottom of the letter he drew a picture of a heart.

Stevenson spoke to University of Illinois students who had organized a Young Democrats group. Some of the students were disappointed in his speech and even more disappointed in his backstage maneuvering. Stevenson attended a meeting of party workers in the courthouse. The students recently had tried to unseat the county chairman. He had defeated them. Stevenson now told the party workers that if elected he would channel patronage through them. This reassured the county chairman but dismayed the students, one of whom has recalled, "We were idealists. We didn't like it. He saw this and sent word to us to meet him in his hotel room. I can't honestly say he said he didn't mean it—but he had us there to give us that impression, to make us think that we were his really true friends." Next day he was at Lincoln, speaking to a noonday crowd at the Logan County Fair, Republican territory, and he spoke from the judges' stand facing the grandstand but with the horse-racing track between him and the crowd. Every few minutes horses would race past, raising clouds of dust and drowning out Stevenson's voice. He cut his speech short, saying he couldn't see his audience, they couldn't hear him, and in any case he couldn't win any votes among horses. That evening he went to the Adams County Fair at Mendon, far west near the Mississippi River, and the following day to Carthage in Macomb County and the Hancock County Fair at Augusta ("Fun for All! Bring the Family"). He spent the night at Nauvoo on the Mississippi River, the town from which the Mormons had been driven, arriving about 10 P.M. after an exhausting day, and he had ordered a Tom Collins and opened his briefcase and half undressed in a sweltering hotel room when a local politician arrived and told him that Nauvoo was proud of its wine and the candidate must visit all five taverns on the main street. They did.

The biggest fair of all was the Illinois State Fair at Springfield. Wednesday, August 18, was "Democratic Day" there. Alben Barkley delivered the principal speech. Stevenson used several paragraphs of reminiscence Lloyd Lewis had drafted, but added material on agriculture from his standard county fair speech and sharpened the political attack. Tagge of the *Tribune* reported "Democratic gloom" over election prospects showed in Stevenson's comment that the Democrats would win "or break our hearts in the attempt" instead of flatly predicting victory. In private correspondence Stevenson was saying he was far ahead of Truman and would win unless Truman lost the state by 400,000 or 500,000 and pulled Stevenson down with him. The Democratic State Convention met again, this time at the Coliseum in Chicago on August 26. Stevenson met that morning with the platform committee at the Morrison Hotel and spoke that night to the convention. He once said he played a leading role in writing the platform, keeping out of it any federal issues. His speech was almost entirely a withering attack on the Green administration and closed with a rousing rally peroration.

Stevenson admirers who later thought that his presidential campaign in 1956 was conducted at a lower level than in 1952 because "professional politicians" ran it, who believed that Stevenson himself was incapable of writing a low-level political rally speech, were mistaken. That 1948 rally speech was written in longhand by Stevenson himself. It does not follow that he admired such speeches. Indeed, he deplored them. But he thought them necessary to fire up the party workers.

The day after the convention Stevenson wrote to Alicia Patterson:

My darling—
This is all I can find to write on in my brief case. I'm on a train as usual.

I'm tired, nervous, harassed and miserable. I felt I could cry when you said you couldn't come on the telephone. And now I've just read your letter posted last night from the airport while I was driving wearily home after that horrible ordeal in the state convention at 98°.

I don't like the sad note of parting, of misgiving, in your letter. Of course our lives are complicated. If they were not we wouldn't be we! Ah, what the hell am I saying. But you understand—we must look forward gaily, happily, hopefully—not backward, over just a few months—with 30 years to come. Or is it 30 days—I feel that way at the moment & I haven't even commenced the horrible Sept-Oct grind. It starts Sunday—day after tomorrow—in Pontiac—I'd like to throw the whole damn thing out the window and catch a plane to Wyo & you—dream in the purple twilight; sing in the first mornings. There I go again—off the rails! . . .

He finished the letter later:

Now I'm home with my horrible, bulging brief case and my bewitching John Fell. Ellen & Borden have gone to dinner parties & I should like to spend the sultry insect noisy night writing useless thoughts to you and talking endless things with him. But I can't—with that ghastly brief case—and tomorrow—staring at me.

He had just read a piece about her newspaper career and said:

I marvel at you more and more. . . . You've made a great success—in the very field I had once dreamed of working. . . . I don't suppose love and envy can meet—but I can't help wishing I was on the beam as you are. Maybe I'm confused with wanting any direction. Or perhaps its wanting you rather than your objective. Anyway the love is hard enough without the other, whatever it is.

My 4 counties a day itinerary for Sept. is almost complete and in a word I will be in Chi Sept 12, 13, & 14 & that's all until Oct. Then I'll be working out of here until election. The 12th I'll be busy all day at the Riverview Democratic "picnic." . . . If you could come the night of the 13th it would be perfect. . . .

As to the campaign—the breaks are all my way—Charley Wheeler of the News . . . thinks I'm going to win in spite of Truman & Green's money. . . . And why the hell do I want to win & get into that hideous mess for 4 years of solitary agony & heartbreak. I must be nuts—or I'm in love like an adolescent. No thats you—not—A

As August ended, Stevenson tried to prepare for the September-October "ordeal" by asking his staff to reorganize all speech material by topic. They produced a compendium of some 175 pages, several paragraphs or several pages on each of 128 topics, inadequately indexed for quick reference. Stevenson again consulted experts on several issues. The distemper he mentioned to Alicia showed in a letter to a man at the University of Chicago Law School written August 28: "I have had a hideous summer and have been in Chicago hardly at all. . . . I had hoped originally to have a small group of advisors on substantive things and have failed utterly both to organize it and take advantage of it, largely due to the fact that the merciless managers have given me almost no time in Chicago." Like other political figures, Stevenson always complained about campaign managers who forced on him a schedule so arduous that he had no time to do any substantive thinking.

16

As the fall campaign, the real campaign, began, the St. Louis (Missouri) *Post-Dispatch* was thundering almost daily with front-page attacks on Green. On September 1, for example, its expert investigative reporter, Ted Link, wrote in a story from Peoria, "Gamblers, slot machine operators and punch-board distributors in at least six counties were 'shaken down' for nearly $100,000 for Gov. Dwight H. Green's 1944 political campaign," while an editorial asked, "How much longer will Gov. Dwight Green be able to evade or ignore the civic resentment which is sweeping Illinois over commercialized gambling and its attendant gangsterism and graft?" And the paper's prize-winning cartoonist, Daniel Robert Fitzpatrick, drew savage cartoons depicting Green as the creature of the gambling rackets just as he had earlier drawn powerful cartoons on the Centralia mine disaster.

Stevenson set forth downstate on his fall campaign on the last day of August, speaking at noon to the Bloomington Young Men's Club and at night to a Democratic rally in Spring Valley. He moved on to the Du Quoin State Fair, to the Vandalia homecoming—many small towns in Illinois had "homecomings" in September, and Stevenson attended. From Pinckneyville to Pana to the Grundy County Fair to Bloomington—he sent a postcard to Alicia Patterson: "Four counties a day is fine education but I don't recommend it for human beings." On Monday, September 6, Stevenson went far south to a town in the East St. Louis (Illinois) area called Brooklyn, inhabited only by Negroes, and delivered one of the most eloquent speeches of his life, a ringing commitment to civil rights. Sydney Hyman drafted it. Ending it, Stevenson said:

"We all dream, of course, of going to sleep at night and waking the next day to find that all the ills of the world are suddenly cured.

I wish things happened that way—that with a single stroke of the pen I could bring to this state the realization of humanity's highest aspirations for a life of dignity, a life of peace, plenty and order. But you and I know that things do not come to pass except by laborious, tedious and backbreaking and sometimes heartbreaking effort.

"Instead of a promise of a miracle, I can promise you only that same laborious effort towards the ultimate goal of man—which is to live as brothers under the law of God. When Christ issued his injunction to men: 'Be ye perfect,' he knew that men were not perfect and that the fallibilities of our nature would prevent us from ever being perfect. But he also understood that the salvation of many lay in striving for perfection. And so it is in the political as well as the spiritual dimension of life. I am going to be your next Governor and I mean here in Illinois to strive for that perfection—and day in and day out, month in and month out, we shall lay brick against brick, plank against plank, to form the structure of life which will bring us a bit nearer to the society of our dreams."[16]

He flatly promised, if elected, to ask the next session of the legislature to pass a Fair Employment Practices Act, to codify existing laws protecting civil rights, to establish a civil rights division in the attorney general's office, and to take steps to end discrimination in schools and hospitals.

Next day he neglected to call on a judge at Red Bud who as a boy had met Stevenson's grandfather; a state Representative told Stevenson the judge was "boiling mad" and asked Stevenson to write to him to get both of them out of "the dog house," and Stevenson did. Stevenson returned to Chicago for the big Democratic fund-raising picnic at Riverview amusement park and made a low-level political speech, a heavy-handed across-the-board attack on "the Green gang" couched in such language as this: "The whole thing smells to high heaven," "gamblers and hoodlums with back-door keys to the State House," and "new revelations of kickbacks and shakedowns." He repeatedly referred to Green, whose nickname was Pete, as "Parlor Car Pete." He said, "Parlor Car Pete . . . has petered out." He said, "They've had enough of greed, grime and Green." He would "fumigate the state capital." Stevenson liked the speech; he noted on it, "Send copy to Lloyd Lewis," who, with Jim Mulroy, probably wrote the basic draft. Stevenson had rewritten it extensively, putting in some of the low-level language himself.

On September 15 he went down to his home town, Bloomington, for a "homecoming." Ellen and the boys went too. It was a high-

[16] More of the speech will be found in Appendix B.

water mark of the campaign. The Bloomington Stevenson-for-Governor Committee organized a torchlight parade resembling the political torchlight parades of the last century when Stevenson's grandfather was running for Vice President. The parade was a mile and a half long, complete with youngsters carrying kerosene torches, horse-drawn hayracks carrying cornstalks and girls in sunbonnets, a float with teen-agers wearing 1890s costumes and sitting on bales of hay and waving Stevenson signs, townsfolk dressed in the costumes of the nineties, 15 floats, 60 horses and 37 motorcycles. Some 22,000 people were present. Mrs. Ives rode in a wagon and wore a Quaker bonnet and dress that were heirlooms. Stevenson rode in a 1904 Reo, Ellen in a 1913 Ford that broke down as the parade ended. His old friends and some of his father's friends were there. The parade started at Franklin Park in front of the homes of his grandfather and Governor Fifer and moved downtown to the courthouse square. There Stevenson, introduced by a Republican lawyer, spoke and afterward sat with his wife and John Fell, watching square dancing and listening to singing. In a picture, he appears relaxed and happy, Ellen distant and a trifle glum, John Fell unmoved.

Stevenson had worked hard on his speech. It was an important one, sure to receive wide coverage, and not an easy one, either—a man's small home town is likely to be more critical than the city. Lloyd Lewis and Jim Mulroy had given him a draft that was lofty in tone, devoted almost entirely to Bloomington, almost devoid of politics, never mentioning Green. Just as Stevenson had made their low-level, heavy-handed political speeches even lower, so did he now make their high-level Bloomington speech even loftier. They had written an opening sentence which said, "I am here tonight, receiving honor at your hands, only because of what Bloomington taught me as a boy." He changed it to read, "I am here tonight, receiving honor at your hands, only because of what I owe to Bloomington." It was the Stevenson touch. That touch and tone shone through all the changes he made. They had used the phrase "Our Town" frequently; Stevenson struck it out, creating his own town. They had written, "My great-grandfather, Jesse Fell, wanted a better Bloomington because he had learned at his mother's knee that civilization marches, never stands still," then had continued for three more sentences about Fell. Stevenson, who constantly used Jesse Fell in speeches elsewhere, sensed that Bloomington people might be sick of Fell; he struck Fell's name entirely from the speech and spoke instead of "our ancestors." They had written, "No matter where you go, if you say that you come from Bloomington, Illinois, there rises immediately in your listeners' minds the picture of a truly

American city." He substituted this: "What is unique and different and very dear to us may not be to others. I don't know whether Bloomington is really unique and different. But I do know that it is a truly American city." Then he picked up with little change a passage they had written: "I do know that it is not too big, not too small—not too rich, not too poor, not too radical, not too conservative—a city half rural, half industrial—a city with all the modern devices but without the overcrowded lonesomeness of the great cities." And so on—it was an "image speech," as speechwriters say, not an "issue speech," and the image had to be precisely his own, and he made it that way, made it more subtle, more oblique, more complex, than it had been, and at the same time a little understated. A less intelligent, less sensitive politician, or one of less integrity, never could have gotten away with it. Stevenson did. "The lights on this old square [he inserted the word 'old,' no doubt for rhythm] were once flares blazing over coonskin caps—and then they were gaslights shining on hats of silk or straw, and then they were the new and naked electric bulbs shining on derby hats—and now they are neon and some of us no longer wear any hats at all—but it is only the lights that have changed—we, the people, have always been the same. I can walk this square tonight and feel just as I felt forty years ago, thirty years ago. How often in the dusk of evenings in remote places at the end of bitter days of struggle and anxiety in war and peace I have sat and thought about the great, cool sanity that was lying on my home town among the cornfields." Only near the end did he touch politics: "And my home town taught me that good government and good citizenship are one and the same, that good individuals make a good town—and that nothing else can. I was taught here that what was wrong between private citizens is doubly immoral between public officials and private citizens. These are not the only lessons I took away from Bloomington. Here I learned from my parents and my grandparents, from the immortal Joe Fifer, the friend of my boyhood, and from many of you, that good government is good politics, and that public office doubled the responsibility that a man felt in his own home, his own neighborhood, his own town. I hope and pray that I can remember the great truths that seem so obvious in Bloomington, but so obscure in other places. If ever a man felt proud of his home town, it is I, and if ever a man wished that he could measure up to it in terms of self-respect, humanity and friendliness, I wish it tonight. I should be doing honor to you, not you to me." He added that final sentence himself, as he had added the sentence mentioning the Republican Fifer.

The speech was a great success. Indeed, it is not too much to say that, for the first time in his life, Adlai Stevenson made it in his own home town. He only did it twice again—in 1962 when, during the Cuban missile crisis, he arraigned the Soviet delegate in the court of world opinion at the UN; and in 1965, when he died.

17

Somehow in this campaign all the tattered loose ends of his life heretofore were drawing together—his love of Illinois, his ambition, his politicizing, the UN, his love of Alicia Patterson, his marital difficulties, everything. Now as never before he was focusing. Nearly everything previous had been tentative and ambiguous. No more— he was single-mindedly running for Governor, and he put into it all he had learned and been and inherited.

October was the critical month. Chicago politicians say that nobody really gets interested in a campaign until after the World Series. The Cook County machine does little until then. Frequently candidates think the party is letting them down, so late does it go to work. After the Series, ward meetings start, precinct captains begin canvassing, the great engine moves the machine. Stevenson, having spent September downstate, would spend most of October in Chicago and suburbs. He went to a few ward meetings in Chicago but spent more time in the suburbs—as a good-government candidate with Republican friends, he could expect to run well in such normally Republican suburbs as Winnetka on the North Shore and Glen Ellyn to the west.

The machine had its big campaign lunch for precinct captains in the Terrace Room of the Morrison on October 6. Jack Arvey said he saw in the precinct captains' faces "a resurgence of the spirit which has won in Cook County for twenty years." Mayor Kennelly said he wanted to disprove a newspaper report that Arvey wouldn't be able to deliver Kennelly to the meeting. "That's settled," he said. "I'm here." Then the Mayor said he was glad to be sitting "alongside the next Governor of Illinois," adding, "If he thinks he's going down there [to Springfield] alone, let me tell him that if his experience is like mine he'll never be alone." Senator Brien McMahon of Connecticut urged the party workers to tell the voters that "Harry Truman has not deserted." The party that had been badly split in the spring was pulling itself together remarkably well.

The *Pantagraph* had long since endorsed Stevenson for election, not, it said, because of but in spite of his connection with it. But it endorsed the Republican opponents of Paul Douglas and Truman. Stevenson wrote immediately to Bud Merwin, saying the *Pantagraph* had embarrassed him with his fellow candidates. Merwin said he was sorry but could not help it. The Chicago *Daily News* endorsed Stevenson in an editorial that praised him highly and attacked the Green administration heavily. The *News* called itself independent but usually endorsed Republican candidates; its endorsement gave the Stevenson campaign a lift. Moreover, coming early, on October 7, it enabled the Stevenson Committee to reprint and broadcast it all over the state. The *Sun-Times* endorsed Stevenson later.

The *Tribune* was plugging Green hard. But the cumulative effects of the Stevenson campaign and the press attacks were beginning to tell. Governor Green was obliged to defend his record. His campaign was not helped when, past midnight of October 7, William John Granata, a member of Green's State Industrial Commission, was killed, probably with an ax, on the sidewalk of Randolph Street in the heart of Chicago's Loop. He was a brother of State Senator Peter Granata, a leader of the West Side Bloc in the state legislature, the political action arm of the Chicago crime syndicate. The St. Louis *Post-Dispatch* said Granata was a Green payroller who did little or nothing for his $5,000-a-year salary—"Dwight Green had the cynicism to appoint a gangster associate." Stevenson picked up the issue, calling the killing another example of the "sordid leadership" of the Illinois Republican Party. He said, "Granata started his political career by stealing a ballot box in a class election at Urbana [at the University of Illinois]. He advanced rapidly. He was Republican ward committeeman and on Governor Green's payroll. His chauffeur, an ex-convict, also was on the Green payroll. His brother Pete is Republican leader in the legislature and distinguished himself in the last session by helping to kill the Crime Commission bills. Another brother was bookkeeper for the late gang chieftain, Frank Nitti," who, some thought, had succeeded to Al Capone's power until he killed himself. A few days later the press reported that the FBI was investigating letters threatening death by strangulation to Stevenson and John Fell. Mulroy told Stevenson about the letters but said Stevenson disregarded them.

On the same day that Granata died, Stevenson and Green appeared together at the Stevens (later the Conrad Hilton) Hotel grand ballroom to discuss constitutional reform before the Illinois League of Women Voters. It was an important occasion. Reform of Illinois's antiquated constitution was of deep concern to good-government groups of all kinds. The League, which favored reform, had much prestige with the independent press. In their speeches Stevenson and Green agreed that the present constitution was inadequate and pledged support for a constitutional convention. They differed, however, on the role the Governor could play in getting one. Stevenson said flatly, "The genuine and wholehearted support of the Chief Executive of the state spells the difference between success and failure in this high enterprise." Green, on the other hand, said, "Certainly the support of the Governor's office is vital to the success of the resolution but it certainly is no guarantee of its passage."

Next day, October 9, Stevenson unveiled a fifteen-point program he would undertake if elected. It was, in effect, a summary of his attack recast in affirmative language. Wally Schaefer and others had prepared it. From here to the end of the campaign, Stevenson repeated it in various forms. It was carefully drafted. Stevenson promised to redistribute "some" of the tax money to local communities —but he did not say how much or which tax monies, although the press that supported him wanted the sales tax distributed. He did not promise flatly to take the state police out of politics but rather contented himself with a general commitment to "offer security—as nearly as that is possible—to all competent civil servants." Again, he did not say how much aid to the schools would be "adequate" nor did he take a strong position on enactment of a Fair Employment Practices Act with teeth in it. Finally, he did not promise a constitutional convention that would write a new constitution but only to "rewrite the state constitution," which could mean merely amending the existing constitution, not replacing it. Several of the fifteen points were little more than pious homilies. The program, in sum, represented not the program of a flaming liberal reformer but of a prudent, rather conservative good-government candidate.

On October 11, Governor Green made a major tax proposal. Incredibly, Mayor Kennelly endorsed it. Stevenson scheduled an appointment with Kennelly the following day. On October 12, Stevenson went down to Danville, in the middle of the state, and joined President Truman's campaign train and rode it to Springfield, as did Senator Lucas. (On an earlier swing Paul Douglas but not Stevenson had joined Truman.) At each whistle stop en route Truman urged the election of Stevenson, Douglas, and Democratic congressional candidates. In Springfield the President laid a wreath on Abraham Lincoln's tomb, attended a $25-a-plate dinner, and, after a torchlight parade, delivered a major address on farm policy at the Springfield Armory. He also said, "Never within my memory has any party offered your state a finer team than Adlai Stevenson and Paul Douglas."

On the day Truman spoke in Springfield, the *Tribune* made its first head-on editorial attack on Stevenson. Though this may be taken as an indication that the *Tribune* thought Green was in danger, the *Tribune* chose, as it often did, to employ a light touch at the outset, poking fun at "Adlai" before heavily attacking the substance of Stevenson's campaign. "Adlai just does not know the score. The Democratic machine that pulled him away from his United Nations chores to front for it does know the score, and at all times. With him in the executive mansion, the boys from Chicago would make [former Governor] John Stelle's notorious Hundred Days look like a reform regime." Stevenson told Alicia Patterson, "This lousy, contemptible edit[orial] really makes me mad. . . . It's the worst for inconsistency and dishonesty I've seen yet."

Stevenson "made the wards" in Chicago—on October 13 he visited several ward meetings and attacked Green as changing from "the character of Mr. Do-nothing to Mr. Fix-it." But he continued to court the independents and Republicans—spoke next day to a Chicago Commonwealth Club lunch on "Adventures in Politics." He found time that day to thank a Chicagoan for a twenty-dollar contribution (the man had written that this was the largest contribution he had ever made): "Some of us cannot translate into dollars what we think, feel and believe in, but we try to make up for it by a type of support which I hope money will never buy." Stevenson always attracted a good deal of this kind of support.

Stevenson spoke on October 15 at the New Trier Township High School in Winnetka—upper-middle-class people, educated, homeowners, interested in good government, many commuting to LaSalle Street, suspicious of politicians, most usually voting Republican but priding themselves on their "independence" and given to saying, "I vote for the man, not the party." They were the kind of people Stevenson now and later thought of as the "independent voters," the "swing voters" who decide American elections. (He was wrong. The swing voters are people of all sorts. There simply are not enough Winnetkans in the United States to produce the enormous presidential swings of 1956 and 1964.)

Two weeks to go. The *Tribune* published a cartoon headed "One-World Preoccupation" showing Stevenson with his head in the clouds and "Old Man Illinois" trying to pull him down to earth by one leg. Jack Arvey predicted that the entire Democratic ticket, including Truman, Stevenson, Douglas, would win—Truman had made "tremendous strides" in Illinois in the past ten days. *Newsweek,* dated October 18, said Democrats felt they had in Stevenson and Douglas the best candidates in many years but feared a Dewey tidal wave would swamp them. Stevenson told Alicia Patterson, "If you see the Newsweek piece don't give up—I'm running better than they realize —particularly downstate." It was a postscript to a short letter which said, "My love—Thanks for the note & I don't mind the mood at all! It came just in time. I was going to take this moment to write you a very bitter little reminder that I'm in my 'agony' & at least you could do was to relieve my anxiety with an occasional post card! I think I gave you that feeling because I too had some miserable days just after you were here—but I couldn't slow up. You're quite right that those feverish snatches at each other are awkward and uncivilized —but they're better than nothing! I wish we could have a few of those lyric days in Ga. . . . ."

To a Polish-American banquet Stevenson gave an inflammatory speech that said, "Where were the McCormicks, Brooks and Green when the Nazis were murdering Poland? I'll tell you where they were. They were against aid to the Allies." Stevenson ran a rough campaign.

Stevenson called Jack Arvey on Sunday, October 24, appeared before a League of Women Voters group on the Gold Coast on Monday afternoon, and late in the afternoon went to the Crystal Ballroom in the Blackstone Hotel to attend a reception in honor of President Truman. Truman's visit to Chicago was the highlight of the campaign in Chicago. After dinner the President led a motorcade out to the Chicago Stadium, largest indoor hall in Chicago, and the *Tribune* reported that between 250,000 and 300,000 people lined the parade route. True, the precinct captains had turned out thousands. But more thousands had come spontaneously. And what was more remarkable was the enthusiasm of all—even the precinct captains. Kennelly and Kelly rode with the President. In the second car were Congressional Medal of Honor winners. Behind them came Stevenson, Douglas, Lucas, Arvey, and others. Ellen Stevenson rode in a car with Mrs. Truman, Mrs. Kelly, and two others. The Stadium was packed—25,000 people. The machine did not look moribund that night. Stevenson, in his speech, praised Truman—"that humble courageous fighting man"—but by implication admitted Truman had made mistakes. He gave the roaring precinct captains raw red meat, but before even them he courted Republican votes.

The *Tribune* reported next day, "President Truman aroused a crowd packing Chicago Stadium last night as he charged that a Republican victory next Tuesday would pave the way for a totalitarian state in America. Touching on subjects usually taboo in a Presidential campaign, Mr. Truman played upon the emotions of hate and fear as he accused his G.O.P. opponents of stirring up racial and religious prejudice. He compared 'powerful forces' behind the Republican party to the interests which raised Hitler, Mussolini and Tojo to power. . . . The crowd responded with deeptoned roars.

. . . When he mentioned 'the crackpot forces of the extreme right wing' he interpolated: 'We have a representative of those forces right here in Chicago!' The crowd cheered and booed." The rally was a shouting success. Next day the tables were turned: Governor Dewey packed the Stadium, while Stevenson spoke at Bloomington and three Chicago meetings.

It was the middle of the final week. Stevenson was feverishly busy. On Thursday the Democratic organization held its final luncheon of precinct captains at the Morrison Hotel, and Alben Barkley predicted victory, and Stevenson said, "I told you that I would tear the striped pants off little Pete Green on November 2. Well, they're slipping fast." He put a note on his calendar pad for Friday: "Call each ward committeeman to thank them" and "statement on stealing votes." He made several appearances that day. The *Tribune* kept hammering away. Its George Tagge reidentified Stevenson as a "socialite and former New Deal diplomat" who intimated he favored a state income tax. On Saturday, Stevenson issued a statement urging a large vote: "The important thing is not my victory but that the citizens of Illinois exercise their right to vote. . . . Win or lose, I shall be content if the people vote in full strength."

On the final Sunday, Stevenson, together with Paul Douglas and John S. Boyle (candidate for Cook County State's Attorney), spoke to seven party rallies. At one, in the Negro ghetto, he said he was proud to be on a ticket headed by Truman. In spite of all the frenzied activity at the end of the campaign, that curious streak of detachment in Stevenson enabled him to write a letter the day before to the wife of a faculty member at the Choate School who, with her husband, lived in the house where Borden lived. And at about the same time, he wrote to Alicia Patterson: "E—You have neglected me shamefully—and I'm getting suspicious of that man Sandburg! When are you leaving—exactly—and when will you be back—exactly. I wish you were going to be here Tues—to share in the confusion around headquarters. . . . There's no question about my election—IF we can get an honest count which will be difficult in many downstate counties." He enclosed a *Tribune* cartoon called "Sucker Bait" and wrote, "I'm the bait on the right—in case you get confused. And you're my bait—you wretched, faithless, beloved witch!"

The public campaign was over. On the last weekend the machine made its final canvass. Jack Arvey believed that Stevenson was going to win big. "I'd noticed the enthusiasm at the time of the Stadium speech—it was tremendous. We thought Truman was creeping up and might win but the final canvass showed he would lose by fifty to sixty thousand votes. We put extra money in all the Negro wards. I got the money from Smith and Ronan and I convinced Ned Brown [Edward Eagle Brown] we were going to win and told him that we might need another forty or fifty thousand dollars and asked if we could pay it back after the election. He would have loaned us the money but we didn't need it." Stevenson himself was confident. He told Ed McDougal, "The reports from downstate are good and I think I'll win by quite a large majority." McDougal recalled, "I was surprised because the talk around town was otherwise. I remember going in to a friend of mine the morning after the election and telling him Truman had won. He said, 'I can't believe it—do you mind if I call my broker to verify it?'" Stevenson had told another man, "May I remind you that I would like very much to have $1,000 of that 3 to 1 money on Green if you can possibly get it for me."

The *Tribune*'s Sunday editorial, entitled "Mark It Straight Republican," discussed the national and congressional races at length but spent only one sentence on the state campaign: "It is evident that Gov. Green and the other Republican nominees for state office will win easily, as they deserve." Clearly Republicans were counting on Dewey to carry Green and Brooks in. The *Daily News* on Monday advised voters to split—vote for Dewey and Stevenson. Stevenson and Green made final radio speeches on Monday. Green said the Democrats had given up on Truman but were making every effort to capture the Statehouse as a haven for federal payrollers. Stevenson predicted his own victory with Republican support.

On Election Day, November 2, Stevenson cast his ballot in a country school at the town of Half Day near Libertyville at 10 A.M. (More experienced politicians vote earlier to ensure getting their pictures in the afternoon papers.) He, Ellen, John Fell, and the campaign staff listened to the early returns at his headquarters at 7 South Dearborn. It became clear early that he was winning. He went over to Democratic headquarters at the Morrison Hotel where, in an inner room, Arvey and other party leaders were receiving returns at a table full of telephones. Stevenson listened for a half hour as Arvey called out the returns. Arvey and other party leaders seemed almost unable to believe the magnitude of the victory. Stevenson went back to his own headquarters and stayed past midnight. Dutch Smith, Lou Kohn, Jim Mulroy, Jane Dick, Lloyd Lewis, and all the rest were there. The early edition of the *Tribune* announced that Dewey was elected. But as time passed Truman began to pull even. Young Adlai, at Harvard, got into a fist fight with another student that night in an argument over Truman. When Stevenson's victory became apparent, he issued a statement saying he was "at once gratified and humbled by the size of the majority," thanking the voters "from the bottom of my heart," and going on to say: "But I realize, just as you do, that I am only the instrument through which the people of our state have expressed their desire for better government, for cleaner government, for the kind of government which will make the name of Illinois famous once more in the states of the Union. I would like to say tonight how pleased I am that the voters of Illinois have responded to my vision of a better Illinois. But the truth is that I caught the vision from the people themselves." Green, conceding late, said, "I accept the verdict of the people, rendered in the American way."

The size of Stevenson's victory was truly astonishing. Only three other Democrats had been elected Governor of Illinois since the Civil War. Stevenson won by the largest plurality any candidate for Governor ever received—a plurality of 572,067 votes (out of a little less than 4,000,000 cast). Almost assuredly he pulled Truman in with him—Truman carried Illinois by only 33,612. This meant that more than a half million people split their tickets, voting Democratic for Governor and Republican for President. It was a remarkable tribute to Stevenson's pulling power with independents and Republicans against Green. He led the ticket; he got 2,250,074 votes, Paul Douglas got 2,147,754, Secretary of State Edward J. Barrett got 2,120,832, and the rest of the state candidates received slightly more than 2,000,000, while Truman got 1,994,715. Stevenson carried Cook County by 1,386,642 to Green's 840,218, a plurality in Cook County alone of 546,424. What is more astonishing, Stevenson, a Democrat, carried downstate Illinois, something nobody had thought possible—carried it by 863,432 to 837,789. He carried Peoria County, where the *Post-Dispatch* had exposed gambling scandals. He carried Marion County, where the Centralia mine had blown up, a normally Republican county. He carried Sangamon County, where Springfield is located. He even carried the county where he grew up, McLean, which almost never goes Democratic. (But he failed to carry Lake County, where Libertyville is located. It has been said that at that time only one Democrat had ever been elected to county office in Lake County since the Civil War, and it had taken him a good part of his term—and a court fight—to get the keys to his office.) Stevenson's was a phenomenal victory. That he won big may be attributed to his own campaigning, the Democratic Cook County machine, the heavy support of three big newspapers, and a number of smaller but influential ones downstate, and, perhaps above all, the fact that he, who could readily play the role of a good-government candidate, had the good fortune to run against a vulnerable incumbent whose scandal-ridden administration had turned many of his own party against him. In 1948 everything went right for Stevenson. But it was, after all, a state, not a national, election; and it caused him to overvalue the independent vote and later caused Truman to overvalue Stevenson's national vote-getting ability.

The day after the election Ellen received friends in her mother's house on Lake Shore Drive. Stevenson wrote to Alicia Patterson:

> I carried Illinois . . . never anything like it in history. . . . Now I'm really in trouble! But there are years and years and years ahead for us. I'll think no other way, if you don't mind. Please, please take it easily and don't get nervous, excited, tired. I know you were here amid the fantastic frenzy Tuesday night. I can't begin to send you the clippings, pix etc. Someday we'll thumb them all over together when this silly little tumult has subsided and all is tranquil and peaceful. Goodbye my little bird—fly back again and we'll talk of many things—I want to write & write; instead I must go to a victory lunch & receive the blessings of the thankful—And I don't owe anyone anything—political or financial. I'll be in the cabin with you—& sometime embodied, not disembodied. Aha! for 5 days of rest & reverie and—
>
>   A

PART TWO
BECOMING

CHAPTER SEVEN

The Governor, the Divorce, and the Presidential Draft 1948-1952

For the first time in his life Adlai Stevenson was his own man. In his early years he had been dominated by his mother and sister. In the late twenties and the 1930s his life had been run by the demands of his wife, Lake Forest, the Gold Coast, and LaSalle Street. World War II, and specifically Frank Knox, had set free his impulses toward public affairs, but during the war years and immediately thereafter he had worked as someone's assistant or alternate. In government there are two kinds of men—the man who runs something, such as an embassy or a cabinet ministry, and the man who helps him. Until now, Stevenson had been a helper, had never had even a bureau in the bureaucracy to run himself. Now all that was past. In the governance of the state of Illinois, he was number one.

In government, in another sense, there are two kinds of men—those elected, and those appointed by the elected. The appointed men may last longer—in the State Department career service, they may last a lifetime—and they may be given something to run, such as an embassy or a ministry. But they serve at the pleasure of the man who appoints them, power drains away from them when he loses it, and they must pursue his policies whether they agree with them or not. They are, in brief, forever his men, never quite their own. A high elected official, on the other hand, stands at the pinnacle of power. The people themselves—or a substantial number, in this case more than two million, of them—have set him on high, have either voted for him or acquiesced in his election. He is free to set policies, to take decisions, to decide great issues, to lead—that is what the people chose him to do. True, he owes political debts, he has made campaign promises, and all power contains its own limits.

In a few years he must face re-election, and so elective political power is ephemeral. But while it lasts it is incandescent. In all of politics, nothing is quite like election to high public office in a democracy.

In Stevenson's case, the limitations on his power were remarkably few. His margin of victory had been so huge that no single group could claim credit for it. He had won votes all over the state, many of them Republican votes. With more justice than most victors he could claim to be the governor of all the people. Although he had maneuvered for the nomination, during the campaign he had declared so often that he had not sought the nomination that he probably believed it; and in a sense it was true: the machine had turned to him because it needed him. No wonder his exultant cry to Alicia: "And I don't owe anyone anything—political or financial." He was indeed, as much as any man ever is—and more than he had ever been or would be again—his own man.

Governors, like Presidents, can be judged by several standards. Among them are these: Were his appointments good? Did he exert wise policy leadership—propose policies that met the people's needs (and here we deal with budgets, programs, and vetoes)? Was he able to get his program through the legislature? Was he an effective party leader? What of the tone and style of his leadership, of his relations with the people? Was his administration honest and upright or corrupt and scandal-ridden? Did he keep his campaign promises? And was he effective—did he know what needed doing and get it done?

The Governor of Illinois, unlike many Governors, has immense power. He has—or had at that time—at his disposal some 30,000 jobs. He can appoint his Cabinet and all manner of important boards and commissions—even the Parole and Pardon Board—that in many states are non-political, that is, are under civil service and untouchable by politicians. He could appoint every state policeman. He has power of life and death—can extend clemency to condemned criminals. As the chief executive officer of the state he was responsible for recommending the expenditure of and for spending well over nine billion dollars every two years; for the care of more than 50,000 people in public institutions; for proposing and working to enact such fundamental changes in state government as constitutional reform; for setting priorities among such diverse claimants to public funds as highways, schools, mental hospitals, prisons, and what Stevenson liked to call "building a bridge over Catbird Creek" —local improvements. As the head of government, he can use the press as a powerful lever to move the state, and he can speak directly to the people. As the leader of his political party, he can use his power to reduce the influence of corrupt elements in the party, get good candidates on the ticket, strengthen the party organization, and align it behind his own purposes.

Balanced against his great powers are great obstacles to his purposes. A hostile legislature can be one. So can all manner of special interests and their lobbies. So can corruptionists in both political parties—and in Illinois, their criminal allies, the Syndicate—whose interests honest government threatens. So can incompatible elected officials. So can tradition—the ancient Chicago-downstate rivalry. So can an indifferent public, a hostile press, and the reluctance of good men to enter government; and, finally, the sheer inertia of government—the vast immovable inherited bureaucracy of government of a big state.

Until 1948, Adlai Stevenson had known little about these problems. His interest had been in foreign affairs. To one who had been on the fringe of world events, gasoline tax policy might not seem of vital importance. Now, however, for better or worse, he confronted a state's panoply of problems; and we shall inquire how he faced up to them. During his governorship, we shall witness the climax in one crisis of his private life. Thus we shall observe a tightening of the tension between the inner man and the outer man, a tension that had begun long ago and would persist to the end.

2

Hopes were high. Midwest newspapers expressed congratulations —and expectations. Arthur Krock predicted in the New York *Times* that the "new" Democrats in states essential to the national victory —Frank Lausche of Ohio, Hubert Humphrey of Minnesota, Paul Douglas and "especially" Stevenson—would wield immense influence in the national Democratic Party: "Quite naturally, after such a triumph in the vital state of Illinois, Mr. Stevenson is being surveyed as a possible Presidential candidate of the Democrats in 1952," Krock wrote, and, in a private note to Stevenson a little later, he said, "I meant it most seriously, Adlai, and shall nudge the ball along from time to time." At the end of 1948, *U. S. News and World Report* said that the Democratic split might produce a "compromise" presidential candidate in 1952 such as Chief Justice Fred M. Vinson, General Eisenhower, or Stevenson.

Stevenson received a great many letters and telegrams congratulating him on his victory. Mrs. Roosevelt cabled from Paris, where the

UN General Assembly was meeting, and he replied warmly, saying, "It's all your fault!" Supreme Court Justice William O. Douglas sent "wonderful congratulations" and Stevenson replied, "I wish a few of us could get together and discuss some of the formidable responsibilities our party has, not to mention its great new opportunity." James Roosevelt congratulated him, and Stevenson replied, "We have a great opportunity and I wish there was some way we could have a meeting like the British parties do to formulate a long term party program in general terms." It was a question that vexed him henceforward. Among others who congratulated him were John Foster Dulles, Ed Stettinius, John Rockefeller, Joseph Grew, Bernard Baruch, and Chester Bowles, his schoolmate at Choate who had just been elected Governor of Connecticut. In answering letters from abroad, he reminisced about earlier days in England or Europe. He was seriously considering going to France to help Secretary Marshall at the UN and to see Alicia Patterson. Marshall, however, said the Assembly would finish its work before mid-December and it would not be worth his while to get involved for so short a period. It might have hurt him politically—would have invited the charge that he was neglecting the business the people had set him to.

3

Instead of going to Paris, he went to the Morrison Hotel headquarters of the Cook County machine—went there on November 4, two days after the election, for a three-hour victory celebration. The *Tribune* quoted Secretary of State Eddie Barrett as saying, "Labor was our precinct captain." The *Tribune* consistently attempted to picture the Democratic Party as the captive of the CIO, a label Stevenson feared. Stevenson, asked at a press conference what would happen to the 30,000 state employees, said, "My disposition will be to appoint Democrats where qualifications are equal."

On November 8, at a victory dinner in Springfield, State Chairman George Kells said, "Illinois will supply the next President of the United States—Governor Stevenson." Stevenson said, "It was the people who won this victory for good government. The people and principles triumphed over money and machines." V. Y. Dallman told Stevenson that the meeting was "a real thriller" and passed on a request that Stevenson speak to the North Central Weed Control Conference. It contrasted sharply to thoughts of Paris.

Stevenson was making preliminary moves toward organizing his government. Preparing to leave for a vacation at Southern Pines, he asked John S. Miller to recommend men for his Cabinet. He considered his "most difficult and important positions" the directors and assistant directors of the Departments of Revenue, Finance, Welfare, and Public Works and Buildings. En route, he stopped briefly in New York and Washington and wrote Alicia Patterson, "I wish I could fly right on to Jax"—Jacksonville, Florida, the airport nearest Alicia's plantation in Georgia; he was fantasying, for she was in Europe at the time—"& find you waiting with dogs & station wagon and then head for the forest and solitude—and you. . . ." Ernest Ives met him at the airport at Raleigh, North Carolina, and on the way to Southern Pines, Stevenson fell asleep in the car. Soon after arriving he fell asleep again on the porch—he was exhausted.

The political writers of the three leading Chicago newspapers accompanied Stevenson to Southern Pines—Tagge of the *Tribune,* Dreiske of the *Sun-Times,* and Wheeler of the *News.* Stevenson played golf with them one day and talked with them often. Once he took them coon hunting. When by 10 P.M. the dogs had not treed a raccoon, Stevenson proposed that the newspapermen go home and rest while he continued the hunt with more expert help. Dreiske wrote, "Well, the rest of the story is a familiar Stevenson climax. He got his coon, of course." Dreiske went on, "Adlai Stevenson plays as hard as he works. Muttering, 'This game is a terrible time-waster,' he plays low-80 golf. He's horsey too and loves to ride, but, with all his love for sports, he is definitely not the playboy type. As you see Stevenson relaxing in that almost grim, businesslike way of his, you have the feeling his serious responsibilities are constantly pressing down upon him. . . . Don't cry for Stevie. He'll tree his coon."

Bud Merwin suggested he resign as vice president and director of the *Pantagraph* "as part of a policy of disassociating yourself with all business connections during your tenure as Governor." Stevenson did. He wanted Mrs. Ives to take his place but Merwin demurred.

On Monday, November 22, Stevenson went to Washington. There he told newspapermen he was "not interested" in becoming the Democratic presidential candidate in 1952, adding, "I will have all I can do to handle state affairs." He called on James Boyd, director of the Federal Bureau of Mines, to discuss mine safety. He called on the Federal Works Administration to talk about Illinois's highway problems. He wrote to Alicia Patterson:

I don't like your note of apprehension and foreboding. I hope there will be a letter awaiting me in Chicago saying all is well

—that you've seen everything and everyone and are fit and happy. Perhaps you will also say that it was silly, shameful, brutal to have even thought of never writing or seeing me again. It had never occurred to me and came as a shock and I'm glad such a gloomy cruel resolve was short-lived. Of course we are going to see each other. . . . There's nothing we can't do if you want to enough and are wise enough. . . . What with all your traffic with the great men I wonder if you'll find your heart as full of me when you come home. Pray God you do, now and always. . . . Somewhere the sun is shining—and you're in it—in a pool of bright light, your hair is glistening and reddish & tumbling all about your shoulders, your delicate little face serene—and your eyes half shut in reverie. And in a moment I'm going to kiss you and you're going to be all alive again—and so am

I

Stevenson took a train home on November 23. Two big problems and two lesser ones faced him. The big ones were staffing the government and preparing his program. The lesser ones were covering the campaign financial deficit and arranging the inauguration.

The Governor's Cabinet consisted in the heads of thirteen "code departments" established under the state administrative code. They ranged from the Department of Aeronautics, with sixty-five or seventy employees and a budget of a few hundred thousand dollars, to the Department of Public Welfare, with more than ten thousand employees and a budget of about $100 million. Under the Governor, too, were some 105 boards and commissions, ranging from the Bee Keepers Commission with two employees to the Illinois Public Aid Commission with two or three thousand employees and a budget of $150 million.

One evening—it was probably December 2—Stevenson and Wally Schaefer went to Dutch Smith's home in Lake Forest and went through the statute books, listing appointments that Stevenson had to make. Stevenson was determined to get the best people possible for the top jobs, especially those jobs that were politically sensitive. It would not be easy—department heads received only $8,000 (the Governor himself received $12,000, compared to $25,000 in California and New York and $20,000 in Massachusetts and New Jersey), and he was looking for men now earning between $50,000 and $100,000. The problem was not only money—it was also reputation. Carl McGowan once said, "Stevenson didn't take over a going concern. He took over an operation that—well, I suppose government had come as close to a full stop in Illinois as we've ever seen.

Just compare taking over New York after it had been run by Lehman and Roosevelt and Smith and taking over Illinois after eight years of Green—and the last part of the Horner administration too. We've had a hell of a low tradition of government here in Illinois."

All through December, Stevenson consulted with Schaefer, Smith, Lou Kohn, Steven Mitchell, Jim Oates, and others. Stevenson himself once said there were three ways to choose key men—to appoint whomever the political party recommended, to pick the best of the people actively seeking the job, and to "go out and try to find your own men." He preferred the third way. But it took time—a great deal of time. When he had been in the office nearly three months he said, "I suspect I spent far too much time" at it. Applicants presented themselves—107 for a single seat on the Court of Claims, for example. Stevenson interviewed men personally only after his aides and friends had checked them out. He was always suspicious when an applicant seemed to have organized support. He received some 250 telegrams urging him to appoint one Leonard Schwartz Director of Conservation and suspected political chicanery. But he found that the telegrams were from sportsmen and Schwartz was all right. Stevenson appointed him. Of his first ten appointees, three were Republicans. He offered one department directorship to nine men before one took it. After he appointed a man to head a downstate institution, a Republican member of the Senate showed him evidence that the man had been indicted for rape years earlier and convicted of carrying concealed weapons. He stopped, at the last moment, another important appointment because he was not quite satisfied with his record; sure enough, the Bureau of Criminal Identification found a record on him in 1934 in connection with graft in the awarding of contracts. Driscoll O. Scanlan, the mine inspector who had repeatedly warned the Green administration that the Centralia mine was dangerous, had made campaign speeches for Stevenson and expected to be appointed Director of Mines and Minerals. But Stevenson was under contrary pressures from the two miners' unions, the two coal operators' groups, and "John Lewis watches every move you make," as Stevenson once said. He finally persuaded another man to take the job only after inducing his company, through a "very devious device," to make up the difference between his state salary and the salary it was paying him—and after three weeks in office he died. Stevenson began the search all over again, and seventeen names came before him. The best-qualified man had a wife who refused to move to Springfield, and the second-best-qualified man had a brother in the slot machine business in Macoupin County and a brother-in-law who ran a betting handbook in East St. Louis. He finally appointed Walter Eadie, mine manager of the New Orient Mine at West Frankfort—and near the end of 1951 the New Orient Mine blew up, killing 119 men, even more than had died at Centralia.

At least three of Stevenson's appointments turned out badly, causing scandals that embarrassed his administration seriously. One of these was of cabinet rank. By and large, however, Stevenson's Cabinet, and the heads of his boards and commissions, were men of stature, experience, and ability higher than is usual in Illinois government.[1]

Stevenson made two cabinet appointments that appeared to be purely political. He named Frank Annunzio Director of Labor, a man who had made his career in the United Steelworkers and the CIO and was, at the time of his appointment, secretary-treasurer of the Illinois CIO-PAC. The appointment infuriated the rival Illinois Federation of Labor, the state AF of L organization. Some people had substantive misgivings about Annunzio, among them Guy E. Reed of the Chicago Crime Commission. Stevenson told him, "I have

[1] Roy Yung, Director of Agriculture, had been born on a farm, had graduated from the University of Illinois College of Agriculture, had worked for a federal farm credit agency in Illinois, had received several promotions there, and had become manager of the Farm Service Department of the Citizens National Bank of Decatur. Stevenson's friends, Gene Funk, Henry Capen, and Don Forsyth, helped recruit Yung. George Mitchell resigned as an officer of the Chicago Federal Reserve Bank to become Director of Finance; previously he had been a consultant to the Bureau of Internal Revenue in Washington, director of research for the Illinois Tax Commission and member of the commission, a deputy director of the State Department of Revenue, a lecturer on economics at Northwestern University, and an instructor and research assistant at the University of Iowa and University of Chicago. Harry B. Hershey, the Director of Insurance, had been a downstate Democrat of probity and a friend of Stevenson's, the party's candidate for Governor in 1940 and, before that, general counsel to the Department of Insurance. Fred K. Hoehler resigned as executive director of the Chicago Community Fund to become Director of Welfare, the state's biggest department; before that he had been director of welfare and director of safety in Cincinnati, had gone abroad in 1943 as chief of the Division of Relief and Rehabilitation of the North African Economic Board under General Eisenhower, had served in London and continental Europe with the U. S. State Department and a United Nations agency, had been president of the American Public Welfare Association and of the National Council of Social Work, and had written two books and many articles on welfare and social work. Charles P. Casey, Director of Public Works and Buildings, had worked in the department under Governor Horner and had held several federal jobs, including director of the Illinois unit of the WPA, regional administrator of the OPA, Illinois Director of the War Manpower Commission, and consultant to the Federal Works Administration.

had a heart-to-heart talk with Annunzio and so have Sam Levin and Philip Murray." But Reed was right—Annunzio turned out badly.

Stevenson's other "political" appointment proved to be one of his best—that of Richard J. Daley as Director of Revenue. Daley was a Democratic career politician from a ward near the Chicago Stockyards. He had been elected to the state House of Representatives in 1936 and to the state Senate in 1938. He had been Minority Leader in the Senate in 1941, 1943, and 1945. He had long been county comptroller of Cook County. He was rising rapidly in the Cook County machine, would replace Arvey as county chairman, and later would become mayor of Chicago. The Director of Revenue is a key man in Springfield, never more so than in this administration, in view of Stevenson's campaign promises to return more state revenue to "starving" local governments. Daley knew the subject, and he knew state and city politics. He served Stevenson well. When he was appointed, Pete Akers, in the *Sun-Times,* publicly congratulated Stevenson and the state on Daley's appointment: "Daley, still a comparatively young man, has come to exemplify the best in politics. . . . If Adlai Stevenson can induce a few more men of Daley's unique qualifications—ability, political experience and integrity—to associate themselves with him for the next four years he will do much to assure the success of his administration."

Arvey once told Stevenson, "As far as your major appointments go, I wouldn't even make a suggestion if you asked me to. As to the rank and file, you'll have to get help somewhere—you won't know enough people to fill all the jobs—and if you need help I'll give it to you." If finding good men for the Cabinet was difficult, hiring 30,000 employees without incurring grave risks was next to impossible. Yet it must be done. If power is the ability to reward and punish, an important source of the Governor's power in Illinois lies in those 30,000 patronage jobs. Now in December, Stevenson talked to Arvey, Lucas, Kells, and other Democratic leaders. The fiction has arisen, encouraged by Stevenson's own insistence that he was a citizen and not a politician, that Stevenson stood aloof from the Democratic politicians. But Carl McGowan once said, "His relations with the Democratic politicians were pretty good. He really didn't give the Chicago organization much trouble about appointments. They feared a Steve Mitchell who would denounce them and refuse to discuss contracts. Stevenson had no problem with this. Starry-eyed friends of Stevenson would find it hard to understand why Stevenson thought it was a necessary part of the game. I've seen him standing around the Mansion with Joe Gill and Al Horan and he was enjoying it and so were they. Botchy Connors"—his leader in the Senate—"especially. You know how politicians operate. A guy in a precinct wants a job as a state weighmaster. Horan wouldn't let him around his house with the safe open—but he will recommend him to the Governor. Maybe also Horan will say to Stevenson on the phone, 'This doesn't mean a thing to me.' Stevenson appoints someone else. The fellow complains to Horan and Horan can always say he did his best for him. This is the way it works. You know Chicago ward leaders—what have you done for me today? They always grouse. But their average with Stevenson on patronage and contracts was very high. He pressed his people to hire Democrats. He had Maude Myers [executive secretary of the Civil Service Commission] make monthly reports to him. He felt good when he got 500 Republicans fired and 500 Democrats hired. He had Maude make a table comparing the speed with which Democrats replaced Republicans under him and under Governor Horner. If a politician complained to him about patronage, he'd pull out this list."

Adlai III has recalled that his father used to tell a story about a Chicago politician, probably Al Horan, who had an insurance company that wrote casualty insurance for the state. A downstate insurance man whom Stevenson knew asked why he couldn't bid on the insurance. Stevenson talked to Horan, and Horan said, "Sure, if you can get a better deal, go ahead and do it." Stevenson discovered he could not. "It left him bewildered," Adlai III said. An Arvey protégé, Bill Rivkin, once said, "Arvey used to say it made him look good and feel good to be identified with Stevenson." Stevenson liked Arvey, according to Newton Minow, because Arvey always told him the truth straightforwardly and because Arvey never asked Stevenson for anything. This last was not quite literally true but it was nearly so.[2]

Patronage was divided equally between Cook County and down-

[2] On December 8, Arvey told Stevenson, "One of the Ward Committeemen who should be considered for appointment is William Milota of the 23rd Ward. He has proven himself a great political leader. Beyond that, he is a prominent leader of his Nationalistic group (Czechoslovak). . . . I do not know what position he would be most fitted for, but I do suggest that you have a talk with him." On December 31, Arvey told Stevenson that the Screening Committee, a committee of the Cook County Democratic Committee headed by Joe Gill and containing three other powerful Chicago politicians, Joseph T. Baran, the Negro Congressman William L. Dawson, and Al Horan, with Eddie McCabe as executive secretary, had unanimously recommended that Milota be appointed a member of the Liquor Control Commission or secretary of it. This was a sensitive commission—liquor and bars in Illinois were often closely connected with organized crime. Stevenson did not appoint Milota to the Liquor Commission.

state. Stevenson once described the Screening Committee and his patronage troubles to the Commercial Club: "The patronage pressure is incessant and dreadful. It is not like organizing a business. It is not like going out and getting the best men you can for the money—the way you would do with any position in your business—because you are dealing in an area that is quite dissimilar. You are dealing with a political party. You are dealing with a legislature. You have to have the legislature or all the best intentions in the world will come to naught, and the pressure from them to put inadequate people and unsatisfactory people into positions is incessant." He finally worked out an elaborate system: each job description went to the screening committees in Springfield and Chicago, the committees invited recommendations from the county chairmen, then screened the applications and sent the best to the department director, who had final hiring authority, subject to Stevenson's veto. For a time, one of Stevenson's staff members sat with the Chicago Screening Committee. But Eddie Barrett, the elected Secretary of State, dominated the downstate committee and was building his own machine independent of both Stevenson and the regular Democratic organization. After about a year the downstate committee was disbanded, and thenceforward Lawrence Irvin handled patronage for Stevenson. By then Barrett's friends had grabbed all the good jobs.

Stevenson told the Commercial Club that his first instruction to department heads was to eliminate "deadheads," or payrollers, state employees who did not work, and also part-time employees. He found that by the time he took office "thousands of people" had already been dropped from the payroll. By March 1, he said, he had eliminated 1,563 more, saving the state $35,000 a month in salaries. "Now, that seems to you all to the good . . . but every time one of these men is discharged . . . you get a repercussion from somewhere. Usually it is from his Republican sponsor, who usually is a member of the state legislature, and generally he comes in to you and says, 'You are making a great mistake. You are going to need my vote for this or for that.' I do not see any way to trifle with the thing. You simply go ahead and do it, and that is what we have attempted to do. We have kept on a good many Republican employees. . . . That is always hard to explain to people of your own party. . . . I am shameless about it. . . . What we do is keep a black book. . . . We watch how this Senator or Representative who sponsors this particular Republican job-holder votes. If he votes badly you always have the threat of reprisal that his patronage will be fired; if he goes along with you, you will keep him. Perhaps it is not a very worthy way to do it, but somebody has got to show me a better way."

In the final weeks of 1948 backstage maneuvering had begun over who would be Speaker of the House. Paul Powell, from far downstate Vienna, was the leading candidate, opposed by another downstater and a Chicagoan. Now Paul Powell was a formidable figure. He was almost surely the most powerful downstate Democratic politician. A rangy man with a southern Illinois drawl, given to using slang, possessor of a loud florid oratorical style, a man of undistinguished appearance, when he arose on the floor of the House of Representatives he suddenly became a commanding presence that dominated the House. He had been born poor in Vienna—pronounced there as Vy-*an*-na—in 1902, had graduated from Vienna High School, had run the high school for six years, then been elected mayor. He had first run for the legislature in 1934 and had been re-elected every two years since. He had been in charge of the 1948 downstate campaign, with headquarters at the St. Nicholas Hotel in Springfield. After Stevenson's victory, Paul Powell had said that "the Democrats smell the meat a-cookin'." Powell was a man of great native ability and intelligence. He knew every highway and byway in Springfield, especially the byways. He was a fearsome alley fighter, a slashing, devastating debater. He knew every pressure point in the Illinois legislature, knew what made each vote turn. He sought power, and it flowed to him. He was, in a sense, a dishonest Lyndon Johnson. Over the years Powell had become identified with some of the most unsavory downstate spoilsmen. One was John Stelle, who had succeeded briefly to the governorship when Henry Horner died October 6, 1940. Stelle was considered a spoilsman and a party wrecker. Although his power had declined, he was still a man to reckon with downstate, and Stevenson was obliged to reckon with him though he found it distasteful. Stelle was a foe of Senator Lucas, and on December 18, Stevenson conferred with Lucas about Paul Powell's candidacy. (Stevenson and Lucas themselves were never really close, and at one point, several years later, Lucas became angry with Stevenson for denying him a favor.) Stevenson decided to remain neutral in the secret struggle over the Speakership, a blow to Powell, who had indicated previously that he had Stevenson's support. Powell, nonetheless, was elected Speaker. Carl McGowan once said, "Stevenson had great regret that Paul Powell couldn't be more helpful. He had been hopelessly compromised long before. He couldn't afford to be in the Stevenson orbit—it cost him a hell of a lot of money to be Speaker that year, he should have been making it all back in one year, as he saw it. Stevenson never had a venomous feeling toward Powell. It was one of regret." Abraham Lincoln Marovitz blamed Stevenson for his failure to work with Powell. He has said, "He could have gotten Paul Powell, too, the same way he did Botchy Connors, by asking his help, but he didn't want to be obligated. You can always say no." After Powell died in 1970, investigators found some $800,000 in cash in shoeboxes, envelopes, and a bowling bag in the closet of Powell's suite at the St. Nicholas and in his office safe.

4

Stevenson's other major task in December was to prepare a legislative program. Wally Schaefer was in charge. Shortly after the election, Schaefer had received from Kenneth Sears, of the University of Chicago Law School, a letter containing several proposals, including a constitutional convention. He hoped Stevenson would try to put the question of calling a constitutional convention to the voters by the "party circle method"—the proposal would be printed on the ballots beneath the party circles, so that people voting either straight Democratic or straight Republican would automatically vote for the proposal, thus improving its chances of approval. (In the past the proposal had been printed on a separate ballot, and a voter had to make a special effort to vote for it.) Lou Kohn drafted memos, or passed on memos from others, suggesting legislation and warning of perils—one warned against graft in the Industrial Commission. Fred Hoehler submitted a long report on reorganizing the state Welfare Department. Stevenson conferred with the regional director of the Federal Security Agency. A delegation of mayors called on him to ask for more money for the cities. He conferred with the superintendent of schools in Chicago. A Jewish agency offered Stevenson advice on a Fair Employment Practices Commission (FEPC) law. Such was the range of his concerns.

Aside from his two big problems, appointments and program, Stevenson had two smaller ones. On December 10 the Stevenson-for-Governor Committee sent out a letter to contributors saying that unaudited figures showed a deficit of about $30,000 and asking them to help meet it. The money came in mostly in large sums. Soon the purpose of money-raising changed. To begin with, it turned out there really was no deficit, in the sense of unpaid bills. Beyond this, however, Stevenson had begun to realize that he would need more money than his state salary to run his office. He told John S. Miller, "There are many expenses—salary supplements, contributions to this and that which a governor has to incur, and for which he needs some outside funds. I am told, in short, that there is always a deficit, and I do not propose to make up these continuing funds out of arbitrary assessments, shakedowns, etc." Out of this evolved the idea of continuing the Stevenson fund and using it to pay Stevenson's expenses and to supplement low state salaries in order to help attract and hold able people. Through a few close friends, therefore, including Dutch Smith, he continued to solicit funds during his governorship. It was done quietly, even secretly. In context, the plan was innocent enough. But his opponents might claim that by accepting such funds he was putting himself under obligation to the donors and creating a serious conflict of interest. And indeed this special fund would make much mischief when it came to light during the 1952 presidential campaign.

Stevenson's other concern was the inauguration. He made John S. Miller chairman of the Inauguration Committee. Other committee members included both Stevenson's friends and politicians. When it came to the ticket committee, where politicians' feelings can be hurt, the subcommittee was dominated by Arvey.

During December, Stevenson was almost frantically busy. He was having appointments nearly every half hour each day and sometimes nearly every fifteen minutes. He was seeing politicians, his personal friends, his staff, candidates for jobs, and a host of people important to his administration—the state officials elected with him, newspapermen and newspaper publishers, budget experts, prison wardens, state Representatives and state Senators, labor leaders, the *Time* magazine staff, judges. He attended numerous functions—a Church Federation dinner, an IVI meeting, a press dinner, the Chicago Bar Association's Christmas show, the old Sidley law firm's annual party, a dinner honoring Mayor Kennelly, a meeting of the Illinois Manufacturers Association, and others. On December 11 he attended the Gridiron Dinner at the National Press Club in Washington, and Arthur Krock reported that, among all the prominent persons assembled there, Stevenson was "of unusual interest." He had hoped to see Alicia Patterson but she was apparently still in Europe. He wrote to her. He really did seem to prefer Washington to Illinois. Or was he simply grumbling? About Christmas he wrote again:

> Darling—It is very late and I am propped up in bed desolate, weary, harassed and sad. Its been a ghastly six weeks. The boys are all home and I've had a few good hours with them, but this job is murder and I need help, understanding and encouragement & I have none.
>
> I've read your letter again & again; it makes me a little sick— Ah ye of little faith! "Tried to fall in love in Berlin!" How can you

write such things to me, let alone do them? Yes, we must talk and soon. And the Mansion is as good a place as any—or Chicago. The Inauguration is the 10th; the smoke will clear away soon and then I'll settle down to my hideous ordeal—alone. Ellen will be staying here in Libertyville with John Fell.

Come to me when you can. I need you, and ask God to give you faith and heart and courage—and please, please don't write such distracted, miserable letters to your lover—yes, and your best friend!

A

On January 3, Stevenson wrote to her:

E darling—I feel better this morning. I've just read your letter —and I hope I was with you New Years even by your black river! You were very much with me—at John Cuneo's! Let me know as far in advance as possible when you are coming. . . .

Commencing Sunday of this week—the 9th—my address is Executive Mansion, Springfield, Ill—lest you've forgotten. Write guarded letters for awhile until I get the secretarial situation down there under control.

I'm desperate—but no compromises yet! Difficulties that would make a volume of "Innocents abroad in Politics." Sometimes I'll tell you about them—I hope. Meanwhile my hours are vanishing & I haven't even written my inaugural. I wish you were to be there smiling at me—because I love you—A

He also sent a note on Morrison Hotel stationery: "I'm in my hide out trying desperately to write my inaugural message—wish you were editing the wretched stuff as it drips from the desk."

5

Steve Mitchell told a friend that the mood of the inaugural was bright, gay, and exciting. Stevenson, accompanied by Ellen and Adlai III and John Fell, leading Democratic politicians and several close friends, went down to Springfield in a private railroad car the day before, January 9. (Borden was away at school.) Next morning they went to the Governor's Mansion where Governor and Mrs. Green greeted them, then all drove in a procession to the Armory. A cold drizzle was falling. Nonetheless, several hundred people lined the route, only a few blocks long. Stevenson rode in the first car, bearing official license plate Number 1, with Governor Green and the adjutant general. Inside, the Armory was packed—the entire legislature was there in joint session. The men and women entered separately. Mayor Kennelly came down the aisle alone and was applauded. Ed Kelly slipped into a seat at the rear of the hall; he was discovered and taken to a seat on the platform with other party leaders. After Supreme Court Chief Justice William J. Fulton swore him in, Stevenson, wearing a dark blue suit, smiled slightly and stood aside while the state office holders elected with him were sworn in. An American Legionnaire presented flags, Stevenson delivered the inaugural address, and Carl Sandburg spoke.

The inaugural speech of the Governor of Illinois is at once an inaugural speech and a State of the State message. In it he lays out his legislative program. Stevenson proposed a long program, perhaps too long, some of his associates came to feel. But they had believed that, with his huge plurality, he was at the peak of his prestige and influence. By the time the legislature next met two years later in 1951, some of that prestige and influence would have been eroded, they feared. (They were wrong, as it turned out. But they thought: Better get everything he could now.)

His speech was sober, containing but a single humorous note. Despite his big majority, he did not employ in his speech language that could be considered peremptory. His tone was conciliatory. He began by referring to Illinois's history since 1848—Illinois formerly had been isolated but was no more, almost any event in the world affected Illinois, and the world was engaged in "a long trial of strength between individualism and collectivism." Our task, therefore, was to demonstrate for all to see that representative democracy was healthy, vigorous, and best.

After such preliminaries, he set forth his program. He first said, "Consistent with maintaining the state's credit and discharging its own prior responsibilities for the general welfare, our greatest single challenge lies in finding the means for better financing of schools, roads and local services." He then asked for—

—more state aid for common schools;

—more state aid for municipalities and other local government units;

—a constitutional convention;

—higher pay for top state officials;

—revision to tighten the civil service law;

—legislation to require disclosure of state payroll information to discourage patronage abuses and to encourage an expanding merit system;

—integration of the Department of Public Welfare and the Illinois Public Aid Commission;

—increased aid to old-age pensioners and the blind;

—improved care of mental hospital patients and a shift of emphasis from institutional care to home care;

—increased workmen's compensation and at the same time reduction of employers' contribution rates;

—consideration of extending unemployment compensation to workers in establishments employing fewer than six people;

—consideration of the "advisability" of the state's taking "an affirmative role in the settlement of labor disputes";

—consideration of FEPC;

—more money for highways;

—a "quick-taking law" to permit the acquisition without delay of land for slum clearances;

—reorganization of the Department of Mines and Minerals;

—conservation to be put in the hands of a non-political commission;

—the state police to be put under a "merit system";

—lengthened and staggered terms of members of the Illinois Commerce Commission and raised pay for them.

The speech was noteworthy not only for its extensive program but for what it omitted. Steve Mitchell thought the speech cautious. The legislators listened quietly. Later Senator Wallace Thompson, Republican leader of the Senate, said the speech was good but its lack of specific recommendations would require further study. Senator Botchy Connors, Stevenson's Minority Leader in the Senate, said the speech was "high in purpose and ideals." In the House, Speaker Paul Powell said the speech was "one of the most liberal ever delivered" to the legislature. Representative Reed Cutler, the huge old-fashioned slashing Republican Minority Leader in the House, said, "He has some great ideas, many of which will be impossible to carry out."

After the speech, the Stevensons and the Greens and about seventy friends of the Stevensons went to the Mansion for lunch. The daughter of former Governor Fifer and the son of former Governor Dunne were there too. So were three old ladies from Bloomington. Mrs. John S. Miller has recalled, "At the Mansion, Ellen went upstairs and refused to come down. We stood around in the receiving line downstairs waiting for her. Finally Buffie said, 'Let's go to lunch.' Poor Adlai just stood and stood. Finally she did appear."

Luncheon at the Mansion lasted till about 4 P.M. Most of the guests returned a little past 7 P.M. for dinner. Other dinner parties were being held all over town. About 9 P.M. more politicians and friends of Stevenson crashed the Mansion. Then all hands went to the

Armory for the Inaugural Ball. The *Tribune* reported, "The governor and his wife, looking as pretty and flushed as if it were at her own debut ball, led the parade onto the stage, with Mrs. Stevenson's stunning gown of pink and gray slipper satin, made slightly off shoulder and with a bouffant skirt, setting the pace. . . . A whole new cross-section of Lake Forest and Libertyville residents undoubtedly will become familiar with the [Mansion]." A society columnist said that during the inaugural ceremonies Ellen had "remained aloof."[3] A photograph of Ellen taken at the inaugural shows her looking unhappy, a glazed expression on her face. Others who were there, however, have remarked how radiantly beautiful she looked—and how handsome Stevenson was—as they danced the first dance alone.

6

Springfield was at that time a place of some 82,000, in character neither a town, really, nor a city. It has a life of its own—quiet shaded residential streets, outlying barbecue stands to which teenagers drive their fast automobiles, movies downtown, a country club, pool halls and beer parlors down by the railroad tracks, industry—Sangamo Electric, Donald Funk, president, was the biggest—farm equipment sales lots, the offices of lawyers and insurance men around the courthouse square. Its biggest industry sometimes seems to be Abraham Lincoln. He is buried here, the only house he ever owned is here, signs on street corners point out to tourists the way to his shrines. But the state Capitol, whose dome can be seen for miles around on the prairie, dominates Springfield, and so does the fact that Springfield is the seat of Illinois government. The state is a big employer. Its buildings are the city's biggest. More, the town really came to life only every two years, when the legislature was in session from January to June 30. (Under the constitution, it met only every two years and was required to end its session by June 30. A new constitution has since provided otherwise.) The Capitol

[3] The columnist said that many friends of Stevenson from Lake Forest, finding no room in the Governor's box, formed a "rump party backstage, draping themselves over stage props and some rickety old chairs and proceeded to have a merry party." Among them were the John Kelloggs, the Ralph Hineses, the Steve Hords, the Dick Bentleys, Mrs. Solomon B. Smith, the Gaylord Donnellys, the Dutch Smiths, and the William McCormick Blairs.

stands on high ground, broad steps mounting to an enormous façade, and inside, despite the coffee and cigarette machines and filing cabinets in corridors, its marble and gilt somehow manage to retain an air of grandeur. Here hang the portraits and here stand the statues of former governors and legislative giants. Here school children come to stand in the great rotunda and gaze upward at the lofty dome. Here, most of all, can be found the offices of the governor and his aides, the offices of his cabinet ministers, the dusty hot committee rooms, and the two chambers of the Illinois legislature—the large chamber of the House, where debate sometimes resembles a street-corner argument, and the smaller quieter chamber of the Senate, presided over by the Lieutenant Governor (or in his absence the president pro tempore), where debate sometimes resembles debate.

A few blocks up a wide brick street, under a viaduct, stood at that time the Abraham Lincoln Hotel, usually considered the Republican hotel (and since closed), and a few blocks away stood the St. Nicholas Hotel, usually called the Democratic hotel. The Leland Hotel was considered neutral. Behind the Abraham Lincoln stands the Governor's Mansion, a graceful house on a rise of land, white, Southern in style, a reminder that Springfield stood midway between what had been in Civil War days Northern and Copperhead country, a gentle house nestled against a gentle slope, a driveway curving up to its basement entrance, a porch atop the porte-cochere, trees shading the sloping lawn. Here, and in the Capitol, and in the hotel rooms the legislators occupied, is power. On soft May and June evenings one can see the Senators and Representatives standing shirt-sleeved outside the hotel entrances, or in the hotel bars and lobbies, talking about pending legislation. It is here, and in committee rooms, and in whispered conferences on the floor, and perhaps most of all in hotel rooms where of an evening the most powerful of the legislators meet, sometimes with each other, sometimes with lobbyists, that the fate of bills is decided. It happens, but not often, that when a bill comes up on the floor for final passage, having wound its tortured way through various readings and committee procedures in both houses, votes change. But usually by the time a bill reaches final passage a close watcher can predict the outcome. In those days only a few legislators—Paul Powell was one—possessed the power to actually change votes during final debate.

The people of Illinois, like the people of most states, pay little heed to their state legislature. Most Americans, indeed, know more about the United States Congress than about their state legislature. Yet the legislature every session enacts laws that directly affect the life of every person in the state. The 1949 session considered legislation as important as the writing of a new constitution and legislation as trivial as restraining cats from running at large. It considered bills or resolutions dealing with adoption, alcoholic liquor, amusement devices, assault and battery, Bangs disease, banks, bastards, birds, blind persons, bookmaking (gambling, not publishing), cancer, chiropody, cigarettes, civil rights, civil service, the coal industry, Communism, conservation, credit unions, cuspidors, drainage districts, elections, employment, fish, floods, fur-bearing animals, habeas corpus, highways, horse racing, hospitals, housing, husband and wife, I Am An American Day, judges, juries, lakes, libraries, marriage, memorials, mentally ill persons, mining, motor vehicles and traffic regulation, naturopathy, obscene literature, old-age pensions, parks, penitentiary, pensions, perjury, police, railroads, real estate, rent, the Rose Bowl game, sanitary districts, schools, seditious activities, sheriffs' fees, slaughterhouses, soldiers and sailors, state building and contracts and employees, syphilis, taxation, tornado, townships, unemployment compensation, villages, waterworks, wells, women, workmen's compensation, the York Community High School Band, youth, and more. The 1949 legislature levied taxes on all citizens. It appropriated nearly a billion and a half dollars of their money. It frustrated Adlai Stevenson by refusing to pass some of his bills, and it obliged him by passing others.

The members of the Illinois legislature were—and are—by and large neither as good as they claim nor as bad as most citizens think. One of them once said, "We got the best Senate money can buy," but it is a canard: the Senate, and the House, too, may seat some men whose votes can be bought but it also has many whose votes cannot. In Illinois at that time the ordinary citizen tended to think that all horse races were fixed, that all policemen and legislators were corrupt. This is not surprising, considering the examples that were held up to the citizens from time to time, and indeed, upon occasion, government in Illinois did sink low. But at the same time the legislature contained men of probity and ability. They were a diverse lot. The Senate in 1949 contained 21 lawyers, 6 farmers, 5 insurance men, 2 merchants, 2 men in the printing business, and one each who listed themselves as "broker—railroad," building material, caterer, civil engineer, director CYO, home and sales promotion, investments, manufacturer, pharmacist, publisher, real estate broker, theater owner, and retired.

The House contained 29 lawyers, 10 insurance men, 9 farmers, 5 men in real estate and insurance, 4 merchants, 3 each of "homemakers," "legislators," and retired men; 2 each of men in the electrical business, farming and livestock, hatchery, manufacturers, pharmacists, real estate, "real estate broker, mortgage, insurance," real estate investments, "vice presidents"; and one each of a great variety of occupations.[4] It seems fair to say that the legislature was weighted rather heavily with lawyers, professional politicians, small businessmen, and farmers, though many of the farmers had moved to town and taken up shuffling real estate papers.

The legislators, so often attacked as clumsy or wrongheaded or downright corrupt, tend to draw together. They room together in the hotels to cut expenses. They dine and drink together in the hotels and night clubs. They like to reminisce about legislative giants of long ago. They are by and large kind and courteous to one another. They protect and defend one another. Their natural enemies are in the Governor's Mansion and the press room. Yet many a member has pronounced the solemn words, "I have an appointment with the Governor," in tones that sound as if he were on his way to a war zone on a presidential mission. And many court the press outrageously, for while publicity can hurt, so can it help re-elect.

7

The legislature at that time met only in odd-numbered years. It had convened and organized itself and was lying in wait for Stevenson when he was inaugurated January 10. It had first met on January

---

[4] "Accountant, insurance and real estate," appraiser and tax examiner, automobiles, automobiles and implements, banking and insurance, bonds, bowling alleys, building maintenance supplies, businessman, chief deputy coroner, chiropodist, "cigars, tobacco," civil engineer, "civil service employee, Sanitary District of Chicago," civilian and uniform tailor, consulting engineer, dean of law school, direct mail advertising, "Director of Research, Assessor's Office, Cook County," editorial work, electrical engineer, farm equipment dealer, "farm implement—gasoline dealer," "farm management and insurance," "farm and federal tax consultant," "farmer, livestock dealer and auctioneer," "farmer and salesman hybrid seed corn," "farmer, salesman and ex. School supt.," "farming and banking," "Ford salesman and educator," fuel oil, funeral director and farmer, hardware and implement store, hotel, inspector, insurance, real estate and editor, "Int. Rep. (UAW-CIO)," "investigator (City Clerk)," lawyer and banker, manufacturers sales agent, merchandise representative, merchant and farmer, musician, newspaper publisher, "gas station, real estate," operating engineer, physiotherapist, pipe organ installer, pressman, probation officer, publisher, "publisher, insurance and real estate," "railroad foreman and farming," real estate broker and farmer, real estate and clerical, "real estate, insurance, small loans and merchant," schools and office supplies, secretary, sheet metal and air condition shop, superintendent of recreation, tax accountant, "tombstone manufacturing—attorney," trucking contractor, ward superintendent of streets.

5. That day Senator Wallace Thompson of Galesburg, the ranking Republican, was elected president pro tempore of the Senate over Senator Botchy Connors, the Chicago Democrat, on a straight party vote, 32 to 18. Connors became Minority Leader of the Senate. On the same day the House convened and elected Paul Powell Speaker. None of this surprised anyone. That same day Governor Green sent to the Senate a list of thirty appointments to various positions and asked its concurrence. (Stevenson told a friend, "They 'pulled a fast one.' And to get my nominations confirmed we had to withhold any protest about theirs." It was a part of his initiation into the world of Springfield.) This and other business concluded, the Senate moved over to the larger House chamber to canvass the votes cast in the November election and to hear the farewell address required of Governor Green. The legislature then adjourned until inauguration day.

The legislature customarily met infrequently and only perfunctorily in the first half or even two thirds of its session. To an outsider it appeared that the legislators were wasting most of the session. Actually, however, during this period they studied bills that were introduced, had bills of their own drawn and introduced; the leaders could line up votes and plan strategy, the lesser members could see which way the wind was blowing; and the Governor had time to prepare his budget, delivered in April. Until then, most of the legislators merely commuted to Springfield a day or two a week and waited for the Administration and the legislative leaders to move events.

8

Stevenson's personal staff assembled. In the beginning Mulroy, the beefy ex-newspaperman from Chicago and campaign manager, carried the highest-ranking title—executive secretary to the Governor. He dealt with both appointments and program, worked with members of the legislature in trying to get Stevenson's program enacted, and served as over-all administration strategist. The rest either carried the title of "administrative assistant to the Governor" or were tucked away on some department's payroll. Wally Schaefer worked on the legislative program. Lou Kohn sat at a desk in the anteroom of the Governor's office in the Statehouse, talking to people who besieged it, giving some appointments with him and turning others over to aides, serving as a buffer and, as he liked to say, as "the Governor's lobbyist" with legislators. Irvin handled patronage. Bill Flanagan was press secretary. Don Hyndman, a former newspaperman who had written speeches for Governor Green, stayed on to do the same for Stevenson. Ed Day, who had been a member of Stevenson's old Sidley law firm, arrived a few months later to work on legislation and other matters. After the legislative session Lou Kohn returned to his law practice and Schaefer to Northwestern University. Early in September, Carl McGowan replaced Schaefer. Later on William McCormick Blair, Jr., joined the staff to handle Stevenson's personal appointments and Richard Nelson came down to work on political matters. All these men were young, most in their thirties. The Governor's staff meetings were inclined to be lively, relaxed, and funny.

Stevenson liked to work at the Mansion. He set up his own office in its basement, or ground, floor. Carol Evans and another secretary, Margaret Munn, had an office guarding his. Across the hall was, at the outset, Wally Schaefer, later McGowan and Blair. Stevenson seldom went to the Governor's official office in the Statehouse. The rest of his staff, headed by Mulroy, was there. This created a certain amount of friction—it was generally believed, probably justly, that Mulroy and Schaefer were closer to the Governor and more influential than the others, Schaefer physically and Mulroy as executive secretary. At different times Schaefer and Blair lived in the Mansion. Having written many speeches himself, Stevenson tended to unfairly discount Hyndman's contribution. Having been close to the press all his life, he frequently dealt directly with newspapermen and did not always take Bill Flanagan, one of his most devoted aides, into his confidence. (This was probably more true in the 1952 presidential campaign than during the governorship. At various times during the rest of his life, Stevenson had several press secretaries; he never took any of them completely into his confidence, and so made their tasks inordinately hard.) By mid-1950 the two staff men at the Mansion were Bill Blair and Carl McGowan, and they remained throughout the governorship. In the 1952 presidential campaign, they would be Stevenson's closest advisers.

McGowan found Stevenson easy to work for. "He never complained about your inadequacies or bawled you out." Schaefer thought Stevenson enjoyed being Governor, though there is ample evidence that during that first spring he often felt badly "rattled," as he himself put it. He worked hard at the job. Schaefer has said, "I had always worked hard myself but I was amazed at the way he worked—night after night after night he worked. If there were guests, we'd go up for cocktails and dinner and then he would excuse himself and he and I would go back down to work. He almost never spent a full evening with anyone. He read the papers or talked about some state matter at breakfast." He had little recreation. "We talked about getting the tennis courts fixed up but we never did. We went horseback riding a couple of times. We went home every weekend in a National Guard plane. Once we drove up to a little town to visit a family Stevenson knew and play tennis. There were always problems of security. Adlai would sit working at a desk right in front of a window in the basement office. He was a perfect target. But he insisted." Stevenson was always impatient of his state police guard. He was not, however, impatient of his big capable state police driver, Everett Van Diver. Mrs. Van Diver was housekeeper at the Mansion.

Education and the state parks interested Stevenson. "He had a feel for the outdoors and parks," McGowan has said. He was determined to see to it personally that the government ran well. Shortly after taking office he made a surprise inspection tour of state buildings on a Sunday morning. At least once he visited the Lincoln State School for retarded children unannounced, taking Joe Bohrer of Bloomington with him. Bohrer has recalled, "We spent four or five hours going through it. He'd look in every ward. I never saw such patience." He did everything that way. Bohrer went on, "Buffie and Adlai bought a farm down here and I drove him down to look at it. He crawled up into the hayloft and looked at every beam. It didn't do much good, because he didn't know much about it—but he was so very thorough." He reversed previous practice and ordered the display of his photograph in public places reduced. He never stopped worrying about what the Chicago *Tribune* said about him. McGowan recalled, "I told him his life would be happier if he'd just quit reading it. They'd clip him, then he'd waste time being nice to them. It was the same as some of his Lake Forest friends. They were really his enemies."

Stevenson took his job seriously and saw it in a larger perspective. He once said, "The job of creating a sense of respect for public office and public officeholders among our young is the most important work we have in hand." A Chicago advertising executive suggested he keep a diary with a view to writing an account of how government really worked. The idea intrigued Stevenson greatly but he never got it done because, he said, of inadequate staff.

One of his powers as Governor was to commute a death sentence. He took it hard. Jane Dick once wrote, "There was the night that Adlai, my husband, and I sat alone in his office on the first floor of the Mansion waiting for the clock to strike midnight, at which time a condemned Illinois prisoner was to die in the electric chair. Adlai was personally opposed to capital punishment, but the law of the state provided for it, and this man had been convicted of a particularly heinous crime, and had exhausted his last appeal—except to the Governor. The telephone kept ringing wildly in all of the offices, and the Governor's administrative assistants talked to priests, relatives, drunks in bars, and emotionally wrought-up citizens, all making desperate last-minute pleas for the prisoner. Despite his aides' urging that he go to bed and not subject himself to the ordeal—for he had spent hours going over the record and had concluded that justice had indeed been done and must now take its course—Adlai insisted on talking to the prisoner's hysterical mother himself, hoping, I believe, that somehow something new might be developed that would enable him to stay the execution. But the heartbreaking conversation was useless. Finally the calls stopped. A deathly silence invaded the dimly lit offices, when at long last the old grandfather clock on the Mansion stairs started tolling out its twelve interminable strokes. I glanced at Adlai, and then had to look away because I know he was sitting in that electric chair himself that night. When it was over, we all went up to bed without speaking."

Stevenson continued to make important appointments for months. He appointed his friend Stuyvesant Peabody, Jr., a coal executive, to head the Illinois Racing Board, a body subject to pressure from corrupt elements in horse racing. He appointed Jane Dick to the five-member Board of Public Welfare Commissioners. He appointed Ralph Budd, a railroad executive, to head the Chicago Transit Authority. He put a University of Northwestern law school professor, W. Willard Wirtz, on the Liquor Control Commission and Wirtz went on to become Stevenson's law partner and then Secretary of Labor in the Kennedy and Johnson administrations. He made Joseph Lohman, a University of Chicago sociologist, chairman of the Parole Board, another sensitive spot. He put Don Forsyth, the Springfield insurance man, on the Veterans' Commission.

The Director of Public Safety holds a job posing potential danger for a Governor, for he controls the state police, the prisons, the Bureau of Criminal Identification and Investigation, and the Parole Board, all subject to heavy political pressure. Stevenson gave the job to Don Walsh, Jim Mulroy's brother-in-law, who had been representing Stevenson in patronage matters. Walsh brought in a Chicago police captain, Thomas J. O'Donnell, and he enlisted the aid of experts, including the FBI, to improve police training and standards. Formerly the state police had been taxi drivers for the state legislators, taking them to night clubs, waiting for them, and then driving them to their homes all over the state. One man forgot his eyeglasses and a relay of state police cars delivered them. (Stevenson once had a state police car retrieve his own toothbrush and shaving materials from the home of a friend where he had left them. But he did not make it a habit.) Walsh recalled, "One night Senator Traeger wanted to go home from the Lake Club in Springfield— home to Peoria," about seventy-five miles. "I told him to take a cab and I'd pay for it out of my own pocket." This and other incidents did not help Stevenson's relations with the legislature. Walsh got into a quarrel with Speaker Paul Powell over a patronage appointment, Powell tied up the House, Jack Arvey and Al Horan intervened, and Stevenson himself had to help make peace. Once Walsh blocked the appointment of a prison farm warden who owned a liquor store in town. Stevenson supported him.

As Director of Public Welfare, Stevenson appointed Fred Hoehler. More than half the state's total budget goes into welfare institutions and public aid. The Welfare Department employs more than a third of all state employees. It administers mental hospitals, correctional institutions, children's hospitals, and schools for the blind and deaf, containing more than 50,000 people. At the outset, Hoehler told Stevenson he knew a good deal about welfare but nothing about politics and might get Stevenson into trouble with the politicians. He gave Stevenson a list of jobs that needed professionals—doctors, psychiatrists, and others—and told him those jobs could not be filled by political patronage. Stevenson agreed. "It hurt," Hoehler once said. "Lots of those jobs had been filled on a patronage basis in the past. He had to resist all sorts of pressure. And he had to fight the battle over and over—those political fellows never give up. I found forty or fifty payrollers in the department. I fired a Democratic state central committeeman. You can imagine the heat that put on the Governor. But he made it stick. I fired a Chicago precinct captain and there was all kinds of hell to pay. The man was a slave to his political sponsor. His sponsor had got him into a job he wasn't able to do." (In these circumstances, a suspicion exists that the man was obliged to kick back a part of his salary to his sponsor.)

Hoehler once learned that the inmates of a small state institution, including chronic alcoholics, were allowed to buy drinks on credit in town. This is illegal. Local politicians had prevented the superintendent from stopping it. Hoehler told Stevenson about it, and Stevenson said, "Go ahead—I don't care who gets hurt."

For years state institutions had paid top-grade prices for fourth-grade meat and fed it to the inmates. They had fed them rotten potatocs from bags marked "Grade A." One day, visiting an institution, Hoehler noticed apples piled up everywhere. A truck arrived loaded with more apples. The superintendent, a Hoehler appointee, said, "Wait a minute—I don't think we need any more apples." The driver said, "Oh, you'll take 'em. I been bringin' apples here for years. You'll learn." The superintendent said, "Well, if I do I'll learn from him," and gestured toward Hoehler. The driver said, "Well, they told me to bring the apples here. They always tell me that. If I can't get rid of 'em anywhere else I dump 'em here and the fellow here knows how to get rid of 'em. I been doin' it for years." Hoehler said, "Well, you don't leave this load here." Apparently a Chicago fruit dealer with political connections had been dumping overripe stock onto state institutions for years.

In addition to playing policeman, Hoehler persuaded several good men to join the Department. He brought in Dr. Percival Bailey, a neurosurgeon, to take over the Research Department. Bailey was reluctant; Hoehler argued that Bailey's prestige would attract other good men and took Bailey to see Stevenson. Stevenson drew him into a long conversation, listening attentively, and finally said, as he nearly always did, "Thank you so much—you've been a tremendous help to me." Bailey took the job. He in turn brought in several outstanding research men, including Dr. Harold Hemwich, an authority on nerve and brain metabolism. Dutch Smith once said, "You see how it works? You get a man like Adlai at the top and he can get a man like Hoehler to come in. [Dutch Smith had recommended him.] Hoehler can get Dr. Bailey. And Dr. Bailey can get Dr. Hemwich. It works all down the line that way."

To run the sprawling Public Aid Commission, which administers relief funds, Stevenson brought in a Chicago lawyer friend. Henry Tenney encountered Stevenson at a cocktail party. Stevenson told him, "The dirtiest job I have to give out is chairman of the Illinois Public Aid Commission." Tenney asked, "What's that?" Stevenson said, "All I can tell you is that it's the biggest headache in state government," and asked Tenney to visit him in Springfield. Tenney did. "I stayed with the Governor. After they give you a certain amount of that, you can't get out of it. We had dinner in the garden —you know that terrible little garden at the Governor's Mansion. Stevenson, Ed Day, Schaefer, McGowan, and I—they were going over bills and deciding what to veto. They'd be sitting around and one of them would say, 'Well, let's veto it,' and they would. The others left after dinner. When Stevenson finished working, about ten or eleven o'clock, he yelled to me and I got my suitcase and he said,

'Let's see if we can find a bed for you,' and we went upstairs in the elevator. It was pitch dark. We felt our way around. Finally we found a bedroom. He said, 'Guess this is all right.' There was nobody in the house. The footsteps were echoing in that old barn, I couldn't believe it." Tenney took the job. "When I went back to Chicago, my law partner, Dick Bentley, told me I was crazy. I agreed. I knew nothing about the job. The first meeting of the commission I went to, there were pickets and cops all over the place—we were about to run out of relief money. I had to fight my way in. They gave me a check to sign. It was for several million dollars—the appropriation for one month. I said, 'My God, are we giving away money like this?' I was shocked. But I signed it."

A LaSalle Street lawyer friend congratulated Stevenson on his "very outstanding appointments for key positions." Others did the same. Carl McGowan, a closer observer, has said, "The Cabinet was spotty. As they go, I suppose it was above average. George Mitchell was a key figure in the Cabinet and so was Daley. Stevenson was high on Leonard Schwartz of Conservation. He didn't think much of Charlie Casey," Director of Public Works. "Fred Hoehler was a key man. I thought he was overrated. George Mitchell in Finance was interested in the government's finances and in good budgeting, not in operating functions like purchasing. Joe Pois was more interested in operations. For purchasing agent, Stevenson's first choice suddenly began to show signs of indiscretion—a flashy car, women, and so on. We got rid of him."

After the first few months Stevenson held few formal cabinet meetings, preferring to talk to directors individually. In January and February, however, he entertained his Cabinet and legislative leaders at dinners in the Mansion. Memories of Ellen's behavior at these dinners vary. Wally Schaefer: "She was superb. I've never seen a woman so charming, gracious, witty. She had those legislators lying down on the floor for her to walk over." But Mr. and Mrs. Funk: "Ellen insulted them—she looked down her nose at them." Carl McGowan said, "I attended one dinner for legislators and she was a great success. The next time she sulked." Stevenson's relations with her were worsening steadily that spring. One night at the Mansion alone with Flanagan he described "what a hell of a life he'd had with her," as Flanagan put it.

Ellen spent most of her time in Libertyville, going to Springfield occasionally when her presence was required by official functions. Stevenson often went home weekends to Libertyville. But he was alone in the Mansion a great deal of the time.

9

Stevenson used the Governor's Chicago office as little as possible. When he did visit Chicago, he stayed overnight several times with Mr. and Mrs. John Miller and many times with Harriet Welling and her husband. He always had a key to the Wellings' home. His Lake Forest and Gold Coast friends were frequent overnight guests at the Mansion. At Christmastime Stevenson gave big festive parties for his children and their friends. Family and family friends attended too. Stuyvesant Peabody, Jr., visited the Mansion with his wife and sometimes took Stevenson goose hunting at his lodge in southern Illinois. Dutch Smith, Ed McDougal, Jim Oates, the Magnusons, John Paulding Brown, Glen Lloyd—especially after his divorce, Stevenson, lonely in the Mansion, wanted old friends around him.

He had friends in Springfield, some like the Funks going back to his own schoolboy days. Funk once said, "He liked to get out of the Mansion once in a while. One time he just stopped by in the middle of dinner and asked if he could eat with us."[5] Nearly all his Springfield friends were Republicans. Mrs. Funk's parents had been friends of Stevenson's parents. The Rev. Richard Paul Graebel, pastor of the First Presbyterian Church of Springfield, was a friend of Stevenson—and remained one the rest of his life and conducted the funeral service in National Cathedral in Washington when Stevenson died. After the divorce, Buffie Ives often acted as Stevenson's hostess at the Mansion. She knew the Springfield people intimately—who had helped whom become head of a company, who drank too much, who had divorced whom, whose children were a trial, who was good at parlor games, who "had her eye on" Stevenson. Mrs. Ives has said, "Once Ronald Tree and Marietta came to the Mansion. She couldn't get the pitch. There was this group from Springfield at the piano. Adlai adored it, he liked charades, imitations, someone doing something gay and funny." Once Stevenson

[5] Among his other Springfield friends were Mr. and Mrs. Robert C. Lanphier —he was vice president of Funk's Sangamo Electric; Dr. and Mrs. Thomas D. Masters—he was a nephew of the poet, Edgar Lee Masters; Mr. and Mrs. Langdon Robinson—he was with a feed and grain company and his daughter Sally had been a Stevenson volunteer; Mr. and Mrs. James Patton—he worked at Sangamo and had been a friend of Stevenson as a boy in Springfield; Mr. and Mrs. Herbert B. Bartholf—he was an insurance executive; Mr. and Mrs. Oliver Keller—he owned the local radio station.

and a group from Springfield got into a bus and went to Elkhart for a New Year's Eve party at the home of one of the great landowning families of central Illinois.

People who were Stevenson's friends there thought he loved Springfield. Others in his life thought he liked their particular corner of the world. Mrs. Ives has said, "He loved Charlevoix," but he stopped going there and went instead to Desbarats with the Dutch Smiths. As he lived out his years, from Princeton on to death, he alighted from one way station to another. Lake Forest had been one. Springfield was another. It is hard to believe he "loved" Springfield. There can be no doubt he loved Illinois and enjoyed Springfield's historicity and the power of the governorship. But it is doubtful he would have chosen to live in Springfield had he never been elected Governor, and even while Governor he spent his free time elsewhere—weekends at Libertyville or Chicago, trips to New York or Washington. Springfield has its charms but it can also be flat and suffocating, a town with narrow horizons. The view is parochial, inward-turned. Don Forsyth once said the Illinois delegation wanted to nominate Stevenson for President in 1952 in order to get him out of Illinois, an extremely narrow view of a complex political movement, and one Springfield woman seems convinced that President Kennedy deliberately executed the Bay of Pigs disaster in order to "hurt Adlai," a view no historian would subscribe to. Loyalties are fierce here; so are antipathies. One wonders how Stevenson could have immersed himself in the minutiae of state government or endured Springfield's pettiness and crudities. Talking to his friends here—and to his friends in Lake Forest and everywhere else—one is struck by the fact that he seems to have been elusive. He influenced many people's lives deeply. He formed deep and lasting friendships. And yet some of his most perceptive friends felt that, while he often seemed to give his confidence, "you never really got through to him," as George Ball has said. Like many others, Ball noted that Stevenson often asked advice of people when he really did not want it. Sometimes he had already made up his mind but simply wanted to hear the arguments on the other side to strengthen his own. Sometimes he was winning friends, gaining confidences, even playing devil's advocate. Ball has said, "He always had an enormous capacity for dramatizing himself. The thing that fascinated me about Adlai was that he accepted so easily the idea that he was a great historical figure moving back and forth on the scene. I think he always had Abraham Lincoln on his mind a good deal." In later years, talking about him after his death, some of Stevenson's liberal friends wondered why they forgave him what they considered his shortcomings—his old remarks about Jews, his clear intellectual rather than passionately emotional commitment to civil rights, his loyal defense of policies of Presidents Kennedy and Johnson in which they thought he did not believe. George Ball, asked why, replied, "Because of his gaiety, his wit, his style, and his guts. And because he had integrity. And he was a friend—that was his great quality. He would do almost anything for a friend."

10

Stevenson and Ellen went to Washington to the inauguration of President Truman, sharing their private railroad car with Jack Arvey and his wife. Arvey thought it a good opportunity to bring the Chicago ward leaders back to shake hands with Stevenson and did so. "It went pretty well," Arvey has recalled, "until suddenly Mrs. Stevenson said, 'I'm going to get out of here and go to bed,' and left abruptly." Retiring that night, Mrs. Arvey said to her husband, "That marriage won't last."

Stevenson had tried to arrange to meet Alicia Patterson there but she said Washington was "far too complicated" and she would visit him in Springfield (which he referred to as "this hell hole"). Returning, Stevenson told Alicia that Washington had been "busy, weary, exciting": "We might have had few minutes, but not enough. So, tho disappointed, I guess it was just as well, except, of course, you missed the opportunity to see me ride down the street in an open car bowing courteously and smiling benignly on the subjects." He was planning to have both Alicia and Marquis Childs, the columnist, at the Mansion next weekend, January 30: "I don't know what Ellens plans are this week. She never makes them far enough in advance to help, but I very much doubt if she will be there for the week end in any event. Why don't you come a day or so early—telephone from Chi & I'll describe the situation up to date—and stay a day or so longer than Mark. If its embarrassing or boring or dangerous in *your* judgment, I won't try to persuade you to stay. But I'm really all alone there & people and guests come & go at a great rate. . . . What a job; what a life; why?" Stevenson told his brother-in-law Ralph Hines, "I am very much alone."

Much of his work had to do with his legislative program. On January 27 a member of his staff gave him a memorandum on the status of the program. A joint resolution calling for a constitutional convention—universally termed Con-Con—together with a "party circle" bill would be ready for introduction by next Tuesday, February 1, the deadline Stevenson had set. An FEPC bill had been drafted by interested groups and a Stevenson staff man would meet with them on Saturday. The Unemployment Compensation Advisory Board was trying to agree upon recommendations. Bills increasing workmen's compensation had already been introduced into both houses. Bills removing the ceiling from old-age pensions and blind relief were ready for introduction. An expert was drafting legislation to consolidate the Welfare Department and Public Aid Commission. No legislation had yet been prepared on the Conservation Department or the Mines and Minerals Department. And so on—such, such were the joys.

Stevenson was getting a good press. Mark Childs, after his visit to the Mansion, wrote several columns, nationally syndicated, about him. One on February 3 said that Stevenson had made excellent appointments and was wrestling with the problem of his own salary and expenses—his salary was $12,000 a year but it cost him about $50,000 to maintain himself in office. The London *Economist* said Stevenson seemed "apprehensive" and no wonder—he was a liberal internationalist in a conservative isolationist state, and while he was intellectually "the most brilliant Governor" Illinois had had in fifty years and his initial appointments had been excellent, it was less clear that Illinois liberals, accustomed to the role of opposition, could govern effectively. Stevenson invited Helen P. Kirkpatrick and Doris Fleeson, another columnist, to stay at the Mansion. Throughout his political career, Miss Fleeson was his partisan. If he did not always please local reporters, he took care to cultivate the national correspondents.

Stevenson made it clear he would enforce the weight limitations on trucks, thus earning the enmity of the powerful truckers' lobby. He asked Jane Dick to analyze the Board of Vocational Education. He received the Grand Exalted Ruler of the Elks. He led a day-long observance of Lincoln's birthday—spoke eloquently at Lincoln's tomb, presided over ceremonies at the Statehouse, gave a dinner for Vice President Barkley and Senator Lucas, and introduced Barkley, who spoke at the high school auditorium. His speeches that day were heavily laden with Illinois history and current Illinois politics. Twice he spoke of Lincoln's place in history and his own concern with civil rights, the latter not lost on members of the legislature about to be confronted with his FEPC bill. Dumas Malone, the Columbia University historian, attended and later told Stevenson, "My little visit was a memorable one for a student of history, since it made me aware of the Lincoln country in a way that I never was before." Perhaps mindful of the advice he had given Governor Horner long ago—to associate oneself with Lincoln was to associate oneself with Illinois—Stevenson encouraged, indeed, sometimes almost forced, his guests to visit Lincoln's tomb and home. Almost no one visited Adlai Stevenson at Springfield without coming away feeling a new appreciation of "the Lincoln country" and, somehow, vaguely connecting Stevenson with it.

On February 17 he wrote to Alicia Patterson in response to a letter of hers saying she wanted to end their relationship:

My dear *"Friend"*—

I have averaged less than 6 hours sleep a night with lunch on the desk for all but two days since you were here. Today a friend arrived from out of town—for no other purpose than to make me go out and walk with him for 20 minutes.

I'm glad I did. I felt much better. But when I got back my next appointment was Mr. Lincoln of Cleveland with a most heart-rending story about his son in the Joliet penitentiary and pleas for a pardon. You remember that celebrated case. My heart died within me, but I said "no." Then a feeble little attack on that appalling pile of mail, reports etc that haunts my nights—and near the top, your letter—opened, neatly spread out. . . . I took a hasty look at the conclusion expecting that exultant feeling when its hard to swallow & keep composed—things like "I've never loved anyone before" etc—things that blessed adolescents say. Instead —"Okay, Lets be friends The whole business is kaput."

I think I behaved well—Dictated a little longer & then took the elevator upstairs. Now I'm in my room—I've read it all and I'm a little sick. Moreover Adm. Jones of Great Lakes & some Generals are downstairs waiting for dinner and then another meeting—and all the time this one and the last one are in my pocket and I'm talking animatedly and interestedly of their silly problems—and all the time about all I've known of love and genuine interest and personal concern for 10 years is—Kaput!

Very well, Alicia, I guess I didn't understand. I guess I never will. Maybe we are cut of different cloths as you say. I'm not resentful—I'm deeply grateful for even a few months of what was to be forever. And don't worry about me. Work has been my refuge for many years—now it will be for many more. I only regret that we couldn't talk. I tried to start that first night here—and again the second but that failed. You *had* drunk too much, altho the hours were precious for talking—wisely, soberly.

Don't be angry—don't be hurt or prideful. If there's love, there's forgiveness—and I thought there was much, much love. So perhaps I've transgressed by not writing as I would rather do than anything else—as you well know—but there's only so much time, only so much strength—and now thats run out all over the floor —and I'm a mess and the butler's knocking—

A

It was one of the most revealing letters he ever wrote. It cut very deeply, perhaps deeply enough to unconsciously refer, in the sentence about his strength having "run out all over the floor," to his having accidentally killed a child as a boy. (This, of course, is pure specu-lation; many other interpretations are possible.) He let show, as he rarely did, the loneliness, the emptiness, of his inner life.

That letter must have crossed one from her, for on February 22, five days later, he wrote to her at Kingsland, Georgia:

Darling!

Now I have your letter and I feel very contrite after writing you that long self righteous explosion. I sent it to Newsday. It must have crossed yours and I hope you haven't seen it. When you do please don't read it—just tear it up & let's bury this curious little incident [language that again recalls the killing of the child].

I hadn't realized [that your visit to] Springfield was such a failure. Of course with Mark about I was behaving, play acting, the casual indifference of an old friend, not badly I suspect. I was a little miserable Tuesday night I confess. I had counted rather on that night—and when you've had too much to drink you are de-finitely not not charming!—nor is anyone else.

But I loved every moment of your visit—it gave me a forgotten supressed excitement feeling for days before you came and a won-derful foolish sort of exultation while you were here. But I'm afraid I didn't behave naturally. Perhaps I was rattled, nervous & I know I'm always trying desperately to condense so much in so little time.

Enough of that—perhaps even at our age the course of true love never runs smoothly. At all events I'm glad you had your little fit of ugly temper, tho I can hardly say I liked it and I think it was the worst 3 days in many years until your sweet letter came. Lets have no more of those—and please spank me roundly if my own petulance gets the best of me.

Do I love you? It seems a strange question and it embarrasses me a little to say I do, because it makes me feel that you might think that I've been a hypocrit all this time—that with all thats happened you're still in doubt. I can hardly believe the line between love and play could be so obscure. I'm going to sleep—I don't know what I'm saying or writing and its 1 AM and its been a hideous day. I wish I didn't feel so alone & with nothing but this little blue envelope and this precious scrap of paper and this splendid cut of a lovely bright eyed bird by the microphone.

In a moment I'll be asleep and then I won't be alone—and I'll whisper to you in the dark and there will be no doubt—

Oh Lord, let me be an instrument of thy peace; where there is injury let me sow pardon; where there is hate, love; where there is *doubt,* faith [a quotation he used later in a famous speech].

But do you love *me*—even if I am a (very wobbly) big shot?

A

Thus Stevenson, tormented by the hopelessness of marriage, faced with public burdens and responsibilities far beyond anything he had ever encountered, was threatened with the loss of the woman he loved. That his relationship with Alicia Patterson was serious there can be no doubt. He once told Carl McGowan's wife and others, including Marietta Tree, that Alicia "was the one"—the one he loved and should have married. Several people thought Stevenson was afraid of Alicia—"afraid of the Patterson toughness in her," Marietta has said; "she drank a lot." Susie Zurcher, a girl he squired around in the 1950s, once said, "He would say 'good old Alicia—she's a wonderful old war horse, isn't she'?" Mrs. Ives thought he might have gotten along well with Alicia as his wife; Alicia could have "shared" with him, she thought. Adlai III has said, "In later years while he was at the UN he talked to me about getting married. He seemed to want the opinion of his children about several prospects for marriage and mentioned a few friends—some he really loved, like Ruth Field. I gradually suspected that he really didn't want to marry anyone for fear of having to give up the friendship and help of others.

"He had loved Alicia Patterson. He knew her from childhood and admired her success. She was a person in her own right. She intrigued him. He knew where she stood. Alicia was a great love. So, for a time, at least, was Jane Dick, but she was happily married. In the end it was Marietta Tree.

"All were attractive, interested in politics and his career, but he never brought himself to remarry. Perhaps he was gun shy after his marriage to my mother. He would not be an easy husband. He needed an outdoor type, someone to care for the Libertyville house, to entertain and to travel and accept long absences—it was a difficult life he offered—and he knew it.

"He needed a wife, but also his freedom. He must have had trouble in his mind fitting someone into that frenetic life, or himself into another's—except for Marietta toward the very end when he was tired."

Whether Alicia considered marrying Stevenson as seriously as he considered marrying her is uncertain. Ruth Field, a friend of both, said, "Alicia had a heart as big as all get out. She'd growl at you but she'd do anything—till it interfered with her newspaper. She was loyal, loving, humorous. She was good-looking and appealing and tough and bright. Once she kissed somebody good-by and Adlai flounced out angrily. She told me one time, 'We'd have torn each other apart.' "

11

His official schedule at this time was heavy, as it had been ever since the Truman inaugural. The pressure was worst on days when Stevenson went to his official Statehouse office; everybody descended on the anteroom. His aides could control the pressure better in his Mansion office, for not everybody who felt he had a right to walk into the Statehouse anteroom would make bold to walk into the Mansion. Some meetings were important—dinner at the Mansion for Dick Daley, Senator Botchy Connors, Representative Jimmy Ryan, Speaker Paul Powell, and Wally Schaefer; a 3 P.M. meeting with Daley and Director Mitchell on the budget. And toward the end of March, as the time drew near when Stevenson must present his budget, the pressures increased. On March 11 his friend Laird Bell wrote, "You are doing fine. But I hear you are trying to do too much."

Into the waiting hostile legislature, several important administration bills and resolutions had already been introduced—a bill creating a constitutional convention to write a new constitution; a bill increasing old-age pensions and blind assistance; the Crime Commission's anti-crime bills; civil service reform; FEPC; and a bill establishing a state reformatory at Sheridan. (Although Stevenson favored the last, its principal sponsor was a Republican.) Commerce Commission reform would go in on April 6. And so would a cluster of bills intended, their sponsor Paul Broyles, a downstate Republican, said, to combat Communism—the Broyles bills, considered by liberals "little McCarthy" bills. More bills, both administration bills and bills it opposed, were in the works. A mass of non-controversial legislation had been disposed of. The budget was near, and Stevenson had already vetoed two bills, one with a witty message, a bill prohibiting cats from running at large in order to protect birds.[6]

On March 8, Steve Mitchell asked to see Stevenson to give his recommendation for public administrator for Cook County, the most lucrative patronage post at the Governor's disposition, usually worth about $75,000 a year in fees for handling the estates of people who die without leaving wills. Mitchell once said that Stevenson had offered Mitchell himself the job but that he had turned it down because he did not want to accept political largesse. Stevenson went to Washington for the White House Correspondents' dinner on March 5. Returning, he told Alicia Patterson, "I was the only gov. at the head table—the Pres was very cordial." He wrote lyrically to Alicia of their relationship. He referred to her letters as "those breathless precious bits." "Bits" of love was an idea that persisted till his death. He met her secretly about the weekend of March 19 in Chicago at her old family residence at Ogden Avenue and Menominee Street, a neighborhood once fashionable.

Stevenson spoke in Chicago on March 28 at a luncheon in his honor given by the Commercial Club at the Chicago Club. Com-

---

[6] The bill had been introduced in previous sessions and, as Stevenson said in his veto message, had been "the source of much comment." He could not believe there was a "widespread public demand" for the bill or that it could be enforced. "Furthermore, I cannot agree that it should be the declared public policy of Illinois that a cat visiting a neighbor's yard or crossing the highway is a public nuisance. It is in the nature of cats to do a certain amount of unescorted roaming. Many live with their owners in apartments or other restricted premises, and I doubt if we want to make their every brief foray an opportunity for a small game hunt by zealous citizens—with traps or otherwise. I am afraid this Bill could only create discord, recrimination and enmity. Also consider the owner's dilemma: To escort a cat abroad on a leash is against the nature of the cat, and to permit it to venture forth for exercise unattended into a night of new dangers is against the nature of the owner. . . . We are all interested in protecting certain varieties of birds. That cats destroy some birds, I well know, but I believe this legislation would further but little the worthy cause to which its proponents give such unselfish effort. The problem of cat versus bird is as old as time. If we attempt to resolve it by legislation who knows but what we may be called upon to take sides as well in the age old problems of dog versus cat, bird versus bird, even bird versus worm. In my opinion, the State of Illinois and its local governing bodies already have enough to do without trying to control feline delinquency. For these reasons, and not because I love birds the less or cats the more, I veto and withold my approval from Senate Bill No. 93. Respectfully." In preparing this veto message and others, Stevenson may have had some help, in this instance probably Ed Day or Lloyd Lewis.

fortable in these Republican surroundings, he spoke off the cuff and was in good form. "Mr. Chairman and fellow Democrats, if any," he began, "I was asked by somebody a moment ago upstairs if anything funny had happened to me since I have been in office, and as he said that I reflected on something that did happen to me within forty-eight hours after I was inaugurated. A flood, a very serious flood in southern Illinois, came along, as you know, from the Little Wabash and the Big Wabash and the Muddy River, and a number of other rivers in southern Illinois, and we had to send out the National Guard and do a lot of things. Well, I said to myself, 'I am going to be different from all Governors. I am going to take a personal interest in the affairs of these poor, wretched, homeless people in the affected areas.' So I promptly seized the phone one morning and started to call the Mayors of all the cities affected by the flood. I disposed of the Mayor of Carmi pleasantly and agreeably, pledging him all of the support of all of the state agencies. And then I asked the girl to get me the Mayor of Murphysboro. She said, after a few minutes. 'The Mayor is on the phone.' I picked it up and said, 'How do you do, Mayor. This is Adlai Stevenson, Governor Stevenson in Springfield.' 'Oh, how do you do, Governor? Well, I never had a Governor call me before.' I said, 'I have been so alarmed about your condition down there. How are you?' 'Oh, fine. I never was better. How are you, Governor?' Finally I said, in desperation, 'Well, we want to do everything we possibly can for you,' having been previously informed that the flood was almost up to the foundations of the waterworks. And I said, 'Mayor, how is your water?' He said, 'My water! What the hell are you talking about? My water is fine. How's yours?' This exchange of epithets went on, each of us getting more and more indignant, and finally I said, 'Say, who the hell am I talking to? Is this the Mayor of Murphysboro?' He said, 'No, this is the Mayor of Murraysville, and my water is fine.' Bang." Stevenson, as he often did, embroidered the incident and used it as a peg on which to hang an old political story, pretending it had happened to him.)

Stevenson went on to say that at a dinner for the Senators his wife had offered to kiss any Senator who voted against the investigation of Communism at the University of Chicago. "The next day she came down with the mumps. She sent a telegram to the Majority Leader of the Senate and said that in her present condition she would have to alter her proposal and she would now kiss any Senator who voted for the investigation." Then he described his legislative program.

12

Now in April the legislature was beginning to move. An administration bill to increase old-age pensions had passed the House late in March; on April 5 it passed the Senate. More controversial were five bills sought by the Chicago Crime Commission to combat organized crime. One would permit courts to extend the life of a grand jury in Chicago by thirty days. Although it was an administration measure, Stevenson's Senate leaders from Chicago did not sponsor it. And when it came up for final vote in the Senate on April 5, Botchy Connors voted against it, as did other Chicago Democrats—Roland V. Libonati, an old fox from the Chicago West Side ghetto whence came men who became infamous as gangsters, and Christopher Wimbish, a Negro from the South Side black ghetto. The criminal syndicate had great power. The bill passed, however, 31 to 12, and went on to the House. Another Crime Commission bill made it easier to convict of perjury; it passed the Senate March 22 and on April 7 was sent to the House Judiciary Committee. Another empowered a grand jury or court to compel reluctant witnesses to testify by imposing immunity on them; it too passed the Senate and was sent to the House Judiciary Committee on April 7. The two other Crime Commission bills died in the Senate.

At midnight on the day the grand jury bill passed the Senate, Stevenson wrote to Alicia Patterson: "I wish I could crawl off somewhere and evaporate. Yesterday I was at it for 17 consecutive hours—today 16, and 26 legislators for dinner which was the hardest part of all. Early in the morning I must waste some precious time to fly down to Effingham where there has been a ghastly hospital fire —as tho I could do any thing. I'm getting so damn tired of this job I can't even decide whether to sign or veto the bill investigating Communism at the U of Chicago & Roosevelt College. If only you were here you would have all the answers—and besides I'd get to bed earlier! . . . Do you think you'd love me as much if you saw me more? How could you love a soft, fat, bald old man? I brood too much about the improbability of this mysterious dream that's enveloped me for a year and a half. Are you quite sure you're sane? I'm not at all. But come back soon and we'll make some scientific tests of sanity—and love."

On April 7 he went up to Chicago to speak to the Democratic Jefferson-Jackson Day dinner in the Stevens Hotel, emphasizing as he had before, "Fewer and fewer men and women vote Democratic or Republican merely because their fathers and mothers did. We have reached political maturity," and he went on to discuss honesty in state government and his program, including eliminating corruption and taking "idlers" off the public payrolls, much of it anathema to many in the Cook County machine. He closed, "I want to do honor to the party that has honored me and my forebears. I want to be a good Governor of Illinois—and that's all I want."

On Monday morning, April 11, "winging through the bright spring sky back to Springfield and my miseries," Stevenson told Alicia Patterson how he had spent Sunday at home—two sets of tennis with Ellen Smith, work on the budget in the afternoon and a canoe trip "with my precious John Fell"—"I love him so much it hurts. And I think he really loves me—he and you and who else?" Stuyvesant Peabody had given him four tickets to the Kentucky Derby—would she and her husband like to come—or she alone? "I am reasonably confident that Ellen will refuse. She has never cared for anything like that." He wrote, "My constitutional convention resolution comes up for a vote on Wed. in the House. It takes ⅔ & of course if it carries it will be a great triumph. I've worked like the devil for it. Keep your fingers crossed."

It was a critical legislative week. Outside his inner dream world lay the other world, often hostile. Not only was the constitutional convention resolution coming to a vote in the House on Wednesday; in the House too were the three Crime Commission bills and the three anti-Communist bills of Senator Broyles. All these, and others too, would become entangled with the question of the constitution. That Monday night Stevenson held a legislative strategy meeting at the Mansion. On Tuesday he gave a large legislative dinner. The first test of his effectiveness as Governor was at hand.

Otto Kerner, a Democrat who later became Governor, once said, "Stevenson was a good governor but he didn't accomplish as much as he had hoped because he didn't realize the give-and-take of the legislative process. He was suspicious of people here. He'd heard stories about graft. Bill Connors [Senator Botchy Connors] told Adlai to tell him what he wanted. Connors had been in the Senate long enough so that both Republicans and Democrats owed him something. Lyndon Johnson was shrewd enough and experienced enough in the legislative process to get his programs through by compromise and give-and-take, where Adlai was not. In his first legislative session he stood off and thought that just because something was good it ought to pass. That's not the way it works. For example, Connors and the state police merit system—it never would have passed if Connors hadn't had the authority to negotiate so that half of the state policemen would be Republican and half Democrat. So he got the bill."

Botchy Connors always called Stevenson "the little fella." He would tell other legislators, "The little fella needs help—give me a vote on this one." Don Walsh said, "Connors was doing things for nix that he used to get a good stipend for. He didn't understand it himself." Connors once remarked, almost in awe, "That little son of a bitch is making an honest man out of me." Jack Arvey has said, "I tried to do for Stevenson something I tried with Kennelly—but Kennelly wasn't smart enough to let me do it. The Governor was. I tried to be a buffer between him and certain men in our organization that I am not very proud of. He turned to me when he had to deal with them. Kennelly would talk to them himself and he would lie to them. You can't lie in politics. It's different from business. In politics your word is your bond." Arvey went down to Springfield about once a week during the 1949 session of the legislature. He has said, "The Governor was having trouble getting his program through. My mere presence there—I tried to impress upon them that Stevenson, while not of the organization, had the full support of the organization."

Arvey understated it; his power was enormous. In the Senate, Stevenson had Botchy Connors and Abraham Lincoln Marovitz helping him. Behind the scenes he also had Dick Daley, his Director of Revenue. Marovitz has said, "Stevenson's greatest weakness was that he was unwilling to talk to the politicians. I told him to call Botchy Connors in. I told him, 'Tell him you don't care what he's done, you need him. You talk to him.' You don't send somebody else to see Botchy Connors. If you want to see him, you go see him yourself. You have to compromise sometimes for the greater good. Stevenson never would. I'd put deals together—he'd say no. He'd say, 'It's a good bill—why don't they vote for it?' " This is the orthodox view of Stevenson, the principled amateur, and it contains truth but is not entirely true. It was probably truer in 1949 than during the 1951 legislative session—by 1951, Stevenson had learned more about political compromise.

Carl McGowan once said, "He had a good knack of facing up to problems. For example, if some legislator was raising hell about an appointment at Manteno [State Hospital], he could have strung him along—but he didn't, he'd meet him head on. I was surprised. If Paul Powell or a county chairman came in to see him, he faced up to the problem and told them what he could do and couldn't do. I might have fuzzed it up a little bit more." Paul Powell, as Speaker of the House in 1949, should have been Stevenson's man there but was not.

A young liberal legislator who came along later, Abner Mikva, once recalled that later, in 1961, Paul Powell, Speaker once more, told the Democratic caucus, "Now, boys, this here Governor Kerner is a real governor—not like Stevenson. If you got problems you can come in and talk to him. He won't give you that highfalutin' talk." Mikva has said that Al Horan, Joe Gill, and Bill Milota, all powerful Chicago machine leaders, felt that way toward Stevenson. In the House in 1949, Stevenson's floor leader was Jimmy Ryan, a Chicago Democrat. Arvey and Daley could be expected to influence Ryan. But the House is unruly, and Ryan had nowhere near the influence that Speaker Powell or the Republican Reed Cutler had.

The state of Illinois was operating under a constitution adopted in 1870. Many lawyers and good-government groups considered it outmoded. It provided for the election of judges, prohibited a state income tax, gave Chicago and its suburbs an unfairly small voice in the legislature, denied home rule to Chicago and other cities, and was difficult to amend. Only seven amendments had ever been adopted, none since 1908, and none changing the constitution materially.

Stevenson had made a constitutional convention the keystone of his legislative program. In December, at Stevenson's request, Samuel W. Witwer, Jr., a Republican lawyer of high reputation, had submitted a legislative program for Con-Con and recommended that Stevenson make it a non-partisan effort. He gave Stevenson the names of four leading Republicans in the House and four in the Senate who were favorably disposed. Through the late winter and early spring, the Illinois Committee for a Constitutional Convention propagandized and lobbied. A Joint Committee for Calling a Constitutional Convention was established.

On February 1, House Joint Resolution 9 was introduced, the constitutional convention resolution. An identical resolution was submitted in the Senate the same day but was allowed to die. While the most powerful Democrats in both houses sponsored the resolutions, the most powerful Republicans in both houses did not. A Chicago lawyer warned Stevenson of hidden opposition from Republican legislators who feared Con-Con would mean redistricting and the loss of their seats. Solid proof of opposition came on February 12, when the Illinois Republican State Central Committee formally opposed the "party circle" bill and so notified all Republican legislators. Stevenson told Clay Tate of the *Pantagraph* that he hoped the *Pantagraph* would explain the "party circle" measure editorially, as the Chicago *Sun-Times* and the Decatur newspaper were already doing. The president of the Chicago Bar Association told Stevenson that the lawyers of Illinois were overwhelmingly in favor of a Constitutional Convention and the "party circle" bill. So did a committee of the League of Women Voters. The Illinois Education Association offered its support. Barnabas Sears, chairman of the State Bar Association's committee on constitutional reform, announced that his committee as well as the board of governors of the association endorsed both Con-Con and the "party circle" bill. Sears also told Stevenson privately that he had found "considerable opposition" among downstate lawyers.

Stevenson himself took the issue to the people on March 9. It was Stevenson's first radio speech as Governor, and he devoted it to constitutional reform. The people, he said, had helped him get his job; "now I want you to help me *do* the job." He was not asking them to "approve" anything; all he was asking was that the legislature give the voters a chance to decide in 1950 whether a constitutional convention should be held.

His fan mail was not huge but was gratifying. Stevenson planned another speech for a week later, and Lou Kohn proposed that Flanagan ask all networks to carry it. Stevenson asked Sam Witwer to talk with a Republican Representative, Noble Lee; Lee agreed to speak on the radio in support of constitutional reform. On March 16, Stevenson himself went back on the radio, speaking at a dinner of the Merchants and Manufacturers Club at the Merchandise Mart in Chicago, disregarding Sam Witwer's advice that he attack the opponents of the "party circle" bill, and sought rather to allay their fears. The Chicago City Council adopted a resolution calling for a constitutional convention. Six days later, on March 22, Con-Con came out of Executive Committee in the House with a recommendation it pass.

On March 29, Stevenson wrote to several people soliciting support. One of them, a woman in Rockford, reported violent opposition from the Chamber of Commerce and said she felt like a voice in the wilderness. Stevenson told her, "Never be afraid to feel a little lonesome." To a friend in St. Charles, Stevenson wrote, "I hope you manufacturers get wise" and realize that constitutional reform was the only hope for efficient and less costly government. Stevenson sounded out Leverett Lyon of the Chicago Association of Commerce and Industry, but Lyon said his board of directors had never taken a position on the constitutional convention. A Peoria lawyer told Stevenson he favored it but could not say so because his clients opposed.

In Springfield, Dick Daley was pushing the political drive for votes. All over town now in early April the pressures were mounting, the meetings being held, the deals being arranged. Working through intermediaries, the West Side Bloc of legislators offered Stevenson a deal: if he would drop his support for the three Crime Commission bills, they would vote for the constitutional convention. The Crime Commission bills were on the move. The perjury bill and the immunity bill had passed the Senate on March 22, gone to the House on March 23, and on April 4 been sent to the Judiciary Committee. The grand jury bill passed the Senate on April 5 and went to the House on the seventh. (Oddly enough, such civil libertarian groups as the American Civil Liberties Union had found themselves aligned with the West Side Bloc, for they feared the bills might endanger individual liberty.) Frequently the West Side Bloc could be counted on to vote for purely governmental measures, such as Con-Con, that did not directly affect their interests. Indeed, in 1945, when Con-Con had been proposed, Jimmy Adducci, Johnny D'Arco, Andrew Euzzino, Robert Petrone, and Peter Granata (whose brother was chopped to death on Randolph Street) had voted for it. But now they seemed to be against it—unless Stevenson would drop the Crime Commission bills. The vote on Con-Con promised to be close. Not only the votes of the five members of the Bloc were involved but other votes they might swing their way in other trades. Nonetheless, Stevenson refused the deal.

Stevenson visited the Dutch Smiths in Lake Forest and Mrs. Smith later recalled, "He sat down at the edge of the lake and just stared at it. I asked him what was the matter. He said, 'I'm discouraged. I sometimes wonder if I can do it if I keep turning down deals. Now I'll probably lose both the Crime bills *and* Con-Con. How am I going to do anything useful? Maybe it'd be better to go ahead and make deals like that.'" Fred E. Inbau, a Northwestern professor who favored both strict law enforcement and constitutional reform, told Wally Schaefer on April 14 he hoped Stevenson would rebuff the West Side Bloc and expose it—compromise with the Bloc would lead Stevenson down the same road Dwight Green had followed. Schaefer replied they had no intention of compromising.

Con-Con would come to a vote in the House on April 13. That morning at eight-thirty Stevenson met with Jack Arvey, Don Walsh, and State Chairman Kells. Tagge of the *Tribune* wrote in that morning's paper that Jack Arvey was "leading the scramble for votes to put 'con-con' over the top." He quoted the House Minority Leader, the huge shrewd troglodytic Reed Cutler, as saying, "I'm surprised to see the capitol dome intact. The con-con lobbyists have traded everything else away." Tagge said that some Republicans were being tempted to vote for the constitutional convention by being told they could keep their friends on the state payroll. He said Democratic leaders had sent word to the president of the Cook County board that he could not expect favorable action on bills he was interested in unless he rounded up Republican votes for Con-Con. The United Mine Workers lobbyist had reversed his position and was lobbying for Con-Con. Representative G. William Horsley of Springfield, who sometimes wore an Abe Lincoln costume, had been counted for Con-Con but the day before the vote he said on the House floor that Stevenson should answer two questions before the Con-Con vote—"Do you believe that any teacher or professor should be permitted to advocate Communism?" and "Do you believe that any public official or employee should draw pay while belonging to the Communist Party?" With such controversial measures as constitutional reform, all sorts of other issues become entangled; behind every "aye" and "nay" vote lie the most varied motives and interests. At last on Wednesday, April 13, Speaker Powell called HJR 9 to a vote on first reading. It needed 102 votes to pass, a two-thirds majority. The first name called on the roll, James J. Adducci, showed that the Administration had refused the deal with the West Side Bloc: he voted nay. So did D'Arco and Euzzino, both Democrats, breaking Democratic ranks. The final tally showed 97 for Con-Con including the Speaker—five votes short. (The West Side Bloc had five votes.) Seven members had sat silent or been absent; Stevenson thought he could only get two of them. Jimmy Ryan immediately moved to postpone further consideration of the bill; this saved Con-Con for another try. In general, the vote had followed party lines, with Democrats for constitutional reform and Republicans opposed. Speaker Paul Powell loyally voted for it. And 19 Republicans, including such good-government people as Mrs. Bernice Van Der Vries, left their party to vote for it. Among the Democrats, only D'Arco and Euzzino left their party to vote against it, though one other was silent. Thus the Democrats maintained almost perfect solidarity, and nearly enough Republicans voted with them to win—but not quite enough.

How did Stevenson react? While the House was voting, he was dictating a letter to a friend in Rockford, saying, "We are optimistic." After the vote, Stevenson issued a statement: "The people and better government in Illinois lost a preliminary skirmish today. . . . I hope that members of the House who may have been doubtful will see the wisdom and necessity for joining in the fight for progress. . . . I am proud of the fidelity of almost all of the Democratic members and most grateful for the support of 19 Republicans." He sent telegrams of thanks to three Representatives who had come to

Springfield especially to vote for Con-Con. He watched newspaper reaction closely. The Chicago *Sun-Times,* in an editorial headed, "How They Beat the People," said Con-Con had failed its first test because of "a combination of political blackmail and blind partisanship." The Chicago *Tribune* was delighted with the result. It said, "This was the turning point. Narrow as was the victory, it was the first victory scored in a long time against those who are driving the world toward enslavement and war. This was a victory for the republican form of government. This was a victory for free men. They have been driven into retreat for the last time. Now they are on the march. We call it a victory even tho the traitor forces refused to accept defeat and postponed the final decision until [later]. . . . The arch-manipulator for 'con-con' was and is Arvey. . . . Gov. Stevenson, who played his minor part in the evil conspiracy to conceal the guilt of the Roosevelt crooks, was found once again on the side of those seeking to overthrow republican government everywhere. But this time he didn't get away with it. This time he encountered the resistance of a gallant band of legislators who couldn't be intimidated, blackmailed, or bought. They saved freedom in Illinois. They rallied its defenders. From this beginning, the greater struggle to rescue the United States from communism and corruption will be carried forward to victory."

Whatever one thinks of describing the West Side Bloc as members of "a gallant band," or of characterizing as "traitors" legislators who voted as the Bar Associations and League of Women Voters wished, the *Tribune* had hit two of the three themes the Republicans would use to win the presidency three years later—Communism and corruption. It had been a long time since the *Tribune* had tasted victory. The 1948 election of Truman and Stevenson had been only the bitter climax to sixteen years of *Tribune* defeats. Now, in the defeat of constitutional reform, the *Tribune* saw nothing less than the opening salvo in a victorious counterattack. And, though probably few believed so at the time, it was right.

The *Tribune*'s editorial infuriated Stevenson. The day it appeared he sent it to Alicia Patterson with a letter saying, "I thought you would enjoy your distinguished cousin's [McCormick's] comments on my heartbreaking effort to give the people at least a chance to vote on whether they would like a constitutional convention. . . . I guess my honeymoon with that medieval SOB is over & its OK by me!" The tone of the letter showed that by now Stevenson, who had been only mildly interested in state government a year earlier, had become vitally engaged. As a lawyer, he knew the importance of constitutional reform. As somebody who cared about Illinois, he

cared about its government. And as most people do, he had become convinced of the importance of what he was working at day and night.

Earlier in the session, several Republican leaders had proposed, as an alternative to a constitutional convention, a constitutional amendment called the Gateway Amendment. It would make it easier to amend the constitution—it provided that amendments to three articles of the constitution could be submitted to the voters simultaneously instead of only one, as provided in the 1870 constitution. Stevenson had considered Gateway but chosen instead to try for Con-Con. After the April 13 defeat of Con-Con, virtually the entire Republican leadership of the Senate introduced a liberalized Gateway Amendment. It passed the Senate on April 27 and went to the House on May 3.

During these weeks Stevenson had been trying to round up more support for Con-Con. It proved hard going. On May 2 he decided on a second try—told Jimmy Ryan to ask the House to take a final vote on Con-Con tomorrow. He also asked that the "party circle" bill be dropped. He told Ryan, "If it is defeated tomorrow we will carry the issue to the voters." Clearly he did not think he had the votes. He was right—the House definitively killed Con-Con on May 3.

Stevenson promptly endorsed Gateway—"we cannot wait forever." Gateway was "only a stopgap" and he would continue his efforts for a constitutional convention at the next session. Meanwhile, he would ask Democrats to support the Republican Gateway. Thus did Stevenson seize the political initiative. Gateway promptly passed the House on May 11. Stevenson took every opportunity to educate the voters on it. It did pass in the referendum of 1950, and subsequently several constitutional amendments passed too. Not until after Stevenson's death was a constitutional convention held and a new constitution written. But he had helped lay the groundwork.

13

A struggle such as that over constitutional reform always snarls up the orderly process of legislation, especially in the House, and it embitters members. In the charged atmosphere of mid-April, only six days after the first defeat of Con-Con, Stevenson was obliged to present his budget. It is one thing to promise, during a campaign, to increase aid to schools and municipalities, to increase old-age pensions and rehabilitate highways while at the same time deploring

tax increases; it is quite another to draw up a budget that will accomplish those purposes—and in a state whose constitution forbids deficit financing. In his budget message to the legislature, Stevenson said he was proposing for the biennium—July 1, 1949, to June 30, 1951—a total budget of $1,055 million, from state sources, an increase of $132 million over the past two years and one due to additional aid to schools, dependents, and municipalities and to soldier bonus bond payments. Since no control was possible over the increase in debt service and little over the public assistance programs, aid to schools and municipalities caused the main problem—the budget was in "precarious balance." A major increase in taxes could be avoided only by appropriating the remainder of the treasury surplus, extending the sales tax to occupations previously excluded, and reducing construction. Operating costs accounted for nearly one third of the proposed budget; he had made economies. His proposed aid to common schools represented an increase of 70 per cent, the largest in the state's history. Stevenson said, "Our future citizens need good schools even more than they need costly schools." Turning to the plight of the municipalities, he said they must rely primarily on the property tax and were having difficulty in meeting mounting demands for services. He proposed a new allocation of $40 million for aid to municipalities. To care for the 56,000 people in state institutions, Stevenson proposed about the same amount of money as in the past biennium. He likewise proposed little increase in appropriation for highway construction—bad as the state's roads were, the state "simply cannot afford" construction now. He proposed a 10 per cent increase in the salaries of state employees.

It was, all in all, a conservative budget, proposing no new taxes except for the broadening of the sales tax and no heavy new expenditures except for increased aid to schools and municipalities. The *Tribune,* nevertheless, entitled its editorial, "Another Democratic Spendthrift." Stevenson sent Alicia Patterson *Tribune* clippings and said, "The honeymoon is definitely over! But ours has just begun! Love in haste."

14

His friend and neighbor at Libertyville, Lloyd Lewis, suddenly died of a heart attack on April 21. Stevenson went to the memorial service. It was a Quaker ceremony, with meditation and extemporaneous speeches, one by Marc Connelly, the playright. Stevenson was called on. He said:

"I have been asked to share too in these farewells to a friend.

"I think it is a good day for this meeting. It is April now and all life is being renewed on the bank of this river that he loved so well. I think we will all be happy that it happened on this day, here with the sky so clear, and the wind so warm and fresh.

"He was my neighbor. He was the neighbor of many of you. He was a very good neighbor who was quick in time of misfortune; he was always present in times of mirth and happiness and trouble.

"I think Mr. Connelly was right when he said he was the most successful man he ever knew. I don't know much about the riches of life, of which I suspect few of you have found the last definition, but I do know that neighborliness and friendship are the richest rewards, the greatest enrichments that I have found.

"Everyone loved this man. Everyone was his friend who knew him or who read him. Why was that? Why is he the most successful man that many of us will ever know? The answers will be different. It depends who says them. For me it was humility, gentleness, wisdom and wit, all in one, and most of all a great compassionate friendliness.

"I think it will always be April in our memory. It will always be a bright day, a soft one and with renewed life. Perhaps nothing has gone at all—perhaps only the embodiment of the tender thing precious to all of us, and that is a friendship that is immortal and doesn't pass along, will be renewed for me, much as I know it will be for all of you."

It was one of the simplest and loveliest of all Stevenson's speeches. He told Alicia Patterson, "He was my dearest friend—my comfort and encouragement and help in need more than I can tell you. I loved him like I've loved no other man. Catherine [Kathryn Lewis] asked me to speak at his funeral I choked up like a silly ass and made a fool of myself on top of everything else. I shall never have such another friend."

15

More administration bills were being introduced in the legislature. On April 6, Jimmy Ryan introduced a bill to reorganize the Commerce Commission and take it out of politics—a campaign promise. On April 12, Republicans introduced bills in both houses to broaden the sales tax, and Stevenson supported them. On April 26, Jimmy Ryan introduced bills to put the state police under a merit system and Stevenson issued a statement arguing that their passage would take the state police out of politics, another campaign promise. Actually, the bills represented a political compromise, not a clean-cut break with politics—from the all-Republican police force he had inherited from Green, Stevenson was weeding out what he considered "the least qualified Republicans" and replacing them with Democrats so that by January 1, 1951, there would be about 250 Republicans and 250 Democrats on the force. After that, only merit, not politics, would control selections. (The regular Democratic organization had proposed the compromise.) On April 27, Senator Botchy Connors, joined by two Republicans, introduced a bill that would raise the gasoline tax from three cents to five cents per gallon and establish a complicated system of distributing the proceeds among the state, the cities, the counties, and local governments. Stevenson did not publicly endorse it, though it was clear he would need it if he was going to do anything about highways. Connors and the two Republicans introduced a bill increasing license fees for trucks based on their weight and size. Jimmy Ryan and Sam Shapiro in the House and Botchy Connors and Thaddeus Adesko in the Senate introduced bills to codify the public assistance laws and to put the Illinois Public Aid Commission under the Department of Public Welfare. On May 12, Jimmy Ryan and others introduced a House bill empowering Chicago to impose a tax on business. (The *Pantagraph* opposed it—"opens the door to unlimited taxation of business for revenue.") Three of the Broyles bills, the anti-Communist bills, were recommended favorably by a House committee.[7]

Patronage problems plagued Stevenson's staff and code directors. The old ways were hard to change. Roy E. Yung, Director of Agriculture, complained to Jim Mulroy that the Democratic county chairman of Grundy County wanted to assess an Agriculture Department field investigator 2 per cent of his salary for the county committee. Mulroy promptly asked State Chairman Kells to tell the county chairman to desist. An employee of the Anna State Hospital complained to Civil Service that "my Central Committeeman has asked me to pay him 2% of each check" and asked whether he

---

[7] They authorized the dismissal of any teacher who advocated "any doctrine designed to undermine by force or violence the form of government of this State or of the United States," declared ineligible for public office or employment as a teacher anyone who advocated unlawful overthrow of the government, and provided that "any person who is communist or who by oath knowingly subscribes to the aims, principles, and program of communism, or who pays dues to or carries a membership card in any communist or communist front organization is guilty of a felony" and could be imprisoned for from one to five years.

should pay. Maude Myers, executive secretary of Civil Service, told him he was not yet certified under Civil Service but was only a provisional employee, a common device politicians had used in the past to enable them to extract contributions. She passed the letter on to Director Hoehler, who told the employee that the Governor had "discouraged" such solicitation but only he could decide whether to pay.

While the Cook County organization handled patronage fairly smoothly, downstate matters were more difficult. Letters to Stevenson from job seekers were referred to Larry Irvin. Most had worked in the campaign. Some were from Bloomington, and Mrs. Ives intervened. Most of the jobs Irvin handled were low-salaried and most were in the Welfare Department. The correspondence between Irvin and Director Hoehler showed Hoehler's desire to cooperate but his stout resistance to candidates for jobs, no matter how strong their political backing, if he thought someone better qualified could be found. This caused Irvin endless difficulties but he usually refrained from going over Hoehler's head. On one occasion, however, Irvin decided that Hoehler's personnel chief was incompetent and wrote a memo saying so, which reached Stevenson. It provoked an angry reply from Hoehler. The school for delinquent girls and the one for delinquent boys, both near Chicago, had been the subject of periodic scandals; Hoehler, in taking great care to choose their superintendents, was protecting not only the professional integrity of his department but also Stevenson. Sometimes the correspondence over a single applicant dragged on for months and filled a thick file.

Inevitably Stevenson himself became involved. His personal friends sometimes asked him to give needy and worthy people jobs. Irvin kept a list of appointments county by county; Stevenson scrutinized it closely—and sometimes used it to placate disgruntled politicians. When a Democratic leader from the industrial suburb of Berwyn complained that Berwyn "received nothing," Stevenson looked it up, sent him the figures, and sent a copy to Arvey. Once Stevenson asked Irvin, "What is the situation with respect to Valentine Felsenthal who worked so diligently in my campaign office? I keep getting notes from Lou Kohn that they seem to be unable to find a place for him. . . . Should I write to Dick Daley and insist that he find a job for him, even if he has to make one?"

Senator Christopher Wimbish, a Negro from Chicago's ghetto, asked him for more patronage for Negroes. Stevenson replied, "I know you are having your troubles. Everyone is. My only comfort and justification is that we have turned over far more of the jobs already than most people realize and are percentagewise far ahead of the first year of Governor Horner's administration or Governor Green's." He went further—told Arvey that Wimbish "seems discontented" about Negro patronage and "tells me he has twenty-six precinct captains without jobs, Dawson twenty-nine and Campbell somewhat the same number." Stevenson also asked Irvin to help Wimbish make applications and he saw Wimbish personally in Chicago. On Stevenson's instructions Irvin also corresponded with State Chairman Kells about employing Negroes in "conspicuous" positions, particularly in Springfield and Chicago. It was a matter of continuing concern and Stevenson handled it, for both humanitarian and political reasons, in the pragmatic way that most Northern politicians do.

16

On May 1, Stevenson wrote Alicia Patterson, "Its Sunday night —12:45 AM—& I've just come up to my bedroom from my cell & my hideous work to reread your last letter from your sleepless bed. . . . Why am I spending my life & health on these damn politicians when they're newspaper men—and newspaperwomen!" Jane and Eddie Dick had come down for the weekend, bringing their son and "my enchanting John Fell," and they had opened the baseball season, Stevenson throwing out the first ball. He gave her his schedule—and Ellen's—for May, hoping she could meet him alone in Springfield, Chicago, St. Louis, or Washington.

Guy Reed of the Chicago Crime Commission told him on May 4 that some legislators felt they did not have easy access to him. They felt that his influence was greater than he knew and that, unless he exerted it, "the wrong crowd" would win—Reed was eager to get the Crime Commission bills out of committee. Stevenson replied, "It has been more than I could handle, and I am afraid I have missed many opportunities to cultivate some people usefully." On May 7, Stevenson issued a statement endorsing the three Crime Commission bills still languishing in committee, then left for the Kentucky Derby, returning on Sunday to Springfield. On Thursday, May 19, Stevenson told Alicia Patterson he was flying to Washington on Saturday and would stay at the Statler—"The President has summoned me for 3:30." Marquis Childs had invited him to attend the Gridiron Club dinner that day. Stevenson told Alicia Patterson he hoped "there's at least a glimpse of you in store for me." Back at the Mansion, he wrote: "Darling—even a glimpse was good—if you did look a little tired and harried. I thought I was going to be dreadfully self-conscious & awkward, but I didn't feel that way. Did you? Indeed I think we're getting adjusted—if I only didn't want to seize you in a somewhat unconventional way. I hope you appreciate my remarkable self-control!"

Why had President Truman "summoned" him? At the time, Stevenson merely told the press he and Truman had met at Blair House and had discussed taxes and the legislative session in Illinois and Washington together with economic and international affairs in general. But it is possible that at this early date— May 21, 1949—Truman first suggested to Stevenson that Stevenson might run for President in 1952. All accounts of that proposal date it at January 22, 1952, and it is true that Truman did make a concrete proposal at that time. He may, however, have held an exploratory talk with Stevenson on May 21, 1949. He had been interested in Stevenson ever since the 1948 election. Stevenson's landslide victory, set alongside Truman's own narrow margin in Illinois, had impressed him. Jack Arvey once recalled, "Several times before 1952 the President asked me, 'How's your Governor doing?' The President was tremendously impressed with Stevenson's big majority in 1948."[8]

17

Back in Illinois on Monday, Stevenson made a radio speech to the people. He said he could have had a constitutional convention on a deal "but I don't think that is right and I don't believe you think so either." He blamed Con-Con's defeat on the Republicans and urged support for Gateway. Only about thirty legislative days remained. To date 126 bills had passed, compared to 54 at the last session. FEPC had passed the House and was on its way to the Senate. While taking note of businessmen's objections to FEPC, Stevenson endorsed it: "For one American to discriminate against another because of

[8] Truman later wrote in his *Memoirs* that he had decided not to run for re-election in 1952 as early as the day of his inauguration in 1949. He said he had written a memorandum to himself "on May 8"—giving no year—saying:

"Now if we can find a man who will take over and continue the Fair Deal, Point IV, Fair Employment, parity for farmers and a consumers protective policy, the Democratic Party can win from now on.

"It seems to me that the Governor of Illinois has the background and what it takes. Think I'll talk to him."

Internal evidence suggests that Truman wrote that memorandum sometime after April of 1950 but he could have written it earlier.

color or religion is a blow at the very foundation of our democracy, which is faith in equality of opportunity for all. We must not play into the hands of the Communists by giving them propaganda material about democratic hypocrisy." Stevenson argued at length for other Administration measures, especially the need for increased aid to schools and cities. He closed: "It's a large, ambitious program. . . . It would have been far easier for me to sit still, administer the state as I find it. . . ."

It was Stevenson's effort to go over the legislature's head to the people. Legislators now knew what he considered his highest priorities—FEPC, state police reform, consolidation of Welfare and the Illinois Public Aid Commission, the intertwined sales tax broadening and aid to schools and cities, and, at a somewhat lower level of priority, workmen's compensation, unemployment compensation, the Crime Commission grand jury bill, mining legislation, a strengthened civil service. By setting these priorities he, by inference, indicated he would not press for an increase in the gasoline tax or a more equitable distribution of its revenues, several other tax proposals, an increase in truck license fees, salary raises for state employees, reorganization of the Commerce Commission, a Little Hoover Commission on governmental efficiency, a new state reformatory for boys, an increase in old-age pensions, and two of the remaining Crime Commission bills. Thus he took the pressure off several controversial bills, relieving members of the need to vote for them and, by implication, asking them in turn to vote for what he considered most important.

18

It was spring, the grass on the sloping lawn in front of the Statehouse was green. And now the legislature was coming into the home stretch. It had disposed of most of its non-controversial bills. It had chewed over the controversial bills already introduced and those—including appropriation bills—about to be introduced. The bellwether politicians had made their positions known. Lesser members were, for the most part, prepared to follow one leader or another. The House and Senate were "ready to vote," as their members put it.

On June 1 the House Judiciary Committee reported out the three Crime Commission bills—reported them out with a recommendation that they not pass. Proponents of the bills made a floor fight on one of them, the bill extending the life of Cook County grand juries, moving to override the Judiciary Committee. They lost. All three bills were tabled—that is, lost for this session. The West Side Bloc had rounded up enough votes, by what deals who could say, to defeat legislation that had the support of the Administration, law enforcement officers, good-government groups, and much of the press. Stevenson had indeed lost both Con-Con and the Crime bills, as he had feared.

Next day Representative W. O. Edwards, a downstate Democrat who was an expert on school legislation, introduced, along with more than a score of others in both parties, ten bills that comprised the school program. They had been drafted after months of work by experts and pressures from all sides. They appropriated $100,319,000 to the common school fund—Stevenson had asked for $112,000,000 and the bill was amended to increase the appropriation to $111,-467,000—changed the method of apportioning the common school fund, moved toward consolidation of rural school districts, and withheld money from segregated schools. The day the bills were introduced, June 2, Stevenson sent a special message to the legislature, urging their passage. That same day six House members, four Democrats and two Republicans, introduced two bills to increase workmen's compensation.

In the midst of all this Stevenson gave what became his famous deposition in the trial of Alger Hiss. Hiss, it will be recalled, had been a young lawyer in the AAA when Stevenson was there, had entered the State Department in 1936 and attended international conferences on the UN along with Stevenson, had later become president of the Carnegie Endowment for International Peace, and had maintained a desultory correspondence with Stevenson. In August of 1948, Whittaker Chambers, an editor of *Time* who had confessed to having been a secret Communist courier, accused Hiss of having helped transmit classified government documents to Russians. Hiss denied the charges and was indicted by a federal grand jury in December of 1948 on two counts of perjury. The case was a *cause célèbre*. In January, Governor Stevenson had been visited by Ross Randolph, the Springfield FBI man, who, on instructions, asked for Stevenson's correspondence with and about Hiss. Stevenson gave it to him. Now Hiss's attorneys proposed to put on the witness stand various character witnesses and to introduce the sworn depositions of other character witnesses who could not testify in person. They first asked Stevenson to testify in person. He refused, pleading the urgency of state business. They then, on May 24, got a court order directing that his deposition be taken. On June 2 the U. S. Commissioner at Springfield went to the Mansion and put the questions for the defense and the cross-questions for the prosecution, as directed by the Court.

In replying to the defense questions, Stevenson said he had known Hiss since June or July of 1933 when they served together in the legal division of the AAA in Washington. "We were working on different commodities. Our contact was frequent but not close nor daily." He had next seen Hiss in 1945 when he went to work for the State Department. That spring Hiss was occupied with arrangements for the San Francisco UN Conference. "I was engaged in other matters and met him mostly in intradepartmental meetings and in connection with some aspects of the plan for the San Francisco Conference, largely relating to matters pertaining to the handling of the press at the conference." At the conference itself Hiss was Secretary General of the conference and Stevenson was attached to the United States delegation. "Our paths did not cross in a business way but we met occasionally at official social functions." Back in Washington in July, they conferred several times on ratification of the UN Charter by the Senate. Stevenson resigned from the Department early in August and "so far as I recall" did not meet Hiss again until he came to London in January 1946, with the United States delegation to the first General Assembly. "We had offices nearby each other and met frequently at delegation meetings and staff conferences." Stevenson returned to the United States in March 1946 and "I do not believe" met Hiss again until the UN General Assembly in New York in 1947. By then, Hiss was with the Carnegie Endowment; Stevenson conferred with him once or twice on the UN budget. "I have not seen him since." Stevenson said he had known other persons who knew Hiss. The next question was: "From the speech of those persons, can you state what the reputation of Alger Hiss is for integrity, loyalty and veracity?" Yes, Stevenson said. "Specify whether his reputation for integrity is good or bad." "Good," Stevenson replied; and he replied the same to questions about Hiss's loyalty and veracity.

In response to cross-questions put on behalf of the prosecution, Stevenson said he had never been a guest in Hiss's home, had never before 1948 heard the charges that Hiss in 1937 and 1938 "removed confidential and secret documents from the State Department and made such documents available to persons not authorized to see or receive them," and had never before 1948 heard reports that Hiss was a Communist or "a Communist sympathizer."

Subsequently, Stevenson came under heavy Republican attack for having given this deposition. He defended his doing so on the ground that in a democracy it is the fundamental duty of all citizens, but especially of lawyers, to give testimony in court. Stevenson could have declined to answer the questions. In that case, he might—or might not—have been subpoenaed. He had considered the matter carefully. Wally Schaefer had advised him to answer the questions. Carl McGowan has said in retrospect, "He probably got [political] credit with the wilder liberals. I thought he was poorly advised, however, and shouldn't have done it. I also thought Hiss was wrong to ask him. Stevenson hardly knew Hiss, except that his reputation was good. If this was all Hiss was asking for, what he was really asking for was the use of Stevenson's name to impress the jury—then if something went wrong, he was jeopardizing an important political career. Stevenson should have been shrewd enough to see that. But it came at a time when it was hard *not* to stand up. Stevenson's succumbing is a tribute to his decent instincts—not to his analytic ability." It may be added that other eminent men, including Supreme Court Justices Felix Frankfurter and Stanley Reed, also testified to Hiss's reputation, Frankfurter going further than Stevenson in vouching for Hiss's reputation. But the Hiss deposition would haunt Stevenson's political career in the next few years.

It did not seem important at the time. On June 3, the day after he made the deposition, he wrote to Alicia Patterson without mentioning it.

19

The relationship between Stevenson and his wife had been deteriorating rapidly ever since his election. Even earlier, during the campaign, she had threatened to divorce him. Their relationship worsened further as he became more and more deeply engrossed in state affairs. They saw each other with increasing infrequency, and their time together was not happy. They discussed separation or divorce. They decided on divorce, and on the weekend of June 4–5, Stevenson went up to Chicago to confer with Richard Bentley, his old friend and the lawyer he chose to handle the divorce. On Monday he asked Brown Brothers Harriman to prepare an inventory of his securities. He made a note to himself to check on the boys' securities, Ellen's securities, and her possessions in a safety deposit box. Bentley kept working through June, seeing Stevenson three times and conferring with Ellen's lawyer, William C. Boyden, partner of Benjamin B. Davis, considered the best divorce lawyer in Chicago, and, on July 1, with Ellen herself and Boyden. They were trying to keep the divorce secret for the time being.

When Mrs. Ives learned that the Stevensons had decided on divorce, she was shocked. She telephoned him, asked a Christian Science practitioner, Mrs. A. Jacqueline Shaw of Brookline, Massachusetts, to help him, and sent him a long letter saying how troubled she was that she could not help him more. She sent him religious advice and recalled to him his inheritance, all to bolster him in his difficulty. His children loved him, she said, and so did his wife though she did not know it now.

Various friends had tried to save the marriage that spring. Some continued to try during the summer. Their next-door neighbor, Glen Lloyd, told Ellen, "Why not stay—nothing is perfect. You've got three children, he's the Governor, you write well." She replied that she had wanted out of the marriage since 1941.

Their old Lake Forest friend, Ruth Winter, has recalled, "I got worried when Ellen began talking at dinner parties," that is, talking about Stevenson. "I had had some experience with mental illness. I went to her mother, Mrs. Carpenter, and begged her to get professional help for Ellen. She said, 'You don't understand—when the divorce is over, she'll be all right. It's killing her.' Ellen was so critical of Adlai. He did not want this divorce. He felt only the greatest sense of failure. He had no idea what was going on. I could only figure that he was so absorbed in his own particular interest that he really did black out on this particular relationship which was just disintegrating." Another friend thought that when Stevenson said he was surprised by the divorce he probably meant that he had thought their marriage was on solid ground once more after Ellen's interest in another man had "blown over." Jane Dick thought that the key to the breakup of their marriage was Stevenson's moving into the limelight—Ellen, jealous, could not stand to take second place to him.

The boys were not surprised by the divorce. Adlai III once recalled, "My mother told me about it in my bedroom in Libertyville that summer. She thought it would be worked out amicably. There would be joint custody. It was not an emotional thing for me because I had known it was coming. I'd overheard enough. I thought it was overdue. There hadn't been a good relationship for a long time. I remember her as the unreasonable one, not only with Dad, but with us and with servants. I was embarrassed about her peremptory way with servants. But Dad may have been innocent enough about women to think this behavior was not out of the ordinary." Adlai III said his father consulted him about the custody of the children. Ellen proposed joint custody, young Adlai has said, but

Stevenson was dubious. He went along with joint custody on the advice of young Adlai.

20

Back in Springfield on Monday, June 6, Stevenson held a long legislative meeting in the Mansion. From now until the end of the session he saw a constant stream of legislators and politicians, as many as twenty or thirty a day. Important bills were moving; others were being introduced. On June 6 a bipartisan bill was introduced to set up a Little Hoover Commission to study the organization of the state government; it sailed through both houses with Stevenson's approval. On the same day the Administration's long-waited series of bills reorganizing the Department of Mines and Minerals was introduced. Hammered out in many difficult meetings among mine owners, labor leaders, and mining experts, they were intended to strengthen mine safety regulations.

On June 8 the administration bills broadening the sales tax passed the House and were sent to the Senate. At the same time Stevenson announced a cut in the budget. That day, too, a bill to increase unemployment compensation from $20 to $25 a week was introduced into the House, though without the sponsorship of Jimmy Ryan. It passed the House quickly and went to the Senate. On June 10, administration bills to increase workmen's compensation passed the House and were sent to the Senate.

The Administration's tax on businesses passed the House June 15 after difficulty; it faced heavy going in the more conservative and Republican Senate. And so did FEPC. It was an emotional issue. Not just the Illinois legislature but Congress and the nation were at that time deeply divided over civil rights. The Democratic Convention had split over the issue the year before. This was not the first time FEPC had been introduced in the Illinois legislature, and the battle lines were drawn before Stevenson took office. In general, Democrats, Negroes, Jews, liberals, some good-government groups, and part of labor supported FEPC; Republicans, much of the white majority, and employers opposed it. But such an issue cuts across normal groupings—in past years, organized employer groups had joined with the AFL to oppose the bill.

Not long after the 1948 election the Commission on Law and Social Action of the American Jewish Congress in Chicago said the prospects for FEPC were good in view of Stevenson's commitment to it and his huge electoral majority but predicted that his "real task" would be to "hold his own party members in line." The analysis said that in the past employers had used a retailers' association as a "front" and pointed out that the association was financed almost entirely by "the multimillion-dollar department store industry" centering on State Street in Chicago. Ed Day once said that it was frequently remarked around Springfield that the financial support for lobbying against FEPC was second only to the slush fund used to oppose the gas tax bill. Downstate Illinois has a strong Southern overlay and many legislators have Southern segregationist leanings (the Ku Klux Klan had been strong in several counties some years earlier). In his campaign, and in subsequent speeches and statements, Stevenson had made FEPC one of his principal proposals. His bill had been carefully drafted and, when it was introduced on February 16, it had fifty-eight sponsors headed by Jimmy Ryan and including both Republicans and Democrats as well as the West Side Bloc and members usually identified with good-government bills.

Stevenson received a good many letters opposing the bill. A doctor wrote, "I heartily agree with you that discrimination does not have a place in the American ideals, but I do not believe that legislation can prevent it." One man wrote, "This bill has vociferous support from do-good organizations, socialists, communists, and large numbers of people resentful of their station in life." An official of a Chicago builders' association said that Negroes were "not ready for forceful equality in employment." The *Pantagraph* opposed FEPC.

On the other hand, influential groups lined up behind the bill—CIO unions, the League of Women Voters, IVI, the Church Federation of Greater Chicago, the Catholic Youth Organization, many more. Their lobbyists, sometimes working with Wally Schaefer, mapped out strategies, counted votes, testified at committee hearings. Pressure was brought to bear to bring the AFL into line. Urged by William Green, president of the AFL, the Illinois AFL reversed its 1947 positon of opposition—a major victory, releasing several members of the House who felt obliged to follow the AFL line.

All spring as the bill made its way through the House with difficulty, the pulling and hauling backstage continued. Finally, on May 18, after immense effort Jimmy Ryan and Paul Powell won—the House passed the bill and sent it to the Senate. The vote was close —81 yes (it had to have 77), 43 no. The prevailing majority consisted in 70 Democrats and 11 Republicans. Joseph D. Keenan, director of Labor's League for Political Education, an AFL affiliate, wrote to Stevenson from Washington, expressing the League's "elation"—it would "strengthen the liberal movement all over the country."

The Senate Judiciary Committee began hearings on FEPC June 1 and reported it out favorably. It came up on second reading in the Senate on June 9 but on motion of the Republican leader, Senator Thompson, was set down as a special order of business on June 14. That day a bitter debate occurred. A Republican offered several amendments to weaken or destroy the bill. Senator Connors led the fight against them. He succeeded, but the votes were close— 25 to 24. On June 16 the bill came up on third and final reading, again as a special order of business. The Senators debated for nearly three hours, then voted. They killed the bill, 23 to 25. All but one Democrat, a downstate farmer, voted for the bill, and so did seven Republicans. It needed 26 votes, a constitutional majority, to pass. Thus it fell three votes short.

Stevenson immediately issued a statement blaming the Republicans: "I had hoped that the state of Lincoln would be a leader." Jack Arvey had worked hard to hold the Democrats in line for FEPC, not only because it was an administration measure but because he believed in it. Many years later he recalled, "After the vote I went into the minority leader's office, tired and discouraged, with all that work gone down the drain. A Negro Senator had made a great speech for FEPC. He came in and I congratulated him on his fine speech. He said, 'That's all right, boss, it's better this way—look at the good issue we've got.' I never supported him again."

21

On the same day the Senate killed FEPC, the House passed the bill to end segregation in the state militia and on June 24 the Senate passed it too. Next day the Senate passed the bill, already passed by the House, increasing workmen's compensation. Despite the mounting tempo of the legislature, Stevenson on the weekend of June 18 left for the annual Governors' Conference at Colorado Springs, Colorado, taking all three of his sons with him. In a speech there, Stevenson staked out a pragmatic position on state-federal relationships that emphasized both states' rights and states' responsibilities. The growth of the centralized federal government since 1932 had long troubled him, and still did, but he had a somewhat altered view of it since he had himself faced state problems. He said, "There are certainly those of us who feel that the rapid extension of federal grants-in-aid is threatening the integrity of the states and the federal system. . . . [But] the industrial age has created problems of health, housing, education, transportation, and employment which inexorably flow over state boundaries. . . . We must face the fact that in many instances the states either won't or couldn't begin to cope with these vast industrial problems. . . . To demand greater state autonomy and control requires that we place our own house in order." It was the starting point from which he later moved on the question of states' rights.

Flying back to Springfield on Wednesday, June 22, with "my tall and handsome son Adlai beside me," Stevenson described the Governors' Conference to Alicia Patterson—"a very de luxe affair, contributing an hour of fine trout fishing, a short sun bath by the pool, a series of long dinners and divertisements and very little education for a conscientious young governor." He could not "figure out" what Ellen was going to do. "She casually informed me Sat night . . . that she had changed lawyers!" He resumed the letter at Thursday midnight: "I've had a harrowing day watching the legislature destroy my fine program in its last convulsive agony."

The legislature had indeed slashed up a good deal of his program, but not all of it. The House passed the mining bills and they sailed through the Senate. On June 20, too, the Senate passed the state police bills unanimously, a miracle attributable largely to Senator Botchy Connors' skill. A bill increasing the Governor's salary from $12,000 to $25,000 passed; Stevenson let it become law without his signature. The Senate was finally ready to vote on the gasoline tax bill. For weeks it had been under heavy attack both from oil lobbyists and from cities quarreling over distribution of the revenue. Any significant highway program depended on the bill. Senator Connors had exerted almost heroic efforts to save it. Now on June 21 the Senate debated the bill for three hours. In the middle of debate, Connors read on the floor a letter from Stevenson endorsing the bill, the first time he had publicly accepted responsibility for the tax increase, a step the Republicans had awaited. The bill needed 26 votes. When the roll call ended and the clerk announced the results, the bill had received only 25 votes, one short. But two Democrats changed their votes, and the bill passed. Only one Democrat voted no. Stevenson's letter changed no Republican votes but may have helped change those of the two Democrats. Now the bill must go to the House with only seven legislative days remaining.

Next day the truck lobby showed its power. The bill introduced in April to increase license fees for trucks came to a final vote. It got the votes of only its three sponsors plus three others—6 yeas, 35 nays. Senator Edward P. Saltiel, a Chicago Republican, moved to reconsider it next day, June 23. The truck lobby was busy that night; so were people who resented its influence. In the morning at 11 A.M., Senator Saltiel saw Governor Stevenson, then went to the Senate chamber and switched his vote. So did six others. But this gave the bill only 13 votes, half what it needed. Stevenson issued a statement deploring the vote.

On the other side of the Statehouse, Speaker Powell was calling big bills. He called the entire group of school appropriation bills, key measures in Stevenson's entire program; and they passed the House and were favorably received in the Senate. It looked as though the school bills would have clear sailing.

Every day Stevenson was seeing his legislative leaders, such key department directors as Dick Daley, such political advisers as Jack Arvey and George Kells, and Senators and Representatives from both parties. On June 23 an administration bill to tax out-of-state corporations passed the House. A House bill giving the State Department of Public Safety additional powers to control fire hazards, introduced after the Effingham Hospital fire, had passed the House and now on June 23 passed the Senate. An administration tax bill, empowering Chicago to tax businesses for revenue purposes, had passed the House, but now on June 23 the Senate killed it. Next day the Senate passed the unemployment compensation bill unanimously (it already had passed the House). It passed another House bill unanimously, one increasing the amount of gasoline tax funds that could be used to build and maintain city streets.

But the Senate struck savagely at the heart of the Administration's sales tax program to help schools and cities. The House, with some difficulty, had passed three bills to broaden the tax. Now on June 23 a Republican offered an amendment to one of them which would make it unconstitutional. Senator Libonati moved to table the amendment. In a vote that followed party lines, the Senate voted against tabling and then adopted the amendment. When the vote was announced, Senator Libonati shouted, "There goes the common school fund." "Let it go," yelled a Republican Senator from East Moline. Stevenson had warned that his $112 million state school aid program would have to be cut if the sales tax bills were not passed. That same day the House passed the school aid bills and sent them to the Senate. George Tagge of the *Tribune* wrote that Stevenson had been outmaneuvered: by passing the school bills, the House had relinquished control of them to the Senate, which would not cut them but now had all but killed the sales tax bills needed to finance them.

Stevenson had been outmaneuvered on another issue. He had let it be known that he might cut his $34-million bill for aid to the cities if his revenue program was not passed—but the aid-to-cities bill was also out of the hands of the Democratic House and was approved that same day by the Senate Appropriations Committee. Clearly the Republicans were out to embarrass the Governor— they would vote for more aid to schools and cities but they would kill bills to provide the money to pay for the aid. Stevenson knew what they were up to.

On June 24, a Friday, the Senate amended his bills to put the Illinois Public Aid Commission under the Department of Welfare and appeared about to kill them. At the same time the legislature was passing, or was about to pass, a large number of bills for local improvements that one or another legislator wanted—"pork barrels bills," they were called in the U. S. Congress, "Christmas tree bills" in Springfield. On June 25, Stevenson issued a statement threatening to veto bills that called for appropriations over the budget. Coming as it did almost at the end of the session and with bills crucial to his program still pending, it was not a politic statement.

Withal, he seemed to be of good cheer. He invited friends from Lake Forest to come down for the closing days of the legislature —"to witness the concluding holocaust," he told one. The Iveses were there, and Mrs. Ives was fascinated by the spectacle yet sensitive to his private heartbreak. The Mansion housekeeper was rude to her, she thought. Concerned about her brother's marital troubles, she drove back to Bloomington to weep.

22

On Monday, June 27, the start of the last week, Stevenson moved his office and staff from the Mansion to the Statehouse. There he received a legislator or political leader every few minutes each day. And he listened in his office to a loudspeaker broadcasting the debates and votes from the floor, keeping track of proceedings, sending aides to round up votes, while Paul Powell and Lieutenant Governor Sherwood Dixon put to final votes key parts of his program.

On Tuesday, June 28, the Senate decisively killed, 25 to 18, the administration bill to put the Illinois Public Aid Commission under the Department of Welfare. On Wednesday the House killed the Broyles "anti-Communist" bills, which Stevenson had opposed all spring. That same day the bill to tax out-of-state corporations fell five votes short of the Senate votes it needed. Worst of all, the Senate Republicans killed the bills broadening the sales tax. Some of them were voting against their own recommendations—a Revenue Laws

Commission appointed in 1947 by Governor Green had recommended the sales tax broadening program. Stevenson was put on the spot: now, the day before the session was to end, the Senate was about to pass his bills increasing aid to schools but had killed the bills that would provide the money. Stevenson ordered the school bills recalled from third (final) reading to second reading in the Senate for amendment. The amendments reduced the appropriations from $111,467,000 to $100,419,000. The Republicans resisted fiercely. When on Thursday, the final day of the session, the Senate voted on the amendment, the vote was tied, 24 to 24. The Democratic Lieutenant Governor, presiding, cast the deciding vote, and the amendment passed, saving the school bills. Stevenson signed them the same day.

The day before, amid all the uproar, Stevenson had written Alicia Patterson, "Darling—I'm sitting in my office at the [Statehouse] while the clamor goes on unabated in the House & Senate & messenger boys & pols run in and out to get my orders on every damn thing. In a few minutes the extension of the sales tax will come to a vote in the Senate & I'll know whether the Rep. program of months to embarrass me if they can has worked. . . . Kennelly has run out on me on the gas tax increase and all in all things are in a mess and so am I! I wish you were here for the last 24 hrs of this fantastic show—and I wish you were here for sundry other reasons!!" He wrote about plans to meet and said, "Things at home are getting more involved. E. has a new lawyer & now wants me to sue her for divorce in Waukegan. As tho I didn't have enough on my hands."

Although Senator Connors had succeeded in passing the gasoline tax bill in the Senate, now, on the final day of the session, Thursday, June 30, the House killed the bill decisively. This meant insufficient money for the highway program. Scores of bills died and scores were passed that day. Stevenson's bill to reorganize the Commerce Commission was finally passed. So were his bills to increase state employees' pay, strengthen civil service, increase the salaries of all department directors but one, and establish a state reformatory —incredibly, Illinois had none. All day long and on into the night emissaries hurried back and forth between the two chambers, trying to reach agreements on amendments that one house or the other had adopted. They hurried, too, from the Governor's office to the anterooms of the chambers.

The Republicans had anticipated earlier that Stevenson would veto a large number of "Christmas tree bills." Furthermore, they had become embittered by the controversies. The legislature normally adjourns June 30, although frequently when midnight arrives the houses stop the clocks and continue on into the early morning hours to wind up their business. The Governor has ten days in which to sign or veto bills; if he does neither, they become law without his signature. In order to give the legislature a chance to override his vetoes, Senator Thompson, the powerful Republican leader, had introduced a resolution on June 21 providing that, when the two houses adjourned on June 30, they do so not *sine die,* that is, permanently, as is customary, but instead adjourn only until July 18. Now on the last day the Senate promptly adopted the resolution and sent it to the House.

Stevenson, after consulting with Schaefer and other advisers, decided to prorogue the legislature—end its session by executive order, a step derived from English constitutional history, buried in the Illinois constitution, and not attempted in Illinois in the twentieth century. Intricate maneuvering began, with Schaefer in charge. The Governor could only prorogue the legislature if the two houses disagreed on adjournment. The Democratic House voted to non-concur in the Senate resolution. Past midnight, the House adopted a resolution offered by Jimmy Ryan that the legislature adjourn *sine die*. The Senate refused to concur. After further maneuvers, Jimmy Ryan offered a resolution certifying to the Governor that the House and Senate were in disagreement on adjournment. It passed. Thereupon, at 5:30 A.M. on July 1, Stevenson issued a proclamation declaring the legislature adjourned until January 3, 1951. A Stevenson aide once said, "I'll never forget the look on Thompson's face in the Senate when the Lieutenant Governor read the proclamation. He jumped to his feet and started hollering and he was still hollering when the gavel banged and it was all over."

Stevenson appraised the legislature's work in a lengthy radio report to the people. He began with the old joke that "Congress has adjourned and the Republic is safe for another year." He said, "I was surprised to see to what an extent party politics influenced legislative decisions. I believe in the two-party system. . . . But the basic divisions between Democrats and Republicans on national issues have little bearing upon state and municipal problems. . . . I saw Republican Senators vote against legislation they themselves had recommended. I saw Republicans vote *against* measures *I* proposed who had voted for identical proposals made by Governor Green. And, finally, I think I saw the summit of legislative irresponsibility and ruinous partisanship when Republican Senators, after protesting loudly about the budget, killed the revenue bills but voted all of my appropriations and a lot more besides. . . . I suppose their motive was to embarrass me. But fortunately some of the Republican Senators would not follow their leaders. They practiced what they preached and, thanks to their help, we carried the day and brought the budget almost into balance. I can do the rest by vetoes."

He said the legislature had enacted about two thirds of his program. "Maybe we tried to do too much all at once. Probably we did, but I think campaign talk should be more than sweet, deceitful words." He then summed up his defeats and victories.

First, his defeats. At the top of the list he put Con-Con, then FEPC, then aid to the cities, including Chicago, then other measures—"I also lost under an avalanche of Senate votes a bill to increase truck license fees. The lobbies were very active in Springfield."

He turned to his successes. First he listed aid to schools—more money than ever before. Next he listed the state police bill. Then he mentioned reorganization of the Commerce Commission, the fire protection bill, the mining bills, the increase in workmen's compensation and unemployment compensation, cost-of-living increases in old-age pensions and blind assistance, increases in the salaries of state employees and officers, strengthening civil service, reorganizing county assessment procedures, codifying the public assistance laws, authorizing a state reformatory, and establishing a Little Hoover Commission.

"Maybe," he said, "I can summarize the results by saying that of the major measures in which the Administration was particularly interested some 21 were passed and 13 defeated. . . . I think it was a good start," and he expressed his gratitude to Speaker Paul Powell, Lieutenant Governor Dixon, Representative Jimmy Ryan, and Senator Botchy Connors. He said the legislature had passed 829 bills. He would sign most, veto some. "That's my next job; some 550 still to be acted on, many appointments to make to boards, commissions, and offices, and then I hope we can settle down to the cold, hard, day-to-day job running this enormous business—the state of Illinois —more efficiently and economically than it has ever been run before. That's my ambition and that's what you sent me here to do."

23

Stevenson set to work on the bills. Some 692 Senate bills and 1,133 House bills had been introduced, a total of 1,825. Of these, according to a press release, the legislature passed 833, the most in modern times. (Another source puts the total passed at 772.) The bills passed were sent to the Attorney General's office to be checked for constitutionality, to the Legislative Reference Bureau to be checked for typographical and other errors, and then to Wally Schaefer and Ed Day, who prepared digests of them, comments on them, and gave them to Stevenson to decide whether to sign or veto them.

Stevenson signed 751 bills, allowed 16 to become law without his signature, vetoed certain sections of 5, and vetoed 61 outright. He vetoed some as unnecessary or duplicating other bills or laws. He vetoed some to balance the budget. He vetoed some as unconstitutional or of doubtful constitutionality.[9]

At the same time he was working on vetoes, Stevenson was trying in other ways to balance his budget. He told department directors to analyze all jobs and eliminate every one possible. He ordered agencies under his control to limit their operating expenses to 10 per cent less than their appropriations.

24

The 1949 legislature had been Stevenson's initiation into state politics, indeed, into elective politics. How did his record look?

His record of legislative achievement was neither really outstanding nor really poor. Governors more experienced in politics some-

---

[9] He vetoed a bill authorizing the creation of roadside lakes and ponds because no funds were available. In the name of economy, he vetoed appropriations of $40,000 to maintain the Senate and House chambers while the two houses were not in session. He vetoed a bill appropriating $750 to a man whose airplane had been wrecked during maneuvers of the Illinois Reserve Militia. He vetoed a $93,000 appropriation to build a road connecting three small coal towns—he had no doubt the road was needed but so were others and he did not want to establish the precedent of using general revenue funds for building local roads. He vetoed a bill providing that narcotics addicts could be imprisoned long enough to "cure" them, though not more than one year—no existing institution was prepared to treat them, addicts should not be treated as criminals. He vetoed a bill increasing the *per diem* fees of clerks of city courts—"the fee system . . . is an anachronism." He vetoed a controversial bill, frequently introduced, regulating, if not putting out of business, currency exchanges which drove armored cars to factory gates and cashed workmen's checks—he considered it unreasonable governmental regulation. He vetoed a bill lowering teachers' qualifications because "our progress must be toward higher standards of qualification, not lower."

times are more effective; his Republican successor, for example, William Stratton, by insisting on the passage of only what he considered absolutely indispensable, passed more of his bills. (He had a Republican legislature, however.) Stevenson, by refusing to compromise, was less effective. Principle is admirable; it can also be costly.

Beyond the confines of Illinois, Stevenson emerged in the minds of a few important people as a liberal Democratic Governor. His liberal credentials included his oppositon to the Broyles bills and his espousal of FEPC and labor legisation (and his Hiss deposition). He could lay claim, also, to standing for good government. He was charged later with indecisiveness but he showed little indecision in proroguing the legislature. He was charged later, too, with spending too much time on substance and not enough in cultivating the politicians, and the charge had some basis.

Roscoe Drummond, then chief of the Washington Bureau of the *Christian Science Monitor,* wrote that probably neither Truman nor Dewey would be nominated for President in 1952 and that Stevenson and Warren of California were outstanding possibilities to replace them. He said that two columnists, Thomas L. Stokes and Doris Fleeson, saw Stevenson "projected into the spotlight of national politics." Stokes wrote that Stevenson had come through his "ordeal" with his legislature better than Governors Bowles of Connecticut and Mennen Williams of Michigan.

25

As the session ended and summer began, Stevenson had other things on his mind. He wrote to Alicia on July 8, "Now its 12:30 & I must to bed & early rise for a days travail in Chicago & then the crisis with Ellen & her lawyer at home on Sunday. She's getting very demanding about money & in her present abnormal, irrational state of mind I suppose she could be very difficult which would mess things up not only for us but for the children for years to come. . . . Pray God it doesn't end on the front pages! . . . I know what you mean by being alone. Perhaps I don't need it as much as you. I've never had much opportunity to pull up & run off anywhere alone. But I have developed sort of an exile & retreat in turmoil. Latterly with life becoming more & more involved I've retreated to my shadows & solitudes a little too much perhaps."

Dick Bentley, Stevenson's lawyer, had been discussing the divorce with William Boyden, Ellen's lawyer. By July 7, in a letter to Bent-

ley, Boyden put in writing Ellen's proposals.[10] Negotiations between
the lawyers dragged on all summer and into the early fall. Ben Davis, Boyden's partner, entered the negotiations on Ellen's behalf. Frequently Stevenson met with Bentley. Stevenson himself made endless
computations of his expenditures on the house and Ellen and the
children over the years of their marriage. He made further computations of investments, inventories of their belongings, long detailed
lists of items that came to bald totals on an adding machine but
which were the trivia of a joint endeavor that had turned into heartbreak—$80 for "tutoring Adlai," $125 wages for the farmer, $7.50
to the Onwentsia Club on some forgotten occasion, $375 for "Adlai
to Canada," $13.25 for eyeglasses, $50 for "Camp—Borden," $4.01
for "auto repair," $75 for "Winter Club"; doctor bills, utility bills,
repair bills, teeth-straightening bills, telephone bills, school bills,
railroad tickets, Christmas presents, club dues, clothing bills, insurance premiums, taxes, taxicab hire—all the minutiae of twenty years
of living together. True, it had not been much of a marriage. But
few marriages are easy to sunder. Stevenson made his computations
in longhand on scratch paper, alone in the Mansion, long columns
of figures; and interspersed among them in his bulging "Divorce
File" were such notes to himself as this:

[10] Ellen would sue in Illinois on the ground of desertion; Stevenson would
get the house and furniture in Libertyville but would either pay her $10,000
per year for ten years for her share in them (half of that if she remarried)
or would pay her $20,000 for them plus $50 a month in alimony until she
remarried; Stevenson would educate and support the children; custody would
be joint for all children or Stevenson would take the two older children and
Ellen would take John Fell. Boyden, for all his experience, found the situation extremely difficult. In all their protracted correspondence, the two
lawyers avoided using either Stevenson's name or Ellen's, no doubt to preserve
secrecy. After consulting with Stevenson that weekend, Bentley accepted the
proposals for Stevenson's ownership of the house and furniture (except for
a Degas which belonged to Ellen) and Stevenson's education and support
of the children. He said, however, that he thought an Illinois divorce impossible in these circumstances; that neither of the custody arrangements
was satisfactory; that Stevenson had not contemplated paying Ellen anything
more than the $20,000 for the furniture; that Ellen already had substantial
means and would inherit more from her mother, and that Stevenson felt
that, to safeguard both Ellen's future and the children's, a substantial part of
her assets should be put in a trust to conserve them.

Bentley then made a counterproposal on Stevenson's behalf: Stevenson
would pay $20,000 outright for the furniture and the cash surrender value
over $8,000 of Ellen's mother's life insurance; alimony until she remarried
of 15 per cent of his gross income over $20,000 a year; Ellen would put in
trust for her life one half of her interest in her mother's Lake Shore Drive
property and also $150,000 in securities.

Ellen wants:

1. Custody of J. F.—me to pay school expenses.
2. Use of house until she makes final living plans—indefinite period.
3. 4,000 per year—total 75,000—as "settlement, not alimony."
4. I have "forced" her to get divorce—I'm at fault.

Interspersed among the computations, too, were notes from Mrs. Ives—a quotation from the Thirty-fourth Psalm, a quotation from Emerson, advice about Ellen, family reminiscences.

Stevenson asked Ellen's mother, now in North East Harbor, Maine, to go to Ellen. She thought it unwise until Ellen "knows *what* she is going to do." She had talked to Ellen several times on the telephone. Stevenson retained her friendship, but not Ellen's, the rest of his life. A few friends came down to Springfield to visit him. It was as though past, present, and future mingled and folded in on one another—his mother, his wife, his sister, Alicia, his friends, his work, solace of friends and religious advice, his mother's writing the Laddie letters, his mother's and sister's religiosity, his father's fumbling efforts to guide him, his Princeton friends' condolences now, concern about the proprieties in time of disaster, all ebbing and flowing to and fro in time of deepening private crisis and rising public stature. He was, essentially, alone.

26

An old man in Chicago told him that Mark Twain once had attended a lunch with Grandfather Stevenson and had said:

> *Philologists sweat and lexicographers bray.*
> *But the best they can do is to call him Ad-lay.*
> *But at longshoremen's picnics—where accents are high—*
> *Fair Harvard's not present—so they call him Adlai.*

Stevenson sent the verse to Mrs. Ives and told the old man he was "enchanted." A correspondence ensued, and each of the old man's letters was longer and more arch than the one preceding it, until finally Stevenson told Carol Evans to reply in his stead. More than once Stevenson fell into profitless correspondence, and even made speech commitments, because he was "enchanted" with strangers' letters. He made several speeches in July.[11]

[11] On July 11 he attended a luncheon in Chicago for Dr. Albert Schweitzer, the physician, philosopher, and musician who won world reknown as a hu-

Adlai III was spending the summer in Springfield working on the newspaper there. He remembers occasional official trips with his father to mental hospitals, penitentiaries, and to make speeches. "He was always very eager to have the kids along with him." Stevenson told Alicia Patterson on July 16, "If we can work out a settlement . . . she will then go to Nevada or somewhere in late Sept [to divorce him]. Its all very painful and difficult, but I'm long since reconciled to it as the only solution. If only she hadn't talked so much & so irrationally it could be done quietly and with dignity. But there seems to be no way to suppress her talk. . . . I know you won't say a word. I've taken almost no one into my confidence except some of her friends—or our friends to whom she has talked." At Mrs. Ives's request, Mrs. Shaw, the Christian Science practitioner, again sent him religious counsel.

He asked the director of public health to arrange with the U. S. Public Health Service for "an efficiency analysis" of his staff but privately told Jane and Edison Dick that he suspected "there is a sort of fraternity among public health people and instead of finding a lot of unnecessary jobs they will recommend more!" He was always prowling around the government, trying to tighten it like a tympanist while an orchestra tunes up. He was considering "a vigorous effort" to defeat obstructionist Republicans in the Senate. He issued a statement commenting on a public complaint by Mayor Kennelly about state aid to Chicago. More than once he met with Chicago officials who wanted a special session of the legislature.

On August 11 he went to an Old Settlers' Picnic at Metamora, where Grandfather Stevenson had gone in 1858 to practice law. It was a sentimental journey for him, and although any orator would have spent a good part of his speech on Illinois history on such an occasion, it had a special meaning for Adlai Stevenson, and he spoke movingly of Illinois's heritage. His historical references were not ones dug up for the occasion; they were always on his mind.

---

manitarian in Africa and became an idol of certain American liberals. A few years later Stevenson visited Schweitzer in Africa and admired him greatly. Stevenson spoke to the Veterans of Foreign Wars in Springfield on July 5, striking a familiar theme: citizens first, veterans second. It was Stevenson's reaction to pressure-group politics, and he showed it over and over. On July 15 he attended a performance of *Abe Lincoln in Illinois* at New Salem State Park, where Lincoln's home town as a young man had been reconstructed. On July 2 he attended the dedication of a Pillsbury Flour plant in Springfield. On the twenty-eighth he spoke at a Soldiers and Sailors Reunion in Salem. On July 31 he went up to Camp McCoy, Wisconsin, where the Illinois National Guard was training, and spoke on peace.

Driving about the state, accompanied by one of his sons or by a friend, he was forever pointing out some obscure historical site and delivering a lecture—or, rather, telling yarns—about it. He had, one dares suggest, always loved Illinois; but never realized how much he loved it until he became Governor and, as such, its custodian for a brief time. That he cared came through to audiences. And he enjoyed presiding over the State Fair that opened next day.

It is illustrative of two aspects of Stevenson's role as Governor that on August 19 Vincent Sheean suggested that he invite Nehru to Springfield during the Indian Prime Minister's forthcoming visit to Chicago, and that on the same day Stevenson, having received from Jack Arvey a complaint from a downstate county chairman that he wasn't getting enough patronage, told Mulroy to find out "exactly where we stand" with respect to having replaced Republicans with Democrats in order to arm Stevenson against "this restlessness and criticism" among the county chairmen.

Stevenson was secretly preparing a major move against organized gambling in Illinois. In confidence he told Irving Dilliard, editorial writer on the St. Louis *Post-Dispatch,* that he wished local citizens and law enforcement officers would "give us a chance" to intervene in counties wide open to gambling. But, he said, only this week the sheriff and state's attorney of Lake County, a Republican county, had "blandly" advised him that they had received "*no* complaints of gambling in that county," which was wide open. He wrote, "I would like to tell you in confidence what we are trying to do to get on top of this vexatious business in the open counties where we can get no cooperation from the local officials. What we are trying to do must be done quietly and without publicity or it won't work." Before long he moved.

With all bills signed or vetoed and the State Fair over, Stevenson, after changing his mind several times, made vacation plans: he would simply spend a long Labor Day weekend either with the Dutch Smiths in Canada at Desbarats or the Sidleys in Wyoming. Finally leaving for Desbarats with Adlai III and Tim Ives, Stevenson told Alicia Patterson: "My domestic situation is clarifying and altho I hate to give her so much money I must do it I suppose to have an end to this business. I suppose she will go west after Oct. 1. Meanwhile the boys are all at home after their scattered summer and the house is gay and beautiful. Its heartbreaking to see it all collapse for no reason I can understand. But I guess it better so."

27

He was back in Springfield on September 8. Carl McGowan now joined his personal staff, replacing Wally Schaefer. McGowan, a tall slender young lawyer with a bony face, deep-set eyes, and an almost excruciatingly incisive mind, had, with his wife, visited Stevenson during a weekend in June. McGowan recalls, "He asked us down to see the lovely old Mansion, to see the tomb," that is, Lincoln's tomb, "and all that. While we were there, Stevenson told me that Schaefer wanted to go back to the Northwestern Law School. He told me that I had been there a year so I was not leaving them high and dry. Well, the upshot of it was, I took the job with him to start on Labor Day of 1949." Stevenson had been trying to get him for a long time. He was right. On substance, on policy, and on questions of principle versus political expediency, McGowan became Stevenson's most valuable adviser throughout the remainder of his governorship and the 1952 campaign. One man close to Stevenson went so far as to say that McGowan was "Stevenson's conscience," and although some Stevenson admirers might find it difficult to entertain the idea that Adlai Stevenson needed someone to supply a conscience, the fact is that any politician does, or at least needs someone to prod his conscience. McGowan performed the further invaluable function of saying no to Stevenson, a role not common around public men. Now in Springfield McGowan and Ed Day were the two staff members with offices next to Stevenson's own basement office in the Mansion. (A little later, Bill Blair replaced Ed Day.) Lou Kohn had returned to his Chicago law practice. Mulroy still headed the staff at the Statehouse.

Stevenson wrote to Alicia Patterson: "Ellen leaves Sat for Boston to see the boys all put away in school & then back here the end of the month to pack up, close up the settlement & leave for the west—and there will end the first volumes of two lives that could have been easily happy & successful. Why did it end in Greek ghastliness? I don't know, in spite of harrowed hours of prayer & search. Am I mad? Is she? I don't know—but nothings left & the eyes are dry, and I'm staggering on & on this fantastic routine without the faintest idea where I'm going or why? Come when you can." He printed the signature "A" upside down, almost as though to symbolize his own confused emotions.

He was developing a disarming approach to his audiences, many of which were predominantly Republican. Speaking September 27 to the Litchfield Chamber of Commerce, he began: "I don't feel much like a politician tonight and not at all like the Governor. So I hope you will not be disappointed if I am quite informal in my remarks, and if I don't attempt to be profound about taxes, the cold war, the high cost of living, or any of the other weighty issues of the day. Not that I don't have some opinions on those questions, but I have little reason to think they are any more competent than your own. And furthermore, I thought you might prefer that I chat with you on a more personal, intimate basis—that you would be interested in hearing about some of the experiences I have had and the impressions I have gained about the governorship of Illinois since I took office last January. After all, we are virtually next-door neighbors and there's nothing wrong with neighbors chatting over the back fence for a few minutes!" People, he said, imagined he could do anything. "A great many people seem to have the idea that all I have to do is snap my fingers and magical things will happen; that a bridge will be built, a new highway will go in, or even that I can get your federal income taxes or your rent reduced—or that an airport will appear. I am happy to say, by the way, that we hope to be of some help to your Litchfield airport." He received, he said, about 500 letters a day, except during a legislative session, when the volume soared. Eight or ten letters a day invited him to attend public functions. Some letters amazed him. "Just this week a woman wrote me a letter suggesting I compel her ex-husband to pay her $1,200 back alimony. A man wrote to ask whether I thought it was true that Sam Houston once shot an Indian at five thousand yards, and shooting over a hill at that! . . . A fifth-grade farm boy wrote to ask whether he could be compelled to 'walk further than my mailbox' to catch the school bus."

Having warmed up his audience, he moved into substantive matter. He said, "I want more than I have ever wanted anything to improve the quality of public administration in Illinois." He spoke at length of the growth of the state and the demands on its government. He talked about the budget and the reasons for its growth. And finally he came to what he really wanted to say to them: that the gasoline tax had to be increased if Illinois wanted to avoid a "complete breakdown" of its highway system. He made the case at length, building public support against the next legislature. He closed with an optimistic view of Illinois's future and a statement that partisanship was becoming "less and less important at the state and local level." It was a speech he made over and over, with variations, during his term, amusing, even funny, but always at its core an issue or a cause for which he pleaded in a reasoned and frequently non-partisan way. And always with an insistence that his only aim was to arouse citizens' interest to help him give Illinois good government. It was a strong position and a credible one—it suited his personality, and he believed it.

Bud Merwin told Stevenson on September 23 that Mrs. Ives had caused an uproar in the *Pantagraph* office by going there and loudly criticizing the staff, causing the society editor to flee the room weeping and later, together with her husband, the paper's best city reporter, to offer to resign. Bud Merwin sent Mrs. Ives a strong letter of protest, with a copy to Stevenson, telling Stevenson that one of the girls on the staff said, "She always speaks to us as though we were hirelings and the very dust under her queenly feet." Stevenson sent the correspondence to Ernest Ives, calling it "very distressing"— Stevenson needed nothing more distressing just now—and asking his advice. Ives reported that Mrs. Ives had sent her regrets to Bud Merwin, and Ives himself had talked to Merwin and they had agreed to drop the matter. Stevenson told Ives, "I am sure she does not realize the effect on the staff of the Pantagraph."

As he did to so many special interest groups, Stevenson told the state convention of the AFL, "Although you have banded together to advance the interests of labor, you are first of all citizens."

On September 29 he flew to Chicago to speak to a Conference on State Government Reorganization. On the way he wrote to Alicia Patterson—he would spend "a critical, harrowing day of finalities at home." As usual, Stevenson's state of mind about the divorce showed through most clearly in the letter to Alicia: "I'm a little bruised but utterly emancipated now."

That night, in editions dated next day, the divorce story became news. The *Herald-American,* the Chicago Hearst paper, had heard of the divorce earlier and its city editor had called Stevenson, who asked him not to print the story until he issued a statement. Bill Flanagan had told the *Herald-American* there was a chance of reconciliation. George Tagge of the *Tribune* now called, and Stevenson told him he had nothing to say and said he hoped for "the same consideration" from the *Tribune* that he had received from the *Herald-American.* About 2 A.M. Bill Flanagan got a call from a St. Louis newspaper. He realized the story could not be held and called Stevenson's bedroom in the Mansion. Flanagan has said that Stevenson was badly upset and his first reaction was to "blast the *Tribune.*" Flanagan saw him at breakfast at 6 A.M. and persuaded him to issue a calm statement instead. Actually, the *Tribune* story was not objectionable. Indeed it went out of its way to attribute the divorce to "growing incompatibility of temperament of

Mrs. Stevenson's distaste for public life and the publicity attendant upon the Governor's political career," to say the negotiations had been "friendly," to say both Stevenson and his wife were determined that the divorce be obtained "fairly and honestly and according to law" and without false evidence common in Illinois, to say that none of the usual grounds for divorce in Illinois such as desertion or cruelty existed, and to say "the Stevensons are in harmony on all questions of property settlement." It added, "Mrs. Stevenson has had no interest in public honors for herself and has steadfastly avoided, whenever possible, the publicity attending the Governor's official life. . . . Stevenson, on the other hand, has been equally insistent upon following up his political career vigorously. He regards his career and political activities as civic duties." The Chicago *Sun-Times* carried a shorter story.

Stevenson's statement said: "I am deeply distressed that due to the incompatibility of our lives Mrs. Stevenson feels that a separation is necessary. Although I don't believe in divorce I will not contest it. We have separated with the highest mutual regard." A photograph of him taken that day showed no expression on his face unless it was a trace of forbearance. Stevenson, in some agitation, wrote out telegrams in longhand. He sent one to Mrs. Carpenter at Beverly, Massachusetts, begging her to persuade Ellen to abide by a commitment to say nothing, even privately. (She reassured him.) He sent another to Borden at the Choate School, who apparently had been told nothing: "Mother has been unhappy and feels that we must be divorced. The story came out prematurely in today's papers. You boys will divide your vacations with mother and me and I will keep the farm. Please do not worry. Everything is all right. Love and best luck. Dad." School officials notified Borden. He was badly upset. John Fell had just entered Milton, and Adlai III told him about it at Aunt Lucy's house in Cambridge, shortly before the *Tribune* broke the story.

Stevenson once told McGowan that Ellen had felt "hemmed in and couldn't find self-expression," adding, "I don't understand it but that's what she said." McGowan admired Stevenson's fortitude. "He never did complain about his family situation's deterioration. Or about times the boys were disappointing. He took it as the way it is." For a time after Ellen vacated the house, Stevenson continued to go home to Libertyville weekends. "He was a lonely guy," his secretary, Margaret Munn, said. Later he leased the house to the young Marshall Fields and spent weekends with friends in Lake Forest or the Near North Side of Chicago.

Stevenson's frame of mind at the time the divorce story broke is clear in a letter to Alicia Patterson written the following weekend: "Darling Elisha—Its Sunday night and all is still in my gloomy mansion, after a frenzied, feverish week. I've read & reread your two letters. They were better than you think and gave me what I needed when I needed it most. . . . You must not grieve for me, my darling. I was long since reconciled to it as I told you. There's much that I don't understand about life and human relationships, but there was little left for us, except the children, I know—whatever the reasons or the justice or injustice. I feel no resentment or bitterness or pain and as for the bewilderment, I've surrendered to the inscrutable. But I *am* troubled about Ellen & her future." He related how the *Tribune* had refused to hold the story as the *Herald-American* had. "It was a 'typical Tribune' performance, but I must say the story was good. . . . Anyway the first ordeal is over and now if we can only finish it with dignity!"

Stevenson and his wife, through their lawyers, reached agreement on terms on October 19—he would keep the house, he would pay her $32,000 in a lump sum for her interest in it, she would remove certain articles from it, Stevenson would turn over the life insurance policy on Mrs. Carpenter's life to Ellen. Custody of the children would be joint, and their education Stevenson's responsibility. There remained the dreary business of settling odds and ends— Stevenson sent Bentley a list of household furnishings Ellen was to remove. And he gave Ellen a demand note for the $32,000. (He paid it December 23, having sold securities to raise the money.)

From Nevada in November, Ellen wrote friendly notes—she had had her Thanksgiving dinner, a club sandwich beside the swimming pool; she was "horrified" that she had thrown away various household articles before learning he wanted them; she proposed deferring Christmas plans until the boys came home because "some persons might consider it heartless of you to demand all three boys for Xmas and leave me alone in Lib. my LAST Xmas there," and she added, with a touch of venom, "But apparently that idea has not occurred to you—or was of no importance." Years later Ellen told Jane Dick, "Do you remember the last thing I said to you? 'Please take care of Adlai. Just do anything to make him happy so that I won't feel guilty.' Well, you've certainly lived up to it and I thank you." On December 8, addressing him as "Dear Ad" and signing herself "Aff. Ellen," Ellen said, "The time has gone very quickly. I rented a typewriter and a radio and they let me use the hotel piano. The press is after me now but I think they are going to be well behaved. . . . At least I have had over five weeks of peace and a wonderful rest. . . . Hoping all goes well with you."

On December 12, 1949, she received her divorce decree. The ground was, routinely, "mental cruelty." Bentley telegraphed Stevenson, who was at the Metropolitan Club in Washington at the time, "Operation successfully completed this morning. Prognosis for patient is good." He and Boyden examined a certified copy of the decree and found it satisfactory. The cleanup of legal details went on for several weeks. The commotion over lesser matters went on longer— the following May, Stevenson, having given friends permission to use the Libertyville house for six months, visited it and wrote Ellen, who by then had moved to 1362 North Astor Street, asking the whereabouts of "the miscellaneous spices" and the Waring mixer, card tables, "large nickel plated cork screw in bar," and "my green rubber boots." He wrote, "I think the purpose of the list was to eliminate any misunderstandings. . . . I found the flat silver in the clothes box and am storing it in a safe. Thanks for wrapping it up." One recalls "the family silver" of yesteryear. And the next day he wrote a touching note (though he probably did not intend it that way): "Referring to the inventory of things to be removed from the house, I also find that the Cheese Ventor painting, which you will find listed at the bottom of page 4, was to stay in the house. I did not see it when I was there on Sunday and if it is put away somewhere, please leave it out so I can hang it. I think I would like it just where you had it, inside on the north wall of the living room." He addressed her as "Dear Ellen" and closed, "Yours." Problems with Ellen went on till the end of his life.

28

On October 5, Hubert H. Humphrey, then national chairman of Americans for Democratic Action, asked Stevenson, along with many others, to sign an ADA-sponsored public statement attempting to strengthen President Truman's hand in forcing steel companies to come to terms with their striking workers. Carl McGowan advised against it and against even acknowledging the request.

He was making a good many speeches in Illinois that fall. His most important speech, however, he would make in New York at the *Herald Tribune* Forum on Monday, October 24. He had worried about the speech beforehand. He also had made complicated plans around the occasion. He would go to Choate to visit Borden on Saturday. On Sunday he would go to New York and on Monday attend President Truman's laying of the cornerstone at the UN building. The *Herald Tribune* Forum would be held Monday night. He asked Alicia to attend. He wrote a first draft of the Forum speech in longhand on odd scraps of paper, had it retyped, revised and revised it. It was his first political speech to a national audience. He was nervous about it. And it came just a few days after the final settlement with Ellen. His reading copy was heavily revised, probably at the last moment.

The assigned topic was, "The Kind of Democrat I Am." In his speech he said people cared little about party labels. He was not sure what kind of Democrat he was but was sure what kind he was not: "I'm not one of those who believes we should have a Democratic regime because it is good for the Democratic Party. If the Democratic Party is not good for the nation, then it is not good for Democrats or for me." He went on, "I have no fixed principles by which every issue is to be automatically resolved. I do not identify big government with good government. I entertain no ambition for the Democratic Party to set the track record for what President Hoover recently called the last mile to socialism. I think government should be as small in scope and as local in character as possible. But it is the job that needs doing that must shape and delimit the area of governmental activity." He then said that "perhaps the best way to find out what one is is from what one does," and he candidly recounted his record in Illinois.

Then he went on, "I'm an internationalist. . . . I think that peace is the most important unfinished business of our generation; that we are going to be in this brutal cold war for a long time to come." He elevated the level of discourse: "I don't like doles. I don't like subsidies. I don't like any interference with free markets, free men and free enterprise. I like freedom to succeed, or to fail. But I also know that there can be no real freedom without economic justice, social justice, equality of opportunity and a fair chance for every individual to make the most of himself. And I know that there is little the man on the assembly line or the plow can do to affect the chain of events which may close his factory or foreclose his mortgage."

It was a good speech, lucid, well structured, sensible. In the context of the embittered partisan politics of that time, when Truman was President and Congress was opposing much of his program, when China was falling under Communist rule and setting the stage for a red-hunt in the State Department, it sounded statesmanlike indeed. It was, moreover, an excellent statement of Stevenson's basic political position—a middle-of-the-road Democratic liberalism with appeal to "independent" voters yet holding such bastions of his party's voting strength and intellectual content as FEPC and labor legislation. From this position he seldom deviated.

He worked over a list of priorities for the 1951 legislature, more than a year away, listing nineteen major topics. At the top of the list were additional general revenue, good roads, constitutional reform, and gambling. McGowan, in a letter over Stevenson's signature, instructed all administration leaders to prepare bills they wanted introduced and to submit them to Stevenson by September 1. McGowan was taking hold.

Stevenson began to move against organized gambling—issued a statement on November 4 threatening a statewide gambling crackdown if local law enforcement failed. He told Alicia Patterson, "I'm getting in deeper and deeper here and I have a premonition that I'm going to skin my nose. I meant to send you clippings from today's papers, but left them in the car—'Stevenson Threatens Gambling Crackdown' etc. I think I hear a muffled, hollow laugh from Cairo to Wis!" She evidently went to Springfield; he wrote to her briefly on November 25 about her visit there.

After the Thanksgiving weekend he held a series of political meetings and gave a dinner for the Supreme Court justices. On Friday, December 9, he attended a meeting of the Board of Managers of the Governors' Conference in Chicago, spoke to the CIO State Convention about his past and future legislative program, and left for Washington to attend the winter dinner of the Gridiron Club, a luncheon sponsored by the Citizens Committee for the Hoover Report, and a reception and dinner for former President Hoover at the Shoreham. It was at this time that Stevenson renewed a friendship with Dorothy Fosdick.

Dorothy Fosdick was the daughter of Harry Emerson Fosdick, the well-known Protestant minister in New York. A rather small, attractive, quick and bright young woman, she was at that time a member of the Policy Planning Staff of the State Department and moved in high circles of the United States Government. Stevenson had known her at least since the San Francisco Conference which wrote the United Nations Charter and had seen her later in Washington and London. Now in December of 1949 they saw each other again and began a relationship which lasted until sometime in the summer of 1952. She wrote him many long letters which were a mélange of love letters, religious counsel, political advice, information on foreign policy and national security. At the time they began, he was, so to speak, on the rebound from his divorce. As he became immersed in presidential politics, the letters stopped.

He saw her on December 10, and the following Monday he delivered a long thoughtful speech at the Hoover Commission luncheon on state-federal relationships. That was the day Stevenson received the telegram from his attorney that he was divorced. He went back to Springfield and wrote to Alicia Patterson—he had telephoned her repeatedly but been unable to reach her. He was exhausted and irritated by his heavy schedule. He had sat at the head table at the Gridiron Dinner—"was introduced for a bow with Lausche and a crack about '52." He asked her to plan a rendezvous in January. He ended, "Ellen got her divorce yesterday & I felt as though it was the end of an era & a dismal failure for me—and all of us." There it was again—that curious ambivalence about the divorce, a sense of bewilderment, almost as though he and Ellen had stumbled down the road that ended in Nevada, that deep sense of failure which smothered any thought he might have had of a future with Alicia Patterson. One wonders whether he ever seriously intended to remarry.

Back in Illinois he carried on with his speeches and official business. On December 22 he gave a Christmas party for his staff though he felt no real enthusiasm for it. Things improved—his sons arrived; and the day after Christmas he told Alicia Patterson, "Its been a glorious holiday. All three boys have been here, my sister & brother in law & their boy—and Ellen *sent* them, I didn't beg. . . . So it all worked wonderfully & I've had 3 dream days—no work and all play. Buffy did most of the appalling Christmas work. I don't know what I'd have done without her what with all the presents, all the traditional entertaining etc—and its not over yet. On Wed we're having a dance!" He was planning to visit her in Georgia on January 11. "Forgive this wretched scrawl—John Fell is sitting on the desk & in my lap mostly and wonders what I'm doing."

A dance at the Mansion on December 28 was a great success. Mrs. Ives conceived it, remembering how she and Stevenson had gone to the Mansion when they were young and Dunne was Governor, and she made the arrangements. Stevenson wrote letters to the parents of the girls invited. Inviting the Dicks' daughters, he asked Jane Dick to "sort of manage to herd them all onto the same train." Of 155 invited, 94 accepted. The girls stayed at the Mansion. Stevenson vacated his own bedroom and moved into the servants' wing for the night. It was a happy time, a good end to a hard year. On New Year's Eve, Mrs. Welling wrote to him, "Life being apparently a continuous test of character, you go to the head of the class. For almost never have I seen anyone take such tough tests so well, with such maturity. . . . I'm *glad* you've been having such fun with your boys lately—And I trust that the first half-hundred years will prove to have been the hardest. . . . Bless you—you're doing fine!" She was a good friend. He went to the New Year's Eve party at the Kelloggs'.

29

In 1950, Stevenson began to get on top of the job of governing. Carl McGowan has said, "As his name became better known the politicians knew they were stuck with him. When I went to Springfield in 1949, in the bars around town I'd hear five or ten people saying, 'Of course he's an accident, a one-termer.' Within six months, surely by the next summer, you *never* heard this. They recognized they couldn't keep him from being nominated for a second term. This means they recognized the fact of his political power. It was due to his own hard work, his radio speeches, his appearances. All this began to affect the people. The man in the street operates on net impressions. They'll say so-and-so is a good President but they couldn't give you one reason why they think so. The moment comes when people start to say, 'That fellow Stevenson seems to be all right.' This happened early in 1950 for Stevenson. He was accepted by the people. He had great political power. He was an organization man—he believed in the Democratic Party and the Democratic organization. He wanted to give jobs to Democrats and to see the party strong. He didn't want to ignore the party leadership. At this time he was greatly preoccupied with the Horner story. I was living in the Mansion. This was September of 1949 to May of 1950. There was just the two of us living there. We'd go for a walk in the late afternoon, we ate together, at night he'd be working in one side office and I'd be in the other. He was haunted by the Horner story. He thought that because Horner had gotten himself at odds with the Chicago organization, therefore to win he had to turn to the downstaters who were worse than anyone in Chicago—John Stelle and the rest of them—and therefore Horner's whole ability to work in the public interest was compromised. Nobody in the Chicago organization ever seemed as evil as John Stelle or Paul Powell. Stevenson felt it was vital not to be driven into the arms of the southern Democrats. It ruined Horner's life. Horner was a county judge, an educated man, a Lincoln scholar, he had money, he was a man about town, he came from an upper-class Jewish family. This was *really* on Stevenson's mind. Some Democrats were thinking about opposing him in the primary of 1952. He was damned interested in running again. Harry Hershey would come over and talk about it on the glass porch of the Mansion. He would tell us how John Stelle used to live across the street and Horner used to stand here and look at Stelle's house and say, 'I'm determined to keep them out. I've got to stop them.' It made a great impression on Stevenson."

McGowan had quickly become Stevenson's right-hand man. Most of the other staff members—Flanagan, Irvin, Hyndman—accepted this, but Jim Mulroy felt displaced. McGowan said, "I never could understand Jim. He was very insecure. He had won a Pulitzer Prize and started out as a whiz kid. Then he fell on leaner days, probably related to drinking. When he came to the Stevenson campaign he was flat. Suddenly they won. Mulroy felt he had fallen into something beyond his wildest hopes. He thought of himself as the No. 1 guy. Because of his basic insecurity, it bothered him to see bright young men show up. Ed Day and I were at the Mansion. He was at the Capitol. It hurt him. He wasn't up to being Adlai Stevenson's brain trust. It got worse and worse—Mulroy got unhappier and unhappier—he drank a lot—the whole thing was unsatisfactory. I liked him—he was an engaging Irishman. In later days he was not figuring in the decisions. He hung around with legislators in order to seem important." It led to his ultimate downfall.

On January 2, Stevenson broadcast his first year-end report to the people on "my first year in office, and also my first year in politics!" Some people contended it was a mistake to make these radio reports, he said, but he felt that "one of our gravest problems" was the lack of discussion of local and state government. Much was said about the danger of concentrating too much power in Washington. The best antidote was effective state government. "Too many of the problems of states' rights have been created by states' wrongs." He reviewed the past year and said his biggest headache had been organized gambling. It could only exist where local officials tolerated it. He had been asked to move in with the state police. He resisted this—it would cost money, it meant asking a higher level of government to do what a lower one should. But gambling must be attacked, and he proposed to act. He argued at length for an increase in the gasoline tax, then moved to the budget—"talking about the budget is tiresome, I know, but it is very important to you who have to pay the bill." Then, "Politicians often speak of 'giving' the people good government. But one can't really give good government to the people. Good government is not a gift; it is an achievement. It has a price—the price that must be paid in time and energy and mental sweat in order to understand and to inform others of our problems; the price of examining all sides of public issues; the price of subordinating your own immediate interest to the long-range welfare of the whole people. That's the price of good government. But the price of poor government is infinitely higher."

Those who knew Stevenson only in his later years at the United Nations might be surprised at his interest in state problems. But while he was Governor he was absorbed in them. McGowan has said, "He was a man who liked his job and was very happy in it. Part of this was his old historical sense. The traditions of Illinois—his roots were there—the old Governor's Mansion—the thought he was doing an important job. He went about it with a style you don't find in Governors. The little things—inviting all the living daughters of former Governors to a weekend at the Mansion. He *made* Springfield a different place. The natives there felt when he was there that life was brighter and more sparkling—it was a reflection of the feeling he had himself—'God, isn't it great that I and my family who have lived here and in Bloomington for all these years now am sitting in the Governor's chair?' The efforts to have a Lincoln play put on at New Salem were connected with this. He got a lift when he rolled over the highways in that old Cadillac, seeing this, seeing that, talking to the people and so on. He wanted people to be interested in the problems of the state. The press didn't cover state problems but it began to give him more coverage because he had flair."

30

It was an election year—not only all Congressmen and many local officials were up for election but also, in Illinois, United States Senator Scott Lucas, President Truman's floor leader. Stevenson delivered a Jackson Day Dinner speech in Missouri January 7. By 1900, he said, the Republican Party had "lost its bearings." It had "cast its lot with power, money, big business and the employer. . . ." One by one the Republican Party deserted the farmer, the working man, the small businessman; they deserted the people, and at last the people deserted them. Now the Republicans were deeply divided between yearning for the "dear, dead past" and expedient "me tooism." He summed up American progress in the first half of the twentieth century and claimed credit for the Democratic Party —it had had faith in the ordinary man. He asked what of the next half century, when our quest for peace, prosperity, and equality must extend to millions around the world. He said he did not know whether we could afford all the things we would like to do to improve the lot of the average man, but "anguished cries of 'statism,' 'welfare state,' and particularly 'socialism'" had been heard before: from those who opposed FDR's reforms. He described prosperity under the Democrats. But, "If we can't balance our national budget now, when will we? And I hope and pray that history will never record that the Democratic Party foundered on the rocks of fiscal irresponsibility after leading America boldly, wisely, courageously, through two world wars and the most extensive social revolution in the shortest period of time in history." It was a characteristic Stevenson stance— and syntax. He praised the two-party system. "In the present critical days when so much of the world's destiny depends on our being right, it is particularly important that there be a strong opposition party which can contribute to the solution of our problems at home and abroad more than epithets and witch hunts."

Epithets and witch hunts—it was an idea that preoccupied Stevenson increasingly as time passed. A little later, on February 9, Senator Joseph McCarthy of Wisconsin made his famous speech at Wheeling, West Virginia, in which he said the State Department was full of Communists and he and the Secretary of State knew their names. By spring McCarthy was a "towering figure," as Richard Rovere has pointed out. Ultimately, he held two Presidents captive or nearly so, had an enormous impact on American foreign policy, cowed Senators contemptuously, ruined careers, helped defeat for re-election Senators who opposed him, all but destroyed George C. Marshall and other patriots, accused the Democratic Party of presiding over "twenty years of treason," and presented to the world a picture of an America that had lost its mind in mad pursuit of shadows. Rovere wrote that McCarthy had thrown the State Department into such a panic that it fired people he accused and that Secretary Acheson "spent a large part of 1950 and the ensuing years explaining to Elks, Moose, Women Voters, Legionnaires, Steel Workers, and the rest that he was not corrupt, that he was opposed to Communism, and that he did not hire traitors."

Stevenson increasingly feared that a party too long out of power, as the Republican Party had been, might succumb entirely to irresponsible "epithets and witch hunts," as he put it now in Missouri. It was an early warning.

Returning to Illinois, Stevenson flew to Lawrenceville to inspect flooded areas, then went to Alicia Patterson's plantation at Kingsland, Georgia, on January 11 and spent five days. Returning, he ran into a series of problems—patronage, gambling, inadequate public relief funds, and pressure to call a special session of the legislature to provide aid to Chicago. He went up to Chicago twice in January to make a string of speeches. It was almost as though he were campaigning, and, in a way, he was—his continuing campaign to educate the public. But something more was involved. Bill Flanagan once recalled, "Going back to the beginning, I thought this guy was presidential timber and I felt I was in a position to do something about it. And I began about 1950. He'd give a speech on welfare, and I'd locate people all over the country interested in welfare and I'd send them a copy of the speech. He gave me a list of his friends in Washington, too, for example, Eric Sevareid," the radio and television commentator. "I'd send them speeches. The Guv knew I was doing it. I started it but he knew. But he was talking on state subjects. I began losing my audience. I said to him, 'You've got to talk more on foreign affairs and national issues.' He said, 'I don't have time to work on it. Who can I get to write them?' I said, 'I don't know—don't you know anybody?' He said, 'I'll think about it.' One day Mulroy calls and says, 'You better go over and talk to the Governor. He's going to bring a guy from the UN here and that will kill him.' I was going to bring it up the next morning but Stevenson did—it was Porter McKeever. I said, 'I don't know—it might not look too good.' The UN was unpopular out here then. He said, 'He can live in the Mansion and nobody needs to know that he is here.' I said, 'You can't hide the guy. You're taking a big risk.' He said, 'I don't know.' A couple of days later he said, 'I won't do it. I'll have to do it myself.' So he started making speeches like that."

At the ADA's Roosevelt Day Dinner, he spoke of larger questions and Roosevelt's place in history: "He knew that at the time he became President he was . . . the one man who could mediate between the old epoch that was dying and the new one coming to birth," the seed of an eloquent phrase in his 1952 convention welcoming speech.

On January 23 he wrote to Alicia Patterson about the hidden problems of the governorship and said, "Oh, God, why do we ever leave that fairyland by the Black River!" He wrote again a few days later—he faced political crises. Tomorrow he would have to fire a state official he had appointed "& its going to be nasty. . . . Its going to raise political hell, but, ho hum, what do I care. I'm just going to be the best one term Gov. I can & then to hell with it."

His birthday party at the Mansion February 4–5 was the first of sixteen. Stevenson told Alicia that "5 couples of friends arrived from Chicago to help me celebrate—invited themselves—and we had 24 hours plus of undiluted merriment."[12] Every year thereafter until Stevenson's death one of the group would give a birthday party for him; the parties became famous. Stevenson described the "undiluted merriment" to Alicia: "First we all went down to Taylorville— changed into miners clothes accompanied by the usual confusion and female cackles & excitement. After a really fascinating exhibition of most modern electrical equipment at a coal face 5 miles from the foot of the shaft we had 'lunch'—at 4 PM at the Peabody executives club—fried chicken, baked beans and all the usual with liquor, wines and speeches. Back to Sp in time for an elegant dinner preceded by songs around the piano written for this momentous, historical celebration extolling the virtues of 'that wonderful, that wonderful etc. guy, Illinois' governor.' I took it with becoming dignity —I hope—covered with confusion and full of bursting heart. To finish the evening we all ended up at a night club to hear Hildegarde," a fashionable singer of that time. "And she was superb—even treated me with gentleness. Sunday we went to church; lunch & they headed back to Chicago leaving me very happy, surrounded with my letters, telegrams and presents from the Democratic faithful." Stevenson had the origin of the song wrong; it was set to the tune of "A Wonderful Guy," a song from the musical play *South Pacific,* then popular, and its chorus ended: "He's our Guv, he's our Guv, he's our Guv, he's our Guv, he's our Guv, he's a wonderful guy."

31

On February 1, Stevenson told Mulroy to "slow up on patronage except in the special and aggravating cases until after the primary. We may want some patronage left to take advantage of the change of circumstances." Stevenson told Paul Powell, "I am constantly baffled about the 'Republican holdovers' I hear so much about." On February 15, Powell told Irvin (misspelling his name) he had a request to fire a guard at Joliet penitentiary and another state employee at Joliet. Irvin, asking Stevenson's advice, said the Chicago organization had also been firing state employees for political reasons. Stevenson said he had authorized one of Powell's requests but added, "There must be NO vicing [firing for political reason] without consulting me by Chicago organ. or anyone else." Mulroy asked Steven-

---

[12] The guests included Mr. and Mrs. McDougal, Mr. and Mrs. Oates, Mr. and Mrs. John Dern (he had been a partner at the old Sidley law firm), Mr. and Mrs. Dutch Smith, Mr. and Mrs. Dick.

son if Irvin would covertly ask all department directors whom they could spare for political work in the primary, as was customary. Stevenson replied, "Yes. . . . We must be *very* careful not to let it be conspicuous—control the numbers sharply & give no general release for political activity." Thus did Stevenson covertly violate, for a limited period—about one month—his frequently reiterated insistence on a full day's work for a day's pay by state employees.

On February 7, Stevenson went down to Centre College at Danville, Kentucky, and delivered a commencement address. It was a sentimental occasion—his Grandfather Stevenson had been a student at Centre nearly a hundred years ago and had married the daughter of its president, Dr. Lewis Warner Green. "The power, for good or for evil, of the political organization which goes by the name of the United States of America is virtually beyond measurement," he said. "The decisions which it makes, the uses to which it devotes its immense resources, the leadership which it provides on moral as well as material questions, all appear likely to determine the fate of the modern world." The decision to build the hydrogen bomb carried responsibility "virtually immeasurable."

He adjured them: "Don't be afraid to learn; don't ever stop learning because at the very best you can know very little. And don't be afraid to live, to live hard and fast; not dissolutely and badly, but hard, fast and fearlessly. Because it is not the years in your life, but the life in your years that count. You'll have more fun, you'll do more good and you'll get and give more satisfaction the more you know, the more you've worked and the more you've lived. For this is a great and glorious adventure at a stirring time in the annals of man. Take it standing up boldly, not sitting down complaining, yawning and waiting for a pension. You have a better chance than many to give a lot, and therefore, take a lot out of life. If we can't look to people like you for leadership, for good judgment, for wise directions for yourselves and the convictions of our society, where can we look? For here at Centre which for a hundred and thirty years has transmitted from one generation to the next the riches of Western civilization you have gotten some grasp of the basic principles on which our culture is founded—the concept of supremacy of the individual, the worth of the individual, the worth of the individual human being and the necessity for a climate of freedom in which these values may find means of expression."

He then proceeded to his familiar survey of the first half of the twentieth century, ending with the competition between democracy and Communism. Our success in that competition hung upon our ability to win the allegiance of millions of uncommitted people throughout the world. Their choice would be shaped by our performance. "It will turn upon such things as our ability to avoid the disruptions of depression, to guarantee equality of opportunity, to narrow the gulfs separating economic status, to preserve freedom of thought and action, to make democracy accord in practice with its premises and professions of faith. We won't resist the Soviet impact on the Western world with a schizophrenic society which protests its devotion to democratic ideals while it indulges in undemocratic practices. If Western civilization is to save its body, it must save its soul too."

He urged them not to stand aside from the great decisions of their time. Only responsible citizens could make government good. "For these tasks and these exciting opportunities, use the equipment that God and this college have given you, and that your own industry each day improves. Use your heart and your head, and not your prejudices. You are more than the social animal Seneca spoke of. Man is a moral agent with the power of making choices affecting not only himself but countless others. And man can hope. Not animals, only mankind, can hope. It is because we are more than animals that we can blow ourselves off the face of this planet in the next fifty years. But it is also because we are more than animals that we can make this world a better place than it has ever been before."

Stevenson made many commencement speeches during the rest of his life but none better than this. It foreshadowed the eloquence, the lofty thought, the complex syntax, the idealism, the appeal to reason and to the best in human nature that, a little more than two years later, moved millions.

A national coal crisis had been building up for months. Now the miners went on strike. The federal government fought them with an injunction and contempt proceedings. In Illinois, Stevenson intervened and after difficult negotiations achieved a settlement. He told Alicia Patterson angrily "that damn Tribune" gave him no credit for it though he had "done more than any northern governor in the country to keep his state going."

He congratulated young Marshall Field on his engagement to Kay Woodruff and invited them to Springfield for a "Democratic indoctrination." More than a social visit was involved—in his 1948 campaign for the governorship, Stevenson had had the support of Marshall Field III, young Marshall's father; but now young Marshall was taking over the *Sun-Times,* and it was by no means certain that he was as enthusiastic about Stevenson as his father or, for that matter, about the Democratic Party and liberalism generally. At about this time, Dutch Smith was trying to arrange for Marshall Field III and his wife, Ruth, to visit Stevenson in Springfield. He succeeded on April 19. Stevenson attended a party for Kay Woodruff at the Casino Club in Chicago on April 28 and the wedding reception when she married young Marshall on May 12. Dutch Smith worked it all out, cementing the relationship between Stevenson and both generations of Fields, a relationship that would figure importantly in Stevenson's affairs until his death—he never had a more loyal friend than Ruth Field.

He continued his appointed rounds—big speeches, lesser speeches, a television appearance, meetings with staff and state officials and politicians and legislators, visits to a hospital and a penitentiary, policy meetings on highways and aid to Chicago, and ceremonial occasions, the most important of which was the installation of Dick Daley as county clerk of Cook County, a powerful political job. On March 21, after a weekend in Chicago and Libertyville, during which he rode Glen Lloyd's horse ("as happy an hour . . . as I've had in a very long while"), he left on a two-week trip East and South. He spoke that night on the role of the states at the Fourth Annual Forum of the Philadelphia *Bulletin,* and a *Bulletin* man told him that he and others in the audience favored him for President in 1952. Stevenson went to Washington for what he called "a confused & rather fruitless day," hoping to see Dorothy Fosdick, then left the next day, March, 23, for Florida and a visit to Alicia Patterson in Georgia.

32

During this period two U. S. Senate investigations were starting that represented potential threats to Senator Lucas. Senator McCarthy followed his West Virginia speech with others and, on February 20, delivered a six-hour speech to the Senate describing what he called Communist influence in the State Department. Although as Richard Rovere has pointed out, McCarthy had come upon the "communists in government issue" almost by chance, and although not even the first part of his famous sentence at Wheeling was true ("I have here in my hand a list of 205 [persons] that were known to the Secretary of State as being members of the Communist party and who, nevertheless, are still working and shaping policy in the State Department")—he had no list of any kind in his hand—and although during these early sallies he kept mentioning at various times 205, 57, and 81 Communists, nevertheless after the Senate speech something had to be done. On February 21, Senator Lucas offered and the Senate unanimously adopted a resolution calling for an investigation. Senator Millard E. Tydings of Maryland became its chairman, and it held thirty-one days of hearings between March 8 and June 28, in the course of which McCarthy charged ten individuals by name with Communist activities. During that time the country seemed to be paying little attention to anything else. The Democratic majority of the Tydings Committee reported on July 20 that McCarthy's charges were false and said, "We have seen the technique of the 'Big Lie,' elsewhere employed by the totalitarian dictator with devastating success, utilized here for the first time on a sustained basis in our history." This did not end the matter. Although the Korean War, which began that summer, for a time took the headlines away from McCarthy, he recaptured and held them, off and on, for five years. McCarthy worked to defeat Senator Lucas for re-election that November, and many people gave him considerable credit for doing so (and many people also thought he was almost single-handedly responsible for the defeat of Senator Tydings).

The other investigation was into interstate crime, led by Senator Estes Kefauver of Tennessee. The Kefauver Committee held hearings across the nation from May 26 to the end of the year, attracting wide attention. After three days of closed hearings in Chicago in October, Kefauver said the Capone Syndicate still was powerful and he had found "evidence of gangsters muscling into legitimate business and of political ties between gangsters and politicians of both parties." Moreover, he obtained testimony from the Democratic candidate for sheriff of Cook County, already head of the state's attorney's police, that "I have been a gambler at heart." The candidate became known as "the richest cop in the world," with a net worth of some $360,000, money amassed (he said) by gambling in stocks and betting on football, prize fights, and elections. Newspapermen obtained part of the testimony; its publication hurt Senator Lucas more than the McCarthy hearings, most politicians thought, though Lucas himself was not shown to have ties to criminals.

Adlai Stevenson had anticipated the Kefauver hearings by moving against gamblers. Now, Illinois, especially Chicago, had a long tradition, going back to before prohibition, of organized crime and corrupt politicians. The Syndicate, as the heirs of Al Capone were collectively called, continued to control gambling, prostitution, and other rackets long after Capone himself was imprisoned. By the 1940s they had moved into labor unions and legitimate businesses. They controlled such things as the distribution of towels to office buildings, the sale of bottled water and certain beers and liquors to taverns, the sale of chalk to horse-betting handbooks. By murder they took over the nationwide system of telegraphic transmission of racing news, of which Chicago had long been the center. By murder or threats of murder they took over the numbers, or policy, racket. Their leaders always denied it but they were believed to have taken over the narcotics trade, at least in later years. Later, too, they went into the loan-shark business. They corrupted politicians and law enforcement officers. They contributed to the campaigns of politicians of both parties.

About 1944 the Chicago Syndicate made an alliance with a gang in the East St. Louis area for the purpose of extending its empire throughout the state, particularly its gambling network. Downstate gambling had been dominated by the downstate Shelton gang. In many counties it had run wide open; the gamblers paid off the local law enforcement officials. The St. Louis *Post-Dispatch* had criticized Governor Green harshly for permitting it. The collision of forces between the Chicago-East St. Louis gangs and the Shelton gang had produced the murder at Peoria of Bernie Shelton at the height of the 1948 political campaign. That murder had led to the disclosure of wide-open gambling, links between downstate politicians and gamblers, links between gamblers and Governor Green's state police, and the indictment, later dismissed, of a *Post-Dispatch* reporter by a supporter of Green.

In the 1948 campaign Stevenson's denunciation of corruption had helped elect him. He once said that as Governor he was besieged by requests from citizens to suppress gambling that local authorities ignored, but it seems more likely that he felt the pressure of his own campaign promises. His was a curious dilemma. He had been elected with the support of a political organization which, in some places, made deals with gamblers; he had also been elected with the support of newspapers and good-government groups which abhorred the crime-politics alliance. He abhorred it himself. Once, speaking at a country club, he discovered that the slot machines had been hidden in anticipation of his arrival; he told his audience that the last time he had visited the club a child had handed him a card to autograph and, turning it over, he had seen that it bore a statement worded so that, when he had signed, it would read in effect: "The slot machines in this club are for members only and meet with my approval. Adlai E. Stevenson." He once addressed the state convention of the American Legion on slot machines in Legion posts. He disliked the double-standard morality of respectable citizens who denounced corruption but played slot machines in their private clubs. Under Green, gambling, including roulette, had been wide open at the Lake Club, a night club outside Springfield frequented by legislators. After the election of Stevenson and a likeminded county prosecutor, it stopped.

During 1949 he and his Attorney General, Ivan Elliott, had quietly brought pressure to bear on local law enforcement officials. They had been only partly successful. In some counties gambling had stopped, in others it had stopped for a time then resumed, and in others it had continued unabated. Now in the spring of 1950 he began to move against the gamblers. He sent the state police to make gambling raids in Madison and St. Clair counties—the East St. Louis area—and in other counties where local officials refused to act. In moving, Stevenson was disturbing delicate political balances. Many politicians, including Dick Daley, opposed his doing it. Stevenson himself had misgivings about the state's doing what local authorities ought to do. But he went ahead. He met frequently that spring with Carl McGowan and the head of the state police, Captain O'Donnell. From time to time when raids were conducted, he issued statements. In a few months his police entered about 75 towns and raided about 300 gambling houses. The *Sun-Times* and *Post-Dispatch* ran encouraging editorials.

In September the Section on Criminal Law of the American Bar Association devoted its annual meeting in Washington to the menace of organized crime, and Stevenson delivered what may be considered his definitive speech on law enforcement. He said the state police raids had been "widely heralded as a 'crackdown'" on commercialized gambling but he regarded it as a "breakdown" as well—"the breakdown of local law enforcement, the breakdown of decency in government in many parts of the state, the triumph of greed, corruption and, perhaps worst of all, cynicism. In ordering these raids I did not feel the joyful exhilaration of a knight in shining armor tilting with the forces of darkness. I felt more like a mourner at a wake. For something had died in Illinois—at least temporarily. And what has happened in Illinois is by no means unique."

What could be done to improve law enforcement? he asked. Securing better personnel was part of the answer. Crime and politics had to be divorced; police forces severed from partisan political control. Policemen must be trained as professionals and paid adequate salaries. The Governor should be empowered to remove any local law enforcement officer who failed to do his duty. The Bar Association should disbar any lawyer who, holding a public law enforcement position, failed to do his duty. Congress should bar from interstate commerce slot machines and racing information. (Stevenson noted wryly that all the slot machine manufacturers were located in Chicago.)

The greatest obstacles, however, were "public indifference and cynicism." It was unfair to put the entire blame on the crime-politics alliance and assume that ordinary citizens were mere bystanders. "The respectable businessman who falls for the myth that a wide-open town is good for business is just as effective an accomplice of the criminal as is the politician. . . . The solid citizen who thinks that illegal slot machines are just fine for his country club but bad for the corner saloon does not realize what difficulties he is making for the persons he has elected to enforce the laws." Of 2,700 gambling machines now registered in Illinois, less than one third were in public places; 1,900 were in country clubs, fraternal organizations, veterans' clubs, army posts, and similar places.

Senator Kefauver congratulated Stevenson on his speech and put it into the Congressional Record. It was reprinted in the Bar Association *Journal,* widely praised in newspaper editorials and letters from lawyers, and Stevenson's staff distributed it widely. On October 5, Senator Kefauver, whose committee was holding closed hearings in Chicago, invited Stevenson to appear. He did, describing what he was doing about gambling in Illinois and recommending federal legislation. His raids continued.

In a sense, the state police gambling raids represented a turning point in Stevenson's governorship. In undertaking them, Stevenson was exerting a kind of leadership new to him. He had undertaken the raids only as a last resort. Doing so was politically risky, bringing him into conflict with local politicians whose support he would need in the next legislature and election. On the other hand, it redeemed a campaign pledge and consolidated the support of good-government groups and the press. Moreover, the raids may be taken as proof of what Carl McGowan said: that by 1950 Stevenson had established enough citizen support to command the respect of politicians. They knew he was not a "freak" or a "political accident" or a "one-term governor." That he made the raids indicates that he knew they knew—he was strong enough to move.

33

Eric Sevareid did a national radio broadcast from Springfield about Stevenson: "He is that rare creature, a reformer who was elected with the support of the hard-bitten political machine. . . . And therefore his position today is a rare one, exposed, dangerous, and exhaustingly difficult. But his ultimate record will be of consequence not only to this hitherto graft-ridden state, but perhaps to other Midwest states struggling to clean their political stables. Every governor in the land, like every crook in Illinois, is watching Stevenson." He delivered a highly favorable recitation of Stevenson's record to date, said Stevenson was not a dramatic reformer but a steady improver, described his troubles with the machine, and said his only hope was to reform so fast and effectively that he would bind the people to him and, like FDR, become stronger than the machine.

Stevenson kept making speeches, that is, going to the people almost incessantly. He told Alicia Patterson "I'm in another tailspin with no light in sight until May 8. Each time I wonder if I'm going to make it. Somehow I always do so I suppose I'll get thru this pressure crisis too. I'm enclosing a priceless E. B. White just in case you may have missed it." Somehow these letters seemed to have lost the deep love and the deep need for love that earlier letters to her had shown. On May 2 he dictated a letter to Dorothy Fosdick, replying to one from her, and saying he had suggested her as a speaker to the Chicago Council on Foreign Relations. On May 8 she sent him a statement by George Kennan on McCarthy for his speech material file. He urged her to continue sending him State Department material—"it all transports me to another world, albeit harrassed and difficult even as mine"—and he hoped she would visit him if she came to Illinois to speak, as he urged many others.

The Democrats were planning an elaborate national "Jefferson Jubilee" in Chicago for May 13–15. To publicize it, Stevenson emphasized the election contest between Senator Lucas and Everett Dirksen. He said the foreign policy issue was clearly drawn—Lucas was a "staunch supporter" of the Marshall Plan while Dirksen was an isolationist. Because of this, and because Lucas was Truman's Majority Leader, the election would attract national and international attention. Stevenson said he doubted McCarthy's charges would have any important effect on the campaign. "My own opinion is that the average man doesn't believe that Senator McCarthy has substantiated his wild charges."

On May 12, Stevenson told George Kells, who was retiring as state chairman, how valuable he had been. Whether Stevenson knew it or not, George Kells was a frightened man. During the preceding three years Mayor Kennelly had been at great pains to divorce himself from the Cook County machine. An honest man himself and a well-intentioned one, Kennelly wanted to remain above the battle. But Ed Kelly, his predecessor, had known it was impossible. Kelly once had said, "I've got to run the machine, or it will run me." He was right. While Kennelly was mayor, presiding at ribbon-cutings and other ceremonial functions, the worst elements of the machine, including some with Syndicate connections, had had a free hand. Members of the West Side Bloc had begun taking over new wards. One was George Kells's ward. Kells never said so publicly but he must have received threats, perhaps one of the miniature black coffins that the mob sent to people it wanted to intimidate, and one day he turned up at City Hall and, white-faced, resigned from politics.

Stevenson wrote his letter to Kells the day before the Jefferson Jubilee began. The Jubilee program was extraordinarily elaborate, even for such occasions, and much of the hullabaloo bore the mark of Barney Hodes. On the first day, a Saturday, the Democratic National Committee met in the main ballroom of the Blackstone Hotel and the public was invited. Stevenson attended a reception for the president of the national Young Democratic Clubs and a buffet supper for visiting dignitaries. On Sunday morning he entertained for visiting governors at breakfast in the Blackstone Hotel. He went to a luncheon of the Anti-Defamation League in the Palmer House, then to the Civic Opera House where the Truman Cabinet met, with the public invited. He attended a panel discussion on civil rights, a reception for dignitaries, and spoke at a banquet in honor of Vice President Barkley. At noon on Monday there was a luncheon for President Truman at the Blackstone Hotel, at 5 P.M. a reception, and at 6:30 P.M. a gigantic parade down Michigan Avenue and westward to the huge Chicago Stadium with President Truman leading the parade. In the great smoky Stadium, Stevenson spoke:

"Mr. President, we welcome you to Illinois which gave Abraham Lincoln to the world—and many other men and women who have added luster to our nation's history—including the Majority Leader of the United States Senate who is here tonight. But I dare not call him by name lest it be thought that there is something political about this celebration. . . .

"To do our honor on the one hundred and fiftieth anniversary of his election to the presidency, we meet in this hall which has witnessed in our time so many fateful events in American political history—including a hot night just six years ago when a senator from Missouri was nominated vice president of the United States. We are proud it happened here!"

And then he delivered a passage he had used before and which two years later would galvanize the Democratic National Convention and the nation:

"And, Mr. President, while we refresh our memory of Jefferson's implacable faith in the people, in life, liberty and the pursuit of happiness for all alike, may I remind you that until two years ago only three men of the political faith of Jefferson had been elected Governor of Illinois since the Civil War. The first was John Peter Altgeld—the eagle forgotten—a German immigrant; the second was Edward F. Dunne, but one generation removed from the old sod of Ireland; the third was Henry Horner, son of an immigrant and beloved in the memory of all those here tonight. May I remind you, Mr. President, that John Peter Altgeld was a Protestant, that Edward F. Dunne was a Catholic, that Henry Horner was a Jew.

"That is the American story; that was the dream of Thomas Jefferson. And here, Mr. President, in the city of Chicago, on the prairies of Illinois his descendants believe in human freedom; we believe in equal opportunity for all; we believe in special privilege for none; we believe in the democratic institutions; we believe in our Chief Executive; we believe in you, Mr. President!

"In the age-old struggle against tyranny over the bodies and minds and the souls of men we know there can be no respite, no rest, no hesitation, no turning back for you or for us.

"For

> *On the plains of hesitation*
> *Bleach the bones of countless thousands*
> *Who, on the eve of victory, rested—*
> *And resting, died.*

"As each day, in the tradition of Jefferson, you forge a broader shield for free men everywhere, we join our prayers to yours that out of the ugly clamor and conflict there will come your heart's desire and ours—peace on earth.

"Mr. President, you are very, very welcome to Illinois!"

The speech was Stevenson at his best. He knew it was good; he used the Altgeld, Dunne, Horner litany many times. Barney Hodes told him later, "It was the universal judgment of those at the Stadium . . . that you sounded the high note of the occasion." President Truman sent him a warm letter. Lou Kohn told him, "So many people have said 'You stole the show.'" Raymond T. O'Keefe, a Chicago Democratic politician, sent congratulations on his show-stealing and added, "I have heard from many Democrats who attended this affair that you are real presidential timber." Stevenson marked the last sentence.

34

Stevenson spent the weekend of May 26 in Chicago with Alicia Patterson. Ten days later, on Tuesday, June 6, he had to make a speech in Washington; he invited Dorothy Fosdick to return to Springfield with him by plane, and she accepted, all "agog."

It was her first visit to the Mansion. In a later letter she recalled the occasion and said Stevenson had said, "Nobody's ever kissed me like that before." Miss Fosdick apparently went up to Chicago next day, Wednesday, June 7, to an engagement at the Council on Foreign Relations, occupied herself during the rest of the week, and met Stevenson there that weekend—they stayed with the Edward K. Welleses in Lake Forest. Their relationship immediately became serious. He was, she felt, seeking support because of his divorce and because of some basic insecurity, an insecurity she thought probably related to his accidental shooting of the child. She felt she was giving him that feminine support.

35

At about this time, in June, Bill Blair joined Stevenson's staff. A tall lean young man of thirty-three, Blair was the son of a wealthy investment banker who was a cousin of Colonel McCormick of the *Tribune,* one of the wealthiest and most distinguished families of the Chicago area, with a town house on Astor Street and a large lakefront estate in Lake Bluff. Educated at Stanford, Bill Blair had taken his law at the University of Virginia, been admitted to the Illinois bar in 1947, and joined the firm of Wilson & McIlvaine. He was interested in the Chicago Council on Foreign Relations, the Juvenile Protective Association, and the other civic enterprises that Stevenson and so many of his associates were interested in. He had known and admired Stevenson since the days of the William Allen White Committee. He was urbane, witty, intelligent. Though he gave the appearance of one who would be more at home at an Astor Street tea than in the lobbies of the legislature, he quickly developed great political skill. Blair became Stevenson's appointments secretary. It is a powerful position; the appointments secretary decides who sees and who does not see the Governor. More, he became Stevenson's confidant and almost constant companion for the next ten years. He was his buffer to the world. He said "no" for him. He arranged his schedule. He persuaded him to do things Stevenson must do but did not want to do. He went nearly everywhere with him. Though Carl McGowan continued to help make policy and was as close to Stevenson as ever, Blair was probably Stevenson's closest confidant longer than anyone else. Indeed, in the sense of total commitment, he was almost Stevenson's only friend. Blair was wholeheartedly devoted to him; he served Stevenson's interests and nothing else for ten years. Stevenson usually repaid him with grumbling. But Stevenson knew his worth—he once told Harriet Welling that Bill Blair was "the best friend a man ever had." Some of Stevenson's political friends felt that the Lake Forest crowd sometimes hurt Stevenson in politics. Blair had a breadth of vision that enabled him to see that Stevenson's Lake Forest friends could be a handicap as well as a help; he had an adaptability that enabled him to leave the Lake Forest world for the political world. Sometimes he acted as a buffer between Stevenson and his Lake Forest friends, some of whom resented it when, because of Blair, their well-intentioned but misguided advice never reached Stevenson.

On June 12, Dorothy Fosdick told Stevenson she had been called upon in the State Department's Planning Staff meeting to report on her impressions of Illinois. Secretary Acheson was going to Chicago; she and Stevenson were eager that he speak to a group of "people who are not already converted." Stevenson wrote to Alicia Patterson on June 13, "E darling—I'm in the dumps again, tho I've reread your letter & feel a little better. I've had or rather am having another very difficult affair with Kennelly & the Chicago boys. . . . They insist on a special session of the legislature. . . . It will surely end up in more recriminations and more trouble for all of us in a campaign year."

On June 15 he issued a proclamation calling a special session of the legislature. He met with various legislators, spent Saturday in Lake Forest with all three boys, and on Sunday went to the University of Illinois to deliver a commencement address attacking McCarthyism: "We are behaving . . . like nutty neurotics. We . . . are nervously looking for subversive enemies under the bed and behind the curtains. We exchange frenzied, irresponsible accusations of disloyalty. 'Guilt by association' has been added to our language. The slanderer is honored. The shadow of a nameless fear slopes across the land. There is talk of thought control among Jefferson's people."

Next day the legislature met in special session, and Stevenson addressed it at 1 P.M. He had called the session "with great reluctance," he said. He had limited the call to four subjects—rent control, aid to cities, the Illinois Public Aid Commission appropriation, and an appropriation for the Mount Vernon Tuberculosis Hospital. (In a special session, the Illinois legislature could consider only subjects contained in the Governor's call.) Rent control might be moot—only that morning the Congress seemed about to extend federal rent controls. Chicago was approaching a financial crisis; he could not recommend invading potential new sources of state revenue for Chicago's use; instead he recommended the programs rejected by the 1949 session. As to the Illinois Public Aid Commission, it needed deficiency appropriations. Finally, construction of the state tuberculosis hospital at Mount Vernon had progressed so rapidly that it would be ready to open in September if the special session would appropriate an additional $250,000.

After delivering the message, Stevenson met at the Mansion with Mayor Kennelly, legislative leaders, and his own people. Stevenson, presiding, said the meeting had been called at the request of Kennelly, then he turned the meeting over to Kennelly. Kennelly talked aimlessly awhile. Finally Senator Thompson said, "What's your program?" Kennelly admitted he had none—he would leave it to the legislators. "Stevenson—who always liked to be prepared—almost fell off his chair," according to Carl McGowan. Convinced that Kennelly was hopelessly inept, Stevenson thereafter gave him little help. Kennelly, in turn, blamed Chicago's difficulties on Stevenson.

Stevenson held a series of meetings all next day and evening with his Finance Director, Kennelly, and legislative leaders. Not much resulted. The atmosphere was becoming acrimonious. Mrs. Ives had planned a party at the Mansion but had to postpone it. On Wednesday, Stevenson went to Washington to join several governors for lunch with President Truman and to see Dorothy Fosdick alone. She afterward sent him a letter saying she had spent all day at the Department on Korea—the Korean War had begun. The Department had had the air of wartime excitement—military men all around, sleepy civilians who had worked all night. She had attended the Secretary's meeting. The Russians, she thought, had acted decisively because the United States had been stiffening and the North Koreans could not win by infiltration. She had read his University of Illinois commencement address; she was impressed by his analysis of "the Age of Anxiety." She was sending him a speech she had made. She urged him to see an Italian movie, *The Bicycle Thief.*

The special session ran through the following week, adjourning Friday, June 30. During it Stevenson was in meetings repeatedly, through long days that ended near midnight. The session accomplished little. Chicago had relied mainly on the bill, defeated in the 1949 legislature, that would permit it to tax business. But with businessmen and many politicians opposed, the bill failed. Senate Republicans proposed a complicated alternative; it failed. As to welfare appropriations, Ed Day once said that they were rejected largely because the West Side Bloc resented the firing of a state police lieutenant. As it turned out, the economic upturn during the Korean War reduced public assistance rolls. The legislature did appropriate money for the tuberculosis hospital.

The session, held as it was during an election year, took place in a highly charged political atmosphere. Stevenson accused Republican legislators of trying to embarrass Kennelly and, in his semi-annual radio report to the people, said he had considered his proposals "non-controversial and non-political" but he had been wrong: "Politics was here in a big way, as usual!" The Chicago *Daily News,* noting rumors that Stevenson might succeed Secretary of State Acheson, said it would oppose such a move because "his chief difficulties as governor have come from indecision and vacillation." The editorial bothered Stevenson. He drafted a long reply in the form of a "Letter to the Editor" for someone else to sign, defending himself with vehemence against the charges. They were charges that would follow him. Carl McGowan once said, "He could drive you crazy on whether he would accept an invitation or not—but on the really big things he didn't do it. It was only a tangential thing. I don't remember once that he was indecisive about something on his desk as Governor. He would grumble like hell because Mrs. Ives kept serving eggplant for lunch, but he never grumbled or vacillated about the Broyles bills or the state police raids on gambling. You might say that President Kennedy proved extremely indecisive at the time of the Bay of Pigs —more indecisive than Stevenson ever had on a major question."

36

Stevenson's mind was not entirely on the special session. Two days before it closed he sent a typed letter to Dorothy Fosdick suggesting she stop in Springfield July 10 on her return to Washington from Missouri. He added, "I am palpitating with apprehension about Korea." Stevenson entertained the children of former governors at the Mansion on June 30, a Friday, attended a performance of *Abe Lincoln in Illinois* at New Salem on Sunday evening, and that night back at the mansion wrote to Alicia Patterson, addressing her as "Dearly beloved." He signed the letter with a drawing of a tiny animal and a note, "That's a rat—you louse!" (Dorothy Fosdick signed her love letters with a drawing of an angel.) By now he was sending longhand notes to her too. She wrote, "I'm sure the American people have the stuff to back up what may be a prolonged military operation in Korea. Our UN proved its worth, didn't it!" She was only reflecting the general feeling of relief then widespread that "at last" Truman had "done something" about the Communists. It was hard to imagine that only two years later the American people would have become so weary of the Korean War that they would defeat Stevenson on, in part, that very issue.

On the Fourth of July, Stevenson went to Vincennes, Indiana, to speak at the hundred and fiftieth celebration of Indiana Territory, renewing his friendship with Governor Schricker, a popular gentle man. He spoke of the Midwest's past and of today's world problems: "So while we meet today at this shrine of freedom . . . we do so with a prayer in our hearts—a prayer that this cynical unprovoked aggression in far-off Korea with all its appalling possibilities may soon end, a prayer that we can march forward again toward a long future when no one rattles a saber and no one drags a chain." The last clause, in modified form, brought the Democratic Convention of 1952 to its feet and became a trademark of his first presidential campaign. He had used it before.

His prerecorded semi-annual report to the people was broadcast on July 5—the budget, taxes, highways, all the state issues. To one who praised the speech, he replied, "I find nothing more difficult than reducing my writing to the simplest possible terms and I still feel that it is a little complicated and highbrow sounding." At the end of the week Dorothy Fosdick arrived and, according to his appointment book, stayed two days. Stevenson planned to meet Alicia Patterson at the fashionable Ambassador East Hotel in Chicago three weeks later, on Friday, July 28, and would try to keep most of the weekend clear. He addressed the Lions International Convention at the Chicago Stadium that Sunday, July 16, laying heaviest emphasis on Korea. All summer his speeches touched that theme. Dorothy Fosdick sent him a love letter on July 20 speaking of Elizabeth Barrett Browning. She was planning to go to Springfield. She wrote, "This is a very risky period just ahead, tho, especially in terms of Soviet reactions, and our Soviet experts like George Kennan and Chip Bohlen are crystal ball gazing like mad. We talk interminably." In lieu of a signature she appended a series of "x" 's. She wrote again on July 29, a love letter. That weekend Stevenson saw Alicia Patterson in Chicago.

He was traveling almost ceaselessly over the state in July. One trip took him to a region he loved, far southern Illinois, a poor region of hills and eroded land, worked-out coal mines and worn-out soil, the most wildly beautiful part of the state. The South was ever present here, in people's speech, in architecture, and because of his heritage it was always just beneath the surface in Stevenson too.

Dorothy Fosdick wrote to him again from Maine on August 4. She was counting the days until she went to Springfield. She wrote a long abstract discussion of love and speculated on why his marriage had failed. She called him "darling." There was more, much more, about love. On the back of the envelope Stevenson penciled the names Boyle, Peabody, and Stelle, probably having in mind the Scott Lucas election campaign.

37

The State Fair opened Friday, August 11, and ran until August 20. Guests descended on the Mansion. Mrs. Ives was Stevenson's hostess. Dorothy Fosdick got in ahead of the crush—signed the guest book first, on August 10. More than fifty others signed the book during the Fair.[13] The Stevenson boys were there part of the time. Stevenson went through the usual round of ceremonies. He seemed to enjoy it. Introducing Barkley, he pleaded for party unity, assailed Republicans, and asked, "Is the battle of our times with our own State Department or is it with world Communism? Partisanship is suffocating patriotism. . . . Tell the people that the enemy is without, not within, that we are outnumbered already, that the shadows are creeping over Asia and that our problem is to fight Communism, not windmills. . . . Tell them that this is a battle for survival, not a witch hunt! The eyes of the world are on Illinois. . . . Senator Lucas is Majority Leader of the Senate, he is the spokesman of your party. He must not lose."

Dorothy Fosdick, back in Washington, wrote to him on August 15: "Darling. I miss you in a funny sort of agonizing way. Tonight when

13 Among them were Eunice Kennedy (sister of John F. Kennedy) and Sargent Shriver (they were not yet married), Fowler McCormick, Judy Mansure, Wally Schaefer and his wife, Vice President Barkley (who came to speak on the nineteenth, Governor's Day) and his wife Jane; Lester Armour, Stuyvesant Peabody, Jr., and his wife; Lou Kohn, Mr. and Mrs. Daggett Harvey, Steve Hord, Jane and Edison Dick, Ruth Winter, William C. Boyden (Ellen's divorce lawyer); and there were others who came but did not sign.

I came home I wanted to fall into your arms, to hug and kiss you fondly, and to be hugged and kissed." Next day, August 16, Stevenson wrote to Alicia Patterson: "I wish there was some place we could meet in mountains or valleys, fish a bit & lie under a blue sky by a rushing torrent."

38

After the State Fair, Stevenson went to Wyoming for a long vacation with the boys. In later life Adlai III said it was "about the only long time we had with Dad that I remember" during these years. "He had loved Wyoming from his own boyhood." Stevenson himself described the trip to Alicia Patterson:

> My beloved cow girl [and drew a picture of one]
> I tumbled down the last weary mountain Sat afternoon. Sunday we all spent a hilarious day motoring thru the Yellowstone & Monday we flew back to Springfield—brown, burned, fit, lean, happy. It was glorious—the boys all to myself for the first time for almost 2 whole blessed weeks. Marvelous scenery, superb fishing in Bridger Lake, perfect weather, good food, a fascinating old cook, fine guide & jolly wrangler—and no misfortunes *except*— saddle sores on poor little John Fell's rump that looked like the black plague. But he didn't seem to mind & I daubed him dutifully & lovingly with zinc ointment which he promptly rubbed off. We caught countless big, fat cutthroat trout and smoked a lot of them in an improvised smokehouse.
> Back here a day—wriggled thru the accumulated mountain of work & I felt I had never been away. The boys took off to Chicago and Ellen & I was desolate again. . . . What a life!

He had tried unsuccessfully to meet Alicia in Wyoming.

Dorothy Fosdick had continued to write to him every few days while he was in Wyoming, a thick sheaf of letters containing biblical quotations, information on Soviet thrusts, United States military unpreparedness, Truman's mistakes, lack of White House leadership, Paul Nitze, jokes for speeches, a description of her new haircut which made her look like his daughter, Kennan's parting advice to the Planning Staff, gossip about a feud between Secretary Acheson and Secretary Johnson and rumors that Harriman and McCloy might succeed them, chitchat about her family, and, nearly always, declarations of love and drawings showing her as an angel and Stevenson as a devil or a wolf. They would meet in Washington on September 17, when he would be there to address the Bar Association. She wrote a long essay on U.S.-Soviet relations and suggested he might use it in speeches. She wrote about the General Assembly, her work, Acheson's speeches, which she compared unfavorably with Stevenson's. She was the first of a number of women who over the years sent him both personal letters and speech material, sometimes in the same letter. Their letters show that they yearned to help him and that they enjoyed him as well.

39

After Labor Day the political season began. Stevenson had complained to Bud Merwin about an editorial critical of the Truman administration. Merwin defended it and said the *Pantagraph* would withhold endorsement from Everett Dirksen for Senator Lucas' seat until satisfied Dirksen was not an isolationist. Stevenson, in a carefully drafted reply on September 12, said Dirksen was inconsistent and demagogic, disagreed with Merwin's view that Lucas had been a mere "errand boy" for Truman, and denied that Secretary of the Air Force Thomas K. Finletter was preventing the rebuilding of naval and marine aviation, an idea that had become almost an obsession with Bud Merwin's brother Dave. He then said, "I will intervene no more on the Lucas-Dirksen situation." No more now as Governor, than formerly as minority stockholder, could Stevenson control *Pantagraph* editorial policy, nor could he later.

In September, Stevenson made several speeches. At the Democratic State Convention in Chicago, he replied to a speech Dirksen had made attacking Stevenson for his Alger Hiss deposition: "What would Mr. Dirksen have said? Would he have told a lie? I thought *his* reputation for veracity was good too, but I am beginning to wonder."

Still, it was a relaxed time. He talked to his department directors at the Mansion, talked to legislators, visited downstate friends for an afternoon, had John Fell down to the Mansion, visited state parks and state institutions, entertained Chicago and Lake Forest friends and the British consul general, went to a University of Illinois football game. Carl McGowan was doing most of the work on the legislative program. Citizens working for the passage of Gateway urged Stevenson to set up a committee to recommend amendments to the 1951 legislature; Stevenson, cool to the idea, let it slide. None of these concerns was central; he was not focused on them. And all the while he was continuing his round of parties and non-partisan speeches and football weekends and plans to meet Dorothy Fosdick and Alicia Patterson on into October, Scott Lucas was fighting for his political life and the next session of the legislature was only three months away. Though Stevenson complained of it, his schedule was not really heavy—and a good deal of it was unnecessary. One gets the impression that he was distracted, that he was doing a good deal of traveling and seeing a great many people, but all to little purpose. As at other times in his life, he seemed to lack direction. Though he had great capacity for leading, in the behind-the-scenes labor of running a government or a campaign it was always hard to get him to focus on a problem until he really must; and sometimes then it was too late. During a legislative session, when a key vote impended, he fastened on the problem tenaciously and did not spare himself or others. But between crises he drifted, fretted more about future planning than he planned, left it to his staff. And this pattern persisted throughout his presidential campaigns and his UN ambassadorship.

Stevenson announced his support of a proposal to lower the voting age to eighteen, another example of his being ahead of his time. He issued a statement denying a Republican charge that campaign contributions were being solicited from state employees. He apparently met Alicia Patterson in St. Louis October 9.

On October 20 guests arrived at the Mansion—Mr. and Mrs. Donald Welles, Mr. and Mrs. Donold Lourie, and James Reston of the New York *Times*. On Saturday, Stevenson took them to the Illinois-University of Washington football game, and that day Reston dropped off the guest list and Dorothy Fosdick replaced him. It was a long-planned trip. She wrote to him a few days later, "Whenever I am with you I feel as tho I am somehow living fully, am more aware of my world, and everything has extra and poignant meaning, is somehow a-light and a-glow." A good many people felt that way about Stevenson. At about the same time in another letter she mingled affection with a recommendation that he read Reinhold Niebuhr, whose ideas did indeed come to influence Stevenson's, particularly on the conflict between American ideals and the employment of American power and on America's attitude toward an impoverished world. She and Mr. and Mrs. Niebuhr were close friends.

Joseph P. Kennedy, the father of John F. Kennedy, invited Stevenson to the Notre Dame-North Carolina game; Stevenson could not go but urged Kennedy to come to Springfield; Kennedy said he would, and added that he was "very much impressed" by Bill Blair. (Blair had come to know the Kennedy family after the war; theirs was a long close association.) Ed Kelly died, and Stevenson delivered a eulogy: "Here was a leader! . . . He will be mourned by thousands. And he will be studied by students of American politics as a leader who was never afraid to lead."

The political campaign was nearing its end. To a Chamber of Commerce luncheon on October 24, Stevenson read a speech for Senator Lucas, who was ill, and spoke to a rally in Champaign. The rest of the week, however, he did little. Dorothy Fosdick wrote that a Columbia University professor had told her that Eisenhower, who was then president of Columbia University, knew nothing about Columbia, knew nothing about domestic problems, would make a disastrous President, was filled with illusions about politics, probably sensed this about himself "and really feels happier at the prospect of a military job." She said that "election night I will be positively drooling for Lucas."

That Saturday, October 28, Stevenson took friends to the Illinois-Indiana football game and on Sunday went up to Chicago for the final week of the campaign. He joined the Republican leader of the Senate, Wallace Thompson, in a bipartisan radio plea for adoption of Gateway. In the evening he spoke to the Polish American Democratic Dinner at the Sherman Hotel. He made three appearances in western suburbs on Tuesday evening. On Wednesday he recorded a broadcast with William Rivkin, a Young Democrats leader, attended a cocktail party on the Near North Side for Congressman Sidney Yates, and that night made four speeches in Republican suburbs for the ticket.

Stevenson spent Thursday at Libertyville, working on a speech for the next night at the climactic rally of the campaign, held in the Coliseum. The principal speaker was Vice President Barkley but Stevenson made a long speech, a straight partisan rally speech, attacking Dirksen, praising Lucas, predicting victory, and saying the burden now lay on the Democratic precinct workers to get out the vote in Cook County.

Next day, November 4, the last Saturday before the election, Stevenson went to Bloomington with Senator Lucas to attend another football game and make three speeches. At 5 P.M. he went to Rock Island for a dinner, a speech to a rally, a broadcast, and a speech to the Belgian American Club, finally returning to Springfield at midnight. He spent Sunday quietly writing letters. One to Alicia Patterson said, "They may not like me too much but the politicians can't say that I haven't done my bit for 'the ticket' & then some, but they probably will! One day this week I spoke 8 times between 10

A.M. & midnight in Chicago and suburbs—and now, thank God, its all over."

That same day Stevenson asked his sons and their schools to arrange for all of them, plus Tim Ives, to meet him in New York and go to Princeton for the Princeton-Harvard game and to the theater in New York. The show he wanted to see was *South Pacific,* a romantic musical play about a middle-aged French planter's love for a young American nurse during the war in the Pacific. Milton refused to let John Fell go.

On Tuesday, Stevenson went home to vote, then returned to Springfield. He had invited Democrats to the Mansion for a victory celebration that night. It was instead a wake: Dirksen beat Lucas by nearly 300,000 votes—1,951,984 to 1,657,630. It was a disaster— Lucas even lost Cook County. (But Richard J. Daley survived—was elected county clerk.) The Republicans elected their entire state ticket—state treasurer, superintendent of public instruction, and clerk of the Supreme Court. They won control of both houses of the legislature. Their sweep was not confined to Illinois—the Democrats lost twenty-eight seats in the U. S. House of Representatives and five in the Senate, though they retained narrow control of both houses. They lost seven governorships.

Across the country the Republicans had campaigned aggressively on the issues of inflation, Korea, Communism, and corruption. Truman had made but one speech during the campaign. Senator Robert A. Taft of Ohio said the Democrats were responsible for high prices, high taxes, the "loss of China" to the Communists, and the Korean War. Senator McCarthy's charge of Communists in government was an important issue. In California, Representative Richard M. Nixon defeated Representative Helen Gahagan Douglas and won a seat in the Senate. In the campaign Nixon accused Mrs. Douglas of having voted frequently with Representative Vito Marcantonio of New York, whose voting record, Nixon said, coincided with the Communist line. Labor had made an all-out effort to defeat Senator Taft for re-election; Taft had won by nearly half a million votes. In Illinois, Dirksen had campaigned as a conservative and had flirted with isolationism. The magnitude of his victory, nearly 300,000 votes, is clear when one recalls that Stevenson had won the governorship two years earlier by 572,000—on the face of it, a reversal of 872,-000 votes.[14] Losing Lucas was more than losing just another Senate

[14] Actually, the reversal was less than that—the total turnout in 1950 was 300,000 less than in 1948.

seat—he had campaigned as President Truman's Majority Leader. His defeat was a heavy blow. Truman never forgave Kefauver for it.

The day after the election Stevenson issued a statement which said nothing at all about Lucas or the national election but focused entirely on state matters and, especially, on the Illinois House. He asked members of both parties to "put the state's welfare ahead of petty party triumphs." The only consolation for Stevenson was that Gateway had passed, receiving a "yes" vote of 2,512,323 to a "no" vote of 735,903.

Stevenson told Alicia Patterson what he thought of the election. On November 9 he wrote, "E darling—Bruised but not bloody, I take my pencil in hand to report that the Demos got the pants trimmed off 'em here. If my life's been hell so far, I've seen nothing yet, when that Rep. legislature goes to work on me in Jan. Ho Hum—guess I asked for it, and no complaints. Sorry to lose Lucas & I'll hope for the best from Dirksen who can probably reverse himself again & make some sense—but for how long with your esteemed kinsman pulling wires? Sunday the 19th looks OK." He was writing to Alicia aboard a train to Chicago for a midnight meeting with Jack Arvey and Paul Douglas and a subsequent meeting with Mayor Kennelly— "I'm going to begin asserting myself a little & see if I can't get a decent guy, *my* guy, in as County Ch. in Cook County & start rehabilitating that organization. Arvey stubbed his toe badly & must quit anyway on account of his health. Douglas will go along with me & if that pompous Mayor will step down from his icy, lonesome throne we'll get a new shake & a new look in that groggy outfit—but I'll have to strike quickly. Then I'm going to jump on a plane & go East —gather up the boys & take them to the Harvard-Princeton football game—keep out of town & out of reach a couple of days & let the dust settle—I hope!" Alicia Patterson had asked about Dorothy Fosdick. Stevenson added a postscript: "Fosdick's a bright little lass— of 35–40—who worked for me in England. What have you heard— I'm bewildered!"

On Friday, November 10, at 1 P.M., he left for New York and his Princeton–New York weekend.

40

In six weeks the legislature would convene. On Tuesday, Stevenson met with several department heads. This was the weekend he had asked Alicia Patterson to join him. He went to Chicago, spoke to the CIO and the Chicago Crime Commission and the University of Chicago Law School Alumni, and conferred with machine leaders —a Chicago alderman, Al Horan, Dick Daley, others. It was part of the effort he had mentioned to Alicia Patterson to rebuild the machine.

Though it was almost December, little more than a month until the legislature met, still Stevenson scattered much energy on cocktail parties, social dinners, football games, and minor appointments. Sporadically he buckled down to work on his program—held budget meetings at the Mansion, had a luncheon on unemployment compensation, met with Senator Wallace Thompson, the Republican leader. He told Alicia on December 2: "Looks as tho the 'organization' & Kennelly were going to insist on Arvey staying—To work!!" Arvey moved up to Democratic national committeeman, filling the vacancy caused by Mayor Kelly's death, and Joe Gill took Arvey's place as Cook County chairman.

In a speech on December 8, Stevenson announced a new fiscal policy. Earlier that year he had spoken of the states' need to find new sources of revenue. Now he proposed that, in view of the Korean War and resulting inflation, the states tighten their belts. Controlling inflation was "our major problem" next to "insuring a peaceful world." States should "postpone all but their most essential new building construction." It was a speech that Dorothy Fosdick had suggested.

She had been writing him every Sunday. He had asked her to write a piece for him on prayer, and she did. She wrote to him about Korea, "a ghastly mess." On the back of one letter Stevenson penciled a note to himself: "Wire Gill re Stengel—He is a fine speaker, fine man, fine Democrat & would make a great Governor." Stengel was Richard Stengel, a tall young state Representative from Rock Island, a lawyer and former assistant U.S. attorney. He had been elected at the same time as Stevenson. In the legislature he was becoming a leader of the young liberal good-government Democrats who, with Stevenson's encouragement, were trying to create a countervailing force to Paul Powell and the old guard. Stengel did run for Senator in 1956, with Stevenson's blessing, though unsuccessfully. But why Stevenson put him down as a candidate for Governor as early as 1950 is mysterious. Was Stevenson really considering seriously the possibility that he might replace Acheson before he had finished his first term as Governor? (He and Dorothy Fosdick had discussed it.) Was he considering so early the possibility of running for President in 1952? Was it a part of his efforts to increase his influence with the Cook County machine—that is, was he considering threatening not to run for a second term in order to increase his bargaining power with the machine and seeking to give the threat plausibility by suggesting an alternative candidate to Joe Gill, the new Cook County chairman? Or was he promoting Stengel for Democratic leader in the House? Who knows? Carl McGowan once said, in ruminating on the responsibility for decisions, "Nobody but the top guy *really* knows. In Springfield there were things in Stevenson's head that he couldn't convey adequately even to me. Why he was checking with someone—what someone might think. With a guy like a President or a Governor, running a public-political operation, he's got a lot of fish to fry that never get through to the staff." But McGowan doubted that Stevenson was seriously considering Stengel for the governorship in 1952.

The holidays passed with considerable uproar, parties and dinners with his sons, staff, and friends. He sent gifts and thanked people who had sent gifts to him. On Christmas Eve, Dorothy Fosdick wrote about his gifts to her, her feelings for him, Acheson, the Christmas party at the State Department, the "growing conviction" that we must *"free* ourselves from Chiang," Reinhold Niebuhr, religion, her father, and her almost motherly concern over Stevenson's health ("Try a long hot bath at night, an occasional walk around the Mansion to fill your lungs with real air, and get to bed at a decent hour whenever you can.") She spent New Year's Eve alone, writing to him and standing by the fireplace drinking a toast to him.

That same New Year's Eve, Stevenson wrote to Alicia Patterson, "The tumult & the shouting have subsided. . . . This afternoon I really got to work & last night finished the first draft of my message to the legislature—70 pages. Horrors! Now for the editing job, tomorrow the annual New Years reception—thousands—and next week the legislature—le deluge. And in Georgia there are quail and enchantments soft and prickly, tender and sharp, gentle and petulant —? ? ? ? I don't know just why I presume to send you this photo of the Stevenson guys on Christmas—except that I'm proud of the boys and love them and want you *to too!"* He sent the same photograph to Dorothy Fosdick and a number of friends.

41

The Republican majorities organized both houses of the legislature. Once again Senator Thompson was president pro tem of the Senate. The Speaker of the House was a downstate Republican, Warren Wood, a neat, rather slight, astute, reasonable man, an exponent of good government, who was serving his seventh term in the House, who was endlessly fascinated by the intricate workings of the Illinois House, and who cared deeply about its reputation and believed deeply in its function as an instrument of the popular will.

Stevenson addressed a joint session of the legislature on January 3, 1951. He asked for and offered cooperation. He said he could only propose, history's verdict would depend on what the legislature did. This legislature had a rare opportunity to modernize the constitution and restore the highways. But danger loomed—the struggle between individualism and collectivism had accelerated into the Korean War, our forces were "engaged in unequal combat" and our public opinion "confused and divided" while inflation threatened our economy and controls would threaten our liberties. Thus did he seek to strike an attitude acceptable to Republicans, place the burden of responsibility on them, and present himself as a wartime Governor. He then set forth his program—no increase in taxes, except for highways, in order to permit Illinois to "contribute fully to the national struggle" and to spare taxpayers at a time when they faced "steep increases" in federal taxes. "I would emphatically recommend that no state dollars be spent at this time which can be conserved. Our job is to hold the line." He recommended, among twenty-three items, tighter control of and heavier taxes on trucks, legislative study of several proposed constitutional amendments, increased common school aid, more taxing power for cities, the Crime Commission bills to spur the attack on organized crime, FEPC, several bills wanted by organized labor, and a requirement that mental hospital patients or their families pay for their care if they were able.

It was, as Stevenson said, a "formidable program." Yet it was realistic, even conservative. It broke little or no new ground. By asking for no new taxes except for highways, Stevenson immediately deprived the Republicans of one of their mightiest weapons—the charge that a Democratic Governor was a "big spender." Although much of the program could be termed liberal, such as FEPC and labor legislation, not all was—for example, the proposal to oblige mental patients to pay for their own care. Much of what he asked for had been previously denied, such as the Crime Commission bills, aid to the cities, FEPC, and the gasoline tax increase. These, together with truck license fees and constitutional amendments, promised to be the most controversial measures. Stevenson had been campaigning for most of them ever since he ran for governor. And for the most part they cut across party lines. Despite Republican domination, the prospects of success seemed fairly good. On January 11 he told Alicia Patterson his message had been "very well" received—the *Tribune* had approved two proposals and disapproved one, the *Post-Dispatch* had given him "top marks," and downstate papers had shown their "usual erratic behavior"—"I'm always interested by the way one editor can be enthusiastic about something and the editor in the next town equally disapproving—and generally neither of them know much about it or evidently make any effort to find out. . . . Also why the hell do they presume to express considered views on *everything?* . . . The Republicans, by the way, beat the crooks by 1 vote on the election of a speaker in the House which helps me a *little*. But it will be assassination in the Senate—its the campaign of '52 already apparently."

42

On January 11, Stevenson delivered his fourth semi-annual radio report to the people. He stood at exactly the halfway point of his term. He reviewed his past accomplishments and disappointments, emphasizing that "most of all we are raising the moral tone and public respect" for Illinois government. He outlined his new legislative program. He concluded, "I'm not omniscient. There may be better ways to solve the problems I've mentioned. . . . The legislature is Republican; the Administration Democratic. So what? We're all Americans; we're all sworn to serve Illinois." He was going over the heads of the legislators, not in acrimony but in reasonableness, to the people. He received a good deal of fan mail, evidence that McGowan was right—Stevenson had run away from his party and established a personal position with ordinary citizens.

The budget he submitted on April 10 implemented his opening message. It was a conservative budget, calling for no new general purpose taxes. It contained only a 3 per cent net increase in general-fund appropriations. Stevenson's close control of spending had made it possible to avoid new or increased general-purpose taxes, as in all other big states. Anticipating the legislators' desire for pet projects, Stevenson urged "your rigorous restraint." Most Democratic legislators and some Republicans praised the budget; Senator Thompson dissented.

Stevenson told Alicia Patterson, "I'm done with the ordeal for 2 years—or forever!" And, "The press reception has been very good and your esteemed cousin has chosen to ignore it—but not me! The last was an edit this week charging me with a conspiracy to capture the criminal vote because I approved a commutation of sentence of some prisoner on the Pardon Boards recommendation!" (The *Tribune,* always a hard-liner on law enforcement, later that year printed an editorial entitled "Murderers' Governor" and said Stevenson had "no serious rival for the title of murderers' best friend" and had extended clemency to "200 or more convicts." Stevenson, stung, issued a statement in rebuttal.)

43

Throughout the spring Stevenson used speeches to argue for his legislative program. He used radio more than any previous Governor. And as the session moved into the home stretch, on May 31, Stevenson again took to the radio to plead for money to restore Illinois's highways—the key gas tax and truck license bills were in danger. The truck bill, he said, had passed the Senate on May 1 by a vote of 42 to 7. But it had been stalled in a House committee for five legislative weeks. The truck lobby had been so crass that members of the House from both parties had formally requested an investigation. While the truck bill was bogged down in the House, the Senate was refusing to act on the gas tax. If the bills failed "it would be a major tragedy for Illinois." Truck fees had not been changed since 1917 and were "about the lowest fees in the country." He concluded, "I am obliged to say that unless the will of the people is made clear now, unless the legislators know you want and expect action, there is real and present danger that Senate Bill 96 will be emasculated or defeated. Thank you for listening to me. It is *your* money and they are *your* roads."

This was a different Stevenson from the harassed, troubled Stevenson of the 1949 legislative session. True, his divorce was behind him. But something else seemed to have happened. He had begun to understand his own political power. He was making bold to go directly to the people. He was focusing hard on the key issues—his budget and the truck and gas tax bills. He was, in a few words, exercising powerful political leadership. He told Alicia Patterson in April, "Life is tough but I think I'm seeing the light at last—even enjoying my job more."

He was operating more effectively in quieter ways. He talked to more legislators. He held meetings that included both his legislative leaders and his own staff. He saw both Paul Powell and the Republican Speaker, Warren Wood, often. He had his picture taken time and again with legislators, Democratic and Republican alike, when he signed bills they had sponsored—pictures that helped them in their home districts. Carl McGowan, acting as field general for the legislative program, talked with legislators, drafted and redrafted bills, rounded up votes, identified key members, prepared periodic reports for Stevenson on the status of his legislation. Stevenson used his Statehouse office more than in 1949, was more accessible to the legislators. He started his heavy schedule of appointments with them early in the session. He seemed no longer to fear or suspect them, seemed eager to speak their language. He had strong staff work and used it well. He involved himself directly in legislative battles. He was, briefly, running the show far more than he had in 1949.

He established priorities—decided which bills were most important and which could be dropped. He held back some bills, such as the Crime Commission's immunity bill, until difficult related bills were passed, such as the Crime Commission's bill to extend the life of Cook County grand juries. He got some bills passed early in the session— the grand jury bill, defeated in 1949 by the West Side Bloc, passed the House on March 20 and the Senate March 28. The other three law-enforcement bills—to prohibit the sale of liquor in gambling places, to prohibit the manufacture of slot machines, and to force immunity on reluctant witnesses—failed to pass. No evidence proves a trade, but the Cook County grand jury bill was more important than the slot machine and liquor bills, and the immunity bill was opposed not only by the West Side Bloc but by civil libertarians.

Stevenson early involved himself personally in key bills. When it appeared almost at once that the gas tax might founder because of rival claims on how it was to be distributed—a quarrel between downstate and Chicago that had killed the bill in 1949—Stevenson called a meeting of those interested for 8:30 P.M. on April 4, told them they must compose their differences if they were to get any bill at all, and kept them in the Mansion until past 2 A.M. when they finally reached agreement. He told Alicia Patterson it was his "major triumph of the session"—"I kept the warring wolves here in the Mansion 6 hours and 20 minutes straight. Exhaustion overtook them & they began to crack. We had arranged to have the press—15 of them—on hand and they stood by all night. Before anyone could leave I called them in and announced the terms of the agreement before any of the conferees could reverse himself! The exhaustion technique I learned from the Russians and it seems to work just as well in Springfield as in London." This did not end the controversy over the gas tax and truck bills. The truck lobby continued the fight. So did other special interests. They sought to reopen the down-state-Chicago split and involve all sorts of irrelevant problems, such as the consolidation of rural school districts, hoping for a stalemate and no legislation at all. Stevenson mobilized powerful newspaper support for his program. Toward the end of the session the press exposed the lobbies. Stevenson encouraged Representative Dick Stengel and others to introduce a resolution calling for an investigation of lobbying. Six days after Stevenson went to the people with his radio warning of May 31, the truck bill began to move in the House, and the following week the Senate passed the gas tax. Both bills eventually became law, the gas tax at the very end of the session. When the truck bill passed, Stevenson thanked Paul Powell and Powell replied, "I'm mighty glad to have your thanks, Governor, because it cost me $50,000."

In the end, Stevenson's legislative program fared better in 1951 than in 1949, especially if one considers what was important and difficult to pass—the gas tax, stiff penalties for overweight trucks and higher truck license fees, increased school aid, amendment of the revenue article of the constitution, the Crime Commission's grand jury bill.[15]

[15] Other Stevenson bills which the legislature passed included a cigarette use tax; civil defense (though it cut his request from $500,000 to $200,000); creation of a new category of disabled persons eligible for public assistance; codification of the mental health laws, with patients to pay their own way in state mental hospitals if able; shifting the expense of medical care of the indigent from Cook County to the state (Stevenson had rejected this Republican proposal in 1949 but made it part of his program in 1951); permitting downstate cities to adopt the city manager plan of government; increased workmen's compensation and unemployment compensation; tighter enforcement of the law regulating wages on public works; repeal of the margarine law; congressional redistricting; and a cost-of-living increase in salaries of state employees. The legislature raised the gas tax only a penny immediately, postponing the two-cent increase Stevenson had asked until 1953, and delayed a fair distribution until 1953.

The legislature failed to pass other administration measures—to establish a legislative commission on proposed constitutional amendments; to adopt amendments to the legislative reapportionment and judicial articles of the constitution (but it set up a commission on the judicial article to report in 1953); to consolidate control of higher education; to prohibit the sale of liquor in gambling places; to prohibit the manufacture of slot machines; to force immunity on reluctant witnesses; to provide for temporary disability insurance; to integrate employment services; to broaden and strengthen the minimum wage law; FEPC; to consolidate the primary ballot to re-enact the county assessor law. In his original message to the legislature Stevenson had asked for revision of the parole laws, traffic safety laws, and military and naval code but no such bills were introduced. He had called for revision of the mining laws but both unions and operators had opposed and no bills had been introduced. The legislature had, on its own, enacted laws to permit Chicago and downstate cities to increase taxes and to have the state assume certain expenses of Chicago. It had also increased the penalties for narcotics peddling. It had passed 78 of 166 bills introduced to reorganize the state Administration as recommended by Schaefer's Little Hoover Commission but the most important rearrangements were not among those passed.

In a radio report on July 15, Stevenson called the session's results "highly gratifying and encouraging"—"the good far outweighs the bad and this was certainly the most productive session of the legislature in many years." More than a thousand bills were passed, he said. The achievements were all the more remarkable considering prophecies that a Republican legislature and a Democratic Administration would deadlock, he said. He concluded by praising Senator Connors and Paul Powell and "many Republicans" in both houses and by saying, "We have made much progress in Illinois of late only because we have had a great deal of public interest and support. For that support and encouragement I am deeply grateful. . . . We are on the way to something better in Illinois."

44

Stevenson vetoed 134 bills and vetoed others in part and allowed still others to become law without his signature. He vetoed bills appropriating money for special projects above his budget, including roads or bridges in legislators' home towns, and "Christmas tree bills" appropriating funds for such private groups as a specific veterans' organization. Dutch Smith once said that Stevenson vetoed $42 million worth of pork barrel bills. When the Veterans of Foreign Wars met in state convention at Springfield, Stevenson explained his vetoes and said, "The appropriation of public funds to carry on the normal functions of private organizations, be they veterans or any other, is both illegal and in my opinion it is wrong to give public funds to some organizations and not to others." The last session of the legislature had passed one big omnibus Christmas tree bill lumping together appropriations to assist various veterans and other organizations. He had allowed it to become law but had warned the organizations that they should arrange other financing before this legislature met. The legislature had paid no attention and had passed six or eight little Christmas tree bills. "So no one should be surprised when I veto all of these bills, as I intend to do. And at least no one can say that they didn't have two years' warning."

No veto message he ever issued attracted more attention than Stevenson's veto of a Broyles bill, which made it a felony to belong to any subversive group and required a loyalty oath of public employees and candidates for office. Senator Broyles had introduced anti-Communist bills previously; this one now had passed. In view of the uproar over Communists in Washington at that time, it might have been considered difficult to veto. Carl McGowan has recalled, "It was no problem at all. We had no doubt about it. He told me that on one trip to Washington he had gone to see J. Edgar Hoover or someone in the FBI and been told that state anti-subversive bills, though they couldn't say so publicly, did not help a damn bit— they got in the way of the FBI, actually, and sometimes state officers were arresting FBI agents who had infiltrated subversive organizations. Broyles asked to see Stevenson during the veto period. I sat in. The legislature was still in session. We knew they would try to override the veto. Broyles explained how important this was to the country and how he'd been working on it for ten or fifteen years. Stevenson listened attentively and said he would consider the matter very carefully. I was full of foreboding and nervousness. It didn't faze Stevenson. We never sat around and debated the veto. After Broyles left, we said that's that, and vetoed it."

In his veto message Stevenson wrote:

"The stated purpose of this bill is to combat the menace of world Communism. That the Communist Party—and all it stands for—is a danger to our Republic, as real as it is sinister, is clear to all who have the slightest understanding of our democracy. . . . Agreed upon ends, our concern is with means." Was the bill needed in light of existing legislation? Might it not be a two-edged sword, more dangerous to ourselves than to our foes? Stevenson then wrote that the Supreme Court had affirmed the conviction of the twelve top leaders of the Communist Party under the Smith Act. The federal government had indicted twenty-one more persons. The FBI had identified and placed under observation "virtually every member of the Communist Party and every serious sympathizer." And under existing laws of Illinois, it had been since 1919 a felony to advocate the violent overthrow of the government. Moreover, the bill obliged local prosecutors to present to grand juries all information obtained by a special assistant attorney general, presumably including rumors. "I can see nothing but grave peril to the reputations of innocent people." Furthermore, the bill provided that a person seeking to teach school or work for the state must himself carry the burden of proving that he was not subversive. The burden was even shifted to those already employed. "Irreparable injury to the reputation of innocent persons" was likely. Such state laws had caught no subversives. Finally, the bill provided for a loyalty oath, and Stevenson asked:

"Does anyone seriously think that a real traitor will hesitate to sign a loyalty oath? Of course not. Really dangerous subversives and saboteurs will be caught by careful, constant, professional investigation, not by pieces of paper.

"The whole notion of loyalty inquisitions is a natural characteristic of the police state, not of democracy. . . . The history of Soviet Russia is a modern example of this ancient practice. The democratic state, on the other hand, is based on the consent of its members. The vast majority of our people are intensely loyal, as they have amply demonstrated. To question, even by implication, the loyalty and devotion of a large group of citizens is to create an atmosphere of suspicion and distrust. . . .

"Basically, the effect of this legislation, then, will be less the detection of subversives and more the intimidation of honest citizens. But we cannot suppress thought and expression and preserve the freedoms guaranteed by the Bill of Rights. That is our dilemma. In time of danger we seek to protect ourselves from sedition, but in doing so we imperil the very freedoms we seek to protect. . . .

"We must fight traitors with laws. We already have the laws. We must fight falsehood and evil ideas with truth and better ideas. We have them in plenty. But we must not confuse the two. . . .

"Finally, the states are not, in my judgment, equipped to deal with the threat of the world Communist movement which inspired this bill. Communism threatens us because it threatens world peace. The great problems with which Communism confronts us are problems of foreign relations and national defense. Our constitution wisely leaves the solution of such matters to the national government.

"In conclusion, while I respect the motives and patriotism of the proponents of this bill, I think there is in it more of danger to the liberties we seek to protect than of security for the Republic. . . .

"I know full well that this veto will be distorted and misunderstood, even as telling the truth of what I knew about the reputation of Alger Hiss was distorted and misunderstood. . . . But I must, in good conscience, protest against any unnecessary suppression of our ancient rights as free men. Moreover, we will win the contest of ideas that afflicts the world not by suppressing these rights but by their triumph. We must not burn down the house to kill the rats."

What caught the eye of both friends and enemies was that his veto was a classic statement of liberal opposition to Senator McCarthy and "McCarthyism." Senator McCarthy had apparently made little impact on ordinary men—a responsible survey even as late as 1954 showed that less than one per cent of the people interviewed said they were worried about either the Communist threat or civil liberties, and nearly one third could not name a single Senator or Congressman who had taken a leading part in the investigation of Communists. But McCarthy and McCarthyism were grievous afflictions to liberals, intellectuals, writers, editors, publishers, professors, and high government officials, and particularly that academic-intellectual group that formed a small but articulate and influential segment of the Democratic Party. Stevenson had long possessed credentials as a liberal in foreign affairs, dating at least from his combat with the isolationists. As Governor, he had been developing domestic liberal credentials by espousing FEPC and labor legislation. But it was his veto of the Broyles bill, taken together with what they considered his courage in "speaking out" on Alger Hiss, that endeared him to the liberals of the nation when, less than a year later, he was proposed for the presidency. At the time, liberals wrote and telephoned to urge him to veto the bill and McGowan has said, "They were not needed. He flattered some of them by asking them to draft veto messages. But they were not important. The Broyles bill simply violated his instincts—and moreover he thought it was a lot of bullshit—the state has a lot of important things to do and why bother with this." More than once it was Stevenson's fate to be surprised by plaudits he did not expect—and to be hurt by attacks he did not deserve.

The Republicans in the Senate sought to override his veto. They failed by four votes—by now, Stevenson's relations with the legislators were so good that he even got Republican Senators to vote to uphold his veto.

45

Archibald MacLeish visited Stevenson. "It was cold. I arrived late for diner. The Mansion was locked. A state policeman let me in and an aged Negro butler took me through dark empty halls. I found Adlai at the end of a big reception room with obviously political types who were haranguing him. Adlai was looking forlorn and lost and miserable. We had dinner, then I went to the frozen train. The whole evening left me with an impression of forlornness and misery. I had a dreadful feeling that even more than resentment of Ellen he felt a longing for her—he still loved her. If ever a man needed a wife, Adlai did."

Ellen was living at 1362 Astor Street and, in the summer, in a rented place at Half Day, not far from Libertyville. John Fell has said, "Borden and I spent more time with her than with Dad." Attending Milton, John Fell often went to lunch in Cambridge at the home of "Aunt Lucy," Mrs. Kingsley Porter, Ellen's great-aunt and an eccentric who lived in the James Russell Lowell house and used candles instead of electricity. Stevenson visited her too. Visiting the boys, Stevenson stayed with friends. Mrs. Ives often acted as Stevenson's hostess at the Mansion. Later on their relations became somewhat difficult. At the Governor's Mansion, however, Mrs. Ives was helpful, and Stevenson relied on her for many things. Some of his longhand notes to her have survived. One reads, "Mrs. Ives —if you could draft reply it would be very welcome." Another: "Dear Buff—Please note & return. I suppose its OK. But *please* don't spend any more—it's killing me!—$36 on drawer *handles* when I need essentials at my office." Always a penny pincher, he used to go around the Mansion turning off lights. He once lectured Jane Dick for having brought up her children improvidently: her son, then thirteen, had been invited to a house party at the Mansion, and Stevenson went looking for him and found him asleep in his room with "every light in his room ablaze." From Charlevoix at the end of August, Mrs. Ives wrote a long letter, telling Stevenson how proud she was of him but going on to say she wished he would talk to her more and ended by saying she would not return to the Mansion to live until he asked her.

"I always thought Stevenson was naïve about people," Carl McGowan once said. "He took them at face value. He was always accessible—much too easy. Odd characters attached themselves. He was not as impatient as I was for him. Maybe this explains the women," that coterie of women who surrounded Stevenson during the UN years, called "Adlai's harem." "If you wanted to attach yourself to Adlai, you could. He never got brusque. I used to think he was a nicer fellow than I. He treated everybody as God's creatures. He brought in nuisances and wasted time."

Some of Stevenson's associates sometimes suspected he did not know what was important. McGowan has said, "I thought he spent too much time answering letters. Maybe it was a kind of relaxation. I always thought, too, that he had an exaggerated idea of what a speech could do for him. He spent too much time on speeches. On the other hand, as Governor, he was conscious of the fact that he needed to be planning initiatives, conceiving projects—a congenital fiddler would not. He was a good administrator, he was conscious of the importance of problems. He had visitors come to stay—not only the Dutch Smiths and the others from Lake Forest, but prominent people from around the country—authors, politicians, John Mason Brown, John Gunther, and so on. Foreigners, too. That's why it was so much fun in Springfield. We had all the benefits of small-town life, with the attractions of seeing big people from all over the world. Once Ralph Bunche spoke at the high school and stayed at the Mansion. Allan Nevins came. There was a big dinner, and Sandburg and Nevins and all the Lincoln scholars were there. Bob Hope was always turning up. Joe Liebling"—A. J. Liebling, then a well-known *New Yorker* writer—"came out and did a piece on Springfield and stayed at the Mansion. Artur Rubenstein gave a recital in Springfield and the Governor had a party afterward for him. These people got a kick out of it. They went away and talked about this guy. It all helped," that is, helped politically by spreading Stevenson's name around the country, particularly in intellectual circles. "He worked hard at keeping this kind of thing going. It was hard—he had no wife. I thought it added a drain on his time. He made life so much more exciting and interesting for a lot of people. Springfield people loved being invited to the Mansion with someone from the outside world. This compares with the ladies in New York—he made their humdrum lives more exciting and interesting."

At the Mansion, as throughout his life, Stevenson had books around him. But McGowan has said, "He was not a heavy reader." Newt Minow once said, "I never thought of him as an intellectual. He was not a great reader. Not a great student. He complained that he never had time to read a book but the fact is that he did not want to read a book. But he knew it was important to read books." Stevenson was an aural person, learning more by listening to what people said than by reading what they wrote. A lonely man after his divorce, he did not occupy his free time by reading but, rather, by seeing people. He always had people around him, was never alone if he could help it (despite his repeated protestations that what he wanted was quiet time, time to be alone, time to read, time to think). He was remarkably lacking the internal resources that enable men to live alone and think and read. Despite his powerful appeal to intellectuals, he was not really himself an intellectual.

His guest list that spring was, despite the legislature, long and impressive, and so were his own comings and goings. He went to the Kentucky Derby and stayed with Barry Bingham of the *Courier-Journal;* the Duke and Duchess of Windsor came to dinner at the Binghams' with Stevenson and other guests. Stevenson was an excellent host, seeing personally to his guests' comfort. His greeting was hearty, sometimes almost effusive. In his Mansion office, he usually worked in a pair of slacks, a sport shirt and blazer or a tweed jacket with patched elbows. If his guests arrived while he was still at work and if he saw them, he would look startled, drop his work, greet them, see them upstairs, make them comfortable, then return to finish work before rejoining them for a drink on the glassed-in sun porch.

Jane Dick once recalled taking a female penologist from New Jersey to Springfield. The penologist was nervous at the prospect of meeting the Governor. As they approached the door, Stevenson chanced to cross the hall and see them. He opened the door himself, picked up their suitcases, and carried them upstairs. Once, when he was inspecting a mental hospital with the welfare commissioners, their car broke down. He got out and crawled under it, why is not clear, since he was unskilled at mechanics. The board members hailed a taxi; the driver was reluctant to take them until one board member pointed to Stevenson's feet, which were sticking out from under the car, and said, "That's the Governor." Not surprisingly, the taxi driver did not believe it—they were near a mental hospital—until Stevenson emerged and the driver recognized him. George Ball once wrote of Stevenson's "sense of decency and proportion, humility and infallible good manners which led him so often to understatement, particularly when he spoke of himself."

46

Dorothy Fosdick was sending him love letters constantly that spring. He wrote her and sent her photographs of himself and his sons. She sent him an idea that one of the Planning Staff had propounded—that the United States was moving "from our Greek period to our Roman period" and that the trouble with Acheson was that "he is too much of a Greek, when what the people now instinctively want is a Roman!" She also wrote that "two of our best" students of Russia said that the Soviet Union's purpose in Korea seemed to be to embroil the United States in war with China in order to "drain our resources," make China "completely dependent militarily on the Soviet Union," and encourage us to bomb Chinese cities and industries, "thus weakening China as a potential threat to the Soviet Union." We were walking into the Soviet trap. "The basic instincts of the American people are correct on this—we don't want to get sucked into a war against China." Stevenson used nearly all of this and more, some of it verbatim, in a speech a little later at Northwestern University. She sent him comments on the United Nations which he used, in part, verbatim, in another speech. And he used other materials she supplied.

He and Dorothy Fosdick kept three dates in ensuing weeks—on the weekend of January 12, in Southern Pines, North Carolina; on February 11 in Washington; and on March 3 in Springfield. She sent him love letters which indicate that their relationship was loving and was physical. Stevenson's letters to Alicia Patterson at this time lacked the almost desperate yearning and ardor of a year or two earlier; one can hardly imagine his having ended a letter then, as he did now, with "Cheerio." A year or two years earlier he had been going through torment—his marriage was ending, his life as Governor beginning, he was deeply shaken, he needed Alicia Patterson greatly. Never before or after did he write letters so self-revealing, so self-questioning, so deeply searching. Now all that was behind him.

He wrote to Alicia January 31, sending a copy of his Northwestern speech and saying, "I would have to say that Stalin is right and no war with Russia is in sight. But as for the Rep. party—how Hoover & Dewey can ever find common grounds I can [not?] see, but meanwhile Taft will be floundering around doing his intellectual contortions somewhere between them, capitalizing every discontent, proposing everything and nothing, and acting like 'Mr. Republican' for sure, and they call this leadership!" It was a political, friendly letter, not a love letter. And he had Dorothy Fosdick. She wrote to him at least once a week and sometimes oftener. Once she discussed the UN. The United States' approach to the UN had been "an idealistic, moralistic" one. This had been useful in launching the organization but now seemed immature. "Lack of such maturity accounts for much of disillusionment today—expressed in despair & rejection of UN because it is not proving a full blown collective security system able to maintain peace. . . . Internationalism now [is] a life and death matter; not a matter of good will and idealism. We should look at UN, as we do other political instruments, see what it is *not,* disabuse ourselves of any illusions, and appreciate how useful it still can be." Stevenson used this material, much of it verbatim, in a speech to the American Association for the United Nations on February 26.

Once he told Alicia Patterson, "As to Eisenhower & Stevenson—I've heard of the former, but whose the latter? Now about resigning as Gov. and being chancellor of U of C [University of Chicago]? That's more my alley I think! Love XX A"

On March 15, Stevenson left Springfield for the East to pick up Borden and John Fell and take them to Southern Pines. Dorothy Fosdick spent four days there with them. Afterward, she wrote thanking him almost humbly. She wrote at length about the boys—Borden was "an absolutely dear and loving and warm-hearted boy" scarred by his mother's rejection; John Fell should have a jeep to help the farmer at Libertyville, a place he loved. She wrote about their own future. Her April 1 letter discussed that future, Illinois politics, Stevenson's staff, and Reinhold Niebuhr, who had found the editorial board of the St. Louis *Post-Dispatch* interested in the possibility that Stevenson might run for President or Vice President next year. The *Post-Dispatch* was thinking of putting up some trial balloons soon. This, it must be remembered, was in April of 1951, much earlier than the date usually given for the launching of Stevenson's 1952 presidential candidacy. And at Southern Pines Stevenson had talked about running for President.

Dorothy Fosdick's letter of April 7 contained the outline of a foreign policy speech: history had thrust world power on the United States, the United States must now, reluctantly or not, concern itself "with the fate of the whole free world," the Soviet system in the long run carried within itself the seeds of its own decay, we must "rediscover our own revolutionary tradition," the Kremlin had betrayed its own revolution and converted it into "a strategy of imperialism," "we must make clearer not *only* to the oppressed peoples, but to the uncommitted peoples and our allies the kind of program we stand for." She commented, "The *hazard* in this type of speech is to formulate our revolutionary tradition honestly (primarily for independence) and relate it creatively to contemporary revolution movements," to which Stevenson added, "which are partly for independence from colonial control, for independence from Soviet imperialism & tyranny and also for social justice."

It was a position that Stevenson, Kennedy, Johnson, and other Democrats would develop in the next fifteen years. Her letters indicate the intellectual ferment of the 1950s. Ideas were in the air— were in her mind, in Acheson's, in Kennan's, in Niebuhr's, in those of many others, however much they might otherwise disagree. What they needed was a political figure to bring them into the open arena, to give them currency, to make them issues. Using Stevenson, Dorothy Fosdick began this process. He was isolated in Illinois; his energies were going into such issues as the gasoline tax. She helped him keep him in touch. McCarthy and General MacArthur were transitory preoccupations; so, in a sense, was the Korean War. But the larger vision of an America committed to revolution, to playing a role on the world stage, to competing with Communist imperialism, to capitalizing on its own revolution to help other peoples make theirs—this was in the air in Washington in the early 1950s, and it came to inform U.S. policy through the 1950s and 1960s. Stevenson spoke for it in 1952 and 1956, unsuccessfully; Kennedy spoke for it in 1960 successfully; Johnson spoke for it after 1964 until, perverted, it led him to disaster. Whatever the vision's validity, Dorothy Fosdick put it to Stevenson, early; he articulated it at the time as best he could and, later, elaborated it; and it became a part of the national intellectual atmosphere and evolved as living doctrine, misguided or not.

On May 1, Stevenson sent Alicia Patterson an editorial from the *Tribune* entitled "The Party of Acheson, Stevenson, and Hiss." (Stevenson, having previously "rushed to the defense of Hiss," had now issued a statement supporting Truman's dismissal of MacArthur.) Stevenson wrote, "Ho! Hum! Its a grizzly life." He began the note quite differently: "E dearest—When will we meet? The Lord knows," and he outlined his schedule and asked her to visit him. "My miseries are many even as yours. But we're making a little progress in spite of the level of politics that prevails in this sovereign state, paced by the Chicago Tribune. . . . Are you well, happy working hard, having a good time at the ANPA etc etc etc?" But there was not much fire in it. And it was she who would have to go to him, not he to her (as he was going to Dorothy Fosdick). And by now it seems likely he was considering marrying Dorothy Fosdick, as once he had considered marrying Alicia Patterson. Nevertheless, a certain longing for Alicia—or was it nostalgia?—remained. On May 16 he wrote a letter about a *Saturday Evening Post* piece about her, ending, "It's late, I'm dog tired & you're in the sun by the black river and I wish I was; but I'm happy, unmarried and don't give a damn anymore!!! Love A."

On June 6, Stevenson left to go to Wallingford, Connecticut, for Borden's graduation from Choate; then went to Washington to spend the weekend, returning to Chicago and Springfield on Sunday, June 10. He saw President Truman on June 9 but said only that he had discussed federal appointments and invited the President to visit the Illinois State Fair. He apparently met Dorothy Fosdick during that trip. She wrote a little later about his running for re-election, a decision he must make during the next six months. She thought Truman was sure to run for re-election and could beat Taft but not Eisenhower. If Truman ran against Taft, Stevenson should risk "making yourself available for the national scene in one spot or another," she thought, but if Truman ran against Eisenhower, Stevenson should run for Governor, a seat he probably could hold even though Eisenhower beat Truman. She wrote, "I love you with a decidedly gay and excited heart."

Alicia Patterson suddenly complicated Stevenson's already complicated life and even alarmed him—she told him she intended to divorce Harry Guggenheim. He replied on July 16, using his most endearing salutation, "Elisha dearest," and saying, "I am sorely distressed by this turn of events." He had been under the impression "that things were going better with you & Harry" and so was "shocked. . . . I wish I knew what to suggest, and about all I *can* suggest is *deliberation*. Certainly to seek a divorce impetuously would be, I should think, a great mistake. Indeed I should think it would be your last recourse. Three [divorces] is quite a lot—even for a brave free spirit! Or a 'tough character.' . . . And then there's your child to think about—Newsday! . . . And then of course you have *him* to consider, whether you want to or not. So I must say, for what it's worth, that I think you should take your time, go back East when tempers have cooled and spirits mended, talk it out and think it out before you attempt to come to any decisions. My guess is that things will look better after a bit. . . . At least I hope so, I pray so, because you are very dear to me and I want the peace & serenity that has eluded you so long to come to you even as its coming to me out of the chaos, confusion and misery of the past few years. Perhaps we can meet in Chicago or here on your way east. Keep me posted."

It was a curious letter. The logic on divorce was odd—he had been divorced and now was finding peace and serenity; he wanted peace and serenity for her but advised against divorce. He offered her nothing except advice to temporize. Indeed, whereas a year or two earlier he had thought of marrying Alicia, now he seemed downright alarmed that she might make it possible. There is a pattern here—he was most tender to those unattainable, and coolest to those close. He showed the letter to Jane Dick, asking her advice, and she, en route to Europe, wrote to him on July 18, "The more I think about that letter from A [Alicia] the more I think you'll have to be very wary and *much* firmer and more forthright than is your natural wont. . . . You know, I've known her well. I like her as a friend, I like her loyalty—(to everyone but her husband—meeow!). I admire her incisive mind and her point of view about many things; but to say that she is temperamentally unstable, self-centered and demanding puts it very mildly. Qualities that may be interesting, amusing, even appealing in a friend are often not those that work out very satisfactorily in a more intimate sort of relationship. . . . Anyway, just remember—BEWARE AND BE FIRM. I suppose *one* reason why I feel such a responsibility about all these women pursuing you is that it is axiomatic that the smartest most brilliant men are the most naive and gullible about women."

47

All spring, whether spurred by friends, by his own ambitions, by concern with the deepening national crisis over Korea and domestic Communist hunts, by his own feeling of mastery over the governorship and hence freedom to address himself to his first love and first concern, Stevenson had been making speeches on foreign policy. He launched himself on that track on January 28, 1951, with his major speech to the Northwestern University Centennial. After speaking briefly in defense of students and their university against "strong, arrogant men who burn books and bend thought to their liking," he discussed Russian "imperialism," "an inscrutable, ruthless conqueror," words he would use in his presidential campaign next year. He warned against both isolationism and war with China, which would drain our resources, make China completely dependent militarily on Russia, and strengthen Russia. He said that military force alone "cannot win the day for us in Asia." Asia was colored, desperately poor, revolutionary, "struggling to shake off the shackles of white colonialism. . . . It will take great patience, great insight, great restraint for us . . . to win confidence and faith in the great uncommitted areas of Asia." When freedom had been young, it had been a fighting faith. But now it was old and looked pale beside imperial Communism. In the long run, however, Communism could not "cure the disease of this anxious age."

The speech attracted the first heavy fan mail he ever received on a speech. Many people asked for copies, and Bill Blair and Jim Mulroy sent out even more. The speech's reputation, and Stevenson's, spread beyond Illinois. Many wrote in the spirit of a man from Mattoon: "I sincerely believe you to be presidential timber." The response came from Republicans, independents, academicians, journalists, ordinary people who were strangers. Moreover, he had managed to return to comfortable ground—the apostle of American world commitment in an isolationist wilderness, ground he had occupied in the days of the William Allen White Committee. But now, as Governor, he had a platform of power.

He had no intention of sticking to Illinois in his speeches. He spoke to the University of Chicago Round Table on national security and individual freedom. In speaking to the American Association for the United Nations at Chicago, he used again the passage Miss Fosdick had suggested about the need to think about the UN in a mature and realistic way and he denounced a resolution pending in the Illinois legislature calling upon the United States to withdraw from the UN. "Of course, the UN is not a full-blown collective security system and it is dangerous to think of it and operate within it as if it were. It's a council table, not a police force." To the Chicago World Trade Conference, he reviewed America's postwar contributions to European recovery and defense, praised the U.S. role in Korea, warned against reliance on military strength alone and against too volatile a public opinion, and said we had gradually built up a number of policies, one for each of the areas of the world, born out of necessity, not out of any world view, whereas the Soviet Union approached foreign policy from a world view—we must develop an "adequate world policy" of our own. In dedicating a new chapel at a boys' correctional school, Stevenson took occasion to speak not only of the rehabilitation of juvenile delinquents but also of America's place in the world. On Veterans' Hospital Day at Danville, he defended Truman's Korean policy of checking aggression.

At a twenty-dollar-a-plate Jefferson-Jackson Day dinner in the Springfield armory on May 24, Stevenson gracefully recited the party's history and heritage, said it was harder to maintain unity in office than in opposition, and went on to declare that "epithets and slander are not a substitute for principles and policy." He asked if the Republicans disapproved of "a relentless policy of peace through international organization and cooperation" or proposed "returning to a bankrupt isolationism" or "all-out war in the bottomless quicksands of Asia." He said the people knew that peace could be won only by strengthening the Western Alliance, determined resistance to Communist aggression, and using any necessary means to that end, "while patiently avoiding, if possible, the precipitation of a third world war." Nearly all his speech was on Democratic wisdom and Republican bankruptcy in foreign affairs. Such a speech would have been unthinkable during his first session of the legislature, only two years earlier.

During his trip to Washington the weekend of June 8, Stevenson saw Averell Harriman and subsequently wrote to Harriman (misspelling Averell), with a copy to Dean Acheson, "I agree emphatically that Dean should . . . take the initiative and exploit the advantage. . . . I think the formal speech . . . less effective than informal discussions . . . with smaller groups of editors, publishers, educators, commentators."

When he delivered the commencement address to the University of Illinois professional schools in Chicago on June 15, he divided his speech between state problems and international ones, talking about overweight trucks, gambling, the Kefauver investigation, and tying them to moral questions, then bridging to the morality of "political charlatans and false prophets" who promised easy solutions to world problems: "Of course there are no painless solutions to war, inflation, revolution, communism, imperialism, hunger, fear and all the diseases of a world in convulsive transition. . . . The baffling difficulty of it all may explain one of the most unwholesome manifestations of our current disorder—which is called 'McCarthyism' . . . this hysterical form of putrid slander." And he quoted a line from King Henry IV, Part I, that was a favorite of his: "But I tell you, my lord fool, out of this nettle, danger, we pluck this flower, safety."

48

Mayor Kennelly was up for re-election that spring. Stevenson exerted his power in Illinois politics as never before. In March an Illinois Supreme Court justice died, and, Stevenson, anticipating pressure from the Democratic organization to appoint one of its own, moved swiftly and skillfully to head it off—appointed Wally Schaefer immediately to fill the vacancy. Furthermore, he insisted on slating him to run for a full nine-year term in the judicial election in June. Carl McGowan has said, "He really put the hammer on the organization to slate him. This was really hard. It made no sense. Schaefer was a renegade Catholic and he didn't even live in Chicago. The Governor gave the orders and Dick Daley loyally carried them out. This was worth a whole batch of appointments of nonentities. It was a clear case of pure political leadership. He was interested in political power." Stevenson spoke at a testimonial dinner for Schaefer, putting his own prestige on the line. Schaefer was elected and was still on the bench when Stevenson died in 1965, widely respected by lawyers and other judges as "a judge's judge."

On March 26, Stevenson addressed a Young Democrats' luncheon in Chicago on behalf of Mayor Kennelly's re-election. "The whole nation," he said, "is watching this election," though newspapers were, rightly, calling the campaign dull. "This election is in the nature of a vote of confidence in one of the most distinguished and, by its very nature and locale, one of the most spectacular efforts at municipal improvement in American political history." Kennelly's defeat would be a blow to good government everywhere. Kennelly was re-elected easily.

Stevenson had friends in the Chicago press. One was Ed Lahey, of the Chicago *Daily News,* who wrote a long piece which ran under the headline, "Adlai Stevenson, A Story of Integrity." He wrote that

Stevenson had been offered up for defeat in 1948 as a "sacrificial goat" by the Democratic leaders only to surprise them with a sensational upset. Lahey thought the governorship was important and said Stevenson did too. By now, he wrote, it ought to be easy to dig up "derogatory information" about Stevenson. But nobody in Springfield would "utter a truly nasty word" about him. "For the first time in the memory of those of us in middle life, there is not even any barroom gossip about corruption in the state administration." Lahey wrote, "There are . . . 35,000 people on the state payroll. Stevenson is ever conscious of the possibility that somewhere along the line, despite his painstaking efforts . . . personal corruption might take root. If anything does go wrong under Stevenson, it will not be for any lack of vigilance on his part." Lahey had been around a long time and he was a skeptical man but he loved Stevenson.

49

A Negro family tried to move into Cicero, an industrial suburb of Chicago, and some 4,000 people, many of Eastern European origin, rioted, and Stevenson sent in the National Guard to restore order. Friends congratulated him, Harold Ickes saying, "That, too, took courage." Ickes also praised Stevenson's veto of the Broyles bill and said he wanted to talk to Stevenson about the 1952 election. Ralph Bunche of the United Nations congratulated Stevenson on his courage in dealing with the riots.

With the legislature gone home, the usual round of summer comings and goings began. Frequently he received letters about the presidency—Allan Nevins said he had heard talk of a possible presidential contest next year between Stevenson and Eisenhower. Larry Irvin told Stevenson he felt strongly that Stevenson should start moving to elect delegates to the Democratic National Convention who were loyal to him. Stevenson agreed, said he did not know how to proceed, and asked Irvin to consult Mike Seyfrit. But, just back from visiting the Smiths in Desbarats and about to open the State Fair, Stevenson let the matter slide. More than a month later, Irvin suggested to Carl McGowan that the question be taken up at the regular Thursday morning staff meeting, called "skull practice."

Senator Douglas too was interested in the composition of the Illinois delegation. Larry Irvin met with Doug Anderson, Senator Douglas' patronage man, to arrange a meeting between Douglas and Stevenson. Other intermediaries became involved—Clifton and Frayn Utley, who had been Stevenson's friends at the Council on

Foreign Relations, and Bob Merriam, the young alderman from the University of Chicago area, a protégé of Douglas and a friend too of Stevenson. Finally, after many phone calls and letters, a secret meeting between Stevenson and Douglas was arranged for October 13–14 at the Utleys' cottage in the Indiana dunes. By this time, for a variety of reasons, some going back to the 1948 campaign and others coming down to judgeships, patronage, and China policy, relations between Stevenson and Douglas were strained. Utley recalls, "The real difficulty between Stevenson and Douglas was differences in their temperament. I kept telling both of them, 'You two represent the same thing and shouldn't be fighting each other.' The emotion was more on Paul's side." Douglas had originally intended to run delegates of his own in most downstate districts. But, at Utley's and Merriam's urging, he reached agreement with Stevenson that each would pick ten to twelve delegates, leaving from four to six to the downstate Stelle-Barrett faction. They began discussing names but soon gave up and agreed to submit lists to each other—Larry Irvin and Doug Anderson would negotiate the lists on November 1. Both men left the dunes meeting thinking the question settled.

The agreement, however, somehow became derailed. Douglas always felt he had been double-crossed and became embittered toward Stevenson. According to Douglas, only eight of the twenty-six delegates and only two of the nineteen alternate delegates jointly agreed upon by Irvin and Anderson actually filed in the primary. Irvin once explained that the arrangement failed when the list reached district chairmen—they considered it a suggestion, not a directive, and put up the candidates they themselves preferred. Most of these turned out to be Stevenson men. The affair dragged on throughout the next spring. In the end only two of those elected delegates were on the original Douglas list and only five from the Stevenson-Douglas agreed slate. And when the state convention met in May, Douglas asked for the right to name four delegates at large but was given only two delegates and an alternate.

In retrospect it appears that the whole affair was mismanaged. Stevenson himself, though he had agreed in October to carry out his arrangement with Douglas, simply did not focus on it. He left it to Irvin but failed to tell Irvin that he had a firm agreement with Douglas, and Irvin, only partially informed, failed to use the power of the governorship to impose the Stevenson-Douglas agreement on the downstate county leaders. The episode again illustrated a failing of Stevenson's—a failure to focus on a purely political question if no one brought it forcibly to his attention (and sometimes not even then).

50

On August 24, Stevenson went to the Midwest Conference of Democrats at French Lick, Indiana, where his friend, Governor Henry Schricker, was host. His performance there, and subsequent events, so impressed Paul Butler, a member of the Indiana Democratic State Committee from South Bend, that he wrote to Stevenson urging him to become a candidate for the presidency. As talk grew about Stevenson for President or Vice President, the *Tribune* increased its attacks on him. He had invited attack by referring again, in a speech on Governor's Day at the State Fair, to his Hiss deposition. The *Tribune* promptly printed an editorial, "We're Glad You Brought It Up, Governor." Stevenson wrote an indignant letter to the editor: "The attached editorial says I told a lie," and said he had simply told the truth about Hiss's reputation. The *Tribune* printed his letter on August 31 and along with it another editorial. One wonders why Stevenson kept bringing up the Hiss deposition. To anticipate attack? To please liberals in his party? Because he thought he was right and could not stop saying so? Perhaps—he so indicated to Alicia Patterson. Or because, simply, he was thin-skinned—extraordinarily, for a politician, sensitive to criticism.

51

It is said to be true of Presidents, and may be true too of Governors, that their third year is their worst. Certainly the last half of Stevenson's third year was his worst. Now in the late summer and the fall of 1951, just as serious talk was commencing of his presidential potential and after his spring political triumphs with the legislature, the Wally Schaefer appointment, and the Kennelly election, he heard the first rumors of trouble in his own administration. Other Illinois Governors with White House ambitions and excellent records had been undone by last-minute scandals. Now it was Stevenson's turn.

Late in August newspapermen, including Lahey of the Chicago *Daily News,* who had written so glowingly of Stevenson's untarnished governorship but had warned that someone might have been corrupted, began checking information uncovered by the Kefauver Crime Committee and found that several members of the Illinois legislature held jobs at Chicago Downs, a harness racing association which ran races at Sportsman's Park in Cicero. Gamblers associated with the old Capone gang had been connected with Sportsman's Park years earlier. In 1949 a special bill had been introduced in the House to repeal a prohibition in the Illinois Harness Racing Act against conducting harness race meetings within five miles of racing on the flat. It had passed easily. The newspapermen found that stock in Chicago Downs had been purchased for ten cents a share by several legislators or their wives, Chicago politicians, and state employees. This ten-cent-a-share stock had, in a few months, paid dividends of $1.75. One of the stock purchasers had been Jim Mulroy, Stevenson's aide. He had bought 1,000 shares for $100 and received $1,750 in dividends. Among other stockholders were a man who once loaned money to Paul "The Waiter" Ricca, a leader of the mob; and the son of William H. Johnston, the operator of Sportsman's Park and of Florida dog tracks, whom the Kefauver Committee report had called "a longtime associate of the Capone gang." Paul Powell had not sponsored the bill legalizing Sportsman's Park but he was considered the man behind it. Carl McGowan said, "Paul was smart enough to figure out that he could get Mulroy involved—and it would be good to have him involved if it blew up. Paul Powell was an old fox." What Mulroy had done was not illegal. He had bought the stock after the bill had passed. The bill's unanimous passage in the Senate argued against any deal. The stock had been highly speculative.

Nevertheless, the affair blemished the spotless Stevenson administration. The *Sun-Times* said, "Racetrack operators don't cut people into their profits without a reason" and "if Mulroy doesn't understand he's not smart enough to be assistant to the governor." Stevenson, asked at a press conference about the affair, replied, "I have a very high personal regard for Mr. Mulroy, and I have no further comment whatever at this time about him." He wrote Alicia Patterson, "Mulroy, the damn fool, put $100 in the Chicago Downs race track & of course told me nothing about it. Now there's hell to pay. . . . In addition I now find he bought a house from a man who is a big contractor with the state. That may break tomorrow. Nice eh! And the worst of it is that Mulroy is guiltless of any wrongdoing— other than enormous stupidity. . . . I haven't summoned the courage to fire him and the hotter it gets the more embattled and stubborn he gets about resigning. What a job!" Stevenson talked to Mulroy several times and on November 2 released an exchange of letters in which he accepted with regret Mulroy's resignation "because of ill health," expressing "my personal appreciation for the devotion you have given your work and me." "Stevenson was heartbroken and heartsick," Schaefer said. Mulroy died a few months later, heartbroken too. His wife became embittered.

Newspapermen were on the trail of other scandals. Johnson Kanady, at that time the *Tribune*'s Springfield correspondent and a good one, wrote on September 26 that E. Todd Wheeler, an assistant in the division of architecture and engineering who handled bids on state construction contracts, had resigned in order to escape political pressure from contractors, organized labor, manufacturers, politicians, and bureaucrats. He made it clear that he had never been offered a bribe but said he wanted to be "an architect and not a politician." At about the same time the state purchasing agent, David H. Cummings, resigned, and Kanaday wrote that Cummings had been forced out because he had differed with Finance Director Pois (who had replaced Mitchell). A little later the Chicago *Daily News* reported that Pois had appointed eleven outstanding purchasing agents in private business to act as an advisory committee; the *News* congratulated Stevenson and Pois. It appears that a general tightening up of the administrative machinery was taking place.

But one of the most notorious scandals of the Stevenson administration was building up. In the summer, Roy E. Yung, Director of Agriculture, reported rumors that beef, inspected by state inspectors, was being adulterated with horsemeat to make hamburgers. Stevenson told him to investigate. Yung turned it over to Charles W. Wray, Superintendent of Foods and Dairies. Wray reported nothing was wrong. Stevenson saw Yung as early as July 23 and Wray the next day. The rumors persisted. Later that fall investigators for the federal Office of Price Stabilization reported they felt certain that horse meat was being sold as beef with the connivance of state inspectors. Stevenson met Wray and Yung regularly. Then on January 10, a Thursday, he turned the whole thing over to Carl McGowan. (He also talked to Ross Randolph, the FBI man in Springfield.)

McGowan asked Director Yung to call the inspectors to Springfield. Yung also invited their superior, Wray. On Saturday two assistant attorneys general went to the Fairgrounds, where the Agriculture Department is located, and questioned the inspectors. They resumed questioning them on Sunday. That afternoon at three o'clock Stevenson left Springfield to attend a wedding in Bloomington and a dinner with the Marshall Fields in Chicago. An hour after he left, one of the attorneys general called McGowan and asked him to join them at the Department of Agriculture. Wray himself, the Superintendent of Foods and Dairies, had fallen under suspicion. This was almost unthinkable. Stevenson had personally picked Wray for his job. He had done so because he had been under heavy political pressure to appoint another man and had suspected this meant the job was a possible target for bribery. Flanagan said there was pressure because there was graft in the job. For example, if a bottler could use an inferior substitute preservative for cherries in pre-mixed manhattan cocktails, he could save a great deal of money—but he could only do it if the state food inspector let him. So informed, Stevenson had chosen for the job Charles Wray, a man who had been active in politics in Lake County, where Libertyville is located, who had been recommended by farmers and businessmen, and whom Stevenson had known slightly as a fellow commuter. His family had been honored as a "typical farm family of Illinois."

McGowan has said, "By seven o'clock it was clear that something was wrong. The Governor was due from Chicago at eight. Then Wray said he wasn't going to say anything else until he talked to his lawyer. I told him, 'You have every right to talk to your lawyer but if you leave now, I'm going to the Mansion at eight o'clock and tell the Governor that it looks like there's something wrong, that you left town to see your lawyer—and what do you think the Governor will think?' Wray was a rather simple man greatly devoted to the Governor. He's not a racketeer. He didn't know what to do. He asked if he could telephone his lawyer. I told him, 'Sure—but the minute you pick up the telephone we'll all leave the room and you'll have crossed the line, you'll no longer be in the family.' Well, it was a very difficult thing. He paced around the room. He wept. It was most painful."

Wray made a statement, and Director Yung fired him. He was in fear of his life; McGowan sent him home under state police protection. McGowan reported to Stevenson and turned Wray's statement over to the Lake County state's attorney. Wray was indicted in Lake County on charges of bribery. Subsequently he was acquitted. The case was never entirely clear. McGowan has said, "I never could figure it out. It was a case of organized crime. There were indications of it elsewhere in the United States. After all, hamburgers and cigarettes"—another racket soon to be investigated—"are much bigger than prostitution and gambling and narcotics. If the mob can get control of them, they're really in the big money."

The Chicago Syndicate was involved and had set up a slush fund for payoffs amounting to $600,000. The profits of the racket ran into the millions. Murders were blamed on horse meat racketeers. Late that spring police, seeking an ex-convict who had been involved in the hijacking of a load of beef, found in his apartment a piece of paper on which he had written "horse meat" in Italian. The investigation continued through the spring. The *Tribune* referred to

"Adlaiburgers." One man, told that his bail was fixed at $30,000, said, "Thirty thousand! They must think I ground up Man o' War." Gamblers whose handbooks were closed at about the same time said, "If we can't bet on 'em, we might as well eat 'em." Butchers asked housewives, "How do you want your hamburger—win, place, or show?"

No scandal in his administration hurt Stevenson more, probably because he himself had chosen Wray—he considered it a personal betrayal. When McGowan told him about it, he put his head in his hands and said, "My God, if Wray goes sour, I don't know, what can you depend on?" McGowan recalls, "He just sat there looking at his desk. He was really quite upset." (Wray, of course, was later adjudged not to have gone sour.) Later Stevenson was able to joke about it publicly, as when he said on a television program on February 3, 1952, "It looks like I'll be on a steady diet of horse meat from now until November." But privately he spoke of it with a gravity he did not give to any other problem of his administration. So late as the 1960s, talking with friends, he mentioned the "pain and grief" the horse meat scandal cost him. Shortly after the scandal, Stevenson appointed Ross Randolph, the FBI man, an administrative assistant. Actually, Randolph was Stevenson's personal investigator, and when Stevenson received complaints about state officials, he gave them to Randolph, not to the department concerned.

52

Early in September, Stevenson went to Washington to try to persuade the federal government to buy Illinois coal, thus helping the chronically depressed coal mining region, and Flanagan, still promoting him for President, arranged a party for the Washington press corps. The *Tribune* accused him of demagogy, saying he must have known his coal scheme would fail, and had only been seeking miners' votes.

Adlai III was going back to Harvard as a senior. "It startles me somehow," Stevenson told Alicia Patterson, "to think he's grown up & will be of age this fall—when only yesterday—But such reflections do no good and for me are very painful. Did I ever tell you that I'm a sickly sentimentalist and that I love my boys so that it literally hurts. Perhaps that's why I haven't been a better father." He said that he loved her too.

A Princeton classmate from Wall Street told Stevenson he had

"motored" through Illinois recently and had asked everybody he
met what they thought of the Governor—"I think you should know
how much your people love you." He added, "I have no hesitation
in predicting that you will be president some day." The president
of the University of Hawaii suggested the time had come for Stevenson to announce his candidacy for Vice President on a ticket with
Truman. Stevenson replied, "I am afraid your proposals do not
coincide either with the realities here or my own ambitions." On
September 30, Stevenson went to a Governors' Conference at Gatlinburg, Tennessee. There he delivered a speech on the states' responsibilities in the Korean War—his "hold the line" fiscal policy, the
National Guard, civil defense. Carl McGowan recalled, "At those
meetings he was invariably one of the two or three who stood out
markedly from the rest. His performances there, founded upon the
deep and absorbing interest he had in his job, had a lot to do with
the swift growth of his national reputation."

Stevenson saw General Marshall, who was visiting Gatlinburg and
whom Stevenson admired greatly. And he met privately with Governor Dewey of New York and Governor Driscoll of New Jersey and
perhaps other governors of big Northern states about a problem they
had in common—the counterfeiting of state cigarette tax stamps. As
McGowan said, cigarettes (and horse meat) were much bigger business than prostitution and gambling. Nearly everybody smoked (and
ate hamburgers). If the criminal syndicate could skim off a profit
from every pack of cigarettes, it need do little more. Revenue officials in Illinois and other states had known for some time that they
were losing state tax revenue. Stevenson, with McGowan's advice,
decided to do something about it. He moved quietly. He appointed
Ben W. Heineman, a Chicago lawyer, a special assistant attorney
general. Heineman, working with McGowan, conducted an investigation, using a firm of private detectives.

Illinois taxed cigarettes at three cents a pack. The state collected
the tax in part by using meters manufactured by the Pitney Bowes
Company and allocated to cigarette wholesalers by the state Department of Revenue. With his meter, the wholesaler printed the state
tax stamp on the bottom of each package of cigarettes. The meter
counted the number of packs printed with the tax stamp. A wholesaler had to go to the state revenue office and pay in advance the
tax for the number of packages he intended to stamp. When he
paid, the state sealed the meter; when the meter had printed the
assigned number of stamps, it stopped functioning, and the wholesaler had to take it back to the Revenue Department and pay to
have it reset.

Late in 1950 cigarette wholesalers had complained to Stevenson that their competitors were cutting prices below normal competitive possibilities. This suggested that their competitors were not paying the state tax. Moreover, the cigarette tax income started dropping off in the fiscal year 1950 and dropped still more the next year—yet cigarette consumption was increasing. Stevenson once estimated the state was losing $10 million (but later said it had been less).

Heineman's investigators bought 361 cartons of cigarettes in 125 stores in and near Chicago. Of these, 130 cartons contained counterfeit tax stamps. Further inquiry showed that about three out of every ten packs sold in the Chicago area had a counterfeit stamp. Moreover, the racket had been going on at least since 1947. It had begun with crude efforts to forge the tax stamps with a hand rubber stamp and with hijacking truckloads of cigarettes. It had become big business late in 1949, when four of the tax meters were stolen. From these machines, the counterfeiters made new dies and plates. They were expert—each legitimate meter had an assigned number and its plate had distinguishing characteristics known only to the Pitney Bowes Company; the counterfeiters in making their new plates used numbers already assigned to legitimate distributors.

Heineman sent investigators to Pitney Bowes, which trained them to recognize counterfeit stamps. The investigators traced cigarettes bearing counterfeit stamps to several wholesalers in the Chicago area. On November 27 fifty state policemen raided the wholesalers without notifying the Chicago police or anyone else, just as earlier they had raided gambling houses. They collected samples of the wholesalers' stock and took them to a Pitney Bowes expert, who said that the stamps had been counterfeited in every case but one. In one place the police found a homemade tax meter. State and city police charged several men with violating the cigarette tax act. They were subsequently freed. On the day of the raids, November 27, Stevenson held a press conference in Chicago. He called the raids "eminently successful" and ordered the investigation continued. Subsequently several state tax collectors were fired. On December 2, Stevenson went on television, together with Heineman and the Director of Revenue, to explain what had happened.

Stevenson's political opponents lumped the cigarette tax case as a "scandal" with the Mulroy and horse meat scandals. The *Daily News* referred to the case that way, and Stevenson wrote a letter to the editor denying it and pointing to an advertisement (probably inspired by a Stevenson supporter) of the Chicago Association of Tobacco Distributors thanking Stevenson for exposing the tax stamp affair. He also referred to praise by the director of the Chicago Crime

Commission. He said he considered the investigation "not a 'scandal' but a great success."

Stevenson himself once said of the tax stamp affair, "We got on top of that one quickly and decisively." Carl McGowan said some years later, "Stevenson was the victim of the fact that he was the one state Governor who did something about it. This made it look like he was the only one that had a scandal. The Governors of New York and Pennsylvania and New Jersey knew for sure that the same thing had been going on there for a long time. It's still a problem in many states. This was one area where Stevenson got the unfair burden of seeming to have a scandal. I thought it was one of the best things he did."

53

On October 5, Stevenson spoke to the Young Democratic Clubs of America at St. Louis. This speech suggested why Stevenson always had a powerful appeal for young people. He began by saying that some of the young Democrats had been in politics much longer than he, and he hoped to learn more about politics from them than he had learned from the old politicians at the Governors' Conference. He talked about the youth of his own staff, including Dick Nelson (who was elected national president of the Young Democrats at this convention). Then he launched into his familiar argument that, to succeed, representative democracy demanded and deserved the thoughtful participation of an informed electorate—and young blood: "more young men and women who have a positive concern for our public affairs and the health of our democratic system."

He moved to a partisan account of the history of the two parties—the GOP had lost its way at the turn of the century, the Democratic Party had remained the party of the people. Today the Republicans were deeply divided, especially on foreign policy, "the one all-important issue. . . . General Eisenhower, if he is a Republican, is just as far or even farther from Taft [than Dewey]—assuming anyone knows where Taft stands." And then, "It seems to me a sad thing that America, at the height of her power, influence, and well-being, should be ringing with slander, epithet, ill temper, and the counsels of political desperation. . . . A misbegotten breed of political demogogue . . . impugns the loyalty of patriotic men, especially Democrats. . . . On the eve of another national election campaign, we find the same Republican die-hards uttering the same old accusations and alarms. . . . They say confidently that the Democrats are licked, but struggle mightily to induce a great general and be-loved American to do the job for them."

He attacked the *Tribune* scornfully. He quoted Charles Dickens' *American Notes.* He quoted Abraham Lincoln. He flattered his au-dience with loftiness. "Perhaps it isn't the right thing to say at a party political convention, but who wins or loses the next elections in your states, in the nation—even in Illinois!—is less important than what wins: Will we stand fast and pay the price, whatever it be, for free-dom? Will we follow the course charted by Roosevelt and Truman, the course of resistance to the Soviets and assistance to our friends? Or will the counsels of retreat, withdrawal, and isolation prevail? . . . These are the questions that must be answered in the political arena of America next year. . . . Our party's record is good. Of course there have been mistakes and there will be more. But the policy, the objectives, the goal, have been consistent and clear. . . . It will be a big year. Make the most of it."

Thus Stevenson spoke, only a few months before he himself was nominated for President. It was a good political speech yet pitched at the high level where Stevenson was comfortable. Parts of it were a paste-up of previous speeches, as were so many of his speeches dur-ing these years—he lacked the staff to contrive a wholly new speech for each occasion and, moreover, he had certain ideas in his head, certain things he believed in and considered important, and he kept saying them, improving them with each refurbishing. This inevitably lent a consistency and coherence to his various speeches. And if they echoed the past, so did they portend the future—when he said, "What the elections decide is more important than who is elected," he was foreshadowing a passage in his welcoming speech to the 1952 National Democratic Convention.

The political atmosphere was heating up that fall. At one of the regular Thursday staff meetings, Stevenson's staff presented him with a pair of track shoes and a bulletproof vest, articles he would need in running for re-election next year. With Stevenson's stature in-creasing, with the presidential-gubernatorial year of 1952 coming up, and with scandals breaking, Stevenson's opponents increased their attacks. On October 7, Johnson Kanady of the *Tribune* wrote that members of Stevenson's administration "have the jitters over what has been called the 'October revolution'"—the firings and cabinet changes already noted. Kanady said Stevenson already had ap-pointed more directors than Governor Green in eight years. Ed Day undertook to rebut the charge. Some criticized Stevenson for having failed to stop gambling. Others criticized him for having stopped it with state police.

54

Mrs. Ives sent Stevenson some advice: if he decided to marry Dorothy Fosdick, he should forget about running for re-election as Governor—she was too careerist and aggressive to be comfortable in politics. He would have to abandon political life; perhaps he could enter diplomacy, which was her field and his.

About this same time, on October 16, Stevenson sent Alicia Patterson a long letter about 1952 presidential politics. He wrote, "Ike would, of course, be a very strong candidate. By saying that he would divide Reps, I didn't say that he would lose. The point I was trying to make . . . was that Taft vs. Truman would present the foreign policy issue much more clearly than Ike vs. HST. The Bertie [McCormick] wing of the Reps on this issue would have nowhere to go in Ike vs Truman. . . . As to whether Ike could beat HST, yes I think he would, but perhaps not so overwhelmingly as one would surmise in the present state of Trumans popularity. . . . I strongly suspect Taft can't be stopped among the regulars and I would feel much better about the future if he is not and the Dems. could nominate Ike—thus presenting the only really important issue in clear colors and letting Harry off. As you know he really does not want to run & takes very seriously the *principle* of the 2 term constitutional limitation on presidential terms. But I suppose that is too much to hope for. As for me I don't want any national business, nor do I intend to run for reelection *unless* I can be sure that the Dem. organ. in Ill & Chicago will give me a really good candidate for states attorney of Cook County, and some more things I will have to insist upon to make 4 more years of this hell endurable. I believe you'll agree that I should use the large bargaining power I now have to the utmost to accomplish some of the less conspicuous and more important long range objectives I have—i.e. better people in this business to make it a better business. I've done it in the administrative branch, with great difficulty, and before I get out I would like to help the party save itself and the system, at least in a small way. . . . I'm distracted and feel futile & ineffective all the time. And out doors the soft indian summer sun is shining, the skies are blue and all I want to do is roll in the leaves—Love Adpai," as he often signed himself to her.

On October 4, Stevenson tried to fly to Wausau, Wisconsin, to address the Democratic State Convention but bad weather grounded him. The speech he had prepared mounted a heavy attack on Senator Joseph McCarthy in his home state.

55

The wife of Lieutenant Governor Dixon gave a tea at the Mansion for women working on the Community Fund, and afterward Stevenson entertained Mrs. Dixon and her mother (it was her seventieth birthday) at dinner and put them up overnight. It was a characteristic generous gesture. On October 31 he gave a dinner for the heads of state mental institutions and Dr. Karl Menninger of the Menninger psychiatric clinic in Kansas. Menninger, at Fred Hoehler's invitation, had been inspecting Illinois hospitals. The visit made a lasting impression on both Stevenson and Menninger. Hereafter Stevenson seemed to take more interest in mental illness. A week earlier Mary Lasker's National Mental Health Committee had asked him to urge President Truman to increase the budget for the National Mental Health Institute, since only research could combat the rising cost of custodial care. Immediately after Menninger's visit, Stevenson did so. But he had only a loose grip on the problem of mental illness—a few weeks later he addressed the first annual convention of the National Association for Mental Health, and his speech was filled with empty rhetoric, betrayed an unfamiliarity with his subject, and adopted old-fashioned and vague ideas about "early diagnosis and treatment."[16]

On November 4, Stevenson went to Chicago for the first of a once-a-month series of Sunday television broadcasts called "Governor's Open House" and designed, as he said, "to get more people in Illinois interested in their state government." On camera, a secretary brought him some letters and read one, criticizing his "leniency" in paroling criminals; he launched a long defense of his parole policies, saying he had commuted only one death sentence. Another letter asked him to make wrestling a sport, not an exhibition, and to recognize lady wrestlers. He said, "This man is an optimist indeed if he thinks a mere Governor can purify and glamorize the wrestling business." Another letter protested his criticism of slot machines in private clubs, another said the Cicero riots had shamed Illinois. Stevenson denounced "bigotry and violence."

[16] Although Stevenson's partisans claimed he greatly improved Illinois's mental hospitals, it must be understood that they were among the nation's worst when he took office and after he left, they were still terrible.

On November 5 the Independent Voters of Illinois (IVI, the Illinois counterpart of the ADA) presented an award to Stevenson. His quarterly radio report to the people was broadcast on November 9, dealing with welfare, finance, gambling, highways, and trucks. That same day he went to New York and attended a Friars Club dinner at the Waldorf Astoria in honor of Jack Benny, the comedian. Stevenson had understood the dinner was a small affair and he need not speak. He was startled to discover 2,000 people on hand and himself at the speakers' table, unprepared. Dinner concluded, George Jessel, master of ceremonies, said he would call on the dignitaries to say a few words before calling on the professional entertainers, so the politicians would not have to follow the professionals. Jessel, however, called on all the dignitaries except Stevenson, then called on Fred Allen, a leading comedian of the time. As Stevenson later told the story, Allen unfolded his menu and inside it Stevenson, who had observed with some relief that none of the other speakers seemed to have prepared speeches, was horrified to see a speech text carefully underlined and ready for delivery. Allen delivered it, and the applause was great. Jessel immediately called on Stevenson. Stevenson said later, "I was never so absolutely terrified in my life." As he arose, some in the audience were still tittering at Allen's remarks. Stevenson said later, "I did the only thing I could think of. I said, 'Ladies and gentlemen, during the course of the dinner Mr. Allen and I were discussing what we would say here tonight. We traded manuscripts so that each of us could take a look at the other's speech. You have just heard Mr. Allen deliver my speech. And I must say he delivered it very well. As for Mr. Allen's speech, I have it here but I don't think it would amuse you.'" The crowd loved it. It was the beginning of an affinity between Stevenson and people in show business.[17]

Next day Stevenson went up to Cambridge for the Harvard-Princeton game. He returned to Springfield Monday, November 12. On November 13 he saw Bill Glasgow, a *Time* magazine staff writer from Chicago. Flanagan had been encouraging *Time* to do a cover story on Stevenson. Glasgow had been doing research in Bloomington and had run across the accidental killing of the child long ago. Glasgow asked Stevenson about it. "Stevenson looked away for a moment and then said: 'You know you are the first person who has talked to me about that since it happened—and this is the first time I have spoken of it to anyone.' I asked the Governor whether he minded

[17] Stevenson once said he had heard of someone else's having used the same dodge.

telling me the story. 'No,' said Stevenson, 'I'll tell you everything I can remember about it.' Then he told me the whole story, in a matter of fact way."

Flanagan's proseletyzing at *Time* was a part of his effort to get the presidential nomination for Stevenson. Lou Kohn was working to the same purpose. He urged Stevenson to make plans for the convention —if nothing else, Stevenson, as Governor of the host state, would have to welcome the delegates. Stevenson told him on November 14, "I think from now on you are my 'convention coordinator,' and some time you should tell me in detail what you have in mind that I should do. I think I could probably borrow someone's apartment in town, which, together with my [Chicago] office, should make a hotel suite unnecessary."

On November 18, Stevenson went to Washington and en route wrote to Alicia Patterson:

I'm in a dreadful travail about politics. I literally don't know whether I could physically survive another campaign and 4 more years. Yet if I slow up as everyone advises, I dread the possibility of the administration slipping back, losing the momentum and the public confidence I've gained. And it all seems to depend on me— the pace, the tone, the everlasting pressure, and the public preaching about the state govt. and good govt. Moreover if Ike runs and it turns into a landslide as well it might I'm not sure I could win against the deluge. If I quit now the record would be excellent and how many politicians quit at the peak of popularity; I might save not only the record, but my health and even make money somehow which I've neglected for 10 yrs plus, or be available for some other govt service. Meanwhile I'm playing strong and silent, and turning on the pressure for good candidates which, if I get them, will prove my theory that men can influence political organizations, no matter how big and powerful, rather than the converse—and you don't have to be a political "boss"—to do it. All of which is another way of saying that the people—which means public opinion, which means the "press"—can still run the democratic system and run it right if it is fair and honest. But that's oversimplifying. On a grander scale Ike illustrates this point. . . . I'll have to make up my mind before long. . . . I have to confer with the State Dept. Tuesday—then back to Spfd—but I don't think I'll call on Truman, altho to put him in a position of asking me to run might have future value. But the press & therefore public reaction would be "pledging support" etc. which wouldn't do me any good in Ill. among the people, where he is hardly popular to say the least. [Clearly Stevenson was thinking of himself as a presidential candidate long before he emerged as one publicly.] I'm glad you're having Buffy to dinner. . . . She's a difficult person for me—little actual knowledge, very possessive and self confident about whats right and wrong for me, but irrationally loyal and loving, and sensitive about me. Besides I love her very much! And you too, my beloved—

A

56

At Gettysburg, Stevenson delivered a short, tightly written, eloquent speech that began with language reminiscent, perhaps too reminiscent, of Lincoln's:

"We are met here today on the field of a bloody, shattering battle. And we meet in reverence for the tall, gaunt man who, standing here eighty-eight years ago, mindful of the dead and the cause for which they here died, phrased in words, clean of all ornament, the duty of the living to continue the striving. The struggle did continue, the high fever that was Gettysburg passed, and the democratic experiment survived its mortal crisis.

"More than the survival of the American Union was at issue here in Gettysburg. Upon the fate of the Union hung the fate of the new dream of democracy throughout the world. . . . America was democracy's proving ground. The masses of other lands looked to us with hope. If our experiment proved successful, they too might win self-government. . . .

"Lincoln saw the war in its global dimensions. . . . Americans were dying for the new, revolutionary idea of the free man, even as they had died at Bunker Hill and Yorktown. They were dying to save the hope of all people everywhere. . . .

"The war ended. The nation, reunited, once again offered hope for liberal yearnings everywhere. Inspired by the example of America, democracy made striking headway throughout the world, even among the so-called backward peoples of the earth." The same struggle for freedom, he said, had been made against the Kaiser and against Hitler and was being repeated in Korea.

The *Tribune* termed Stevenson's thesis "preposterous": "Lincoln, the great nationalist apostle of the indestructibility of the Union, emerged under the Stevenson treatment as a One Worlder who fought the Civil war to make the world safe for 'democracy'. . . . Furthermore, Adlai declaimed, Lincoln would have indorsed the

Truman excursion into Korea. We should enjoy a little textual proof of this unique theory, which seems to carry us back four score and seven red herrings ago." It quoted a Lincoln letter saying "we have forborne from taking part in any controversy between foreign states"; and said, "Well, we should not have expected Adlai to understand Lincoln very well—not when his Democratic grandfather stumped the state of Illinois for Gen. McClellan against Lincoln in 1864."

The editorial galled Stevenson. He sent it to Alicia Patterson with a note: "Here's Bertie's last—trying to cut Lincoln down to a nationalist with no vision of the implications of the Civil War to democratic aspirations beyond the U.S. The historians are contra." Next day he talked to Dutch Smith about the editorial. Smith sent the editorial to Benjamin P. Thomas, a Lincoln scholar, and suggested an article or editorial in rebuttal.

Nor did the matter rest there. A Chicagoan named Harry G. Green told Stevenson that his researches did not support the *Tribune*'s statement that Stevenson's grandfather had campaigned for McClellan. Encouraged by Stevenson, Green wrote a letter to the editor of the *Tribune*. Still Stevenson carried the question on, writing to his aunts, who sent him old clippings and other materials. And on December 13, speaking in Chicago at an important Democratic National Committee dinner, Stevenson said, according to the *Tribune,* "The Tribune is entitled to its views of the world, but pray God they don't prevail now any more than they did in 1863, when the publisher said we could not win the Civil war." The *Tribune* published a long story about the controversy, saying, "Gov. Stevenson, self-confessed friend and 'believer in' Alger Hiss, convicted traitor, is the grandson of a pro-slavery, pro-southern Democrat who was shown to have been an Illinois Copperhead and member of anti-northern secret organizations in 1863 and 1864 . . . who hired a substitute when ordered to service in the northern armies in 1864." It quoted at great length from ancient editorials, letters, and affidavits. It is difficult to believe that any of this mattered to the *Tribune*'s readers or Stevenson's constitutents. But it mattered to Colonel McCormick and Governor Stevenson, and so they continued their dubious battle. Stevenson told Alicia on December 19, "That lousy Tribune has now and for the third time taken to attacking Grandfather. The absurd charges in this story which were trumped up in the 1908 campaign were all disproved then which the Tribune overlooks now. They have also carefully overlooked any mention of Jesse Fell who probably had more to do with Lincoln's nomination—" and so on. He disclaimed interest: "However I've become so serene and indifferent I don't react any more." What makes this episode remarkable is that Stevenson at the time had more than enough on his hands—the cigarette tax raids, far-reaching political decisions, and a crowded calendar.

He saw Joe Gill and Dick Daley in Chicago on November 26. He told John Miller, "I wish I could make up my mind about whether to run again." He told Irving Dilliard of the *Post-Dispatch,* "I am very loathe—and getting more so—to run again, and I need the sober counsel of a wise man and a good friend." The *Illinois Public Official,* a small political newspaper, said that Stevenson was under pressure to run from Democrats in both Illinois and Washington and if he refused he would be accused of deserting his party when it needed him and of putting his own welfare above the public good.

Arguments existed against running. Stratton, the probable Republican candidate, was a good campaigner. Stevenson would be in a weaker position than in 1948—he could not attack, would have to defend his record, including the scandals, and he had made enemies as well as friends while Governor. Moreover, the Truman administration, plagued by Korea and scandals, was unpopular. It looked as though 1952 would be a Republican year. If Eisenhower ran for President as a Republican, he might win in a landslide, and Stevenson might lose the governorship in the landslide. On the other hand, if Stevenson retired to private life, he would be abandoning the program he had begun and the people who had supported him. Most likely Eddie Barrett, the Secretary of State for whom he had no use (nor Barrett for him), would be nominated, a prospect that disheartened Stevenson. And what, realistically, lay ahead? He was nearly fifty-two. Practicing law would seem dull. A high position in the State Department would almost surely be impossible if Eisenhower became President. He had passed beyond the time to take a job at the UN Secretariat. And, finally, public affairs had been his lifelong interest. It is hard to believe that he seriously came close to deciding to retire. Nevertheless, throughout December he continued to appear undecided. By doing so, he could demand that the party put forward a good ticket in return for his consent to run.

Did the party want him? He had enemies in the party, to be sure. But for the party to deny him renomination would have been almost impossible—it would be to repudiate its own record, to appear as the enemy of its own good-government candidate, and to risk almost certain defeat. Moreover, if 1952 promised to be a bad year for Democrats, the party could be expected to nominate its strongest candidate for Governor, and Stevenson was surely that.

57

During the first week in December he made a report to the people on television, attended a Northwestern reception, spoke at the dedication of a temple, attended the Chicago Bar Association's annual Christmas party, and held a series of political meetings, taking time out for a hunting trip and hospital tests. Dorothy Fosdick reported a new scandal in the Truman administration, perhaps fatally damaging to the Administration, she said. Some people thought it would encourage the Republicans to nominate Taft, whom they wanted, instead of Eisenhower, whom they had thought they needed—any Republican could win now.

Marietta Tree and her husband stayed at the Mansion the nights of December 7 and 8. Jane Dick was there too, and they played charades. Marietta invited Stevenson to stay with them in New York and to visit them in Barbados, where they had a beautiful winter place. On Sunday after their visit, December 9, Stevenson went to Washington and saw Dorothy Fosdick. Lou Kohn was trying to put together a book of Stevenson's speeches to be published during the spring and promote his presidential candidacy; Miss Fosdick sent him, on his request, speeches Stevenson had made at the UN.[18]

Back in Chicago on December 13, Stevenson spoke to the Democratic National Committee. It was an important occasion, bringing together party leaders from around the country. He spoke sarcastically about the divisions in the Republican Party and the differences between Taft and Dewey, between Taft and Eisenhower. He attacked McCarthy. He took note of charges of Democratic corruption and quoted Charles Evans Hughes on Teapot Dome: "Guilt is personal and knows no party," then said, "If there is Democratic dirt let us clean it up and turn the flashlight into every dark corner." He returned to the attack: "May responsible Democrats never ape the political charlatans and false prophets who promise us painless solutions of the painful problems that bedevil our world. There are no painless solutions to war, inflation, Communism, imperialism, hunger, fear, and all the diseases of a tormented world." Those themes would recur later.

---

[18] Kohn approached the present author about editing the book. It became not a collection of speeches but a short biography that Harper & Brothers published after Stevenson was nominated.

Stevenson spent the rest of the week in Chicago. On Friday he attended a ceremony at the Merchandise Mart and had lunch with its owner, Joseph Kennedy. Sargent Shriver, who managed the Mart and later married Kennedy's daughter Eunice, told Stevenson that "your girl friends and ardent admirers, Eunice and Jean [her sister], were overjoyed to see you." Sending Stevenson a copy of Joseph Kennedy's speech, Shriver said, "My boss may not agree one hundred per cent with you on matters covered in this speech, but he certainly enjoyed his lunch & tells me you are one of the very few office holders who might do a real job as Democratic candidate for you know what! Hope you agree & decide to do so—NOW!" Stevenson, replying, made no comment on the idea that he might run for President. (Later, Shriver offered to join Stevenson's staff to help organize his candidacy for President. Stevenson told him, as he told others, that he would run in 1952 not for President but for re-election as Governor.)

Stevenson signed a note to Alicia Patterson, "The Waif of Ogden & Menominee!"—her family home in Chicago where they had met in secret. It seemed a long time ago. He wrote to her again on the nineteenth, describing his hospital tests and saying they gave him "no good and sufficient reasons to thumb my nose at the pols for keeps." He hoped to visit her in Georgia at the end of January. He told her, "I've been in fiendish travail trying to decide what to do. The party wants and needs me desperately this time. But where does it all lead? Four more years of this and, if I'm still alive, where am I? 4 yrs older, feebler, completely out of touch with the international field, no job, no security (damnable word), and no use, except in politics for 'higher office', which I don't want. In short, it would seem to me that now is the time to get out and during the remaining year of my term when my availability would be known look about for something else to do. However I'm sure to succumb to the [illegible] I suppose. Meanwhile I'm using my bargaining power for all its worth to get as good candidates as I can—particularly in Chicago. As to the national, Tafts professional political backing seems to be growing apace, and Ike is in the unhappy position of coming back, changing clothes, and at once losing much of his reverential following or staying in Europe awaiting the draft that may never come, especially as the word gets around that Truman won't run. If I were Ike and wanted the nomination I would stay in Europe, keep up the impression that Taft can't win & hope the hungry leaders would ditch Taft at the convention to be sure of a winner."

A round of Christmas parties began in Springfield. On Friday, the twenty-first, Stevenson gave a children's party at 4:30 P.M. and a

staff party at 6 P.M. That day a coal mine, the New Orient Mine No.
2 at West Frankfort, blew up, killing 119 men, more than were
killed at Centralia. Next morning Stevenson flew to the scene. He said
later that "it was about the most distressing experience in war and
peace." The dead men left 100 widows and 162 children under
eighteen. Stevenson said, as he reconstructed it later, "This is a sad
Christmas. I came down to West Frankfort to see if the state is doing all it can to help. All of the state's trained rescue teams are on
the job and the rescue work is proceeding as rapidly as possible.
. . . I hope people will send me contributions for the dependents of
the dead and the injured at this Christmas season. Illinois was on
the eve of a national all time safety record—only one fatality per
one and a half million tons of coal mined this year. The cause of the
explosion must have been gas, but the place was inspected in usual
routine only an hour and a half before the accident took place.
. . . I hope the disaster was not due to anything a modern mine
safety code would have prevented. I presented one—the work of
months—at the last session of the Legislature, but neither the unions,
the operators nor the Senators from Southern Illinois would support
it."[19]

He ordered an investigation headed by Walter Eadie, Director
of Mines and Minerals, and asked Harold Walker of the University
of Illinois to work with the investigators "on my personal behalf." A
federal investigation began.

The federal safety code was stricter than the state. But federal
inspectors had no power to force coal companies to comply with
their recommendations. State inspectors did have the power. The
last full state inspection of New Orient No. 2, made less than two
weeks before the disaster, had found ventilation "good" and rock-
dusting "fair." (When methane gas is present in a mine, as it was at
New Orient No. 2, its explosiveness is decreased by ventilation.
Coal dust is also highly explosive. To reduce its combustibility, rock
dust is mixed with it. Any local explosion in a mine may throw into
the air clouds of coal dust, and if rock-dusting has been insufficient,
the clouds of dust will in turn explode, thus throwing more dust into
the air, and so on, propagating the explosion throughout the mine in
a chain reaction, turning what might have been only a small local explosion into a great disaster. Existing law set forth precisely how
much rock dust must be applied.) In addition to periodic full inspec-

[19] Stevenson's mining bills had passed the 1949 session of the Legislature
but he was unable to persuade the coal operators, unions, and downstate
legislators to agree to revisions he requested in 1951. They would probably
not have prevented the explosion.

tions, each coal company had its own mine examiners, union members who went into the mine every day before each shift started to work. Only a short while before the explosion at New Orient No. 2, the mine examiners had found nothing abnormal.

Stevenson, in a radio talk, said that "either present safety measures are not enough or their enforcement by the industry and the state is not good enough, or both." Stevenson prodded the Mining Commission to hold hearings on the New Orient No. 2 disaster and a new Mining Code. It was reluctant. An operator's representative said, "In the mining fields we think the thing to do is let a thing like this settle down, not stir it up." A union man concurred.

The various investigations were unable to determine precisely what had caused the explosion at New Orient No. 2. Several theories were put forward. Harold Walker of the University of Illinois said that, whatever had caused the initial explosion, it had been propagated through the mine "because of the inadequacy of rock-dusting." It had been precisely this that had caused the Centralia disaster. Director Eadie now thought that visual examination alone was not adequate to determine the need for rock-dusting. Eadie, before Stevenson appointed him Director, had been mine manager of New Orient No. 2. McGowan sent a letter to Director Eadie over Stevenson's signature asking about methods other than visual inspection. Eadie replied that in doubtful cases an inspector could collect dust samples and send them to the state laboratory but the New Orient Mine No. 2, largest underground coal mine in the world, contained about sixty miles of entries and rooms which needed rock-dusting and it would be impossible for an inspector to collect dust samples from so large an area. The state inspector at New Orient No. 2, James Wilson, had recommended rock-dusting at New Orient No. 2 three times in 1951; each time the company had complied. During 1951 state mine inspectors throughout the state had taken 2,051 dust samples; Wilson had taken only four. Eadie wrote, "Mr. Wilson has apparently depended too much upon visual examinations. . . . I did have confidence [in him]." In June, Wilson was fired for neglect and incompetence. He told the Chicago *Tribune* that, at Director Eadie's request, he and other inspectors had contributed to the Democratic campaign fund in 1950. A Stevenson staff member said that Stevenson had disavowed the 1950 campaign contributions at that time.

Stevenson's opponents likened the New Orient disaster to the Centralia disaster. There was the one similarity—inadequate rock-dusting. On the other hand, the differences were greater. The cause of the Centralia disaster was clear and it could have been avoided; the cause of New Orient No. 2 was less clear and it could less clearly have been avoided. The inspector at Centralia had repeatedly warned that the mine was dangerous and the company had ignored his warnings; the inspector at New Orient had seemed satisfied that the mine was safe and the company had followed his recommendations. (Indeed mining men talked about New Orient No. 2 as a "model" mine.) The Centralia miners had repeatedly asked the Department of Mines and Minerals to force the company to comply with the law and once had appealed to Governor Green himself to save their lives; no such steps had been taken at New Orient No. 2. An investigation after the Centralia disaster had disclosed that some inspectors (not the one at Centralia) had solicited campaign contributions from coal mine operators; no evidence other than Wilson's accusation after he was fired followed the New Orient disaster.

Stevenson's opponents criticized him for not having pushed the Legislature to rewrite the mining law. Carl McGowan once said, "If Stevenson had wanted to play tongue-in-cheek politics and public relations up to the hilt, he could have introduced that bill—but he knew it wouldn't pass, so introducing it would have been an empty gesture." In retrospect it appears that, while the Stevenson administration was far less culpable than the Green administration, it deserved at least as much criticism as it received. One searches Stevenson's letters to Alicia Patterson in vain for any indication that the New Orient disaster grieved him or, indeed, for any mention of it less unfeeling than this: "Christmas chaos, politics, decisions, explosions, crises, presents, children—and now a horse meat scandal! Ugh!"

Christmas Eve Stevenson attended midnight services at the Presbyterian Church with Mr. and Mrs. Ives, Tim Ives, and Attorney General and Mrs. Elliott. Stevenson's sons arrived and he gave the annual Christmas dance for them. The Edison Dicks arrived for a family New Year's Eve party. He canceled another party. Dorothy Fosdick thought he was right to go ahead with the boys' party despite the mine disaster.

58

Newspapers were speculating now that he might not run for reelection. Friends and relatives besought him to. One, however, warned that good government could not depend on a single man. Stevenson replied, "I suppose I will capitulate—and probably live to regret it."

Stevenson was hanging back chiefly in order to pressure the machine into dumping John Boyle, the Cook County state's attorney. Stevenson was on a first-name basis with Boyle. But Boyle had not been a successful state's attorney, and the press opposed his re-election. The *Daily News* said he had not convicted any important gangsters and attempted to prosecute few. He had retained Captain Dan Gilbert as his chief investigator despite Kefauver Committee disclosures about Gilbert. The Kefauver Committee had also shown that, before his election, Boyle had done legal work for a racing service with gangster connections. (So had other lawyers.) Worse still, one of Boyle's investigators, Mike Moretti, had shot three young men, killing two, during an off-duty drinking spree, and Boyle, the *Sun-Times* said, had railroaded the case past a grand jury. The *Sun-Times* had demanded the case be reopened, and it had been. Ultimately, despite powerful political connections, Moretti had been convicted, but only by special prosecutors, and Boyle had said, "I suppose I'll have Moretti around my neck for a long time." Finally, a grand jury had returned indictments in the Cicero riot which a court subsequently dismissed, and Boyle was blamed.

For all these reasons, and perhaps others, Stevenson had decided to get rid of Boyle. Carl McGowan pointed out, "When Stevenson did decide to cross the organization it needed courage, because the spectre of Horner was always there—is it worth it to dump John Boyle? It might jeopardize more important things." The state's attorney's office is one of the most important and sensitive of county offices. To a considerable extent the state's attorney decides who will be indicted and who will not. Boyle had deep connections in the machine; dumping him was not easy. Stevenson, however, accomplished it. Boyle struck back: "Stevenson will not turn his back on Alger Hiss but he will on the State's Attorney of Cook County. What is this?" Stevenson replied, "What does Mr. Boyle mean? Would he, a lawyer, refuse to tell what he had heard about the reputation of a defendant in a criminal trial for fear the defendant might later be convicted? . . . Mr. Boyle should direct his political attack at the Democratic Committee, not at me. They make the decisions. I was told long ago that they would not endorse him for reelection. I am sorry that he is angry at me. Personally, I like him very much."

In Boyle's stead, the machine slated Judge John Gutknecht, an upright man though a rather lackluster campaigner. Boyle ran against him in the primary and lost badly. In all fairness, it must be said that Boyle was not entirely to blame for everything that had gone wrong while he was state's attorney. Early the summer before, Boyle had told Stevenson he thought he saw a chance to prosecute Anthony J. Accardo, generally considered the head of the Chicago Syndicate, and he had asked Stevenson to help him get Accardo's income tax records for 1949 and 1950. Stevenson had written to President Truman, requesting access to the returns. Some six weeks later President Truman said that he could not comply with the request—the returns could be used only in connection with the administration of tax laws. (Accardo's returns themselves were under federal investigation at the time.)

On January 5, almost immediately after Boyle attacked him, Stevenson issued his announcement that "after long and prayerful consideration" he himself had decided to run for re-election as Governor. "That office, like many others, has its heavy burdens. But the burdens are also opportunities to give Illinois the kind of government it ought to have. . . . And I take great satisfaction in the progress we have made since 1949. But I have learned that the road is long and we have far to go before any of us, myself included, can in good conscience stop and rest. I invite the Republican Party to nominate the best man it can find. It is of little importance whether the next Governor of Illinois is named Adlai Stevenson; but it is of the highest importance that he finish what we have started. No matter then who loses, the people will win."

59

On Friday, January 18, Stevenson met with a "planning group" to organize a campaign committee. On February 6, Stevenson sent Steve Mitchell a $5,000 check to open the Stevenson-for-Governor account. He appointed Donald Funk its downstate chairman and Don Forsyth, the Springfield insurance man, his personal campaign manager. Forsyth recalls, "Things went well—we started to raise money early and we had $300,000 by convention time."

Early in February an important Republican politician from the West Side of Chicago, Charles Gross, was shot dead. Great uproar ensued, and Republicans began purging from public payrolls everybody from hoodlum-dominated wards. Democrats did not. On February 8, Stevenson said, "I'm glad Chicago has awakened to this menace. I hope it stays awake until we are rid of this creeping cancer. I have never bowed to these people and I never will. If any of them have crept onto the state payroll, I want to know it." He offered to meet with leaders of both parties on how to destroy "hoodlum political power." (No such meeting was held, and when reporters later questioned Stevenson about it, he denied he had called such a meeting himself and said he had merely offered to make his office and himself available for such a meeting but no one had responded.) Three days later he announced he had discussed the question with Mayor Kennelly and Dick Daley, by now vice chairman of the Cook County Democratic Committee. Several things could be done, he said. Organized gambling could be "virtually eliminated" in Cook County. Better methods of selecting judges could be devised. Redistricting would eliminate "rotten burroughs" and "undesirable influences" in the legislature—the West Side Bloc. He had ordered an investigation of state employees in Chicago and if any hoodlums were found on the state payroll they would be fired, regardless of sponsorship. Nobody who was "a part of this criminal conspiracy" should be on the public payrolls.

On February 15, Kanady of the *Tribune* asked Larry Irvin for a "progress report" on getting rid of payrollers sponsored by the West Side Bloc. Irvin said he had asked the departments for a report on employees who came from hoodlum-dominated wards but added that "no innocent people will be fired just because they happen to live in a particular ward." The purge would be selective, not total. On February 20, Stevenson told Irvin that state employees were doing patronage screening at Democratic State Committee headquarters and told him to get them off the state payroll promptly. Stevenson, having announced his candidacy, was moving quickly to put his house in order.

In his year-end radio report to the people on January 10, he discussed state problems and looked back over his three years. He said a "vast new program of highway reconstruction" had begun. Dr. Menninger had reported that Illinois had made "tremendous progress" with its mental hospitals. Nationally, industrial accidents had increased 14 per cent in 1951; in Illinois they had declined by 1 per cent. Two clinics for the treatment and rehabilitation of narcotic addicts had been opened in Chicago. The Illinois Commerce Commission, with a staff reduced by one third, had done 30 per cent more work than formerly. The Liquor Control Commission had ended large-scale bootlegging from Cairo, Illinois, to dry states. The new Commission on Human Relations was "spearheading a promising program for greater interracial understanding in Illinois." The State Employment Service had abolished racial designation in applications for employment; the Attorney General had created a new branch of his office to deal with violations of civil rights; the charter of the "infamous" White Circle League had been revoked; many cities had formed new human relations groups; the state Chamber of Commerce was conducting an educational campaign to eliminate racial discrimination in employment.

The state police, freed from politics, had performed well in cigarette tax and gambling raids, Stevenson went on. The state's financial position was good. "The new year is always a time for looking ahead. . . . It [1952] will be a political year. . . . I hope that partisanship and the intemperance which is so characteristic of campaigns will not obscure truth and the broader interests of the nation and of Illinois."

60

Before this month of January 1952 was out, Stevenson was involved in presidential politics. Although he continued to govern Illinois for another full year, increasingly national politics took his time this spring and, after the convention, of course, the campaign took all of it. This, therefore, may be a good time to assess his record as Governor.

Stevenson himself, in notes made for a Jackson Day dinner speech in East St. Louis on February 26, wrote: "Record—Not all successes—many disappointments, failures and shattered illusions: But more successes & satisfactions," and he noted his successes starting with schools and the state police.

More formal appraisals were prepared by his partisans during 1952. They claimed that he had been "a strong advocate of progressive measures," a foe of crime and corruption and favoritism, and a "great and economical administrator." They praised his appointments and said that under him Illinois "has been a low tax, low spending state." Ed Day, in a tract on the Stevenson record, emphasized his frugality and his belief that government should do as little as possible. He made no claim to liberalism for Stevenson save a single reference to his support of civil rights. To a reporter who asked him that spring what he considered his major accomplishments, Stevenson himself put at the top of the list "a higher moral tone" in government and "more people around the Statehouse with a sense of mission." Bill Rivkin prepared a memorandum claiming that Stevenson had fired 1,300 payrollers, including 50 affiliated with newspapers, but added that Stevenson had increased employment in the Highway Department and state police. The Agriculture Department prepared a "fact sheet" listing fifteen measures Stevenson had taken to promote economy. Other departments did likewise during the campaign. Press releases were prepared to show that Illinois had the "second lowest tax burden in the Nation."

On the other hand, the *Tribune,* in an editorial four years later, contrasted the Stevenson administration with that of his Republican successor, Stratton, showing that it was Stratton, not Stevenson, who had pushed reapportionment through the legislature, improved the mental hospitals, "brought honesty" into food inspection, provided cash for schools, held more civil service examinations, and prevented prison riots (a serious riot occurred at Menard Penitentiary in the fall of 1952).

All these were partisan appraisals, the favorable ones made in 1952 to promote Stevenson's presidential campaign, the unfavorable one made to help Stratton and Eisenhower in their 1956 campaigns. Other appraisals made years later after Stevenson's death have the advantage of perspective. Stevenson's son, Adlai III, once said, after he himself had sat in the Illinois House of Representatives and been elected State Treasurer, "After I went to the House, I realized that my father might have been an even greater Governor. He had a chance to change permanently the government of Illinois. It's easy in hindsight but I don't think he fully understood the power he had. No Governor of Illinois has recognized this power. He told me he thought I ought to practice law, make a name in the community, and go into public life late and at a high level, the way he did it. I think there's something to be said for going into politics early and going up the ladder and learning how to get along in politics. Dad might have gotten along better if he had known politics and politicians better in those early years. The politicians usually resent a man who suddenly comes in at the top. Resentment is something you can do without in public life. In my life, his was often a voice of caution— understandably for a father weary of many fights and worried about the pitfalls awaiting a young man. But he may have been overly cautious. But he gave the state good government. He was a good judge of character and I suppose that is the most important ability of a good administrator. But I think if he had had more experience in politics and he had better understood the dimensions of his power, he might have done more to reform the government and the party. He didn't discover the real dimensions of the office in time. The Governor is the most powerful man in the state of Illinois. I mean favors, patronage, press, all the rest. He didn't use it to remake the party and change things at the grass roots. There's a great opportunity there for any Governor—to get patronage into the hands of his friends, to get better candidates and a better legislature. If he had been a politician he'd have been more than a match for the Eddie Barretts and Paul Powells. He was improving government at the top on the theory that it would trickle down. But you've got to start from the bottom up too. He was learning, and learning fast, when his own term expired."

Abner Mikva, the young lawyer from the 5th Ward, the University of Chicago district, got interested in state politics because of Stevenson. He had been a law clerk to Supreme Court Justice Minton and had considered entering the federal government. In 1952, however, he returned to Illinois and went to work for Stevenson. "And I became aware how important state government could be. Because Stevenson was the first active state leader that could excite young people. Horner never did." Later, Mikva was elected to the state House of Representatives and the Congress, sometimes opposing the machine, sometimes supported by it. He exemplified the bright young liberal college men whom Stevenson attracted to the party. He has said he considered Stevenson's greatest accomplishment, in his entire life, the record he made as Governor. "I went to Springfield under the impression that he was an ineffective Governor. This was a myth created by Paul Powell. But the truth is that to this day you can't turn anywhere in Illinois without seeing his mark. For example in the police. In gambling, there was always the threat of the state police coming in after Stevenson. So all the gambling became sneak stuff. For another example, the Department of Finance. Joe Pois made it the Governor's internal audit and fiscal agent of Illinois—and it still is. For example, the budgeting process—it is still terrible but it's better than most states. There are other examples of how he pushed things—FEPC, Con-Con, reapportionment. He was ahead of his time. These were all basic things, and they were all first pushed by Stevenson. And Stevenson was the first Governor with a concept of civil liberties. His reforms in mental health did not stick—but later in 1960 it became the issue that elected Kerner. It's hard to think that he was only Governor for four years. He had a profound influence."

Carl McGowan, who worked more closely with Stevenson on substance than anyone else during most of his governorship, once said, "The big criticism of him as Governor was that he didn't think in terms of spending enough money. Though he made a great record for fiscal responsibility, this is not necessarily good. Illinois needed more money for mental hospitals. His instinct was to be a low-budget man. If he'd gone on being Governor, he would have had to go for increased revenues and spending. I think he'd have found it a lot harder than to veto the Broyles bill. But the Governors that are remembered built stuff. It's no more fun to live poor as a Governor than in a private family." Stevenson should have done more to help Chicago and education, McGowan thought. "We didn't really anticipate what was going to be needed in education. He did not want to contemplate a tax increase. I think this was wrong. If he needed more money, he should have gotten it—recommended a tax increase. People loved Governor Dever [of Massachusetts] after he built a highway around Boston. They began to say, 'That Governor's pretty good, after all, isn't he—he's doing stuff.' Horner passed a sales tax at the bottom of the depression and got away with it. It's good politics to do stuff. The AFL-CIO always yells about increasing taxes, especially the sales tax, but they didn't really care. Of course, you have to understand that under Green there had been a spending orgy. Stevenson had to see what the urgent needs were. If he had had a second term, all this might have changed. Those who said they were for Eisenhower solely for reasons of fiscal responsibility knew not whereof they spoke. They voted against the man who was, if they could but have known, their dream candidate."

McGowan adds, "On the whole, though, he was a pretty damn good Governor. His growing acceptance around the state—with politicians as well as with the League of Women Voters—was based on the skill with which he handled them. Even some of the Chicago pols came to like him. The only bitterness came when real economic interests clashed. On patronage they had nothing to complain about. Stevenson did not shake up the system." Was Stevenson a federalist? McGowan said, "The more he got interested in state government, the more he felt state governments had greater potentialities than they were realizing. He took the line that there were things that we could do—some things—better than Washington could do them. He never was a confirmed states rightist—never thought that everything Washington did was bad. But he felt the state could have a more significant function and his experience in Washington led him not to be starry-eyed about Washington."

Stevenson's hardest decision as Governor was to send the state police against gambling, McGowan thought. As to Stevenson's liberal credentials, McGowan cited the Broyles bill veto and the Hiss deposition, though he considered the latter a mistake. "He would say that what he was spending a lot of time on was trying to upgrade mental hospitals—this was a bigger contribution to the world than sitting around brooding about free speech all the time."

As Governor, Stevenson worked hard. By the start of his third year he ran the state with a sure hand. Ironically, it was during that very year that the scandals began. Every one of the scandals was connected with the Chicago Syndicate. The governorship was Stevenson's initiation into the alliance between criminals and politicians, a rough initiation in a rough state.

While Governor, he was moderately successful in getting his program through the legislature, more than moderately so if one considers that the Senate was Republican during both his sessions and the House during one. The program itself was far from revolutionary. And as McGowan said, he adopted an unduly tight-fisted fiscal policy, partly by instinct and partly for political reasons, fearing the *Tribune*'s "big spender" label. Nearly every one of the lists of Stevenson's "accomplishments" prepared in 1952 by his supporters stressed his frugality. But his frugality did not advance Illinois.

As a political leader, Stevenson was not outstanding. True, he forced the slating of Wally Schaefer for Supreme Court justice and the dumping of State's Attorney Boyle. And he attracted bright young liberals to his party. But he did little more to improve his party and the quality of its candidates. Whether he could have is debatable. The Cook County machine is hard to budge, and so are the downstate county chairmen. Stevenson was more effective as a leader of the people. His sensitivity to newspaper criticism helped him use the press skillfully. He conceived his role as one of "preaching" to the people, of educating them and urging them to pay attention to state government; and he was at his best when he went over the heads of legislators and parties and spoke directly to the people. By this means, and by bringing good men into government, he did indeed improve the tone, or spirit, of state government. This, in a state as big and corrupt as Illinois, is no small accomplishment. He displayed his talents as an administrator chiefly by appointing good men. All this may have been his greatest achievements as governor. While Stevenson was Governor, Springfield and the Statehouse seemed somehow cleaner and brighter than before or since. A fresh wind was blowing. If it did not work permanent change in many areas, if it did not cleanse every dark corner of the moldy Capitol, at least for a time it brought new promise to a capital that too often forgets that Abraham Lincoln is more than a tourist attraction.

Stevenson's term as Governor, indeed, only its first three years, comprised the last period of his life when he was primarily an Illinoisan. From the spring of 1952 he moved to a wider stage, first national, then international. It was Illinois that shaped him and prepared him to try to shape his world. First Bloomington, then Lake Forest and Chicago, then Springfield—these were the places where he was formed. During his time as Governor, too, he passed through one of the great crises of his private life, his divorce. As Governor, as well as earlier and later, he presented the appearance of a man gay and insouciant, funny and brave. The inner man was at times unhappy, frustrated, lonely, self-doubting. His private life up to now, despite his love affairs, contained more than its share of misery. As a child, he had suffered the agonies of quarreling and sick parents and a sometimes dominating mother and older sister; and he had himself accidentally killed a child. While he was Governor, Mrs. Ives competed with his women friends for possession of him, just as she had competed with Ellen and, earlier, their mother. The tension between his inner and his public life showed clearly while he was Governor. It would continue the rest of his life. The public man masked the inner sufferer. Rarely the suffering broke through, and people spoke, sometimes mockingly, of a "man of sorrows." But he was one. And in a way, just as when as a child he had been the vehicle of his parents' disagreements, so now in 1952 he became the vehicle of the agonized struggles of the Democratic Party. Seen thus, he was more the creature than the creator of history. Destiny placed many events beyond his control—the rearrangement of the Democratic Party after the Roosevelt years, the struggle in the Republican Party that produced an unbeatable Eisenhower, the hydrogen bomb. He may have sensed the crushing weight of destiny during his governorship. It was, really, the only time he was ever his own man. Only a year or two—1951 and, to a lesser extent, 1950. Perhaps he knew it; that might explain why at the outset he seemed nervous and rattled, so anxious about the details of running the state government. Although he sought the friendship of the Presbyterian minister in Springfield, and although he received endless religious advice from both Mrs. Ives and Dorothy Fosdick, he was not really a religious man. Carl McGowan once said, "Religion didn't mean much to Stevenson."

So seen, Stevenson appears more the vehicle than the driver, a victim of destiny. Nevertheless, just as Illinois shaped him, after he moved to the wider stage he helped to shape his nation and the world. Indeed, history may judge his public life triumphant—if history goes his way, toward peace through internationalism.

61

On January 8, 1952, at a press conference at the Mansion, Stevenson was asked if he would be a candidate for the presidency of the United States. He replied, "I would not have announced for Governor unless I meant to run for the office. There are only three things that could take me out of the race—death, health, or higher office. As to death, only God knows. As to health, I'm feeling fine. And as to higher office, I have no ambition except to be Governor."

Others, however, had other ambitions. In December of 1951 or early January of 1952, a small group—only five at first, then seven, then a few more—of leaders of the Independent Voters of Illinois decided that a leadership vacuum existed in the national Democratic Party and that Stevenson ought to fill it. Marshall Holleb was one of its leaders. He was a young lawyer and the law partner and brother-in-law of Congressman Sidney Yates, who had first been elected in 1948 with Stevenson and had been re-elected from Stevenson's own Gold Coast and slum district. Working with Holleb were Leo Lerner, a neighborhood newspaper publisher; Richard R. Meyer and Paul Berger, young businessmen; and Don Petrie, a young lawyer, as well as Florence Medow and Gwen Glasser. Petrie later dropped out, thinking it was not right to promote Stevenson for President without his permission.

As a leader of IVI and the American Civil Liberties Union, Holleb had known Stevenson slightly as Governor—had presented to him the views of the IVI and ACLU on the Broyles bills and other issues. He had heard Stevenson deliver the Centennial speech on foreign policy at Northwestern University and had "reacted emotionally." "The IVI and ACLU and AVC—American Veterans' Committee—were always looking for heroes. Early in 1952 we met almost daily in the IVI office on Jackson Boulevard and formed a Stevenson committee. These were intelligent, intuitive, energetic people." At first they were all IVI people. Others joined later—Hubert Will, a young lawyer, later a federal judge; Bob Ming, a young Negro lawyer; Walter Johnson, a University of Chicago history professor. Leo Lerner became chairman. Lerner, former IVI chairman, was the philosopher of the postwar liberal movement in Chicago. Holleb has recalled, "In those early days we pulled together a pathetic little handful, raised a little money, printed letters and Stevenson buttons. It seemed so obvious to us that a genuine political vacuum did exist and that Adlai Stevenson was clearly the right man to be nominated. But only the innocents had the unblurred vision to see it that way and to act on it. The sophisticates, the professionals, couldn't or wouldn't recognize that possibility. They turned away from the inconceivable—an unmanaged political event. It was childlike, so beautiful, to have such unspoiled faith." They gravitated to Stevenson—whom they knew but slightly—because of his success as Governor, his freshness on the political scene, and his liberal position on the Broyles bills. "Compared to anybody else who had been in office as Governor, he was an enlightened man, and we equated this with liberalism because there was a possibility of a dialogue between us." They tried to get in contact with Stevenson. He sent word he wanted them to abandon their efforts.

This was the nucleus of the group that, despite Stevenson's disavowals, persisted all through the spring in trying to draft him, conducting what Lerner called "the campaign without a candidate," and that later set up a Stevenson headquarters—despite Stevenson's public annoyance—at the Democratic National Convention. This volunteer group, however, cannot be credited with "drafting" Stevenson singlehanded, or almost singlehanded, as has sometimes been claimed. A great many forces were at work.

One was Bill Flanagan. For some time he had been assembling data on Stevenson and having it mimeographed—Stevenson's family history, his record as Governor, biographies of his staff assistants and of his department and commission directors. He distributed it to the press as background material. A man from the Philadelphia *Bulletin* referred to "Flanagan's twenty-pound packet." The packet became famous. "I started to get press from Philadelphia to San Francisco and everywhere else coming in here, because he was beginning to be talked about. I started the Stevenson wit thing, had it mimeographed. And I was working on the *Time* cover story."

Another influence was that of Stevenson's friends. On January 3, two days before he announced for re-election, Jane Dick wrote to him about the presidential nomination. She phrased several hypothetical presidential non-candidacy statements, dismissing all except one that said he was committed to the people and had a job to finish in Illinois. She went on, "As for 1956—I'm afraid that I *do* think if you run [for Governor], win, & make an equally fine record for the next 4 years, your refusal to take the next step at that time would be just that much harder." Illinois, she thought, would gain "immeasurably" if he would run for re-election as Governor, removing himself unequivocally from 1952 presidential consideration.

In another letter, she questioned whether he could "survive" the presidency, considering his temperament and conscience, and pointed out that the presidency entailed "complete lack of privacy," "constant glare of publicity," "misinterpretation of your motives by your political foes," "soul-destroying flattery by political friends," "pomp, protocol, 'flap,'" and added that all this would be "preceded by a *grueling* no-holds-barred, smear type of campaign which you might very well lose," especially in 1952, considering Truman's unpopularity and the widespread demand for a new administration. A little later, however, she said that if the presidency really sought him he should run for it.

Many of Stevenson's friends were less concerned about his personal fortunes and strongly urged him to run for Governor. Some were Republicans who felt they could support him for Governor but not for President. Some simply did not want him to "desert" the state. When he announced his gubernatorial candidacy, John Miller told him his decision was both brave and right. Miller, noting that the *Sun-Times* was supporting Eisenhower for the presidency and would support Stevenson for Governor, and that the New York *Times* and New York *Herald Tribune* were also supporting Eisenhower, thought that attitude widespread among independent voters. Stevenson replied, "I hope that I can hold some of the independent support I had in 1948, but I am quite conscious of the hazards in the national situation. What's more, the everlasting agitation about the President business—mostly coming from the East—causes me discomfort and no excitement." He thanked Irving Dilliard for a *Post-Dispatch* editorial about his re-election and said he admired the paper's editorial on Eisenhower: "I have been a little surprised by the impetuous endorsement of so many newspapers."

That Stevenson was toying with another wholly different idea seems apparent in a letter from Dorothy Fosdick, saying she had "investigated the problem of an aging Austin on your behalf." Austin was still United States ambassador to the UN. She concluded that Austin was not old or ill enough to resign, that many people in the State Department would like to see him replaced by Stevenson but felt obligated to remain loyal to him, and that if Stevenson was interested he should make his interest known.

The Republican situation was clarifying rapidly in January of 1952. Governor Dewey of New York had removed himself in 1950 as a candidate and said he would support Eisenhower "if he would accept the draft." In September of 1951, Eisenhower's old friend, Roy A. Roberts of the Kansas City *Star,* had said Eisenhower had told him he was "a good Kansas Republican." During the fall Senator Taft, Governor Warren, and Harold Stassen had announced their candidacies but Eisenhower had remained silent. On January 6, 1952, however, Senator Henry Cabot Lodge returned from a visit to Eisenhower in Paris and announced that Governor Sherman Adams of New Hampshire had asked him to enter Eisenhower in the New Hampshire Republican primary. He had assured Adams that Eisenhower "is in to the finish." He said he was speaking for Eisenhower. Next day in France Eisenhower corroborated Lodge, said he would not seek nomination but indicated he would accept if it was offered. Ten days later Eisenhower supporters actively campaigned at a meeting of the Republican National Committee and state chairmen in San Francisco. His name was filed in New Hampshire.

On January 13, Dorothy Fosdick told Stevenson that Edward Weeks of the *Atlantic Monthly* and Walter Lippmann were "all for Eisenhower." Friends, however, told her that Eisenhower was ill equipped for the presidency—that he "thinks rigorously about military problems but that he thinks about political problems largely in terms of principles and hope." She said that a *Time* reporter was interviewing Stevenson's old friends in Washington. In another letter she made plans to be with him in Washington on January 22.

62

At 2 P.M. on Sunday, January 20, Stevenson left Chicago for New York and Washington, a fateful trip. Lloyd Garrison, his distinguished lawyer friend, had arranged the New York part of it months earlier. Garrison has said, "He was not known in New York. I thought it would be good for him to be acquainted there." Garrison, who was president of the National Urban League, an organization devoted to improving the Negro's lot, invited principal staff members of the Urban League to his office Monday morning to meet with Stevenson. "He was just great with them," Garrison has recalled. "He asked questions, was very eager to learn. They were immensely pleased." Garrison had arranged lunch for about 45 people in various fields; Stevenson gave a talk that was "witty and charming, gay and amusing and friendly." After lunch Garrison and other Urban League leaders took Stevenson on a tour of Harlem, inspecting housing—"an experience which I shall not soon forget," Stevenson said. The Urban League's annual dinner was held that night in the main ballroom of the Waldorf Astoria, and about 2,000 attended, and Stevenson delivered the principal speech. Stevenson had worked hard on the speech, putting it through several revisions, using some old material but writing out much new material in longhand, including several phrases that a few months later he made famous, such as, "Self-criticism is democracy's secret weapon." He said that "our illiteracy in human relations" was "perhaps our foremost domestic problem" and "a democracy qualified by color will win no hearts in Africa and Asia." He traced progress in race relations, said the Supreme Court had recently modified its earlier "separate but equal" doctrine, said the South was "unmasking the Ku Klux Klan and extending the suffrage," said segregation was diminishing throughout the nation, and warned against solving problems by violence.

It was, for Stevenson, a strong civil rights speech, establishing for Stevenson a position in the liberal wing of the Democratic Party and doing so in New York City, where civil rights was an important issue. The *Herald Tribune* praised the speech and said it indicated why Stevenson was being mentioned for President, and James A. Farley commended Stevenson. So did Lloyd Garrison at the time: "I have heard nothing but praise of you from all hands. . . . I am yours to command in all things to achieve your future." Actually, Garrison thought the speech left the audience "a little cold"—"it didn't have quite the insights and warmth and awareness that was needed. A little conventional—the sort of thing we'd heard so many times. While they were pleased, it did not have the incandescence I'd hoped for." Afterward, Stevenson and Garrison walked around the Biltmore block, talking about Stevenson's future. He told Garrison he was going to take a night train to Washington and see President Truman. "He knew Truman was going to put the bite on him to run for President. He was torn. I pressed him very hard to keep himself in readiness for the party. When a man goes into public office, he ceases to belong entirely to himself, he has to be responsive to the needs of the party. I hoped he'd subordinate his personal preferences. He wanted to continue as Governor and finish what he'd started."

In Washington on Tuesday afternoon he discussed coal mine safety with John L. Lewis of the United Mine Workers. And that night he saw President Truman.

Truman's popularity was low. The Korean War, begun the summer of 1950 with high hopes and national unity, had gone badly. After initial success, General MacArthur's troops had crossed the 38th Parallel and moved on to the Yalu River in North Korea, only to be thrown back by a massive Chinese counterattack. MacArthur had urged Washington to carry the war to the Chinese mainland. While the war itself seesawed, MacArthur had disagreed with Truman's and the Joint Chiefs' instructions, and Truman had fired him. In June of 1951 the Soviet Union had proposed a truce. But the truce talks had limped along, and so had the fighting. By early 1952, Korea had become a divisive sore, contaminating the political atmosphere at home, hampering American diplomacy abroad, and undermining Truman's entire position. Moreover, during this same period Senator McCarthy, along with Senators Jenner and McCarran and others, and with the aid and comfort of Senator Taft (who once advised McCarthy that if one of his "cases" didn't work he should try another), had been conducting guerrilla warfare against Truman, Secretary Acheson, and various officers of the State Department.

Truman had fought back courageously, once calling McCarthy "untruthful, pathological and a character assassin." It all was poisonous. Finally, a series of scandals involving Truman administration officials had enabled Republicans to charge the Administration with corruption and "cronyism." In sum, Truman's political position early in 1952 was extremely weak, and Republicans sensed that they had their best chance of winning the presidency in twenty years. Many Democrats and independents agreed.

President Truman himself said in his *Memoirs* not only that he had decided not to run for re-election in 1952 as early as his inauguration in 1949 but that on April 16, 1950, he had written a memorandum to himself saying so, that he had locked it away, that he had read it to his White House staff in March of 1951, and that during 1951 he had come to the conclusion that Chief Justice Vinson was "the most logical and qualified candidate." Truman wrote that he had first approached Vinson in the summer of 1950, that Vinson had declined to run, that he had talked with him again in the fall of 1951 at Key West and urged him to run, that Vinson had "finally" said he would talk to his wife about it, and that, after Truman had returned to Washington, Vinson had declined.[20]

---

[20] Clark Clifford, a Washington lawyer and adviser to Presidents Truman, Kennedy, and Johnson (and Secretary of Defense under President Johnson), one of the ablest, most acute, and polished men in Washington as well as one of its most successful lawyers, recalled a somewhat different version. He said, "One Sunday evening early in 1952, or possibly in late December of 1951, President Truman and Chief Justice Vinson and I had Sunday evening supper. After a pleasant meal, reminiscing, it was a warm and friendly atmosphere, President Truman said flatly that he was not going to run. I had the distinct impression that he had thought it out with the greatest of care, talked it out with Mrs. Truman. He had served as President for seven and one half years, there was a psychological factor about the two-term amendment, and he had pulled off the political miracle of the century in 1948. There seemed to be no sound reason for going on, considering the enormous burdens of the office and considering that he was getting older and older. He thought he had served his country well as Senator and Vice President and seven and one half years, hard, tough years, as President—and the time had come to turn the burdens of office over to someone else. I don't think he had given any thought to what the competition was going to be, win or lose—he didn't get to that point in his thinking. Mrs. Truman, who had enormous influence on him, very much wanted him to quit. Power didn't affect Truman. He was forthright and simple and considerate. He accepted advice well. There was nothing devious about him. Vinson and I accepted what he had said.

"The reason for the supper was to tell us in strictest confidence that he was not going to run. After a well-prepared presentation, he told Vinson that he had thought it out and he had concluded that Vinson ought to be

Truman wrote that after Vinson refused he canvassed the possibilities and came to consider Stevenson "the best all-around candidate" and said so in the May 8, no year, memorandum. Truman wanted someone who would "continue the Fair Deal, Point IV, Fair Employment, parity for farmers and a consumers protective policy. . . . I liked Stevenson's political and administrative background. I admired him personally. I liked his forthright and energetic campaign for the governorship. He proved in that contest that he possessed a knowledge and 'feel' for politics, that he understood that politics at its best was the business and art of government, and that he had learned that a knowledge of politics is necessary to carry out the function of our form of free government. I had an especially high regard for Stevenson's many contributions to the federal government as special assistant to many agency heads and Cabinet members. His work on the United Nations and in the State Department demonstrated that he had a clear grasp of the role of this country as the leader among nations and of our program to secure the peace."

One can only admire Truman for turning to Stevenson. After all, Stevenson, a political nobody nationally, had dared campaign in Illinois in 1948 almost without mentioning Truman's name. True, since then he had praised him at party gatherings, and had introduced him glowingly to a big Chicago rally (and almost stolen the show). But they were very different men, and it is a tribute to Truman's loyalty to his party and his program and his country that he turned to Stevenson despite their differences.

---

the candidate. I think it came as very much of a surprise to Vinson. He started to list some reasons why he was not the man—he had been out of politics a long time—he had no base—he had not lived in Kentucky for many years—he had a limited acquaintance with Democrats around the country. He said he would think it over with care and report back. He left.

"The President told me, 'Wait a couple of days, then drop up and see Fred [Vinson] and help him make up his mind. He's honest, able, and I've worked with him. We need him.'

"A few days later I did go to lunch with Vinson and made the pitch. He voiced very considerable doubt. There was a question as to whether he was up to the campaign. He had talked to his wife. He came up with a new reason. He liked the job he had. He was enjoying it, he felt he was making a real contribution, he had helped to bring unity and cohesion to the Court. I got the impression that the answer was no. I told the President so. In a few days Vinson told the President no. It was after this that Truman offered the nomination to Stevenson.

"Truman attached considerable significance to the fact that Stevenson's grandfather had been Vice President. He came from a good, strong political family. He had received a marvelous 1948 majority. He was honest, clean, decent."

Precisely how their meeting came about is difficult to discover. At the time it was variously speculated that Joseph Rauh, executive director of ADA, and James Loeb, Jr., a former ADA director then working in the White House for Charles S. Murphy, President Truman's special counsel, called Stevenson to Truman's attention; that Arvey arranged the whole thing; that former Senator Lucas did it to block Kefauver. Arvey, however, has denied having any part in it. It is not unlikely that several people got the same idea at the same time, as frequently happens with reasonable ideas.

Jim Loeb has written that he considered Stevenson a possible presidential candidate in the fall of 1951. Late in 1951, Loeb told Arthur Schlesinger that the White House was looking for a candidate, should Truman decide not to run, and was interested in Stevenson. Schlesinger told Loeb what he knew about Stevenson and suggested he get in touch with George Ball, Stevenson's old friend who was practicing law in Washington. Ball, however, was in Europe, and Loeb was reluctant to see him anyway, since his doing so might be misinterpreted at the White House. He asked Mrs. Violet Gunther, then political secretary of ADA, to see Ball. Loeb himself brought up Stevenson's name in White House staff political meetings. The reaction was favorable, especially from David Lloyd, who had accompanied Stevenson on his wartime mission to Italy and was by now another assistant to Charles Murphy. At a December meeting Murphy asked what "you liberals" thought of Stevenson. William Batt, Jr., assistant to the Secretary of Labor, said Stevenson was one of three governors who were most cooperative with the Labor Department on unemployment problems. Loeb made what he later called "a nominating speech," saying he considered Stevenson the only feasible alternative if Truman was not going to run. Murphy asked what he knew about the Lieutenant Governor of Illinois. Loeb knew nothing and asked why Murphy was interested. Murphy suggested that Stevenson might be brought to Washington for some important job with "even higher office" in prospect. Loeb and David Lloyd guessed the job was Attorney General—"the mess in Washington" was becoming a national issue.

In January, Mrs. Gunther saw George Ball and arranged for him to meet with Loeb after Loeb cleared it with Murphy. Ball has said he served as intermediary between Stevenson and the White House. Early in January, David Lloyd told him that he and Murphy had talked to President Truman about Stevenson. Truman had not authorized Murphy and Lloyd to approach Stevenson directly on his behalf but had indicated he would not object if they did it on their own initiative. After several conversations, Lloyd asked Ball to arrange for Stevenson to come to Washington and talk to the President. Ball telephoned Stevenson in Springfield and "found him totally cold to the idea." He had just announced his own candidacy for re-election. Running for President would be "an act of bad faith." He had unfinished business in Illinois. He would not "let down" his Illinois supporters, many of whom were Republicans. He would not behave "like the garden variety of opportunistic pol." Ball has recalled, "After several telephone calls and considerable persuasion on my part, he did, however, concede that he had official business in Washington that could provide an occasion for a visit," his need to discuss mine safety with John L. Lewis and Secretary of the Interior Oscar Chapman. By this time President Truman, through Murphy, was letting his staff know that a Democratic Governor could not visit Washington without calling on the Democratic President. Truman's memoirs indicate that he himself asked Stevenson to visit him. An appointment was made with the President for Tuesday evening, January 22.

Stevenson, after seeing Lewis in Washington, went to Ball's house for dinner that evening. The meeting with Truman was to be secret. Stevenson was dismayed to learn that Carleton Kent of the Chicago *Sun-Times* Washington Bureau had been calling Ball and knew that something was afoot. The story was leaking rapidly. Loeb had leaked it in part to Marquis Childs, the columnist. Bill Flanagan has recalled that he himself had leaked the story, though not, he says, to any newspaperman. The *Time* cover story had appeared on sale that Monday. The previous Thursday, before leaving Springfield, Stevenson, at the regular staff meeting, told Flanagan, as Flanagan later remembered it, "I'm going to be gone the first part of next week. But I don't want you to ask me any questions about where I am." Flanagan agreed. "But then," Flanagan said later, "I got to thinking —Jesus, *Time* is coming out. If he is going to Washington and talking to Truman, this might be just what we need to really blow this off the ground," that is, to give Stevenson's presidential candidacy a real lift. "I think McGowan or Blair or someone told me, 'He's going to Washington to see Truman but we're not supposed to know about it.' On Saturday—*Time* went to press that night—on Saturday morning I called Bill Glasgow and told him that Stevenson had gone to Washington to see Truman. I told him he could tell only his office and that they couldn't pin it on me. He said okay."

George Ball recalled, "Dinner was hasty, and Adlai was droll but preoccupied. How could he best explain to President Truman that he wished to remain Governor of Illinois without seeming ungrateful or disrespectful of the office of the presidency? I drove Adlai to Blair

House, where President Truman was then in residence. I waited while he argued with the guards, who had never heard of him."

It is hard to reconstruct precisely what happened at that meeting, though the general sense of it is clear enough. President Truman said:

"I told him that I would not run for President again and that it was my opinion he was best-fitted for the place. He comes out of a political family. His grandfather was Vice President with Grover Cleveland in the campaign and the election of 1892. The grandfather had been on the ticket with Winfield Scott Hancock in 1880. [The last is erroneous]. He had served in Congress.

"Adlai's father had been connected with the government of the State of Illinois. Adlai had served the country in the State Department and the United Nations. He had made an excellent Governor of Illinois.

"When I talked with him, I told him what I thought the Presidency is, how it has grown into the most powerful and the greatest office in the history of the world. I asked him to take it and told him that if he would agree he could be nominated. I told him that a President in the White House always controlled the National Convention. Called his attention to Jackson and Van Buren and Polk. Talked about Taft in 1912, Wilson in 1920, Coolidge and Mellon in 1928, Roosevelt in 1936, 1940, 1944. But he said: No! He apparently was flabbergasted."

Jack Arvey once said that Stevenson's answer had angered Truman. "He couldn't understand it. How a man could dillydally around with a thing like the presidential nomination." Clark Clifford said, "During the spring the President felt some uneasiness [about Stevenson]. He had such a high regard for the office that it was hard for him to see how a man when presented with an opportunity could debate within himself. He understood Vinson—he was older and out of politics and he was Chief Justice. The President and Stevenson were about as different as two men could be. Truman had the kind of mind that saw issues very clearly. He divided things into black and white. Stevenson had gray areas. Truman's decisions were sharp and final. As individuals they didn't hit it off too well."

Carl McGowan received a different impression. "When he came back he told me that Truman had talked to him about the nomination and Stevenson had deprecated his interest in it, but left it that he would think it over. Truman said that he was going to quit if he could find a suitable successor. Stevenson came back full of admiration for Truman. He told me about going to Blair House and said the President was sitting in front of a fire reading the Bible. The President said he always did that, had done it all his life. Stevenson was impressed with this self-contained, internally secure man that Truman was. A simple man of great strength. Stevenson, with his own churning around, was impressed with the calm, serenity, self-contained quality."

Scotty Reston of the New York *Times* recalled that Stevenson telephoned him at eleven-thirty that night in Washington, said he had to leave at nine the next morning, he was at the Roger Smith Hotel, and wanted to talk. Reston recalled, "He was terribly agitated. He said that Truman wanted him to run for President. He was very upset. I asked if he was going to do it. He said, 'What are you trying to tell me? That it's my duty to save Western civilization from Ike Eisenhower? In the first place I don't want to do it—I want to stay on and be Governor and I don't want to be a caretaker for the party. In the second place I'm not at all sure we ought to win this election—the Republican Party has been out of power for twenty years. The time has to come when they get back into power, Eisenhower believes in collective security, I have no question in my mind about who's going to win. If he's nominated he's a cinch.' Truman was furious—but Stevenson didn't commit himself. Truman's approach was simple. He never liked Stevenson. He thought that anointing him should be enough. But instead of being grateful, he was getting brushed off."

Yet even before his meeting with Truman, Stevenson had given more than passing consideration to the idea. Wally Schaefer once recalled having been on a train with Stevenson between Chicago and Springfield about the middle of January. "Adlai was in the drawing room. I went in and talked to him. He said the President wanted him to come to Washington next week 'and I think I know what he wants—he wants me to be a candidate for the presidency.' Then he said, 'I'm not qualified to be President, or equipped.' I said, 'That's utter nonsense—who is? Who's better equipped? Nobody but God is really equipped to be President.' He said, 'Can you and Harry Hershey come over for dinner.' [Hershey was on the Illinois Supreme Court with Schaefer.] We went to dinner and Adlai went on in the same vein. Harry took the same position I did. At one point Adlai said, 'If I become a candidate for President will you run for Governor?' I said, 'Yes.' Which I shouldn't have done. He didn't mention it again."

George Ball recalled that Stevenson telephoned him the morning after he saw Truman. "He had, he said, 'made a hash' of his talk with the President, who had not understood his feelings at all, and no doubt thought him a complete idiot. He was satisfied that President

Truman had written him off as hopeless and that the incident was closed. It was not an accurate appraisal, for I immediately began receiving calls from newspaper correspondents who had been alerted by the White House that Stevenson had spent the previous evening with the President."

Stevenson had a breakfast appointment that Wednesday morning with Newton Minow, a young round-faced lawyer, intelligent, able, with a mind not unlike Carl McGowan's. Minow had met Stevenson briefly in 1948 when Minow had been chairman of the Law Students for Stevenson at Northwestern University Law School. In late 1951 he was at the Supreme Court in Washington as Chief Justice Vinson's law clerk. McGowan had been urging Stevenson to build up his staff with promising young lawyers. McGowan had first approached Minow about going to work for Stevenson. He had told him Stevenson was coming to Washington and would interview Minow himself. Bill Blair made Minow's appointment with Stevenson —7 A.M. breakfast at the Metropolitan Club. Minow later recalled, "I told him I'd worked in the 1948 campaign. He was very reluctant to have a large personal staff but Carl McGowan had been telling him he needed someone to help draft legislation and work with the legislators and develop a program. The new man would work more with Carl than with the Governor. I said I was interested. There was no talk of compensation. I said I couldn't come until the court term was over in June. Stevenson said, 'I'm running for Governor and I want you part of the summer. I want to develop a program and use it in the campaign. If I offer you this job is there any reason why you wouldn't take it?' I said, 'There's only one—Chief Justice Vinson is periodically mentioned as a candidate for President in the papers. Should he run for President and ask me to remain with him, I would want to do that.' Stevenson looked at me quizzically and said, 'I just don't think that is very likely.' I said, 'I don't either but if—' Stevenson said, 'Okay, but it's not likely.' We finished. I went to the Court and got the New York *Times* and saw the headlines: 'HST Offers Stevenson Nomination: Vinson Out.'" Minow took the job on Stevenson's staff and asked Vinson's permission to leave early enough to attend the Democratic Convention. Vinson said, "Okay, but I have news for you—your boy's out. I was with President Truman last night and he's tired of Stevenson's procrastination and indecision and he's going to back Barkley." Later Minow became one of Stevenson's most trusted and valuable advisers, his law partner, and, under President Kennedy, chairman of the Federal Communications Commission.

Stevenson had lunch that day with George Ball, David Lloyd, and

Jim Loeb. Stevenson told them of his meeting with Truman. The President, he said, had indicated his own and Mrs. Truman's desire that he not run again, gone over all possible candidates, told Stevenson he had first offered it to Vinson but Vinson had refused, said he was determined that Kefauver would not be nominated, said he liked Senator Kerr but his voting record made him vulnerable, and concluded that Stevenson was the only alternative to himself. To the others at lunch, Stevenson did not appear reluctant that day—although he did not say he would run, he discussed the dates of various primaries with them, and Loeb "had the feeling that he talked very much like a candidate."

The *Time* piece and the newspaper stories blew up a tremendous storm. On Wednesday, January 23, Stevenson sent Alicia Patterson a telegram, "Bedevilled with emergencies. Must return to Illinois heartbroken and exasperated." He left Washington next day, Thursday, arriving in Springfield at 3:30 P.M., and told Alicia Patterson he had spent Wednesday "dodging around from hotels to homes to clubs trying to avoid all my 'dear old friends' of the press. . . . Then things broke in Spfd & there was nothing for it except to get home as fast as I could. So, instead of the black river, sun and thou, I have miseries here . . . and great distress of soul and mind about this sudden clamor about the Presidency—in which, thanks to a loving publisher, even Newsday has joined. The phone rings from near and far, newspaper characters are arriving and asking hideous questions and departing with crumbs. Instead of a rest I've had an advanced case of traumatic exhaustion—and what's more I don't know what the devil its all about. If its true and Eisenhower is a lost cause and the only hope of the rationals is Stevenson, we're in a hell of a fix. Besides Stevenson wants nothing except to be Gov. of Ill. again—and his heart won't break if the people deny him that. But I suspect it will all blow over and I can relax a little before long." Would she be in Georgia about February 17?

His telephoning Reston seems at first glance to contradict his telling Alicia that he had tried desperately to dodge the press. Yet perhaps it does not—perhaps he dodged the press selectively. (In this case, he had promised Reston he would call him the next time he was in Washington.) One of the "homes" he hid out in, as he told Alicia Patterson, was that of Dorothy Fosdick, who congratulated him on having avoided the reporters. She was saving clippings—"I'm going to have to retire from my job to keep up with the news of you. . . . Loving you the way I do I would not wish the Presidency upon you, because of its burden." She would support whatever he decided but suggested tentatively that if Taft was nominated Stevenson should run, but if Eisenhower was nominated or if a Republican victory seemed inevitable, "why not let Truman assume responsibility for defending his record and do the best he can?"

The *Time* piece was favorable. It summed up Stevenson's record as Governor, stressed his independence and his insistence on good government, related his ancestry and his career, speculated whether Truman had "summoned" him to Washington to ask him to run as Vice President or as President or merely to seek his advice, and concluded, "Whatever the truth behind the rumors, this much was evident: in a cold season for the Democrats, Adlai Stevenson is politically hot, and Harry Truman feels the need of a little warmth."

After the *Time* piece, Bill Flanagan recalled, "we were really off the ground—so far off the ground that he really got frightened. It all looked like we were really running. Back in Springfield he told me, 'I think you've gone too far.' I told him no. Then the tension and heat increased. I was making phone calls to people in politics outside of Illinois. We had a goddam good thing going because newspapermen from out of state began coming in. They would ask if he were going to run and I would say I didn't know. But I would also say, 'If it's not Stevenson, who would it be? Look at the competition—Kerr, Harriman, and so forth.' They'd say, 'You've got something there.' Well, the feeling got hotter."

Two days after their meeting President Truman held a press conference, and the first question concerned his own plans to run again and the next concerned Stevenson. Truman said, "I didn't offer him anything in particular, except to talk about the general political situation—worldwide, national, and Illinois. . . . He is very much interested in mine safety, just as I am. And we had a very pleasant visit all around." The next question was, "You didn't offer him higher office?" The President said, "How could I?" Another questioner asked if Truman had invited Stevenson to come to Washington to talk to him. Truman replied, "Governor Stevenson came to Washington to discuss mine safety. Of course, when any Democratic Governor comes to Washington, he always asks for an interview with the President. That is the way it happened." Another questioner asked, "Did you have any part in inflating all these trial balloons? Would you say that the Governor was a favorite in case you decide not to run?" Truman replied, "No. I had no hand in it. That is surmise." The President also said he knew what he was going to do about running for re-election but would announce it when he chose. Truman wrote to Stevenson on the twenty-ninth: "I am glad you are pleased with the manner in which I had to handle the interview between us at the Press Conference" and, "I hope that sometime in the not too distant future we may have further conversations on the subject in which we are both interested."

In Cambridge, Dean Griswold of the Harvard Law School, who knew that Stevenson had flunked out of Harvard Law and who admired Stevenson and wanted nothing to embarrass him, took Stevenson's grade record out of the cabinet in the secretary's office and put it in a locked cabinet in his own office. Later a faculty member protested vehemently and demanded that Griswold show him the record. Griswold refused.

63

In the next few weeks Stevenson made numerous public appearances and he nearly always discussed state issues. But most of his time was taken up with the question of the presidential nomination. Hardly a day passed that a national newspaper reporter or magazine writer did not come to the Mansion.[21] Photographers swarmed over the place. Stevenson even visited the *Tribune* offices to sit for a color photograph. One day the despairing secretary in his Chicago office, Phyllis Gustafson, wrote in his appointment book, "There were various photographers and newsmen in during the afternoon. I don't know how many of them saw the Governor."[22] Politicians came too —Secretary of the Interior Chapman, Alan Cranston of California, Governor Schricker of Indiana, Senator Humphrey of Minnesota. So did Walter Reuther of the United Auto Workers. So did his old friends, especially Jane Dick and Dutch Smith. And he met frequently with other members of the Stevenson-for-Governor Committee and with downstate and Cook County leaders.

His own writings, unwittingly or not, fed the national fires—he published an article on gambling in the *Atlantic Monthly* and one defending Truman's Korea policy in *Foreign Affairs*.

A great deal of Stevenson's time was taken up with answering letters about a presidential candidacy. Now as never before he was

[21] Among them were such photographers as Arnold Newman of *Life* and such writers as Max Gilstrap of the *Christian Science Monitor*, Richard Rovere of *The New Yorker*, Ernest K. Lindley of *Newsweek*, Cabell Phillips of the New York *Times*, John Gunther, James Wechsler, Joe Alsop, and Roscoe Drummond. Two men arrived to write books about Stevenson, Noel Busch and John Bartlow Martin.

[22] Miss Gustafson later became secretary to Adlai III when he was State Treasurer and U. S. Senator. Bill Flanagan served Adlai III, too, and so did Dan Walker and Juanda Higgins, a secretary active in Stevenson's presidential campaigns and in his law office between campaigns.

receiving fan mail, great mounds of it from strangers, including a good many who wanted to correspond about genealogy. He left much of it to his staff. But he could not, or would not, leave to staff letters from old friends and important new ones. He thanked Michael Straight, editor of the *New Republic,* for an editorial. He thanked Arthur Krock of the New York *Times* for defending Stevenson on the Hiss issue. (Krock told him privately that "one or two intimates of the President said . . . the Hiss deposition was poison.") In replying to a letter from Douglas Fairbanks on February 2, Stevenson said professional politicians believed Taft would be nominated and so the Democrats should make "the best fight possible." Even if Eisenhower were elected, he thought, Republican isolationist leaders in the Senate and House would be more powerful than Eisenhower. To an Alaskan politician who asked permission to try to persuade the Alaskan delegation to the Democratic National Convention to vote for Stevenson on the second ballot, Stevenson wrote, "I have no ambitions for the Democratic nomination and will do nothing to further such a project." (The Alaska delegation stayed with Kefauver to the end.) He went on Edward R. Murrow's television show on February 3 and repeated that the governorship was "the full measure of my strength and capacity—and then some."

Cynics thought that if Stevenson really did not want to run for President he would not accept such invitations as Murrow's. They forgot he was running for Governor and such publicity did him no harm. Every place he went in private, however, he seemed to want to talk about the presidency. On February 3, visiting Lou Kohn's apartment in Chicago, where Mrs. Kohn presented him with a birthday cake (two days early), he asked Bill Rivkin's advice on what to do. Rivkin, then president of the Young Democrats of Cook County, later recalled, "He was acting like he thought I was some sort of a professional. I was only thirty-three years old. He was dressing me up in these clothes that didn't fit me and asking my advice— who didn't have any. His mind was long since made up." In retrospect, many people felt that Stevenson asked their advice only rhetorically, as a courtesy to flatter them or as a tactic to draw them out, without really intending to pay heed to their advice, or perhaps as a way of thinking out loud himself.

From Louisville, Wilson Wyatt wrote on February 4 that he was meeting with Barry Bingham and Mark Ethridge to discuss Stevenson's situation and see "how we could help." Dutch Smith talked to Stevenson in Stevenson's Chicago office on February 5, Stevenson's fifty-second birthday, and told him he was in a strong bargaining position for the presidential nomination because he was not seeking it. Smith advised him not to become a candidate without assurance of enough Northern and Southern support to be nominated and further assurance that he would have Southern support in the campaign. Smith named the following situations in order of undesirability:

1) *To be definitely avoided*—to be an unsuccessful candidate for the nomination, running for governor as a second choice

2) *Also to be avoided*—to be nominated and running for Pres. without full party support

3) *Acceptable*—to be nominated & running on the right terms, & with full support

4) *Preferable*—to run for Gov. in 1952 & president in 1956.

Smith went on to tell Stevenson that he should seek assurance of Southern support "promptly," and Stevenson said he would consider seeing or telephoning James Byrnes while at Chelsea, Marshall Field's plantation.

He asked the advice of many friends. Jane Dick, in a voluminous correspondence, was first refusing to advise him, then urging him not to run for President this year. She also advised, "And for goodness sake—don't call on Byrnes if you still have any idea of running for Gov. 400,000 Negro votes lost in Chicago could be too many!" She told him the grave decision he faced could not be properly made in an atmosphere of conflicting advice and she suggested other places suitable for reflection, then reiterated a theme not uncommon with her, asking him to consider her views: *"Please*—if you value [the advice of] the McGowans & Dicks of your life as much (I'm being a little sarcastic here, but I don't mean it that way) as the Balls, etc." Jane Dick sometimes disagreed with Stevenson's Eastern friends but she was trying to help him, and in the end she said, ". . . your judgment is just as good as anyone's—*far better,* in my opinion. Your intuition is as good or better than others. Have faith in yourself, in Life, in God, in the eventual rightness of whatever course appears to you right at this time."

The *New Republic* of February 18 carried a cover drawing and story on Stevenson. *Newsweek* of February 4 ran a story on him. Stevenson complained at length to Ernest K. Lindley, its Washington editor, that it had unfairly portrayed him as more liberal than he was. *Newsweek* said later that, while Stevenson had strongly supported the Truman foreign policy, he had "significant reservations" about parts of the New Deal-Fair Deal programs, was "orthodox" on fiscal policy, and feared excessive federal power.

Tom Finletter, Secretary of the Air Force, wrote on February 6, "May [1952] give you what you want, whatever that is, you being a very sensible fellow." Seymour Harris, professor of economics at Harvard, inquired whether Stevenson was the same Stevenson who had been a student of his at Princeton in 1920–21. (He was.) He added that he had had "fine reports" on Stevenson from Paul Douglas and Arthur Schlesinger, Jr. Harris soon became an important adviser to Stevenson. Schlesinger, the Harvard history professor who was becoming a leader of the academic liberal wing of the Democratic Party, was enthusiastic about the Stevenson candidacy. Reinhold Niebuhr, speaking for a group of academics, urged Stevenson to run and asked leave to come to Springfield or Chicago to urge their views on him. The ADA leader, Joseph L. Rauh, went to Springfield with Jim Loeb and Libby Donahue, also of ADA, and spent an "inspiring" day urging Stevenson to run. Loeb thought that for the first four hours of their visit, including lunch, Stevenson "talked very much like a candidate." But later he remarked, to their dismay, that race problems could be more easily solved if the NAACP would stay out of them, then said he would not run for President. His friend John S. Miller of Chicago suggested that Stevenson's friends persuade people not to come out for Eisenhower until they were certain Stevenson would not run— Meyer Kestnbaum had already declared for Eisenhower and, while friendly toward Stevenson, now might find it difficult to switch. This did indeed become a problem—to this extent Stevenson's delay was costly.

On February 13, Stevenson went to Chelsea, Marshall Field's plantation in South Carolina, and to Alicia Patterson's plantation, Kingsland, Georgia. Flying back to Springfield on February 20 from her place, he wrote to her: "As always it was a charmed moment by the blessed black river with you. I feel reborn, well, strong and peaceful. You are right that nature gets things back into perspective quickest. But how long will it last in that high voltage area in Illinois. Long enough, I think, to decide what to do and how—as to the Gov-Pres. business. . . . Arribe Eisenhower!

"Adpai the addlepate."

Back in Springfield he sent a thank-you note to Marshall Field at Chelsea: "That glimpse of another world—a tranquil, relaxed world —lifted me so quickly and so far from present ugly realities that it is hard to resume the debate 'to be or not to be.' Quail seem so much more important than politics! . . . I don't know whether it is your gentle, diffident way of talking, intuition, or just great 'understanding,' but it has always been the same and I come away from a talk with you wiser, surer and *very* thankful!"

Dorothy Fosdick told Stevenson she had found the best possible man to advise him and research and write foreign policy speeches for him—Bob Tufts, "the best man on the Planning Staff, economist, . . . under forty, . . . pure security record . . . wise and imaginative, . . . the man George Kennan & Paul Nitze both respect the most." Bob Tufts did go to work for Stevenson after Stevenson was nominated, and proved during the campaign that he was everything Miss Fosdick had said and more.

Rexford Tugwell told Stevenson February 19 that FDR had known he would have to fight a depression if elected and, "Our next President will have something even worse—guidance toward coexistence with a ruthless, powerful and almost inscrutable equal power in the world," and he urged Stevenson not to regard himself too modestly— he was up to the job. Stevenson replied, "My modesty is not false. I just feel that the difficulties are beyond my limited capacity, and moreover, I have become so preoccupied with this job . . . that I am loathe to leave to go to sea without a chart."

On February 20, Roger W. Straus, Jr., president of Farrar, Straus, and Young, a publishing house, told Stevenson he had heard from Alicia Patterson that she and Stevenson had discussed the possibility of a biography of Stevenson. Straus was "keenly interested." He proposed a book of about 300 pages, half a short biography and the other half a statement by Stevenson himself. He would ask Barry Bingham or Mark Ethridge to write the biographical section. He had heard (inaccurately) that the present author, John Bartlow Martin, was writing an article on Stevenson for the *Saturday Evening Post*. Stevenson told Straus that Martin was working on "sort of a 'collection of state's papers,' I gather." He had sent word to "my friends who are evidently backing him in this work" that Martin should call on Straus in New York around March 10. He had no objection to Straus's project "but I hardly see how I could either find the time or the wits to write a long statement." But his previous speeches might be of use.[23]

[23] Actually, Lou Kohn had proposed to Martin around February 1 that he edit and publish a collection of Stevenson's speeches. Martin had made a contract with Harper & Brothers for this book, had agreed to write a long biographical introduction, and had started assembling the speeches and researching the introduction. Informed of this, Farrar, Straus and Young interested Noel Busch, a journalist, in producing a book that was approximately half biographical sketch and half Stevenson documents. Busch's book and Martin's were competitive commercial ventures. Stevenson erred in thinking anyone was "backing" Martin except the publisher, Harper. As events unfolded, Martin and Harper decided to expand the biographical introduction and print the speeches as an appendix, but in the end the speeches were dropped and the biographical introduction expanded to make the book. Martin delivered his manuscript to Harper in mid-April, when it was un-

On February 21 the IVI group in Chicago that was trying to draft Stevenson published a full-page ad in the *Sun-Times* announcing the launching of the Draft Stevenson movement, printing a list of sponsors, and urging others to join. Stevenson had known about the ad in advance and done nothing to stop it, but after it was published sent word he disapproved. The IVI Draft Stevenson movement, from this time through August, deposited in its bank account $20,-300.91 and ended up with a balance of $507.13, which it contributed to Stevenson's campaign fund.

At about this same time, but entirely independently, George Ball set up a "Stevenson information center" in his Washington law office. He had visited Stevenson in Springfield and "wheedled" him into consenting. He raised several thousand dollars, sent a man to Springfield to research Stevenson's career, and hired people to write press releases about Stevenson, his family, his governorship, his views on issues. Arthur Schlesinger, Jim Loeb, and others were working too. Ball took a friend, Bernard DeVoto, who then wrote "The Easy Chair" column in *Harper's* magazine, to Springfield, and DeVoto wrote an "Easy Chair" on Stevenson. DeVoto's piece, entitled "Stevenson and the Independent Voter," was an eloquent essay that, being written by a liberal of DeVoto's stature and published in a prestigious magazine, persuaded many thoughtful liberals to Stevenson's cause.

George Ball wrote a long letter to Stevenson on February 20. He began by saying that he would not blame Stevenson if he renounced presidential nomination, in view of the fact that the campaign "will tend to seek a low level" and because the next President "will have little but sweat and tears." Stevenson had asked Ball in Springfield if he thought Stevenson the indispensable man. On reflection, Ball now said the Eisenhower boom had been "badly deflated," even if Eisenhower were nominated he would probably have Congress largely against him, and Eisenhower's experience was not relevant to the presidency. Taft was the most likely candidate, and his very election would "fracture the Atlantic Alliance. . . . On the Democratic side I think the choice is either you or the President." Kefauver had "very little chance," he lacked professional political support. Kerr was a "Southerner" hampered by his oil and gas record. In the light of all this, "I do consider you indispensable." (Stevenson checked that passage and the one about the Atlantic

---

certain that Stevenson would run for President. Harper held the manuscript until the eve of Stevenson's nomination on July 25.

Alliance.) Ball thought the problem should be resolved soon, the sooner the better. He advised Stevenson to arrange a secret conversation with President Truman about mid-March. If they agreed that Stevenson would not run, he could make his position unequivocally clear. If he was to run, time was needed for a "build-up" so that he would not "appear hand-picked." It was for this last reason that Ball had been trying to "generate as much national publicity for you as possible." A "substantial" amount of writing was in progress. Joseph Alsop's interview should appear in the *Saturday Evening Post* in early April. Allen Harris was assembling a *Look* article and needed Stevenson's help in locating family photographs. *Collier's* was preparing an article, though Ball had had nothing to do with it. All would appear about the same time as DeVoto's *Harper's* piece. Ball said that Harris and Libby Donahue had gotten together a detailed brochure intended for national distribution; Ball would send it to Stevenson for checking. He asked if Stevenson wanted him to desist from all this.

Stevenson replied next day. He had heard "some alarming reports about the activities of Mr. Harris with various magazines in the East." Publishers "seem to be confused as to whether or not he is my spokesman, and I hope you can restrain him. I thought his purpose was to look over the speech material to write something, but not to do any promotional work." Stevenson said, "The unwilling candidate becomes more unwilling daily!" But he said nothing about Ball's desisting.

Ball replied he did not know how Harris' activities had become known. "However, to be on the safe side, I have put Harris in a corner and covered him with a rug." Ball enclosed the brochure; it was intended as a background fact sheet, and Ball proposed sending it to editors and librarians of major friendly newspapers throughout the country. It needed sponsorship; perhaps the IVI group would do it. "If this whole idea appalls you, please let me know and I shall behave accordingly."[24] Ball said that *Harper's*

[24] The brochure, or one like it, was distributed later by the IVI group, which by then had become the "National Committee, Stevenson for President" and had as its co-chairmen Walter Johnson and George Overton. The brochure had a prefatory note: "Entirely on our own initiative as a group of Illinois citizens, this material has been prepared by the National Committee, Stevenson for President." It contained quotations from newspaper editorials and columnists around the country, a statement of Stevenson's administrative record and one of his legislative program, and a biographical sketch.

"has been persuaded" to send advance galleys of DeVoto's piece to a list of friendly newspapers.

On February 27, Stevenson replied, "I have your letter and have marked it well. I am sorely troubled. My heart is here and my head not far behind. We will see." In a postscript he asked for changes in the DeVoto column, good though it was, to make it completely accurate. DeVoto promised to telephone them to the magazine, even though the article had been set in type, put in pages, and locked into forms. Stevenson never hesitated to ask for changes in pieces about him however laudatory they were or however eminent their authors or however difficult mechanically the changes were.

On February 15, Arthur Krock told Stevenson that Ellen had been "talking very foolishly in these parts" about the reasons for the divorce. Krock warned that she had "threatened" to write a letter to the Chicago papers denying that Stevenson's entry into public life had caused the divorce—she had intended to divorce him anyway. Krock thought this harmless "if it is added that you never wanted the divorce." It worried Stevenson, however. He told Krock that he found Ellen's talking "very disturbing." He wrote, "Perhaps it is a disguised blessing and will add another cogent reason why Stevenson should not be considered for President! I only hope it isn't a sufficiently cogent reason to eliminate him for Governor too!" He wrote to Dutch Smith and to Ellen's sister, Mrs. Ralph Hines, in New York, about Ellen's "wild and threatening talk in Washington, New York, etc."

The kind of advice he was getting about the presidency, and his frame of mind at this time, can be glimpsed in several letters the last week in February. To John Miller February 21: "I have no ambition beyond this job." To Lady Spears,[25] "I will continue in this job if the people will let me, and I find it the full measure of my capacity." Archibald MacLeish wrote on February 21 that a man's friends could not tell him his duty but could help him see himself clearly—and although the idea that he might be President must seem to him "a grotesque hallucination," the fact was that he was "in every way qualified by character and experience and ability" to be President. "Whatever you decide, God bless you." So many of Stevenson's good friends closed their letters with similar simple and fervent affection. Stevenson replied with a direct quotation from Tugwell's letter about what the next President would have to face, not attributing it to Tugwell.

[25] Lady Spears was Mary Borden, aunt of Ellen Borden Stevenson. She lived in England, was an author, and was married to Brigadier E. L. Spears.

Arthur Schlesinger, Jr., sent Stevenson a long letter: "I feel that the best way over the next four years to maintain a strong and positive foreign policy abroad and to preserve and advance American liberalism at home would be to have you in the White House." The problem was, he thought, that President Truman would not withdraw until he thought Stevenson could win; he would not be convinced of that until he saw evidence of Stevenson's "national strength"; this was hard to show unless Stevenson became a national candidate, and Stevenson could not become a candidate until Truman withdrew. Schlesinger thought he saw a "break in the circle—with the help of Ball, Rauh, Loeb, and others like them, Stevenson could become a figure. But in the final analysis, Stevenson must himself decide he wanted to be a candidate; nobody could do it for him.

64

Stevenson saw Frank Annunzio, Director of the Labor Department, on February 25 and March 3. Between those dates, he fired Annunzio, the first member of his Cabinet to become involved in scandal. Annunzio had embarrassed Stevenson about a year earlier by becoming acting ward committeeman of the First Ward—the Loop—in Chicago. At Stevenson's insistence, he had resigned as committeeman. Now he embarrassed Stevenson more seriously. In the investigation of the murder of the Republican Chicago ward committeeman, Charles Gross, it became known that Annunzio had formed an insurance agency with John D'Arco, a rising member of the West Side Bloc and a man who had been a state Representative from the same district as Senator Libonati and Representatives Andrew A. Euzzino and Peter C. Granata when the West Side Bloc had helped kill Con-Con and the Crime Commission bills in 1949. By 1952, D'Arco was alderman and Democratic First Ward committeeman, powerful positions. He and Annunzio had formed Anco, Inc., the insurance agency, at about the time Annunzio became acting First Ward committeeman. Annunzio was president, D'Arco vice president. Another officer was a man who had been wounded when gangsters killed Hymie Weiss in the Capone days. He had also had been convicted of vote fraud in 1928. Selling insurance is a Chicago politician's favorite way of getting rich. Annunzio had sold his stock in Anco and resigned as its president when he resigned as acting ward committeeman. But now under the pressure of the Gross investigation it was suspected that he had used his position as a member of Stevenson's Cabinet to promote his political and financial fortunes. At Stevenson's request, Annunzio resigned, setting forth the facts, denying wrongdoing, and saying, "I personally feel that I am being persecuted only because of my nationality and nothing else." Stevenson himself once said that Annunzio had done nothing illegal but had simply exercised bad judgment.

By the first of March the national political situation was still uncertain. Among the Republicans, Eisenhower, Taft, and Stassen were entered in the New Hampshire primary, to be held March 11. As for the Democrats, Senator Kefauver had announced his candidacy on January 23, the day after Stevenson's talk with Truman at Blair House, and he was entered in the New Hampshire primary. He criticized the Truman administration for not doing "nearly enough" to eradicate corruption. Arthur Krock reported on January 14 that Supreme Court Justice William O. Douglas had told Truman he had decided neither to seek nor accept presidential or vice-presidential nomination. On February 6, Senator Kerr of Oklahoma announced he would enter the Nebraska primary unless President Truman became a candidate for re-election. Democratic leaders in California, Pennsylvania, and at a thirteen-state Midwest conference promised to support Truman. A Gallup poll in January showed him first choice among Democratic voters but far behind Kefauver among independents. On January 31, President Truman said he would withdraw his name from the New Hampshire primary because primaries were just "eyewash." A few days later, after pleas by New Hampshire Democrats, he reversed himself and permitted his name to stay on the ballot. On February 28, Senator Richard B. Russell announced his candidacy. Political writers speculated that Russell might end up leading a third-party movement of Southern Dixicrats, dissidents who had left the party in 1948 on the civil rights issue.

It was in this atmosphere that, at 11 A.M. on March 4, Stevenson left Springfield for St. Louis and there, using the assumed name of his appointments secretary, Bill Blair, boarded an airplane on a secret trip to see President Truman. He had asked for the appointment himself. George Ball had been attempting the difficult task of maintaining communication between the White House and Stevenson; Truman's aides, Charles Murphy and David Lloyd, had told him the President's patience was wearing thin. En route, Stevenson stopped to meet Barry Bingham at the Louisville airport. Bingham urged him strongly to keep himself available to a presidential draft. Stevenson spoke of the difficulty of raising his children in the publicity glare of the White House.

In his *Memoirs,* Truman quoted a memorandum he made at the time: "'On March 4 Governor Stevenson came to see me again, this time at his request, to tell me that he had made a commitment to run for reelection in Illinois and that he did not think he could go back on that commitment honorably. I appreciated his viewpoint, and I honored him for it. . . .' But I felt that in Stevenson I had found the man to whom I could safely turn over the responsibilities of party leadership. . . . I would not pressure him [but] I felt certain that he would see it as his duty to seek the nomination." Carl McGowan once said, "He told Truman no. And the whole thing— Truman immediately tightened up. It wasn't much of an interview. Truman was still bemused by 1948 and thought no Republican would ever be elected. He thought the laying on of hands meant electing the President, and saying no was an insult to the office if not to himself."

65

Stevenson returned to Springfield the next day, arriving at 1 P.M. Short though the trip was, he had seen Dorothy Fosdick. He spent a crowded week with journalists, photographers, and Illinois politicians. Dutch Smith's wife, an emotional but sensible woman, sent him a long letter: "In the emotional stress of political discussions I have been most unhappy. . . . Suddenly, this evening, all my unhappiness and indecision about what I stand for in my own mind has evaporated. I was reading aloud to Dutch the Bernard DeVoto article, and at the end, in all those quotations from your speeches, I realized that *there* were the positive things I wanted for this country, and that only with you as president . . . could I be happy inside. So I hope you will run for President." Stevenson replied, "Ellen dear: I have read and re-read your letter. It touches me deeply and is more persuasive than the talk of a gross of pundits and political leaders. But it is hard for me to see how I can desert this commitment . . . the prairies of Illinois."

An old friend from Princeton, Richard K. Stevens, a prominent Philadelphia lawyer, offered to participate in a "build-up" in Philadelphia. Stevenson on March 5 thanked him but declined. A friend told Stevens that Stevenson's former wife would cause trouble if Stevenson ran. Stevens reported this to Stevenson. Stevenson sent Stevens' letter to Ellen. Ellen told Stevens, "It seems to me that if [his friend] . . . et al, kept their mouths as tightly closed as I have kept mine—your candidate would be better off! Adlai has a moral obligation here in Illinois. Most of the Independents who worked and voted for him for governor will feel betrayed if he accepts Truman's equivocal blessing. I count myself among them."

Despite all his reluctance, Stevenson on March 10 sent George Ball a long list of family photographs *Look* had wanted. That day too he went on a television show, though warned in advance he would be asked about the presidency. Next day, Tuesday, March 11, he left Chicago for Washington. The New Hampshire primary was held that day, and Kefauver defeated Truman while Eisenhower defeated Taft.

Stevenson attended a meeting of a Governors' Conference committee with the Senate Ways and Means Committee, then on Thursday went up to New York and Boston to see young Adlai and Borden and pick up John Fell, whose spring vacation was starting. Flying from New York to Boston, Stevenson told Alicia Patterson he had been pressed in Washington to tell Truman he would run, particularly after the New Hampshire primary, "and I escaped in utter exhaustion and mental distress. I just don't want to go out for it; I wouldn't be honest with myself if I did and I attach importance to the inconsistency of being a candidate for Gov. of Ill. and publicly or even privately running for Pres. I just can't seem to get over that hurdle which no one seems to understand—even if I wanted to run for Pres. which I don't. . . . [I will return] to Chicago, with my resolve hardened, I hope, that I will keep out of this thing and concentrate on *being* and *running* for Gov. unless the Democratic convention should nominate me which would seem very unlikely." It was the first time he had said he would accept a draft.

In Cambridge, Stevenson saw Arthur Schlesinger, Jr. Schlesinger wrote him a little later that Robert Sherwood, the playwright, hoped he would run and, "You appear the only solution," a sentence Stevenson underlined. He added that his wife reported that her hairdresser had announced she was for Stevenson, "whereupon," Schlesinger wrote, "an expensively-dressed woman in the next chair said, 'Why I'm for Stevenson too.' It looks as if you could count on support in all classes."

From Massachusetts, Stevenson had intended to go to Florida, taking John Fell with him. But on Friday, March 14, Charles Murphy, who was in Key West with President Truman, telephoned Jim Loeb and told him he and the President were coming to Washington and the President was eager to have Murphy talk with Stevenson. Stevenson reluctantly agreed. Loeb met Truman's plane. Murphy said the President wanted him to discuss two things with Stevenson—the timing of President Truman's announcement of his own plans, and the California primary. Loeb and Stevenson had dinner with Ball; Murphy came in after dinner. Ball recalls, "The discussion did not go well."

That was understating it. In addition to being reluctant to run, in addition to saying sharply that he couldn't see why he should have to make the sacrifice just because Truman happened to dislike Kefauver, Stevenson also made it clear that he did not believe in the Fair Deal program. Almost defiantly and angrily, he outlined his views on various issues. He said he was opposed to the principle of public housing. He said he did not favor repealing the Taft-Hartley labor law—he favored amending it. He said that if he were President the country would face a crisis, with strikes everywhere, for he would be tough on stabilization issues. He said he did not favor federal aid to education—it was a state problem—but at the same time he believed that if the states failed the federal government must help. He said he opposed what he called "socialized" medicine and thought Truman wrong. He said he did not understand well the Brannan Plan for agriculture (farm subsidies without the purchase and storage of surplus) but that, in so far as he did understand it, he opposed it. On civil rights, he said it was the states' responsibility to act and the federal government ought not "put the South completely over a barrel." He said he considered himself an orthodox economist and could not ignore the rising national debt. He wanted economy in government. He denounced the notion of a steadily rising standard of living. As for corruption, he criticized the President by saying that wrongdoers should be not only fired from government but prosecuted. Only on foreign policy did he indicate admiration for the Truman administration. He said he thought he would be a bad candidate and a poor President. After the meeting Loeb considered reporting to his ADA colleagues that the ADA ought to prevent, not promote, Stevenson's nomination. George Ball recalled, "Murphy told me afterward that he was deeply discouraged—reflecting, I assume, President Truman's own view of Stevenson's continued obduracy."

That Saturday, leaving Washington for Florida, Stevenson telephoned Dorothy Fosdick. She sent him a clipping from the Washington *Post* mentioning her and him but told him not to worry.

At that time President Truman and some of his staff were vacationing at Key West. On Monday, March 17, from New Smyrna Beach, where he and John Fell were visiting Hester Ayers (Bud Merwin's sister) and her husband, Stevenson wrote to Charles Murphy in care of President Truman at the U.S. naval base at Key West. (He wrote in longhand and reconstructed the letter when he returned to Springfield.) He said:

14. Another society-page photograph of Ellen Borden Stevenson. Photographs of her varied amazingly—some show her looking pert and lovely, others gloomy and almost austere, depending on her mood.

15. Stevenson and Ellen at their place in Libertyville, outside Chicago. Stevenson rode horseback and played tennis there and lived the life of a gentleman farmer. He loved that home and so, for a time, did Ellen.

16. The United States delegation to the second regular session of the United Nations General Assembly at Flushing Meadows, New York, on September 16, 1947. Left to right in first row: John Foster Dulles, Eleanor Roosevelt, Herschel V. Johnson, Warren R. Austin, and Secretary of State George C. Marshall (delegation chairman). Stevenson, one of four U.S. alternate representatives, is seated behind John Foster Dulles.

17. September 15, 1948, a high spot of the Stevenson campaign for Governor of Illinois: a homecoming torchlight parade in his home town, Bloomington. He delivered a lofty eloquent speech on small towns and the real America.

18. Dorothy Fosdick in 1949, the year she became Stevenson's intimate friend. He was Governor, recently divorced; she was on the Policy Planning Staff of the State Department and unmarried.

19. Stevenson, running for Governor, had made a coal mine disaster at Centralia a major issue. Elected, he discovered mine safety elusive. Here he talks with survivors of a mine fire in 1949. Still later in his term a mine at West Frankfort blew up, killing 119 men, more even than had died at Centralia.

20. When Stevenson was Governor he gave Christmas dances for his three sons at the Governor's Mansion in Springfield. Here he is in 1951 with (left to right): John Fell, 16, home from Milton Academy; Borden, 20, home from Harvard; Adlai III, 22, then a second lieutenant in the U. S. Marines, now United States Senator from Illinois.

22. Governor Stevenson and his sister Buffie in the Governor's Mansion, Springfield. The date was July 2, 1952. Three weeks later he was nominated for President.

21. In 1952 the Democratic Party's efforts to draft Steven-son for President provoked this cartoon, whose author sent him the original. Note Stevenson's striped pants—his oppo-nent for Governor in 1948 had called him a "striped pants diplomat" and as late as 1952 the label stuck. The draft was genuine—Stevenson wanted to run for President but not in 1952 and not against Eisenhower.

23. Adlai Stevenson III, in Marine training at Quantico in 1952, reading *Daily News* article on Democratic Party's efforts to persuade Adlai Stevenson II to run for President.

24. Stevenson and the youngest of his three sons, John Fell Stevenson, at their Libertyville home, in 1952, a few weeks after he was nominated for President. They are outside the porch and below the sun deck, two of Stevenson's favorite places on earth.

25. Jane Dick was one of Adlai Stevenson's oldest and closest friends in Lake Forest, Illinois. She campaigned for him for Governor in 1948, became co-chairman of the national Volunteers for Stevenson in 1952 (when this picture was taken), and worked with him in his last years at the United Nations.

26. Near the end of the 1952 campaign Stevenson stopped courting independent voters and began calling the Democrats home. Here he visits his good friend Eleanor Roosevelt at Hyde Park, where he laid a wreath on her husband's grave.

27. Alicia Patterson, one of the great loves of Adlai Stevenson's life, gave
a party for him in New York during his presidential campaign. A Stevenson
aide called it one of the worst nights of the campaign—all the guests were
rich Republicans. With them here at the party is William McCormick
Blair, Stevenson's able and loyal adviser.

"We must look forward to great tomorrows"

STEVENSON

28. President Truman campaigns for Stevenson for President. The quotation is from Stevenson's welcoming speech at the Democratic National Convention in 1952. They were vastly different men and their relationship was never so close and comfortable as both probably wished.

I have been thinking about our confused talk the other night at George Ball's house, on Friday, March 14. Let me try to summarize it as I see it:

1. I do not want to be a candidate for the nomination; I do not want to run for President, and I do not want to be President at this time. I have been in "politics" only three years and while I have learned a great deal, I have a great deal more to learn. My ambitious program in Illinois is well under way but there is still much to be done. I should like to do it, or at least try to do it, if the people of Illinois will let me.

2. I am the unopposed candidate for re-election and loathe to abandon an objective I *do* want to work for, for one which I *do not* honestly want. Even if I *did* want to run for President in these extraordinary circumstances, I would find it difficult to carry water on both shoulders and run for the nomination while ostensibly running for Governor. . . . (Perhaps I should inject here my conviction that I will be a much stronger candidate in Illinois for Governor than for President due to large independent and Republican support.)

To the foregoing I *could* add misgivings about my strength, wisdom and humility to point the way to coexistence with a ruthless, inscrutable and *equal* power in the world [Rex Tugwell's phrase]. That I am the best available man, aside from President Truman, to assume this monstrous task, seems to *me* grotesque [MacLeish's word]. But I will quickly concede that *that* decision is for the President, and the many others who have written and talked to me and share his view.

To the foregoing I *must* add, however, that my children seem to me altogether too young and undeveloped to subject to the pitiless exposure of a national campaign, let alone the presidency. Nor do they have the advantage of a strong and stable family life.

You will see, then, that there are many considerations which inhibit me at this time. . . .

Another four years as Governor of my beloved Illinois, and many of these obstacles will have vanished. As a more seasoned politician, with my work in Illinois behind me, creditably, pray God, I might well be ready and even eager to seek the presidency, if I then had anything desirable to offer.

But you will say now is the opportunity and now is the time— "The moving finger writes and having writ moves on." Indeed, you may say "Now is the time that need and events converge in duty." The President has explained the situation to me with compelling logic. . . .

The disintegration of the grand alliance, among other possible consequences, is an appalling reflection for me as it is for so many.

Our talk Friday perplexed me a little because I was under the distinct impression from my last visit with the President [on March 4], that given my Illinois situation, he was quite reconciled to run again himself. If I misunderstood him, or that is no longer the case and the question is whether I would accept the nomination at Chicago and then do my level best to win the election, I should like to know it. In that event, about the only solution I can see, in sincerity and good conscience, would be for me to say publicly, and I would like to say it before he announces his intention not to run, if such is his decision, that all I want is to carry on my work in Illinois, that I have no other ambition, desire or purpose; that I do not want and will not seek the nomination; that if my party should nominate me anyway I would accept proudly and prayerfully, of course, as should any American in good health with convictions about this tormented world. I am sure the people of Illinois would release me from my undertaking to run for Governor in order to run for President if I neither wanted nor sought it.

. . . Also, the problem of choosing a replacement as candidate for Governor is a difficult [one]. . . .

Now, if you have waded this deep, and the President should feel that a nomination I did not seek is a plausible solution, I should, of course, like to know so that I could reach a final decision and inform him at whatever time he prescribes. His confidence and interest in me is a compliment few Americans have ever received, and I pray that he—and you—understand, even if you may not wholly sympathize with my torment.

Murphy replied at once, in a letter dated March 18 at Key West:

Dear Governor—

I received your letter this morning and have talked with the President about it. He was much impressed by what you had to say—impressed in the sense that it confirmed and strengthened the high regard he already had for you. I do think it helped a great deal to clarify your situation in his mind. He said that he would like to think the matter over for a few days, and would then talk to me about it again. Until he does, there is little I can add about his views.

I would, however, like to add something on my own behalf. First, let me say I am honored that you should have written me such a letter. I have read it and reread it with great care. I have read it with my heart as well as my head.

The reasons you give for not wishing to seek the nomination are very compelling. I honestly wish I could say that you ought to be left alone. But the more I think about it, the more I am driven to the conclusion that if the President "propositions" you, on the basis indicated in your letter, you should accept. The reasons for this are more than compelling. They are overwhelming. I am not going to try to set them out here—you know most of them better than I do.

I will say this. If the President's final decision is not to run, it will be because he thinks such a decision is in the best interest of the country. . . .

And in such a case, you are just "it." Circumstances converge on you. I would be glad for your sake to see the call put off for four years. But this will be one that can't wait. It will be a matter of duty, as I see it.

One word about a practical aspect of this matter. We get considerable information here . . . that you stand well enough in the eyes of your countrymen so that you would be the strongest candidate the Democrats could have, except, perhaps, the President himself. You can't ignore that either.

In reading this exchange, one should bear the New Hampshire primary in mind. Kefauver had won all eight delegates and an important symbolic victory. To challenge an incumbent President is rare; to challenge him successfully even rarer. True, the President had not campaigned in New Hampshire. Kefauver had campaigned hard, and his street-corner handshaking style was well received. Truman's press secretary had said that the results would have no influence on Truman's decision on whether to run. Many people, however, thought that Truman declined to seek re-election because Kefauver beat him in the New Hampshire primary. But the President has said that he had decided much earlier not to run. It is possible that, had Truman defeated Kefauver decisively in New Hampshire, he might have changed his mind and run. Viewed that way, Kefauver was the man who all unintentionally brought about the Stevenson nomination. That is to say, his New Hampshire victory clinched Truman's decision not to run, which in turn created the vacuum that the choice of Stevenson ultimately filled. The Minnesota primary was held on March 18, the day Charles Murphy received and replied to Stevenson's letter. Senator Humphrey got 98,-704 votes and all twenty-six delegates as a favorite son; Kefauver had 19,783 write-in votes; Truman 3,602. But what made political scientists call Minnesota a "thunderclap" was that more than 100,-000 voters wrote in Eisenhower's name. On that same day, the Democratic national chairman, Frank McKinney, issued a statement asking that President Truman's name be withdrawn from the important June 3 California primary.

As Stevenson was preparing to leave Florida, he received another phone call from Key West, and on March 23 another Truman aide, David Lloyd, who had gone to Italy with Stevenson long ago, wrote to Stevenson from Key West, a personal letter written without Truman's knowledge and saying directly:

> I sincerely hope that when the President sees you or calls you again, after this Key West visit, you will tell him that you will take on the responsibility of running, if he asks you to. . . .
>
> I have been too close to this Presidential job to have many illusions about it. In terms of peace of mind, or personal convenience, or a civilized mode of existence, it is terrible. Your reluctance to consider taking it on does great credit to your common sense and good judgment. . . .
>
> . . . The President said to me on the beach the other day, "If I had been as ambitious as I ought to have been, I never would have become President" . . . I think of an acquaintance of ours who planned and missed because he planned too wisely and rationally. That is Bill Douglas [Justice William O. Douglas], who would probably have been the candidate today if he hadn't agreed with his very able advisers in 1948, when the President offered him the Vice Presidential candidacy, that the chances for a liberal would be better in 1952. The chances for a liberal *are* better in 1952, but the chances for Bill Douglas are few. . . . This is a job that you do not seek, and that you do not refuse. [Stevenson underlined that last sentence.]
>
> The other aspect of this matter that weighs heavily on my mind is the position of President Truman. Anybody who works closely with that man loves him, so I am prejudiced, and think, like the others, that he ought to have what he wants. Because of all he has put into the job, because of the way he has given himself to it, because of the things he has done for us all, I feel that if he wants to quit, and wants you to take the job, he ought to have his way. This may sound a little rough on you. But there is more to it than my personal feeling about him. We have to support him because of the things he represents, which are the things we believe in. If we don't support him, then we signify to the world that we aren't really tak-

ing seriously the things we talk about and work for, and the world will cease to take us seriously. . . .

I don't have to tell you that I think you have the equipment, the brains and the temperament and the character, for the job. Neither do I have to go into the question of whether you would win if nominated. I would trust the President's judgment on that. Of course, anybody can lose in this business. But I am convinced, after 1948, that these decisions are not to be made on the basis of careful calculations about victory or defeat. There is more to history than public opinion polls or sales charts.

Stevenson did not reply for ten days, and then only briefly, saying "you have touched me deeply," and then, "I emphatically agree that some decisions are not to be made on the basis of careful calculations of victory or defeat. That has never been and is not my problem."

66

On March 20, the day after he returned to Springfield, Stevenson delivered a long introduction of Senator Humphrey, the main speaker at a Jackson Day dinner in the Springfield Armory, and said, "This is the season of our political cycle when men dream dreams and see visions—mostly of the White House. Well, I'm not one of them. I want to run for Governor of Illinois—and that's all." The Illinois primary was less than three weeks away. Stevenson asked support for the ticket and talked about state issues.

An Ohio judge offered to go to Springfield to outline the Ohio political situation and invited Stevenson to speak in Ohio. Stevenson declined. An Iowa state Senator and others were circularizing Iowa legislators, newspapers, and others on Stevenson's behalf. Richard Jenkins of Sasabe, Arizona, who had met Stevenson that preceding June at Jim Douglas' house in Lake Forest, reported interest in Stevenson's national candidacy in the Arizona Democratic organization. (It was to Jenkins' ranch that Stevenson went after the November election.) Clay Tate, editor of the *Pantagraph,* took a poll of *Pantagraph* employees and found that among them Taft would beat Truman narrowly and Eisenhower would beat him badly while Stevenson would overwhelm Taft and beat Eisenhower narrowly. Stevenson commented he hoped he'd do as well for Governor.

Stevenson was telling friends he felt "the noose" tightening around his neck—that is, felt he was being drafted and was almost sure to lose to Eisenhower.

The pressure grew. Adolf A. Berle, Jr., asked Stevenson to speak to the Liberal Party dinner in New York on May 28, saying that the Tammany Hall Democratic machine was ineffective, that probably no Democratic candidate could carry New York State without Liberal Party support, and that his appearance at the Liberal Party dinner would indicate that the Liberal Party preferred him to Harriman. Stevenson declined. Scotty Reston wrote on March 26 that Stevenson "had informed President Truman that he would not seek" the nomination but had refused to discuss whether he would accept a draft and added several of his "intimate associates" in Chicago said he would. Professional politicians in Chicago, Reston wrote, were making contingency plans on a substitute candidate for Governor. Reston said Truman was under pressure from liberals to make a decision soon and Reston expected much talk about all this in Washington this weekend—Democrats would hold their annual Jefferson-Jackson Day dinner on Saturday, and President Truman, Stevenson, and other Democratic politicians would attend. *Newsweek* propounded three questions to Stevenson and on March 27 he made his answers public: He was not a candidate for the Democratic nomination for President. He would not be even if President Truman were to announce that Stevenson was his choice. If he were offered the nomination by the Democratic Convention would he run? "I can't cross a bridge as remote as that, and I don't expect to be confronted with that decision."

That same day Jack Arvey sent him a letter he had received from John J. Nangle, Democratic national committeeman from Missouri and therefore, because he was from Truman's home state, of more than ordinary importance. Nangle said that he had a feeling that Truman would announce at the Jefferson-Jackson Day dinner he would not be a candidate and, if so, that Stevenson was the most promising candidate. Stevenson scribbled an undated longhand note to Arvey: "Assume you will say nothing about my plans until I make an announcement A E Stevenson."

Reinhold Niebuhr wrote that the Republican Party was still deeply divided on foreign policy and that he hoped Stevenson would allow himself "to become a rallying point" for liberals. Stevenson replied, "Were I drafted, or threatened with a draft, I should have a most difficult decision to make."

On March 28, Bill Rivkin and Angelo Geocaris, young Chicago Democrats, gave a confidential memo to Jack Arvey and Dick Nelson. It said that Stevenson-for-President clubs were now functioning in Massachusetts, California, New York, Pennsylvania, Indiana, Wisconsin, Iowa, Michigan, Ohio, Florida, New Jersey, Minnesota, Washington, Connecticut, Illinois, and Oregon, and at least ten more would announce "momentarily." But now money was needed—each group needed a paid executive director and two paid field organizers. Money could not be raised if Stevenson continued to be "adamant." "Therefore," they asked, "can you determine whether he would accept a truly bona fide draft."

On the next day, Saturday, March 29, Stevenson left for Washington to attend the Jefferson-Jackson Day dinner. He would go on national television on "Meet the Press" next day. It was one of the important weekends of his life. The vast cavernous Armory was packed. This, in a presidential year, was the Democrats' big spring meeting. Democratic leaders—and potential Democratic candidates —from all over the country were there. It was a black-tie dinner. Arthur Schlesinger wrote in his journal, "When the head table guests were introduced, Acheson received by far the loudest applause; a standing ovation. Farley and Stevenson came in next. The speaking was indifferent. The Armory was too vast for people to feel much involvement in what was going on. Rayburn gave a speech with a nice human quality. Barkley was loud and vigorous. The meeting warmed up a bit when the President began. It was a good, fighting campaign speech, I thought; nothing new, but lively, and delivered with humor and composure. Libby [Donahue], bored, whispered to me toward the end, 'This is the most utterly meaningless speech I have ever heard.' At that moment, the President announced that he would not be a candidate for reelection, would not seek the nomination. The audience was stunned and confused. Some people reacted automatically by applause (as Adlai said in the car later, 'They applauded with really macabre enthusiasm'); others shouted 'No.' I found myself shouting 'No' with vigor; then I wondered why the hell I was shouting 'No', since this is what I had been hoping would happen for months. Still the shouts of 'No' seemed the least due to the President for a noble and courageous renunciation. He hurriedly finished the speech and disappeared, leaving the audience still stunned. Half the people did not seem to know what had happened." And immediately, almost before President Truman had finished speaking, photographers and reporters rushed to Stevenson as though pulled by wires.

What Truman had said was, "I shall not be a candidate for reelection. I have served my country long, and I think efficiently and honestly. I shall not accept a renomination. I do not feel that it is my duty to spend another four years in the White House." Truman had not included the announcement in his advance text released to the press. Even Jack Arvey has said that he—and Frank McKinney too—were taken by surprise.

Arvey was "tremendously impressed" by the rush to Stevenson. Averell Harriman, as the dinner began, had invited Stevenson and Schlesinger to have a drink with him afterward. Schlesinger wrote in his journal, "Finally we pulled him out and got into Averell's car. Also present were Senator Green, Mr. Ives (Adlai's brother-in-law), Daisy Harriman. Adlai told me, while waiting for the car, that he was completely astonished by the President's decision. Averell told me later that Adlai seemed rather angry about it all. 'The President put me in a hell of a spot,' he said, indicating that he would have much preferred for the President to wait another few weeks (presumably long enough to eliminate all thought of Adlai's going into primaries)."

Stevenson "did not feel he could" go to Harriman's house so, after dropping off Senator Green and the ladies, the remaining men went to the Metropolitan Club, where Stevenson was staying. George Ball was lurking in the doorway, having just left a note for Stevenson, and Stevenson found many other messages, including one from Joseph Alsop, the columnist, saying, "Call me any time tonight." The bar was closed so they went upstairs to talk. George Ball discussed what Stevenson should say on "Meet the Press" next day, and Harriman joined in. They then turned to the candidacy. Harriman and Stevenson had known each other casually for years but this was the first time they had talked privately at length. Harriman once recalled, "There had been talk but I didn't take it seriously about how I had to try for it. I told Adlai he had to run. He said, 'No, I won't.' He was very firm. I did everything I could to persuade him—he was a liberal, he'd been elected, it was his duty. He said no. I said, 'Then I think I'll make a stab at it.'" Schlesinger noted in his journal, "Adlai, looking very tired, tending to bury his head in his hands, was obviously appalled at the great abyss opening up before him. He kept saying that he didn't want to be a candidate. Running against Taft was one thing; but he wasn't certain that Eisenhower would ruin the country. Averell at this point became very eloquent." Eisenhower's nomination, Harriman urged, would remove foreign policy as an issue but that would only make domestic policy more important, and Eisenhower was "far to the right of Taft," as Schlesinger put it, and so were most of the men around him. "Averell went on to say how much a successful foreign policy depended on a successful domestic policy, and how unreliable an Eisenhower administration would be. Adlai simply groaned. Finally Averell said,

'For the sake of the party and of the nation, Adlai, you've just got to run. There isn't anybody else.' Adlai groaned, looked as if he were going to cry, put his head in his hands, and finally said, half humorously, half agonizedly, 'This will probably shock you all; but at the moment I don't give a god damn what happens to the party or to the country.' Averell, who was not shocked, correctly ascribed these sentiments to fatigue, confusion, an impending cold; and we shortly afterwards dispersed." Before they dispersed, however, Harriman said that he was a favorite son candidate only to hold the New York delegation together and would throw all his strength to Stevenson. Stevenson replied that Harriman was "the best of all candidates," in Schlesinger's words, and he would throw the Illinois delegation behind Harriman. Harriman did not ask him to.

Schlesinger went home with Harriman for—finally—a drink. Harriman would be New York's favorite-son candidate. Schlesinger told him that, if Stevenson took himself out, liberals would have to support Harriman. Harriman said, "It would be idiotic to nominate a man who has never run for office before," but did not look displeased.

Next day Stevenson attended a lunch in a private room at the Shoreham given by Francis Biddle. Schlesinger was there, and so were such leaders of the liberal wing of the party as Humphrey, Lehman, Rauh, Loeb, Jim Carey, Jack Kroll, a representative of David Dubinsky, and Monroe Sweetland. The lunch was cheerful and animated and Stevenson was far more composed and buoyant than the night before. None of them took Kefauver seriously. Humphrey was far more worried over what he called the Russell-Kerr coalition. Everyone present assumed that Stevenson represented the Democrats' only hope of winning. For a long time he remained silent. Finally he said, "I think we are now getting down to specifics. As I understand it, none of you thinks I should say anything before the Illinois primaries. None of you thinks I should go into the primaries at any point. But you do say that I must, sometime after April 8 [the date of the Illinois primary], and the sooner after the better, either state publicly, or communicate privately to key figures, that I will accept the nomination if offered it." Everyone agreed, Biddle saying he would much prefer that he say it publicly. The meeting broke up on an optimistic note.

Stevenson hurried off to appear on "Meet the Press." He said he had never watched the program and did not know what it was like. On "Meet the Press" several journalists joined Lawrence Spivak each Sunday in questioning a public figure. At that time such programs were bear-baiting sessions, intended less to elicit information than to determine which reporter could most discomfit the guest. The panel Stevenson faced was, however, by and large, friendly—Roscoe Drummond, Ed Lahey, May Craig of the Portland (Maine) *Press-Herald,* and Richard Wilson of the Des Moines *Register,* a Cowles newspaper. In addition to the wide public, many important politicians were watching—Jack Arvey had called Mayor David Lawrence of Pittsburgh, the most powerful Democrat in Pennsylvania, and told him to watch.

Mrs. Craig asked if Stevenson didn't think it was "dangerous to the country" for one party to stay in power so long. Not unless it resulted in the destruction of the two-party system, Stevenson replied, and that wasn't happening. She asked if "the revelations of corruption" didn't show that the Democrats had been in too long. Stevenson replied that corruption had been revealed in the first three years of the Harding administration. The exchange between them became testy.

Wilson asked about the mood of the people and what they wanted. High moral standards in public life, Stevenson said, and they were concerned about taxes and "the long frustrating ordeal in Korea." There was, he thought, "general unrest in the country." Asked what should be done about it, Stevenson said, "I think that the moral aspect of your question is very much like a pump, that you will pump in the government precisely what you pump out of the people . . . that the level of morals in public life can never be very much different from the level of morals in civilian life. I think therefore that our problem about improving the moral tone of public life is pretty much a reflection of the spiritual difficulties which we seem to be encountering in this anxious age of two devastating wars. I think government, however, must take the lead. . . . It must be like Caesar's wife, unimpeachable." The tax burden, he thought, was due largely to the national defense effort. As to Korea, he believed in the postwar policy of resistance to Communist expansion, and assistance to the free world. What would have happened had the United States and UN not gone into Korea? We would probably have disillusioned our friends both in Asia and in Europe, they would have appeased the Communists, and we would have found ourselves almost alone—we had to go in.

Drummond asked if postwar foreign policy, including the Greek-Turkish loan, the Marshall Plan, the North Atlantic Treaty, Mutual Assistance, all of which had largely been supported by both parties, was an issue in the coming election. Stevenson said foreign policy should be bipartisan, he did not know what Republican policy would be, he knew what Democratic policy would be, he hoped the campaign would remove confusion and misunderstanding among the people about our responsibilities and our self-interest.

Lahey asked, "To what avail is all this talk if you insist on shunning a role in national politics, Governor?" Stevenson agreed he had said he was "a candidate for Governor of Illinois and that's all." Lahey said, "Wouldn't your grandfather, Vice President Stevenson, twirl in his grave if he saw you running away from a chance to be the Democratic nominee in 1952?" "I think we will have to leave Grandfather lie," Stevenson replied. Spivak asked if his position was the same as Truman's—that he would not seek the nomination or accept a draft. Stevenson answered, "I'm an announced candidate for Governor of Illinois. We haven't even had our Illinois primary. I have no other ambitions than to be Governor of Illinois. I do not seek, I will not seek, the Democratic nomination for the presidency. A man cannot run for two offices at the same time," and he talked about his accomplishments in and his hopes for Illinois—"a state in which my people have lived for over one hundred and twenty years." Spivak pursued it: "Are we to understand from what you have just said that you are requesting that your name not be presented to the convention for the Democratic nomination and that if it is presented that you will ask that it be withdrawn, sir?" Stevenson replied, "Mr. Spivak that's a bridge that's more than four months hence, isn't it? It certainly is a bridge that I will not attempt to cross now." They tried to corner him but with little success.

They sought his views on national issues, starting by asking if he was for or against the Taft-Hartley Act, the labor relations law passed in 1947 over President Truman's veto. Stevenson said, "There are about more than a hundred provisions, I think, sections, subsections, in the Taft-Hartley law. I couldn't answer am I for or against it." Spivak said, "Would you say generally that it has helped or hurt?" "I think in some respects it's helped and in other respects it's hurt. And if you would give me ten minutes, I'd try to discuss it. I think the Taft-Hartley law needs revision, needs substantial amendment. I don't think it should be repealed." Spivak said, "Where do you stand on a compulsory FEPC?" and Drummond, "Or on civil rights generally." Stevenson said, "You haven't any easy questions you'd like to ask me first, have you?" Then, "I'd say this. I personally feel that the states should regulate as many of the public affairs of this country as they possibly could. I'm a very strong believer that the government concentration of authority in Washington to the extent that that's possible should be arrested. . . . I would hope very much that the problem of civil rights could be administered by the states. . . . To that end I have tried in the past two sessions of the Illinois legislature to get an FEPC bill passed in Illinois. If, however . . . it's impossible for the states to do this job and do it properly, then I would say the federal government must because I think ultimately it's imperative that we move on progressively to realize in practice our professions of faith, and one of our professions of faith is the equality of opportunity of every man, woman, and child in this country irrespective of race, color, and creed. I think democracy knows no color line."

And then Mrs. Craig raised the Hiss question and drew forth one of his most eloquent replies: "Pursuant to an order of [the trial] court, some questions, interrogatories as they are called, were sent out to me in Springfield . . . and the question in effect was: From what you heard from others, that is, from what others told you, what was Mr. Hiss' reputation for loyalty, integrity, honesty, as of that time, in 1948? My answer was that it was good. . . . That was the question that was asked me. From what you have heard from others, what is his reputation? And I would say this if I might, if you will permit me to speak a word longer. I'm a lawyer. I think that one of the most fundamental responsibilities, not only of every citizen, but particularly of lawyers, is to give testimony in a court of law, to give it honestly and willingly, and it will be a very unhappy day for Anglo-Saxon justice when a man, even a man in public life, is too timid to state what he knows and what he has heard about a defendant in a criminal trial for fear that defendant might later be convicted. That would to me be the ultimate timidity." They questioned him further about Hiss but what remained when it was over was his defense of Anglo-Saxon justice.

Asked about the McCarran investigation "to find out how deep the roots of Communism go," Stevenson replied, "I don't condemn that. I do very much condemn the danger of very broad accusation, unsubstantiated charges, which not only endanger the reputation of an individual, but they actually do an injustice to the Republic, because we can't let hysteria, in our anxiety to prevent any injury to the Bill of Rights, destroy the Bill of Rights itself." Soon they ran out of time.

Stevenson's performance could justly be termed a triumph. He seemed calm, thoughtful, intelligent, and forceful, especially when he dealt with the Hiss issue. Arvey was delighted, Mayor Lawrence of Pittsburgh greatly impressed, as were members of the National Press Club. The program helped advance Stevenson toward the nomination.

That night he had dinner with George Ball and Walter Lippmann. Lippmann suggested that Stevenson should not run because he could not possibly beat Eisenhower. According to Ball, Stevenson bridled and said: "What do you mean? Why are you so sure I can't beat Eisenhower?" Learning this, Schlesinger concluded, "I think he is on the toboggan slide." Schlesinger, complimenting Stevenson on his "Meet the Press" appearance, suggested that he favor enlarging the civil rights section of the Justice Department, which would "cheer up the North without offending the South," and that he place more emphasis on the need to amend Taft-Hartley in order not to offend labor. A few days later Schlesinger and Bernard DeVoto, at George Ball's request, wrote a draft statement intended to launch Stevenson's presidential candidacy.

Stevenson returned to Chicago on Monday, March 31, and at the airport cast a disavowal of presidential candidacy in jocular tone. With Director of Welfare Hoehler, Stevenson inspected the State Hospital at Manteno, taking Adlai III and Borden, home for spring vacation, then went to Springfield and immediately wrote to President Truman:

"I was stunned by your announcement Saturday night after that superb speech. I can only accept *your* judgment that the decision was right, although I had hoped long and prayerfully that it might be otherwise. As for myself, I shall make no effort to express the depth of my gratitude for your confidence. I hope you don't feel that I am insensitive to either that confidence or the honor you have done me."

Truman replied promptly. He "appreciated most highly" Stevenson's letter. He "sincerely" hoped "that we can find a man who will carry on the Foreign Policy of the United States as it was established in 1938 by President Roosevelt and carried through by me, to the best of my ability. . . . We must also have a President who believes in the domestic policies which have made the Foreign Policy possible," for the two were so linked that the failure of one meant the failure of the other. Finally: "I sincerely hope you will not take yourself completely out of the picture."

67

President Truman's withdrawal had created a leadership vacuum in the Democratic Party which only Stevenson could fill. Conceivably the Southern right wing might capture the party; but that would reverse the whole course of the party for the past twenty years. In the liberal wing, Harriman, although one of the best and nicest men in public life, had never held elective office and was not widely known. Kefauver, somehow, seemed implausible despite his primary victories—his candidacy was narrowly based on crime busting and he had a folksy mountaineer style, all of which seemed irrelevant to such grave issues as Korea; moreover, the party leaders, such as Truman and Arvey, opposed him. Chief Justice Vinson had taken himself out. Kerr was vulnerable because of his record on oil and gas legislation. Russell, a Southerner, would forfeit the Negro and pro-civil rights vote in the North. Such a Northern favorite son as Hubert Humphrey was too liberal on civil rights to hold the South. And so on—each of the possible candidates had fatal liabilities.

Stevenson, on the other hand, was the choice of virtually every major faction in the Democratic coalition. The Northern liberals supported him. The Southern conservatives could accept him. He was thought to have the backing of President Truman, Chairman McKinney, Senator (and former New York Governor) Herbert Lehman and Harriman and state chairman Paul Fitzpatrick of New York, Senator Benton and Senator Brien McMahon[26] of Connecticut, Senator Humphrey of Minnesota, Senator Murray of Montana, Governor Dever of Massachusetts, Governor Schricker of Indiana, Governor Byrnes of South Carolina, Governor Williams of Michigan, former Senator Alexander of New Jersey, Mayor Lawrence of Pittsburgh, Jack Arvey of Illinois, and party leaders in California, Missouri, Oregon, and Ohio. In short, Stevenson had the support of the professionals as well as such amateurs as his own independent and Republican friends and such amateurs-professionals as the IVI and ADA.

Stevenson was receiving calls from Jack Arvey telling him that various leaders around the country were saying they would not "go out on a limb" for Stevenson if he might later refuse the nomination. Flanagan, fearing that Arvey might be "cooling them off," suggested to Arvey that he tell other leaders, "Sure, he'll accept." Mayor Lawrence of Pittsburgh called Arvey several times. So did Eleanor Roosevelt.[27]

Arvey has said, "This went on all spring. I'd never seen anything like it before. Horan, Gill, and Daley kept asking me, 'Will he

---

[26] McMahon was ill and died two days after the Democratic Convention started.

[27] Among others who telephoned Arvey were James Roosevelt, Carmine De Sapio of the New York City machine, Governor Dever, Tracey McCracken of Wyoming, Calvin Rawlings of Utah, Paul Fitzpatrick of New York (though Fitzpatrick swung to Harriman when Harriman announced his candidacy on April 22). An aide to Senator Russell told Arvey that Stevenson would get the Georgia delegation when Russell withdrew.

run?' They thought I knew something, that it would be okay. When I said this wasn't so, Horan said, 'Well, goddammit, why don't you make him say yes or no?' I said, 'I can't do it. I think he'll be nominated and I think he'll take it. I can't conceive of a man with his great desire to do something worth while for the world turning this down if you offer it.' I said this on TV, in the press, and in private. I'd call Stevenson or go to Springfield and tell him, 'You don't have to say yes but don't discourage people.' I feared a Sherman statement.[28] I told him, 'You can't do that. You can't say no. You're running for re-election.' " Arvey did not really believe this last; he knew that Stevenson could issue a Sherman-like statement on the presidency and still run for re-election as Governor; but he so advised him nonetheless. "I want to make it clear that Stevenson was not a party to the draft. He made it clear to me time and again that he didn't want it." Arvey once said that he never spent a nickel for a telephone call or three cents for postage to help along the Stevenson draft, and while this may not be quite literally true, it is nearly so: he did not need to.

A Stevenson-for-President Club was organized in Iowa early in April. The Indiana Draft Stevenson for President Club sent a letter to county chairmen. A member of the Indiana House of Representatives offered assistance in adjoining states. Dick Nelson, though he wanted Stevenson to run, had the job of discouraging such efforts: "He has asked me to . . . express his appreciation for your good wishes. However, it is still his hope to continue as governor of Illinois." A state Senator from California offered to help draft him. A long list of students and faculty members at Yale sent Stevenson a telegram. (They were also in touch with George Ball and George Overton.) Immediately after the Jefferson-Jackson Day dinner, Leo Lerner, Marshall Holleb, and their friends converted the IVI movement into a national committee. They invited Jim Loeb to head it, but Loeb said the candidate's approval was lacking and a little later went over to Harriman.

Stevenson at this time did not seem dismayed or tormented. The present author made a trip with him to southern Illinois on April 1, the day after he returned from Washington, accompanied by Borden and Adlai III, to inspect Menard Penitentiary and the hospital for insane criminals at Chester and to speak to Rotarians at Nashville. He was, as always, interested in everything—the hospital and

[28] In 1884, General William Tecumseh Sherman told the Republican National Convention, "If nominated, I will not accept. If elected, I will not serve."

prison, their shortcomings, their inmates; the countryside and its natural beauty and its history; the people he met. And presidential politics—being driven back to Springfield in the ancient official Cadillac
he insisted on using, he listened to the day's primary returns from
Wisconsin and Nebraska. The radio was full of politics—recorded
statements by Senator Kefauver, Senator Kerr, and Senator Russell,
and Stevenson said, "Let's hear Dick Russell." Listening to the Wisconsin returns, Stevenson said quietly, "That knocks Taft out." (It
didn't, though at the time it seemed to.) He fell to talking to the
boys about their friends, their entry into the armed forces, and
John Fell's summer plans. Eisenhower's voice came on the radio,
talking about NATO, and Stevenson said, in a voice that sounded
almost awed, "I never heard him speak before," and listened closely.
Back at the Mansion he found Bill Blair listening to election returns
on the radio. Blair gave him a copy of *Collier's* containing a photograph of Kefauver's young children in a bathtub and said, "They
want to do one on you next week, they want to get Borden and
Adlai and John Fell and you all in a bathtub, think that can be arranged?" Stevenson laughed. Adlai III asked how many write-in
votes his father had received in Nebraska. Blair said, "Two. Cousins,
I suppose." Stevenson seemed tired but relaxed, even enjoying his
position, complex and difficult though it was.

Kefauver won the Wisconsin primary without serious opposition,
taking twenty-eight firmly pledged delegates. The Nebraska delegation split five for Kefauver, four for Kerr, one for Russell, and two
uncommitted. (The two uncommitted went for Stevenson on the first
ballot at the convention.) On April 8, in the Illinois primary, which
does not bind delegates but simply indicates voters' preferences,
Kefauver was the only presidential candidate on the ballot and received 526,301 votes. Stevenson was not on the ballot for President
but received 54,336 write-in votes. And Eisenhower received 6,655
Democratic write-ins. Taft won the Republican primary overwhelmingly with 935,867 votes. Eisenhower got 147,518 write-ins. In the
primary for Governor, Stevenson, unopposed, received 708,275.
His leading Republican opponent, William G. Stratton, opposed by
four candidates, got 716,000 votes. Eddie Barrett, unopposed for
Secretary of State, received 709,646, slightly more than Stevenson.
At the time the Illinois primary was considered virtually meaningless.
It seems worth noting, however, that Stevenson ran slightly behind
his running mate, Barrett; that the total vote for Governor in the Republican primary greatly exceeded Stevenson's vote; that Taft received more votes for President than either Stevenson or Stratton received for Governor; and that Eisenhower got a combined write-in

total from both parties of 154,173 compared to only 54,336 write-in votes for Stevenson. True, Stevenson's name on the ballot for Governor may have reduced his write-ins for President, and he had publicly discouraged write-ins; true, local contests in the Republican Party brought out a heavy vote. Nonetheless, the vote does seem to contain a warning of Stevenson weakness and remarkable Eisenhower pulling power.

68

During the first half of April, Stevenson was making speeches and working on his state political problems as well as considering the presidency. To the Rotarians at Nashville on April 1 he talked about the budget. To the Life Underwriters Association in Springfield next day he talked about good government. He made ceremonial appearances and introduced Abba Eban at an Israel Freedom Festival. He devoted his TV "Open House" on April 6 to conservation. He tried to stay out of local factional fights over the selection of state committeemen, especially a quarrel in McLean County (Bloomington).

The old Stevenson-for-Governor Committee had been reactivated. Its chairman was Dutch Smith; Jane Dick, Fred Hoehler, and others were heavily involved. Smith has said, "He really wanted another term as Governor. I held his hand a good deal through this. We told him we'd rather have him for Governor, though I did tell him that maybe he would have no choice." Smith thought Stevenson wanted to run against Taft but not against Eisenhower. Once Stevenson sought the advice of Henry Tenney, head of the Public Aid Commission. Tenney said if he didn't want to run for President he should "tell them to go to hell." Stevenson replied, "You can't in this business—if you say that, you're through."

Bill Rivkin once said, "I am convinced that Stevenson did not want to run in 1952 because he thought it was time for a change—that the system was breaking down—that a party out of power for twenty years could only become more irresponsible—apart from the fact that he thought he couldn't win. A friend of mine in England got very excited about Stevenson. He wrote to me and told me that the whole thing reminded him of a great story about cricket. There was a match between South Africa and England. In baseball parlance, it was the last of the ninth, the pitcher was up to bat, the bases were loaded, he hadn't made a hit in two years, he went to the plate with the score tied, and the crowd booing, and he turned to the crowd and said, 'Cometh the hour, cometh the man.' Then he swatted a home run. I mailed this to Stevenson in August of 1952 after he was nominated. I didn't get an answer. Then in November, the week after Eisenhower had won the election, he wrote to my friend and sent me a carbon, saying in effect, 'I want to say that I think you were quite right—cometh the hour, cometh the man.' "

Abner Mikva, who left his clerkship at the Supreme Court at about the same time Newton Minow did and went to work for Stevenson, once recalled the dilemma Stevenson supporters in Illinois were in that spring: "We wanted him to stay here but he was also too good not to share with the rest of the United States." Lou Kohn has said, "I don't think he wanted it in '52 but he was trapped." Kohn did not think Stevenson could win against Eisenhower.

Why, really, was Stevenson so reluctant to run? Carl McGowan has said, "I myself had taken the position that I would give him my opinion on everything except whether to run for President. It was too intensely personal a decision. His own reluctance went back to the basic thing: Stevenson knew better than Truman or the organization that Truman did not have the power to pass the presidency on, and that, with things shaping up as they were, the worst thing would be to have a distinguished Republican running against Truman's man. This was a shrewd political judgment. He knew the temper of the country well enough to know that if he marched out of Blair House and said, 'Mr. Truman has kindly asked me and I have agreed to run,' it would be devastating. He was not being indecisive. Mind you, Stevenson never told me this. But he was no fool about politics. He knew that our friends in Washington had been misled by 1948. They thought no Republican would ever be elected. They didn't realize how unpopular Truman really was out in our part of the country. Truman himself didn't realize it. Out on the prairie they weren't thinking of Truman in the terms the Eastern Democrats were thinking. Truman started off too humble and ended too cocky. If Stevenson had any chance at all to win, he *had* to stand on his own feet and not be a passive Truman candidate. Joe Rauh and others came out to Springfield. They were completely out of touch with reality. George Ball too. They shouldn't have urged him to run. Stevenson was smarter than they were. Even if he had known completely that this was what he wanted to do—that is, run for President—he should have played it the way he did. It gave him his minuscule chance to win. When Eisenhower was nominated, even that was gone.

"I thought all of this at that time. He didn't say it to me. He'd say, 'You can't say no to Truman.' I would say, 'Why not? What's the reason? He is not a political force, though he is a great man.'

He'd say, 'The Democrats are in bad shape.' He had a sneaking feeling, too, as an American, that maybe a little change would be good. He also felt strongly that bitterness built up needs to be blown out—or the Republicans would become irresponsible and tear the country to pieces. The Republicans were getting mean. They had been so disappointed in 1948. He thought that if he won he couldn't accomplish anything.

"There was also the thing that he hated to give up being Governor of Illinois. He liked the job. Things were just beginning to fall into place. Then personally—his family situation was in a snarl. There were a lot of things operating that made perfect sense to me as to why he seemed to be reluctant."

Could he have avoided the nomination in 1952 and run in 1956? McGowan has said, "I don't know. Maybe the time had come and he had to relax and enjoy it. But on the other hand, I don't believe in this theory that the party will say no next time if you say no now. I don't know if he could have avoided '52 and taken '56. But such a parlay is dangerous. When the mysterious tide that carries you to the presidency sets in, you had better go if you want it."

McGowan did not consider the IVI draft efforts important. "We were never conscious of those guys. It always seemed to me that as things developed during the spring the Governor was going to be nominated if he would let himself be. No one could change that. The Governor had given strict injunctions to the staff against associating with these activities. Only Flanagan violated this. If the Governor had known of Flanagan's activities, he'd have kicked his ass out. Flanagan was beglamorized. I thought the nomination was right in Stevenson's lap. So all this activity by the IVI didn't matter. The reality was: Truman decided that Stevenson would be the best candidate and the most likely to win. Truman had no alternative—he couldn't stomach Kefauver, Barkley was too old. Truman was driven into a corner. The convention was going to do whatever Truman said. I'm not sure he was wrong to run. But I did resent the callousness of the group from Washington. They said, 'He's got to run.' For example, Joe Alsop, who wouldn't even support him. Dewey at the Governors' Conference urged him and said, 'You've got to do it.' He put it on high ground—'We need an alternative to Taft.' But it was pretty shrewd—it gave them ammunition for Eisenhower and against Taft."

Flanagan did indeed disregard Stevenson's instructions. Without Stevenson's knowledge, he wrote to politicians around the country. One of them telephoned Stevenson and said enthusiastically, "We're for you," and Stevenson remonstrated with him, then, learning that

Flanagan was responsible, "gave me hell," as Flanagan put it, "and clamped down on me." Flanagan told Arvey what he was doing and asked him to try to get the leaders of state delegations to support Stevenson. Arvey said, "I can't—I've given my word to him that I won't." Flanagan felt certain Stevenson would run if nominated; he had talked to Stevenson about it.

Flanagan was also engaged in another maneuver. One of the nastiest false rumors of the campaign had started: that Stevenson was homosexual. It sought credibility from the fact that Bill Blair, a bachelor at that time, lived in the Mansion with Stevenson and from newspaper speculation about the reasons for Stevenson's divorce. Mrs. John Miller once said that the rumor was begun by her Republican friends. Arvey suspected that former Governor Green, bitter at his defeat, had started the rumor. The rumor reached the White House. Early in 1952, Frank McKinney went to Chicago at President Truman's request and inquired about the rumor of Arvey and others. His report allayed the President's misgivings. Flanagan, cognizant of the rumor, planted a counter rumor with the press: that a romance existed between Stevenson and Dorothy Fosdick. This probably accounted for the several newspaper items about them. Flanagan did it in all innocence—he simply knew that she had known Stevenson in his UN days and had visited him a few times in Springfield. When the newspaper stories started appearing, Stevenson asked Flanagan if he had started the rumor and told him, "You've got to do something about this—she's engaged to someone else."

On April 10, Ben Cohen told Stevenson, "There is a tide in the affairs of man and when it comes, one must ride out to sea." Stevenson replied, "Perhaps I have lived too long on the prairies to understand the tides." To Senator Benton, who had told him that the labor leader Jacob Potofsky, among others, was for Stevenson, he wrote, "I am sorely troubled, but I feel strongly that my commitment, my duty and my opportunity lie here." The *Newsweek* cover story came out in the issue dated April 14, and Alfred A. Knopf, the publisher, describing himself as "a black, reactionary Republican," sent high praise for the interview. Increasingly, people around the country, a certain kind of people, liberals, intellectuals, writers, academics, amateur-professional politicians, were talking to each other about Stevenson. Robert E. Sherwood, the playwright and Roosevelt associate, had been talking with Barry Bingham and Herbert Agar, for example, and on April 14 told Stevenson he was the Democrats' strongest candidate. On that same day others wrote similar letters.

These letters arrived as Stevenson was drafting a formal public statement taking himself out of the running. On April 16 he issued it.

It said that he was a candidate for Governor, that he could not run for two offices at the same time, that his duties as Governor precluded his running for the presidential nomination, and that because of his prior commitment to run for Governor and his desire—and the desire of many who had helped him—to complete unfinished work in Illinois, he "could not" accept nomination for any other office that summer.[29]

Stevenson sent copies of the statement to numerous persons, including President Truman, whom he told: "This is the hardest thing I have ever had to do, but, as I told you at Blair House, I could see no best way out of my dilemma, and this seemed to me the right way in all the circumstances. Further agonizing debate since your announcement has only fortified this condition. I know you will be dis-

[29] The full text of the statement reads:

"I have been urged to announce my candidacy for the Democratic nomination for President, but I am a candidate for Governor of Illinois and I cannot run for two offices at the same time. Moreover, my duties as Governor do not presently afford the time to campaign for the nomination even if I wanted it.

"Others have asked me merely to say that I would accept a nomination which I did not seek. To state my position now on a prospect so remote in time and probability seems to me a little presumptuous. But I would rather presume than embarrass or mislead.

"In these somber years the hopes of mankind dwell with the President of the United States. From such dread responsibility one does not shrink in fear, self-interest or humility. But great political parties, like great nations, have no indispensable man, and last January, before I was ever considered for the presidency, I announced that I would seek reelection as Governor of Illinois. Last week I was nominated in the Democratic primary. It is the highest office within the gift of the citizens of Illinois, and its power for good or ill over their lives is correspondingly great. No one should lightly aspire to it or lightly abandon the quest once begun.

"Hence, I have repeatedly said that I was a candidate for Governor of Illinois and had no other ambition. To this I must now add that in view of my prior commitment to run for Governor and my desire and the desire of many who have given me their help and confidence in our unfinished work in Illinois, I could not accept the nomination for any other office this summer.

"Better state government is the only sound foundation for our Federal system, and I am proud and content to stand on my commitment to ask the people of Illinois to allow me to continue for another four years in my present post.

"I cannot hope that my situation will be universally understood or my conclusions unanimously approved.

"I can hope that friends with larger ambitions for me will not think ill of me. They have paid me the greatest compliment within their gift, and they have my utmost gratitude."

appointed with me. That you are is my greatest distress—and also my greatest honor. I pray that some time I can serve your confidence better."

Truman replied six days later:

"I appreciated your letter of the sixteenth very much with the attached statement which I didn't appreciate so much.

"I am sorry that you felt it necessary to make this statement, although you are your own best judge of what you should do. I am very certain that if you had left the door open there would have been no difficulty about your nomination and I think you could be elected.

"Best of luck to you in whatever you do."

69

It was not a Shermanesque statement, closing and locking the door to a draft. Jack Arvey pointed out that Stevenson said he "could" not accept rather than "would" not. (Curiously Dwight Eisenhower, in his statement of January 1948, declining nomination, had used the same word "could.") Thus closely were politicians reading the omens —watching the meaning of a single letter in a subjunctive verb. They were right. Carl McGowan had given Stevenson a draft statement saying, "I cannot and will not accept the nomination." It came back from Stevenson with "cannot and will not" changed to "cannot, in good conscience, accept." This convinced McGowan that Stevenson would in fact accept the nomination and he told him that he might as well drop "in good conscience." Whether Stevenson intended it to or not, the statement did have the effect of leaving the door ajar for a draft and at the same time of cutting himself loose from Truman, so that if a draft did occur he would appear to be the choice of a free convention, not the hand-picked choice of an unpopular President.

The day after he issued the statement he went to New York to speak at the Democratic State Committee dinner for Averell Harriman at the Waldorf. Paul Fitzpatrick, state chairman, had asked Jack Arvey to persuade Stevenson to speak. Arvey had called Bill Blair, and he had accepted for Stevenson. Fitzpatrick was inviting everybody being considered for President. But now Stevenson, having issued his statement the day before, told Fitzpatrick he would not appear. Fitzpatrick telephoned Arvey, "frantic"—Stevenson was "my chief drawing card." Arvey told Stevenson he owed it to the party to go. Mrs. Roosevelt was to be there; a rumor was going around that Stevenson might marry her. (Once, when someone suggested he do, he replied that he was too old for her.) Stevenson agreed to go but only if Arvey too went—Stevenson wanted to take him to Harriman's home.

For a man who maintained he appeared only because he wanted to help Harriman, Stevenson said remarkably little about Harriman in his speech, and he stole the show. His speech was in part drawn from earlier speeches. He said, "The burdens of the presidency dwarf the imagination. And the next President will have something more to face than most any of his predecessors—guidance toward co-existence in this world with a ruthless, inscrutable, and equal power in the world," Tugwell's line. Stevenson said again, "Perhaps it isn't exactly the thing to say to a partisan meeting, but who wins this fall is less important than what wins—what ideas, what concept of the world of tomorrow, what quality of perception, leadership, and courage." He said the omens were good for the Democrats. "The Republican Party is bereft of common purpose, policy, principles, or program—as usual." Democrats had made mistakes. "But the objectives, the goals, at home and abroad, have been consistent and clear —and, to the everlasting credit of Franklin D. Roosevelt and Harry S. Truman, they have been right!" Then, "We can be proud of our twenty years of faith and service in the American way. But we must look forward, not back. Rather we lose this election than mislead the people by representing as simple what is infinitely complex, or by representing as safe what is infinitely precarious. For there are no painless solutions to war, inflation, Communism, imperialism, hunger, fear, intolerance, and all the hard, stubborn problems that beset us."

Arvey considered it a "brilliant" speech. When it was over he told Stevenson so and said, "Please don't take me to Harriman's home tonight. He was dull and inarticulate and if he can't inspire me he can't inspire people who don't feel any obligation to the Democratic Party." As Arvey was leaving the banquet hall, Congressman Emanuel Celler of New York stopped him and said, "Jack, you've got to make that man run. This is our only hope, our only salvation." The Democratic state chairman of New Jersey told Stevenson he was the "only one who can save our party."

A few days after the Harriman dinner, on April 22, Harriman, having first obtained the approval of President Truman, announced his candidacy. (Truman told him he had no objection but at the convention wanted him to help nominate "the man, whoever he is," adding that he himself was committed to Stevenson.) Stevenson at the convention took the position that he himself was committed to Harriman in order to beg off nominating Barkley. Actually his commitment seems to have been nothing more than what he said at the Metropolitan Club after the Jefferson-Jackson Day dinner.

The three months remaining to the convention were a strange period. Stevenson's April 16 statement seemed to restore the vacuum Truman had created, yet it did not really. A Gallup poll released April 24 showed that Stevenson still was the favorite of Democratic county chairmen by two to one over Kefauver. A poll of fifty Washington correspondents on May 26 showed Stevenson the most likely candidate. Very late, on May 29, Vice President Barkley announced his candidacy with President Truman's blessing. All the candidates were campaigning. Each in his own way performed a valuable function. Harriman, promising to carry on the programs of Roosevelt and Truman, held together the liberal wing of the party. Kefauver held liberals who liked Truman's programs but did not like Truman. Democrats on the right who liked Truman but not his programs gravitated toward Barkley. Senator Russell held together responsible Southerners and promised to prevent a Dixiecrat third-party movement. But none of these candidates, nor the various favorite sons, seemed himself a real possibility. What was happening, really, during these three months was that the Democratic Party, bereft of the Roosevelt-Truman leadership continuity, was rearranging itself. For just as the leadership chain was broken, so was, to some extent, the old Roosevelt coalition shattered, and its various pieces had to rearrange themselves. And all this rearranging had to take place around a man—and he was absent in Illinois. It was symptomatic of the problem that Truman, asked about Stevenson's statement of April 16, reportedly said, "I haven't seen it and I don't intend to look at it."

Stevenson's statement shocked Democrats; his performance at the Harriman dinner excited them. The statement deflated both amateurs and professionals who had hoped he would run. Professionals do not want to get committed to a non-candidate; most of the amateur clubs became quiescent. Almost alone, the IVI group in Chicago continued what seemed a forlorn quest. Other groups disbanded and some of their leaders went to work for Harriman. In American politics, programs and ideals are not enough; one needs a candidate.

70

During this same period public interest shifted to the Republicans' struggle over Taft and Eisenhower. By the end of April, with 716 of

1,206 delegates selected, the Associated Press reported that Taft seemed assured of 274, Eisenhower 270. Taft won the Ohio primary as expected. In Oregon on May 16, Eisenhower won eighteen delegates and an important psychological victory. Then occurred the famous struggle in Texas. Though outnumbered and outvoted at the county conventions in the larger Texas counties, the Taft men were able to control the state convention—but Eisenhower supporters held a rump session, and when both conventions picked delegate slates, it was clear that the Texas delegate fight would go into the convention. Taft won the last primary he contested with Eisenhower on June 3, in South Dakota. He got thirty-two delegates in Indiana on June 7 and ten more in Illinois on June 23. With his nomination far from assured, Eisenhower returned from Europe after the Texas fight. He made his first political speech at Abilene, Kansas, on June 4. It was a dispiriting affair. He retired to the house in Morningside Heights he had occupied as president of Columbia University and there received state delegations almost up to the convention. The infighting for delegates was bitter, especially in Texas. Eisenhower himself spoke at Dallas on June 21 and accused Taft's supporters of betraying the Republican Party and stealing "the Texas birthright." To this Taft men replied that Texas Democrats had tried to nominate the weakest Republican candidate. A Gallup poll of June 19 showed that Esienhower led Stevenson 59 to 31 and that he led Kefauver by 55 to 35 but that both Stevenson and Kefauver led Taft, Kefauver by 50 to 41 and Stevenson by 45 to 44.

Stevenson's own frame of mind seems clear in a letter he wrote to Alicia Patterson while returning from the Harriman dinner:

> Elisha my love
> En route back to Illinois after an almost frightening 24 hrs in NY. for the big Democratic clam bake at the Waldorf. . . . I like Ill more & more & my once maddening problems there are positively inviting after these forays into the outside world. Its been another awful week—agonizing last minute conferences & pressures from everywhere to "announce"; the zero hours of decision, writing the statement . . . then N.Y. & now back I hope to 48 hrs of peace & serious work over the weekend—then to Dallas on Monday for a full dress foreign affairs speech (not yet written); back just in time for the State Convention where they have threatened to adopt a resolution repudiating my "statement"; declaring me still the "favorite son" & starting up the whole wretched business all over again.

He thought he had spoken well at the Harriman dinner—"too well for my own peace & security from renewed pressure." Kefauver, he said, had not distinguished himself "& got a little tight afterward to boot, I'm told." He thought Harriman had done well but had not pleased the politicians—he would make a "very good" President but probably could not even beat Taft, let alone Eisenhower. Lloyd Garrison and others had rebuked Stevenson for making his statement.

> I hope you, at least, agree that it made some sense. . . . Your precious letters and prayerful, loving, understanding of my journey in the wilderness were a great comfort, Elisha darling. I don't get wisdom, perspective, objectivity and love in single packages & I'm praying that you will never think the worse of me for what I've done. . . .
> Love my darling and big, big, x x x s

A

His statement had brought a flood of mail. Vice President Barkley telegraphed praise for his "lofty motives." Ben W. Heineman of Chicago said it was a first-rate courageous statement—"now let's go to work and beat Stratton." To a sprightly Republican lady Stevenson wrote, "Your good wishes for Governor satisfy me wholly. It has been my only ambition." He told many others the same thing. Arthur Schlesinger regretted but respected the statement; he would go to work for Harriman. Stevenson himself told Harriman he would see what he could do to keep the Illinois delegation uncommitted. Jack Kroll, director of the CIO Political Action Committee, expressed his "deep regret" at what he regarded as Stevenson's "wrong decision." Various "Students for Stevenson" groups refused to desist.

Arthur Krock told Stevenson, "I think you may face the prospect of one of the few true drafts in our political history." Stevenson replied, "You terrify me." But he told Ed McDougal he would have to respond to a draft.

Stevenson gave his reasons for not wanting the nomination *ad infinitum*. That he did not want it is doubtful. There are few men in public life who do not want to be President. That he felt he was not worthy is open to question, too. He knew the problems the new President would face; and they were formidable. But although the idea that he might become President only four years after first assuming public office may have shocked him at first, by spring he had accepted the idea as a possibility. What else? That he had a prior commitment to Illinois and his friends was a valid reason and it grew out of his character. That the Republicans needed to win fits his character too. That he could not run for two offices at the same time was pure nonsense—no one expected him to. As for his sons, there is no reason to think this was uppermost in his thoughts. Vague stirrings of guilt, and fear of worse problems with his former wife, may have prompted concern about the boys.

He took many things into consideration, and it was a complex decision. It was, however, essentially a political decision. If he could run against Taft, he would replay the old debate of the William Allen White Committee days and he could be comfortable and probably win. But if he must run against Eisenhower, he had lost the foreign policy issue, he faced a national hero, and he would probably lose.

Newspaper columnists during the campaign and later repeatedly referred to him as a "Hamlet" who could not make up his mind. A woman who knew him in the 1960s, Mrs. John B. Currie, once made notes on several conversations with him, and she wrote, "Indecision and Hamlet—This was a very sore point. He was bitter on this. . . . And, he added, putting the tag of 'indecisive' on Hamlet was a gross over-simplification of *that* young man. . . . There was no indecision in 1952. He did not want to run and said so, but he did not feel a man should refuse a draft and he said so."

His reluctance during the spring had, as most political choices have, effects both good and bad. On the one hand, he was able to divorce himself from an unpopular President. On the other hand, his reluctance fed the myth that he was "indecisive," and it permitted independents, such as the *Sun-Times,* to go to Eisenhower. (He never forgave young Marshall Field.) His instinct told him to run against Taft but not against Eisenhower, and his instinct was right. But events controlled. Once again he seemed more the creature than the creator of history; once more the role of chance seemed large. When he was a child, the death of his mother's father and his own accidental shooting of a child combined to start the family's traveling. In the 1930s his mother's death, Bud Merwin's replacing Dave Merwin at the *Pantagraph,* and Stevenson's work at the Council on Foreign Relations all served to liberate him. The *Daily News* purchase failed and left him free but with no place to go—until a most unlikely political event, Mayor Kennelly's election, paved the way for Stevenson's otherwise most unlikely candidacy for Governor, ultimately forcing him into a course that ended in defeat for the presidency. Thus did chance sometimes operate in his favor and sometimes not.

71

For a non-candidate, he was remarkably active. In the three months between his withdrawal statement and the Democratic National Convention, he went to Dallas, to Oregon and California, to Washington and Virginia.[30] And many Democrats remained unconvinced of his non-candidacy, though President Truman turned to Barkley.

In Dallas on April 22 he delivered a speech on Korea, drafted in part by Dorothy Fosdick, to the Dallas Council on World Affairs. (Stevenson drafted in longhand a page of comment on offshore oil and another on civil rights, both important issues in Texas at the time, though it is not clear whether he intended to use them in his speech or in anticipation of newspapermen's questions. On both issues he took positions that would be unpopular in Texas.) His defense of Truman's Korea policy was powerful and eloquent—and it came naturally: Korea was, he said, the first occasion in world history that the United Nations or any international organization used military force to turn back aggression. A Texan told him that he was the "overwhelming choice" of liberal Democrats in Texas and "a most acceptable candidate" to the conservatives—"the man behind whom the Democratic Party of Texas will reunite."

He returned to Chicago next day, April 23, and met at the Commercial Club with a group of friends to discuss his campaign for Governor and the private fund he had been using to supplement the pay of his aides. One of these friends would expose the "slush fund" during his presidential campaign that fall. Stevenson entertained Governor and Mrs. Schricker of Indiana, then left for a trip of nearly two weeks to the West Coast, departing Springfield April 30 and returning to Chicago May 12. He took Dick Nelson with him. In Portland on May 1 he told the Oregon Democratic State Committee's Jefferson-Jackson Day dinner he would take his name off the ballot in the Oregon primary if he could and requested that Oregon voters disregard his name. He went down to San Francisco and on May 5 spoke before one of the most attentive and prestigious audiences in America, the Commonwealth Club. He delivered a civilized address on politics and on morality in government. None of what he said was new. But he was a national figure now, speaking in a faroff state. He

---

[30] The state paid for some of his travels, audiences he addressed paid for others, and he paid for the rest himself.

spent several more days in California, visiting friends and meeting with Edmund Brown, called "Pat," then Attorney General of California and later its Governor and a Stevenson supporter.

72

While Stevenson was away, the Illinois State Democratic Convention adopted a resolution saying that if he was nominated for President by the national convention "we hereby pledge our wholehearted militant and enthusiastic support."

On May 5 a Minnesota delegate sent Stevenson a closely reasoned three-page letter urging him to reconsider. He declined. But when a man urged that the nation needed him worse than Illinois did, Stevenson replied, curiously, "I wish I could approach the appalling prospect with more enthusiasm," almost as though he anticipated his nomination.

Stevenson was feeling the pressure. To Alicia Patterson, abroad, he wrote on May 15 that from Portland to Pasadena "the newsmen and photographers closed in 3 or 4 times a day with the inevitable—'Will you accept a draft?' . . . I'm being pounded to death by mail, wire, telephone & quick visit on the damn nomination. I thought I had it all settled and for keeps but it seems to be hotter than ever now and I wonder if I have to issue a Gen. Sherman. Its a cocky, contemptuous distasteful thing to do and I hate to earn a place in the history books by saying I *won't* do something honorable that has come to few people. Please advise me promptly—shall I say 'No' again and more sharply & decisively; shall I keep still; shall I indicate privately that I would accept a genuine draft—i.e.—not let them down if it comes? Help. Help. . . . Ike has plenty of trouble still ahead for all I can see or hear, but I think he's ahead of Taft in spite of the figures."

Dorothy Fosdick wrote from Washington on May 17 that John Foster Dulles, Eisenhower's foreign policy adviser, envisaged no more limited wars but "the real and complete thing if the Russians make one more move anywhere." She thought that as the Soviets increased their atomic power a major war would become increasingly intolerable and "we may not want to put all our eggs in the one basket of *the great retaliation,*" as Dulles advocated, "but develop such strength at points of tension and develop the *types* of power so that we could have the option of handling local incidents locally if the enemy let us," thinking that, while not original with her, was finding its way into Stevenson's thought and, later, President Kennedy's.

What was happening was that Harriman's campaign had not really gotten off the ground and Kefauver was inexorably picking up delegates, worrying the party leaders and causing them to turn again to Stevenson. The Oregon primary was held May 16, and Kefauver took all the delegates. An Associated Press tabulation on May 27 showed that Kefauver had 117 votes—615½ were needed to nominate—Harriman had 85½, Russell 66½, Governor Williams of Michigan 40, Kerr 35½, Stevenson 30½, followed by Barkley, Humphrey, and eleven others, with the views of 328 delegates unknown.

Harriman was trying to rebuild the old Roosevelt coalition. He spoke on "liberal issues," such as FEPC, and on foreign policy. He came to Chicago to speak at Roosevelt College on May 28, and Stevenson introduced him. If Stevenson really hoped to escape the draft, his best chance was to promote Harriman. He glowingly recited Harriman's record. Then he said, "If Presidents are chosen for their vision, their courage and conviction, for their depth of understanding of the meaning of this revolutionary era and the mission of America, you will find them all in our honored guest, Averell Harriman." It was high praise but not a flat endorsement.

While all this was going on, Stevenson had been making numerous speeches around Illinois, speeches a candidate for Governor makes—to the Illinois Congress of Parents and Teachers, to the Lithuanian Chamber of Commerce in Chicago, at the dedication of KAM Temple's Community House and chapel in Chicago, at a commencement, at a political dinner in Bloomington, to the Springfield Manufacturers' and Employers' Association, and to the National Conference of Social Work in Chicago (where he stirred up an angry controversy by speaking well of a law making public the names of people on relief and the amounts they received, a proposal anathema to social workers but one he thought helpful in putting down "irresponsible rumors" that welfare rolls were loaded with the undeserving).

Occasionally he touched national issues, as when in Bloomington he jibed at Republican division and praised twenty years of Democratic rule or, at Vandalia, defended our Korean policy. But for the most part, as he continued his almost ceaseless speeches on into June, he stayed on state issues.

Mrs. Ives asked Mrs. Shaw, the Christian Science practitioner, to give Stevenson religious counsel and she did, on June 3. Stevenson as usual paid her little heed. Of more tangible help the same day was a letter from an old Princeton friend in Philadelphia, who reported that Jim Finnegan, the powerful Philadelphia Democratic leader, had told him that the big Pennsylvania delegation would vigorously support a Stevenson draft. If Lawrence of Pittsburgh and Finnegan of Philadelphia supported him, Pennsylvania was his, a key state. A little later another Philadelphia friend reported that Finnegan said sixty-two out of the seventy Pennsylvania delegates were already for Stevenson. Stevenson asked his old friend in Bloomington, Joe Bohrer, "Isn't it possible to persuade anyone that I *do not* want the nomination and I *do* want to be Governor?"

On June 8 he went to Washington—he was to give the commencement address at Hampden-Sydney College in Virginia. Before leaving, he told Flanagan to issue a press release saying he would meet with the general manager of the Atomic Energy Commission in Washington to encourage the construction of a billion-dollar atomic energy plant in southern Illinois. This would allay rumors that his trip East was political.

Stevenson returned to Chicago on June 10. He had spent both evenings with Dorothy Fosdick. He was not feeling well. The day after he got back he made two political speeches, one at Freeport and one at Rockford, returned to Springfield ill about 11 P.M., and went directly to a hospital. Miss Fosdick wrote to him on June 14, concerned about his illness, wishing he had specialists from Chicago or St. Louis in attendance, urging him to make certain the X rays were read correctly. She also recommended he do a speech on "freedom of the mind" which he had spoken of to her. She said that to write such a speech was more important than to "shake a few extra hands," words that would have set his political advisers' teeth on edge a little later. And she sent him a biblical quotation from Matthew 26:39, he had asked for: "O my Father, if it be possible, let this cup pass from me: nevertheless, not as I will, but as thou wilt." It was the quotation with which, in a variant version, he opened his speech accepting the nomination for President a little more than a month later. (She did not intend it for use in a public speech but to help him come to terms with his dilemma.)

Ruth Winter wrote to Mrs. Carpenter to say she was deeply worried not about Ellen herself but about what damage Ellen might do to Stevenson and his children. Word had reached her that Ellen, at a dinner party, sitting next to a New Yorker whom she had just met, had denounced Stevenson viciously, saying outrageous things about his private life, and indicated she intended to do so publicly. The man thought her irrational and did not believe her—but similar things had happened repeatedly in Washington, New York, and Chicago, as Mrs. Carpenter knew. Moreover, a Chicago newspaper reporter had recently said Ellen told him much more than he had printed. Ruth Winter thought all this, and more, indicated that Ellen was planning what amounted to a slanderous public campaign against Stevenson. She seemed to be out of control and wholly irrational and had been so for a number of years. Only Mrs. Carpenter could constrain her, Ruth Winter thought—could not Mrs. Carpenter persuade Ellen to go and stay with her for a time? It would be best for all concerned, including Ellen herself, whom Ruth Winter once had loved dearly when Ellen was herself.

Thus poor Stevenson—a Governor facing a re-election campaign, troubled by a decision on the presidency, sick in a hospital, and with a former wife making trouble. On the night he returned from the East he wrote to Alicia Patterson, "Birdie mine—Ho hum, quelle vie!" and described his heavy schedule. "Meanwhile no summer plans for the boys, Ellen on the rampage in the East I hear, no decision on the damn President business, my Governor campaign bogged down—and and and—well what the hell!" Of the presidential nomination he wrote, "I really don't want to do it now any more than I did 4 months ago. But I hate to say some further words that may look or sound as tho I deprecate the affair or the duty or whatever it is, and, you're right too, that I might well want to try it four years hence. Meanwhile I've hoped, prayed and expected that the draft idea would blow over and that Harriman or Kefauver would emerge the winner & I could sit aloof and run like hell for Governor and try to find a little time for the children. But it doesn't seem to work that way. . . . I don't know what to do—still!—except to sit tight and hope to get out at the last minute, quietly if possible. Somehow I got the impression in my 24 hrs in the east that it looks like Taft still thanks to the monkey business in Texas & the south. Personally I think Ike has done darn well and his press conferences with impressive sincerity and warmth and good humor. But somehow the Dems. grow more confident as the Rep. division hardens aided and abetted by those fine papers you live off of! Nasty!! . . . I wish we could have a long uninterrupted talk—I feel peculiarly devoid of a philosophy about life and work . . . meanwhile there is the haunted harassed sense of 'a naked runner in a storm of spears.' "

73

Stevenson had entered Memorial Hospital with a kidney stone attack on June 11 and stayed briefly. He made a note on his calendar pad next day to call Governor Schricker of Indiana. He spent the following week in Springfield, much of it seeing visiting journalists and photographers and writing letters. The draft movement continued. Steve Mitchell was helping it—on June 11 he sent Bill Blair a letter from a Massachusetts delegate who said he agreed with Mitchell's hope that in the end Stevenson would be prevailed upon to run. Massachusetts was an important state at the convention; its Governor Dever would be the keynote speaker.

Stevenson was having trouble at home: despite the mounting national clamor for him to run, his own newspaper, the *Pantagraph,* served notice upon him that it would not support him for President. Bud Merwin, in a letter he typed himself to keep it secret, said the *Pantagraph* had "enthusiastically" supported Stevenson for Governor in 1948 and because of his "splendid" record would support him for re-election but that Merwin and his editorial board felt unanimously and strongly that "there MUST be a change in our national administration" and accordingly would support the Republican candidate even if the Democrats drafted Stevenson. Merwin thought it "only fair" to tell him so now. He wanted the *Pantagraph* to hurt Stevenson as little as possible, however—*Life* was preparing a story on Stevenson and its photographers would take pictures in the *Pantagraph* office; Merwin proposed that he and Stevenson try to "manage" the *Life* story.

Stevenson told John Miller on June 14, "I am apprehensive that if I don't get out—all the way out—before the Republican Convention I will never be able to get out regardless of whom they nominate. I have lived from day to day with the confident hope and expectation that it would blow over and that a genuine draft was literally impossible, but now I begin to have my doubts—particularly as Taft's nomination seems to become more certain." On June 16 he told a friend, "I hope I can avoid any involvement, but I would be less than frank if I didn't admit I have been flattered by the support and encouragement of so many." To a man who reported that many Maryland delegates wanted to vote for him: "I had thought to remove myself from the presidential discussion utterly, but it seems to persist. . . . At the same time the threat of Taft is occasion for anxiety for all of us. Why did I ever leave the law business!" Attorney General Pat Brown of California urged him to accept the nomination if it was offered even though it might prove impossible to defeat Eisenhower. Philip B. Perlman, the U. S. Solicitor General, urged Stevenson on June 19 to announce he would accept a draft. Stevenson refused—to do so would invite a draft.

On June 20, Drew Pearson wrote in his column that "the most cogent" reason why Stevenson did not want to run was "his family."

He said that Stevenson was "reported to be in love with Miss Dorothy Fosdick" and went on to say that no divorced man had ever occupied the White House and that Catholic voters might tolerate a divorced man but not one who remarried, "especially if his new wife was the daughter of Harry Emerson Fosdick, an outstanding Protestant cleric." Stevenson promptly issued a statement: "The newspapers have married me to three ladies in the last few months. I guess they think the plural of spouse is spice. And now Mr. Pearson has added still another. It is all very flattering to me—if not to the ladies! I apologize to them for any embarrassment the writers may have caused them." The next night, Saturday, June 21, after delivering a commencement address at the John Marshall Law School, Stevenson entered Passavant Hospital in Chicago and the following day underwent surgery to have a kidney stone removed from the left ureter. At least it gave him a short rest from reporters.

On Monday, June 23, Jay McMullen wrote in the *Daily News* that Ellen said she was opposed to "another four years of the 'New Deal'" even if Stevenson were President. McMullen quoted her as saying, "It wasn't just because of politics in general as they said at the time. Although I have voted for the Democrats, I am going to vote Republican in the next election no matter who is running. One party has been in power too long." Another newspaper reported that she said, "Not seeing eye-to-eye on the New Deal was one reason for our divorce. There were other reasons."

Stevenson stayed in the hospital till June 25, then returned to Springfield. A Rockford publisher told him his nomination might be inevitable. Stevenson replied, ". . . perhaps you are right." He told an old friend, "It is only now, at long last, that I feel some confidence about this job, which I feel is the full measure of my ability. At the same time, I don't want to be a coward or evade my destiny." Was he weakening, speaking thus of "destiny"?

On the twenty-sixth he wrote to Alicia Patterson: "I want so much to stay here and do this job . . . but at the same time if the country really needs me, if theres a touch of destiny about the draft business, then I don't want to thwart it and make a tragic mistake. . . . I can't or don't want to tell them if its Taft yes, Ike no. That's a deadly thing to do politically."

"Ellen's behavior has been most distressing," he wrote to Ruth Winter, "as you well know, but Adlai has taken an active part in the situation now I have hopes, reasonable hopes, that she will take a different view of things for the children's sake and her own self interest."

Stevenson held a press conference on Saturday, June 28. He dodged all questions about the presidency and stayed on state issues. George Ball was at the Mansion overnight and advised him on a statement he planned to make at the Governors' Conference in Houston. He talked by telephone to Tom Matthews of *Time,* seeking advice, but Matthews, like McGowan, left him alone with destiny, which is where he was anyway and had been for some time. That same day Stevenson told Jane Dick, "I'm trying my best to do just what you say about saying nothing more about my availability so that I can get out if its Ike and go if its Taft and there is a genuine demand for me and I feel I must etc." It was as close as he came to an explicit statement that he was trying to so maneuver that he could run against Taft but not against Eisenhower.[31]

[31] At various times during the spring Stevenson himself wrote out drafts which he discarded. One of them said:

"1. I would not accept the nomination if offered me.

"The burdens of this office, the demands of leadership and the solemnity of the decisions confronting the next President dwarf the imagination. I (feel no confidence) do not feel that I have the strength, the wisdom or the humility (reverence) (grace) (courage) (self confidence) (resources of the spirit) (serenity) (goodness) (virtue) (divine guidance) to lead the way (guide us) to coexistence with an inscrutable, hostile and *equal* power in the world. (I marvel that any one does) (has such self confidence) This is a new and fearsome position for Am. Its Pres. will be sorely tried.

"I [illegible] that the Presidency is a duty from which no American should shrink in fear or reject in his own self interest except in the most extenuating circumstances. But even if I had the self confidence and desire to aspire to (for) that dread office I could not accept the Democratic nomination because I (have committed myself to run) am a candidate for reelection as Governor of Illinois. That undertaking I have proudly and gladly accepted and intend to discharge to the best of my ability. After the most careful consid I accepted that undertaking before I was seriously considered for the Presidency. I wish to discharge that resp to the best of my ability.

"2. I do not wish to be nominated for the Presidency. I have made a prior commitment. I am a candidate for reelection as Gov. of Ill.

"My only ambition is to continue (as Governor of Illinois.) I have much unfinished business to do as I have repeatedly said (in that position which is the full measure of my strength and ability.)

"As I have repeatedly said my only amb. is to be reelected Gover of Ill. I have a lot of unfinished business here in Ill. which I think is in the public interest I want to stay with it and discharge (satisfy) to the best of my limited ability the confidence that many people of both parties have given me. My family have lived & prospered here in Ill. almost since this state was admitted to the Union. I love it, and I mean to do something for it, something good and enduring, if I possibly can. With a renewal of that confidence I think I can. That is the limit of my ambitions and probably the full measure of my competence too.

Next day, Monday, June 30, in Houston for the Governors' Conference, Stevenson held a press conference and issued a statement reiterating that he was not a presidential candidate and, as for a draft, "I have not participated, nor will I participate, overtly or covertly, in any movement to draft me. Without such participation on my part, I do not believe that any such draft can or will develop. In the unlikely event that it does, I will decide what to do at that time in the light of the conditions then existing."

A few hours later Governor Schricker of Indiana told newspapermen, "I'd say Governor Stevenson is definitely available. And I'd like to ask how any man could possibly turn down a sincere draft." Stevenson's Houston statement was widely interpreted as making him available to a draft. The fire was fed by Flanagan, albeit inadvertently—he had told his Springfield office to mail a bundle of mimeographed biographical material to him in Houston and by chance it arrived just as Stevenson's press conference was ending and Flanagan distributed it to the reporters. "It looked like a put-up job," Flanagan later recalled.

Stevenson's semi-annual "Report to the People" was broadcast by radio and television on July 1. It was a dull speech on a dull subject, Illinois problems, and Stevenson was right when he remarked that asking people to listen to it was like asking a small boy to keep on with his piano lessons while a big fire was raging down the street.

Dorothy Fosdick wrote: Chip Bohlen and others were greatly disappointed in Eisenhower. Dean Rusk had told her that Eisenhower's rejection of Dulles' hard line on foreign policy was worded so as to permit him to backtrack later. Dulles hoped to replace Acheson as Secretary of State—"O horrors!" She again recommended Bob Tufts for Stevenson's staff, and in doing so seemed almost to assume Stevenson's nomination for President.

The St. Louis *Post-Dispatch* reported from Washington on July 3 that President Truman had "quite definitely cooled off" on Steven-

---

"If I disappoint those who feel (wish to see me President) that I am qualified for the Presidency I am both sorry and full of gratitude. I hope they can understand my sense of obligation to fulfill the commitment I have made here in Illinois.

"I do not wish to be nominated for the Presidency. I am a candidate for reelection as Gov. of Ill. That is my only ambition. I have much unfinished business in that position which I think is in the public interest. I want to satisfy the confidence that many people in Ill, of both parties, have given me.

"Would I accept the nomination of the Dem Party. Yes, I would I don't suppose one can refuse except in the most extenuating circumstances. And I suppose the friendly people of Ill. would release me from my commitment in that event which would not be of my making."

son, that Truman's friends quoted him as saying that Stevenson "is too damn coy," and that the President intended to throw his influence behind Harriman—"Hell, he's the only New Dealer and Fair Dealer we have got." The President let it be known that he would indicate his preference only at the time of the first ballot, when he would instruct his alternate delegate, an old political friend from Kansas City named Tom Gavin, whom to vote for. In his *Memoirs,* however, Truman himself wrote that "about two weeks" before the convention Barkley "let it be known" that he would like to be a candidate. Truman told him that Stevenson had refused to run and if Barkley was "serious" Truman would support him. Jack Arvey has said that the White House asked him to persuade Stevenson to nominate Barkley. Stevenson refused because of his "commitment" to Harriman, Arvey said.

74

Shortly before Houston, Stevenson in his private correspondence had been increasingly inclined to let destiny overhaul him and to permit himself to be drafted, and in his public statement there had all but said so. After Houston, however, in his correspondence he reverted to his earlier aversion to being drafted.

What had happened to harden his determination to avoid a draft? Eisenhower, on July 11, had been nominated. The contest between him and Taft, bitter before the convention, worsened there. The party was deeply divided. Senator Dirksen of Illinois at one point shook his finger at the New York delegation below the speaker's rostrum and on national television spoke directly at Governor Dewey: "We followed you before and you took us down the path to defeat." An uproar ensued; a delegate collapsed and was carried off the floor, the convention dissolved into booing and shouting. The division in the party took the form of a struggle over contested delegations from Georgia, Louisiana, and Texas. By Wednesday night Eisenhower's managers had won those contests. Taft had gone into the convention only seventy or eighty votes short of what he needed; his best chance had been to show enough strength to swing those votes from the 120-odd uncommitted delegates; but after he lost the contested delegate fights he had little chance. Eisenhower received 595 votes on the first ballot, Taft 500, Warren 81, Stassen 20, MacArthur 10. Eisenhower was nine votes short. Minnesota changed its vote—it had given 9 votes to Eisenhower and 19 to its favorite son, Harold Stassen—and it was all over at 12:45 P.M.

Stevenson went to Bill Flanagan's house in Springfield to watch Eisenhower's nomination. Television at that time was rare in Springfield, for only broadcasts from St. Louis reached Springfield and not many people had television sets. Stevenson rarely watched television and knew little about it—yet he was about to become the presidential candidate in the first televised presidential campaign in history. After Eisenhower's nomination Flanagan issued a statement on Stevenson's behalf: "He is a candidate for re-election as Governor of Illinois, and as he has often said, wants no other office. He will ask the Illinois delegation to continue to respect his wishes and he hopes all of the delegates will do likewise." His son Adlai III joined the Marine Corps and left that week for Quantico, Virginia.

The IVI Draft-Stevenson Committee, now down to its last hundred dollars, sent a letter on July 12 to all delegates and alternate delegates: "We have no doubt Governor Stevenson, devoted as he is to public service, will respond to the call."

Walter Reuther spent three hours with Stevenson that day. He and others who saw Stevenson at this time came away with conflicting impressions about whether he would run. Stevenson went to Camp Ripley, Wisconsin, on Sunday, July 13, to review the National Guard. On the parade ground, he was approached by a man who said he was a delegate from Minnesota and wanted to know what Stevenson would do if the convention drafted him. "I'll shoot myself," Stevenson replied. The delegate had neglected to say he was also a journalist; the story appeared across the country.

75

The Democratic Convention, to be held in Chicago, was only one week away. For the first time in twenty years the Democratic Convention would be an open convention. Always after 1932 the delegates had simply renominated an incumbent President. Not now—it was open—uncomfortably open, for some party leaders. Not only was there no clear-cut leading candidate but there was every prospect of a fight on civil rights. With 1,230 votes in the convention, 615½ were needed to nominate. An Associated Press poll of July 19 showed Kefauver had 257½ delegates committed, Russell had 161½, Harriman had 112½, Kerr 45½, Stevenson 41½, while other candidates and favorite sons had 231½ votes and 380 were undecided, uncommitted, or disputed, including 52 from Texas and 18 from Mississippi. The Alsops thought Truman could swing at least 400 votes to any candidate. But Truman entered Walter Reed Hospital on Wednesday, July 16, and was incommunicado for several days.

Work started on the platform. This, and the Credentials Committee report, promised to be divisive because of civil rights, although Chairman McKinney told the press on July 14 that the Platform Committee's chief purpose would be to "remove the disunity that existed in 1948," when the Dixiecrats walked out. Francis Biddle, chairman of ADA, however, said that 654 delegates would support not only a civil rights plank as strong as the one of 1948 but also a plank calling for an end to Senate filibusters. If one wanted unity, it was not a promising start. All through the week before the convention, sometimes on television, sometimes behind the closed doors of hotel suites, the struggle went on.

On Tuesday, July 15, Stevenson sent a telegram to Walter Johnson of the IVI Committee: "Have just seen circular letter to delegates and am very much disturbed in view of my unwillingness to be candidate. . . . I do not want to embarrass you and I am grateful for your good will and confidence but my attitude is utterly sincere and I desperately want and intend to stay on this job, with your help I hope." Jack Arvey that day publicly rebuked the IVI Committee for disregarding Stevenson's wishes and said, "I don't think the convention will nominate Stevenson unless it receives some indication from him and I don't think that indication will come."

On Wednesday, July 16, Senators Russell and Kefauver issued statements calling for repeal of the Taft-Hartley Act. Labor leaders immediately accused Senator Russell of trying to "perpetrate a hoax" —he had voted for the bill and voted to override President Truman's veto. Kefauver's statement further alarmed the middle-of-the-road Democratic leaders and tended to drive him further into the left wing of the party. Vice President Barkley opened headquarters, occupying in effect the right wing. These divisions deepened through the week, leaving the broad center empty and thereby increasing the suction of the vacuum for Stevenson.

On Wednesday too the IVI Committee opened headquarters, not without difficulty—since Stevenson was not a candidate, no space had been allotted him at convention headquarters, the Conrad Hilton Hotel; the committee finally obtained a small three-room suite only because one of its members was a friend of Conrad Hilton's lawyer. It paid $150 a day for the suite. It had only an ordinary house telephone in each room. For a time it made badges by hand out of paper. Then it had a thousand "America Needs Stevenson For President" buttons manufactured. These quickly disappeared. The committee cautiously ordered two thousand more and two days later another two thousand. The rooms were always full of people, mostly young people, milling about. They were put to work hand-painting signs, making up slogans as they went along: "Madly for Adlai," "Gladly for Adlai," and so on. One day the organized wholesale gladioli growers delivered thousands of gladioli in huge tin tubs, filling the suite entirely. Journalists came to the headquarters and so did delegates, always asking, "But will your man run?" Al Weisman, a young public relations man at the second level of the committee, recalled, "We were all volunteers. Everybody else, all the other candidates, had a switchboard. We had just our telephones. We had one room to see the delegates in." On Saturday, John Fell Stevenson wandered in, hoping to pick up some campaign buttons, and somebody quickly shut the door to conceal his presence; but a *Life* photographer and reporter disguised as pages discovered him. Leo Lerner and Walter Johnson talked to party leaders. Marshall Holleb, Bob Ming, Hubert Will, and others talked to delegates. Will began a delegate count. Al Weisman recalls, "Our object was to have a place where delegates could come and pick up propaganda. We had a couple of mimeograph machines. There was a lot of running around telling everybody he would run, telling everybody to ignore the statements from Springfield." The mere opening of the headquarters attracted considerable attention in the press. On the day it opened James A. Hagerty, then a New York *Times* staff member, wrote that Stevenson "can be drafted"—two of his "intimate friends" had told Hagerty so, but only if the draft was a "genuine one."

On Thursday, July 17, Archibald Alexander, former Undersecretary of the Army who was campaigning in New Jersey for the United States Senate, went to the Stevenson Committee's headquarters and offered to make the nominating speech for Stevenson. To Tom Finletter's wife in Washington, who had telegraphed Stevenson urging him to "please keep your foot in the door," Stevenson wrote on Friday the eighteenth, "I have been trying to shut the door and keep it shut for months but the newspapers have their own way of interpreting everything I say. I have been sorely tried." Arthur Krock told Stevenson he was going to be drafted, the first "real" draft Krock had ever seen. Bill Flanagan told Stevenson he thought a draft inevitable. Stevenson asked what could be done to avoid it. Flanagan thought nothing and asked, "What are you going to do if they tell you on the second ballot that you'll be nominated—are you going to say, 'I will not run'?" Stevenson replied, "Oh, God, no—I couldn't do that."

Stevenson arrived in Chicago on July 18, the Friday before the convention opened, and at the lake-front airport smiled and bantered with reporters, saying he hoped his name would not be placed in nomination. From the airport he drove to his Chicago office and met with Arvey and other machine leaders. They pressed him to say he would accept a nomination; he refused.

He and his staff moved into the Blair family's town house at 1416 Astor Street in Chicago. Astor Street was a staid street of brownstone houses only starting to give way to apartment buildings, one of the few remaining islands of what was left of the old Gold Coast. Ellen lived a few doors away. After Stevenson moved into "Blair House," as it quickly came to be called, the place became, in Flanagan's words, "a shambles." Reporters, photographers, and television crews trampled the tiny lawn. Bright lights blazed evenings. Temporary telephone booths were set up out in front. Telephone wires and television cables were strung everywhere. Television trucks were parked on the narrow street. Astor Street's dignity was shattered. This was Stevenson's own old home ground, suddenly now transformed by the clamor that attends public life.

The full National Committee met on Saturday, July 19, to deliberate on the seating of contested delegations, especially the Mississippi delegation led by Attorney General J. P. Coleman and the Texas delegation led by Governor Allan Shivers (Shivers had replied ambiguously to questions about whether he would loyally support the platform and candidates). Jack Arvey played a key role in working out a formula to seat them temporarily when the convention opened but then oblige them to "reaffirm" their loyalty to the platform and candidates. On Saturday, too, Walter Johnson and another IVI leader met with Jim Finnegan and other leaders of the Pennsylvania delegation. Finnegan gave them money to pay for more Stevenson buttons and said some of the Pennsylvania delegates would emerge from the state caucus next day wearing them. By this time, however, Barkley seemed to be emerging as the candidate of a coalition between the South and big-city bosses who opposed either Kefauver or Harriman, and Reuther thought Kefauver and Harriman should work together in Stevenson's behalf lest a conservative, probably Barkley, be nominated. They were not yet ready to do it.

Sunday was the day most delegates arrived in Chicago. Few events in American political life—or for that matter political life anywhere—provide the drama and excitement of a national party convention. The Republican Convention in the same city, the same hotel, and the same auditorium two weeks before had offered the spectacle of two massive forces in collision, those of Taft and Eisenhower. The Democratic Convention now presented a picture of total confusion. Bands played, parades marched to and fro, young people carrying banners and wearing their candidates' buttons demonstrated enthusiastically on Michigan Avenue and in hotel lobbies. Delegates wandered across Balbo Drive between the Conrad Hilton and Blackstone hotels, asking anybody wearing a Stevenson button, "But will he run?" Newspapermen, magazine writers, columnists, photographers, radio and television men were everywhere. The elevators of the massive Hilton were hopelessly jammed. The din was awful. Candidates held press conferences, their agents passed out press releases, their volunteers passed out buttons and bumper stickers.

But the principal candidate was missing, hidden out on Astor Street. Sunday morning he went to church at the fashionable Fourth Presbyterian Church on upper Michigan Avenue, where he had been married twenty-three and a half years earlier, and the New York *Herald Tribune* reported that the sermon deplored indecision. He attended various preconvention receptions. One, a reception for Paul Douglas at the Windermere Hotel on the South Side, was a painful social occasion, for it was Stevenson, not Douglas, who was the center of attention. Scotty Reston of the New York *Times* and his wife called on Ellen Stevenson, whom they had known in London. Reston has recalled, "She talked about Stevenson in the most outrageous way—said he was not qualified for the presidency, almost suggested that he wasn't a very good husband, was bitter about what agony he had brought on her by his political career, and she was being followed everywhere. She took a pistol out of her purse and said, 'I feel I have to keep this with me wherever I go.' Finally I said, 'It's a good thing you're talking to a guy from the New York *Times* and not the New York *News*. I'm saying this not as a reporter but as a citizen—I think it's dreadful to talk about him this way to any reporter."

Stevenson's friends were still giving him advice. On that Sunday, John S. Miller wrote to him, saying Stevenson need not accept a draft if in his "heart of hearts" he did not want to, if he had "some personal reason" for not running, if he felt "the welfare of the country would be best served by Eisenhower's election," or if he felt convinced that Eisenhower would win.

But events were moving that night, events that set others in train and ultimately carried the decision beyond Stevenson's control. The state delegations were caucusing—meeting to decide whom to support for President. At 4 P.M. at the Morrison Hotel, Stevenson attended the Illinois caucus as a delegate. Reporters, eavesdropping behind a partition, heard him say, they later wrote, "I do not deem myself fit for the job—temperamentally, mentally, or physically. And I ask therefore that you all abide by my wishes not to nominate me, nor to vote for me if I should be nominated." Arvey told the caucus he wanted to do whatever Stevenson wished and accordingly would respect Stevenson's request that Illinois not nominate him but went on to say that should Stevenson's name be placed in nomination he would personally vote for him on the first ballot. He said, "When that happens I consider I am relieved from any promise I have made not to further his candidacy. He cannot take away from me my right to cast my ballot as I wish to cast it. If I am convinced that a vote for Stevenson is a vote to unify the party and win the election in November, I will vote for him." The delegation cheered. When the caucus ended reporters asked Stevenson if he would accept a draft in the event of a deadlock. He replied, "Show me the deadlock first." Arvey has since said, "Everybody thought it was an act—he was being reluctant and I was pushing. But it wasn't an act at all. That night after the caucus Stevenson came to my apartment and said, 'You got me into this, now get me out.' " Arvey has since said, "During the spring, I had been working on the California, New York, Pennsylvania, and Minnesota delegations. I knew we had the South—of course Dick Russell wanted to run but he would have to get out and as soon as he did Stevenson would have the Southern delegations."

At almost the same time and also at the Morrison, the Pennsylvania delegation was caucusing. It took no binding vote but an informal count showed Stevenson 32, Kefauver 14, Truman 7, and 17 scattered. That evening the hotel lobbies were filled with delegates, many wearing newly acquired Stevenson buttons. The IVI Committee sent people to find the leaders from Pennsylvania, Indiana, New Jersey, and Kansas, where Stevenson strength lay, and invite them to a meeting at eleven o'clock that same night. Hubert Will from the IVI Committee said he calculated that Stevenson would receive 178½ votes on the first ballot. A Pennsylvanian asked how many they were counting on from Pennsylvania. Thirty-five and a half, Will replied. It was about what the caucus had just voted. How many did they think they had from Indiana? Governor Schricker asked. Twenty-five out of 26, with one for Kefauver, Will said. Right again. Jim Finnegan suggested that Mayor Lawrence become Stevenson's floor leader. Lawrence declined and recommended former Senator Francis J. Myers. Myers had been Majority whip in the U. S. Senate. All present agreed he should serve. Who would nominate Stevenson? David Lawrence told Schricker he should do it. (Walter Johnson has said that Governor Schricker had telephoned him from Indianapolis several days earlier to ask who the committee was. Schricker said an Indianapolis paper had said he was going to

nominate Stevenson and, while he would be glad to do it, nobody
had asked him; whereupon Johnson asked him.) Schricker at first
demurred, saying they needed to know whether Stevenson would
accept the nomination if it was offered. He promised to consult his
delegation and let them know next day. They would meet at 4 P.M.

76

The convention met for its first session at noon that Monday in the
enormous Amphitheater at the Chicago Stockyards on the South
Side. The delegates sat on chairs on the floor facing a high, crowded
speakers' platform bedecked with flags. Balconies rose in tiers to the
high dim ceiling. Smoke swirled in the spotlights. A scaffolding rose
in the center of the hall, containing television cameras aimed re-
morselessly at the rostrum. For some time during recent weeks, *Life*
magazine had been preparing a cover story on Stevenson. Stevenson
had expressed misgivings about it, telling Flanagan, "If this comes
out before the convention it will look like I'm really a candidate."
Flanagan had asked *Life*'s Chicago bureau chief to promise not to
publish it if Eisenhower was nominated. The day after Eisenhower
was nominated *Life* called Flanagan and indicated it wanted to publish. Flanagan told Stevenson, "I don't know what to do about *Life*.
It's a helluva piece. It's part of my job. It goes against the grain to
tell them not to print it. Why don't you tell me to let them go ahead?
Anyway if all the papers and magazines stopped publication you'd be
nominated anyway. This piece won't make any difference." Stevenson said, "Okay, tell them to go ahead." Flanagan has recalled, "So
this issue of *Life* was on the seat of every delegate when the convention opened. The timing was fantastic—and I don't mean that
I planned it that way. It's the way it worked out."

Chairman McKinney called the convention to order at noon.
Ordinarily the first session of a convention is dull but today was
different, for the address of welcome, usually a perfunctory affair,
was to be given by Adlai Stevenson as Governor of Illinois; and
when McKinney introduced him at twelve thirty-one, a demonstration began that lasted at least ten minutes, while delegates applauded
and marched and milled about, waving signs and yelling, "We want
Stevenson." He replied almost inaudibly: "You can have him if——"

As he waited for the demonstration to subside and several times
began, "Mr. Chairman—" in a voice so high-pitched it was almost
squeaky, he seemed a small figure, surrounded by party officials,
nearly hidden by the big rostrum and the microphones, facing all

alone the enormous hall and the massed thousands, holding up his hand to wave tentatively and smile quickly, then fiddle with his glasses or his speech manuscript.

The welcoming speech was short, only fourteen minutes long. Flanagan had the impression that McGowan had written it, but McGowan has said Stevenson did it "very much himself." The evidence indicates that someone, perhaps McGowan or Hyndman, had written a first draft, drawing on former Stevenson speeches, and that Stevenson had edited it heavily, inserting the Altgeld-Dunne-Horner passage and writing out in longhand some of the great applause lines of the speech, including the last six paragraphs. The Rev. Dr. Graebel of Springfield had loaned him his notes from a sermon on "The Heaven-Rescued Land," a phrase from "The Star-Spangled Banner" Stevenson used in his speech. Edgar Bernhard had sent him a draft, and Stevenson told him he had "lifted some morsels" from it. And he had eliminated a final paragraph that he himself had drafted which came close to foreclosing the nomination—"And, in any case, come back in 1956. If you do I hope to have the privilege of welcoming you again—as Governor of Illinois."

Flanagan had had the speech mimeographed and distributed to the press the night before, and a member of the IVI Committee had read it to the Pennsylvania and other delegates at that night's meeting. Riding out to the Amphitheater with Stevenson Monday morning, Flanagan told him, "This speech is going to cause a riot." Stevenson had replied, "I don't think so."

Now from the rostrum, in a voice edged with strain but growing stronger as he progressed, Stevenson delivered it to the delegates and guests and to the national television audience. After preliminary welcoming remarks, he said,

"Here, my friends, on the prairies of Illinois and of the Middle West, we can see a long way in all directions. We look to east, to west, to north and south. Our commerce, our ideas, come and go in all directions. Here there are no barriers, no defenses, to ideas and to aspirations. We want none; we want no shackles on the mind or the spirit, no rigid patterns of thought, and no iron conformity. We want only the faith and conviction that triumph in fair and free contest.

"As a Democrat perhaps you will permit me to remind you that until four years ago the people of Illinois had chosen but three Democratic Governors in a hundred years. One was John Peter Altgeld, whom the great Illinois poet, Vachel Lindsay, called the Eagle Forgotten, he was an immigrant; one was Edward F. Dunne, whose parents came here from the old sod of Ireland; and the last was

Henry Horner, but one generation removed from Germany. John Peter Altgeld, my friends, was a Protestant, Governor Dunne was a Catholic, Henry Horner was a Jew.

"And that, my friends, is the American story, written by the Democratic Party here on the prairies of Illinois."

He recounted the accomplishments of the past twenty years of Democratic rule, starting with those of President Roosevelt. He jibed at the bitterness of the Republican Convention held in this same hall a little earlier. He said he hoped the Democratic Convention would be businesslike and dignified, befitting "the solemnity of the hour in history in which we meet. For," he went on, "it is a very solemn hour indeed, freighted with the hopes and fears of millions of mankind who see in us, the Democratic Party, sober understanding of the breadth and the depth of the revolutionary currents in the world. . . . They see in us, the Democratic Party, that has steered this country through a storm of spears for twenty years, an understanding of a world in the torment of transition from an age that has died to an age struggling to be born."

He took note of charges that the Truman administration was corrupt: "Where we have erred, let there be no denial; and where we have wronged the public trust, let there be no excuses. Self-criticism is the secret weapon of democracy, and candor and confession are good for the political soul. But we will never appease, we will never apologize for our leadership of the great events of this critical century all the way from Woodrow Wilson to Harry Truman!

"We glory rather in these imperishable pages of our country's chronicle. But a great record of past achievement is not good enough. There can be no complacency perhaps for years to come. We dare not just look back to great yesterdays. We must look forward to great tomorrows.

"What counts now is not just what we are against, but what we are for. And who leads us is less important than what leads us— what convictions, what courage, what faith—win or lose. A man does not save a century or a civilization, but a militant party wedded to a principle can."[32]

The audience interrupted twenty-seven times during the speech with both applause and cries of "We want Stevenson." And when he finished the convention hall broke up in a storm of applause and cheers. Arvey, watching from the platform, said, "Nobody will believe me when I tell them that this is all spontaneous. He asked me

[32] The full text, transcribed from a recording of his actual voice, is printed in Appendix C.

not to have anything like this and I kept my word. He will have to change his mind." Flanagan too had been right: when Stevenson finally left the platform, he could not take his seat on the floor with the Illinois delegation, delegates converged on him and milled about, and the "riot" Flanagan had predicted ensued. Flanagan has said, "He broke up the convention. We had to get out."

The welcoming speech was an excellent example of Stevenson oratory, containing humor, serious substance, sharp political attack (against McCarthyism), and sheer shimmering eloquence. Many people (including the present author) considered it then and consider it in retrospect a better speech than the more widely acclaimed acceptance speech later that week. It would be too much to compare it with William Jennings Bryan's Cross of Gold speech, which stampeded the Chicago convention of 1896 and was considered to have directly caused Bryan's nomination. (Curiously, if one listens to a reading of Bryan's Cross of Gold speech and of Stevenson's welcoming and acceptance speeches, they bear considerable resemblances, less in their ideas and phrasing than in their tone and emotional impact.) Nevertheless, the welcoming speech without question played an important part in the draft-Stevenson movement. That is to say, after all the months of pulling and hauling, had Stevenson delivered an uninspiring, disappointing welcoming speech, he would have considerably deflated the boom. Instead, he rose to the occasion with a speech that exhilarated the delegates and gave additional momentum to the draft. It has been said that great occasions make great speeches, not the other way around, and this occasion was great, for the delegates had been searching for Stevenson a long time and here suddenly he appeared before them in the flesh, and his speech, including passages he had been uttering for several years almost unnoticed, such as the Altgeld-Dunne-Horner litany, delivered now in this charged setting and on national television, confirmed him almost instantly as a national figure.

77

Outside the convention hall, other events important to the nomination had occurred early that morning. Vice President Barkley had met with a group of labor leaders, seeking their support. President Truman wrote later in his *Memoirs* that he and his aides had advised Barkley to see the labor leaders one at a time. Instead, he arranged a breakfast with sixteen of them. They unanimously refused to support him. This was a disaster. That afternoon, Truman wrote, Barkley called him in Washington and told him he was going to withdraw as a candidate. Truman urged him not to, but Barkley said he had already given his decision to the press. This removed an important roadblock in the way of the Stevenson draft, since it left Truman once more without a candidate. At the suggestion of Secretary of Commerce Charles Sawyer, Truman telephoned McKinney and suggested Barkley make a farewell speech. Barkley did, on Wednesday, July 23, an old-fashioned political stem-winder, and received what Truman termed "one of the greatest ovations ever accorded anyone at a national political convention." (Eight years later, at the Los Angeles convention of 1960, it was Stevenson who received a great ovation but no nomination. Ovations are what conventions give when they cannot give votes.)

On Monday, behind the rostrum during the opening session and later in the Hilton, Chairman McKinney met with other party leaders to try to find a compromise in the "loyalty fight," as the struggle over the seating of the Texas and Mississippi delegations was called. Substantial agreement was reached that the Shivers Texas delegation and the Coleman Mississippi delegation would be seated temporarily and would voluntarily refrain from voting until permanently seated. But an ADA statement on a "loyalty pledge" issued late Monday afternoon threw the Southern delegations into an uproar.

At 4 P.M. on Monday afternoon the IVI Draft-Stevenson Committee met with their friends in the party hierarchy. They met in the law office of Marshall Holleb and his brother-in-law Sid Yates, for they wanted privacy and their small suite in the Hilton was full of reporters."[33] Governor Schricker of Indiana agreed to place Stevenson's name in nomination. He had talked to Stevenson at a breakfast for Democratic Governors that morning and, although Stevenson had reiterated that he was a candidate only for Governor, Schricker was convinced he would not refuse a presidential draft. They decided to announce that night that Senator Myers of Pennsylvania would be Stevenson's floor leader and to announce the next day that Schricker would nominate him. Myers and Finnegan suggested that everyone work from the IVI Committee's headquarters in the Hilton. Myers would seek Stevenson votes from key people in each delega-

---

[33] At the meeting were Myers and Finnegan of Pennsylvania, Schricker and Butler of Indiana, Anderson and John Young of Kansas, Alexander of New Jersey, Jonathan Daniels of North Carolina (who had been trying to compose the civil rights fight), Joe Gluck, national committeeman from Washington State, and, from the IVI, Lerner, Yates, and Johnson.

tion and maintain contact with such party leaders as Arvey. The committee would order 1,500 placards with sticks attached.

At the evening session of the convention on Monday, Governor Dever of Massachusetts delivered a long keynote speech and then, after efforts had failed to produce a successful compromise on civil rights, the convention stayed in session until 2:05 A.M. quarreling over civil rights. The liberals won that round.

At 7:22 A.M. on Tuesday morning, the second day of the convention, Stevenson wrote out in longhand a note to Barkley:

> Dear Alben—I've just read your statement. I'm distressed that you found it necessary to do this.
>
> It is a noble statement which perhaps no one else in our country could write. Charity, candor and courage are the firm rock on which you've stood for a long time. And you have again made the rock more visible to many lesser men, this one included.
>
> God bless you—
>
> Adlai
>
> P.S. But you have made it very hard for me!!!

On Tuesday, July 22, at Harriman's request, Schlesinger talked to Stevenson. Stevenson was considering issuing a statement flatly rejecting nomination but did not want to do it because he felt it would end his political career. He had instructed his alternate to vote for Harriman but was receiving discouraging reports about Harriman's strength. Stevenson said he did not want the nomination but if he had to take it he hoped it would be offered by all the other candidates after a deadlock which none of them could break. He was unhappy about the civil rights and strongly opposed to doing anything that might drive the South out of the party—the party needed unity against Eisenhower, and Harriman was a "disunity" candidate. Schlesinger, who had been sent by Harriman to seek Stevenson's support for Harriman, concluded that Stevenson would reluctantly run himself. A little later he learned that Carl McGowan and Stevenson were already thinking ahead about the campaign to come—considering designating Wilson Wyatt national chairman.

Stevenson spent Tuesday at his office in the State of Illinois Building. He talked briefly to reporters, denying he had told Governor Schricker he would not refuse a draft. Among his callers were Arvey's law partner, Barney Hodes, and Congressman John F. Kennedy of Massachusetts. Stevenson spent the evening at Blair's, watching the convention on television.

At this very time, on Tuesday, the Stevenson boom was moving. Some of the big uncommitted delegations were showing signs of going over to Stevenson early—Pennsylvania, Illinois, Indiana, New Jersey, Massachusetts, Connecticut, Missouri, Kansas. Even in the New York delegation defection from Harriman was detected. Schricker's announcement that he would nominate Stevenson produced a movement in the Illinois delegation to vote for Stevenson on the first ballot. Arvey himself disavowed any such purpose because of his "personal promise" to Stevenson. (A persistent Chicago political legend has it that the men of the Cook County machine—not including Arvey—wanted to nominate Stevenson for President in order to get him out of the governorship. It seems unlikely.) Governor Carvel of Delaware, who had arrived as a Barkley supporter, told his delegation Tuesday morning he was for Stevenson. By Wednesday morning some of his delegates knew that he would somehow participate in placing Stevenson's name in nomination.

On Tuesday morning, too, the IVI Committee's little headquarters on the fifteenth floor of the Hilton suddenly expanded from three rooms to fourteen. Al Weisman recalled, "Leo Lerner suddenly went to a meeting with Reuther and some others. He had suddenly become important. Later he gave me some notes he'd made and said to me, 'Destroy these notes' and I flushed them down the toilet. Somebody ordered Andy Frain ushers [professional ushers who handle crowds at conventions and baseball games] but I thought the idea was to get people in, not keep them out. We had had bum food to offer newspapermen who had expense accounts. On Tuesday morning Dave Lawrence moved in. I don't know what it was but something happened Monday night." (It was the meeting in the Holleb-Yates office when Schricker agreed to nominate Stevenson.) "The first thing I noticed was the presence of a switchboard on Tuesday and everybody ordering room service. That was when I realized we'd made it. Their publicity man from Pennsylvania came in and told me, 'Let's get some food up here,' and picked up the phone and by God there was food for everybody. And a switchboard. And we were pro. We were first class. Jack Kennedy and Sid Yates were in our room. So were the Shrivers. They were buttonholing delegates. We were big time." That evening John F. Kennedy of Massachusetts, Mike DiSalle of Ohio, who was campaigning for the Senate, Alexander of New Jersey, and a Congressman from Utah asked Democratic leaders to sign a statement that the Stevenson draft was spreading through the nation and calling upon the convention to nominate him.

During Tuesday, too, the civil rights fight was becoming even worse. The Southern delegations caucused angrily, and when Eleanor Roosevelt was introduced to the convention she received a tremendous standing ovation—but Governor Shivers' delegation remained seated, and Senator Harry F. Byrd of Virginia walked out of the convention hall. The platform committee worked all through the night, and finally at five-thirty next morning its exhausted members, under McKinney's prodding, compromised its differences.

Throughout all these days and nights, Stevenson alone among the candidates was able to avoid the controversy. Such Southern leaders as Senator Russell were driven further and further into the far right wing of the party; such Northerners as Harriman—and Kefauver too —were driven further and further into the far left wing. Increasingly, as the party rearranged itself, the broad center continued to open up for the Stevenson bandwagon. As active candidates, the others were obliged to take positions on issues and, doing so, inevitably lost support. But for Stevenson the only issue was, "Will he run?" He alone remained unscarred so that in the end he emerged not only with his previous attractions untarnished but also in the role of the only man who could unify the convention.

While Stevenson remained silent in Blair's house on Astor Street, the swirling struggle continued all through Wednesday—over the platform, over credentials, over rules, all relating to civil rights. In the midst of it Senator Kefauver violated an ancient tradition by appearing on the convention floor with his aged father; a demonstration for him, probably prearranged, started and continued for twenty-five minutes before he left the hall remarking disingenuously, "My father and I wanted to sit in and listen to the proceedings. I didn't expect a demonstration. I was pleased, though, that so many people wanted to give me a hand." It was rather irrelevant and somewhat akin to the ovation given Barkley: Missouri, Indiana, and New Jersey were caucusing and the Missouri delegation, including President Truman's alternate, let it be known it would support Stevenson, while New Jersey gave 28 of its 32 votes to Stevenson and Illinois gave him at least 46 of its 60 votes, Joe Gill, the delegation chairman, saying, "We are not going to nominate or second anybody. We're respecting Governor Stevenson's wishes in that regard."

Still Stevenson was reluctant. He had breakfast on Wednesday in Ed McDougal's apartment (where the Iveses were staying) with Oscar Chapman, the Secretary of the Interior who often performed political chores for President Truman. Neither Stevenson nor Chapman would tell the press what happened at the breakfast. Stevenson spent the day at Blair's house. Not until past midnight did the convention at last adopt the platform and adjourn. Shortly before it did, around midnight, Jack Arvey said to Governor Schricker on the convention floor, "You're not going to nominate him, are you?

He doesn't want it." Schricker said he would decide for himself. Arvey said, "Didn't the Governor ask you not to do it?" Schricker replied, "No, he didn't. Adlai Stevenson said to me: 'I don't want you to do it but I can't stop you.'" Arvey said Stevenson had asked Governor Carvel of Delaware not to nominate him, but Carvel was going to anyway, and Delaware came ahead of Indiana in the roll call. And it might hurt Stevenson if his name was offered by an Easterner. After complicated negotiations that lasted all night and involved Arvey, Paul Butler of Indiana, and Walter Johnson of the IVI, Arvey arranged a compromise: when the roll was called, Carvel's Delaware would yield to Indiana; Schricker would deliver half the nominating speech, and then Carvel would deliver the second half.

That day, Thursday, July 24, the day candidates were to be placed in nomination, Stevenson telephoned President Truman. The President later wrote, "He said that he called to ask whether it would embarrass me if he allowed his name to be placed in nomination. I replied with a show of exasperation and some rather vigorous words and concluded by saying to Stevenson, 'I have been trying since January to get you to say that. Why would it embarrass me?' . . . I transmitted instructions to my alternate on the Missouri delegation, Thomas J. Gavin, to get behind the Illinois candidate." Donald Funk of Springfield wrote to Don Forsyth about dissolving the Stevenson-for-Governor Committee.

78

The convention came to order—of a sort—at noon on Thursday, July 24, to start the nominating process. Alabama, at the top of the alphabetical roll, yielded to Georgia, and Georgia nominated Senator Russell. Alaska yielded to Tennessee, and Tennessee nominated Kefauver. Arizona yielded to Oklahoma, and Oklahoma nominated Kerr. Arkansas nominated Fulbright. California, which favored Kefauver, passed. Colorado yielded to New York, and New York nominated Harriman and Oscar Ewing. Senator William Benton of Connecticut nominated Senator Brien McMahon (who, from his deathbed, had told President Truman that Connecticut would switch early to Stevenson). All this took hours. Not until past five o'clock was Delaware called, and Delaware yielded to Indiana, whose Governor Schricker arose and nominated Stevenson.

Mr. and Mrs. Ives, Stevenson's elderly Aunt Letitia, and Dutch and Ellen Smith were watching from Stevenson's box. Smith later wrote, "It was very good fun, as the box was pretty much the center of the Stevenson activities with reporters, radio people, etc., coming up to interview Mrs. Ives in particular." Just before Schricker began his nominating speech, the band leader sent a messenger to the box to ask what Stevenson's favorite song was. Ellen Smith thought of the parody set to the tune of "A Wonderful Guy" from *South Pacific,* and written two years ago by Ed Day for Stevenson's fiftieth birthday party. She scribbled out an amended version of the words and sent it to the band leader, and when the curious Schricker-Carvel dual nominating speech was finished and a demonstration broke out on the floor, the band played the song:

> He's as honest as Abraham Lincoln,
> He's the man no money can buy,
> He's the best guy on earth,
> So let's sing to his worth.
> He's our gov, he's a wonderful guy.
> Now he's called to head up the nation,
> Look at his record and you will know why
> He's the man that we need.
> We'll all follow his lead.
> He's our Adlai our Adlai our Adlai our Adlai our Adlai's a
>   wonderful guy.

For the first time in her life, Ellen Smith would vote Democratic for President. That night she asked Stevenson to sign her impromptu lyric, and he did.

The demonstration for Stevenson was "easily the biggest, noisiest, longest and most spontaneous outburst of this long day of nominating speeches," a Baltimore *Sun* correspondent wrote. Felix Belair of the New York *Times* said of the Stevenson nomination, "It was then that the convention really went wild." Carvel delivered most of his speech to a tossing sea of Stevenson placards parading around the hall. Amid the demonstration, Missouri caucused, and President Truman's alternate announced publicly that he had been instructed by the President to vote for Stevenson. Stevenson, watching on television at Blair's house, issued a statement: "I had hoped they would not nominate me, but I am deeply affected by this expression of confidence and good will."

The Stevenson demonstration over, the roll call proceeded. Idaho yielded to Michigan, which nominated Governor G. Mennen Williams. At six fifty-five Louisiana was called and yielded to Virginia. And the floor fight over the seating of South Carolina, Virginia, and Louisiana broke out all over again. Sam Rayburn, Speaker of the

House, now presiding, ruled that the South Carolina, Virginia, and Louisiana delegations had not complied with the convention rules and continued the roll call. Maine passed. Maryland was next, and Rayburn immediately recognized a Maryland Congressman who moved that the delegations of Virginia and South Carolina be seated, a motion from which South Carolina was almost immediately dropped, and Rayburn quickly began to gavel the motion through but was interrupted by loud demands for a roll call, and once more the civil rights fight broke out noisily on the floor. As the roll began, many delegates did not know what they were voting on. They milled about while such liberals as Franklin D. Roosevelt, Jr., Senator Humphrey, Senator Paul Douglas, and Governor Orville Freeman of Minnesota tried without much success to concert their efforts. By the end of the first reading of the roll, some sixteen confused delegations had passed, including several big ones. Illinois had voted 45 to 15 against seating Virginia. This made it appear that the Stevenson supporters wanted to keep Virginia, South Carolina, and Louisiana out of the convention. But Pennsylvania voted 57 to 13 in favor of seating Virginia. Confusion prevailed, and Illinois delegates, recognizing a serious danger to Stevenson, sent out hurriedly for Joe Gill, Jack Arvey, and Scott Lucas, all of whom had gone to dinner. At the end of the first roll call the vote was 351½ in favor of seating Virginia, 462½ against, and 416 still deciding. Delegations caucused.

Arvey said later, "It suddenly dawned on us what was happening." Kefauver's strategy and that of the Northern liberals was to make impossible demands on the Southern delegates and force them to walk out of the convention. If the total convention vote was thus reduced, Kefauver would have a better chance of winning. Perceiving this, at 8:50 P.M. Illinois declared its "confidence in the Governor of Virginia" and changed its vote to 52 to 8 in favor of seating Virginia. This was decisive. For more than an hour delegations switched. At one point South Dakota walked out of the hall but walked back in. At 9:55 P.M. the recording clerk announced the result as 615 in favor of seating Virginia, 529 against, and 86 not voting. (The correct total, which gave 650½ in favor, 518 against, 17½ abstaining, and 34 not voting, was not finally determined until a year later.) What had happened was that the Kefauver and Harriman supporters had failed to capture the convention from party leaders, and the Southern and border-state delegations had thrown in with the party leaders and avoided a Dixiecrat walkout that would have split the party.

The roll call for nominations resumed, and Governor Dever, Senator Humphrey, and Vice President Barkley were put in nomination. But delegates and journalists continued to talk about the meaning of the vote on Virginia, and a suggestion got about that the South had defeated the liberals with the help of Stevenson men in Illinois and Pennsylvania, and this in turn suggested a deal on a Stevenson-Russell ticket. By 10:30 P.M., Stevenson was being quoted on the television networks as having specifically denied any personal role in the Illinois switch. Nevertheless, now for the first time he had been drawn into the bitterly divisive controversy—and on the side of the so-called Arvey-Dixiecrat alliance. The affair looked dangerous to his nomination.

Stevenson was at Blair's house. Dutch Smith later told his daughter, "We got up there about nine o'clock and found Astor Street between Schiller and Burton absolutely jammed, not only with people, but with all kinds of equipment such as sound trucks, telephone trucks, klieg lights, etc. A row of telephone booths had been installed along the fence of the garden between Mrs. Bowen's and the Blairs', which looked exactly like sentry boxes. We were glad to see our good friend, Captain Van Diver [Stevenson's driver] . . . at the door and he let us in where we found a very quiet scene with about half a dozen people watching television. It was a warm evening so the shades were up, and we could see the crowds and lights and movie cameras, giving a very unreal effect. Adlai would listen for a while, and then wander away to get some rest or to confer with someone."

At the convention, liberal leaders consulted hurriedly. Kefauver's and Harriman's supporters were seeking adjournment or, if that proved impossible, a fight to prevent South Carolina and Louisiana from being seated on the Virginia precedent. Governor Battle of Virginia moved that South Carolina and Louisiana be seated. Paul Douglas of Illinois moved to adjourn; another Illinois delegate moved to table Douglas' motion and demanded a roll call; and reluctantly at midnight Rayburn began the roll call. It lasted more than an hour and was generally regarded as a "stop-Stevenson" delaying move. Amid great confusion—again, many delegates did not know what they were voting on—Douglas' motion to adjourn was tabled. And the roll call for nominations resumed. When at length it was completed, Representative John McCormack, temporarily holding the chair, reminded the convention that Governor Battle's motion to seat South Carolina and Louisiana was still before it. Senator Long of Louisiana and Governor Byrnes of South Carolina arose to give assurances that the convention's presidential and vice-presidential nominees would be on the ballot in accordance with the laws of their states but, like Governor Battle of Virginia, they did not say that the nominees' names would be on the ballot as the nominees of the state Democratic Parties as well as of the national Democratic Party. Delegates promptly began to question Byrnes closely on the subject. Byrnes fell back on his previous statements. They pressed him hard. He held firm and declared he refused to be cross-examined further; and at that point a fire broke out on the crowded floor not far from where Byrnes was standing. The floor of the convention, after thirteen hours of continuous session, was covered with papers. After an anxious moment, the fire was extinguished without panic, and Governor Byrnes said, "Mr. Chairman, I want to announce that I did not set the place on fire." And the obscure struggle resumed, with Senator Paul Douglas striving to keep the Kefauver candidacy alive. Finally, after another unsuccessful attempt at a roll call, the South Carolina and Louisiana delegations were seated; and at 2 A.M. the convention adjourned.

This was, really, the end of the Kefauver candidacy. After the convention at large made peace with the South, Kefauver was isolated as the leader of a bitter-end leftist faction, angrily opposed not only to the South but to most of the party's leaders. It was not so clear at the time, however, and Kefauver made an effective though late-at-night television appearance, protesting the boss-ridden convention, denouncing the fake draft of Stevenson, and calling on viewers to telegraph and telephone their delegates to support Kefauver. Watching, Schlesinger became convinced Harriman should meet with Stevenson and told him so, and Harriman, after consulting his political advisers, agreed. Schlesinger and Jim Loeb tried for some twenty minutes to telephone Stevenson at Blair's house but the phone was busy, so they hurried down to the street and got a taxi and arrived at Blair's house after two-thirty. The house was dark. In front were several policemen and a patrol car. Loeb and Schlesinger persuaded them to allow them to ring the doorbell. No answer; the house was silent. They tried telephoning again, and this time succeeded in rousing Bill Blair. Blair said Stevenson was asleep; he would call in the morning. They returned to the hotel and reported to Harriman, then went to the Congress Hotel where five or six hundred people were rallying to the liberal cause at Hubert Humphrey's call. Many of them opposed Stevenson, considering him allied with the Dixiecrats. They expected Humphrey to lead a stop-Stevenson movement. Instead he said resisting the South was one thing, opposing Stevenson was another, and three candidates were acceptable to liberals—Harriman, Kefauver, and Stevenson. Then FDR, Jr., delivered a militant speech damning Rayburn and calling

Stevenson a "Northern Dixiecrat." (Schlesinger shared the irritation with Stevenson that many present felt. He assumed, incorrectly, that Stevenson had directed the switch of the Illinois vote on seating Virginia.) Schlesinger went to bed at 6:30 A.M. At nine-thirty Harriman and Bill Blair called him and arranged a breakfast meeting with Stevenson. It was held at 10:15 A.M. in Ed McDougal's apartment—Harriman, a political adviser, Schlesinger, and Stevenson.

Harriman said that the previous night's events had identified Stevenson with the worst elements in the party—Dixiecrats, Northern city bosses, and the national committee. It had produced a real danger of a new swing to Barkley. Stevenson said he had not countenanced any pressures on his behalf, he had not sought the nomination, did not want it, and if he had to take it wanted it only as a genuine draft. He wanted to repair his relations with liberals but at the same time spoke of "labor leaders who have wormed their way into the inner councils of the party." They discussed the vice presidency, Stevenson mentioning Kefauver, Sparkman, Mike Monroney, and Barkley. He seemed to think that Kefauver would add the most campaign strength but would make trouble in office, that Sparkman and Monroney would be excellent Vice Presidents but would create political problems, and that Barkley could have it if he wanted it but Stevenson hoped he would not be interested. He also mentioned Russell. He repeatedly indicated concern about losing the South. He intended to get rid of McKinney as national chairman and was considering Sparkman, Oscar Chapman, or Wilson Wyatt to replace him. Stevenson was clearly worried about his relations with Truman and seemed to want to disassociate himself from him. In the end, Harriman said he was not ready to abandon his own candidacy but that he preferred Stevenson to any other candidate and would, if necessary, use his strength to support Stevenson against Barkley or Kefauver. The entire conversation seemed almost to assume that Stevenson would be nominated and would accept. Humphrey and Governor Williams of Michigan telephoned Stevenson to say they would withdraw in his favor and urged Kefauver upon him for Vice President. They thought he reacted favorably.

The convention met at noon to nominate its candidate for the presidency. The balloting began at 12:20 P.M. Many delegates demanded that their delegations be polled individually, some because they genuinely felt the vote as cast did not represent their views, some because for the first time in their lives they had a chance to be seen on national television. When the Missouri delegation was polled, President Truman's alternate voted for Stevenson. At about that same time the President was leaving Washington with Mrs. Truman aboard the plane Independence, and a television network showed a split-screen picture of both events, the President's departure from Washington and his alternate's vote in Chicago. The President watched the convention on television aloft.

Stevenson was watching at Blair's house. Blair and Dutch Smith suggested that he invite some of his closest associates, and he did, including, among others, Walter Fisher, Henry Tenney, Wally Schaefer. Ellen Smith kept a running tally of the balloting. Smith wrote, "Adlai would come into the room every so often, very quietly take a look at [Mrs. Smith's] score sheet, sit down for a few minutes, and then go back to see somebody or to make a telephone call."

The first ballot, which ended at 4:14 P.M., gave Kefauver 340 votes, Stevenson 273, Russell 268, Harriman 123½, Kerr 65, Barkley 48½, and others 111, with 1 not voting. Stevenson's biggest bloc of votes came from four states—New Jersey (28 of its 32 votes), Pennsylvania (36 of 70 votes), Indiana (25 of 26), and Illinois (53 of 60). New York gave most of its big delegation to Harriman, California gave its to Kefauver. Stevenson got all 16 of Connecticut's votes, only 13 of Ohio's 54 (Kefauver got 29½). All Michigan and Wisconsin votes went to Kefauver. The second ballot began promptly, and President Truman arrived at the Blackstone Hotel during it, having been met at the airport by Mayor Kennelly and Chairman McKinney, and went to work on his own speech. The second ballot ended about 6 P.M. Kefauver and Russell had gained a little, Harriman held steady, Kerr lost all his delegates (with his approval), and Stevenson increased by 50 votes—but Barkley also increased with 30 more, and his friends began to think he might be nominated by a deadlocked convention. Dutch Smith wrote, "At the end of the second ballot, I think we all felt considerably let down as the feeling on Thursday was that Adlai would be nominated either by shifting the votes at the end of the first ballot or perhaps the second ballot, and we had the feeling that his 'band wagon' had slowed down pretty much." The convention recessed for dinner.

Jack Arvey has recalled that while he was having dinner in a private dining room at the Stockyards Inn with President Truman, Chairman McKinney, Governor Dever, Speaker Rayburn, and others, an usher brought him word that a man named Fitzpatrick wanted to see him urgently. Arvey went to the door and Paul Fitzpatrick, the New York State chairman, told him that Harriman was ready to withdraw and throw his support to Stevenson. Arvey told him to wait, and reported the news to Truman and Rayburn. They arranged that Rayburn would recognize Fitzpatrick and then Dever would release Massachusetts and that would start the bandwagon. Arvey has said, "So Stevenson's old commitment to Harriman paid off. It broke the deadlock."

The convention met at 8:48 P.M. Immediately Rayburn recognized Franklin D. Roosevelt, Jr., who announced that Paul Fitzpatrick was on his way to the rostrum to make an important announcement. Fitzpatrick read Harriman's withdrawal in favor of Stevenson. He had prepared it that afternoon while his staff was away and his wife had run it off on the mimeograph machine. Rayburn then recognized Governor Dever, and Dever announced his own withdrawal and asked his supporters, 30½ votes, to switch to Stevenson. At 9:07 P.M. the third roll call began. Dutch Smith wrote that things were "very tense" at Blair's house—"nobody said much, particularly Adlai, who would appear and disappear very quietly. Meanwhile the crowd outside had grown tremendously, and in the darkness with the illumination of the klieg lights, the setting was most dramatic and reminded me of a scene from a movie. The crowd was very good-natured and sometimes would call out questions or give a little cheer, but it made me shudder to think of a similar situation with a threatening crowd."

Arkansas switched to Stevenson—a Truman staff member had called Governor Sid McMath of Arkansas. And Senator Kefauver and Senator Douglas walked arm in arm toward the rostrum, clamoring for recognition and apparently wanting to withdraw Kefauver's name in favor of Stevenson; and an uproar commenced in the hall, slowly swelling, but Rayburn, angry at Kefauver, refused to recognize him and let him withdraw gracefully, but instead gaveled through the roll call grimly, accordingly to the scenario arranged at dinner, while Kefauver and Douglas sat silent on the platform. At the end of the roll call at 12:18 A.M., Stevenson had 613 votes, 2½ short of a majority. Only then did Rayburn recognize Kefauver, and Kefauver withdrew and conceded to Stevenson. So did Senator Russell. Rayburn then recognized Utah, and Utah shifted its 4½ remaining votes to Stevenson, giving him the nomination with 617½. At that point the vote stood: Kefauver 275½, Russell 261, Barkley 67½, 6½ for others, and 1½ not voting. Orville Freeman moved the nomination be made unanimous, and it was. Television reporters told Stevenson at Blair's house, and Stevenson said he would accept.

"Cometh the hour, cometh the man"—he went immediately out the front door of Blair's house into the bright lights and the cheering crowd, walked down Astor Street to Mrs. Bowen's, Bill Blair's grandmother's, and went through her house to a little platform overlooking her garden and facing the Blair house. Dutch Smith wrote, "He stood there for a few minutes while eight movie and television cameras took some pictures and as he read a brief statement. He then walked through the garden, back into the house and immediately out the front door." He had said he regretted the inconvenience the reporters had suffered, said he was "deeply moved" by what had happened and appalled by the responsibilities of the presidency. "I did not seek it. I did not want it. I am, however, persuaded that to shirk it, to evade it, to decline, would be to repay honor with dishonor." He would now go to the convention hall to accept. It had been a long road from Bloomington, to Princeton, to Chicago and Lake Forest and LaSalle Street and Libertyville, to Washington and San Francisco and London, back to Chicago and on to Springfield. And now, once more to Chicago.

McGowan had written a first draft of Stevenson's acceptance speech. He and Stevenson had worked at it off and on through the week. Stevenson spent more time on it than usual. McGowan has said, "There are some sections in it that were mine. But really it was more of a personal production of his. The biblical quotations were all his—I don't know where that crept in. I thought it was a terribly false note. I blame myself, I should have spotted it"—for McGowan, like a great many people (including the present author), did not like the opening biblical quotation, which had been supplied by Dorothy Fosdick. "After I wrote the draft he went to work and wrote a lot of stuff. What survived of mine was not the frills—it was more the substance. We worked in a bedroom on the second floor of the house. The acceptance was more his than speeches he gave later in the campaign."

Now the time had come. Stevenson went out of Blair's house and got into his car. He sat in the back seat with Carl McGowan, Jodie McGowan between them. Dutch Smith and his wife and a security guard—from now on Stevenson would have U. S. Secret Service with him—were in the jump seats. In front with the driver were Bill Blair and Jane Dick. Dutch Smith recalled, "The crowd was so thick that the car could not move for awhile." People in the crowd called out to him, and one woman asked who would be his vice-presidential candidate, and he asked whom she would recommend, and she replied, "Anybody but Kefauver." "We finally got under way," Smith wrote, "with a motorcycle police escort. There were crowds almost the whole way from Astor Street to the Amphitheater," a distance of several miles, though it was long past midnight. "[Mrs. Smith] made some comment about it being a most wonderful experience and Adlai replied 'I'm glad somebody is enjoying it!' On the way down we had a discussion about possible candidates for Vice President, and I expressed some special enthusiasm for Sparkman. . . . As soon as we got to the Amphitheater, [Ellen Smith] got out right after the Secret Service man, just ahead of Adlai." In the car, Stevenson had a "frog" in his throat, and Ellen Smith feared he might lose his voice.

President Truman and Stevenson met briefly, then at 1:45 A.M. Truman and Stevenson entered the convention hall together, and at the rostrum Truman held up Stevenson's hand in a victory sign, Truman grinning, Stevenson half turning away with a wry grimace, almost as though embarrassed by the President's embrace; and the delegates roared. They had been getting restless, but now, weary as they were, they came to life. They finally quieted down, and Truman spoke, then introduced Stevenson as "the next President of the United States" and they came roaring to their feet again, and, alone, he faced them, small, waving and smiling tentatively, clearing his throat nervously, holding his shoulders back like a small boy told to stand erect, fiddling with his glasses and his manuscript. Mrs. Ives was sitting in a front-row box with Mrs. Truman, Mrs. Roosevelt, Mrs. Lehman, and Mrs. Chapman. Late though it was, millions were watching on television, and, crossing the Atlantic aboard the *Mauretania,* Stevenson's old friend Jim Oates stayed up alone most of the night listening and next day got together "a bunch of Princeton people" for a shipboard celebration.

In the crowded littered smoky convention hall, blinded by lights, Stevenson spoke, his voice high, his delivery jerky and at first slow, chopping up his own long complicated sentences. His first sentence brought them to their feet again: "I accept your nomination—and your program." It was the answer to the question they had been asking all week, indeed, all spring. Then he went on: "I should have preferred to hear those words uttered by a stronger, a wiser, a better man than myself. But after listening to the President's speech, I even feel better about myself.

"None of you, my friends, can wholly appreciate what is in my heart. I can only hope that you understand my words. They will be few.

"I have not sought the honor you have done me. I *could* not seek it because I aspired to another office, which was the full measure of my ambition. And one does not treat the highest office within the gift of the people of Illinois as an alternative or as a consolation prize.

"I *would* not seek your nomination for the presidency because the burdens of that office stagger the imagination. Its potential for good or evil now and in the years of our lives smothers exultation and converts vanity to prayer.

"I have asked the merciful Father—the Father of us all—to let this cup pass from me. But from such dread responsibility one does not shrink in fear, in self-interest, or in false humility. So, 'if this cup may not pass away from me, except I drink it, Thy will be done.'"

He said he believed he would win but then reverted to the notion that better men than he were available. He paid special tribute to Alben Barkley, "my kinsman." He praised the delegates' conduct of the convention and their platform: "You have restated our party's record, its principles and its purposes, in language that none can mistake, and with a firm confidence in justice, freedom and peace on earth that will raise the hearts and the hopes of mankind for that distant day when no one rattles a saber and no one drags a chain."

He anticipated Republican charges that the Democrats were "the war party," or socialists, and the Republican slogan, "It's time for a change." He said the workingman, the farmer, and "the thoughtful businessman" all knew they were better off than ever before, thanks to the anti-depression measures of the Democrats. He said he did not fear the death of the two-party system and did not believe the Democratic Party was old and tired: "After one hundred and fifty years it has been old for a long time; and it will never be indolent as long as it looks forward and not back, as long as it commands the allegiance of the young and hopeful who dream the dreams and see the visions of a better America and a better world."

He argued that "change for the sake of change has no absolute merit in itself." He said it was unwise to change for change's sake to "a party with a split personality; to a leader, whom we all respect, but who has been called upon to minister to a hopeless case of political schizophrenia." As for corruption, he quoted Charles Evans Hughes—guilt was personal and knew no party. He referred to the campaign as "this great quadrennial opportunity to debate issues sensibly and soberly," as a "great opportunity to educate and elevate a people." He went on, "And, my friends, even more important than winning the election is governing the nation. That is the test of a political party—the acid, final test. When the tumult and the shouting die, when the bands are gone and the lights are dimmed, there is the stark reality of responsibility in an hour of history haunted with those gaunt, grim specters of strife, dissension and materialism at home, and ruthless, inscrutable and hostile power abroad."

The ordeal of the twentieth century was far from over, he said.

"Sacrifice, patience, understanding and implacable purpose may be our lot for years to come. Let's face it. Let's talk sense to the American people. Let's tell them the truth, that there are no gains without pains, that we are now on the eve of great decisions, not easy decisions, like resistance when you're attacked, but a long, patient, costly struggle which alone can assure triumph over the great enemies of man—war, poverty and tyranny—and the assaults upon human dignity which are the most grievous consequences of each. . . .

"The people are wise—wiser than the Republicans think. And the Democratic Party is the people's party, not the labor party, not the farmers' party, not the employers' party—it is the party of no one because it is the party of everyone.

"That, I think, is our ancient mission. Where we have deserted it we have failed. With your help there will be no desertion now. Better we lose the election than mislead the people; and better we lose than misgovern the people. . . .

"I ask of you all you have; I will give you all I have, even as he who came here tonight and honored me, as he has honored you—the Democratic Party—by a lifetime of service and bravery that will find him an imperishable page in the history of the Republic and of the Democratic Party—President Harry S. Truman.

"And, finally, my friends, in the staggering task that you have assigned me, I shall always try 'to do justly, to love mercy and to walk humbly with my God.' "[34]

79

Adlai Stevenson had survived, if not always prevailed over, many trials—the accidental killing of a child, his parents' unhappy marriage, a loving but sometimes difficult sister, a glamorous marriage that ended in divorce, the struggles with the state legislature and the Democratic machine, all the tribulations that came to him in his trial by fire in Illinois. He was ready, if he ever would be, for the nation.

That night down in Bloomington, his old friend, the insurance man, Heinie Capen, was giving a little party, a convention television party.

[34] The full as-delivered text will be found in Appendix D. It is worth noting, with respect to the final religious quotation, that in 1927, Alfred E. Smith wrote an article for the *Atlantic Monthly* which concluded with "a fervent prayer that never again in this land will any public servant be challenged because of the faith in which he has tried to walk humbly with his God."

He and his guests were watching television, Joe Bohrer, who had played with Stevenson as a child at Charlevoix, among them. Finally the convention adjourned at 2:27 A.M.; they turned off the television set; and Joe Bohrer went home: "And on the way home I saw that half the houses in Bloomington were still lit up. I realized then that Bloomington had lost him. He'd moved on to a higher step than this. This town is normally 3 to 2 Republican. I'll never get over the fact that those houses were lighted. Over half of them," he said in awe. "This is a ten o'clock town during the week. We wished him well. We knew he could no longer be a part of our lives." Joe Bohrer was right.

CHAPTER 8

The Campaign for President
1952

There was a campaign to organize, staff to find, quarters to rent, people to call, itineraries to plan, speeches to write, organizations to set up, issues to consider, positions to take, people to court and people to shun, strategy to plan. How does it get done? Unlike most candidates who get nominated, Stevenson, since he had not campaigned in the primaries, found himself without a staff, strategies, position papers, programs, speaking schedule, organization. When he was nominated, the election itself was only three months and nine days away. Jim Farley, FDR's national chairman who had become chairman of the board of the Coca-Cola Export Corporation, with offices in New York, told Stevenson on July 29 that he and Herbert Bayard Swope were in agreement on the campaign and therefore, of course, in New York everything was under control. Things were certainly not under control in Springfield.

Immediately upon returning there from the convention on July 28, Stevenson began going through rituals expected of a candidate. That day he spoke to a crowd at a hastily organized "homecoming celebration" at the courthouse. His years as Governor had been "years of toil and tears and struggle for me. . . . They have been hard years, but . . . rewarding. I wanted four more. . . Actually, I had only now come to enjoy my job. That beautiful, revered old house, the Mansion, has just now begun to mean more to me than a prison or a salt mine. . . . I have now been called upon to perform a task—the most formidable task in the modern world at the crossroads of history. My heart is not light here today. I feel no elation."

He went alone at night to sit silently in Lincoln's old home not far from the Mansion. Urged by Eleanor Roosevelt, he wrote to Bernard Baruch and later arranged to see him—it was a ritual, too, in those years for a presidential nominee to call on both Baruch and Cardinal Spellman of New York, and Stevenson did both. (It was also ritual that if elected he would immediately announce that he would retain J. Edgar Hoover as head of the FBI. Likewise the press usually announced that "Lewis Douglas,[1] a Democrat of long standing, announced that he could not support the Democratic candidate this year.") Stevenson also held a press conference, as was traditional, but his was a rather unconventional press conference. Reporters from all over the nation had already—it was Wednesday, July 30—flocked to Springfield. He began by saying, "Well, it seems our press conference has outgrown the office. If we could always promise this kind of weather, I would be appropriately dressed. This suit was sent to me from Spain. It is not more than four inches too long in the trousers." A reporter asked if Sears Roebuck had a store in Spain. Another asked who had sent the suit. An artist, Joseph Allworthy, Stevenson said. "Friend of yours?" asked a reporter; and another, "Enemy?" Stevenson: "He's a friend. Or was."

This is how it began, the famous campaign of 1952. This set the tone, the tone that made those who were directly involved in it and millions who watched it remember it so fondly. There was a gaiety, a spontaneity, a freshness, an insouciance about it that was extraordinarily appealing to countless people weary of pompous politicians. It endeared him to the reporters who crisscrossed the nation with him that fall, and some of them lost their objectivity and, though they worked for Republican newspapers, ardently wanted him to win. It attracted to his cause, too, great numbers of intellectuals. It made him seem an extraordinarily appealing civilized human being— which he was.

2

The convention had not quite ended with Stevenson's acceptance speech. After delivering it late Friday night, he had met in a small room behind the speakers' platform with President Truman, Sam Rayburn, and Chairman McKinney to decide who should run for Vice President. Stevenson was leaning toward Kefauver. Truman proposed Senator John Sparkman of Alabama. The question was: Which defeated wing of the party needed to be conciliated—

[1] Douglas, a conservative businessman with a rigid adherence to laissez-faire economics, had been an early adviser to FDR but had soon broken with him because he thought the New Deal was headed toward "the Collective State" and by the 1936 election was trying to defeat Roosevelt. He later became ambassador to Great Britain under Truman.

Kefauver's Northern liberals or Russell's Southerners? Stevenson's liberal credentials seemed better than his Southern credentials. Hence the South must be conciliated. Senator Russell had no broad base, would be unacceptable to the Northern liberals, and probably wouldn't take it anyway. Kefauver, though from Tennessee, was anathema to Southerners. The conferees decided to eliminate anybody who had been a presidential contender. Thus they turned to Senator John Sparkman of Alabama who, though he had in the Senate voted as a Southerner on civil rights, had built up a record on other issues as a liberal and had few enemies in the party. On Saturday morning he was nominated by acclamation. Stevenson appeared with him, and the convention adjourned at two-twenty Saturday afternoon.

That morning, at six-forty o'clock, President Truman had written in longhand on Blackstone Hotel stationery a letter to Stevenson and sent it to him by hand:

Dear Governor:—Last night was one of the most remarkable I've spent in all my sixty eight years. When thousands of people— delegates and visitors—are willing to sit and listen to a set speech and an introduction by me, and then listen to a most wonderful acceptance speech by you, at two o'clock in the morning, there is no doubt that we are on the right track, in the public interest.

You are a brave man. You are assuming the responsibility of the most important office in the history of the world.

You have the ancestral, political and the educational background to do a most wonderful job. If it is worth anything to you, you have my whole hearted support and cooperation.

When the noise and shouting are over, I hope you may be able to come to Washington for a discussion of what is before you.

On the back of the envelope Stevenson penciled, "Dever at 10," apparently a reminder that he had an appointment with Governor Dever. He did not get around to answering Truman's generous letter until July 29, the following Tuesday. He said: "I am deeply touched. . . . I am grateful beyond expression for your charity and good will. . . . I am literally staggering under the new and unfamiliar burdens I have so abruptly assumed." He would be "delighted" to call on the President—"most any time" would be convenient for Stevenson.

The acceptance speech was widely acclaimed, although some people felt that Stevenson's quoting Christ's words at Gethsemane was sacrilegious. Cardinal Stritch of Chicago, however, thought the speech "fine." (A nineteenth-century Spanish general and politician had once used the same phrasing, referring to high office as a "bitter cup," leading a British diplomat to refer to him as "the vainest man I ever met with.") Press reaction to Stevenson's nomination was mixed.

The New York *Times* would still support Eisenhower but welcomed Stevenson's candidacy, since it would elevate discussion of issues. London newspapers were pleased that both parties had nominated good candidates. The sentiment of "two good candidates" was widespread on both sides of the Atlantic—too widespread for Stevenson's good—and was strong among Stevenson's Lake Forest friends—many of them voted for Eisenhower. Stevenson received congratulatory messages from a great many people, including General George C. Marshall, Secretary of State Acheson, Dean Rusk, and Archibald MacLeish, who offered help with speeches. (Stevenson asked him for a draft for the American Legion Convention on August 17—speech scheduling was already starting.) To several people Stevenson expressed dismay that he could no longer write all his own speeches.

En route to Springfield on Monday, July 28, Stevenson wrote to Alicia Patterson:

Alicia dear I finally got your note in the madness & mess at the house—but not until Sunday. Why didn't you come to the house—Blair House as we called it!—during the week? Everyone else did I think. I wanted so much a final glimpse and word and—But nothing's *final*. I refuse to believe that my life is over. . . . Its hard for me to think of myself as a candidate for Pres. & it gives me a wan & weary smile. I'm on my way to Spfd by train with a full carload of reporters, police etc—triumphal stop in Bloomington & then parade, civic celebration and speech in Spfd. Oh Lord deliver me! I don't know how long I can last!

> Love ever & ever
> Adpai!

He added, "The line to emphasize is that I am *not* Truman's candidate. He asked me and I turned it down. Then he turned to Harriman, then Barkley, but the convention turned to me after I had repeatedly said I was not a candidate and didn't want it."

It was a final glimpse of the old Stevenson, the man he had been before he suddenly became a national and international figure. He seemed himself to feel that "my life is over." His private life was indeed over. From now on to his death, he would never again be a truly private person.

3

At the press conference which began with a discussion of the length of his pants, a reporter asked if he intended to resign as Governor. He did not and, his enormous curiosity engaged, asked the reporters if Governor Roosevelt had resigned in 1932, if Governor Wilson had in 1912—"I am curious to know. This is new to me." No response. A reporter asked whom he had seen and talked to on the telephone, if Bill Flanagan or Bill Blair could hold twice-daily press briefings, if Stevenson himself could hold press conferences as often as possible "with adequate notice of four or five hours," and if the reporters could be given schedules in advance. It was a long question, rather formally worded, and Stevenson responded, "The proposals sound entirely reasonable. Do you suppose we should appoint a collective bargaining committee?" A reporter asked, "Should we submit our proposal to Bill Flanagan?" Stevenson said, "Very well. What are the penalties for a breach?" "We'll all leave town," a reporter said. Would he comment on newspapers' opposition to him? "I can only express regret, and . . . do my best" to earn their support. (He soon changed this line and attacked the "one-party press in a two-party country.")

Did he expect to do any campaigning in the South? "I don't know what the itinerary will be." Would he comment on press reports that Louisiana, Virginia, Mississippi, and South Carolina would not support him? No—he hadn't read the story. Would he keep Frank McKinney on as national chairman? They pressed him on this, and rightly, for it presented him with a difficult problem since McKinney was Truman's national chairman, and he finally said he had asked McKinney to stay on "temporarily" and would consult Senator Sparkman and others before taking a final decision. Did he expect foreign policy to "play an important part in your campaign?" Yes—"public education" was desirable. Did he agree with the agricultural plank in the platform? He did. How did he reconcile his own views on the Taft-Hartley Act and the platform's position, which called for repeal? This was another thorny problem. The Taft-Hartley Act had become a symbol, almost a bloody barricade, dividing capital and labor, conservatives and liberals, and, speaking generally, Republicans and Democrats. Because it forbade the closed shop and because it had been passed in an atmosphere hostile to labor, labor leaders were denouncing Taft-Hartley as a "slave labor" law, while businessmen were calling it the salvation of the free enterprise system.

Stevenson now replied that he had previously said that Taft-Hartley needed "substantial revision" which could be accomplished through amendment, that the Democratic platform called for outright repeal, that he thought this "more a question of form than of substance," and that "maybe it is better to remove the political symbolism of the name, 'Taft-Hartley,' by repeal."

A reporter asked about the reduction of taxes and armaments, as General Eisenhower had proposed. He said, "I feel very strongly that foolish or irresponsible promises of substantial tax reduction can be very misleading, and I hope that neither candidate nor either party would offer hopes that are forlorn and at the same time be demanding a defense establishment adequate to our . . . international security." They pressed him—"would you say Eisenhower's remarks are foolish?" He would not. Would he call Eisenhower's remarks "false promises" and "misleading"? He avoided a direct answer. Then a reporter asked if he thought President Truman's campaigning "would help you." He replied, "I don't know what the present campaign plans are. I have never heard them discussed by anyone." On this too they pressed and, again, rightly, for it was another difficult problem for Stevenson. Then, would he campaign from Springfield? He would, at least temporarily. If elected, would he retain Secretary of State Acheson? He would not discuss cabinet posts until after the election.

Whom did he favor to succeed himself as candidate for Governor of Illinois? Lieutenant Governor Dixon would be logical. Was Dixon reluctant to run? "From my experience with reluctance, I think he could be persuaded." Was he himself still a reluctant candidate? "No, I get more aggressive all the time." What part would former Senator Myers play in his campaign? "Who?" he asked, incredibly, since Myers had been his convention floor manager. A reporter asked, "Do you think that divorce will be a political liability?" He said, "I can't comment on that. I don't know. I wouldn't have thought it would be." What did he think would be his biggest campaign problem—not being well enough known? Probably—though that might be an advantage as well. Would he use television a lot? "To the extent that we can pay for it."

Some people had said he would continue the New Deal but others had said he represented "a different philosophy"—"do you intend to put on your own personal stamp?" "Oh, definitely," he said airily. They pressed him—asked if he favored the Administration's national health program, and he flatly said, "No." They repeatedly came back to differences between him and Truman. The platform called for a federal FEPC, while he had said that the states had primary responsibility. He fell back on an old proposal that the federal FEPC relinquish jurisdiction to states that had FEPCs of their own. What about the filibuster? "I suppose the President might properly be concerned with the rules of the Senate. . . . I should certainly want to study it. . . . I am told that it has disadvantages as well as advantages. There are other considerations involved in unlimited and free debate that must not be overlooked in our anxiety to advance in one field alone." It was a characteristically Stevensonian answer that his friends would call "thoughtful" and his enemies would call "indecisive."

The next question was, "You have made superb speeches. Are they written wholly by you?" He said, "I am blushing—becomingly, I hope," and then said, "I had some things to say to you, if it is my turn." He announced plans to ensure continuity of state administration during the presidential campaign. He was withdrawing as a candidate for Governor. He had a dental appointment in Lake Forest and wanted to buy some clothes, "now that I am on parade. Maybe I should get a price list first." Was he planning a vacation? He'd like to.

A reporter asked if he felt it necessary to keep "certain areas of foreign policy" out of the campaign, as FDR and Dewey had agreed to do in 1944. Stevenson thought it "worthy of serious consideration," believed Eisenhower's views on Western Europe were substantially his own, and said, "I would hope that we would say nothing during the campaign which would be calculated in any way to diminish the allegiances of our allies." A reporter asked, "Are you going to wage a 'give them hell' campaign?" "I don't believe I am gifted with talents of that kind."

4

Springfield, that quiet brick-paved midland town with the Lincoln shrines, was jammed as never before with reporters, national politicians, labor leaders, Senators, business leaders, writers, and professors of national renown drawn there by Stevenson. Every hotel room and many rooms in private homes as well were filled. The telephone and telegraph companies sent men to work frantically to expand facilities. Stevenson's aides worked in a frenzy day and night to get organized. Once Dick Nelson went to meet Walter Reuther of the United Auto Workers and found eight other important people arriving at the same time. While Reuther talked with Stevenson at the Mansion, newspapermen clustered around outside the doorway under the portico, grumbling because they were not admitted to the Mansion and because they would have to interview Reuther on the spot when he emerged, scribbling notes on paper held against the whitewashed stone and brick wall, getting whitewash on their suits, no chairs or benches to sit on; and one warned that when fall came and the weather turned cold and wet Stevenson would start getting "a bad press" if he did not provide more comfortable facilities. Joseph Alsop went to see Stevenson, expecting to be treated as a privileged character, but was not and resented it. Stevenson had friends in the press, however, and made more, especially such people as Alistair Cooke, though he never quite got the hang of handling the working press that covers the day-to-day "hard news"—he was more at home with the columnists and editorial writers.

Stevenson himself had no idea of how huge, how complex, and how disorderly a presidential campaign is, or what demands it would make on him personally. When he prepared to leave in mid-August for a brief Wisconsin vacation, he sent word to reporters he would rather have them stay in Springfield, "apparently," the *Tribune* correspondent wrote, "not realizing that many newspapers and the press associations traditionally cover Presidential candidates in the same manner they follow the President." Newt Minow once recalled, "Let me give you the Governor's idea of a campaign headquarters. He called in Ed Day and said, 'Find us a headquarters.' Ed found a little house on South Fifth Street, two blocks from the Mansion. It would be for Carl and Bill and Ed and Stevenson and me. The Governor went through it. He went through the upstairs and said, 'These fellows we're bringing out from the East can sleep upstairs—it'll save hotel bills. They can eat here too.' Then he said, 'Well, maybe we should get an extra telephone.'" In a few weeks Flanagan alone had taken over most of that house and it was still inadequate, a press room had to be set up in a ballroom of the Leland Hotel.

Minow was sleeping in Carl McGowan's house and working at a desk in McGowan's office in the Mansion. Others were working on corners of desks there. Workmen were installing a switchboard in the kitchen of Flanagan's little house on South Fifth Street. On a sunporch Flanagan had a desk where he wrestled with the logistics of transporting newspaper reporters by plane. He had gone off the state payroll and did not know whose payroll he was on now. His wife thought he'd better find out. Stevenson and his staff would travel in one chartered airplane, the press in another, both DC-6s or DC-6Bs, four-engined propeller planes—jet aircraft were not yet in use—chartered from and manned by crews of American Airlines. Telephones were ringing everywhere. National reporters, accustomed to Washington, complained about inadequate telephone and telegraph facilities, infrequent plane and train schedules to Springfield, slow mails, and the absence of magazines and newspapers. They felt suddenly cut off from the outside world. They were outraged if Flanagan kept them waiting; thought they should have a press room in the Mansion, preferably in Blair's office; demanded "closer liaison" with Stevenson; said Flanagan seldom knew what Stevenson was doing (which was true to some extent because Stevenson simply did not keep Flanagan fully informed and did not permit him to make announcements on his own).

Journalists and publishers overwhelmed Flanagan with requests for help on articles and books. The publishers, Simon and Schuster, wanted Stevenson to write a book; he had no time, nor did anyone else; the proposal was passed from hand to hand and finally disappeared into someone's files. The publisher of a campaign biography agreed to furnish copies to the Stevenson Volunteers at cost; nothing ever came of it. Porter McKeever at the Volunteers in Chicago wanted 200 copies of Ed Day's summary of the Stevenson administration as Governor; a staff member in Springfield found a huge stack of them outdoors on the back porch of Flanagan's house, piled up with the Congressional Record and unopened cartons of documents, counted out 200 and set them on a filing cabinet and told a girl to get a messenger to dispatch them, found them still on the filing cabinet a few days later, got a box and string and wrapped them himself and sent them off by messenger to the post office, only to discover they were too heavy to go by parcel post, so asked someone to call Railway Express; the box finally disappeared.

Edward L. Bernays, the publicist, volunteered to advise Stevenson but despite many telephone calls and meetings with Stevenson's staff and volunteer leaders, little came of it. He and hundreds of other prominent and able people sent letters and memoranda to Springfield; most ended up in the files. Countless ideas, some good, some bad, went that way. Stevenson never saw them. It always happens in a presidential campaign, more so than usual in the Stevenson campaign of 1952. Stevenson seemed bewildered as the headquarters sprawled out all over town—in the Mansion, in the South Fifth Street house, the Elks Club, two floors in the Leland Hotel, and many rooms in the Leland, Abraham Lincoln, and St. Nicholas hotels. Rooms could not be held vacant; when Stevenson's campaign plane returned from a swing around the country, the first thing his staff had to do was find beds. In the end, Springfield came to resemble a disaster area, a haven for refugees from a flood.

This was the first presidential campaign in which television played an important role. Without it, Stevenson could not have become known nationally in so short a time. Nevertheless, he used television poorly. His rehearsals were inadequate. Time and again he was cut off the air before he finished his speech. His staff agonized when he went on the air. George Ball came to the conclusion that Stevenson would have been better off if he had run earlier, when only radio was available. "There was a vibrant eloquence in his words and in his oddly cadenced voice, but he obstinately refused to master the skills of the effective television performer." Stevenson attracted people in television, including Ed Murrow, and they tried to coach him, but he was their despair. More than once he missed press coverage completely by withholding his speech for further polishing beyond newspaper deadlines. Moreover, he had no established speaking pace—sometimes he would start slowly, then race near the end when he discovered he could not finish; sometimes he would start fast, then suddenly slow down. He had little sense of prose structure. George Ball often told him, "You are a fine poet, but a lousy architect. You say the right things and say them eloquently, but you don't let the structure of your speeches show through. Consequently, your listeners cannot recall what you have said or that you have recommended anything specific." Eisenhower's speech writers regularly put into his speech an "eight point program" or a "ten point program" to solve a problem; Stevenson would go to the heart of the matter but never tick off his recommendations in systematic form. Such criticism irritated Stevenson and he rejected it. He was in this, as in other matters, incorrigible.

5

Few enterprises anywhere are as frenzied, confused, and exciting as an American presidential campaign. It is an undertaking of such vast proportions as to be almost unimaginable. It must be put together in days or weeks, to be used for only two or three months. It must somehow draw together the most disparate people in a heterogeneous population scattered across a continent. Thousands upon thousands of people were suddenly working for Adlai Stevenson, some performing the most menial of tasks, such as stuffing envelopes, some practicing the arcane rites of speech writing and money raising and television production.

Confused and chaotic though the campaign seemed, it was basically organized into three sections.

First, the Democratic National Committee, with headquarters in Washington, the only one of the three that was permanent, worked with the Democratic State Central Committees in all forty-eight states and, through them, with the myriad county and city and village, ward and precinct and block organizations throughout the nation. This was the indispensable permanent regular Democratic organization composed of professional Democratic politicians.

Second, the Volunteers for Stevenson, with headquarters in Chicago, grew out of the old Stevenson-for-Governor Committee, sought the votes and active support of "independent voters" and Republicans, set up state and local volunteer committees in states outside the South, and worked exclusively for Stevenson (thus sometimes coming into conflict with local regular Democratic organizations which worked for state and local Democratic candidates as well as for Stevenson).

Third, Stevenson's personal staff, based in Springfield, worked directly with him, arranging his itinerary, advising him on issues and people, giving him ideas, answering his mail, dealing with the press, traveling with him.

Stevenson's relations with the National Committee were complicated by his relations with Truman and the choice of a national chairman. His relations with his personal staff were better, though tainted with his aversion to having anybody write speeches for him. His relations with the Volunteers were probably the most comfortable of all, since the Volunteers were headed by Dutch Smith and Jane Dick, but, again, complicated by the misgivings of old Lake Forest friends about any national Democratic candidate.

In addition to these three basic groups, there were, of course, thousands of others working for Stevenson—national, state, and local labor groups most importantly, but also the campaign organizations of Democratic candidates for Governor and Senator and Congressmen and local offices; the ADA; the Liberal Party of New York; and all manner of special groups, some local, some national, some well-organized fronts set up by the Volunteers; some spontaneous helter-skelter citizens' groups catalyzed by the enthusiasm Stevenson generated, such as the Women's Democratic Club of Southeast Lake County, Stevenson's home county. But the central structure of the campaign was three-legged—the Democratic National Committee in Washington, the Volunteers for Stevenson in Chicago, and Stevenson's personal staff in Springfield.

6

The National Committee—on August 4, President Truman sent Stevenson a warm letter, inviting him to the White House the following week, telling him it was "of vital importance that you know exactly what the foreign situation is every minute," and offering to arrange a confidential briefing for Stevenson. The President wrote, "You have made a grand impression since the nomination. . . . Whatever I can do I am at your command." That same day Stevenson held another press conference, but although he tried to get it off on a humorous note again, this time the reporters had harder questions. Whom did he want for chairman of the National Democratic Committee? Stevenson replied that McKinney would be back from a vacation at the end of the week and he would see him. The reporters pressed him hard, mentioning men who had been candidates for the job, but he would only say that at least a dozen names had been mentioned. The reporters had other hard questions. Was it true that "the ADA or far left wing" of the party had "taken [him] over"? ("Nonsense.") What was his position on tidelands oil? (He had taken none yet.) Would he support other Democratic candidates whose views differed from his own on foreign policy? (No.) Would he support cloture in the Senate to shut off filibusters? (Not sure.) Did he favor the "parallel point proposition" in the Reciprocal Trade Agreement Act? ("You would have to educate me.") What did he think of the civil rights plank in the platform? ("Excellent.") What were his views on Taft-Hartley? (He would give them during the campaign.) Where would he campaign most heavily? (He didn't know.) Had he been "in consultation with" Truman since the convention? (No.) Would Sparkman cost him "the Negro vote"? (No.) How did he propose to end "the stalemate in Korea"? (He would discuss it during the campaign.)

Stevenson's choice of Steve Mitchell for Democratic national Chairman was one of the most important and controversial moves of the campaign. Stevenson was almost universally advised to pick an Irish Catholic, in accordance with Democratic tradition (the theory being that the Democrats needed Irish Catholic votes and, having been unable in 1928 to elect a Catholic President because of prejudice, were obliged to pick one as national chairman). Stevenson's divorce made a Catholic even more imperative. Carl McGowan has said, "The first post-nomination conflict between Truman and Stevenson was over the national chairman. Truman wanted to keep

Frank McKinney. It was hard going for Stevenson. But to rid himself of Truman he could not keep McKinney." Once Stevenson said, "Goddammit, can't anyone think of a Catholic?" and McGowan thought of Jim Doyle of Wisconsin but could not reach him by phone. Finally Stevenson said, "I was lying awake last night and thought of Steve Mitchell. Mitchell is a Catholic, loyal to me, gives me an alternative to McKinney."

Mitchell himself once wrote that Stevenson asked him to take the job as early as August 1. Mitchell asked for twenty-four hours to think it over. (Stevenson asked him to hold the job until his inauguration, an indication of Stevenson's inward confidence.) When Mitchell telephoned Stevenson to accept, Stevenson said he was under pressure to pick John Bailey of Connecticut. Mitchell offered to back out, but Stevenson said he needed someone he knew and could trust. They agreed Mitchell's appointment could be announced about August 8 or 10. On August 6, Stevenson, accepting President Truman's invitation to lunch on Tuesday, August 12, told him rather cavalierly he had found an old friend, a Catholic, who would be a suitable replacement for McKinney. McKinney was due in Springfield on the tenth. On August 7, Stevenson told Mitchell that Oscar Chapman had been enthusiastic about Mitchell but that President Truman "took a very definitely negative attitude." McKinney, he said, was "very anxious" to keep the job. Stevenson asked Mitchell to come to Springfield next day, Friday, so that, when McKinney arrived on Sunday, they could present him with an accomplished fact. Mitchell wanted to discuss Cardinals Stritch and Spellman but Stevenson said he had enough to worry about without adding the Church.

On Friday, Stevenson sent a letter to Senator Sparkman informing him that he had chosen Mitchell. Wilson Wyatt reported that he had cleared Mitchell's selection with four members of the Executive Committee of the Democratic National Committee. Stevenson talked to David Lawrence of Pittsburgh and that night announced Mitchell's selection. Thus by the time McKinney arrived in Springfield he was indeed confronted by an accomplished fact. When Stevenson informed McKinney, McKinney called the White House, and Truman or someone speaking for him called Stevenson to try, unsuccessfully, to reverse the decision and rescue McKinney.

Jack Arvey found the whole thing incredible. He had felt previously that earlier Mitchell had tried to "use the Church" to get himself appointed United States district attorney and now had done the same thing again. Arvey has said, "I wasn't consulted: I was told." Arvey was in Beverly Hills. Stevenson called and said he wanted to appoint Mitchell as national chairman. Arvey said, "My God, you can't do that. He's had no political experience. He doesn't know one national committeeman. The chairman's job is to get the national committeemen to work for you." Stevenson said, "He's close to the cardinal." Arvey belittled that notion and said, "If you get rid of McKinney, you'll displease Harry Truman and why break up a winning team?" Stevenson said, "I've already done it." Arvey said, "Then why call me?" Stevenson said, "Call a meeting of the National Committee and you nominate him." Arvey said, "You're asking me to do something that I don't agree with." Stevenson insisted, and Arvey said, "Okay, boss." They used to kid about the *Tribune*'s calling Arvey his boss. Arvey recalls, "So I called McKinney, I had him call a meeting of the Executive Committee, and we did it. Dave Lawrence kids me about it to this day. I went to Washington and nominated Mitchell. Lawrence was a trained politician. In his home state he himself was not doing well. Oh, God, all for Stevenson, all for Stevenson."

Arvey thought Mitchell gave Stevenson bad advice on Catholics. Catholic ward committeemen and Catholics generally "detested" Stevenson, Arvey thought, picturing him as an intolerant Presbyterian. Mitchell, Arvey said, advised Stevenson to decline to attend the Al Smith dinner, an important Catholic function in New York run by Cardinal Spellman. Arvey told Stevenson that, as a Protestant and a divorced man, he dared not turn down Spellman. But he did, and, Arvey said, Spellman never forgave him.

Carl McGowan agreed that Catholics were disaffected but attributed it to the divorce, to the Communists-in-government issue—which the Hiss deposition may have aggravated—and to what some Catholics regarded as Stevenson's sanctimonious Lake Forest Presbyterian background.

Harry Truman wrote in his *Memoirs,* "Stevenson's attitude toward the President he hoped to succeed was a mystery to me for some time, and I believe Stevenson made several mistakes. . . . The first mistake he made was to fire the Chairman of the Democratic National Committee and to move his campaign headquarters to Springfield, Illinois, giving the impression that he was seeking to disassociate himself from the administration in Washington, and perhaps from me. How Stevenson hoped he could persuade the American voters to maintain the Democratic party in power while seeming to disown powerful elements of it, I do not know. . . . Another mistake in the 1952 campaign was that there was little or no co-ordination between Washington and Springfield. . . . It was an unfortunate situation that could have been avoided."

There is, of course, another side to this story—Mitchell's. Mitchell was a friendly man, clean-cut in appearance, wearing bow ties, looking like anything but a professional politician. He later wrote a book, *Elm Street Politics,* describing how to organize neighborhood political clubs, in suburbs as well as cities, to complement and sometimes supplant old-fashioned party machines. After Stevenson's death, he wrote a chapter entitled "Adlai's Amateurs" in a book of reminiscences about Stevenson. After all, Mitchell, together with Lou Kohn and Dutch Smith, was one of the men who in 1947 had urged Stevenson on Jack Arvey and the machine. Stevenson wanted him in 1952 precisely because he was not a professional politician and because he was Stevenson's man, not Truman's. Stevenson, remembering his own appeal in 1948 as an amateur, an almost non-partisan man, was now striving to give not only his personal campaign staff but the National Committee itself a "new look." Mitchell was part of that effort.

7

The Volunteers—on July 31, Don Forsyth sent a letter to contributors to the Stevenson-for-Governor Committee asking them whether they wanted their $300,000 refunded, turned over to Sherwood Dixon's gubernatorial campaign fund, or turned over to Stevenson for his presidential campaign fund.[2] Most contributors told him to turn the money over to the presidential campaign, though some Republicans did not. On August 4, Stevenson telephoned Dutch Smith, vacationing in Canada at Desbarats, and asked him to set up a national independent group along the lines of the old Stevenson-for-Governor Committee. Smith returned to Chicago and a few days later met in Springfield with Stevenson, Jane Dick, Lou Kohn, George Ball, James Alley, Wilson Wyatt, and Steve Mitchell and laid out plans for the national Volunteers. Back in Chicago, Smith met with Leo Lerner, Marshall Holleb, and other IVI men who had helped draft Stevenson. They established contact with independents and Republicans around the country. John Paulding Brown, Stevenson's eccentric friend from long ago, turned up and went to work. Smith has said, "We were absolute babes in the woods, but we were able to get money and give an amateur quality to it and I really think this did a hell of a lot of good. Someone would say he knew a state well and

[2] Dixon, Lieutenant Governor under Stevenson, was defeated for Governor that year.

we'd tell him to handle it. It was all personal. We probably had thirty states organized. We had very little trouble with the National Committee because I knew Steve Mitchell well."

The Stevenson-for-Governor headquarters at 7 South Dearborn suddenly expanded into several more rooms and became national Volunteer headquarters. Desks were pushed into the big bare rooms helter-skelter, piles of literature and buttons and ribbons littered the floor, and everybody was scurrying about and talking on telephones, Leo Lerner saying to a friend who had canceled his vacation to go to work for Stevenson, "So many people are giving up their summer." Lou Kohn was handing people newspaper clippings from his pockets. A few blocks away, in a quiet plush suite of offices at 105 West Monroe, George Ball, Porter McKeever, and Dick Babcock (who had come over from the Stevenson-for-Governor Committee) were working on a draft statement setting forth the purposes of the Volunteers—a "why I am for Stevenson" statement.

Dutch Smith was chairman of the Volunteers and Jane Dick co-chairman. George Ball was executive director (though he soon gravitated to Stevenson's personal staff); and Porter McKeever was publicity director. At Ball's urging, Roger Stevens became finance chairman. Stevens, the attractive New York real estate man and theatrical producer, once said, "I thought it'd be nice to see politics—I'd made the Empire State Building deal and there didn't seem to be much more to do in real estate. Well, it was a very frustrating seventy-five days." Campaign strategists decided the Volunteers would pay for and sponsor Stevenson's television programs. They had to pay cash for TV. An hour-long nationwide "simulcast"—simultaneous radio and television broadcast—cost about $85,000. Stevens has said, "A couple of times I kept banks open" to furnish the actual cash at the last minute to pay for a TV broadcast.

The Volunteers reported they collected $749,812.32 between August 11 and the election on November 6, repaid loans of $25,120, and spent $729,306.56, leaving a bookkeeping surplus of $45,-625.76. Of their total expenditures, $421,575.13 went for radio and television. At a rate of $85,000 an hour, this would have paid for about ten half-hour programs. The entire total expenditure reported by the Volunteers was only a little more than three quarters of a million dollars, an astonishingly low figure. This, of course, was the figure for the Volunteers alone. It did not include money spent by the Democratic National Committee, labor unions, and other groups. Campaign spending is virtually impossible to calculate. In that year, however, for what it is worth, Congressional Quarterly said that the two major parties officially reported spending at the national level $12.2 million for Eisenhower and less than half that, $5.1 million, for Stevenson.

Political money is extremely difficult to trace. Executives of many of the largest corporations give money to both parties, much as gamblers do, to cover all eventualities, but only two or three of the highest corporate officers know about it, and often much of it never reaches the candidate at all but ends up in the pockets of lawyers, public relations men, or other go-betweens. Often big contributors want promises in return or at least an opportunity to present their views to the candidate. One man offered to contribute $10,000 but insisted he would give it only to Bill Blair or Stevenson himself. Roger Stevens has said, "You have to call on the large contributors in person. If they contribute two or three thousand, you have to listen to their ideas about what the candidate should do. A really large contributor usually wants to talk to the candidate himself. In the whole campaign I never made a commitment or a promise. I used to say that Adlai told me 'No commitments.' Later, in 1956, when he asked me to get into it again, he said, 'I want you to do it because I don't think you'll make any commitments on behalf of me, not even for embassies—which is a habit of most fund raisers.'" Stevenson himself hated fund raising. Stevens said, "He had a funny respect, a bourgeois feeling, for money. He was always very worried about running over the budget. I think now he should have talked to more of his large contributors."

The Volunteers solicited the help of people around the country who had offered their support to Stevenson. Many were bright young people, some in the advertising or public relations business, who found no place in the regular Democratic organization or on Stevenson's personal staff. Throughout the campaign they generated ideas, some of which finally filtered up to the candidate, more of which died along the way. Marshall Holleb organized Volunteer committees in Colorado, Oregon, Washington, and other states. Such agents as Holleb always had to be sure the local regular Democratic organization understood that the Volunteers were not competing with them. Nevertheless, friction was inevitable. During the fall, as Stevenson traveled the country, in order to generate local publicity involving people who were not a part of the regular Democratic organization, Volunteer agents would introduce their local committee people to him. Holleb has recalled, "I remember him being constantly harassed—and looking it. But he carried them off well. Sometimes he would terminate the interview too soon—the schedule was frantic. The local people were worshipful so they forgave him." Volunteer groups sprang up all over the country, some spontaneously out of abortive spring efforts. Some attracted outstanding people—John Hersey, the novelist, was chairman of the Connecticut Volunteers, and Archibald MacLeish was honorary chairman in Massachusetts. So rapid and confused was the growth of the Volunteers that two months after the movement started Dutch Smith said he had no way of knowing how many local groups existed—they were springing up so fast that any count would be out of date before it was completed. The Volunteers published leaflets and pamphlets, wrote magazine articles and "letters to the editor," produced placards and buttons and bumper stickers, purchased newspaper ads, organized youth groups and other groups, and provided speakers.

When Stevenson was nominated, Jane Dick had told him, "I can't say that I'm glad for you that things have happened this way. But I can genuinely say that I am *very very very* proud for you (and for me!) and very very glad *and* proud for the American people. I think you are a great man, Adlai. I thought so 25 years ago . . . and now America is just discovering something that I've known all that time!" It was, understandably, a constant theme of hers and of other old friends. And another theme appeared in her letters, a mystic and religious one: "You will be the people, and the people will be you. And—keeping your hand in the hand of God—you will come to know that you are not facing alone a formidable and impossible task. . . . And just a personal word," and here the first theme more strongly: "keep close to your old friends—those whom you love and trust and who love and respect you. Keep them in your political life and in your personal life. Other forces—the professional politicians, the self-seekers . . . will seek you out and try to take you over."

Several times during the campaign Mrs. Dick and Mrs. Ives had minor quarrels, despite their long-standing mutual affection and esteem. As co-chairman of the Volunteers, Mrs. Dick occasionally was asked to accompany Stevenson on campaign trips and sometimes appeared beside him on the back platform of his campaign train at whistle stops, as did Mrs. Ives. After all, he had no wife, and a candidate needs ladies around him. But Mrs. Ives feared Mrs. Dick's presence would be misunderstood. Mrs. Ives recalled, "I told Jane to be careful because of gossip. Adlai froze up. He said, 'You tell me these things, but I reject it.'" Other women devoted to Stevenson criticized Mrs. Dick and each other. Sometimes Stevenson became embroiled in these battles among his female admirers. They continued throughout his life.

Marietta Tree had gone to work for the Volunteers at their New York headquarters in the Waldorf. Stevenson spoke briefly to the

Volunteers there, and Bill Blair told her that Stevenson wanted to see her privately. She later recalled, "I thought, who, me? He was in some hotel, the Biltmore, I think, and when I went to see him he said, 'Dulles has just said that Eastern Europe should be liberated. What do you think of this?' Well, I was so staggered to be asked what I thought of this that I went on and on about it and how I thought this should be denounced and all that sort of thing, but I was really staggered." Why had Stevenson asked her view? "Eden and Attlee did the same thing—asked the advice of people whose opinions they did not value on large questions. It was a technique to ingratiate themselves with the people they were talking to. I did not think it very nice." Stevenson went on to say he was surprised to find Marietta working in the campaign. "He thought of me as the wife of the stylish Ronald Tree. He didn't know that I'd been a vice chairman of the CIO-PAC and had been a shop steward once."

8

Early in August, Stevenson appointed Wilson Wyatt his "personal campaign manager," the third leg of the campaign, and Wyatt set up headquarters in Springfield. Wyatt, an able Kentucky lawyer of forty-six, had been elected Mayor of Louisville in 1941 and appointed housing expediter and administrator of the National Housing Agency in 1946 by President Truman. In 1947 he had been a founder and the first national chairman of the ADA. He had been national chairman of the Democratic Party's Jefferson-Jackson Day dinners in 1948 and 1949. He had known Carl McGowan for several years. In 1952, Wyatt had gone to the national convention as a Kentucky delegate favoring Barkley but he had considered Barkley's candidacy hopeless and so had turned to Stevenson, urging him to run and urging him on the other Kentucky delegates.

Dick Nelson went over from Stevenson's staff to work with Wyatt. Clayton Fritchey, of President Truman's staff, came out from Washington to work with Wyatt. Phil Stern, a young man who had worked as a legislative assistant to then Congressman (later Senator) Henry M. Jackson of Washington and Senator Paul Douglas, came out to work for Fritchey. Neale Roache, a thirty-nine-year-old Democratic National Committee man who had worked on the itinerary of Vice President Barkley during the off-year campaign of 1950 and worked with Wyatt in 1948 and 1949 on the Jefferson-Jackson Day dinners, went to help Wyatt on scheduling and itineraries. Louis G. Cowan became Stevenson's television adviser. Victor A. Sholis, a former

Chicago newspaperman who had been an assistant to Harry Hopkins and was now director of a Louisville radio and television station, came up to help Wyatt with radio and television. George Ball spent a good deal of time with Wyatt. Charles Brewton, of Senator Lister Hill's staff, came out to handle mail. Thousands of letters had come in since the convention, and Don Hyndman, in the Statehouse, had tried to handle them. It was hopeless—letters got lost; an offer of help from Dore Schary, the motion picture producer, lay around for weeks. Brewton and another man took space at the Leland Hotel and set up a letter-answering and letter-analysis section. Though he had handled political mail for years, he had never seen letters like these—fervent, touching, yet sensible.

Wyatt, Carl McGowan, Oscar Chapman, Jim Lanigan (formerly with Harriman, now working with Wyatt), and Neale Roache, together with Steve Mitchell, devised Stevenson's itineraries and speaking schedules. Scheduling is, really, the heart of any political campaign. Only scheduling brings together the candidate, the issues, and the audience. It involves—or should involve—the highest political strategy. Will you try to win the South or write it off? Are you weak in the big Northern industrial cities? How strong are you in California? Among Negroes? Farmers? Is it wise to maximize your Democratic vote or should you fight for independent and Republican votes (with the danger of stirring them up to vote against you when they might stay home)? How well can you do in Republican suburbs? What kind of audience are you best with—students, labor, businessmen, who? What kind of audiences do you want early in the campaign—party workers, independents, what? What issues do you want to discuss? Will you speak mostly to special interest groups, such as veterans and labor? Or on national television, directly to the people? Will you attack or propose programs? Are you stronger than the party, or vice versa? Do you hope to carry a state by riding the coattails of a popular Governor or Senator? Or should you help a weak one? And so on. Innumerable pressures are brought to bear on schedulers by local politicians. Sometimes geography controls— Stevenson canceled a trip to Huntsville, Alabama, Senator Sparkman's home town, because his airplane could not land at its airport.

On August 4, Stevenson sent a memo to Wilson Wyatt saying he had heard that Eisenhower's over-all strategy was to make foreign policy the "No. 1" issue with emphasis on the Far East, to have Nixon "push hard on the Hiss business," to make "every effort" to appease the conservative Taft wing of the Republican Party, to make "a big play" for the farmers. "According to [Leonard] Hall, one of Ike's advisers," Stevenson wrote, "the plan is to let me develop as a

shining knight until October and then hit me with horse meat, cigarette tax scandals, and whatever else they may have."

Early in August the basic strategy of the Stevenson campaign was
worked out. It was done as most things are done in a campaign—at
a series of meetings, usually unplanned, sometimes downright haphazard, at breakfast or lunch or dinner or over drinks, occasionally
more formally with Stevenson in the Governor's Mansion. It was
done by various people, including Stevenson, McGowan, Blair, Wyatt,
Mitchell, Ball, Bob Tufts, Schlesinger, and David Bell, who was on
loan from the Truman staff. The basic strategy was for Stevenson to
spend the first half of the campaign setting forth his views on the issues and establishing his competency, since neither he nor his views
was well enough known, then to shift over to attack Eisenhower
during the second half. He would begin in the East at the American
Legion convention late in August but the campaign would open officially with a Labor Day speech in Detroit. After that he would make
a Western trip, then an Eastern trip, then a Midwest trip. He would
go into the South at least once. He would go West and Southwest
again, into the Midwest again, and end with a heavily scheduled
trip through the thickly populated East, whistle-stopping home from
the Atlantic seaboard to Chicago to end the campaign.

By near the end of August the strategists had worked out a full
schedule of speeches for the entire campaign, with topics selected
and writers and researchers assigned—"September 12, Challenge of
the Future, Los Angeles"; "September 20, Liberal Tradition,
AF of L"; "October 28, Why Liberals and Independents Should Vote
Democratic." Many of these proved illusory. Who wrote what was almost wholly unpredictable, subjects changed till the last minute before the speech, places were dropped and others substituted, sometimes the campaign managers were uncertain where they'd be next
week. (The Eisenhower campaign was so well organized it could
publicize detailed itineraries two weeks in advance.) Nevertheless,
the broad geographical outline of the Stevenson campaign trips held
up, and so did its basic strategy—affirmative and expert in first half
of campaign, attack in second.

The strategy seems sound. But during the first part of the campaign it resulted in a feeling that Stevenson was talking furiously
about the world's problems and nobody was listening, while Eisenhower was getting the crowds by saying nothing. More than once
Stevenson complained, "I can't hold a debate with a man who
isn't there." The strategy sought to cast Stevenson in the role of the
experienced Governor with all the answers and to cast Eisenhower
in the role of the ignorant fumbler who knew all about military mat-

ters but nothing about government. Eisenhower's early speeches fit the role perfectly. But the strategy did oblige Stevenson to discard an asset that had served him well in 1948—that of the upright citizen and political amateur from Lake Forest who proposed to go down to Springfield and clean up a political mess. Since many people, especially suburban voters, were disillusioned about politicians, and since many new voters were being almost driven to the polls by the heavy television coverage, what had been a powerful position for Stevenson in 1948 proved to be one again in 1952—for Eisenhower. Moreover, the role of the man with all the answers was not congenial to Stevenson, who had doubts about most things. Nonetheless, given Eisenhower as his opponent, he probably had no choice. A Republican slogan was, "Time for a Change." Stevenson himself considered the people's deep desire for change after twenty years of Democratic rule the most dangerous issue and devoted an early major speech on national television to it but remained dissatisfied with his handling of the issue and returned to it time and again through the campaign.

Within the over-all scheduling framework, Wyatt and his aides worked out detailed itineraries, advised on the technical and political side by Lou Cowan and Neale Roache and on the substantive side by Schlesinger and others. They took the schedules to McGowan and Stevenson, who throughout the campaign consistently complained that the schedule was too heavy. The schedule kept changing, sometimes at the last minute. Wyatt, a friendly gregarious man, spent hour after hour on the telephone, consulting people all over the country about where Stevenson ought to go. Wyatt was an extremely attractive man, excellent on issues, less strong on organization. A little later Wyatt brought Jim Rowe out from Washington to help with scheduling, advance, and strategy.

Minow thought it unfortunate to have two headquarters—Wyatt's in Springfield and the Democratic National Committee's in Washington—and considered that as a result the campaign was loosely coordinated. When Stevenson was in town, he worked on speeches, not organization. One night Bill Blair and Minow persuaded him to go to a movie. He walked out after ten minutes to go back to work. Minow has said, "Confusion was inevitable—there was no discipline because people aren't motivated that way. You can't fire people the way you can at U. S. Steel. Albert Lasker used to say that half of every advertising dollar is wasted but nobody knows which half. In politics about eighty-five per cent is wasted." Carl McGowan, asked why Stevenson chose to have two campaign headquarters, once said, "The idea of running from Springfield was at the bottom of it.

Also keeping away from Truman. We recognized the administrative difficulties. But now we know that it was not inefficiency that lost the election. I still think, from a political standpoint, it helped, on balance."

Once the schedule for a campaign trip was set, an advance man went to each town where the candidate was to appear. Working with both the local Democratic organization and the local Volunteers—which sometimes proved impossible—he had to see that a good crowd, equipped with banners and hats and signs and sometimes a band, met Stevenson at the airport, that a string of automobiles and press buses would be waiting at the airport, that the route of the motorcade was marked out carefully to take the candidate through the politically most useful sections of the city (often the slums), that a police escort was provided, that an overflowing crowd filled the hall where he spoke, that the public address system worked, that the candidate had a hotel suite where he could change clothes and receive local politicians and volunteer leaders, and, if it was an overnight stop, that there were hotel rooms for the staff and the press and the accompanying and visiting dignitaries, a press room, and all manner of other facilities. Problems were endless. In the motorcade, who would ride with the candidate? Who would be in the second car? The third? Who would sit on the speakers' platform? Who would introduce him? Who would introduce the introducer? Who else would speak? Would the local party sponsor the affair or the Volunteers? Which local heroes and local candidates should the candidate mention in his speech? Which ones avoid? Whom should he see privately before or after his speech—labor leaders, Jewish leaders, Negro leaders, party leaders, Volunteers, businessmen, civic leaders, big contributors? Must he visit his local Volunteer headquarters? A factory? A local shrine? The job of the advance man was a thankless one. If a newspaperman lost his suitcase, or if some local politician was offended, the advance man was blamed. If everything went well—which it almost never did—he got no credit. Some of the advance men were experts sent out by the National Committee. Some were amateurs, or nearly so, sent out by Wyatt's headquarters—men like Bill Rivkin of the Chicago Young Democrats. It was the advance man's duty, above all, to represent Stevenson's interests in each place he visited, for often zealous but misguided local people would urge him to do something helpful to them but damaging to him. Oscar Chapman stayed out in advance of the candidate, but his work was at a high political level. Jim Rowe for a time followed Chapman and stayed one day ahead of Stevenson, until called to Springfield to help Wyatt. Advancing was not in 1952 developed into the high art it became in the 1960s, when dozens of experts did nothing else. Consequently, Stevenson often found himself addressing half-empty auditoriums, or giving the wrong speech to the wrong audience, or mentioning the wrong name of a local hero (he once resoundingly endorsed for Congress a man who was chairman of a meeting he addressed, only to discover later that the man was running for nothing at all, and he once thanked "the people of Allentown" in Bethlehem, Pennsylvania, for a warm welcome). All this contributed to the over-all impression that Stevenson's was a haphazard amateurish campaign, not a bad impression politically.

9

On Monday, August 11, Senator Kefauver visited Stevenson, Mitchell, and Wyatt in Springfield and afterward told the press he would do what he "appropriately" could for Stevenson. He would do "some" speaking himself. A reporter suggested he did not sound very enthusiastic. "Well, I've been through a long campaign," Kefauver said. He was the coolest of Stevenson's callers who came to demonstrate party unity. The same day the *Pantagraph* published an editorial questioning whether Stevenson could bring about the change in Washington which the country demanded.

It was against this background of presidential irritation at Mitchell's appointment, Kefauver's lack of enthusiasm, and the *Pantagraph*'s editorial that Stevenson went to lunch with President Truman on Tuesday, August 12. He took with him Mitchell, Wyatt, McGowan, Flanagan, Blair, and Nelson. He spent more than three hours in the White House. The President had arranged an elaborate briefing on foreign affairs.[3] Sparkman joined them. The full Cabinet attended a lunch, then Truman talked politics privately with Stevenson and Sparkman. (It was at this time that Truman loaned Stevenson two of his staff aides, Clayton Fritchey and David Bell, and that they went back to Springfield with him.) Emerging from the White House with the President, Stevenson found about fifty newspapermen waiting; and Truman pointed to the microphones and said, "That's your point of contact right there, Governor." "Am I to ad-

[3] Among those present were Secretary of State Acheson; the chairman of the Joint Chiefs of Staff, Omar N. Bradley; Averell Harriman, Mutual Security Administrator; John R. Steelman, acting Defense Mobilization Director; General Walter Bedell Smith, director of CIA; Leon H. Keyserling, chairman of the President's Council of Economic Advisers.

dress the multitude now?" Stevenson asked, then said he had enjoyed his lunch though another such might make him "so fat I won't be able to campaign"; had enjoyed a tour of the White House escorted by the President, had had a briefing "on the international situation" and had "a very satisfactory and reassuring and gratifying talk with the President about the campaign. I am deeply grateful to him for his proffer of cooperation in every respect and in every degree." Republicans criticized the briefing. Truman invited Eisenhower to a similar briefing but Eisenhower declined: "It is my duty to remain free to analyze publicly the policies and acts of the present administration." Truman was understood to have offered to undertake a nationwide whistle-stop speaking tour on Stevenson's behalf. Stevenson, returning to Springfield, wrote to Truman: "My understanding is that we can count on you for speeches in October in the East and possibly Pittsburgh and St. Paul, winding up in St. Louis; and also for a trip to the Northwest if that seems necessary. I know how sincere you are about helping us and of your almost limitless energy, but we shall try not to impose on you unreasonably." The press, most of which supported Eisenhower, continually emphasized Stevenson's efforts to disengage from Truman. Truman wrote later in his *Memoirs,* "By alienating many influential Democratic leaders at the outset Stevenson may have thought he was attaining full freedom of action. But in reality he needlessly sacrificed basic political backing and perhaps millions in votes. . . . When it seemed to me almost too late, Stevenson asked me to get into the campaign, which I did as soon as I could, and I gave it all I had."[4]

Stevenson asked Minow not to let his state legislative program slide, even though it was not to be presented to the legislature until January. But much of the legislative program devolved upon young Dan Walker (later Governor of Illinois), for Minow found other chores more pressing—finding a place for the writers to live, hiring secretaries, answering reporters' questions, writing statements, reading mail, answering telephones, talking to people in Illinois with state government problems. Stevenson introduced Minow to his Cabinet and told them to call him with their problems while Stevenson was absent, campaigning. Minow was twenty-six. "They got to calling me Governor. When you're twenty-six you have no consciousness of your limitations." He was, in effect, the head of Illinois government for a few months. He urged Stevenson to challenge Eisenhower to a television debate. Stevenson refused.

As always, Stevenson was resisting pressure from special interest

---

[4] More on the AES-HST controversy will be found in Appendix E.

groups, and his resistance to labor—and to Jewish groups—seemed stronger than his resistance to business. When Walter Reuther visited him in Springfield, they argued over repeal of Taft-Hartley. McGowan has recalled, "It irritated him to be pressed. One of his great fears was that the Democratic Party would turn into the labor party. But the only big money was coming from labor. Steve Mitchell said if it was not for labor and the Jews he'd have to close headquarters in a week. Stevenson thought this was unhealthy. So if Reuther started shoving him around, he bridled. He was never close to Reuther. Few people were."

Jack Arvey once explained Stevenson's reluctance to address Jewish groups somewhat differently: "Stevenson refused to be a demagogue. He felt he might become President and if he did he might do a great deal to ease tensions between the Arabs and the Jews but he couldn't do it if he was a partisan on one side. I remember my own dinner in 1954. He made a speech and I was satisfied with it. But the professional Jews didn't like it—he didn't go far enough for Israel. He went far enough to satisfy me and it was my dinner."

10

That August there was something kinetic in the atmosphere in Springfield. Dozens of young liberal writers arrived, some invited, some not, all drawn by the Stevenson magnet. They became the speech writers. They worked in the Elks Club, surely an incongruity —mail came there addressed "Professor Arthur M. Schlesinger, Jr., Elks Club, Springfield, Illinois." They became known as the Elks Club Group. Since Stevenson's speeches attracted so much comment, and since he attached so much importance to them, the Elks Club deserves special treatment.[5]

On August 13, the day after Stevenson's meeting with Truman, with writers already crowding the Mansion and more coming, Ed Day rented space in the Elks Club for them, a large workroom and four adjoining bedrooms. The Elks Club was a brick building two or three blocks from the Leland Hotel and the Governor's Mansion. The writers worked—and some of them slept—on the third floor. Their workroom was a big bare room with a long table running down its middle where the secretaries spread out neatly typed speech

---

[5] The present author was a member of the group. It was his first experience at writing speeches or participating in a political campaign. In the following account he is referred to as Martin.

drafts and incoming documents and where the writers gathered to work collectively on speeches. Against the walls were the desks. Often as many as ten people were at work here. One was a researcher and fact checker, Mary Helen Wood. The rest were writers.

The first to arrive, invited by Stevenson, was Arthur M. Schlesinger, Jr., professor of history at Harvard, biographer of Andrew Jackson and Franklin Roosevelt, Pulitzer Prize winner, ADA leader. Schlesinger was thirty-four, with a high forehead and getting bald, alert eyes and liquid face, glasses; a funny and gay man, articulate, sometimes acid, gregarious, with a quick intelligence and broad knowledge. He was rapidly becoming a leading American intellectual (and later joined John F. Kennedy's White House staff). He knew intellectuals and politicians around the country. He carried on an astonishing correspondence and an astonishing telephonic dialogue. He could, seemingly, simultaneously hold a telephone conversation, write a speech, read source materials, and talk to somebody across the desk. He wrote rapidly and well. He wrote basic drafts on major speeches, did heavy rewrite on other people's drafts, and, from his friends around the country, obtained dozens of drafts. Schlesinger had been somewhat troubled by the acceptance speech and considered it his duty to make Stevenson's speeches "simple and militant," not "complex and philosophic." He agreed with Harriman's thesis that the Democrats could win only by carrying on the fight for New Deal and Fair Deal issues. He feared Stevenson was too conservative and sought to push him leftward. He thought Stevenson too pro-Southern and insufficiently committed to civil rights and labor, indeed, even anti-labor and anti-Truman. He believed Stevenson overvalued the independent Republican vote—it had helped elect him Governor but would oppose him for President, and he should concentrate on getting every Democratic vote that existed. He wrote, "What Adlai must understand is that the central domestic issue is still the fight between the business community and the rest of the country. . . . All of us will have to do a lot of work on him in the next few months." He urged James Wechsler, editor of the New York *Post,* to "worm your way" into Stevenson's confidence and become his foremost political adviser on New York questions.

W. Willard Wirtz was probably the oldest Elk, forty, and one in whom Stevenson had great confidence, in part because, more than the others, he encouraged Stevenson to do what he wanted to do. He had been with the War Labor Board and the National Wage Stabilization Board, had taught law at Northwestern University, and had sat on the Illinois Liquor Control Commission while Stevenson was Governor. A big crew-cut man from Winnetka who later became Secretary of Labor in the Kennedy and Johnson administrations, Wirtz was tense, abstemious, almost painfully loyal to Stevenson, and he kept to himself more than other members of the Elks Club Group. A labor expert, he was originally brought in to handle labor speeches but, like the others, wrote drafts on all sorts of subjects and rewrote other people's speeches, sometimes more than they thought necessary. Bob Tufts, a friend of Dorothy Fosdick, an economist from Oberlin College who had worked in the Office of Strategic Services during the war and later in the Department of State, was thirty-six, short, strongly knit, tough-minded and clear-minded. Tufts was a good writer and a precise one, writing painstakingly in longhand, a small cramped script. He wrote all, or nearly all, the basic drafts on foreign policy but he also wrote on other subjects. Dave Bell, thirty-three, tall, blond, affable, and outwardly calm, with a wide knowledge of government and politics, had been in the Bureau of the Budget for two years and had been a member of Truman's staff since 1947. Bell rarely wrote first drafts himself but, rather, rewrote everybody else's first drafts, to the dismay of some writers, especially Sydney Hyman. Those four—Schlesinger, Bell, Tufts, and Wirtz—were the ones officially listed as comprising the "research staff" in an early publicity release. Bell had administrative responsibility.

In addition to those four, several others worked at the Elks Club —Bill Reddig, a Kansas newspaperman who produced good ideas but not much Stevensonian language with the exception of "the one-party press in a two-party country"; John Kenneth Galbraith, the Harvard economist, a very good writer with no hesitancy about rewriting other people's drafts, who worked at the Elks Club steadily during the early part of the campaign before returning to Harvard; John Fischer, editor of *Harper's,* who stayed through September and most of October; Bernard DeVoto, the historian and writer, who worked on conservation and public lands; Sydney Hyman, a Washington writer who worked at the Elks Club through the campaign but somehow saw most of his drafts heavily rewritten; John Bartlow Martin, a journalist originally asked to help Flanagan, who gravitated to the Elks Club in mid-September and stayed full time; Phil Stern, nominally an assistant to Clayton Fritchey who in turn was Wilson Wyatt's assistant, who also gravitated to the Elks. Herbert Agar of the Louisville *Courier-Journal* joined the Elks Club for a time. So did Eric Hodgins, an editor of *Fortune,* though he was not entirely happy there. David Cohn, a Southern writer, came to Springfield, and for a time he and the Elks Club Group tried to work together, but Cohn and Schlesinger—and Cohn and McGowan—did not get along. Cohn insisted on delivering speeches directly to Stevenson, instead of working with the Elks Club, and soon he formed a schismatic group of writers at the St. Nicholas Hotel, and to him gravitated Hodgins and Agar, though Agar later rejoined the Elks Club. McGowan termed the Cohn group the "moonlight and magnolia team"; it produced several speeches that Stevenson used in the South. At least once the Elks assumed that the Cohn group had already written all the speeches for a Southern trip, only to discover at the last minute that it had not. Some of the Elks, such as Schlesinger and Bell, had highly developed political instincts. Others, such as Hyman, Cohn, and Agar, were more interested in the prose of a speech than in its political effectiveness.

On any given day one could usually find in the main workroom Schlesinger, Bell, Tufts, Reddig, and Martin. Wirtz usually worked in one of the bedrooms, as did Hyman and Fischer. Scattered about were piles of magazines and newspapers, the Democratic National Committee's basic campaign fact book, the Democratic platform, fact sheets on each speech locale—its economy, political leaders, local color, issues—supplied by the National Committee, voting records of Senators Nixon and McCarthy and others, an analysis of the Republican platform, research papers on Eisenhower's speeches, issue papers, Stevenson's record as Governor (though the writers never made as much use of it as they would have liked, mainly because Stevenson balked; he also disliked giving the expected speech, for example, a speech on natural resources in the Pacific Northwest, but found he had to do it). Scattered about, too, were the World Almanac—someone once said that no campaign could be run without an Almanac and the Bible—collections of quotations, and copies of the Elks' own books. Throughout the campaign, speech drafts and position papers, solicited and unsolicited, came to Stevenson and the Elks from a wide variety of people.[6] Most of them were

---

[6] Seymour Harris, professor of economics at Harvard, contributed numerous drafts and memos on economic policy. James P. Warburg contributed them on national security. James Wechsler of the New York *Post* contributed a draft for the Liberal Party convention which contained so many good jokes that the Elks mined it throughout the campaign. At Stevenson's request, Robert Sherwood and Samuel Rosenman wrote drafts; though they would have been excellent for Franklin Roosevelt, they were not in Stevenson's idiom. Schlesinger asked Ben Cohen to work on foreign policy drafts. Rexford G. Tugwell wrote a memorandum on conservation. Professor Stuart Gerry Brown of Syracuse University did a draft on state and local government. Professor Walter Johnson of the University of Chicago did a draft on the American liberal tradition and solicited other drafts from other Chicago faculty members. James R. Arnold of the University of Chicago's

transmitted to the Elks, though Stevenson kept on reserve in his briefcase a few drafts or memoranda that he received directly. Some material sent in from outside found its way into speeches, though usually in altered language. As the campaign went on, the Elks discovered that a speech had to be written on the spot and almost the night before it was delivered. It is nearly impossible to write a campaign speech away from the candidate or long in advance.

As each week's schedule became available, the Elks would meet in one of the bedrooms and divide the schedule up among themselves, each taking an assignment because he knew the place or the topic or both. Sometimes they would decide the subject of each speech themselves. Sometimes McGowan would bring word that Stevenson wanted to give a speech soon on a certain subject—say, "time for a change"—and to discuss where it might be given. The writer assigned to a speech usually telephoned local people for advice on issues and local problems, researched the topic, then wrote a rough draft and turned it in to Dave Bell. Bell would either rewrite it himself or give it to someone else for rewrite. If it was a major speech, several Elks would gather around the big table and work on it collectively. It was not unusual for a speech to go through

---

Institute for Nuclear Studies, Byron S. Miller, a Chicago attorney, and Aaron Novick of the Institute of Radiobiology and Biophysicians at Chicago did a draft on atomic energy. Henry Heineman, a Chicago lawyer, did a draft on civil liberties and the McCarran immigration act. Thomas H. Eliot of Washington University did a draft on the revitalization of state government. Norman Cousins of the *Saturday Review* sent several drafts to Stevenson and was rewarded by a letter saying "your material is by far the best that I receive" (though it is not certain that Stevenson himself wrote the letter, and Cousins was not the only one so rewarded). Randolph Paul of Lloyd Garrison's New York law firm contributed papers on tax policy. Schlesinger asked Raymond Swing, a former radio commentator then with the State Department, to "try your hand at" a draft on coexistence with Russia. Joe Lohman of Stevenson's state Parole Board did a civil rights draft. Art Moore, who had worked on the *Pantagraph,* wrote farm speech drafts. Leon H. Keyserling, chairman of the Council of Economic Advisers, sent in papers on fiscal policy. Jack Fischer asked Stuart Chase for material on economic policy. Professor Eugene Rostow of Yale sent in material on anti-monopoly legislation. John Palfrey of the Institute for Advanced Study at Princeton contributed a memorandum on atomic energy. James Otis of the Illinois Commerce Commission submitted notes on public power, Fred Hoehler supplied material on Social Security and welfare. Professor Henry Steele Commager of Columbia put everything aside to prepare material for an education speech; not until mid-December did Stevenson get around to thanking him (and telling him he was "mortified" that he had "concluded not to speak on the subject"). No women were among these contributors.

half a dozen drafts, and some went through more. Rewriting sometimes merely honed language; sometimes it changed policy.

An evening or two before Stevenson was due to leave town for a campaign trip, McGowan would come to the Elks Club and pick up the speeches, going over the major ones with the Elks if there was time, then taking the speeches to the Mansion. There he would go over them himself, sometimes rewriting them extensively. More than any other single person, McGowan shaped the substance of the campaign. His draft would go to Stevenson, who would sometimes deliver it almost as he received it, sometimes edit and rewrite it heavily. Stevenson was a good writer but not a good editor. When he went off on a campaign trip, one and usually two Elks accompanied him. Except for this, the Elks' contact with Stevenson was almost entirely through McGowan, though Schlesinger saw Stevenson alone occasionally.

The Elks referred to themselves as "speech researchers" who were "doing basic research work." For they understood that Stevenson was pained at the thought of "ghost writers." Only once or twice did they meet as a group with Stevenson, and the meetings were inconclusive, as large meetings usually are. The Elks got instructions on policy by osmosis. "Ghost candidate," seemed a better phrase than ghost writers, from the Elks' viewpoint. They rarely knew, except by a cryptic sentence from McGowan, what subject Stevenson wanted to talk about or what he wanted to say on it. Usually they did not even know what he thought of the speeches they turned in, though he used a good many almost as submitted. Sometimes, traveling with him, they would literally slip the speeches under his hotel room door in the middle of the night, in order that when he awoke in the morning he might find an anonymous draft on the floor, pick it up, and, rewriting it, make it his own. It was his way. He really wished the writers weren't there. He was proud of his own writing and once told a friend he wished more than anything else he had been a writer. It irritated him that writers were indispensable to him. No one could say the Elks advised him; they hardly talked to him. It was all the more curious that Stevenson attacked Eisenhower for merely mouthing speeches written for him by someone else—but Stevenson himself was not accused of uttering a word that was not his own. Incredibly, newspapermen did not challenge him. Mere arithmetic—how many words he uttered daily, how many hours there are in a day—would have shown them how impossible it was. Schlesinger thought that Stevenson overvalued the reputation he had as the author of his own speeches.

The Elks went to work about 10 A.M. They usually went to lunch

together about 2 P.M. at the Sazerac, an obscure saloon a block or
two beyond the Leland Hotel, to avoid the press. Walking there,
they would stop at the *State Register* office and read the bulletins
written in crayon on newsprint and hung in a window. Walking past
Coe's bookstore, they looked for copies of their own books in the
window, almost never seeing them. The Sazerac was small and dingy,
with a round table beside the jukebox. Once when somebody started
to put a nickel in the jukebox, Galbraith said to him, "I'll give you a
dime if you don't play it." Their waitress was a pretty girl too young
to vote. She never had chocolate sauce for their ice cream and
finally Schlesinger, Tufts, and Martin refused to leave until she had
sent out for a can. They seldom drank liquor at lunch. Bell always
ordered two bottles of milk. After lunch they went back to work at
the Elks Club.

Phones there rang constantly, usually long distance. Bell and
Schlesinger were on the phone much of the time; the others wrote
more rough drafts. They went to dinner together at seven-thirty or
eight, usually stopping at the Elks downstairs bar for a drink, and
Dave Bell would look longingly at the bowling alley. They dined at
Stevie's, a steak house some distance away, or at some other out-
of-the-way place, again to avoid the press. Afterward they worked,
always till midnight, sometimes—the night before Stevenson left on
a campaign trip—till 2 or 3 A.M. or later. Two or three evenings
that fall some of them took an evening off—once went to a party at
the rented house of Jim Lanigan; once went to a movie; played pool
down by the railroad tracks. There was little to do in Springfield.
At lunch and dinner they talked about almost nothing but the campaign. Once Bell fell to talking about President Truman, whose independence he admired greatly; some of what Bell said found its
way into Stevenson's speech in Kansas City.

They quickly came to despise Eisenhower because he refused to
renounce the support of Senators McCarthy and Jenner, because he
reached an accord with Senator Taft, because, as they saw it, he
was sacrificing principles for votes and knew little or nothing about
politics and government. They came to think his election would be a
national disaster. When they heard that Eisenhower, in a speech on
fiscal policy, had referred to "the Federal Reserve System and stuff
like that," they invented an elaborate Stuff Theory of Fiscal Policy.
They fell into possession of a document outlining the Republican
plan to saturate the country with radio and TV spot announcements,
selling the candidate (as the Elks put it) the way one sells soap; they
resented it. They became prisoners of their own propaganda. They

knew it, and feared it, and resorted to telephoning their wives back home to ask how the campaign was progressing.

On some sensitive issues such as offshore oil, Stevenson outlined his stand and McGowan wrote the language. But the Elks' casual talk at lunch and dinner also produced policy. One evening at dinner Galbraith said, "It seems to me our farm policy is simple—the Democratic Party is the farmer's friend. And we're for price supports." Tufts added, "And we can talk about Sparkman as a tenant farmer." All agreed. Galbraith drafted a speech, and Art Moore drafted one, and the Elks put the two together and gave them to McGowan for Stevenson: his major speech on agriculture. It was not always so casual. They discussed long and earnestly a speech on Communism and one in New York on civil rights, drafting and redrafting language as strong as they thought he would accept. They were serious men. They cared about the issues and believed the rhetoric.

Stevenson said early that he did not intend to campaign against Herbert Hoover, as the Democrats had been doing ever since 1932. The Elks, feeling that the Democratic Party was stronger than its candidate and wanting to reawaken the party's ancient anti-Republican feelings, frequently tried to slip anti-Hoover material into his speeches at the last minute, as well as material that made Stevenson sound more liberal than he was. Years later he confided to a friend that he sometimes found himself saying things on TV he did not believe; upset and angered, he would stop in mid-sentence and stare blankly at the lectern; it contributed to his bad "TV image," he felt. Sometimes he would try to ad-lib and become confused by "the re-entry problem"—the problem of finding his way gracefully back into his text after ad-libbing. He said he was more conservative than his writers. He said his adolescence had been marred by his mother, who thought she knew better than he what was best for him; just so was his 1952 campaign marred by managers who thought they knew better than he.

After the campaign ended, Stevenson and his aides, editing a book collecting his speeches, omitted some of the most effective ones—the rally speeches, those rousing highly political speeches delivered to highly partisan Democratic rallies, such as the one at the Cow Palace in San Francisco. Schlesinger, Wirtz, and Martin wrote a good many of them. Schlesinger has said, "They had a gay, rollicking quality. Stevenson loved giving them, but he hated them beforehand and after. Jane Dick or somebody would reproach him for attacking the Republicans."

Stevenson was always more interested in foreign affairs issues than domestic issues. Agriculture policy bored and mystified him, labor policy bored and troubled him. He was much more interested in education and natural resources. Schlesinger, when he first arrived in Springfield and met with Stevenson, came away thinking him the most conservative Democratic presidential candidate since John W. Davis. He thought Stevenson intended to aim his campaign at Southern Democrats and high-minded Republicans in Lake Forest, groups for whom Schlesinger had little use and who were not numerous enough to elect a President. Stevenson seemed far more anxious to see Richard B. Russell than Averell Harriman. He once indicated he was considering appointing John J. McCloy Secretary of State if he won. Still, Schlesinger acknowledged that Stevenson was the one man in politics who struck an authentically fresh note. Eisenhower uttered the clichés of the right, Harriman the clichés of the left; Stevenson spoke for the future. And Carl McGowan reassured Schlesinger, "You fellows get too much worried by some of the Governor's off-the-cuff reactions to issues—they don't mean anything. I know that, as soon as you get down to cases with the Governor, he will do everything that needs to be done." Schlesinger thought the logic of the situation would force Stevenson leftward as the campaign progressed. He was right.

The Elks considered Senator McCarthy a sinister figure running all through the campaign, and when McCarthy attacked Schlesinger and DeVoto, Schlesinger feared his presence was damaging Stevenson. Bill Rivkin told them how one night, after debating with McCarthy, he had driven McCarthy and his aides to a railroad station, and McCarthy had said to one, "Pass me the medicine," and one of his henchmen had handed him a medicine bottle and, drinking, he had said belligerently to Rivkin, "I suppose you think this is bourbon— well, it is." All their talk had been of liquor and women, possibly for Rivkin's benefit. McCarthy meetings in Milwaukee and Chicago produced heckling, with some hecklers forcibly ejected; the Elks recalled Hitler's beer-hall brawling. The Elks may have known that McCarthy was a mere adventurer but they were obliged to take him seriously, nor could they help blaming Eisenhower for tolerating McCarthy. They usually referred to President Truman as "the President," not as "Harry" as so many Americans did, and to Stevenson as "the Governor" or "the candidate," or simply "he," almost never as "Adlai."

After several weeks of campaigning, Tufts felt that, although Stevenson actually had discussed the issues thoroughly, little residue remained of what he had said. In fact, he could recall more of what Eisenhower had said, vapid as it was. Why? Perhaps, he thought, the speeches were honed too much and became too smooth, not sufficiently blunt and forceful. When an Elk accompanied Stevenson on a trip, he called the other Elks in Springfield nearly every day, and they always asked, "How did the whistle stops go?" and "How were the crowds?" and "Did he use our stuff?" and "Did they like him?" They were almost pathetically concerned about the fate of the candidate, who ignored them. When Stevenson told Martin he was grateful for the work he'd done on a recent campaign trip, Martin was astonished. When Stevenson told Wirtz that the Cow Palace rally in San Francisco was so good he wished he'd written it himself, Wirtz remarked to a friend, "That's the first kind word of the entire campaign." Neither heard more. Yet Stevenson did appreciate their work, as he subsequently showed.

The Elks worked together in remarkable harmony. They worked too hard. One day Bell collapsed at the Elks Club. The others put him to bed in one of the bedrooms and called a local doctor, who talked to him for some time, then emerged and announced that it "wasn't anything much, maybe chronic appendicitis, too much work, he'll be okay." Tufts asked if he had given him an antibiotic, and he said, "That's a good idea," and went back and gave him penicillin. (Thereafter Tufts was called Dr. Tufts.) Bell told Schlesinger he wasn't satisfied with the doctor, and the Elks got another doctor who put Bell in a hospital, and one of the Elks called Bell's wife and she came to Springfield. Bell recovered in a few days and returned to work, and on that day Reddig collapsed. Then, getting off the campaign plane, Schlesinger injured a knee; it became infected and he went briefly to a hospital. Later Tufts collapsed in Philadelphia and had to be left behind. All suffered from overwork. Yet they found time to joke. Once they composed an imaginary farm speech which began:

"Good afternoon, peasants:

"I have during this campaign traveled the length and breadth of this broad land, looking upon the smiling faces of Americans everywhere, and I can tell you in all sincerity that I have never seen anywhere such a bunch of ignorant, shiftless, selfish, greedy people as you farmers."[7]

---

[7] Fischer composed one on offshore oil:

"Good morning, my friends in Dallas:

"I come before you to tell you plainly my position on the question of the tidelands—the title, that is, to [offshore] oil which is thought to lie beneath the submerged lands along your seacoast. It has been called to my attention that some of you have been asserting a claim to those lands.

"Well, I tell you in all candor that if I am elected I will make it my business to see to it that any such dream you may entertain will come to

Behind this, and other mock speeches they wrote, lay their delight in and occasional concern about Stevenson's unorthodox approach to audiences—his habit of telling them what they did not want to hear. He warned the American Legion against flag-waving; he told labor unions he was not their captive. Schlesinger said years later, "It was a brilliant device to establish Stevenson's identity. As a permanent device, it was an error." As the campaign progressed, journalists picked up a word—Joseph and Stewart Alsop were credited with printing it first—to describe Stevenson and his advisers: eggheads. The word may originally have been suggested by Stevenson's baldness and by the intellectual background of the Elks. It became, as Senator McCarthy and Senator Nixon increased their attacks, a word of opprobrium, well suited to the anti-intellectual climate of 1952.

11

It is impossible to make a general statement about "who wrote Stevenson's speeches." One can only say how a particular speech was written. A good example is the speech Stevenson delivered October 9 to a Democratic rally at Kiel Auditorium in St. Louis.

From the beginning it was considered a major speech with national television, and its topic was listed as "Missouri Valley." Early drafts and memos were submitted by Galbraith, Bernard DeVoto, Leon Keyserling, and others. Tufts reshaped them into a draft on the Missouri Valley and the expanding economy. Dissatisfied with his draft, he asked Martin to rewrite it. Martin proposed to incorporate into it a summing up of all positions Stevenson had taken thus far— the speech would be given about halfway through the campaign— a statement of Stevenson's view of the proper role of government, and a vision of the future that would take off from St. Louis' historic position as the gateway to the Western frontier. Martin wanted the speech to become Stevenson's vision of "the New Frontier for America." (The phrase became John F. Kennedy's principal 1960 campaign theme, though unwittingly.) While they were working, Stevenson was traveling. They got the speech to him almost at the

---

nothing. Why, you seceded from the Union in 1860, we whipped the bejesus out of you and dragged you back into the Union; and I intend to treat you like a conquered province, an occupied territory, which in truth is precisely what you are. You prate of your rights. Well, don't you come whining to me about your so-called rights. You deserve nothing, and from me you'll get nothing. So far as I am concerned you have no right to anything, not to the tidelands nor to anything else."

last minute. He delivered it poorly but, worse, it was the wrong speech for the audience—too thoughtful for a rally. It should have been delivered earlier in the campaign (if at all), before the crowds became enthusiastic—October crowds are always hotter than September crowds.[8]

12

Some candidates arrive at a political meeting armed with a speech text, realize the text is inappropriate for the crowd they face, and discard the text and speak extemporaneously. Not Stevenson—he plowed doggedly through his prepared speeches. Thus he disappointed many an enthusiastic audience. Moreover, he refused to speak extemporaneously, even at whistles stops. Most candidates develop a standard extemporaneous speech that they give repeatedly at whistle stops and even to large audiences, getting it firmly fixed in their minds and delivering it with good timing. Stevenson, however, almost always refused to give the same speech twice, even when he was making ten or more a day. As a result, he sometimes seemed not to have mastered the speech and delivered it poorly. Moreover, the effect of his speeches was diffuse, and his campaign lacked the impact of simple repetition. It may explain why Tufts thought little residual impression remained. But repeating a speech bored him, and he feared it would bore the reporters traveling with him. No doubt it would have; but on the other hand many of them complained at the huge quantity of material they had to handle daily.

All these problems, taken together, may explain why so many people, by mid-September, were accusing Stevenson of "talking over the heads of the people." No complaint was more widespread among Stevenson's own supporters. The Elks felt that each person who complained believed he understood the speech but others did not. This was Stevenson's own view. Before the campaign proper began, Stevenson told the Rev. Dr. Graebel, "I want to keep my literary effort on as high a level as I can." Carl McGowan thought that one speech, largely written by Herbert Agar and delivered at the Mormon Tabernacle in Salt Lake City, may have been "over the people's heads" but really amounted to nothing. McGowan thought the rest of the speeches good. "These were things—talking over the heads of the people and his wit—conceived by people to denigrate him." The *Tribune* repeatedly criticized Stevenson's wit, com-

---

[8] A detailed exegesis of the speech is printed in Appendix F.

paring "Adlai the side-splitter" to Abraham Lincoln "the rail-splitter." McGowan has said, "His wit was not as great as it was popularly assumed to be, but it was not as damaging as was believed, either. He always had a risky sense of humor—some of it was not funny at all." Politicians criticized Stevenson for spending time polishing speeches that he should have spent talking with local politicians. McGowan has said, "There's truth and non-truth in that. Yes, he might have inspired a greater effort by the politicians. But Stevenson's peculiar asset was speeches; so maybe it was okay. It's one of those irreconcilable demands on your time. It's too bad—his personality was good and local leaders always liked him." McGowan thought the Elks Club "very successful" and filled with talent. "But Stevenson had an exaggerated idea of what a speech can do. And I must say he did a hell of a lot with speeches."

13

Conservative Republicans viewed Stevenson as either a man dangerously liberal himself or as the captive of the ADA and big labor. Democrats considered Stevenson a liberal. How liberal was he?

On his record, he had taken a strong liberal position on foreign affairs in the Midwest context, leading the fight against isolationism. In domestic affairs, while Governor he had sponsored but failed to pass FEPC and had vetoed the Broyles bill but had pursued conservative fiscal policies and had not liked the drift of power to Washington. His instincts were conservative. Schlesinger considered Stevenson illiberal on civil rights and economic issues but nevertheless a liberating influence. Schlesinger once said, "No one in politics is a creative thinker. But some incite creativity around them. Even FDR was not an original thinker, though he had a questing mind, probably more than Stevenson had. He chose liberals for political friends because he liked them and could learn from them. He questioned the clichés and made people around him think that they could take a fresh look at things. So he was the cause of creativity in others. Kennedy was the same. No one in politics is an intellectual. But Stevenson and Kennedy enjoyed intellectuality. Politicians live in the world of power. Kennedy and Roosevelt relished power. Stevenson understood the world of power better than he conceded. He enjoyed it, it was his world, but somehow the thought of exercising it made him feel guilty." Schlesinger speculated that guilt might spring from the childhood shooting in which Stevenson had been involved. He went on, "The creative politician is the one who picks up fresh ideas and acts as a broker of ideas. They are alert to ideas, they incite them, even though they have to abandon cherished ideas of their own." When Stevenson became a national figure in the Democratic Party, which was dominated by liberals at that time, he had to abandon conservative ideas he had picked up in Bloomington and Lake Forest. He abandoned them reluctantly. More than once during the 1952 campaign Schlesinger protested to Stevenson strongly about John Sparkman's remarks on civil rights. Stevenson seemed unmoved. More than once Schlesinger and others tried to push him into a strongly pro-labor position. But Stevenson seemed convinced that Truman was in trouble because he was regarded as the captive of labor. Repeatedly Stevenson wanted to say in speeches that he himself was not labor's captive, while Schlesinger and others urged him to try to get labor to work for his election. "It depends on who you think your audience is," Schlesinger said, "the people in Lake Forest or the people that are going to work for you. He finally refused to say that he favored repeal of the Taft-Hartley Act. The formula became 'repeal and replace' it." Carl McGowan once said that after the convention several liberal members of the Truman administration came out to Springfield from Washington to discuss their views with the man who might become their leader. Some of them went back to Washington dazed and shocked by what they regarded as Stevenson's conservatism. As the years passed, Stevenson's positions became increasingly liberal. But he never was a dedicated—or even a convinced—liberal ideologue. He remained skeptical.

Dave Bell acted as liaison between Stevenson and Truman. When Stevenson set forth on his first campaign swing, Bell took the speeches to the White House, a diplomatic mission. From time to time Bell checked speeches with David Lloyd or Charles Murphy of Truman's staff. Early in the campaign Clark Clifford, another Truman adviser, met with Stevenson to tell him how Truman had won in 1948.

McGowan has said, "Perhaps Truman's vanity was hurt because Stevenson did not telephone him all the time. But there was no time." At the outset Truman seems to have made every effort to help Stevenson. On August 16, four days after Stevenson had visited him, Truman told him, "I am more than happy that you enjoyed the visit to Washington and that it was of some service to you. The only objective that I have in mind is to see that you are elected President of the United States." He said he feared the Republicans would try to make foreign policy a "partisan" issue. He went on, "I've been in elective public office thirty years and I think there comes a time when every politician, whether he be in a County,

State, or Federal office, should retire. Most of them find it impossible to do that—they either have to be carried out feet first or kicked out." Stevenson did not get around to answering for a week. He said he was "a little alarmed" at the Republicans' efforts to make foreign policy a partisan issue. "Little by little I am learning the ropes—and I hope the knots! It has been difficult for me and I hope you will be patient with me and also point out my mistakes. There will be many I am afraid."

One mistake had already occurred. The editor of the *Oregon Journal* of Portland, Oregon, had asked Stevenson, "Can Stevenson really clean up the mess in Washington?" "The mess in Washington" was a Republican campaign slogan. Carl McGowan had drafted a reply for Stevenson to sign: "As to whether I can clean up the mess in Washington, I would bespeak the careful scrutiny of what I inherited in Illinois and what has been accomplished in three years." The *Journal* published it. Republican leaders gleefully picked it up, saying that Stevenson had admitted that the Truman administration was riddled with corruption. It became a national issue. President Truman, asked about it at his press conference, said: "I have no comment, because I know nothing about any 'mess.'" Stevenson called Truman to apologize. Truman reassured him graciously. McGowan thought the incident a mistake and took the blame for it. He had dictated the letter and failed to put the phrase into quotation marks or say "what you characterize as the mess in Washington." At the time, people in the campaign thought the fault lay not with McGowan but with the typist, who omitted the quotation marks.

Stevenson tried to divorce himself not only from Truman but from the architect of Truman's foreign policy, Secretary of State Dean Acheson. In the campaign, Stevenson gave Acheson's Korean policy all-out support—but he never, or almost never, mentioned Acheson's name.

Carl McGowan once said, "It's unfortunate if Truman and Acheson look back upon the campaign with bitterness. Stevenson gave the Administration's controversial foreign policy, for example, 100 per cent support. He never mentioned cabinet officers by name, however. This was a deliberate tactic to counter the charge that Stevenson was hand-picked by Truman to continue his administration unchanged. The 'time for a change' issue was tough enough without this. We thought it was more important to defend policies than persons. We assumed that the persons involved were sufficiently sophisticated politically to see what was up, and to accept it as conceived solely as something that might help to win the election."

George Ball has said, "Acheson was absolutely dedicated to

Harry Truman. He felt in 1952 that, one, Stevenson never said a word about Acheson and, two, Stevenson was trying to disassociate himself from Truman. To Acheson this was treason. So Acheson thought that Stevenson had no gonads and wouldn't stand up and fight. They should have been friends—they were both stylists and believed in lots of the same things." Although they had had personal ties for many years, Acheson broke with Stevenson subsequently, and once said, "You will not find me an admirer of Stevenson."

Several years later Arthur Krock wrote that during the 1952 campaign "an important Stevenson manager" suggested to Truman that it would be helpful if Secretary Acheson were to resign "and got a violent reaction from Mr. Truman." Stevenson asked Steve Mitchell if this was true. Mitchell said that, after consulting Stevenson carefully, he had twice suggested to Truman that Acheson state publicly that his government service would end with Truman's term and he would not accept reappointment by Stevenson. Truman hesitated to suggest it to Acheson because he was "as touchy as a high school girl" about his position, according to Mitchell. Mitchell tried again through two other men, without result. Shortly after the campaign ended, Acheson's wife told Lloyd Garrison that during the campaign a high Democratic Party official had suggested to Acheson that he announce he would retire at the end of Truman's term. Acheson had refused, had been hurt, and would feel better, his wife thought, if he were satisfied that Stevenson had had nothing to do with it. Garrison asked McGowan (though he assured McGowan he need not reply if Stevenson would prefer not). McGowan consulted Stevenson, then gave Garrison "unequivocal assurance" that no such mission was undertaken by anyone with Stevenson's "prior knowledge or approval." By 1960, Acheson seems to have moderated his resentment of Stevenson, for he later told McGowan he had worked to get Stevenson nominated for President that year.

14

Stevenson was getting a bewildering amount of advice, some from members of the Truman administration, some from other Democratic leaders around the country, some from his own friends. Not all pleased him. Jane Dick passed on some criticism of him she had heard and on August 8 he replied, "Frankly your letter amazes me. This is the first time I've ever detected that the Tribune line—the ex-

treme partisan line—could affect your judgment. . . . That ———
and ——— [two friends whose names Mrs. Dick has suppressed]
et al could fall for the idea that I was a puppet in the hands of Wyatt
& a young writer Schlesinger is exactly the equivalent of the idea the
opposition will also spread that I'm a puppet of Truman. . . . It
makes me despair of 'friends,' just as you say. . . . Forgive me—
but just remind them and yourself that *I'm* the candidate and if
they don't know me & what I stand for and I thought had demonstrated then perhaps Eisenhower is their best bet who doesn't know
what he stands for and is surrounded with people that have neither
depth of intellect or convictions that my friends have ever shown any
affinity for."

Carroll Sudler of Chicago told Stevenson he had supported Eisenhower but now was switching to Stevenson because he had seen
what one man, Stevenson, could do to change the whole tone of
government. He praised a Stevenson speech deploring the drift of
power to Washington. He would work in the Volunteers. But many
of Stevenson's well-intentioned Lake Forest friends, inexperienced
in politics, sometimes caused problems for his staff throughout the
campaign. Once during the campaign a friend excitedly told Jane
Dick he had just heard that the Republicans were spreading a
rumor that Stevenson was a homosexual. He declared he would
issue a statement denying it. Mrs. Dick told him not to, it would
only make gossip worse. Stevenson was right in thinking he must
appeal to the millions of "independent" voters—those voters who
swing from one party to another, producing, for example, the extremely close election of 1960 and the enormous landslide of 1964.
But he was wrong if he conceived, as at times he seemed to, the "independent voter" as being a thoughtful affluent educated resident of
Lake Forest.

In early August the attacks on Stevenson's defense of Alger Hiss
began. A Maryland lawyer told him that Governor McKeldin had
"blasted" Stevenson and offered to rebut McKeldin. McGowan
sent him the facts. Stevenson thought Dulles' prominence in the
Eisenhower campaign would make it impossible for Republicans to
attack Stevenson or Hiss—Dulles himself had been associated with
Hiss. Stevenson was wrong.

Civil rights continued to percolate. Governor Byrnes of South
Carolina carefully explained his position to Stevenson. He had told
the state Democratic Convention that the Democratic electors on the
South Carolina ballot should be pledged to Stevenson and Sparkman.
Inasmuch as electors pledged to Eisenhower might not be on the
ballot, a slate of independent electors should be put on it. If the

election were held today, he himself would vote for Stevenson but "with some misgivings" because of the "platform Stevenson had accepted." He added his "genuine personal affection" for Stevenson. Stevenson, thanking him, sought common ground—they were "in complete accord" as to "the concentration of power in Washington." Dorothy Fosdick warned him against being a perfectionist about speeches—sleep and relaxation would in the long run be more productive than phrasing. Written August 20, it was the last complete letter from her that survived in Stevenson's files.

15

A continuing concern of Stevenson and his staff was his former wife. She talked publicly about a book she intended to write "exposing" him; its title would be *The Egghead and I*. (A popular book at the time was *The Egg and I*.) A columnist who saw her later recalled, "[She] said he had no right to run for President, she was going to expose him, he was unfit. I said, 'You can't do that. It will ruin you and not him.'" Vincent Sheean suggested that Ellen be persuaded to leave Chicago or leave the country. Stevenson passed the letter on to Harriet Welling, who, with her usual good sense, said she wished she had kept a count of people who had made the same futile suggestion. A Chicago *Daily News* series of articles on Ellen's relationship with Stevenson contained nothing sensational and indeed quoted her as saying that no ill feeling attended their divorce and she hoped the divorce would not influence anyone's vote. Years later Stevenson told a friend that he thought the divorce had cost him "a number" of votes though not so many as people thought.

A man posing as an FBI agent called on a friend of a member of Stevenson's staff and said he was investigating the homosexuality of Stevenson and the staff. Crude scurrilous literature circulated. Bud Merwin sent Mrs. Ives a piece of it from Bloomington. It called Mrs. Ives "very high-hat," said Ellen had divorced Stevenson because he was incompetent and incapable of supporting her, said he had killed a young girl "in a jealous rage" because she was interested in another boy, said he had been dismissed from school because of poor grades and had never finished Princeton law school (Princeton has no law school), said his political career had been launched by Arvey and Dawson (Arvey was "Communistically saturated and a scoundrel," Dawson was "a Negro, and a Communist"). Merwin and Joe Bohrer ran down the source of the piece, an inconsequential man with, Merwin said, a "reputation as a screwball." Merwin considered answering it in the *Pantagraph* but Bill Blair and Carl McGowan dissuaded him. Members of Stevenson's staff discussed rumors that Eisenhower had been involved with a woman not his wife, and some of them felt that if the Stevenson rumors persisted the Eisenhower rumors should be spread. Nothing was done about it. All in all, the campaign was less contaminated with underground calumny than many.

Stevenson's two younger sons, Borden and John Fell, left with a friend by automobile early in August to visit the John P. Kelloggs in British Columbia. In the fall John Fell returned to Milton and Borden to Harvard but joined their father several times on campaign trips. Stevenson wanted them around him but at the same time did not want to exploit them. Wyatt encouraged them—a candidate in America needs a family. Stevenson's was a lonely campaign.

Dave Merwin visited Eisenhower, and the wire services described the visit, inaccurately, Merwin told Stevenson—he had submitted questions on national defense to Eisenhower and now submitted the same questions to Stevenson. Stevenson replied that he was not offended and said he had neither the competence nor the time to answer his questions intelligently. Bud Merwin referred to the incident as "that goddam story about Dave." Merwin went on to say, "Believe me, I have been going through some of the worst mental anguish of my lifetime on this question of what the Pantagraph should do in relation to your candidacy." He wrestled with his conscience all fall. Finally on October 18 he wrote to Stevenson, "The enclosed editorial—scheduled to run next Wednesday—is the result of the most painful decision in which I have ever participated. . . . I had desperately hoped that a way might be found for the Pantagraph to justify a switch in its position so we could support you in this election. . . . I've tried to word this editorial with complete honesty and the least possible hurt to you. If you detect anything unfair I hope you'll say so." The editorial said, "This year, for the first time in its history,[9] the PANTAGRAPH will not endorse either candidate in the presidential election. We will not make a choice because we feel that we are much too close to one of the candidates." Stevenson, the editorial said, was qualified for the presidency. At the same time, the *Pantagraph* thought it now time for a change. So it would "sit this one out." Four years later, in 1956, the *Pantagraph,* disillusioned with Eisenhower and feeling Stevenson was free of Truman, endorsed Stevenson.

[9] This was erroneous: the *Pantagraph* had endorsed no one in 1892, when Stevenson's grandfather ran for Vice President.

16

Stevenson opened his campaign unofficially on August 14 on Governor's Day at the Illinois State Fair. In his introduction of Alben Barkley, campaign themes emerged—the argument that change for the sake of change was not necessarily wise, that "there are many fine people in the Republican Party" and he was conducting no "crusade"—Eisenhower's word—to "exterminate" Republicans, and his declaration of independence of city bosses, the CIO, the Dixiecrats, President Truman, Wall Street, and the ADA. "Then next week I'll probably read in a paper that I'm the 'captive' of a girl named Ada." Stevenson deliberately referred to Eisenhower as "the General." Later, probably at Schlesinger's suggestion, he changed it to "the General of the Army." The theory was that most Americans don't like generals and that Eisenhower lacked experience in civil government. But Eisenhower's disarming confession of ignorance of politics overcame these feelings, if they existed; his approach was similar to that of General Ulysses S. Grant's 1868 campaign song: "And now let politicians wait, there's work for men to do."

Five days later, on August 19, Stevenson flew aboard a state-owned plane to the summer home of a Chicago friend, Dr. Clark Finnerud, in northern Wisconsin. Ellen Smith, Dutch Smith's wife, had invited him to Desbarats, but he said he was forbidden to leave the United States. Carol Evans went along, and a Chicago lawyer and his wife were among fellow guests, as were Jane and Edison Dick. The house was located in a pine forest, and a newspaper reported that Stevenson's bedroom had a glass ceiling through which one could observe the stars. Stevenson held a press conference there. Asked for comment on President Truman's recent remark that Stevenson must run on the Roosevelt-Truman record, which made Truman "a key figure" in the campaign, Stevenson replied, "Of course, I approve and applaud the vast accomplishments for the public good under Democratic leadership." He said he was pleased to read that "the General" considered those social gains now above politics. He said Truman "or any President" was "a key figure." He was asked for comment on Eisenhower's recent remarks that "terrible blunders" had preceded the Korean War but if the United States had not reacted as it had "we might have been involved in a far more serious thing"; that "some people" advocated all-out war with China but "no one I know of has presented any pos-

sible plans for attacking China." Stevenson replied that he was glad
"the General" had "approved" President Truman's action in Korea.
The Chicago *Tribune,* which had favored Taft's candidacy and was
still not reconciled to Eisenhower's, poked fun at Eisenhower's "five
star syntax."

Stevenson returned to Springfield that night, August 22, a Friday.
He was due to go East for the American Legion speech five days
hence. Meanwhile he faced several policy decisions which could not
be postponed, including developing positions on offshore oil (often
called tidelands oil), Israel, and labor. Next day, August 23, Governor Allan Shivers of Texas was coming to see him about offshore
oil. Although soon nearly forgotten, offshore oil was an important
issue in 1952, particularly in Texas, Louisiana, and California.
Whether the states or the federal government owned the oil de-
posits thought to exist beneath submerged lands off the coast had
been in controversy for years. President Truman, by proclamation
and executive order, asserted federal jurisdiction over submerged
areas beyond low tide. Truman acknowledged that the states owned
the actual tidelands, land covered by high tide; what he federalized
were mineral resources of the continental shelf, submerged land con-
tiguous to the continent and covered by no more than 600 feet of
water. The states, however, disputed his doctrine. Texas claimed it
was entitled to territory extending into the sea three Spanish leagues
—about ten and a half miles—on the historical ground that the an-
nexation statute permitted Texas to keep the public lands of the Republic of Texas, originally measured as the Mexicans had measured
them. Other coastal states claimed the three-mile limit. Truman's
Attorney General had brought suit in 1945 to force a test case. In
1947 the United States Supreme Court had held that the federal
government had "dominant rights" and reaffirmed the principle twice
in 1950. Congress, urged on by the oil lobby, passed a resolution
giving the title to Texas, Louisiana, and California. On May 29,
1952, Truman vetoed the resolution, declaring it would unwisely
and improperly transfer an asset belonging to all the people of the
nation to a few coastal states. The issue promptly became one for
the national campaign, and it became entangled publicly with other
emotional issues, such as "states' rights" which, at that time, was
often a Southern euphemism for "white supremacy." And it became
entangled in the Byzantine politics of Texas.

Governor Shivers of Texas led the 1952 fight for state ownership.
On July 30 he asked Stevenson for an appointment to discuss "our
Tidelands." Stevenson replied cordially, said he was "woefully igno-
rant about the Tidelands business," would welcome Shivers' views,

and invited him to Springfield in the hope that "sober consideration" would remove "some of the passion" from this issue. In the following weeks Stevenson sought the views of various people and also received much unsolicited advice. Toward the end of August so strained had relations become between Stevenson and regular Texas Democrats that about a hundred pro-Stevenson Democrats gathered in Austin to plan a campaign secretly—they were convinced that Shivers and the regular Democrats would do nothing for Stevenson. Stevenson, examining the complexities of the tidelands question itself, discovered that Mexico had a strong claim to some of the area in question. And there were other possible political ramifications— the Chicago *Daily News,* for example, asked Stevenson to explain how he would, if elected, differentiate between submerged lands in the Great Lakes and the oceans. Moreover, the question seemed to go to Stevenson's integrity and to his relations with Truman: would he seek tidelands state votes and repudiate the Truman position, or would he turn his back on Texas and uphold Truman and the Supreme Court? Finally, Eisenhower had come out in favor of state claims.

With some difficulty, Jack Arvey arranged an appointment for Shivers with Stevenson on Saturday, August 23. In preparation for the meeting, McGowan drafted a statement. In McGowan's mind the case had been closed long ago, ever since the Supreme Court had held for the federal government. McGowan said later, "Shivers was no friend of Adlai." Shivers spent most of August 23 with Stevenson. He left empty-handed: Stevenson issued a statement saying that he would "accept and abide by" the Supreme Court decision, that the present question was merely one of "wise national policy in the disposition of the national assets," that he did not think it wise to cede national assets to the states, and "I agree, therefore, with the President's veto." In a paragraph that might have given Shivers some comfort had he chosen to take it, Stevenson went on, "At this moment there is a legislative stalemate, however, which is harmful to both the states and the nation. It should be broken by enactment of legislation providing equitable arrangement for the administration of these lands and the disposition of their proceeds." Thus he did not close the door to legislation that might rebate to Texas and other states a part of the proceeds from the lands. He added, "Governor Shivers naturally found my views disappointing" but recognized "that I should reach my conclusions honestly" and according to "my best judgment regardless of the possible effect on electoral votes. Whatever our differences of opinion, I am sure I am in agreement on this principle with all my friends in Texas, among whom I continue to include Governor Shivers." Back in Texas, Shivers said he could not vote for Stevenson because of his stands on offshore oil and civil rights. (He and Stevenson had barely discussed civil rights.) Price Daniel, Texas Attorney General and Democratic candidate for the Senate, said he would not campaign actively for Stevenson because he had followed the "Truman line" on tidelands. Lyndon Johnson, according to James Rowe, Jr., a shrewd Democratic politician and Stevenson supporter, was "also somewhat cross about the Governor's stand on Tidelands Oil because he thinks he unnecessarily gave Shivers a weapon to beat Johnson over the head in Texas." A little later Stevenson, preparing to campaign in Texas, talked to Speaker of the House Sam Rayburn, sent him copies of his tidelands statement and a speech on civil rights, invited suggestions, and said he thought efforts had been made to reassure oil men that their existing leases would not be repudiated.

In retrospect, McGowan thought Stevenson's position on tidelands had mainly cost him Texas money. "The Texas national committeewoman was for Stevenson—she was an oil lady—and she hoped he'd come out the other way. She couldn't do anything for him after the Shivers interview." He laughed. "I remember getting a letter one day from Beeville, Texas, in a plain envelope and I opened it and a check fell out on the floor. The letter said that the Communists had taken over the country and the Democratic Party was infiltrated, but because he was a Democrat he was enclosing a contribution. I didn't think it worth reaching down to pick it up, but I did and it was a check for $5,000." Wealthy Texas friends of the present author refused in strong language to support Stevenson. Schlesinger thought Stevenson's handling of the issue good. The night after the Shivers meeting, McGowan, weary, visited the Elks Club and said that at last it was settled, though Stevenson might lose Texas as a result. Bell said, "If we lose Texas we'll lose the election —a shift of 15 per cent of the vote is needed there, and if that many shift it means a real drift to Eisenhower and enough of a shift elsewhere to win for him." Bell, after studying Stevenson's statement, said, "He sure runs a tough campaign." He meant Stevenson need not have endorsed Truman's veto; he need only have stood by the Supreme Court decision. Bell thought the statement wholly consistent with Stevenson's character and principles. "But the question is, can he make it that way?"

17

On the evening of Tuesday, August 26, there was an air of excitement in Springfield. Tomorrow at 6 A.M., Stevenson would leave for the East on his first campaign trip. The Leland Hotel was crowded with staff and press people, all happier than in weeks, relieved that at last the campaign proper was getting started (although the "official" opening was still Labor Day in Detroit). Stevenson, dining at the Mansion with Blair, McGowan, Schlesinger, Carol Evans, and Ernest Ives, seemed cheerful and unconcerned. He did seem upset by Eisenhower's belligerent foreign policy speech to the American Legion national convention in New York setting forth John Foster Dulles' line of "liberation" of peoples in the Soviet satellite countries of East Europe. Not all of Stevenson's speeches for the trip were finished, and Bill Flanagan had to provide typing and mimeographing materials for the chartered airplane. Early next morning Stevenson took off. McGowan and Schlesinger went with him.

Stevenson's first stop was the Legion convention, the most difficult and important speech of the trip.[10] The day was beautiful in New

---

[10] The speech had gone through many drafts. More than two weeks earlier, Archibald MacLeish had said that the importance of the speech and the audience dictated the subject: patriotism, the ideal which held the Legion together but the mask concealing much evil, including Senators McCarthy and Jenner. Stevenson agreed and suggested adding "the idea of Americans first and veterans second" and material on peace and national security. In a revealing note on his approach to speeches, he told MacLeish, "I get so sick of the everlasting appeals to the cupidity and prejudice of every group which characterize our political campaigns. There is something finer in people; they know that they *owe* something too. I should like to try, at least, to appeal to their sense of obligation as well as their avarice." He sent MacLeish a copy of his veto of the Legion-backed Broyles bill. MacLeish produced a draft. Stevenson had also asked Professor Walter Johnson to try a draft independently, and he did, submitting it on August 17 to Schlesinger. Meanwhile, at the Elks Club, Schlesinger and Tufts had been working on drafts. They submitted their second draft to Stevenson on August 18. He made a few desultory changes. They reworked it three times, introducing some of MacLeish's language on patriotism. Stevenson himself worked hard on Draft 5a, which was submitted August 22 after extensive work by all the Elks. He inserted the line "After all, we are Americans first and veterans second," a strong denunciation of Communism, and a passage to balance MacLeish's denunciation of unnamed "inquisitions." As work progressed, the speech grew sharper and more and more politically charged, draft by draft. Stevenson worked carefully on Draft 6, inserting, "The anatomy of patriotism is complex. But surely intolerance and public irresponsibility cannot be cloaked in the shining armor of true patriotism. Nor can the denial of the right to hold ideas that are different—the freedom of man to think as he pleases. To strike freedom of the mind with the fist of patriotism is an old and ugly subtlety." He also wrote in longhand, "The tragedy of our day is the climate of fear in which we live, and fear breeds repression." All this survived the final Elks Club rewrite, Draft 7, which became the speech as delivered. Stevenson made few changes in his reading

York. Observing the waiting police escort at the airport, Stevenson remarked, "It is hard to tell whether I am going to be received or arrested." The crowd at the Legion convention was large. Eisenhower had spoken two days earlier, outlining what *Life* called a "new foreign policy," the policy of liberation, and had marched in the Legion parade, as had Nixon running for Vice President with Eisenhower. The Legion had adopted resolutions calling for the removal of Dean Acheson, an end to the Manchurian "sanctuary" of Chinese Communists fighting in Korea, military victory in Korea, improved relations with Spain, a strengthened NATO, and a warning to Russia to stay out of the Middle East and Southeast Asia. It was in this atmosphere that Stevenson delivered his speech in huge Madison Square Garden, looking far less comfortable than Eisenhower in his Legionnaire's cap. He expressed his "warm respect" for Eisenhower's "military achievements," described his own World War I experience as "a worm's eye view," suggested he had made important decisions in World War II, praised the Legion's past efforts "to awaken America" to the need for preparedness to assume her proper role in the world rather than retreat into isolationism, and then launched into his speech on patriotism. Patriotism, he said, was not "short, frenzied outbursts of emotion, but the tranquil and steady dedication of a lifetime." It meant putting country before self. This excluded lobbying by special interests. Stevenson said he had in the past resisted pressures from special organized groups, including veterans, when they conflicted with the public interest; he would do so again.

Patriotism, he said, should never be used as a club to attack other Americans. "What can we say for the self-styled patriot who thinks that a Negro, a Jew, a Catholic, or a Japanese-American is less an American than he?" Moreover, some men proclaimed themselves patriots, then for political reasons attacked the patriotism of public servants—even including General Marshall. This was "the last refuge of scoundrels. . . . To strike freedom of the mind with the fist of patriotism is an old and ugly subtlety. . . . Most all of us favor free enterprise for business. Let us also favor free enterprise for the mind."

Many of the threats to our freedoms today, he said, arose from "a healthy apprehension" about Communism. He protected his flank:

---

copy, none of substance. The final draft was an amalgam of Stevenson, MacLeish, McGowan, and the Elks Club, with biting language from Schlesinger and Galbraith. Nothing survived from the two Walter Johnson drafts. Only one paragraph from MacLeish's original draft survived virtually intact. But the basic theme, and the approach to it, were his.

"Communism is abhorrent. It is the strangulation of the individual; it is the death of the soul. Americans who have surrendered to this misbegotten idol have surrendered their right to our trust. And there can be no secure place for them in our public life. Yet, as I have had occasion to say before, we must take care not to burn down the barn to kill the rats," almost a direct quotation from his Broyles bill veto. Too often "sinister threats" to the Bill of Rights were concealed under "the patriotic cloak of anti-Communism. . . . There is no justification for indiscriminate attacks on our schools and the sincere, devoted, and by no means overpaid teachers who labor in them. If there are any Communist teachers, of course they should be excluded, but the task is not one for self-appointed thought police or ill-informed censors."

Near the end he launched a paragraph of MacLeish's rhetoric: "When an American says that he loves his country, he means not only that he loves the New England hills, the prairies glistening in the sun, the wide and rising plains, the great mountains, and the sea. He means that he loves an inner air, an inner light in which freedom lives and in which a man can draw the breath of self-respect."

Then, "Men who have offered their lives for their country know that patriotism is not the fear of something; it is the love of something. Patriotism with us is not the hatred of Russia; it is the love of this Republic and of the ideal of liberty of man and mind in which it was born and to which this Republic is dedicated."

It was a remarkable speech, given the occasion and the climate of the times. The Legion was politically rightist, inclined to sympathy with red-hunts at home and military conquest of Communism abroad. Many of its members had applauded McCarthy and Jenner. A far safer speech for Stevenson would have been one on defense policy. David Lawrence, in the New York *Herald Tribune,* said Stevenson "may have pulled the biggest 'boner' of his Presidential campaign" by taking a "soft" line on Communism and embracing "the 'Left Wing' line that freedom of thought is endangered by the effort being made to rid our government of Communistic influences." A few days later Nixon declared that Stevenson had "made light of the menace of communism" and "demonstrated a shocking lack of understanding" of the problem of subversion.

Stevenson's followers thought the speech a great success. McGowan, looking back years later, called it "the best day of the campaign." The immediate audience responded well. More important, Stevenson reached the national audience with a high-level speech that stamped him as a man of courage, unafraid to tell his audiences what they did not want to hear. McGowan said, "It did a lot to create the idea of a new kind of man. You were not going to get those Legion votes anyway, so you might as well get credit for courage." New York City responded to Stevenson as many places did not. McGowan has said, "Whatever may have been that speech's impact upon the Legionnaires—and it was surprisingly favorable—it set that cynical and sophisticated town by the heels." New York's long and lasting love affair with Stevenson really began that day.

That evening Stevenson motorcaded to northern New Jersey, and the *Herald Tribune* reported that his motorcade went ninety miles an hour on the New Jersey Turnpike, where the limit was sixty, and seventy miles an hour on other highways where the limit was between twenty-five and fifty. At Freehold, a car in the motorcade killed a dog. Stevenson later wrote a letter to its owner expressing his "deep regret." It was a nightmare of the staff that someday a motorcade would kill somebody—all too often the cars were driven by inept volunteers. Stevenson spoke to a Democratic rally at Jumping Brook Country Club near Asbury Park, New Jersey, attacking the "divided" Republican Party as unable to govern, declaring the country was well off after twenty years of Democratic rule, warning that the future's problems were complex and difficult, and praising at length the Democratic senatorial candidate, Archibald Alexander. Next day he gave three speeches in New York. The New York Volunteers gave a lunch for him in the Grand Ballroom of the Waldorf Astoria Hotel sponsored by, among others, Lloyd Garrison, Sam Rosenman, Robert Sherwood, George Ball, and James Alley, and Averell Harriman introduced Stevenson. Dorothy Schiff, publisher of the New York *Post,* wrote that Tallulah Bankhead, the actress, was there and said "that she never had been so thrilled about a man as she was about Stevenson since she had first met John Barrymore more than 20 years ago." Mrs. Roosevelt sent a message praising Stevenson's courage.

His second speech was to the New York State Democratic Convention. The subject was "equal rights." He praised John Sparkman, whose nomination New York liberals had opposed, as a leader of "the new" South and recited his liberal voting record on housing and other issues. Civil rights, he said, meant equal treatment before the law, equal opportunity for education, employment, and decent living conditions. More than laws was needed. "The fight for equal rights must go on every day in our souls and our consciences, in our schools and our churches and our homes, in our factories and our offices as well as in our city councils, our state legislatures and our national Congress. . . . And this is a job for the East, the North, the West, as well as the South." True, "the problem is more serious" in the South than elsewhere. But "things are taking place in the South today that would have seemed impossible only a few years ago." He believed in strong state and local government. In Illinois he had worked for a state FEPC. The Democratic platform favored a federal FEPC, "particularly, I assume, when states fail to act and inequalities of treatment persist." (The platform said no such thing.) He was "very favorably impressed" by a bill in Congress that created a federal FEPC empowered to act only in states without state FEPCs and gave enforcement power to the courts, not an administrative body. Perhaps the bill could be improved by giving the states a "reasonable" time in which to act. Thus Stevenson on FEPC, mindful of his Southern running mate, determined to say nothing in liberal New York that he could not later repeat in the South. He was equally cautious on the filibuster and he knew it— said, "If there are those who disapprove, I will be sorry but not surprised."

He seemed to be saying they would have to take him as he was. No doubt it was a far weaker statement than the New York Democratic Party would have liked or would have heard from an Averell Harriman. But it was Stevenson, pulled in one direction by his Southern ties and antecedents, by his stubborn insistence that results count for more than oratory, by his instinctive mistrust of big government; pulled in the other direction by Northern liberals, by his own intellectual sense of fair play, by his determination not to take contradictory positions in different parts of the country and, above all, to try to serve as a bridge between what was at that time presented as a question, not of black versus white, but of North versus South, to use the political process to resolve what he (and many others) already recognized as the most divisive issue in modern American political life.

That same evening he gave the New York State convention of the Liberal Party a speech more to its liking. Its subject was faith in liberalism, and it was based almost entirely on a draft by James Wechsler, editor of the New York *Post*. It was an eloquent funny rally speech and contained some of the lines that made Stevenson the darling of the nation's liberal intellectuals. He said, "I hope that alert members of the press will note that I arrived here under my own power. I was escorted, not dragged, to the platform. I am standing on my own feet and, to the best of my knowledge, I have been neither drugged nor hypnotized. I offer these testimonials in advance since, as you know, I am alleged to be in a state of multiple captivity and you either are or soon will be on my list of distinguished jailers.

I have been much interested in the continued debate raging in the newspapers as to whether I am headed left, center, or right. I think it would be more relevant to ask: Is the man moving forward or backward, or is he grounded?"

Of political platforms: "The real question is whether a platform represents the clicking of a ghost's typewriter or the beating of a human heart." The Republicans had shamelessly plagiarized past Democratic platforms, he said. "The season when Republican hearts regularly throb with such thoughts is, of course, the autumn of a presidential year. This is indeed a truly remarkable interval, a sort of pause in the Republican occupation that should be known as the liberal hour." He handled Eisenhower carefully: "I don't envy the General having to listen to all the conflicting advice about how to treat the slanderers [McCarthy and Jenner] of his dear friend and senior officer, General Marshall . . . the middle-of-the-gutter approach. There is low comedy in this minor Republican spectacle, but there is symbolic tragedy too. For everything the General has accomplished in his great service to his country is imperiled by many men who propose to ride to Washington on his train. They are the men who hunt Communists in the Bureau of Wild Life and Fisheries while hesitating to aid the gallant men and women who are resisting the real thing in the front lines of Europe and Asia. . . . They are, finally, the men who seemingly believe that we can confound the Kremlin by frightening ourselves to death."

He staked a claim to intellectualism: "You of the Liberal Party will perhaps understand me best when I vigorously disclaim infallibility. For it seems to me that an authentic humility, an awareness of the complexity of men's choices, a tolerance for diverse opinions, and a recognition of the need for brave experimentation are the heart of any liberal faith." On the filibuster he said, "I yield to no man, if I may borrow that majestic parliamentary phrase, in my belief in the principle of free debate, inside or outside the halls of Congress. The sound of tireless voices is the price we pay for the right to hear the music of our own opinions. But there is also a moment at which democracy must prove its capacity to act. Every man has a right to be heard; but no man has the right to strangle democracy with a single set of vocal cords."

He closed: "The challenge to all of us is to prove that a free society can remain free, humane, and creative, even when it is under heavy and ruthless fire; that it can combat poverty, injustice, and intolerance in its own midst, even while resisting a monstrous foreign despotism. . . .

"We shall be accused of idealism or some such crime for projecting so optimistic a vision. To which the only truthful answer is that we are guilty. This is not to say that we guarantee a happy ending; it is only to say that we retain our confidence in man's ability to achieve the triumph of decency and compassion in our lifetime.

"After all, there was a man named Hitler, and it looked for a while as if he were invincible. Yet we despised and decadent peoples are still talking—and he hasn't made a speech in seven years. . . . So let the demagogues beware. I believe we are living in the twilight of the totalitarian gods; beyond the fury and turmoil of our time lies an horizon of new hope for embattled humanity. With liberal faith, with cool heads, with warm hearts, we shall make that hope real for our nation and for our century, and I thank you from the bottom of my heart."

18

It had been his first foray into the East, and a highly successful one, establishing him on the national scene as an eloquent, funny, courageous liberal. He told reporters he was "very much pleased" with the trip. John Crosby, radio and television editor of the *Herald Tribune,* wrote that Stevenson was "a television personality the like of which has not been seen ever before." He was setting a pace that would be hard to maintain. "The speech before the Liberal Party might be taken as a model of televised political oratory . . . delivered to the accompaniment of an almost continual gunfire of laughter." President Truman told Stevenson the Legion speech "rang the bell": "We have the Republicans on the run," and he repeated his offer to do whatever Stevenson wished. Stevenson sent Lewis Douglas several of his speeches on foreign policy. Douglas responded by saying he would support and assist Eisenhower.

On September 1, Labor Day, Stevenson went to Michigan to officially open the campaign, a gesture to organized labor. He started in the morning at Grand Rapids, Republican territory, with a speech praising the late Republican Senator Arthur Vandenberg and the bipartisan foreign policy he had supported. Then he went to the traditional Democratic labor rally in Cadillac Square in the heart of Detroit. In Michigan the Democratic Party was to a great extent dominated by the United Auto Workers, led by Walter Reuther (as the Republican Party was largely dominated by automotive management). The day was hot, the huge square only partly filled by a crowd which police estimated, probably generously, at 30,000. Here Stevenson had to face the issue of the Taft-Hartley Labor Relations

Act. No issue of the campaign vexed him more, no speech was more heavily rewritten, on none did he and McGowan work harder. The basic draft was Wirtz's and it included several key phrases that stayed in virtually intact—a description of Taft-Hartley as "a tangled snarl of barbed wire law," and "I don't say that everything in that act is wrong; I don't think it is. I don't think it was a 'slave labor act,'" which was precisely what Reuther and other labor leaders were calling it. And, "I do say that it was a politically inspired legislative act and that as such we ought to wipe it out and start over," the closest Wirtz thought Stevenson would come to meeting the unions' demands that he call for "repeal." By the time Draft 5 went to Stevenson, the sentence declaring that Taft-Hartley was not a "slave labor" law had been deleted at the Elks; Stevenson restored it.

Governor G. Mennen Williams introduced him as a "great friend of labor." He started lightly, saying he was "a fugitive from a sweat shop" in Springfield, where "the speed-up is in full force," introducing Borden and Adlai III, pointing out Adlai's boot-camp haircut: "He's a private in the Marine Corps and he looks to me like he escaped from a chain gang." Then he said he had come to talk about the relationship between the Democratic Party and "the working people" and plunged straight into this passage: "Contrary to the impressions fostered by some of the press, you are not my captives, and I am not your captive. On the contrary, I might as well make it clear right now that I intend to do exactly what I think right and best for all, for all of us—business, labor, agriculture—alike. And I have no doubt that you will do exactly what you think at the election." He labored the point for several paragraphs. Then he listed three "sets of common interests"—equality of work opportunity for everyone, control of inflation, and the process of collective bargaining. After dealing with the Taft-Hartley law,[11] he outlined five "general prin-

[11] On Taft-Hartley, he used this language:

"The only legitimate purpose of a federal labor relations law is to make private bargaining work better. And that purpose has not, in my judgment, been served by the Taft-Hartley Act.

"Now, in 1947, we needed some revisions of the old Wagner Act. We needed some new rules for labor peace. Well, we got a new law all right— a tangled snarl of legal barbed wire, filled with ugly sneers at labor unions and built around the discredited labor injunction.

"I don't say that everything in the Taft-Hartley Act is wrong, it isn't. And moreover, I'll say frankly that I don't think it's a slave labor law, either. But I do say that it was biased and politically inspired and has not improved labor relations in a single plant.

"We must have a new law and my conclusion is that we can best remedy the defects in the old law by scrapping it and starting over again. What

ciples" as the basis for a new labor relations law.[12]

Stevenson took occasion to lecture the union members: "And speaking of industrial democracy, let me say that you, too, have a responsibility to participate in the affairs of your unions. The union exists for your benefit. If there is anything wrong with it, if you don't approve of the officers, if you don't like the union's policies, if there are racketeers or Communists, then it's up to you and your fellow members to do something about it. . . . But you can't do it by sitting at home and complaining." He closed as the apostle of labor peace: "It's hard to remember that here in Detroit fifteen years ago a mighty industry was paralyzed, and fighting in the streets between bitter men was an imminent possibility. Today the automobile companies and the workers have a five-year contract, giving the nation an assurance of labor peace infinitely firmer than any Congress could ever supply."

From Cadillac Square, Stevenson went to Hamtramck, an enclave in Detroit populated by persons of East European extraction, and attacked Eisenhower's "liberation" speech on Eastern Europe. "His speech aroused speculation here and abroad that if he were elected some reckless action might ensue in an attempt to liberate the peoples of Eastern Europe from Soviet tyranny." The plight of the people behind the Iron Curtain and the anxieties of their relatives in the United States ought not become a "false campaign issue. Even if votes could be won by it, I would not say one reckless word on this matter during this campaign. Some things are more precious than votes. The cruel grip of Soviet tyranny upon your friends and relatives cannot be loosened by loose talk or idle threats. It cannot be loosened by awakening false hopes which might stimulate intemperate action that would only lead your brothers to the execution squads," a warning prophetic of the later uprising in Hungary. "My opponent is an honorable man. . . . I hope that recent statements by him and his advisers have been misunderstood."

On he went to Pontiac. The weather had turned bad, a storm was imminent, and it broke just as he began to speak at Murphy Park. About a thousand persons were huddled together. He said, "I'm not

---

should be retained from the old law can best be written into the new law after the political symbolism of the Taft-Hartley Act is behind us."

[12] The law "must accept labor unions, like employer corporations, as the responsible representatives of their members' interests"; unions in turn "must conform to standards of fair conduct and equal protection in the exercise of their stewardship," including membership and seniority rights regardless of color; the law "must reject the labor injunction"; and "new methods must be found for settling national emergency disputes."

going to talk to you about labor policies. I'm not going to talk to you about foreign policies. In fact, I'm not going to talk to you about a thing, because of this damned rain. Good-by." The crowd laughed and broke up, and Stevenson and his motorcade moved on to Flint for another Labor Day rally. Here he spoke on Social Security and health insurance, poking fun at Eisenhower and arguing that Republican leaders in Congress had been fighting Social Security ever since it was enacted in 1935. It was here at Flint that the famous photograph was taken of Stevenson sitting beside Governor Williams, his legs crossed, a hole in the sole of one shoe.

From Flint he went back to Springfield. It had not been a good day. The Cadillac Square speech had pleased hardly anyone. It was one thing to write off the American Legion vote and gain broader support by kicking the Legionnaires; it was quite different to kick organized labor, the "automatic Democratic" vote. Truman, by contrast, speaking the same day to a labor audience in Milwaukee, said the Republicans didn't seem to pay much attention to Labor Day, recited the Democratic record, denounced Taft-Hartley, and warned that when the Republicans talked about "time for a change" they were really talking about dismantling Social Security and other New Deal-Fair Deal advances. Stevenson, on the other hand, finally yielded to pressure and came out for repealing and replacing Taft-Hartley, but he did it so grudgingly that he earned little credit with labor and, at the same time, he alienated businessmen since he had "swallowed the labor line." His old friend Arthur Krock broke with Stevenson because he thought Stevenson had surrendered to labor; Stevenson resented it. Scotty Reston became Stevenson's contact with the New York *Times*. But even he wrote, the day after the Cadillac Square speech, that Stevenson was "moving slowly but steadily to the Left." The New York *Herald Tribune* gave Stevenson credit for the "courage to admit" that Taft-Hartley was not a "slave labor" law but said that on balance he had adopted Truman's vehement call for repeal.

Newt Minow, who accompanied Stevenson to Cadillac Square, said privately, "That's when, if I had any remaining hope of winning, I knew it was lost. There were plenty of people but there was no real enthusiasm—no real fire—no real confidence. It was a defeated group."

19

Stevenson spent most of the rest of the week in Springfield preparing for his first big Western trip. He wrote to Philip Noel-Baker, his British friend in Parliament, "The Republican talk about 'liberation' in Eastern Europe of late has disturbed me, as it doubtless has you." Senator Dirksen came to Springfield and in a speech to Republican women said he would fight to defeat Stevenson on the "Red, moral and Federal issue as well as the issue of fake prosperity." The *Daily Worker,* the American Communist Party newspaper, said that Stevenson had picked three "corporation lawyers" as his closest campaign aides—Blair, Wyatt, and McGowan—and said that Stevenson's own law partners before he became governor "were considered Chicago's closest parallel to the blue-chip Wall Street firms." Ed Austin thought it a compliment and circulated the clipping to the Sidley partners.

On Thursday, September 5, Stevenson wrote to Alicia Patterson:

Dear—your note just arrived in the midst of ghastly turmoil re speeches, visitors, getting off tomorrow. . . . Now this about Jane!! What's it all about? *Please, please* tell me. She's been my friend of 25–30 years, my indispensable help with Ellen, my loyal supporter in my political adventures. Is her reward for that gossip? —with a devoted husband who is also my close friend of years and three children whom I practically count my own. I would do anything not to harm her after all she has done for me. What have I done? What can I do? . . . Naturally I don't want her to drop out of the campaign in Chicago. . . . Help Help.

Later, returned from his Western trip, he found a reassuring letter from Alicia.

John F. Kennedy from Hyannisport relayed an invitation to Stevenson to attend a "Coke party" when he campaigned in Massachusetts. Bill Blair replied that they would try to go. Blair told Larry Irvin to decline an offer of a $750 dictating machine from a friend—"he just cannot in his present position accept gifts of value." Madame Tussaud's museum in London decided to add a wax figure of Stevenson to its gallery of famous people and sent a questionnaire asking his description and measurements. Carol Evans provided most of his measurements except for that of his "seat" and sent the questionnaire to Blair with a note: "Bill—Sometime during a serious moment in the Gov's life will you measure his 'seat' for Mme Tussaud?" Blair told her to call Stevenson's tailor.

He left Springfield Friday morning, September 5, for the three-and-a-half-hour flight to Denver. Throughout most of the campaign Stevenson and his staff flew aboard planes chartered from American Airlines. The accompanying press, about a hundred strong by Octo-

ber, flew in one or two other DC6s, taking off after Stevenson did
and landing before him so that if he crashed they would be on the
ground to report the accident. Stevenson usually sat in a cabin at
the rear fitted with a desk. With him were McGowan and Bill Blair,
Mr. and Mrs. Ives and sometimes their son Tim, sometimes visiting
notables or candidates, Wyatt or Ball if they were aboard. Sometimes if his cabin became crowded Stevenson slipped into the toilet
and shut the door to work alone on a speech. The Elks aboard rode
up front with the typewriters and mimeograph machines and the
rest of the staff.[13]

The atmosphere was friendly. When Stevenson approved a speech
aloft, one of the secretaries typed it on the speech typewriter (with
oversize type) and another cut a mimeograph stencil. They ran off
copies from the stencil, then assembled the speech—put, say, seven
dinner trays onto seven seats, stacked about 200 copies of each of
the seven pages onto the trays, and then passed them down the line
page by page to a man at the end who stapled them. Frequently
they were still assembling a speech when the plane landed; sometimes Flanagan had to distribute copies to the press while Stevenson was delivering it, which irritated newspapermen—they had no
time to digest the speech and find the heart of it, and they needed
time; for, unlike speeches which contained four-point programs, Stevenson's speeches were structured with complexity. Sometimes the assembly line on the plane was frantic; more than once a visiting Congressman or even a Senator was pressed into service.

The stewardesses, Helen Renk, a vivacious and good-looking
blonde, and Dorothy Berry, a quieter brunette, served coffee, milk,
drinks, and food whenever anybody wanted them. The pilot, Fred
Jeberjahn, was American Airlines' senior pilot, a big steady-eyed
middle-aged man. Once when in mid-flight Jeberjahn left the flight
deck and strolled back through the cabin, only to be followed in a
moment by the first officer, Flanagan cried, "For Christ's sake, who's
steerin'?" They kept the door to the flight deck open during landing,
and after touchdown, while the plane was running the runway, en-
gines reversed; everybody aboard applauded the landing or, if it
was rough, booed. And stared out the window, asking, "How's the
crowd?"—that is, was the crowd to greet Stevenson large? Everybody
else disembarked before he did, hurrying past the reception committee to find cars in the motorcade, and sometimes the crowd mis-

[13] Flanagan and his secretary, Mary Watt; Stevenson's own secretaries,
Carol Evans and Margaret Munn; such other staffers as might be along,
including Phil Stern, Vic Sholis, Clayton Fritchey, and visitors.

takenly applauded Wyatt, whose bald head resembled Stevenson's. Being greeted on the ground, surrounded by local officials and reporters and cameramen, Stevenson always looked confused and harried, a man alone among hungry strangers. He rode in the first car behind the security cars, accompanied by a candidate or an incumbent or both. Behind his car was the "wire car"—a car containing the reporters for the three wire services and sometimes a "pool" reporter, representing the rest of the press, and behind that car a truck carrying photographers. Several official cars followed, containing local and itinerant dignitaries, and behind them came the press buses, then the Stevenson staff cars and the cars of lesser dignitaries. The last cars always jockeyed a good deal to avoid getting directly behind the buses' exhaust fumes. The Elk along usually stayed aboard the plane or in a hangar or airline office, working on the upcoming speeches, or, if he went into town for an overnight stop, worked in his hotel room. Flanagan and his secretary once compared the color of the wallpaper in Albuquerque to that in Oregon —airports and hotel rooms were about all they ever saw of the great nation they crisscrossed.

In Denver, Stevenson had lunch privately with political leaders of the eleven Western states, spent the afternoon at the Brown Palace Hotel, and attended a dinner sponsored by the Volunteers where he delivered a major broadcast on "time for a change" over nationwide radio and television. He was, as always when beginning a speech, nervous. He ran his hand down his lapel. His voice was high-pitched. Instead of looking into the TV camera or at the audience, he looked down at his manuscript, reading his speech. After seeking to identify with independent voters by recalling that they had helped elect him Governor in 1948—"my first venture into political life"—he said demands for change would be coupled with such words as "crime, corruption and cronies; bossism, blundering and bungling; stupidity and socialism." But specifically what did the Republicans propose to change? What would be their new foreign policy, unless it would follow "the reckless suggestion of a war of liberation in Europe." He said, "I confess it's all a little perplexing." His audience seemed perplexed; he did not have them with him. He plowed ahead, asking which party best understood the meaning of change in the modern world. He was glad that Eisenhower "has apparently embraced" the changes wrought by the New Deal but declared that "the Old Guard" of the Republican Party had not— Colonel McCormick of the *Tribune* and Senator Taft. "I shall not argue that it is necessarily fatal to change horses in midstream. But I doubt if it is wise to jump on a struggling two-headed elephant trying to swim in both directions in rough water." (Arthur Schlesinger once said that Stevenson's writers got through the first half of the campaign on the two-headed elephant phrase, the second half on "the Munich of Morningside Heights" which was their description of a meeting in New York between Eisenhower and Taft. They also got a lot of mileage out of the traducers of General Marshall, he said.)

Stevenson attacked "time for a change" as a slogan "designed to get action without reflection" and said, "This may not be too serious when all that is at stake is whether to buy one cake of soap or another, but I don't think it furnishes a sound basis for deciding a national election." Democrats too, including Truman, wanted a change and had proved it by nominating him.

He turned next to corruption. Corruption in high office was "treason," whether committed by Democrat or Republican, and if elected he would expose and punish it as "ruthlessly as I've done in Illinois." And he knew more about crooks' methods than Eisenhower because he had succeeded eight years of corrupt Republican rule in Illinois. "I resent the charges that imply that either my honesty or my fidelity to the public trust would be diminished by election to an office I revere. I had not expected that from the General."

Governor Fuller Warren of Florida told Stevenson, "You really detonated a depth-charge at Denver." But to many the speech seemed defensive, amorphous, and fancy, almost tortured, in its reasoning, less effective than Truman's blunt warnings that the Republicans' idea of change was to destroy Social Security.

From the Volunteers' dinner that night Stevenson went to a Democratic rally in the Denver Municipal Auditorium and delivered a rousing rally speech telling jokes, kidding himself, praising John Sparkman, kidding "the two Republican parties," picturing Eisenhower as a "very distinguished" soldier being torn to pieces by warring Republican factions, forced to fall back on the corruption issue because nothing else pleased both factions. He approached the Truman technique by accusing the Republicans of wanting to scuttle slum clearance, rural electrification, public power, reclamation, and public lands management, "issues that separate the men from the boys."

That first day of the Western trip had been relatively light. The next day, Saturday, September 6, was different. The schedule called for Stevenson to leave the hotel in Denver at 6:20 A.M., fly to Minneapolis, change to a smaller plane, fly to Rochester, Minnesota, motorcade to a farm at nearby Kasson where the national plowing contest was being held, inspect farm equipment, have lunch, deliver a major farm policy speech at 3:30 P.M., fly back to Rochester and Minneapolis, and fly to Cheyenne for a speech to a rally in a high school auditorium, then fly on to Billings, Montana, arriving at the Northern Hotel there at 1 A.M. It was a long day, most of it wasted aloft, for it would produce only two speeches though it would carry Stevenson 2,105 miles and keep him on the move for nearly twenty hours (assuming he stayed on schedule). Stevenson said, "I think I am the only man in history . . . that ever decided to go to Cheyenne [from Denver] by way of Minneapolis."

At Kasson he set forth an agricultural policy. (Eisenhower spoke there that same day.) It was considered one of the most important speeches of the campaign, and Stevenson stuck closely to the prepared text. Although he said, "I am here today as a candidate for public office—not masquerading as a dirt farmer, but as a politician," he went on to describe his antecedents "in the heart of the Farm Belt," to say he owned "farm land" in Illinois, to recount his service with the AAA in Washington during the depression and as Governor "of a great agricultural state." He was running now on the Democratic platform without equivocation. It called for government support of basic agricultural commodity prices at not less than 90 per cent of parity. By contrast Republican policy was "aimed" at 100 per cent of parity. "How good is their aim anyway?"

When Stevenson's plane arrived over Cheyenne, it circled fifteen or twenty minutes so the Cheyenne speech could be finished and mimeographed. At the high school auditorium Stevenson recalled at length vacations he had spent at Wyoming ranches, then said that in Minnesota that day Eisenhower had "made off with the farm plank of the Democratic platform in broad daylight."

He flew on to Billings to spend the night. Next morning, Sunday, the Billings *Gazette* carried a long front-page story on Eisenhower's farm speech at Kasson but its only reference to Stevenson's farm speech was a single sentence in the Eisenhower story: "Gov. Adlai E. Stevenson of Illinois also spoke." Stevenson had a private breakfast that morning with Montana party leaders, attended the Presbyterian church, and after lunch flew to Lewiston, Idaho. The Lewiston stop was on the private advance schedule but the press thought the stop was made on the spur of the moment because Stevenson wanted to attend a rodeo. He landed and drove around the arena in an open car followed by a posse of cowboys, one of whom lassoed him. He complimented the cowboy and put on a ten-gallon hat and said, "This is the first fun I've had since I got into this thing." He and his staff had headed for the Northwest determined not to let anybody put an Indian headdress on him but resigned to cowboy hats.

His plane headed for Portland, Oregon, and, en route he presided over a birthday party for Margaret Munn, bringing the cake down the plane aisle and leading the singing. He spent the night at Portland, spent Monday morning, September 8, working on speeches and meeting separately with labor leaders, farm leaders, Volunteers, and Democratic Party leaders. He told a longshoreman, "They tell me I laugh too much. I don't see how in hell you could do this job without laughing about it occasionally."

He spoke at a lunch given by Oregon newspaper editors, publishers, and radio broadcasters at the Benson Hotel. After paying tribute to the objectivity and fairness of most newspapers in their news columns, he said that in their editorial columns "the overwhelming majority of the press is just against Democrats . . . automatically, as dogs are against cats." He said, "I am, frankly, considerably concerned when I see the extent to which we are developing a one-party press in a two-party country," a phrase that became widely known. He elaborated it, not with vehemence as Truman had in 1948, but with reasoned argument.

He answered questions from the editors. One asked whether, after the Korean War ended, the United States should recognize the People's Republic of China. "I must say, in response to that, that it would seem to me there would be very considerable objection, and perhaps of long duration, to that recognition. On the other hand I point out to you that once we have resolved our difficulties with our enemies in this and in previous wars, notably in the case of Italy, we recognized them rapidly." Should the UN give Peking the permanent Chinese seat on the Security Council? "There again I don't think the time will come when this country will view with any equanimity acceptance of any nation that shoots its way, so to speak, into the United Nations."

From Portland, Stevenson flew to Seattle, Washington, and there drove in an open-car motorcade through downtown streets, then spoke to a Democratic rally in the Civic Ice Arena, a major address on natural resources. He began by telling a story about his grandfather who, campaigning the state of Washington sixty years earlier, had found that the big issue of the day was whether the mountain near Seattle was to be named Mount Tacoma or Mount Rainier. "The views were in emphatic disagreement and it seems that my adroit grandfather solved this difficulty by giving each audience from the rear platform of his train an eloquent speech about the beauties of this close mountain, and then he went on to say, 'And I want everyone to know, all of you good people, that I emphatically agree that this magnificent mountain should be named—' and just then they pulled the whistle on the train and it started with a huff and a puff, and the old man bowed to the audience graciously and they cheered ecstatically." He then spoke at length on the growth of the Northwest and the development of its resources for the benefit of all.

John Fell, who had been visiting friends from Lake Forest in British Columbia, joined Stevenson in Seattle. From there, Stevenson flew on Tuesday, September 9, to San Francisco, met with labor and farm leaders in the afternoon, attended a reception, and, after resting at the Fairmont Hotel overlooking the bay and the beautiful city, went to Veterans' Memorial Auditiorium to deliver a foreign policy speech, broadcast live over the CBS national radio-television networks.

At Stevenson's request, Bob Tufts was along to work on this speech. He had intended to go only as far as Denver. But he had no opportunity to talk to Stevenson before Denver—Stevenson worked on the Denver speech almost until he delivered it. After the speech McGowan told Tufts that Stevenson was concerned about the San Francisco speech and wanted Tufts to continue as far as Minnesota. The same thing happened. And again beyond Minnesota—not until he was aboard the plane from Seattle to San Francisco did Stevenson begin to read the San Francisco speech, to be delivered that night. When he finished reading it, McGowan told Tufts, "The Gov thinks this is too pious," and gave it to Tufts, who worked on it and gave it back to Stevenson. Stevenson rewrote it and gave it to the secretaries to mimeograph. The speech, therefore, was mimeographed before Tufts saw it in final manuscript form, which horrified him—he had had no opportunity to consult with Stevenson or to check the final draft for error. As it turned out, Tufts worried needlessly.

This was Stevenson's first major speech on foreign affairs. He said that "my honored opponent" had set forth a ten-point foreign policy program, including three proposals to "throw the Democratic rascals out" and seven which recited the same goals the Democrats had been pursuing for years. But the most powerful wing of the Republican Party would not support the Truman-Eisenhower program. (He did not name Truman or Eisenhower.) Eisenhower had spoken approvingly of foreign trade. But the Republicans in Congress had been trying for years to wreck the Reciprocal Trade Agreements program. "Now then, can a disunited party unite the country for the hard tasks that lie ahead? I don't think it can." America was threatened "as never before." America was "freedom's foremost champion, indeed her shield and sanctuary." War was not inevitable. But if it came, America must have the strength to win. At present, the Soviet Union fixed the level of our defense expenditures and thus our tax rates. The solution was to end the armaments race by negotiation. "Coexistence is not a form of passive acquiescence in things as they are. It is waging the contest between freedom and tyranny by peaceful means." He spoke of the Marshall Plan, NATO, and other efforts to "build patiently for peace" in Europe.

Asia was a different case, he said. "Across the continent of Asia more than a billion of the world's peoples are churning in one of history's greatest upheavals. . . . The causes behind the upheaval are many and varied. But there is nothing complicated about what the people want. They want a decent living—and they want freedom." The Soviet Union posed as their champions while in reality pursuing czarist expansionist aims. It proclaimed its sympathy for the goals of national liberation and independence, promised human and social equality, offered land and two bowls of rice a day. "When we think of Communism we think of what we are going to lose. When many of the Asian peoples think of Communism they think of what they are going to gain." The Communists had failed to incite Western European workers to revolution or to divide the Western Allies. But they might well believe that in Asiatic nationalism they had found the key to world power. With Asia under their control, they could confront "a weakened, frightened Europe" with new resources. "There is active fighting in Malaya and Indo-China. Have we given fitting recognition to the hard, bitter, and prolonged efforts by the British, French, and native Malayan and Indo-Chinese forces? . . . What will the defensive task require of us in these areas? . . . In Korea we took a long step toward building a security system in Asia. As an American I am proud that we had the courage to resist that ruthless, cynical aggression; and I am equally proud that we have had the fortitude to refuse to risk extension of that war despite extreme Communist provocations and reckless Republican criticisms. . . . I believe we may in time look back at Korea as a major turning point in history—a turning point which led not to another terrible war but to the first historic demonstration that an effective system of collective security is possible."

He continued, "It would seem to me that the Republican critics could better demonstrate the good faith of their concern for Asia by doing something about India today rather than talking about China yesterday"—and he spoke at length about developing India, proposing to send agricultural experts, engineers, and other trained people there. "The answer to Communism is, in the old-fashioned phrase, good works—good works inspired by love and dedicated to the whole man. . . . Some will say to you that this is visionary stuff. . . . It was Woodrow Wilson, with his dream of the League of Nations, who was the truly practical man—not the Old Guard who fought him. And in the fateful summer of 1940 it took the vision of a Churchill to see beyond Dunkerque to victory. I say that America has been called to greatness."

California was important and worth fighting for. It was a big state with 32 electoral votes, equal to Pennsylvania and surpassed only by New York. The Republican vice-presidential candidate, Richard Nixon, had gone to the U. S. Senate from California and the Republicans hoped he would help carry the state. Stevenson had ties there too—he had been born there, had written marketing agreements for the AAA there, had worked with the UN delegation there. All his life Stevenson loved California, especially San Francisco.

Politically, California was and is divided into three main areas—the San Francisco Bay area, the Central Valley, and the Los Angeles area; plus San Diego. Stevenson could expect to do well in the San Francisco area. But Southern California was dangerous, more conservative, less sophisticated, considered Nixon country, especially Orange County; and Southern California would cast nearly half the votes in the entire state. The Central Valley was a different problem. Toward its northern end, around Sacramento, its Democrats tended to be liberal, perhaps because of the influence of the three *Bee* newspapers, owned by the McClatchy family, some of the few newspapers to endorse Stevenson. (They did so at least in part because he adopted the orthodox liberal Democratic position on public power and natural resources, issues which the McClatchys considered paramount. Stevenson carried only eight of California's fifty-eight counties; seven of those eight were in *Bee* territory.) But as one moved farther south into the San Joaquin end of the Central Valley, the "Valley Democrats," as they were called, tended to be conservative, many of them transplanted Oakies and Arkies, driven from Oklahoma and Arkansas during the dust storms and depression of the 1930s; and Bakersfield Democrats, some of them oil men from Texas, more conservative than Eastern Republicans. Stevenson therefore had serious problems in California both in the Valley and in the Los Angeles area.

The night of his speech in San Francisco—presidential candidates always seemed to speak on foreign policy in San Francisco—Stevenson stayed overnight at the Fairmont Hotel, one of America's

great hotels and one of its most magnificently situated. He made a
Democrat out of the hotel's owner, Ben Swig, a rich man who lived
in a penthouse atop the hotel and who was named after a Republican President, Benjamin Harrison. Swig remained a friend of Stevenson—and later of his son John Fell—and a contributor and fund
raiser in all of Stevenson's campaigns and later those of other Democrats.

The next day, Wednesday, September 10, Stevenson set out early
in the morning to whistle-stop by train down the Central Valley. It
was a hot dusty daylong trip. Between stops Stevenson tried to work
on speeches on the jolting train. At each stop local politicians got
aboard to ride to the next stop to appear with him or introduce
him. At each stop the crowd would gather around the open rear platform of the ancient observation car, newspapermen would get off
and mingle with the crowd, and Stevenson would speak briefly. He
made eight speeches that day. The train was scheduled to leave San
Francisco at 7:30 A.M. and arrive at Los Angeles at 10:40 P.M.
Each stop was scheduled for ten minutes except Fresno and Bakersfield, which were allotted fifteen minutes each. It was only a half
hour between some stops, an hour or more between others, and the
last five and a half hours, from Bakersfield to Los Angeles, were
entirely wasted. It was not good scheduling.

Even at these brief stops Stevenson insisted on having a prepared
speech text, though he departed from it more freely than usual.
Some candidates have been masters of whistle-stopping—Roosevelt
with his jaunty confident grin and wave and thanks to the crowd and
then move on, Truman with his short blunt "the Republicans will
get you if you don't watch out" speech, Robert F. Kennedy with his
wry jokes at the expense of the crowd and himself and politics itself and then a single hard-hitting slashing point, his straightforward request: "I ask your help in this election." But Stevenson did
not like whistle-stopping, was not comfortable at it, sometimes
seemed almost apologetic, and usually did it poorly.

At the first stop that day, at San Jose, he began, "I have to confess
to you that this is the first whistle stop I ever made. In fact, practically everything I have done for the past several weeks is the first
time I ever did it." He was "flattered indeed by this enormous turnout at such an unconscionable hour in the morning." He spoke without conviction of the Democratic "philosophy." "Be that as it may,
all we can do is to promise you the same conscientious effort to continue this general philosophical approach to the human welfare of
people of all of our groups in the future that you have observed in
the past. We want our government clean, we want it honest, we

want it efficient, we want it responsive to the needs of our people. Basically our greatest responsibility in this generation is peace on earth, as you all know. We feel that we have had a positive program. There have been mistakes, to be sure. There will probably be more mistakes. I suppose mistakes are inevitable in the ordering of any human society. But we can give you our heart, we can give you our heads, we can give you our best. No more than that can you ask of any man."

The train pulled out for Tracy, and here Stevenson said he was "in favor of" the Central Valley water project. Water was at that time the paramount issue in California. The problem was that most of the state's water was in the north while most of its people lived in the south, and to get the water to the south required costly government expenditures supported, in general, by the Democrats and opposed, in general, by the Republicans. Stevenson said that if big irrigation projects threatened to unbalance the federal budget we must go slow. But self-liquidating projects served the public interest "magnificently."

The train turned southward, headed down the Valley into Stanislaus County, a rather conservative area, and stopped at Modesto; and here Stevenson spoke of his experiences in writing marketing agreements for the AAA for Valley crops, defended the Central Valley water projects against Republican attacks, skirted the sensitive difficult issue of price supports for perishable farm products, again accused Eisenhower of having "completely taken over" the Democratic farm platform plank, and said Eisenhower reminded him of an Australian bushman "who got a new boomerang, and he spent the rest of his life trying to throw away the old one." He closed with a characteristic plea for support: "I hope . . . that you will not only register to vote but that you may look with some favor on the Democratic candidates for office come November."

The train stopped briefly at Merced, and again Stevenson spoke of the Central Valley. He also praised Governor Earl Warren, a liberal Republican popular throughout California. As at most stops he was presented with gifts of local products, this time salted almonds and fruit. At Madera, he said, "I say that I am proud of my party. I am. There have been mistakes." It was a basic dilemma of his entire campaign (as it would be of Hubert Humphrey's in 1968: how to identify with the Democratic Party without embracing an unpopular incumbent President and an unpopular war).

The next stop was Fresno, the biggest city in the San Joaquin Valley. He used a favorite line: "I have been thinking that I would make a proposition to my Republican friends. . . . That if they will stop telling lies about the Democrats, we will stop telling the truth about them." He spoke a little longer than at earlier stops but largely on the same topics.

At Tulare he talked about cotton and trade. At conservative Bakersfield he took two positions that were courageous if perhaps impolitic: drew the Democratic-Republican party line sharply on a liberal-conservative basis (to these conservative Democrats) and attacked (to these Democrats of Southern origin) racial discrimination. Characteristically, too, where other candidates loudly predict their own victory, Stevenson said only, "My prospects are improving every moment, I think." So the day ended; he rode the train to Los Angeles and went to bed at the sprawling Ambassador Hotel on Wilshire Boulevard.

Stevenson began his day of campaigning in Los Angeles that Thursday, September 11, with a meeting with party leaders and a visit to his own birthplace. Los Angeles press agents had prepared an elaborate scenario for the visit which said in part:

11:00—Arrival of cavalcade at birthplace.

11:00–11:05—Stevenson dismounts from car in front of walk leading to porch. Crowd and party is held back in order to allow Governor to walk alone up the steps and to the front door. This should be done with reasonable reverence, in such a manner as to give camera men a dramatic shot of an historical figure returning to the place of his birth.

Stevenson is met at the door by Miss Bertha Mott, current occupant of the house who says, "Since I was a little girl, it has been my ambition to fetch a glass of water for a President. May I have that honor now?" (all this in light, friendly vein.)

Stevenson accepts and enters the house. When he enters those outside shout: "We want Adlai" at the same time; those actively participating in the ceremony take their positions on the front porch and, as Adlai comes out (and waves to the crowd) they usher him to his seat on the porch.

11:05–11:07—Congressman Cecil King, master of ceremonies, quiets the crowd and gives a brief history of the house, Adlai's birth and early Los Angeles childhood. He then introduces—

11:08–11:09—Elizabeth Snyder who in short speech reveals that Stevenson's great-grandfather, Jesse W. Fell, was Lincoln's campaign manager. . . .

There was more, much more. When Bill Flanagan discovered it, he ordered all mimeographed copies destroyed but by then newspapermen already had copies. Los Angeles press agents were the bane

of his—and Stevenson's—existence. In Los Angeles more than anywhere else in the nation, political campaigns always resembled
Hollywood extravaganzas. When Stevenson arrived at his birthplace
he ignored the script. Miss Mott greeted him and held a glass of water
in her hand throughout the meeting. Afterward she told the press she
didn't offer it to him "because they," the Los Angeles press agents,
on Flanagan's instructions, "told me not to." Stevenson made a few
brief remarks.

He had two major speeches scheduled that day—one at a Town
Hall luncheon at the Biltmore Hotel, the other at a night Democratic
rally at the Shrine Auditorium. He had been dissatisfied with the
speech prepared for the Town Hall lunch and had wired Newt
Minow back in Springfield, "Please wire text of my speech at
Philadelphia Bulletin forum in 1950 to me at Ambassador Hotel
as quickly as possible. Regards from the weary pilgrims." It seems
incredible that nobody aboard the Stevenson plane had a copy of the
Bulletin Forum speech. Minow telegraphed it.

That night at the Shrine Auditorium, Stevenson spoke on the
American future. In the speech the phrase, "this new America,"
which became "the New America" theme of the 1956 campaign, first
appeared. He also spoke of "new frontiers." The speech was a
thoughtful eloquent statement, hardly capable of setting a Democratic rally in Los Angeles on fire.

He left early next morning, Friday, September 12, for Phoenix,
Arizona, where he lunched with party leaders and spoke to a rally
in the Fox Theater about the two-headed elephant, agriculture, conservation, and natural resources. He gave nearly the same speech
later that afternooon at Tucson, a stop not on his advance schedule.
Then he flew on to Albuquerque to address a Democratic rally in
the National Guard Armory that night, what he called "my last
stop on my first major tour as a presidential candidate; eight states,
thirty speeches—good, bad and indifferent," and said, "I confess I
am tired but I have been having a lot of fun and I am not ashamed
of it."

During the day, across the country in New York, one of those
breaks occurred that occurs in every campaign: General Eisenhower
and Senator Taft conferred at Morningside Heights and afterward
Taft issued a statement announcing his support for Eisenhower: "I
am completely satisfied that General Eisenhower will give this country
an administration inspired by the Republican principle of continued
and expanding liberty for all as against the continued growth of New
Deal Socialism which we would suffer under Governor Stevenson,
representative of the left wingers, if not a left winger himself." As to

foreign affairs, "I cannot say that I agree with all of General Eisenhower's views . . . but I think it is fair to say that our differences are differences of degree." Both, he said, were determined to battle Communism "throughout the world" and to keep expenditures on armament and foreign aid low enough so as not to wreck the economy. Eisenhower had also assured Taft, according to Taft, that he believed in constitutional limitations on executive power, believed in "the basic principles" of the Taft-Hartley law, and favored a limited role for the federal government. In making appointments, Eisenhower would not punish anyone because he had supported Taft.

Many Stevenson partisans, Archibald MacLeish among them, thought Taft's statement astonishing—thought it would lose Eisenhower countless independent votes and erode his whole position. But it was an experienced politician, Jim Rowe, who pounced on the statement immediately and, through Arthur Schlesinger, suggested to Stevenson that he attack at once—and did so in time for Stevenson to insert an attack passage in his Albuquerque speech on the same day Taft spoke. Stevenson said, of the "two-headed elephant": "One head huffs and puffs and announces that it is fighting mad at the Democrats, while the other head claims credit for all of the Democratic achievements of the past twenty years. I understand the elephant put its two heads together today in New York for a peace conference. They must have eaten crow for luncheon. And if they did make peace, I wonder what happened to all of those declarations of undying principle we heard from both sides while they were calling each other nasty names in Chicago—names, by the way, that they usually reserve only for Democrats. Now, after seeing the announcement . . . I am tempted to make a very profound comment: it looks as if Taft lost the nomination but won the nominee."

Schlesinger thanked Rowe: "One of the triumphs of the campaign." Stevenson returned to the theme time and again. It seemed an important turn in the campaign. It gave Stevenson an issue he badly needed and one he could use to attack, thus freeing him from forever defending the Truman record. Taft and Eisenhower were, of course, trying to unite the Republican Party. But the way they did it, the deep bitterness of their earlier struggles, the conviction with which they had asserted principles, the wide gulf between an isolationist Taft and an internationalist Eisenhower, between a conservative Taft and a moderate Eisenhower, dramatized the split in the party. A different candidate from Stevenson probably would have attacked savagely, accusing Eisenhower bluntly of abandoning principle for political expediency. It is in this manner that issues are made. But at Albuquerque, Stevenson hit the issue almost gently, with humor. Soon in his lexicon—and probably from Schlesinger's typewriter—the Taft-Eisenhower conference became "the Munich of Morningside Heights"—a perhaps oversubtle formulation intended to suggest that Eisenhower had appeased Taft's Old Guard wing as Chamberlain had tried to appease Hitler at Munich.

While in Albuquerque, Stevenson found time to visit a hospital to see a law-school classmate, Nelson Wettling. He did not want the visit publicized. It is hard to think of another recent presidential candidate who would take precious time out to do it. It was the kind of act that Stevenson's admirers called noble, that his detractors called foolish.

20

Stevenson returned to Springfield on Saturday to learn that Senator Wayne Morse had announced he would not campaign for Eisenhower. (Later Morse left the Republican Party and became a Democrat.) After dinner that night Stevenson met with Wyatt, McGowan, Blair, Bell, Schlesinger, Galbraith, Jack Fischer, and Syd Hyman to review the campaign. He said the liberal record had been made on the Western trip; now was the time to get back to the middle of the road. "We haven't said a damn thing about cost of government, efficiency, economy, anti-socialism, anti-concentration of power in Washington. The impression is that we are moving more and more to the left. Now I want some good hard licks on the conservative side. I don't want to be euchred out of that position. We mustn't let them pre-empt the position of fiscal responsibility." He wanted to declare his independence of labor at the AF of L convention, and when Schlesinger suggested this might jeopardize AF of L endorsement, Stevenson said, "It seems to me much more important to tell them what I really think than to deceive them in order to get their endorsement."

Stevenson attended Dr. Graebel's church on Sunday and rested afterward. He remained in Springfield, writing letters and speeches and holding a press conference, until the following Thursday, September 18, nearly a week. The Rev. Dr. Graebel had received numerous requests for a statement on Stevenson's religious views and pressed Stevenson for one. A statement was released September 15.

James P. Warburg, Raymond Swing, Samuel Rosenman, Ambassador Eugenie Anderson, President Truman, and a host of strangers congratulated him on his Western trip, Truman writing, "Don't let anybody inveigle you into changing your style of approach on these subjects. I think you are making a campaign that will be successful and I am only urging you to keep it up. . . . The campaign is one of the dirtiest I've been in, from a personal standpoint. . . . But do not let it bother you. It won't bother me. . . . I've had some very constructive conversations with the new Chairman [Steve Mitchell]. He impresses me as a good man and a man of common sense." Carl McGowan said some years later that the first Western trip was a good one. "It had a lot to do with his catching on with people. But I'm not sure it's as important to make two swings around the country as we thought it was."

In a private letter to Harriet Welling, Stevenson seemed far less enthusiastic about the first Western trip: "It has been a hideous strain with such ghastly pressures, but I believe we learned some brutal lessons in the West which will not be repeated." This sounds like more than the usual Stevensonian grumbling. Tufts, who had been on the Western trip, reported that the California whistle stops had been disastrous. Stevenson had been ill at ease and disliked the whole business. As the train slowed down for one whistle stop, Stevenson had sighed and got to his feet and said, "Well, I have to go face my tormentors." Tufts had been shocked; had newspapermen overheard it, they could have crucified him. Reading the whistle-stop speeches years later, one is struck by their great length. (But, then, speeches became shorter in the 1960s. A half-hour televised speech was not unusual in the 1950s. By 1972 it was rare.)

On Sunday, Wilson Wyatt met with about twenty members of the staff to discuss the lessons of the first Western trip and plan the second Eastern trip. They considered abandoning whistle stops altogether but reached no clear-cut decision. Bob Tufts wrote a memorandum on questions for discussion. Would it be possible to keep firmly scheduled at least two weeks in advance? Could the writers know what the audience would be and whether there would be TV and radio coverage? (It makes a vast difference whether a rally is televised. A speech written to please a highly partisan Democratic rally is likely to offend independent home TV viewers; a moderate, reasoned speech calculated to interest TV viewers is likely to bore a partisan rally crowd, leading the press to write that Stevenson cooled off another audience.) Had not Stevenson established his competence on major issues? Should he not now attack the opposition? Was there not some danger that Stevenson would become known as a jokester?

General Eisenhower came to Chicago on Monday, September 15, and, in brief speeches to large crowds in nearby Republican towns, rebuked Stevenson for his humor: "Is there anything funny about the fact that they have fumbled and bungled away the peace and even gotten us into a war in Korea? . . . And I see nothing funny or deserving of wisecracks in federal spending of 85 billions a year —that's crazy!" Senator A. S. Mike Monroney of Oklahoma replied that Eisenhower was "telling America to wipe that smile off its face."

Joseph Alsop, in the Midwest at this time, wrote that, while it was considered Taft country, Eisenhower was making headway, mainly because he was already well known and inspired "warm affection." The slogans "I like Ike" and "time for a change" had helped him, Alsop wrote, for to date he had made but a single "reasonably specific, full-dress discussion of a major national issue," his farm speech—and in that speech he had abandoned the Republican platform and embraced the Democratic plank of high, fixed parity. Stevenson was still "a dim figure," Alsop thought.

On Monday, September 15, Stevenson held a press conference with Wyatt at his side. Wyatt had announced that "a new campaign wrinkle" would be tried out that night: the NBC television network would broadcast a report on the Western trip at 10:30 P.M. while a similar program, using excerpts from Stevenson's speeches, would be broadcast over a Mutual Broadcasting System network. Stevenson told the press that he was looking forward to seeing the TV show: "I have been told that possibly some of you would like to come over to the Mansion to see it, too, on the set we have over there. I should be delighted to have all of you. The trouble is I just made inquiry this morning and that set is in the small room, the library, in which we can get only a few people, and it can't be moved."

It was really incredible that, at the opening of the television age in politics, a presidential candidate should be thus handicapped.

Stevenson then turned to the real reason for the press conference. He had decided that his response at Albuquerque to the Eisenhower-Taft meeting had been inadequate. He now read a formal statement on it. He said the "Great Crusade," as Eisenhower termed his campaign, had become the "Great Surrender." "Hitherto, I have had to address myself to the rival policies of both Republican parties because it was not certain whether Taft or the General would end up in the command post. It now appears brutally clear that Senator Taft has taken over. This puts an entirely new aspect on the campaign and the election. I suspect many people like myself will be genuinely alarmed by the reduction of their differences on foreign policy to 'differences of degree.' . . . Senator Taft says he has not abandoned his views. Has the General abandoned his? And finally, we will welcome the many Republicans whose hopes for new leadership in their party have been dashed." He then announced the schedule of his forthcoming Eastern trip.

The reporters did not let him off lightly. Gone was the good-natured banter of the pre-campaign press conference in July. A reporter asked if the Democratic Party was not as deeply divided as the Republican Party. Stevenson said only on civil rights, a division he did not consider as serious as the Republican divisions. A reporter asked if he thought Senator Richard B. Russell of Georgia would agree with that. Stevenson said he would have to ask Russell. They pressed him—Russell had recently been complaining that Stevenson was moving left. Stevenson said, "I have the utmost personal regard for Senator Russell as a splendid public servant." Did he plan to go into Texas, where Governor Shivers was withholding his support? Stevenson thought so. Was he worried about "the apparent defections in the South," especially Texas and Louisiana? "Not in the least. I expect Texas, Louisiana, and Florida—all of them—to go Democratic, and overwhelmingly." Did this mean he might lose other Southern states? No. But how could he hold the Dixiecrats? He would try. Did he plan, in fact, "any major, extensive campaign" in the South at all? He wasn't sure. "What about supporting the Democratic ticket from top to bottom in every state?" He said, "I can't answer that." What about Senator Byrd of Virginia? "I have the utmost regard for him as a conscientious public servant." "Is the relationship between you and Senator Byrd much different from the relationship between Eisenhower and Senator Taft?" Stevenson said, "I don't know." What about Senator McCarran of Nevada? Stevenson fell back on, "I am afraid you will have to forgive me. In the first place, I must confess to you I have never met Senator McCarran of Nevada face to face, and I just don't know." But they pressed him: "Are you acquainted with his views?" He said, "I am acquainted with his views to some extent, perhaps not as well as I should be." What about his own relations with President Truman? How often had they been in touch? What had been said? Again Stevenson floundered. Had he apologized to the President for having used the phrase "the mess in Washington" in replying to the Portland editor? No, he had sent him the correspondence. Was he "in favor of" the President's current whistle-stop tour to the West Coast? "Well, yes. I am not—he is making his own decisions, and I would certainly approve of whatever he chose to do with respect to his campaign on my behalf." They pushed him on taxes and the budget until he admitted that there was no difference between him and Eisenhower. And then, having been pressed hard, he stumbled badly: A reporter suddenly asked whether as President he would appoint an ambassador to the Vatican. Stevenson said, "I think I will not propose the appointment of an ambassador." Why not? "I think the matter in this country has become—the feeling in this country is that it constitutes an official recognition of a religion—of a denomination—and this is highly incompatible with our theory of the separation of the church and the state, and so on. That is not to say that we must not take advantage of the sources of information that are available at the Vatican, as at any other national capital, so to speak. I have not been able to see that there is any great disadvantage in the system that existed previously of a special representative of the President at the Vatican. This is a subject that I have not heretofore discussed in the campaign. I may have occasion to later. I haven't encountered it previously." The reporter pressed on: "Since other nations do have representatives at the Vatican, is there any inconsistency there, do you think?" Stevenson said, "Yes, I suppose there is."

He had one or two friendly questions but failed to take full advantage of them. It had been a rough press conference. He held no more. Some Stevenson partisans suggested the press resented his attack on the "one-party press in a two-party country." But it was more than that. This was the Washington press corps, tough and knowledgeable; Stevenson had attacked Eisenhower head on for his pact with Taft; the reporters justly pressed him hard about divisions within his own party. This was the abrasive give-and-take of national politics. He would have been better advised to make his partisan attack on Eisenhower-Taft in a speech or by reading a statement and refusing to answer questions. Instead, accustomed to the easygoing relations with reporters that he had enjoyed as Governor, he had thrown himself to the wolves. Stevenson was already in deep trouble with Catholics. Now at his press conference he had made it worse. Flanagan said privately, and rightly, that Stevenson ought not ad-lib on so delicate an issue.

Ten days after the press conference Schlesinger sent a memorandum to Wyatt and McGowan saying that the one important element in the old FDR coalition that now threatened to defect was the Irish Catholic vote—because of McCarthy, Hiss, the divorce, and the absence of leading Irish Catholics from the Springfield headquarters and the campaign plane. "This is a serious situation." To remedy it, Schlesinger proposed "a full-dress anti-Communist speech," the activation of Irish Catholic campaigners, the visible attachment of Jim Rowe or some other Irish Catholic to the Stevenson headquarters, invitations to such Catholic Senators or Congressmen as John Pastore of Rhode Island to accompany Stevenson on his trips, and the release of a letter by Stevenson explaining his position on the Vatican issue.

The night of the press conference, Stevenson entertained the entire campaign staff—typists as well as strategists—at cocktails and a buffet supper at the Mansion. More than 100 people were there, and butlers served drinks in the garden, and the guests ate at card tables indoors. Few of the guests looked older than forty; many were in their twenties and early thirties. After supper some gathered around the piano and sang college songs; more knew "Hail to the Orange, Hail to the Blue" than the "Illinois Loyalty Song." Stevenson sat at a big table in the state dining room, and all evening people hovered around him, cornering him. Mrs. Ives wore white. She had been receiving counsel from the Christian Science practitioner, Mrs. Shaw, for she was worried about having to make speeches herself. At nine-thirty Stevenson and others watched the television show of his Western trip. Several of the Elks thought it poor and ineffective, not worth the cost, probably about $75,000. It was not done again during the campaign.

Through it all, Stevenson worked on. He seemed remarkably equable. Carl McGowan recalled, "He went along on a pretty even plane. I never discussed with him whether we were going to win. He was always running to stay alive. He kept bucking ahead. He did not seem to get difficult under pressure. He never was that way to work for." Robert Sherwood sent him a long memo proposing that he face the Korean War squarely in a major speech. Stevenson asked him for a full draft. Stevenson met with the Wisconsin Democrat who was running against Senator Joe McCarthy and issued a statement asking, "Does anyone have true freedom of speech when not only his views but his very character and reputation are to be subjected to irresponsible, distorted attack by others?" Stevenson told Dutch Smith he was "vastly heartened" by everything he had heard about the Volunteers. He congratulated Alicia Patterson on her courage in defending Jimmy Wechsler, under rightist attack because he had been a member of the Young Communist League while in college though he had left the party in 1937 and fought Communism ever since. Stevenson also tried to arrange to see Alicia during his forthcoming trip to New York. He told her his Western trip had been "a great success politically, but very tiring for an amateur." He was still receiving maddeningly even-handed letters from friendly independent voters who admired both him and Eisenhower.

He talked with Sam Rayburn, who reported that Lyndon Johnson was working hard in Texas, that the big money there was going to the Republicans, that Texas looked discouraging but the dissidents

might return to the party by election time. Rayburn urged Stevenson
to visit Texas about mid-October. Stevenson sent Rayburn his tidelands statement and FEPC speech. He told Senator Richard B.
Russell, "I am disturbed that you feel that I am 'reaching to the
left.' . . . Thus far, I do not feel that I have yielded any positions
which are inconsistent with my own views, nor do I intend to. But
because I value so highly your own judgment I should like to be
informed about my mistakes when your convenience permits." Senator Paul Douglas wrote from Italy that he was returning "ready to
give my best to your campaign." He was pleased with Stevenson's
positions on offshore oil, civil rights, Taft-Hartley, and foreign policy.
He regretted past misunderstandings and hoped for future fruitful
and happy cooperation. It was a generous letter.

Steve Mitchell suggested Stevenson meet with groups of Southern
and Eastern leaders. Sargent Shriver sent, on request, advice on what
Stevenson should and should not do in Massachusetts—should emphasize that "Jack Kennedy is Stevenson's kind of a man" and had
fought for minimum wage laws, decent housing, civil rights; that
Kennedy was "independent of special interest groups"; that he agreed
with Stevenson on offshore oil; that he was courageous. Shriver noted
that Kennedy, not Nixon, had obtained the first successful perjury
citation of a Communist labor leader—"up here this anti-Communist
business is a good thing to emphasize." Shriver advised Stevenson to
avoid two subjects: Senator Joe McCarthy and isolationism.

The night before Stevenson was to leave for the East, Tufts and
other Elks were tired, gloomy, and grumbling while having drinks in
the bar next to the Elks Club bowling alley. That day Eisenhower
had been loudly cheered when he told the AF of L he would sign a
loyalty oath daily. Tufts thought Eisenhower read Senator McCarthy's
recent primary triumph as proof of his national appeal and that "the
lower Eisenhower sinks, the harder he gets to beat." Tufts argued
that every demagogue in the last thirty or forty years had won, that
Americans were tired of crises and eager to dump their problems in
the lap of anybody who said he'd solve them, that Eisenhower's
embrace of McCarthy might get Stevenson independent votes but
might cost him far more so-called automatic Democratic labor votes,
who would succumb to demagogy. George Ball had come down from
Chicago and said they were "over the hump" in organizing the
Volunteers. (A few days earlier the Volunteers had not even been
listed with New York telephone information.) Stevenson told Ball
he was deeply worried about how many speeches he would have to
give in the East. He suspected darkly that good material was coming
to Springfield but being withheld from him. It was possible that Ball

might join the Elks. This dismayed some of the Elks but Schlesinger assured them Ball was amiable and would make no trouble—it might make it easier for everybody if Stevenson felt he had his own man at the Elks.

21

At Bridgeport that Thursday, September 18, Stevenson began a motorcade through New Haven and eight Connecticut mill towns that ended with a major evening speech in Hartford. At Bridgeport, before an enthusiastic noontime crowd of 20,000, he spoke on good government, the Taft-Eisenhower détente, Social Security and the Republican Old Guard, and his own sense of humor. His audience at New Haven was "unusually responsive," the *Herald Tribune* reported, and he plugged hard for the re-election of Senator Bill Benton and the election to the Senate of Abraham Ribicoff, then a Congressman. His motorcade moved on to Derby, to Ansonia, to a Mayor's reception at Seymour, to Beacon Falls and Naugatuck, all the way up the Naugatuck Valley, accompanied by Benton and Ribicoff, plugging them and the local congressional candidates, telling jokes with local references, talking for a few minutes about prosperity and full employment. He spoke longer at Waterbury, attacking Taft for calling Korea "Truman's useless war," drawing the party line sharply.

He devoted his major speech that night at Hartford to atomic energy. It was a part of his plan to set forth his views on important issues; he chose Hartford for atomic energy because the late Senator Brien McMahon of Connecticut had been chairman of the Joint Committee on Atomic Energy. He discussed arms control and the development of atomic energy for peaceful uses and said it was dangerous to make the atomic bomb the center of our defense strategy—it could not be our only answer to aggression. Before getting into substance, however, he sharpened his attack on "the General" for supporting all state and local candidates on the Republican ticket regardless of their views and records.

Wyatt, Minow, the Elks, and others dined that night at the Mansion back in Springfield. Schlesinger said labor leaders felt Stevenson didn't really care about them and would support him but not work for him: Stevenson should telephone them. Wyatt disclosed a "highly confidential" poll that he considered encouraging, though it showed that the main issues were Korea, Communism, and corruption—the Republican issues. Wyatt had reports of big crowds that day in Connecticut; his face lit up when he described them. Other reports were less glowing. Stevenson had returned from the Western trip complaining that he was speaking too much and not well enough, so the Eastern schedule had been loosened up—and everybody now feared it was too loose, no whistle stops after Connecticut, long gaps between major speeches.

But during the day something far more important occurred, the second big break of the campaign: the Nixon slush fund scandal. On the preceding Sunday, September 14, Nixon had been approached by a good though not widely read Washington columnist, Peter Edson, who told him that ever since the convention a story had been "kicking around" that Nixon was getting money from a special fund set up by wealthy Californians. Nixon had suggested he check with a Pasadena lawyer named Dana Smith. Dana Smith had been Nixon's finance chairman when he ran for the Senate in 1950 and now was Southern California chairman of Citizens for Eisenhower-Nixon. Edson had telephoned Smith and written his story, and Edson's syndicate had distributed it to his clients for release on Thursday, September 18. It was not written as a sensational exposé; it was a low-keyed matter-of-fact account. By itself, it probably would have aroused little attention. Drew Pearson, a more widely read and more sensational columnist, had already passed it up. But that same Thursday that Edson's column was released, the New York *Post* broke the story with a big splash; and almost overnight it mushroomed into the biggest story of the campaign. The *Post* headline said: "Secret Nixon Fund" and the subhead: "Secret Rich Men's Trust Fund Keeps Nixon in Style Far Beyond His Salary" and the opening paragraph read, "The existence of a 'millionaires' club' devoted exclusively to the financial comfort of Senator Nixon, G.O.P. vice presidential candidate, was revealed today." The story said the Pasadena lawyer, Dana Smith, boasted that during the past two years he and several friends had collected some $16,000 or $17,000 to help pay Nixon's political expenses, such as travel, postage, office maintenance. Nixon, Smith said, was "the best salesman against socialization and government control of everything in the country today" and since Nixon lacked the money to "do the kind of job he wanted to do and that we wanted him to do," Smith and his friends got the money for him. Contributions were sought from regular Republican Party contributors, were limited to $500 per person, were paid into a trust fund administered in Pasadena by Smith as trustee, and were independently audited.

Word of the story reached the Eisenhower train that Thursday night while it was rolling through the Midwest. Eisenhower had been doing well. Lately his crowds at whistle stops had been two or three times as big as Stevenson's. He seemed to have got the hang of campaigning and to be enjoying it. The latest poll by George Gallup had shown 51 per cent for or leaning toward the Republican Party to 42 per cent for the Democrats, with 7 per cent undecided. At the same point in 1948, Dewey had had 46½ per cent to 44½ per cent, with 9 per cent undecided. Most people felt that Eisenhower was pulling ahead. Thus the impact of the Nixon fund scandal was all the greater on Eisenhower and his associates. Eisenhower later wrote in his memoirs, "The storm of criticism that broke was of hurricane proportions." *Time* reported, "Almost instantly the words 'Nixon' and 'millionaires' club' zipped through [Eisenhower's] train." Steve Mitchell demanded that Eisenhower require Nixon's resignation from the ticket. Eisenhower later wrote in his memoirs that his own people "bombarded" him with contradictory advice— to dump Nixon, to keep him.

Nixon himself was whistle-stopping in California. He issued a statement confirming the existence of the fund but saying the money had been used for postage, travel, printing speeches, and clerical help in his Senate office. According to *Newsweek,* his explanation "satisfied neither Eisenhower nor his aides." Arthur E. Summerfield, Republican national chairman, put in a call to Nixon. That same Thursday night Eisenhower, speaking in Omaha to a big enthusiastic crowd, "clearly showed his distress," according to *Newsweek,* then went to bed aboard his train while his aides conferred far into the night en route to Kansas City. Journalists aboard were almost unanimous in thinking that unless he dropped Nixon as his running mate his "crusade" was doomed. One difficulty with dropping Nixon was that the Republican National Committee would have to convene to choose a replacement, probably touching off a party struggle that might also ensure defeat. About 10 A.M. next day, Friday, James C. Hagerty, Eisenhower's press secretary, read an Eisenhower statement in the press car: "I have long admired and applauded Senator Nixon's American faith and the determination to drive Communist sympathizers from offices of public trust. There has recently been leveled against him a charge of unethical practices. I believe Dick Nixon to be an honest man. I am confident that he will place all the facts before the American people fairly and squarely. I intend to talk with him at the earliest time." A reporter asked whether Eisenhower's announced subject in Kansas City that night would still be corruption. Hagerty said yes. An Eisenhower adviser, Senator Fred Seaton, dropped off the train in Nebraska to try to suggest to Nixon in California that he break off his campaign and come to Eisenhower to explain, could not reach him, and left word for him to call Eisenhower in Kansas City. Nixon, heckled that day in Marysville about the $16,000, shouted angrily, "Hold the train!" and when it stopped said, "You folks know the work that I did investigating Communists in the United States. Ever since I have done that work the Communists and the left-wingers have been fighting me with every possible smear. . . . And believe me, you can expect that they will continue to do so. They started it yesterday." He went on to say that he had paid his office expenses out of private contributions, not out of public funds, and that by contrast other Senators put their wives on the public payroll.

The counterattack did not go down well. The Washington *Post* and even the Republican New York *Herald Tribune* prepared editorials for Saturday morning's papers saying that Nixon should resign from the ticket. "This one really hit me," Nixon wrote later. "I had been hit by a real blockbuster." He consulted with his advisers, Murray Chotiner and William P. Rogers (a lawyer who later became Secretary of State under President Nixon). Rogers was shaken, Chotiner furious at what he regarded as Republican treason. Nixon telephoned Eisenhower in Kansas City, but Eisenhower was motorcading through confetti downtown, so Nixon dictated a message to Eisenhower—promised to make a full accounting of the fund, said the whole issue had "developed as a deliberate smear attempt," and assured Eisenhower that the "public-spirited citizens" who contributed to his fund had asked or received nothing from him. Eisenhower's advisers conferred at length, and Eisenhower prefaced his speech on corruption by reading the Nixon statement, then adding on his own behalf, "Knowing Dick Nixon as I do, I believe that when the facts are known to all of us they will show that Dick Nixon did not compromise with what is right."

Next day, Saturday, in Oregon, Nixon was heckled at nearly every stop. He received word that "an aura of gloom" had settled over the Eisenhower train and later wrote, "If that was so, it was nothing compared to the despair on the 'Nixon Special.'" Editorials across the nation were 2 to 1 against Nixon. At Nixon's request, Dana Smith made public the names of contributors to his fund, which totaled $18,235, and an accounting of what the money had been spent for, and Nixon himself issued a more formal statement; but the Nixon statement went almost unnoticed amid the uproar over whether Eisenhower would or would not dump Nixon. When he reached Portland that night, Nixon found a message asking him to call Sherman Adams on the Eisenhower train. He told Chotiner to tell Adams he would talk to no one but Eisenhower. That same day Eisenhower called in reporters and repeated his belief in Nixon's honesty but added that Nixon would have to prove his honesty to "fair-minded" people and said, "Of what avail is it for us to carry on this crusade against this business of what has been going on in Washington if we, ourselves, aren't clean as a hound's tooth?" Nixon and his advisers were considering national television to take his case to the people. Eisenhower telephoned Nixon Sunday night, and they agreed he should go on television. A broadcast was arranged for Tuesday, and on Monday Nixon flew down to Los Angeles to deliver it.

What was Stevenson doing about it? He had said nothing on Thursday in Hartford, the day the story broke. On Friday morning he spoke briefly at two Hartford suburbs, then went to Springfield, Massachusetts, to address a noonday crowd in front of the City Hall. Still he was silent on Nixon. He followed Shriver's advice—praised John Kennedy as "my type of guy" and the man who had obtained the first citation of a Communist for perjury. He also did as he had done in Connecticut—talked about his own humor and the Republicans' humorlessness, attacked Taft and the Old Guard. He went on to New York to rest before heading south on Saturday and there he wrote out in longhand a statement on the Nixon scandal. The important questions, he said, were: "Who gave the money, was it given to influence the senator's position . . . and have any laws been violated." He went on, "I am sure the great Republican Party will ascertain these facts, will make them public, and act in accordance with our best traditions. . . . Condemnation without all the evidence, a practice all too familiar to us, would be wrong." The press at the time believed that Stevenson issued so mild a statement in order to leave the door open for a full-scale attack after the Republicans had finished dealing with the matter. Actually, Stevenson may have been cautious because he knew that he, while Governor, had established a fund to augment the state salaries of some of his aides.

On that Saturday, Stevenson flew to Washington National Airport and went on to Quantico to speak at graduation exercises at the U. S. Marine Base—Adlai III was one of the graduates. In a short speech, one of the most eloquent since the acceptance speech, he talked about the reasons for the Korean War:

"Why must you defend your country when your country seems to lie in peace around you? Is it because of some mistake made in the past by those older than yourselves—some failure of foresight or decision? Is it for that you must offer the sacrifice of the young years of your lives?

"Certainly there have been failures and mistakes. The course of human history is a record, in tragic part, of things done which should not have been done, things not done which should have been done. Our own history is like the rest. But of one thing I, for myself, am certain and I think you also can be certain.

"It is not to make good the errors of the past that you are here but to make good the promise of the future. The fighting in which we are now engaged in Korea is fighting undertaken in the name of the common collective security of the great majority of the nations of the world against the brutal aggressiveness of one or more of them. . . .

"We and our friends found the courage to resist two years ago. It is to press that courage home, to affirm and to establish the faith that a peaceful world can in truth be built, that you and the thousands upon thousands of young men like you have been asked to serve your country with the hope and promise of your lives."

At Quantico he made no mention of the Nixon fund. He motorcaded to Richmond, stopping briefly at Fredericksburg, where he said, as he had on arriving at Washington National Airport, that he would make no political speech because this was the Jewish New Year. When he got to Richmond, he said, on the steps of the Capitol, "I hope you will forgive me if I don't cut the enemy to ribbons. For the moment they seem to be taking care of that themselves." *Newsweek* called his reception in Richmond "puzzling." The crowds along the streets watched his motorcade to the Capitol almost in silence. But that night when Governor John S. Battle warmly introduced him in the city-owned Mosque Auditorium for a major speech on civil rights, the crowd interrupted him more than forty times with loud applause and friendly rebel yells. The decision to speak at the Mosque had been difficult. By law, meetings there had to be segregated. Stevenson dared not address a segregated audience. But his schedulers had made the arrangements before learning of the law. The night the Nixon fund scandal broke, Wilson Wyatt and others in Springfield were preoccupied with the Mosque problem. There were local assurances that Richmond authorities would wink at the law, rumor had it that Republicans might file a formal complaint. Yet it would be embarrassing to move the meeting outdoors (where it could be desegregated). In the end, Stevenson spoke indoors, and to an unsegregated overflow crowd. The meeting was a great success, despite the conspicuous absence of segregationist leaders of the powerful Byrd machine. Byrd himself let it be known he was busy picking apples. Stevenson made no mention of the Nixon fund but stuck to his prepared text. The crowd applauded loud and often when, early in his speech, he described how the Democratic Party had set the South on its feet. Applause diminished when he declared his position on civil rights. But the crowd came roaring to its feet when he added: "I should justly earn your contempt if I talked one way in the South and another elsewhere." He went on to say that we should grant all men their rights, not because discrimination gave Soviet Russia a propaganda weapon, but because discrimination was wrong; that he rejected "the reckless assertions that the South is a prison in which half the people are prisoners and the other half are wardens"; that "human character will never free itself entirely from the blemish of prejudice, religious or racial," especially in places where a minority was large, as in the South; but that "I do not attempt to justify the unjustifiable, whether it is anti-Negroism in one place, anti-Semitism in another—or for that matter, anti-Southernism in many places. And neither can I justify self-righteousness anywhere." He said the South had made "great strides" toward equal treatment of all and denounced the exploitation of both racial aspirations and racial prejudice to catch votes.

Stevenson flew back to New York. Sunday he attended church, then went to lunch with Cardinal Spellman. That night Alicia Patterson gave a private dinner for him at the expensive River Club. Carl McGowan years later described that dinner as a low point of the campaign: "If he was going to take a night off campaigning, he should have gone to bed. He let her set up a dinner party. It was a great coup for her. We walked in—and there were all his enemies: Gardner Cowles, Clare Boothe Luce, all whooping it up for Eisenhower. Before we sat down, she said that she had a telegram from her husband, Harry Guggenheim. She read it. It said something like, 'Sorry can't be there. Tell Adlai glad to have a Democrat like Stevenson in the White House provided Eisenhower is the host.' Everybody laughed. He put up with an awful lot of guff from his Republican friends." It was Lake Forest all over again, and worse.

On Monday, while Nixon was flying to Los Angeles to prepare for his television broadcast, Stevenson addressed the American Federation of Labor convention in New York. The Federation had not endorsed a presidential candidate since its Executive Council supported Robert LaFollette's third-party candidacy in 1924. But since passage of the Taft-Hartley Act, David Dubinsky of the garment workers and other leaders had tried to push the Federation into endorsing a Democrat. Eisenhower had addressed the convention a few days earlier. It had received silently his declaration that he favored amending Taft-Hartley, not repealing it. Stevenson now hoped to win the Federation's endorsement. Characteristically, he said at the outset, "Now, I have been told that I should try here today to make you roar with enthusiasm. Why, I would not do that even if I could. After all, you are the responsible leaders of organized labor. . . . And I, in turn, am a candidate for the most important individual responsibility in the world. . . . So you will, I hope, understand that what little I have to say, or rather to add, to the many speeches you have dutifully listened to, is intended for your heads and not your hands. And, if I don't start any cheers, I hope at least that I shall not stop any minds." And then: "First I should like if I may to dispose of this matter of the Taft-Hartley law. The Democratic platform says that the Taft-Hartley Act is 'inadequate, unworkable, and unfair,' and should be replaced by a new law. I developed, on Labor Day, the five basic respects in which the present law seems to me defective and I outlined some five principles to guide the writing of a new one. How to get a new one? The method, whether by amendment of the existing law or replacement with a new one, has, frankly, seemed to me less important than the objective. But, because the required changes are major changes, because the present law is spiteful, and because it has become a symbol of dissension and bitterness, I urge, therefore, as I did on Labor Day, that the Taft-Hartley Act be repealed." The audience shouted its approval. As he went on, attacking Republicans, it whistled and shouted, "Pour it on, Steve." After the speech the Executive Council announced its support of Stevenson.

By Monday, while the Republicans were still grappling with the Nixon fund, Stevenson was picking up steam. Then the counterblow fell, delivered by one of Stevenson's old friends in Lake Forest, Kent Chandler. (Chandler was an officer of the A. B. Dick Company, the company of Edison Dick, Jane Dick's husband, though they, of course, had nothing to do with Chandler's telegram and were outraged by it.) His letters to Stevenson while Stevenson was Governor had been addressed "Dear Adlai" and signed "Kent." He had been present at the Commercial Club when Stevenson said he had used a private fund to supplement state salaries. Now, on this same Monday that Stevenson addressed the Labor Federation in New York, Chandler sent a telegram to Stevenson in Springfield, saying that in view of Steve Mitchell's attack on Nixon it was Stevenson's responsibility to admit publicly that as Governor of Illinois he had personally promoted a similar fund, contributed by private individuals and paid to his aides to supplement state salaries. Chandler called on Stevenson to divulge the names of all contributors to his fund, the amount each contributed, and the names of, and amounts received by, each appointed state official. Chandler added that Stevenson enjoyed a private income and said he saw nothing improper about aiding other men not so "blessed." Chandler released his telegram to the press.

A few hours after the Kent Chandler story broke, Stevenson, in New York, wrote out in longhand a statement saying he had not yet received Chandler's telegram but confirming that he had collected a fund "to reduce the financial sacrifice" of those entering public service. It was no secret, he said. The money had come from private contributions and money left over from the 1948 governorship campaign. It had gone to his own appointees. A reporter asked Flanagan, who distributed the statement, for the names of contributors, recipients, and amounts. Flanagan said a fuller statement would be issued soon.

On this same day, Monday, September 22, reporters pressed Newt Minow and others in Springfield. Minow simply said there was nothing wrong with the Stevenson fund. Minow warned McGowan that Stevenson probably would be met by questioning reporters at the Springfield airport Wednesday.

Stevenson went to Baltimore on Tuesday, the twenty-third, and delivered an address on inflation at the Armory. That same night Nixon delivered his nationwide TV defense of the Nixon fund, a speech that became known, at least among Democrats, as "the Checkers speech," since he mentioned his dog, Checkers. He began, "I come before you . . . as a man whose honesty and integrity have been questioned." Then he launched into a personal appeal for sympathy and vindication, relying on domestic details—his wife's wardrobe ("a respectable Republican cloth coat"), his debts, his assets, his house, his 1950 car, his insurance and mortgages, his children, his dog. He counterattacked briefly, challenging Stevenson to explain his own fund to the people as Nixon was doing, challenging Sparkman to likewise explain his wife's presence on the government payroll, saying the country was endangered by Communism, corruption, and Korea, and only Eisenhower could save it. But by and large it was a purely emotional speech about himself, and he staked his political life on it. His wife sat near him as he spoke. Despite pressure brought to bear just before broadcast time by Eisenhower's advisers, he did not end by resigning from the ticket. Instead, he said he did not believe he ought to quit. ("I am not a quitter. And, incidentally, Pat is not a quitter. After all, her name was Patricia Ryan and she was born on St. Patrick's Day, and you know the Irish never quit.") The decision, however, was not his, he said. He would do nothing to hurt Eisenhower's chances. Therefore, he was submitting the decision to the Republican National Committee through this broadcast and he was asking the television viewers to write the National Committee "to help them decide. . . . Regardless of what happens, I am going to continue this fight. I am going to campaign up and down America until we drive the crooks and the Communists and those that defend them out of Washington. And remember, folks, Eisenhower is a great man. Folks, he is a great man, and a vote for Eisenhower is a vote for what is good for America."

The Elks who heard it were not impressed. Democrats called it soap opera. But millions of Americans were sympathetic. Eisenhower and his wife watched the speech in Cleveland while an audience of 15,000 in the Public Auditorium, waiting for Eisenhower to appear there, heard it over radio. When Eisenhower appeared, he began his speech by saying, "I have been a warrior and I like courage. Tonight I saw an example of courage," and the crowd roared. Next day Nixon flew to Wheeling, West Virginia, where Eisenhower was campaigning, and Eisenhower went up the steps to Nixon's plane and told him, "You're my boy." They drove to a rally at a football stadium where Eisenhower formally re-embraced Nixon; Nixon wept and put his head on the shoulder of Senator William Knowland of California; and as Nixon resumed campaigning he was greeted as a hero.

If Nixon was out of trouble, Stevenson was getting in deeper. Nixon in his Checkers speech had demanded that Stevenson and Senator Sparkman make a full accounting of their finances. Stevenson, leaving the Baltimore Armory, refused to comment on the Nixon speech. Of all the men he encountered in public life, Stevenson despised none as he did Richard Nixon. (Stevenson, indeed, despised few men, and his friends sometimes wished he were a better hater.) He once told a friend that Nixon was the one man in public life he would have to say he "really loathed." He thought that if Nixon had any principles at all they were certainly "very easy principles." His friend noted, "The very thought of Nixon in the White House made him ill. His loathing went back to what he considered Nixon's despicable early campaigns in California against Jerry Voorhis and Helen Gahagan Douglas. He was sure that Nixon's election [in 1960] would have been an unparalleled catastrophe." (Stevenson did not live to see Nixon elected in 1968.) He felt differently about Joe McCarthy, whom he regarded as "a sick man." He thought Nixon had done a great deal to make McCarthyism possible. Once in 1964 at a party at the U. S. Mission to the UN, someone mentioned Nixon's views on Vietnam, and Stevenson said, "Please! Not while I'm eating!" Stevenson thought no statement of Eisenhower's more "unbecoming" than his declaration that "Dick's my boy." Later on,

Chairman Khrushchev described to Stevenson his conversation in 1959 with Nixon (which Nixon made much of in the 1960 campaign as his "kitchen debate" with Khrushchev), and made it plain that he, Khrushchev, held Nixon in contempt.

None of this made any difference now, however. Stevenson was in trouble with his own fund. True, several years earlier he had discussed his fund openly in a speech at the Commercial Club. But now suddenly, in the Nixon context, the national press treated Stevenson's fund as a scandal and demanded explanation. On Wednesday morning, the day after the Checkers speech, Stevenson breakfasted with a group of Volunteers at the Sheraton-Belvedere Hotel in Baltimore and talked about his fund. He described the difficulty of recruiting able men for government service at low state salaries. He said that, as Governor, he had considered several methods of supplementing key officials' salaries, including gifts by public-spirited citizens directly to the state of Illinois or to a foundation created for the benefit of the state, but had concluded that the only feasible way was through gifts by himself, usually near Christmas. The money came from his campaign fund, supplemented by additional contributions. No official knew the source of the money he received, nor any donor the identity of the recipient. To identify them now would be a breach of faith.

Journalists asked Stevenson to hold a press conference. Instead, he flew to Springfield, arriving at 1 P.M. The newspapers that morning quoted Fred Hoehler as saying he never had heard of the Stevenson fund and neither had Ed Day. The Public Works Director and the Director of Mines and Minerals said they knew nothing about the fund. The Public Safety Director said he had heard Stevenson discuss it. The Illinois Republican National Committeeman, C. Wayland Brooks, said Stevenson should abandon his campaign for the presidency. When Stevenson arrived at the Springfield airport, reporters asked whether he would make public the list of donors to his fund. He said, "I don't know. I'd have to check with them."

By this time most of Stevenson's principal aides in Springfield—including George Ball, Wilson Wyatt, Arthur Schlesinger, Newt Minow, Ed Day—recognized how dangerous the issue was. Just as Eisenhower had called his campaign a "crusade" against "the mess in Washington," so was one of Stevenson's greatest assets his reputation for probity. The press was clamoring for an accounting. The *Tribune,* always expert at keeping the pressure on, daily ran a page-one story with a bold-faced insert: "5 [the number changed daily] days have passed since Gov. Stevenson was asked for an account of his special fund."

On Thursday, September 25, Wally Schaefer, by now an Illinois Supreme Court justice, said he had received a $500 check from Stevenson's fund while on Stevenson's staff. Another former aide, William J. McKinney, who had resigned as state purchasing agent in 1950, told a newspaper that "upwards of $100,000" had been collected from 1,000 business corporations, including state suppliers, and the money used to pay Stevenson's charitable contributions, entertainment, and other expenses. Fred Hoehler changed his story—told reporters he had indeed been a beneficiary of the fund, but declined to say by how much. Dutch Smith said he had turned over some $450 to Stevenson's fund, contributed by two men who did not want their names disclosed. Reporters were digging the story out by bits and pieces. Sherman Adams, with Eisenhower, accused Stevenson of trying to brazen his way through the controversy. Stevenson's campaign was stalled, could not resume until the fund was explained. Finally, on Thursday, Wilson Wyatt announced that Stevenson would make a further statement.

That day Robert W. Notti, a young campaign aide, received a telephone call from Helen Mulroy in Chicago, the widow of Jim Mulroy. She said newspaper reporters had been tipped off that she had a list of contributors to Stevenson's 1948 campaign and that the lobby of her apartment contained so many reporters she couldn't go out. Notti, after checking with Wyatt, hastened to Chicago that night. To avoid reporters, he entered her apartment building by a rear door. He and Mrs. Mulroy found two big suitcases on a closet shelf. Notti carried them into the living room, dumped their contents on the floor, and soon found a list of contributors, about 1,000 names. Notti took the list to Wyatt in Springfield next morning, Friday, September 26. Stevenson himself was already aboard his plane, about to take off for Evansville, Indiana. Wyatt gave the list to his staff to check, telephoned the airport, asked that Stevenson's plane be held, then took Notti to the airport with a police escort. Aboard the plane, they told Stevenson that Notti and Helen Mulroy had hastily scanned the list, that it looked all right, that it would be checked further, and that, if the list was "clean," it should be released to the press. Staff aides began telephoning the 1948 contributors, asking permission to make public their names and contributions, and began checking suspect names.

The audit of 1948 contributions and expenditures had been completed in the spring of 1949. It showed that, as of February 28, 1949, the net balance left in the checking account of the Stevenson-for-Governor Committee was $18,744.96. This $18,744. 96 was turned over to Stevenson by the Stevenson-for-Governor Committee accompanied by a letter stating the funds should "be subject to withdrawal for such purposes connected with the office of the Governor as Mr. Stevenson shall determine." This $18,744.96 was the beginning of the Stevenson fund.

During his first year in office Stevenson used the money to supplement the meager state salaries of his personal staff—Schaefer, Day, Flanagan, Mulroy, McGowan, and Irvin—and two members of his Cabinet, Hoehler and Mitchell, by a total of $13,500. He also used it to provide Christmas presents to his office and household staffs and police, to give a party for Springfield children, to buy uniforms for the Governor's female and male bowling teams, to contribute to charities and buy tickets to benefits and send flowers to sick friends. He hoped to find ways to defray such expenses during the rest of his term. On September 29, 1950, he wrote to Dutch Smith: "I think it better to write this in long hand. For your private information the supplementary payments last year were about as follows," and he tabulated the individual payments to his staff and cabinet members, added his incidental expenses, and concluded, "There seems to be *literally* almost no limit to what one can spend this way." He hoped to increase his supplementary payments to his staff and estimated he would need contributions of from $20,000 to $25,000 per year to "enable me to do what we have talked about without robbing the children!" or tapping regular political funds that he would need if he ran for re-election or wanted to help someone else run. "I hope this will give you something of what you need for the purposes we discussed the other morning." He authorized Smith to show the letter to John S. Miller in order to help him convince prospective Republican contributors that the money was for Stevenson's use in improving Illinois government and was not to help Truman or Democratic candidates. It was not easy, however. On November 16, 1950, John S. Miller told Stevenson he and Smith had talked to Ned Brown, the banker, and that Brown's "reactions to our program were negative and firm." On December 15, 1950, Stevenson thanked Miller "for the checks." The records showed that five Chicago businessmen contributed $2,900 to the fund. The original fund left over from the governorship campaign, plus the businessmen's contributions, came to $21,644.96. The records showed that, during his term as Governor, Stevenson supplemented his aides' salaries by a total of $18,150.

As Stevenson left for Evansville, George Ball and Wilson Wyatt hoped to compile a full accounting of Stevenson's political receipts and expenditures during his term in office. They worked through the night. They worked under heavy time pressure—disclosure must be made quickly, there was no time for a proper audit. A full audit would have been impossible anyway—records were incomplete. Ball and Wyatt sought them, fruitlessly. What records did exist dismayed Ball and Wyatt, for they suggested that the Stevenson fund was bigger than supposed and that, to some extent, Stevenson had used some of it for questionable purposes.

The work sheets of Ball, Wyatt, and others show that to the original $18,744.96 additional sums were added in 1950, 1951, and 1952 totaling $65,281.60—a grand total of $84,026.56. They do not show where that money came from. Certainly all of it did not come from public-spirited Chicago businessmen. No doubt most of it came from the usual sources of political contributions. (One item was a personal check for $10,542.59, written out in longhand by Stevenson himself, signed by him, drawn on his personal bank account, and made out to the Stevenson-for-Governor Committee on September 26, 1952, long after the Stevenson-for-Governor Committee had disbanded—and on the precise day that Stevenson was preparing to issue his fund accounting. The work sheet characterized the item as representing a return of an advance which had not been disbursed. It was most unusual for Stevenson to write out a check in longhand; Carol Evans usually typed checks, and he signed them. Perhaps he was repaying to the fund money it had spent on a mixture of his political and personal affairs.)

What had all that $84,026.56 been spent on? A work sheet which appears to be an early draft of the statement Stevenson was to issue later said that $18,150 had been paid to supplement Stevenson's aides' salaries; $35,037.19 had been turned over to Sherwood Dixon's campaign; and $17,410 had been given to campaigns of other Democratic candidates in 1950 and 1951. This left $13,429.37 unaccounted for. The draft said it "was expended for miscellaneous political purposes, long customary in the use of such a fund by Illinois Governors," and it listed:

Travel	$3,821.57
Charities	2,356.48
Back bills of 1948 headquarters	713.38
Office supplies and expenses for political uses	1,292.87
Annual Christmas parties	1,925.59
Gifts for news men	1,266.35
Refund of a political contribution	250.
Advertising & tickets for political programs	747.90
	$13,608.07

The work sheets show a long list of detailed disbursements, including these: $96.04 for "bowling costumes for girls"; $10 to the Lake

County Tuberculosis Association in 1949 (Lake was Stevenson's home county; one might have expected him to have made this contribution himself, and indeed he claimed the $10 contribution as a deduction on his personal income tax return); $193.67 in 1949 for hams as Christmas gifts from Stevenson to newspapermen; $125 to reimburse Stevenson for his expenses to the Gridiron dinner in Washington in 1950; $286 for an orchestra to play at the Christmas dance at the Mansion for Stevenson's sons in 1949 and $20.25 to the Abraham Lincoln Hotel for "rooms for boys at Stevenson boys dance"; $10 as a Stevenson donation to the church in Bloomington; $10 to pay Stevenson's dues in the American Legion's 40 and 8 Club; $25 in 1951 to reimburse him for a contribution to the Salvation Army; $167 for his share of the cost of a wrist watch given to Paul Powell; $13.14 to the Metropolitan Club in Washington, December 5, 1951. Sizable contributions were made directly to various political campaigns—$500 to Scott Lucas in 1949, $250 each to George Kells and Dick Daley in 1950, $500 each to four candidates for the Illinois Supreme Court. The last check in these work sheets was dated October 17, 1951. Thus these work sheets do not show disbursements made at Christmastime, 1951, nor do they show disbursements made in 1952.

Some of these items were clearly political, such as Christmas hams for newspapermen, the girls' bowling costumes, and Stevenson's trip to the Gridiron dinner—expenses Stevenson would not have incurred had he not been Governor. A few appear somewhat questionable, such as the money spent on the boys' Christmas dance. At law, a political contribution is a gift and becomes the sole property of the man it is given to. If he spends it for political purposes, it is not taxable. If, however, he spends it for non-political purposes, thereby in effect diverting it to his personal use, it becomes taxable income. The Internal Revenue Service never made a claim that Stevenson had made non-political use of any political contributions. It would therefore be unwarranted to conclude that he had diverted any of the money to his personal use.[14]

[14] A wholly different set of work sheets gives a wholly different picture of the fund—shows it, in fact, to have been far larger than any other set of figures shows. It starts out, as do other computations, with the $18,744.96 left over from the 1949 campaign. It then lists contributions shown on ledgers and bank statements totaling $67,397. And it also shows something called "Departmental contributions" for 1950 of $44,691.01. This last sounds as though state employees of the various departments were required, or at least encouraged, to make campaign contributions in that campaign year, as was the practice in Illinois at that time. The grand total is $146,219.57.

George Ball and the others, realizing it would be impossible to compile a full accounting, certainly not quickly, recommended to Stevenson that he release a summary, omitting details, and that he also make public his income tax returns for recent years. Reluctantly, he agreed. Initially, Stevenson had planned to make no statement until his fireside chat the next Monday. Schlesinger protested strongly that this would lower Stevenson to Nixon's level and delay would only make things worse. McGowan agreed, and convinced Stevenson: they would issue a statement as soon as the facts were assembled. Stevenson left for Evansville.

The plane was a Convair, smaller than the DC-6 Stevenson ordinarily used, so it was crowded, with little room for the secretaries to work. Margaret Munn's speech typewriter had broken; a man had repaired it that morning and she fastened it to a desk on the plane herself.

In Evansville, the airport crowd was small. The motorcade made a couple of stops where Stevenson walked through factories. He was greeted by workmen holding up "I Like Ike" signs. Here, as elsewhere, as the motorcade passed slowly through town, small groups, mostly children, stood at street corners where the motorcade slowed to turn and held up "I Like Ike" signs. About 8,000 to 10,000 people were at the courthouse square. When Stevenson was introduced, they just stood there. Traditionally Evansville crowds are cold (years earlier vaudeville troupes avoided Evansville). Their loudest noise consisted in calls that they "couldn't hear," and groups of children shouted repeatedly, "I Like Ike."

The Elks had been told in advance that the crowd would be made up of workingmen, so had written a speech discussing unemployment and prosperity after production for Korea stopped—Evansville had had a long history of wartime-peacetime boom-and-bust employment cycles. The speech was too long and too complicated for an outdoor noonday courthouse crowd. Stevenson seemed to sense it. Nearing the end, he departed from his text to tell an irrelevant joke, then had trouble returning to his text. It read, at that point, "We don't want Senator Taft to write our labor laws. We don't want Senator Taft to conduct our foreign affairs. And we dare not trust Senator Taft to see to it that we still have jobs after we have won the peace." Instead, Stevenson ad-libbed, "I say to you, my friends, that we don't want—no labor bosses are ever going to boss me, and I think that goons and violence and property damage is as wrong and as intolerable in labor disputes as it is anywhere else." He tried

---

One obscure notation suggests that various contractors made contributions. The work sheets show cash disbursements to the "Mansion" totaling $15,574.

to recoup by adding, "I also say that I shall never be bossed by any group of industrialists either" and by returning to the prepared attack on Taft. But the damage was done. He had in effect attacked big labor; worse, he had used the word "goon," a Chicago *Tribune* epithet for labor organizer, a word universally hated by union leaders. After this trip, McGowan and the Elks discussed the problem at length; one of them warned Stevenson that while his remarks had attracted little attention, since they had been made in a minor speech, they might have cost him the national labor vote had he delivered them elsewhere; and thereafter whenever the Elks wrote a speech involving Taft and labor policy, Dave Bell would say, "Remember what he did to us at Evansville" and try to find language that Stevenson could bring himself to deliver. But the problem continued through the campaign. On October 5, for example, Stevenson gave Wirtz a memo saying that he wanted to say again that he would "be bossed neither by big labor nor big industry and that I deplore disorder, violence, law violation and property damage in labor disputes as much as in anything else." The memo was prompted by a letter from a Chicago friend.

From the Evansville courthouse, Stevenson went to the Vendome Hotel for lunch with about 200 local party workers. He spoke briefly but the way he said it touched his audience deeply. At the courthouse he had seemed stiff, ill at ease, distracted. Here he seemed warm, friendly, burdened, tired, kind. The courthouse had been a near disaster; the Vendome was a small triumph. It happened often during that campaign. He had good days and bad days, like all candidates, but most of his days were mixed, partly good, partly bad. He reacted strongly to crowds. And to distractions and difficulties. On the plane that day what distracted him was the Stevenson fund: he would have to issue a statement on it that night. He had already delayed too long; the fund was drawing attention away from his campaign. And tomorrow he would go to Louisville for a major speech on Korea. He had to get rid of the fund tonight, before Louisville.

In Indianapolis his motorcade drew big crowds in the Negro districts, bigger, a policeman said, than Eisenhower's. (At this time the press was filled with comparisons of Eisenhower's crowds—very big —and Stevenson's—small.) At the Fairgrounds, Stevenson spoke on economy in government. One of the Elks had hit upon the idea that when the Republicans talked about the budget they always talked about money, whereas Democrats talked about what government expenditures accomplished for people—"the budget with a heart speech," the Elks called it.

After the speech Stevenson went with Governor Schricker to the

Governor's Mansion. The Elk who happened to be on this trip, the present author, Martin, had been working on the Korea speech. Since the Republicans were making Korea one of their three main issues—C_2K_1, as they said, Communism, corruption, and Korea—Stevenson's first major speech on Korea was of national importance. The Korean speech had gone through many drafts, and late the night before Tufts had talked with Stevenson about the final draft and found him dissatisfied with it. Tufts had returned to the Elks Club and worked until 6:30 A.M. rewriting the speech. He left it on his desk for Martin to take aboard the plane, together with a note that it could not be delivered until its facts were rechecked. Now in Indianapolis, while Stevenson was speaking at the Fairgrounds, and while Wyatt, Ball, and others were working on the fund, Martin telephoned Tufts. Checking, as always, proved difficult. The Democratic National Committee in Washington had only two researchers, and the Elks' own researcher, Mary Helen Wood, kept one of them overloaded. (Late in the campaign, the Elks discovered to their horror that for some time Miss Wood had been doing her checking by simply calling up Phil Stern in Wilson Wyatt's office, reading him a passage in a speech, and asking if it sounded all right. The Elks were young, new to campaigning; they learned later that many campaigns do even less checking. The safest solution is to omit facts.)

Martin made the corrections Tufts wanted. He finished the next morning's speech for Paducah and took both speeches to Stevenson. Stevenson liked Paducah and made few changes in the first two thirds, then said, "Now I've got to start cutting." Martin pointed out that the Paducah speech was really three speeches—an attack on the Republicans, a statement of the Democratic record, and a passage about the new frontier in Kentucky to be created by atomic energy—and asked which of the three speeches he wanted to use. Stevenson preferred the promise of the future. They turned to Korea.

Stevenson read it slowly and carefully, moving his lips. On nearly every page he raised questions of fact about the history of United States involvement in Korea. Once or twice he muttered that he wondered how careful with their facts "they" were at the Elks Club. Martin reassured him. They worked about an hour. Stevenson thought the speech "very good." Martin would ask Tufts to check facts with the State Department and would shorten the speech. Stevenson seemed pleased. But he also seemed tired and distracted. He asked how the others at the Claypool Hotel were getting along with their work on the fund. Martin said they expected to be finished by midnight. It was already past midnight. Bill Blair came in and told Stevenson they were having a hard time with the accounting because the bookkeeping had been poor. For example, they needed to know how much money Joe Gill, the Cook County machine leader, had contributed. Stevenson couldn't remember. He seemed harassed and put upon. Here he was, working on a speech on Korea, a fateful event for America and, for him, a fateful speech— and he had to worry about how much a ward leader had contributed to his fund. And indeed he did have to.

At 4 A.M., Flanagan awakened the newspapermen and gave them Stevenson's statement on the fund, together with annexes. (Some newspapermen accused Flanagan of deliberately and unnecessarily awakening them in the middle of the night out of spite, because they had badgered him so for the statement. He pleaded innocence.) Stevenson's long-awaited statement repeated what he had said previously about the difficulty of getting good men into state government and his device of making Christmas gifts to key executives. The total amount he gave them, he said, was $18,150. The money came from the $18,744.96 balance left over from the Stevenson-for-Governor Committee and the Chicago businessmen's subsequent contributions of $2,900.00. He was reluctantly making public both the list of 1948 Stevenson-for-Governor contributors and the subsequent contributors. He was also reluctantly making public the names of recipients. He said his sole purpose had been to improve the quality of public administration in Illinois and he did not consider public interest in the matter "a smear or unfair" but, on the contrary, "entirely healthy." Finally, as soon as possible, he would make public his personal income tax returns for the past ten years. So would Senator Sparkman.

Exhibit A accompanying the statement was the list of contributors to the 1948 Stevenson-for-Governor Committee. Exhibit B showed "Supplemental Contributions by Chicago Businessmen" as follows:

H. D. "Dutch" Smith	$ 100.00
H. D. Smith (for others undisclosed)	350.00
Clarence Ross	350.00
Rawleigh Warner	100.00
Kenneth F. Burgess	2,000.00
	$2,900.00

No dates were given for these contributions.

Exhibit C listed the donations to men in the Administration:

William I. Flanagan—eight payments ranging between $400 and $1,000 each	$ 7,900
Fred Hoehler—two payments of $1,000 each	2,000
George Mitchell—one gift of $1,000	1,000
J. Edward Day—two gifts of $1,000 each	2,000
Carl McGowan—two gifts of $1,500 each	3,000

Lawrence Irvin—one gift of $250, one gift of $500   750
Walter V. Schaefer—one gift of $500   500
Thomas J. O'Donnell (Supt. of State Police)—one gift of
  $1,000   1,000
           $18,150

Again, no dates were given.

In his statement in Indianapolis, Stevenson said, "There have been assertions that there were other political contributions made during my administration. Of course there were. Nineteen-fifty, 1951, and 1952 were all election years in Illinois. Campaign contributions were received in all these years—and they were spent for political purposes. No one during my administration ever had to make a political contribution to do business with the State of Illinois or to work for it. The balance remaining when I was nominated for President has been turned over to my successor candidate on the Democratic state ticket." It would appear that the Stevenson statement and exhibits dealt only with the 1948 surplus and contributions made shortly after that campaign. They did not deal with 1950, 1951, or 1952. Johnson Kanady, the *Tribune* reporter, harassed Flanagan about this throughout the rest of the campaign. He later wrote, "No newspaper was ever able to get details of the 1950 and 1951 Stevenson funds, and so far as I know no newspaperman with Stevenson, except me, tried very hard. . . . There was never an opportunity to ask Stevenson about the matter personally. . . . To my mind he never held a press conference after September 15, and certainly never after the fund controversies broke."

While Stevenson's statement and accompanying exhibits amounted to less than a full disclosure, they satisfied most of the press. And on Sunday when, back in Springfield, he made public his income tax returns, the press published the news widely; his disclosure of his income overshadowed the fund, and Stevenson was home free. Even David Lawrence, the columnist who supported Eisenhower, wrote, "Now that Gov. Stevenson and Sen. Nixon have made a clean breast of it . . . maybe the candidates will concentrate on the important issues of the campaign."

It seems clear Stevenson had done nothing illegal or clearly improper, but that he made only partial disclosure and that he had handled some of the funds unwisely. He never got over resenting the press's equating his fund to Nixon's.

22

Stevenson left Indianapolis that morning, Saturday, September 27, for Paducah. The motorcade went from the airport to Vice President Barkley's home, called The Angles, a Kentucky country estate, and everybody ate fried chicken and ham, sitting on the grass under the trees. McGowan and a TV commentator discussed Stevenson's speeches, agreeing that Stevenson was not coming across as the warm human being they knew him to be. The speeches were closely reasoned, brilliant, even, but they lacked warmth and humanity. Eisenhower, on the other hand, was not saying much but was coming across as a likable friendly man. It was a problem never solved.

From Barkley's the party motorcaded to the courthouse in Paducah. The crowd was large but not responsive. In his speech Stevenson praised Barkley lavishly, recited the Democratic record, attacked the Republicans, and spoke of the "new frontier" that would be opened up in Kentucky with atomic power. Again, it was too graceful and complicated a speech for a courthouse square, which must be more than a mere "hello" at a whistle stop but must stop short of a reasoned substantive speech for a thoughtful indoor audience. Nor can it be a rousing rally speech for a hot partisan audience. A courthouse speech must be simple, blunt, black and white, partisan enough to arouse enthusiasm among Democrats but not so partisan as to offend Republicans in the crowd. It is primarily an "image" speech, not an "issue" speech; if it is to contain an issue, it should contain only one, and that one should be presented in simple terms. There is little room for lyricism on courthouse steps. Although the Elks enjoyed writing lyric speeches, and Stevenson enjoyed delivering them, they did not make votes.

On to Louisville, arriving at 5 P.M., and by motorcade to the Seelbach Hotel, where McGowan and Martin made final cuts on the Korean speech, determined that this time Stevenson would finish before his TV time ran out. Outside, a carnival atmosphere prevailed, crowds, noise, confetti, searchlights. They motorcaded to the auditorium, and Barkley began a long introduction of Stevenson, an old-fashioned ad-libbed stem-winder speech, jaw chomping, arms flailing, his hog caller's voice booming, reciting the glories of the Democratic Party and reading the great names, Jefferson, Jackson, Wilson, FDR, Truman, running through the litany once, then starting it a second time, only to be given a cue that Stevenson's air time was at hand, and somehow extricating himself from a long sentence that began with Jackson and ended by introducing Stevenson. It was almost as though Stevenson's own grandfather, Adlai Stevenson I, the Vice President, were introducing him; the contrast between Barkley's exhortations and Stevenson's lawyerlike defense of the Korean policy could not have been greater.

Stevenson had considered declaring in a speech that if elected he would go to Korea personally. He had discussed it at the Mansion with McGowan. They had decided against it. Years later McGowan recalled, "We had just thought that it was thinking ahead to the time when Adlai would be elected, the same as talking about cabinet appointments would be premature. This was no great strategy decision on our part. I think it was Stevenson's own idea, thrown out casually. To us it seemed slightly ridiculous." It did not seem ridiculous a little later, when Eisenhower made the pledge. But Stevenson's making it would have had less impact than Eisenhower's, since Eisenhower was a general. Stevenson himself, reminiscing years later, said he had not done it because he feared it would seem an obvious attempt to catch votes. He also feared it would weaken his bargaining position as President.

Stevenson's speech in Louisville contained no such dramatic proposal. Instead, it was a point-by-point rebuttal of a recent Eisenhower speech on Korea, plus a broad outline of the American policy of containing Communism. He began, "I have been increasingly disturbed about the tone and spirit of the campaign. Ugly, twisted, demagogic distortion neither educates nor elevates." Then the rebuttal, which listed five points of variance between him and Eisenhower.

First, he said, Eisenhower accused the Administration of having underestimated the Soviet threat. But at the end of the war Eisenhower himself had said he saw "no reason" why the Russian and the Western systems "could not live side by side in the world."

Second, he said, Eisenhower had criticized the Truman demobilization. But Eisenhower had said in 1946, "Frankly, I don't think demobilization was too fast."

Third, Stevenson said, Eisenhower charged that the Administration had withdrawn American forces from Korea. But while Eisenhower was Chief of Staff, the Chiefs of Staff had recommended withdrawal.

Fourth, Eisenhower charged that the Administration abandoned China to the Communists. But Eisenhower knew "in his heart" that in the past six years nothing except sending an American expeditionary force to China could have prevented Communist victory.

Fifth, Eisenhower charged the Administration with "writing off"

Korea and condemned Secretary Acheson's excluding Korea from
our defensive perimeter in 1950. (Here for the first time Stevenson
defended Acheson, though he did not name him.) Eisenhower, he
said, failed to point out that this defense perimeter was a line developed by the military, not the Secretary of State.

Stevenson said that shortly after Eisenhower returned to the United
States he said, "There had been built up behind the Yalu River
a very definite air strength that would make very dangerous any attempt to extend the war at this moment, until we have a bigger
build-up of our own." Three months later Eisenhower was saying,
"I have always stood behind General MacArthur in bombing those
bases on the Yalu from which fighter planes are coming." Stevenson
demanded, "What kind of straddle is this?" Stevenson said he had
thought Eisenhower would agree that the greatest threat to American freedom was world Communism. But now he had adopted
Taft's theory that the greatest threat to liberty was the cost of our
own federal government. A year ago Republicans wanted to both cut
the defense budget and expand the war in Asia. Today they wanted
to reduce our aid to our allies in Europe and speak with "cold
finality" to the Soviet Union. "This is the policy of tougher words
backed up with smaller armies." He said scornfully, "Differences of
degree, indeed!" and asked if it was a difference of degree to be for
or against the North Atlantic Treaty, to blame the Korean War on
Stalin or on our own President, to be for or against strengthening our
allies? "Strength is the road to peace. Weakness is the road to war."
The Democratic Party was the party of strength. The Republican
Party was the party of weakness, obsessed with the idea that we
must fear not the Kremlin but our own government. Korea had
proved that Communism could go no further without risking world
war; it had helped save Indochina, Japan and Formosa; it had
"mightily strengthened" our defenses around the world; it had "kept
faith with our solemn obligations."

23

Harold W. Dodds, president of Princeton, wrote (a few days before the Stevenson fund stories appeared), "You are in the best
Princeton tradition." Stevenson was greatly pleased, pleased, too,
when the daughter of Woodrow Wilson told him his speeches reminded her of her father's. It seems gallant, or muddleheaded, of
Stevenson to take time during a presidential campaign to answer
her letter; but he cannily passed it on to Clayton Fritchey with the

suggestion that she might make a radio broadcast in his behalf. (George Ball released her letter to the press.)

It was about mid-point in the campaign, September 28. Public opinion polling in 1952 had not yet become as highly developed or awe-inspiring as it became in the 1960s. But it was heeded. A Gallup poll of August 9 had shown Eisenhower 47 per cent, Stevenson 41 per cent, with 12 per cent undecided. By September 30, Eisenhower had opened up a big lead—53 per cent to 39 per cent, with 8 per cent undecided. Gallup thought the undecided voters were overwhelmingly Democratic; distributing them 3 to 1 in favor of Stevenson, he still came out with Eisenhower 55 per cent, Stevenson 45 per cent.

That Sunday, September 28, Stevenson, looking rested, met around the long T-shaped table in his office with McGowan and some of the Elks. They agreed they must henceforward stick to the main issues—corruption, inflation, Communism, war and peace. They discussed the whistle-stop and courthouse problems. One suggested the Elks merely provide Stevenson with notes for each town and let him extemporize; he refused and asked for an all-purpose whistle-stop and an all-purpose courthouse speech. He said that if he attacked he must attack from the record specifically. He felt that in the main he must make "positive" speeches. (From time to time Schlesinger would see Stevenson and report to the Elks that "the Governor is feeling positive," then Eisenhower would say something Stevenson considered outrageous, or McCarthy would slash away, and Schlesinger would report that Stevenson was "in a belligerent mood and wants to attack like hell.") Schlesinger suggested that the days of the two-headed elephant were over; that the new line should be that the Old Guard was in control. All agreed. It had been proposed that Stevenson challenge Eisenhower to a TV debate. He was reluctant—he might "win" but his glibness and quick wit would only reinforce the subtle unfavorable impression of him as a lightweight and of Eisenhower as a solid, capable man. The debate never came off. They discussed specific speeches coming up, especially the next night's nationwide television "fireside chat"—a phrase from the FDR days. Although it was not much more than twenty-four hours away, they still did not know what the subject or format should be. One man suggested Stevenson should answer letters he had received on various issues, mainly Communism, corruption, and Korea. Another suggested he add warmth to his public image by talking about his family, his origins, and his record as Governor. He seemed interested but resisted the idea of talking about himself. The meeting broke up, some Elks to hunt for letters and write a speech answering them, others to try drafts along different lines.

In retrospect, it seems curious that Stevenson and everyone else by now assumed that Stevenson must talk about corruption, Communism, and Korea. All three were Republican issues. He could, instead, have swung over to the attack on obstructionist Republicanism and Eisenhower's lack of experience with civilian problems and warned that the Republicans would dismantle Social Security and other domestic programs and, abroad, either withdraw into a new isolationism or risk war by fanatic opposition to Communism. But Stevenson and McGowan and the Elks seemed preoccupied with Republican issues.

Eisenhower was coming to speak at the courthouse in Springfield October 2. Stevenson sent a telegram inviting him and his wife to have lunch at the Mansion or to visit him during the day. Eisenhower thanked him courteously but declined—his schedule would not permit. On Monday afternoon, September 29, Stevenson went to Chicago and delivered his TV "chat" live from an NBC studio. He began—unwisely, it seems in retrospect—by explaining his gifts as Governor to members of his administration, a long, uninteresting, defensive passage. He must have lost a good part of his audience right there. He then described how he had tried to fulfill his promise to "talk sense to the American people" by seriously discussing issues; he was disappointed that "my opponent" had not. He had read some of the "thousands" of letters he had received and knew what was troubling people: Korea, Communism in America, prosperity, and integrity in government. He undertook to answer some. On corruption, he said, "Behind every crooked tax collector is a crooked taxpayer." On prosperity, he explained dull policy. On Communists in government, he spoke briefly about the need for "quiet professional work" by the FBI rather than a need for "slandering innocent people." He talked about Korea and "the men in the Kremlin." Then he launched a rhetorical passage, his expression intense, on television outlined harshly in black and white: "A campaign addressed not to men's minds and to their best instincts, but to their passions, emotions, and prejudices, is unworthy at best. Now, with the fate of the nation at stake, it is unbearable; with the darkest evil, the mightiest force ever gathered on earth arrayed against us and our friends, this is not time for such talk. . . . Mankind and its hundreds of millions is on the march, toward what good and with what destruction on the way no man can foretell. Whole nations have sunk out of sight behind iron curtains; whole peoples have disappeared from view. . . . While the anti-Christ stalks our world, organized Communism seeks even to dethrone God from His central place in this Universe. It attempts to uproot everywhere it goes the gentle and restraining influences of religion, of love and peace. One by one the lamps of civilization go out and nameless horrors are perpetrated in darkness. All this is done by an enemy of a kind that we have never faced before. He is primitive but he is also advanced. He goes with a piece of black bread in his hand, but in his mind he carries the awful knowledge of atomic energy. He is careful, cool, calculating, and he counts time not impatiently like we do, not by the clock, but by decades, in terms of centuries. . . . The problems of a tortured, convulsive humanity stagger the nation. Unprecedented times demand of us unprecedented behavior. The task that confronts us will try our souls. . . . Whose task is this? It is inescapably your task."

The speech produced by far the biggest volume of fan mail yet. It seemed impressive at the moment; if one reflected, it was really an exercise in rhetoric. More importantly, the TV broadcast revealed a new Stevenson. He was not the same easygoing, friendly, warm, doubting, tentative, somewhat fretful and harassed man his friends knew. Instead, he seemed hard, determined, forceful, ruthless even, a man sure of himself and intent upon rousing the crowd. In private life he was given to beginning sentences by saying, "It seems to me" or "I may be wrong but I think"—a man aware of the complexity of public questions, always subject to doubt, testing his opinions. On television now, he seemed dark and forceful. Thus many around the country who admired him from afar were admiring somebody his friends had never known. From the night of the Chicago fireside chat—which became known as the "strange things happening in the dark speech"—onward, Stevenson's public impression was increasingly that of a cold remote man. It was as though somewhere about here, in mid-campaign, he decided, perhaps subconsciously, that "if you're going to lead you've got to lead" and put aside the charm that had been his in private and, previously, in public life.[15]

Now at mid-campaign, Stevenson returned to Springfield and spent nearly all the rest of the working week there. Few presidential candi-

[15] Bob Tufts, disturbed, put it a little differently. He concluded it was a natural function of politics, that "great men withdraw"—that is, that great men become surrounded by countless people, some with selfish purposes of their own, and, in self-protection, withdraw, become remote and suspicious. Thus Stevenson became, as the campaign progressed, more like all professional politicians who often strike non-politicians as false, cold, hard, unreachable, unable to permit their emotions to become involved, lest they not survive the ordeal of power.

dates in modern times, and none who were underdogs, have spent
so much time so late in the campaign at home.

Henry A. Kissinger, then editor of the Harvard University *Con-
fluence,* later President Nixon's and President Ford's Secretary of
State, told Schlesinger that, although he had earlier favored Eisenhower, he had been alienated by the crudity and primitivism of Eisenhower's campaign. Nevertheless, he said, unless Stevenson gained
rapidly, Eisenhower might win by a landslide. He thought Stevenson's campaign too often a rebuttal of charges. Stevenson should
switch to the attack, especially on foreign policy, challenging Eisenhower to say where he stood on specific questions. He should attack
Republican campaign tactics directly. Kissinger could not agree with
Stevenson's reiteration that it did not really matter who won so long
as the campaign was on a high plane. Stevenson should make his
points few and clear, establish Democratic positions instead of letting
Republicans choose the battleground. It was one of the most cogent
letters of advice received. Others, including Eric Sevareid, feared
Eisenhower would win because of his father image and advised Stevenson to attack Eisenhower hard.

The Elks were busy drafting speeches for the next trip. Stevenson, Schlesinger informed them, now thought Eisenhower's election
would be a "disaster" and was willing to attack him—but felt that
the Eisenhower myth was still so strong that it was wiser to say he
had "fallen among thieves" than to attack him frontally.

24

On Friday, October 3, Stevenson set forth on a two-day swing
through Ohio, Iowa, and Minnesota. He went first to Cincinnati,
pausing at Covington and Newport, Kentucky, across the Ohio River.
In Cincinnati he spoke at a Democratic lunch at the Netherland
Plaza Hotel, a strong highly partisan attack on Senator Taft and the
Old Guard. He went on to Columbus to speak on welfare, racial
discrimination, housing, slum clearance, rural electrification, hospitals, medical care, education, Social Security.

On Saturday, Stevenson went into Fort Dodge, Iowa, for a noonday speech into which an enormous amount of work had gone; it
dealt with farm policy. The writers had disagreed as to whether it
should be a flat statement of agricultural policy or a warmer, more
human speech. Stevenson himself had sent the Elks a memo saying
he wanted to talk about the farmer as a "whole man"—father,
husband, and so on, not just as farmer. McGowan did not want to

commit Stevenson on price supports for perishable commodities. It had been long past midnight when the Elks' draft went to the Mansion, and Stevenson and McGowan rewrote it extensively during the trip. Stevenson delivered it in a cornfield to almost empty temporary bleachers in freezing weather with a bitter wind and a balky public address system. On perishables he said, "The Democratic platform pledges the party to continue its search for practical methods of supporting perishables. . . . I have no easy solution to offer. But I do ask: on the basis of the record, which party can you trust to seek a fair solution?"

From Fort Dodge, Stevenson went up to Minneapolis and St. Paul. His chances of carrying Minnesota looked good. The Democratic-Farmer-Labor Party, which had grown out of old progressive movements of the Northwest and had sent Hubert H. Humphrey to the U. S. Senate and seemed about to put Orville Freeman in the Governor's chair, was near the peak of its power. Although Stevenson had long since said he refused to run against Herbert Hoover, he did it in Minneapolis and St. Paul. The Minneapolis speech was delivered to a hot Democratic-Farmer-Labor Party rally. The crowd received it with wild enthusiasm, and newspapermen friendly to Stevenson said that at last he had delivered a fighting speech.

The St. Paul speech became something of a model for rally speeches. In it, Stevenson heavily attacked the Old Guard and Senator Taft, and listed New Deal reforms they had opposed. "They have always been against. They have always cried: 'It costs too much,' or 'It is socialism,' or 'It is regimentation,' or, more simply, 'Ruin, ah ruin.' " Again he recalled the Great Depression:

"When FDR took office in 1933, the farmers of the Northwest were burning their wheat in their stoves because they couldn't sell it for the price of coal. The land lay barren, just gray-black dirt, and thistles blew across it, and farm wives canned the green thistles to have something to eat. And they headed out of the worst depression in memory into the worst drought. Well, FDR had been in office just two weeks when he asked Congress to act. I remember it very well; I had a hand in the early days of the old triple-A.

"In those terrible days your Farmers Union co-ops were actually sending relief trains carrying food out of the Twin Cities to feed the farmers who were starving west of here—starving on the richest land on God's earth. Today those trains are running in the opposite direction—year after year they bring to the Twin Cities a harvest of food greater than any ever known.

"And I want to recall, also, that when the Democrats took over, the mines were shut, the factories were dark, the workingmen in the cities stood in breadlines. . . . Today your industries are busy and prosperous, you all have jobs and money to buy the things your children need.

". . . The Democratic Party wrote into the law of the land the biblical injunction that we are indeed our brother's keeper—the principle that individual men and women ought not to be required to bear alone the burdens and disasters of life—flood and drought, depression and unemployment, sickness and old age—the principle that calamity to one is calamity to all."

He returned to the attack: "Unfortunately, the Old Guard orators have never understood any of this. And their candidate seems to be rapidly forgetting what he must have known about it. . . .

"So perhaps we'd better start the General's education by telling him of the Murderers' Row[16] that would control the standing committees of the Senate if the General's 'top to bottom' endorsement of all Republicans should carry weight with the American people," and he went on to name and denounce them.

"To the farmer who should know the record we say 'beware.' To the workman who should know the record we say 'beware.' "

During the end of that week Eisenhower, too, had been working the Midwest. Here he ran head on into the McCarthy problem. Stevenson had been somewhat embarrassed at being obliged to embrace Governor Frank Lausche of Ohio, a maverick conservative Democrat, but this was nothing compared to Eisenhower's McCarthy dilemma. Earlier he had tried to deal with it by saying he would support all Republican candidates but would not give a blanket endorsement to any who violated his "conception of what is decent, right, just, and fair." This had not been enough. Now Eisenhower was going to Wisconsin. His advisers leaked a formula that had been worked out: McCarthy would introduce Eisenhower in McCarthy's home town, Appleton, Wisconsin, but otherwise would be kept in the background; while at Milwaukee, Eisenhower would make a strong speech on Communism which would emphasize civil liberties and reiterate his admiration for General Marshall.[17] But professional Republican politicians were putting pressure on Eisenhower to give McCarthy an all-out endorsement. Thursday night McCarthy flew to Peoria, Illinois, to join the Eisenhower train. Next morning at Green Bay, Wisconsin—while Stevenson was in Cincinnati and Columbus—

[16] The New York Yankees' powerful batting line-up was then called "Murderers' Row."

[17] McCarthy had denounced Marshall as "a man steeped in falsehood." Senator Jenner of Indiana had called him "a living lie" and "a front man for traitors."

Eisenhower called for the election of the entire Republican ticket and said that the differences between him and McCarthy were well known but applied to "method," not objectives. McCarthy appeared on the rear platform at the whistle stops. Campaigning from Green Bay through Fond du Lac, Eisenhower repeatedly said he wanted Wisconsin voters to return McCarthy to the Senate. At Milwaukee that night, Friday, October 3, Eisenhower's crowd was unusually small and unenthusiastic. Before Eisenhower arrived to speak, McCarthy spoke for ten minutes amid cheers and jeers—several men were ejected by the police. He described Eisenhower as "a great American who will make a great President" and said that, although they did not agree "entirely on everything . . . I shall continue to call them as I see them, regardless of who is President." The advance text of Eisenhower's speech contained no defense of General Marshall. A rumor spread that he would ad-lib it; he did not. Instead he made a strong attack on persons who had let themselves be duped by Communist propaganda. He attacked Truman and Stevenson (without naming them) for treating the Communist danger lightly.

The United Press reporter, Merriman Smith, began his report, "Dwight D. Eisenhower, speaking in the company of Sen. Joseph R. McCarthy, tonight flatly accused the Truman administration of 'treason.'" (The UP soon deleted that first paragraph and substituted a softer one.) Advisers of both McCarthy and Eisenhower denied that McCarthy had asked Eisenhower to omit the praise of Marshall. Local Republicans assured Eisenhower that his handling of McCarthy would win Wisconsin; some of his aides feared the reaction of independents elsewhere. Stevenson, in his St. Paul speech next day, said, "[My opponent] has disappointed even myself—though none of us was prepared for yesterday's melancholy spectacle. That spectacle can leave no doubt in anyone's mind that the General is hopelessly the captive of the Old Guard. And we all know where the Old Guard stands." Eisenhower increased his own attacks. He issued a long, sarcastic statement directly counterattacking Stevenson's Louisville speech on Korea. He again criticized Acheson for declaring early in 1950 that South Korea lay outside the American defense perimeter. And in downstate Illinois he said that if there must be war in the Far East "let it be Asians against Asians with our support on the side of freedom." Soon Nixon would say that Stevenson "holds a Ph.D. degree from Acheson's school of the three C's— Cowardly Communist Containment." When Eisenhower stopped in Springfield, Stevenson had released state employees for an hour to hear him. It was virtually his last chivalrous act of the campaign, and no wonder.

25

Newsweek said that, with only a month to go, the Democrats had decided to sharpen their attacks on Eisenhower. President Truman, whistle-stopping eastward on the second leg of his cross-country trip, "was blowing two shrill notes," the magazine said: "Dwight D. Eisenhower didn't amount to much after all. And besides, the voters should think of their pocketbooks." Stevenson, too, was increasingly criticizing Eisenhower. Last spring, *Newsweek* said, Stevenson had considered Eisenhower a great and historic figure, but since then had changed his mind because of Eisenhower's rapprochment with Taft, his embrace of Senators Jenner and McCarthy, and his increasing criticism of the Korean War. But Stevenson was motorcading through almost empty streets. The polls showed Eisenhower ahead but were still calling the contest "wide open" and saying that a "very large proportion" of voters were still undecided. The Gallup poll "if the election were held today" showed Eisenhower leading in New York 50–43, in Illinois 47–42, in California 54.5–40.5. *Newsweek,* noting Stevenson's appeal to reason, quoted Carl McGowan as saying, "If you win elections this way, we'll win. If you don't, we'll lose. There's no point in trying to change the Governor's personality and methods. He'd be miserable and make a mess of it."

Stevenson would leave Tuesday and keep on the move almost continuously till the election. Senator J. W. Fulbright of Arkansas had come to Springfield to bolster the amateurs, according to the press. Steve Mitchell said Stevenson's chances looked better daily, despite a shortage of money.

Some of the banter with the press continued. Wilson Wyatt held a press conference in the big bare press room in the Leland Hotel littered with coffee cups. He announced Stevenson would cover eight states that week, traveling about 4,350 miles and making about twenty-three speeches in quest of 111 electoral votes. They would leave tomorrow and return Saturday night "at the usual eleven fifty-five." "Approximately," a reporter said. Wyatt said, "That is approximately. It could be eleven fifty-six." Reporter: "Or one fifty-six." The Detroit speech would be "one of the most important speeches in the campaign," for in it Stevenson would deal with "the entire subject of Communism." Reporter: "How long is he going to talk? Five hours?"

That night Wyatt, Ball, and Clayton Fritchey went to the Elks

Club. They had dinner with Stevenson and reported he wanted to attack and didn't mind "corn"—saying, for example, he had a son in the Marines. Wyatt was happy about the schedule for the last ten days, which ended with a whistle stop from the East Coast to Chicago—"I can see that whistle stop the last day across Ohio and Indiana as a triumphal tour."

26

Stevenson and the party left Tuesday, October 7, for the eight-state swing through the Midwest and the South. He had a heavy schedule the first day—six appearances in Michigan during the day, followed by his major address on Communism that night. He started in the Municipal Auditorium at Saginaw, a long speech on economic issues. Young hecklers interrupted him repeatedly with shouts of "I like Ike." Heckling continued at Ypsilanti, and once an airplane roared overhead, drowning out his words, and Stevenson observed, "Republican pilot." He tried out a new all-purpose whistle stop the Elks had prepared, dealing at length with education, alluding to foreign policy, recalling the depression, raising labor issues, attacking Eisenhower as the captive of the Old Guard. He did it well, and the crowd responded enthusiastically. From Ypsilanti, the motorcade went to Detroit, stopping en route at Willow Run Village, Wayne, River Rouge (where, years earlier, Walter Reuther and others of the CIO had been beaten savagely by Ford guards and thugs at the giant Ford plant). Such Democrats as Governor G. Mennen Williams carried Michigan by winning the union vote and the Negro vote in Detroit and other auto cities plus votes in the faraway Upper Peninsula; the vast geographical bulk of the state was Republican. Labor was the key. But at Wayne, Stevenson repeated the Evansville fiasco—discarded his carefully prepared all-purpose whistle stop and declared belligerently, to workers leaving a factory gate at 5 P.M., "I will never be bossed by big labor and I will never be bossed in any way, shape, or form by big industry. I should like to say to you, too, that I deplore violence, disorder, lawlessness in labor disputes just as much as I deplore it anywhere else." He called Congressman Lesinski "Lesnicki." Back in the motorcade, Schlesinger, depressed, asked McGowan to speak to Stevenson before the next stop, and he did, and Stevenson improved.

From his last stop, a union hall, he motorcaded to the Detroit-Leland Hotel, attended a buffet supper with party and labor leaders, and went to his hotel suite before delivering his major speech live on national television and radio. The idea of a full-dress speech on Communism had been debated throughout September by the Stevenson staff. Finally the decision had been taken to deliver it. Wirtz had written an early draft; Schlesinger had rewritten it; others had contributed. Dave Bell had cleared parts of it with the White House. With Nixon and McCarthy arguing that Stevenson was "soft on Communism," it was a crucial statement.

He began, "I want to talk to you tonight about a disease. It is a disease which may have killed more people in this world in the last five years than cancer, than tuberculosis, than heart disease—more than all of these combined. It has certainly killed more minds, more souls, more decent human hopes and ambitions, than any corruption—including the darkest days of Hitler." He would discuss what the United States was doing to resist Communism in America. He would, he said, dispel "fog and confusion" created by Communists and "political demagogues, who are hunting for votes much more than they are for Communists."

Twenty years ago, he said, the Great Depression had presented Communism with its best opportunity. A Democratic administration had defeated the depression. It had gone on to rally the free world against Communism abroad—over the entrenched opposition of the Republican Old Guard. Moreover, Democratic leadership had built an internal security system to protect against subversion. Under the Smith Act, Truman's Department of Justice had convicted thirty-one leaders of the American Communist Party. During the war, over 1,500 people had been denied federal employment because of doubtful loyalty. In 1947, Truman had set up "a new and tighter" federal loyalty program. Truman's Attorney General had established an official list of subversive organizations. In 1948 and 1949 the Department of Justice had convicted Communist leaders.

All this had happened before Joe McCarthy began "his wild and reckless campaign against the integrity of our government itself." McCarthy had yet to produce evidence leading to the conviction of a single Communist agent. "Catching real Communist agents . . . is not a job for amateurs. . . . It is a job for professionals," and he related the FBI's record. Eisenhower, "I'm sorry to say," implied that the federal government was deliberately concealing Communists. "What would he do? Would he fire J. Edgar Hoover? Would he fire General Bedell Smith, head of the Central Intelligence Agency and the General's own former Chief of Staff? Would he discharge General Smith's deputy, Allen Dulles? . . . I think we are entitled to ask, is the Republican candidate seriously interested in trying to root Communists out of the government, or is he only interested in scaring the American people to get votes? . . . And let me say one more thing, so there will be no shadow of a doubt. If I find in Washington any disloyal government servant, I will throw him out ruthlessly, regardless of place, position, or party. . . . Let us never forget that tension breeds repression, and repression, injustice and tyranny. Our police work is aimed at a conspiracy, and not ideas or opinion. Our country was built on unpopular ideas, on unorthodox opinions. My definition of a free society is a society where it is safe to be unpopular. I want to keep our America that way."

Reaction to the speech was mixed. The immediate audience liked it. Harry Truman considered it a mistake—too defensive. Senator Benton, who had been one of McCarthy's earliest critics and was now running for re-election in Connecticut, praised the speech. Senator Tydings of Maryland called it "a masterpiece." The conservative columnist, David Lawrence, thought it indicated that Stevenson was uninformed or had decided to ignore the facts in order to get votes.

Stevenson stayed overnight in Detroit and flew next morning to Madison, Wisconsin. Small street crowds greeted him; the university field house had a capacity of 14,000 but only about 9,000 were present; and cries of "I like Ike" arose. Undismayed, Stevenson attacked Senator McCarthy (without naming him) here in his own state.

"The pillorying of the innocent has caused the wise to stammer and the timid to retreat. I would shudder for this country if I thought that we too must surrender to the sinister figure of the Inquisition, of the great accuser."

From the university field house in Madison, Stevenson went to the Hotel Loraine and spoke briefly. After lunch he spent the afternoon motorcading from Madison to Milwaukee, largely a waste of time, with two unimportant stops. Milwaukee was Newt Minow's home town; he had advanced the trip. He introduced his parents to Stevenson. Minow had arranged for Stevenson to have dinner with the editorial board of the influential Milwaukee *Journal.* Stevenson, Minow later recalled, was "great" at the dinner, and the *Journal* subsequently endorsed him, one of the few major newspapers to do so.[18] After dinner Stevenson addressed a Democratic rally at the Arena. In praising candidates for the Senate and Congress, he jibed: "Let it be clear that I speak of these men because I admire

[18] Others were the St. Louis *Post-Dispatch,* Bingham's Louisville *Courier-Journal* and *Times,* and the New Orleans *Item.*

them—and not just because they are Democrats. If I were ashamed of them—so that I could not bring myself even to speak their names —I would not ask you to vote for them. My opponent has been worrying about my funnybone. I'm worrying about his backbone." It was one of the sharpest personal attacks yet on Eisenhower—yet even this was touched with wit. He took up several issues one by one —agriculture, labor, inflation, prosperity, Communism, American policy in Europe—and on each stated the Democratic position, then attacked "the General" or "the General of the Army" or "the Republican candidate" or "the Republican leaders" for either having no position or one which was, he argued, inimical to the public interest. He was, thus, developing a "shopping list" speech, an all-purpose speech covering a long list of issues for a partisan rally.

The speech was a great success. Stevenson's crowds in Milwaukee, both on the sidewalk and in the Arena, were bigger than Eisenhower's. Stevenson left early next morning, Thursday, October 9, for St. Joseph, Missouri, where, at a morning airport rally, he talked about the Republicans' multimillion-dollar campaign "on trains, and even on confetti, and on balloons, and on television, and on radio." He endorsed a "Mr. Welch" for Congress, and a voice from the crowd called, "Mr. Richardson to the Congress," and Stevenson said, "Oh, Mr. Richardson. I apologize, Mr. Richardson. I sometimes forget which congressional district I am in."

From St. Joseph, Stevenson flew to Kansas City where, at a Democratic luncheon, he praised President Truman as a man of independence. (Truman's home was in nearby Independence, Missouri.) By contrast, he said, Eisenhower was not. "When the General of the Army spoke in Kansas City, he said something which troubled me very much. He said, 'Between the Democrat and the Republican parties, there are deep differences. They are irreconcilable differences.' I would hope that no differences in our great democracy become irreconcilable—because irreconcilable differences lead only to one thing, and that is bitterness and division when unity and strength are the goal. Irreconcilable differences led to the Civil War." It was a characteristic remark. The crowd, a big one, responded enthusiastically.

Afterward Stevenson met privately with Democratic leaders and spoke briefly and extemporaneously, saying, "I believe we Democrats are on the right side this time of everything, and I think that is going to have its ultimate manifestation on Election Day, depending, of course, on how much you get out and get them registered, and get them into the precincts and get them into the polling places." He should have done more of this everywhere.

A classmate in Massachusetts told Stevenson that neither the Democratic State Committee nor the National Committee was yet active there in his behalf—candidates were campaigning for themselves, not mentioning Stevenson's name. If this was true nationally at this point, Stevenson was in serious trouble. No candidate can win a presidential election alone, however brilliant his personal performance. He requires the support of local, state, and national party organizations—they raise money, prepare campaign materials, recruit party workers, get out the vote, and buy billboard and newspaper space and radio and television time, and so on. If Stevenson was indeed chasing around the country all alone, his effort was doomed.[19]

From Kansas City, Stevenson flew to St. Louis and motorcaded across the Mississippi River into the Democratic stronghold of southern Illinois, the drab gray industrial crime-ridden slum, making short stops at Alton, Wood River, Granite City, Brooklyn, and East St. Louis. The Elks had prepared a package of speeches for these stops. They hoped he could read through the package as the motorcade started; between stops he could reread the piece for the one coming up, and when the motorcade halted he could speak almost extemporaneously. It was another attempt to solve the whistle-stop problem. But the motorcade was late, the arrangements poor, the crowds pressed in too close, and, worrying about his big evening speech, he sometimes said little more than hello. The motorcade was no success but it was no disaster either—a so-so afternoon.

That night in St. Louis at the Kiel Auditorium to an overflow crowd, he delivered on nationwide TV and radio the speech on "America's New Frontier"—what role the government should play in developing the United States. He also summed up the positions he had taken on ten issues during the first half of the campaign.[20] It would have been a good September speech, was not fiery enough for October's hot crowds.

Stevenson stayed that night in St. Louis and left early next morn-

---

[19] The organization's failure need not be due to indifference or hostility. In 1968, years of neglect of the Democratic National Committee, plus state and local factionalism, plus a lack of funds, contributed to Hubert Humphrey's defeat. In 1952, when reporters saw the small crowds that greeted Stevenson's motorcade, what they may really have been witnessing was a failure of the local organization and the advance men to turn out crowds. Crowds are seldom automatic, except at such places and times as New York's garment district or Los Angeles' Broadway at noontime.

[20] A fuller account of this speech will be found in Appendix F.

ing, Friday, October 10, for Oklahoma City, eating breakfast aloft. In Oklahoma City he spoke at a rally, then at a lunch at the Skirvin Hotel sponsored by the Oklahoma Democratic Organization. His speech was brief, direct, and good. He said "the General" had "admitted that he does not know very much" about domestic economic policies so had deferred to Taft. He spelled out Democratic domestic programs. He said the road to peace lay through building strength and unity with our allies. He said Republican proposals to slash the defense budget and aid to allies might well be disastrous. Eisenhower had forsaken the bipartisan policy of strength and joined Taft. Republican policy of talking tough while simultaneously weakening our defenses and alliances was "a sure road to disaster." It was not a notably eloquent speech. But it was about as straightforward, crisp, and clear a statement of the issues as he ever managed. It was the kind of speech that evolves from a candidate's having made dozens of speeches and being obliged, in relaxed surroundings and without the pressures of national television, to state briefly what he thinks the campaign is all about. It went unnoticed.

After it, Stevenson and his party flew to New Orleans, coming over it just at dark, with the red afterglow of the sun westward over the crescent curve of the Mississippi. The airport crowd was big, one of the biggest yet, with a Dixieland band. Democratic leaders from ten Southern states greeted Stevenson, including the Governor of Louisiana, who had announced he supported Eisenhower. The motorcade was wild, weaving on a four-lane highway, clashing fenders, raising dust and scattering animals and people all the way to the Roosevelt Hotel. As always, there was a terrible jam at the registration desk, rooms having been reserved for people who were not in the party and not having been reserved for people who were. Stevenson had a fantastic suite, enormous, with onyx tables and free-form sculpture and complete bar—but no electric lights: they wouldn't turn on. McGowan lit a candle in one room: Blair moved about in the shadows; Stevenson sat in the living room with several men in the dark. And a crisis arose.

A Negro newspaperman, James Hicks of New York, traveling with Stevenson, had talked to Flanagan a day or two earlier about what would happen when they reached New Orleans: the law there forbade unsegregated hotels. Flanagan had planned for Hicks to stay with a professor from a Negro college. Schlesinger, warned by Ralph McGill of the Atlanta *Constitution* and Harry Ashmore of the Arkansas *Gazette,* consulted Flanagan. Hicks refused to go to the professor's home and, refused admission to the hotel, held a press conference.

Now newspapermen were trying to ask Stevenson about it. Flanagan and McGowan took the calls and refused to let them speak to Stevenson. Flanagan told them Stevenson had not known about the affair; that he, Flanagan, was responsible, and that since a law existed nothing could be done. Actually, by the time Stevenson left the hotel to make his speech at Beauregard Square, Stevenson knew all about the incident. McGowan and Flanagan stayed behind at the hotel, trying to decide what, if anything, Stevenson should do. Martin, who happened to be on this leg of the trip, sought advice from the Elks. Dave Bell recommended that Stevenson move out of the hotel forthwith; this was what Truman would do, he said. Martin doubted Stevenson would do it and asked for other suggestions. After a long conversation they outlined a statement Stevenson might issue: that Stevenson deeply regretted the incident, that before leaving Springfield he had given instructions that Negroes traveling with him should have the same quarters as everyone else, that Louisiana law prevented this, that he looked forward to the time when such racial barriers would be struck down. The Elks considered the incident serious. At that time Dewey was disseminating in Harlem a Democratic primary ballot from Alabama—the home state of Stevenson's running mate, John Sparkman—which read, "White Supremacy Ballot." The Elks feared that if Stevenson failed to act now in New Orleans he might lose New York and Illinois with their large Negro votes.

Flanagan thought they should do nothing—sit tight and ride out the storm. In accordance with the Elks' view, McGowan and Martin drafted a statement. It would be issued only if the incident received big national publicity. McGowan felt that any dramatic gesture such as leaving the hotel would not genuinely advance human rights and might be construed as demagogic; that the best course, if possible, was to do nothing. Stevenson concurred. It was a characteristic decision. It turned out that the incident received relatively little publicity, and McGowan decided to do nothing. Throughout the campaign he carried far too heavy a burden. Everybody turned to him. It was no wonder that he sometimes seemed distracted; the wonder was that he was able to focus clearly on such a matter as the Hicks incident, where demands were being made for immediate action but where large ethical, legal, and political questions were inextricably entangled. Every campaign has its McGowan; few have anyone so good.

Stevenson returned to the hotel from the Beauregard Square speech looking happy, rested, strengthened. The crowd had been large, the speech successful. Most of its rhetoric had been drafted by

David Cohn. But its substantive heart, Stevenson's definitive statement on offshore oil, had been done by McGowan—offshore oil
was a major issue in Louisiana. Stevenson took a firm position. The
Supreme Court had ruled that the offshore lands belonged to the
federal government, not to state governments (as Louisiana claimed).
Such national assets should be used to benefit all, not given away to
individual states. But the next President should press Congress to
enact legislation which would provide for "fair" arrangements for
dividing the proceeds between state and federal governments.[21]
The main body of the speech dealt with foreign aid, taking the
orthodox liberal free-trade position. Stevenson also spoke directly on
civil rights: "As you know, I stand on the Democratic Party platform
with respect to minority rights. I have only one observation to make
on this subject; one that must sadden you as it saddens me. It is that,
after two thousand years of Christianity, we need discuss it at all."
After the speech a local politician took some of the staff and press to
cabarets in New Orleans' Latin Quarter. They were up all night.
It was probably the only night "on the town" during the entire campaign. Others on the staff stayed up all that night, too, working on
the Miami and Tampa speeches.

That night Richard Nixon said in a speech of his own, "Stevenson himself hasn't even backbone training, for he is a graduate of
Dean Acheson's spineless school of diplomacy which cost the free
world 600 million former allies in the past seven years of Truman-
ism." Repeatedly Nixon talked about "more Alger Hisses, more
atomic spies, more crises" and suggested that Stevenson's judgment was bad, that he would be a weak President, and that he had
demonstrated weakness in giving the Hiss deposition.

The Stevenson party had to get up at 5:30 A.M. so their baggage
could be collected; the plane was due to leave at seven. The Miami
speech, to be delivered that midday, needed inserts; they had to be
written aloft. Stevenson approved them, and the girls typed and
mimeographed the speech and finished assembling it just before the
plane touched down. Stevenson was speaking that day in Bayfront
Park, where an assassin had missed Franklin Roosevelt but killed
the Mayor of Chicago years ago, and McGowan was concerned
because some of Stevenson's bodyguards—he usually had two, a
Chicago policeman and a Secret Service man—looked as though
they had been up all night. The crowd at the Miami airport was

---

[21] He pointed out that in some cases 37½ per cent of the revenue from
other public lands went to the state where the lands were located but said
he did not know whether that formula should be used in this case.

small. He was late. On the radio in the motorcade one could hear an announcer at Bayfront Park filling in time. By the time Stevenson arrived, half his radio time was gone. And when he began speaking, the public address system failed. But the crowd was friendly and enthusiastic; it applauded often. He hurried back to the airport and flew to Tampa, where, after having been presented with a large-mouth bass which bit him—he had not known it was alive— he delivered a speech to a football stadium that was at least two thirds empty and where most of his audience was seated behind him. The crowd was noisy, the presentation of local politicians interminable. When at last Stevenson spoke, it was clear that the crowd was not with him, that they did not understand what he was saying, or that they were simply cold and unsympathetic. He became rattled and tried to insert jokes, but they fell flat. Only once did he get any enthusiastic applause: when he promised to repeal and replace Taft-Hartley. The rest of the speech was a failure, if success is judged by crowd response. En route back to the airport McGowan, while acknowledging Stevenson had been in poor form, said he simply did not know what to think of political crowds. If they were enthusiastic, one was pleased, of course. But perhaps the silent crowds were listening and thinking about what was being said; maybe that was better. Moreover, newspaper coverage of a passage on Social Security would reach people too old to go to the rally. The speech had lacked the applause lines and heavy-handed repetition always necessary in an outdoor speech. The plane took off for Nashville.

The flight that night was beautiful, high above a solid overcast with the sun setting far beyond the western rim of the clouds, a kind of half-night. Many aboard were sleeping or drinking, exhausted; it was near the end of the trip. The weather was bad at Nashville; the captain made an almost unbelievable landing, breaking through the overcast at five hundred feet while flying visually because the instrument landing system was out of order, then suddenly making a forty-five-degree turn and changing runways because what had looked from the air like a runway was not and the one he had to use went off at an angle; he landed without a jolt. Despite the rain the crowd at Nashville—at the airport, along the motorcade route, around the downtown hotel, and at the War Memorial Auditorium where Stevenson spoke—was one of the biggest and most enthusiastic he had yet seen. Harry Ashmore and the David Cohn group had written the speech. Like all Southern speeches, it was very long and contained a recitation of Stevenson's Southern ancestry; the crowd expected and liked it. He talked at great length about the Democratic Party and the South, calling the people home to the party of their fathers. He recalled their heroes, John C. Calhoun and Cordell Hull and Andrew Jackson. He called the roll of Southern Democrats who presided over powerful Senate and House committees. He recalled how Southern voters had rallied behind Woodrow Wilson, FDR, and Harry Truman. He praised Southern valor under arms. He praised Southern internationalism and resistance to isolationism. He declared that what the Republicans denounced as Big Government had accomplished much—including TVA; he reminded them that Eisenhower had pledged "there would be no more TVAs" if he was elected. Yet he was careful to say balance must be maintained between economic security and personal liberty and to say that as a Governor he had learned the virtues of states' rights "as a bulwark against Big Government." It was a skillful speech.

After the speech and a reception, the Stevenson party flew on to Springfield, arriving at midnight. Wyatt or someone else had arranged to have a large crowd, probably mostly state employees, greet Stevenson at the Springfield airport, and Stevenson was surprised and touched to see them. Johnson Kanady of the *Tribune* seized Fred Hoehler and demanded to know who had arranged the crowd and said he would not accept any baloney about its being spontaneous. (Kanady, a good reporter, never let up.) The weeklong trip had been a mixed one, hence the crowd to hearten Stevenson. It was Saturday night, October 11. Three weeks to go.

27

Alicia Patterson was in a New York hospital; Stevenson sent her a sympathetic note and wrote of "this endless pilgrimage." She might be, she thought, fatally ill; she prepared to return Stevenson's letters to him with a note saying she thought them beautiful and hoped that, with his sense of history, he would not destroy them— how good it would have been, she thought, had Lincoln written to Ann Rutledge and had his letters been preserved; and she reaffirmed her love. (The letters apparently were not delivered to him until 1963, the year of her death.)

John Mason Brown had sent Stevenson a quotation uttered by Cromwell just before the Battle of Dunbar, "I beseech ye in the bowels of Christ, think that ye may be mistaken." (Stevenson used it.) He thanked Marshall Field III for his support—he had personally endorsed Stevenson, but his newspaper, the Chicago *Sun-Times,* run by his son, had endorsed Eisenhower. In another letter he referred to "my dreary speeches." To a woman concerned about his religious beliefs, he wrote, "I have had some faith from childhood, and more and more in later years, because I have known sorrow, trouble and severe testing. Only in Him will we find 'peace at the end.'" Stevenson was still meticulous about Illinois affairs. In signing a printing contract he instructed Newt Minow not to process it until he had checked it carefully. At long last twenty-two prominent attorneys, both Democrats and Republicans, issued a statement defending Stevenson's involvement in the Hiss affair. At the same time Nixon launched a vehement attack on Stevenson.

The Elks spent the weekend preparing for the second Western trip. It would begin Tuesday, October 14. It was considered extremely important. Eisenhower had just been West and seemed to be doing better there than in the East. The election was considered close in California. Stevenson was in trouble in Texas. This would be his last chance to win the West; after this he would have to concentrate in the industrial East and Midwest. The schedule was backbreaking—more than two dozen speeches in five days in seven states. Stevenson met with the Elks on Sunday. He seemed prepared to attack. He was angry at the Nixon-McCarthy attacks and at reports of a climactic Republican radio-TV blitz. He was prepared to reply to McCarthy or Nixon or both. The Elks, divided over the wisdom of doing so, argued the question far into the night on Monday, the night before Stevenson was to leave. Because of the heavy work load en route, two Elks would accompany Stevenson—Bill Wirtz and Martin.

28

Tuesday morning, October 14, was bright and cold, and the planes took off on schedule at 8:45 A.M. for Casper, Wyoming, flying low because of headwinds up high, seeming to barely skim the prairies and Great Plains sloping up to the Rockies. Stevenson would speak that day at Casper and Salt Lake City. Everyone thought it foolish to go a second time to Wyoming, a state with only three electoral votes. Stevenson was going because Senator O'Mahoney was in trouble and asking help. It is a measure of the confidence of Stevenson and his managers that they could spend a part of a day in an effort to rescue a Senator.

On the plane that morning, Wirtz and Martin, having reread the Salt Lake Tabernacle speech, a lofty rhetorical speech to be broadcast on national TV, concluded it would be inappropriate to insert into it a defense of Stevenson's actions in the Hiss case and an attack on Nixon. McGowan agreed. Martin wrote an insert for the Pendleton, Oregon, speech endorsing the Hell's Canyon Dam on the Snake River. It was a controversial issue. Truman had recommended it, but Congress had refused to act. The private power lobby was against it. Senator Wayne Morse, leaving the Republican Party for the Democratic, was for it. Dave Bell strongly urged that Stevenson be for it—it was a sound project and an administration measure and it offered Stevenson an opportunity to sharply contrast his own position on natural resources development with Eisenhower's. Martin took his insert to McGowan and argued for it, presenting documents and Bell's arguments. McGowan resisted stoutly. He didn't think that Stevenson should commit himself to any such project without knowing more about it, since doing so was tantamount to putting it in his first presidential budget. It was an example of the almost hopelessly high-minded—or, some would say, highly responsible—approach that McGowan and Stevenson took to campaign issues. McGowan finally agreed to present it to Stevenson, and during the day he, Wirtz, and Martin worked on language on Hell's Canyon. They also worked on "the Indians"—Eisenhower had been telling the Indians that the government was keeping them in slavery, Dave Bell had reported, and they believed it, and so Stevenson should propose gradual withdrawal of federal services to increase their freedom without endangering their prosperity.

It was cold and snowy in Casper, high in the mountains. The crowd at the airport and along the motorcade route was small but at the courthouse square, where both Eisenhower and Taft had spoken in the preceding forty-eight hours, Stevenson's crowd was as big as Eisenhower's and far bigger than Taft's. The prepared speech was too transparently an appeal for votes for Senator O'Mahoney, plus a brief "shopping list" of Democratic positions and an attack on Old Guard obstructionism; the crowd did not respond. Stevenson seemed to sense it. When he finished his prepared text, he continued extemporaneously, uttering one of the most eloquent personal passages of the campaign:

"I am grateful to you for coming here on this cold day to welcome me in Casper. You have been very good to me; you are very courteous and you have been very hospitable. The job which I have undertaken is not an easy one, traveling across our country from coast to coast, urging people to support my party, our principles and myself, but it has been a very rewarding experience. It has accorded me an opportunity to see so much of our country; to see so much of it rapidly. As it unfolds rapidly like a motion picture, you get some impression of the enormity, the variety, the might, the majesty of this United States of America.

"It is a humbling experience. To confront the possibility of being responsible for at least the execution of its policies and the suggestion of its programs—to do that and to do it well—to do it in the interests of all of the people, with so many conflicting views and such a variety of interests, is a job that staggers the imagination, the human mind, human patience. . . .

"I just say to you here that our hope, my friends, we think lies in our party; we think the record establishes it; we think the projection of our future on the basis of these policies of the past make it manifest. But whichever party—whoever is assigned this ghastly responsibility can only succeed—he and your congressmen and your Senators—with the support, the confidence, the good will and, I must add, the patience of the people—people like you.

"You have been very good to me. I am very grateful to you for coming here to see me.

"Thank you."

Delivering that passage, he changed the tenor of his voice. He seemed to be putting himself into it. More than at any previous time in the campaign the inner warmth of his personality came through. The crowd responded with cheers. The day had been cold and bleak and damp and gray, and Margaret Munn, enthralled by Stevenson's extemporizing, exclaimed that when he began it the sun came out.

The party flew to Salt Lake City. En route, McGowan, Wirtz, and Martin went back to Stevenson's cabin. Stevenson had been reading a book on Lincoln; it lay beside him on the seat. Looking out the window at the mountains below, Stevenson said the Los Angeles rally speech was in a state of confusion. He wanted to talk about Korea there. He said he had been informed in a confidential briefing from the Joint Chiefs of Staff that the United States was in a dangerously weak military position in Korea and elsewhere. Stevenson thought that everybody was "entirely too complacent" about it. He also said, "I want to get off this slap-happy idea that we've got all the answers. We haven't." He was angry at Eisenhower's campaign, particularly at what Eisenhower was saying about Korea. He felt the country faced problems of almost terrifying urgency and Eisenhower was evading them. He asked for suggestions for Los Angeles. Wirtz proposed a discussion of all issues. Martin suggested putting it in terms of problems the country faced—rather than as campaign issues—and making an almost non-political speech. Nothing was settled. Stevenson told them to think about it.

Salt Lake City came up over the high mountain range. The crowds along the motorcade route and around the hotel were enormous, and they were enthusiastic. Local politicians in the motorcade said they had never seen anything like it. At the hotel about 5 P.M., McGowan and Martin set to work independently to shorten the Mormon Tabernacle speech, to be given that evening. The Tabernacle speech is an important traditional one for both candidates, given in every recent presidential campaign. It was to be nationally televised. McGowan and Martin were anxious that, for once, Stevenson finish on time. The speech had already been mimeographed and released to the press; their cuts would appear only in Stevenson's reading copy. They would not merely mark optional cuts, as they had at Louisville and St. Louis—he had not taken the cuts and had run overtime; now they would mark firm cuts.

About six o'clock Martin took his manuscript to the suite which McGowan shared with Stevenson. Neither was there. Jim Daley, Stevenson's Chicago bodyguard, was joking about a pretty girl at the door. Tim Ives said McGowan and Stevenson had gone to a reception. Soon Blair and McGowan came in, then Stevenson. Stevenson had a drink with the others. He was tired and a little annoyed at having had to attend the reception; he complained again that he had no time to work on speeches. He wondered whether he should have a second drink—"I won't know what I'm saying tonight." But he had a second, one of the few times during the campaign that he did. He dined in his suite with McGowan, Blair, Daley, Tim Ives, and Martin. Stevenson's spirits revived. He chided McGowan for ordering flounder instead of local rainbow trout; he ate with gusto; he did not mind that nobody knew how he should address the president of the Mormon Church. He said he wanted to talk to McGowan and Wirtz and Martin later about the speeches for the rest of the week, especially Los Angeles. McGowan told him that Speaker of the House Sam Rayburn had invited them to visit John Nance Garner at Uvalde, Texas. McGowan recommended it, and not only for reasons of Texas politics: ever since the Hicks hotel segregation incident at New Orleans, they had feared a similar incident at Dallas and so had decided to make part of the Texas trip by train and sleep aboard the train instead of in a Dallas hotel—going to Uvalde provided an excuse.

Stevenson said, "Why can't they [the Negro reporters] go somewhere else? Are they just trying to embarrass us?"

The others told him it was deeper than that, the reporters felt strongly about it and were determined to make an issue of it as a matter of conscience.

Blair proposed that, on Election Day, Stevenson tour the South Side of Chicago, the Negro ghetto, not a noisy motorcade but a tour by the Governor of Illinois dropping around on his way to cast his own vote in Libertyville. Blair thought it would "do you some good."

Stevenson said, "A hundred thousand dollars would do more good."

Blair said, "But do you have the hundred thousand dollars? No. So you do the next best thing."

The Chicago *Defender,* a Negro newspaper, had just endorsed Stevenson; he sent a wire to its publisher thanking him. McGowan said that the New York *Times* had reported that Stevenson had called up John L. Lewis of the United Mine Workers of America. McGowan said, "Now we have it all—Garner and the evil whisky-drinking crowd and John L. Lewis." (This referred to Lewis' remark several years earlier that Garner was "an evil, whisky-drinking, poker-playing old man.")

Stevenson, laughing, said, "Now everything's in balance." Then, seriously, "I never should have done that. That was that man Alinsky." Saul Alinsky, who had in the past acted as an intermediary between Lewis and President Roosevelt, had recently suggested that Stevenson telephone Lewis in an effort to head off a proposed coal strike. Stevenson regretted that news of the call had leaked; he instinctively disliked being linked closely to labor leaders. He recurred to the upcoming speeches and asked who had written them. He talked about which newspaperman had written which story in recent days. His spirits became almost high—he talked to the waiters, bantered with his staff.

Finishing dinner, Stevenson asked about the cuts on the Tabernacle speech. He would have to leave the hotel no later than eight-ten to go to the Tabernacle, and it was already past seven. He, McGowan, and Martin began going over the speech together. Earlier, Stevenson had been cutting a copy of his own. It turned out that the three of them, working independently, had made almost identical cuts, including two paragraphs attacking Eisenhower. In several places Stevenson had made drastic cuts; McGowan and Martin showed him how to gain the same space by numerous small cuts. Stevenson worked hard and fast, with the deadline approaching. They finished just at the time he had to leave. He was pleased with the speech. He went off to deliver it. He praised "the great confident majority of Americans" and said Republican speechmakers served them ill when they pictured Americans as half defeated, half bankrupt, self-pitying, isolationist, indifferent to the fate of man, even "dupes and fellow travelers." He recalled the war, when it had been "a noble experience to be one of the American people. . . . But a cold war leads the timid and the discontented into frustration. . . . American power is not just our forests and our mountain ranges, and the huge meandering rivers of our central plains, and the high dry cattle country, and this lucky land of yours between the mountains and the ocean. It is not even all these things plus 160 million people. It is these things, plus the people, plus the idea! . . .

"What is this 'American idea' which we so justly venerate? I suggest that the heart of it is the simple but challenging statement that no government may interfere with our conscience, may tell us what to think. . . . Let us lift up our hearts."

The speech was well received. But newspapermen emphasized that Stevenson had omitted two paragraphs of attack on Eisenhower, and were skeptical of Stevenson's staff's explanation that the cuts had been made solely for length. While Stevenson was speaking at the Tabernacle, McGowan told Wirtz and Martin that Stevenson considered the draft for the Los Angeles fireside chat terrible—"just a lot of moonlight and magnolia by Cohn"—and they would have to redo it. They had a draft on Korea by Tufts, and Stevenson had some miscellaneous drafts in his briefcase, but McGowan thought they ought to start afresh. Wirtz left for his own room to rewrite Schlesinger's draft for the next night's rally at the Cow Palace in San Francisco. McGowan was polishing the Spokane speech, due the next noon. Stevenson returned from the Tabernacle about 10 P.M. McGowan followed him into his bedroom and in a few minutes told Wirtz and Martin that Stevenson was too tired to do more tonight. They said he had to—deadlines were close. Presently Stevenson came into McGowan's bedroom wearing a shirt and shorts and socks. He looked exhausted. He sat down on the bed, and they asked him about the Los Angeles fireside chat, and he said he was too tired to think about it. McGowan finally asked him if he would at least read the Tufts draft on Korea before going to sleep. He promised to take it to bed with him.

Next morning the party flew to Spokane and motorcaded downtown, and the crowds were bigger and hotter than Truman's in 1948. Something was happening. Stevenson's speech, carried over statewide radio, attacked the Republican Old Guard for opposing the development of natural resources, and Eisenhower for claiming credit for their development. They flew to Pendleton. Dave Bell had warned Martin not to let anybody put a war bonnet on Stevenson for a photograph, and Martin had passed the word on to McGowan, noting that at Pendleton he was supposed to be greeted by an Indian beauty queen. The speech there was at the airport, a midafternoon prop-stop, and somebody did drape an Indian blanket around Steven-

son but not a war bonnet. He took his position on the Hell's Canyon
Dam:

"The General had some nice things to say the other day about
upstream storage on our rivers, to hold back floodwaters and release them later for power development. So have I. But the General
carefully avoided discussing the biggest storage dam proposed in the
Pacific Northwest—Hell's Canyon Dam, over on the Oregon-Idaho
line. Of course the General couldn't be for Hell's Canyon Dam—
everyone out here knows that dam has been bitterly opposed by
his supporters.

"I don't know when we can afford to build that dam, but I do
know that the controversy is really over the full development of
great resources by government and their partial development by private utilities. And that in turn reflects the difference between the
approach of the two parties.

"I think you know the Democratic Party stands for full development of our resources for the good of all the people. Where private
enterprise can do the job, I am for it. Where the job cannot be done
by private enterprise, the job should be done by government as fast
as possible consistent with what we can wisely afford."

He then took his position on the Indians—advocated full development of the Indians' timber resources, urged that we "reconsider
laws denying to Indians rights that are enjoyed by other citizens,"
and urged that we integrate into society those Indians who wanted
integration.

On they flew, arriving at San Francisco about dark and going to
Ben Swig's Fairmont Hotel. Stevenson went off after dinner to deliver his speech at the Cow Palace. McGowan, Wirtz, and Martin
had dinner in Stevenson's suite and listened to the speech on the
radio. The crowd was roaring at almost every line. Scotty Reston of
the New York *Times* called it one of the great rally speeches of
the times. It contained a poem, "Ode to the Old Guard."

> Nixon, Dirksen and Taft one night
> Sailed off in a lead canoe,
> Freighted with cargoes of woe and fright
> Just like in '32.

> "Oh, what are you hunting as if you would bust?"
> The old Moon asked the three.
> "We are hunting for issues all covered with dust—
> And national policies heavy with rust;
> To win this election its clear that we must,"
> Said Nixon and Dirksen and Taft.

The speech praised FDR and Truman and Democratic programs. It attacked "Old Guard" Republican Senators who had opposed those programs and now had perverted Eisenhower's Great Crusade. It said:

"No one can question the General's integrity or the excellence of his intentions. But does anyone think he would really stand a chance against this team of isolationists and cutthroat reactionaries?

"My friends, it *is* time for a change. . . .

"We Democrats have always fought for change—for change toward a new and better world."

In speech after speech Stevenson struck this "time for a change" theme, the central theme of the Republican campaign. It was almost an unconscious suicidal impulse. But that night in San Francisco the mood was gay, and after his speech Stevenson went off to Chinatown, then back to his hotel to talk to friends and to work. During the day, aloft, and on the plane on the ground at Spokane and Pendleton, and at the Fairmont that night, Martin had written the next day's speech for Los Angeles; now he and McGowan went over it and made final changes. They gave it to the typists page by page; Stevenson had to clear it that night; the next day would be too crowded for him to write. Stevenson went over it, making numerous changes, more for sentence rhythm than for substance. He added a Negro dialect joke and Martin protested to McGowan—Los Angeles in 1952 was a strong civil rights city. McGowan agreed, but Stevenson had gone to bed. They deleted the joke on their own initiative, one of the few times during the entire campaign when anybody overruled Stevenson on a speech passage. McGowan would point out the deletion to Stevenson so that he would not ad-lib it.

Next morning, Thursday, October 16, Stevenson motorcaded around the East Bay Area, across the bay from San Francisco, with stops at Berkeley, Richmond, and Vallejo, then went on to Sacramento for a noontime speech on the steps of the state Capitol. He attacked Eisenhower and such Republicans as Nixon who campaigned with praise for farm price supports and the Central Valley Project but between elections voted against them in the Senate. Several times he talked about his earlier years in California and about his cleanup of government in Illinois, and he praised Governor Warren. He lost time on the morning motorcade. By the time he finished his speech at Sacramento, he looked worn out. And he still had a long day ahead of him. When he boarded his plane to fly to Los Angeles, it was overloaded. With him in his rear cabin were McGowan, Wirtz, Martin, the Iveses, and motion picture people—Lauren Bacall and her husband Humphrey Bogart, and Mercedes McCambridge. It was the practice of presidential candidates to take actors and actresses campaigning with them, sometimes helping to draw a crowd or warm it up. Mrs. Ives looked askance. Once she asked Martin, "How long are we going to have to put up with them?" Later she came to understand their worth. And the fact was that these three were decent people and that each in his own way loved Adlai Stevenson. Although from now on Stevenson would be associated with many actors and actresses, including Marlene Dietrich, Ava Gardner, Bette Davis, and Tallulah Bankhead, none was more devoted to him than these early three.

Aloft that day, the staffers worked on speeches, their faces drawn, while Mercedes McCambridge chatted gaily. By this time McGowan was saying, when he finally cleared a speech with Stevenson, "There's another one gone." For by now what had begun as a lark had become exhausting; the staff was feeling the strain that Stevenson had felt earlier. It happens in every campaign and in the final weeks drudgery can be dangerous. As someone said, "We make our most important decisions when we are the most tired."

The crowds at Los Angeles were the biggest yet. The crowd at the airport was vast; people lined the streets nearly all the long distance from the airport to the Biltmore Hotel. They jammed the hotel. Nor did they just stand and stare as Stevenson passed by; they waved and yelled and screamed at him. They were out to see him. Martin was not the only one who suddenly became sure Stevenson was going to win the election. *Newsweek* wrote: "Adlai Stevenson's campaign finally had caught fire. . . . He created as much enthusiasm as Dwight D. Eisenhower. . . . Just what it meant was anybody's guess. The governor's advisers naturally interpreted the crowds as evidence that what they had been predicting for so long— a switch from Eisenhower to Stevenson—at last was under way." *Newsweek* thought Stevenson's eloquence, party and labor organization work, and reawakened memories of the depression had finally brought out the crowds. En route to the hotel, the motorcade made an unscheduled stop, and Mexicans and Negroes pressed so close that the cars could not move. This would become common in the John F. Kennedy campaign of 1960 and the Robert Kennedy primary campaign of 1968; now it was happening to Stevenson for the first time.

From the Biltmore, Stevenson went to the KTTV studio to deliver, at 7:30 P.M., his fireside chat. He had chosen for his subject, after all, Korea. He praised American and UN resistance to Communist aggression there and attacked Republican proposals that we withdraw our forces—"the policy of scuttle and run." To do so would be to invite new Communist aggression in Asia, especially in Indochina "where the French have fought so long, so valuably and so expensively." One by one allies would fall and "we would wait for the blow to fall on us." Some Republicans, including Eisenhower, advocated letting Koreans do the fighting. America had long been training South Korean soldiers, but the best military opinion held they could "never" replace American troops until fighting ended. He criticized equally MacArthur's proposal to extend the war to China. Stevenson himself could offer "no miracles." He would not extend the war to new areas, would "continue to press" the negotiations, would keep troops in Korea until settlement was reached, would continue to train South Korean troops and to rotate American soldiers.

From the TV studio he went straight to the Shrine Auditorium. Attacking the Old Guard, calling Eisenhower Taft's puppet, praising Truman, recalling the depression, reading the shopping list of Democratic issues with heaviest emphasis on the economy, his speech was aimed at a rally crowd, and it succeeded. They seemed to be expecting him to say certain things, to be waiting for him to say them, and to explode into applause and cheers when he did say them. *Newsweek* was right; he was no longer the unknown Governor. He was getting the kind of response that FDR had gotten when he used the "Martin, Barton, and Fish" line. It was the kind of response a potential winner gets.

From the Shrine Auditorium, Stevenson went to Los Angeles International Airport to fly to San Diego to spend the night at a rambling old resort hotel, the Del Coronado. It had been a grueling day but a good day, the third in a row.

Next morning, Friday, October 17, Stevenson spoke at the plaza. In this area where prosperity depended on defense contracts, Stevenson spoke on foreign trade, prosperity, internationalism, and the danger to all three if Republicans were elected. From San Diego they flew to Forth Worth, Texas, a long flight, nearly five hours, over desolate dry country. The Fort Worth and Dallas speeches for that day were in good shape. Houston, for the next, was not, and Martin, meeting Jack Fischer in Forth Worth, rewrote it. Stevenson's Fort Worth speech, introduced by Senator Lyndon Johnson, was designed to call quarreling Democrats home to their party, using conservation and agricultural policy as the lure and recalling the Great Depression. Stevenson went by motorcade to Dallas, and at Fair Park spoke on offshore oil, repeating, substantially, his New Orleans statement.

That night Stevenson boarded a special train bound for Uvalde, the desolate cactus-grown home of John Nance Garner, former Vice

President with Roosevelt, an aging cantankerous man on whom Democratic candidates of the time paid courtesy calls as, later, in the 1960s, they called on Harry Truman. Stevenson breakfasted with Garner, Rayburn, and others, said a few words from Garner's porch, then got back on the train. As it headed north, McGowan, Wirtz, and Martin were still working on Houston. Fischer tried to coach Stevenson on how to pronounce a few words of Spanish at the next stop, San Antonio. The writers finished as the train pulled into San Antonio. Stevenson left the train to speak at Milan Square, the public market, brief remarks aimed entirely at Mexican-American voters, promising a Good Neighbor policy within our own borders, then went to Alamo Plaza, where, to a Democratic rally, he compared the Battle of the Alamo with Korea. He crossed the street for a reception and lunch at the Manger Hotel. Meanwhile, back at the train, McGowan, Wirtz, Martin, and the stenographers grabbed mimeograph machines, paper and ink and typewriters, and got into a taxi and hurried to the San Antonio airport where they mimeographed and assembled the Houston speech, to be delivered that same afternoon. They finished as Stevenson arrived at the airport and all hands boarded the planes for the short flight to Houston. There Stevenson went to a hotel, cleaned up, and went to deliver his speech to an outdoor rally, running against "Hoover hogs," calling Texans home to the Democratic Party, and delivering a long serious passage on foreign trade. It went well. He went back to the hotel for a reception. The crowds everywhere were substantial. Martin, resting alone in a hotel room during the reception, answered the phone, and a voice which sounded like that of a young Negro said, "Mr. Stevenson?"

"No, he's in a meeting. I'm a member of his staff. Who's calling?"

"Robert Hall."

"Who?"

"Robert Hall."

The name meant nothing. "Can I help you?"

"I wanted to talk to Mr. Stevenson."

"Are you a relative or a friend of his?" (Often during the campaign Stevenson's staff received such calls.)

"No."

"Well, we'll give him the message if you want to tell me what it is, I'll be glad to pass it on to him."

He hesitated, then said, "Tell him I'm for him. I saw him on television and I'm for him."

Martin thanked him and said Stevenson would be pleased.

"Where can I write him? At the White House?"

"You mean now?"

"Yes."

"You'd better write him now in Springfield at the Executive Mansion."

The caller hung up. Martin and other staffers to whom he told the story were moved and cheered by the incident. Somehow it seemed to them that this young Negro spoke for the great unseen masses they had been trying to reach by radio, television, and newspapers; to this one, at least, they had gotten through.

They made the long flight home to Springfield, Stevenson sitting with McGowan and the writers. It was Saturday night, October 18. They talked about the final two-week Eastern-Midwestern trip that would start on Tuesday. The schedule would be almost unbearably heavy. They decided to take along virtually the entire Elks Club, including the typists. This Western trip had been hard; the Eastern swing would be worse. Stevenson was exhausted that night. But when he arrived at Springfield airport he found a small crowd gathered, late though it was, and he introduced the crew of his plane and the stewardesses, Helen and Dottie, recounted the campaign, then said:

"I wish I could tell you what is in my heart. I will make no attempt to. I just want to thank you—thank you from the bottom of a very full heart indeed—you, my neighbors, who have been so patient, so understanding, and so good to me here in Springfield for so long. Good night and bless you all."

Then he added: "Before you leave—or before I leave—may I introduce to you my sister, Mrs. Ives, and my aunt, Letitia Stevenson, who is over seventy, and who is the best campaigner of us all. What is more, they make speeches everywhere they go. I think if they made all the speeches and I made none of them, it would be all over."

Then he and the others went home to bed.

29

Although in retrospect Carl McGowan thought the second Western trip anticlimactic, at that time it seemed a great success. The polls showed Stevenson gaining. They also showed a startlingly high percentage of undecided voters—16 per cent, according to Elmo Roper. Gallup reported that among independents 54 per cent favored Eisenhower, 25 per cent Stevenson, with 21 per cent undecided. He distributed the undecided vote two thirds for Stevenson, one third for Eisenhower (based on his 1948 experience) and came out with Eisenhower 61 per cent, Stevenson 39 per cent. But that was among the independents only. A full national Gallup poll showed that Stevenson was closing the gap. On September 30 the poll had stood 53 per cent Eisenhower, 39 per cent Stevenson, with 8 per cent undecided. On October 9, Eisenhower's percentage had shrunk to 50 per cent, Stevenson had held almost even at 38 per cent, and the undecideds had risen to 12 per cent. It appeared that Stevenson was pulling voters away from Eisenhower and that most of them were going into the undecided group. And this poll was taken October 9, before the second Western trip. A Gallup poll taken on October 25 showed that Eisenhower was slipping badly—he was down to 48 per cent, while Stevenson was back to 39 per cent and the undecideds had risen to 13 per cent. That was only ten days before the election. Thus instead of decreasing as the election drew near, the undecideds were increasing. True, a two-thirds–one-third distribution of the undecideds in that October 25 poll would still give Eisenhower victory, 52.33 per cent to 47.66 per cent. But it was a chancy calculation. In any case, now, with the election only a little more than two weeks off, everybody agreed that Stevenson had at last caught fire and was gaining. Two weeks left. Enough? This was the question around Springfield that weekend as Stevenson and his staff prepared for the final trip.

On Sunday evening McGowan and Fritchey met with the writers at the Elks Club. They discussed speeches of the forthcoming week, especially one on nationwide TV from Chicago on Tuesday. It had been proposed that several women appear with him and ask him questions in order to achieve warmth and appeal to women. (It is curious that toward the end of many presidential campaigns everybody begins to worry about how to appeal to women.) McGowan liked the idea because it was the only way to get Stevenson to speak extemporaneously. Fritchey feared it would seem contrived. Eventually it was abandoned. On Monday, Stevenson recorded several radio broadcasts aimed at women. That night he spoke on the Illinois election to a Democratic rally in the Springfield Armory. He had caught cold and was coughing badly. He looked very tired, working on his speech in a corner backstage at the Armory, surrounded by a score of politicians. Next morning, Tuesday, October 21, exactly two weeks before Election Day, he set forth on his final trip. He would campaign without letup; he would not return to Illinois until the Saturday night before the election. In those two weeks he would make some ninety-five speeches.

He left at noon by special train from the old railroad station in Springfield, bound for Chicago, with whistle stops en route. At 8:30 P.M. on national television and (later) on radio, he delivered his third fireside chat. His subjects were peace, Communism, and Korea. He spoke of the roots of war—poverty, ignorance, and political instability—and of the need for a "war against poverty." Then he went to the Studebaker Theater in Chicago to participate in the New York *Herald Tribune* Forum on national radio and TV. The speech, termed non-political, sounded like one he might have made in the old days at the Council on Foreign Relations. Eisenhower spoke on the same program, pledging cooperation with America's allies, seeking to recapture his original supporters. One of them, Walter Lippmann, wrote that Eisenhower was not, as they had hoped, an effective leader of his party; but that, in spite of his appeasement of Taft, he was not the captive of the Old Guard either.

30

Stevenson's "Democratic Presidential Campaign Special" pulled out of Chicago on the New York Central system early next morning, Wednesday, October 22. The train was old and rickety. Stevenson worked and ate and slept in the last car and spoke from its back platform. That car contained a dining room and staterooms for Stevenson, McGowan, Blair, and a bodyguard. The furniture was old and overstuffed. The woodwork was ancient and darkened with the varnish of years; the lights were dim and oppressive. The Iveses, Margaret Munn, Carol Evans, and others were in car No. 2, Schlesinger and others in car No. 3, Wirtz and Tufts and Jane Dick and two Elks secretaries, Nona Cox and Rita Coleman, were in car No. 4. The Elks wrote speeches in crowded bedrooms, scrambling along the train's swaying corridors between Stevenson's car and the typists. Jane Dick took care of local Volunteer leaders who came aboard at each stop just as Blair, McGowan, and others took care of local politicians.

He stopped first at South Bend, Indiana, an hour and a half out of Chicago, and spoke briefly from the back platform, then left the train and motorcaded to Notre Dame University, where he talked about the depression and "ridding the world of the disease of Communism." Back to the train and the next stop, a brief one about 10:30 A.M. at Elkhart, Indiana, where Stevenson praised Governor Schricker, good-naturedly sought Republican votes, praised Elkhart farmers, and warned that if Republicans were elected to Congress

they would cut our defenses and imperil prosperity. Next stop, To-
ledo; and here Stevenson left the train and drove to the courthouse
square in the early afternoon. (He should have arrived at noon to
get the lunch-hour crowd.) He stopped at Sandusky and Elyria,
Ohio, for about ten minutes each and spoke from the rear platform.
From Elyria he rode the train four hours undisturbed to Buffalo,
New York, where he addressed an enthusiastic evening rally in the
overcrowded Memorial Auditorium. And in this city with a large
East European population, he called the Eisenhower-Dulles proposal
to liberate Eastern Europe "a cruel hoax"—it might mislead Poles
into insurrection, for which they would pay dearly (as actually would
happen a few years later in Hungary). He said a Polish general of
World War II, General Bor-Komorowski, considered the "liberation"
policy "a great mistake." (After the election, the general denied it
to Stevenson.)

Stevenson spent the night at the Statler Hotel in Buffalo and next
morning, Thursday, October 23, whistle-stopped in the corner where
Ohio, New York, and Pennsylvania come together. He spoke from
the back platform at Dunkirk, New York, at Erie, Pennsylvania,
and Ashtabula, Ohio. Youngstown, a steel town and workingman's
town, was the first important speech of the day; he motorcaded to
the public square downtown but again arrived too late for the lunch-
hour crowds. He attacked Republican efforts to frighten the voters
—then himself warned of depression if the Republicans were
elected. He recalled, "Youngstown was not, in 1932, a pleasant
place to work or to live—and Youngstown was typical of most of the
cities of America. The steel mills here in the Mahoning Valley
were working at thirty-one per cent of capacity. One Youngstown
workingman out of every three was unemployed. There was no
unemployment compensation. The other two men worked at poverty
wages. There was no minimum wage law. Those men worked in
silence beside the furnaces. There was no collective bargaining act.
The foreman's word was law. . . . At the end of life's work when
you could no longer work, there was nothing. There was no Social
Security. You only knew that one day—and you never knew when—
there would be a pink dismissal slip in your envelope, and that
would be all. If it was bad at the mill, it was infinitely worse in the
street and in the home. Youngstown was one of the first cities to start
soup kitchens." He recited the record of twenty Democratic years
begun by FDR. It was a long way from Cadillac Square on Labor
Day.

After a brief stop at Ravenna, Ohio, and a rally at Akron, he
went on to the Cleveland Arena for the big speech of the day—on

nationwide television and radio about the Hiss case. Schlesinger and Ben Heineman had written the first draft, a somewhat awkward collaboration, since they knew each other but slightly and since Schlesinger habitually wrote rough drafts on the typewriter while Heineman dictated. Senator McCarthy's speech, scheduled for next Monday, had been highly publicized. Stevenson and his staff suspected he would discuss Stevenson and the Hiss case; the Cleveland speech was intended to discount McCarthy's in advance. Backstage at the Arena, waiting to appear, Stevenson worked on the speech with McGowan at a bare wood table under an overhead bulb, Carol Evans sitting beside them poised to type if they rewrote pages heavily, Schlesinger and Heineman and Bill Blair talking softly and nervously in a corner. The time came, and he was introduced and began to speak. He seemed unusually nervous. When he had gone through only a few sentences a heckler shouted hoarsely, "Okay, Steve, tell us what *you* believe." For a moment he seemed thrown off stride, and his aides feared he might not regain it. But he did, and soon was speaking with passionate earnestness and intensity, and it became evident that the audience was transfixed.

He said Eisenhower had embraced not only the Republican Old Guard but Senator Jenner, who had called General Marshall "a living lie," and Senator McCarthy, who had called Marshall "a living falsehood" and had proposed going aboard Stevenson's campaign train with a club "to make a good American out of me." Nixon was leading this campaign of "innuendo and accusation." Acidly, Stevenson denounced Eisenhower himself for not restraining "those who would slander me." He made a lawyer-like defense of his Hiss deposition. Then he said, "I would never have believed that a presidential contest with General Eisenhower would have made this [present] speech necessary." And "It may well be that the General has been misled by his lack of experience in civil life. This is not a war; it is a political contest in a free democracy; and the rules are different. . . . I resent—and I resent bitterly—the sly and ugly campaign that is being waged in behalf of the General, and I am deeply shocked that he would lead a so-called 'crusade' which accepts calumny and the big doubt as its instruments." He ended by declaring his opposition to Communism at home and abroad and discussing how to combat it.

It is debatable whether, as Truman thought, the Cleveland speech was a political mistake. But it is hardly debatable that it was a stirring speech. Some speeches must be given simply because candidates feel they must give them, not for politics but for themselves. This speech was one such. He received a tremendous ovation.

31

Not only Nixon and McCarthy were hitting Stevenson hard on Hiss; so was much of the press, and not just the Chicago *Tribune*. *Life* magazine gave a full page to an editorial entitled "Softness Toward Communism." It said, "Many Americans, including Adlai Stevenson, are extremely touchy—and no wonder—about the charge of 'softness toward Communism.' It rests not against the whole Democratic party but against its Acheson faction. Other members of this faction are Philip Jessup, Eleanor Roosevelt and a host of lesser fry, including until recently John S. Service and Owen Lattimore. . . . On the periphery of this faction one finds the trail of Alger Hiss. . . . The Acheson faction," *Life* said, had watched Chairman Mao's victories "with feelings ranging from complacency to connivance," had "defended subversives in the U.S. government with cries of 'red herring' and 'witch hunt,'" had been responsible for U.S. foreign policy while Communism "enslaved" 600 million people, and, since "treason was afoot during this calamity," McCarthyism legitimately stood on "grounds for wholesome doubt." Stevenson had aligned himself with the Acheson faction, *Life* said.

Stevenson spent the night on the train after his Cleveland speech and next day, Friday, October 24, whistle-stopped his way across upstate New York, a long day with a dozen stops en route to Albany, defending Korea, attacking the Republican Old Guard.

The Republicans were keeping up their own attack. Nixon attacked Stevenson on Hiss. But far more important was Eisenhower's own speech that night, October 24. Speaking in Detroit, he declared that, if elected, "I shall go to Korea." Emmet John Hughes, an editor of *Life* on loan to Eisenhower's staff, had conceived and written the speech. The effect on the country was electric. George Ball once recalled that he and Stevenson had read the advance text with no great concern—Stevenson, and his advisers, had considered and rejected the same idea. Only a day later, when they saw how great the impact of a military hero's promise had been, did Stevenson realize he must do something. Some Stevenson staffers proposed to tell the truth—that Stevenson had discarded the idea earlier. This was, wisely, abandoned. It is impossible to judge how many votes Eisenhower's pledge made. Some people thought it turned a victory into a landslide.

The Stevenson party spent the night on the train in Albany. Everybody aboard was exhausted. They were crammed into bedrooms with their baggage, files, and typewriters. Unable to bathe, often sleepless, they had grown moody and depressed. The whistle stops had, as usual, not gone well. Stevenson stuck his head into the dining room where McGowan and others were working, said he was "going off to charm the multitudes," and left for Troy. He was in better spirits, weary as he was, than the others, perhaps because he was averaging about six hours' sleep a night, more than most. McGowan was beginning to detect signs of slippage. He believed, in retrospect, that Stevenson would have done better if the nation had voted on October 25 instead of November 4. "He had sky-rocketed into the minds and consciousness of a lot of people. There's a point where you hit a maximum. We crossed over that point by one week."

Next morning, Saturday, October 25, the Stevenson train left Albany early. It stopped at Hyde Park station at eight-ten, a small station beside the Hudson River, and Mrs. Roosevelt and FDR, Jr., met Stevenson, and a little band on the platform played "Happy Days Are Here Again," and the party drove up a winding road to a plot of ground enclosed by evergreens at the rear of FDR's house, flower beds bordering a green lawn, and in the center a headstone. Stevenson, walking to President Roosevelt's grave with Mrs. Roosevelt, her son, her daughter-in-law, Mrs. Ives, and John Fell Stevenson, laid a wreath on it—then had to re-enact it for the photographers, while a dog, the successor to FDR's Fala, barked at them. They drove to Val-Kill, where Mrs. Roosevelt was living, and had breakfast, then went on to Poughkeepsie, a few miles away, where a small crowd was waiting in front of the Nelson House hotel. Stevenson spoke from a second-floor balcony. Schlesinger, biographer of FDR, had written the speech, an eloquent one on the Roosevelt legacy; but the crowd was apathetic, seeming to care not at all about Roosevelt—or Stevenson, for that matter. It was one of the most disappointing occasions of the campaign.

From Poughkeepsie, Stevenson headed into Massachusetts, where John F. Kennedy was running for Henry Cabot Lodge's Senate seat. At Pittsfield, after Kennedy boarded his train, Stevenson attacked Republican campaign tactics. At Springfield, to a huge crowd, he interpolated into his speech a passage declaring he was no man's captive, including trade unions'. It was a labor audience, and Schlesinger groaned—but to his astonishment the crowd roared its approval. Stevenson knew best, Schlesinger concluded. The principal Massachusetts speech came that night in Boston at Mechanics Hall, a Democratic rally broadcast nationally. In it, he gave his answer, drafted by McGowan and Tufts, to Eisenhower's Korea pledge:

"The General has announced his intention to go to Korea. But the root of the Korean problem does not lie in Korea. It lies in Moscow. If the purpose of the General's trip is to settle the Korean War by a larger military challenge, then the sooner we all know about it, the better.

"The Korean War must end and will end, as we all know, only when Moscow is convinced that the people of this country—Republicans and Democrats alike—are united in unshakable determination to stand firm—which is the only background against which honorable and final settlements can ever be reached. This is my purpose."

Next day was Sunday; both candidates had eschewed campaigning on Sundays but now, with the election only ten days away, Stevenson made several appearances—at a veterans' breakfast and a Volunteers meeting, went to church, had lunch, drove with Governor Dever to a hospital dedication and then went to two teas sponsored by Mrs. Joseph P. Kennedy, mother of the future President. (Kennedy teas and coffees later became famous.) He spent the night again at the Statler.

That day Jack Arvey appeared on "Meet the Press." Martin, in New York working on the final big speech for Saturday night at the Chicago Stadium, asked Arvey for suggestions. Arvey was worried about Eisenhower's promise to go to Korea. He thought Stevenson should cast doubt on what Eisenhower might do there—widen the war? The Commander-in-Chief should be a civilian. Arvey said a friend of his who was close to Eisenhower had told him that Eisenhower would soon meet dramatically with General Douglas MacArthur. (Martin and Dave Bell, whom he informed, were gleeful at what they saw as a mistake. It turned out, however, that Arvey's information was wrong.) Arvey thought Stevenson would win. He said he would have answered differently two weeks earlier. But now he was sure Stevenson had New York; California looked close but hopeful; he was about ready to believe the Pennsylvania Democratic leaders who kept telling him Stevenson would carry that state; Michigan was doubtful; Stevenson would certainly carry Illinois; he would lose Indiana but win Minnesota; and the South was safe, including Texas.

On Monday, October 27, the final week of the campaign, Stevenson started out from Boston by train. He made morning whistle stops at Quincy, Brockton, and Attleboro, Massachusetts, talking mostly about Korea and peace. He was working almost feverishly on those speeches. It was as though now at the end he was desperately eager to squeeze the last drop out of every audience. At midday in

Providence, Rhode Island, he spoke from the City Hall steps on Communism. Back on the train he spoke from the rear platform at Woonsocket, Rhode Island; then at Putnam, Norwich, New London, and New Haven, Connecticut. At New Haven, Schlesinger recalled, "we finally got the Governor to disown Senator McCarran." (He had resisted attacking McCarran because McCarran, as chairman of the Senate Judiciary Committee, would be powerful in the next four years.) That evening at Bridgeport he addressed a rally in Kline Auditorium—Communism and Korea again, and Eisenhower's promise to go to Korea.

In New York, at the 125th Street station, he got off and drove to 125th Street and Seventh Avenue, near the heart of Harlem. Some of Stevenson's friends thought that the key to New York State might lie in Harlem, and that the key to the election might lie in New York State. The Elks had worked hard on this speech. Stevenson had resisted the speech from the beginning, as he always resisted making appeals to minority groups or special interests. The speech was given to him only a few minutes before he arrived. He didn't like it and threw it away. He was worn out, had nearly collapsed at one of the Connecticut stops. He was late. He refused to talk more than five minutes, even though a tremendous crowd had been standing in the cold, waiting for him. He ad-libbed a five-minute speech, filled with generalities, making only a mention of civil rights and going out of his way to praise his running mate, Senator Sparkman of Alabama. It was Evansville all over. He arrived at the Biltmore in midtown Manhattan long past midnight.

Heineman, Wyatt, Ball, Steve Mitchell, and others had gathered to discuss McCarthy's long-awaited speech, which had been delivered that night. McCarthy had said, "Let me make it clear that I'm only covering [Stevenson's] history in so far as it deals with his aid to the Communist cause and the extent to which he is part and parcel of the Acheson-Hiss-Lattimore group." Waving "documents" and "exhibits," McCarthy had associated Stevenson's advisers, including Schlesinger, DeVoto, and MacLeish, with organizations which he said were either fronts for Communist subversion or whose members were also members of other organizations which had been termed fronts by various congressional committees. Most of it was old stuff and rather dull. Stevenson's advisers decided to abandon plans to have someone answer McCarthy. Stevenson himself was utterly spent. McGowan said later it was the worst night of the campaign. For the first time Stevenson seemed physically beaten; he questioned whether he could go on. He went to bed, and

McGowan and Schlesinger stayed up until 4 A.M. revising the next day's speeches. That same day a riot had begun at the Illinois State Penitentiary at Menard.

32

On Tuesday morning, October 28, with the election exactly one week away, Stevenson talked at breakfast with political and business leaders, then left the Biltmore at noon and went to the garment district. The crowds were enthusiastic beyond belief, someone said the biggest and wildest ever seen in New York. In the heaving sea of people Stevenson could speak only briefly and almost inaudibly. David Dubinsky of the garment workers' union introduced him. Now in the closing days he was, again, calling the Democrats home. Twenty years ago crowds on the street were looking for work, he said; now the signs all read "Men at Work," owing to "two great Presidents—to New York's beloved Franklin Roosevelt, and to his stouthearted successor—Harry Truman." He dropped, too, any hesitancy about proclaiming the liberal faith and asking for the labor vote. In other speeches in the New York area he sought the Catholic vote, the Italian vote, the labor vote.

That night Stevenson spoke at Madison Square Garden, New York's traditional Democratic windup rally. As they had on other occasions, his aides had debated whether the speech should be a pour-it-on speech for the immediate audience or a more thoughtful speech aimed at the great television audience. Schlesinger had written a good rally speech based on a Wechsler draft; Wirtz had written a more serious speech. McGowan combined them, emphasizing the thoughtful note. The crowd was red hot, tense with expectancy. Such speakers as Averell Harriman and such Hollywood and Broadway stars as Lauren Bacall were warming it up. As TV time approached, the senatorial candidate, John Cashmore, was speaking and refused to stop. Somebody cut off his microphone; he continued talking; Senator Lehman and others tried to soothe him, but long after Stevenson had started to speak on national television those in the Garden could still see Cashmore waving his arms, surrounded by a little knot of men trying to quiet him. Stevenson came on at ten-thirty, and the crowd, by now taut as a drum, went wild.

But the speech, one of reasoned partisanship, disappointed them. Stevenson was tired and delivered it poorly. From the Garden he went to spend the night on his train in Hoboken. Past midnight he wrote to Alicia Patterson:

E dearest—I'm back in Hoboken on the train after a hideous day beating my way through the crowds in N.Y. and N.J. and speaking speaking speaking ad nauseum—for them as well as for me I fear. When Oh when will this ghastly ordeal end! I had hoped for a moment alone to call you but the throng never opened and now you're asleep and so am I, or should be. The note at the Hotel when I arrived late last night from Conn. via Harlem was a warm blessing & relief. . . . The campaign is going well—I guess —at least measured by crowds and hysteria which seem to be the politicians yard stick. Indeed it looks almost too good, with virtually every state at least a battle ground and many "safe"—as the wise guys say. And woe to him who wins. Why oh why did I do it? I had to, didn't I?

I must to bed—or die—and sometimes I wish it was both.

Love & blessings to Madam Rat

A

P.S. I did a poor rally speech at the Garden tonight—but it was intended to be different than the usual rally, pour it on, conventional type of thing. But always, always too little time to prepare!

His train pulled out long past midnight; his first stop was scheduled in Scranton, Pennsylvania, at 7:55 A.M., Wednesday, October 29. This was coal country, and Stevenson time and again went after the labor vote, the vote of John L. Lewis' United Mine Workers. It was Johnny Mitchell Day in the anthracite fields, a day commemorating an early leader of the miners. Stevenson laid a wreath on Mitchell's monument in the snow and in his speech faithfully recited Mitchell's history, denounced the rich, praised the unions, reminded his audience of the Great Depression.

It was the same all day—at Wilkes-Barre, Allentown, Bethlehem, Hazelton: bread-and-butter issues, plus anti-Communism, anti-"liberation," anti-Taft-Hartley, anti-Old Guard. Once when people in the crowd shouted "I like Ike," Stevenson said, "Well, I like him, too, but I would ask you fellows to listen a minute." He related how a writer on *Life* had written Eisenhower's pledge to go to Korea and said, "My friends, there you have it. A speech writer from a slick magazine cooked up an idea to catch votes by playing upon our hopes, our desperate hopes for a quick end to the Korean War— and the General accepts the idea immediately . . . a cynical search for votes." He talked about his ancestor, Jesse Fell, and life in pioneer Pennsylvania.

He went into Philadelphia in the afternoon, spoke briefly at Independence Hall, crossed the river into Camden, New Jersey, spoke briefly, then went back to Philadelphia and a motorcade at rush hour through big crowds, and a Volunteers' meeting where he talked as usual about good government in Illinois. The main rally that night was at Convention Hall, with local TV and radio, and he said, "The war won't be settled in Korea; the right address is Moscow. . . . The men in Moscow are not yet ready for an armistice. And why do you think that is? . . . . They have been following our election campaign, too. They have heard the Republican candidate and the highest Republican leaders say first one thing about the Korean War and then another. They have heard, in other words, sounds of disunity—and disunity means weakness. . . . It is tragic—it is tragic, it seems to me, that the Republican Party has chosen to divide and to confuse for political purposes, and so to injure our chances for an early peace."

Meanwhile calls were coming in from Illinois: the riot at Menard prison was in its fourth day and getting worse; rebellious inmates were holding seven guards hostage; Newton Minow had sent Michael H. Farrin, Stevenson's investigator, there; Mike Seyfrit, Director of Public Safety, had gone too. Minow would keep McGowan and Stevenson informed at each stop the next day. Thursday, October 30: Stevenson's train left Philadelphia early to cross the mountains to Pittsburgh. It was a beautiful fall day, and the train wound its way past blazing red oaks on the hillsides, a far-off smudge of smoke on a range of hills, past the stone houses of Pennsylvania, the foothills and mountains, rich black-dirt valleys, a clean white church, a long winding steely river, ducks winging in. When the train passed factories, men's faces appeared at the window; in railroad yards, track workers paused and looked up.

When the train pulled into the station at Harrisburg on an elevated roadbed, the street below was jammed with people standing packed tightly together from building to building as far as it was possible to see. They were on rooftops, on car tops, on telephone poles; they were everywhere. Newspapermen who had jumped off to hear the speech scrambled back aboard as the train pulled out and said they had been with Truman in 1948 and had witnessed the same phenomenon in the last week—something had happened, something was in the air, people by the thousands were pouring out to see not a candidate but the man they were sure was going to be the next President of the United States. (At Harrisburg, of course, the Governor had released state employees so they could hear Stevenson.)

After three stops, the major speech was at Pittsburgh that evening in Hunt Armory. Three Pennsylvania labor leaders spoke, and so did Philip Murray, president of the CIO. Stevenson was introduced by Mayor David L. Lawrence of Pittsburgh. He was running late, barely arriving in time for his TV-radio appearance and beginning his speech by apologizing for being out of breath. "It has been a most exciting day for me," he said, and spoke feelingly of the crowds, for he too had caught the scent of victory, widespread among his companions since New York's garment district. He attacked hard. "It looks as though the great crusade has become the great masquerade—or should I say the great rout—as one principle after another, one pledge after another, one plank after another is discarded in the scramble."

Throughout the day, at the whistle stops, McGowan had been talking to Springfield about the Menard riot. By now, Joseph D. Lohman, chairman of the Parole Board, and Lieutenant Governor Sherwood Dixon were at Menard. Minow told McGowan that officials at Menard intended to give the inmates a chance to release the guards unharmed; if the inmates refused, state police were going in after them with guns the next morning. Although unable to consult Stevenson, McGowan told Lieutenant Governor Dixon that Stevenson would go to Menard that night. Late in the afternoon he told Stevenson what he had done and said, "I assume you'd want to be there." Stevenson said, "There's no question about it." McGowan thought Stevenson's attachment to the state police, whom he had tried to professionalize and who had served him well in the cigarette tax and gambling raids, helped him decide to go to Menard. McGowan has recalled, "If the convicts did not give up peaceably, the state police would have to storm the prison. He had a strong emotional feeling that his place was there, not campaigning. Also, if he was on the scene, the prisoners would see that there was no one else to appeal to."

The decision to go to Menard, taken thus so automatically, looked to outsiders extremely difficult. Some Stevenson aides felt he had little to gain and everything to lose. If he compromised with the inmates, he would be criticized for "coddling convicts." If he ordered the state police to storm the cell blocks, hostages or state policemen might be killed, and Stevenson might be accused of playing politics with people's lives. The most he could accomplish would be to quell the riot. He would get little credit for that. And furthermore, Lieutenant Governor Dixon did not want Stevenson to go, for Dixon, running for Governor, had tried to quell the riot and failed; if Stevenson now succeeded, Dixon would be hurt politically.

But Stevenson was still Governor, campaign or no campaign, and the responsibility was inescapably his. In any case, after the Pittsburgh speech, late that final Thursday night, October 30, five days before the election, Stevenson, McGowan, Blair, Flanagan, Ball, Schlesinger, and a few newspapermen left by plane. Menard, located near the Mississippi River in far downstate Illinois, was probably the worst penitentiary in Illinois. Guards were hired on a spoils politics basis. Some sold contraband to the inmates and stole from the state. They and the warden ran the prison loosely. Favored inmates, or inmates with money, could buy special privileges. Many inmates were idle. The psychiatric section caused unrest in the prison at large. Homosexuality was widespread. Stevenson had tried to tighten up Menard. There were reports that old-time guards who resisted change told inmates, "This is your chance," that is, their chance to make trouble while Stevenson was campaigning for President.

Several inmates, according to plan, had created a disturbance in the dining hall, then, in cell house E, had seized seven guards and locked them in on the high seventh tier—350 convicts locked in with seven guards. Inmates in the psychiatric division seized other guards. The warden demanded their release. The inmates refused and, flashing knives, threatened to kill the guards. Lieutenant Governor Dixon and the Director of Public Safety, Michael Seyfrit, talked to them. They said they wanted to talk to newspapermen about their grievances—they wanted a new warden, several guards fired, better food, easier parole. Dixon and Seyfrit promised reform if the convicts would release the guards. The convicts refused. Chaplains and others tried to mediate, to no avail. At this point, Stevenson went to Menard.

During the night state police had been brought into the prison and hidden behind the chapel in the prison yard. Stevenson, arriving about 4 A.M., went over the plans. Seyfrit, backed by armed force, would read an ultimatum; Stevenson and McGowan helped draft it. At 6 A.M., still dark, state police went into the prison chapel, facing cell house E, carrying submachine guns, shotguns, and revolvers. About 100 prison guards, some armed, some carrying clubs, went into the prison yard. At ten-five Stevenson himself stepped into the prison yard with the police and guards and stood there while Seyfrit read the ultimatum over a loudspeaker: "We are going into the cell house with state police armed with guns, we will use whatever force is necessary to restore order." Then he and Stevenson went to the E-house north door, Seyfrit repeating over and over, "You'd better bring those guards out and you'd better bring them down unharmed." He told the troopers to cut the north and south doors open with acetylene torches—the inmates had barricaded them with chains. They did. Seyfrit kept saying over the loudspeaker, "Get back to your cells, get back to your cells," and "Bring the guards out, bring them out." The state police went into the cell house yelling at the prisoners, telling them to get off the galleries and into their cells or they'd be killed. The police fired a few shots. Some prisoners started to shout, some waved white sheets or undershirts, some walked around idly, armed with clubs. One prisoner yelled, "It's just bird shot," and Seyfrit announced, "That'll be the last of the bird shot." At ten twenty-five the first two hostage guards came out of the north door. Five minutes later a third hostage came out. A prisoner struggling with a guard was shot (and later died). A few minutes later the rest of the hostages came out. Seyfrit told the inmates to return to their cells; only then would they get their first hot meal in five days. Troopers entered the cell house in force, followed by guards with clubs. By ten forty-two they reported "all secure," the prisoners locked in their cells. Stevenson walked the high tiers of cells, walking along the steel galleries, saying not a word to the prisoners. He went to the prison hospital to talk to the guards. Then he flew back East.

33

Meanwhile, that day, Friday, October 31, Stevenson's campaign train went to New York. Everybody aboard felt lost. Dignitaries quarreled over who would make his speeches. Stevenson was scheduled to make two rally speeches in Manhattan that afternoon, to deliver a TV broadcast in the evening, to speak at a rally at 8:15 P.M., and to make a major speech in the Brooklyn Academy of Music at 9:15 P.M. As the afternoon passed, the meetings were canceled, one at a time. When darkness fell, his staff began to fear he would not be able to get to New York at all: LaGuardia was fogged in, his plane circled awhile, then went back to Philadelphia to refuel, then took off again. Planes were stacked up thick over LaGuardia. Stevenson's staffers in New York called aviation authorities in Washington and received permission for Stevenson's plane to land ahead of the stack. He landed at six fifty-one and in a police car raced to the city, arriving at a TV studio just as Adolf Berle of the Liberal Party was introducing him. He arrived at the Academy of Music in Brooklyn about five minutes before he was due to speak on Korea.

From Brooklyn, Stevenson and his party went to their train. Mary Lasker, the widow of Albert D. Lasker, who had made a fortune in advertising, gave Stevenson $16,500. It was the beginning of a long relationship. The train pulled out about midnight. For better or worse he was finished with the East. The next day was the final Saturday, November 1. Stevenson would spend it whistle-stopping across Ohio and Indiana and on to Chicago. While he slept his writers worked all night on the Chicago Stadium speech. They had been working on it for a week or more; they worked on through the day while he made the whistle stops. Martin had written a draft of which only the ending was usable. Wirtz had written a draft of which only a portion of the middle was usable. Finally Schlesinger, Ball, and Wyatt put together a draft, using some of a Wechsler draft, Wirtz's middle, and Martin's ending—and, Schlesinger noted, "the result, to our considerable astonishment, was a bang-up speech. It was the last that any of us had in us."

Now he was finished with Ohio. Crossing into Indiana with Governor Schricker, he stopped at Fort Wayne where the *Journal-Gazette* had endorsed him, and said, "This has been a wonderful day for me. We have had happy crowds all along the way. There is a feeling of victory in the air." His train rolled on across northern Indiana and stopped at dusk at Gary, the smoky steel city on the lake, and Stevenson reminded the crowd that this once had been a company town with all its evils, multiplied by the Great Depression.

And so to Chicago. The crowds around the Conrad Hilton and Blackstone hotels were dense that night. In his suite in the Hilton, Stevenson, showering and resting before the speech, clad only in shorts, told Schlesinger, "Of course, I'm going to win. I knew it all the time. That is why I was reluctant to run. . . . I figure that I will get about 366 [electoral] votes. I don't see how I can lose. But I have been giving some thought to what I should say if I happen to lose. I thought that I would use the old story Abraham Lincoln used to tell—the one about the boy who stubbed his toe in the dark, who said that he was too old to cry but he couldn't laugh because it hurt too much."

Barney Hodes had arranged one of his torchlight parades from the Loop to the Stadium for the final Saturday night rally. The motorcade left from Balbo Drive, between the two hotels, and moved slowly westward, with floats and marching bands. The sidewalks of skid row, West Madison Street, were almost deserted. Now and then a drunk would stagger into the street and wave one hand limply, then fall down in the gutter. Stevenson's staff was disturbed— where were the crowds? Absent. A crowd milled around the Stadium; inside, all seats were taken except those in the topmost balcony; Democratic ward leaders were trying to drive the milling precinct captains and hangers-on up to the highest seats but they kept going in one door and out another, they did not want to climb so far. The Stadium was vast. A smoky haze hung in the air, as it had at the Amphitheater during the convention in July. The crowd rose out of sight among the beams and rafters. Stevenson, Illinois candidates and party leaders, and visiting dignitaries took their places on the platform. This was the climactic rally of the campaign, carried live from 9:30 to 10 P.M. on national TV and radio, and arranged by the powerful Cook County Democratic machine. Lieutenant Governor Dixon was introduced as the hero of the Menard prison riot. He introduced Stevenson.

Stevenson began by urging the election of Dixon and by thanking "every Democratic precinct worker" and every Volunteer who had worked in the campaign. Then he launched into his prepared text: "Tonight we have come to the end of the campaign, and a long, long journey—and I have come home to old friends and to familiar surroundings." He wondered if there hadn't been some easier way his friends in Illinois could have gotten rid of him. The crowd laughed. "It has been a great campaign. I have enjoyed every minute of it. . . . It has not only been a great campaign for me—it's also a winner," then, "It sounds as though you are surprised." The crowd roared "No." The crowd was hot, ready to applaud and laugh and boo, and did so, in part because it was cued by a klaxon onstage. He went on: "There has been an electric feeling of victory in the air all the way home." He poked fun at the Republicans, rising to the crowd's response. He had chosen to ignore advice to eschew humor; he was off to a rollicking start; the speech was working. He turned to Eisenhower. In the Midwest, Stevenson said, Eisenhower had identified himself with the Old Guard; in New York and California with New Deal-Fair Deal social gains. "We have been offered a strange picture of an anguished, reluctant, respected figure reciting distasteful words, shaking hands that make him shudder, walking in strange, dark alleys, caught in a clamor of conflicting voices. . . . Can independents really believe that victory would strengthen progressive Republicans?" Far from it—if Eisenhower were elected, Taft and McCarthy would run the country.

He ended with: "I have seen an America where all of the signs read 'Men at Work.'

"But we have much to do in this century in this country of ours before its greatness may be fully realized and shared by all Americans. As we plan for change let us be sure that our vision is high enough and broad enough so that it encompasses every single hope and dream of both the greatest and the humblest among us.

"I see an America where no man fears to think as he pleases or say what he thinks.

"I see an America where slums and tenements have vanished and children are raised in decency and self-respect.

"I see an America where men and women have leisure from toil—leisure to cultivate the resources of the spirit.

"I see an America where no man is another's master—where no man's mind is dark with fear.

"I see an America at peace with the world.

"I see an America as the horizon of human hopes.

"This is our design for the American cathedral, and we shall build it brick by brick and stone by stone, patiently, bravely and prayerfully. And, to those who say that the design defies our abilities to complete it, I answer: 'To act with enthusiasm and faith is the condition of acting greatly.' "

He had reached his closing litany—the "I see an America" passage—close to the end of his TV time. The crowd had begun to applaud at the end of each sentence but he had held up his hands to stop the applause so he could finish on time. At the end the crowd "took the roof off the place," as one Stevenson staffer put it. Some had tears in their eyes. And when he finished the press arose and applauded him, a rare event. Next morning's New York *Times* carried his "I see an America" litany on page one.

34

That day, at Eniwetok, the United States had detonated its first hydrogen "device"—the hydrogen age had begun. Stevenson flew to Springfield to spend the night. Some of his staff went with him, some stayed in Chicago, some scattered to their own homes across the country. Schlesinger and Tufts spent the night with Martin in Highland Park, a Chicago suburb, and the Dave Bells joined them. Late at night after the Stadium rally they talked about how many electoral votes Stevenson would receive; they talked about starting a pool, each putting in five dollars and his guess. All—except for Fran Martin—thought Stevenson would win. She said Stevenson was doing fine, though of course he would lose Illinois. Schlesinger called his wife in Cambridge, and she said Stevenson was doing fine although of course he would lose Massachusetts. Sunday at the airport in New York, Schlesinger encountered Max Lerner, who said that everything looked great for Stevenson except of course he would lose New York. It was at this point, Schlesinger recalled later, that he realized what was really going to happen.

Stevenson drove to Bloomington on Sunday, attended church and a reception, and drove back to Springfield in the late afternoon. On Monday he flew to Chicago where he made his final speech on national TV and radio at 9:30 P.M. Election Eve. Stevenson rewrote the speech heavily and it became too long. It was a summary of the campaign, a graceful speech but not a good political speech, almost sad in tone. He did not deliver it well, seemed ill at ease. "He fooled with it too much," McGowan said. He was cut off the air before he finished. Wilson Wyatt said it was the only time he ever saw Stevenson lose his temper. After Stevenson had gone off the air, Dutch Smith and others hurriedly bought a few minutes of TV time later that evening so Stevenson could deliver the remainder of his speech. Dutch Smith once recalled, "It was ghastly. After that he spent the night at our house. He was tired. We had very little conversation. I never thought he was going to win." Eisenhower's final television show was, by contrast, a smooth production.

On Tuesday morning Stevenson went out into the Smiths' kitchen to thank their cook, then went to Libertyville to vote. It took him a long time. (He said it was because there was a long constitutional amendment on the ballot and he read every word of it, but he may have been splitting his local ticket.) The polling place was a country schoolhouse. The PTA had set up a tent and was serving coffee and doughnuts to the Stevenson staff and press. Stevenson chatted with the school children and greeted old friends and neighbors. He made a little speech to the children: "I would like to ask all of you children to indicate, by holding up your hands, how many of you would like to be Governor of Illinois, the way I am." They did. He said, "Well, that is almost unanimous. Now I would like to ask the Governors here if they would like to be one of you kids." Whereupon he himself cheered. He went on, "I don't know whether you understand what is going on here this morning very well. I am not sure I do myself. But what you see here is something that does not happen everywhere in the world. Here are a lot of your parents and your neighbors going over to the schoolhouse there to cast their vote. That means they are deciding for themselves who is going to lead them. You understand that? . . . In other words, what that means is, we decide who governs us. It is not everybody in the world who can do that. These are the things you read about in the history books, that your ancestors have been struggling for for generations—not only to get the right to govern themselves, but to keep it. Anyway, I think you are going to remember today for one thing only, and that is you got a half day off from school. I am sure I have enjoyed this as much as you have. What I would like to do is spend the recess this morning playing in the yard, but I don't know what we would play. What would we play?" They shouted, "Baseball, football." He said, "The same old fight between the cattlemen and the sheepmen. Wouldn't anybody like to have a little mock game of politics?" One boy said, "We don't like mud fights." He laughed and talked a few minutes more, then said, almost sadly, "Good-by, kids. I hope you will all come over and see me on St. Mary's Road, but I am not over there very often any more. Good-by."

His motorcade went to O'Hare Field and, with his staff and friends, he flew to Springfield. On the plane, the five-dollar electoral vote pool was completed. Two hundred and sixty-six electoral votes were needed to win. Schlesinger's guess had been 325, Tufts's about 450, Martin's about 400. Fran Martin felt she couldn't put down a losing number, so she put down the bare minimum Stevenson needed to win. Stevenson himself guessed 325 (350, according to Schlesinger). On the plane Stevenson seemed calm and confident. But the rest were quiet, subdued. Even Oscar Chapman, who had been optimistic all along, was not cheerful. In Springfield a good crowd met them. Stevenson went to the Mansion. His staff scattered to the St. Nicholas Hotel, the Elks Club, Flanagan's headquarters.

The last Sunday and Monday before an election are hard for a candidate and his staff, and Tuesday is hardest of all. They are exhausted, there is little to do; it is a time of nervous waiting, waiting for the great mysterious body of the American people to heave and speak. Everybody asks everybody, "What do you think?" Rumors fly—the vote is extraordinarily heavy in a certain state. Is that good or bad? The weather forecast is for rain. Is that good or bad? The final polls show many undecided. What does that mean?

Dore Schary had sent Stevenson a telegram on Monday: "If you do not win, then I, as so many others, ask only 'when do we fight again and how can we help?'" John Cowles, an old friend whose publications had nonetheless supported Eisenhower, wrote that he was going to vote for Eisenhower but had "nothing but respect and admiration for the way you have conducted yourself under extremely difficult circumstances." Stevenson replied coolly—and waited until December 8 to reply at all. Carl McGowan had given Stevenson a handwritten note on Monday: "I don't know who is going to win *tomorrow*, but it is clear to me that *today* all of the honest and sensitive and intelligent people in this country know who should. Who can say, then, that victory has not already come?" McGowan did not think Stevenson would win. Most of those close to Stevenson thought

Stevenson believed he would. George Ball once recalled that near the end of the campaign he and Wyatt had insisted he pay a call on "a powerful leader of a minority group who he thought was a charlatan"; Stevenson, annoyed, had said, "Don't you characters believe that we are going to win with such a big vote that that kind of noxious business isn't necessary?"

In retrospect, the Elks and Stevenson seemed wildly optimistic. But at the time it did not seem so. The polls called the election close. Eisenhower's margin had shrunk in the Gallup poll from 53–39 on September 30 to 50–38 on October 9 to 48–39 on October 25, with 13 per cent still undecided. With the undecideds distributed 3 to 1 for Stevenson, the October 25 poll would give Eisenhower 52 per cent, Stevenson 48 per cent. The various polls contained so many anomalies that some experts mistrusted all—Gallup gave Stevenson only 38 per cent in California but the Field poll gave him 43.1 per cent there; all polls showed an unusually high percentage of undecideds. *Newsweek* said, "The guessing is closer, and the 'experts' are more genuinely confused than in any other election of our times."

Election Day afternoon, Ball and Wyatt took a long walk through Springfield. Neither of them, Ball recalled years later, thought Stevenson would win. Now they said so for the first time. Wyatt said, "It hasn't worked. We haven't had time to turn it around." Dutch Smith and his wife, Jane Dick and her husband, the John Millers, and other friends of Stevenson were at the Mansion. About 6 P.M. several of the Elks gathered in a restaurant for drinks and dinner. About seven, a few scattered returns began to come in over the radio. When they came in unfavorably from industrial areas of Connecticut, the Elks were worried. Having dined and heard more discouraging returns, they went to the Leland Hotel. The ballroom had been taken over for an election returns headquarters. At one end of the room was a big blackboard; Jim Lanigan and others were chalking up the returns as they came in state by state. TV cameras had been set up, TV lights flared, TV cables were strung snakelike everywhere. Nobody was saying much. The atmosphere was one of defeat. Aging John L. Lewis walked alone in the crowded room; no one thought to speak to him. People kept shuttling back and forth from the Mansion. By eight-thirty, Virginia, where Harry Byrd had refused to work for Stevenson, seemed to be breaking the solid South of the old Roosevelt coalition: it gave Eisenhower a 48,000 to 34,000 lead. And in Florida, Eisenhower not only was leading in the big resort cities but was running only slightly behind Stevenson in industrial Democratic Jacksonville. On the other hand, a predominantly Jewish precinct in Philadelphia gave Stevenson a bigger lead than it had given Truman four years earlier. As early as seven forty-five the Hartford, Connecticut, *Courant* gave Connecticut to Eisenhower— industrial Democratic Bridgeport had gone Republican for the first time since 1924. By 8 P.M. the Republican national chairman, Arthur Summerfield, was predicting a landslide. By nine-thirty Senator Benton had conceded defeat and predicted an Eisenhower sweep. In Maryland, with half the votes counted, Eisenhower had a 55 per cent majority. But Georgia and South Carolina held fast for Stevenson, and so did Philadelphia, with more than half the districts in. At the same time Eisenhower was opening a wide lead in New Jersey. Rome, the first New York town to report completely, went to Eisenhower; it had gone narrowly to Truman in 1948. Cleveland was going 2 to 1 for Eisenhower. In Massachusetts the Boston *Post* declared victory for Eisenhower at 9:45 P.M. He had taken a long early lead in Indiana. Illinois looked bad.

Suddenly the ticker showed a splurge of Democratic votes from Minnesota and the farm states, and Stevenson staffers thought Stevenson might repeat Truman's upset of four years ago. They had been saying, "Just wait till we hear from Ohio" or "Indiana" or "Michigan and Illinois." As the night wore on they kept moving their predictions westward, ending with, "Just wait till we hear from California."

By ten-thirty the Mansion was deadly quiet. About fifty people, Stevenson's friends and close staff and a few people from his gubernatorial administration, such as Fred Hoehler, were sitting around in little groups close to several radios. Mrs. Ives asked a staffer what he thought. He thought it looked very bad. People would walk by, stop to listen to the radio, shake their heads. Once Jim Oates went down to Stevenson's ground-floor office. Stevenson was working there. "I was pretty sunk," Oates recalled. "He said, 'What the hell's the matter with you—don't you realize this is going to save me a hell of a lot of work?'" By ten-thirty CBS' Univac computer predicted that Eisenhower would win with 314 electoral votes to 217, a popular vote of 27 million to 24 million. At ten forty-five Chairman Summerfield said flatly, "Dwight Eisenhower has been elected President of the U.S." Not quite. Stevenson was running well in Cook County, though probably not well enough to overcome the heavy Republican downstate vote, and he was getting about 61 per cent of the vote in Detroit, and he was still ahead in Pennsylvania. He would need them all and more: Eisenhower took New York.

McGowan joined Stevenson in his office. Bill Flanagan was bringing in news from the ticker. Stevenson saw the trend early and wanted to concede at once, but Steve Mitchell dissuaded him—premature concession might imperil Democratic congressional and senatorial candidates. By midnight it was clear that the Eisenhower sweep was moving westward—Ohio, Oklahoma, Kansas, Wisconsin, and Minnesota fell, and just before midnight Jack Arvey conceded Illinois. The first returns began coming in from the West Coast. They were all for Eisenhower. So was Mobile—Republican for the first time since Grant carried it in 1872. Steve Mitchell said just after midnight it wasn't over, Stevenson would carry Ohio and Pennsylvania; but a little later the Ohio state chairman conceded, and the New York *Times* said Eisenhower had carried Pennsylvania. Stevenson would wait no longer. At 12:40 A.M. he went to the Leland Hotel headquarters. A crowd of floodlit townspeople standing on the Mansion lawn watched him leave and gave him a small cheer.

Stevenson had written out in longhand his telegram to Eisenhower. "The people have made their choice and I congratulate you. That you may be the servant and guardian of peace and make the vale of trouble a door of hope is my earnest prayer. Best wishes. Adlai E. Stevenson." The longhand draft contained no corrections. Eisenhower replied, "I thank you for your courteous and generous message recognizing the intensity of the difficulties that lie ahead it is clearly necessary that men and women of good will of both parties forget the political strife through which we have passed and devote themselves to the single purpose of a better future this I believe they will do. Dwight D. Eisenhower."

At the Leland, on nationwide TV, Stevenson made his concession speech:

"The people have rendered their verdict and I gladly accept it.

"General Eisenhower has been a great leader in war. He has been a vigorous and valiant opponent in the campaign. . . .

"It is traditionally American to fight hard before an election. It is equally traditional to close ranks as soon as the people have spoken.

"From the depths of my heart I thank all of my party and all of those independents and Republicans who supported Senator Sparkman and me.

"That which unites us as American citizens is far greater than that which divides us as political parties.

"I urge you all to give to General Eisenhower the support he will need to carry out the great tasks that lie before him.

"I pledge him mine.

"We vote as many, but we pray as one. With a united people, with faith in democracy, with common concern for others less fortunate around the globe, we shall move forward with God's guidance toward the time when His children shall grow in freedom and dignity in a world at peace."

His prepared text ended there; he extemporized a paragraph:

"Someone asked me, as I came in, down on the street, how I felt, and I was reminded of a story that a fellow townsman of ours used to tell—Abraham Lincoln. They asked him how he felt once after an unsuccessful election. He said he felt like a little boy who had stubbed his toe in the dark. He said that he was too old to cry but it hurt too much to laugh."

Stevenson's sense of history was operating. He put a note to Carol Evans on his concession speech: "I hope this time we are *keeping* carefully my statement on election night & my telegram to Ike." Returning to the Mansion, Stevenson paused to say good-by to the TV men who had set up equipment there in case he won: "And I do want to tell you how sorry I am to have put you to all this unnecessary trouble." He told a friend, "No one needs to feel sorry for me, I've been spared a great ordeal." One wonders whether Stevenson had bet on his own election: some time later, to a man who said he had lost a $100 bet on Stevenson, Stevenson replied, "I can assure you that *you* got off easy!"

Inside the Mansion he found several staffers, mainly Elks, on the ground floor preparing to leave; they had thought he would want to be alone with his family and close friends. He asked, "Where's everybody going?" They told him. He said, "Come on upstairs and have a drink; let's celebrate my defeat." Upstairs were his Lake Forest friends and others. Minow once recalled, "Almost all of them had voted for Eisenhower. One of them had a big diamond Eisenhower pin on." One woman said, "Governor, you educated the country with your great campaign." Stevenson replied, "But a lot of people flunked the course." To a group of them he said he had no taste for political wakes, "especially when I'm the corpse." He asked his butler to bring out the champagne. He proposed a toast to Wilson Wyatt, "the most *successful* campaign manager ever to manage an *un*successful campaign." Fran Martin, to whom he offered the first glass, had won the electoral pool; she gave the money to Stevenson, telling him it was an early contribution to the 1956 campaign fund. He said, "I take it shamelessly," and put it in his pocket. He was by far the most composed man in the room—many of his supporters were tearful. Most of the guests left about 2 A.M., though some stayed up in hotel rooms, talking, until 4 or 5 A.M.

35

What can one say of Adlai Stevenson's 1952 presidential campaign?

First, he lost overwhelmingly—carried only nine states, all Southern or border states. He received only 89 electoral votes to Eisenhower's 442. The popular vote was closer: Eisenhower 33,936,234, or 55.1 per cent, to Stevenson's 27,314,992, or 44.4 per cent, according to Congressional Quarterly. But Eisenhower's percentage of the popular vote was bigger than any Democratic victory since Roosevelt's 60.8 per cent victory in 1936. It had been little short of an electoral revolution.[22]

What had happened?

At the time, analysts said that the old Roosevelt coalition was broken, perhaps permanently—the once solid South had split, farmers had forgotten FDR's soil conservation and Truman's price supports and had deserted their party, blue-collar workers had forgotten the union struggles of the 1930s which the Democrats had so powerfully aided, Catholics had defected, and many people whom the New Deal had set on their feet had moved to the suburbs and now were voting Republican in the hope that, if they emulated their banker neighbors, they too might become bankers. But in retrospect, while these defections did occur, it appears that a deeper tide was running. Not all the Roosevelt coalition defected—Negroes and Jews, for example, supported Stevenson stoutly, and much of FDR's South held solid for him. No, 1952 was, quite simply, a Republican

[22] Stevenson carried only Alabama, Arkansas, Georgia, Kentucky, Louisiana, Mississippi, North Carolina, South Carolina, and West Virginia. He had carried Illinois for Governor in 1948 by 572,000; he lost it for President in 1952 by 443,407 (and carried only four counties out of 102). In the nation, he lost such Democratic strongholds as New York and lost them big—Eisenhower had a plurality of 848,212 and 55.5% of the votes in New York, a plurality of 357,711 and 56.8% in New Jersey, a plurality of 320,872 and 55.4% in Michigan, a plurality of 99,086 and 55% in Florida, a plurality of 208,800 and 54.2% in Massachusetts (but John F. Kennedy won Lodge's Senate seat). Pennsylvania came closer to holding the line— Eisenhower won only 52.7% of the votes, a plurality of 269,520. But he won Texas with 53.1% and a plurality of 133,650; he won that volatile critical state which seemed so friendly to Stevenson, California, with 56.3% and a plurality of almost 700,000. He broke the solid South—carried Texas, Florida, Virginia, Oklahoma, Tennessee. Eisenhower even carried the most Democratic state of all, Rhode Island, with 50.9%. And if any doubts had existed about Wisconsin, he dispelled them—he got 61% of the vote there.

presidential year, and Eisenhower was, quite simply, a national hero, and the American people were, quite simply, weary of twenty years of challenge—of struggle against domestic depression and foreign totalitarianism—and wanted to disengage from the struggle, to be let alone, to hand their problems over to someone who promised them not more trouble (as Stevenson did) but surcease (as Eisenhower did). The issue that cut deepest was Korea, an unpopular war. "Time for a change" cut too, a slogan that summed up a generation's malaise. Communists-in-government moved fewer votes, though it did touch Catholics and blue-collar workingmen. Corruption was probably less effective than had been anticipated.

That it was an Eisenhower victory can be demonstrated by the results in Congress. The Republicans gained only twenty-two seats in the House, three more than they needed to control. In the Senate, Republicans gained only one seat, just enough for a majority.

Could Stevenson have won in 1952? Almost nobody thinks so. The tide was too deep and powerful. Yet in terms of pure politics it was not a very good campaign, and many mistakes were made. Steve Mitchell, handicapped at the outset, did not inspire important state leaders to maximum effort. Many professionals, feeling left out of the Stevenson campaign, concentrated on local candidates. Most of the old-time big-city machines failed to produce for Stevenson—he even lost Cook County, Illinois.[23] Across the country, the Volunteers

---

[23] In California the organization was split several ways. In Cleveland, September registration figures showed that such Republican strongholds as suburban Shaker Heights had all but 2 to 4% of their voters registered, while in heavily Democratic wards in Cleveland as much as 35 to 40% was unregistered. In Ohio as a whole the organization was split, with Governor Lausche running his own private organization and the party leader in Cleveland tending to favor Senator Richard B. Russell for President. Among big-city machines, the outstanding exception was Philadelphia. There the ADA claimed credit for turning a 1948 majority of 7,000 for Truman into a 160,000 majority for Stevenson. But Jim Finnegan, Democratic city chairman of Philadelphia, contributed a thoughtful analysis of the 1952 election that may have helped induce Stevenson to choose Finnegan to manage his campaign in 1956. Finnegan wrote that the Philadelphia campaign was led by the city Democratic organization and that it was fresh, had come to full power only in 1951, and so lacked the problems which beset older machines—loss of able workers through appointment to public office, increasing dependence on organized labor, and a tendency to lose contact with large segments of voters, especially independents. Moreover, most of Finnegan's city committeemen did not want public payroll jobs; many were businessmen and professional men. The organization's strategy had been to make the bread-and-butter issues overriding and to exploit Stevenson's courage, independence, and good-government record in Illinois. The organization had decided early that Stevenson was assuredly "the best

and the machines refused to cooperate. Wyatt and others had made mistakes in scheduling; it was probably foolish to go once to Wyoming, let alone twice. Stevenson ensured Catholic defections in New York by ignoring the Al Smith dinner. Many Democratic leaders, such as Senator Kefauver, did little or nothing to help. And Stevenson himself had made mistakes. He spent too much time polishing speeches and not enough talking to important local political leaders. He misapprehended the nature of the "independent" vote. He mishandled the Truman problem. He never mastered the whistle stop. Governor Williams of Michigan, one of the few Democrats to survive the disaster, thought Stevenson had botched the campaign—was bothered by heckling, made a poor impression, was not good at handling crowds. Stevenson contrived to spoil nearly all his nationwide TV appearances. His technique of telling audiences what they did not want to hear was arresting; but he overdid it. Perhaps worst of all, Stevenson permitted himself to be thrown on the defensive and to fight on Eisenhower's grounds—time for a change, corruption, Communism, Korea.

To say that it was a Republican victory is to raise the question whether Stevenson could have defeated Taft. Samuel Lubell, the political analyst, thought not, and Carl McGowan said, "I'm not so sure. The extent of defection from Truman and the Democratic Party was very deep. The tide was running toward the Republican Party. It is cyclical. You add Korea to that and add mink coats and the tax increase and you have a problem. Taft might have won. There is a tendency to give Eisenhower too much credit."

Stevenson received a huge amount of mail from political analysts, both professional and amateur, and in his replies can be found hints of what he thought defeated him. To one he wrote, "We ran out of poor people and we ran into Korea and a few other rather solid obstacles." To Ernest Gruening of Alaska he stressed the importance of Korea, especially toward the end, but added, "of course there were other factors too." He told Schlesinger that Korea hurt more than any single issue. He said he liked Truman greatly as a person

---

thing we had to sell," and its radio commercials concentrated on him, not on local candidates. Finnegan saw no substantial Catholic defection as in Massachusetts, Rhode Island, and Connecticut. He thought the Volunteers had been too glib and clever. He thought Truman's campaigning helped Stevenson. Notes of defeatism in some Stevenson speeches, such as his final speech of the campaign, had hurt him. Finnegan thought the national election results showed that Americans were not yet a "genuinely mature people" capable of world leadership but were still "impetuous, intolerant of delay or impasses, clamoring for quick decisions."

but "I wish to hell he had stayed at home." To Claude Bowers, historian and ambassador to Chile, Stevenson wrote that the old Democratic coalition in the South had little reason for further existence, new party leadership was needed in many places, the New York organization was "woefully weak," the Republicans had spent an "appalling" amount of money, but the most important element in the Republican victory was the impression Eisenhower created that he could settle the Korean War promptly. He took comfort in his campaign: he told a friend, "After all, one has to live for oneself, and the satisfactions of a proper race seem to me greater than victory."

What made his campaign so gloriously memorable to his followers? Several things, really. His wit and humor—George Ball said, "He simply punctured the arrogance of power." His self-deprecation, for another; although this may have looked to the great mass like weak leadership, it was a becoming humility to his devotees. His often-repeated declaration that he would rather lose the election than mislead the people helped create the picture of a man of high principle (though to some politicians it sounded like defeatism). His appeal to the intellect, his eloquence, his elevation of the level of political discourse captured the imaginations of academic people and other intellectuals who remained his devoted followers, and the admiration of millions of less-educated people. He was, indeed, an off-trail candidate, a sport, a man who behaved and talked unlike almost any other candidate in recent memory. There was about him a certain superficial resemblance to the Senator Eugene McCarthy of 1968 whose campaign against the Vietnam War that year produced success in the New Hampshire primary. (But McCarthy later behaved in a careless, offhand, eccentric, erratic way, as when he relinquished his seat on the Senate Foreign Relations Committee. Stevenson was more responsible. In 1972, Senator George McGovern's idolators compared him to Stevenson. But McGovern's campaign was vastly inferior to Stevenson's, nor did he himself stand up nearly so well as Stevenson in the blinding spotlight of a presidential campaign.) Such men attract followers who become idolators; but it is an appeal to a narrow segment of the population; such men do not get elected President. Robert F. Kennedy went about as far as a politician can go in the direction of unconventionality and still hold broad-based support (and we shall never know if he would have been elected President though his friends, including the present author, thought so). President John Kennedy, a politician to his fingertips and in many ways a rather conventional one, was much closer to FDR than was Robert Kennedy or Adlai Stevenson.

What was the significance of the 1952 campaign?

George Ball called that campaign Stevenson's highest achievement. Stevenson himself told a friend years later that it had been "a high point" of his life, "one of his most glorious experiences." Once a young woman friend told him of the thrill she had felt when she had made her first public speech and at its conclusion the audience had risen to applaud. Stevenson said, "You've felt it too, then, haven't you? You know how it is." Ed McDougal said, "He rose to the challenge as he should have. By doing so he raised the standard of political life." McDougal contrasted Stevenson's acceptance of defeat with Nixon's press conference of 1962, when, having lost the governorship of California, he told reporters, "You won't have Nixon to kick around any more." McGowan remarked that Stevenson uniquely "stirred the interest of people, especially young people, who were jaded or not interested in politics." Schlesinger wrote, "Adlai won widespread respect and response because of the high intellectual and moral standards of his campaign. He created the image of something new, fine, and exciting. . . . What we confronted this time was an upsurge of natural forces. Our number was up—and very little we could have done would have altered the outcome. But . . . the Governor did establish himself as a great national leader—gallant and honorable and dedicated."

It is true that Stevenson elevated the political dialogue, that he stirred new interest, that he carried political debate to new heights not only of eloquence but of responsibility. But important as those things were, they were rather impermanent. The conclusion seems inescapable that the real significance and the lasting importance of the 1952 campaign was that it made Stevenson a national, even an international, figure. Without it, he would have been just another Illinois Governor, better than most; but no more. With it, he was able to reach higher, to go on to help to shape his party and his country, and his times, in the 1950s and 1960s.

The day after the election, a cold day with pale hard sunshine, McGowan took the Elks and Newt Minow to lunch at a restaurant on the edge of town, a rather melancholy affair, then, back at McGowan's office in the Mansion, talked desultorily with Ball and others about Stevenson's future. People suggested he ought to teach, or take a university presidency, or go around the world, or go back to Libertyville and read and write and speak occasionally. George Ball said, "He could always come into my law firm." But the others wanted him to find a public forum from which to expound the liberal Democratic faith during the Eisenhower years. Nobody had a good idea. All agreed it was arranged much better in England, where he would have become the leader of the parliamentary opposition. They talked about his running again in 1956, and somebody suggested a parallel with Bryan—several times a loser for President, finally appointed Secretary of State. After a time everybody went away.

That bleak November day in Springfield after the election, it did not seem so but the truth is that the best years of Adlai Stevenson's leadership lay ahead.

APPENDIXES

APPENDIX A

Of the total contributions to Stevenson's 1948 gubernatorial fund, $21,-053 was anonymous. Among the remainder, these are worth noting: Graham Aldis of Lake Forest and his wife and company, $350; J. D. Allen, $1,000; the Amalgamated Clothing Workers of America, $2,000; Frank Annunzio, Secretary of the Illinois State CIO-PAC, $2,500 (a woman who gave her address as care of Annunzio contributed another $750); Lester Armour, $1,000; Max Ascoli of New York, $500; George Ball, $100; Ralph Bard and his wife, $150; Morton A. Barker of Springfield, $1,000; Laird Bell and his wife, $1,800; Dick Bentley and his wife, $265; William Benton of New York, $100; Edgar Bernhard and his wife, $65; Barry Bingham, editor of the Louisville *Times* and the *Courier-Journal*, $250; Blair and his family, $185; Leigh Block of Inland Steel, $500; Joe Bohrer, $50; Randolph Bohrer, $1,000; Edward Eagle Brown, $500; Edward Burling, Jr., the Washington lawyer, $25; William Burry, Jr., and his wife, of Lake Forest, $925; Stevenson's mother-in-law and her husband, John Alden Carpenter, $150; Fred B. Caron of Danville, $1,000; the Central Iron and Metal Company of Springfield, $1,000; Bennett Cerf, the New York publisher, $10; John S. Clark, Cook County assessor, $1,000; Elmer M. Crane of Chicago, $1,000; Joseph B. Crowley of Chicago, $1,000; Henry Crown, $5,000; Mrs. Honore W. Cudahy of Lake Forest, $25; Mrs. Walter Cummings, Jr., of Lake Shore Drive, $8; V. Y. Dallman of Springfield and his wife, $100; Mr. and Mrs. Leonard Davidow of Highland Park, $20; Benjamin B. Davis, a prominent Chicago lawyer, $50; Ralph DeMange of Bloomington, $50; Edison and Jane Dick, $2,250; W. M. Duncan of the Duncan Machine & Foundry Company of Alton, $1,000; the 11th Ward Democratic Organization of Chicago, $250; Alex Elson, $25; three members of the Ewing family of Bloomington, $400; Mrs. Francis C. Farwell III of Lake Bluff, $6; Marshall Field IV, $7,100 (plus more included in the anonymous list); Richard J. Finnegan, editor of the *Sun-Times*, $100; Walter T. Fisher of Hubbard Woods, $100; Edward J. Fleming, $5,000; the 14th Ward Regular Democratic Organization of Chicago, $1,000; Max Fuhrer of Chicago, $500; Donald Funk of Springfield, $400; Joe Gill's company, $2,500; Freda R. Goelitz, $1,000; the law firm of Arthur Goldberg, $100; Frank E. Harmon of Chicago, $750; Mrs. Paul V. Harper, a neighbor of Stevenson's in Libertyville, $5; Irving B. Harris, $100; Daggett Harvey and his wife, $325; Ben W. Heineman, $50; Lillian Herstein, a woman active in labor and civil liberties causes, $10; Ralph J. Hines of New York, the second husband of Ellen's sister, $250; Fred K. Hoehler, $25; Al Horan, $2,500; Steve Hord and his wife, $50; Lawrence Houghteling, $500; Mr. and Mrs. R. W. Ickes of Winnetka, $15; Local 777 of the Illinois State Barbers & Beauticians, $700; Charles F. Jarrard of the Allied Structural Steel Company, $1,000; Walter Johnson of the University of Chicago, $25; Sam Katzin of Chicago, $500; G. P. Kelley of Lake Worth, Florida, $1,000; Phelps Kelley, $1,000; John and Mickey Kellogg of Libertyville, $75; James T. Kelty of Springfield, $1,500; Mayor Kennelly, $500; Mrs. Otto Kerner of River Forest, $5; Meyer Kestnbaum of Hart, Schaffner & Marx, and his wife, $375; Phillip Klutznick, $50; Mrs. Frank Knox, $20; Ferd Kramer, $100; Mrs. J. M. Lebolt, $10; Morris I. Leibman, $200; Lloyd Lewis and his wife, $350; Walter Lichtenstein, $15; Benjamin Lindheimer, $3,000; Glen Lloyd, $1,100; Leon Mandel, the merchant, $500; William B. McIlvaine, $100; H. L. McKay, $1,000; Donald McKellar of Lake Forest, $20; Mrs. George D. McLaughlin of Ritchie Court on the Gold Coast, $25; Mrs. George F. McLaughlin of Lake Forest, $20; Mrs. Harriet McLaughlin of Lake Forest, $25; Mrs. Herbert McLaughlin of Lake Forest, $50; Mrs. Hollis Letts McLaughlin of Lake Forest, $25; Mrs. Donald R. McLennan of Lake Forest, $25; Ward McNally of East Walton Street on the Gold Coast, $10; Mrs. Robert C. McNamara of Winnetka, $10; I. J. Meites, $1,000; Bud Merwin, $500; Dr. Karl Meyer of Cook County Hospital, $500; John S. Miller, Astor Street, Chicago, $1,150, and his wife, $10; H. S. Morgan of 2 Wall Street in New York, $100; Paul Scott Mowrer, $100; John H. Murray of the Murray Supply Company in Springfield, $1,500; D. K. Olin of the Goldenrod Ice Cream Company, $200; Stuart Otis and his wife of Lake Forest, $75; George W. Overton, $75; Chris Paschen and his company, which did construction work for the city, $350; Alice H. Patterson of Lake Shore Drive, Chicago, $50; Stuyvesant Peabody, Jr., of the Peabody Coal Company, $500 (in addition to his company's $1,000); Joseph S. Perry of Wheaton, $1,000; the Regular Organization of the Democratic Party of Cook County, $10,000; Mr. and Mrs. W. B. Requa of Lake Shore Drive, Chicago, $10; E. L. Richardson of Milwaukee, a relative of Stevenson, $100; Sam Rothberg, $3,500; S. D. Ruby, $1,000; Mrs. Donald Ryerson of Lake Forest, $100, and Mrs. Joseph T. Ryerson of Astor Street, Chicago, $50; Jack A. Schram of Highland Park, $20; C. K. Schwartz of La Salle Street, Chicago, $1,500; Ulysses S. Schwartz, $150; Samuel H. Shapiro of Kankakee, $100; William P. Sidley, $250; Edward A. Simon and Matt E. Simon of the Ashland Construction Company, $1,000; Oliver O. Smaha, $500; Dutch Smith, $1,000, and his wife, $42.85; Mrs. Solomon B. Smith, of Lake Forest, $100; Mrs. Modie J. Spiegel, Jr., of Glencoe, $25; Mr. and Mrs. Lawrence Stein of Highland Park, $35; Sydney Stein, Jr., $400; David B. Stern of Lake Shore Drive, $200; David B. Stern, Jr., $100; E. R. Stettinius, Jr., of New York, $100; Stevenson's aunt, Letitia E. Stevenson, $200; his cousin, Dr. E. M. Stevenson of Bloomington, $50; Carroll Sudler, Jr., and his wife of Lake Forest, $225; Joseph R. Sullivan, $1,000; John Stuart, $1,250; Herbert Bayard Swope, $250; Wayne Chatfield Taylor of Washington, $200; Henry F. Tenney, $100; Harold E. Thomas, $400; Floyd E. Thompson, a prominent lawyer, $250; Ben Thoron, of Washington, $50; the United Auto Workers, $2,500; the United Steelworkers, $2,500; Clifton Utley, $50; the Carl Vroomans, Stevenson's cousins, $500; Mrs. W. G. Walling of Hubbard Woods, $10; Mrs. J. Harris Ward of Lake Forest, $25; David Weil, $100; Marvin Welfeld, $500; Mr. and Mrs. Edward K. Welles and Mrs. Donald P. Welles, of Lake Forest, $700; Harriet Welling, $650; John Hay Whitney of New York, $250; F. E. Windish of Galesburg, $500; Mrs. Edwin W. Winter of Lake Forest, $25; Samuel W. Witwer, Jr., a prominent Republican lawyer, $65; Quincy Wright, of the University of Chicago, $10; Philip K. Wrigley, owner of the Chicago Cubs and the chewing gum company, $1,000.

APPENDIX B

Stevenson said at Brooklyn, Illinois:

"The men who helped found Brooklyn some one hundred and eleven years ago were of that handful who look beyond today and tomorrow and can see not alone what men are but what men are meant to be. Brooklyn, as places go in America, is not very large or important. And yet, as things go in America, great principles seem to have a habit of taking root in small places, and in time, they cast their shadows over the land. That was true of a farming village called Lexington where political freedom was born in this hemisphere. It was true of a crossroads town called Gettysburg where human freedom was victorious. And it is true right here in Brooklyn, Illinois.

"Here, in Brooklyn, your forebears and mine didn't merely establish another settlement in America. They established a *special kind* of settlement—one formed by people who by choice turned their backs on slavery and by choice accepted the risks of being free men. It is not an easy choice to make now. It was equally difficult then. . . . And even after the choice was made, those who traveled the underground route to Brooklyn ran risks and endured hardships as great as those faced by any man who escaped Hitler's Europe to join the legions of free men.

"It is right and proper that we should recall the courage of the men who founded this community. . . . It is equally right and proper to ask:

"What tasks should command our efforts today in the historic struggle to foster the growth of mankind?

"The outline of that task was graphically expressed for me by a minister of your color. Before the Civil War, he said, a high wall was built around the Negro and the whites said to him: 'You can't get out.' But since the Civil War, the minister continued, the whites have built a high wall around themselves and said to the Negro: 'You can't get in!' Will there ever be a time, the minister went on to ask, when we shall be able to live side by side without these prison walls?

"My great-grandfather, Jesse Fell—a close friend of Lincoln and Elijah P. Lovejoy—helped tear down the walls the whites had built around the Negro. I would be unworthy of my heritage if in my own day I too failed to help tear down the walls whites have built around themselves. For that task summons us both—whites and Negroes alike. We have no strength to waste on the vice of bigotry and prejudice. . . .

". . . I am aware of the existence in this country of sinister forces like the Ku Klux Klan and the Silver Shirts. I am aware of the Jim Crow laws and of the lynchings and discriminations at the polls. I am aware that Theodore Bilbo once sat in the Senate of the United States. I am aware that Henry Wallace, whose right to speak his mind, whatever his views, is the same as my right, or yours, has been egged and stoned, assaulted by men who claim Thomas Jefferson as their political saint. . . .

"I do not minimize any of these facts. They are all ugly sores on the body of our nation. They threaten not only Negroes, but they threaten every other citizen in the land. And the sooner that threat is met and mastered, the sooner we will be able to stand forth before the world as champions of human freedom, without exposing ourselves to the charge of hypocrisy.

"Those of you who followed the proceedings of the Democratic National Convention know that the Democratic Party had the courage to bring the issue of civil rights out into the open. . . .

"As an American, I am proud of President Truman for the courage he has shown on this issue. I was proud to have had an active part in that fight as a member of the Illinois delegation to the convention and I am proud of the Illinois delegation which, united all the way, led the fight all the way. I am proud that I belong to the Democratic Party which has cleaned house and shouted to the nation:

"The rights of safety and security of person belong to *all* Americans, not just to some of them!

"The rights to citizenship and its privileges belong to *all* Americans, not just to some of them!

"The right to freedom of conscience and expression belongs to *all* Americans, not just to some of them!

"The right to equality of opportunity belongs to *all* Americans, not just to some of them! . . .

"And here in Illinois the Democratic Party has also spoken out for fair and equal treatment."

APPENDIX C

The full text of Stevenson's welcoming speech to the 1952 Democratic Convention, transcribed from a recording of his voice, follows:

"Mr. Chairman, delegates and guests of the convention:

"I thought I came here to greet you, not you to greet me.

"I'm grateful for your courtesy but I have an assignment here this morning as Governor of the host state to welcome the 1952 Democratic Convention. And in the name of nine million of the people of Illinois, I extend to you the heartiest of greetings.

"Chicago and Illinois are proud that once again the party conventions by which we restate our principles and choose our candidates for the greatest temporal office on earth are held here in Chicago—at the crossroads of the continent.

"Here, my friends, on the prairies of Illinois and of the Middle West, we can see a long way in all directions. We look to east, to west, to north and south. Our commerce, our ideas, come and go in all directions. Here there are no barriers, no defenses, to ideas and to aspirations. We want none; we want no shackles on the mind or the spirit, no rigid patterns of thought, and no iron conformity. We want only the faith and the conviction that triumph in fair and free contest.

"As a Democrat perhaps you will permit me to remind you that until four years ago the people of Illinois had chosen but three Democratic Governors in a hundred years. One was John Peter Altgeld, whom the great Illinois poet, Vachel Lindsay, called him the Eagle Forgotten, he was an immigrant; one was Edward F. Dunne, whose parents came here from the old sod of Ireland; and the last was Henry Horner, but one generation removed from Germany. John Peter Altgeld, my friends, was a Protestant, Governor Dunne was a Catholic, Henry Horner was a Jew.

"And that, my friends, is the American story, written by the Democratic Party here on the prairies of Illinois.

"You are very welcome here in the heartland of the nation. Indeed, we think you were wise to come here for your deliberations in this fateful year of grace. For it was in Chicago that the modern Democratic story began. It was here, just twenty years ago this month, in the depths of shattering national misery at the end of a dizzy decade of Republican rule, that you commenced the greatest era of economic and of social progress in our history. It was here, my friends, just twenty years ago, that you nominated Franklin Roosevelt; twenty years during which we fought total depression to victory and have never been more prosperous; twenty years during which we fought total war to victory, both East and West, and have launched the United Nations, history's most ambitious experiment in international security; twenty years, my friends, that close now in a grim contest with the Communist conspiracy on every continent of the globe.

"But our Republican friends have said it was all a miserable failure. For almost a week pompous phrases marched over this landscape in search of an idea. And the only idea they found was that the two great decades of progress in peace, and of victory in war, and of bold leadership in this anxious hour, were the misbegotten spawn of bungling, of corruption, of socialism, of mismanagement, of waste and of worse. They captured, they tied, and they dragged that ragged idea here into this hall and they furiously beat it to death for a solid week.

"After listening to this everlasting procession of epithets about our misdeeds I was even surprised the next morning when the mail was delivered on time! I guess our Republican friends were out of patience, out of sorts and, need I add, out of office.

"But we Democrats were by no means the only victims here. First they slaughtered each other, and then they went after us. And the same vocabulary was good for both exercises, which was a great convenience. Perhaps the proximity of the stockyards accounts for the carnage.

"My friends, the constructive spirit of the two great Democratic decades must not die here on its twentieth anniversary—it must not die here in destructive indignity and disorder. And I hope and pray, as you all do, that we can conduct our deliberations with a businesslike precision and a dignity befitting our responsibility and the solemnity of the hour in history in which we meet.

"For it is a very solemn hour indeed, freighted with the hopes and fears of millions of mankind who see in us, the Democratic Party, sober understanding of the breadth and the depth of the revolutionary currents in the world. Here and abroad they see in us awareness that there is no turning back, and that, as Justice Holmes said, 'We must sail sometimes with the wind, sometimes against it; but we must sail and not drift or lie at anchor.' They see in us, the Democratic Party, that has steered this country through a storm of spears for twenty years, an understanding of a world in the torment of transition from an age that has died to an age struggling to be born. They see in us relentless determination to stand fast against the barbarian at the gate, to cultivate allies with a decent respect for the opinion of others, to patiently explore every misty path to peace and security—which is the only certainty of lower taxes and a better life.

"This is not the time for superficial solutions and for endless elocution. This is not the time for frantic boast and foolish word. For words are not deeds and there are no cheap and painless solutions to war, to hunger, to ignorance, to fear, and to the new imperialism of the Soviet Union. My friends, you know full well that intemperate criticism is not a policy for the nation; and denunciation is not a program for our salvation. Words that are calculated to catch everyone may catch no one. And I hope that we can profit from their mistakes, not just for our partisan benefit, but for the benefit of all of us, Republicans and Democrats alike.

"Where we have erred, let there be no denial; and where we have wronged the public trust, let there be no excuses. Self-criticism is the secret weapon of democracy, and candor and confession are good for the political soul. But we will never appease, we will never apologize for our leadership of the great events of this critical century all the way from Woodrow Wilson to Harry Truman!

"We glory rather in these imperishable pages of our country's chronicle. But a great record of past achievement is not good enough. There can be no complacency perhaps for years to come. We dare not just look back to great yesterdays. We must look forward to great tomorrows.

"What counts now is not just what we are against, but what we are for. And who leads us is less important than what leads us—what convictions, what courage, what faith—win or lose. A man does not save a century or a civilization, but a militant party wedded to a principle can.

"So I hope that our preoccupation here is not just with personalities but with objectives. And I hope that the spirit of this convention is a confident reaffirmation that the United States is strong, resolved, resourceful, and rich; that we know our duty and the destiny of this heaven-rescued land; that we can and we will pursue a strong, consistent, honorable policy abroad, and meanwhile preserve the free institutions of life and of commerce at home.

"What America needs and what the world wants is not bombast, abuse, and double talk, but a sober message of firm faith and of confidence. St. Francis said: 'Where there is patience and humility there is neither anger nor worry.' And that might well be our text.

"And let us remember that we are not meeting here alone. All the world is watching and listening to what we say, what we do, how we behave. So let us give them a demonstration of democracy in action at its best—our manners good, our proceedings orderly and dignified. And above all, let us make our decisions openly, fairly, not by the processes of synthetic excitement or mass hysteria. Let us make them, as these solemn times demand, by earnest thought and by prayerful deliberation.

"And thus can the people's party reassure the people and vindicate and strengthen the forces of democracy throughout the world."

APPENDIX D

The full as-delivered text of the acceptance speech of 1952 follows:

"I accept your nomination—and your program.

"I should have preferred to hear those words uttered by a stronger, a wiser, a better man than myself. But after listening to the President's speech, I even feel better about myself.

"None of you, my friends, can wholly appreciate what is in my heart. I can only hope that you understand my words. They will be few.

"I have not sought the honor you have done me. I *could* not seek it because I aspired to another office, which was the full measure of my ambition. And one does not treat the highest office within the gift of the people of Illinois as an alternative or as a consolation prize.

"I *would* not seek your nomination for the presidency because the burdens of that office stagger the imagination. Its potential for good or evil now and in the years of our lives smothers exultation and converts vanity to prayer.

"I have asked the merciful Father—the Father of us all—to let this cup pass from me. But from such dread responsibility one does not shrink in fear, in self-interest, or in false humility. So, 'if this cup may not pass away from me, except I drink it, Thy will be done.'

"That my heart has been troubled, that I have not sought ths nomination, that I could not seek it in good conscience, that I would not seek it in honest self-appraisal, is not to say that I value it the less. Rather it is that I revere the office of presidency of the United States.

"And now, my friends, that you have made your decision I will fight to win that office with all my heart and my soul. And with your help I have no doubt that we will win.

"You have summoned me to the highest mission within the gift of any people. I could not be more proud. Better men than I were at hand for this mighty task, and I owe to you and to them every resource of mind and of strength that I possess to make your deed today a good one for our country and for our party. I am confident, too, that your selection of a candidate for Vice President will strengthen me and our party immeasurably in the hard, the implacable work that lies ahead of all of us.

"I know you join me in gratitude and in respect for the great Democrats and the leaders of our generation whose names you have considered here in this convention, whose vigor, whose character, whose devotion to the Republic we love so well have won the respect of countless Americans and have enriched our party. I shall need them, we shall need them, because I have not changed in any respect since yesterday. Your nomination, awesome as I find it, has not enlarged my capacities. So I am profoundly grateful and emboldened by their comradeship and their fealty, and I have been deeply moved by their expressions of good will and of support. And I cannot, my frinds, resist the urge to take the one opportunity that has been afforded me to pay my humble respects to a very great and good American, whom I am proud to call my kinsman, Alben Barkley of Kentucky.

"Let me say, too, that I have been heartened by the conduct of this convention. You have argued and disagreed, because as Democrats you care and you care deeply. But you have disagreed and argued without calling each other liars and thieves, without despoiling our best traditions. You have not spoiled our best traditions in any naked struggles for power.

"And you have written a platform that neither equivocates, contradicts nor evades. You have restated our party's record, its principles and its purposes, in language that none can mistake, and with a firm confidence in justice, freedom and peace on earth that will raise the hearts and the hopes of mankind for that distant day when no one rattles a saber and no one drags a chain.

"For all these things I am grateful to you. But I feel no exultation, no sense of triumph. Our troubles are all ahead of us. Some will call us appeasers; others will say that we are the war party. Some will say we are reactionary. Others will say that we stand for socialism. There will be the inevitable cries of 'throw the rascals out'; 'it's time for a change'; and so on and so on.

"We'll hear all those things and many more besides. But we will hear nothing that we have not heard before. I'm not too much concerned with partisan denunciation, with epithets and abuse, because the workingman, the farmer, the thoughtful businessman, all know that they are better off than ever before and they all know that the greatest danger to free enterprise in this country died with the great depression under the hammer blows of the Democratic Party.

"Nor am I afraid that the precious two-party system is in danger. Certainly the Republican Party looked brutally alive a couple of weeks ago, and I mean both Republican parties! Nor am I afraid that the Democratic Party is old and fat and indolent. After one hundred and fifty years it has been old for a long time; and it will never be indolent as long as it looks forward and not back, as long as it commands the allegiance of the young and the hopeful who dream the dreams and see the visions of a better America and a better world.

"You will hear many sincere and thoughtful people express concern about the continuation of one party in power for twenty years. I don't belittle this attitude. But change for the sake of change has no absolute merit in itself. If our greatest hazard is preservation of the values of Western civilization, in our self-interest alone, if you please, is it the part of wisdom to change for the sake of change to a party with a split personality; to a leader, whom we all respect, but who has been called upon to minister to a hopeless case of political schizophrenia?

"If the fear is corruption in official position, do you believe with Charles Evans Hughes that guilt is personal and knows no party? Do you doubt the power of any political leader, if he has the will to do so, to set his own house in order without his neighbors having to burn it down?

"What does concern me, in common with thinking partisans of both parties, is not just winning this election, but how it is won; how well we can take advantage of this great quadrennial opportunity to debate issues sensibly and soberly. I hope and pray that we Democrats, win or lose, can campaign not as a crusade to exterminate the opposing party, as our opponents seem to prefer, but as a great opportunity to educate and elevate a people whose destiny is leadership not alone of a rich and prosperous, contented country as in the past, but of a world in ferment.

"And, my friends, even more important than winning the election is governing the nation. That is the test of a political party—the acid, final test. When the tumult and the shouting die, when the bands are gone and the lights are dimmed, there is the stark reality of responsibility in an hour of history haunted with those gaunt, grim specters of strife, dissension and materialism at home, and ruthless, inscrutable and hostile power abroad.

"The ordeal of the twentieth century—the bloodiest, most turbulent era of the whole Christian age—is far from over. Sacrifice, patience, understanding and implacable purpose may be our lot for years to come. Let's face it. Let's talk sense to the American people. Let's tell them the truth, that there are no gains without pains, that we are now on the eve of great decisions, not easy decisions like resistance when you're attacked, but a long, patient, costly struggle which alone can assure triumph over the great enemies of man—war, poverty and tyranny—and the assaults upon human dignity which are the most grievous consequences of each.

"Let's tell them that the victory to be won in the twentieth century, this portal to the Golden Age, mocks the pretensions of individual acumen and ingenuity. For it is a citadel guarded by thick walls of ignorance and of mistrust which do not fall before the trumpets' blast or the politicians' imprecations or even a general's baton. They are, my friends, walls that must be directly stormed by the hosts of courage, of morality and of vision, standing shoulder to shoulder, unafraid of ugly truth, contemptuous of lies, half truths, circuses and demagoguery.

"The people are wise—wiser than the Republicans think. And the Democratic Party is the people's party, not the labor party, not the farmers' party, not the employers' party—it is the party of no one because it is the party of everyone.

"That, I think, is our ancient mission. Where we have deserted it we have failed. With your help there will be no desertion now. Better we lose the election than mislead the people; and better we lose than misgovern the people. Help me to do the job in this autumn of conflict and of campaign; help me to do the job in these years of darkness, of doubt and of crisis which stretch beyond the horizon of tonight's happy vision, and we will justify our glorious past and the loyalty of silent millions who look to us for compassion, for understanding and for honest purpose. Thus we will serve our great tradition greatly.

"I ask of you all you have; I will give you all I have, even as he who came here tonight and honored me, as he has honored you—the Democratic Party—by a lifetime of service and bravery that will find him an imperishable page in the history of the Republic and of the Democratic Party—President Harry S. Truman.

"And finally, my friends, in the staggering task that you have assigned me, I shall always try 'to do justly, to love mercy and to walk humbly with my God.' "

APPENDIX E

When President Truman wrote his *Memoirs,* he sent proof sheets to Stevenson before publication; and on January 10, 1956, in a letter to Truman, Stevenson commented on "mistakes" which Truman thought he had made in the 1952 campaign. Stevenson said that if it was a mistake to choose a personal friend as national chairman, it was a mistake "that the great majority of Presidential candidates have traditionally made." He had set up his own headquarters in Springfield, he said, because he was Governor of Illinois—"It was my capital, and my continuing responsibility was there throughout the campaign." As to alienating influential Democratic leaders and thus losing perhaps millions of votes, Stevenson said that Governors Shivers of Texas and Kennon of Louisiana were alienated only because of his position on tidelands oil, a position that both he and Truman had defended, and that Governor Byrnes of South Carolina and Senator McCarran of Nevada had opposed him on principle. Truman spoke of the poor coordination between Washington and Springfield; Stevenson said he had been unaware of it at the time, though he had since learned it was true and regretted it. Truman wrote that Stevenson went "on the defensive in Cleveland and other cities on the question of so-called Communists in Government"; Stevenson said that, if Truman was right, "I can only say that my words served my intentions very poorly." Truman thought that if Stevenson had accepted "in good faith" his original proposal to run for the nomination he would have received three million more votes; Stevenson commented: "I don't see how I could have done it—in good faith—even if I had wanted to, because I had already asked the people of Illinois to re-elect me Governor."

APPENDIX F

A detailed anatomy of the speech delivered October 9 at Kiel Auditorium in St. Louis follows:

The St. Louis speech had a long history. The documents that went into its preparation filled more than half a file drawer. From the outset it was considered a major speech. The tentative schedule drawn up September 18, three weeks before the speech was to be delivered, showed its subject listed as "Missouri Valley." Bell was the assigned Elk; drafts were expected from DeVoto, Galbraith, and Keyserling. A revised schedule a week later showed that the subject had become "Expanding Economy-

Missouri Valley," that drafts were now expected from Galbraith, DeVoto, Keyserling, Randolph Paul, Walter Blum, and Schlesinger, and that it was scheduled for nationwide television and radio broadcast. About October 1, Tufts took the speech in hand. He spent a couple of days going through the mass of material that had accumulated and began talking about the speech to other Elks. Martin had done research for a magazine article some years earlier in the Plains States and now was struck by several ideas—the Mississippi and Missouri rivers, the Missouri Valley Authority, the liberalism of the St. Louis *Post-Dispatch,* and the expanding economy, which he saw not as statistics but as the sweep of land westward from the St. Louis gateway and the promise of the future.

At about this time a stranger in New Hampshire sent Martin a leaflet arguing that the United States should approach foreign aid in a religious spirit. On the leaflet was a quotation attributed to De Tocqueville: "I sought for the greatness and genius of America in her commodious harbors and her ample rivers, and it was not there; in the fertile fields and boundless prairies, and it was not there; in her rich mines and her vast world commerce, and it was not there. Not until I went into the churches of America, and heard her pulpits aflame with righteousness, did I understand the secret of her genius and power. America is great because she is good, and if America ever ceases to be good, America will cease to be great." Martin wrote a memo recommending the quotation as a starting point for a foreign policy speech and at a speech meeting of the Elks, in one of the bedrooms, suggested that the idea might fit into the St. Louis speech. Tufts said, "A sort of Mississippi Valley and the World speech," and went to work. He finished on Monday, October 6, and another Elk rewrote it, and Schlesinger took the result with him when he left with Stevenson on the morning of Tuesday, October 7. The campaign plane was headed for Michigan, Wisconsin, and for Missouri on the ninth, then on to Oklahoma and the South.

Nobody had liked the St. Louis speech and Schlesinger had planned to work on it en route. On the morning of Tuesday, the seventh, Tufts gave Martin his first draft, which he thought better than the revised draft Schlesinger had taken with him. Martin thought the substance of Tufts's draft weak, some of the prose soaring. Martin wanted to harden the passage on today's problems and the future's promise, to lay out Stevenson's view of the proper role of government in realizing that promise, and to sum up a program. On the last point he had in mind Tufts's remark that no residue remained from Stevenson's previous speeches. Since this speech was being delivered approximately halfway through the campaign, it should be the occasion for summing up the positions Stevenson had taken in September, opening the way for an attack in October. Martin proposed these changes to Tufts, Tufts liked them, and they set to work separately. During the day Martin, in making notes, hit on the phrase "new frontier": "Theory of a frontier that never closes. 1890 they said frontier closed. They were men who dealt with figures. We say never. New frontier. New frontier for America." Going over their notes, Tufts and Martin decided that this would be "the New Frontier speech— Adlai Stevenson's New Frontier, his vision of an America to be." (Eight years later, of course, John F. Kennedy delivered his own New Frontier speech in accepting the Democratic nomination for President, and his administration became known as the New Frontier. Ted Sorensen, Kennedy's principal writer, was unaware of Stevenson's use of the phrase.) Martin drafted a three-point outline of the role of government in the expanding frontier—that of a "policeman" to restrain greed and monopoly, that of support for new enterprises much as the Spanish queen gave Columbus his ships and as the federal government built TVA, and that of creating an economic climate where enterprise could flourish by developing safeguards against depression. Tufts was drafting a "tenpoint program of Adlai Stevenson"—a summing up of the positions already taken. That night they pasted their three drafts together—Tufts's original one, his program of today, and Martin's paragraphs on the proper role of government and the New Frontier—plus an attack on the Republican Old Guard's assertion that the nation's prosperity was based on war.

While they were working, McGowan and Schlesinger telephoned from Detroit. They discussed changes in the next two days' speeches with Bell and Tufts, then Tufts said he and Martin had produced a better St. Louis draft than the one Schlesinger had with him—he would mail it tonight so it would be at the Milwaukee hotel when Schlesinger arrived.

Martin and Tufts went back to work on the St. Louis speech. Nona Cox, one of the three secretaries, stayed to work with them. The last plane would leave at 2:45 A.M. They persuaded the post office to hold the mail at the post office until 2:25 A.M. Very late they finally got a draft, handing it to Miss Cox page by page. She finished typing at 2:20 A.M. and, with five minutes to go, ran to the post office, three blocks away. (At the last minute Tufts and Martin deleted the peroration quoting De Tocqueville because they could not find the passage in their copy of De Tocqueville. Throughout the rest of the campaign, Martin tried to fit the quotation into a speech but he never was able to locate the original quotation and feared to use it unchecked. On the final night of the campaign, Election Eve, Tufts and Martin again suggested that Stevenson close with the De Tocqueville quotation. Stevenson did not. That was fortunate, for Eisenhower, speaking too on national television on Election Eve, did use it. He did not attribute it directly to De Tocqueville but to a young French writer visiting our shores. It would have startled the public had both candidates uttered the same last words on the same climactic night.)

Next day, Tufts and Martin telephoned Schlesinger in Milwaukee; he had the speech and liked it. The opening paragraphs on the Louisiana Purchase and the American future were DeVoto's as reworked by Tufts; the peroration was derived from Cohn; and the rest, the central substance of the speech, was from the Tufts-Martin draft. The central substance began, "I would speak to you tonight about our opportunities. I would speak to you of America's new frontier." It discussed America's prosperity, the need to spread that prosperity wider, and the proper role of government. The central passage read:

". . . And what is the proper role of government?

"This is one of the great questions on which our two political parties divide.

"It seems to me that the answer is this: government has three roles.

"First, government is an umpire, denying special privilege, ensuring equal rights, restraining monopoly and greed and bigotry, making sure that the game is played according to the rules. On this point, the Republicans agree—so long as they write the rules.

"Second, government has the duty of creating an economic climate in which creative men can take risks and reap rewards, so that our economic life will have a continuous flow of fresh ideas and fresh leadership; and, of course, it means the building of solid defenses against the greatest threat to that flow—depression. . . .

"The Republicans are against depression just as much as we Democrats are—and especially during September and October of election years! But the rest of the time they are busy opposing and denouncing most of these defenses against depression as 'socialistic.'

"Third, government has the duty of helping the people develop their country.

"The federal government made the Louisiana Purchase, and on that land a nation grew to greatness. No private corporation would have built Grand Coulee Dam, yet in the Grand Coulee country people are building their homes and establishing their private businesses, and farmers are converting desert into garden.

"And this is only one of the frontiers that government has helped the people open in recent years. The Republicans disagree on this. They say that such activity is interference with private enterprise. But the fact is that it is this very activity of government which enables private enterprise to flourish.

"Have any great frontiers in human history ever been opened without the help of government? Christopher Columbus discovered the New World, but it was the Queen of Spain who provided his ships. The American government not only bought the Louisiana Territory but subsidized the railroads that spanned it, opened government lands to homesteaders, built TVA so the middle South could lift itself out of the quagmire of want. Government achieved the miracle of atomic power which is the new dimension for both good and evil in the world of tomorrow. [Stevenson inserted that last sentence.]

"It is this partnership of government with free and daring men that we need today."

The speech went on to discuss the opportunities of the future and

Stevenson's ten-point program on the issues—"repeal and replace" Taft-Hartley, support agricultural prices, widen and expand Social Security, eradicate racial discrimination, "move ahead on our well-established housing programs," "meet our most pressing educational needs," combat inflation, "review" tax policy, encourage small business, and develop and conserve national resources.

Before the speech was delivered, Schlesinger, McGowan, Martin, and Stevenson himself made further minor changes, shortening the speech slightly, transposing several paragraphs, changing government's role from that of "policeman" to that of "umpire," softening the educational program by inserting "most" before "pressing" educational needs, recasting the Taft-Hartley paragraph to Stevenson's liking, and removing some of the rhetoric from the peroration. Stevenson delivered the speech substantially as it left the Elks Club.

Martin joined the Stevenson party in St. Louis a few hours before the speech was to be delivered. With a National Committee radio and television technician, he timed the speech; it was twenty-eight minutes, too long, allowing no time for introduction, applause, local celebrities, and so on. He made some cuts; McGowan agreed but expected difficulty in persuading Stevenson to adopt them since he liked the speech as it was. Martin thought at the time that historians would rely heavily on the St. Louis speech, since it contained the clearest exposition of Stevenson's views of the proper role of government and of the 1952 Democratic program. This proved not to be so; the speech was virtually forgotten. It was also badly received—Stevenson delivered it slowly, he did not take the cuts Martin had marked, he seemed tired and distracted, his timing was off, the historical section was much too long, the hot partisan audience was waiting for a chance to cheer and instead of giving it to them Stevenson was giving them a lecture on government. He did not finish on time; the networks cut him off before he reached the eloquent peroration. Stevenson, returning to the hotel, felt he had spoiled an excellent speech by poor delivery—he had been tired from a long and unsuccessful day of whistle-stopping followed by entertaining about twenty-five people at dinner. Actually, it was not really Stevenson's fault: It was the wrong speech for the audience.

SOURCE NOTES

The principal sources I have used in writing this book are Adlai Stevenson's public and private papers. They exist, for the most part, in four locations. Most of those relating to his governorship, and some of the early family letters, are at Springfield, Illinois, in the Illinois State Historical Library. Those relating to his ambassadorship are in the Department of State archives in Washington, D.C., and in the chancery of the United States Mission to the United Nations in New York. The rest are in Firestone Library at Princeton University in Princeton, New Jersey. In addition, his family and friends retain possession of a relatively small number of papers.

Some of Stevenson's papers are in the process of being published in a multi-volume Selected Papers under the editorship of Walter Johnson.

I have interviewed most of the principals in Stevenson's life and used miscellaneous other papers. Transcripts of the interviews are in my possession. In these notes I will locate the miscellaneous papers.

Often the source of a sentence in the book is stated explicitly in the text, as when Stevenson wrote a letter to a certain person on a given date. It would be tedious to repeat such citations in these notes. Moreover, individual documents cannot at this time be precisely located for scholars within libraries; the documents are in the process of being rearranged by archivists. Scholars will readily find ordinary material, such as the proceedings of the United Nations, Stevenson's speeches during the presidential campaign, or Stevenson's letters. And of course, on matters of general knowledge, I have used such standard reference works as Who's Who, the Columbia Encyclopedia, and various publications by the U. S. Government and the United Nations and Congressional Quarterly; scholars will not need citations to them. Therefore, in these notes, I shall in the main cite only unusual sources, such as private journals or interviews—material not readily identified or found.

One caveat: The system just explained results in a certain distortion. That is to say, by far the most important sources of this book are AES' own speeches, correspondence, official papers, diaries, statements, press conference transcripts, and so on. Since, as I say, I am not citing them here, a cursory inspection of the Source Notes would suggest that interviews and several private journals other than AES' own had an importance far greater than they actually do have. One should remember that the basic sources are AES' own utterances.

In citing sources below, chapter by chapter, section by section, I have used the following abbreviations:

AES-Adlai Ewing Stevenson, Governor of Illinois, 1949–53; presidential candidate, 1952 and 1956; Ambassador to the United Nations, 1961–65.

AESVP-his grandfather, Adlai Ewing Stevenson, Vice President of the United States, 1893–97.

HDS-his mother, Helen Davis Stevenson.

LGS-his father, Lewis Green Stevenson.

ESI-his sister, Elizabeth Stevenson Ives.

EBS-his wife, Ellen Borden Stevenson.

AES III-his eldest son, Adlai Ewing Stevenson III, United States Senator from Illinois, 1971– .

BS-his second son, Borden Stevenson.

JFS-his youngest son, John Fell Stevenson.

PFL-Princeton Firestone Library.

ISHL-Illinois State Historical Library.

DOSA-Department of State archives.

JBMA-my own archive.

Certain newspapers are cited thus:

NYT-New York *Times.*

NYHT-New York *Herald-Tribune.*

CT-Chicago *Tribune.*

CDN-Chicago *Daily News.*

CST-Chicago *Sun-Times.*

On an important Stevenson speech, I have used, if it was available, a transcript of AES's words as actually uttered. As a second choice, I have used his reading copy; as a third, the mimeographed text released to the press in advance; as a fourth, the text as subsequently published in a book.

CHAPTER 1: 1900–1916

SECTION ONE:
ESI interviews.

SECTION TWO:
ESI, Joseph Bohrer, Loring C. Merwin, et al. interviews

SECTION FOUR:
Loring Merwin interviews; Sarah M. Fell, *Genealogy of the Fell Family*

in America . . . published by An Association of the Fell Family in Western Pennsylvania (Philadelphia, 1891), pp. 139–40; Robert Dale Richardson, *Abraham Lincoln's Autobiography* . . . (Boston: Beacon Press, 1948); Francis Milton I. Morehouse, "The Life of Jesse W. Fell," *University of Illinois Studies in the Social Sciences,* Vol. 5, June 1916; Loring C. Merwin, "McLean County's Newspapers— Particularly the Pantagraph," *Journal of the Illinois State Historical Society,* Vol. 51, spring, 1958; *Daily Pantagraph,* Bloomington, Ill., Feb. 12, 1947.

SECTION FIVE:

Letters of W. O. Davis and his wife Eliza Fell Davis are collected in a bound volume of transcripts prepared by ESI and Loring Merwin, 1947 (copy in the possession of AES III); Loring Merwin interview; Harold Sinclair, ed., "The Autobiography of William Osborne Davis," *Journal of the Illinois State Historical Society,* Vol. 39, Sept. 1946.

SECTION SIX:

Letter to AES from ESI, Apr. 22, 1946 (copy in possession of ESI); copies of early family letters are at PFL, ISHL, and in possession of AES III and ESI; ESI and Mrs. John F. Wight interviews; Rev. Samuel Harris Stevenson et al., *A History and Genealogical Record of the Stevenson Family from 1748 to 1926,* n.d., n.p.; W. U. Hensel, *Life and Public Services of Grover Cleveland . . . with a Sketch of the Life and Public Services of Adlai E. Stevenson* (Edgewood Publishing Company, 1892); *Addresses Delivered at the Inauguration of Rev. Lewis W. Green, D.D., as President of Transylvania University and State Normal School, Nov. 18, 1856* (Frankfort, 1856); *In Memoriam . . . Letitia Green Stevenson—Adlai Ewing Stevenson,* n.d., n.p.; Plymouth *Reporter,* Plymouth, Wisc., July 28, 1892; *Daily Pantagraph,* Oct. 3, 1881; Nov. 15, 1950; miscellaneous clippings re AESVP are in a family scrapbook in the possession of AES III.

SECTION SEVEN:

W. O. Davis letters; Loring Merwin interview; unpublished MS on the life of W. O. Davis, by ESI and in her possession; Harriet Fyffe Richardson, *Sketch of the Life of Eliza Brown Fell Davis* (unpublished MS in the possession of ESI); *Bloomington and Normal Illinois . . .* (Bloomington, Pantagraph Printing and Stationery Company, 1896); Bloomington Club Constitution.

SECTION EIGHT:

Letters from Grover Cleveland to AESVP, July 24, Sept. 13, 1892 (copies in the possession of AES III); W. O. Davis letters cited above; other family letters cited above; ESI interview; Hensel, op. cit., pp. 333–43; *Judge,* Vol. 23, Sept. 10, 1892; *Courier-Journal,* Louisville, Aug. 28, 1892; *Weekly Times,* Biddeford, Me., July 28, 1892; other contemporary newspaper accounts.

SECTION NINE:

AES speech to Daughters of the American Revolution, Mar. 30, 1943;

early family letters; Ida Hinman, *The Washington Sketch Book* . . .
(Washington: Hartman & Cadick, 1895) pp. 48–51; *National Parent-
Teacher,* Feb. 1951; San Francisco *Chronicle,* July 20, 1893; San
Francisco *Examiner,* Jan. 28, 1894; other contemporary clippings in
the family's possessions.

SECTION TEN:

Letter to AES from AESVP (in the possession of AES III); other early
family letters; ESI and Mrs. Wight interviews; Hinman, op. cit.,
p. 49.

SECTION ELEVEN:

Early family letters and papers; Samuel Eliot Morison and Henry Steele
Commager, *The Growth of the American Republic* (New York:
1942); New York *Journal,* Oct. 17, 1900.

SECTION TWELVE:

Letter to AES from ESI, Nov. 18, 1935; early family letters; W. O.
Davis letters; Joseph Bohrer, Hesketh Coolidge, ESI, Loring Merwin,
Newton N. Minow, Mrs. Ronald Tree (Marietta), Mrs. John F.
Wight interviews; Joseph Lash, *Eleanor and Franklin* (New York:
Norton, 1971), pp. 238–39, 512ff.; a collection of letters relating to
LGS Scott farm management is at Syracuse University.

SECTION THIRTEEN:

Letters from AES to Mrs. Stone, undated "first" letter; AES to LGS,
undated [Mar. 1, 1907]; AES to HDS, Jan. 27, 1910; Lydiard H. W.
Horton to AES, Nov. 28, Dec. 30, 1934; other early family letters;
ESI and Joseph Bohrer interviews.

SECTION FOURTEEN:

AES/Grandfather Davis: ESI interview, AES speech to Daughters of
American Revolution, Washington, D.C., Mar. 30, 1943, at PFL.

AESVP speeches and library: 4-page typescript entitled "Historical
Riches—1897—Priceless Mementoes Collected by A. E. Stevenson,"
in possession of ESI; AES letter to Dr. E. M. Stevenson, Mar. 4,
1937, at PFL.

AESVP 1908 campaign: early family papers and contemporary news
clippings at PFL.

AES early childhood: ESI, Joseph Bohrer, Hesketh Coolidge, Loring
Merwin interviews.

AES/ESI relationship: letter from ESI to AES, Dec. 5, 1935; Stevenson
family trip to Europe: early family letters at PFL.

AESVP/Wilson: letter from Wilson to AESVP, Nov. 7, 1912, in possession of AES III.

Shooting accident: ESI, Hesketh Coolidge, Bohrer, L. Merwin, et al. interviews; early family letters.

AES letters to Alicia Patterson Guggenheim are in possession of Alice
Albright Arlen.

CHAPTER 2: 1916–1927

AES to HDS from Europe, summer 1920, at PFL.

AES meeting with LGS at Folies Bergere: ESI–Hildegarde Dolson, *My Brother Adlai* (New York, 1956), p. 141; interview with a confidential source.

AES/European mountain climb: AES to HDS, Sept. 5, 1920, at PFL.

AES/LGS letter is in longhand and in possession of ESI.

SECTION FOUR:
AES' enigmatic personality: Oppenheimer interview.

AES/1920 political campaign: *Daily Princetonian,* Oct. 27, 1920.

SECTION FIVE:
AES/fellow students at Harvard Law: Francis T. P. Plimpton interview.

AES–HDS correspondence during Harvard Law years, copies at PFL.

Eleanor Roosevelt/Jews: Lash, op. cit.

AES/grades at Harvard Law: Erwin N. Griswold, Dean, to JBM, May 12, 1967.

SECTION SIX:
David F. Houston pamphlet in LGS scrapbook, in possession of AES III; press release for June 22, 1924, papers from Houston Information Center, copy in possession of ESI.

AES/*Pantagraph: Merwin v. Stevenson,* 246 Ill. App. 342 (copy of decision at PFL with other papers relating to controversy); ESI and Loring Merwin interviews.

SECTION SEVEN:
AES/traveling and writing on Italy and Mussolini: *Daily Pantagraph,* Nov. 27, 29, 1926.

CHAPTER 3: 1927–1934

SECTION ONE:
AES/Cutting, Moore & Sidley: Edwin C. Austin, Roswell Chrisman, Edward D. McDougal, Jr., Mrs. Ruth Winter interviews.

AES/income from law firm: firm's records; Robert Diller (firm historian) interview.

AES' income tax records are at PFL.

SECTION TWO:
AES/links to Gold Coast and Lake Forest: ESI, Mrs. Welling, James Douglas, James Oates, Hermon Dunlap Smith, Jane Dick interviews.

AES' life in late twenties: Stephen Y. Hord, Ed McDougal, Mrs. Ruth Winter, Jane Dick, Dutch Smith, Mrs. John S. Miller, Mrs. Welling, ESI interviews; Jane W. Dick, *A Personal Look at A.E.S.* (unpublished MS in possession of Mrs. Edison Dick).

SECTION THREE:

AES' courtship and wedding: Mrs. Welling, Mrs. Winter, Mrs. Dick,
Mrs. John S. Miller, James Douglas, Marietta Tree, AES III, ESI,
Roswell Chrisman interviews; AES to HDS, July 31, 1928, at PFL;
contemporary newspaper articles.

SECTION FOUR:

AES' early marriage years: Mrs. Welling, Mrs. Dick, Mrs. Winter,
Donald Lourie, Stephen Hord, William McIlvaine, Mr. and Mrs.
Merwin, Joe Bohrer, Ed Austin, Dutch Smith, AES III interviews;
HDS to EBS, undated fragment (1929?) at PFL; AES to HDS, Feb.
1, 1929, at PFL; other AES–HDS correspondence at PFL.

SECTION FIVE:

AES/father's death, etc.: LGS to ESI, Feb. 1929, at PFL; LGS to
HDS, Mar. 4, 14, 24, 1929, copies at PFL; AES to HDS, Mar.
26, 1929, at PFL; LGS notes to AES about burial, at PFL; ESI to
AES and HDS, Apr. 26, 1929; *Pantagraph* clippings on LGS funeral
in LGS scrapbooks, in possession of AES III.

SECTION SIX:

AES/family silver: AES correspondence at the time, at PFL; Loring
Merwin, ESI, Joe Bohrer interviews.

AES/Dave Merwin/*Pantagraph:* a huge volume of *Pantagraph* correspondence is at PFL; Loring Merwin interview.

SECTION SEVEN:

AES' income tax return for 1929 at PFL.

AES/John Borden's financial affairs: AES–Borden correspondence,
1935–39, at PFL.

AES/investments: Newton N. Minow, William Benton, Stephen Hord
interviews.

AES/duties at law firm: McDougal, Chrisman, and Austin interviews;
law firm records in possession of law firm; AES to Newton Rogers,
Sept. 11, 1941, at PFL.

SECTION EIGHT:

AES/Council on Foreign Relations: Mrs. Welling, McDougal, and Mr.
and Mrs. Clifton Utley interviews; AES' article on the Council published in an unidentified local Chicago magazine, 1932, MS at PFL.

SECTION NINE:

AES/Ives's Foreign Service experiences: correspondence between AES
and ESI, and AES and Ernest Ives, 1931, at PFL.

SECTION TEN:

AES/beginning in politics: Jane Dick and Austin interviews; AES to
HDS, Dec. 1932, at PFL; AES to John Cowles, July 21, 1932; AES
to Henry Horner, Aug. 15, 1932; AES to James Hamilton Lewis,
July 17, 1933 (?), letters at PFL; AES to HDS, Jan. 1933, at PFL.

SECTION ELEVEN:

AES/AAA: AES to Newton Rogers, Sept. 11, 1941, at PFL; AES AAA/files, 1933–34, at PFL; AES–EBS correspondence, 1933–34, at PFL; AES–HDS correspondence, 1933–34, at PFL; Francis Plimpton, George Ball, and Arthur Krock interviews; AES speech, Legal Club, Chicago, Feb. 11, 1935, typescript at PFL.

AES/Jerome Frank: AES to EBS, Wednesday [July 1933?], at PFL; EBS to AES, July 19, 1933, at PFL.

AES/EBS life in Washington: Laura Magnuson interview; AES to HDS, Sept. 1933, at PFL; EBS–AES correspondence.

SECTION TWELVE:

AES/Dave Merwin and *Pantagraph:* AES to Merwin, Aug. 3, 1933, Apr. 12, 1934; Dave Merwin to AES, Mar. 18 (1933), July 25, 27, 1933, Nov. 13, 1933, April 7, 1934, all at PFL.

SECTION THIRTEEN:

AES/move from AAA to FACA: AES' speech, Legal Club, Chicago, Feb. 11, 1935, typescript at PFL.

AES/the proper role of government: AES' speech to Legal Club cited above.

CHAPTER 4: 1934–1941

SECTION TWO:

AES/duties at law firm: Cutting, Moore & Sidley records in possession of firm; Robert Diller interview.

John Abt appointment to Justice Department: AES to Victor Rotnem, Mar. 6, 1935, at PFL; Rotnem to AES, Feb. 25, 1935, at PFL.

AES/U.S. district attorney appointment: AES to J. Hamilton Lewis, Mar. 18, 1935; AES to George Peek, Mar. 18, 1935; AES to Stanley F. Reed, Mar. 19, 1935; AES to Harold Ickes, Mar. 19, 1935; AES to Louis FitzHenry, Mar. 19, 1935; J. Hamilton Lewis to AES, Mar. 21, 1935; Stanley F. Reed to AES, Mar. 27, 1935; Ickes to AES, Mar. 25, 1935; FitzHenry to AES, Mar. 20, 1935; all at PFL.

AES/enjoying the law: Ed McDougal interview.

Dispute over rented Washington house: Cornelia P. Mayo to AES, Oct. 30, 1934, and related correspondence, at PFL.

AES/neighborhood garbage collection: Janet A. Fairbank to AES, Jan. 9, 1935; AES to Edward J. Kelly, Jan. 11, 1935; Kelly to AES, Jan. 15, 1935; all at PFL.

SECTION THREE:

AES/HDS' illness and hospitalization: voluminous correspondence, sanitarium reports and medical records, during 1934 and 1935, at PFL.

SECTION FOUR:

AES/James B. Alley/RFC: voluminous correspondence in the spring of 1935; at PFL.

AES/Davis and Loring Merwin at *Pantagraph:* Loring Merwin interview.

SECTION FIVE:

AES/presidency of Chicago Council on Foreign Relations: Council records in possession of the Council; AES introductions of speakers at PFL: Ed McDougal, Mrs. Winter, Mrs. Welling, Mr. and Mrs. Utley, George W. Ball interviews; Walter Lichtenstein to AES, Mar. 12, 1937, at PFL.

SECTION SIX:

Furnishings of Libertyville house reconstructed from insurance claims when it burned (documents at PFL); description of study is as it was at time AES died.

AES life there: Mr. and Mrs. AES III interviews.

SECTION SEVEN:

HDS illness: medical records and correspondence at PFL.

ESI's account of EBS at time of HDS funeral: ESI interview.

AES/HDS' death: ESI to AES, Nov. 18, 1935, at PFL; AES letters to Dr. Merle Q. Howard at Milwaukee sanitarium, Oct. 24, Dec. 9, 1935, at PFL.

SECTION EIGHT:

AES/proper role of government: Glenn McHugh to AES, Nov. 20, 1935; AES to McHugh, Dec. 3, 1935; at PFL.

SECTION NINE:

AES/Democratic leaders: Otto Kerner, Jacob M. Arvey, Mrs. Welling interviews.

SECTION TEN:

AES/Mr. and Mrs. Ives's career and Mrs. Ives's health: Ernest Ives to AES, Mar. 10, 1936, at PFL.

AES/Horner correspondence is at PFL.

SECTION ELEVEN:

AES/Democratic fund raising: Austin and Mrs. John S. Miller interviews; Kelly correspondence at PFL.

AES/1936 campaign bet: AES to W. R. Joslyn, Oct. 29, 1936, at PFL.

AES income tax return is at PFL.

SECTION THIRTEEN:

AES/Brownlow: AES to Louis Brownlow, Nov. 27, Dec. 13, 1937, at PFL.

SECTION FOURTEEN:

AES/fire: Glen Lloyd and AES III interviews; AES to Parker C. Hardin, Feb. 18, 1938, at PFL.

AES/financial loss from fire: AES 1938 income tax returns at PFL.

AES/income, 1938: income tax returns at PFL.

AES/family life at Libertyville: AES III, Glen Lloyd, and Marietta Tree interviews.

AES/Pirie departure for New York: AES notes at PFL.

EBS' appearance at Chicago society functions in late thirties: AES' file of newspaper clippings and pictures, some at PFL, some in possession of AES III.

EBS/talents, activities, relations with friends and family: ESI, Mrs. Winter, Mrs. Welling, Mrs. Dick, Mrs. Magnuson, JFS, Marietta Tree interviews.

SECTION SIXTEEN:

AES/House of Commons visit: AES to Laird Bell, June 13, 1939, at PFL.

Subletting house on Astor Street: AES to Vesta Channon, Aug. 24, 29, 1939; Vesta Channon to AES, Aug. 25, Sept. 8, 1939; at PFL.

Financing Omaha gas company: George Ball interview.

SECTION SEVENTEEN:

Subletting house on Astor Street: AES to Vesta Channon, Nov. 17, 27, 1939; Channon to AES, Nov. 21, 1939; at PFL.

ESI's dispute with Merwins: ESI to AES, [Dec. 5? and Dec. 11?], 1939, at PFL.

AES speech at Town Meeting of the Air, Feb. 23, 1940: typescript at PFL.

SECTION EIGHTEEN:

Material on Midwest isolationism is drawn from JBM's files accumulated as a free-lance writer in the 1930s and 1940s. A few fragments appeared in an article in *Harper's* magazine, July 1944.

AES/liberalism: George Ball and Mrs. Welling interviews.

AES/friends' reaction to William Allen White Committee: Mrs. Welling, Mrs. Ed McDougal, Mrs. Dick interviews.

AES'/law firm's reaction to White Committee involvement: Clifton Utley, Ed Austin interviews; AES to Mrs. Stanley McCormick, Dec. 17, 1940; AES files on William Allen White Committee, at PFL.

AES'/activities at White Committee: the committee's own files are at PFL, separate from the AES collection; AES' own committee files are at PFL, as part of the AES collection.

America First Committee: Manfred Jonas, *Isolationism in America 1935–1941* (Ithaca, 1966), pp. 19, 23, and others.

AES/platform plank on foreign affairs submitted to Democratic National Convention, 1940, is at PFL.

SECTION NINETEEN:

AES/White Committee: AES' committee files (at PFL); George Ball and Ed Austin interviews; contemporary newspaper clippings; AES' speech text, Chicago Coliseum, Sept. 18, 1940, at PFL.

SECTION TWENTY:

AES' White Committee files at PFL.

AES/religious aspect of White Committee support: AES to M. J. Spiegel, Jr., Nov. 15, 1940, and related correspondence, at PFL.

AES/social pressure from friends against White Committee: McGowan interview.

AES/*Pantagraph*'s political endorsements: AES to Merwin, Oct. 21, 31, 1940; Merwin to AES, Oct. 23, 25, 1940; at PFL.

AES/Ambassador Bullitt's speech to Council on Foreign Relations: AES to FDR, Oct. 22, 1940; FDR to AES, Oct. 26, 1940; at PFL.

AES/Dutch Smith dispute over Willkie: Dutch Smith to Charlotte Carr, Nov. 1, 1940; AES to Smith, Nov. 4, 1940; Smith to AES, Nov. 4, 1940, at PFL.

SECTION TWENTY-ONE:

AES/White Committee under attack; AES to editor, Chicago *Daily Times,* Dec. 20, 1940; AES to editor, Chicago *Daily News,* Dec. 23, 1940.

AES/considered replacement for William Allen White: AES White Committee files at PFL; White Committee's own files, also at PFL.

CHAPTER 5: 1941–1946

Principal sources are AES' diaries, speeches, and correspondence, all at PFL, plus JBM's interviews.

SECTION ONE:

AES relations with Knox: James Douglas, Archibald MacLeish, Carl McGowan, and a columnist who requests anonymity interviews.

AES/EBS correspondence is at PFL.

SECTION TWO:

Paul Douglas senatorial campaign 1942: Paul Douglas interview.

SECTION THREE:

AES/EBS life in Washington: AES III, JFS, Mrs. Welling, Glen Lloyd, ESI, Mrs. Winter interviews.

SECTION FOUR:

AES/Carl McGowan: Carl McGowan interview.

AES job generosity: George Ball interview.

SECTION FIVE:

AES/MacLeish: Archibald MacLeish interview.

AES Caribbean trip 1942: handwritten notes made on the stationery of "Office of the Secretary of the Navy" (headnoted "Caribbean inspection tour with Paul C. Smith 6/24–7/1–1942"), at PFL.

AES income: AES income tax returns at PFL.

AES Washington life: AES handwritten entries in brown leather notebook, embossed "1943 Year Book" and "Adlai E. Stevenson" at PFL.

SECTION SIX:

AES 1943 South Pacific trip with Knox: "1943 Year Book" at PFL.

AES/Henry Crown: Crown interview.

SECTION EIGHT:

AES/oil industry: Rowland Evans and Robert Novak, *Lyndon B. Johnson: The Exercise of Power* (New York: New American Library, 1966), pp. 16–71.

SECTION NINE:

AES 1943 Italy/North Africa trip: handwritten entries in brown spiral notebook, 5″ by 8″, first page headnoted "Notes on Mission to Italy Dec.–Jan. 1943–4," at PFL. *Major Campaign Speeches of Adlai E. Stevenson 1952,* with an introduction by the author (New York: Random House, 1953), p. xviii; copy of the trip report to Leo Crowley is at PFL.

SECTION TEN:

AES' political future: Barney Hodes interview.

AES' sons' early lives: AES III and BS interviews.

Knox death/AES effect: ESI diary is in her possession.

AES Navy Dept. career after Knox: Carl McGowan, George Ball interviews.

Daily News files are at PFL.

SECTION ELEVEN:

AES III boarding school life: AES III interview.

SECTION TWELVE:

1944 Strategic Bombing Survey trip: handwritten entries in coverless notepad with blue back, 3½″ by 5″, headnoted "U.S. Strategic Bombing Survey 1944," at PFL; handwritten entries in brown spiral top turning notebook, 5″ by 8″, first page headnoted "AEStevenson US Strategic Bombing Survey," at PFL; Doyle, Edward P., editor, *As We Knew Adlai* (New York: Harper & Row, 1966), p. 141; George Ball interview.

SECTION THIRTEEN:

AES job offers: AES job list at PFL.

AES on returning to law practice: AES handwritten jottings at PFL; Ed Austin interview.

AES/1945 State Dept. public relations problems: AES proposed draft of victory in Europe radio broadcast is at PFL; Marietta Tree interview.

San Francisco Conference: *Report to the President on the Results of the San Francisco Conference by the Chairman of the United States*

Delegation, the Secretary of State, June 26, 1945, Dept. of State Publication 2349, pp. 28–29. AES' copy is at PFL.

AES at San Francisco Conference: Arthur Krock, James Reston interviews; AES speech, Commonwealth Club, Jan. 22, 1947 (as transcribed, 1959, from original longhand text), at PFL.

SECTION FOURTEEN:

AES/London UN meeting: typescript of AES London diary is at PFL.

SECTION FIFTEEN:

AES/London UN meeting trip: typescript of diary of London trip is at PFL; Marietta Tree interview.

AES/EBS family life in London: AES III interview; AES appointment calendar; AES correspondence at PFL.

AES appointment as U.S. UN ambassador: Newton Minow interview.

JFS childhood: JFS interview.

AES/London UN meetings: Stoneman article, *CDN* Oct. 17, 1945; AES speech, Commonwealth Club, Jan. 22, 1947 (as transcribed, 1959, from original longhand text), at PFL.

Argentine job offer: AES speech, Commonwealth Club, Jan. 22, 1947, at PFL.

SECTION SIXTEEN:

AES suggests Hiss for job: AES to Dulles, May 31, 1946.

AES/Hiss/CT, Chicago *Tribune,* Oct. 15, 17, 1952; Nov. 12, 1952.

SECTION SEVENTEEN:

First UN General Assembly: AES diary, typed, Oct./Nov. 1946 at PFL, loose sheets.

AES/McDougal proposed law firm: AES to McDougal, Oct. 31, 1946, and a file of related correspondence, at PFL.

AES/ADA: Jim Loeb interview; letter, Loeb to JBM, Dec. 19, 1971; Arthur M. Schlesinger, Jr., letter to JBM, Jan. 11, 1972.

AES/Illinois politics: Dick interview.

AES/Marietta Tree meeting: Mrs. Ronald Tree (Marietta) interview.

CHAPTER 6: 1947–1948

Principal sources are interviews, AES letters and diaries and speeches, and contemporary newspaper accounts of the 1948 campaign, plus official vote tallies.

SECTION ONE:

AES discontent Jan.–Feb. 1947: longhand private diary notes on looseleaf sheets, PFL; Harriet Welling interview.

SECTION TWO:

AES' diarizing Jan.–Feb. 1947: longhand private diary notes on looseleaf sheets, PFL.

AES' introduction of Mrs. Roosevelt, Chicago Council on Foreign Relations, Mar. 3, 1947, PFL.

Other AES/UN: speech at PFL labeled "Commonwealth Club, Jan. 22, 1947 (As transcribed, 1959, from original long hand text)."

AES–Gov. Kim Sigler, "Your Right to Say It," WGN's Public Service Debate Series, Apr. 27, 1947, "Should the Communist Party Be Banned in America?" typed transcript at PFL.

SECTION THREE:

Arvey background: Jacob M. Arvey interview.

Arvey/Democratic organization: Arvey interview.

Arvey/JFK quote: Arvey interview.

Arvey/AES: Arvey–AES correspondence at PFL; Arvey interview.

Success of Kennelly formula/AES' slating: Arvey, William R. Rivkin interviews.

AES/Louis A. Kohn: JBM observation; Hermon Dunlap Smith, Louis Kohn interviews.

Steve Mitchell/Democratic organization: Arvey and Rivkin interviews.

Arvey/Byrnes/Lucas: Doyle, ed., op. cit., pp. 50–51.

Kohn letter campaign: Kohn files in possession of JBM.

Merwin letter to newspaper friends: Kohn files in possession of JBM.

SECTION FOUR:

AES/"heaviest pressure" from Secretary Marshall: Kohn files in possession of JBM.

Truman/Palestine: Harry S. Truman, *Memoirs,* Vol. II, *Years of Trial and Hope* (New York: Doubleday & Co., 1956), p. 158.

SECTION FIVE:

Richard Bentley/AES candidacy: Kohn files in possession of JBM.

"Discovering" AES: Marovitz, Hodes, Arvey interviews.

Arvey/Stevenson-for-Senator Committee meeting: Arvey and Dutch Smith interviews.

Arvey–AES lunch at which Arvey suggests governorship: Arvey and Smith interviews.

Form letter urging AES for Senate: Kohn files in possession of JBM.

Clifton Utley view of Democratic organization's preference for AES as governor: Utley interview.

Paul Douglas/Senate-Governor slate making: Douglas interview.

Glen Lloyd's advice to AES on Senate-Governor slate making: Lloyd interview.

Harriet Welling/advice to AES on Senator Governor: Mrs. Welling interview.

Ed Austin's advice to AES to run for Governor: Austin interview.

Smith-Arvey conversation on AES' candidacy: Dutch Smith interview.

AES III/AES' candidacy: AES III interview.

Arvey's concern over AES' reluctance to run for Governor: Dutch Smith interview.

AES/Kennelly: Henry Tenney interview.

Smith/Arvey consultations before AES' "last-minute" decision: Dutch Smith interview.

Douglas notified of senatorial slating: Paul Douglas interview.

Lloyd Lewis/night of AES' slating for Governor: Kathryn Lewis interview.

New Year's Eve, 1947: Jane Dick interview.

SECTION SIX:

The sources for this section are JBM interviews with political and civic leaders and other public figures, plus JBM previous magazine articles and books, and JBM's experience of living and writing in Chicago and the Midwest.

SECTION SEVEN:

Stevenson-for-Senator/Governor Committee: Kohn files, in possession of JBM.

Mulroy/AES' campaign manager, 1948: Don Walsh and William Flanagan interviews.

Campaign money and staffing problems: Walsh and Flanagan interviews.

AES/McGowan: McGowan interview.

AES/Walter Schaefer: McGowan interview.

AES/Paul Douglas: McGowan, Walsh, Flanagan interviews; JBM observation.

Good new young men in 1948 campaign: Lou Kohn interview.

AES/neighbors in Libertyville: Lloyd interview.

Socialites in 1948 campaign: Mrs. John S. Miller interview.

Blair/election night 1948: Mrs. Lloyd Lewis interview.

EBS/1948 campaign: Mrs. Lewis, Mrs. Dick, Mrs. Winter interviews.

AES/downstate support in campaign: Don Forsyth, Donald S. Funk, Margaret Munn interviews.

AES/1948 campaign: Donold Lourie interview.

Burgess view that AES would lose: Henry Crown and Arvey interviews.

Sidley view that AES would lose: Arvey interview.

AES' acceptance speech, 1948 nomination: Arvey interview.

1948 campaign off to slow start: Henry Tenney interview.

CIO contribution/appointment of Director of Labor: Arvey interview.

AES' desk calendar, at PFL, shows how campaigning claimed all his time.

Henry Crown campaign contribution: Crown interview.

Audit of 1948 campaign books is at PFL.

Mitchell on campaign financing: Doyle, ed., op. cit., p. 73.

SECTION EIGHT:

1948 campaign speeches are at PFL. Green speeches are in contemporary newspapers.

AES opens 1948 campaign in Bloomington: Ernest Ives to Ellen Carpenter, Feb. 24, 1948, at PFL.

SECTION NINE:

EBS' attitude during '48 campaign: Ernest Ives to Ellen Carpenter, Feb. 24, 1948, at PFL.

SECTION TEN:

Centralia disaster: JBM, "The Blast in Centralia No. 5," *Harper's,* Mar. 1948.

Democratic Party/Truman/Eisenhower: Arvey interview, Truman *Memoirs,* contemporary newspapers.

Eisenhower Democratic possibilities: Arvey interview.

AES 1948 primary work: folder marked "Cook County Chicago Ward Meetings 1948," at PFL.

AES to Jane Dick: correspondence in Mrs. Dick's possession.

SECTION ELEVEN:

Alicia Patterson background: Mrs. Jane Dick, Mrs. Welling, and other interviews, *Newsday* obituary.

AES/Alicia Patterson relationship: Mrs. Ronald Tree (Marietta), Mrs. Dick, and other interviews.

AES letters to Alicia Patterson are at PFL, hers to him are in possession of Alice Albright Arlen.

SECTION THIRTEEN:

Truman re-election: Truman, *Memoirs,* Vol. II, Chap. 13.

AES campaign promises, 1948: Peru *Daily News Herald* letter to JBM, in his possession.

SECTION FOURTEEN:

Convention/AES/1948 civil rights platform: Carl McGowan and Arvey interviews, contemporary newspapers.

SECTION FIFTEEN:

AES/EBS impending divorce: Mrs. Utley, Mrs. Dick interviews.

AES campaign: AES III and Kohn interviews.

Libertyville county fair: Mrs. Lewis interview.

University of Illinois students' dsappointment with AES: Howard Schuman interview.

AES/state platform: AES to H. Clay Tate, Sept. 27, 1948, at PFL.

SECTION SIXTEEN:

AES/Bloomington torchlight parade: *Pantagraph,* Sept. 16, 1948.

SECTION SEVENTEEN:

Final campaign days: Arvey, Ed McDougal, Smith, Kohn, Mrs. Dick interviews; contemporary newspapers.

CHAPTER 7: 1948–1952

Most of AES' speeches during his governorship were issued as mimeographed press releases and a few, such as his inaugural address, were
printed as pamphlets; copies and related documents are to be found
at PFL. Official documents while he was Governor are at ISHL.
His private correspondence for the period is at PFL (except for
certain private letters which are in the possession of AES III). On
legislative matters, I have used the printed Illinois Bluebook, House
and Senate Legislative Digest and Legislative Synopsis and Journals,
Statutes, Constitution, Budgets and Budget Messages, and Vetoes, all
at ISHL. AES' appointment books and calendars are at PFL. The
Mansion Guest Book is at PFL. On the 1952 Democratic National
Convention, the party's Proceedings are useful as is *Presidential
Nominating Politics in 1952,* prepared by Paul T. David, Malcolm
Moos, Ralph M. Goldman, and others, in five volumes, published at
Baltimore by the Johns Hopkins Press in 1954. AES' welcoming
speech and acceptance speech are at PFL in various forms. For the
most part, I shall not cite below the foregoing sources or contem-
porary newspaper articles.

SECTION TWO:
AES considers going to UN in Paris to help Secretary Marshall: AES to
Alicia Patterson, Nov. 12, 1948; George Marshall to AES, Nov. 26,
1948; at PFL.

SECTION THREE:
Organizing government: Smith interview.
Illinois's government coming to a stop during Green administration:
McGowan interview.
AES' method of organizing his administration: AES speech, the Com-
merical Club of Chicago, Mar. 28, 1949, at PFL, ISHL.
Biographical background material on AES' cabinet members: William
Flanagan press release, Springfield; at PFL.
Arvey's advice to AES on his appointments: Arvey interview.
AES/relations with Illinois Democratic politicians: Arvey, McGowan,
Adlai III, Minow, Rivkin, other politicians interviews.
AES/patronage: speech to Commercial Club, Chicago, Mar. 28, 1949, at
PFL, ISHL.
AES' system to screen job applicants: Don Walsh and Lawrence Irvin
interviews.
Paul Powell and other downstate politicians' background: JBM, "Back-

stage at the Statehouse: What Those Politicians Do to You!" *Saturday Evening Post,* Dec. 12, 19, 26, 1953; other JBM writings and interviews; contemporary newspaper clippings.

AES/Paul Powell: McGowan, Marovitz interviews.

SECTION FOUR:

Files on legislative program, campaign fund audit, and inaugural plans are at PFL.

AES schedule at PFL.

SECTION FIVE:

Inaugural festivities: Stephen Mitchell to William L. Ayers (?), Jan. 14, 1949, at PFL; Mrs. John S. Miller, Mrs. Kohn, Louis Kohn, Mrs. Welling interviews.

SECTION SIX:

Springfield description and legislature: See "Backstage at the Statehouse," cited above, and other JBM published articles in the *Saturday Evening Post* and *Harper's.*

". . . best Senate money can buy": Clyde Traeger interview, 1953.

SECTION SEVEN:

Green's last-minute nominations: AES to Guy Reed, Jan. 13, 1949, at PFL.

SECTION EIGHT:

AES' personal staff: Schaefer, Kohn, Irvin, Flanagan, Hyndman, McGowan, Walsh, Blair, Joe Bohrer interviews.

AES/public service for youth: AES to Sheldon J. Howe, Jan. 13, 1949, at PFL.

AES/commutation of death sentence: Jane Dick, *A Personal Look at A.E.S.,* unpublished MS, copy at PFL.

Director of Public Safety appointment: Walsh interview.

Director of Public Welfare appointment: Fred Hoehler and Dutch Smith interviews, 1952.

Public Aid Commission appointment: Henry Tenney interview.

Quality of AES' Cabinet: McGowan interview.

EBS' attitude toward Cabinet: Schaefer, Mr. and Mrs. Funk, McGowan, Flanagan interviews.

SECTION NINE:

AES' way of life in early governorship: Mrs. John S. Miller, Mrs. Welling, Jane Dick, the Dutch Smiths, the Donald Funks, ESI interviews.

Liberals later "forgave" AES: George Ball and Arthur M. Schlesinger, Jr. interviews.

SECTION TEN:

EBS' attitude toward Democratic politicians: Arvey interview.

AES relationship to Alicia Patterson: Mrs. Carl McGowan, Marietta Tree, Mrs. Zurcher, ESI, AES III, Mrs. Field interviews.

SECTION ELEVEN:

AES schedule: appointment books are at PFL.

SECTION TWELVE:

AES accomplishments as governor: Otto Kerner, Don Walsh, Arvey, Marovitz, McGowan, Abner Mikva interviews.

AES' soliciting support for Con-Con: AES to Mrs. Thomas D. Schmidt, Apr. 25, 1949; AES to J. McWilliams Stone, Apr. 25, 1949; at PFL.

AES discouraged with legislative prospects: Mrs. Dutch Smith interview.

SECTION FIFTEEN:

Downstate patronage: Larry Irvin files, in his possession.

SECTION SIXTEEN:

AES/Truman: Arvey interview; *Harry S. Truman, Memoirs,* Vol. II; James Loeb, unpublished MS.

SECTION EIGHTEEN:

Alger Hiss background: Alistair Cooke, *A Generation on Trial, U.S.A. v. Alger Hiss* (New York: Alfred A. Knopf, 1950).

AES' Hiss deposition: mimeographed text is at PFL; McGowan interview.

SECTION NINETEEN:

Impending divorce: ESI diary, in possession of Mrs. Ives; Glen Lloyd, Jane Dick, Ruth Winter, AES (1952), Mrs. Welling, AES III interviews.

SECTION TWENTY:

Lobbying against FEPC: typewritten pamphlet prepared by J. Edward Day, 1952, to cite accomplishments of AES' administration, copy at PFL.

Arvey/FEPC: Arvey interview.

SECTION TWENTY-ONE:

Closing days of the legislature: ESI diary, in possession of Mrs. Ives.

SECTION TWENTY-TWO:

Legislative session: Schaefer, McGowan, Irvin interviews.

SECTION TWENTY-FIVE:

Terms of divorce: copies of documents in AES' files at PFL.

SECTION TWENTY-SIX:

AES/official trips accompanied by sons: Adlai III interview.

SECTION TWENTY-SEVEN:

AES/McGowan: McGowan interview.

Newspaper coverage of divorce: contemporary newspaper clippings; Flanagan interview.

AES' reaction to divorce: McGowan, Margaret Munn interviews.

Final divorce settlement: copy of property settlement agreement and divorce decree supplied by law firm which represented AES— Tenney, Bentley, Howell, Askow & Lewis—courtesy of AES III.

SECTION TWENTY-NINE:

AES strengthening governorship: McGowan interview.

AES/Jim Mulroy: McGowan interview.

AES/absorption in state government: McGowan interview.

SECTION THIRTY:

Emergence of Senator Joseph McCarthy: Richard H. Rovere, *Senator Joe McCarthy* (New York: Harcourt, Brace and Company, 1959).

AES as potential presidential candidate: Flanagan interview.

SECTION THIRTY-TWO:

McCarthy "Communists in government" issue: Rovere, *Senator Joe McCarthy,* cited above.

Chicago Syndicate/downstate gambling: JBM, "The Sheltons: America's Bloodiest Gang," *Saturday Evening Post,* Mar. 18, 1950; JBM, *Butcher's Dozen* (New York: Harper & Brothers, 1950).

AES/state gambling raids: AES speech to American Bar Association, Section on Criminal Law, Washington, D.C., Sept. 19, 1950, at PFL.

SECTION THIRTY-THREE:

Eric Sevareid broadcast on AES: CBS network, 10 P.M., Apr. 12, 1950, Springfield; typescript at PFL.

AES/radio interview by Clifton Utley: NBC network, Friday, May 12, 1950, 9:45 P.M.; typed outline and notes at PFL.

George Kells: JBM, "How Corrupt Is Chicago?" *Saturday Evening Post,* Mar. 31, 1951.

SECTION THIRTY-FIVE:

AES/Blair: Mrs. Welling interview.

AES/Mayor Kennelly: McGowan interview.

AES/"indecision and vacillation": McGowan interview.

SECTION THIRTY-NINE:

Blair-Kennedy relationship: Blair interview.

SECTION FORTY:

AES/Stengel as gubernatorial candidate: McGowan interview.

SECTION FORTY-ONE:

Wood: JBM "Backstage at the Statehouse," cited above.

SECTION FORTY-THREE:

Powell/truck bill: AES III interview.

SECTION FORTY-FOUR:

AES explains vetoes: speech to State Convention, Veterans of Foreign Wars, Springfield, July 13, 1951; at PFL.

AES/Broyles bills: McGowan interview.

1954 public survey on Communist threat: Samuel A. Stouffer, *Communism, Conformity and Civil Liberties* (New York: Doubleday & Co., 1955), as quoted in Earl Latham, *The Communist Controversy in Washington* (Cambridge: Harvard University Press, 1966).

SECTION FORTY-FIVE:

AES/life alone in Mansion: MacLeish interview.

EBS/life with sons: John Fell Stevenson interview.

AES relations with ESI: Adlai III interview; AES notes to ESI, at PFL.

AES' accessibility: McGowan interview; Jane Dick, *A Personal Look at A.E.S.*

EBS/life with sons: John Fell Stevenson interview.

SECTION FORTY-EIGHT:

Schaefer appointment to Supreme Court: McGowan interview.

Ed Lahey article on AES: Chicago *Daily News,* June 21, 1951.

SECTION FORTY-NINE:

Cicero race riot, July 1951: contemporary newspaper clippings.

Move to elect AES convention delegates: Larry Irvin memorandum to AES, Aug. 7, 1951, at PFL.

AES-Paul Douglas meeting, Indiana dunes: Irvin, Utley, McGowan interviews.

SECTION FIFTY-ONE:

AES/Jim Mulroy and race-track scandal: McGowan and Schaefer interviews; JBM journal; AES interviews (1952).

AES/Charles Wray and horse meat scandal: McGowan interview; AES interviews (1952) JBM journal.

SECTION FIFTY-TWO:

Washington press corps party: Flanagan interview.

AES/Governors' Conference: McGowan interview.

AES/cigarette tax stamp scandal: McGowan, Dutch Smith (1952), and AES (1952) interviews.

SECTION FIFTY-FIVE:

AES/*Time* magazine interview on childhood killing: Noel F. Busch, *Adlai E. Stevenson of Illinois* (New York: Farrar, Straus and Young, 1952).

SECTION FIFTY-SEVEN:

Social evening at Mansion: Marietta Tree interview.

Shriver/AES: Shriver to JBM, Feb. 15, 1973.

Reports of the various investigations of the New Orient mine disaster, and related documents and correspondence, are at PFL.

SECTION FIFTY-EIGHT:

AES/State's Attorney John Boyle: McGowan interview; JBM, "The Moretti Case," *Saturday Evening Post,* Dec. 6, 13, 20, 1952; AES press release, Springfield, Jan. 4, 1952, at PFL; AES to Boyle, Aug. 13, 1951, AES to HST, June 18, 1951, HST to AES, Aug. 8, 1951, all but JBM in AES collection at PFL.

SECTION SIXTY:

AES' record as Governor: AES notes for Jackson Day dinner speech,

Feb. 26, 1952; Ed Day pamphlet cited above; Rivkin memorandum on payrollers; Agriculture Department "fact sheet"; Chicago *Tribune*, Feb. 13 (?), 1958; all at PFL. Plus AES (1952), AES III, Otto Kerner, Abner Mikva, McGowan, William Benton interviews.

SECTION SIXTY-ONE:

AES/Independent Voters of Illinois: Marshall Holleb interview; JBM and Eric Larrabee, "The Drafting of Adlai Stevenson," *Harper's,* Oct. 1952; Leo Lerner interview (1952).

Distribution of AES background material: Flanagan interview.

Republican situation: Paul David et al., *Presidential Nominating Politics in 1952* (5 vols., 1954). This is the best and fullest account of the 1952 nominations; I have used it at various places and cite it below as *PNP*.

SECTION SIXTY-TWO:

AES trip Jan. 20, 1952, to see Truman: Lloyd Garrison, Clark Clifford, Arvey, George Ball, Flanagan, McGowan, Reston, Schaefer, Newton Minow interviews; HST, *Memoirs,* cited above; Jim Loeb, unpublished MS in possession of Loeb; Doyle, *As We Knew Adlai; Time* magazine, Jan. 28, 1952; Griswold to AES III, Mar. 24, 1967.

SECTION SIXTY-THREE:

AES/Korea: *Foreign Affairs,* April 1952, Vol. 30, No. 3.

Decision to run for presidency: Rivkin, Dutch Smith interviews, Joseph Rauh to AES, Feb. 8 (?), 1952; AES to Rauh, Feb. 11, 1952, at PFL.

AES/Independent Voters of Illinois: JBM, Larrabee, *Harper's* article cited above.

SECTION SIXTY-FOUR:

AES/Annunzio scandal: JBM journal; AES and McGowan interviews, 1952.

AES secret visit to Truman: George Ball interview; Harry S. Truman, *Memoirs,* cited above; Barry Bingham, Sr., to JBM, Dec. 16, 1971.

SECTION SIXTY-FIVE:

Ellen Smith to AES, AES to Mrs. Smith, Mar. 5, 1952, both at PFL.

EBS' attitude toward AES candidacy: EBS to Richard K. Stevens, undated; Stevens to AES, Mar. 5, 1952; AES to Stevens, Mar. 10, 1952; AES to Stevens, April 22, 1952, copies supplied by Mr. Stevens.

Schlesinger to AES, Mar. 25, 1952, re candidacy, at PFL.

AES/meeting with Murphy in Washington: Jim Loeb, unpublished manuscript in his possession; George Ball's account in *As We Knew Adlai,* cited above.

SECTION SIXTY-SIX:

Rivkin-Geocaris confidential memo to Arvey, Mar. 28, 1952: copy supplied by Mr. Rivkin.

Jefferson-Jackson Day dinner, Truman announcement not to run: Schlesinger journal in his possession; Truman, *Memoirs,* cited above; Harriman and Arvey interviews; Harriman to JBM, Dec. 22, 1971.

AES/"Meet the Press," Mar. 30, 1952: transcript is at PFL.

AES/Lippmann dinner: Ball interview; Schlesinger journal in his possession; Schlesinger to AES, April 1, 1952, at PFL.

SECTION SIXTY-SEVEN:

Vacuum: Larrabee and Martin in *Harper's,* cited above.

National party leaders' concern at AES hesitancy: Flanagan, Arvey interviews.

IVI converted to national committee: Holleb and Leo Lerner (1952) interviews.

Southern Illinois trip April 1; JBM journal.

SECTION SIXTY-EIGHT:

Stevenson-for-Governor Committee: Dutch Smith interview.

AES decision to run for presidency; Don Forsyth, Henry Tenney, Rivkin, Mikva, Arvey, Lou Kohn, McGowan, Flanagan interviews.

AES/homosexuality charge: Flanagan, Mrs. John Miller, Arvey, Mrs. James Mundis interviews.

SECTION SIXTY-NINE:

AES statement, April 16, 1952: Arvey, McGowan interviews.

Harriman dinner and candidacy: Arvey interview; Truman, *Memoirs.*

SECTION SEVENTY:

Republican maneuvers: *PNP.*

AES/Hamlet: Beth Currie notes on conversations with AES, in the 1960s, unpublished MS in possession of Mrs. Currie.

SECTION SEVENTY-ONE:

AES' longhand notes on Texas issues are at PFL.

SECTION SEVENTY-TWO:

AES/Pennsylvania support: Lewis M. Stevens to AES, June 3, 1952; Lawrence M. C. Smith to AES, June 26, 1952; both at PFL.

EBS' attitude damaging to AES and sons: Mrs. Winter to Mrs. Carpenter (undated), 1952, at PFL.

SECTION SEVENTY-THREE:

EBS' interview, Chicago *Daily News,* June 23, 1952: Lou Kohn files in possession of JBM.

AES/EBS' behavior: AES to Mrs. Winter, June 27, 1952, at PFL.

AES/candidacy: AES to Jane Dick, June 29, 1952, handwritten original in possession of Mrs. Dick.

AES/Houston Press conference: Flanagan interview.

AES/Barkley candidacy: Truman, *Memoirs;* Arvey interview.

SECTION SEVENTY-FOUR:

AES watches Eisenhower's nomination: Flanagan interview.

AES-Walter Reuther meeting: Schlesinger's journal in possession of Schlesinger.

SECTION SEVENTY-FIVE:

AES/IVI draft: Walter Johnson's *How We Drafted Adlai Stevenson* (New York: Alfred A. Knopf, 1955) provides a useful if partial account of how AES was drafted. Marshall Holleb, Reston, Arvey, Leo Lerner, Arthur Krock, Flanagan, Al Weisman interviews; *PNP*.

AES/convention: JBM journal in possession of JBM; Schlesinger journal in possession of Schlesinger; McGowan, Reston, Arvey interviews; Larrabee and Martin article in *Harper's*.

SECTION SEVENTY-SIX:

AES/convention opening: JBM observation; Flanagan and Arvey interviews.

SECTION SEVENTY-SEVEN:

Barkley withdrawal: Truman, *Memoirs; PNP.*

IVI Committee meeting: Holleb interview.

AES/Harriman at convention: Schlesinger journal.

AES boom: JBM journal, *PNP.*

IVI Committee expansion and activities: Al Weisman interview.

Civil rights, Arvey/Schricker: *PNP,* McDougal and Arvey interviews, JBM journal.

AES/HST telephone conversation on July 24: Truman, *Memoirs.*

SECTION SEVENTY-EIGHT:

Nominations: *PNP.*

Description of AES box at convention: Dutch Smith letter to his daughter, July 28, 1952, copy supplied by Mr. Smith.

Ellen Smith parody of "He's a Wonderful Guy," copy with AES autograph, supplied by Mrs. Smith.

Kefauver convention strategy: Arvey interview; Schlesinger journal; *PNP.*

Description of "Blair House": Dutch Smith letter to his daughter, cited above.

Final convention maneuvers resulting in AES' nomination: Schlesinger and JBM journals; *PNP;* notes made at the time by Ellen and Dutch Smith, in possession of the Smiths; Blair, Arvey, Schaefer, Tenney, Walter Fisher, McGowan, Mrs. McGowan, James Oates interviews.

Religious quotation at end of acceptance speech: Alfred E. Smith, "Catholic and Patriot, Governor Smith Speaks," *Atlantic Monthly,* May 1927.

SECTION SEVENTY-NINE:

AES/Bloomington: Joe Bohrer interview.

CHAPTER 8: 1952

Principal sources for the 1952 campaign are AES' statements, speeches, press conference transcripts, political files, correspondence, all at PFL; Arthur Schlesinger, Jr.'s journal, in his possession; contemporary newspaper articles; JBM's journal and campaign files, including schedules, in his possession. The speech files at PFL are voluminous, containing early drafts and memoranda, final drafts, reading copies, mimeographed texts released to the press, and recordings of some of the as-delivered speeches.

SECTION ONE:

AES/Lincoln's old home in Springfield: Carl McGowan interview; McGowan to JBM, Dec. 20, 1971; Blair to JBM, Dec. 21, 1971.

SECTION TWO:

Spanish general: Raymond Carr, *Spain 1808–1939* (New York: Oxford University Press, 1966), p. 251.

SECTION FOUR:

AES naïveté on running a presidential campaign: Newton Minow interviews; JBM journal.

AES/television campaign: George Ball interview.

SECTION SIX:

AES/National chairman controversy: McGowan and Arvey interviews; memorandum re AES-1952 campaign by Mitchell, at PFL.

Stephen A. Mitchell, *Elm Street Politics* (New York: Oceana Publications, 1959). Stephen A. Mitchell, "Adlai's Amateurs," in Doyle, *As We Knew Adlai,* pp. 62–92.

SECTION SEVEN:

AES campaign switch—Governor to President: Don Forsyth, Dutch Smith interviews; JBM journal.

AES early campaign finances: Roger Stevens, Jane Dick interviews.

Vounteers organization: JBM journal; Holleb, Lerner, Kohn interviews.

AES close supporters: letter Jane W. Dick to AES, "Thursday," on Racquet Club notepaper, marked "Personal, via Mr. Blair," in possession of AES III; Mrs. Ives, Kathryn Lewis, Marietta Tree interviews.

SECTION EIGHT:

AES staff: Flanagan's biographical sketch of AES staff, at PFL; JBM journal.

AES campaign, early strategy: JBM journal; McGowan, Schlesinger, Blair, Rowe, Minow, Ball interviews.

AES campaign, operation: JBM journal; Minow, McGowan, Ball, Rivkin, Rowe interviews; *Major Campaign Speeches of Adlai E. Stevenson, 1952* (New York: Random House, 1953), Intro., p. xiii.

SECTION NINE:
AES campaign in Truman's opinion: Truman, *Memoirs,* Vol. 2, pp. 498–99.
AES legislative program: Minow interviews.
AES/special interest groups: McGowan, Arvey interviews.

SECTION TEN:
AES speech writers: JBM journal; Schlesinger journal; Edward Day's memos at PFL; speech files at PFL; Schlesinger, McGowan interviews.
AES bad TV image: Beth Currie, notes in her possession.

SECTION ELEVEN:
AES speeches being written: JBM journal.
New Frontier phrase: Theodore Sorensen to JBM letter, Jan. 20, 1972.
Speech anatomy: JBM journal.

SECTION TWELVE:
AES speechmaking: JBM journal, McGowan interview.

SECTION THIRTEEN:
AES political stance and conservative instincts: Schlesinger, McGowan interviews; JBM journal.
AES/Truman relations: McGowan, Ball, Krock interviews.
AES/Acheson relations: Ball, McGowan, Schlesinger, Minow interviews; Mitchell, AES, Mrs. Acheson, Garrison, McGowan correspondence.
AES/firing Acheson: letter, Garrison to McGowan, Dec. 2, 1952, at PFL; Schlesinger interview.

SECTION FOURTEEN:
AES receiving bewildering advice: letter, AES to Jane Dick, Aug. 8, 1952; Jane Dick interview.
AES/Hiss: AES letter to Carroll Binder, Aug. 21, 1952, at PFL.

SECTION FIFTEEN:
AES/EBS relations: Walter Lippmann interview; Mrs. Currie's notes in her possession.
FBI/AES staff investigation: JBM journal.

SECTION SIXTEEN:
AES/the "General": McGowan, Schlesinger interviews; JBM journal.
AES/Shivers/tidelands oil: *Public Papers of the Presidents of the United States—Harry S. Truman 1952–53.* (Washington: United States Government Printing Office, 1966), item 146; Arvey, McGowan interviews; JBM journal.

SECTION SEVENTEEN:
AES/first campaign trip: JBM journal.

AES/Legion speech: Schlesinger's journal; McGowan interview.
Motorcade fears: JBM journal.
Liberal Party speech: JBM journal.

SECTION EIGHTEEN:
Michigan trip: Truman, *Public Papers;* Schlesinger journal, JBM journal;
contemporary clippings; Arthur Krock, Newton Minow interviews.

SECTION NINETEEN:
Daily Worker comment: Austin memo and clipping, at PFL.
Dictating machine gift: Blair memo at PFL.
AES in wax: Carol Evans memo at PFL.
AES Western trip: JBM journal; AES schedules at PFL; AES speeches
at PFL.
California: JBM journal; AES speeches at PFL; Fred Dutton, C. K.
McClatchy, Flanagan interviews; letter, Ben Swig to JBM, Dec. 22,
1971; LA press agent scenario at PFL.
Sen. Taft for DDE: contemporary clips; Schlesinger journal and inter-
view; Schlesinger letter to James Rowe, Sept. 21, 1952.

SECTION TWENTY:
Getting back on the middle of the road: JBM journal.
Western trip: Carl McGowan interview; JBM journal.
Planning second Eastern trip: JBM journal and files.
Taft/DDE pact press conference: JBM journal; Schlesinger memo, Sept.
25, 1952 at PFL.
AES campaign attitude: McGowan interview.
Elks gloomy: JBM journal.

SECTION TWENTY-ONE:
Connecticut trip: JBM journal, AES speeches at PFL.
Nixon slush fund: contemporary clips; Richard M. Nixon, *Six Crises*
(Garden City: Doubleday & Co., 1962), pp. 73–101; JBM journal.
AES reaction to slush fund: AES speeches at PFL; contemporary clips;
JBM journal; McGowan interview.
AES fund: Chandler telegram; Flanagan interview.
Checkers speech: Richard M. Nixon, op. cit., pp. 113–17.
AES trouble after Checkers: contemporary clippings; AES speeches at
PFL; Dutch Smith memo, Oct. 1, 1952, at PFL; Robert W. Notti
memo at PFL; press release, Sept. 27, 1952, at PFL; AES Fund
accounts at PFL; AES check at PFL; George Ball, Dutch Smith,
Minow, Wyatt, McGowan interviews; work sheets on accounts at
PFL; AES to Dutch Smith letter, Sept. 29, 1950, at PFL; John S.
Miller letter to AES, Nov. 15, 1950; AES letter to Miller, Dec. 15,
1950; Schlesinger journal; JBM journal.
AES in Evansville and Indianapolis: JBM journal.
AES statement on his fund: JBM journal; contemporary clippings; Flan-
agan interview; AES tax returns, longhand, at PFL.

SECTION TWENTY-TWO:
AES visit to Barkleys: JBM journal.
Korea trip pledge: JBM journal; McGowan interview.

SECTION TWENTY-THREE:
October campaign strategy: JBM journal; letter, Kissinger to Schlesinger,
    Oct. 2, 1952, at PFL.
Attack: JBM journal.

SECTION TWENTY-FOUR:
Fort Dodge speech and trip: JBM journal; AES speech at PFL; McGowan
    interview.
DDE/McCarthy problem: JBM journal.

SECTION TWENTY-FIVE:
Last month of campaign trips: JBM journal.
Wyatt press conference: transcript at PFL.
AES doesn't mind "corn": JBM journal.

SECTION TWENTY-SIX:
AES heavy schedule: AES schedules at PFL.
AES full-dress Communism speech: JBM journal; AES speech at PFL.
AES in Madison: JBM journal; AES speech at PFL.
AES in Milwaukee: JBM journal; AES speech at PFL.
AES in southern Illinois: JBM journal.
AES in Oklahoma City: JBM journal.
AES in New Orleans, Miami, Tampa: JBM journal.

SECTION TWENTY-SEVEN:
AES meticulous on Illinois affairs: memorandum from Minow, Oct. 13,
    1952, at PFL.
Second Western trip: JBM journal.

SECTION TWENTY-EIGHT:
Second Western trip: JBM journal.

SECTION TWENTY-NINE:
AES final trip plans: JBM journal.
Third fireside chat: Schlesinger journal.

SECTION THIRTY:
Last campaign trip: JBM journal.
Cleveland speech: Truman, *Memoirs,* Vol. 2; Schlesinger journal and in-
    terview; text at PFL.

SECTION THIRTY-ONE:
Eastern whistle-stopping/Korea pledge: contemporary clippings; Schle-
    singer and JBM journals; George Ball, Theodore H. White, Schle-
    singer interviews.
Arvey on "Meet the Press": JBM journal.
Final week of campaign: AES speeches at PFL; McGowan and Schle-
    singer interviews; JBM and Schlesinger journals.

SECTION THIRTY-TWO:

Campaign's last week: JBM journal.

Menard prison riot: JBM journal; Schlesinger journal; contemporary clippings; McGowan, Minow interviews; John Steele's file, in his possession.

SECTION THIRTY-THREE:

Middle Atlantic States whistle stops: Schlesinger and JBM journals; Mary Lasker to AES, Oct. 31, 1952, at PFL.

Last Midwest campaign: JBM and Schlesinger journals; AES texts at PFL.

SECTION THIRTY-FOUR:

Campaign's last weekend: JBM and Schlesinger journals; Schlesinger interview.

Last campaign speech: McGowan and Smith interviews; JBM journal; contemporary clippings.

Last day before election: JBM journal; handwritten note, McGowan to AES, Nov. 3, 1952, at PFL; Ball interview.

Election Day: JBM journal; McGowan, Ball, Minow, Smith, Jane Dick, Jim Oates interviews; letter, AES to Mrs. S. Spaeth, May 20, 1954, at PFL; Jane Dick poem with cover letter to Schlesinger from Carol Evans, Feb. 10, 1954, at *PFL.*

SECTION THIRTY-FIVE:

AES campaign recapitulation: CQ; JBM journal; McGowan, Minow, Arvey interviews; contemporary clippings; Williams letter at PFL; Finnegan memo to Stephen A. Mitchell, Feb. 24, 1953, at PFL.

What made campaign memorable: Ball, McGowan, Minow, Schlesinger interviews; JBM journal.

Significance of '52 campaign: contemporary clippings; Mrs. Currie's notes in her possession; Ed McDougal, McGowan, Lippmann interviews; Schlesinger and JBM journals.

Index